Hemmings
Vintage Auto Almanac
14th EDITION

Illustration by Russ von Sauers

Publisher & Editor-in-Chief – *Terry Ehrich*
Vice President – *Perez Ehrich*
New Products & Publications Director – *Doug Damerst*
Editor – *Richard Lentinello*
Technical Editor – *Dave Brownell*
Managing Editor – *Mary Pat Glover*
Editorial Assistant – *Wendy Bissonette*
Listings Preparation – *Nancy Bianco*
Technical Assistance – *Mary McGuinness*
Retail Sales – *Kathy Ryder*
Circulation/Fulfillment Manager – *Heather Hamilton*
Assistant Manager of Circulation/Marketing – *Marian Savage*
Customer Service/Fulfillment Supervisor – *Linda Bump*

Customer Service – *Carol Dewey, Lisa Knapp,*
Kelly Kwasniak, Amy Mooney, Merri Moore,
Melissa Telford, Freda Waterman
Advertising Sales Manager – *Lesley McFadden*
Advertising Sales – *Laurie Mulbern, Randy Shannon*
Art & Production Manager – *Edward Heys*
Art & Production Staff – *Suzy Anderson, Nancy Bianco,*
Danielle Brownell, Donna Elwell, Anita Finney, Karen Gaboury,
Don Hicks, Adelaide Jaquith, Linda Knapp, Paige Kwasniak,
Shelley Lantz, Peg Mulligan, Rob Randall, Dawn Rogers,
Abby Shapiro, Nancy Stearns, Peg Stevens, Bonnie Stratton,
Dick Warner, Carol Wigger, Pat Woodward

FRONT COVER PHOTOGRAPHS

Foreground picture: 1965 Pontiac GTO *by Richard Lentinello*

Background pictures left to right: 1948 Indian *by Richard Lentinello*,
1940 Modified Ford Coupe *by Harley Koopman*, 1931 Model A Ford Deluxe Delivery *by David Newhardt*

BACK COVER PHOTOGRAPHS

Clockwise from top left: 1976 Triumph TR-6 *by Don Spiro*,
1950 Willys Jeepster *by Dennis L. Tanney*, 1970 Corvette LT-1 convertible *by Richard Lentinello*,
1935 Packard *by Mike Scott*, 1948 Cadillac *by Bud Juneau*,

WHOLESALE INFORMATION:

Dealers, vendors, newsstands:

Wholesale copies for resale, contact:
Kathy Ryder, *Hemmings Vintage Auto Almanac*, PO Box 945, Bennington, Vermont 05201
or phone 1-800-227-4373, Extension 552

A publication from Hemmings Motor News, © 1999
PO Box 256, Bennington, Vermont 05201 • 1-800-227-4373
www.hemmings.com
Published and printed in the U.S.A.

ISBN 0-917808-35-5
ISSN: 0363-4639
LCCN: 76-649715

Hemmings' Vintage Auto Almanac ™

is brought to the collector-car hobby by:

Dear Reader,

Welcome to the *Almanac's* family!

Our **Vintage Auto Almanac** is the world's most complete directory to the old auto hobby. Here are over 3,000 listings for clubs, dealers, vendors, salvage yards, services, and individuals serving the hobbyist. And there's much more, including the most complete listing of old car museums you'll find anywhere.

This edition of the *Almanac* also contains 92 listings for Legislative Watch Organizations. These groups were formed to take on the vital chore of protecting the interests of the collector car hobby/industry. From what threats should we be protected? So-called "Clunker Bills" and related governmental actions that threaten to reduce or eliminate the supply of old cars & parts, and legislation or regulation that would impose additional costs or restrictions on our enjoyment of old cars. Become involved! These important listings begin on page 565.

To old hands, this *Almanac's* excellence is no surprise – it's an offshoot of *Hemmings Motor News* and *Special Interest Autos*, two of the most respected publications in the hobby.

Hemmings Motor News is known as "the bible" of the collector-car hobby. *"HMN"* has been published monthly since 1954, and now serves over 700,000 readers (paid circulation over 260,000 monthly, average 2.8 readers per copy). We also serve tens of thousands of advertisers worldwide. *Hemmings Motor News* is literally The World's Largest Collector-Car Hobby Publication.

HMN is about 98% advertising of collector cars for sale and related items down to the most obscure and hard-to-find parts, literature, services, tools, supplies, and more. During 1999, *HMN* averaged over 800 pages per month! That's a fat package for the annual subscription price of just $26.95.

www.hemmings.com – *Hemmings Motor News* online is the world's largest "E-Community center" for antique, vintage, and special-interest cars and trucks, parts, services, car show dates and info, car clubs, automobilia collectibles, and more! Our searchable database makes it easy to locate, buy or sell, by make, model, year and location. Plus, you can visit Car Club Central, kick tires in Dealers' Showrooms nationwide, convene your own virtual Online Car Show, E-mail a friend, or shop our Motor Mall for the latest in die-cast collectibles and other automobilia. It's easy, it's fun, it's FREE!

Visit www.hemmings.com to see why we're the fastest growing E-Community center for the collector car and truck hobby.

Thirty years ago, when finned Cadillacs, porthole T-birds, side-curtained MGs, and Ram Air GTOs were just used cars (selling for less than a years' insurance premium on a new car today) *Special Interest Autos* became the hobby's authoritative source of in-depth collector car information.

Special Interest Autos is the world's only automobile magazine specializing in present–day road tests of vintage cars, trucks, and other uncommon and unique collector vehicles you won't discover elsewhere. From Brass Era beauties to computer controlled muscle machines of the eighties, each issue features driveReports on at least four collector cars,

tracing developmental histories and including complete driving impressions of restored or fine original examples of the cars – information which helps you choose which collector car will suit you and informs you all about the collector cars you and your friends already own.

SIA's exclusive comparisonReports face off two, three or four collector cars of similar vintage & price against each other – and we pull no punches! You'll also find valuable insights to the hobby via such new columns as *Sleepers, Market Driven, Value Timeline* and *Motor Books* – the kind of information, facts & figures, and stunning photography, you'll enjoy reading.

Just $19.95, buys a one-year subscription (six issues) of *Special Interest Autos* mailed directly to your home. So come along and cruise with us in style as we explore the collector car hobby of the 21st century.

ACCESS for Street Rod & Custom – *Hemmings* reaches out to Street Rod, Custom Car and Muscle Car enthusiasts with *ACCESS*, a yellow page directory of aftermarket manufacturers, suppliers and specialists. From mechanical and electrical parts to body kits, billet wheels and chrome accessories, each issue is a powerhouse of more than 200 pages listing who's who in the world of custom and performance cars and trucks. If it's go-fast and look-good parts you want, you'll find 'em in *ACCESS*. Each copy costs just $3.00 for shipping and handling, or visit the *Hemmings* tent at a car show swap meet near you for a free copy.

Hemmings Bookshelf offers a wide & carefully selected list of old car books to aid, educate, and entertain the restorer and enthusiast. Titles offered cover how-to topics, value & investment guides, interchange manuals, marque histories, and more – everything from old farm tractors to '60s and '70s muscle cars, from low-bucks hobby cars to Ferraris & Duesenbergs. We ship promptly, and we refund promptly if you're not satisfied. See our monthly ads in *HMN*.

We welcome visitors to our Bennington, Vermont, offices, and at our Hemmings Motor News Sunoco Filling Station & Store at 216 Main Street (Vermont Route 9) in downtown Bennington, and we're always glad to hear from readers through the mail.

Your "feedback" and opinions are critical to us, because our long-established goal is to make all our publications useful, comprehensive, and a good value for the dollar! Please help us know how we're doing by writing us at PO Box 256, Bennington, Vermont 05201, or by calling us at 1-800-CAR-HERE. Thank you!

Sincerely yours,

Terry Ehrich

Publisher & Editor-in-Chief

***P.S. Check out our new web site
at www.hemmings.com***

How To Pick A Restoration Shop

By Richard A. Lentinello

Clean, organized facilities are a clear indication that the shop will produce a quality end product, as shown by the tidy conditions surrounding these two Duesenbergs undergoing body-off restorations at Al Prueitt & Sons in Glen Rock, Pennsylvania.

Restoring old cars, regardless of make or model, is a very expensive proposition. It is also an extremely time-consuming process that requires a considerable amount of skilled labor. It's a big investment, eclipsed only by a homeowner's mortgage and a child's college education.

Before engaging in a restoration, considerable thought must be given to the end product: what you want it to be and how you will use it. Are you looking for a 100-point, concours-perfect automobile or a really nice street restoration? Whichever you choose, you must decide how you want your vehicle restored before your search for a restorer begins. There are many different kinds of shops, each with a different level of work quality.

Ideally we would all like to restore our beloved cars ourselves, but few of us have the necessary skills, tools, facilities and time. This is why most people commission shops to either carry out an entire restoration or perform several of the more specialized tasks involved that are beyond the scope of even the more experienced enthusiast. Your financial resources will dictate whether you can carry out a full mechanical rebuild at the same time as a complete body/chassis rebuild.

Let us assume that you are looking for a shop to perform a complete ground-up restoration to show quality. It is important to choose a shop that provides clear and accurate communication with its clients and is aware of the many unique problems involved in such a venture. By doing so you will avoid conflict later on, or at least keep it to a minimum.

To ascertain which restoration facilities offer the best service and quality, you should visit at least three or four different shops during working hours. This will give you a good idea of how a restoration shop operates and the skill level of its work force. Soon you'll be able to separate the good from the bad.

Rule number one when looking for a restorer: Never, ever, go to a local garage or body shop, even if they advertise a restoration service. They simply do not have the skill or knowledge necessary for such a job. They only know tune-ups and collision work. They haven't the faintest idea about the intricacies of a true restoration, especially if they try to assure you that there is nothing magical about it. Always keep in mind that restoration firms are not body shops and body shops are not restoration firms. They are two distinctly different types of businesses.

Like any business that relies solely on a skilled work force to produce a finished product (as opposed to a manufacturer or retailer), a restoration business is very difficult to run due to the extensive use of hand labor, which always limits the cash flow. By understanding the numerous problems that a shop proprietor has to deal with, you will be able to comprehend why he has to perform certain tasks, charge for each of those tasks accordingly and expect you to make payments promptly.

To get the best job for your money, it is important to deal with a shop that specializes in your particular car make and/or model. No one knows everything there is to know about a particular vehicle and its parts, nor can they successfully solve all its inherent problems in a timely manner. If they've never worked on your type of vehicle before, your car or truck may be the experimental vehicle they are looking to learn on.

Dealing with non-specialists will result in higher restoration costs because they take longer to do things due to their unfamiliarity with the car. When you are being charged by the hour, every minute counts. Also, the end result will likely not be of the same quality, nor will the car be restored to the correct specifications.

To obtain the services of a quality restoration facility, see "Restoration Shops" in Section Two. There are more than 17 pages of listings to meet all your restoration needs, from complete body-off show quality restorations to partial driver restorations. Make an appointment to visit a few of the shops listed that are located near you to see if their work meets with your approval.

When you think you have found the proper facility to restore your car, don't be afraid to ask the shop owner questions about his experience and the techniques he uses. If he is honest and his business has a good reputation, he will gladly answer all your questions. Ask him about his background and how long he has been in the restoration business. Ask about his employees and their individual experience in the field. Take the time to inspect the workshop, and take a detailed look at the work being performed on the cars under restoration.

The ideal restoration facility will have all the necessary tools and equipment needed to carry out its work in the most efficient manner with the best results. Besides standard hand tools, a bead blast cabinet, lathe, half-ton press, metal brake, and a full complement of both gas and MIG welding equipment are essential items that every good shop should have. A self-contained spray booth is another crucial item. Not only will the paint-work be of a higher quality, but it also makes the work place safer for the employees and lessens the damaging effects of toxic paint fumes on our environment.

It is also important for you to inspect a couple of vehicles that the restorer has completed. Ask for at least three references from former customers. Call them and ask about their dealings with the shop. By knowing as much about the restorer as possible, you will know what to expect, which will let you negotiate the contract accordingly.

Because no two cars are alike and no two cars are in the same condition when their restorations begin, it would be unjust for you to compare your estimate with that of another vehicle. Because each restoration is unique, a program must be outlined that is tailored to the specific requirements of the car and its owner.

It is often very difficult for the shop owner to provide an estimate that will hold true throughout the length of the restoration process. Because the restorer doesn't have X-ray eyesight, he simply cannot judge the amount of rust and body repair that might be required without disassembling the entire vehicle

and inspecting every component. And because they cannot foresee every single problem, most restorers have a clause in their contracts that states an additional charge will be incurred if extra work is required.

Specialized restorers who have extensive experience with a particular model car or truck already know exactly how many hours of labor it will take them to strip and paint that vehicle, restore its frame and rebuild the suspension. This will allow them to charge a flat rate for each job because the work really doesn't vary much from car to car, no matter if it's a 1967 Camaro or a 1969 Camaro. However, if extra repair work is necessary to the body or frame due to a car's below-average condition, then the customer will be charged for the additional work.

Most of the big-dollar restoration shops that specialize in highly collectible cars, such as Bugattis, Ferraris and Packards, bill their clients on a time-plus-material basis due to their ability to pay for a true, perfect, 100-point restoration. Being charged an hourly rate is the most expensive way to pay for a restoration. But if you want the absolute highest quality possible there is no alternative, particularly

Some shops are more specialized than others, especially those that have coachbuilding abilities. This hand-made Ferrari Testa Rossa body, and its egg crate grille, are outstanding examples of the panel beater's craft.

from the restorer's perspective, since he will have to put in endless hours of labor until every single aspect of the car is perfect.

Be very skeptical of the shop that will restore your vehicle for a price that seems too good to be true. Once they have your car apart, if the work is much more extensive that they anticipated (and it usually is), you can be sure they will cut corners in places you won't notice. This can lead to a dangerous situation if they decide not to replace fatigued brake lines or a weak suspension support bracket.

After both parties have agreed to terms, you must provide a deposit so the restorer can begin working. This not only shows your genuine intention, but it lets the shop start ordering the parts and supplies they will need during the next few weeks. The better-run shops will invoice you on either a weekly, bi-weekly or monthly basis, depending on what you have agreed to. Each invoice statement should include detailed labor descriptions, a listing of all purchased parts and a brief outline of the progress that is being made. Invoices will also vary in amount depending on how much time was put in and which parts were bought during that period.

Most restoration shops usually require a substantial deposit before work begins. This varies among shops, but it can be as much as half the total estimate. Since most people are a little wary of leaving such a large sum of money, finding a restorer who is understanding and flexible is almost as important as finding one who is qualified in the first place.

If you have any questions regarding the shop's invoices, inquire at once. If the restorer can not justify his expenses, order him to stop all work immediately and iron out the problem before the charges get out of hand. If all charges are realistic, pay your bill promptly. Should you fail to pay your bills in a timely manner, the shop has the right to stop work and your project will get pushed aside, only to lose its spot in line when you decide to pay what is owed. Up-to-date accounts always receive top priority.

Assuming the cost of a continuous restoration is beyond your means, you should set a budget with the shop owner prior to the start of the project. The restorer will then work against advanced installments until all the money is used up. Should you take more than thirty days to furnish additional money, a nominal monthly fee for storage and interest charges may be incurred. This is only fair, as space costs money.

One often-overlooked item is insurance. Although the law states that all shops must be insured, you really don't know how much coverage they carry. It is therefore wise, especially if your vehicle is rare and highly valuable, to carry full coverage on the car while it's being restored at the shop and while it is being transported.

It is also important for you to take photographs of the entire restoration. This documentation will be extremely valuable when you need to substantiate your claimed ground-up restoration should you decide to sell the vehicle at a later date or to make an insurance claim. Detailed photos showing the car before and during the rebuild are most important. The "before" photos will greatly assist the restorer later should any doubts arise about how to install a piece of trim or reassemble a particular component correctly. The photos showing the work in progress will prove how extensive the rebuild really was.

The photos will also provide documentation on the parts status. Prior to delivering the vehicle to the restorer's workshop, you should inventory each and every part and note if it is good, broken or missing. Take note of the condition of all the glass, including all scratches and chips. This will help avoid misunderstandings between you and the restorer later on.

Since restoration is a labor-intensive craft, most cars and trucks will take more than a year to restore. The vehicle with a solid, rust-free body will take less

time, of course, but it all depends on whether you want perfection or if you can tolerate minor flaws. The final fitting of the windshield, bolting on the bumpers and installing all the delicate chrome trim pieces are painstaking procedures that take a lot of time. One slip of the screwdriver and your new paint is ruined. It is also impossible to avoid delays waiting for parts that may be on back order. Searching for a rare part that is missing or not available as a reproduction will also contribute to delays. Parts are expensive and they add up rather quickly, so don't forget to include them in your budget.

When your vehicle is complete, it should be handed over to you after the restorer has given it an extensive road test to see if everything performs as it should. There should be no problems at all. The car must be satisfying to drive and provide the same level of responsiveness that it did when it was new. Only then will you know if the restoration was a success. Remember, a fine restoration is substantially more than just cosmetics.

In conclusion, whatever estimate you're given for the work, add a minimum contingency of 25 percent. This way when the time comes to pay the bills, you won't be surprised. During the restoration, keep in touch with the shop and try to visit as often as possible.

Be friendly to the people who are rebuilding your car and let them know how much you appreciate their work. Make sure everything you want is in writing and shoot as many photographs of the restoration as possible. You should also get some sort of a warranty on mechanicals and body and paint. It's usually 10,000 miles and one year, respectively.

And before you take your "new" vehicle out on the road, get it appraised by a professional, then have it properly insured. There are more than one hundred appraisers throughout the country listed in Section Two who will appraise your vehicle professionally. Then insure it for what the restoration cost, not its stated value. This way all your restoration expenses will be covered should anything unfortunate happen; there are more than a dozen insurance companies listed in Section Two that specialize in collector cars, trucks, motorcycles and street rods. They will gladly put together a liability package to meet your specific needs.

Good luck and happy motoring.

Reprint courtesy of Petersen Publishing

Hemmings' Vintage Auto Almanac©   Fourteenth Edition

CONTENTS

Section One – Specialists by Make or Model *(2,775 listings)*

Organized alphabetically by make or model, this section includes all vendors, dealers and suppliers concerned with the following specific vehicles 13

Section Two – Generalists *(4,047 listings)*

Organized alphabetically by subject, this section lists businesses offering specific types of parts or services for a range of automotive marques 191

Section Three – Clubs *(3,653 listings)*

A comprehensive listing of clubs and organizations, divided into **sub-sections** for Multi-Marque Clubs, Marque Clubs, Registries, Specialty Clubs, Legislative Organizations and State or Local Clubs.
....455

Section Four – Publications & Information Sources *(156 listings)*

Section Five – Salvage Yards *(71 listings)*

Section Six – Museums *(183 listings)*

Section Seven – Useful Lists and Compilations

Index to this Almanac

Index to Display Advertisers

Section One:
Specialists by Make & Model

2,775 listings

Section One provides a comprehensive roster of specialists in one or a limited number of particular car makes. Marques are presented alphabetically, and vendors offering parts, supplies, literature, services or cars appear alphabetically under every marque in which they specialize. Certain extremely popular models, such as Corvette and Thunderbird, are presented as separate categories following the appropriate main marque category.

The taglines in the right-hand box of each listing offer a quick guide to the primary services or products offered by each marque specialist.

Vendors who specialize in several marques will have an abbreviated listing under each pertinent marque category with a cross reference to the vendor's full listing. This full listing appears under the category of that vendor's most significant concentration.

Hobbyists seeking services or products appropriate to a variety of car marques should also consult Section Two, which lists vendors by general product or service categories.

FAZA/Al Cosentino
Box 1917
Thousand Oaks, CA 91360
818-707-2301

books
information

Mail order only. UPS, Federal Express, air cargo, truck, sea freight. Unlimited information for Fiat group and Abarth from 1932.

Highway One Classic Automobiles and Highwayone.com Classic Classifieds
1035 California Dr
Burlingame, CA 94010
650-342-7340; FAX: 650-343-0150
E-mail: djboscacci@msn.com

classic automobiles

Open shop only. Monday-Friday 9 am to 6 pm, Saturday by appointment. Buying, selling and marketing of classic automobiles. Web site: www.highwayone.com

British Wire Wheel
1650 Mansfield St
Santa Cruz, CA 95062
831-479-4495; FAX: 831-462-1517

hubs
tires
wire wheels

See full listing in **Section One** under **Austin-Healey**

Cobra Restorers Ltd
3099 Carter Dr
Kennesaw, GA 30144
770-427-0020; FAX: 770-427-8658

parts
restoration
service

See full listing in **Section One** under **Cobra**

Finish Line
3593 SW 173rd Terr
Miramar, FL 33029
954-436-9101; FAX: 954-436-9102
E-mail: e.dlibrandi@worldnet.att.net

parts
supplies

See full listing in **Section One** under **Cobra**

Healey Lane
5920 Jones Ave
Riverside, CA 92505
800-411-HEALEY (4325)
FAX: 909-689-4934
E-mail: healeylane@aol.com

parts
restoration
service

See full listing in **Section One** under **Austin-Healey**

JWF Restorations Inc
11955 SW Faircrest St
Portland, OR 97225-4615
503-643-3225; FAX: 503-646-4009

restoration

AC restoration specialist. 40 years' experience. Partial to full restorations done to street or concours standards.

Ragtops & Roadsters
203 S 4th St
Perkasie, PA 18944
215-257-1202; FAX: 215-257-2688
E-mail: info@ragtops.com

bodywork/painting
British automobiles
engine rebuilding
vintage race prep

See full listing in **Section Two** under **restoration shops**

Alfa Heaven Inc
2698 Nolan Rd
Aniwa, WI 54408-9667
715-449-2141

parts

Mail order and open shop. Monday-Friday 8 am to 5 pm, Saturday by appointment only. Specializing in new and used parts, transmission and brake rebuilding, performance parts, fiberglass repro parts for 1975 thru current models Alfa Romeo. Museum houses mostly Alfa Romeo, but also has one Maserati, a Ferrari and a Lancia. We also have the prototype Giulietta

Spider and specialize in first of Series Alfas. Specializing in 1970s Japanese motorcycle parts. Web site: www.alfaheaven.com

Alfas Unlimited Inc	engine rebuilding
89 Greenwoods Rd W, Rt 44	parts
Norfolk, CT 06058	restoration
860-542-5351; FAX: 860-542-5993	service
E-mail: alfasun@esslink.com	

Repair and restoration shop and mail order parts. Monday-Saturday 10 am to 6 pm. Authorized Alfa Romeo dealer. Vintage Alfa restorations for racing or street. Also repair shop for modern Alfas. Complete restorations including body, paint, engine and any other mechanical components. Twenty years' experience in Alfas. Many new, NOS and used parts for sale as well as vintage and modern Alfas for sale, for race or street. Member VSCCA, SVRA, AROC.

Algar	parts
1234 Lancaster Ave	
Rosemont, PA 19010	
800-441-9824, 610-527-1100	
FAX: 610-525-0575	
E-mail: algarferrari.com	

See full listing in **Section One** under **Ferrari**

Centerline Products	cars
Box 1466	parts
4715 N Broadway	
Boulder, CO 80306	
303-447-0239; FAX: 303-447-0257	

Mail order and open shop. Monday-Friday 9:30 am to 5:30 pm. Specializes in Alfa Romeo parts, new and used, and used Alfa cars. Deals in all models, Giulietta, Giulia thru 164. Web site: www.centerlinealfa.com

Concours Cars of Colorado Ltd	accessories
2414 W Cucharras St	parts
Colorado Springs, CO 80904	service
719-473-6288; FAX: 719-473-9206	

See full listing in **Section One** under **BMW**

FAZA/Al Cosentino	books
Box 1917	information
Thousand Oaks, CA 91360	
818-707-2301	

See full listing in **Section One** under **Abarth**

Grand Prix Classics Inc	racing cars
7456 La Jolla Blvd	sports cars
La Jolla, CA 92037	
619-459-3500; FAX: 619-459-3512	

See full listing in **Section Two** under **racing**

Healey Lane	parts
5920 Jones Ave	restoration
Riverside, CA 92505	service
800-411-HEALEY (4325)	
FAX: 909-689-4934	
E-mail: healeylane@aol.com	

See full listing in **Section One** under **Austin-Healey**

International Auto Parts Inc	accessories
Rt 29 N	parts
PO Box 9036	
Charlottesville, VA 22906	
800-788-4435, 804-973-0555	
FAX: 804-973-2368	

Mail order. Monday-Friday 8:30 am to 8 pm, Saturday 9 am to 3 pm EST. Parts and accessories for Alfa Romeo, Fiat and Lancia, concentrating on 1966-on US spec cars. Since 1971. Most orders shipped the same day. Catalog is free in USA, $6 worldwide. Web site: www.international-auto.com

The Italian Car Registry	information source
3305 Valley Vista Rd	
Walnut Creek, CA 94598-3943	
925-458-1163	

See full listing in **Section Four** under **information sources**

Mac's Euro Motorcars & Transport	Alfa Romeos
1520 Burr Oak Rd	parts
Homewood, IL 60430	transport
708-799-3469	

Alfa Romeo cars and parts for sale and trade, 1954-1974. Giulietta, Giulia cars, Series 750-101-105-115, all models. I also do auto transport for Alfa Romeos and all other makes of cars, trucks, motorcycles, tractors and parts.

Orion Motors European Parts Inc	parts
10722 Jones Rd	
Houston, TX 77065	
800-736-6410, 281-894-1982	
FAX: 281-849-1997	
E-mail: orion-yugo@yugoparts.com	

Mail order and retail store. All parts for Alfa Romeo, Fiat, Yugo. Direct importer of parts from country of origin and other sources. Web site: yugoparts.com

Rayce Inc	parts
4656 SW 75th Ave	
Miami, FL 33155	
800-426-2221, 305-261-3355	
FAX: 305-261-3615	

Parts for Alfa Romeo, Fiat, Peugeot, Saab, Volvo, Yugo only, (1968-1996). Web site: www.rayce.com

Replicarz	books
99 State St	kits
Rutland, VT 05701	models
802-747-7151	videos
E-mail: replicarz@aol.com	

See full listing in **Section Two** under **racing**

Garry Roberts & Co	cars
922 Sunset Dr	parts
Costa Mesa, CA 92627	service
714-650-2690; FAX: 714-650-2730	
E-mail: garryroberts@fea.net	

See full listing in **Section One** under **Ferrari**

Doug Schellinger	automobilia
13717 W Green Meadow Dr	books
New Berlin, WI 53151	sales literature
414-786-8413	toys
E-mail: dsac@execpc.com	

See full listing in **Section One** under **Fiat**

Sports Car Tours Inc	back road tours
PO Box 265	
Batesville, VA 22924	
804-823-4442	
E-mail: napol@rlc.net	

See full listing in **Section Two** under **special services**

Voss Motors Inc	service manuals
21849 Virginia Dr	
Southfield, MI 48076	
888-380-9277 toll-free	
248-357-4750; FAX: 248-354-6577	
E-mail: vossmotors@aol.com	

See full listing in **Section Two** under **literature dealers**

Brady Ward-Scale Autoworks   models
313 Bridge St #4
Manchester, NH 03104-5045
603-623-5925
FAX: 603-623-5925 ext 66
E-mail: bradyward@mediaone.net

See full listing in **Section Two** under **models & toys**

Wolf Steel   Alfa Romeo body
1 Ballerina   parts
Frelighsburg, QC Canada J0J 1C0
450-298-5078; FAX: 450-298-5088
E-mail: allenhal@citenet.net

See full listing in **Section One** under **Jaguar**

All American Rambler   manuals
11661 Martens River Cir #M   parts
Fountain Valley, CA 92708
714-662-7200
E-mail: rambler411@aol.com

Mail order and open shop. Monday-Friday 9 am to 5 pm, Saturday by appointment only. Specializes in parts for 1958-1963 Rambler Americans. Also tech service manuals for all Ramblers, tail lenses for most Ramblers. Buy, sell, trade. If we don't have it, we will help you find it. Bob (Mr Rambler) Pendleton. Web site: http://members.aol.com/rambler411/private/rambler.html

American Parts Depot   accessories
409 N Main St   parts
West Manchester, OH 45382
937-678-7249; FAX: 937-678-5886

Mail order and open shop. Monday-Friday 8 am to noon and 1 pm to 6 pm. We supply new, used, reproduction and NOS parts and accessories for AMC and Rambler vehicles. 176 parts cars in stock. Web site: www.americanpartsdepot.com

American Performance Products   parts
675 S Industry Rd
Cocoa, FL 32926
407-632-8299; FAX: 407-632-5119
E-mail: amc@oldcarparts.com

Mail order and open shop. Monday 9:30 am to 8:30 pm, Tuesday-Friday 9:30 am to 5:30 pm. Specializing in American Motors Corp vehicle parts for all AMC including AMX, Javelin, Spirit, Gremlin, Hornet and Jeep, performance and stock.

AMX Connection   literature
David Simon   parts
19641 Victory Blvd
Reseda, CA 91335-6621
818-344-4639

Mail order and open shop by appointment only. Dealing in NOS and used parts and original literature for the 1968-1970 American Motors AMX. Some 1971-1974 Javelin/AMX parts and literature available. Also AMC, Nash and Rambler original unused and used shop manuals, owner's manuals, parts books and sales literature. Also owner's manuals (domestic) pre-1980 unused and used originals.

AMX Enterprises Ltd   information source
7963 Depew St
Arvada, CO 80003-2527
303-428-8760

Larry Mitchell, owner. AMC performance and handling expert. Custom sway bar packages, 4-wheel disc brakes, one-piece solid

axles and more. Specialty in AMX, Javelin and other AMC performance cars. Also full restoration services and restoration parts. Service and technical help on all AMC cars. Since 1974. Brokerage and finding service available. Web site: www.am-xperience.com

Blaser's Auto, Nash, Rambler, AMC   NOS parts
3200 48th Ave
Moline, IL 61265-6453
309-764-3571; FAX: 309-764-1155
E-mail: blazauto@sprynet.com

Mail order only. Monday-Friday 9 am to 5 pm CST. Specialize in new old stock Nash, Rambler and AMC parts for most 1949-1987 model cars. Offer the largest and most complete stock of new parts for these fine cars. Our 55 years of experience makes us the best choice for your one stop shopping. Also offer quality reproduction windshield and back glass gaskets for select 1961-1969 models. All major credit cards accepted along with UPS COD shipping. Do not offer a catalog but your one call does it all and we look forward to helping you.

Dom Corey Upholstery &   carpets/conv tops
Antique Auto   dash covers
1 Arsene Way   door panels
Fairhaven Business Park   headliners
Fairhaven, MA 02719   seats
508-997-6555   upholstery

See full listing in **Section Two** under **interiors & interior parts**

Doc & Jesse's Auto Parts   literature
PO Box 30   models
Guilderland, NY 12084   parts
518-399-2889
E-mail: ajg@nyserda.org

Specializing in AMC memorabilia, literature, scale models, NOS and hard to find parts, accessory items, V8 motor parts and 1954-1975 AMC/Rambler cars (all models). We buy, sell and swap AMC. Proud sponsors of the free Northeast AMC-Rambler Meet, held at the Days Inn, Glenmont, NY, every year during the last weekend of June. Hope to see you there.

Dennis DuPont   automobilia
77 Island Pond Rd   literature
Derry, NH 03038   parts
603-434-9290

See full listing in **Section One** under **Studebaker**

Elliott's Car Radio   radio repairs
313 Linfield Rd   speaker kits
Parkerford, PA 19457
610-495-6360; FAX: 610-495-7723

See full listing in **Section Two** under **radios**

For Ramblers Only   accessories
2324 SE 34th Ave   parts
Portland, OR 97214
503-232-0497
E-mail: ramblers@teleport.com

Mail order and open shop. Weekdays 10 am to 2 pm and weekends 10 am to 6 pm. Specializing in parts and accessories, NOS and used, for 1958-1969 Rambler and AMC. Carpets and trunk mats for Ramblers only. Windshield gaskets for most Ramblers. Wiper motors and fuel pumps.

Doug Galvin Rambler Parts   parts
7559 Passalis Ln
Sacramento, CA 95829
916-689-3356

Mail order only. Specializing in new and used parts, including reproduction items and literature for 1958-1988 Ramblers and AMCs. No Jeep or Metropolitan.

Hidden Valley Auto Parts 21046 N Rio Bravo Maricopa, AZ 85239 602-252-2122, 602-252-6137 520-568-2945; FAX: 602-258-0951	**parts**

See full listing in **Section One** under **Chevrolet**

Jahns Quality Pistons 1360 N Jefferson St Anaheim, CA 92807 714-579-3795, 800-225-0277 FAX: 714-524-6607	**piston rings** **pistons**

See full listing in **Section Two** under **engine parts**

Kennedy American Inc 7100 State Rt 142 SE West Jefferson, OH 43162 614-879-7283	**parts**

Mail order and open shop. Monday-Friday 9 am to 6 pm. New, select used and reproduction parts for American Motors, Rambler, AMX, Javelin and Jeep vehicles from 1950s to present.

Master Power Brakes 254-1 Rolling Hills Rd Mooresville, NC 28115 704-664-8866; FAX: 704-664-8862	**brake products** **conversion kits**

See full listing in **Section One** under **Chevelle/Camaro**

Mike's Auto Parts Box 358 Ridgeland, MS 39158 601-856-7214	**ball/roller bearings** **engine parts** **wall calendars** **water pumps**

See full listing in **Section One** under **Chrysler**

NASHional Auto Parts & Cars 2412 Lincoln Ave Alameda, CA 94501 510-522-2244; FAX: 510-864-8151	**cars** **parts**

See full listing in **Section One** under **Nash**

Garth B Peterson 122 N Conklin Rd Veradale, WA 99037 509-926-4620 anytime	**accessories** **parts** **radios**

See full listing in **Section Two** under **comprehensive parts**

Eddie Stakes' Planet Houston AMX 3400 Ocee #1601 Houston, TX 77063 713-785-1375 E-mail: planethouamx@pdq.net	**parts** **parts locator**

Mail order only. Monday-Friday 11 am to 1 pm CST. Specializing in 1968-1974 AMX and Javelin. Buy, sell, trade. Used, reproduction and NOS parts and literature. Also buy single parts or entire collections and inventories; AMC related literature, toys, promos, models, films, press photos, etc. Current catalog ($7) lists paint, trim, VIN codes, national AMC clubs, local chapters, markets, production figures, huge 120+ AMC/Rambler vendors list, AMC websites and more. Sponsor AMC Southwest Regional every summer and AMC AMO International Convention Houston 2001. Web site: www.planethoustonamx.com

Peter Stathes 51 Twin Lawns Ave Hicksville, NY 11801-1817 516-935-5298, 10 am to 10 pm EST E-mail: statamc@hoflink.com	**parts**

Mail order only. Specializing in AMC and Rambler vacuum wiper motor rebuilding, door locks, beltline fuzzy window sweeps, rubber window channels, reproduction rubber door, trunk seals and rubber parts, reproduction truss rods. SASE. Visit our web site for our online catalog. Web site: www.geocities.com/motorcity/garage/3222

Treasure Chest Sales 413 Montgomery Jackson, MI 49202 517-787-1475	**parts**

See full listing in **Section One** under **Nash**

Pat Walsh Restorations Box Q Wakefield, MA 01880 781-246-3266; FAX: 781-224-3311 E-mail: pwalshrest@aol.com	**literature** **rubber parts**

See full listing in **Section Two** under **rubber parts**

Webb's Classic Auto Parts 5084 W State Rd 114 Huntington, IN 46750 219-344-1714; FAX: 219-344-1754	**NOS parts** **reproduction parts** **service manuals** **used parts**

Mail order and open shop. Monday-Friday 8 am to 5 pm, weekends by appointment. Specialize in NOS, used and repro parts for Rambler and AMC from 1950 and newer. Large line of AMX/Javelin parts. Large selection of technical service manuals and parts books for Nash, Hudson, Rambler, AMC, Jeep and 83-up Renault. Many aftermarket parts available for AMC and other makes. Send SASE with your needs. Discover, Visa, MC and AmEx accepted. Web site: www.angelfire.com/in/webbsclassic

Wenner's 5449 Tannery Rd Schnecksville, PA 18078 610-799-5419	**NOS parts**

Mail order only. Evenings and weekends. Large inventory of AMC, Rambler and Nash parts. Specializing in NOS plus some used and aftermarket parts available.

Wymer Classic AMC Mark & George Wymer 340 N Justice St Fremont, OH 43420 419-332-4291 419-334-6945 after 5 pm	**NOS parts** **owner's manuals** **repairs** **service manuals** **used parts**

Mail order and open shop. Monday-Friday 8 am to 5 pm EST. An American Motors dealership from 1958-1982. Repairs all AMC and Nash cars. Still has a large supply of NOS and used parts from our AMC, Rambler, salvage yard from 1958-1982 and all the specialty tools to repair the cars. Selection of technical service manuals, service literature, specification books and owner's manuals from 1955-1982 for Nash, Hudson, Rambler, AMC, Jeep, Renault, Metropolitan. Can do repair work on Packard cars. Have some Packard literature and memorabilia.

Golden Mile Sales Inc J DeAngelo 2439 S Bradford St Allentown, PA 18103-5821 PH/FAX: 610-791-4497, 24 hours	**NORS parts** **NOS parts** **sheetmetal**

1930-1940 American Austin/Bantam vehicles, NOS, NORS parts, sheetmetal. Buy, sell, trade. All services. World's largest active source. SASE appreciated. Visit Fall Hershey Chocolate annex, spaces C4W19-22. MasterCard/Visa.

Heinze Enterprise 7914 E Kimsey Ln Scottsdale, AZ 85257 602-946-5814	**instrument** **restoration**

Mail order and open shop. Free list of items for sale for American

Austin, Bantam and Crosley. Also instrument restoration and refacing. Reproducer of vintage auto parts. Mechanical temperature gauge rebuilding. Send SASE for listing.

Gordon Imports Inc	parts
14330 Iseli Rd Santa Fe Springs, CA 90670-5296 562-802-1608, 714-523-3512 FAX: 562-404-1904	

Mail order and business open Monday-Friday 8 am to 5:30 pm. Call for weekend hours, special appointments available. Amphicar parts for all years of Amphicars.

Anglia Obsolete	parts
1311 York Dr Vista, CA 92084 760-630-3136; FAX: 760-630-2953 E-mail: enfo1948@aol.com	

Mail order only. New, used, reproduction parts for English Fords, 1939-1959, 8 hp and 10 hp cars and commercial vehicles. Models include: 7W, 7Y, Anglia, Prefect, Popular, Thames, E93A Series, 100E Models and some 105E Series. Web site: http://members.aol.com/enfo1948/index.html

Cockermouth Motor Museum	museum
The Maltings Brewery Ln Cockermouth Cumbria England 01900 824448	

See full listing in **Section Six** under **England**

JAE	parts service tech info
375 Pine #26 Goleta, CA 93117 805-967-5767; FAX: 805-967-6183 E-mail: jefforjay@jaeparts.com	

See full listing in **Section One** under **Lotus**

Kip Motor Company Inc	literature parts restoration
2127 Crown Rd Dallas, TX 75229 972-243-0440; FAX: 972-243-2387 E-mail: kipmotor@aol.com	

See full listing in **Section One** under **Austin**

S-E Autoparts	NOS parts reproduced parts
Jarpbo 4 78193 Borlange Sweden +46 243 221297 FAX: +46 243 221298 E-mail: s-e.autoparts@ebox.tninet.se	

Mail order and open shop. Daily 8 am to 10 pm, 24 hour fax. We have a large selection of NOS and reproduction parts for European Ford cars, all models, 1940-1975, and Mustang. Ship worldwide. Possibility to deliver in person to US post office if requests are up to a reasonable quantity. Will accept all orders small or large.

Dick Ames Stainless Steel Exhaust	exhaust systems
4850 Fallcrest Cir Sarasota, FL 34233 941-923-8321; FAX: 941-923-9434 E-mail: dickamesfl@aol.com	

See full listing in **Section One** under **Jaguar**

British Wire Wheel	hubs tires wire wheels
1650 Mansfield St Santa Cruz, CA 95062 831-479-4495; FAX: 831-462-1517	

See full listing in **Section One** under **Austin-Healey**

British Wiring Inc	wiring accessories wiring harnesses
20449 Ithaca Rd Olympia Fields, IL 60461 PH/FAX: 708-481-9050	

See full listing in **Section Two** under **electrical systems**

Charles S Crail Automobiles	auto sales
36A Calle Cesar Chavez Santa Barbara, CA 93103 805-568-1934; FAX: 805-568-1533	

See full listing in **Section One** under **Rolls-Royce/Bentley**

Drummond Coach and Paint	painting restoration
531 Raleigh Ave El Cajon, CA 92020 619-579-7229; FAX: 619-579-2128	

See full listing in **Section One** under **Ferrari**

The Fine Car Store	car dealer
1105 Moana Dr San Diego, CA 92107 619-223-7766; FAX: 619-223-6838	

See full listing in **Section One** under **Ferrari**

Kensington Motor Group Inc	consignment sales
PO Box 2277 Sag Harbor, NY 11963 516-537-1868; FAX: 516-537-2641 E-mail: kenmotor@aol.com	

See full listing in **Section One** under **Mercedes-Benz**

Lake Oswego Restorations	restoration sales
19621 S Hazelhurst Ln West Linn, OR 97068 PH/FAX: 503-636-7503	

Sales and restoration for 1950s and 1960s Aston Martins, XK Jaguars and other European sports cars.

Ragtops & Roadsters	bodywork/painting British automobiles engine rebuilding vintage race prep
203 S 4th St Perkasie, PA 18944 215-257-1202; FAX: 215-257-2688 E-mail: info@ragtops.com	

See full listing in **Section Two** under **restoration shops**

Rolls-Royce of Beverly Hills
11401 West Pico Blvd
Los Angeles, CA 90064
800-321-9792, 310-477-4262
FAX: 310-473-7498
E-mail: smrr64@aol.com

parts

See full listing in **Section One** under **Rolls-Royce/Bentley**

Royal Coach Works Ltd
2146 Lunceford Ln
Lilburn, GA 30047
PH/FAX: 404-249-9040

appraisals

See full listing in **Section Two** under **appraisals**

Steelwings
229 Railroad Dr
Ivyland, PA 18974
215-322-7420 parts/service
PH/FAX: 215-322-5517 sales

parts
sales
service

Mail order and open shop. Monday-Friday 8 am to 5 pm, open most weekends (call to confirm). Specializing in Aston Martin Lagonda. Pre-war to current. Large selection of cars for sale. Advice on sales or service freely given. Web site: www.steelwings.com

Vintage Restorations
The Old Bakery
Windmill Street, Tunbridge Wells
Kent, TN2 4UU England
UK 1892-525-899
FAX: UK 1892-525499

accessories
instruments

See full listing in **Section Two** under **instruments**

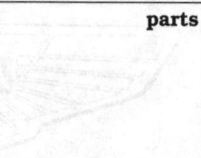

Cape Cod Classic Cars
Pete Harvey
PO Box 280
Cataumet, MA 02534
508-548-0660; FAX: 508-457-0660

car dealer

See full listing in **Section One** under **Cadillac/LaSalle**

Guild of Automotive Restorers
PO Box 1150
44 Bridge St
Bradford, ON Canada L3Z 2B5
905-775-0499; FAX: 905-775-0944
E-mail:
webmaster@guildautomotive.on.ca

restoration
sales
service

See full listing in **Section Two** under **restoration shops**

Interesting Parts Inc
Paul TerHorst
27526 N Owens Rd
Mundelein, IL 60060
PH/FAX: 847-949-1030

appraisals
gaskets
parts
storage
transport

See full listing in **Section Two** under **comprehensive parts**

Lincoln Highway Packards
Main St
PO Box 94
Schellsburg, PA 15559
814-733-4356; FAX: 814-839-4276

engine rebuilding
restoration

See full listing in **Section One** under **Packard**

McLellan's Automotive History
Robert and Sharon McLellan
9111 Longstaff Dr
Houston, TX 77031-2711
713-772-3285; FAX: 713-772-3287
E-mail: mclellans@worldnet.att.net

books
factory literature
magazines
memorabilia
press kits/programs
sales literature

See full listing in **Section Two** under **literature dealers**

Motor Foundry & Tooling Inc
7382 Doniphan Dr
Canutillo, TX 79835-6601
915-877-3343; FAX: 915-877-7071

brake drums
castings
exhaust manifolds
water pumps

See full listing in **Section One** under **Packard**

Northeast Classic Car Museum
NYS Rt 23
24 Rexford St
Norwich, NY 13815
607-334-AUTO (334-2886)
FAX: 607-336-6745
E-mail: neccm@ascent.net

museum

See full listing in **Section Six** under **New York**

John's Car Corner
Rt 5, PO Box 85
Westminster, VT 05158
802-722-3180; FAX: 802-722-3181

body parts
car dealer
mechanical parts
restoration service

See full listing in **Section One** under **Volkswagen**

Austin Works East
PO Box 1997
Sandwich, MA 02563
PH/FAX: 508-833-3109
E-mail: austnworks@aol.com

parts
service

Mail order and open shop. 7 days a week 6 am to 10 pm. Specializing in parts for pre-war English Austins and engine and gearbox rebuilding for American and English Austin. 1922-1954 English Austin parts and service plus engine and gearbox rebuilds for 1929-1940 American Austin and 1922-1954 English Austins.

BritBooks
PO Box 321
Otego, NY 13825
PH/FAX: 607-988-7956
E-mail: britbook@dmcom.net

books

See full listing in **Section Four** under **books & publications**

British Auto Shoppe
1909 5th Ave
Moline, IL 61265
309-764-9513; FAX: 309-764-9576

parts
service

See full listing in **Section One** under **MG**

Don Flye 5 Doe Valley Rd Petersham, MA 01366 978-724-3318	parts

See full listing in **Section One** under **Austin-Healey**

Pete Groh 9957 Frederick Rd Ellicott City, MD 21042-3647 410-750-2352; FAX: 410-466-3566 E-mail: petegroh@yahoo.com	original British keys

See full listing in **Section One** under **Jaguar**

Kip Motor Company Inc 2127 Crown Rd Dallas, TX 75229 972-243-0440; FAX: 972-243-2387 E-mail: kipmotor@aol.com	literature parts restoration

Mail order and open shop. Monday-Friday 9 am to 6 pm, Saturday 9 am to 12 noon. Parts, service, restoration, manuals and literature, etc, for British orphans: Austin, Berkeley, English Ford, Hillman, Humber, Metropolitan, Morris, Riley, Sunbeam-Talbot, Singer, Triumph Herald, Vauxhall, Vanden Plas, etc. Free catalogs. Complete restoration shop.

Mini Mania 31 Winsor St Milpitas, CA 95035 408-942-5595; FAX: 408-942-5582 E-mail: info@minimania.com	parts service

Mail order and open shop. Monday-Friday 8 am to 6 pm, Saturday 8 am to 2 pm. Mechanical, performance and restoration parts and services for Austin Minis, Morris Minors, Austin-Healey Sprite, MG Midget, all years. Parts and accessories for all makes and models British made autos. Free separate monthly flyers *Austin Mini*, *Morris Minor*, *Sprite/Midget* and *British Parts Source*. Web site: www.minimania.com

Mini Store PO Box 7973 Van Nuys, CA 91409-7973 PH/FAX: 818-893-1421 E-mail: jorn@aol.com	cars repairs restorations

Open by appointment only. Specializing in restored Minis, restorations of Minis and complete mechanical repairs. Also bench labor available for Austin, Morris Mini, Cooper and Cooper S cars.

Patton Orphan Spares 52 Nicole Pl West Babylon, NY 11704 516-669-2598	parts

See full listing in **Section One** under **Renault**

Seven Enterprises Ltd 802 Bluecrab Rd, Ste 100 Newport News, VA 23606 800-992-7007; FAX: 800-296-3327 E-mail: seven@7ent.com	accessories parts

Mail order and open shop. Monday-Friday 10 am to 6 pm. Parts and accessories for Mini Cooper and MGB. Competition parts also for Mini-Mini Coopers 1959-present, MGB 1962-1980. Web site: www.7ent.com

Victory Autoservices Box 5060, RR 1 W Baldwin, ME 04091 207-625-4581	parts restoration

See full listing in **Section One** under **Austin-Healey**

West of England Transport Collection 15, Land Park Chulmleigh Devon EX18 7BH England 01769 580811	museum

See full listing in **Section Six** under **England**

1 CAAT Limited Co 1324 E Harper Ave Maryville, TN 37804 423-983-7180 E-mail: jhenriks@icx.net	restoration

See full listing in **Section Two** under **restoration shops**

Absolutely British II 1720 S Grove Ave, Unit A Ontario, CA 91761 PH/FAX: 909-947-0200	restoration service

See full listing in **Section Two** under **restoration shops**

American-Foreign Auto Electric Inc 103 Main St Souderton, PA 18964 215-723-4877	parts rebuilding

See full listing in **Section Two** under **electrical systems**

Austin Works East PO Box 1997 Sandwich, MA 02563 PH/FAX: 508-833-3109 E-mail: austnworks@aol.com	parts service

See full listing in **Section One** under **Austin**

Automotive Artistry 679 W Streetboro St Hudson, OH 44236 330-650-1503 E-mail: dale@cmh.net	restoration

See full listing in **Section One** under **Triumph**

Automotive Artistry 4311 Mennonite Rd Mantua, OH 44255 330-274-8699	restoration

See full listing in **Section One** under **Triumph**

BMC Classics Inc 828 N Dixie Freeway New Smyrna Beach, FL 32168 904-426-6405; FAX: 904-427-4570 E-mail: bmcar1@aol.com	parts repair restoration

See full listing in **Section Two** under **restoration shops**

British Auto Parts Ltd 93256 Holland Ln Marcola, OR 97454 541-933-2880; FAX: 541-933-2302	parts

See full listing in **Section One** under **Morris**

British Auto Shoppe 1909 5th Ave Moline, IL 61265 309-764-9513; FAX: 309-764-9576	parts service

See full listing in **Section One** under **MG**

British Car Keys | keys
Rt 144 Box 9957
Ellicott City, MD 21042-3647
410-750-2352
E-mail: britishcarkeys@hotmail.com

Mail order only. Specializing in original Wilmot Breeden keys for British cars. Keys have letters and numbers on side of key. For early British cars, Jaguar, MG, Triumph, Austin, 1949-1969.

British Car Magazine | periodical
343 Second St, Suite H
Los Altos, CA 94022-3639
650-949-9680; FAX: 650-949-9685
E-mail: britcarmag@aol.com

See full listing in **Section Four** under **periodicals**

British Car Specialists | parts repairs restoration
2060 N Wilson Way
Stockton, CA 95205
209-948-8767; FAX: 209-948-1030
E-mail: healeydoc@aol.com

Specializing in service, repairs, parts, restorations for British cars, MG, Jaguar, Austin-Healey, Triumph, Rover. Web site: http://members.aol.com/healeydoc/pubpage.htm

British Miles | accessories literature parts restoration
9278 Old E Tyburn Rd
Morrisville, PA 19067
215-736-9300; FAX: 215-736-3089

See full listing in **Section One** under **MG**

British Parts NW | parts
4105 SE Lafayette Hwy
Dayton, OR 97114
503-864-2001; FAX: 503-864-2081
E-mail: bpnw@onlinemac.com

See full listing in **Section One** under **Triumph**

British Racing Green | new parts rebuilt parts used parts
30 Aleph Dr
Newark, DE 19702
302-368-1117; FAX: 302-368-5910
E-mail: info@brgparts.com

See full listing in **Section One** under **MG**

British Restorations | car dealer restoration
4455 Paul St
Philadelphia, PA 19124
215-533-6696

See full listing in **Section One** under **Jaguar**

British Wire Wheel | hubs tires wire wheels
1650 Mansfield St
Santa Cruz, CA 95062
831-479-4495; FAX: 831-462-1517

Mail order and open shop. Monday-Friday 8 am to 5 pm. 22 years in the business serving British car owners. We sell and service Dayton and Dunlop wire wheels, hubs, adapters, knock-offs, conversions and related wheel care items for all wire wheeled cars. Tires too, both radial and bias-ply in many top brands: Avon, Dunlop, Michelin, Vredestein, plus others. Worldwide shipping of properly mounted and balanced tire and wheel assemblies, ready to put on your car. Web site: www.britishwirewheel.com

British Wiring Inc | wiring accessories wiring harnesses
20449 Ithaca Rd
Olympia Fields, IL 60461
PH/FAX: 708-481-9050

See full listing in **Section Two** under **electrical systems**

Cambridge Motorsport | parts race tuning
Caxton Rd
Great Gransden, NR Sandy
Beds SG19 3AH England
0044 1767 677969
FAX: 0044 1767 677026
E-mail:
cambridge.motorsport@dial.pipex.com

See full listing in **Section One** under **Triumph**

Classic Showcase | classic vehicles restorations
913 Rancheros Dr
San Marcos, CA 92069
760-747-9947, 760-747-3188 sales
FAX: 760-747-4021
E-mail:
management@classicshowcase.com

See full listing in **Section Two** under **car dealers**

Doug's British Car Parts | accessories parts
2487 E Colorado Blvd
Pasadena, CA 91107
818-793-2494; FAX: 818-793-4339

See full listing in **Section One** under **Jaguar**

Don Flye | parts
5 Doe Valley Rd
Petersham, MA 01366
978-724-3318

Mail order and open shop by appointment only. Specializing in British used parts for Austin-Healey 100-6 thru BJ8, Austin America, MG TD, A, Midget and B, Triumph TR3-TR6.

Fourintune Garage Inc | restoration
W63 N147 Washington Ave
Cedarburg, WI 53012
414-375-0876; FAX: 414-675-2874

Open shop. Monday-Friday 9 am to 5 pm CST. Specialize in Austin-Healey restoration. Can locate and restore to your specifications.

Harbor Auto Restoration | restoration
1504 SW 3rd St
Pompano Beach, FL 33069
954-785-7887; FAX: 954-785-7388
E-mail: harbor@harbor-auto.com

See full listing in **Section Two** under **restoration shops**

Healey Coop | parts restorations sales service
400 Harding St
Exeter, PA 18643
717-693-2248

Mail order and open shop. Monday-Friday 9 am to 5 pm, Saturday 8 am to 12 noon. For 100, 100-6, Mk I, Mk II, Mk III and 3000 models. Ground-up restorations, including acid dipped frames and lacquer painting.

Healey Lane | parts restoration service
5920 Jones Ave
Riverside, CA 92505
800-411-HEALEY (4325)
FAX: 909-689-4934
E-mail: healeylane@aol.com

Austin-Healey restoration, parts, service, sales for all years and Marks made 1953-1967.

Healey Surgeons Inc | parts restoration
7211 Carroll Ave
Takoma Park, MD 20912
301-270-8811; FAX: 301-270-8812

Mail order and open shop. Monday-Friday 9:30 am to 5 pm. Parts and restoration for Austin-Healey 100-4, 100-6, 3000, 1953-1967.

Heritage Motor Centre
Banbury Rd
Gaydon
Warwichshire CV35 0BJ England
01926 641188; FAX: 01926 641555

| | museum |

See full listing in **Section Six** under **England**

Heritage Upholstery and Trim
250 H St, Unit 8110
Blaine, WA 98231
604-990-0346; FAX: 604-990-9988

| interior kits |
| trim |
| upholstery |

Classic British car upholstery and trim using original materials, Connolly Leather, Wilton Wool. Interior kits to a very high standard. Concours show quality.

Jahns Quality Pistons
1360 N Jefferson St
Anaheim, CA 92807
714-579-3795, 800-225-0277
FAX: 714-524-6607

| piston rings |
| pistons |

See full listing in **Section Two** under **engine parts**

Lake Oswego Restorations
19621 S Hazelhurst Ln
West Linn, OR 97068
PH/FAX: 503-636-7503

| restoration |
| sales |

See full listing in **Section One** under **Aston Martin**

McLean's Brit Bits
14 Sagamore Rd
Rye, NH 03870
800-995-2487; FAX: 603-433-0009
E-mail: sam@britbits.com

| accessories |
| parts |
| sales |
| service |

See full listing in **Section One** under **MG**

Mini Mania
31 Winsor St
Milpitas, CA 95035
408-942-5595; FAX: 408-942-5582
E-mail: info@minimania.com

| parts |
| service |

See full listing in **Section One** under **Austin**

Mini Motors Classic Coachworks
2775 Cherry Ave NE
Salem, OR 97303
503-362-3187; FAX: 503-375-9609
E-mail: 104306,114@compuserv

| parts |
| restoration |
| sales |
| service |

Mail order and open shop. Monday-Friday 8 am to 5:30 pm, evening/weekend appointments available. Typically 15-20 restorations ongoing. Services: body fabrication, paint, interior, mechanical service, parts and sales, custom parts casting and manufacturing. In business for 20 years, specializing in British cars and other collectibles. Ask about our 5-speed transmission conversion for Sprite/Midgets and factory replica hardtops for Austin-Healey Mk I Sprites.

Moss Motors Ltd
PO Box 847
440 Rutherford St
Goleta, CA 93117
800-235-6954; FAX: 805-692-2525

| accessories |
| parts |

See full listing in **Section One** under **MG**

Motorhead Ltd
2811-B Old Lee Hwy
Fairfax, VA 22031
800-527-3140; FAX: 703-573-3195

| parts |
| repairs |

Parts, repairs and restoration of British sports cars. Please ask for parts catalogs on MGB, Sprite, Midget, Spitfire, TR6, TR250, TR7, TR8. Web site: motorheadltd.com

NOS Locators
587 Pawtucket Ave
Pawtucket, RI 02860
401-725-5000

| parts |

See full listing in **Section One** under **MG**

Omni Specialties
10418 Lorain Ave
Cleveland, OH 44111
888-819-6464 (MGMG)
216-251-2269; FAX: 216-251-6083

| parts |
| restoration |
| service |

See full listing in **Section One** under **MG**

Ragtops & Roadsters
203 S 4th St
Perkasie, PA 18944
215-257-1202; FAX: 215-257-2688
E-mail: info@ragtops.com

| bodywork/painting |
| British automobiles |
| engine rebuilding |
| vintage race prep |

See full listing in **Section Two** under **restoration shops**

Rogers Motors
25 Leverett Rd
Shutesbury, MA 01072
413-259-1722
E-mail: akor@ent.umass.edu

| used parts |

See full listing in **Section One** under **Jaguar**

Scarborough Faire Inc
1151 Main St
Pawtucket, RI 02860
800-556-6300, 401-724-4200
FAX: 401-724-5392

| parts |

See full listing in **Section One** under **MG**

Smooth Line
2562 Riddle Run Rd
Tarentum, PA 15084
724-274-6002; FAX: 724-274-6121

| body panels |
| removable hardtops |

See full listing in **Section Two** under **tops**

Sports Car Haven
2-33 Flowerfield Industrial Pk
St James, NY 11780
516-862-8058
E-mail: sch94@aol.com

| race prep |
| restorations |
| service |

See full listing in **Section One** under **Triumph**

Sports Car Haven
3414 Bloom Rd, Rt 11
Danville, PA 17821
570-275-5705

| parts |
| restoration |
| service |

See full listing in **Section One** under **MG**

Sports & Classics
PO Box 1787
512 Boston Post Rd, Dept H
Darien, CT 06820-1787

| parts |

See full listing in **Section Two** under **body parts**

The Registry
Pine Grove
Stanley, VA 22851
540-778-3728; FAX: 540-778-2402
E-mail: britregstry@aol.com or
oldwregistry@aol.com

| periodical |

See full listing in **Section Four** under **periodicals**

Triple C Motor Accessories
1900 Orange St
York, PA 17404
717-854-4081; FAX: 717-854-6706
E-mail: sales@triple-c.com

accessories
models

See full listing in **Section One** under **MG**

Victoria British Ltd
Box 14991
Lenexa, KS 66285-4991
800-255-0088, 913-599-3299

accessories
parts

See full listing in **Section One** under **MG**

Victory Autoservices
Box 5060, RR 1
W Baldwin, ME 04091
207-625-4581

parts
restoration

Mail order and open shop. Monday-Friday 8 am to 5 pm.
Restoration and parts for post WW II British cars, particularly
Austin-Healey, Jaguar, Alvis, MG, Triumph. Magneto ignitions
(new and used) is a specialty also.

Von's Austin-Healey Restorations
10270 Barberville Rd
Fort Mill, SC 29715
803-548-4590; FAX: 803-548-4816
E-mail: vons@vnet.net

parts
repairs
restoration

Mail order and open shop. Monday-Friday 8 am to 5 pm.
Specializing in Austin-Healey restoration, repair and service.
Also do mail-in repair service and parts sales. Although Austin-
Healey is our specialty, we do restore all British cars. Web site:
www.vonsaustinhealey.com

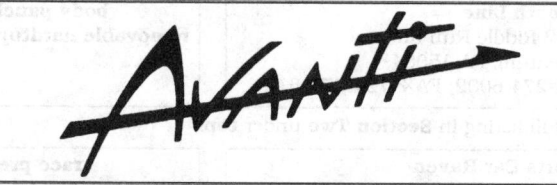

Avanti Auto Service
Rt 322, 67 Conchester Hwy
Glen Mills, PA 19342-1506
610-558-9999

repair
restoration

See full listing in **Section One** under **DeTomaso/Pantera**

Motorcar Gallery Inc
715 N Federal Hwy
Fort Lauderdale, FL 33304
954-522-9900; FAX: 954-522-9966

car dealer

See full listing in **Section One** under **Ferrari**

Nostalgic Motor Cars
47400 Avante Dr
Wixom, MI 48393
248-349-4884, 800-AVANTI-1
800-AVANTI-X; FAX: 248-349-0000

car dealer
parts

Mail order and open shop. Avanti dealer, cars and parts. World's
largest manufacturer and supplier of 1963-1985 Avanti parts.

Penn Auto Sales Co
Dr Roger Penn
7115 Leesburg Pike, #113
Falls Church, VA 22043
703-538-4388

car dealer
parts
service

Mail order and shop open by appointment only. Avanti sales. All
years. Avanti factory franchised dealer since 1970. Parts and
service, 1963-1991. Also will provide information on restoration
and parts.

Regal International Motor Cars Inc
PO Box 6819
Hollywood, FL 33081
305-989-9777; FAX: 305-989-9778

car dealer

See full listing in **Section One** under **Rolls-Royce/Bentley**

Southwest Avanti Sales & Service
7110 N Red Ledge Dr, Ste #147A
Phoenix, AZ 85253
PH/FAX: 602-948-7853
E-mail: wfsf602@aol.com

parts
repairs
sales

Mail order and open shop. Monday-Saturday 8 am to 6 pm.
Complete Avanti store. Sales, repairs, parts, restorations of all
Avantis, 1963-1991.

Studebaker Parts & Locations
228 Marquiss Cir
Clinton, TN 37716
615-457-3002
E-mail: studebaker_joe@msn.com

parts
parts locator

See full listing in **Section One** under **Studebaker**

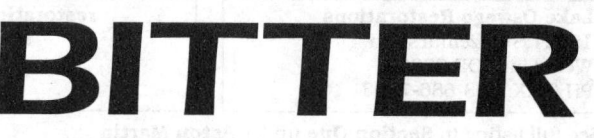

Ed Swart Motors Inc
2675 Skypark Dr Unit 104
Torrance, CA 90505
310-530-9715; FAX: 310-530-9786

cars
parts
restoration

Open shop. Monday-Friday 9 am to 6 pm. Specializing in sale of
auto parts and race car parts and restoration of Bitter automobiles and Chevron race cars.

Aase Bros Inc
701 E Cypress St
Anaheim, CA 92805
714-956-2419; FAX: 714-956-2635
E-mail: sales@aasebros.com

salvage yard

See full listing in **Section Five** under **California**

Asom Electric
1204 McClellan Dr
Los Angeles, CA 90025
310-820-4457; FAX: 310-820-5908

electrical systems
rebuilding

See full listing in **Section Two** under **electrical systems**

The Auto Doctor Inc
23125 Telegraph Rd
Southfield, MI 48034
248-355-1505, FAX: 248-355-3460

mechanical parts
service repairs

Mail order and open shop. Monday-Friday 7 am to 6 pm,
Saturday 9 am to 3 pm. Mechanical parts and service repairs for
BMW, Jaguars, Saab, Audi, VW and Porsche.

Bavarian Autosport
275 Constitution Ave
Portsmouth, NH 03801
800-535-2002; FAX: 800-507-2002

accessories
parts

Telephone orders: Monday-Thursday 8 am to 9 pm, Friday 8 am

to 7 pm, Saturday 9 am to 4 pm; catalog showroom open
Monday-Friday 9 am to 5:30 pm, Saturday 9 am to 4 pm. When
your BMW mechanic says he can't get it, chances are we can.
Our 3-story warehouse contains thousands of parts and accessories for 1600, 2002, 2800, 3.0, Bavaria and all others. Same
day shipping of in-stock items. FedEx 3-day Express Service is
standard. Free 100-page color catalog. Web site:
www.bavauto.com

BCP Sport & Classic Co 10525 Airline Dr Houston, TX 77037 281-448-4739; FAX: 281-448-0189	parts service

See full listing in **Section One** under **MG**

Bentley Publishers 1734 Massachusetts Ave Cambridge, MA 02138-1804 800-423-4595; FAX: 617-876-9235 E-mail: sales@rb.com	books manuals

See full listing in **Section Four** under **books & publications**

Best Deal 8171 Monroe St Stanton, CA 90680 800-354-9202; FAX: 714-995-5918 E-mail: bestdeal@deltnet.com	accessories parts

See full listing in **Section One** under **Porsche**

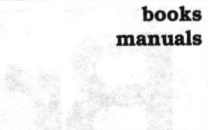

Bimmer Magazine 42 Digital Dr #5 Novato, CA 94949 415-382-0580; FAX: 415-382-0587	magazine

See full listing in **Section Four** under **periodicals**

Blitzen Enterprises Inc 8341 E Evans Rd, Suite 104 Scottsdale, AZ 85260 888-254-8936 toll-free FAX: 602-991-6301 E-mail: mbparts@blitzen.com	parts

See full listing in **Section One** under **Mercedes-Benz**

Concours Cars of Colorado Ltd 2414 W Cucharras St Colorado Springs, CO 80904 719-473-6288; FAX: 719-473-9206	accessories parts service

Concours Cars, established in 1978. Provides professional service, parts, select accessories and performance tuning on
European automobiles. We service all European cars from
Britain, Italy, Germany, Sweden and France. We are a Bosch
authorized service center and all our technicians are ASE Master
techs.

CSi 1100 S Raymond Ave, Suite H Fullerton, CA 92831 714-879-7955; FAX: 714-879-7310 E-mail: csila@compuserve.com	parts

Mail order and open shop. Monday-Friday 9 am to 6 pm.
Specializing in new and used parts, accessories for BMW and all
Japanese marques, of all years.

Dashboards Plus 336 Cottonwood Ave Hartland, WI 53029 800-221-8161; FAX: 414-367-9474	restoration parts wood dash overlays

See full listing in **Section One** under **Jaguar**

European Parts Specialists Ltd PO Box 6783 Santa Barbara, CA 93160 800-334-2749, 805-683-4020 FAX: 805-683-3689 E-mail: epsparts@impulse.net	accessories parts

See full listing in **Section One** under **Mercedes-Benz**

Foreign Motors West 253 N Main St Natick, MA 01760 508-655-5350; FAX: 508-651-0178	car sales

See full listing in **Section One** under **Rolls-Royce/Bentley**

Griot's Garage 3500-A 20th St E Tacoma, WA 98424 800-345-5789; FAX: 888-252-2252 E-mail: info@griotsgarage.com	car care products paint tools

See full listing in **Section Two** under **tools**

Hjeltness Restoration Inc 630 Alpine Way Escondido, CA 92029 760-746-9966; FAX: 760-746-7738	restoration service

See full listing in **Section Two** under **restoration shops**

JAM Engineering Corp PO Box 2570 Monterey, CA 93942 800-JAM-CORP, 831-372-1787 E-mail: jam@redshift.com	carburetors

See full listing in **Section Two** under **carburetors**

Maximillian Importing Co PO Box 749 Parkton, MD 21120 800-950-2002; FAX: 410-357-0298 E-mail: max2002cs@aol.com	parts

Mail order. New, used and reproduction parts for classic BMW
models from 1928-present. Specialist in the 2002, 3.0 CS,
Bavaria models, as well as seemingly unique/hard to find parts.

Motorcars Ltd 8101 Hempstead Houston, TX 77008 800-231-6563; FAX: 713-863-8238 E-mail: info@britishparts.com	parts

See full listing in **Section One** under **Jaguar**

Motorcycle Hall of Fame Museum 13515 Yarmouth Dr Pickerington, OH 43147 614-882-2782 info 614-856-1900 office FAX: 614-856-1920 E-mail: afitch@ama-cycle.org	museum

See full listing in **Section Six** under **Ohio**

Northern Motorsport Ltd PO Box 508, Rt 5 Wilder, VT 05088 802-296-2099; FAX: 802-295-6599	repair restoration sales service

See full listing in **Section Two** under **restoration shops**

Ottorich 619 Hammond St Chestnut Hill, MA 02467 617-738-5488 E-mail: rdmfm@mediaone.net	restoration

See full listing in **Section One** under **Mercedes-Benz**

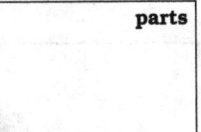

Paul Padget
7641 Reinhold Dr
Cincinnati, OH 45237
513-821-2143

sales

See full listing in **Section One** under **Mercedes-Benz**

Peninsula Imports
3749 Harlem Rd
Buffalo, NY 14215
800-999-1209; FAX: 905-847-3021
E-mail: imports@ican.net

accessories
parts
trim

Mail order and open shop. Monday-Friday 8 am to 5:30 pm,
Saturday 8 am to 2 pm. We specialize in distribution of hard
parts, accessories and trim, including starters, alternators,
European lighting, Weber carburetors, ignition, fuel system,
exhaust, gaskets, filters, radiators, rubber parts, steering
wheels, suspension, tops, bras, car covers, transmissions,
engines, cams, pistons, bearings, brakes, clutch and hydraulic
parts, carpet kits, interior panels, body panels, glass, etc. For
Audi, BMW, Mercedes, VW, Porsche, Saab, Volvo, MG, Triumph,
Jaguar, Alfa Romeo, Fiat, Ferrari, Lamborghini, Maserati,
Honda, Mazda, Hyundai, Toyota, Mitsubishi, Nissan, etc. Web
site: www.peninsulaimports.com

John T Poulin
Auto Sales/Star Service Center
5th Ave & 111th St
North Troy, NY 12182
518-235-8610

car dealer
parts
restoration service

See full listing in **Section One** under **Mercedes-Benz**

Replicarz
99 State St
Rutland, VT 05701
802-747-7151
E-mail: replicarz@aol.com

books
kits
models
videos

See full listing in **Section Two** under **racing**

Restoration Services
16049 W 4th Ave
Golden, CO 80401
303-271-0356

restoration

See full listing in **Section One** under **Porsche**

Paul Russell & Company
106 Western Ave
Essex, MA 01929
978-768-6919; FAX: 978-768-3523
E-mail: info@paulrussellandco.com

car dealer
mechanical service
parts
restoration

See full listing in **Section Two** under **restoration shops**

Vintage Auto Parts
PO Box 323
Temple, PA 19560-0323
610-939-9593

car dealer
new/used parts

Mail order or by special appointment. 10 am to noon, 5 pm to 7
pm, answering machine. Specializing in BMW 300, 600 and 700,
Crosley, Corvair, Citicar (EV), Fiat 500 and 600, Honda 600 and
Civic, 1950 Jeepster, Metro, NSU, Panhard, Subaru 360, VW II,
III, IV and 181 and LeCar. Also Zundapp cycle and NSU.
Thousands of new parts for Subaru 360 cars. SASE for info. 100
vehicles, restore or parts, no list. Plan on selling out by end of
1999, including lot, available offers over $75,000.

Willow Automotive Service Inc
29870 Hwy 41
Lake Bluff, IL 60044
847-785-8080; FAX: 847-785-8106

sales
service

See full listing in **Section One** under **Mercedes-Benz**

J Wood & Co Auctioneers
RR 1 Box 316
Stockton Springs, ME 04981
207-567-4250; FAX: 207-567-4252
E-mail: jwoodandco@mindspring.com

auctions

See full listing in **Section Two** under **auctions & events**

World Upholstery & Trim
PO Box 2420
Camarillo, CA 93011
805-988-1848; FAX: 805-278-7886
E-mail: worlduph@mail.vcnet.com

carpet
tops
upholstery kits

See full listing in **Section Two** under **interiors & interior parts**

Bricklin

Bob's Brickyard Inc
1030 N Hickory Ridge Tr
Milford, MI 48380
248-685-9508; FAX: 248-685-8662
E-mail: bobsbrick@aol.com

parts

Mail order parts and total restoration. Specialize in Bricklin
parts and service. Free parts list.

Bricklin Literature
3116 Welsh Rd
Philadelphia, PA 19136-1810
215-338-6142
E-mail: bricklin.literature@excite.com

collectibles
literature

Mail order only. Carry a variety of collectible items such as literature, books, toys, magazines, video and other unique items
related to the Canadian made Bricklin automobile made during
1974-1976. Please send a SASE for a complete listing of items
available. All items guaranteed for satisfaction. Web site:
www.inc.com/users/bricklin.html

The Gullwing Garage Ltd
Bricklin SVI Specialists
5 Cimorelli Dr
New Windsor, NY 12553-6201
914-561-0019 anytime

appraisals
literature
parts
service

Telephone calls accepted until 10 pm, 7 days a week. Parts service, appraisals, prepurchase assistance literature for Bricklin
SVI, 1974-1975-1976. Over 7,000 original genuine Bricklin parts
(1974-1975-1976) with access to thousands more. Aftermarket
items such as: consoles, carpet sets, seat covers, fiberglass panels, air scoops, ground affects, gas shocks, antennas, radios,
wheels, s/s exhaust pipes. Specializing in air door systems,
headlight systems and door glass track system repairs. Prompt,
personal, friendly service. Will travel to repair your Bricklin.

Auto Europa
221 Berrellesa St
Martinez, CA 94553
925-229-3466; FAX: 925-313-0542

painting
restorations
woodworking

See full listing in **Section Two** under **restoration shops**

Blackhawk Collection	acquisitions
1092 Eagles Nest Pl	sales
Danville, CA 94506-3600	
925-736-3444; FAX: 925-736-4375	
E-mail: info@blackhawkcollection.com	

See full listing in **Section One** under **Duesenberg**

Charles S Crail Automobiles	auto sales
36A Calle Cesar Chavez	
Santa Barbara, CA 93103	
805-568-1934; FAX: 805-568-1533	

See full listing in **Section One** under **Rolls-Royce/Bentley**

Paul Foulkes-Halbard	brass age cars
Filching Wannock Eastbourne	parts
Polegate	
Sussex BN26 5QA England	
011 441323 487838	
011 441323 487124	
FAX: 011 441323 486331	

Specializing in Bugatti and related vehicles and brass age cars.
Maker of alloy wheels and many related parts for Bugatti and
other makes, all years. Anything before 1950.

Guild of Automotive Restorers	restoration
PO Box 1150	sales
44 Bridge St	service
Bradford, ON Canada L3Z 2B5	
905-775-0499; FAX: 905-775-0944	
E-mail:	
webmaster@guildautomotive.on.ca	

See full listing in **Section Two** under **restoration shops**

LMARR Disk Ltd	wheel discs
PO Box 910	
Glen Ellen, CA 95442-0910	
707-938-9347; FAX: 707-938-3020	
E-mail: lmarr@ibm.net	

See full listing in **Section One** under **Rolls-Royce/Bentley**

Midbanc Financial Services	financing
PO Box 20402	
Columbus, OH 43220	
614-442-7701; FAX: 614-442-7704	
E-mail: patricia@midbanc.com	

See full listing in **Section Two** under **financing**

Northern Motorsport Ltd	repair
PO Box 508, Rt 5	restoration
Wilder, VT 05088	sales
802-296-2099; FAX: 802-295-6599	service

See full listing in **Section Two** under **restoration shops**

Paul Russell & Company	car dealer
106 Western Ave	mechanical service
Essex, MA 01929	parts
978-768-6919; FAX: 978-768-3523	restoration
E-mail: info@paulrussellandco.com	

See full listing in **Section Two** under **restoration shops**

Valley Wire Wheel Service	wheel restoration
14731 Lull St	wheels
Van Nuys, CA 91405	
818-785-7237; FAX: 818-994-2042	

See full listing in **Section Two** under **wheels & wheelcovers**

Viking Worldwise Inc	leather jackets
190 Doe Run Rd	
Manheim, PA 17545	
800-842-9198; FAX: 717-664-5556	
E-mail: gkurien@success.net	

See full listing in **Section Two** under **apparel**

120 Thornton Drive, Hyannis, MA 02601
- *Sales:* (508) 790-2566
- *Restorations:* (508) 775-8131
- *Fax:* (508) 790-2339

Located in picturesque Cape Cod, Massachusetts, Hyannis Restoration has been in the business of restoration and sales of all marque automobiles for over twenty years. Awards have been given from the world famous Pebble Beach Concours in California to the prestigious Louis Vuitton Concours at Bagatelle, in France.

The Amster family (Bruce, Gary, and their father Sonnie), along with twenty other dedicated employees, does every aspect in connection with the restoration of automobiles. Their knowledge of the pre-1900's to the present both gasoline and electric powered autos have made Hyannis Restoration world known for our diversity in handling any marque restoration needed.

Brady Ward-Scale Autoworks	models
313 Bridge St #4	
Manchester, NH 03104-5045	
603-623-5925	
FAX: 603-623-5925 ext 66	
E-mail: bradyward@mediaone.net	

See full listing in **Section Two** under **models & toys**

Antique & Classic Cars Inc	bodywork
328 S 3rd St	machine work
Hamilton, OH 45011	painting
513-844-1146 in OH	parts
800-798-3982 nationwide	service

Mail order and open shop. Monday-Friday 9 am to 5:30 pm.
Services Cadillacs, Packards, Oldsmobiles and Buicks, have a
machine shop for engines and drivetrain, will replace rings and
grind valves, also can machine parts for old cars. Complete paint
and body shop and frame straightening. Also will look for parts
for old and unusual cars. Sales of classic cars and some vintage
automobiles. Will try and find special classic cars for collectors.

Art's Antique & Classic Auto Services	restoration
1985 E 5th St #16	
Tempe, AZ 85281	
602-966-1195	

Open Monday-Friday 9 am to 5 pm, Saturday 10 am to 3 pm.
Restoration of Buick cars, 1950s and 1960s. Also other GM cars.

Bicknell Engine Company	**parts**
7055 Dayton Rd	**repair**
Enon, OH 45323	**restoration**
937-864-5224	

Mail order and open shop. Evenings and weekends only. Repair service for antique, classic and special interest cars. Specializing in Buicks and independent make cars from the 1920s-1950s. Services include: engine rebuilding, transmission rebuilding (manual and automatic), any mechanical or electrical work. Buick parts, mostly used, some NOS. Appraisal service.

Bill's Speed Shop	**body parts**
13951 Millersburg Rd	
Navarre, OH 44662	
330-832-9403; FAX: 330-832-2098	

See full listing in **Section One** under **Chevrolet**

Bob's Automobilia	**accessories**
Box 2119	**parts**
Atascadero, CA 93423	
805-434-2963; FAX: 805-434-2626	
E-mail: bobsbuick@thegrid.net	

Mail order only. 1920-1956 Buick parts, accessories, manuals, hubcaps, hood ornaments, floor mats. Electrical, rubber, trunk lenses. Catalog available.

Boyer's Restorations	**parts**
Skip Boyer	**repairs**
1348 Carlisle Pike	**restorations**
Hanover, PA 17331	
717-632-0670	

Mail order and open shop by appointment only. Exclusively Buick parts, new and used as well as reproductions, servicing primarily 1937-1974. Manifolds and machine turned dashes a specialty, as well as interior plastic parts, 1937-1950. 1940-1942 Buick dash restorations and partial restorations and repairs for 1937-1974.

Buick Bonery	**parts**
6970 Stamper Way	
Sacramento, CA 95828	
916-381-5271; FAX: 916-381-0702	

Mail order and open shop. Monday-Friday before 9 am and after 12 noon PST. Specializing in Buick new, used and repro parts. Full scope stainless restoration for any make. 150+ parts Buicks, 1936-1975. Restored and better Buicks warehoused.

The Buick Nut-Joe Krepps	**repro parts**
2486 Pacer Ln S	
Cocoa, FL 32926-2606	
PH/FAX: 407-636-8777	
E-mail: buicknut@palmnet.net	

Mail order. Reproductions 1928-1955. Specializing in 1940-1947 instrument plastics and 1929-1935 high speed differential gears.

Buick Specialists	**parts**
1311 S Central Ave #G	
Kent, WA 98064	
253-852-0584; FAX: 253-854-7520	

Mail order and open shop. Specialists in 1946-1979 Buicks. New, used and NOS parts for all models.

Cape Cod Classic Cars	**car dealer**
Pete Harvey	
PO Box 280	
Cataumet, MA 02534	
508-548-0660; FAX: 508-457-0660	

See full listing in **Section One** under **Cadillac/LaSalle**

Chevrolet Parts Obsolete	**accessories**
PO Box 0740	**parts**
Murrieta, CA 92564-0740	
909-279-2833; FAX: 909-279-4013	
E-mail: spo@att.net	

See full listing in **Section One** under **Chevrolet**

Chief Service	**parts**
Herbert G Baschung	**restoration**
Brunnmatt, PO Box 155	
CH-4914 Roggwil Switzerland	
PH/FAX: 0041-62-9291777	

See full listing in **Section Two** under **restoration shops**

Chrome Masters	**chrome plating**
1109 W Orange Ave, Unit D	**pot metal restoration**
Tallahassee, FL 32310	
850-576-2100; FAX: 850-576-2772	

See full listing in **Section Two** under **plating & polishing**

Clark's Corvair Parts Inc	**carpets**
Rt 2, #400 Mohawk Tr	**headliners**
Shelburne Falls, MA 01370	**upholstery**
413-625-9776; FAX: 413-625-8498	**weatherstrips**
E-mail: clarks@corvair.com	

Request our free 24 page catalog of 1963-1965 Buick Riviera upholstery and interior items. Also weatherstrips and rubber parts. Web site: www.corvair.com
See our ad on page 55

Classic and Muscle	**reproduction parts**
Muscle Car Restoration Parts	**restoration parts**
PO Box 657	
Elmsdale, NS Canada B0N 1M0	
902-883-4489; FAX: 902-883-1392	
E-mail: classicmuscle@sprint.ca	

See full listing in **Section One** under **Chevrolet**

Classic Buicks Inc	**custom parts**
4632 Riverside Dr	**high-performance**
Chino, CA 91710-3926	**parts**
909-591-0283; FAX: 909-627-6094	**literature**

Mail order and open shop. Monday-Friday 8 am to 5 pm,

Saturday 8 am to 11:30 am. Specializing in parts and literature for 1946-1975 Buicks. Our specialty is quality USA made engine and high-performance, rubber and weatherstrips, brake, chassis, carpets and restoration parts. Web site: www.classicbuicks.com

Classic Car Works Ltd	restoration
3050 Upper Bethany Rd	
Jasper, GA 30143	
770-735-3945	

See full listing in **Section Two** under **restoration shops**

The Clockworks	clock service
1745 Meta Lake Ln	
Eagle River, WI 54521	
800-398-3040; FAX: 715-479-5759	
E-mail: clockworks@juno.com	

See full listing in **Section Two** under **instruments**

JA Cooley Museum	museum
4233 Park Blvd	
San Diego, CA 92103	
619-296-3112	

See full listing in **Section Six** under **California**

Coopers Vintage Auto Parts	parts
3087 N California St	
Burbank, CA 91504	
818-567-4140; FAX: 818-567-4101	

See full listing in **Section One** under **Cadillac/LaSalle**

CR Plastics Inc	bumper filler parts
2790 NE 7th Ave	
Pompano Beach, FL 33064	
800-551-3155	

See full listing in **Section One** under **Cadillac/LaSalle**

Glenn Curtiss Museum	museum
8419 St Rt 54	
Hammondsport, NY 14840	
607-569-2160; FAX: 607-569-2040	

See full listing in **Section Six** under **New York**

JB Donaldson Co	castings
2533 W Cypress	steering wheels
Phoenix, AZ 85009	wood parts
602-278-4505; FAX: 602-278-1112	

See full listing in **Section Two** under **steering wheels**

Durabuilt Automotive Hydraulics	hose assemblies
808 Meadows Ave	pumps
Canon City, CO 81212	top cylinders
PH/FAX: 719-275-1126	valves
E-mail: durabuilt@ris.net	

See full listing in **Section Two** under **tops**

Egge Machine Company Inc	bearings
11707 Slauson Ave	pistons/rings
Santa Fe Springs, CA 90670	timing components
800-866-EGGE, 562-945-3419	valve train
FAX: 562-693-1635	
E-mail: info@egge.com	

See full listing in **Section Two** under **engine parts**

Elliott's Car Radio	radio repairs
313 Linfield Rd	speaker kits
Parkerford, PA 19457	
610-495-6360; FAX: 610-495-7723	

See full listing in **Section Two** under **radios**

Faxon Auto Literature	literature
3901 Carter Ave	manuals
Riverside, CA 92501	
800-458-2734; FAX: 909-786-4166	

See full listing in **Section Two** under **literature dealers**

GM Obsolete	parts
909 W Magnolia St	
Phoenix, AZ 85007	
602-253-8081; FAX: 602-253-8411	
E-mail: info@gmobsolete.com	

Mail order and open shop. Monday-Friday 8 am to 6 pm, Saturday 9 am to 2 pm. Specializing in Buick, Oldsmobile and Cadillac parts, 1950-1990. Web site: www.gmobsolete.com

Green Valentine Inc	car dealer
5055 Covington Way	woodies
Memphis, TN 38134	
901-373-5555; FAX: 901-373-5568	

See full listing in **Section Two** under **car dealers**

Hamel's Automotive Inc	restorations
RR 2 Box 61	
Wingdale, NY 12594	
914-832-9454	
E-mail: startnagan@aol.com	

See full listing in **Section Two** under **restoration shops**

Hampton Coach Inc	fabrics
6 Chestnut St	top kits
PO Box 6	upholstery kits
Amesbury, MA 01913	
888-388-8726, 978-388-8047	
FAX: 978-388-1113	
E-mail: lbb-hc@greennet.net	

See full listing in **Section One** under **Chevrolet**

Harbor Auto Restoration	restoration
1504 SW 3rd St	
Pompano Beach, FL 33069	
954-785-7887; FAX: 954-785-7388	
E-mail: harbor@harbor-auto.com	

See full listing in **Section Two** under **restoration shops**

Harnesses Unlimited	wiring harnesses
PO Box 435	wiring supplies
Wayne, PA 19087	
610-688-3998	

See full listing in **Section Two** under **electrical systems**

Inline Tube	brake lines/cables
33783 Groes Beck Hwy	choke tubes
Fraser, MI 48026	flex brake hoses
800-385-9452 order	fuel/vacuum lines
810-294-4093 tech	transmission lines
FAX: 810-294-7349	
E-mail: kryta@aol.com	

See full listing in **Section Two** under **brakes**

Integrity Machine	brake masters
383 Pipe Stave Hollow Rd	clutch masters
Mount Sinai, NY 11766	wheel cylinders
888-446-9670; FAX: 516-476-9675	

See full listing in **Section Two** under **brakes**

J & C's Parts	parts
7127 Ward Rd	
North Tonawanda, NY 14120	
716-693-4090; FAX: 716-695-7144	

Offer new and used 1953-1976 Buick stock and high-performance engine parts and services to include engine, carburetor, and distributor rebuilding. Also new and used restoration parts are available for 1965-1976 Buicks. Offer distributors and carburetors for 1953-1974 GM, Chrysler and Ford cars to include popular and hard-to-find numbers. Electronic ignition conversion service and kits available. ROA, GSCA, BCA member.

JECC Inc PO Box 616 West Paterson, NJ 07424 973-890-9682; FAX: 973-812-2724	**chassis parts** **gaskets** **transmissions**

Mail order only. Specializing in torque ball seal kits, transmission gaskets and seal kits for Buicks 1934-1960. Revulcanizing torque balls for 1939 Buicks. U-joint seal kits for Chevys 1929-1954. Packard flywheel ring gears (new), 1937-1953.

Jerry's Automotive c/o Jerry Cinotti 431 S Sierra Way San Bernadino, CA 92408 909-884-6980; FAX: 909-884-7872	**brake repair**

See full listing in **Section Two** under **brakes**

K&W Kollectibles 220 Industrial Pkwy S #6 Aurora ON Canada L4G 3V6 416-410-7741; FAX: 905-727-5771 E-mail: kwkoll@sympatico.ca	**parts** **repair** **restoration**

Mail order and open shop by appointment. Parts, repair, restoration for 1963-1965 Riviera, Skylark. Web site: www3.sympatico.ca/kwkoll

Lares Manufacturing 13517 Hwy 65 NE Ham Lake, MN 55304 800-334-5749; FAX: 612-754-2853 E-mail: sales@larescorp.com	**power steering** **equipment**

See full listing in **Section One** under **Ford 1954-up**

Lectric Limited Inc 7322 S Archer Road Justice, IL 60458 708-563-0400; FAX: 708-458-2662	**parts**

See full listing in **Section One** under **Corvette**

Legendary Auto Interiors Ltd 121 W Shore Blvd Newark, NY 14513 800-363-8804 FAX: 800-SEAT-UPH (732-8874)	**soft trim**

See full listing in **Section One** under **Chrysler**

Lloyd's Literature PO Box 491 Newbury, OH 44065 800-292-2665, 440-338-1527 FAX: 440-338-2222	**literature**

See full listing in **Section Two** under **literature dealers**

M & H Electric Fabricators Inc 13537 Alondra Blvd Santa Fe Springs, CA 90670 562-926-9552; FAX: 562-926-9572 E-mail: sales@wiringharness.com	**wiring harnesses**

See full listing in **Section Two** under **electrical systems**

Motor Foundry & Tooling Inc 7382 Doniphan Dr Canutillo, TX 79835-6601 915-877-3343; FAX: 915-877-7071	**brake drums** **castings** **exhaust manifolds** **water pumps**

See full listing in **Section One** under **Packard**

Normans' Classic Auto Radio 7651 Park Blvd Pinellas Park, FL 33781 888-222-3433, 727-546-1788	**custom sales**

See full listing in **Section Two** under **radios**

Opel GT Source 18211 Zeni Ln Tuolumne, CA 95379 209-928-1110; FAX: 209-928-3298 E-mail: opelgts@opelgtsource.com	**parts** **service** **technical info**

See full listing in **Section One** under **Opel**

Opels Unlimited 871 E Lambert Rd #C La Habra, CA 90631 562-690-1051; FAX: 562-690-3352 E-mail: opelsunl@opelsunl.com	**parts** **service**

See full listing in **Section One** under **Opel**

Dennis Portka 4326 Beetow Dr Hamburg, NY 14075 716-649-0921	**horns** **knock-off wheels**

See full listing in **Section One** under **Corvette**

Precision Pot Metal/Bussie Restoration Inc 1008 Loring Ave #28 Orange Park, FL 32073 904-269-8788	**pot metal** **restoration**

See full listing in **Section Two** under **plating & polishing**

Raine Automotive Springs Warehouse 425 Harding Hwy Carney's Point, NJ 08069 609-299-9141; FAX: 609-299-9157	**springs** **suspension parts**

See full listing in **Section Two** under **suspension parts**

REM Automotive Inc 2610 N Brandt Rd Annville, PA 17003 717-838-4242; FAX: 717-838-5091	**interior parts** **trunk lining**

See full listing in **Section Two** under **restoration aids**

Robertson Bros & Sons Restoration PO Box 5678 Sevierville, TN 37864-5678 423-970-1655; FAX: 423-908-6838 E-mail: classicbop@aol.com	**NOS parts** **restoration parts** **used parts**

See full listing in **Section One** under **Oldsmobile**

Harry Samuel 65 Wisner St Pontiac, MI 48342-1066 248-335-1900 E-mail: hsamuel1@aol.com	**carpet** **fabrics** **interiors** **upholstery covers**

See full listing in **Section Two** under **interiors & interior parts**

E J Serafin Valley Rd Matinecock, NY 11560	**manuals**

See full listing in **Section One** under **Cadillac/LaSalle**

Special Auto Restoration 689 Fern Dr Merritt Island, FL 32952 407-453-8343, 407-783-4758	**restoration**

See full listing in **Section One** under **Chevelle/Camaro**

Tags Backeast PO Box 581 Plainville, CT 06062 860-747-2942 E-mail: dataplt@snet.net	**data plates** **trim tags**

See full listing in **Section Two** under **special services**

Tom's Classic Parts 5207 Sundew Terr Tobyhanna, PA 18466 800-832-4073	**parts**

See full listing in **Section One** under **Chevrolet**

Howard Whitelaw 29249 Bolingbrook Rd Pepper Pike, OH 44124 216-721-6755 days 216-464-2159 evenings & weekends FAX: 216-721-6758 E-mail: howardwhitelaw@prodigy.net	**fenders**

See full listing in **Section One** under **Mopar**

AAAC-Antique Automobile Appraisal & Consulting PO Box 700153 Plymouth, MI 48170 PH/FAX: 734-453-7644 E-mail: aaac@ameritech.net	**appraisals Cadillac parts consulting**

Mail order and open shop by appointment. Cadillac parts from 1953-1970 including some NOS. Specializing in 1957-1960. Appraisal and consulting service by appointment for antique, custom and special interest vehicles. Detailed and comprehensive reports with 35mm photographs. Appraisals accepted by major insurance companies. Also service for sellers, buyers, divorce, estate settlement, loans and charitable contributions. Over twenty years in the old car hobby.

Aabar's Cadillac & Lincoln Salvage & Parts 9700 NE 23rd Oklahoma City, OK 73141 405-769-3318; FAX: 405-769-9542 E-mail: louanne1@juno.com	**parts**

Open Monday-Friday 9 am to 5:30 pm, some Saturdays 9 am to 12 pm. Mainly used parts but some NOS and NORS. 600 Cadillac cars standing, 1939-1994, and 300 Lincoln cars standing, 1941-1994, plus many parts off. Satisfaction guaranteed. Credit cards accepted. Free advice anytime. If you write, send SASE or no negative answers.

Dennis Akerman 19 Gulf Rd Box 107 Sanbornton, NH 03269 800-487-3903; FAX: 603-286-2761 E-mail: dennis@caddyparts.com	**literature parts**

Open shop by appointment. New and used Cadillac parts and literature, 1937-1976. Call, e-mail or fax your requirements. Visa/MC. Fast, courteous service. Ship worldwide. Web site: www.caddyparts.com

Antique Auto Battery 2320 Old Mill Rd Hudson, OH 44236 800-426-7580, 330-425-2395 FAX: 330-425-4642 E-mail: sales@antiqueautobattery.com	**batteries battery cables**

See full listing in **Section Two** under **batteries**

Antique & Classic Cars 1796 County Rd 7 Florence, AL 35633 205-760-0542	**car locator**

Mail order only. I find antique and classic cars for a finders' fee.

My minimum fee is $150 or 3% of the purchase price and $25 deposit for pictures and postage.

Archive Replacement Parts 211 Cinnaminson Ave Palmyra, NJ 08065 609-786-0247	**parts**

Mail order only. Stainless steel water outlet replacements for 1936-1948 flathead V8 Cadillac/LaSalle.

Art's Antique & Classic Auto Services 1985 E 5th St #16 Tempe, AZ 85281 602-966-1195	**restoration**

See full listing in **Section One** under **Buick/McLaughlin**

Auto Advisors 14 Dudley Rd Billerica, MA 01821 978-667-0075	**appraisals**

See full listing in **Section Two** under **appraisals**

Auto Europa 221 Berrellesa St Martinez, CA 94553 925-229-3466; FAX: 925-313-0542	**painting restorations woodworking**

See full listing in **Section Two** under **restoration shops**

Automobile Appraisal Service Steve Cram 1080 Eddy St #607 San Francisco, CA 94109 415-567-1087, 619-584-4678 FAX: 415-567-1245	**appraisals**

See full listing in **Section Two** under **appraisals**

C E Babcock 619 Waterside Way Sarasota, FL 34242 941-349-4990	**1941, 1942, 1946, 1947 Cadillac parts**

A+ 1941-1947 Cadillac parts (all models): NOS, gently used and remanufactured parts (specialist). 35 years hobbyist accumulation (over 10,000 items) available. Exclusive exact reproduction of 8 pc floorboards, body braces, trunk floors, inner splash guards, stainless and chrome trim parts, battery boxes, rocker panels, special rocker clip, horn parts, large or small, I will assist you or advise. This is not a junk yard. Most parts have been on dry shelves for several years.

Be Happy Automatic Transmission Parts 414 Stivers Rd Hillsboro, OH 45133 800-416-2862; FAX: 937-442-6133	**trans rebuild kits**

See full listing in **Section Two** under **transmissions**

Binder's Auto Restoration and Salvage PO Box 1144 1 Mile Maud Rd Palmer, AK 99645 907-745-4670; FAX: 907-745-5510	**salvage yard**

See full listing in **Section Five** under **Alaska**

Caddy Central 11117 Tippett Rd Clinton, MD 20735 301-234-0135; FAX: 301-234-0140 E-mail: cadlocator@aol.com	**cars locating service parts**

One stop shopping for Cadillacs, 1956-1970. Huge selection of bumpers and body parts in dry storage. Specializing in consolidation of orders for cheaper overseas delivery. Honest and reliable. Locating service also available.

Caddytown™/Pawl Engineering Co | memorabilia parts toys
4960 Arrowhead
PO Box 240105
West Bloomfield, MI 48324
PH/FAX: 248-682-2007
E-mail: pawl@earthlink.net

Mail order only. Specializing in Cadillac memorabilia, parts, toys, specialties, especially 1973 Cadillac Eldorado Indy pace car, decals, registry, authenticity. All years of special built Cadillacs, limos, celebrity cars.

Cadillac Crazy | parts
687 N Loudoun St
Winchester, VA 22601
540-665-2027

Mail order and open shop. Monday-Saturday 9 am to 6 pm, Sunday by appointment. We sell used and NOS mechanical, body, trim, etc. parts for 1963-1978 Cadillacs. Specializing in the 1967-1978 Eldorado. We also keep some cars for sale in good restorable condition.

Cadillac International | chrome interiors moldings sheetmetal
32 Kinney St
Piermont, NY 10968
914-365-8290; FAX: 914-398-0085
E-mail: cadintl@aol.com

Mail order and open shop by appointment only. Specializing in Cadillac parts and restoration services for 1940s-1990s. Rust-free sheetmetal, moldings, chrome, interiors, rubber repro parts, rebuilt power brake units, new floor pans, etc.

Cadillac Motor Books | books
PO Box 7
Temple City, CA 91780
626-445-1618

Mail order only. Publishers of *Cadillacs of the Forties*, *Guide to*

Cadillac 1950-1959, *Cadillacs of the Sixties*, plus other Cadillac/LaSalle hardcover books. Also reprints of rare sales catalogs from the classic era. Send for complete list and information.

Cadillac Parts & Cars Limited | car dealer literature parts
46 Hardy
Sparks, NV 89431
775-826-8363

Mail order and open shop. Any day by appointment, 8 am to 8 pm. Offers new and good used and reproduction 1938-1980 Cadillac parts, manuals, literature and collector cars for sale. Presently have 8,000 square foot facility for parts and maintain 15-20 collector car inventory of extra clean, low mileage cars.

California Collectors' Classics (CCC) | parts restoration
PO Box 2281
Irwindale, CA 91706
818-962-6696

Mail order and open shop. Specializing in restoration, parts, rebuilding of most major components for Cadillac, Lincoln and Thunderbird 1961-1985. Parts, restoration and service by appointment. Mail order sales, locating and inspection for buyer and seller of cars for sale.

Cape Cod Classic Cars | car dealer
Pete Harvey
PO Box 280
Cataumet, MA 02534
508-548-0660; FAX: 508-457-0660

Open shop by appointment only. Quality collector cars only in good condition for 1930-1970 big cars as Cadillac, Packard, Buick. Also classic mahogany runabouts 1920-1960. Complete good condition collector. No parts.

Chevrolet Parts Obsolete | accessories parts
PO Box 0740
Murrieta, CA 92564-0740
909-279-2833; FAX: 909-279-4013
E-mail: spo@att.net

See full listing in **Section One** under **Chevrolet**

Chewning's Auto Literature | literature manuals
2011 Elm Tree Terr
Buford, GA 30518
770-945-9795

See full listing in **Section Two** under **literature dealers**

Ed Cholakian Enterprises Inc | museum parts
dba All Cadillacs of the 40's and 50's
12811 Foothill Blvd
Sylmar, CA 91342
800-808-1147, 818-361-1147
FAX: 818-361-9738

Mail order and open shop. Monday-Friday 8 am to 5:30 pm, weekends by appointment. Specializing in parts and service for all Cadillacs, 1940-1958. Museum open year round, Monday-Friday 8 am to 5:30 pm. 60 Cadillacs from 1940-1958 on display. Many of the cars have been used in movies or on the Discovery Channel and TNN.
See our ad on page 627

Chrome Masters | chrome plating pot metal restoration
1109 W Orange Ave, Unit D
Tallahassee, FL 32310
850-576-2100; FAX: 850-576-2772

See full listing in **Section Two** under **plating & polishing**

Classic Auto Air Mfg Co | air conditioning heating parts
2020 W Kennedy Blvd
Tampa, FL 33606
813-251-2356, 813-251-4994

See full listing in **Section One** under **Mustang**

The Clockworks	clock service
1745 Meta Lake Ln	
Eagle River, WI 54521	
800-398-3040; FAX: 715-479-5759	
E-mail: clockworks@juno.com	

See full listing in **Section Two** under **instruments**

Convertible Service	convertible parts
5126-HA Walnut Grove Ave	manufacture/service
San Gabriel, CA 91776	top mechanism
800-333-1140, 626-285-2255	
FAX: 626-285-9004	

See full listing in **Section Two** under **tops**

JA Cooley Museum	museum
4233 Park Blvd	
San Diego, CA 92103	
619-296-3112	

See full listing in **Section Six** under **California**

Coopers Vintage Auto Parts	parts
3087 N California St	
Burbank, CA 91504	
818-567-4140; FAX: 818-567-4101	

Mail order and open shop. Monday-Friday 8:30 am to 5:30 pm, Saturday 8:30 am to 4 pm. Large inventory of new and used parts for GM cars. Full stock of weatherstripping, mechanical, brake, suspension, trim, manuals, carpet sets, etc.

The Copper Cooling Works	radiators
2455 N 2550 E	
Layton, UT 84040	
801-544-9939	

See full listing in **Section Two** under **radiators**

CR Plastics Inc	bumper filler parts
2790 NE 7th Ave	
Pompano Beach, FL 33064	
800-551-3155	

Specializing in bumper filler parts, also known as extensions, for Cadillac 1977-1992, rear for Coupe deVille, Sedan deVille, Fleetwood, rear wheel drive. Cadillac Eldorado 1975-1985 front and rear. Cadillac Seville 1976-1985 front and rear. Buick Regal 2-dr 1981-1987 rear. We manufacture them and sell them. ABS plastic, lacquer primed, complete satisfaction guaranteed. The price war continues. Web site: www.crplastics.com

Tom Crook Classic Cars	car dealer
27611 42nd Ave S	
Auburn, WA 98001	
206-941-3454	

See full listing in **Section Two** under **car dealers**

Dash Specialists	interiors
1910 Redbud Ln	
Medford, OR 97504	
541-776-0040	

Mail order only. Rebuilding dash pads, door panels that are molded, armrests, consoles for all makes and models of automobiles from 1956-present. Both foreign and domestic. 25 years' experience.

JB Donaldson Co	castings
2533 W Cypress	steering wheels
Phoenix, AZ 85009	wood parts
602-278-4505; FAX: 602-278-1112	

See full listing in **Section Two** under **steering wheels**

Driving Passion Ltd USA	cars
Marc Tuwiner	parts
7132 Chilton Ct	salvage yard
Clarksville, MD 21029	
PH/FAX: 301-596-9078	
E-mail: mt.tees@erols.com	

Mail order and open shop. Monday-Saturday 7 am to 6 pm. Specializing in 1959 and 1960 Cadillacs, parts, cars and locating services. Tons of trim and stainless. Rare Eldorados and convertibles, parts, glass, interior parts.

Durabuilt Automotive Hydraulics	hose assemblies
808 Meadows Ave	pumps
Canon City, CO 81212	top cylinders
PH/FAX: 719-275-1126	valves
E-mail: durabuilt@ris.net	

See full listing in **Section Two** under **tops**

Edgerton Classics Ltd	restoration
9215 St Rt 13	woodworking
Camden, NY 13316-4933	
315-245-3113	

See full listing in **Section Two** under **restoration shops**

Egge Machine Company Inc	bearings
11707 Slauson Ave	pistons/rings
Santa Fe Springs, CA 90670	timing components
800-866-EGGE, 562-945-3419	valve train
FAX: 562-693-1635	
E-mail: info@egge.com	

See full listing in **Section Two** under **engine parts**

Elliott's Car Radio	radio repairs
313 Linfield Rd	speaker kits
Parkerford, PA 19457	
610-495-6360; FAX: 610-495-7723	

See full listing in **Section Two** under **radios**

Faxon Auto Literature	literature
3901 Carter Ave	manuals
Riverside, CA 92501	
800-458-2734; FAX: 909-786-4166	

See full listing in **Section Two** under **literature dealers**

FEN Enterprises of New York Inc	parts
PO Box 1559	restoration
1324 Rt 376	
Wappingers Falls, NY 12590	
914-462-5959, 914-462-5094	
FAX: 914-462-8450	

Suppliers of the finest in restoration parts and products. Combined with a full in-house restoration shop, our firm has the insight needed to help you with getting the correct parts for your restoration. Our full service restoration shop has upholstery, mechanical, body and paint, chrome and stainless. Our customers receive the same quality parts that are used on our national award winning restorations. Also have an in-house appraisal service for classic cars and will travel to inspect the vehicle. Frank R Nicodemus is our licensed and bonded appraiser.

From Rust To Riches	appraisals
16643 Rt 144	car dealer
Mt Airy, MD 21771	repairs
301-854-5900, 410-442-3637	restoration
301-854-5956; FAX: 301-854-5957	
E-mail: tatrabill@aol.com	

See full listing in **Section Two** under **restoration shops**

GM Obsolete | parts
909 W Magnolia St
Phoenix, AZ 85007
602-253-8081; FAX: 602-253-8411
E-mail: info@gmobsolete.com

See full listing in **Section One** under **Buick/McLaughlin**

Grand Touring | engine rebuilding
2785 E Regal Park Dr | machine shop
Anaheim, CA 92806 | restoration
714-630-0130; FAX: 714-630-6956 | suspension

See full listing in **Section Two** under **restoration shops**

Hand's Elderly Auto Care | repair
2000 Galveston St | restoration
Grand Prairie, TX 75051
PH/FAX: 972-642-4288

See full listing in **Section Two** under **restoration shops**

Harbor Auto Restoration | restoration
1504 SW 3rd St
Pompano Beach, FL 33069
954-785-7887; FAX: 954-785-7388
E-mail: harbor@harbor-auto.com

See full listing in **Section Two** under **restoration shops**

Justin Hartley | reprinted literature
17 Fox Meadow Ln
West Hartford, CT 06107-1216
860-523-0056
860-604-9950 cellular
FAX: 860-233-8840

Mail order only. Cadillac and LaSalle shop manuals, parts books, service bulletins, owner's manuals, body manuals, data books. 1902-1995. Republished full size with care, pride and

love. Prompt delivery. Recommended by Cadillac club judges and restoration shops. Money-back guarantee. Electronic improvement of pictures. Layflat binding. Started in 1912. References in 50 states and worldwide. MC, Visa, AmEx.
See our ad on this page

Holcombe Cadillac Parts | parts
2933 Century Ln
Bensalem, PA 19020
215-245-4560; FAX: 215-633-9916

Mail order and open shop. Monday-Friday 9 am to 5:30 pm. Specializing in Cadillac parts, NOS, used and reproduction for 1949-1983 Cadillacs, all models. NOS parts a specialty, with over 11,000 part numbers stocked. Carry a full line of used body and trim parts as well as an extensive inventory of rubber weatherstripping, air conditioning, brake and general mechanical and electrical parts as well as body fillers.

Honest John's Caddy Corner | parts
PO Box 741 | restoration
2271 FM 407 W | service
Justin, TX 76247
888-592-2339 toll-free
FAX: 940-648-9135
E-mail: honestjohn@website

Mail order and open shop. Monday-Friday 9 am to 5 pm. Parts, sales, service and restoration for 1941-1991 Cadillacs. Rebuilding and fabrication also. Online parts catalog. Accept MasterCard, Visa, Discover and American Express. Web site: www.honestjohn.com

Horsepower Sales | limousines
130 Cardinal Dr
Waynesville, NC 28786
516-532-7605 mobile, NY

See full listing in **Section Two** under **limousine rentals**

Hubcap Mike | hubcaps
26242 Dimension Ste 150 | wheelcovers
Lake Forest, CA 92630
949-597-8120; FAX: 949-597-8123

See full listing in **Section Two** under **wheels & wheelcovers**

Interesting Parts Inc | appraisals
Paul TerHorst | gaskets
27526 N Owens Rd | parts
Mundelein, IL 60060 | storage
PH/FAX: 847-949-1030 | transport

See full listing in **Section Two** under **comprehensive parts**

Jacks Wholesale Division | limousines
250 N Robertson Blvd, Ste 405
Beverly Hills, CA 90211-1793
310-839-9417; FAX: 310-839-1046

See full listing in **Section One** under **Lincoln**

Jesser's Classic Keys | automobilia
26 West St, Dept HVA | keys
Akron, OH 44303-2344
330-376-8181; FAX: 330-384-9129

See full listing in **Section Two** under **locks & keys**

John's Auto Classics | appraisals
6135 N 79 Dr
Glendale, AZ 85303
602-872-8695

Appraisals for antique, classic and collectibles. Appraisals for banks, insurance companies and personal use. Specializing in Cadillacs.

Keleen Leathers Inc | leather hides
10526 W Cermak Rd
Westchester, IL 60154
708-409-9800; FAX: 708-409-9801

See full listing in **Section Two** under **interiors & interior parts**

Lares Manufacturing
13517 Hwy 65 NE
Ham Lake, MN 55304
800-334-5749; FAX: 612-754-2853
E-mail: sales@larescorp.com

| power steering equipment |

See full listing in **Section One** under **Ford 1954-up**

Lectric Limited Inc
7322 S Archer Road
Justice, IL 60458
708-563-0400; FAX: 708-458-2662

| parts |

See full listing in **Section One** under **Corvette**

Mahoning Auto
11110 Mahoning Ave
North Jackson, OH 44451
330-538-3246; FAX: 330-544-0242

| chrome interiors motors |

Mail order and open shop. Saturdays 9 am to 11 am and by appointment. Cadillac autos and parts for 1938-1978. Chrome, dashes, interiors, skirts, motors and more. Located near I-80 and I-76 in NE Ohio.

Mastermind Inc
32155 Joshua Dr
Wildomar, CA 92595
PH/FAX: 909-674-0509
E-mail: mike@mastermindinc.net

| new/used parts restoration |

Mail/catalog orders and open shop. Please call for appointment. Specialize in restoration and repro parts for 1957-1960 Cadillac Eldorado Broughams. Also other 1950s and 1960s Cadillac parts and restoration, stainless molding repair, loads of new and used parts, misc services, expert air suspension rebuilding. Major emphasis and specialization in Eldorado series cars. Many unique parts and services unavailable elsewhere. Quality is our major concern. Web site: www.mastermindinc.net

Maximum Torque Specialties
PO Box 925
Delavan, WI 53115
414-740-1118; FAX: 414-740-1161

| high-perf parts restoration parts |

Mail order only. Specializing in high-performance and restoration parts for 1968-1976 Cadillac 472-500 cid engines.

Mid-Jersey Motorama Inc
1301 Asbury Ave
PO Box 1395
Asbury Park, NJ 07712
PH/FAX: 732-775-9885
beeper: 732-840-6111
E-mail: sjz1@aol.com

| car dealer |

Open by appointment. Specializing in Mercedes, Cadillac, Land Rover, Rolls-Royce, Jaguar, Lincoln.

Motor Foundry & Tooling Inc
7382 Doniphan Dr
Canutillo, TX 79835-6601
915-877-3343; FAX: 915-877-7071

| brake drums castings exhaust manifolds water pumps |

See full listing in **Section One** under **Packard**

Normans' Classic Auto Radio
7651 Park Blvd
Pinellas Park, FL 33781
888-222-3433, 727-546-1788

| custom sales |

See full listing in **Section Two** under **radios**

North Yale Auto Parts
Rt 1, Box 707
Sperry, OK 74073
918-288-7218, 800-256-6927 (NYAP)
FAX: 918-288-7223

| salvage yard |

See full listing in **Section Five** under **Oklahoma**

OEM Glass Inc
Rt 9 E
PO Box 362
Bloomington, IL 61702
309-662-2122; FAX: 309-663-7474

| auto glass |

See full listing in **Section Two** under **glass**

Ohio Limo and Coach Sales
PO Box 681
Bellefontaine, OH 43311
937-592-3746; FAX: 937-593-3299
E-mail: ohiolimo@ohiolimo.com

| car dealer |

See full listing in **Section Two** under **car dealers**

Old Air Products
4615 Martin St
Ft Worth, TX 76119
817-531-2665; FAX: 817-531-3257
E-mail: sales@oldairproducts.com

| air conditioning |

See full listing in **Section One** under **Corvette**

ORF Corp
Phil Bray
8858 Ferry Rd
Grosse Ile, MI 48138
734-676-5520; FAX: 734-676-9438
E-mail: carolbray@yahoo.com

| ring and pinion gears |

See full listing in **Section Two** under **special services**

Original Auto Interiors
7869 Trumble Rd
Columbus, MI 48063-3915
810-727-2486; FAX: 810-727-4344
E-mail: origauto@tir.com

| upholstery |

See full listing in **Section Two** under **upholstery**

The Parts Place
217 Paul St
Elburn, IL 60119
PH/FAX: 630-365-1800
E-mail: pplace9594@aol.com

| parts |

See full listing in **Section One** under **Chevrolet**

Piru Cads
402 Via Fustero Rd
Box 227
Piru, CA 93040
805-521-1741

| cars parts restoration |

Mail order and open shop. Monday-Saturday 10 am to 6 pm. Cadillac and LaSalle restoration 1937-1970, 1980-1992 parts, heavy in 1938-1953. Sales also, project cars, plus restored.

Dennis Portka
4326 Beetow Dr
Hamburg, NY 14075
716-649-0921

| horns knock-off wheels |

See full listing in **Section One** under **Corvette**

**Precision Pot Metal/
Bussie Restoration Inc**
1008 Loring Ave #28
Orange Park, FL 32073
904-269-8788

| pot metal restoration |

See full listing in **Section Two** under **plating & polishing**

Precision Rubber
Box 324
Didsbury, AB Canada T0M 0W0
403-335-9590; FAX: 403-335-8100

| rubber parts |

See full listing in **Section Two** under **rubber parts**

Sam Quinn Cadillac Parts
Box 837
Estacada, OR 97023
503-637-3852

parts

Mail order only. Parts supplier for Cadillac/LaSalle, 1937-1977.
NOS, rebuilt water pumps 1937-1977, Mopar 1952-1975. New
AC fuel pumps, fender skirts, oil pumps 1949-1962. Motor
mounts 1954-1964. Transmission mounts 1949-up. Ignition
parts. Body parts. Locator service.

**Raine Automotive Springs
Warehouse**
425 Harding Hwy
Carney's Point, NJ 08069
609-299-9141; FAX: 609-299-9157

springs
suspension parts

See full listing in **Section Two** under **suspension parts**

Harry Samuel
65 Wisner St
Pontiac, MI 48342-1066
248-335-1900
E-mail: hsamuel1@aol.com

carpet
fabrics
interiors
upholstery covers

See full listing in **Section Two** under **interiors & interior parts**

Sea Yachts Inc
2029 N Ocean Blvd #410
Fort Lauderdale, FL 33304
PH/FAX: 954-561-8389
E-mail: seayachts@aol.com

parts

Mail order only. Collects 1954-1958 Cadillacs only as a hobby.
Extra parts for sale.

E J Serafin
Valley Rd
Matinecock, NY 11560

manuals

Mail order only. Exact reproductions of owner's and shop manuals for 1930, 1931, 1934, 1935, 1936, 1940, 1941, 1947, 1949,
1957, 1959, 1961 Cadillacs and 1937 Buick.

Dick Shappy Classic Cars
26 Katherine Ct
Warwick, RI 02889
401-521-5333; FAX: 401-421-9480

parts

Cadillacs 1930-1933 parts. Specializing in V16 but have parts
also for 8 and 12 cylinder cars.

Showroom Auto Sales
960 S Bascom Ave
San Jose, CA 95128
408-279-0944; FAX: 408-279-0918

car dealer

See full listing in **Section One** under **Mercedes-Benz**

SMS Auto Fabrics
2325 SE 10th Ave
Portland, OR 97214
503-234-1175; FAX: 503-234-0651

upholstery

See full listing in **Section Two** under **interiors & interior parts**

Robert H Snyder
PO Drawer 821
Yonkers, NY 10702
914-476-8500
FAX: 914-476-8573, 24 hours
E-mail: cohascodpc@earthlink.net

literature
parts

Mail order only. 1941-1949 Cadillac Fleetwood Series 75, 76 and
86 only. Free catalog available of revolving inventory of original
parts only, principally small trim, garnish, fittings and miscel-
lany. No heavy mechanical parts. Literature and collectibles of
every description. All want lists invited. Web site:
http://home.earthlink.net/~cohascodpc/index.html

Special Auto Restoration
689 Fern Dr
Merritt Island, FL 32952
407-453-8343, 407-783-4758

restoration

See full listing in **Section One** under **Chevelle/Camaro**

TA Motor AB
Torpslingan 21
Lulea S 97347 Sweden
+46-920-18888
FAX: +46-920-18821

accessories
parts

Mail order and open shop. Monday-Friday 8 am to 5 pm.
Specializing in parts and accessories for Cadillacs 1940-1970.

Tags Backeast
PO Box 581
Plainville, CT 06062
860-747-2942
E-mail: dataplt@snet.net

data plates
trim tags

See full listing in **Section Two** under **special services**

Tom Taylor
PO Box 129
Guinda, CA 95637
530-796-4106

NOS parts

See full listing in **Section One** under **Mopar**

Tom's Classic Parts
5207 Sundew Terr
Tobyhanna, PA 18466
800-832-4073

parts

See full listing in **Section One** under **Chevrolet**

Town Auto Top Co
111 Clinton Rd
Fairfield, NJ 07004
973-575-9333; FAX: 973-808-8366

convertible repairs
interiors

See full listing in **Section Two** under **restoration shops**

U S Oldies & Classics
Vunt 3
Holsbeek 3220 Belgium
3216446611; FAX: 3216446520

car dealer
parts

See full listing in **Section Two** under **car dealers**

Valley Wire Wheel Service
14731 Lull St
Van Nuys, CA 91405
818-785-7237; FAX: 818-994-2042

wheel restoration
wheels

See full listing in **Section Two** under **wheels & wheelcovers**

Waldron's Antique Exhaust Inc
PO Box C
25872 M-86
Nottawa, MI 49075
616-467-7185; FAX: 616-467-9041

exhaust systems

See full listing in **Section Two** under **exhaust systems**

West Coast Sheetmetal
Lawrence M Camuso
219 S 20th St
San Jose, CA 95116
408-286-6537

body parts

See full listing in **Section Two** under **body parts**

CHECKER

Ace Antique Auto Restoration
65 S Service Rd
Plainview, NY 11803
516-752-6065; FAX: 516-752-1484

**air conditioning
body rebuilding
restoration
wiring harnesses**

See full listing in **Section Two** under **restoration shops**

Blackheart Enterprises Ltd
305-12 Knickerbocker Ave
Bohemia, NY 11716
516-935-6249; FAX: 516-752-1484

**parts
restoration**

Checker taxi and Marathon parts. Thousands in stock. NOS, used and many reproduction parts only available from us. Sales and service of Checker cars and complete restoration services. Web site: www.blackheart.net

Checker Motors
1314 Rollins Rd
Burlingame, CA 94010
650-340-8669; FAX: 650-340-9473
E-mail: tonyleo@pacbell.net

**cars
parts
rentals**

Specializing in Checker taxi cabs, Checker Marathons and Checker station wagons. Cars for sale or rent for movies, commercials or print ads. Checker locator service for cars and parts.

Danchuk Mfg
3201 S Standard Ave
Santa Ana, CA 92705
714-751-1957; FAX: 714-850-1957
E-mail: info@danchuk.com

**accessories
parts
restoration**

See full listing in **Section One** under **Chevrolet**

Pollard Co
Joe Pollard
9331 Johnell Rd
Chatsworth, CA 91311
PH/FAX: 818-999-1485

parts

Specialize in parts for Checker station wagons and sedans, 1960-1982.

Turnpike Checker
Erich Lachmann Jr
495 North St
Middletown, NY 10940-4526
914-343-4322, 5 pm to 5:30 pm EST
FAX: 914-343-2224, 8 am to 5 pm EST

**parts
repairs**

Mail order only. Specializing in parts and repairs for 1960-1982 Checker taxi cabs and Marathons. The last factory authorized Checker cab dealer. Front end parts, reproduction rocker panels, taxi decals, taillight lenses, vent shades.

CHEVROLET

4-Speeds by Darrell
PO Box 110
3 Water St
Vermilion, IL 61955
217-275-3743; FAX: 217-275-3515

transmissions

See full listing in **Section Two** under **transmissions**

60 Chev Sam
2912 Wright Rd
Hamptonville, NC 27020
336-468-1745

parts

Mail order and open shop. 6 days a week 12 am to 9 pm. 1959-1960 parts, all NC good parts, 348 engine parts, rebuild differential 1955-1964.

A & M SoffSeal Inc
104 May Dr
Harrison, OH 45030
800-426-0902
513-367-0028 service/info
FAX: 513-367-5506
E-mail: soffseal@soffseal.com

**rubber parts
weatherstripping**

See full listing in **Section Two** under **rubber parts**

A-1 Street Rods
631 E Las Vegas St
Colorado Springs, CO 80903
719-632-4920, 719-577-4588
FAX: 719-634-6577

parts

See full listing in **Section Two** under **street rods**

Accessoryland Truckin' Supplies
10723 Rt 61 S
Dubuque, IA 52003
319-556-5482; FAX: 319-556-9087

**accessories
foglights/spotlights
mounting brackets
parts**

Mail order and open shop by appointment. Specializing in 1941-1959 GMC and Chevy truck parts. NOS, reproduction and good used (parts for other years available). Parts and project vehicles. Catalog available. Another specialty, Unity spotlights, foglights, mounting bracket kits and repair parts for most vehicles 1930s-present, with many obsolete parts available. We also have nostalgic accessories such as Blue Dots, headlight visors, aftermarket hood ornaments, curb feelers, plus many more. Serving your parts needs since 1976.

Adler's Antique Autos Inc
801 NY Route 43
Stephentown, NY 12168
518-733-5749
E-mail: advdesign1@aol.com

**auto preservation
Chevrolet knowledge
parts
repair
restoration**

See full listing in **Section Two** under **restoration shops**

Air Flow Research
10490 Ilex Ave
Pacoima, CA 91331
818-890-0616; FAX: 818-890-0490

cylinder heads

Mail order only. Manufacturing aftermarket small block Chevy aluminum cylinder heads for all V8 small block Chevys from 1950-present.

AKH Wheels
1207 N A St
Ellensburg, WA 98926-2522
509-962-3390
E-mail: akhwheel@eburg.com

**Rallye wheels
styled steel wheels
vintage aluminum**

See full listing in **Section Two** under **wheels & wheelcovers**

All American Chevys
7950 Deering Ave
Canoga Park, CA 91304-5063
818-887-0550; FAX: 818-884-1343
E-mail: mail@challengeweb.com

publication

Publish bi-monthly *All American Chevys*. 1955-1973 coverage of all Chevrolet cars and trucks. Technical how-tos, restoration, high-performance and street machines. Subscription: $16.95/year. Web site: www.challengeweb.com

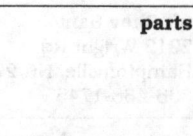
All Chevy/Canadian Impala | parts
404 Allwood Rd
Parksville, BC Canada V9P 1C4
250-248-8666; FAX: 888-248-1958
E-mail: canimp@nanaimo.ark.com

Mail order and open shop. Specializing in reproduction parts for full-size 1955-1970 Chevy! Impala specialists. Emblems, weatherstrips, interiors, literature, reproduction body parts. Books and manuals.

Alpha Omega Motorsport | parts
15612 New Century Dr | repairs
Gardena, CA 90248 | restorations
310-366-7993; FAX: 310-366-7499
E-mail: aomotor@pacbell.net

See full listing in **Section One** under **Pontiac**

American Autowire Systems Inc | battery cables
150 Heller Pl #17W | electrical systems
Dept HVAA99 | switches/compo-
Bellmawr, NJ 08031 | nents
800-482-9473; FAX: 609-933-0805
E-mail: facfit@erols.com

See full listing in **Section Two** under **street rods**

American Classic Truck Parts | parts
PO Box 409
Aubrey, TX 76227
940-365-9786; FAX: 940-365-3419
E-mail: americanclassic@airmail.net

Mail order only. Order by fax, phone, mail or shop online at our web site. Business hours are 9 am to 17:30 pm CST. Stock a very large inventory of antique pickup parts for Chevy and GMC trucks, 1936-1972. New old stock and reproduction. Weatherstripping, sheetmetal, rubber, trim, emblems, chrome, electrical, wiring, moldings, interior trim, mats, upholstery and

much more. Accept Visa, MasterCard, Discover, American Express, money orders and prepaid checks. Catalogs are free within the USA (we need to know the year and type of truck that you are working on as we have different catalogs). Web site: www.americanclassic.com
See our ad on this page

Andover Automotive Inc | parts
PO Box 3143 | seat belts
Laurel, MD 20709
410-381-6700; FAX: 410-381-6703
E-mail: andoauto@clark.net

See full listing in **Section One** under **Corvette**

Antique Auto Battery | batteries
2320 Old Mill Rd | battery cables
Hudson, OH 44236
800-426-7580, 330-425-2395
FAX: 330-425-4642
E-mail: sales@antiqueautobattery.com

See full listing in **Section Two** under **batteries**

Antique Auto Fasteners | fasteners
Guy C Close Jr & Son | hardware
13426 Valna Dr | hose clamps
Whittier, CA 90602 | molding clips
562-696-3307

See full listing in **Section Two** under **hardware**

Antique & Classic Cars | car locator
1796 County Rd 7
Florence, AL 35633
205-760-0542

See full listing in **Section One** under **Cadillac/LaSalle**

Antique Radio Doctor | radio repairs
Barry Dalton
196 Kilborn Dr
Grants Pass, OR 97526
541-474-2524 evenings

See full listing in **Section Two** under **radios**

Authentic Automotive | power brakes
529 Buttercup Trail | power steering
Mesquite, TX 75149
972-289-6373; FAX: 972-289-4303

Mail order only. Monday-Friday 9 am to 5 pm CST. Power steering parts and complete power steering kits for 1955-1964 Chevys; power brake parts and complete power brake kits for 1955-1958 Chevys. Also ps and pb component restoration and new reproduction parts that pertain to ps and pb. Wholesale and retail. Free brochure, state year. American Express, MasterCard, Visa, Discover.

Auto Custom Carpet Inc | carpets
Jeff Moses | floor mats
PO Box 1350, 1429 Noble St
Anniston, AL 36201
800-633-2358, 205-236-1118
FAX: 800-516-8274
E-mail: info@accmats.net

Auto Custom Parts Inc, the world's leading manufacturer of aftermarket floor coverings, has a product line covering vehicles from 1940s-1990s. Available from ACC is complete line of molded carpet sets, cut and sew carpet sets, vinyl and rubber molded floor coverings, trunk mats and custom floor mats. Furthermore, ACC products meet or exceed OEM specifications. Web site: www.accmats.com

Auto Hardware Specialties | hardware fasteners
3123 McKinley Ave
Sheldon, IA 51201
712-324-2091; FAX: 712-324-2480
E-mail: rweber@rconnect.com

Mail order only. Specializing in original type hardware for 1929-

1941 GM cars, including: screws, nuts, bolts, molding clips, hinge pins, tube nuts, anchor nuts, step bolts, hose clamps, gas caps and related items. Illustrated catalog, $2.

| **Avanti Auto Service**
Rt 322, 67 Conchester Hwy
Glen Mills, PA 19342-1506
610-558-9999 | **repair
restoration** |

See full listing in **Section One** under **DeTomaso/Pantera**

| **B & T Truck Parts**
906 E Main St
PO Box 799
Siloam Springs, AR 72761
501-524-5959; FAX: 501-524-5559 | **pickup parts** |

See full listing in **Section Two** under **trucks & tractors**

| **Bay Ridges Classic Chevy**
1550 Bayly St #38A
Pickering, ON Canada L1W 3W1
905-839-6169; FAX: 905-420-6613 | **accessories
parts** |

Authorized dealer for Danchuk Mfg, Ol' 55 and C&P Auto. Specializing in 1955-1957 Chevy parts and accessories, new and used, including interiors, tires, suspension parts, batteries, car covers and car care products.

| **Bentley Publishers**
1734 Massachusetts Ave
Cambridge, MA 02138-1804
800-423-4595; FAX: 617-876-9235
E-mail: sales@rb.com | **books
manuals** |

See full listing in **Section Four** under **books & publications**

| **Bill's Speed Shop**
13951 Millersburg Rd
Navarre, OH 44662
330-832-9403; FAX: 330-832-2098 | **body parts** |

Mail order and open shop. One of the foremost suppliers of obsolete and current body repair panels. Our main interest is obsolete panels from 1949-up. Also in stock, a few NOS fenders and quarters.

| **Bob's Radio & TV Service**
238 Ocean View
Pismo Beach, CA 93449
805-773-8200 | **radios** |

See full listing in **Section Two** under **radios**

| **Bow Tie Chevy Association**
PO Box 608108
Orlando, FL 32860
407-880-1956; FAX: 407-886-7571
E-mail: chevy55@ao.net | **parts** |

Mail order and open shop. Monday-Friday 8 am to 5 pm EST. Sell parts for 1955-1972 Chevys. Web site: www.ao.net/chevy55-72/

| **Bow Tie Reproductions**
7297 Maple St
Mentor, OH 44060
PH/FAX: 440-974-8384 (call first) | **parts** |

Reproduction parts for 1929-1932 Chevrolets. Quality die-formed steel fenders, aprons, other sheetmetal is our specialty.

| **Boyds Hot Rods & Collectable Cars**
8400 Cerritos Ave
Stanton, CA 90680
714-220-9870; FAX: 714-220-9877
E-mail: sales@boydshotrods.com | **car dealer** |

Open shop. Monday-Friday 9 am to 6 pm, Saturday 9 am to 4 pm, Sunday 11 am to 4 pm. Sell hot rods, classic cars and muscle cars. Web site: www.boydshotrods.com

| **Brasilia Press**
PO Box 2023
Elkhart, IN 46515
FAX: 219-262-8799 | **models** |

See full listing in **Section Two** under **models & toys**

| **Brothers Truck Parts**
4375 Prado Rd #105
Corona, CA 91720
800-977-2767; FAX: 909-808-9788
E-mail: sales@brotherstrucks.com | **accessories
parts** |

See full listing in **Section Two** under **trucks & tractors**

| **Bumper Boyz LLC**
2435 E 54th St
Los Angeles, CA 90058
800-995-1703, 323-587-8976
FAX: 323-587-2013 | **bumper repairs
reconditioning
sandblasting** |

Mail order and open shop. 7 am to 6 pm PST. Specializing in reconditioning all makes and models. GM, Ford, Chrysler. Also foreign bumpers. Repair, sandblast and triple plate bumpers. Carry accessories, bumper guards, fender wing tips plus grilles, exchange or outright. Ship nationwide also overseas. Web site: www.bumperboyz.com

| **Burrell's Service Inc**
PO Box 456
Keego Harbor, MI 48320
248-682-2376 | **parts** |

Mail order only. Specializing in service and parts information for 1976-1981 Chevy and Ford vans with the Vemco VX4 4-wd conversion.

| **Butch's Trim**
W-224 S-8445 Industrial Ave
Big Bend, WI 53103
414-679-4883, 414-662-9910 shop | **molding
polishing
trim restoration** |

Mail order and open shop. Monday-Saturday 9 am to 4 pm. Restoration of aluminum trim, body side moldings, headlamp bezels, grilles. Dents and scratches removed. Polishing and anodizing. Stocking NOS and used for 1958-1967 Chevy.

| **C & P Chevy Parts**
50 Schoolhouse Rd
PO Box 348VA
Kulpsville, PA 19443
215-721-4300, 800-235-2475
FAX: 215-721-4539 | **parts
restoration supplies** |

Mail order and open shop. Monday-Friday 9 am to 5 pm. Parts and restoration supplies for 1955-1957 Chevrolets and 1955-1959 Chevrolet truck. Visit our web site: www.1chevy.com

| **Cal West Auto Air & Radiators Inc**
24309 Creekside Rd #119
Valencia, CA 91355
800-535-2034; FAX: 805-254-6120
E-mail: mike@calwest-radiators.com | **a/c condensers
fan shrouds
gas tanks
heaters
radiators** |

See full listing in **Section Two** under **radiators**

| **California Jaguar**
29109 Triunfo Dr
Agoura, CA 91301
800-335-2482; FAX: 818-707-3062 | **auto transport** |

See full listing in **Section Two** under **transport**

| **Camaro Specialties**
112 Elm St
East Aurora, NY 14052
716-652-7086; FAX: 716-652-2279
E-mail: dunlop@wzrd.com | **parts
restoration** |

See full listing in **Section One** under **Chevelle/Camaro**

CARS Inc	interior
1964 W 11 Mile Rd	
Berkley, MI 48072	
248-398-7100; FAX: 248-398-7078	
E-mail: carsinc@worldnet.att.net	

Mail order and open shop. Monday-Friday 8:30 am to 5:30 pm, Saturday 8:30 am to 2 pm. Original style interiors, parts and heavy gauge sheetmetal products for 1955-1972 full-size Chevys, 1964-1972 Chevelle and El Camino, 1967-1976 Camaro, 1962-1972 Nova, 1970-1972 Monte Carlo, 1955-1957 Cameos and 1967-1972 Chevy pickups. Web site: www.carsinc.com

Jim Carter's Antique Truck Parts	truck parts
1508 E Alton	
Independence, MO 64055	
800-336-1913; FAX: 800-262-3749	
E-mail:	
jimcartertruck.parts@worldnet.att.net	

We specialize in quality parts for the 1934-1972 Chevrolet and GMC truck. Our trained, experienced crew knows older GM trucks and what you need in their restoration. We are one of the leaders in this fast growing truck restoration field. Let us help you make your truck just the way you want it to be. Catalogs, $5, includes a $7.50 coupon good towards your first order. Web site: www.oldchevytrucks.com

John Chambers Vintage Chevrolet	parts
PO Box 35068, Dept VAA	
Phoenix, AZ 85069	
602-934-CHEV	

Mail order and open shop by appointment, customer pick-up by appointment. 1955, 1956 and 1957 Chevrolet parts: chrome parts, lenses, wiring harnesses, weatherstripping, sheet metal, interiors, mechanical items, rubber parts. Large selection of rust-free used parts from the Southwest.

Chernock Enterprises	trailers
PO Box 134	
Airport Rd	
Hazleton, PA 18201	
570-455-1752; FAX: 570-455-7585	
E-mail: jim@chernock.com	

See full listing in **Section Two** under **trailers**

Chev's of the 40's	parts
2027 B St, Dept HVA	
Washougal, WA 98671	
800-999-CHEV (2438)	
FAX: 360-835-7988	

Mail order only. The world's most complete supplier of 1937-1954 Chevrolet car and truck parts.

Chevi Shop Custom Casting	custom castings parts
338 Main Ave	
Box 75	
Milledgeville, IL 61051	
815-225-7565; FAX: 815-225-7616	

Retail sales of 1933-1957 Chevrolet parts. Manufacturer of custom castings in zinc aluminum alloy using spin casting and investment casting techniques. Some iron and aluminum castings (sandcastings) also done. Will custom cast for dealer or individual, one part or many, with painting or plating available also. No 1941-1954 parts and no sheetmetal. Catalog, $2. Free quotes on parts.

Chevrolet Parts Obsolete	accessories parts
PO Box 0740	
Murrieta, CA 92564-0740	
909-279-2833; FAX: 909-279-4013	
E-mail: spo@att.net	

Mail order only. Carry over 50,000 NOS General Motors parts and accessories, 1965-1985. We also purchase discontinued and obsolete GM parts. When calling, please provide part numbers if possible.

Chevy Duty Pickup Parts	pickup parts
4319 NW Gateway	
Kansas City, MO 64150	
816-741-8029; FAX: 816-741-5255	
E-mail: trucks@sky.net	

Mail order and retail parts store. Monday-Friday 9 am to 5:30 pm, Saturday 9 am to 12 noon. Specializes in parts and restoration supplies for 1947-1972 Chevy and GMC pickups. We have 4 fully illustrated catalogs, complete with descriptions and prices for you to order from. Web site: www.chevyduty.com

Chevyland Parts & Accessories	accessories parts restoration
3667 Recycle Rd #8	
Rancho Cordova, CA 95742	
916-638-3906; FAX: 916-638-0302	
E-mail: chevylnd@concourse.net	

See full listing in **Section One** under **Chevelle/Camaro**

Chewning's Auto Literature	literature manuals
2011 Elm Tree Terr	
Buford, GA 30518	
770-945-9795	

See full listing in **Section Two** under **literature dealers**

Cheyenne Pickup Parts	body panels bumpers carpet weatherstripping
Box 959	
Noble, OK 73068	
405-872-3399; FAX: 405-872-0385	

See full listing in **Section Two** under **trucks & tractors**

Classic and Muscle	**reproduction parts**
Muscle Car Restoration Parts	**restoration parts**
PO Box 657	
Elmsdale, NS Canada B0N 1M0	
902-883-4489; FAX: 902-883-1392	
E-mail: classicmuscle@sprint.ca	

Mail order and open shop located at home. High quality reproduction parts and new factory GM restoration parts for 1958-1972 Chevrolet Impala, 1964-1972 Chevelle, El Camino, 1970-1972 Monte Carlo, 1967-1981 Camaro, 1962-1974 Chevy II/Nova, 1964-1972 Pontiac GTO and LeMans, 1964-1972 Buick Skylark and GS, 1964-1972 Olds 442 and Cutlass, 1966-1974 Dodge/Plymouth. An authorized Year One dealer in Nova Scotia, Canada.

Classic Auto Air Mfg Co	**air conditioning**
2020 W Kennedy Blvd	**heating**
Tampa, FL 33606	**parts**
813-251-2356, 813-251-4994	

See full listing in **Section One** under **Mustang**

Classic Auto Restoration Service Inc	**restoration**
381 National Dr	
Rockwall, TX 75032-6556	
972-722-9663	

Open Monday-Friday 8 am to 5 pm CST. Specialize in Chevrolet 1955-1972 cars and pickups. Also Ford and Mustang 1958-1968.

Classic Chevy International	**modified parts**
PO Box 607188	**repro parts**
Orlando, FL 32860-7188	**used parts**
800-456-1957, 407-299-1957	
FAX: 407-299-3341	
E-mail: cciworld@aol.com	

Mail order and open shop. Monday-Friday 8 am to 5 pm, Saturday 9 am to 3 pm. Phone orders: Monday-Friday 8 am to 11 pm EST, Saturday 9 am to 6 pm EST. Specializing in reproduction, modified, used parts and selected restoration services for 1955-1972 Chevrolets. Call for a catalog and more information. Web site: www.classicchevy.com

See our ad on pages 38 and 40

Classic Industries Inc	**accessories**
Nova/Chevy II Parts and Accessories	**parts**
Catalog	
17832 Gothard St	
Huntington Beach, CA 92647	
800-854-1280 parts/info	
FAX: 800-300-3081 toll-free	
E-mail: info@classicindustries.com	

Largest selection of Chevy II/Nova parts and accessories ever assembled in one catalog. Nearly 400 full color pages of the finest quality restoration products and accessories. Only $5, refunded on first order. Call our 24-hour toll-free catalog hotline, 888-GM-CATALOG, and receive the industry's most comprehensive parts catalog from the undisputed leader in the industry, Classic Industries. Web site: www.classicindustries.com

See our ad inside the front cover

Classic Industries Inc	**accessories**
Impala/Full-size Chevrolet Parts and	**parts**
Accessories Catalog	
17832 Gothard St	
Huntington Beach, CA 92647	
800-854-1280 parts/info	
FAX: 800-300-3081	
E-mail: info@classicindustries.com	

New from Classic Industries. The largest selection of Impala and full-size Chevy parts and accessories ever assembled in one catalog. Over 400 full color pages of the finest quality restoration products and late model Impala SS accessories. Only $5, refunded on first order. Call our 24-hour toll-free catalog hotline at 888-GM-CATALOG and receive the industry's newest and most com-

prehensive parts catalog from the undisputed leader in the industry, Classic Industries. Web site: www.classicindustries.com

See our ad inside the front cover

Classic Industries Inc	**accessories**
Chevy/GMC Truck Parts and	**parts**
Accessories Catalog	
17832 Gothard St	
Huntington Beach, CA 92647	
800-854-1280 parts/info	
FAX: 800-300-3081	
E-mail: info@classicindustries.com	

New from Classic Industries. Announcing our newest parts and accessories catalog, *Chevy/GMC Truck*, covering all years from 1948-present. You'll find the finest quality restoration products and late model truck accessories. Scheduled for release in early 2000. Call our 24-hour toll-free catalog hotline at 888-GM-CATALOG to be placed on our advance mailing list to receive free, the industry's newest and most comprehensive parts catalog from the undisputed leader in the industry, Classic Industries. Web site: www.classicindustries.com

See our ad inside the front cover

Classic Wood Mfg	**wood kits**
1006 N Raleigh St	**wood replacement**
Greensboro, NC 27405	
336-691-1344; FAX: 336-273-3074	

See full listing in **Section Two** under **woodwork**

Clester's Auto Rubber Seals Inc	**gloveboxes**
PO Box 1113	**molded rubber**
Salisbury, NC 28145	**parts**
704-637-9979; FAX: 704-636-7390	**weatherstripping**

See full listing in **Section Two** under **rubber parts**

Cliff's Classic Chevrolet Parts Co | parts
619 SE 212nd Ave
Portland, OR 97233
503-667-4329; FAX 503-669-4268
E-mail: clifchev@aol.com

Mail order and open shop. Monday-Saturday 9 am to 5:30 pm. Specializing in 1955-1957 Chevrolet passenger car and 1955 2nd Series, 1959 Chevrolet truck parts, new and used. Many rebuilding/restoration services for same. Web site: cliffsclassicchevrolet.com

The Clockworks | clock service
1745 Meta Lake Ln
Eagle River, WI 54521
800-398-3040; FAX: 715-479-5759
E-mail: clockworks@juno.com

See full listing in **Section Two** under **instruments**

Cn'V Corvette Sales | parts / sales / service
2166 E University Dr
Tempe, AZ 85281
602-994-8388; FAX: 602-423-0407
E-mail: sales@cnv-corvettes.com

See full listing in **Section One** under **Corvette**

Coach Builders Muscle Car Parts & Services | interiors / parts / rust remover
PO Box 128
Baltimore, MD 21087-0128
410-426-5567

NOS and reproduction body panels, interiors, convertible and vinyl tops, rechromed bumpers, weatherstripping, Oxisolv rust remover and metal conditioner for 1955-1957 Chevy, Chevelle, Camaro, Impala, Nova, Monte Carlo, GTO, LeMans, Firebird, 442, Cutlass, Charger, Skylark, GS, Roadrunner, GTX, Cuda,

Dart. Pre-purchase inspection service (don't buy the wrong car). Specializing in the past for the future.

The Collector's Guild | models / toys
41 Counter St
Kingston, ON Canada K7K 6C7
800-653-0251; FAX: 613-536-5211
E-mail: cars@collectorsguild.on.ca

See full listing in **Section Two** under **models & toys**

Convertible Service | convertible parts / manufacture/service / top mechanism
5126-HA Walnut Grove Ave
San Gabriel, CA 91776
800-333-1140, 626-285-2255
FAX: 626-285-9004

See full listing in **Section Two** under **tops**

JA Cooley Museum | museum
4233 Park Blvd
San Diego, CA 92103
619-296-3112

See full listing in **Section Six** under **California**

Coopers Vintage Auto Parts | parts
3087 N California St
Burbank, CA 91504
818-567-4140; FAX: 818-567-4101

See full listing in **Section One** under **Cadillac/LaSalle**

CPX-RTS Auto Parts | parts
7552 W Appleton Ave
Milwaukee, WI 53216
414-463-2277; FAX: 414-463-2098

Mail order and showroom sales. Monday-Friday 9 am to 6 pm, Saturday-Sunday and holidays 9 am to 1 pm. Our 26th year as the major discounter of 1955-1975 Chevrolet, Camaro, Chevelle, Nova, Monte Carlo, El Camino parts and accessories, new, used and reproduction. "Why pay more?" Web site: www.cpxrt-sautoparts.uspc.net

Custom Autosound Mfg | CD players / custom radios / speaker upgrades
808 W Vermont Ave
Anaheim, CA 92805
800-888-8637; FAX: 714-533-0361
E-mail: info@custom-autosound.com

Monday-Friday 8 am to 5 pm. Manufacturer and distributor. Custom radios, AM-FM cassettes, CDs, speakers and acc. "No modification fit" for all classic Chevys, Fords, Mopar, GM, AMC, Studebaker, Lincoln Mercury, AMC-Nash, DeSoto, Hudson, imports, and more. Web site: www.custom-autosound.com
See our ad on page 364

Custom Classic Cars | parts / restoration
2046 E 12B Road
Bourbon, IN 46504
219-342-5007; FAX: 219-342-0399
E-mail: customclassiccars@waveone.net

Mail order and open shop. Monday-Saturday 8:30 am to 5:30 pm. Specializing in 1968-1972 Nova and 1969-1981 Trans Am and Firebird parts, also restoration of any make or model, 1929-present. Extensive fabrication work, custom concept, complete, partial, chassis, suspension, body, paint and media blasting. Four-man shop dedicated to your needs. Shop rate is very competitive.

Danchuk Mfg | accessories / parts / restoration
3201 S Standard Ave
Santa Ana, CA 92705
714-751-1957; FAX: 714-850-1957
E-mail: info@danchuk.com

Monday-Friday 7 am to 4 pm, Saturday 8 am to 3 pm. World's largest manufacturer of 1955-1957 Chevrolet restoration parts. Also carry 1964-1972 Chevelle and El Camino and all Corvette

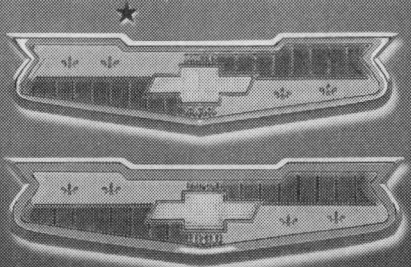

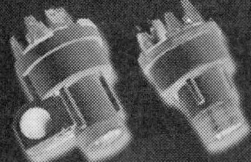

parts and accessories. Call for a catalog , visit our web site or visit our Santa Ana, CA, showroom. Web site: www.danchuk.com

See our ad on page 41

Dave's Auto Machine & Parts Rt 16 Ischua, NY 14743 716-557-2402	accessories machine work parts

Mail order and open shop. Monday-Friday 9 am to 5 pm EST; sometimes closed Friday if at swap meet, please call ahead. Phone hours 10 to 7 EST. Specialize in Chevrolet 1955-1972, all models car and truck parts, NOS, used only. Specializing in hp big and small block dated engine parts and accessories, including carbs, manifolds, trans, etc. Machine shop service available.

Desert Muscle Cars 2853 N Stone Ave Tucson, AZ 85705 520-882-3010; FAX: 520-628-9332	parts

See full listing in **Section One** under **Chevelle/Camaro**

Mike Drago Chevy Parts 141 E St Joseph St Easton, PA 18042 PH/FAX: 610-252-5701 E-mail: dragomdcp@aol.com	Chevrolet parts

Mail order and open shop. Monday-Saturday 8 am to 5 pm. Specialize in classic Chevrolet parts for 1955-1957. Stock a full line of the finest quality reproduction parts available. New old stock as well as good used is available. Show quality chrome plating is also offered. Catalog is available, $4, refundable on first order. Web site: http://members.aol.com/dragomdcp

East Coast Chevy Inc Ol '55 Chevy Parts 4154A Skyron Dr Doylestown, PA 18938 215-348-5568; FAX: 215-348-0560	custom work parts restoration

Mail order and open shop. Monday-Friday 9 am to 5 pm, 1 Saturday per month 9 am to 12 pm (call first for Saturday). Complete inventory new, used and reproduction parts (1955-1957 our specialty). Also restoration services for 1955-1957 Chevrolets. Now stocking 1958-1970. Personal service, parts restoration and custom work.

East West Auto Parts Inc 4605 Dawson Rd Tulsa, OK 74115 800-447-2886; FAX: 918-832-7900	European import parts GM parts

See full listing in **Section Five** under **Oklahoma**

Elliott's Car Radio 313 Linfield Rd Parkerford, PA 19457 610-495-6360; FAX: 610-495-7723	radio repairs speaker kits

See full listing in **Section Two** under **radios**

Engineering & Manufacturing Services Box 24362 Cleveland, OH 44124-0362 216-541-4585; FAX: 216-541-4989	sheetmetal

See full listing in **Section One** under **Ford 1932-1953**

David J Entler Restorations 10903 N Main St Ext Glen Rock, PA 17327-8373 717-235-2112	woodwork

See full listing in **Section Two** under **woodwork**

Bruce Falk 1105 Nichilson Joliet, IL 60435 815-726-6455 E-mail: bbfalk@aol.com	parts

Specializing in all parts, NOS, used and reproduction for 1949-1954 Chevrolets.

Faxon Auto Literature 3901 Carter Ave Riverside, CA 92501 800-458-2734; FAX: 909-786-4166	literature manuals

See full listing in **Section Two** under **literature dealers**

Fifth Avenue Graphics Fifth Avenue Antique Auto Parts 415 Court St Clay Center, KS 67432 785-632-3450; FAX: 785-632-6154 E-mail: fifthave@kansas.net	cooling systems electrical systems fuel systems

See full listing in **Section Two** under **electrical systems**

Fifties Forever 206 Division Ave Garfield, NJ 07026 PH/FAX: 973-478-1306 E-mail: fiftiesforever@webtv.net	Chevy specialist

Mail order and showroom. Monday-Friday 9 am to 6 pm, Saturday 9 am to 1 pm. Complete inventory of new, used and NOS parts for 1955-1957 Chevrolet. Also many hard to find items for 1956-1967 Corvette. Discounted prices, monthly specials, volume discounts.

John Filiss 45 Kingston Ave Port Jervis, NY 12771 914-856-2942 E-mail: johnfiliss@hotmail.com	appraisals

See full listing in **Section Two** under **appraisals**

The Filling Station 990 S Second St Lebanon, OR 97355-3227 800-841-6622 orders 541-258-2114; FAX: 541-258-6968 E-mail: fssales@fillingstation.com	literature parts

Mail order and open shop. Monday-Saturday 9 am to 5 pm; closed Sunday. Chevrolet and GMC quality reproduction parts for: 1916-1964 passenger cars and 1918-1972 trucks. Rubber products including: windshield, vent window, door and trunk seals. Chrome items including: mirrors and arms, hood and grille ornaments, door and window handles. Shop manuals, owner's manuals, sales and restoration literature. Brakes, suspensions and much more. Web site: www.fillingstation.com

Fowlkes Realty & Auction 500 Hale St Newman Grove, NE 68758 800-275-5522; FAX: 402-447-6000	appraisals auctions

Specialize in the appraisal and auctioning of American made classic and antique automobiles. 15 years' experience. Auctions throughout the Midwest.

Ron Francis' Wire Works 167 Keystone Rd Chester, PA 19013 800-292-1940 orders, 610-485-1937 E-mail: rfwwx@aol.com	fuel injection harnesses wiring accessories wiring kits

See full listing in **Section Two** under **wiring harnesses**

George Frechette 14 Cedar Dr Granby, MA 01033 800-528-5235	**brake cylinder sleeving**

See full listing in **Section Two** under **brakes**

Fred's Truck Parts 4811 S Palant Tucson, AZ 85735 520-883-7151	**parts**

Mail order and open shop. Monday-Saturday 8 am to 6 pm.
Specializing in reconditioned, reproduction and used parts for
1947-1959 Chevy pickups.

Garton's Auto 401 N 5th St (at 5th & Vine) Millville, NJ 08332-3129 609-825-3618	**bicycles Ford NOS parts sales literature**

See full listing in **Section One** under **Ford 1932-1953**

Gilbert's Early Chevy Pickup Parts PO Box 1316 470 Rd 1 NW Chino Valley, AZ 86323 PH/FAX: 520-636-5337 E-mail: gilb@goodnet.com	**pickup parts**

See full listing in **Section Two** under **trucks & tractors**

GMC Solutions Robert English PO Box 675 Franklin, MA 02038-0675 508-520-3900; FAX: 508-520-7861 E-mail: oldcarkook@aol.com	**literature parts**

See full listing in **Section One** under **GMC**

Gold Eagle Classics 5990 SW 185th Ave Bldg H Aloha, OR 97007 503-642-2005; FAX: 503-642-0808 E-mail: gldeagle@europa.com	**accessories parts**

See full listing in **Section One** under **Chevelle/Camaro**

Golden Gulf Classics Inc PO Box 490 22530 Hwy 49 Saucier, MS 39574 228-831-2650; FAX: 228-831-1513 E-mail: gudhowdy@datasync.com	**repairs restorations**

See full listing in **Section One** under **Triumph**

Golden State Pickup Parts 4245 Baseline Ave Santa Ynez, CA 93460 800-235-5717, 805-686-2020 FAX: 805-686-2040 E-mail: gspp@gspp.com	**truck parts**

1947-1987 Chevy and GMC truck parts. Lifetime guarantee on
all parts. Web site: gspp.com

Great Lakes Auto "N" Truck Restoration PO Box 251 Mayville, MI 48744 517-683-2614	**parts**

Specializing in 1955-1959 Chevy and GMC trucks and parts,
Chevrolet Cameo trucks, NOS, used, reproduction, Cameo,
Stepside, Fleetside.

Hagerty Classic Insurance PO Box 87 Traverse City, MI 49685 800-922-4050; FAX: 616-941-8227	**insurance**

See full listing in **Section Two** under **insurance**

Hampton Coach Inc 6 Chestnut St PO Box 6 Amesbury, MA 01913 888-388-8726, 978-388-8047 FAX: 978-388-1113 E-mail: lbb-hc@greennet.net	**fabrics top kits upholstery kits**

Antique auto "ready to install" upholstery kits, top kits and fabrics for over 400 models and variations of Chevrolet (1922-1954)
and Buick (1930-1955) vehicles. Free literature with fabric samples and prices available upon request. Worldwide reputation for
quality and service. Web site: www.lebaronbonney.com

Hand's Elderly Auto Care 2000 Galveston St Grand Prairie, TX 75051 PH/FAX: 972-642-4288	**repair restoration**

See full listing in **Section Two** under **restoration shops**

Haneline Products Co PO Box 430 Morongo Valley, CA 92256 760-363-6597; FAX: 760-363-7321	**gauges instrument panels stainless parts trim parts**

See full listing in **Section Two** under **accessories**

Harbor Auto Restoration 1504 SW 3rd St Pompano Beach, FL 33069 954-785-7887; FAX: 954-785-7388 E-mail: harbor@harbor-auto.com	**restoration**

See full listing in **Section Two** under **restoration shops**

Harmon's Incorporated Hwy 27 N PO Box 100C Geneva, IN 46740 219-368-7221; FAX: 219-368-9396 E-mail: harmons1@adamswells.com	**interiors parts**

Celebrating our 27th year of bringing our customers the best
service, largest variety, guaranteed quality and the fairest prices
on Chevrolet restoration parts. Our 1999 catalog has over
18,000 parts for 1955-1972 Chevrolet, 1962-1972 Nova, 1964-
1972 Chevelle, 1970-1977 Monte Carlo, 1967-1980 Camaro and
1947-1980 truck. Also a wide assortment of accessories including books, posters, paints, models and decals. Simply call or
write to above address to order our $5 catalog and receive a 5%
discount coupon. Web site: www.harmons.com

Hidden Valley Auto Parts 21046 N Rio Bravo Maricopa, AZ 85239 602-252-2122, 602-252-6137 520-568-2945; FAX: 602-258-0951	**parts**

Mail order and open shop. Monday-Friday 8 am to 5 pm,
Saturday 9 am to 3 pm. Specializing in classic, antique auto and
truck parts, 1940s-1980s, American and foreign.

Historic Video Archives PO Box 189-VA Cedar Knolls, NJ 07927-0189	**videotapes**

See full listing in **Section Two** under **automobilia**

Bruce Horkey's Wood & Parts Rt 4 Box 188 Windom, MN 56101 507-831-5625; FAX: 507-831-0280	**pickup parts**

See full listing in **Section Two** under **trucks & tractors**

Hubcap Mike 26242 Dimension Ste 150 Lake Forest, CA 92630 949-597-8120; FAX: 949-597-8123	**hubcaps wheelcovers**

See full listing in **Section Two** under **wheels & wheelcovers**

William Hulbert Jr PO Box 151 13683 Rt 11 Adams Center, NY 13606 315-583-5765	**radios**

See full listing in **Section Two** under **radios**

Impala Bob's Inc 4753 E Falcon Dr Dept HVAA14 Mesa, AZ 85215 800-IMPALAS orders 480-924-4800 retail store 480-981-1600 office FAX: 800-716-6237, 480-981-1675 E-mail: info@impalas.com	**restoration parts**

Impala Bob's has everything for the classic Chevrolet restorer. Specialize in 1949-1976 full-size Chevrolet and 1967-1972 Chevrolet/GMC truck. Offer a full line of restoration parts including moldings, emblems, trim, lenses, interior kits, dash pads, convertible parts, weatherstrips, rubber parts, body repair panels, rechromed bumpers, wiring harnesses, radiators, mechanical parts, stereos, OEM tires and batteries, engine decals, books and more. All of our catalogs are free. Mention code HVAA14. Visit our retail store on Falcon Field Airport. Web site: www.impalas.com

Inline Tube 33783 Groes Beck Hwy Fraser, MI 48026 800-385-9452 order 810-294-4093 tech FAX: 810-294-7349 E-mail: kryta@aol.com	**brake lines/cables choke tubes flex brake hoses fuel/vacuum lines transmission lines**

See full listing in **Section Two** under **brakes**

Instrument Services Inc 11765 Main St Roscoe, IL 61073 800-558-2674; FAX: 815-623-6416	**clocks gauges instruments**

See full listing in **Section Two** under **instruments**

Integrity Machine 383 Pipe Stave Hollow Rd Mount Sinai, NY 11766 888-446-9670; FAX: 516-476-9675	**brake masters clutch masters wheel cylinders**

See full listing in **Section Two** under **brakes**

J & K Old Chevy Stuff Ship Pond Rd Plymouth, MA 02360 508-224-7616	**car dealer parts sheetmetal**

Mail order and open shop. Monday-Sunday 8 am to 7 pm. Sell used rot-free Chevy sheetmetal for 1955-1969 Chevys including Novas and Chevelles. Also sell used miscellaneous items for 1955-1957s and Chevy II Novas. Also buy and sell 1955-1969 Chevy cars.

JECC Inc PO Box 616 West Paterson, NJ 07424 973-890-9682; FAX: 973-812-2724	**chassis parts gaskets transmissions**

See full listing in **Section One** under **Buick/McLaughlin**

Jefferis Autobody 269 Tank Farm Rd San Luis Obispo, CA 93401 800-807-1937; FAX: 805-543-4757	**windshield glass kit**

See full listing in **Section Two** under **glass**

Jerry's Automotive c/o Jerry Cinotti 431 S Sierra Way San Bernadino, CA 92408 909-884-6980; FAX: 909-884-7872	**brake repair**

See full listing in **Section Two** under **brakes**

Jersey Late Greats Inc PO Box 1294 Hightstown, NJ 08520 609-448-0526	**documentation service restoration details**

Maintain extensive database of original 1958-1964 Chevrolets. The only source to have completely decoded the Fisher Body cowl tags from 15 different assembly plants. Documentation service provides when, where and with what options a car was built. Also can provide restoration details which differ between plants and date of production.

Jesser's Classic Keys 26 West St, Dept HVA Akron, OH 44303-2344 330-376-8181; FAX: 330-384-9129	**automobilia keys**

See full listing in **Section Two** under **locks & keys**

JR's Antique Auto 21382 E Scherry Ln Claremore, OK 74017 918-342-4398	**chrome parts interiors**

1916-1948 Chevy cars, parts and muscle cars. 1964-1972 Chevy cars, parts, interiors, motors.

J R's Chevy Parts 478 Moe Rd Clifton Park, NY 12065 518-383-5512; FAX: 518-383-2426 E-mail: jrschev@aol.com	**parts**

Mail order only. Specialize in selling parts for 1965-1979 full-size Chevys: Impalas, Caprices, Super Sports, Bel Airs and Biscaynes. Have thousands of parts for these models, NOS and repro. Catalogs available, $4 each, must state year and model.

Kessler's Antique Cars & Body Shop 1616 E Main St Olney, IL 62450 618-393-4346	**parts**

Mail order and open shop. Monday-Friday 8 am to 5 pm. 1928-48 Chevrolet reproduction parts. Some NOS parts. Please call before you come, we travel a lot to swap meets and we're not always there.

Al Knoch Interiors 130 Montoya Rd El Paso, TX 79932 800-880-8080; FAX: 915-581-1545 E-mail: alknoch@flash.net	**carpets interiors tooling services tops**

Mail order and open shop. Monday-Friday 8 am to 5 pm MST. Specialize in seat covers, carpet, door panels, convertible tops, interiors for Chevrolet Corvette. Manufacturer of original quality interiors, tooling services, dielectric, vacuum forming and foam molding.

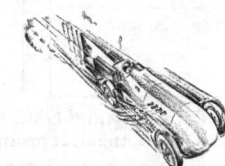

Late Great Chevrolet Association | magazine
Robert Snowden
PO Box 607824
Orlando, FL 32860
407-886-1963; FAX: 407-886-7571
E-mail: chevy55-72@ao.net

See full listing in **Section Four** under **periodicals**

Lee's Classic Chevy Sales | accessories
314A Main St | literature
Glenbeulah, WI 53023 | parts
920-526-3411

Mail order and open shop. Wednesday-Saturday 9 am to 4 pm. Have operated this business in the same location for 24 years and take great pride in selling only quality parts that are guaranteed correct with customers all over the world. Parts, accessories and literature for 1955-1956-1957 Chevrolets (all models).

LES Auto Parts | parts
PO Box 81
Dayton, NJ 08810
732-329-6128; FAX: 732-329-1036

Mail order and open shop. Monday-Saturday 8 am to 5 pm. Specializing in NOS GM parts for Chevrolet Impala, Chevelle, Nova, Camaro, all Pontiacs and Olds and Buick. All car parts 1950-1985.

Lloyd's Literature | literature
PO Box 491
Newbury, OH 44065
800-292-2665, 440-338-1527
FAX: 440-338-2222

See full listing in **Section Two** under **literature dealers**

LMC Truck | accessories
PO Box 14991 | parts
Lenexa, KS 66285
800-222-5664; FAX: 913-599-0323

Mail order catalog. Monday-Friday 7 am to 9 pm, Saturday-Sunday 9 am to 5 pm. Restore or repair your 1/2 or 3/4 ton Chevy truck 1947-1987. Our easy to read, fully illustrated free catalogs, fast service and an on-line computer order system make ordering easy. Large supply of parts and accessories include bed kits, body, interior, heating and cooling, suspension, brakes, electrical, and much more. Web site: lmctruck.com

Lord Byron Inc | fender covers
420 Sackett Point Rd
North Haven, CT 06473
203-287-9881; FAX: 203-288-9456

See full listing in **Section Two** under **car covers**

Lutty's Chevy Warehouse | reproduction parts
RD 2, 2385 Saxonburg Blvd
Cheswick, PA 15024
724-265-2988; FAX: 724-265-4773

Mail order and open shop. Monday-Wednesday 9 am to 7 pm, Thursay-Friday 9 am to 5 pm, Saturday 9 am to 2 pm EST. Specializing in reproduction parts to restore your Chevrolet 1955-1968; Chevelle 1964-1977, including Monte Carlo; Nova 1962-1979; Camaro 1967-1981 and Chevy truck 1947-1972.

See our ad on this page

M & H Electric Fabricators Inc | wiring harnesses
13537 Alondra Blvd
Santa Fe Springs, CA 90670
562-926-9552; FAX: 562-926-9572
E-mail: sales@wiringharness.com

See full listing in **Section Two** under **electrical systems**

Mack Products | parts
PO Box 856 | pickup beds
Moberly, MO 65270
660-263-7444

See full listing in **Section One** under **Ford 1932-1953**

Majestic Truck Parts | parts
17726 Dickerson
Dallas, TX 75252
972-248-6245; FAX: 972-380-8913
E-mail: majestictrk@juno.com

Specializing in top quality parts, NOS, reproduction, used and rare for 1947-1972 Chevy/GMC half to one ton trucks. We have a few good project trucks. Our tall new red and white trailer visits Dallas/Fort Worth Metroplex meets. Visit north Dallas anytime by appointment; phone or fax; we ship. Carry most of your needs, some of your wants and a few of your dreams. The most friendly, helpful people in truckin'.

Marcovicci-Wenz Engineering Inc | Cosworth engines
33 Comac Loop
Ronkonkoma, NY 11779
516-467-9040; FAX: 516-467-9041
E-mail: tedwenz@compuserve.com

See full listing in **Section Two** under **racing**

Martz Classic Chevy Parts | parts
RD 1, Box 199B
Thomasville, PA 17364
717-225-1655; FAX: 717-225-3637

Mail order and open shop. Monday-Friday 8 am to 5 pm. Specializing in sales of NOS and reproduction parts for 1955-1970 full-size Chevrolets, 1962-1974 Novas, 1967-1981 Camaros and 1964-1972 Chevelles.

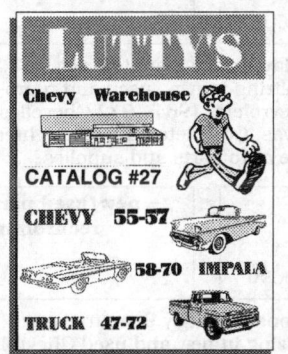 

Master Power Brakes | brake products conversion kits
254-1 Rolling Hills Rd
Mooresville, NC 28115
704-664-8866; FAX: 704-664-8862

See full listing in **Section One** under **Chevelle/Camaro**

Max Neon Design Group | custom face logos glass light-up clocks neon clocks
19807 Sussex Dr
St Clair Shores, MI 48081-3257
810-773-5000; FAX: 810-772-6224

See full listing in **Section Two** under **automobilia**

McCoy's Memorabilia | memorabilia racing literature
35583 N 1830 E
Rossville, IL 60963-7175
PH/FAX: 217-748-6513
E-mail: indy500@soltec.net

See full listing in **Section Two** under **literature dealers**

Merv's Classic Chevy Parts | parts
1330 Washington
Iowa Falls, IA 50126
515-648-3168, 515-648-9675

Mail order and open shop. Specializing in reproduction, NOS and used parts for 1955-1957 Chevy and 1967-1972 Chevy pickups

Mid-America Auction Services | auctions
2277 W Hwy 36, Ste 214
St Paul, MN 55113
612-633-9655; FAX: 612-633-3212
E-mail: midauction@aol.com

See full listing in **Section Two** under **auctions & events**

Mike's Chevy Parts | restoration supplies
7716 Deering Ave
Canoga Park, CA 91304
818-346-0070; FAX: 818-713-0715

Mail order and open shop. Monday-Friday 8 am to 5 pm, Saturday 9 am to 12 pm. Specializing in new, used and reproduction parts for 1955-1970 Chevrolets, 1964-1972 Chevelles and El Caminos, 1962-1974 Novas. Complete frame straightening and front end repair. Antique auto parts and supplies.

Monroe Motorsports Inc | new/used parts rechroming
7138 Maddox Rd
Lithonia, GA 30058
770-482-9219; FAX: 770-482-6690

Mail order and counter sales. Monday-Friday 9 am to 6 pm; Saturday 9 am to 3 pm. Specializing in new and used Chevrolet parts for cars and trucks. Plastic and metal. Rechroming.

Mooney's Antique Chevrolet Parts | engine parts rubber parts
HC 01, Box 645C
Goodrich, TX 77335
409-365-2899, 9 am to 6 pm
409-685-4577, 6 pm to 9 pm
orders only
FAX: 409-685-4711

Zoned for mail order only. Monday-Friday 9 am to 5:30 pm, Saturday 9 am to 12 pm. Counter sales by chance or appointment. Large line of parts for Chevrolets, 1916-1954 passenger cars and 1916-1946 pickups. Complete line of mechanical, transmission, engine, ignition, rubber parts, etc. Free catalog.

Mike Moran | information
1349 Cleveland Rd
Glendale, CA 91202

Mail order only. Technical information on Vegas, including Cosworth, also Mobil Gas economy runs, gasoline economy devices and unusual engines. SASE required.

Moroso Motorsports Park | race track
PO Box 31907
Palm Beach Gardens, FL 33420
561-622-1400; FAX: 561-626-2053
E-mail: racetrack@moroso.com

See full listing in **Section Two** under **racing**

National Chevy Assoc | parts
947 Arcade Street
St Paul, MN 55106
612-778-9522; FAX: 800-785-5354

Mail order and open shop. Monday-Friday 8:30 am to 5 pm. Specializing in new, used, NOS parts for 1953-1954 Chevrolet. You need our catalog! Catalog and sample newsletter, $6.

The National Corvette Museum | museum
350 Corvette Dr
Bowling Green, KY 42101-9134
800-53-VETTE; FAX: 270-781-5286
E-mail: lisa@corvettemuseum.com

See full listing in **Section Six** under **Kentucky**

New England Mustang Supply Inc | accessories parts
1830 Barnum Ave
Bridgeport, CT 06610
203-333-7454; FAX: 203-332-0880

See full listing in **Section One** under **Mustang**

Dave Newell's Chevrobilia | literature memorabilia
PO Box 588
Orinda, CA 94563
510-223-4725

Mail order only. Original literature (sales, service, parts), showroom memorabilia, photos, films, models, jewelry, posters, etc for all Chevy cars and trucks, for all years. Impala, Chevelle, Nova, Camaro, Corvair and Corvette. Please send $5 for latest catalog of my constantly changing inventory.

Charles Noe | broker parts/auto purchases parts/auto sales
64-1/2 Greenwood Ave
Bethel, CT 06801
PH/FAX: 203-748-4222
E-mail: mdchas@aol.com

See full listing in **Section Two** under **brokers**

NorCal Auto | appraisals
615D Saint John St
Pleasanton, CA 94566
888-224-6005; FAX: 925-426-8845
E-mail: mwjohn@hotmail.com

See full listing in **Section Two** under **appraisals**

Normans' Classic Auto Radio | custom sales
7651 Park Blvd
Pinellas Park, FL 33781
888-222-3433, 727-546-1788

See full listing in **Section Two** under **radios**

North Yale Auto Parts | salvage yard
Rt 1, Box 707
Sperry, OK 74073
918-288-7218, 800-256-6927 (NYAP)
FAX: 918-288-7223

See full listing in **Section Five** under **Oklahoma**

Oak Bows | top bows
122 Ramsey Ave
Chambersburg, PA 17201
717-264-2602

See full listing in **Section Two** under **woodwork**

Obsolete Chevrolet Parts Co
524 Hazel Ave
PO Box 68
Nashville, GA 31639-0068
800-248-8785; FAX: 912-686-3056
E-mail: obschevy@surfsouth.com

**engine parts
radiators
rubber parts
transmissions**

Mail order and open shop. Monday-Friday 8 am to 5:30 pm,
Saturday 8:30 am to 12:30 pm. NOS and reproduction inventory
of mechanical, electrical, weatherstripping, sheetmetal, trim
parts, truck bed parts and interior parts. We accept MasterCard,
Visa or Discover or ship COD via UPS. We also accept orders by
fax. Catalogs $3 each and available for 1929-1954 car, 1955-
1957 car, 1958-1972 Impala, Bel Air and Caprice, 1962-1972
Chevy II, Chevelle and Camaro, 1929-1959 truck or 1960-1972
truck. Web site: www.obschevy.com

See our ad on this page

OEM Glass Inc
Rt 9 E
PO Box 362
Bloomington, IL 61702
309-662-2122; FAX: 309-663-7474

auto glass

See full listing in **Section Two** under **glass**

OEM Paints Inc
PO Box 461736
Escondido, CA 92046-1736
760-747-2100

**custom aerosol
colors**

See full listing in **Section Two** under **paints**

Old Air Products
4615 Martin St
Ft Worth, TX 76119
817-531-2665; FAX: 817-531-3257
E-mail: sales@oldairproducts.com

air conditioning

See full listing in **Section One** under **Corvette**

The Old Car Centre
19909 92A Ave
Langley, BC Canada V1M 3B6
604-888-4412, 604-888-4055
FAX: 604-888-7455

parts

See full listing in **Section One** under **Ford 1903-1931**

Old Car Parts
7525 SE Powell
Portland, OR 97206
800-886-7277, 503-771-9416
FAX: 503-771-1981
E-mail: gsnovak@europa.com

parts

Mail order and open shop. Monday-Friday 9 am to 5 pm.
Specializing in GM parts for Chevrolet cars and pickups 1936-
1969.

The Old Carb Doctor
Rt 3, Box 338
Drucilla Church Rd
Nebo, NC 28761
800-945-CARB (2272)
704-659-1428

**carburetors
fuel pumps**

See full listing in **Section Two** under **carburetors**

Old Chevy Parts Store
formally known as Palm Springs
Obsolete Automotive
120 N Pacific A-8
San Marcos, CA 92069
760-752-1479; FAX: 760-752-1528
E-mail: info@oldchevypartsstore.com

parts

Mail order and open shop. Tuesday-Friday 7 am to 5 pm,
Saturday 8 am to 4 pm. Manufacture of 1955/1957 passenger car
fan shrouds, new, reproduction parts for 1955/1957 pass cars,
1958/1972 Impalas. Established in 1983. Catalogs $4 each in

US and $8 out of country, free with purchase. Please state which
model you are working on. Web site: www.oldchevypartsstore.com

Old Dominion Mustang/Camaro
509 S Washington Hwy, Rt 1
Ashland, VA 23005
804-798-3348; FAX: 804-798-5105

parts

See full listing in **Section One** under **Mustang**

Old Tin Australia
PO Box 26
Wendouree Victoria 3355 Australia
03 5336 FORD; FAX: 03 5339 9900

salvage yard

See full listing in **Section Five** under **Australia**

Only Yesterday Classic Autos Inc
24 Valley Rd
Port Washington, NY 11050
516-767-3477; FAX: 516-767-8964

cars

Classic and special interest autos from the 1950s-1960s. We specialize in Chevys, Corvettes, Fords and Pontiacs. We are manufacturers' representatives for the Duesenberg II, ask us about
this fabulous automobile. Tell us your interest and we will help
you locate what you are looking for. Web site: www.oldautos.com

Original Auto Interiors
7869 Trumble Rd
Columbus, MI 48063-3915
810-727-2486; FAX: 810-727-4344
E-mail: origauto@tir.com

upholstery

See full listing in **Section Two** under **upholstery**

Original Parts Group Inc
17892 Gothard St
Huntington Beach, CA 92647
800-243-8355 US/Canada
714-841-5363; FAX: 714-847-8159

accessories
parts

See full listing in **Section One** under **Pontiac**

P-Ayr Products
719 Delaware St
Leavenworth, KS 66048
913-651-5543; FAX: 913-651-2084
E-mail: sales@payr.com

replicas

Specializing in light weight automotive engines, transmissions
and motorcycle engine replicas for Chevrolet, Ford and Chrysler.
Web site: www.payr.com

Packard Farm
97 N 150 W
Greenfield, IN 46140
317-462-3124
800-922-1957 orders only
FAX: 317-462-8891

parts

See full listing in **Section One** under **Packard**

The Paddock® Inc
PO Box 30
221 W Main
Knightstown, IN 46148
800-428-4319; FAX: 800-286-4040
E-mail: paddock@indy.net

accessories
parts

See full listing in **Section One** under **Mustang**

Paragon Reproductions Inc
8040 S Jennings Rd
Swartz Creek, MI 48473
810-655-4641; FAX: 810-655-6667
E-mail:
www.info@corvette-paragon.com

Corvette repro
parts

See full listing in **Section One** under **Corvette**

M Parker Autoworks Inc
150 Heller Pl #17W
Dept HVAA99
Bellmawr, NJ 08031
609-933-0801; FAX: 609-933-0805
E-mail: facfit@erols.com

battery cables
harnesses

See full listing in **Section Two** under **electrical systems**

The Parts Place
217 Paul St
Elburn, IL 60119
PH/FAX: 630-365-1800
E-mail: pplace9594@aol.com

parts

Classic car parts for General Motors vehicles. Specializing in
new, used, reproduction and discontinued parts for 1960-1980.

Parts Unlimited Inc
Todd Bidwell
12101 Westport Rd
Louisville, KY 40245-1789
502-425-3766; FAX: 502-425-0055

interiors
weatherstrips

Manufacturer of quality interior components for many 1955-
1981 GM cars and trucks including seat covers, door panels
(standard, pre-assembled), headliners, sunvisors, top boots,
Windowfelt® brand replacement weatherstrips, package
trays/insulation, trunk dividers, arm rest bases/pads, assorted
trim products, etc. Also: Chrysler seat upholstery, headliners,
Windowfelt®; 1964-1973 Ford Mustang Windowfelt®, door panels. All quality products made in USA. Established 1975. Over
500 dealers. Call 800-342-0610 for the dealer nearest you.

Passenger Car Supply
102 Cloverdale Rd
Swedesboro, NJ 08085
609-467-7966

parts

Both mail order and open shop. Monday-Friday 10 am to 10 pm,
weekends by chance/appt. Full size Chevy resto parts for 1958-
1975 full size Chevrolet, NOS, used, new and repro, all items.

Patrick's Antique Cars & Trucks
PO Box 10648
Casa Grande, AZ 85230
520-836-1117; FAX: 520-836-1104
E-mail: patstrks@aol.com

parts

Mail order and open shop. 7 days a week. Complete engine
rebuild parts and speed equipment for 1937-1962 Chevy/GMC
6s and flathead Ford/Merc V8 1932-1953. Free catalog (specify
Chevy or Ford, please). Visa, MC, Discover, COD orders welcome.

Performance Chevy
2995 W Whitton
Phoenix, AZ 85017
800-203-6621; FAX: 602-254-1094

engine parts
restoration

See full listing in **Section One** under **Corvette**

Pick-ups Northwest
1430 Bickford Ave
Snohomish, WA 98290
360-568-9166; FAX: 360-568-1233

parts
trim

Mail order and open shop. Monday-Friday 9 am to 5:30 pm,
Saturday 9 am to 3 pm. Specializing in weatherstrip, interior,
chrome trim, pickup box parts and wood kits for 1932-1972 Chevy
and 1932-1973 Ford pickup trucks. Restoration or street rod parts.

John E Pirkle
3706 Merion Dr
Augusta, GA 30907
706-860-9047; FAX: 706-860-2723
E-mail: pirklesr@juno.com

electrical parts

See full listing in **Section One** under **Corvette**

Jack Podell Fuel Injection Spec
106 Wakewa Ave
South Bend, IN 46617
219-232-6430; FAX: 219-234-8632

fuel system parts
fuel system
rebuilding

See full listing in **Section One** under **Corvette**

Dennis Portka
4326 Beetow Dr
Hamburg, NY 14075
716-649-0921

horns
knock-off wheels

See full listing in **Section One** under **Corvette**

Power Brake Booster Exchange Inc
4533 SE Division St
Portland, OR 97206
503-238-8882

brake boosters

See full listing in **Section Two** under **brakes**

Power Brake X-Change Inc
336 Lamont Pl
Pittsburgh, PA 15232
800-580-5729, 412-441-5729
FAX: 412-441-9333

parts

See full listing in **Section Two** under **brakes**

**Precision Pot Metal/Bussie
Restoration Inc**
1008 Loring Ave #28
Orange Park, FL 32073
904-269-8788

pot metal restora-
tion

See full listing in **Section Two** under **plating & polishing**

PRO Antique Auto Parts   parts
50 King Spring Rd
Windsor Locks, CT 06096
860-623-8274

Mail order and open shop. Monday-Friday 9 am to 5 pm.
Exclusive distributor of numerous reproduction parts for 1923-
1964 Chevrolets. Catalog, $3.

R & R Fiberglass & Specialties   body parts
4850 Wilson Dr NW
Cleveland, TN 37312
423-476-2270; FAX: 423-473-9442
E-mail: rrfiberglass@wingnet.net

See full listing in **Section Two** under **fiberglass parts**

Red Bird Racing   parts
6640 Valley St
Coeur d'Alene, ID 83815
208-762-5305

Mail order only. Specializing in 1937-1954 Chevy chassis update
parts. Bolt on Saginaw steering adapters, dropped spindles,
Teflon button rear spring kits, front and rear tube shock mounting kits, lowering block kits. All Chevy 6-cyl split manifolds, 216-
235-261 alternator brackets. GMC and Chevy 6-cyl to Turbo
350-400 kits. Inline and flathead V8 speed parts, Fenton headers, Edmunds style air cleaners.

Reproduction Parts Marketing   parts
1920 Alberta Ave   restoration
Saskatoon, SK Canada S7K 1R9   service
306-652-6668; FAX: 306-652-1123

Mail order and open shop. Monday-Saturday 8 am to 9 pm.
Canada's largest stocking GM, Ford and Mopar dealer. All parts
are guaranteed to be the finest available and our prices are the
lowest. Also handling complete restorations. Parts, service, tech
advice, appraisals, locator service.

Restoration Specialties   interiors
John Sarena   restoration
124 North F St
Lompoc, CA 93436
805-736-2627

Open shop only. Monday-Friday 8 am to 5 pm PST. Partial to
1955-1957 Chevrolets and one of the authors of the *CCCI
Restoration and Judging Guidelines Manual*. Shares the love of
all special interest cars of the 1940s-1960s and worked with
Moss Motors for nine years in designing all of their interior kits.
Takes great pride in craftsmenship and it shows in finished interiors. Dealer for CARS reproduction interiors. Specializing in
interior restoration, partial restoration for 1955-1957 Chevys,
American cars of the 1950s and 1960s, and English sports cars.

Rick's First Generation Camaro   accessories
Parts & Accessories   parts
420 Athena Dr
Athens, GA 30601
800-359-7717; FAX: 706-548-8581
E-mail: firstgen@negia.net

See full listing in **Section One** under **Chevelle/Camaro**

Frank Riley Automotive Art   automotive prints
PO Box 95
Hawthorne, NJ 07506
800-848-9459

See full listing in **Section Two** under **artwork**

Riverhill Truck Co   parts
458 Wilde Rd
Jackson, TN 38301
901-988-5079

1967-1972 Chevy/GMC truck parts. New and used.
"Joshua:24:15." Joey Blackmon, owner.

Roberts Motor Parts   parts
17 Prospect St
West Newbury, MA 01985
978-363-5407; FAX: 978-363-2026
E-mail: sales@robertsmotorparts.com

See full listing in **Section One** under **Dodge**

Leon J Rocco   accessories
4125 Loring St   parts
Butler, PA 16001
724-482-4387 after 6 pm

See full listing in **Section One** under **Chevelle/Camaro**

Rock Valley Antique Auto Parts   gas tanks
Box 352
Rt 72 and Rothwell Rd
Stillman Valley, IL 61084
815-645-2271; FAX: 815-645-2740

See full listing in **Section One** under **Ford 1932-1953**

Rod-1 Shop   street rods
210 Clinton Ave
Pitman, NJ 08071
609-228-7631; FAX: 609-582-5770

See full listing in **Section Two** under **street rods**

Ross' Automotive Machine Co Inc   racing engines
1763 N Main St   rebuilding
Niles, OH 44446
330-544-4466

See full listing in **Section Two** under **engine rebuilding**

Saturn Industries   axles/instruments
10-14 Newland St, Coleford   literature
Royal Forest of Dean   nostalgic bits
Gloucestershire GL 16 8AN England   repro parts
01594 834321; FAX: 01594 835456   street rods

See full listing in **Section One** under **Ford 1903-1931**

SC Automotive   parts
Rt 3 Box 9   restoration
New Ulm, MN 56073
800-62-SS-409 (627-7409)
507-354-1958 info
FAX: 800-6477-FAX (647-7329)

348-409 parts. Free catalog listing thousands of parts for your
1958-1964 Chevrolet. Fuel lines, radiators, air cleaners, pistons,
valves, rebuild kits, exhaust, decals, moldings/emblems, electrical, accessories, shop and assembly manuals and more. Simply
the best. Credit card and CODs accepted.

Chuck Scharf Enterprises   parts
1019 N Minnesota St
New Ulm, MN 56073
507-354-4501

Mail order only. Specializing in 348/409 equipped 1958-1965
full size Chevrolets. Offer a full line of engine rebuild parts, 12
different engine kits, 348/409 pistons, +.030, +.040, +.060. One
call does it all, same day shipping. Visa, MasterCard, COD
orders welcome. Free rebuild catalog.

Scotts Super Trucks   parts
1972 Hwy 592 W
Penhold, AB Canada T0M 1R0
403-886-5572; FAX: 403-886-5577

Mail order and open shop. Tuesday-Saturday 10 am to 5 pm
MST. Specialize in 1967-1972 GMC/Chev trucks, but also carry
a full line of new and used parts from 1934-1966 original and
custom parts. Everything to restore your classic truck. Also
many project trucks for sale, 1935-1972.

Sherman & Associates Inc	**body panels**
61166 Van Dyke Rd	**body parts/fenders**
Washington, MI 48094	**floors**
810-677-6800; FAX: 810-677-6801	**quarter panels**

See full listing in **Section Two** under **body parts**

Skimino Enterprises	**body parts**
129 Skimino Rd	**license plates**
Williamsburg, VA 23188-2229	**mechanical parts**
757-565-1422	

See full listing in **Section Two** under **license plates**

O B Smith Chevy Parts	**parts**
PO Box 11703	**tires**
990 New Circle Rd NW	
Lexington, KY 40577	
606-253-1957; FAX: 606-233-3129	

Restoration parts for 1955-1957 classic Chevrolets and 1947-1972 Chevrolet pickups. Catalogs, $3 each.

Lyn Smith Nova Parts	**car dealer**
1104 Countryside Ln	**parts**
Pontiac, IL 61764	
815-844-7852	

Mail order and open shop by appointment only. Specializing in 1962-1967 Chevy Nova parts. Have new, used and reproduction items. Also buy and sell Nova cars. Rust-free fenders, doors, subframes, bezels, moldings, bucket seats, consoles, bumpers, grilles, disc brake set ups, stick shift parts, V8 kits, 4-core radiators. Buy, sell, trade.

Bob Sottile's Hobby Car Auto	**car dealer**
Sales Inc	**restoration**
RD 2 Box 210B, Rt 164	
Martinsburg, PA 16662	
814-793-4282	

See full listing in **Section One** under **Corvette**

Sound Move Inc	**radios**
217 S Main St	
Elkhart, IN 46516	
800-901-0222, 219-294-5100	
FAX: 219-293-4902	

Mail order and open shop. Monday-Friday 9 am to 5 pm, Saturday 9 am to 12 pm. Specializing in AM-FM radios and audio systems that install into original factory location with no modifications. For classic cars and trucks, 1940-1989. Web site: www.soundmove.com

Special Auto Restoration	**restoration**
689 Fern Dr	
Merritt Island, FL 32952	
407-453-8343, 407-783-4758	

See full listing in **Section One** under **Chevelle/Camaro**

Stoudt Auto Sales	**parts**
1350 Carbon St	**sales**
Reading, PA 19601	**service**
800-523-8485 USA parts dept	
800-482-3033 USA sales dept	
610-374-4856, parts info	
FAX: 610-372-7283	

See full listing in **Section One** under **Corvette**

Strader Classics	**parts**
Bill Strader	
2849 Locust Grove Rd	
Elizabethtown, KY 42701	
502-737-5294	

Mail order and open shop. Monday-Friday after 4 pm, anytime on the weekend. New reproduction parts, new old stock, used parts and over 90 parts cars for 1955, 1956 and 1957 Chevrolet cars. If they make it, we can get it. If you need it, we can find it.

Street-Wise Performance	**differentials**
Richie Mulligan	**parts**
Box 105 Creek Rd	**rebuild kits**
Tranquility, NJ 07879	**transmissions**
973-786-6668 days	
973-786-7133 evenings	
FAX: 973-786-7861	
E-mail: richie@goes.com	

See full listing in **Section Two** under **transmissions**

Stringbean's Pickup Parts	**parts**
985 Cushon St	**service**
Johnstown, PA 15902	
PH/FAX: 814-539-6440	
E-mail: s-bean@surfshop.net	

Mail order and open shop. Monday-Saturday 2 pm to 10 pm. Specializing in new, used and repro parts for 1947-1972 Chevrolet pickup trucks. Can also install everything we sell in our full service shop. Web site: www.surfshop.net/users/s-bean/billhome.htm

Tags Backeast	**data plates**
PO Box 581	**trim tags**
Plainville, CT 06062	
860-747-2942	
E-mail: dataplt@snet.net	

See full listing in **Section Two** under **special services**

Bill Thomsen	**salvage yard**
1118 Wooded Acres Ln	
Moneta, VA 24121	
540-297-1200	

See full listing in **Section Five** under **Virginia**

Tom's Classic Parts	**parts**
5207 Sundew Terr	
Tobyhanna, PA 18466	
800-832-4073	

Mail order and pick up. Call for hours. Genuine Chevrolet parts for your Bel Air, Biscayne, Caprice, Impala, Monte Carlo, Nova and others, 1960-present. Have NOS and quality used parts available. Experienced staff to help in your search for parts. MasterCard, Visa, AmEx.

Transgo Performance	**shift kits**
2621 Merced Ave	
El Monte, CA 91733	
626-443-4953; FAX: 626-443-1079	

See full listing in **Section Two** under **transmissions**

Trim Parts Inc	**trim items**
5161 Wolfpen Pleasant Hill	
Milford, OH 45150	
513-831-1472; FAX: 513-248-3402	
E-mail: sales@trimparts.com	

Mail order and open shop. Monday-Friday 8 am to 5 pm. Classic GM restoration, reproduction emblems, lenses, scripts and other trim items for classic GM cars and trucks. 1955-1957 Chevy, 1958-1972 full-size, 1967-1985 Camaro, 1953-1982 Corvette, 1964-1972 Chevelle, 1967-1969 Firebird, 1962-1972 Nova, 1964-1972 El Camino, 1970-1972 Monte Carlo, GTO, Corvair. Web site: www.trimparts.com

The Truck Shop	**parts**
PO Box 5035	
104 W Marion Ave	
Nashville, GA 31639	
800-245-0556 orders	
info: 912-686-3833, 912-686-3396	
FAX: 912-686-3531	

Mail order and open shop. Monday-Friday 8 am to 5 pm. Chevrolet and GMC truck parts. NOS and reproduction 1927-1987. Bed components, weatherstrips, glass channel, hubcaps, handles and controls, headliners, interior parts, emblems and moldings, manuals, mirrors, patch panels, lights, suspension, carpets, mats and much more. Catalog, $5.

Ultimate Spray-On Truck Bedliner   bedliners
115 Garfield St
Sumas, WA 98295
800-989-9869; FAX: 604-864-0207
E-mail: info@ultimatelinings.com

See full listing in **Section Two** under **trucks & tractors**

Ultra Wheel Co   custom wheels
6300 Valley View Ave
Buena Park, CA 90620
714-994-1444; FAX: 714-994-0723

See full listing in **Section Two** under **wheels & wheelcovers**

Unfair Advantage Enterprises   emblems
2219 W Olive Ave #179   trim
Burbank, CA 91506
213-245-8441

See full listing in **Section One** under **Cobra**

Universal Transmission Co   transmission parts
23361 Dequindre Rd
Hazel Park, MI 48030
800-882-4327; FAX: 248-398-2581

See full listing in **Section Two** under **transmissions**

Tom Vagnini   used parts
58 Anthony Rd, RR 3
Pittsfield, MA 01201
413-698-2526

See full listing in **Section One** under **Packard**

Valley Motor Supply   accessories
1402 E Second St   parts
Roswell, NM 88201
505-622-7450

See full listing in **Section One** under **Ford 1954-up**

Vibratech Inc (Fluidampr)   performance parts
11980 Walden Ave
Alden, NY 14004
716-937-3603; FAX: 716-937-4692

See full listing in **Section Two** under **engine parts**

Vintage Books   books
6613 E Mill Plain   literature
Vancouver, WA 98661
360-694-9519; FAX: 360-694-7644
E-mail: vintageb@teleport.com

See full listing in **Section Two** under **literature dealers**

Vintage Ford & Chevrolet   parts
Parts of Arizona Inc
So-Cal Speed Shop
3427 E McDowell Rd
Phoenix, AZ 85008-3845
800-732-0076, 602-275-7990
FAX: 602-267-8439
E-mail: vintageparts@sprintmail.com

See full listing in **Section One** under **Ford 1954-up**

Vintage Parts 411   books
4909 Ruffner St
San Diego, CA 92111
800-MOTORHEAD
FAX: 619-467-0777
E-mail: cars@vintageparts.com

See full listing in **Section Four** under **information sources**

Volunteer State Chevy Parts   accessories
Hwy 41 S   parts
PO Box 10
Greenbrier, TN 37073
615-643-4583; FAX: 615-643-5100

Mail order and open shop. Monday-Friday (Saturday?) 8 am to 6 pm CST. Specializing in obsolete parts and accessories from 1949-1972 passenger cars and trucks, includes Chevelle, Chevy II, Camaro, with special emphasis on 1955-1967 Impalas, etc.

Waldron's Antique Exhaust Inc   exhaust systems
PO Box C
25872 M-86
Nottawa, MI 49075
616-467-7185; FAX: 616-467-9041

See full listing in **Section Two** under **exhaust systems**

Wales Antique Chevy Truck Parts   parts
143 Center
Carleton, MI 48117
734-654-8836

Specializing in 1936-1972 Chevrolet trucks. Windshield, cab, door and hood rubber. Seals, weatherstrip, headlights, parking lights, taillights. Parts, brackets, outside and inside handles. Bed wood, tailgates, front and side panels. Wear strips, angles, repair panels. Books, manuals. Engine and mechanical parts, fiberglass fenders and runningboards. Hubcaps, trim rings, runningboard step plates. Also rebuilds door hinges, refaces and rebuilds gauges. Chrome work and cutting of clear and tinted glass. Used parts for 1947-1955 Chevrolet trucks. Send (2) 33¢ stamps for free catalog, state year of truck.

Ted Williams Enterprises   parts
5615 Rt 45
Lisbon, OH 44432
330-424-9413; FAX: 330-424-9060
E-mail: willitd@valunet.com

Mail order and open shop. Monday 9 am to 8 pm, Tuesday-Friday 9 am to 5 pm, Saturday 9 am to 2 pm, call first. NOS and reproduction parts for 1964-1972 Chevelles and El Caminos, 1962-1972 Nova and Chevy II. Retail and wholesale, mostly mail order, pick up at warehouse available. No showroom. COD available. Accepts Visa and MC. UPS daily. Orders shipped same or next business day. In business since 1975. Web site: www.chevellenova.com

The Woodie Works   woodworking
245 VT Rt 7A
Arlington, VT 05250
PH/FAX: 802-375-9305
E-mail: dkwoodie@vermontel.com

See full listing in **Section Two** under **woodwork**

CHEVELLE
camaro

4-Speeds by Darrell   transmissions
PO Box 110
3 Water St
Vermilion, IL 61955
217-275-3743; FAX: 217-275-3515

See full listing in **Section Two** under **transmissions**

All American Chevys   publication
7950 Deering Ave
Canoga Park, CA 91304-5063
818-887-0550; FAX: 818-884-1343
E-mail: mail@challengeweb.com

See full listing in **Section One** under **Chevrolet**

All Chevy/Canadian Impala 404 Allwood Rd Parksville, BC Canada V9P 1C4 250-248-8666; FAX: 888-248-1958 E-mail: canimp@nanaimo.ark.com	parts

See full listing in **Section One** under **Chevrolet**

American Classics Unlimited Inc PO Box 192-V Oak Lawn, IL 60454-0192 PH/FAX: 708-424-9223	automobilia models toys

See full listing in **Section Two** under **models & toys**

American Restorations Unlimited TA 14 Meakin Ave PO Box 34 Rochelle Park, NJ 07662 201-843-3567; FAX: 201-843-3238 E-mail: amerrest@earthlink.net	restoration parts

See full listing in **Section Two** under **glass**

AMK Products 18600 E 96th St Broken Arrow, OK 74012 918-455-2651; FAX: 918-455-7441	parts

See full listing in **Section One** under **Mustang**

Auto Custom Carpet Inc Jeff Moses PO Box 1350, 1429 Noble St Anniston, AL 36201 800-633-2358, 205-236-1118 FAX: 800-516-8274 E-mail: info@accmats.net	carpets floor mats

See full listing in **Section One** under **Chevrolet**

Auto Decals Unlimited Inc 11259 E Via Linda, Ste 100-201 Scottsdale, AZ 85259 602-220-0800	decals stripe kits

See full listing in **Section Two** under **decals**

Boyds Hot Rods & Collectable Cars 8400 Cerritos Ave Stanton, CA 90680 714-220-9870; FAX: 714-220-9877 E-mail: sales@boydshotrods.com	car dealer

See full listing in **Section One** under **Chevrolet**

Camaro Specialties 112 Elm St East Aurora, NY 14052 716-652-7086; FAX: 716-652-2279 E-mail: dunlop@wzrd.com	parts restoration

Specializing in 1966-1972 GM muscle cars. Offer new, used, reproduction and southern parts. Now booking restorations for 1967-1969 Camaros or Firebirds. Catalogs available for Camaro, Firebird and Chevelle. Web site: www.camaros.com

CARS Inc 1964 W 11 Mile Rd Berkley, MI 48072 248-398-7100; FAX: 248-398-7078 E-mail: carsinc@worldnet.att.net	interior

See full listing in **Section One** under **Chevrolet**

Chevyland Parts & Accessories 3667 Recycle Rd #8 Rancho Cordova, CA 95742 916-638-3906; FAX: 916-638-0302 E-mail: chevylnd@concourse.net	accessories parts restoration

Mail order and open shop. Monday-Friday 9 am to 6 pm,

Saturday 10 am to 3 pm. Specializing in restoration parts and accessories for Camaro, Chevelle, El Camino, Nova and 1967-1972 Chevrolet pickup trucks.

Classic and Muscle Muscle Car Restoration Parts PO Box 657 Elmsdale, NS Canada B0N 1M0 902-883-4489; FAX: 902-883-1392 E-mail: classicmuscle@sprint.ca	reproduction parts restoration parts

See full listing in **Section One** under **Chevrolet**

Classic Coachworks 735 Frenchtown Rd Milford, NJ 08848 908-996-3400; FAX: 908-996-0204	bodywork painting restoration

See full listing in **Section Two** under **restoration shops**

Classic Industries Inc Camaro Parts and Accessories Catalog 17832 Gothard St Huntington Beach, CA 92647 800-854-1280 parts/info FAX: 800-300-3081 toll-free E-mail: info@classicindustries.com	accessories parts

Largest selection of Camaro parts and accessories ever assembled in one catalog. Over 580 full color pages of the finest quality restoration products and late model accessories. Only $5, refunded on first order. Call our 24-hour toll-free catalog hotline, 888-GM-CATALOG, and receive the industry's most comprehensive parts catalog from the undisputed leader in the industry, Classic Industries. Web site: www.classicindustries.com

See our ad inside the front cover

Coach Builders Muscle Car **Parts & Services** PO Box 128 Baltimore, MD 21087-0128 410-426-5567	interiors parts rust remover

See full listing in **Section One** under **Chevrolet**

Competitive Automotive Inc 2095 W Shore Rd (Rt 117) Warwick, RI 02886 401-739-6262, 739-6288 FAX: 401-739-1497	parts restoration

Mail order and showroom. Monday-Friday 11 am to 8 pm. GM restoration supplies. Specializing in complete line of 1967-1981 Camaro and Firebird restoration supplies and parts. New, used, reproduction and obscure parts including body panels, trim, mechanical, suspensions, wiring, interior and upholstery, weatherstripping, lenses, convertibles, windows, literature, decals, fasteners, switches, bumpers, braces, grilles, manuals, emblems, headliners, etc. Also handle all GM muscle cars in 1960s and 1970s.

Custom Autosound Mfg 808 W Vermont Ave Anaheim, CA 92805 800-888-8637; FAX: 714-533-0361 E-mail: info@custom-autosound.com	CD players custom radios speaker upgrades

See full listing in **Section One** under **Chevrolet**

Custom Classic Cars 2046 E 12B Road Bourbon, IN 46504 219-342-5007; FAX: 219-342-0399 E-mail: customclassiccars@waveone.net	parts restoration

See full listing in **Section One** under **Chevrolet**

Desert Muscle Cars	parts
2853 N Stone Ave Tucson, AZ 85705 520-882-3010; FAX: 520-628-9332	

Mail order and open shop. Weekdays 9 am to 5:30 pm, Saturday 9 am to 3 pm. Specializing in restoration supplies and parts for 1955-1970 Chevrolets, 1967-1981 Camaro, 1964-1972 Chevelle, 1947-1972 Chevrolet trucks, 1964-1973 Mustangs, all Corvettes. Deal in weatherstripping, interiors, emblems, moldings, decals, books, etc.

Dynatech Engineering	motor mounts
PO Box 1446 Alta Loma, CA 91701-8446 805-492-6134 E-mail: dynatechengineering@yahoo.com	

See full listing in **Section Two** under **engine parts**

The El Camino Store	parts
57 B Depot Rd Goleta, CA 93117 805-681-8164; FAX: 805-681-8166 E-mail: ec@elcaminostore.com	

Walk-in and phone orders. Monday-Friday 8 am to 5:30 pm. Sell parts for all the Chevrolet and GMC El Caminos ever made from 1959-1987. Carry an extensive inventory of weatherstripping, emblems, chrome, trim, decals, interior parts. Also manufacture our own parts and are a GM Restoration parts licensee.

ETC Every Thing Cars	paint repairs restoration welding
8727 Clarinda Pico Rivera, CA 90660 562-949-6981	

See full listing in **Section One** under **Mopar**

Fire-Aro Restoration Parts Supply Co	accessories parts
9251 Yonge St Unit 8, Ste 108 Richmand Hill, ON Canada L4C 9T3 888-249-4939 toll-free 905-881-7337; FAX: 905-881-2445	

Mail order and open shop by appointment. Monday-Saturday. Retail sales of Camaro, Firebird, Nova, Chevy II, NOS or reproduction parts. Have been supplying the Canadian GM restoration hobby since 1979. Supply everything from emblems to sheetmetal, dash knobs, to complete interiors. Specialize in details and hard to source items. Thousands of satisfied customers are our best advertisement.

Fowlkes Realty & Auction	appraisals auctions
500 Hale St Newman Grove, NE 68758 800-275-5522; FAX: 402-447-6000	

See full listing in **Section One** under **Chevrolet**

Gardner Exhaust Systems	exhaust systems
2 Cedar Ln Rhinebeck, NY 12572 PH/FAX: 914-876-8117 E-mail: gexhaust@aol.com	

Specializing in reproduction GM muscle car exhaust systems for 1964-1972 GTOs, 1965-1972 Nova SS, 1967-1974 Camaro RS, SS, Z-28, 1967-1974 Firebird, Super Duties, 1964-1972 Chevelle SS, 1965-1972 Buick GS, 1965-1972 Oldsmobile 442, 1968-1972 El Camino SS. Web site: www.gardnerexhaust.com

Gold Eagle Classics	accessories parts
5990 SW 185th Ave Bldg H Aloha, OR 97007 503-642-2005; FAX: 503-642-0808 E-mail: gldeagle@europa.com	

Mail order and open shop. Monday-Friday 9 am to 6 pm, Saturday 11 am to 3 pm PST. New and reproduction classic GM auto parts and accessories for 1964-1987 Chevelle and El

Camino, 1967-1981 Camaro, 1962-1972 Nova, 1960-1972 Impala. Web site: www.europa.com/~gldeagle

Guldstrand Engineering Inc	parts
11924 W Jefferson Blvd Culver City, CA 90230 310-391-7108; FAX: 310-391-7424 E-mail: gss@guldstrand.com	

See full listing in **Section One** under **Corvette**

Harmon's Incorporated	interiors parts
Hwy 27 N PO Box 6C Geneva, IN 46740 219-368-7221; FAX: 219-368-9396 E-mail: harmons1@adamswells.com	

See full listing in **Section One** under **Chevrolet**

J & K Old Chevy Stuff	car dealer parts sheetmetal
Ship Pond Rd Plymouth, MA 02360 508-224-7616	

See full listing in **Section One** under **Chevrolet**

JR's Antique Auto	chrome parts interiors
21382 E Scherry Ln Claremore, OK 74017 918-342-4398	

See full listing in **Section One** under **Chevrolet**

The Last Precinct Police Museum	museum
15677 Hwy 62 W Eureka Springs, AR 72632 501-253-4948; FAX: 501-253-4949	

See full listing in **Section Six** under **Arkansas**

Lectric Limited Inc	parts
7322 S Archer Road Justice, IL 60458 708-563-0400; FAX: 708-458-2662	

See full listing in **Section One** under **Corvette**

LES Auto Parts	parts
PO Box 81 Dayton, NJ 08810 732-329-6128; FAX: 732-329-1036	

See full listing in **Section One** under **Chevrolet**

Lutty's Chevy Warehouse	reproduction parts
RD 2, 2385 Saxonburg Blvd Cheswick, PA 15024 724-265-2988; FAX: 724-265-4773	

See full listing in **Section One** under **Chevrolet**

Mac's Euro Motorcars & Transport	Alfa Romeos parts transport
1520 Burr Oak Rd Homewood, IL 60430 708-799-3469	

See full listing in **Section One** under **Alfa Romeo**

Martz Classic Chevy Parts	parts
RD 1, Box 199B Thomasville, PA 17364 717-225-1655; FAX: 717-225-3637	

See full listing in **Section One** under **Chevrolet**

Master Power Brakes	brake products conversion kits
254-1 Rolling Hills Rd Mooresville, NC 28115 704-664-8866; FAX: 704-664-8862	

Manufacturer of power boosters and power disc brake conversion kits. Kits available for Fords, Pontiacs, GM cars and trucks.

Stainless steel sleeving of 4-piston calipers and master cylinders. Web site: www.mpbrakes.com

Mike's Chevy Parts 7716 Deering Ave Canoga Park, CA 91304 818-346-0070; FAX: 818-713-0715	**front end repair** **parts**

See full listing in **Section One** under **Chevrolet**

Muscle Express 509 Commerce Way W #3 Jupiter, FL 33458 800-323-3043 order line 561-744-3043 tech line	**parts**

Molded carpet, weatherstrip and interior kits, body panels plus more reproduction, used, NOS parts. Restorations, installations. Many discontinued parts, full quarter panels, fenders, tach and gauges, consoles, shifters, bucket seats. UPS daily. Credit cards.

National Parts Depot 3101 SW 40th Blvd Gainesville, FL 32608 800-874-7595 toll-free 24 hours 352-378-2473 local	**accessories** **restoration parts**

See full listing in **Section Two** under **comprehensive parts**

Dave Newell's Chevrobilia PO Box 588 Orinda, CA 94563 510-223-4725	**literature** **memorabilia**

See full listing in **Section One** under **Chevrolet**

OEM Glass Inc Rt 9 E PO Box 362 Bloomington, IL 61702 309-662-2122; FAX: 309-663-7474	**auto glass**

See full listing in **Section Two** under **glass**

OEM Paints Inc PO Box 461736 Escondido, CA 92046-1736 760-747-2100	**custom aerosol** **colors**

See full listing in **Section Two** under **paints**

Old Dominion Mustang/Camaro 509 S Washington Hwy, Rt 1 Ashland, VA 23005 804-798-3348; FAX: 804-798-5105	**parts**

See full listing in **Section One** under **Mustang**

M Parker Autoworks Inc 150 Heller Pl #17W Dept HVAA99 Bellmawr, NJ 08031 609-933-0801; FAX: 609-933-0805 E-mail: facfit@erols.com	**battery cables** **harnesses**

See full listing in **Section Two** under **electrical systems**

The Parts Place 217 Paul St Elburn, IL 60119 PH/FAX: 630-365-1800 E-mail: pplace9594@aol.com	**parts**

See full listing in **Section One** under **Chevrolet**

Performance Chevy 2995 W Whitton Phoenix, AZ 85017 800-203-6621; FAX: 602-254-1094	**engine parts** **restoration**

See full listing in **Section One** under **Corvette**

John E Pirkle 3706 Merion Dr Augusta, GA 30907 706-860-9047; FAX: 706-860-2723 E-mail: pirklesr@juno.com	**electrical parts**

See full listing in **Section One** under **Corvette**

Power Brake Booster Exchange Inc 4533 SE Division St Portland, OR 97206 503-238-8882	**brake boosters**

See full listing in **Section Two** under **brakes**

Rick's First Generation Camaro **Parts & Accessories** 420 Athena Dr Athens, GA 30601 800-359-7717; FAX: 706-548-8581 E-mail: firstgen@negia.net	**accessories** **parts**

Mail order and open shop. Monday-Friday 9 am to 5 pm, Saturday 10 am to 2 pm. Restoration parts, new GM, NOS and used parts for 1967-1969 Camaro. Same day shipping. All credit cards, COD welcome. 24 hour order line. Fully illustrated catalog with over 2,600 parts photos. 1967-1969, it's all we do! Web site: www.firstgen.com

Leon J Rocco 4125 Loring St Butler, PA 16001 724-482-4387 after 6 pm	**accessories** **parts**

Mail order only. Specializing in accessories and new, used and NOS parts for 1950s, 1960s, 1970s Chevrolet, Camaro, Chevelle, Nova, Corvair, El Camino. Lights, lenses, bezels, emblems, mirrors, radios, dash knobs, switches, steering wheels, glass triangle Optikleen bottles, door and window handles, bumper jacks, misc.

SC Automotive Rt 3 Box 9 New Ulm, MN 56073 800-62-SS-409 (627-7409) 507-354-1958 info FAX: 800-6477-FAX (647-7329)	**parts** **restoration**

See full listing in **Section One** under **Chevrolet**

O B Smith Chevy Parts PO Box 11703 990 New Circle Rd NW Lexington, KY 40577 606-253-1957; FAX: 606-233-3129	**parts** **tires**

See full listing in **Section One** under **Chevrolet**

Special Auto Restoration 689 Fern Dr Merritt Island, FL 32952 407-453-8343, 407-783-4758	**restoration**

Restoration for Chevelles and Camaros as well as other GM cars.

Steve's Camaros 1197 San Mateo Ave San Bruno, CA 94066 650-873-1890; FAX: 650-873-3670	**parts**

Mail order and open shop. Monday-Friday 8 am to 5 pm; Saturday 10 am to 3 pm. Specializing in 1967-1969 Camaro parts, new, reproduction; 1970-1981 new and reproduction parts. 1967-1969 Pontiac Firebird parts in stock. 1964-1972 Chevelle and El Camino parts.

Street-Wise Performance
Richie Mulligan
Box 105 Creek Rd
Tranquility, NJ 07879
973-786-6668 days
973-786-7133 evenings
FAX: 973-786-7861
E-mail: richie@goes.com

differentials
parts
rebuild kits
transmissions

See full listing in **Section Two** under **transmissions**

Tabco Inc
11655 Chillicothe Rd
Chesterland, OH 44026-1994
216-921-5850; FAX: 216-921-5862

body parts

See full listing in **Section Two** under **sheetmetal**

Tags Backeast
PO Box 581
Plainville, CT 06062
860-747-2942
E-mail: dataplt@snet.net

data plates
trim tags

See full listing in **Section Two** under **special services**

**Tamraz's Parts Discount
Warehouse**
10022 S Bode Rd
Plainfield, IL 60544
630-904-4500; FAX: 630-904-2329

carpeting
upholstery
weatherstripping

Specializing in restoration parts. Sell everything to restore your 1964 and newer Chevelle, Cutlass, GTO, Skylark and 1967 and newer Camaro and Firebird. From bumper to bumper, road to roof. Carry seat upholstery, door panels, sheetmetal, emblems, carpet, weatherstripping, convertible tops and convertible top parts, plus much more.

Trim Parts Inc
5161 Wolfpen Pleasant Hill
Milford, OH 45150
513-831-1472; FAX: 513-248-3402
E-mail: sales@trimparts.com

trim items

See full listing in **Section One** under **Chevrolet**

True Connections
3848 Pierce St
Riverside, CA 92503
909-688-6040; FAX: 909-688-6939
E-mail: trueconnect@earthlink.net

parts

Mail order and open shop. Monday-Friday 9 am to 6 pm, Saturday 9 am to 2 pm. Specializing in 1964-1972 Chevelle, El Camino and Monte Carlo parts. New, used, repro. Web site: trueconnections.com

Vibratech Inc (Fluidampr)
11980 Walden Ave
Alden, NY 14004
716-937-3603; FAX: 716-937-4692

performance parts

See full listing in **Section Two** under **engine parts**

Volunteer State Chevy Parts
Hwy 41 S
PO Box 10
Greenbrier, TN 37073
615-643-4583; FAX: 615-643-5100

accessories
parts

See full listing in **Section One** under **Chevrolet**

Ted Williams Enterprises
5615 Rt 45
Lisbon, OH 44432
330-424-9413; FAX: 330-424-9060
E-mail: willitd@valunet.com

parts

See full listing in **Section One** under **Chevrolet**

CORVAIR

Clark's Corvair Parts Inc
Rt 2, #400 Mohawk Tr
Shelburne Falls, MA 01370
413-625-9776; FAX: 413-625-8498
E-mail: clarks@corvair.com

accessories
interiors
literature
parts
sheetmetal

Mail order only. Monday-Friday 8:30 am to 5 pm. Over 26 years supplying NOS and repro parts, upholstery, carpets, door panels, sheetmetal and accessories for Corvair. Technical assistance by mail or phone. Over 625 page illustrated catalog listing over 14,000 different NOS, used, high-performance and Corvair to VW adapter parts, $6. Web site: www.corvair.com
See our ad on this page

Classic Car Care
4603 Powell Hwy
Ionia, MI 48846
616-527-7173

parts
sales
service

Mail order and open shop. Monday-Saturday 8 am to 6 pm EST. Sales, service, parts, appraisals. Corvair club information for Corvair 1960-1969.

Corvair Ranch Inc 1079 Bon-Ox Rd Gettysburg, PA 17325 717-624-2805; FAX: 717-624-1196	**auto sales** **parts** **restoration** **service**

Mail order and open shop. Monday-Saturday 8 am to 6 pm. Strictly 1960-1969 Corvair only parts, service and restoration facility dedicated to the Corvair auto and truck. Parts inventory includes much NOS and repro in many buildings plus a 375 car salvage yard. Also many complete and restorable projects. Visa, MC, Discover, AmEx. UPS daily.

Corvair Underground PO Box 339 Dundee, OR 97115 800-825-8247, 503-434-1648 FAX: 503-434-1626	**parts**

Specialize in Corvair parts, new, reproduced, rebuilt and used. Largest western supplier of Corvair parts. 300 page mail order catalog for only $5. Free newsletter available. All major credit cards accepted. Celebrating 25 years in 1999! Web site: www.corvairunderground.com

Bill Cotrofeld Automotive Inc US Rt 7 Box 235 East Arlington, VT 05252 802-375-6782	**rebuilding service** **repair service** **restoration**

Monday-Friday 10 am to 6 pm, call for Saturday or Sunday hours. Corvair repair and restoration shop. Corvair restorations, repairs and rebuilding services. Call for brochure. "America's oldest Corvair shop."

See our ad on this page

LES Auto Parts Box 81 Dayton, NJ 08810 732-329-6128; FAX: 732-329-1036	**parts**

See full listing in **Section One** under **Chevrolet**

Maplewood Motors 138 Ogunquit Rd Cape Neddick, ME 03902 207-361-1340	**restoration**

Mail order and open shop by appointment only. Chevrolet Corvair. Over 40 years in the auto business. Complete mechanical restoration in-house and bodyshop at other location.

Dave Newell's Chevrobilia PO Box 588 Orinda, CA 94563 510-223-4725	**literature** **memorabilia**

See full listing in **Section One** under **Chevrolet**

Safari O-Rings 18131 W Lake Desire Dr SE Renton, WA 98058 425-255-6751	**parts** **repair**

Mail order and open shop. Supply Viton O-rings for Corvair and Corvair-related vehicles. Also general repairs for 1960-1969 Corvair and Corvair-related vehicles.

Silicone Wire Systems 3462 Kirkwood Dr San Jose, CA 95117-1549 E-mail: sethracer@aol.com	**ignition wire sets**

Mail order only. Manufacture ignition wire sets for all Corvairs, street and race. 8mm wire is used with special snap-in seals and silicone plug boots. Custom wire sets available. Nine colors available.

The Source Inc 13975 Mira Montana Del Mar, CA 92014-3113 858-259-1520 Voice mail and FAX: 858-259-3843 E-mail: source@adnc.com	**accessories** **parts** **reproduction services**

Orders: 24 hours, 7 days; office hours: Monday-Friday 12 noon until at least 9 pm, some Saturday afternoons. Manufacturer of RS (Replacement Series, heavy duty and US), Ultra Series (severe service/high-performance) parts and accessories for all Corvair powered vehicles. Product bulletins available with quantity price schedules. NOS (new old stock) GM parts. Visa, MasterCard or Discover.

Trim Parts Inc 5161 Wolfpen Pleasant Hill Milford, OH 45150 513-831-1472; FAX: 513-248-3402 E-mail: sales@trimparts.com	**trim items**

See full listing in **Section One** under **Chevrolet**

Vibratech Inc (Fluidampr) 11980 Walden Ave Alden, NY 14004 716-937-3603; FAX: 716-937-4692	**performance parts**

See full listing in **Section Two** under **engine parts**

4-Speeds by Darrell | transmissions
PO Box 110
3 Water St
Vermilion, IL 61955
217-275-3743; FAX: 217-275-3515

See full listing in **Section Two** under **transmissions**

5362 Corvette Place | Corvette parts
4602 Kenbridge Dr
Greensboro, NC 27410
336-852-1011; FAX: 336-852-6107

Reproduction, used and original parts for 1953-1962 Corvettes.

AM Racing Inc | race prep / sales / vintage racing
PO Box 451
Danvers, MA 01923
PH/FAX: 978-774-4613

See full listing in **Section Two** under **racing**

American Restorations Unlimited TA | restoration parts
14 Meakin Ave
PO Box 34
Rochelle Park, NJ 07662
201-843-3567; FAX: 201-843-3238
E-mail: amerrest@earthlink.net

See full listing in **Section Two** under **glass**

Andover Automotive Inc | parts / seat belts
PO Box 3143
Laurel, MD 20709
410-381-6700; FAX: 410-381-6703
E-mail: andoauto@clark.net

Mail order and open shop. Monday-Friday 9 am to 6 pm. Corvette new, used and NOS parts. Seat belt distributor, retail and wholesale for most classic cars and trucks. We also carry partial sets, webbing, bolt kits, along with related items. Free Corvette parts catalog, specify year. Web site: www.andoauto.com

Antique Cars, Parts & Trains | car dealer / literature / parts / trains
Second & Broad Sts
Millville, NJ 08332
609-825-0200

Open shop. Monday-Saturday 9 am to 5 pm. Features Corvettes. Car dealer, parts, automotive literature and trains for sale. 35 miles west of Atlantic City.

Auto Advisors | appraisals
14 Dudley Rd
Billerica, MA 01821
978-667-0075

See full listing in **Section Two** under **appraisals**

Auto Custom Carpet Inc | carpets / floor mats
Jeff Moses
PO Box 1350, 1429 Noble St
Anniston, AL 36201
800-633-2358, 205-236-1118
FAX: 800-516-8274
E-mail: info@accmats.net

See full listing in **Section One** under **Chevrolet**

Auto Quest Investment Cars Inc | car dealer
710 W 7th St
PO Box 22
Tifton, GA 31793
912-382-4750; FAX: 912-382-4752
E-mail: info@auto-quest.com

See full listing in **Section Two** under **car dealers**

Automobile Appraisal Service | appraisals
Steve Cram
1080 Eddy St #607
San Francisco, CA 94109
415-567-1087, 619-584-4678
FAX: 415-567-1245

See full listing in **Section Two** under **appraisals**

Automotive Artistry | restoration
679 W Streetboro St
Hudson, OH 44236
330-650-1503
E-mail: dale@cmh.net

See full listing in **Section One** under **Triumph**

Automotive Design Center Inc | chassis / frames
14135 S Harrison
Posen, IL 60469
708-385-8222

Specializing in round tube chassis and frames for 1953-1962 Chevrolet Corvettes. Customer can purchase frame or chassis, or Auto Design will install.

Avanti Auto Service | repair / restoration
Rt 322, 67 Conchester Hwy
Glen Mills, PA 19342-1506
610-558-9999

See full listing in **Section One** under **DeTomaso/Pantera**

B & B Cylinder Head Inc | cylinder heads
320 Washington St
West Warwick, RI 02893
401-828-4900

See full listing in **Section Two** under **engine parts**

B & B Restorations | parts / restoration / service
Box 591
Elmvale, ON Canada L0L 1P0
715-322-2455
E-mail: bbrestoration@georgian.net

Open shop only. Monday-Saturday 8 am to 8 pm. Complete restoration, parts and service for Corvette only, 1953-1982.

JJ Best & Co | financing
737 Main St
PO Box 10
Chatham, MA 02633
508-945-6000; FAX: 508-945-6006

See full listing in **Section Two** under **consultants**

Bloomington Gold® Corvettes USA | Corvette show
PO Box 457
Marengo, IL 60152
815-568-1960; FAX: 815-568-8650
E-mail: bginfo@bloomingtongold.com

Promotion of annual Corvette show. The granddaddy of Corvette shows, 1999 is the 27th year. The Bloomington Gold certification judging is the standard for Corvettes the world over. Held annually in Bloomington, IL. Web site: www.bloomingtongold.com

Blue Ribbon Products
4965 Old House Trail NE
Atlanta, GA 30342
404-843-8414; FAX: 404-252-0688

> parts

Mail order. Monday-Friday 9 am to 8 pm, Saturday 9 am to noon. New and reproduction parts for 1956-1967 Corvettes. Thousands of parts in stock including weatherstrip, under hood, exterior, interior and chassis parts. Many discontinued 1956-1962 parts available. Visa and MasterCard accepted.

Cal West Auto Air & Radiators Inc
24309 Creekside Rd #119
Valencia, CA 91355
800-535-2034; FAX: 805-254-6120
E-mail: mike@calwest-radiators.com

> a/c condensers
> fan shrouds
> gas tanks
> heaters
> radiators

See full listing in **Section Two** under **radiators**

California Jaguar
29109 Triunfo Dr
Agoura, CA 91301
800-335-2482; FAX: 818-707-3062

> auto transport

See full listing in **Section Two** under **transport**

CBS Performance Automotive
2605-A W Colorado Ave
Colorado Springs, CO 80904
800-685-1492; FAX: 719-578-9485

> ignition systems
> performance products

See full listing in **Section Two** under **ignition parts**

Chevrolet Parts Obsolete
PO Box 0740
Murrieta, CA 92564-0740
909-279-2833; FAX: 909-279-4013
E-mail: spo@att.net

> accessories
> parts

See full listing in **Section One** under **Chevrolet**

Chevyland Parts & Accessories
3667 Recycle Rd #8
Rancho Cordova, CA 95742
916-638-3906; FAX: 916-638-0302
E-mail: chevylnd@concourse.net

> accessories
> parts
> restoration

See full listing in **Section One** under **Chevelle/Camaro**

Chicago Corvette Supply
7322 S Archer Rd
Justice, IL 60458
708-458-2500; FAX: 708-458-2662

> parts

Mail order and open showroom. Monday-Friday 9 am to 6 pm, Saturday 8 am to 2 pm. Specializes in new, reproduction and remanufactured 1953-1982 Corvette parts, accessories and books. Also maintain one of the largest inventories of discontinued NOS (new old stock) parts in the nation. Call for our newest catalog.

Chrome Masters
1109 W Orange Ave, Unit D
Tallahassee, FL 32310
850-576-2100; FAX: 850-576-2772

> chrome plating
> pot metal restoration

See full listing in **Section Two** under **plating & polishing**

Classic Car Research
29508 Southfield Rd, Ste 106
Southfield, MI 48076
248-557-2880; FAX: 248-557-3511
E-mail: kawifreek@msn.com

> appraisals
> consultant
> part locating

See full listing in **Section Two** under **appraisals**

Classic Coachworks
735 Frenchtown Rd
Milford, NJ 08848
908-996-3400; FAX: 908-996-0204

> bodywork
> painting
> restoration

See full listing in **Section Two** under **restoration shops**

Classics 'n More Inc
1001 Ranck Mill Rd
Lancaster, PA 17602
717-392-0599; FAX 717-392-2371

> repairs
> restoration

See full listing in **Section Two** under **restoration shops**

Cn'V Corvette Sales
2166 E University Dr
Tempe, AZ 85281
602-994-8388; FAX: 602-423-0407
E-mail: sales@cnv-corvettes.com

> parts
> sales
> service

Mail order and open shop. Monday-Saturday 8:30 am to 7 pm. Specializing in Corvette sales, service and parts for 1956-1996 Corvettes. Web site: www.cnv-corvettes.com

Corvette & High-Performance
Division of Classic & High-Performance Inc
2840 Black Lake Blvd SW #D
Olympia, WA 98512
360-754-7890

> accessories
> parts

Mail order and open shop. Tuesday-Saturday 9 am to 5:30 pm. Specializing in new and reproduction parts for Corvettes, Camaros, Chevelles and other GM classic cars and trucks. Corvette mechanical service. UPS daily. Major credit cards accepted. Established 1984.

Corvette America
PO Box 427
Rt 322
Boalsburg, PA 16827
800-458-3475; foreign: 814-364-2141
FAX: 814-364-9615, 24 hours
E-mail: vettebox@corvetteamerica.com

> accessories
> fiberglass
> interiors
> leisure items
> parts

A powerhouse in the industry for over 22 years. Offering an unmatched inventory of parts, interiors, accessories, fiberglass and leisure items. Both beginners and pros alike appreciate the thoroughly knowledgeable staff and unmatched service and delivery. Call or fax for a free 1999 master catalog.

Corvette Enterprise Brokerage
The Power Broker
52 Van Houten Ave
Passaic Park, NJ 07055
973-472-7021

> appraisals
> broker
> car locator
> investment planning

Cars shown Monday-Saturday by appointment only. Corvette brokerage offering investment grade classics and new models. SASE for free catalog. Consultations and appraisals. Quality Corvettes always wanted. Look for our comprehensive value guides in fine automotive publications. Over two decades of providing America's best Vettes.

Corvette Mike
1133 N Tustin Ave
Anaheim, CA 92807
800-327-8388, 714-630-0700
FAX: 714-630-0777
E-mail: cvtmike@deltanet.com

> accessories
> parts
> sales
> service

Mail order and open shop. Monday-Friday 9 am to 6 pm, Saturday 10 am to 4 pm, Sunday 11 am to 2 pm. Specializing in Corvette sales, service, parts, accessories and chrome wheels for 1953-1998 Corvettes and occasionally other classics and sports cars like Ferrari, Jaguars, Mercedes-Benz, NSX, Viper, etc. Most trusted name in Corvettes for 20 years. Web site: www.corvettemike.com

Corvette Pacifica
Division of EC Products
PO Box 2360
Atascadero, CA 93423
800-488-7671, 805-466-9261 int'l
FAX: 805-466-4782

> accessories
> parts

Mail order and open shop. Monday-Friday 7:30 am to 5 pm PST. Carries over 10,000 parts and accessories for 1953-1997 Corvettes. Web site: www.corvettepacifica.com

Corvette Rubber Company | rubber products
H-10640 W Cadillac Rd | **weatherstripping**
Cadillac, MI 49601
888-216-9412 toll-free
616-779-2888; FAX: 616-779-9833

Mail order and open shop. Monday-Friday 10 am to 5 pm.
Specializing in weatherstrip and rubber products for 1953-1996
Corvettes.

Corvette Specialties of MD Inc | parts
1912 Liberty Rd | restoration
Eldersburg, MD 21784 | service
410-795-3180; FAX: 410-795-3247

Mail order and open shop. Monday-Friday 9 am to 5:30 pm.
Since 1977, a major supplier of new, used and reproduction
parts, specializing in 1956-1967. Also offer a restoration service
for clocks, gauges, instrument clusters, headlight and wiper
motors. Mechanical service and restoration work is also offered
at our facility. Tune-ups to frame-off restorations. Service all
years.

Corvette World | accessories
RD 9, Box 770, Dept H | parts
Greensburg, PA 15601
724-837-8600; FAX: 724-837-4420
E-mail: cvworld@sgi.net

Mail order and open shop. Monday-Thursday 9 am to 6 pm,
Friday 9 am to 5 pm, Saturday 9 am to 12 pm. This family
owned company has been serving Corvette owners for over 23
years. Handle a complete line of parts and accessories for 1953-
1982 Corvettes, so you can go from start to finish all at one
place. Our 208 page catalog is fully illustrated and contains over
10,000 GM, reproduction and used parts. Call for a free copy of
our catalog today. Web site: www.corvettedept.com

County Corvette | restoration
PO Box 258 | sales
Lionville, PA 19353 | service
610-363-0872, 610-363-7670 sales
FAX: 610-363-5325

Open shop only. Monday-Friday 8:30 am to 5:30 pm, Saturday
10 am to 2 pm. State of the art restoration, service and sales for
Corvettes. Web site: www.countycorvette.com

Custom Autosound Mfg | CD players
808 W Vermont Ave | custom radios
Anaheim, CA 92805 | speaker upgrades
800-888-8637; FAX: 714-533-0361
E-mail: info@custom-autosound.com

See full listing in **Section One** under **Chevrolet**

D&M Corvette Specialists Ltd | parts
1804 Ogden Ave | restoration
Downers Grove, IL 60515 | sales
630-968-0031; FAX: 630-968-0465 | service

Mail order and open shop. Monday-Thursday 8 am to 8 pm,
Friday 8 am to 6 pm, Saturday 10 am to 6 pm. Specializing in
sales, service, parts and restoration for Corvettes 1953-present.
40 car indoor showroom, quality classics and low mileage late
models. Full service, restoration and parts department.

Danchuk Mfg | accessories
3201 S Standard Ave | parts
Santa Ana, CA 92705 | restoration
714-751-1957; FAX: 714-850-1957
E-mail: info@danchuk.com

See full listing in **Section One** under **Chevrolet**

Dashboards Plus | restoration parts
336 Cottonwood Ave | wood dash overlays
Hartland, WI 53029
800-221-8161; FAX: 414-367-9474

See full listing in **Section One** under **Jaguar**

Davies Corvette | accessories
7141 US Hwy 19 | parts
New Port Richey, FL 34653
727-842-8000, 800-236-2383
FAX: 727-846-8216
E-mail: davies@corvetteparts.com

Corvette parts and accessories, all years (used and new).
"Making Corvettes the best they can be since 1953." Web site:
www.corvetteparts.com

Dean's Corvette Wiper | wiper trans service
Transmission Service
Dean Andrew Rehse
16367 Martincoit Rd
Poway, CA 92064
619-451-1933; FAX: 619-451-1999
E-mail: classicvette@home.com

Specializing in 1953-1962 Corvettes. Rebuild your broken wiper
transmissions. Restring your broken cables, replace broken parts.
Price varies. Division of Mary Jo Rohner's Corvette Parts
Collection, 1953-1962. Web site: earlycorvetteparts.com

Desert Muscle Cars | parts
2853 N Stone Ave
Tucson, AZ 85705
520-882-3010; FAX: 520-628-9332

See full listing in **Section One** under **Chevelle/Camaro**

DiSchiavi Enterprises Inc | restoration
1248 Yardville Allentown Rd
Allentown, NJ 08501
609-259-0787

See full listing in **Section Two** under **restoration shops**

Dobbins Restoration Publishing | literature
16 E Montgomery Ave | parts
Hatboro, PA 19040 | restoration
215-443-0779

Mail order and open shop. Corvette service and restoration,
parts and literature. Corvette appraisals.

Doug's Corvette Service | race prep
11634 Vanowen St | repairs
North Hollywood, CA 91605
818-765-9117

Open shop only. Monday-Friday 8 am to 5 pm. Specializing in all
mechanical repairs on all year Corvettes. Restoration and race
car preparation. Fuel injection specialist.

EC Products Design Inc | accessories
PO Box 2360 | parts
Atascadero, CA 93423
800-488-5209
805-466-4703 international
FAX: 805-466-4782

Mail order and open shop. Monday-Friday 7:30 am to 5 pm PST.
Serves all auto businesses throughout the world that deal in
Corvette parts. Business license required, wholesale only.
Specializing in parts and accessories for 1953-1997 Corvettes.
Web site: www.everythingcorvette.com

Eckler's Quality Parts & | accessories
Accessories for Corvettes | parts
PO Box 5637
Titusville, FL 32783
800-327-4868; FAX: 407-383-2059
E-mail: ecklers@ecklers.com

Specializing in parts and accessories for 1953-1998 Corvettes.
One 350+ page color catalog for 1953-1999 models, featuring
enhancement accessories of every description, plus restoration
items including fiberglass body panels, interiors, chassis parts,
fuel systems, electrical items, glass, engine parts, exhaust systems in addition to a complete line of gift and apparel items. Web
site: www.ecklers.com

Elliott's Car Radio | radio repairs
313 Linfield Rd | speaker kits
Parkerford, PA 19457
610-495-6360; FAX: 610-495-7723

See full listing in **Section Two** under **radios**

Fifties Forever | Chevy specialist
206 Division Ave
Garfield, NJ 07026
PH/FAX: 973-478-1306
E-mail: fiftiesforever@webtv.net

See full listing in **Section One** under **Chevrolet**

Florida Caliper Manufacturers Inc | brake systems
1450 SW 10th St #3 | chassis parts
Delray Beach, FL 33444 | suspension parts
561-272-5238

Specializing in Corvette and Harley-Davidson motorcycles. For Corvettes: O-ring brake systems, stainless sleeved; also specializing in differentials, axles, trailing arms, brake and fuel lines, chassis rubber parts, suspension parts, steering, all chassis related drivetrain, brake and steering components for 1963-1996. For Harley-Davidson motorcycles: six piston Harrison billet brake systems, 11-1/2x13" floating stainless discs, front and rear.

Fowlkes Realty & Auction | appraisals
500 Hale St | auctions
Newman Grove, NE 68758
800-275-5522; FAX: 402-447-6000

See full listing in **Section One** under **Chevrolet**

Gemini Racing Systems Inc | race prep
571 N 54th St | restoration
Chandler, AZ 85226
800-992-9294, 602-940-9011

See full listing in **Section One** under **Mustang**

Grossmueller's Classic Corvette | NOS parts
55 Sitgreaves St | used parts
Phillipsburg, NJ 08865
610-258-2028
FAX: 610-258-7013, PA
E-mail: wfg@gccorvettes.com

Specializing in 1953-1962 and 1968-1982 Corvette parts. We constantly have several cars of each year available for parts. We also manufacture many parts for the 1953-1955 cars, including carb linkage, gaskets, accelerator linkage as well as bumper brackets, splash shields and frame brackets for the 1953-1962 cars. Restoration services for all gauges, heater/defroster switches and steering columns are also available. Web site: www.gccorvettes.com

Guldstrand Engineering Inc | parts
11924 W Jefferson Blvd
Culver City, CA 90230
310-391-7108; FAX: 310-391-7424
E-mail: gss@guldstrand.com

Mail order and open shop. Monday-Friday 8 am to 5 pm. The original designers for Corvette suspension and modifications. The 46-page suspension and preparation manual is full of street to racing components, applications for 1953-1999 Corvette and GM A and G-bodies. Web site: www.guldstrand.com

Hi-Tech Software | CD encyclopedia
2 Cooks Farm Rd
Montville, NJ 07045
PH/FAX: 973-402-9710
E-mail: htsoftware@erols.com

Specializing in computer CD-ROM software automobile encyclopedias, *The Anthology* and *The Mustang Anthology*. Web site: www.htsoftware.com

Highway One Classic Automobiles and Highwayone.com | classic automobiles
Classic Classifieds
1035 California Dr
Burlingame, CA 94010
650-342-7340; FAX: 650-343-0150
E-mail: djboscacci@msn.com

See full listing in **Section One** under **Abarth**

Hubcap Mike | hubcaps
26242 Dimension Ste 150 | wheelcovers
Lake Forest, CA 92630
949-597-8120; FAX: 949-597-8123

See full listing in **Section Two** under **wheels & wheelcovers**

Instrument Services Inc | clocks
11765 Main St | gauges
Roscoe, IL 61073 | instruments
800-558-2674; FAX: 815-623-6416

See full listing in **Section Two** under **instruments**

Jesser's Classic Keys | automobilia
26 West St, Dept HVA | keys
Akron, OH 44303-2344
330-376-8181; FAX: 330-384-9129

See full listing in **Section Two** under **locks & keys**

JR's Antique Auto | chrome parts
21382 E Scherry Ln | interiors
Claremore, OK 74017
918-342-4398

See full listing in **Section One** under **Chevrolet**

Al Knoch Interiors | carpets
130 Montoya Rd | interiors
El Paso, TX 79932 | tooling services
800-880-8080; FAX: 915-581-1545 | tops
E-mail: alknoch@flash.net

See full listing in **Section One** under **Chevrolet**

Lectric Limited Inc | parts
7322 S Archer Road
Justice, IL 60458
708-563-0400; FAX: 708-458-2662

Specializing in wire harnesses, battery cables, spark plug wire sets, switches and T3 headlight bulbs for all GM cars. Our particular specialty is Corvette.

LES Auto Parts | parts
Box 81
Dayton, NJ 08810
732-329-6128; FAX: 732-329-1036

See full listing in **Section One** under **Chevrolet**

Long Island Corvette Supply Inc | parts
1445 Strong Ave
Copiague, NY 11726-3227
516-225-3000; FAX: 516-225-5030
E-mail: mail@licorvette.com

Mail order and open shop. Monday-Friday 9 am to 5 pm. Specializing in parts for 1963-1967 Corvettes. The largest and best stocked manufacturer and distributor of 1963-1967 Corvette parts. Send $3 for the biggest and best 1963-1967 Corvette parts catalog. Web site: www.licorvette.com

No artificial
preservatives.

Nothing endures like the real thing. And now it's available at your GM dealer or www.gmgoodwrench.com.
To get our latest catalog, call 888.245.5800.

As real as your passion.

M & H Electric Fabricators Inc	wiring harnesses
13537 Alondra Blvd	
Santa Fe Springs, CA 90670	
562-926-9552; FAX: 562-926-9572	
E-mail: sales@wiringharness.com	

See full listing in **Section Two** under **electrical systems**

Mac's Euro Motorcars & Transport	Alfa Romeos
1520 Burr Oak Rd	parts
Homewood, IL 60430	transport
708-799-3469	

See full listing in **Section One** under **Alfa Romeo**

MAR-K Quality Parts	bed parts
6625 W Wilshire, Ste 2	customizing parts
Oklahoma City, OK 73132	trim parts
405-721-7945; FAX: 405-721-8906	

See full listing in **Section Two** under **trucks & tractors**

Marcel's Corvette Parts	parts
5940 N Sam Houston Pkwy E #319	
Humble, TX 77396	
800-546-2111 order line	
281-441-2111 info line	
FAX: 281-441-3057	

Mail order and open shop. Monday-Friday 9 am to 6 pm CST. Specializes in 1953-1982 Corvette parts of all kinds. New, NOS, used and reproductions.

Master Power Brakes	brake products
254-1 Rolling Hills Rd	conversion kits
Mooresville, NC 28115	
704-664-8866; FAX: 704-664-8862	

See full listing in **Section One** under **Chevelle/Camaro**

Michigan Corvette Recyclers	Corvette parts
PO Box 98	new/used parts
Riga, MI 49276	
800-533-4650; FAX: 517-486-4124	

Mail order and open shop. Monday-Friday 9 am to 4 pm, Saturday by appointment only. Specializing in new and used Corvette parts, 1968-present. We also buy and sell damaged and undamaged Corvettes.

Midbanc Financial Services	financing
PO Box 20402	
Columbus, OH 43220	
614-442-7701; FAX: 614-442-7704	
E-mail: patricia@midbanc.com	

See full listing in **Section Two** under **financing**

Muncie Imports & Classics	repair
4401 St Rd 3 N	restoration
Muncie, IN 47303	upholstery
800-462-4244; FAX: 317-287-9551	
E-mail: mic@netdirect.net	

See full listing in **Section One** under **Jaguar**

Muskegon Brake & Dist Co	brakes
848 E Broadway	springs
Muskegon, MI 49444	suspensions
616-733-0874; FAX: 616-733-0635	

See full listing in **Section Two** under **brakes**

The National Corvette Museum	museum
350 Corvette Dr	
Bowling Green, KY 42101-9134	
800-53-VETTE; FAX: 270-781-5286	
E-mail: lisa@corvettemuseum.com	

See full listing in **Section Six** under **Kentucky**

Dave Newell's Chevrobilia	literature
PO Box 588	memorabilia
Orinda, CA 94563	
510-223-4725	

See full listing in **Section One** under **Chevrolet**

OEM Glass Inc	auto glass
Rt 9 E	
PO Box 362	
Bloomington, IL 61702	
309-662-2122; FAX: 309-663-7474	

See full listing in **Section Two** under **glass**

OEM Paints Inc	custom
PO Box 461736	aerosol colors
Escondido, CA 92046-1736	
760-747-2100	

See full listing in **Section Two** under **paints**

Old Air Products	air conditioning
4615 Martin St	
Ft Worth, TX 76119	
817-531-2665; FAX: 817-531-3257	
E-mail: sales@oldairproducts.com	

Mail order and open shop. Monday-Friday 8:30 am to 5 pm. Specializing in custom air conditioning systems and replacement parts for air conditioning and heating for Corvette, 1955-1957 Chevy trucks and cars, 1972 and back Chevrolet trucks, Ford trucks and cars. Web site: oldairproducts.com

Only Yesterday Classic Autos Inc	cars
24 Valley Rd	
Port Washington, NY 11050	
516-767-3477; FAX: 516-767-8964	

See full listing in **Section One** under **Chevrolet**

Paragon Reproductions Inc	Corvette repro
8040 S Jennings Rd	parts
Swartz Creek, MI 48473	
810-655-4641; FAX: 810-655-6667	
E-mail:	
www.info@corvette-paragon.com	

Mail order and open shop. Monday-Friday 9 am to 6:30 pm, Saturday 10 am to 2 pm. Specializing in 1953-1982 Corvette reproduction parts.

M Parker Autoworks Inc	battery cables
150 Heller Pl #17W	harnesses
Dept HVAA99	
Bellmawr, NJ 08031	
609-933-0801; FAX: 609-933-0805	
E-mail: facfit@erols.com	

See full listing in **Section Two** under **electrical systems**

Performance Chevy	engine parts
2995 W Whitton	restoration
Phoenix, AZ 85017	
800-203-6621; FAX: 602-254-1094	

Mail order and open shop. Monday-Friday 7 am to 3:30 pm. Specializing in Chevy 1955-1997 V8 engine parts and restoration for engines for 1955-1972.

JT Piper's Auto Specialties Inc	parts
PO Box 140	
Vermilion, IL 61955	
800-637-6111, 217-275-3742	
FAX: 217-275-3515	
E-mail: parts@pipersauto.com	

We have one of the largest inventories of used Corvette parts in the world. Used parts for 1954-1986 Corvettes are our specialty, however, we stock a full line of new GM, NOS, discontinued GM and reproduction Corvette parts for the 1954-1986 models. All pricing is done over the phone. So just pick up the phone and give us a call for all your 1954-1986 Corvette parts needs. Web site: pipersauto.com

John E Pirkle | **electrical parts**
3706 Merion Dr
Augusta, GA 30907
706-860-9047; FAX: 706-860-2723
E-mail: pirklesr@juno.com

Specializing in starters, alternators, generators, V regulators, relays for Corvette, Chevrolet and GM cars.

Jack Podell Fuel Injection Spec | **fuel system parts fuel system rebuilding**
106 Wakewa Ave
South Bend, IN 46617
219-232-6430; FAX: 219-234-8632

Mail order and open shop. Daily 7 am to 7 pm. Specializing in the rebuilding and restoration of 1957-1965 Corvette Rochester fuel injection units with over 29 years of satisfied customers worldwide! Units bought, sold, taken in on trade. Massive parts inventory available including steel reproduction air cleaners, restored fi units in stock. Now available, genuine Tetraethyl lead. Boost 93 octane to 99.5 leaded for 15¢ a gallon. Call us first for all your FI needs. Catalog upon request.

Dennis Portka | **horns knock-off wheels**
4326 Beetow Dr
Hamburg, NY 14075
716-649-0921

Mail order only. Two separate businesses. Specializing in rebuilding and sales of GM horns for Corvette and GM cars, 1955-present. Restoration of Corvette aluminum knock-off wheels, enlarged mounting holes remachined to factory specs. Also knock-off wheel wrenches available

Hugo Prado Limited Edition Corvette Art Prints | **fine art prints**
PO Box 18437
Chicago, IL 60618-0437
PH/FAX: 800-583-7627
E-mail: vetteart@aol.com

Specialize in Limited Edition fine art prints of classic Corvettes and Camaros. 1957 Sebring Corvette, 1960 Roman red Corvette convertible, 1963 tuxedo black Corvette Z06, 1965 tuxedo black Corvette, 1966 rally red Corvette, 1967 marina blue Corvette, 1968 tuxedo black Corvette, 1969 Daytona yellow Corvette, 1967 Camaro SS/RS Indy pace car, 1970 Mulsanne-blue Corvette, 1971 Steel Cities gray Corvette, 1990 bright red ZR-1, 40th Anniversary Corvette, 1972 Ontario orange Corvette, 1997 torch red C5 Corvette. Web site: www.hugoprado.com

Proteam Corvette Sales Inc | **car collection car dealer**
PO Box 606
Napoleon, OH 43545-0606
888-592-5086, 419-592-5086
FAX: 419-592-4242
E-mail: proteam@proteam-corvette.com

Corvettes 1954-1996, over 150 in stock, one location. Mostly 1972 and older. Free catalog. Dealers welcomed, worldwide transportation. Visit our web site for complete comprehensive list of Corvettes for sale: www.proteam-corvette.com

RARE Corvettes | **cars parts**
Joe Calcagno
Box 1080
Soquel, CA 95073
831-475-4442; FAX: 831-475-1115

Mail order. Specializing in Corvettes, 1956-1962. Complete cars, project cars, Survivors, drivers, show cars. Parts: new reproduced, used original, NOS, replacement. Technical advice and appraisals. NCRS and Bloomington judge, author, historian. Assisting people with accurate and honest information.

RC Corvette Parts Inc | **accessories parts**
3656 Foothill Blvd
La Crescenta, CA 91214
PH/FAX: 818-541-9710

Specializing in Corvette parts for 1963-1967 Corvettes plus accessories. NOS parts and hard-to-find accessories that are no longer available. Manufacture 1963-1967 gas pedals with correct margins and backside ribs. Only American-made supplier.

Repro Parts Mfg | **parts**
PO Box 3690
San Jose, CA 95156
408-923-2491

Mail order only. Specializing in reproduction and original used parts (body and mechanical) for 1953-1957 Corvettes.

Rik's Unlimited Corvette Parts | **accessories parts**
3758 Hwy 18 S
Morganton, NC 28655
828-433-6506; FAX: 828-437-7166
E-mail: riksvet@riksvet.com

Quality parts and accessories for 1963-1982 Corvettes: emblems, weatherstrips, interiors, brakes, moldings, suspension, bumpers and much more. Our parts catalog is packed full of illustrations and listings to help find the part you need. Call or write for catalog (cost $2). Web site: www.riksvet.com

Frank Riley Automotive Art | **automotive prints**
PO Box 95
Hawthorne, NJ 07506
800-848-9459

See full listing in **Section Two** under **artwork**

Rogers Corvette Center | **car dealer**
8675 N Orlando Ave
Maitland, FL 32751
407-628-8300; FAX: 407-628-8388
E-mail: sales@rogerscorvette.com

Open Monday-Saturday 8 am to 6 pm. Quality, original, low mileage Corvettes of every year.

Tom Rohner | **gauge repair**
16367 Martincoit Rd
Poway, CA 92064
619-674-5777; FAX: 619-451-1999
E-mail: tom_rohner@compuserve.com

Mail order only. Specializing in Corvette gauge restoration and repair. Only work on gauges for 1953-1962 models. Recalibrate, repair, rebuild, rechrome and fully restore all gauges to look and operate just like new. Also rebuild fuel sending units for those years.

Mary Jo Rohner's 1953-1962 Corvette Parts | **parts**
16367 Martincoit Rd
Poway, CA 92064
619-451-1933; FAX: 619-451-1999
E-mail: classicvette@home.com

Mail order only. Specialize in new, used and reproduction Corvette parts, 1953-1962. Many rare and hard-to-find parts. Prices lower than the rest and the quality is the best! Rebuild wiper motors, defroster switches, master cylinders, clocks, full line of used parts including hardtop parts. Web site: earlycorvetteparts.com

Royals' Garage | **NOS parts used parts**
16-24 Calhoun St
Torrington, CT 06790
860-489-4500

Est 1977. Glenn and John Royals, owners. Specializing in Corvette sales, repairs, parts sales, many Corvette franchises (interiors, wheels, chroming, radiators, etc). Also general repair facility, repair any auto or truck, equipment, any year, make or model.

SC Automotive
Rt 3 Box 9
New Ulm, MN 56073
800-62-SS-409 (627-7409)
507-354-1958 info
FAX: 800-6477-FAX (647-7329)

parts
restoration

See full listing in **Section One** under **Chevrolet**

Shines Unlimited
11709 Oakland
Schoolcraft, MI 49087
616-679-4002

car buckles
toys

See full listing in **Section Two** under **models & toys**

Smooth Line
2562 Riddle Run Rd
Tarentum, PA 15084
724-274-6002; FAX: 724-274-6121

body panels
removable hardtops

See full listing in **Section Two** under **tops**

**Bob Sottile's Hobby Car
Auto Sales Inc**
RD 2 Box 210B, Rt 164
Martinsburg, PA 16662
814-793-4282

car dealer
restoration

Mail order and open shop. Monday-Friday 9:30 am to 8:30 pm, Saturday 9 am to 5 pm. Buy, sell, repair and restore Corvettes. All are clean and original. Have a combined 30 years of Corvette sales, repair and restoration experience with parts too. Also do muscle cars and street rods.

Ssnake-Oyl Products Inc
Rt 2, Box 269-6
Hawkins, TX 75765
800-284-7777; FAX: 903-769-4552

carpet underlay
firewall insulation
seat belt restoration

See full listing in **Section Two** under **interiors & interior parts**

Stainless Steel Brakes Corp
11470 Main Rd
Clarence, NY 14031
800-448-7722, 716-759-8666
FAX: 716-759-8688, 24 hr

brake accessories
disc conversion kits
pads/fluid/rotors
parking brake kits
power steering parts

See full listing in **Section Two** under **brakes**

Stencils & Stripes Unlimited Inc
1108 S Crescent Ave #21
Park Ridge, IL 60068
847-692-6893; FAX: 847-692-6895

NOS decals
stripe kits

See full listing in **Section Two** under **decals**

Still Cruisin' Corvettes
5759 Benford Dr
Haymarket, VA 20169
703-754-1960; FAX: 703-754-1222

appraisals
repairs
restoration

Open shop only. Monday-Friday 8 am to 5 pm, Saturday 8 am to 12 noon. Specializing in restoration or repair of Corvettes 1953-1972 and consultant for pre-purchase. Certified appraiser of all collectible cars. Expert witness for court cases. Sales of original, NOS and reproduction Corvette parts.

Stoudt Auto Sales
1350 Carbon St
Reading, PA 19601
800-523-8485 USA parts dept
800-482-3033 USA sales dept
610-374-4856, parts info
FAX: 610-372-7283

car dealer
parts

Mail order and shop open. Monday-Thursday 9 am to 6 pm, Friday 9 am to 5 pm, Saturday 9 am to 3 pm. Sales dept: Monday-Thursday 9 am to 8 pm, Friday 9 am to 5 pm, Saturday 9 am to 3 pm. Huge selection of new, used and repro parts for all years. Over 6,500 parts in stock. 35 Corvettes in stock. Same location for 41 years. Catalog. Web site: www.sevenwaves.com

Straw Church Speed Shop
602 Passaic St
Phillipsburg, NJ 08865
908-454-7487
E-mail: strawchurch_ss@hotmail.com

accessories
engine swaps
parts

See full listing in **Section Two** under **car & parts locators**

Street-Wise Performance
Richie Mulligan
Box 105 Creek Rd
Tranquility, NJ 07879
973-786-6668 days
973-786-7133 evenings
FAX: 973-786-7861
E-mail: richie@goes.com

differentials
parts
rebuild kits
transmissions

See full listing in **Section Two** under **transmissions**

Tags Backeast
PO Box 581
Plainville, CT 06062
860-747-2942
E-mail: dataplt@snet.net

data plates
trim tags

See full listing in **Section Two** under **special services**

Lars Tidblom Automobil
Vegagatan 5-7
Sundbyberg 17231 Sweden
+46-8-293292; FAX: +46-8-982885
E-mail: lt.automobil@swipnet.se

parts
restoration
service

Mail order and open shop. Monday-Friday 7:30 am to 5 pm. Service, restoration to original, trimmings, parts and used parts for Chevrolet Corvette 1953-1999. GM, AC Delco, Ecklers, Corvette Central, Paragon, Zip Products, EC Products, Mid America Vette brakes and products, Lingenfelter and more.

Trim Parts Inc
5161 Wolfpen Pleasant Hill
Milford, OH 45150
513-831-1472; FAX: 513-248-3402
E-mail: sales@trimparts.com

trim items

See full listing in **Section One** under **Chevrolet**

U S Oldies & Classics
Vunt 3
Holsbeek 3220 Belgium
3216446611; FAX: 3216446520

car dealer
parts

See full listing in **Section Two** under **car dealers**

USAopoly Inc
565 Westlake St
Encinitas, CA 92024
760-634-5910; FAX: 760-634-5923
E-mail: allison@usaopoly.com

Monopoly® game

See full listing in **Section Two** under **models & toys**

Vette Dreams Inc
1004 Peconic Ave
West Babylon, NY 11704
516-661-4613; FAX: 516-661-4623

restorations

Specializing in Corvette restorations for 1953-1972.

Vette Vues Magazine
PO Box 741596
Orange City, FL 32774
904-775-8454; FAX: 904-775-3042
E-mail: comments@vettevues.com

magazine

See full listing in **Section Four** under **periodicals**

Vibratech Inc (Fluidampr)
11980 Walden Ave
Alden, NY 14004
716-937-3603; FAX: 716-937-4692

performance parts

See full listing in **Section Two** under **engine parts**

Virginia Vettes Parts & Sales
105 Lindrick St
Williamsburg, VA 23188
757-229-0011
FAX: 757-565-1629, 24 hours
E-mail: www.info@virginiavettes.com

interiors
parts

Mail order and open shop. Saturday 7:30 am to 5 pm. Shop location: 5662 Mooretown Road, Williamsburg, VA 23188. Serve the collector and hobbyist with OEM, reproduction and good used parts. Corvette interiors, carpet, weatherstrip, special fasteners, seat covers and door panels are all made to original specifications. Free catalog showing available parts. Web site: www.virginiavettes.com

Walneck's Inc
7923 Janes Ave
Woodridge, IL 60517
630-985-4995; FAX: 630-985-2750

motorcycles
murals
posters

See full listing in **Section Two** under **artwork**

Wild Bill's Corvette & Hi-Performance Center Inc
446 Dedham St
Wrentham, MA 02093
508-384-7373; FAX: 508-384-9366
E-mail:
wildbillscorvette@worldnet.att.net

parts
rebuilding
service

Mail order and open shop. Monday-Friday 9 am to 6 pm. Specializing in service, parts, consultation, major rebuilding and overhaul for Chevrolet Corvettes 1953-present. With 19 years' experience concentrating on 1963-1982. Member of NCRS.

Wilson's Classic Auto
417 Kaufman Rt 150
PO Box 58
Congerville, IL 61729
309-448-2408; FAX: 309-448-2409

restoration

See full listing in **Section Two** under **restoration shops**

James Wood
1102 E Jefferson St
Mishawaka, IN 46545
219-256-0239; FAX: 219-254-2722

appraisals

See full listing in **Section Two** under **appraisals**

Zip Products
8067 Fast Ln
Mechanicsville, VA 23111
804-746-2290, 800-962-9632
FAX: 804-730-7043
E-mail: zipvette@erols.com

accessories
parts

Mail order and open shop. Monday-Thursday 8:30 am to 6:00 pm, Friday 8:30 am to 5:30 pm, Saturday 10 am to 3 pm. Offer over 16,000 parts and accessories for the repair and restoration of 1956-1997 Corvettes. Stock new and reconditioned items and offer rebuild services for numerous parts. Call or visit our web site to receive a copy of our catalog. You may also shop our online store or e-mail us to receive a quote. Web site: www.zip-corvette.com

A & M SoffSeal Inc
104 May Dr
Harrison, OH 45030
800-426-0902
513-367-0028 service/info
FAX: 513-367-5506
E-mail: soffseal@soffseal.com

rubber parts
weatherstripping

See full listing in **Section Two** under **rubber parts**

American Dream Machines
711 Bowman Mill Rd
Strasburg, VA 22657-2808
PH/FAX: 540-465-9613
E-mail: mopar4me@shentel.net

parts

Mail order only. Used parts for 1960s and 1970s Chrysler A, B and E-bodies.

AMK Products
18600 E 96th St
Broken Arrow, OK 74012
918-455-2651; FAX: 918-455-7441

parts

See full listing in **Section One** under **Mustang**

Antique DeSoto-Plymouth
4206 Burnett Dr
Murrysville, PA 15668
724-733-1818 eves
FAX: 724-733-9884 or
412-243-4556 anytime
E-mail: parts4u@aol.com

Mopar parts

See full listing in **Section One** under **Mopar**

Antique Mopar Auto Sales
5758 McNicholl Dr
Hale, MI 48739-8984
517-257-3123

cars
parts

See full listing in **Section One** under **Mopar**

Brewer's Performance Motor Parts
2560 S State Route 48
Ludlow Falls, OH 45339-9773
937-698-4259; FAX: 937-698-7109

parts

See full listing in **Section One** under **Mopar**

Classic Auto Air Mfg Co
2020 W Kennedy Blvd
Tampa, FL 33606
813-251-2356, 813-251-4994

air conditioning
heating
parts

See full listing in **Section One** under **Mustang**

The Clockworks
1745 Meta Lake Ln
Eagle River, WI 54521
800-398-3040; FAX: 715-479-5759
E-mail: clockworks@juno.com

clock service

See full listing in **Section Two** under **instruments**

The Collector's Guild
41 Counter St
Kingston, ON Canada K7K 6C7
800-653-0251; FAX: 613-536-5211
E-mail: cars@collectorsguild.on.ca

models
toys

See full listing in **Section Two** under **models & toys**

Edgerton Classics Ltd
9215 St Rt 13
Camden, NY 13316-4933
315-245-3113

restoration
woodworking

See full listing in **Section Two** under **restoration shops**

Egge Machine Company Inc
11707 Slauson Ave
Santa Fe Springs, CA 90670
800-866-EGGE, 562-945-3419
FAX: 562-693-1635
E-mail: info@egge.com

bearings
pistons/rings
timing components
valve train

See full listing in **Section Two** under **engine parts**

ETC Every Thing Cars 8727 Clarinda Pico Rivera, CA 90660 562-949-6981	**paint** **repairs** **restoration** **welding**

See full listing in **Section One** under **Mopar**

Jay M Fisher Acken Dr 4-B Clark, NJ 07066 732-388-6442	**mascots** **sidemount mirrors** **windwing brackets**

See full listing in **Section Two** under **accessories**

Glazier Pattern & Coachworks 3720 Loramie-Washington Rd Houston, OH 45333 937-492-7355; FAX: 937-492-9987 E-mail: s.glazier.fam@juno.com	**coachwork** **interior woodwork** **restoration of wood** **bodied cars**

Mail order and open shop by appointment only. Complete new wood for all years Chrysler Town & Country; complete restorations. Structural and concours quality interior woodwork for coachbuilt classics. Rebuild, restore or remanufacture damaged or missing parts. Specialize in Rolls-Royces, Bentleys, Chrysler T&C, etc. Award winning complete restorations.

Green Valentine Inc 5055 Covington Way Memphis, TN 38134 901-373-5555; FAX: 901-373-5568	**car dealer** **woodies**

See full listing in **Section Two** under **car dealers**

Hagerty Classic Insurance PO Box 87 Traverse City, MI 49685 800-922-4050; FAX: 616-941-8227	**insurance**

See full listing in **Section Two** under **insurance**

Hidden Valley Auto Parts 21046 N Rio Bravo Maricopa, AZ 85239 602-252-2122, 602-252-6137 520-568-2945; FAX: 602-258-0951	**parts**

See full listing in **Section One** under **Chevrolet**

Imperial Motors Rt 3 Box 380 Campobello, SC 29322 864-895-3474; FAX: 864-895-1248	**parts**

Mail order only. Chrysler, Plymouth, Dodge parts only. Chrysler parts 1955-1982. Chrysler, Plymouth, Dodge, Imperial, DeSoto, Barracuda parts. Parting out complete running cars. Rust-free sheetmetal. 30 acres of cars and parts. Visa, MasterCard, American Express, Discover. Web site: www.chryslerparts.com

International Towing & Recovery Museum 401 Broad St Chattanooga, TN 37402 PH/FAX: 423-267-3132	**museum**

See full listing in **Section Six** under **Tennessee**

Jeff Johnson Motorsports 4421 Aldrich Pl Columbus, OH 43214 614-268-1181; FAX: 614-268-1141	**accessories** **literature** **parts**

See full listing in **Section One** under **Mopar**

Kramer Automotive Specialties PO Box 5 Herman, PA 16039 724-285-5566; FAX: 724-285-8898	**body parts** **interiors** **sheetmetal**

See full listing in **Section One** under **Mopar**

L & L Antique Auto Trim 403 Spruce, Box 177 Pierce City, MO 65723 417-476-2871	**runningboard** **moldings**

See full listing in **Section Two** under **special services**

Legendary Auto Interiors Ltd 121 W Shore Blvd Newark, NY 14513 800-363-8804 FAX: 800-SEAT-UPH (732-8874)	**soft trim**

Specialists in the manufacturing of authentic reproduction seat upholstery, door panels, molded seat foam, vinyl tops and more for 1957-1979 Chrysler, Plymouth and Dodge cars, Dodge trucks, 1968-1974 AMC Javelin and AMX, and 1964-1972 Buick Skylark, GS and GSX and custom vintage vinyl floormats for General Motors muscle cars 1953-1996. Complete interior trim line including molded carpets, headliners, convertible tops, boots, and well liners, NOS interior items, etc. Catalog $5 US.

Lloyd's Literature PO Box 491 Newbury, OH 44065 800-292-2665; 440-338-1527 FAX: 440-338-2222	**literature**

See full listing in **Section Two** under **literature dealers**

David Martin Box 61 Roosevelt, TX 76874 915-446-4439	**parts**

Mail order only. Specializes in parts for 1946-1947-1948 Chryslers, some DeSoto and Dodge.

Mike's Auto Parts Box 358 Ridgeland, MS 39158 601-856-7214	**ball/roller bearings** **engine parts** **wall calendars** **water pumps**

Mail order. Specializing in Chrysler, Dodge, DeSoto, Plymouth, AMC/Jeep, Nash, Hudson, Willys, GM parts and bearings, universal joints, engine parts, brake parts, ignition parts, starter drives, spark plugs, 6-volt bulbs, tubular shocks, belts, water pumps, fuel pumps, transmission gears, clutches and windshield wipers for all makes. Also collectible wall calendars and memorabilia.

Moroso Motorsports Park PO Box 31907 Palm Beach Gardens, FL 33420 561-622-1400; FAX: 561-626-2053 E-mail: racetrack@moroso.com	**race track**

See full listing in **Section Two** under **racing**

Clayton T Nelson Box 259 Warrenville, IL 60555 630-369-6589	**NOS parts**

See full listing in **Section One** under **Oldsmobile**

North Yale Auto Parts Rt 1, Box 707 Sperry, OK 74073 918-288-7218, 800-256-6927 (NYAP) FAX: 918-288-7223	**salvage yard**

See full listing in **Section Five** under **Oklahoma**

NS-One PO Box 2459, Dept VA Cedar Rapids, IA 52406 319-362-7717	**NOS parts**

Mail order only. NOS Chrysler product parts. Trim, electricals, minor mechanicals, etc, for late 1930s to early 1970s. No catalogs, no lists available. Postpaid prices; COD extra. Easy return policy. No SASE, no answer.

Obsolete Chrysler NOS Parts
4206 Burnett Dr
Murrysville, PA 15668
724-733-1818 eves
FAX: 724-733-9884 or
412-243-4556 anytime
E-mail: parts4u@aol.com

literature
parts

Mail order and open shop. Saturdays 8 am to 5 pm. New old stock Chrysler products, parts. Specializing in chrome trim, medallions, fenders and bumpers, 1930s-1960s. Lots of literature also. Dodge and Plymouth NOS parts for 1938-1958. Satisfaction guaranteed.

Obsolete Parts of Iowa
PO Box 233
Earlville, IA 52041
E-mail: finsrus@mwci.net

NOS parts

See full listing in **Section One** under **Mopar**

OEM Paints Inc
PO Box 461736
Escondido, CA 92046-1736
760-747-2100

custom aerosol
colors

See full listing in **Section Two** under **paints**

Old Air Products
4615 Martin St
Ft Worth, TX 76119
817-531-2665; FAX: 817-531-3257
E-mail: sales@oldairproducts.com

air conditioning

See full listing in **Section One** under **Corvette**

Older Car Restoration
Martin Lum, Owner
304 S Main St, Box 428
Mont Alto, PA 17237
717-749-3383, 717-352-7701
E-mail: jlum@epix.net

repro parts
restoration

See full listing in **Section One** under **Mopar**

P-Ayr Products
719 Delaware St
Leavenworth, KS 66048
913-651-5543; FAX: 913-651-2084
E-mail: sales@payr.com

replicas

See full listing in **Section One** under **Chevrolet**

Plymouth, Dodge, Chrysler, DeSoto Parts
4206 Burnett Dr
Murrysville, PA 15668
724-733-1818 eves
FAX: 724-733-9884 or
412-243-4556 anytime
E-mail: parts4u@aol.com

NOS parts for
DeSoto

See full listing in **Section One** under **DeSoto**

Power Brake X-Change Inc
336 Lamont Pl
Pittsburgh, PA 15232
800-580-5729, 412-441-5729
FAX: 412-441-9333

parts

See full listing in **Section Two** under **brakes**

Power Play, Bob Walker
276 Walkers Hollow Tr
Lowgap, NC 27024
336-352-4866; FAX: 336-789-8967
E-mail: rlwalker@infoave.net

parts

Mail order only. Monday-Saturday 1 pm to 8 pm. Early Hemi engine parts, adaptors and complete engine rebuild service for 1951-1958 Chrysler, 1952-1957 DeSoto and 1953-1957 Dodge Hemi engines. Web site: www.powerplayhemi.com

Precision Rubber
Box 324
Didsbury, AB Canada T0M 0W0
403-335-9590; FAX: 403-335-8100

rubber parts

See full listing in **Section Two** under **rubber parts**

Quality Tire Barn Inc
255 Twinsburg Rd
Northfield, OH 44067
330-467-1284

tires

See full listing in **Section Two** under **tires**

REM Automotive Inc
2610 N Brandt Rd
Annville, PA 17003
717-838-4242; FAX: 717-838-5091

interior parts
trunk lining

See full listing in **Section Two** under **restoration aids**

Restorations By Julius
10101-1/2 Canoga Ave
Chatsworth, CA 91311
818-882-2825; FAX: 818-882-2855
E-mail: julius@cyberweb1.com

restoration

See full listing in **Section One** under **Plymouth**

Roberts Motor Parts
17 Prospect St
West Newbury, MA 01985
978-363-5407; FAX: 978-363-2026
E-mail: sales@robertsmotorparts.com

parts

See full listing in **Section One** under **Dodge**

Don Rook
184 Raspberry Ln
Mena, AR 71953
501-394-7555

parts

Mail order and open shop. Open anytime at home. Specializes in parts for Chryslers and Packards of the 1940s, 1950s and 1960s, mostly Chrysler 300s 1955-1971 and specifically 1965 and 1966. Also many Packard parts from 1941-1956, trim and chrome. No heavy and internal mechanical items. Trim and detail pieces only. Some windshields.

Sherman & Associates Inc
61166 Van Dyke Rd
Washington, MI 48094
810-677-6800; FAX: 810-677-6801

body panels
body parts
fenders/floors
quarter panels

See full listing in **Section Two** under **body parts**

Paul Slater Auto Parts
9496 85th St N
Stillwater, MN 55082
612-429-4235

parts

See full listing in **Section One** under **Dodge**

Totally Auto Inc
337 Philmont Ave
Feasterville, PA 19053
215-322-2277; FAX: 215-322-4755
E-mail: totalyauto@aol.com

parts
restoration
service

See full listing in **Section One** under **Mopar**

Transgo Performance
2621 Merced Ave
El Monte, CA 91733
626-443-4953; FAX: 626-443-1079

shift kits

See full listing in **Section Two** under **transmissions**

Trim Parts Inc — trim items
5161 Wolfpen Pleasant Hill
Milford, OH 45150
513-831-1472; FAX: 513-248-3402
E-mail: sales@trimparts.com

See full listing in **Section One** under **Chevrolet**

U S Oldies & Classics — car dealer / parts
Vunt 3
Holsbeek 3220 Belgium
3216446611; FAX: 3216446520

See full listing in **Section Two** under **car dealers**

Ultimate Spray-On Truck Bedliner — bedliners
115 Garfield St
Sumas, WA 98295
800-989-9869; FAX: 604-864-0207
E-mail: info@ultimatelinings.com

See full listing in **Section Two** under **trucks & tractors**

Ultra Wheel Co — custom wheels
6300 Valley View Ave
Buena Park, CA 90620
714-994-1444; FAX: 714-994-0723

See full listing in **Section Two** under **wheels & wheelcovers**

Universal Transmission Co — transmission parts
23361 Dequindre Rd
Hazel Park, MI 48030
800-882-4327; FAX: 248-398-2581

See full listing in **Section Two** under **transmissions**

Vintage Woodworks — upholstery / woodwork
PO Box 49
Iola, WI 54945
715-445-3791

See full listing in **Section Two** under **woodwork**

Weimann's Literature & Collectables — literature
16 Cottage Rd
Harwinton, CT 06791
860-485-0300
FAX: 860-485-1705, 24 hour

See full listing in **Section One** under **Plymouth**

Wheels & Spokes Inc — Mopar parts / restoration
383 Mopar Dr
Hays, KS 67601
785-628-6477; FAX: 785-628-6834

See full listing in **Section One** under **Mopar**

Enthousiaste Citroen — appraisals / brokerage / consultation / locating
David Allen
HC4, Box 330
Mustoe, VA 24465
540-468-1500; FAX: 540-468-1501

Specializing in brokerage, locating, appraisal, import, export, shipping and consultation for all marque of Citroen automobiles, exclusively. 2CV specialist, all other models only exceptional, rare, collector; no parts.

Bill Stratton — parts / sales / service
Box 153
Exton, PA 19341
610-363-1725; FAX: 610-363-2691

Mail order parts. Citroen CX specialist. Expert service. Cars bought and sold.

Tony D Branda Performance — accessories / decals / emblems / sheetmetal / wheels
Shelby and Mustang Parts
1434 E Pleasant Valley Blvd
Altoona, PA 16602
814-942-1869; FAX: 814-944-0801
E-mail: cobranda@aol.com

See full listing in **Section One** under **Mustang**

California Classic Mustang — steel wheels
1102 Industrial Ave
Escondido, CA 92128
888-320-8929, 760-746-6580
FAX: 760-746-6581
E-mail: mmatt1965@aol.com

See full listing in **Section One** under **Mustang**

Carl's Ford Parts — muscle parts
23219 South St, Box 38
Homeworth, OH 44634
PH/FAX: 330-525-7291

See full listing in **Section One** under **Mustang**

CJ Pony Parts Inc — parts
7441 B Allentown Blvd
Harrisburg, PA 17112
800-888-6473; 717-691-5623
FAX: 888-888-6573, 717-657-9254
E-mail: creed@redrose.net

See full listing in **Section One** under **Mustang**

Classics 'n More Inc — repairs / restoration
1001 Ranck Mill Rd
Lancaster, PA 17602
717-392-0599; FAX 717-392-2371

See full listing in **Section Two** under **restoration shops**

Cobra Restorers Ltd — parts / restoration / service
3099 Carter Dr
Kennesaw, GA 30144
404-427-0020; FAX: 404-427-8658

Mail order and open shop. Monday-Friday 9 am to 6 pm. Largest supplier of parts for Cobra roadsters (replica and original). Restoration and builder of ERA Cobras. Manufacture many parts. Catalog, $5.

Collectors Choice LTD — parts / race preparation / restoration / service
6400 Springfield-Lodi Rd
Dane, WI 53529
608-849-9878; FAX: 608-849-9879

See full listing in **Section One** under **DeTomaso/Pantera**

Drummond Coach and Paint — painting / restoration
531 Raleigh Ave
El Cajon, CA 92020
619-579-7229; FAX: 619-579-2128

See full listing in **Section One** under **Ferrari**

The Fine Car Store   car dealer
1105 Moana Dr
San Diego, CA 92107
619-223-7766; FAX: 619-223-6838

See full listing in **Section One** under **Ferrari**

Finish Line   parts
3593 SW 173rd Terr   supplies
Miramar, FL 33029
954-436-9101; FAX: 954-436-9102
E-mail: e.dlibrandi@worldnet.att.net

Specializing in OEM parts and supplies for Shelby Cobras, OE
and reproductions. Parts and supplies for British Leyland Group
cars. Also run three registries for Mustangs of various years.
Web site: www.cobraaccessories.com

Gemini Racing Systems Inc   race prep
571 N 54th St   restoration
Chandler, AZ 85226
800-992-9294, 602-940-9011

See full listing in **Section One** under **Mustang**

Mark Gillett   car locator
PO Box 9177   sales
Dallas, TX 75209
PH/FAX: 214-902-9258
011-525-559-6240 Mexico City, Mexico
E-mail: autonet@onramp.net

See full listing in **Section Two** under **car dealers**

JWF Restorations Inc   restoration
11955 SW Faircrest St
Portland, OR 97225-4615
503-643-3225; FAX: 503-646-4009

See full listing in **Section One** under **AC**

Marcovicci-Wenz Engineering Inc   Cosworth engines
33 Comac Loop
Ronkonkoma, NY 11779
516-467-9040; FAX: 516-467-9041
E-mail: tedwenz@compuserve.com

See full listing in **Section Two** under **racing**

Operations Plus   accessories
PO Box 26347   parts
Santa Ana, CA 92799
PH/FAX: 714-962-2776
E-mail: aquacel@aquacel.com

Distributor for Unique Motor Cars. Supplier of numerous Cobra
parts and accessories: body, interior, seats, windshield, lighting,
mirrors, hardware, fasteners, steering wheels, seats, wheels, oil
pans, coolers and adapters, knock-off hammers, vinyl graphics
and memorabilia. Web site: www.cobracountry.com/opsplus

Greg Purdy's Mustang Supply   parts
PO Box 784
Forest Hill, MD 21050
410-836-5991

See full listing in **Section One** under **Mustang**

Scarborough Faire Inc   parts
1151 Main St
Pawtucket, RI 02860
800-556-6300, 401-724-4200
FAX: 401-724-5392

See full listing in **Section One** under **MG**

Showroom Auto Sales   car dealer
960 S Bascom Ave
San Jose, CA 95128
408-279-0944; FAX: 408-279-0918

See full listing in **Section One** under **Mercedes-Benz**

Unfair Advantage Enterprises   emblems
2219 W Olive Ave #179   trim
Burbank, CA 91506
213-245-8441

Mail order only. Organized to provide exact, high quality
emblems and trim pieces for specific automotive markets.
Specializing in Cobras, Shelbys 1965-1970, Chevrolets 1955,
1956, 1957.

XKs Unlimited   instruments
850 Fiero Ln   parts
San Luis Obispo, CA 93401   restorations
805-544-7864; FAX: 805-544-1664
E-mail: xksunltd@aol.com

See full listing in **Section One** under **Jaguar**

COOPER

1 CAAT Limited Co   restoration
1324 E Harper Ave
Maryville, TN 37804
423-983-7180
E-mail: jhenriks@icx.net

See full listing in **Section Two** under **restoration shops**

Heritage Motor Centre   museum
Banbury Rd
Gaydon
Warwichshire CV35 0BJ England
01926 641188; FAX: 01926 641555

See full listing in **Section Six** under **England**

Mini Mania   parts
31 Winsor St   service
Milpitas, CA 95035
408-942-5595; FAX: 408-942-5582
E-mail: info@minimania.com

See full listing in **Section One** under **Austin**

Mini Store   cars
PO Box 7973   repairs
Van Nuys, CA 91409-7973   restorations
PH/FAX: 818-893-1421
E-mail: jorn@aol.com

See full listing in **Section One** under **Austin**

Auto World Car Museum by Backer   museum
Business 54 N
PO Box 135
Fulton, MO 65251
573-642-2080, 573-642-5344
FAX: 573-642-0685
E-mail: webacker@ktis.net

See full listing in **Section Six** under **Missouri**

J K Howell
455 N Grace St
Lombard, IL 60148
630-495-1949

parts

Mail order only. Full line of new, used, original and reproduction Cord parts and manuals. Catalog available to owners or restorers.

Lincoln Highway Packards
Main St
PO Box 94
Schellsburg, PA 15559
814-733-4356; FAX: 814-839-4276

engine rebuilding
restoration

See full listing in **Section One** under **Packard**

McLellan's Automotive History
Robert and Sharon McLellan
9111 Longstaff Dr
Houston, TX 77031-2711
713-772-3285; FAX: 713-772-3287
E-mail: mclellans@worldnet.att.net

books
factory literature
magazines
memorabilia
press kits/programs
sales literature

See full listing in **Section Two** under **literature dealers**

Norm's Custom Shop
6897 E William St Ext
Bath, NY 14810
PH/FAX: 607-776-2357

interiors
tops

Mail order and open shop. Monday-Friday 8:30 am to 5 pm, Saturday 8:30 am to 2 pm. Fabrication and installation of automobile tops and interiors, custom or original design using materials of your choice. Many national winners over the past 34 years.

Northeast Classic Car Museum
NYS Rt 23
24 Rexford St
Norwich, NY 13815
607-334-AUTO (334-2886)
FAX: 607-336-6745
E-mail: neccm@ascent.net

museum

See full listing in **Section Six** under **New York**

Edwards Crosley Parts
PO Box 632
Mansfield, OH 44901
419-589-5767

parts

Mail order and open shop. Evenings and weekends. Call before visiting. Shop address: 988 Reed Rd, Mansfield, OH 44903.

Heinze Enterprise
7914 E Kimsey Ln
Scottsdale, AZ 85257
602-946-5814

instrument
restoration

See full listing in **Section One** under **American Austin/Bantam**

Service Motors
PO Box 116
Twelve Mile, IN 46988
219-664-3313

car dealer
parts

Phone hours: 9 am to 5 pm daily. Crosley parts bought, sold and traded. Complete cars for sale. Parts shipped via UPS, COD. We accept Visa, MasterCard and Discover.

Cushman

Dennis Carpenter Cushman Reproductions
PO Box 26398
Charlotte, NC 28221-6398
704-782-1237; FAX: 704-786-8180
E-mail: info@dennis-carpenter.com

accessories
parts

Mail order and over the counter sales. Monday-Friday 8 am to 5 pm. Manufacture and sell obsolete Cushman motor scooter parts, including body and engine parts, accessories and much more. We also buy and sell all makes of vintage motorbikes and motor scooters. Send $4 for catalog. Web site: www.dennis-carpenter.com

Arthur W Aseltine
18215 Challenge Cut-Off Rd
Forbestown, CA 95941
530-675-2773

parts
research
restoration

See full listing in **Section One** under **Stearns-Knight**

Healey Lane
5920 Jones Ave
Riverside, CA 92505
800-411-HEALEY (4325)
FAX: 909-689-4934
E-mail: healeylane@aol.com

parts
restoration
service

See full listing in **Section One** under **Austin-Healey**

Jaguar Daimler Heritage Trust
Browns Ln
Allesley, Coventry CV5 9DR England
0044 (0) 1203 402121
FAX: 0044 (0) 1203 405581

archive services
photographic
records

See full listing in **Section One** under **Jaguar**

Sandringham House Museum & Grounds
Sandringham
Nr King's Lynn
Norfolk PE356EN England
01553-772675; FAX: 01485-541571

museum

See full listing in **Section Six** under **England**

Texas Viper Hotline
5405 Montclair
Colleyville, TX 76034
817-267-1299; FAX: 972-986-1519

Prowlers
Vipers

See full listing in **Section One** under **Dodge**

Barry Thorne
PO Box 246
Dorking
Surrey RH5 5FU England
mobile: 0585-882416

manuals
parts

Mail order and open shop. Anytime, any day. For 1959-1964 Daimler SP 250s and SP 251s (lhd). Also Daimler 2-1/2 V8 and V8 250. All inquiries answered. Free advice. Worldwide shipping.

DATSUN

Banzai Motorworks
6735 Midcities Ave
Beltsville, MD 20705
PH/FAX: 301-937-5746
E-mail: zspert@erols.com

| | pre-purchase insp/consultation parts repairs/restoration service |

Mail order and open shop. Monday-Friday 8:30 am to 6 pm, Saturday 10:30 am to 3 pm. The East Coast's premier Z car restoration shop. From 1970-1996 from oil changes to restorations. We do it all. Banzai Motorworks is the leading supplier of reproduction parts to the Z car hobby. We are also the major reproduction parts supplier to Nissan's 240Z restoration program. Owner Michael McGinnis has more than 29 years' experience servicing Datsuns. We know Z cars. Web site: www.zzxdatsun.com

Stan Chernoff
1215 Greenwood Ave
Torrance, CA 90503
310-320-4554; FAX: 310-328-7867
E-mail: az589@lafn.org

| | mechanical parts restoration parts technical info trim parts |

Mail order only. Specializing in restoration, mechanical and trim parts and technical information for 1963-1970 Datsun roadsters, Models SP(L) 310, SP(L) 311 and SR(L) 311.

CSi
1100 S Raymond Ave, Suite H
Fullerton, CA 92831
714-879-7955; FAX: 714-879-7310
E-mail: csila@compuserve.com

| | parts |

See full listing in **Section One** under **BMW**

John's Cars Inc
800 Jaguar Ln
Dallas, TX 75226
800-866-JAGS (5247) parts orders only; 214-426-4100
FAX: 214-426-3116

| | conversion retrofits parts restoration service |

See full listing in **Section One** under **Jaguar**

KATO USA Inc
100 Remington Rd
Schaumburg, IL 60173
847-781-9500; FAX: 847-781-9570

| | models |

See full listing in **Section One** under **Toyota**

Motormetrics
6369 Houston Rd
Macon, GA 31216
912-785-0275
E-mail:
fzampa@cennet.mc.peachnet.edu

| | used parts |

See full listing in **Section One** under **Triumph**

Motorsport Auto
1139 W Collins Ave
Orange, CA 92667
800-633-6331, 714-639-2620
FAX: 714-639-7460
E-mail: motorsport@worldnet.att.net

| | parts |

Mail order and open shop. Monday-Friday 8 am to 5 pm, Saturday 10 am to 2 pm. Parts and accessories for Datsun 240Z, 260Z, 280Z, 280ZX; Nissan 300ZX. Full line of restoration items for all Z-cars. 144 page catalog now available. Web site: www.zcarparts.com

Smooth Line
2562 Riddle Run Rd
Tarentum, PA 15084
724-274-6002; FAX: 724-274-6121

| | body panels removable hardtops |

See full listing in **Section Two** under **tops**

DE LOREAN MOTOR COMPANY

DeLorean Literature
3116 Welsh Rd
Philadelphia, PA 19136-1810
215-338-6142
E-mail: delorean.literature@excite.com

| | collectibles literature |

Mail order only. Carry a variety of collectible items such as literature, books, toys, magazines, video and other unique items related to the DeLorean automobile made during 1981-1982. Please send a SASE for a complete listing of items available. All items guaranteed for satisfaction. Web site: www.inc.com/users/delorean.html

DeLorean One
20229 Nordhoff St
Chatsworth, CA 91311
818-341-1796; FAX: 818-998-6381

| | bodywork parts service |

Mail order and open shop. Monday-Friday 8 am to 6 pm. Specializes in DeLorean parts, service, bodywork, electrical, suspension and sales for all DeLorean automobiles, 1981-1983.

French Stuff
PO Box 39772
Glendale, CA 90039-0772
818-244-2498; FAX: 818-500-7628
E-mail: frenchap@gte.net

| | accessories engine rebuilding parts transaxle rebuilding |

See full listing in **Section One** under **Renault**

PJ Grady Inc
118 Montauk Hwy
PO Box 7
West Sayville, NY 11796
800-350-7429; FAX: 516-589-6241
E-mail: pjgrady@ibm.net

| | parts restoration sales service |

Sales, parts, service and restoration for DeLoreans.

Al Trommers-Rare Auto Literature
614 Vanburenville Rd
Middletown, NY 10940

| | hubcaps license plates literature/records |

See full listing in **Section Two** under **literature dealers**

Wilson's Classic Auto
417 Kaufman Rt 150
PO Box 58
Congerville, IL 61729
309-448-2408; FAX: 309-448-2409

| | restoration |

See full listing in **Section Two** under **restoration shops**

DeSoto

Antique DeSoto-Plymouth 4206 Burnett Dr Murrysville, PA 15668 724-733-1818 eves FAX: 724-733-9884 or 412-243-4556 anytime E-mail: parts4u@aol.com	Mopar parts

See full listing in **Section One** under **Mopar**

Antique Mopar Auto Sales 5758 McNicholl Dr Hale, MI 48739-8984 517-257-3123	cars parts

See full listing in **Section One** under **Mopar**

Egge Machine Company Inc 11707 Slauson Ave Santa Fe Springs, CA 90670 800-866-EGGE, 562-945-3419 FAX: 562-693-1635 E-mail: info@egge.com	bearings pistons/rings timing components valve train

See full listing in **Section Two** under **engine parts**

Jahns Quality Pistons 1360 N Jefferson St Anaheim, CA 92807 714-579-3795, 800-225-0277 FAX: 714-524-6607	piston rings pistons

See full listing in **Section Two** under **engine parts**

David Martin Box 61 Roosevelt, TX 76874 915-446-4439	parts

See full listing in **Section One** under **Chrysler**

Clayton T Nelson Box 259 Warrenville, IL 60555 630-369-6589	NOS parts

See full listing in **Section One** under **Oldsmobile**

NS-One PO Box 2459, Dept VA Cedar Rapids, IA 52406 319-362-7717	NOS parts

See full listing in **Section One** under **Chrysler**

Obsolete Chrysler NOS Parts 4206 Burnett Dr Murrysville, PA 15668 724-733-1818 eves FAX: 724-733-9884 or 412-243-4556 anytime E-mail: parts4u@aol.com	literature parts

See full listing in **Section One** under **Chrysler**

Obsolete Parts of Iowa PO Box 233 Earlville, IA 52041 E-mail: finsrus@mwci.net	NOS parts

See full listing in **Section One** under **Mopar**

Older Car Restoration Martin Lum, Owner 304 S Main St, Box 428 Mont Alto, PA 17237 717-749-3383, 717-352-7701 E-mail: jlum@epix.net	repro parts restoration

See full listing in **Section One** under **Mopar**

Plymouth, Dodge, Chrysler, **DeSoto Parts** 4206 Burnett Dr Murrysville, PA 15668 724-733-1818 eves FAX: 724-733-9884 or 412-243-4556 anytime E-mail: parts4u@aol.com	NOS parts for DeSoto

Mail order only. Large supply of Mopar parts. Strong in DeSoto and Plymouth. Mostly NOS. DeSoto, Plymouth chrome for 1938-1965. Send SASE with want list for reply. Satisfaction guaranteed.

Power Play, Bob Walker 276 Walkers Hollow Tr Lowgap, NC 27024 336-352-4866; FAX: 336-789-8967 E-mail: rlwalker@infoave.net	parts

See full listing in **Section One** under **Chrysler**

Roberts Motor Parts 17 Prospect St West Newbury, MA 01985 978-363-5407; FAX: 978-363-2026 E-mail: sales@robertsmotorparts.com	parts

See full listing in **Section One** under **Dodge**

U S Oldies & Classics Vunt 3 Holsbeek 3220 Belgium 3216446611; FAX: 3216446520	car dealer parts

See full listing in **Section Two** under **car dealers**

Weimann's Literature & **Collectables** 16 Cottage Rd Harwinton, CT 06791 860-485-0300 FAX: 860-485-1705, 24 hour	literature

See full listing in **Section One** under **Plymouth**

Wheels & Spokes Inc 383 Mopar Dr Hays, KS 67601 785-628-6477; FAX: 785-628-6834	Mopar parts restoration

See full listing in **Section One** under **Mopar**

DeTomaso PANTERA

Avanti Auto Service Rt 322, 67 Conchester Hwy Glen Mills, PA 19342-1506 610-558-9999	repair restoration

Open shop only. Monday-Friday 9 am to 6 pm. General auto repair serving all makes, models and years. Mechanical restoration, front end alignment, computer service, brakes, shocks, tires, etc. 20 years' experience. Specializing in Pantera, Avanti, Corvette and others.

Collectors Choice LTD
6400 Springfield-Lodi Rd
Dane, WI 53529
608-849-9878; FAX: 608-849-9879

parts
race preparation
restoration
service

Mail order and open shop. Monday-Friday 8 am to 5 pm. DeTomaso and Dodge Viper parts distributors. Specializing in DeTomaso Panteras, AC Cobras, GT-40 Fords, Shelbys, Ferraris, Jaguars, Rolls-Royces and Vipers.

DeTomaso Registry
Bill Van Ess
2306 Post Dr NE
Belmont, MI 49306
616-364-1973; FAX: 616-363-2870

book

Mail order only. A registry of all the production models from DeTomaso Automobili SpA Modena. Includes all models of the Pantera, Mangusta, Vallelunga, Longchamp and Deauville. 256 pages, includes pictures and history of each model with production figures and running production changes. Current and past owners and history on the remaining cars, etc. $21 postpaid US; $25 postpaid Europe.

Hall Pantera
15337 Garfield Ave
Paramount, CA 90723
562-867-3319, 562-531-2629
FAX: 562-630-8156
E-mail: hallpantera@msn.com

parts

Open shop. Tuesday-Friday 10 am to 5 pm PST. Specializing in DeTomaso parts, Pantera, Mangusta and Vallelunga parts. Ford SVO dealer. Web site: www.hallpantera.com

The Italian Car Registry
3305 Valley Vista Rd
Walnut Creek, CA 94598-3943
925-458-1163

information source

See full listing in **Section Four** under **information sources**

Pantera Parts Connection
645 National Ave
Mountain View, CA 94043
800-DETOMAS, 650-968-2291
FAX: 650-968-2218
E-mail: larrys@panteraparts.com

parts

Mail order and open shop. Monday-Friday 8 am to 5 pm PST. Specializing in DeTomaso Pantera for 1971-1974. Web site: www.panteraparts.com

Pantera Performance Center
1856 N Park St
Castle Rock, CO 80104
303-660-9897; FAX: 303-660-9159

parts
restoration
service

Mail order and open shop. Monday-Friday 9 am to 5 pm, evenings/weekends by appointment only. Specialize in parts, service and restoration for DeTomaso Pantera.

PI Motorsports Inc
1040 N Batavia Ste G
Orange, CA 92867
714-744-1398; FAX: 714-744-1397
E-mail: pimflash.net

parts
restoration
sales

Specializing in DeTomaso automobiles for sale, parts, restoration and automobilia for 1971-1996 Panteras, Mangusta, Longchamp and Deauville DeTomaso race cars. Web site: www.pim.net

Antique DeSoto-Plymouth
4206 Burnett Dr
Murrysville, PA 15668
724-733-1818 eves, 724-327-2594
FAX: 724-733-9884 or
412-243-4556 anytime
E-mail: parts4u@aol.com

Mopar parts

See full listing in **Section One** under **Mopar**

Antique Mopar Auto Sales
5758 McNicholl Dr
Hale, MI 48739-8984
517-257-3123

cars
parts

See full listing in **Section One** under **Mopar**

Bill's Speed Shop
13951 Millersburg Rd
Navarre, OH 44662
330-832-9403; FAX: 330-832-2098

body parts

See full listing in **Section One** under **Chevrolet**

The Brassworks
289 Prado Rd
San Louis Obispo, CA 93401
800-342-6759; FAX: 805-544-5615

radiators

See full listing in **Section Two** under **radiators**

Brewer's Performance Motor Parts
2560 S State Route 48
Ludlow Falls, OH 45339-9773
937-698-4259; FAX: 937-698-7109

parts

See full listing in **Section One** under **Mopar**

**Coach Builders Muscle Car
Parts & Services**
PO Box 128
Baltimore, MD 21087-0128
410-426-5567

interiors
parts
rust remover

See full listing in **Section One** under **Chevrolet**

Collectors Choice LTD
6400 Springfield-Lodi Rd
Dane, WI 53529
608-849-9878; FAX: 608-849-9879

parts
race preparation
restoration
service

See full listing in **Section One** under **DeTomaso/Pantera**

Dynatech Engineering
PO Box 1446
Alta Loma, CA 91701-8446
805-492-6134
E-mail:
dynatechengineering@yahoo.com

motor mounts

See full listing in **Section Two** under **engine parts**

Egge Machine Company Inc
11707 Slauson Ave
Santa Fe Springs, CA 90670
800-866-EGGE, 562-945-3419
FAX: 562-693-1635
E-mail: info@egge.com

bearings
pistons/rings
timing components
valve train

See full listing in **Section Two** under **engine parts**

ETC Every Thing Cars	paint
8727 Clarinda	repairs
Pico Rivera, CA 90660	restoration
562-949-6981	welding

See full listing in **Section One** under **Mopar**

Fitzgerald Motorsports	Viper dealer
1258 Union Ave	
Laconia, NH 03246	
603-528-1000; FAX: 603-524-2951	
E-mail: snake@fitzmotorsports.com	

Open Monday-Saturday 9 am to 8 pm. Dodge Vipers. The top volume Viper dealer in the world. Visit our new 20 car showroom. Web site: www.fitzmotorsports.com

Bruce Horkey's Wood & Parts	pickup parts
Rt 4 Box 188	
Windom, MN 56101	
507-831-5625; FAX: 507-831-0280	

See full listing in **Section Two** under **trucks & tractors**

Imperial Motors	parts
Rt 3 Box 380	
Campobello, SC 29322	
864-895-3474; FAX: 864-895-1248	

See full listing in **Section One** under **Chrysler**

Jeff Johnson Motorsports	accessories
4421 Aldrich Pl	literature
Columbus, OH 43214	parts
614-268-1181; FAX: 614-268-1141	

See full listing in **Section One** under **Mopar**

Kramer Automotive Specialties	body parts
PO Box 5	interiors
Herman, PA 16039	sheetmetal
724-285-5566; FAX: 724-285-8898	

See full listing in **Section One** under **Mopar**

Legendary Auto Interiors Ltd	soft trim
121 W Shore Blvd	
Newark, NY 14513	
800-363-8804	
FAX: 800-SEAT-UPH (732-8874)	

See full listing in **Section One** under **Chrysler**

Mack Products	parts
PO Box 856	pickup beds
Moberly, MO 65270	
660-263-7444	

See full listing in **Section One** under **Ford 1932-1953**

Jim Mallars	parts
5931 Glen St	
Stockton, CA 95207	
209-477-1702, 9 am to 6 pm	

Mail order and open by appointment only. For 1915-1928 Dodge Brothers 4-cylinder vehicles. New and used parts.

David Martin	parts
Box 61	
Roosevelt, TX 76874	
915-446-4439	

See full listing in **Section One** under **Chrysler**

Clayton T Nelson	NOS parts
Box 259	
Warrenville, IL 60555	
630-369-6589	

See full listing in **Section One** under **Oldsmobile**

Hemmings' Vintage Auto Almanac©   Fourteenth Edition

NS-One	NOS parts
PO Box 2459, Dept VA	
Cedar Rapids, IA 52406	
319-362-7717	

See full listing in **Section One** under **Chrysler**

Obsolete Chrysler NOS Parts	literature
4206 Burnett Dr	parts
Murrysville, PA 15668	
724-733-1818 eves	
FAX: 724-733-9884 or	
412-243-4556 anytime	
E-mail: parts4u@aol.com	

See full listing in **Section One** under **Chrysler**

Obsolete Parts of Iowa	NOS parts
PO Box 233	
Earlville, IA 52041	
E-mail: finsrus@mwci.net	

See full listing in **Section One** under **Mopar**

Older Car Restoration	repro parts
Martin Lum, Owner	restoration
304 S Main St, Box 428	
Mont Alto, PA 17237	
717-749-3383, 717-352-7701	
E-mail: jlum@epix.net	

See full listing in **Section One** under **Mopar**

The Paddock® Inc	accessories
PO Box 30	parts
221 W Main	
Knightstown, IN 46148	
800-428-4319; FAX: 800-286-4040	
E-mail: paddock@indy.net	

See full listing in **Section One** under **Mustang**

Plymouth, Dodge, Chrysler,	NOS parts for
DeSoto Parts	DeSoto
4206 Burnett Dr	
Murrysville, PA 15668	
724-733-1818 eves	
FAX: 724-733-9884 or	
412-243-4556 anytime	
E-mail: parts4u@aol.com	

See full listing in **Section One** under **DeSoto**

Power Play, Bob Walker	parts
276 Walkers Hollow Tr	
Lowgap, NC 27024	
336-352-4866; FAX: 336-789-8967	
E-mail: rlwalker@infoave.net	

See full listing in **Section One** under **Chrysler**

R & R Fiberglass & Specialties	body parts
4850 Wilson Dr NW	
Cleveland, TN 37312	
423-476-2270; FAX: 423-473-9442	
E-mail: rrfiberglass@wingnet.net	

See full listing in **Section Two** under **fiberglass parts**

Restorations By Julius	restoration
10101-1/2 Canoga Ave	
Chatsworth, CA 91311	
818-882-2825; FAX: 818-882-2855	
E-mail: julius@cyberweb1.com	

See full listing in **Section One** under **Plymouth**

Roberts Motor Parts	parts
17 Prospect St	
West Newbury, MA 01985	
978-363-5407; FAX: 978-363-2026	
E-mail: sales@robertsmotorparts.com	

Specializing in Dodge trucks, Chrysler product automobiles.

Chevy and GMC trucks for 1929-1980 and 1933-1960 cars; various parts. Web site: www.robertsmotorparts.com

| **Sherman & Associates Inc**
61166 Van Dyke Rd
Washington, MI 48094
810-677-6800; FAX: 810-677-6801 | **body panels**
body parts
fenders/floors
quarter panels |

See full listing in **Section Two** under **body parts**

| **Paul Slater Auto Parts**
9496 85th St N
Stillwater, MN 55082
651-429-4235 | **parts** |

Mail order and open shop by appointment only. Phone hours are 9 am to 9 pm CST. Specializing in 1966-1974 performance Dodge and Plymouth parts (Roadrunner, GTX, Coronet, Super Bee, Charger, Barracuda, Challenger, Dart, Duster, Demon and some others). Excellent quality used my specialty, but also some NOS parts. More items in every week. Call or write me (send SASE) with your needs. Sorry, no list or catalog. I also buy NOS and quality used parts.

| **Tags Backeast**
PO Box 581
Plainville, CT 06062
860-747-2942
E-mail: dataplt@snet.net | **data plates**
trim tags |

See full listing in **Section Two** under **special services**

| **Texas Viper Hotline**
5405 Montclair
Colleyville, TX 76034
817-267-1299; FAX: 972-986-1519 | **Prowlers**
Vipers |

Specializing in Dodge Vipers and Plymouth Prowlers. Web site: www.viperhotline.com

| **Totally Auto Inc**
337 Philmont Ave
Feasterville, PA 19053
215-322-2277; FAX: 215-322-4755
E-mail: totalyauto@aol.com | **parts**
restoration
service |

See full listing in **Section One** under **Mopar**

| **Ultimate Spray-On Truck Bedliner**
115 Garfield St
Sumas, WA 98295
800-989-9869; FAX: 604-864-0207
E-mail: info@ultimatelinings.com | **bedliners** |

See full listing in **Section Two** under **trucks & tractors**

| **Vintage Motor and Machine**
Gene French
1513 Webster Ct
Ft Collins, CO 80524
970-498-9224 | **auto components**
fixtures
industrial
components |

See full listing in **Section Two** under **machine work**

| **Vintage Power Wagons Inc**
302 S 7th St
Fairfield, IA 52556
515-472-4665; FAX: 515-472-4824 | **parts**
trucks |

Mail order and open shop. Monday-Friday 8:30 am to 5 pm. Specializing in 1939-1970 Dodge Power Wagons, 4-wd trucks and parts.

| **Weimann's Literature &**
Collectables
16 Cottage Rd
Harwinton, CT 06791
860-485-0300
FAX: 860-485-1705, 24 hour | **literature** |

See full listing in **Section One** under **Plymouth**

| **Wheels & Spokes Inc**
383 Mopar Dr
Hays, KS 67601
785-628-6477; FAX: 785-628-6834 | **Mopar parts**
restoration |

See full listing in **Section One** under **Mopar**

| **Auto Advisors**
14 Dudley Rd
Billerica, MA 01821
978-667-0075 | **appraisals** |

See full listing in **Section Two** under **appraisals**

| **Blackhawk Collection**
1092 Eagles Nest Pl
Danville, CA 94506
925-736-3444; FAX: 925-736-4375
E-mail: info@blackhawkcollection.com | **acquisitions**
sales |

Specializing in sales and aquisitions as well as exposition sale events for pre and post-war American and European classics, custom-bodied and one-of-a-kind automobiles. Web site: www.blackhawkcollection.com

| **Collector Car Appraisers LLC**
800 Waterford Dr
Frederick, MD 21702
301-473-8333; FAX: 301-698-4796
E-mail: gfmchugh@netstorm.net | **appraisals** |

See full listing in **Section Two** under **appraisals**

| **Edgerton Classics Ltd**
9215 St Rt 13
Camden, NY 13316-4933
315-245-3113 | **restoration**
woodworking |

See full listing in **Section Two** under **restoration shops**

| **Leo Gephart Classic Cars**
7360 E Acoma Dr, Ste 14
Scottsdale, AZ 85260
602-948-2286, 602-998-8263
FAX: 602-948-2390 | **car dealer**
parts |

See full listing in **Section Two** under **car dealers**

| **Grand Touring**
2785 E Regal Park Dr
Anaheim, CA 92806
714-630-0130; FAX: 714-630-6956 | **engine rebuilding**
machine shop
restoration
suspension |

See full listing in **Section Two** under **restoration shops**

| **Libbey's Classic Car**
Restoration Center
137 N Quinsigamond Ave
Shrewsbury, MA 01545
PH/FAX: 508-792-1560 | **bodywork**
restoration
service |

See full listing in **Section Two** under **restoration shops**

| **McLellan's Automotive History**
Robert and Sharon McLellan
9111 Longstaff Dr
Houston, TX 77031-2711
713-772-3285; FAX: 713-772-3287
E-mail: mclellans@worldnet.att.net | **books**
factory literature
magazines
memorabilia
press kits/programs
sales literature |

See full listing in **Section Two** under **literature dealers**

Northeast Classic Car Museum
NYS Rt 23
24 Rexford St
Norwich, NY 13815
607-334-AUTO (334-2886)
FAX: 607-336-6745
E-mail: neccm@ascent.net

museum

See full listing in **Section Six** under **New York**

ORF Corp
Phil Bray
8858 Ferry Rd
Grosse Ile, MI 48138
734-676-5520; FAX: 734-676-9438
E-mail: carolbray@yahoo.com

ring and pinion gears

See full listing in **Section Two** under **special services**

Restorations Unlimited II Inc
304 Jandus Rd
Cary, IL 60013
847-639-5818

restoration

See full listing in **Section Two** under **restoration shops**

Supreme Metal Polishing
84A Rickenbacker Cir
Livermore, CA 94550
925-449-3490; FAX: 925-449-1475
E-mail: supremet@home.com

**metal working
parts restoration
plating services
polishing**

See full listing in **Section Two** under **plating & polishing**

Valley Wire Wheel Service
14731 Lull St
Van Nuys, CA 91405
818-785-7237; FAX: 818-994-2042

**wheel restoration
wheels**

See full listing in **Section Two** under **wheels & wheelcovers**

**Dennis Carpenter Ford
Reproductions**
PO Box 26398
Charlotte, NC 28221
704-786-8139; FAX: 704-786-8180

parts

See full listing in **Section One** under **Ford 1954-up**

Edsel Associates
2912 Hunter St
Fort Worth, TX 76112
817-451-2708
E-mail: theparts@flash.net

**brakes
sheetmetal
suspension**

Mail, e-mail, telephone orders and open shop. 1958-1960 Edsel parts, new suspension, brake, engine parts, ignition, water/fuel pumps. New and used sheetmetal, interior and exterior trim. SASE for partial list. Keep America beautiful, restore your Edsel.

McCoy's Memorabilia
35583 N 1830 E
Rossville, IL 60963-7175
PH/FAX: 217-748-6513
E-mail: indy500@soltec.net

**memorabilia
racing literature**

See full listing in **Section Two** under **literature dealers**

SMS Auto Fabrics
2325 SE 10th Ave
Portland, OR 97214
503-234-1175; FAX: 503-234-0651

upholstery

See full listing in **Section Two** under **interiors & interior parts**

Tags Backeast
PO Box 581
Plainville, CT 06062
860-747-2942
E-mail: dataplt@snet.net

**data plates
trim tags**

See full listing in **Section Two** under **special services**

Thunderbolt Traders Inc
6900 N Dixie Dr
Dayton, OH 45414-3297
513-890-3344; FAX: 513-890-9403

battery cables

Specializing in battery cables for Edsels 1958, 1959 and 1960. Also fuel additives, real tetraethyl lead, make your own leaded gasoline.

Grand Prix Classics Inc
7456 La Jolla Blvd
La Jolla, CA 92037
619-459-3500; FAX: 619-459-3512

**racing cars
sports cars**

See full listing in **Section Two** under **racing**

JAE
375 Pine #26
Goleta, CA 93117
805-967-5767; FAX: 805-967-6183
E-mail: jefforjay@jaeparts.com

**parts
service
tech info**

See full listing in **Section One** under **Lotus**

Vintage Racing Services
1785 Barnum Ave
Stratford, CT 06497
203-386-1736; FAX: 203-386-0486
E-mail: vrs@vintageracingservices.com

**storage
track support
transportation**

See full listing in **Section Two** under **racing**

Excalibur

Brooks Stevens Auto Collection Inc
10325 N Port Washington Rd
Mequon, WI 53092
414-241-4185; FAX: 414-241-4166
E-mail: apjb@prodigy.net

**parts
restoration
service**

Mail order and open shop. Monday-Saturday 8 am to 5 pm. Excalibur motor cars, service, restoration, parts and general repairs and info for 1965-1985. Dealing in antique, classic, collector, race and special interest autos and auto museum.

Ferrari

Algar 1234 Lancaster Ave Rosemont, PA 19010 800-441-9824, 610-527-1100 FAX: 610-525-0575 E-mail: algarferrari.com	parts

Specializing in parts for Ferrari and Alfa Romeo.

Auto Europa 221 Berrellesa St Martinez, CA 94553 925-229-3466; FAX: 925-313-0542	painting restorations woodworking

See full listing in **Section Two** under **restoration shops**

Automobile Appraisal Service Steve Cram 1080 Eddy St #607 San Francisco, CA 94109 415-567-1087, 619-584-4678 FAX: 415-567-1245	appraisals

See full listing in **Section Two** under **appraisals**

Bassett's Jaguar PO Box 245 53 Stilson Rd Wyoming, RI 02898 401-539-3010; FAX: 401-539-7861 E-mail: www.jagwillie@ids.net	parts restoration service upholstery

See full listing in **Section One** under **Jaguar**

Francois Bruere 8 Avenue Olivier Heuze LeMans 72000 France (33) 02-4377-1877 FAX: (33) 02-4324-2038	artwork

See full listing in **Section Two** under **artwork**

California Wire Wheel 6922 Turnbridge Way San Diego, CA 92119 619-698-8255; FAX: 619-589-9032	rechroming tires tubes wheels

See full listing in **Section Two** under **wheels & wheelcovers**

The Checkered Flag Collection PO Box 806 Millville, NJ 08332 609-327-1505	car dealer

By appointment only. Specialize in investment quality Ferrari, Cobra, Mercedes-Benz and vintage racing cars. For serious collectors.

Collector Car Appraisers LLC 800 Waterford Dr Frederick, MD 21702 301-473-8333; FAX: 301-698-4796 E-mail: gfmchugh@netstorm.net	appraisals

See full listing in **Section Two** under **appraisals**

Collectors Choice LTD 6400 Springfield-Lodi Rd Dane, WI 53529 608-849-9878; FAX: 608-849-9879	parts race preparation restoration service

See full listing in **Section One** under **DeTomaso/Pantera**

DeVito Auto Restorations 470 Boston Post Rd Weston, MA 02493 781-893-4949 ext 142 FAX: 781-899-4900 E-mail: radjr@ix.netcom.com	restorations rust repair

See full listing in **Section Two** under **bodywork**

Drummond Coach and Paint 531 Raleigh Ave El Cajon, CA 92020 619-579-7229; FAX: 619-579-2128	painting restoration

Open shop only. Specializing in Ferrari painting and restoration of paint, interior and chrome for pre-1974 Daytonas, 275 GTB 2 and 4 cam, 365, BB, BB512, California Spyders, PF Series II, Lussos. Also other exotics.

DTE Motorsports 242 South Rd Brentwood, NH 03833 PH/FAX: 603-642-3766 E-mail: ldnh49a@prodigy.com	engines mechanical services race prep transportation

See full listing in **Section One** under **Mercedes-Benz**

Exoticars USA 6 Washington St Frenchtown, NJ 08825 908-996-4889; FAX: 908-996-6938	machine work paint/bodywork restoration/service welding/fabrication

Ferrari, Maserati and Lamborghini. Racing car preparation. Cars located and inspected worldwide. Expert service and restoration, including paint and bodywork, engine rebuilding, interiors, electrical work, engine compartment detailing, motor-vac service and fabrication of parts and pieces. Basket case to First Place is our specialty. Web site: http://exoticars-usa.com

FAZA/Al Cosentino Box 1917 Thousand Oaks, CA 91360 818-707-2301	books information

See full listing in **Section One** under **Abarth**

The Fine Car Store 1105 Moana Dr San Diego, CA 92107 619-223-7766; FAX: 619-223-6838	car dealer

Sale of antique, classic, special interest, collectible, sports, hot rods and vintage race cars. Specializing in collectible Ferrari, Jaguar and Aston Martin automobiles.

Forza Magazine 42 Digital Dr #5 Novato, CA 94949 415-382-0580; FAX: 415-382-0587	magazine

See full listing in **Section Four** under **periodicals**

Mark Gillett PO Box 9177 Dallas, TX 75209 PH/FAX: 214-902-9258 011-525-559-6240 Mexico City, Mexico E-mail: autonet@onramp.net	car locator sales

See full listing in **Section Two** under **car dealers**

Highway One Classic Automobiles **and Highwayone.com Classic** **Classifieds** 1035 California Dr Burlingame, CA 94010 650-342-7340; FAX: 650-343-0150 E-mail: djboscacci@msn.com	classic automobiles

See full listing in **Section One** under **Abarth**

The Italian Car Registry 3305 Valley Vista Rd Walnut Creek, CA 94598-3943 925-458-1163	information source

See full listing in **Section Four** under **information sources**

Kensington Motor Group Inc PO Box 2277 Sag Harbor, NY 11963 516-537-1868; FAX: 516-537-2641 E-mail: kenmotor@aol.com	consignment sales

See full listing in **Section One** under **Mercedes-Benz**

The Klemantaski Collection 65 High Ridge Rd, Suite 219 Stamford, CT 06905 PH/FAX: 203-968-2970 E-mail: klemcoll@aol.com	books photography

See full listing in **Section Two** under **photography**

Kreimeyer Co/Auto Legends Inc 3211 N Wilburn Ave Bethany, OK 73008 405-789-9499; FAX: 405-789-7888	antennas/repair glass/wholesale parts/wholesale radio repair/radios

See full listing in **Section One** under **Mercedes-Benz**

London Stainless Steel Exhaust Centre 249-253 Queenstown Rd London, SW8 3NP England 011-44-171622-2120 FAX: 011-44-171627- 0991 E-mail: 101445.341@compuserv.com	exhaust systems

See full listing in **Section Two** under **exhaust systems**

Marcovicci-Wenz Engineering Inc 33 Comac Loop Ronkonkoma, NY 11779 516-467-9040; FAX: 516-467-9041 E-mail: tedwenz@compuserve.com	Cosworth engines

See full listing in **Section Two** under **racing**

Mercedes-Benz Service by Angela & George/ABS Exotic Repair Inc 700 N Andrews Ave Fort Lauderdale, FL 33304 954-566-7785; FAX: 954-522-0087	sales service

See full listing in **Section One** under **Mercedes-Benz**

Midbanc Financial Services PO Box 20402 Columbus, OH 43220 614-442-7701; FAX: 614-442-7704 E-mail: patricia@midbanc.com	financing

See full listing in **Section Two** under **financing**

Motorcar Gallery Inc 715 N Federal Hwy Fort Lauderdale, FL 33304 954-522-9900; FAX: 954-522-9966	car dealer

Mail order and open shop. Monday-Saturday 10 am to 6:30 pm. Vintage exotic and classic European automobiles of limited production such as Ferrari, Pegaso, Maserati, Lamborghini, Iso, Monteverdi, AC Cobra, Aston Martin, Rolls-Royce, Bentley, Delage, Delahaye, Talbot-Lago, Facel Vega, Mercedes 300S and 300SL, BMW M-1 and 507, etc. Always an excellent selection of 40-50 high quality examples in stock. Trades welcome, pick up/delivery worldwide easily arranged.

Motorcars International 528 N Prince Ln Springfield, MO 65802 417-831-9999; FAX: 417-831-8080 E-mail: sales@motorcars-intl.com	accessories sales service tools

Monday-Friday 8 am to 6 pm, Saturday 9 am to 3 pm. The authorized Lamborghini center. Sales, service, accessories. Pre-owned car sales of Ferrari, Porsche, Mercedes, BMW, Jaguar, Lotus, Rolls-Royce and Bentley. National locating service. Custom financing programs. Over 16 years delivering the experience of fine motoring with recognized excellence. Cash buyers for your car. Enclosed nationwide delivery. Factory authorized service and parts. Concours salon services. Aftermarket accessories specializing in custom fit car covers, floor mats and car care products. Web site: motorcars-intl.com

Orpheograff BP33 72201 La Fleche Cedex France (33) 243452629 FAX: (33) 243452512	prints

See full listing in **Section Two** under **artwork**

Partsource 32 Harden Ave Camden, ME 04843 207-236-9791; FAX: 207-236-6323	parts

Mail order only. Parts importer/distributor. Ferrari parts specialist, 1949-1998. 25 years' experience. Exclusively Ferrari, all models. Web site: www.partsourcenet.com

Peninsula Imports 3749 Harlem Rd Buffalo, NY 14215 800-999-1209; FAX: 905-847-3021 E-mail: imports@ican.net	accessories parts trim

See full listing in **Section One** under **BMW**

Precision Autoworks 2202 Federal Street East Camden, NJ 08105 609-966-0080, NJ FAX: 610-649-3577, PA	restorations

See full listing in **Section One** under **Mercedes-Benz**

Proper Motor Cars Inc 1811 11th Ave N St Petersburg, FL 33713-5794 727-821-8883; FAX: 727-821-0273 E-mail: propermotorcarsinc@email.msn.com	parts restoration service

See full listing in **Section One** under **Rolls-Royce/Bentley**

Replicarz 99 State St Rutland, VT 05701 802-747-7151 E-mail: replicarz@aol.com	books kits models videos

See full listing in **Section Two** under **racing**

RM Auto Restoration Ltd 9435 Horton Line Blenheim, ON Canada N0P 1A0 519-352-4575; FAX: 519-351-1337 E-mail: clark@rmcars.com	panel fabrication parts restoration

See full listing in **Section Two** under **restoration shops**

Garry Roberts & Co 922 Sunset Dr Costa Mesa, CA 92627 714-650-2690; FAX: 714-650-2730 E-mail: garryroberts@fea.net	cars parts service

Specializing in pre-owned Ferrari, sales, service, restorations for Ferrari.

Showroom Auto Sales | car dealer
960 S Bascom Ave
San Jose, CA 95128
408-279-0944; FAX: 408-279-0918

See full listing in **Section One** under **Mercedes-Benz**

Spyder Enterprises Inc | accessories / artwork / automobilia / books
RFD 1682
Laurel Hollow, NY 11791-9644
516-367-1616; FAX: 516-367-3260
E-mail: singer356@aol.com

See full listing in **Section One** under **Porsche**

Thoroughbred Motors | parts / sales / service
3935 N US 301
Sarasota, FL 34234
941-359-2277; FAX: 941-359-2128

See full listing in **Section One** under **Jaguar**

Tillack & Co Ltd | parts / restoration
630 Mary Ann Dr
Redondo Beach, CA 90278
310-318-8760; FAX: 310-376-3392

See full listing in **Section Two** under **restoration shops**

Valley Wire Wheel Service | wheel restoration / wheels
14731 Lull St
Van Nuys, CA 91405
818-785-7237; FAX: 818-994-2042

See full listing in **Section Two** under **wheels & wheelcovers**

Viking Worldwise Inc | leather jackets
190 Doe Run Rd
Manheim, PA 17545
800-842-9198; FAX: 717-664-5556
E-mail: gkurien@success.net

See full listing in **Section Two** under **apparel**

Brady Ward-Scale Autoworks | models
313 Bridge St #4
Manchester, NH 03104-5045
603-623-5925
FAX: 603-623-5925 ext 66
E-mail: bradyward@mediaone.net

See full listing in **Section Two** under **models & toys**

White Post Restorations | brakes / restoration
One Old Car Dr
White Post, VA 22663
540-837-1140; FAX: 540-837-2368

See full listing in **Section Two** under **brakes**

Auto Italia | parts
3350 Woolsey Rd
Windsor, CA 95492
707-528-4825; FAX: 707-569-8717

Mail order only. New, used and reconditioned parts for Fiats, 1968-1988; Lancia Betas; Maserati Bi-Turbo. Used parts for Fiat Spiders and Maserati Bi-Turbos a specialty.

Automotive Artistry | restoration
4311 Mennonite Rd
Mantua, OH 44255
330-274-8699

See full listing in **Section One** under **Triumph**

Bayless Inc | accessories / parts
1111 Via Bayless
Marietta, GA 30066-2770
770-928-1446; FAX: 770-928-1342
800-241-1446, order line
(US & Canada)

Mail order and open shop. Monday-Friday 9 am to 5:30 pm. Spare parts and accessories for Fiats 1953-1989 and Lancia Beta series 1975-1982. Distributors of Magneti Marelli electrical components and Alquati performance parts. Fiat and Lancia factory parts distributors. Expanded 136 page catalog, $4 ($10 international). Worldwide shipping since 1971.

Blint Equipment Inc | parts / tractor rebuilding
2204 E Lincolnway
LaPorte, IN 46350
219-362-7021

See full listing in **Section One** under **Ford 1954-up**

Caribou Imports Inc | parts
26804 Vista Terr
Lake Forest, CA 92630
949-770-3136; FAX: 949-770-0815
E-mail: cariboulh@aol.com

Mail order and open shop. Monday-Friday 9:30 am to 5 pm. Supplies parts worldwide for Fiat, Lancia and Maserati automobiles. Over 22,000 parts available for immediate shipment. We reproduce parts that the factories have discontinued. For Fiat Spiders in particular, we are known as "The Spider Restoration Headquarters." Web site: www.caribou.cc

DeVito Auto Restorations | restorations / rust repair
470 Boston Post Rd
Weston, MA 02493
781-893-4949 ext 142
FAX: 781-899-4900
E-mail: radjr@ix.netcom.com

See full listing in **Section Two** under **bodywork**

FAZA/Al Cosentino | books / information
Box 1917
Thousand Oaks, CA 91360
818-707-2301

See full listing in **Section One** under **Abarth**

Fiat Auto Service | parts / repair / restoration
18440 Hart St, Unit J
Reseda, CA 91335
818-345-4458; FAX: 818-345-6213
E-mail: fiatsteve@aol.com

Specialize in new and used parts. Also full repair and restoration for Fiats, all makes and models, 1960-on.

International Auto Parts Inc | accessories / parts
Rt 29 N
PO Box 9036
Charlottesville, VA 22906
800-788-4435, 804-973-0555
FAX: 804-973-2368

See full listing in **Section One** under **Alfa Romeo**

The Italian Car Registry | information source
3305 Valley Vista Rd
Walnut Creek, CA 94598-3943
925-458-1163

See full listing in **Section Four** under **information sources**

| Linearossa International Inc
3931 SW 47th Ave
Ft Lauderdale, FL 33314
954-327-9888; FAX: 954-791-6555 | parts |

Mail order and open shop. Monday-Friday 9 am to 5 pm. Specializing in Fiat parts, all years for 500, 600, 850, X1/9, 124 models. Only US factory distributor for OEM Fiat parts. Full line of Alfa Romeo 105 parts, 1966-1992 Spider/GT/GTV to 1974. Web site: linearossausa.com

| Motormetrics
6369 Houston Rd
Macon, GA 31216
912-785-0275
E-mail:
fzampa@cennet.mc.peachnet.edu | used parts |

See full listing in **Section One** under **Triumph**

| C Obert & Co
2131-D Delaware Ave
Santa Cruz, CA 95060-5706
800-500-3428 orders
831-423-0218; FAX: 831-459-8128
E-mail: fiatplus@aol.com | parts
repairs |

Mail order and open shop. Monday-Friday 8:30 am to 5:30 pm. Specialize in parts and repairs for Fiat and Lancia. Authorized Fiat/Lancia parts center. Imports parts as necessary from Europe. Hard-to-find Fiat parts from 1955-present. Write or call for free newsletter. Web site: http://we.got.net/~fiatplus

| Orion Motors European Parts Inc
10722 Jones Rd
Houston, TX 77065
800-736-6410, 281-894-1982
FAX: 281-849-1997
E-mail: orion-yugo@yugoparts.com | parts |

See full listing in **Section One** under **Alfa Romeo**

| Rayce Inc
4656 SW 75th Ave
Miami, FL 33155
800-426-2221, 305-261-3355
FAX: 305-261-3615 | parts |

See full listing in **Section One** under **Alfa Romeo**

| Doug Schellinger
13717 W Green Meadow Dr
New Berlin, WI 53151
414-786-8413
E-mail: dsac@execpc.com | automobilia
books
sales literature
toys |

Mail order only. Sales literature, books, toys and automobilia for Fiat, Lancia and Alfa Romeo; also literature and memorabilia for all types of racing and high-performance.

| Smooth Line
2562 Riddle Run Rd
Tarentum, PA 15084
724-274-6002; FAX: 724-274-6121 | body panels
removable hardtops |

See full listing in **Section Two** under **tops**

Ford
1903-1931

| Antique Auto Parts et al
9103 E Garvey Ave
Rosemead, CA 91770-0458
626-288-2121; FAX: 626-288-3311 | accessories
parts |

Mail order only. Phone hours Monday-Friday 9 am to 5 pm.

Parts and accessories for Ford cars and trucks. SASE required for parts information. Dealer wholesale catalog available.

| Antique Auto Parts of Kentucky
PO Box 23070
Lexington, KY 40523
606-548-4016 | parts |

Mail order and open shop by appointment only. Complete line for Model As, limited number for Model Ts and V8s.

| Auto Restoration
8150 S CR 1250 W
Albany, IN 47320
PH/FAX: 765-789-4037 | transmission
conversion kits |

Transmission conversion kits for Model A Fords, 1929-1931.

| Auto World Car Museum by Backer
Business 54 N
PO Box 135
Fulton, MO 65251
573-642-2080, 573-642-5344
FAX: 573-642-0685
E-mail: webacker@ktis.net | museum |

See full listing in **Section Six** under **Missouri**

| Bill's Model Acres Ford Farm
RD 1 Box 283, 8th St Rd
Watsontown, PA 17777
570-538-3200, PA
908-479-4479, NJ | parts
restorations |

Mail order and open shop. Monday-Friday 8 am to 5 pm, evenings and weekends by appointment. Home address: 510 Rt 173, Stewartsville, NJ 08886. Shop address: PO Box 22, Watsontown, PA 17777. Complete line of reproduction and large inventory of used parts for Model As. Reproduction parts for Ford cars and trucks 1909-1972. Complete or partial restoration services for all vehicles. Spin painting of spoke wheels our specialty. Reasonable shop rates.

| Bob's Antique Auto Parts Inc
PO Box 2523
Rockford, IL 61132
815-633-7244; FAX: 815-654-0761 | parts |

Mail order and open shop. Monday-Friday 9 am to 4:30 pm, Saturday 9 am to 12 pm. Specialize in Model T Ford parts, 1903-1927. Quality T parts only. Known as the Model T specialists. Retail catalog upon request. Dealer inquiries invited.

| Boyds Hot Rods & Collectable Cars
8400 Cerritos Ave
Stanton, CA 90680
714-220-9870; FAX: 714-220-9877
E-mail: sales@boydshotrods.com | car dealer |

See full listing in **Section One** under **Chevrolet**

| The Brassworks
289 Prado Rd
San Louis Obispo, CA 93401
800-342-6759; FAX: 805-544-5615 | radiators |

See full listing in **Section Two** under **radiators**

| Bryant's Antique Auto Parts
851 Western Ave
Hampden, ME 04444
207-862-4019 | appraisals
chassis/engine parts
sheetmetal
wiring harnesses |

Mail order and open shop. Monday-Friday 9 am to 5 pm, Saturday by appointment. In business for 28 years. Appraisal within 100 mile area in Maine. Quality Model A and T parts. Call for catalog information.

| Calimer's Wheel Shop
30 E North St
Waynesboro, PA 17268
717-762-5056; FAX: 717-762-5021 | wooden wheels |

See full listing in **Section Two** under **wheels & wheelcovers**

**Car-Line Manufacturing &
Distribution Inc**
1250 Gulf St
PO Box 1192
Beaumont, TX 77701
409-833-9757; FAX: 409-835-2468

chassis parts
engine parts
sheetmetal

See full listing in **Section Two** under **sheetmetal**

Cass County Historical Society
1351 W Main Ave
PO Box 719
West Fargo, ND 58078
701-282-2822; FAX: 701-282-7606

museum

See full listing in **Section Six** under **North Dakota**

Class-Tech Corp
62935 Layton Ave
Bend, OR 97701
800-874-9981

wiring harnesses

See full listing in **Section Two** under **electrical systems**

Classic Wood Mfg
1006 N Raleigh St
Greensboro, NC 27405
336-691-1344; FAX: 336-273-3074

wood kits
wood replacement

See full listing in **Section Two** under **woodwork**

Classtique Upholstery & Top Co
PO Box 278 KH
Isanti, MN 55040
612-444-4025; FAX: 612-444-9980

top kits
upholstery kits

Mail order and open shop. Specializing in 1914-1931 Ford interior upholstery kits, top kits, etc. Original materials, guaranteed workmanship. $1 requested for postage, advise year and body style, standard or deluxe. Established 1959.

Cockermouth Motor Museum
The Maltings
Brewery Ln
Cockermouth Cumbria England
01900 824448

museum

See full listing in **Section Six** under **England**

CT Model A Parts & Service
75 Prospect Ave
West Hartford, CT 06106
860-233-1928; FAX: 860-233-1926
E-mail: ctmap@aol.com

parts
restorations
service

Open shop. Monday-Friday 9 am to 5 pm. A full line of parts and services, full restoration, painting for Model A Fords 1928-1931. Web site: http://members.aol.com/ctmodela/index.htm

Chuck & Judy Cubel
PO Box 278
Superior, AZ 85273
520-689-2734
FAX: 520-689-5815, 24 hours
E-mail: chuckjudy.cubel@cwix.com

wood parts

Call Monday-Friday 9 am to 8 pm. Our parts are made from oak and ash hardwoods. Have been making wood for Fords since 1963. Manufacture wood parts for the standard Ford body styles from 1913-1948. The following information is needed to send the correct catalog: the year and complete body style of the car, your name and mailing address.

**Darrell's Automotive and
Restorations**
2639 N Tripp Ave
Odessa, TX 79763
915-381-7713

repairs
restorations

See full listing in **Section Two** under **fire engines**

Mike Dennis, Nebraska Mail Order
1845 S 48th St
Lincoln, NE 68506
402-489-3036; FAX: 402-489-1148

parts
Trippe mounting
brackets/hardware

See full listing in **Section One** under **Ford 1932-1953**

S D Dennis
708 Pineview Dr
Valdosta, GA 31602
912-242-3084

rebabbitting

Rebabbitting service Ford As, Bs, and Cs.

Bob Drake Reproductions Inc
1819 NW Washington Blvd
Grants Pass, OR 97526
800-221-3673; FAX: 541-474-0099
E-mail: bobdrake@bobdrake.com

repro parts

See full listing in **Section One** under **Ford 1932-1953**

Early Ford Parts
2948 Summer Ave
Memphis, TN 38112
901-323-2179; FAX: 901-323-2195

literature
parts

See full listing in **Section One** under **Ford 1932-1953**

Egge Machine Company Inc
11707 Slauson Ave
Santa Fe Springs, CA 90670
800-866-EGGE, 562-945-3419
FAX: 562-693-1635
E-mail: info@egge.com

bearings
pistons/rings
timing components
valve train

See full listing in **Section Two** under **engine parts**

Fifth Avenue Graphics
Fifth Avenue Antique Auto Parts
415 Court St
Clay Center, KS 67432
785-632-3450; FAX: 785-632-6154
E-mail: fifthave@kansas.net

cooling systems
electrical systems
fuel systems

See full listing in **Section Two** under **electrical systems**

Ford Obsolete
9107-13 Garvey Ave
Rosemead, CA 91770
626-288-2121

chassis parts
engine parts

Mail order and open shop. Monday-Friday 11 am to 5 pm, Saturday 9 am to 3 pm. Full line of new and used chassis and engine parts for trucks and Model As, T and V8 Ford. SASE required for information.

Ford Parts Specialists
Div of Joblot Automotive Inc
98-11 211th St
Queens Village, NY 11429
718-468-8585; FAX: 718-468-8686

parts

Mail order and open shop. Monday-Friday 8:30 am to 4:30 pm. Over 12,000 different new and rebuilt parts. Specializing in the Ford family of cars and trucks 1928-1969. Engine, brake, transmission and clutch, front and rear end, a full line of rubber, electrical, wiring and ignition. Established in 1956. Three catalogs available: 1928-1948 cars and trucks, 1948-1969 F-1/100 thru F-6/600 trucks, 1949-1969 Ford family of cars. Visa, MC and COD, phone or fax orders accepted.

Freeman's Garage
29 Ford Rd
Norton, MA 02766
508-285-6500; FAX: 508-285-6566

parts
restoration
sales
service

Mail order and open shop. Weekdays 8 am to 5:30 pm, Saturday mornings, some evenings, other times by chance or appointment. Sales, service, parts for 1928-1931 Model A and AA Fords. New address but same location since 1957.

Fun Projects Inc	electrical parts
37 W 222 Rt 64, Ste 164	mechanical parts
St Charles, IL 60175	
630-584-1471	
E-mail: piewagon@funprojects.com	

See full listing in **Section Two** under **electrical systems**

Gaslight Auto Parts Inc	accessories
PO Box 291	parts
Urbana, OH 43078	
937-652-2145; FAX: 937-652-2147	

Mail order and open shop. Monday-Friday 8:30 am to 5 pm. 36th year in business. Antique Ford parts, accessories and sheetmetal for Model A, T and early V8.

Good Old Days Garage Inc	engine building
2341 Farley Pl	Firestone tires
Birmingham, AL 35226	parts
205-822-4569; FAX: 205-823-1944	service

Mail order and open shop. Monday-Saturday 8:30 am to 10 pm. Parts and service for Model As. Marlar-built engines and T/A/B engine rebuilding a specialty. Uses KR Wilson tools as the Ford repair shops used. Appointment necessary to watch your block poured and align bored. Have completed 774 A and T engines at this time. Shipped to Germany, England, Australia, Quita Equidore and Santiago, Chile. My 30th year. Honesty and reasonable prices always. A full service Model A shop. Come visit.

Hancock's Engine Rebuilders and Balancing Service	engine rebuilding
2885 Cherokee Rd	
Athens, GA 30605	
706-543-7726; FAX: 706-543-4767	

Open Monday-Friday 9 am to 5 pm. For Model Ts, As, Bs, Cs and early V8s.

Earle C Hartshorn	parts
9 Robert St	
Walpole, MA 02081	
508-688-9319	

Mail order only. Used pre-World War II, some Ford and various other parts.

Henry's Model T & A Parts	parts
52 Poole St	
Deer Park, Victoria 3023 Australia	
03-9363-2869; FAX: 03-9363-5219	

Mail order only. Phone orders 7 days a week. Specializing in reproduction parts for Ford Model T and A and early Ford V8 1909-1954. Carry a large range of Model T and A and early Ford V8 parts and distribute Australia wide. Bank card, Visa and MasterCard facilities available.

Hot Rod & Custom Supply	custom parts
1304 SE 10th St	engine parts
Cape Coral, FL 33990	speed parts
941-574-7744; FAX: 941-574-8820	

See full listing in **Section One** under **Ford 1932-1953**

Howell's Sheetmetal Co	body panels
PO Box 792	sheetmetal
Nederland, TX 77627	
800-375-6663, 409-727-1999	
FAX: 409-727-7127	
E-mail: dhowell@fordor.com	

Mail order and open shop. Monday-Friday 8 am to 5 pm, Saturday by appointment. Specialize in reproduction sheetmetal, body panels, seat frames, patches, aprons for 1909-1940 Fords. Custom parts from your patterns other than Ford. Web site: roadster.fordor.com

International Ford History Project	newsletter
PO Box 11415	
Olympia, WA 98508	
360-754-9585	
E-mail: ifhp@aol.com	

See full listing in **Section Four** under **newsletters**

Joyce's Model A & T Parts	new parts
PO Box 70	NOS parts
Manchaca, TX 78652-0070	rebuilt parts
512-282-1196	

Specializing in parts, new, used, NOS and rebuilt for Ford Model T 1909-1927 and Ford Model A 1928-1931.

Kid Stuff	parts
Larry Machacek	repair
PO Box 515	restoration
Porter, TX 77365	
281-429-2505	

Open Monday-Friday 9 am to 4 pm. Specialize in any stage of restoration and repair for Model A Fords, 1928-1931. Original used parts available for purchase.

Joe Lagana	parts
RD 1, Miller Rd	
Canterbury, CT 06331	
860-546-6000	

Mail order and open shop. Monday-Saturday 9 am to 5 pm, other times by appointment. For Model As. No catalogs, send want list.

Lang's Old Car Parts Inc	parts
202 School St	
Winchendon, MA 01475	
800-TPARTS-1, 978-297-1919	
FAX: 978-297-2126	

Mail order and retail store. Monday-Friday 8:30 am to 5:30 pm EST. Leading supplier of Model T Ford parts. Your one stop mail order and retail store for reproduction, new old stock, and used Model T Ford parts. Toll-free order line, technical support line, and web page with ordering online. Write or call for our 90-page free catalog. Web site: www.modeltford.com

Loyal Ford Mercury Inc	cars
2310 Calumet Dr	parts
New Holstein, WI 53061	
920-898-4248; FAX: 920-898-9705	

See full listing in **Section One** under **Ford 1954-up**

Mac's Antique Auto Parts	literature
1051 Lincoln Ave	parts
PO Box 238	restoration supplies
Lockport, NY 14095-0238	
800-777-0948 US and Canada	
716-433-1500 local and foreign	
FAX: 716-433-1172	
E-mail: mailmacs@aol.com	

Mail order and store. Phone hours: Monday-Friday 8 am to 11 pm, Saturday 8 am to 5 pm. New parts for 1909-1970s Fords from Model T to Mustang and 1909-1948 street rods. 15 free catalogs available. Outside US, $5 each to cover postage. Specify year and model of car to receive correct catalog. Worldwide sales, prompt shipment. MC, Visa, Discover, AmEx, Diners Club, Optima, and COD accepted. Web site: www.macsautoparts.com

Gwyn Machacek	literature
PO Box 515	
Porter, TX 77365	
281-429-2505	

Mail order only. Selling out of print back issues of *The Restorer* and *Model A News* magazines, which are publications of the Model A Ford Club of America (MAFCA) and the Model A Restorers Club (MARC).

W L Wally Mansfield   cars
214 N 13th St   parts
Wymore, NE 68466-1640   trucks
402-645-3546

See full listing in **Section Two** under **comprehensive parts**

Mark Auto Co Inc   parts
Layton, NJ 07851   restoration supplies
973-948-4157; FAX: 973-948-5458

Mail and phone orders only. Phone hours: 10 am to 2 pm; fax orders may be sent anytime. No counter service. Model T and A Ford parts. A comprehensive selection of restoration supplies. Illustrated master catalog free. Visa, MasterCard. Worldwide dealer inquiries welcomed. Wholesale, retail.

McInnes Antique Auto   parts
PO Box 653
Niagara-on-the Lake
ON Canada L0S 1J0
905-468-7779; FAX: 905-468-0759

Mail order and open shop by appointment only. Phone hours: 9 am to 10 pm daily. For 1909-1931 Fords. Price list available on request.

Myers Model A Ford Parts,   parts
Mustang & Car Trailers
17103 Sterling Rd
Williamsport, MD 21795
301-582-2478

Mail order and open shop. Monday-Friday 5:30 pm to 9:30 pm, Saturday 8 am to 4:30 pm. Sell new and used Model T and A Ford parts and cars. Also Mustang and Ford parts up to 1948.

Northeast Ford   parts
Box 66, Rt 9   restoration
East Sullivan, NH 03445
603-847-9956, 800-562-FORD
FAX: 603-847-9691

See full listing in **Section One** under **Ford 1954-up**

Oak Bows   top bows
122 Ramsey Ave
Chambersburg, PA 17201
717-264-2602

See full listing in **Section Two** under **woodwork**

Obsolete Ford Parts Inc   parts
8701 S I-35
Oklahoma City, OK 73149
405-631-3933; FAX: 405-634-6815

See full listing in **Section One** under **Ford 1954-up**

The Old Car Centre   parts
19909 92A Ave
Langley, BC Canada V1M 3B6
604-888-4412, 604-888-4055
FAX: 604-888-7455

Mail order and open shop. Monday-Friday 8 am to 5 pm, Saturday 10 am to 4 pm. 1909-1956 Ford cars and pickups, 1937-1964 Chev parts. Specialize in 1928-1956 Fords. Stock and rod parts. 1955-1957 Chevys. A catalog, $3; V8 catalog, $3; 1948-1956 Ford pickup catalog, $3; Rod catalog, $3; Chev catalog, $1.50.

Original Falcon, Comet, Ranchero,   interiors
Fairlane Interiors   weatherstripping
6343 Seaview Ave NW
Seattle, WA 98107-2664
206-781-5230; FAX: 206-781-5046
E-mail: falcons1@ix.netcom.com

See full listing in **Section One** under **Ford 1954-up**

Original Ford Motor Co Literature   collectibles
PO Box 7-AA   literature
Hudson, KY 40145-0007
502-257-8642; FAX: 502-257-8643
E-mail: whiteb@bellsouth.net

See full listing in **Section One** under **Ford 1932-1953**

Phelan Antique Auto Parts   parts
73 Hillview St
Hamilton
Guelph, ON Canada L8S 2Z3
905-527-0002; FAX: 905-527-5929
E-mail: phelanantiqueauto@hwcn.org

Mail order and open shop by appointment. Monday-Friday 5 pm to 9 pm, Saturday-Sunday 9 am to 5 pm. Phone orders toll free: 877-MODEL-A-T, Monday-Sunday 9 am to 9 pm. Model A, Model T and early V8 parts, new and used for Fords 1909-1948. Can have most parts delivered to your door for the price you pay in the store. Free catalogs by request. We sell Hemmings.

The Plasmeter Corporation   brake drums
173 Queen Ave SE
Albany, OR 97321
541-928-3233; FAX: 541-928-0596

Specializing in brake drums for Ford Model A 1928-1931.

Precision Babbitt Service   babbitting
4681 Lincoln Ave   engine rebuilding
Beamsville, ON Canada L0R 1B3
905-563-4364
E-mail: tkoudys@sprint.ca

See full listing in **Section Two** under **babbitting**

PV Antique & Classic Ford   parts
1688 Main St
Tewksbury, MA 01876
800-MSTANGS orders only
978-851-9159; FAX: 978-858-3827
E-mail: pvford@flash.net

Mail order and open shop. Monday-Friday 9 am to 5 pm, Thursday 9 am to 9 pm, Saturday 9 am to 1 pm. Large inventory in stock of reproduction Model A, 1932-1948 early V8, 1948-1960 F-100 pickups and 1964-1/2-1973 Mustang parts and accessories. Ship UPS daily and accept MasterCard and Visa on all orders. Any catalog above, $2 or free with purchase. Web site: www.pvford.com

Rock Valley Antique Auto Parts   gas tanks
Box 352
Rt 72 and Rothwell Rd
Stillman Valley, IL 61084
815-645-2271; FAX: 815-645-2740

See full listing in **Section One** under **Ford 1932-1953**

Walter E Rodimon   parts
PO Box 353
Pike, NH 03780
603-989-5557

Mail order. Parts department open by appointment only. Antique original Ford parts bought, sold and traded.

Rootlieb Inc   parts
815 S Soderquist
PO Box 1829
Turlock, CA 95380
209-632-2203; FAX: 209-632-2201

Reproduction parts manufacturer: 1906-1937 hoods, 1909-1927 fenders, 1909-1931 runningboards, 1909-1929 splash aprons, Model A and T speedster kits and 1909-1916 Model T bodies. Also engine pans. Chevrolet, Ford and Mopar street rod hoods. Free catalog.

| **S & S Antique Auto**
Pine St
Deposit, NY 13754
607-467-2929; FAX: 607-467-2109 | **parts** |

See full listing in **Section One** under **Ford 1932-1953**

| **Saturn Industries**
10-14 Newland St, Coleford
Royal Forest of Dean
Gloucestershire GL 16 8AN England
01594 834321; FAX: 01594 835456 | **axles/instruments**
literature
nostalgic bits
repro parts
street rods |

Mail order and open shop. Free computer print out price list for individual model containing complete range of parts used in restoration, building hot rods, street rods, customs and kit cars. Shop also sells motoring books, model and toy cars, souvenirs, nostalgic novelty goods. Overseas visitors welcome. Always looking for new suppliers, please send information.

| **William G Shearman**
PO Box 547
Jamestown, NY 14702-0547
716-484-0940 | **windshield frame**
tubing |

Specializing in windshield frame tubing. Steel and brass.

| **Smith & Jones Distributing**
Company Inc
1 Biloxi Square
West Columbia, SC 29170
803-822-8500; FAX: 803-822-8477 | **parts** |

Mail order and open shop. Monday-Friday 8:30 am to 5 pm. A complete line of reproduction parts for 1909-1931 Ford cars and trucks.

| **Snyder's Antique Auto Parts Inc**
12925 Woodworth Rd
New Springfield, OH 44443
888-262-5712, 330-549-5313
FAX: 888-262-5713, 330-549-2211
E-mail: snyantique@aol.com | **parts** |

Mail order and open shop. Monday-Friday 8 am to 5 pm, Saturday 8 am to 12 pm. 1909-1931 Model T and A Ford parts. Also custom builds seat springs for any year or make of vehicle. In business 39 years. Features same day shipping.

| **Special T's Unlimited Corp**
PO Box 146
Prospect Heights, IL 60070
847-255-5494; FAX: 847-391-7666 | **general repair**
parts
restoration
service |

See full listing in **Section One** under **Mopar**

| **Valley Motor Supply**
1402 E Second St
Roswell, NM 88201
505-622-7450 | **accessories**
parts |

See full listing in **Section One** under **Ford 1954-up**

| **Vintage Ford Center Inc**
19437 Harmony Church Rd
Leesburg, VA 20175
888-813-FORD (3673)
FAX: 703-777-3738
E-mail: mdla@masinc.com | **accessories**
parts |

Mail order and open shop. Monday-Friday 9 am to 7 pm EST. Specializing in parts and accessories for Ford 1928-1931 Model A. Web site: www.modelastuff.com

| **Vintage Motor and Machine**
Gene French
1513 Webster Ct
Ft Collins, CO 80524
970-498-9224 | **parts** |

See full listing in **Section Two** under **machine work**

| **Vintage Speed Parts**
9103 E Garvey Ave
Rosemead, CA 91770
626-280-4546 | **parts** |

Mail order and open shop. Monday-Friday 12 noon to 5 pm, Saturday 9 am to 3 pm. For Model Ts, As, and V8s. SASE required for parts information. Catalog, $6. Specify engine, chassis, etc.

| **Vintage Trunks**
5 Brownstone Rd
East Granby, CT 06026
860-658-0353
E-mail: john.desousa@snet.net | **trunks** |

See full listing in **Section Two** under **trunks**

| **Wagon Works**
213 SW Kline
Ankzny, IA 50021
515-964-5085
E-mail: wagonwork2@aol.com | **hardware**
wagon plans |

Mail order only. Depot, Mack and Huckster wagon plans and hardware. Web site: http://members.aol.com/wagonwork2

| **Pete Watson Enterprises**
PO Box 488
Epworth, GA 30541
706-632-7675 | **car dealer**
restoration |

See full listing in **Section Two** under **restoration shops**

| **Wescott's Auto Restyling**
19701 SE Hwy 212
Boring, OR 97009
800-523-6279; FAX: 503-658-2938
E-mail: marykarl@gte.net | **body parts** |

See full listing in **Section One** under **Ford 1932-1953**

| **Wilson's Classic Auto**
417 Kaufman Rt 150
PO Box 58
Congerville, IL 61729
309-448-2408; FAX: 309-448-2409 | **restoration** |

See full listing in **Section Two** under **restoration shops**

| **Wiseman Motor Co Inc**
Bill Wiseman, Owner
PO Box 848
Marion, NC 28752
828-724-9313 | **car dealer** |

See full listing in **Section Two** under **car dealers**

| **A-1 Street Rods**
631 E Las Vegas St
Colorado Springs, CO 80903
719-632-4920, 719-577-4588
FAX: 719-634-6577 | **parts** |

See full listing in **Section Two** under **street rods**

| **Antique Auto Fasteners**
Guy C Close Jr & Son
13426 Valna Dr
Whittier, CA 90602
562-696-3307 | **fasteners**
hardware
hose clamps
molding clips |

See full listing in **Section Two** under **hardware**

Antique Ford V8 Parts 658 Buckley Hwy Union, CT 06076 860-684-3853	**parts** **shock absorbers**

Mail order and open shop by appointment only. Specializing in the rebuilding of Ford shock absorbers and shock related parts for 1928-1948. Also 1932-1948 chassis parts, distributors, water pumps and brake parts.

Antique Radio Doctor Barry Dalton 196 Kilborn Dr Grants Pass, OR 97526 541-474-2524 evenings	**radio repairs**

See full listing in **Section Two** under **radios**

ARASCO PO Box 24, Dept HA14 Newport, KY 41072 606-441-8363	**parts**

Mail order and open shop by appointment only. Custom dual or stock exhaust systems. Specializing in flathead Fords.

B & W Antique Auto Parts Inc 150 W Axton Rd, Unit 2 Bellingham, WA 98226 360-398-9820; FAX: 360-398-9431 E-mail: bwautoparts@bwautoparts.com	**accessories** **parts**

Reproduction and NOS parts for 1932-1979 Ford cars and trucks and 1936-1976 Chev cars and trucks. Web site: bwautoparts.com

Blint Equipment Inc 2204 E Lincolnway LaPorte, IN 46350 219-362-7021	**parts** **tractor rebuilding**

See full listing in **Section One** under **Ford 1954-up**

Bob's Radio & TV Service 238 Ocean View Pismo Beach, CA 93449 805-773-8200	**radios**

See full listing in **Section Two** under **radios**

Boyds Hot Rods & Collectable Cars 8400 Cerritos Ave Stanton, CA 90680 714-220-9870; FAX: 714-220-9877 E-mail: sales@boydshotrods.com	**car dealer**

See full listing in **Section One** under **Chevrolet**

The Brassworks 289 Prado Rd San Louis Obispo, CA 93401 800-342-6759; FAX: 805-544-5615	**radiators**

See full listing in **Section Two** under **radiators**

C & G Early Ford Parts 1941 Commercial St, Dept AH Escondido, CA 92029-1233 760-740-2400; FAX: 760-740-8700 E-mail: cgford@cgfordparts.com	**accessories/chrome** **emblems/literature** **mechanical** **weatherstripping** **wiring**

Mail order and open shop. Since 1978 C & G has offered fine quality, knowledgeable staff, excellent customer service, same day shipping and toll-free order lines. Over 200 suppliers, one call gets them all. Over 13,000 quality parts are listed in our comprehensive catalogs for 1932-1956 and 1957-1970 cars and pickups, $6 each USA $8 foreign, refundable, please state year and model. Web site: www.cgfordparts.com

California Jaguar 29109 Triunfo Dr Agoura, CA 91301 800-335-2482; FAX: 818-707-3062	**auto transport**

See full listing in **Section Two** under **transport**

Car Controls Div 9107-9 E Garvey Ave Rosemead, CA 91770 626-288-2121	**parts**

Mail order and open shop. Daily 12 pm to 5 pm. Phone hours 8 am to 4:30 pm daily. Friction shocks for T, A, V8. Conversion brackets for tube shocks. Catalog, $6, refundable with purchase.

Cass County Historical Society 1351 W Main Ave PO Box 719 West Fargo, ND 58078 701-282-2822; FAX: 701-282-7606	**museum**

See full listing in **Section Six** under **North Dakota**

Chandler Classic Cars 1308 14th St W Bradenton, FL 34205 941-747-3441; FAX: 941-747-9650 E-mail: chandlercars@worldnet.att.net	**Ford products**

See full listing in **Section One** under **Ford 1954-up**

Chernock Enterprises PO Box 134 Airport Rd Hazleton, PA 18201 570-455-1752; FAX: 570-455-7585 E-mail: jim@chernock.com	**trailers**

See full listing in **Section Two** under **trailers**

Class-Tech Corp 62935 Layton Ave Bend, OR 97701 800-874-9981	**wiring harnesses**

See full listing in **Section Two** under **electrical systems**

Classic Carriages 267 County Rd 420 Athens, TN 37303 PH/FAX: 423-744-7496	**repair** **restoration**

Open shop. Monday-Saturday 9 am to 5 pm. Deal in restoration and repair of antique and classic autos and the building of street rods. 1932-1953 flathead Fords and 1950s style hot rods are a specialty, as well as engine conversions and complete chassis work. Will consider all projects.

Collector Car Appraisers LLC 800 Waterford Dr Frederick, MD 21702 301-473-8333; FAX: 301-698-4796 E-mail: gfmchugh@netstorm.net	**appraisals**

See full listing in **Section Two** under **appraisals**

Chuck & Judy Cubel PO Box 278 Superior, AZ 85273-0278 520-689-2734 FAX: 520-689-5815, 24 hours E-mail: chuckjudy.cubel@cwix.com	**wood parts**

See full listing in **Section One** under **Ford 1903-1931**

Alan Darr Early Ford Parts 124 E Canyon View Dr Longview, WA 98632 360-425-2463	**accessories** **parts**

Mail order only. 1932-1953. Some original and reproduction

parts, accessories, collectibles. New and used flathead speed equipment. No catalog. In business since 1968.

Mike Dennis, Nebraska Mail Order 1845 S 48th St Lincoln, NE 68506 402-489-3036; FAX: 402-489-1148	**parts Trippe mounting brackets/hardware**

Ford parts 1926-1970, NOS or used. Mercury original parts, 1939-1965. Classic Trippe driving light brackets with nuts, bolts, wrench. Web site: www.fordoldpart.com

Dependable RV & Auto Service 2619 Rt 11 N Lafayette, NY 13084 315-677-5336; FAX: 315-677-5258	**parts restoration service**

See full listing in **Section Two** under **service shops**

Bob Drake Reproductions Inc 1819 NW Washington Blvd Grants Pass, OR 97526 800-221-3673; FAX: 541-474-0099 E-mail: bobdrake@bobdrake.com	**repro parts**

Mail order and open shop. Monday-Friday 8 am to 4:30 pm. Specializing in reproduction Ford parts for 1932-1948 automobiles and 1932-1966 pickups. Web site: www.bobdrake.com

Durabuilt Automotive Hydraulics 808 Meadows Ave Canon City, CO 81212 PH/FAX: 719-275-1126 E-mail: durabuilt@ris.net	**hose assemblies pumps top cylinders valves**

See full listing in **Section Two** under **tops**

Early Ford Engines George and Marion Hibbard Rt 3 Box 448 Claremont, NH 03743 603-542-6269	**engine rebuilding parts**

Open shop. Specializing in engine building for 1928-1953 Fords. Chassis parts and accessories for 1928-1948 Fords available. Most engine overhauls are complete running engines, customer ready and meet judging standards.

Early Ford Parts 2948 Summer Ave Memphis, TN 38112 901-323-2179; FAX: 901-323-2195	**literature parts**

Mail order and open shop. Monday-Friday 9:30 am to 5:30 pm; Saturday 9 am to 2 pm. New parts for 1928-1959 Ford and Mercury cars and trucks. Catalogs for 1932-1959, $4, specify year and body style. In business full time over 20 years. "Over a million parts." Visa, MasterCard, personal checks accepted.

Early Ford V8 Sales Inc Curtis Industrial Park, Bldg 37 831 Rt 67 Ballston Spa, NY 12020 518-884-2825; FAX: 518-884-2633 E-mail: earlyford@prodigy.net	**parts**

Mail order and open shop. Specializing in new, reproduction and NOS original engine, chassis and body parts for Ford 1932-1956 passenger and pickup. Web site: earlyford.com

Egge Machine Company Inc 11707 Slauson Ave Santa Fe Springs, CA 90670 800-866-EGGE, 562-945-3419 FAX: 562-693-1635 E-mail: info@egge.com	**bearings pistons/rings timing components valve train**

See full listing in **Section Two** under **engine parts**

Engineering & Manufacturing Services Box 24362 Cleveland, OH 44124-0362 216-541-4585; FAX: 216-541-4989	**sheetmetal**

Mail order only. Outer body sheetmetal, specialize in EMS Tail Pan®, fender repair sections for 1935-1954 Ford cars, 1948-1952 Ford pickup trucks, 1935-1948 Chevrolet.

Fairlane Automotive Specialties 107 W Railroad St St Johns, MI 48879 517-224-6460; FAX: 517-224-9488	**fiberglass bodies parts**

Mail order and open shop. Monday-Friday 9 am to 5 pm. The leading manufacturer of high quality replacement panels for Ford trucks (1942-1966) and cars (1935-1936 and 1941-1948). Fairlane is well known for parts that fit like NOS. Check out Fairlane's selection of truck parts: hoods, tilt front ends, front and rear fenders, runningboards and more! Replacement parts available for cars include: hoods, runningboards, front and rear fenders, dashes, fender skirts and much more. Also manufactures a superior 1936 roadster body.

Fifth Avenue Graphics Fifth Avenue Antique Auto Parts 415 Court St Clay Center, KS 67432 785-632-3450; FAX: 785-632-6154 E-mail: fifthave@kansas.net	**cooling systems electrical systems fuel systems**

See full listing in **Section Two** under **electrical systems**

Ford Obsolete 9107-13 Garvey Ave Rosemead, CA 91770 626-288-2121	**chassis parts engine parts**

See full listing in **Section One** under **Ford 1903-1931**

Ron Francis' Wire Works 167 Keystone Rd Chester, PA 19013 800-292-1940 orders, 610-485-1937 E-mail: rfwwx@aol.com	**fuel injection harnesses wiring accessories wiring kits**

See full listing in **Section Two** under **wiring harnesses**

George Frechette 14 Cedar Dr Granby, MA 01033 800-528-5235	**brake cylinder sleeving**

See full listing in **Section Two** under **brakes**

Garton's Auto 401 N 5th St (at 5th & Vine) Millville, NJ 08332-3129 609-825-3618	**bicycles Ford NOS parts sales literature**

Mail order and open by appointment only. 9 am to 9:30 pm. NOS 1932-1975 Ford, Mercury and 1929-1960 Chevrolet parts. Send SASE for free sales literature list on Ford V8, Model A, Studebaker or special interest. Also classic balloon bicycles. Genuine Ford, Mercury parts, literature, etc, bought and sold. Specializes in 1929-1979 fenders, grilles, bumpers, radiators, etc. Send SASE for list of original Schwinn sales literature.

Gaslight Auto Parts Inc PO Box 291 Urbana, OH 43078 937-652-2145; FAX: 937-652-2147	**accessories parts**

See full listing in **Section One** under **Ford 1903-1931**

Leo Gephart Classic Cars 7360 E Acoma Dr, Ste 14 Scottsdale, AZ 85260 602-948-2286, 602-998-8263 FAX: 602-948-2390	**car dealer parts**

See full listing in **Section Two** under **car dealers**

Green Valentine Inc	car dealer
5055 Covington Way	woodies
Memphis, TN 38134	
901-373-5555; FAX: 901-373-5568	

See full listing in **Section Two** under **car dealers**

Hagerty Classic Insurance	insurance
PO Box 87	
Traverse City, MI 49685	
800-922-4050; FAX: 616-941-8227	

See full listing in **Section Two** under **insurance**

Half Ton Fun	NOS parts
Bob Selzam	
166 Toms River Rd	
Jackson, NJ 08527	
732-928-9421	

Mail order and open shop. Specializing in new old stock Ford parts for 1932-1956 pickups and trucks, 1932-1948 passenger cars (mechanical only) and 1932-1953 flathead V8 and 6-cylinder engine and transmission parts. Also stocking new parts such as: heavy duty radiators for V8 and 6-cyl, fiberglass and steel body parts, bed kits and parts, wiring, glass and rubber.

Haneline Products Co	gauges
PO Box 430	instrument panels
Morongo Valley, CA 92256	stainless parts
760-363-6597; FAX: 760-363-7321	trim parts

See full listing in **Section Two** under **accessories**

Bruce Horkey's Wood & Parts	pickup parts
Rt 4 Box 188	
Windom, MN 56101	
507-831-5625; FAX: 507-831-0280	

See full listing in **Section Two** under **trucks & tractors**

Hot Rod & Custom Supply	custom parts
1304 SE 10th St	engine parts
Cape Coral, FL 33990	speed parts
941-574-7744; FAX: 941-574-8820	

Specializing in 1950s speed and custom parts for Ford/Mercury flathead, speed and custom accessories, flathead air conditioning, engine parts. Web site: www.rodncustom.com

Howell's Sheetmetal Co	body panels
PO Box 792	sheetmetal
Nederland, TX 77627	
800-375-6663, 409-727-1999	
FAX: 409-727-7127	
E-mail: dhowell@fordor.com	

See full listing in **Section One** under **Ford 1903-1931**

Integrity Machine	brake masters
383 Pipe Stave Hollow Rd	clutch masters
Mount Sinai, NY 11766	wheel cylinders
888-446-9670; FAX: 516-476-9675	

See full listing in **Section Two** under **brakes**

International Ford History Project	newsletter
PO Box 11415	
Olympia, WA 98508	
360-754-9585	
E-mail: ifhp@aol.com	

See full listing in **Section Four** under **newsletters**

Jefferis Autobody	windshield glass kit
269 Tank Farm Rd	
San Luis Obispo, CA 93401	
800-807-1937; FAX: 805-543-4757	

See full listing in **Section Two** under **glass**

Joblot Automotive Inc	parts
Ford Parts Specialists	
98-11 211th St	
Queens Village, NY 11429	
718-468-8585; FAX: 718-468-8686	

Mail order and open shop. Monday-Friday 8:30 am to 4:30 pm. Over 12,000 different new and rebuilt parts. Specializing in the Ford family of cars and trucks 1928-1972. Engine, brake, transmission and clutch, front and rear end, a full line of rubber, electrical, wiring and ignition. Established in 1956. Three catalogs available: 1928-1972 cars and trucks, 1948-1972 F-1/100 thru F-6/600 trucks, 1949-1969 Ford family of cars. Visa, MC and COD, phone or fax orders accepted. Dealer inquiries invited.

Ken's Carburetors	carburetors
2301 Barnum Ave	distributors
Stratford, CT 06615	parts
203-375-9340	

Mail order only. Specializing in Ford parts. Mainly rebuilding of flathead carbs and ignition distributors and some NOS and used parts. No body parts. Also glass beading and Ford fuel pump rebuilding services.

Kenroy Ford Parts	NOS parts
2 Folwell Ln	
Mullica Hill, NJ 08062	
609-478-2527	
E-mail: duffieldm@aol.com	

See full listing in **Section One** under **Ford 1954-up**

Dale King Obsolete Parts	parts
PO Box 1099	
211 Hilltop Dr	
Liberty, KY 42539	
606-787-5031; FAX: 606-787-2130	

See full listing in **Section One** under **Ford 1954-up**

Knight Automotive Engineering Inc	engine rebuilding
Kettle Cove Industrial Park	
743 Western Ave, Rt 127	
Gloucester, MA 01930	
978-525-3491	

See full listing in **Section Two** under **engine rebuilding**

LeBaron Bonney Co	fabrics
PO Box 6	interior kits
6 Chestnut St	top kits
Amesbury, MA 01913	
800-221-5408, 978-388-3811	
FAX: 978-388-1113	
E-mail: lbb-hc@greennet.net	

Antique auto "ready to install" interior kits, top kits and fabrics for over 300 models and variations of Ford (1928-1954) and Mercury (1939-1951) cars and trucks. Free literature with fabric samples and prices available upon request. Free parts and accessories catalog. Worldwide reputation for quality and service.

Loyal Ford Mercury Inc	cars
2310 Calumet Dr	parts
New Holstein, WI 53061	
920-898-4248; FAX: 920-898-9705	

See full listing in **Section One** under **Ford 1954-up**

Mac's Antique Auto Parts	literature
1051 Lincoln Ave	parts
PO Box 238	restoration supplies
Lockport, NY 14095-0238	
800-777-0948 US and Canada	
716-433-1500 local and foreign	
FAX: 716-433-1172	
E-mail: mailmacs@aol.com	

See full listing in **Section One** under **Ford 1903-1931**

Mack Products	parts
PO Box 856	pickup beds
Moberly, MO 65270	
660-263-7444	

Mail order only. Monday-Friday 8 am to 5 pm. Established in 1973. Die-stamped pickup bed parts, oak bed wood, tailgates. Complete reproduction pickup beds for 1926-1972 Fords and 1928-1972 Chevrolets. Catalog, $1. New items include bed parts for 1933-1947 Dodge, 1941-1955 Studebaker and 1933-1962 Willys.

Mark's 1941-1948 Ford Parts	parts
97 Hoodlum Hill Rd	
Binghamton, NY 13905	
607-729-1693	

Mail order only. Caters to people who feel 1941-1948 Fords are among the best looking Fords ever produced. Deals in rust-free western sheetmetal and cars. Carries vintique reproduction as well. Specializing in NOS, reproduction and used parts for 1941-1948 Ford and Mercury cars. Reproduction catalog $2, NOS parts list $2, free with orders over $100.

Master Power Brakes	brake products
254-1 Rolling Hills Rd	conversion kits
Mooresville, NC 28115	
704-664-8866; FAX: 704-664-8862	

See full listing in **Section One** under **Chevelle/Camaro**

The Masters Company	parts
30 Willow Dr Suite A	tools
Fort Thomas, KY 41075-2035	
800-385-5811; FAX: 606-441-6765	
E-mail: badger@cinternet.net	

See full listing in **Section Two** under **tools**

Max Neon Design Group	custom face logos
19807 Sussex Dr	glass light-up
St Clair Shores, MI 48081-3257	clocks
810-773-5000; FAX: 810-772-6224	neon clocks

See full listing in **Section Two** under **automobilia**

McDonald Obsolete Parts Company	body parts
RR 3, Box 94	chassis parts
Rockport, IN 47635	
812-359-4965; FAX: 812-359-5555	
E-mail: mcdonald@psci.net	

See full listing in **Section One** under **Ford 1954-up**

Medicine Bow Motors Inc	car dealer
343 One Horse Creek Rd	
Florence, MT 59833	
406-273-0002	

See full listing in **Section Two** under **car dealers**

Melvin's Classic Ford Parts Inc	parts
2526 Panola Rd	
Lithonia, GA 30058	
770-981-2357; FAX: 770-981-6207	

See full listing in **Section One** under **Ford 1954-up**

Mercury & Ford Molded Rubber	parts
12 Plymouth Ave	
Wilmington, MA 01887	
978-658-8394	

See full listing in **Section One** under **Mercury**

Miller Obsolete Parts	locator service
1329 Campus Dr	parts
Vestal, NY 13850	
607-722-5371; FAX: 607-770-9117	
E-mail: fordpart@spectra.net	

See full listing in **Section One** under **Ford 1954-up**

NorCal Auto	appraisals
615D Saint John St	
Pleasanton, CA 94566	
888-224-6005; FAX: 925-426-8845	
E-mail: mwjohn@hotmail.com	

See full listing in **Section Two** under **appraisals**

Normans' Classic Auto Radio	custom sales
7651 Park Blvd	
Pinellas Park, FL 33781	
888-222-3433, 727-546-1788	

See full listing in **Section Two** under **radios**

Northeast Ford	parts
Box 66, Rt 9	restoration
East Sullivan, NH 03445	
603-847-9956, 800-562-FORD	
FAX: 603-847-9691	

See full listing in **Section One** under **Ford 1954-up**

Oak Bows	top bows
122 Ramsey Ave	
Chambersburg, PA 17201	
717-264-2602	

See full listing in **Section Two** under **woodwork**

Obsolete Ford Parts Co	parts
311 E Washington Ave	
Nashville, GA 31639	
912-686-2470, 912-686-5101	
FAX: 912-686-7125	

See full listing in **Section One** under **Ford 1954-up**

Obsolete Ford Parts Inc	parts
8701 S I-35	
Oklahoma City, OK 73149	
405-631-3933; FAX: 405-634-6815	

See full listing in **Section One** under **Ford 1954-up**

The Old Car Centre	parts
19909 92A Ave	
Langley, BC Canada V1M 3B6	
604-888-4412, 604-888-4055	
FAX: 604-888-7455	

See full listing in **Section One** under **Ford 1903-1931**

Old Ford Parts	parts
35 4th Ave N	
Algona, WA 98001	
253-833-8494; FAX: 253-833-2190	

Mail order and open shop. Monday-Thursday 8 am to 6 pm, Friday-Saturday 8 am to 2 pm. Specializing in 1932-1948 Ford cars and 1932-1979 Ford trucks parts. Parts, rubber seals, electrical supplies, ie: wiring, bulbs, connectors, trim parts, sheetmetal panels, bumpers, hubcaps, etc.

Old Tin Australia	salvage yard
PO Box 26	
Wendouree Victoria 3355 Australia	
03 5336 FORD; FAX: 03 5339 9900	

See full listing in **Section Five** under **Australia**

Original Falcon, Comet, Ranchero,	interiors
Fairlane Interiors	weatherstripping
6343 Seaview Ave NW	
Seattle, WA 98107-2664	
206-781-5230; FAX: 206-781-5046	
E-mail: falcons1@ix.netcom.com	

See full listing in **Section One** under **Ford 1954-up**

Original Ford Motor Co Literature PO Box 7-AA Hudson, KY 40145-0007 502-257-8642; FAX: 502-257-8643 E-mail: whiteb@bellsouth.net	collectibles literature

Original Ford literature and collectibles. Send SASE with want list.

Patrick's Antique Cars & Trucks PO Box 10648 Casa Grande, AZ 85230 520-836-1117; FAX: 520-836-1104 E-mail: patstrks@aol.com	parts

See full listing in **Section One** under **Chevrolet**

Phelan Antique Auto Parts 73 Hillview St Hamilton Guelph, ON Canada L8S 2Z3 905-527-0002; FAX: 905-527-5929 E-mail: phelanantiqueauto@hwcn.org	parts

See full listing in **Section One** under **Ford 1903-1931**

Pick-ups Northwest 1430 Bickford Ave Snohomish, WA 98290 360-568-9166; FAX: 360-568-1233	parts trim

See full listing in **Section One** under **Chevrolet**

Precision Babbitt Service 4681 Lincoln Ave Beamsville, ON Canada L0R 1B3 905-563-4364 E-mail: tkoudys@sprint.ca	babbitting engine rebuilding

See full listing in **Section Two** under **babbitting**

PV Antique & Classic Ford 1688 Main St Tewksbury, MA 01876 800-MSTANGS orders only 978-851-9159; FAX: 978-858-3827 E-mail: pvford@flash.net	parts

See full listing in **Section One** under **Ford 1903-1931**

R & R Fiberglass & Specialties 4850 Wilson Dr NW Cleveland, TN 37312 423-476-2270; FAX: 423-473-9442 E-mail: rrfiberglass@wingnet.net	body parts

See full listing in **Section Two** under **fiberglass parts**

Recks & Relics Ford Trucks 2675 Hamilton Mason Rd Hamilton, OH 45011 513-868-3489 E-mail: truck@choice.net	truck parts

Ford truck parts for 1928-1979 Ford trucks. Web site: ww4.choice.net/~truck

Red's Headers & Early Ford Speed Equipment 22950 Bednar Ln Fort Bragg, CA 95437-8411 707-964-7733; FAX: 707-964-5434 E-mail: red@reds-headers.com	headers mechanical parts

Mail order and open shop. Monday-Friday 8 am to 4:30 pm. Specializing in headers, mechanical parts and engine machine shop services for 1928-1970 Fords. Headers made and stocked for Model A side valve and ohv, flathead V8 including V8-60; Y-block Fords 272-312 in cars, trucks and T-Birds; 289-302 in Falcons/Comets, Mustangs/Cougars, each different. Crankshaft grinding and balancing, rod work and engine rebuilding for stock and hot rod Fords, since 1964. Web site: bounce.to/redsheaders

Renner's Corner 10320 E Austin Manchester, MI 48158 734-428-8424; FAX: 734-428-1090	bushings/hardware carb/pump kits gauges/gaskets rebuild service

Mail order only. Specializing in reproduction of 1932 hard-to-find 4-cylinder and 8-cylinder repair and rebuild kits for fuel pumps, carburetors, fuel gauges, float level gauges, fuel lines and tank gaskets; steering bushings; engine snubbers; side-mount spares; distributor conversions; dry air silencers and more. Some 1928-1931 kits. Carburetor, distributor, fuel gauge and fuel pump rebuild services. Send SASE for complete list. Parts are exactly as Henry built them or better.

Rock Valley Antique Auto Parts Box 352 Rt 72 and Rothwell Rd Stillman Valley, IL 61084 815-645-2271; FAX: 815-645-2740	gas tanks

Deal in stainless steel gas tanks for most antique and street rod cars and pickups. Makes 1931-1940 passenger, 1941-1954 pickup bumpers for Chevrolet. Offers a full line of 1928-1948 reproduction, used and NOS Ford parts. Call or send for our free brochure.

Rocky Mountain V8 Ford Parts 1124 Clark Cir Colorado Springs, CO 80915 719-597-8375	parts

Mail order and open shop by appointment. Parts for 1932-1960s Ford products. New, used and reproduction. Buy, sell and trade. Large inventory on hand. Parts cars and trucks in yard. Visa/MC, UPS, COD. Send your want list.

Rod-1 Shop 210 Clinton Ave Pitman, NJ 08071 609-228-7631; FAX: 609-582-5770	street rods

See full listing in **Section Two** under **street rods**

S & S Antique Auto Pine St Deposit, NY 13754 607-467-2929; FAX: 607-467-2109	parts

Mail order and open shop. Monday-Saturday 9 am to 6 pm. Specialize in NOS parts, used and repro for Ford cars and trucks.

S-E Autoparts Jarpbo 4 78193 Borlange Sweden +46 243 221297 FAX: +46 243 221298 E-mail: s-e.autoparts@ebox.tninet.se	NOS parts reproduced parts

See full listing in **Section One** under **Anglia**

Sacramento Vintage Ford Parts 2484 Mercantile Dr Rancho Cordova, CA 95742 916-853-2244; FAX: 916-853-2299 E-mail: sacvintage@aol.com	accessories parts street rod products

Mail order and open shop. Monday-Friday 9 am to 6 pm, Saturday 9 am to 3 pm. Specializing in reproduction parts and accessories for Ford automobiles 1909-1947 and Ford pickups 1928-1966. Plus a complete inventory of street rod products. Catalogs available. Web site: www.vintage-ford.com

Sammy's Street Strollers 2725 Chinook Ct Union City, CA 94587 510-489-3502; FAX: 510-489-2994 E-mail: sammy@slipnet.com	baby stroller

Mail order only. We produce a highboy hot rod baby stroller. Web site: www.slip.net/~sammy

Saturn Industries | axles/instruments
10-14 Newland St, Coleford | literature
Royal Forest of Dean | nostalgic bits
Gloucestershire GL 16 8AN England | repro parts
01594 834321; FAX: 01594 835456 | street rods

See full listing in **Section One** under **Ford 1903-1931**

Joe Smith Ford & Hot Rod Parts | parts
2140 Canton Rd, Unit C | service
Marietta, GA 30066
800-235-4013, 770-426-9850
FAX: 770-426-9854
E-mail: hank@joesmithauto.com

Mail order and open shop. Monday-Friday 8:30 am to 5:30 pm.
1932-1948 Ford cars, 1932-1952 Ford trucks. Parts and service.
Web site: www.joesmithauto.com

Dick Spadaro | fiberglass bodies
Early Ford Reproductions | patch panels
PO Box 617, 6599 Rt 158 | rubber products
Altamont, NY 12009 | trim
518-861-5367

Mail order and open shop. 9 am to 5 pm EST. Ford V8 to 1948
and pickup to 1956. Supplier of quality accessories and replacement parts and sheetmetal repair panels. Dealer for Gibbon
fiberglass bodies. Manufacturer of steel 1932 front fenders. NOS
and used parts always in stock. Web site: www.dickspadaro.com

Speedway Motors Inc | parts
300 Speedway Cir
Lincoln, NE 68502
402-474-4411; FAX: 402-477-7476

See full listing in **Section Two** under **comprehensive parts**

Tags Backeast | data plates
PO Box 581 | trim tags
Plainville, CT 06062
860-747-2942
E-mail: dataplt@snet.net

See full listing in **Section Two** under **special services**

Ultra Wheel Co | custom wheels
6300 Valley View Ave
Buena Park, CA 90620
714-994-1444; FAX: 714-994-0723

See full listing in **Section Two** under **wheels & wheelcovers**

Valley Motor Supply | accessories
1402 E Second St | parts
Roswell, NM 88201
505-622-7450

See full listing in **Section One** under **Ford 1954-up**

Vintage Ford & Chevrolet Parts of | parts
Arizona Inc
So-Cal Speed Shop
3427 E McDowell Rd
Phoenix, AZ 85008-3845
800-732-0076, 602-275-7990
FAX: 602-267-8439
E-mail: vintageparts@sprintmail.com

See full listing in **Section One** under **Ford 1954-up**

Waldron's Antique Exhaust Inc | exhaust systems
PO Box C
25872 M-86
Nottawa, MI 49075
616-467-7185; FAX: 616-467-9041

See full listing in **Section Two** under **exhaust systems**

Wescott's Auto Restyling | body parts
19701 SE Hwy 212
Boring, OR 97009
800-523-6279; FAX: 503-658-2938
E-mail: marykarl@gte.net

Mail order and open shop. Monday-Friday 9 am to 5:30 pm,
Saturday 9 am to 5 pm PST. Specializes in fiberglass replacement fenders and bodies and reproduction body parts for 1926-
1948 Ford cars and 1926-1956 Ford pickups.

Wesley Obsolete Parts | parts
116 Memory Ln
Liberty, KY 42539
606-787-5293; FAX: 606-787-7252

See full listing in **Section One** under **Ford 1954-up**

Wilson's Classic Auto | restoration
417 Kaufman Rt 150
PO Box 58
Congerville, IL 61729
309-448-2408; FAX: 309-448-2409

See full listing in **Section Two** under **restoration shops**

Wirth's Custom Automotive | custom accessories
PO Box 5 | fender skirts
505 Conner St | spinner hubcaps
Prairie du Rocher, IL 62277
618-284-3359
E-mail: roywirth@htc.net

See full listing in **Section Two** under **accessories**

James Wood | appraisals
1102 E Jefferson St
Mishawaka, IN 46545
219-256-0239; FAX: 219-254-2722

See full listing in **Section Two** under **appraisals**

The Wood N'Carr | wood parts
3231 E 19th St | woodwork
Signal Hill, CA 90804
562-498-8730; FAX: 562-985-3360
E-mail: suzyq22222@aol.com

See full listing in **Section Two** under **woodwork**

The Woodie Works | woodworking
245 VT Rt 7A
Arlington, VT 05250
PH/FAX: 802-375-9305
E-mail: dkwoodie@vermontel.com

See full listing in **Section Two** under **woodwork**

Ford
1954-up

1958 Thunderbird Convertible | book
Registry
Bill Van Ess
2306 Post Dr NE
Belmont, MI 49306
616-364-1973; FAX: 616-363-2870

See full listing in **Section One** under **Thunderbird**

AKH Wheels
1207 N A St
Ellensburg, WA 98926-2522
509-962-3390
E-mail: akhwheel@eburg.com

| | Rallye wheels styled steel wheels vintage aluminum |

See full listing in **Section Two** under **wheels & wheelcovers**

Alpha Omega Motorsport
15612 New Century Dr
Gardena, CA 90248
310-366-7993; FAX: 310-366-7499
E-mail: aomotor@pacbell.net

| | parts repairs restorations |

See full listing in **Section One** under **Pontiac**

AMK Products
18600 E 96th St
Broken Arrow, OK 74012
918-455-2651; FAX: 918-455-7441

| | parts |

See full listing in **Section One** under **Mustang**

Andover Automotive Inc
PO Box 3143
Laurel, MD 20709
410-381-6700; FAX: 410-381-6703
E-mail: andoauto@clark.net

| | parts seat belts |

See full listing in **Section One** under **Corvette**

Andy's Classic Mustangs
18502 E Sprague
Greenacres, WA 99016
509-924-9824

| | parts service |

See full listing in **Section One** under **Mustang**

Donald Antilla
888 Hulls Hill Rd
Southbury, CT 06488
203-264-8301 evenings
E-mail: dsa0004@ibm.net

| | supercharger parts |

Mail order only. 1957 Ford and Thunderbird supercharger parts bought, sold and traded. Reproductions of hoses, brackets, idlers, fittings. Cast parts machined from ductile iron. Active in 1957 supercharger activities for twenty years.

Antique Radio Doctor
Barry Dalton
196 Kilborn Dr
Grants Pass, OR 97526
541-474-2524 evenings

| | radio repairs |

See full listing in **Section Two** under **radios**

ARASCO
PO Box 24, Dept HA14
Newport, KY 41072
606-441-8363

| | parts |

See full listing in **Section One** under **Ford 1932-1953**

Auto Custom Carpet Inc
Jeff Moses
PO Box 1350, 1429 Noble St
Anniston, AL 36201
800-633-2358, 205-236-1118
FAX: 800-516-8274
E-mail: info@accmats.net

| | carpets floor mats |

See full listing in **Section One** under **Chevrolet**

Auto Krafters Inc
PO Box 8
522 S Main St
Broadway, VA 22815
540-896-5910; FAX: 540-896-6412
E-mail: akraft@shentel.net

| | parts |

Mail order and open shop. Monday-Friday 8:30 am to 6 pm, Saturday 9 am to 12 pm. Specializing in weatherstrip, interior, exterior, engine, wiring, suspension, brakes, hardware, literature. Rebuild parts such as ps control valves for 1964-1973 Mustangs, 1967-1973 Cougars, 1960-1970 Falcons, 1962-1976 Fairlanes/Torinos, 1960-1970 full size Fords, 1958-1976 T-Birds, 1966-1979 Broncos, 1953-1979 F-Series, 1970-1977 Mavericks, 1960-1979 Rancheros. Aftermarket parts and accessories for 1991-1999 Explorers/Expeditions and 1992-1999 F-Series/Rangers. Online ordering available on our web site: www.autokrafters.com

Autowire Division
9109 (Rear) E Garvey Ave
Rosemead, CA 91770
626-572-0938; FAX: 626-288-3311

| | alternator conversions motors/relays switches |

Mail order and open shop. Monday-Friday 9 am to 5 pm. For 1949-1968 Fords, Lincolns and Mercurys. Top motors, relays, window regulators, motors and switches, and alternator conversions for all Fords, 6 and 12 volt. Catalog $6, please specify exact year.

Bill's Speed Shop
13951 Millersburg Rd
Navarre, OH 44662
330-832-9403; FAX: 330-832-2098

| | body parts |

See full listing in **Section One** under **Chevrolet**

Blint Equipment Inc
2204 E Lincolnway
LaPorte, IN 46350
219-362-7021

| | parts tractor rebuilding |

Mail order and open shop. Monday-Friday 8 am to 5 pm, Saturday 8 am to 12 noon. Rebuild Ford tractors 1939 and up. Also have parts for Ford tractors. Work on other makes too, but specialize in Fords. Also work on some cars and trucks, mostly older models. Have a small stock of Fiat parts and repair older Fiat cars.

Boyds Hot Rods & Collectable Cars
8400 Cerritos Ave
Stanton, CA 90680
714-220-9870; FAX: 714-220-9877
E-mail: sales@boydshotrods.com

| | car dealer |

See full listing in **Section One** under **Chevrolet**

Brasilia Press
PO Box 2023
Elkhart, IN 46515
FAX: 219-262-8799

| | models |

See full listing in **Section Two** under **models & toys**

Bumper Boyz LLC
2435 E 54th St
Los Angeles, CA 90058
800-995-1703, 323-587-8976
FAX: 323-587-2013

| | bumper repairs reconditioning sandblasting |

See full listing in **Section One** under **Chevrolet**

Bob Burgess 1955-56 Ford Parts
793 Alpha-Bellbrook Rd
Bellbrook, OH 45305
937-426-8041

| | parts |

Mail order and open shop by appointment. Phone hours: daily 9 am to 9 pm. Specializing in NOS, used and reproduction parts for 1955-1956 Ford, Lincoln, Mercury. Send SASE for free Ford catalog.

Burrell's Service Inc
PO Box 456
Keego Harbor, MI 48320
248-682-2376

| | parts |

See full listing in **Section One** under **Chevrolet**

Butch's Trim — molding / polishing / trim restoration
W-224 S-8445 Industrial Ave
Big Bend, WI 53103
414-679-4883, 414-662-9910 shop

See full listing in **Section One** under **Chevrolet**

C & G Early Ford Parts — accessories/chrome / emblems/literature / mechanical / weatherstripping / wiring
1941 Commercial St, Dept AH
Escondido, CA 92029-1233
760-740-2400; FAX: 760-740-8700
E-mail: cgford@cgfordparts.com

See full listing in **Section One** under **Ford 1932-1953**

California Thunderbirds — parts
Bill Denzel
1507 Arroyo View Dr
Pasadena, CA 91103
626-792-0720; FAX: 626-792-9937
E-mail: teamdenzel@aol.com

See full listing in **Section One** under **Thunderbird**

Carl's Ford Parts — muscle parts
23219 South St, Box 38
Homeworth, OH 44634
PH/FAX: 330-525-7291

See full listing in **Section One** under **Mustang**

Carolina Classics — truck parts
624 E Geer St
Durham, NC 27701
919-682-4211; FAX: 919-682-1286

Mail order and open shop. Monday-Friday 8 am to 5:30 pm,
Saturday by appointment. 1948-1979 Ford truck parts.

Dennis Carpenter Ford Reproductions — parts
PO Box 26398
Charlotte, NC 28221
704-786-8139; FAX: 704-786-8180

Mail order and counter sales. Monday-Friday 8 am to 5 pm.
Manufacture and sell obsolete Ford car and truck parts.
Specializing in weatherstripping, antennas, scuff plates, outside
door handles and much more. For 1932-up Ford cars, 1932-
1979 pickups, 1940-1956 Mercury, 1958-1966 T-Birds, 1960-
1970 Falcons, 1962-1971 Fairlanes and 1966-1979 Broncos.
Catalogs $3, state year and body style.

Cass County Historical Society — museum
1351 W Main Ave
PO Box 719
West Fargo, ND 58078
701-282-2822; FAX: 701-282-7606

See full listing in **Section Six** under **North Dakota**

Chandler Classic Cars — Ford products
1308 14th St W
Bradenton, FL 34205
941-747-3441; FAX: 941-747-9650
E-mail: chandlercars@worldnet.att.net

Specialize in selling Ford products for 1950s and 1960s. Web
site: www.c-it.com/chandler

Chewning's Auto Literature — literature / manuals
2011 Elm Tree Terr
Buford, GA 30518
770-945-9795

See full listing in **Section Two** under **literature dealers**

Class-Tech Corp — wiring harnesses
62935 Layton Ave
Bend, OR 97701
800-874-9981

See full listing in **Section Two** under **electrical systems**

Classic Auto — restoration
251 SW 5th Ct
Pompano Beach, FL 33060
PH/FAX: 954-786-1687

See full listing in **Section Two** under **restoration shops**

Classic Auto Air Mfg Co — air conditioning / heating / parts
2020 W Kennedy Blvd
Tampa, FL 33606
813-251-2356, 813-251-4994

See full listing in **Section One** under **Mustang**

Classic Auto Restoration Service Inc — restoration
381 National Dr
Rockwall, TX 75032-6556
972-722-9663

See full listing in **Section One** under **Chevrolet**

Classic Enterprises — sheetmetal
Box 92
Barron, WI 54812
715-537-5422

See full listing in **Section One** under **Studebaker**

Classic Ford Sales — salvage yard
PO Box 60
East Dixfield, ME 04227
207-562-4443; FAX: 207-562-4576
E-mail: classicford@quickconnect.com

See full listing in **Section Five** under **Maine**

Clester's Auto Rubber Seals Inc — gloveboxes / molded rubber / parts / weatherstripping
PO Box 1113
Salisbury, NC 28145
704-637-9979; FAX: 704-636-7390

See full listing in **Section Two** under **rubber parts**

The Clockworks — clock service
1745 Meta Lake Ln
Eagle River, WI 54521
800-398-3040; FAX: 715-479-5759
E-mail: clockworks@juno.com

See full listing in **Section Two** under **instruments**

Concours Parts & Accessories — parts
3493 Arrowhead Dr
Carson City, NV 89706
800-722-0009; FAX: 800-725-8644

See full listing in **Section One** under **Thunderbird**

Bob Cook Classic Auto Parts Inc — new parts / NOS parts / reproduced parts
2055 Van Cleave Rd, PO Box 600
Murray, KY 42071-0600
502-753-4000, 800-486-1137
FAX: 502-753-4600

Mail and phone orders. Most Ford vehicles 1955-1972. Catalog
price refundable, $5.

Walt Dantzler — parts
1567 Bertrand Dr
Lafayette, LA 70506
318-234-1344, leave message
FAX: 318-233-4113

Mail order and open shop by appointment. NOS Ford 1949-up
parts. Sheetmetal, wheelcovers, emblems, chrome, switches,
lenses, nameplates. Part time hobbyist. Lists available for SASE.

Dearborn Classics — accessories / restoration parts
PO Box 7649
Bend, OR 97708-7649
800-252-7427; FAX: 800-500-7886

The nation's parts source for Ford Ranchero, Falcon, Fairlane and Torino parts and accessories. Moldings, emblems, weather-stripping, interior, engine parts, suspension, brake system and more. Large fully illustrated catalog available or request. Web site: www.dearbornclassics.com

See our ad on this page

Mike Dennis, Nebraska Mail Order 1845 S 48th St Lincoln, NE 68506 402-489-3036; FAX: 402-489-1148	**parts** **Trippe mounting** **brackets/hardware**

See full listing in **Section One** under **Ford 1932-1953**

Greg Donahue Collector Car Restorations Inc 12900 S Betty Pt Floral City, FL 34436 352-344-4329; FAX: 352-344-0015	**parts** **restoration**

Mail order only. Phone hours: Monday-Saturday 9 am to 8 pm, no Sundays or holidays. 1963, 1963-1/2, 1964 Ford Galaxie reproduction and NOS parts: all of the parts needed for any type of Galaxie restoration from the Galaxie restoration authority. Weatherstrip, rubber parts, moldings, carpet, seat covers, dash pads, healiners, exterior and interior chrome, emblems, ornaments, mirrors, mechanical parts, accessories, lenses, sheetmetal, wheelcovers, decals, parts diagrams and shop manuals. We have the largest inventory in the US and handle only 1963 and 1964 Galaxie parts. Current 150 page catalog, $5. Also 100 point concours restorations available. Web site: http://38.212.103.105/gregdonahue-ccr.html

Edward W Drozd 84 Farm Hill Rd Wallingford, CT 06492 203-265-6638 E-mail: ewdrozd@snet.net	**grilles** **moldings**

See full listing in **Section One** under **Mercury**

Early Ford Parts 2948 Summer Ave Memphis, TN 38112 901-323-2179; FAX: 901-323-2195	**literature** **parts**

See full listing in **Section One** under **Ford 1932-1953**

Early Ford V8 Sales Inc Curtis Industrial Park, Bldg 37 831 Rt 67 Ballston Spa, NY 12020 518-884-2825; FAX: 518-884-2633 E-mail: earlyford@prodigy.net	**parts**

See full listing in **Section One** under **Ford 1932-1953**

Egge Machine Company Inc 11707 Slauson Ave Santa Fe Springs, CA 90670 800-866-EGGE, 562-945-3419 FAX: 562-693-1635 E-mail: info@egge.com	**bearings** **pistons/rings** **timing components** **valve train**

See full listing in **Section Two** under **engine parts**

Daniel A Evans 2850 John St Easton, PA 18045 610-258-9542 after 5:30 pm FAX: 610-252-0370 E-mail: evansd@lafayette.edu	**literature** **parts**

Specializing in NOS and restored hard-to-find parts for 1955-1957 Thunderbirds. Buy, sell, trade Ford dual quad and supercharger parts. Also original literature and Ford dealership items.

Falcon's Forever   parts
PO Box 6531
Albany, CA 94206
510-525-9226; FAX: 510-525-2652
E-mail: dr4falcons@aol.com

Shop open weekends by appointment. Specializing in hard to
find parts for 1960-1965 Falcons and Comets. This includes
rust-free California sheetmetal, moldings, trim and mechanical
parts. Also a supply of new rubber parts.

Faxon Auto Literature   literature
3901 Carter Ave   manuals
Riverside, CA 92501
800-458-2734; FAX: 909-786-4166

See full listing in **Section Two** under **literature dealers**

Fifth Avenue Graphics   cooling systems
Fifth Avenue Antique Auto Parts   electrical systems
415 Court St   fuel systems
Clay Center, KS 67432
785-632-3450; FAX: 785-632-6154
E-mail: fifthave@kansas.net

See full listing in **Section Two** under **electrical systems**

John Filiss   appraisals
45 Kingston Ave
Port Jervis, NY 12771
914-856-2942
E-mail: johnfiliss@hotmail.com

See full listing in **Section Two** under **appraisals**

Ford Parts Store   parts
110 Ford Rd, Box 226
Bryan, OH 43506
419-636-2475; FAX: 419-636-8449
E-mail: fordpart@bright.net

Mail and telephone orders only. Monday-Saturday 9 am to 9 pm,
24 hour fax. Since 1978, specializing in 1952-1970 Ford passenger cars. New and reproduction weatherstripping for doors,
windshield, convertible tops, roof rails, wire harnesses, trunk
mats, carpet, scuff plates, plastic emblems, chrome scripts,
owner's and shop manuals. Appears at 18 major swap meets
throughout the year. Catalog available, $3. Web site:
www.fordpartsstore.com

Ford Powertrain Applications   engines
7702 E 96th St
Puyallup, WA 98371
PH/FAX: 253-848-9503

Monday-Friday 9 am to 6 pm, Saturday 9 am to 12 noon.
Specializing in Ford race engines and hp street rod/restoration
engines and related hp engine components, Ford Motorsports,
Blue Thunder heads and manifolds, FPA custom Tri-Y and
shorty Ford headers.

Fowlkes Realty & Auction   appraisals
500 Hale St   auctions
Newman Grove, NE 68758
800-275-5522; FAX: 402-447-6000

See full listing in **Section One** under **Chevrolet**

Gemini Racing Systems Inc   race prep
571 N 54th St   restoration
Chandler, AZ 85226
800-992-9294, 602-940-9011

See full listing in **Section One** under **Mustang**

Randy Goodling   parts
2046 Mill Rd   parts locating
Elizabethtown, PA 17022-9401
717-367-6700

See full listing in **Section One** under **Mercury**

Half Ton Fun   NOS parts
Bob Selzam
166 Toms River Rd
Jackson, NJ 08527
732-928-9421

See full listing in **Section One** under **Ford 1932-1953**

Haneline Products Co   gauges
PO Box 430   instrument panels
Morongo Valley, CA 92256   stainless parts
760-363-6597; FAX: 760-363-7321   trim parts

See full listing in **Section Two** under **accessories**

Bill Heeley   shift assemblies
3621 Mt Olney Ln   shift levers
Olney, MD 20832
301-774-6710

Mail order only. Rebuild/restore original Ford shifters from
1962-1973. Generally have at least one of every Ford V8 4-spd
shifters in stock, five to ten of most, have over 20 varieties of
rechromed shift levers.

Hidden Valley Auto Parts   parts
21046 N Rio Bravo
Maricopa, AZ 85239
602-252-2122, 602-252-6137
520-568-2945; FAX: 602-258-0951

See full listing in **Section One** under **Chevrolet**

Highway Classics   parts
949 N Cataract Ave, Unit J
San Dimas, CA 91773
909-592-8819; FAX: 909-592-4239
E-mail: donnelson@earthlink.net

Mail order and open shop. Monday-Friday 9 am to 5 pm,
Saturday 10 am to 1 pm. Restoration and repair parts for 1960-
1970 Falcon, 1962-1973 Fairlane/Torino, 1967-1973 Cougar,
1964-1973 Mustang, 1960-1967 Comet, 1960-1979 Ranchero.
Web site: highwayclassics.com

Bill Horton   vacuum motors
5804 Jones Valley Dr
Huntsville, AL 35802
256-881-6894

See full listing in **Section One** under **Mercury**

Hot Rod & Custom Supply   custom parts
1304 SE 10th St   engine parts
Cape Coral, FL 33990   speed parts
941-574-7744; FAX: 941-574-8820

See full listing in **Section One** under **Ford 1932-1953**

Hubcap Mike   hubcaps
26242 Dimension Ste 150   wheelcovers
Lake Forest, CA 92630
949-597-8120; FAX: 949-597-8123

See full listing in **Section Two** under **wheels & wheelcovers**

International Ford History Project   newsletter
PO Box 11415
Olympia, WA 98508
360-754-9585
E-mail: ifhp@aol.com

See full listing in **Section Four** under **newsletters**

Jacks Wholesale Division   limousines
250 N Robertson Blvd, Ste 405
Beverly Hills, CA 90211-1793
310-839-9417; FAX: 310-839-1046

See full listing in **Section One** under **Lincoln**

JAE
375 Pine #26
Goleta, CA 93117
805-967-5767; FAX: 805-967-6183
E-mail: jefforjay@jaeparts.com

parts
service
tech info

See full listing in **Section One** under **Lotus**

Jerry's Classic Cars & Parts Inc
4097 McRay Ave
Springdale, AR 72764
800-828-4584; FAX: 501-750-1682
E-mail: jcc@jerrysclassiccars.com

parts
restoration

Mail order and open shop. Monday-Friday 8 am to 5 pm. Specializing in new, used and reproduction parts for 1957-1959 Ford retractables and convertibles. We also restore 1957s-1959s from good drivers to showroom cars. Web site: www.jerrysclassiccars.com

Joe's Auto Sales
5849-190th St E
Hastings, MN 55033
612-437-6787

parts

Mail order and open shop. Monday 9 am to 5 pm, Tuesday-Friday 8 am to 5 pm (closed noon hour during weekdays), Saturday 8 am to 12 pm. Specializing in 1939-1989 Ford and Mercury products, sales of used, rebuilt and new parts. Some repair work and parts rebuilding for customers. Rebuild steering columns: auto, standard and tilt.

K C Obsolete Parts
3343 N 61
Kansas City, KS 66104
913-334-9479; FAX: 913-788-2795

parts

Mail order only. Carries a full line of parts for 1948-1972 Ford pickups and panels. Full line catalog available for $2.

Kenroy Ford Parts
2 Folwell Ln
Mullica Hill, NJ 08062
609-478-2527
E-mail: duffieldm@aol.com

NOS parts

Mail order only. Specializing in NOS FoMoCo parts, 1940-1985. Very low prices, huge inventory: window regulators, lower window channel, exterior molding. 19 years in business.

Dale King Obsolete Parts
PO Box 1099
211 Hilltop Dr
Liberty, KY 42539
606-787-5031; FAX: 606-787-2130

parts

Specializing in NOS hard to find parts and quality reproductions for Ford, Fairlane, Falcon, Mustang, Ford trucks, Mercury and Comet.

Lares Manufacturing
13517 Hwy 65 NE
Ham Lake, MN 55304
800-334-5749; FAX: 612-754-2853
E-mail: sales@larescorp.com

power steering
equipment

Mail order and open shop. Monday-Friday 8 am to 5 pm CST. Power steering gears, manual steering gears, power steering pumps, power steering control valves and power steering cylinders. Web site: www.larescorp.com

Larry's Thunderbird & Mustang Parts Inc
511 S Raymond Ave
Fullerton, CA 92831
800-854-0393 orders
714-871-6432; FAX: 714-871-1883

parts

See full listing in **Section One** under **Thunderbird**

L B Repair
1308 W Benten
Savannah, MO 64485-1549
816-324-3913

restoration

Mail order and open shop. Monday-Saturday 9 am to 7 pm. Specializing in mig welding and subframe installation, all suspension modifications. Special interest: 1953-1956 big window Ford pickups and panels. Drop kit installation on late model pickups, low riders, fiberglass repair, economical restorations.

Lincoln Parts International
707 E 4th St, Bldg G
Perris, CA 92570
800-382-1656, 909-657-5588
FAX: 909-657-4758
E-mail: lincprts@pe.net

parts

See full listing in **Section One** under **Lincoln**

Ed Liukkonen
37 Cook Rd
Templeton, MA 01468
978-939-8126

accessories
parts

Mail order only. Sale of NOS genuine FoMoCo parts, 1949/1979, for Ford full size, Fairlane, Comet, Mercury, Falcon, Mustang. Some used factory high-performance parts for Ford "muscle cars" also stocked.

Lloyd's Literature
PO Box 491
Newbury, OH 44065
800-292-2665, 440-338-1527
FAX: 440-338-2222

literature

See full listing in **Section Two** under **literature dealers**

Loyal Ford Mercury Inc
2310 Calumet Dr
New Holstein, WI 53061
920-898-4248; FAX: 920-898-9705

cars
parts

Mail order and open shop. Monday-Wednesday 7 am to 8 pm, Thursday-Friday 7 am to 8 pm, Saturday 8 am to 5 pm. Specializing in Ford, Lincoln, Mercury, SVT, Saleen vehicles and parts for most years. Roush and Steeda performance vehicles.

Mac's Antique Auto Parts
1051 Lincoln Ave
PO Box 238
Lockport, NY 14095-0238
800-777-0948 US and Canada
716-433-1500 local and foreign
FAX: 716-433-1172
E-mail: mailmacs@aol.com

literature
parts
restoration supplies

See full listing in **Section One** under **Ford 1903-1931**

The Maverick Connection
137 Valley Dr
Ripley, WV 25271
PH/FAX: 304-372-7825

literature
parts

Mail order only. Specializing in parts and literature for 1970-1977 Ford Mavericks and Mercury Comets.

McDonald Obsolete Parts Company
RR 3, Box 94
Rockport, IN 47635
812-359-4965; FAX: 812-359-5555
E-mail: mcdonald@psci.net

body parts
chassis parts

Mail order only. Specializing in body parts and chassis parts, script glass, spotlights and foglights for 1938-1980 Ford, Mercury, Lincoln and trucks. Inventory is 90% NOS. Also dealers of all major quality reproduced parts. Web site: mcdonaldparts.com

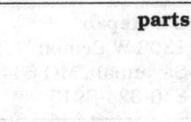
Mean Mustang Supply Inc 201 D St South Charleston, WV 25303 304-746-0300; FAX: 304-746-0395 E-mail: meanstang@aol.com	**parts**

See full listing in **Section One** under **Mustang**

Melvin's Classic Ford Parts Inc 2526 Panola Rd Lithonia, GA 30058 770-981-2357; FAX: 770-981-6207	**parts**

Mail order and open showroom. Tuesday-Friday 8:30 am to 5:30 pm, Saturday 8:30 am to 4 pm, closed Sunday-Monday. Specializing in parts for 1964-1/2-1973 Mustang, 1960-1970-1/2 Falcon, 1962-1979 Fairlane, Torino, Ranchero, 1949-1959 Ford car and T-Bird, 1960-1972 Ford car and T-Bird, 1948-1979 Ford trucks.

Mid-America Auction Services 2277 W Hwy 36, Ste 214 St Paul, MN 55113 612-633-9655; FAX: 612-633-3212 E-mail: midauction@aol.com	**auctions**

See full listing in **Section Two** under **auctions & events**

Miller Obsolete Parts 1329 Campus Dr Vestal, NY 13850 607-722-5371; FAX: 607-770-9117 E-mail: fordpart@spectra.net	**locator service** **parts**

Mail order only. New obsolete (NOS) parts. 1950s-1990s Ford, Lincoln, Mercury vehicles, 70,000 parts in stock. Free nationwide locator service.

Mostly Mustangs Inc 55 Alling St Hamden, CT 06517 203-562-8804; FAX: 203-562-4891	**car dealer** **parts sales** **restoration**

See full listing in **Section One** under **Mustang**

Mustang Service Center 11610 Vanowen St North Hollywood, CA 91605 818-765-1196; FAX: 818-765-1349 E-mail: fmustang@primenet.com	**parts** **service**

See full listing in **Section One** under **Mustang**

Mustangs & More 2065 Sperry Ave #C Ventura, CA 93003 800-356-6573; FAX: 805-642-6468 E-mail: mustmore@aol.com	**parts** **restoration**

See full listing in **Section One** under **Mustang**

NorCal Auto 615D Saint John St Pleasanton, CA 94566 888-224-6005; FAX: 925-426-8845 E-mail: mwjohn@hotmail.com	**appraisals**

See full listing in **Section Two** under **appraisals**

Normans' Classic Auto Radio 7651 Park Blvd Pinellas Park, FL 33781 888-222-3433, 727-546-1788	**custom sales**

See full listing in **Section Two** under **radios**

North Yale Auto Parts Rt 1, Box 707 Sperry, OK 74073 918-288-7218, 800-256-6927 (NYAP) FAX: 918-288-7223	**salvage yard**

See full listing in **Section Five** under **Oklahoma**

Northeast Ford Box 66, Rt 9 East Sullivan, NH 03445 603-847-9956, 800-562-FORD FAX: 603-847-9691	**parts** **restoration**

Mail order and open shop. Monday-Friday 8 am to 5:30 pm. Ford parts for cars and trucks. Our parts include new, used and quality reproductions from 1928-1979. Catalogues available, from 1932-1979, $3 refundable, must specify year and model. We do inspections and repairs, plus we have a complete restoration facility.

Northwest Classic Falcons Inc 1715 NW Pettygrove St Portland, OR 97209 503-241-9454; FAX: 503-241-1964 E-mail: ron@nwfalcon.com	**parts**

Mail order and phone order/pickup. Monday-Friday 9 am to 6 pm PST. Specializes in new, reproduction, NOS and good used parts for 1960-1970 Falcon and Comet. Web site: www.nwfalcon.com

See our ad on this page

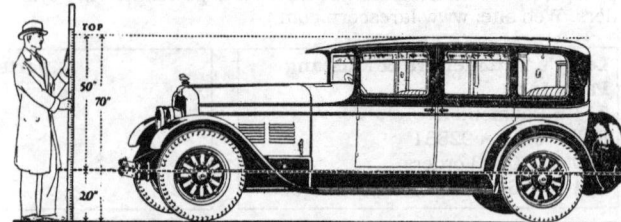

Obsolete Ford Parts Co — parts
311 E Washington Ave
Nashville, GA 31639
912-686-2470, 912-686-5101
FAX: 912-686-7125

Mail order and open shop. Monday-Friday 8 am to 5 pm. Comprehensive stock of NOS sheetmetal, trim, chrome, rubber, accessories, literature for 1949-1979 Ford, Falcons, Fairlanes, Ford pickups, Comets, Cougars. Customers' requests by phone or mail accepted.

See our ad on this page

Obsolete Ford Parts Inc — parts
8701 S I-35
Oklahoma City, OK 73149
405-631-3933; FAX: 405-634-6815

Mail order and open shop. Monday-Friday 8 am to 6 pm, Saturday 9 am to 1 pm. Ford parts for 9 different Ford products ranging from 1909-1979. Offer catalogs for: 1909-1927 T, 1928-1931 A, 1932-1948 car and pickup, 1948-1979 Ford truck, 1960-1970 Falcon, 1962-1972 Fairlane/Torino, 1955-1972 T-Bird, 1949-1972 full-size car and 1949-1972 Mercury. Web site: www.ford-obsolete-parts.com

Joe Odehnal — literature parts
2722 N Westnedge
Kalamazoo, MI 49004
616-342-5509
E-mail: joe.odehnal@wmich.edu

Mail order only. Used parts for 1957-1959 Ford retractables. Literature and magazine ads for the retractable.

Old Air Products — air conditioning
4615 Martin St
Ft Worth, TX 76119
817-531-2665; FAX: 817-531-3257
E-mail: sales@oldairproducts.com

See full listing in **Section One** under **Corvette**

The Old Car Centre — parts
19909 92A Ave
Langley, BC Canada V1M 3B6
604-888-4412, 604-888-4055
FAX: 604-888-7455

See full listing in **Section One** under **Ford 1903-1931**

The Old Carb Doctor — carburetors fuel pumps
Rt 3, Box 338
Drucilla Church Rd
Nebo, NC 28761
800-945-CARB (2272)
704-659-1428

See full listing in **Section Two** under **carburetors**

Old Dominion Mustang/Camaro — parts
509 S Washington Hwy, Rt 1
Ashland, VA 23005
804-798-3348; FAX: 804-798-5105

See full listing in **Section One** under **Mustang**

Only Yesterday Classic Autos Inc — cars
24 Valley Rd
Port Washington, NY 11050
516-767-3477; FAX: 516-767-8964

See full listing in **Section One** under **Chevrolet**

Original Auto Interiors — upholstery
7869 Trumble Rd
Columbus, MI 48063-3915
810-727-2486; FAX: 810-727-4344
E-mail: origauto@tir.com

See full listing in **Section Two** under **upholstery**

Original Falcon, Comet, Ranchero, Fairlane Interiors — interiors weatherstripping
6343 Seaview Ave NW
Seattle, WA 98107-2664
206-781-5230; FAX: 206-781-5046
E-mail: falcons1@ix.netcom.com

Mail order and open shop. Monday-Saturday 9 am to 6 pm. Specialize in new old stock upholstery seat sets as well as produces OEM seat sets, door panels, carpets for 1960-1966 Falcons, Comets and Rancheros, Fairlanes as well as through the 1970s for Rancheros. These models are Sprints, Futuras, Cyclones, Calientes, Mercury S-22 2 and 4-door sedans, convertibles, with a full range of interior goods and weatherstripping.

Original Ford Motor Co Literature — collectibles literature
PO Box 7-AA
Hudson, KY 40145-0007
502-257-8642; FAX: 502-257-8643
E-mail: whiteb@bellsouth.net

See full listing in **Section One** under **Ford 1932-1953**

P-Ayr Products — replicas
719 Delaware St
Leavenworth, KS 66048
913-651-5543; FAX: 913-651-2084
E-mail: sales@payr.com

See full listing in **Section One** under **Chevrolet**

Pick-ups Northwest — parts trim
1430 Bickford Ave
Snohomish, WA 98290
360-568-9166; FAX: 360-568-1233

See full listing in **Section One** under **Chevrolet**

Section One
Marque Specialists

Power Brake Booster Exchange Inc | **brake boosters**
4533 SE Division St
Portland, OR 97206
503-238-8882

See full listing in **Section Two** under **brakes**

Greg Purdy's Mustang Supply | **parts**
PO Box 784
Forest Hill, MD 21050
410-836-5991

See full listing in **Section One** under **Mustang**

PV Antique & Classic Ford | **parts**
1688 Main St
Tewksbury, MA 01876
800-MSTANGS orders only
978-851-9159; FAX: 978-858-3827
E-mail: pvford@flash.net

See full listing in **Section One** under **Ford 1903-1931**

Raine Automotive Springs Warehouse | **springs**
 | **suspension parts**
425 Harding Hwy
Carney's Point, NJ 08069
609-299-9141; FAX: 609-299-9157

See full listing in **Section Two** under **suspension parts**

Rapido Group | **accessories**
 | **parts**
80093 Dodson Rd
Tygh Valley, OR 97063
541-544-3333

See full listing in **Section One** under **Merkur**

Recks & Relics Ford Trucks | **truck parts**
2675 Hamilton Mason Rd
Hamilton, OH 45011
513-868-3489
E-mail: truck@choice.net

See full listing in **Section One** under **Ford 1932-1953**

Red's Headers & Early Ford Speed Equipment | **headers**
 | **mechanical parts**
22950 Bednar Ln
Fort Bragg, CA 95437-8411
707-964-7733; FAX: 707-964-5434
E-mail: red@reds-headers.com

See full listing in **Section One** under **Ford 1932-1953**

Regent Trading Corp | **parts**
Paul Brensilber
15 Stonehurst Dr
Tenafly, NJ 07670
201-541-7718, NJ
FAX: 212-362-3985, NY

Mail order only. Specializing in door striker plates for Ford trucks and automobiles, for Ford truck 1953-1955, Ford truck 1956, Ford passenger car 1949-1956. Also Ford parts.

S & S Antique Auto | **parts**
Pine St
Deposit, NY 13754
607-467-2929; FAX: 607-467-2109

See full listing in **Section One** under **Ford 1932-1953**

S-E Autoparts | **NOS parts**
 | **reproduced parts**
Jarpbo 4
78193 Borlange Sweden
+46 243 221297
FAX: +46 243 221298
E-mail: s-e.autoparts@ebox.tninet.se

See full listing in **Section One** under **Anglia**

Sam's Vintage Ford Parts | **parts**
5105 Washington
Denver, CO 80216
303-295-1709

Mail order and open shop. Monday-Saturday 9 am to 5:30 pm. For V8s, Mustangs and 1949-1970 Fords and Mercurys. Also truck parts.

Harry Samuel | **carpet**
 | **fabrics**
65 Wisner St | **interiors**
Pontiac, MI 48342-1066 | **upholstery covers**
248-335-1900
E-mail: hsamuel1@aol.com

See full listing in **Section Two** under **interiors & interior parts**

Sanderson Ford | **parts**
Jim Ray
6300 N 51 Ave
Glendale, AZ 85301
888-364-3673, 602-842-8663
FAX: 602-842-8637

Mail order and open shop. Monday-Friday 8 am to 6 pm, Saturday 8 am to 4 pm. Specializing in 1965-1973 Mustangs, 1955-1966 Thunderbirds, 1960-1965 Falcons, 1971-1974 Panteras, 1967-1973 Cougars, 1953-1956 F-100, Motorsport parts and late model 5.0 parts. No catalogs. Web site: www.sandersonford.com

Sixties Ford Parts | **books**
639 Glanker St | **new parts**
Memphis, TN 38112 | **shop manuals**
PH/FAX: 901-323-2195, recorder

Mail order only. New parts for 1960-1968 Fords, big Ford, Fairlane, Falcon, Thunderbird, trucks. 90 page catalog, $4, specify year and type of Ford as listed above. In business over 20 years. Visa, MasterCard, personal checks accepted.

SMS Auto Fabrics | **upholstery**
2325 SE 10th Ave
Portland, OR 97214
503-234-1175; FAX: 503-234-0651

See full listing in **Section Two** under **interiors & interior parts**

SoCal Pickups Inc | **parts**
6321 Manchester Blvd
Buena Park, CA 90621
800-SOCAL-49; FAX: 714-994-2584

Mail order and showroom. Monday-Friday 9 am to 5 pm, Saturday 8 am to 3 pm. Specializing in parts for 1953-1956 F-100 pickups. 1948-1966 Ford pickups parts. 25 years in business, the most complete stock of F-100 parts anywhere. Complete wiring harnesses, hubcaps, complete bed kits, bed sides and fronts, new radiators, power steering, disc and power brake kits, complete weatherstripping, in and outside mirrors, crossmounts, headers, chrome and stock bumpers, grilles, runningboards, stainless steel trim, emblems, monoleaf and stock springs, shop manuals, independent front suspension. We have it all. Web site: socalpickups.com

Sound Move Inc | **radios**
217 S Main St
Elkhart, IN 46516
800-901-0222, 219-294-5100
FAX: 219-293-4902

See full listing in **Section One** under **Chevrolet**

Special Interest Cars | **parts**
451 Woody Rd
Oakville, ON Canada L6K 2Y2
905-844-8063; FAX: 905-338-8063

See full listing in **Section Two** under **comprehensive parts**

Specialty Ford Parts
9103 Garvey Ave
Rosemead, CA 91770
626-280-4546; FAX: 626-288-3311

engine parts
speed parts

A, B, C and V8 Ford engine and speed parts. Catalog, $6 USA.

Stencils & Stripes Unlimited Inc
1108 S Crescent Ave #21
Park Ridge, IL 60068
847-692-6893; FAX: 847-692-6895

NOS decals
stripe kits

See full listing in **Section Two** under **decals**

Stilwell's Obsolete Car Parts
1617 Wedeking Ave
Evansville, IN 47711
812-425-4794

body parts
interiors
parts

See full listing in **Section One** under **Mustang**

Tags Backeast
PO Box 581
Plainville, CT 06062
860-747-2942
E-mail: dataplt@snet.net

data plates
trim tags

See full listing in **Section Two** under **special services**

Tech-Art Publications
Jason Houston
Box 753
Ranchero Mirage, CA 92270
760-862-1979

books

See full listing in **Section Four** under **books & publications**

Tee-Bird Products Inc
Box 728
Exton, PA 19341
610-363-1725; FAX: 610-363-2691

parts

Mail order and open shop. Monday-Friday 8 am to 5 pm, Saturday morning by appointment. Specializing in a complete line of parts for 1954-1959 Ford, with emphasis on 1955-1956 cars and 1955-1957 Thunderbirds. We have offered prompt service, competitive prices and customer satisfaction since 1973.

Thunderbird, Falcon & Fairlane Connections
728 E Dunlap
Phoenix, AZ 85020
602-997-9285; FAX: 602-997-0624
E-mail: tbirdconn@aol.com

new repros
parts
used repros

See full listing in **Section One** under **Thunderbird**

Thunderbird Information eXchange
8421 E Cortez St
Scottsdale, AZ 85260
602-948-3996

newsletter

See full listing in **Section One** under **Thunderbird**

Thunderbirds East
Andy Lovelace
140 Wilmington W Chester Pike
Chadds Ford, PA 19317
610-358-1021; FAX: 610-558-9615

parts
restoration

See full listing in **Section One** under **Thunderbird**

Ultimate Spray-On Truck Bedliner
115 Garfield St
Sumas, WA 98295
800-989-9869; FAX: 604-864-0207
E-mail: info@ultimatelinings.com

bedliners

See full listing in **Section Two** under **trucks & tractors**

Ultra Wheel Co
6300 Valley View Ave
Buena Park, CA 90620
714-994-1444; FAX: 714-994-0723

custom wheels

See full listing in **Section Two** under **wheels & wheelcovers**

Universal Transmission Co
23361 Dequindre Rd
Hazel Park, MI 48030
800-882-4327; FAX: 248-398-2581

transmission parts

See full listing in **Section Two** under **transmissions**

Valley Motor Supply
1402 E Second St
Roswell, NM 88201
505-622-7450

accessories
parts

Mail order and open shop. Monday-Friday 8 am to 5 pm. GM, Ford, Chrysler and tractor products. Some parts for all makes, early to present. Many NOS items.

Vintage Ford & Chevrolet Parts of Arizona Inc
So-Cal Speed Shop
3427 E McDowell Rd
Phoenix, AZ 85008-3845
800-732-0076, 602-275-7990
FAX: 602-267-8439
E-mail: vintageparts@sprintmail.com

parts

Mail order and open showroom. Monday-Friday 9 am to 5 pm, Saturday 8 am to 3 pm. Dealing in 1928-1956 Ford car and truck, 1948-1972 Ford truck, 1947-1972 Chevy truck, 1965-1973 Mustang, 1966-1977 Bronco and hot rods. Offer new and used parts. Web site: www.so-calspeedshop.com

Wesley Obsolete Parts
116 Memory Ln
Liberty, KY 42539
606-787-5293; FAX: 606-787-7252

parts

Mail order only. New old stock and reproduction parts for 1949-up Ford, Lincoln, Mercury and Ford trucks.

Dan Williams Toploader Transmissions
206 E Dogwood Dr
Franklin, NC 28734
828-524-9085 noon-midnight
FAX: 828-524-4848

transmissions

Specializing in Ford toploader transmissions. Sales, service, parts. Hurst shifters, Lakewood bellhousings. Web site: www.toploadertransmissions.com

Pat Wilson's Thunderbird Parts
235 River Rd
New Milford, NJ 07646-1721
888-262-1153; FAX: 201-634-1916

parts

See full listing in **Section One** under **Thunderbird**

MUSTANG

A&A Mustang Parts & Mfg Co
105 Fordham Rd
Oak Ridge, TN 37830
423-482-9445

exhaust systems
parts
restorations

Mail order and open shop. Monday-Friday 8 am to 5 pm, Saturday 8 am to 12 noon. Specializing in single and dual exhaust systems, new and used parts and full restorations for 1964-1/2-1973 Mustangs.

American Restorations Unlimited TA — restoration parts
14 Meakin Ave
PO Box 34
Rochelle Park, NJ 07662
201-843-3567; FAX: 201-843-3238
E-mail: amerrest@earthlink.net

See full listing in **Section Two** under **glass**

AMK Products — parts
18600 E 96th St
Broken Arrow, OK 74012
918-455-2651; FAX: 918-455-7441

Mail order only. Offers a comprehensive line of 1965-1973 Mustang and Ford fasteners. Items in our fastener kits feature original manufacturer's markings and the correct grade and finish as specified in Ford's assembly manuals. Your best source for "True to Original" under the hood detailing items such as voltage regulators, starter solenoids, radiator caps, ignition wires, battery cables and alternators. Offer 100% new alternators for popular 1964-1981 applications. Like your Chevy, our products are made in USA. Catalog, $5.

Andy's Classic Mustangs — parts / service
18502 E Sprague
Greenacres, WA 99016
509-924-9824

Mail order and open shop. Monday-Saturday 8 am to 5 pm. Specializing in Mustangs since 1965. New and used parts. Professional engine rebuilding, carburetors, transmissions, differentials. An authority on Mustangs 1965-1973 as to originality and correctness.

Antique Auto Electric — repro wiring
9109 (Rear) E Garvey Ave
Rosemead, CA 91770
626-572-0938

See full listing in **Section Two** under **electrical systems**

Antique & Classic Cars — car locator
1796 County Rd 7
Florence, AL 35633
205-760-0542

See full listing in **Section One** under **Cadillac/LaSalle**

Auto Craftsmen Restoration Inc — appraisals / buyer/car locator / old M-B parts / restoration
27945 Elm Grove
San Antonio, TX 78261
PH/FAX: 830-980-4027

See full listing in **Section Two** under **restoration shops**

Auto Custom Carpet Inc — carpets / floor mats
Jeff Moses
PO Box 1350, 1429 Noble St
Anniston, AL 36201
800-633-2358, 205-236-1118
FAX: 800-516-8274
E-mail: info@accmats.net

See full listing in **Section One** under **Chevrolet**

Auto Decals Unlimited Inc — decals / stripe kits
11259 E Via Linda, Ste 100-201
Scottsdale, AZ 85259
602-220-0800

See full listing in **Section Two** under **decals**

Auto Krafters Inc — parts
PO Box 8
522 S Main St
Broadway, VA 22815
540-896-5910; FAX: 540-896-6412
E-mail: akraft@shentel.net

See full listing in **Section One** under **Ford 1954-up**

JJ Best & Co — financing
737 Main St
PO Box 10
Chatham, MA 02633
508-945-6000; FAX: 508-945-6006

See full listing in **Section Two** under **consultants**

Tony D Branda Performance — accessories / decals / emblems / sheetmetal / wheels
Shelby and Mustang Parts
1434 E Pleasant Valley Blvd
Altoona, PA 16602
814-942-1869; FAX: 814-944-0801
E-mail: cobranda@aol.com

Mail order and open shop. Six days a week 8 am to 5:30 pm. Specializing in Shelby and Mustang parts and accessories for 1965-1970 Shelbys, GT 350 and GT 500. Mustang 1965-1973 parts also available. We deal in parts for restoration such as: decals, emblems, aluminum engine dress-up parts, fiberglass, sheetmetal, wheels, etc.

California Classic Mustang — steel wheels
1102 Industrial Ave
Escondido, CA 92128
888-320-8929, 760-746-6580
FAX: 760-746-6581
E-mail: mmatt1965@aol.com

Styled steel wheels (lowest price in the US) for classic Mustangs. Offer a complete set of styled steel wheels for $499 with center caps and lug nuts. Web site: www.classicmustanginc.com

California Jaguar — auto transport
29109 Triunfo Dr
Agoura, CA 91301
800-335-2482; FAX: 818-707-3062

See full listing in **Section Two** under **transport**

California Pony Cars — parts
1906 Quaker Ridge Pl
Ontario, CA 91761
909-923-2804; FAX: 909-947-8593
E-mail:
105232.3362@compuserve.com

Manufacturer/wholesaler of reproduction 1964-1/2-1973 Mustang parts and restoration supplies. Emblems, suspension, engine, electrical and fiberglass components and 5-speed conversions.

Canadian Mustang — parts
20529 62 Ave
Langley, BC Canada V3A 8R4
604-534-6424; FAX: 604-534-6694
E-mail: parts@canadianmustang.com

Largest and oldest Mustang parts distributor in Canada. Manufacturers, wholesalers and distributors of 1965-1973 Mustang parts. Large Canadian mail order catalog. Web site: www.canadianmustang.com

Carl's Ford Parts — muscle parts
23219 South St, Box 38
Homeworth, OH 44634
PH/FAX: 330-525-7291

Mail order only. Specializing in 1960-1970 Ford muscle parts for all Fords and Mercurys. Carburetor rebuilding, parts locating and engine building services for 390, 406, 428, 427 engines.

CBS Performance Automotive — ignition systems / performance products
2605-A W Colorado Ave
Colorado Springs, CO 80904
800-685-1492; FAX: 719-578-9485

See full listing in **Section Two** under **ignition parts**

CJ Pony Parts Inc
7441 B Allentown Blvd
Harrisburg, PA 17112
800-888-6473, 717-691-5623
FAX: 888-888-6573, 717-657-9254
E-mail: creed@redrose.net

parts

Mail order with a store and showroom. Commitment to quality, price and service is the foundation that CJs is built upon. We've been serving the Mustang restorer for 15 years. We carry a complete line of upholstery, weatherstrip, chrome, sheetmetal, wheels, brakes, suspensions, carpet and accessories. One stop shopping from bumper to bumper. Wholesale and body shop discounts available. Web site: www.cjponyparts.com

Class-Tech Corp
62935 Layton Ave
Bend, OR 97701
800-874-9981

wiring harnesses

See full listing in **Section Two** under **electrical systems**

Classic Auto
251 SW 5th Ct
Pompano Beach, FL 33060
PH/FAX: 954-786-1687

restoration

See full listing in **Section Two** under **restoration shops**

Classic Auto Air Mfg Co
2020 W Kennedy Blvd
Tampa, FL 33606
813-251-2356, 813-251-4994

air conditioning
heating
parts

Mail order and open shop. Monday-Friday 9:30 am to 6 pm. Manufactures exact factory or aftermarket parts and complete systems for all 1955-1973 Ford, GM and Chrysler. Show quality rebuilding services and exact hose duplications. Large NOS stock of a/c and heat parts. Specializing in 1965-1973 Mustang/Cougar, 1949-1979 Rolls-Royce/Bentley and Ford/GM auto temp control systems. Very detailed 1965-1973 Mustang a/c catalog.

Classic Auto Restoration Service Inc
381 National Dr
Rockwall, TX 75032-6556
972-722-9663

restoration

See full listing in **Section One** under **Chevrolet**

Classic Coachworks
735 Frenchtown Rd
Milford, NJ 08848
908-996-3400; FAX: 908-996-0204

bodywork
painting
restoration

See full listing in **Section Two** under **restoration shops**

Classic Creations of Central Florida
3620 Hwy 92E
Lakeland, FL 33801
941-665-2322; FAX: 941-666-5348
E-mail: flclassics@aol.com

parts
restoration
service

Monday-Thursday 9 am to 5 pm, Friday 9 am to 8 pm, Saturday 8 am to 4 pm. Full service restoration and repair facility for all of your classic car needs, whether it is complete or partial. Offering complete welding and fabrications, including quarter panels, undercarriage and all exterior metal. Also offering partial or complete interior service and suspension rebuilds. Carrying a full line of new, used and NOS Mustang parts, accessories and collectibles.

Classics 'n More Inc
1001 Ranck Mill Rd
Lancaster, PA 17602
717-392-0599; FAX 717-392-2371

repairs
restoration

See full listing in **Section Two** under **restoration shops**

Cobra Restorers Ltd
3099 Carter Dr
Kennesaw, GA 30144
770-427-0020; FAX: 770-427-8658

parts
restoration
service

See full listing in **Section One** under **Cobra**

The Collector's Guild
41 Counter St
Kingston ON Canada K7K 6C7
800-653-0251; FAX: 613-536-5211
E-mail: cars@collectorsguild.on.ca

models
toys

See full listing in **Section Two** under **models & toys**

Bob Cook Classic Auto Parts Inc
2055 Van Cleave Rd, PO Box 600
Murray, KY 42071-0600
502-753-4000, 800-486-1137
FAX: 502-753-4600

new parts
NOS parts
reproduced parts

See full listing in **Section One** under **Ford 1954-up**

CT Mustang II
1870 Barnum Ave
Stratford, CT 06614
203-377-4795; FAX: 203-380-0612

parts

Specializing in parts for 1974-1978 Mustang II. Mail inquiries to: PO Box 407, Stratford, CT 06615.

Custom Autosound Mfg
808 W Vermont Ave
Anaheim, CA 92805
800-888-8637; FAX: 714-533-0361
E-mail: info@custom-autosound.com

CD players
custom radios
speaker upgrades

See full listing in **Section One** under **Chevrolet**

Desert Muscle Cars
2853 N Stone Ave
Tucson, AZ 85705
520-882-3010; FAX: 520-628-9332

parts

See full listing in **Section One** under **Chevelle/Camaro**

Dynatech Engineering
PO Box 1446
Alta Loma, CA 91701-8446
805-492-6134
E-mail:
dynatechengineering@yahoo.com

motor mounts

See full listing in **Section Two** under **engine parts**

ETC Every Thing Cars
8727 Clarinda
Pico Rivera, CA 90660
562-949-6981

paint
repairs
restoration
welding

See full listing in **Section One** under **Mopar**

Ford Powertrain Applications
7702 E 96th St
Puyallup, WA 98371
PH/FAX: 253-848-9503

engines

See full listing in **Section One** under **Ford 1954-up**

Fowlkes Realty & Auction
500 Hale St
Newman Grove, NE 68758
800-275-5522; FAX: 402-447-6000

appraisals
auctions

See full listing in **Section One** under **Chevrolet**

Gemini Racing Systems Inc
571 N 54th St
Chandler, AZ 85226
800-992-9294, 602-940-9011

race prep
restoration

Mail order and open shop. Monday-Friday 9 am to 6 pm. Specializing in vintage race car restoration and preparation for

Ford GT-40, Cobra, Shelby GT 350, 1965-1968 Mustangs, 1963-1967 Corvette and late model Mustangs and Corvettes. We are suspension and set-up specialists and fabricate the race and high-performance suspension parts for these cars as well as carry a full line of other aggressive performance parts.

Glazier's Mustang Barn Inc 531 Wambold Rd Souderton, PA 18964 800-523-6708, 215-723-9674 FAX: 215-723-6277	accessories parts restoration service

Mail order and showroom sales. Monday-Friday 8:30 am to 5 pm, Saturday 9 am to 1 pm, other times by appointment. Prize winning restoration shop. Monday-Thursday 8 am to 5:30 pm, Friday 8 am to 12 noon, other times by appointment. Specializing in 1964-1/2-1973 Mustangs and Shelbys. Restorations on other early Fords are considered. Catalog available.

Randy Goodling 2046 Mill Rd Elizabethtown, PA 17022-9401 717-367-6700	parts parts locating

See full listing in **Section One** under **Mercury**

Haneline Products Co PO Box 430 Morongo Valley, CA 92256 760-363-6597; FAX: 760-363-7321	gauges instrument panels stainless parts trim parts

See full listing in **Section Two** under **accessories**

Bill Heeley 3621 Mt Olney Ln Olney, MD 20832 301-774-6710	shift assemblies shift levers

See full listing in **Section One** under **Ford 1954-up**

Bill Herndon's Pony Warehouse 20028 Cinnabar Dr Gaithersburg, MD 20879 301-977-0309; FAX: 301-977-1573	accessories parts

Mail order only. Specialize in factory original options and accessories for 1965-1973 Mustangs and Shelbys. One of the largest selections of new old stock parts, including hundreds of hard to find reconditioned original parts and the best available reproduction parts. Quality reconditioning services available for steering wheels, consoles and radios. Your satisfaction guaranteed. We ship anywhere in the USA, Canada and overseas. Visa/MasterCard. Let us be your number one source for quality parts.

Hi-Tech Software 2 Cooks Farm Rd Montville, NJ 07045 PH/FAX: 973-402-9710 E-mail: htsoftware@erols.com	CD encyclopedia

See full listing in **Section One** under **Corvette**

Highway One Classic Automobiles and Highwayone.com Classic Classifieds 1035 California Dr Burlingame, CA 94010 650-342-7340; FAX: 650-343-0150 E-mail: djboscacci@msn.com	classic automobiles

See full listing in **Section One** under **Abarth**

Bill Horton 5804 Jones Valley Dr Huntsville, AL 35802 256-881-6894	vacuum motors

See full listing in **Section One** under **Mercury**

Hubcap Mike 26242 Dimension Ste 150 Lake Forest, CA 92630 949-597-8120; FAX: 949-597-8123	hubcaps wheelcovers

See full listing in **Section Two** under **wheels & wheelcovers**

Inline Tube 33783 Groes Beck Hwy Fraser, MI 48026 800-385-9452 order 810-294-4093 tech FAX: 810-294-7349 E-mail: kryta@aol.com	brake lines/cables choke tubes flex brake hoses fuel/vacuum lines transmission lines

See full listing in **Section Two** under **brakes**

Kenroy Ford Parts 2 Folwell Ln Mullica Hill, NJ 08062 609-478-2527 E-mail: duffieldm@aol.com	NOS parts

See full listing in **Section One** under **Ford 1954-up**

Dale King Obsolete Parts PO Box 1099 211 Hilltop Dr Liberty, KY 42539 606-787-5031; FAX: 606-787-2130	parts

See full listing in **Section One** under **Ford 1954-up**

Larry's Thunderbird & Mustang Parts Inc 511 S Raymond Ave Fullerton, CA 92831 800-854-0393 orders 714-871-6432; FAX: 714-871-1883	parts

See full listing in **Section One** under **Thunderbird**

Ed Liukkonen 37 Cook Rd Templeton, MA 01468 978-939-8126	accessories parts

See full listing in **Section One** under **Ford 1954-up**

Long Island Mustang Restoration Parts 168 Silverleaf Ln Islandia, NY 11722 516-232-2388; FAX: 516-272-5201 E-mail: tom@l-i-mustang.com	rebuilding services repro parts

Mail order and open shop. Monday-Saturday 1 pm to 6 pm EST. Specializing in 1964-1/2-1973 and 1979-1993 Mustangs (Ford). Convertible specialist, reconditioned consoles, 1,000s new, NOS Ford, finest quality reproduction parts, rebuilding services. Power steering pumps, control valves, slave cylinders, glass beading and general reconditioning. Web site: www.l-i-mustang.com

Loyal Ford Mercury Inc 2310 Calumet Dr New Holstein, WI 53061 920-898-4248; FAX: 920-898-9705	cars parts

See full listing in **Section One** under **Ford 1954-up**

Mac's Antique Auto Parts 1051 Lincoln Ave PO Box 238 Lockport, NY 14095-0238 800-777-0948 US and Canada 716-433-1500 local and foreign FAX: 716-433-1172 E-mail: mailmacs@aol.com	literature parts restoration supplies

See full listing in **Section One** under **Ford 1903-1931**

Master Power Brakes 254-1 Rolling Hills Rd Mooresville, NC 28115 704-664-8866; FAX: 704-664-8862	**brake products** **conversion kits**

See full listing in **Section One** under **Chevelle/Camaro**

McDonald Obsolete Parts Company RR 3, Box 94 Rockport, IN 47635 812-359-4965; FAX: 812-359-5555 E-mail: mcdonald@psci.net	**body parts** **chassis parts**

See full listing in **Section One** under **Ford 1954-up**

Mean Mustang Supply Inc 201 D St South Charleston, WV 25303 304-746-0300; FAX: 304-746-0395 E-mail: meanstang@aol.com	**parts**

Mail order and open shop. Tuesday-Friday 10 am to 5:30 pm EST, Saturday 10 am to 2 pm. Restoration parts, OEM Ford parts, high-performance parts for Mustang 1964-1/2-1999 model years. Parts such as: Ford Motorsport, Eibach, Koni, new Ford parts, Powerdyne and Corbeau seats. Web site: http://members.aol.com/meanstang

Melvin's Classic Ford Parts Inc 2526 Panola Rd Lithonia, GA 30058 770-981-2357; FAX: 770-981-6207	**parts**

See full listing in **Section One** under **Ford 1954-up**

Miller Obsolete Parts 1329 Campus Dr Vestal, NY 13850 607-722-5371; FAX: 607-770-9117 E-mail: fordpart@spectra.net	**locator service** **parts**

See full listing in **Section One** under **Ford 1954-up**

Mostly Mustangs Inc 55 Alling St Hamden, CT 06517 203-562-8804; FAX: 203-562-4891	**car dealer** **parts sales** **restoration**

Mail order and open shop. Monday-Friday 10 am to 9 pm, Saturday 10 am to 5 pm. Sales, restoration and service of Mustangs and sixties and later Ford products. Discounted new and used parts. Free Mustang parts catalog available.

Mustang Classics 3814 Walnut St Denver, CO 80205 303-295-3140	**parts** **restoration** **sales** **service**

Mail order and open shop. Monday-Friday 9 am to 6 pm. Specializing in parts, service, sales and restoration for 1965-1973 Mustang.

Mustang Service Center 11610 Vanowen St North Hollywood, CA 91605 818-765-1196; FAX: 818-765-1349 E-mail: fmustang@primenet.com	**parts** **service**

Mail order and open shop. Tuesday-Saturday 8 am to 5 pm. Specializing in NOS Ford and Mustang parts and service. Web site: www.fordmustangparts.com

Mustang Village 8833 Fowler Ave Pensacola, FL 32534 850-477-8056; FAX: 850-484-4244 E-mail: rmcneal@aol.com	**salvage yard**

See full listing in **Section Five** under **Florida**

Mustangs & More
2065 Sperry Ave #C
Ventura, CA 93003
800-356-6573; FAX: 805-642-6468
E-mail: mustmore@aol.com

parts
restoration

Mail order and open shop. Monday-Friday 9 am to 5:30 pm, Saturday 9 am to 1 pm. Specializing in parts and restorations for 1965-1994 Mustangs, 1962-1973 Fairlanes, 1960-1970 Falcons and 1955-1957 Thunderbirds. Offers the highest quality parts available, original Ford, reproductions and used, to suit your budget and needs. 25 years of experience in Ford parts and restorations enable us to help you with most of your restoration projects. Quality, service, same day shipping and extensive Ford knowledge are our marks of excellence. Free catalog.

Mustangs Unlimited
185 Adams St
Manchester, CT 06040
860-647-1965; FAX: 860-649-1260
E-mail: info@mustangsunlimited.com

accessory parts
performance parts
restoration

Mail order and open shop. Monday-Friday 8 am to 10 pm, Saturday 8 am to 5 pm, Sunday 11 am to 5 pm EST. Second location: 5182 Brook Hollow Pkwy, Norcross, GA 30071, PH: 770-446-1965; FAX: 770-446-3055. Over 30,000 items available for 1965-present Mustang, Shelby and 1967-1973 Cougar. Quality parts at competitive prices with toll free ordering. Ford Motorsport distributor, catalogs available: 1965-1973 Mustang and Shelby, $3; 1974-present Mustang, $3; 1967-1973 Cougar, $3; and Motorsport Performance, $5. Web site: www.mustangunlimited.com

National Parts Depot
3101 SW 40th Blvd
Gainesville, FL 32608
800-874-7595 toll-free 24 hours
352-378-2473 local

accessories
restoration parts

See full listing in **Section Two** under **comprehensive parts**

New England Mustang Supply Inc
1830 Barnum Ave
Bridgeport, CT 06610
203-333-7454; FAX: 203-332-0880

accessories
parts

Mail order. Monday-Friday 9 am to 5:30 pm, closed Thursday, call for showroom hours. 1965-1995 Mustang parts and accessories. Also supplies parts and accessories for classic GM, Ford, Mopar cars and trucks, 1960s-present. Sheetmetal, suspension, soft trim, chrome, weatherstripping and more.

Northeast Ford
Box 66, Rt 9
East Sullivan, NH 03445
603-847-9956, 800-562-FORD
FAX: 603-847-9691

parts
restoration

See full listing in **Section One** under **Ford 1954-up**

OEM Paints Inc
PO Box 461736
Escondido, CA 92046-1736
760-747-2100

custom aerosol colors

See full listing in **Section Two** under **paints**

Old Dominion Mustang/Camaro
509 S Washington Hwy, Rt 1
Ashland, VA 23005
804-798-3348; FAX: 804-798-5105

parts

Mail order and open shop. Monday-Friday 9 am to 5 pm, Saturday 9 am to 3 pm. Specializing in Mustang and Camaro parts. Web site: www.oldominion.com

Original Falcon, Comet, Ranchero, Fairlane Interiors
6343 Seaview Ave NW
Seattle, WA 98107-2664
206-781-5230; FAX: 206-781-5046
E-mail: falcons1@ix.netcom.com

interiors
weatherstripping

See full listing in **Section One** under **Ford 1954-up**

The Paddock® Inc
PO Box 30
221 W Main
Knightstown, IN 46148
800-428-4319; FAX: 800-286-4040
E-mail: paddock@indy.net

accessories
parts

Mail order and open shop. Monday-Friday 8 am to 7 pm, Saturday 9 am to 4 pm, Sunday 12 pm to 4 pm. The original supplier of muscle car parts. Specializing in interior, accessories, sheetmetal, suspension, engine, brake parts and more for 1964-1995 Mustang, 1967-1995 Camaro, 1962-1974 Dodge/Plymouth, 1964-1977 Chevelle, 1970-1988 Monte Carlo, 1962-1979 Nova, 1964-1974 GTO, 1958-1976 Impala, 1964-1977 Cutlass, 1967-1995 Firebird, 1955-1957 Chevy and 1963-1987 Chevy/GMC truck. Three convenient locations. Web site: www.paddockparts.com

Pony Enterprises
PO Box L-1007
Langhorne, PA 19047
215-547-2221; FAX: 215-547-7810
E-mail: ponyent@aol.com

fasteners
hardware

Specializing in hardware items (nuts, bolts, screws, rubber bumpers, springs, clips, clamps, plugs, straps, etc) for 1965-1993 Ford Mustangs. Items sold individually packaged in the quantities proper for use or in bulk. Also private label packages for dealers. Wholesale only. Established in 1981. Member of SEMA and MCA.

See our ad on this page

Pony Parts of America
1690 Thomas Paine Pkwy
Centerville, OH 45459
937-435-4543; FAX: 937-435-4548
E-mail: porshfreek@aol.com

floor boards
frame rails

Mail order and open shop. Monday-Friday 7:30 am to 6 pm,

Saturday 9:30 am to 12 pm. Reproduction body parts for Mustangs. Manufacturer of frame rails and floorboards, 1963-1/2-1969. Also manufacturer of replacement body panels for Porsche 914 and 911. Web site: http://members.aol.com/porshfreek/homepage.html

Power Brake Booster Exchange Inc	**brake boosters**
4533 SE Division St	
Portland, OR 97206	
503-238-8882	

See full listing in **Section Two** under **brakes**

Power Brake X-Change Inc	**parts**
336 Lamont Pl	
Pittsburgh, PA 15232	
800-580-5729, 412-441-5729	
FAX: 412-441-9333	

See full listing in **Section Two** under **brakes**

Greg Purdy's Mustang Supply	**parts**
PO Box 784	
Forest Hill, MD 21050	
410-836-5991	

Specializing in NOS and excellent clean used parts for 1969-1973 Mustangs (all body styles). Options and accessories, convertible parts, glass, performance parts, Mach I and Boss 302/351 pieces, body parts and more. Also a limited supply of 1968-1973 Torino and 1972-1973 Montego GT pieces. Always interested in buying NOS parts. Serving the Ford/Mustang hobbyist for 15 years. Buy, sell, trade.

PV Antique & Classic Ford	**parts**
1688 Main St	
Tewksbury, MA 01876	
800-MSTANGS orders only	
978-851-9159; FAX: 978-858-3827	
E-mail: pvford@flash.net	

See full listing in **Section One** under **Ford 1903-1931**

Rapido Group	**accessories**
80093 Dodson Rd	**parts**
Tygh Valley, OR 97063	
541-544-3333	

See full listing in **Section One** under **Merkur**

Reproduction Parts Marketing	**parts**
1920 Alberta Ave	**restoration**
Saskatoon, SK Canada S7K 1R9	**service**
306-652-6668; FAX: 306-652-1123	

See full listing in **Section One** under **Chevrolet**

Rode's Restoration	**parts**
1406 Lohr Rd	**restoration**
Galion, OH 44833	
419-468-5182; FAX: 419-462-1753	
E-mail: rodes@bright.net	

Mail order and open shop. Rebuilders of mid-1960 Ford steering components, ie: pumps, control valve, steer gears, slave cylinder, complete power steering conversion kits. Rebuilt date coded 302/289s, 1965-1967-1968-1969 engines; welding of Mustang and Fairlane convertibles. Solid welded rolling chassis available, call for detailed quote. Rode's also reproduces unique ps brackets and hoses, Dana products.

S-E Autoparts	**NOS parts**
Jarpbo 4	**reproduced parts**
78193 Borlange Sweden	
+46 243 221297	
FAX: +46 243 221298	
E-mail: s-e.autoparts@ebox.tninet.se	

See full listing in **Section One** under **Anglia**

Sam's Vintage Ford Parts	**parts**
5105 Washington	
Denver, CO 80216	
303-295-1709	

See full listing in **Section One** under **Ford 1954-up**

Sanderson Ford	**parts**
Jim Ray	
6300 N 51 Ave	
Glendale, AZ 85301	
888-364-3673, 602-842-8663	
FAX: 602-842-8637	

See full listing in **Section One** under **Ford 1954-up**

Ssnake-Oyl Products Inc	**carpet underlay**
Rt 2, Box 269-6	**firewall insulation**
Hawkins, TX 75765	**seat belt restoration**
800-284-7777; FAX: 903-769-4552	

See full listing in **Section Two** under **interiors & interior parts**

Stainless Steel Brakes Corp	**brake accessories**
11470 Main Rd	**disc conversion kits**
Clarence, NY 14031	**pads/fluid/rotors**
800-448-7722, 716-759-8666	**parking brake kits**
FAX: 716-759-8688, 24 hr	**power steering parts**

See full listing in **Section Two** under **brakes**

Stilwell's Obsolete Car Parts	**body parts**
1617 Wedeking Ave	**interiors**
Evansville, IN 47711	**parts**
812-425-4794	

Mail order only. Specializing in 1965-1973 Mustang and Ford NOS and reproduction parts. Bumpers, patch panels, upholstery, original fenders, quarter panels, hoods, etc in stock. We stock the finest upholstery and carpets on the market. Catalog, $3.

Tabco Inc	**body parts**
11655 Chillicothe Rd	
Chesterland, OH 44026-1994	
216-921-5850; FAX: 216-921-5862	

See full listing in **Section Two** under **sheetmetal**

Tags Backeast	**data plates**
PO Box 581	**trim tags**
Plainville, CT 06062	
860-747-2942	
E-mail: dataplt@snet.net	

See full listing in **Section Two** under **special services**

Tech-Art Publications	**books**
Jason Houston	
Box 753	
Ranchero Mirage, CA 92270	
760-862-1979	

See full listing in **Section Four** under **books & publications**

TMC (Traction Master Co)	**suspensions**
2917 W Olympic Blvd	
Los Angeles, CA 90006	
213-382-1131	
E-mail: tmcgroup@aol.com	

Mail order and open shop. Monday-Saturday 10 am to 3 pm. High-performance suspensions for 1964-1973 Mustangs. Original supplier to Ford and Shelby, in business since 1953. Free catalog. Web site: http://members.aol.com/tmcgroup

TMI Products Inc | classic car
191 Granite St | interiors
Corona, CA 91719
909-272-1996, 800-624-7960
FAX: 909-272-1584
E-mail: tmiprods@aol.com

See full listing in **Section One** under **Volkswagen**

Transgo Performance | shift kits
2621 Merced Ave
El Monte, CA 91733
626-443-4953; FAX: 626-443-1079

See full listing in **Section Two** under **transmissions**

USAopoly Inc | Monopoly® game
565 Westlake St
Encinitas, CA 92024
760-634-5910; FAX: 760-634-5923
E-mail: allison@usaopoly.com

See full listing in **Section Two** under **models & toys**

Vibratech Inc (Fluidampr) | performance parts
11980 Walden Ave
Alden, NY 14004
716-937-3603; FAX: 716-937-4692

See full listing in **Section Two** under **engine parts**

Vintage Ford & Chevrolet Parts of Arizona Inc | parts
So-Cal Speed Shop
3427 E McDowell Rd
Phoenix, AZ 85008-3845
800-732-0076, 602-275-7990
FAX: 602-267-8439
E-mail: vintageparts@sprintmail.com

See full listing in **Section One** under **Ford 1954-up**

Virginia Classic Mustang Inc | accessories
PO Box 487 | parts
Broadway, VA 22815
540-896-2695; FAX: 540-896-9310

Mail order and open shop. Monday-Friday 8 am to 6 pm, Saturday 8 am to 1 pm. Specializing in parts and accessories for 1964-1/2-1973 Mustang. Our 1964-1/2-1973 Mustang parts catalog has over 900 photos and 208 pages. Full line of parts available including interior, wheelcovers, weatherstripping, chrome, sheetmetal, engine compartment, suspension, hardware, decals, stereo, literature and detail items. We have been offering super quality parts, fast service and reasonable prices for over 18 years.

Dan Williams Toploader Transmissions | transmissions
206 E Dogwood Dr
Franklin, NC 28734
828-524-9085 noon-midnight
FAX: 828-524-4848

See full listing in **Section One** under **Ford 1954-up**

1958 Thunderbird Convertible Registry | book
Bill Van Ess
2306 Post Dr NE
Belmont, MI 49306
616-364-1973; FAX: 616-363-2870

Mail order only. A registry of all the remaining 1958 convertibles.

40 pages includes pictures, Square Bird history, production figures and running production changes, frame differences between hardtops and convertibles, current and past owners and history on the remaining cars. If you love Square Birds, you will enjoy this book. $9.75 postpaid.

Donald Antilla | supercharger parts
888 Hulls Hill Rd
Southbury, CT 06488
203-264-8301 evenings
E-mail: dsa0004@ibm.net

See full listing in **Section One** under **Ford 1954-up**

ARASCO | parts
PO Box 24, Dept HA14
Newport, KY 41072
606-441-8363

See full listing in **Section One** under **Ford 1932-1953**

Auto Krafters Inc | parts
PO Box 8
522 S Main St
Broadway, VA 22815
540-896-5910; FAX: 540-896-6412
E-mail: akraft@shentel.net

See full listing in **Section One** under **Ford 1954-up**

Auto Parts Exchange | NORS parts
PO Box 736 | NOS parts
Reading, PA 19603 | rebuilt parts
610-372-2813 | used parts

See full listing in **Section One** under **Lincoln**

Baker's Auto-SRO Inc | parts
196 Providence Pike | service
Putnam, CT 06260
860-928-7614, 800-962-9228
FAX: 860-928-0749

See full listing in **Section One** under **Lincoln**

Bird Nest | parts
745 SE 9th, PO Box 14865
Portland, OR 97214
503-231-6669
800-232-6378, USA & Canada toll-free
FAX: 503-234-2473
E-mail: info@tbirdparts.com

Mail order and open shop. Monday-Friday 8 am to 5 pm. Specializes in 1958-1966 Thunderbird parts. New, NOS, reproduction and used parts. Parts out approximately one car per week. 25,000-square foot indoor warehouse. Free catalog. Web site: www.tbirdparts.com

Bob's Bird House | parts
124 Watkin Ave
Chadds Ford, PA 19317
610-358-3420; FAX: 610-558-0729

Mail order and retail store. Tuesday-Friday 9 am to 5 pm, Saturday 9 am to 12 pm. Thunderbird specialist 1958-1966, cars, parts. Buy, sell, trade. New, used and reproduction parts. Catalog available, $3. Web site: www.cybertowne.com/bobsbirdhouse/

California Continental & T-Bird Connection | consultant
PO Box 2281 | parts
Irwindale, CA 91706 | repairs
818-962-6696 in CA

See full listing in **Section One** under **Lincoln**

California Thunderbirds
Bill Denzel
1507 Arroyo View Dr
Pasadena, CA 91103
626-792-0720; FAX: 626-792-9937
E-mail: teamdenzel@aol.com

parts

Mail order only. New, used and closeout parts plus complete cars. 1955-1957 Ford Thunderbirds.

Dennis Carpenter Ford Reproductions
PO Box 26398
Charlotte, NC 28221
704-786-8139; FAX: 704-786-8180

parts

See full listing in **Section One** under **Ford 1954-up**

Classic Auto
251 SW 5th Ct
Pompano Beach, FL 33060
PH/FAX: 954-786-1687

restoration

See full listing in **Section Two** under **restoration shops**

Classic Auto Supply Company Inc
795 High St
PO Box 850
Coshocton, OH 43812
800-374-0914; FAX: 800-513-5806

Thunderbirds

Mail order and open shop. Monday-Friday 8:30 am to 5 pm. Full line parts supplier, restorer and manufacturer of parts for 1955-1957 Thunderbirds. Free 72 page catalog. Specializing in 1955-1957 Thunderbirds exclusively.

Classic Coachworks
735 Frenchtown Rd
Milford, NJ 08848
908-996-3400; FAX: 908-996-0204

bodywork
painting
restoration

See full listing in **Section Two** under **restoration shops**

Classic Ford Sales
PO Box 60
East Dixfield, ME 04227
207-562-4443; FAX: 207-562-4576
E-mail: classicford@quickconnect.com

salvage yard

See full listing in **Section Five** under **Maine**

Classic Sheetmetal Inc
4010 A Hartley St
Charlotte, NC 28206
800-776-4040, 704-596-5186
FAX: 704-596-3895

body panels
sheetmetal

Mail order and open shop. Monday-Friday 9 am to 5 pm. Manufacturing sheetmetal body panels for 1955-1971 Thunderbirds. Free catalog. Web site: www.classicsheetmetal.com

Classics 'n More Inc
1001 Ranck Mill Rd
Lancaster, PA 17602
717-392-0599; FAX 717-392-2371

repairs
restoration

See full listing in **Section Two** under **restoration shops**

Classique Cars Unlimited
7005 Turkey Bayou Rd
PO Box 249
Lakeshore, MS 39558
800-543-8691, USA
228-467-9633; FAX: 228-467-9207
E-mail: parts@datasync.com

appraisals
parts
repairs
restorations

See full listing in **Section One** under **Lincoln**

Clean Sweep-Vacuum Windshield Wiper Motor Rebuilding
760 Knight Hill Rd
Zillah, WA 98953
509-865-2481; FAX: 509-865-2189
E-mail: dkjaquith@prodigy.net

motors
repairs
wiper parts

See full listing in **Section Two** under **windshield wipers**

Concours Parts & Accessories
3493 Arrowhead Dr
Carson City, NV 89706
800-722-0009; FAX: 800-725-8644

parts

Mail order and open shop. Monday-Friday 8 am to 5:30 pm, Saturday 8:30 am to 12:30 pm. Parts for 1955-1966 Thunderbirds, 1949-1959 big Ford cars, 1960-1972 Galaxies and 1948-1966 F-1/100 trucks. Web site: concoursparts.com

Bob Cook Classic Auto Parts Inc
2055 Van Cleave Rd, PO Box 600
Murray, KY 42071-0600
502-753-4000, 800-486-1137
FAX: 502-753-4600

new parts
NOS parts
reproduced parts

See full listing in **Section One** under **Ford 1954-up**

Custom Autocraft Inc
2 Flowerfield, Ste 6
St James, NY 11780
PH/FAX: 516-862-7469

restoration
sheetmetal parts

Mail order and open shop. Monday-Friday 9 am to 5:30 pm. Specializing in 1955-1957 Thunderbirds. Concours quality reproduction sheetmetal (18 ga). Braces, rockers, lower rear quarters, doglegs, floor sections (indentations pressed as original), trunk floors, much more. Buy direct from manufacturer. Doing business since 1974. Satisfaction guaranteed. Send SASE for free brochure. See us at Carlisle, PA, Spring Q83, All Ford National K43, Fall Q48-48A.

Custom Autosound Mfg
808 W Vermont Ave
Anaheim, CA 92805
800-888-8637; FAX: 714-533-0361
E-mail: info@custom-autosound.com

CD players
custom radios
speaker upgrades

See full listing in **Section One** under **Chevrolet**

Early Ford Parts
2948 Summer Ave
Memphis, TN 38112
901-323-2179; FAX: 901-323-2195

literature
parts

See full listing in **Section One** under **Ford 1932-1953**

Daniel A Evans
2850 John St
Easton, PA 18045
610-258-9542 after 5:30 pm
FAX: 610-252-0370
E-mail: evansd@lafayette.edu

literature
parts

See full listing in **Section One** under **Ford 1954-up**

Randy Goodling
2046 Mill Rd
Elizabethtown, PA 17022-9401
717-367-6700

parts
parts locating

See full listing in **Section One** under **Mercury**

Hamel's Automotive Inc
RR 2 Box 61
Wingdale, NY 12594
914-832-9454
E-mail: startnagan@aol.com

restorations

See full listing in **Section Two** under **restoration shops**

Hollywood Classic Motorcars Inc   cars
363 Ansin Blvd   parts
Hallandale, FL 33009
800-235-2444, 954-454-4641
FAX: 954-457-3801
E-mail: hcm@tbird.net

Mail order and open shop. Monday-Friday 9 am to 5 pm.
Specializing in Thunderbird cars, parts, and restorations for
1955-1966. Convertible parts such as frames, package trays,
limit switches, doors, fenders, hoods, etc. Also sells Thunderbird
cars. Web site: http://tbird.net

Bill Horton   vacuum motors
5804 Jones Valley Dr
Huntsville, AL 35802
256-881-6894

See full listing in **Section One** under **Mercury**

Jim's T-Bird Parts & Service   parts
710 Barney Ave   restoration
Winston-Salem, NC 27107   service
PH/FAX: 336-784-9363
E-mail: tbirdjims@aol.com

Mail order and open shop. Monday-Friday 8 am to 5:30 pm. One
stop Thunderbird parts and service company. Specializing in
parts, service and restoration for 1955-1979 Thunderbirds.

Joblot Automotive Inc   parts
Ford Parts Specialists
98-11 211th St
Queens Village, NY 11429
718-468-8585; FAX: 718-468-8686

See full listing in **Section One** under **Ford 1932-1953**

Kenroy Ford Parts   NOS parts
2 Folwell Ln
Mullica Hill, NJ 08062
609-478-2527
E-mail: duffieldm@aol.com

See full listing in **Section One** under **Ford 1954-up**

Dale King Obsolete Parts   parts
PO Box 1099
211 Hilltop Dr
Liberty, KY 42539
606-787-5031; FAX: 606-787-2130

See full listing in **Section One** under **Ford 1954-up**

Larry's Thunderbird and Mustang   parts
Parts Inc
511 S Raymond Ave
Fullerton, CA 92831
800-854-0393 orders
714-871-6432; FAX: 714-871-1883

Mail order and open shop. Monday-Friday 8 am to 6 pm,
Saturday 9 am to 1 pm. Specializing in restoration parts and
accessories for 1965-1973 Mustangs and 1955-1966
Thunderbirds. In business over 30 years supplying Mustang and
Thunderbird enthusiasts with extensive product lines of restoration parts. Offer excellent pricing and availability, with most
orders shipped out the same day.

See our ad on this page

Lincoln Parts International   parts
707 E 4th St, Bldg G
Perris, CA 92570
800-382-1656, 909-657-5588
FAX: 909-657-4758
E-mail: lincprts@pe.net

See full listing in **Section One** under **Lincoln**

Ed Liukkonen	accessories
37 Cook Rd	parts
Templeton, MA 01468	
978-939-8126	

See full listing in **Section One** under **Ford 1954-up**

Long Island Mustang Restoration	rebuilding services
Parts	repro parts
168 Silverleaf Ln	
Islandia, NY 11722	
516-232-2388; FAX: 516-272-5201	
E-mail: tom@l-i-mustang.com	

See full listing in **Section One** under **Mustang**

Loyal Ford Mercury Inc	cars
2310 Calumet Dr	parts
New Holstein, WI 53061	
920-898-4248; FAX: 920-898-9705	

See full listing in **Section One** under **Ford 1954-up**

Mac's Antique Auto Parts	literature
1051 Lincoln Ave	parts
PO Box 238	restoration supplies
Lockport, NY 14095-0238	
800-777-0948 US and Canada	
716-433-1500 local and foreign	
FAX: 716-433-1172	
E-mail: mailmacs@aol.com	

See full listing in **Section One** under **Ford 1903-1931**

Bob Marriott	sheetmetal parts
497 Delaware Ave	shop manuals
Delmar, NY 12054	

Mail order only. I am a Thunderbird collector (who's gotten carried away with too many cars!). Having found sources for many of the parts I need, I'm making these available to other collectors. Specializing in sheetmetal repair panels and shop manual reprints for 1961-1966 Thunderbirds. Send SASE with year for free list.

McDonald Obsolete Parts Company	body parts
RR 3, Box 94	chassis parts
Rockport, IN 47635	
812-359-4965; FAX: 812-359-5555	
E-mail: mcdonald@psci.net	

See full listing in **Section One** under **Ford 1954-up**

Mean Mustang Supply Inc	parts
201 D St	
South Charleston, WV 25303	
304-746-0300; FAX: 304-746-0395	
E-mail: meanstang@aol.com	

See full listing in **Section One** under **Mustang**

Miller Obsolete Parts	locator service
1329 Campus Dr	parts
Vestal, NY 13850	
607-722-5371; FAX: 607-770-9117	
E-mail: fordpart@spectra.net	

See full listing in **Section One** under **Ford 1954-up**

Mustang Service Center	parts
11610 Vanowen St	service
North Hollywood, CA 91605	
818-765-1196; FAX: 818-765-1349	
E-mail: fmustang@primenet.com	

See full listing in **Section One** under **Mustang**

Mustangs & More	parts
2065 Sperry Ave #C	restoration
Ventura, CA 93003	
800-356-6573; FAX: 805-642-6468	
E-mail: mustmore@aol.com	

See full listing in **Section One** under **Mustang**

National Parts Depot	accessories
3101 SW 40th Blvd	restoration parts
Gainesville, FL 32608	
800-874-7595 toll-free 24 hours	
352-378-2473 local	

See full listing in **Section Two** under **comprehensive parts**

Northeast Ford	parts
Box 66, Rt 9	restoration
East Sullivan, NH 03445	
603-847-9956, 800-562-FORD	
FAX: 603-847-9691	

See full listing in **Section One** under **Ford 1954-up**

Obsolete Ford Parts Inc	parts
8701 S I-35	
Oklahoma City, OK 73149	
405-631-3933; FAX: 405-634-6815	

See full listing in **Section One** under **Ford 1954-up**

Original Falcon, Comet, Ranchero,	interiors
Fairlane Interiors	weatherstripping
6343 Seaview Ave NW	
Seattle, WA 98107-2664	
206-781-5230; FAX: 206-781-5046	
E-mail: falcons1@ix.netcom.com	

See full listing in **Section One** under **Ford 1954-up**

Power Brake Booster Exchange Inc	brake boosters
4533 SE Division St	
Portland, OR 97206	
503-238-8882	

See full listing in **Section Two** under **brakes**

Power Brake X-Change Inc	parts
336 Lamont Pl	
Pittsburgh, PA 15232	
800-580-5729, 412-441-5729	
FAX: 412-441-9333	

See full listing in **Section Two** under **brakes**

Prestige Thunderbird Inc	appraisals
10215 Greenleaf Ave	radios
Santa Fe Springs, CA 90670	repairs
800-423-4751, 562-944-6237	restorations
FAX: 562-941-8677	tires
E-mail: tbirds@prestigethunderbird.com	

Mail order and open shop. Monday-Friday 8 am to 5:30 pm, Saturday 8:30 am to 4 pm. Specializes in 1955-1957 Thunderbirds. Offers parts, radios, air conditioners, tires and appraisals, along with restorations and car sales. Parts catalog, $2. Web site: prestigethunderbird.com

William H Randel	appraisals
PO Box 173	car locators
Hatboro, PA 19040	
215-675-8969; FAX: 215-441-0960	
E-mail: tbrdnut@bellatlantic.net	

Mail order and open shop. Monday-Tuesday and Friday-Sunday 9 am to 9 pm. Specializing in locating and appraising for 1955-1957 classic Thunderbird automobiles.

Rapido Group 80093 Dodson Rd Tygh Valley, OR 97063 541-544-3333	accessories parts

See full listing in **Section One** under **Merkur**

Regal Roadsters Ltd 301 W Beltline Hwy Madison, WI 53713 PH/FAX: 608-273-4141	replicars restoration

Mail order and open shop. Monday-Friday 8 am to 5 pm. Specializing in the manufacture of the Regal T-Bird and the restoration of domestic and foreign collectibles. The Regal T-Bird is a full size, authentic, fiberglass bodied reproduction of the famed 1955 and 1956 Ford Thunderbird. We manufacture and sell a variety of kits for the hobbyist, ranging from exact reproductions to personalized street rod versions. Also handcraft turnkey Regal T-Birds to your exacting specifications and deliver worldwide.

Frank Riley Automotive Art PO Box 95 Hawthorne, NJ 07506 800-848-9459	automotive prints

See full listing in **Section Two** under **artwork**

Sanderson Ford Jim Ray 6300 N 51 Ave Glendale, AZ 85301 888-364-3673, 602-842-8663 FAX: 602-842-8637	parts

See full listing in **Section One** under **Ford 1954-up**

Sixties Ford Parts 639 Glanker St Memphis, TN 38112 PH/FAX: 901-323-2195, recorder	books new parts shop manuals

See full listing in **Section One** under **Ford 1954-up**

Stilwell's Obsolete Car Parts 1617 Wedeking Ave Evansville, IN 47711 812-425-4794	body parts interiors parts

See full listing in **Section One** under **Mustang**

Sunyaks PO Box 498 Bound Brook, NJ 08805 908-356-0600	NOS parts upholstery used parts

Mail order and open shop. Monday-Saturday 10 am to 10 pm. Specializing in NOS and restored hard to get parts for 1955-1957 Thunderbirds. Over 1,800 items in our catalog. Specializing in convertible top frames, hardtops, original power steering units, power brakes, power windows, and power seat assemblies, dual quads and NASCAR parts along with upholstery and continental kits. Appraisals, and technical help available.

T-Bird Sanctuary 9998 SW Avery Tualatin, OR 97062 503-692-9848; FAX: 503-692-9849	parts

Mail order and open shop. Monday-Friday 8 am to 5:30 pm, Saturday by appointment, closed Sunday, PST. Comprehensive source for NOS, used and reproduction parts for 1958-1979 Thunderbirds. Your T-Bird restoration specialist since 1966. Sheetmetal cut to order. Our parts cars come from the salt-free Northwest and are remarkably well preserved in our mild cli-

mate. Same day shipping on most orders. Call in your order on our toll-free parts hotline: 800-275-2661.

See our ads on pages 110 and 627

T-Bird Specialists	locating service
3156 E President St	parts
Tucson, AZ 85714	parts cars
602-889-8634	repairs

Mail order and open shop. Monday-Saturday. One-man shop with knowledge to repair most any problem on 1955-1976 T-Birds. Have about 100 parts cars, 1958-1976. Also provide locating service for any make and model. Complete service, repairs and parts for 1955-1976 Thunderbirds.

T-Birds By Nick	parts
14649 Lanark St, Unit B	repair
Panorama City, CA 91402	
800-669-1961; FAX: 818-780-8493	

Mail order parts and repair shop. Monday-Friday 8 am to 5 pm. 16 years' repair experience on Ford Thunderbirds, 1958-1966. Huge inventory of new and used parts. Orders shipped worldwide.

Tags Backeast	data plates
PO Box 581	trim tags
Plainville, CT 06062	
860-747-2942	
E-mail: dataplt@snet.net	

See full listing in **Section Two** under **special services**

Tech-Art Publications	books
Jason Houston	
Box 753	
Ranchero Mirage, CA 92270	
760-862-1979	

See full listing in **Section Four** under **books & publications**

Tee-Bird Products Inc	parts
Box 728	
Exton, PA 19341	
610-363-1725; FAX: 610-363-2691	

See full listing in **Section One** under **Ford 1954-up**

Thunderbird Center	parts
23610 John R St	
Hazel Park, MI 48030	
248-548-1721; FAX: 248-548-5531	
E-mail: tbirdcenter@sprintmail.com	

Monday-Friday 9 am to 5 pm. 1955-1956-1957 T-Bird parts sales, NOS, used, new repro. Everything you may need. Web site: tbirdcenter.com

Thunderbird, Falcon & Fairlane Connections	new repros
728 E Dunlap	parts
Phoenix, AZ 85020	used repros
602-997-9285; FAX: 602-997-0624	
E-mail: tbirdconn@aol.com	

Mail order and open shop. Monday-Friday 8:30 am to 5 pm, Saturday 8:30 am to 12:30 pm. Offers the finest in new, used and reproduced items for your 1958-1972 T-Birds, 1960-1970 Falcons and Comets and 1962-1969 Fairlanes. Ford authorized dealer. Offer the finest in quality and service. Write for free updated and illustrated Thunderbird catalog. Order number: 800-TTT-BIRD. In business since 1972. Falcon and Fairlane catalogs also available, $3 each.

Thunderbird Headquarters	accessories
1080 Detroit Ave	literature
Concord, CA 94518	parts
800-227-2174, US	upholstery
FAX: 925-689-1771, 800-964-1957	
E-mail: tbirdhq@tbirdhq.com	

Mail order and counter sales. Monday-Friday 8 am to 5 pm, Saturday 8 am to 11:30 am. Specializing in new and used parts including rubber weatherstrip, convertible tops, literature, a complete line of upholstery, carpets and accessories for 1955-1966 Thunderbirds. Free catalog available on request. Web site: www.tbirdhq.com

Thunderbird Information eXchange	newsletter
8421 E Cortez St	
Scottsdale, AZ 85260	
602-948-3996	

Specializing in the exchange of information about how to enjoy and personalize 1989 and later Thunderbird and Cougar automobiles. The TIX package contains a newsletter with technical tips, want ads, event listings, production figures and model comparisons. The TIX package costs $10 (checks payable to Paul Cornell please).

Thunderbird Parts	parts
1051 Lincoln Ave	
Lockport, NY 14094	
800-289-2473, 716-741-2866	
FAX: 716-741-2868	
E-mail: mailmacs@aol.com	

Phone hours: Monday-Friday 8 am to 11 pm, Saturday 8 am to 5 pm. Parts for big and small Birds. 1955-1957 free catalog with 176 pages; 1958-1966 free catalog with 232 pages. Web site: www.macsautoparts.com

Thunderbirds East	parts
Andy Lovelace	restoration
140 Wilmington W Chester Pike	
Chadds Ford, PA 19317	
610-358-1021; FAX: 610-558-9615	

Mail order and open shop. Monday-Friday 8 am to 5 pm, Saturday 8 am to 12 noon. 1955-1956-1957 Thunderbirds and 1967-1980s Thunderbird parts, new and used. Restorations, partial or complete.

Transgo Performance	shift kits
2621 Merced Ave	
El Monte, CA 91733	
626-443-4953; FAX: 626-443-1079	

See full listing in **Section Two** under **transmissions**

Wilson's Classic Auto	restoration
417 Kaufman Rt 150	
PO Box 58	
Congerville, IL 61729	
309-448-2408; FAX: 309-448-2409	

See full listing in **Section Two** under **restoration shops**

Pat Wilson's Thunderbird Parts	parts
235 River Rd	
New Milford, NJ 07646-1721	
888-262-1153; FAX: 201-634-1916	

Mail order and open shop. Monday-Friday 9 am to 8 pm, Saturday 9 am to 5 pm. Specializing in selling, repairing and rebuilding new and used Thunderbird parts for 1958-1966. Have rebuilt seat and window motors. Buy, sell, trade parts and cars and part out many cars. Member of ITC, VTCI and North Jersey Thunderbird Club. Accept Visa, MasterCard, UPS COD. Call or fax for free 1999 catalog.

FRANKLIN

Air Cooled Motors
2081 Madelaine Ct
Los Altos, CA 94024
PH/FAX: 650-967-2908
E-mail: zmrmn@macconnect.com

car dealers
information
restoration

Specializing in the preservation and restoration of Franklin, Zimmerman automobiles.

Auto World Car Museum by Backer
Business 54 N
PO Box 135
Fulton, MO 65251
573-642-2080, 573-642-5344
FAX: 573-642-0685
E-mail: webacker@ktis.net

museum

See full listing in **Section Six** under **Missouri**

JA Cooley Museum
4233 Park Blvd
San Diego, CA 92103
619-296-3112

museum

See full listing in **Section Six** under **California**

Franklin Museum
3420 N Vine Ave
Tucson, AZ 85719
520-326-8038; FAX: 520-326-6100
E-mail: hhff2@aol.com

museum

See full listing in **Section Six** under **Arizona**

Hasslen Co
9581 Jeske Ave NW
Annandale, MN 55302
320-274-5576

engine parts

New Franklin gasket sets, engine and trim parts. Series 13 and Series 14 through 16 and Olympic hubcaps. Series 10 reserve and supply fittings. Series 5 through 10 mufflers. Series 16 and 18 door handles. Timing chains for most Franklins, porcelain signs and more. Manufactures Franklin parts. Write your needs.

Hildene
PO Box 377
Historic Rt 7A
Manchester, VT 05254
802-362-1788; FAX: 802-362-1564
E-mail: info@hildene.org

museum

See full listing in **Section Six** under **Vermont**

Northeast Classic Car Museum
NYS Rt 23
24 Rexford St
Norwich, NY 13815
607-334-AUTO (334-2886)
FAX: 607-336-6745
E-mail: neccm@ascent.net

museum

See full listing in **Section Six** under **New York**

Odyssey Restorations Inc
8080 Central Ave NE
Spring Lake Park, MN 55432
612-786-1518; FAX: 612-786-1524

parts
restoration

See full listing in **Section Two** under **restoration shops**

Viking Worldwise Inc
190 Doe Run Rd
Manheim, PA 17545
800-842-9198; FAX: 717-664-5556
E-mail: gkurien@success.net

leather jackets

See full listing in **Section Two** under **apparel**

A & M SoffSeal Inc
104 May Dr
Harrison, OH 45030
800-426-0902
513-367-0028 service/info
FAX: 513-367-5506
E-mail: soffseal@soffseal.com

rubber parts
weatherstripping

See full listing in **Section Two** under **rubber parts**

American Classic Truck Parts
PO Box 409
Aubrey, TX 76227
940-365-9786; FAX: 940-365-3419
E-mail: americanclassic@airmail.net

parts

See full listing in **Section One** under **Chevrolet**

Antique Radio Doctor
Barry Dalton
196 Kilborn Dr
Grants Pass, OR 97526
541-474-2524 evenings

radio repairs

See full listing in **Section Two** under **radios**

B & T Truck Parts
906 E Main St
PO Box 799
Siloam Springs, AR 72761
501-524-5959; FAX: 501-524-5559

pickup parts

See full listing in **Section Two** under **trucks & tractors**

Brothers Truck Parts
4375 Prado Rd #105
Corona, CA 91720
800-977-2767; FAX: 909-808-9788
E-mail: sales@brotherstrucks.com

accessories
parts

See full listing in **Section Two** under **trucks & tractors**

Jim Carter's Antique Truck Parts
1508 E Alton
Independence, MO 64055
800-336-1913; FAX: 800-262-3749
E-mail:
jimcartertruck.parts@worldnet.att.net

truck parts

See full listing in **Section One** under **Chevrolet**

Chevy Duty Pickup Parts
4319 NW Gateway
Kansas City, MO 64150
816-741-8029; FAX: 816-741-5255
E-mail: trucks@sky.net

pickup parts

See full listing in **Section One** under **Chevrolet**

Cheyenne Pickup Parts
Box 959
Noble, OK 73068
405-872-3399; FAX: 405-872-0385

	body panels
	bumpers
	carpet
	weatherstripping

See full listing in **Section Two** under **trucks & tractors**

Classic Industries Inc
Chevy/GMC Truck Parts and
Accessories Catalog
17832 Gothard St
Huntington Beach, CA 92647
800-854-1280 parts/info
FAX: 800-300-3081
E-mail: info@classicindustries.com

	accessories
	parts

See full listing in **Section One** under **Chevrolet**

Dash Specialists
1910 Redbud Ln
Medford, OR 97504
541-776-0040

	interiors

See full listing in **Section One** under **Cadillac/LaSalle**

The Filling Station
990 S Second St
Lebanon, OR 97355-3227
800-841-6622 orders
541-258-2114; FAX: 541-258-6968
E-mail: fssales@fillingstation.co

	literature
	parts

See full listing in **Section One** under **Chevrolet**

Gilbert's Early Chevy Pickup Parts
PO Box 1316
470 Rd 1 NW
Chino Valley, AZ 86323
PH/FAX: 520-636-5337
E-mail: gilb@goodnet.com

	pickup parts

See full listing in **Section Two** under **trucks & tractors**

GMC Solutions
Robert English
PO Box 675
Franklin, MA 02038-0675
508-520-3900; FAX: 508-520-7861
E-mail: oldcarkook@aol.com

	literature
	parts

Mail order and open shop. Monday-Friday 9 am to 5 pm. GMC truck parts, NOS, NORS, used, literature, factory training films and materials for pre-1955 GMC light and medium duty. GMC only. 1947-1955 GMC Technical Advisor, National Chevy/GMC Truck Association. Licensed copyright for General Motors. Ship via UPS daily, worldwide.

Golden State Pickup Parts
4245 Baseline Ave
Santa Ynez, CA 93460
800-235-5717, 805-686-2020
FAX: 805-686-2040
E-mail: gspp@gspp.com

	truck parts

See full listing in **Section One** under **Chevrolet**

Hagerty Classic Insurance
PO Box 87
Traverse City, MI 49685
800-922-4050; FAX: 616-941-8227

	insurance

See full listing in **Section Two** under **insurance**

Hamel's Automotive Inc
RR 2 Box 61
Wingdale, NY 12594
914-832-9454
E-mail: startnagan@aol.com

	restorations

See full listing in **Section Two** under **restoration shops**

Impala Bob's Inc
4753 E Falcon Dr
Dept HVAA14
Mesa, AZ 85215
800-IMPALAS orders
480-924-4800 retail store
480-981-1600 office
FAX: 800-716-6237, 480-981-1675
E-mail: info@impalas.com

	restoration parts

See full listing in **Section One** under **Chevrolet**

Jahns Quality Pistons
1360 N Jefferson St
Anaheim, CA 92807
714-579-3795, 800-225-0277
FAX: 714-524-6607

	piston rings
	pistons

See full listing in **Section Two** under **engine parts**

Majestic Truck Parts
17726 Dickerson
Dallas, TX 75252
972-248-6245; FAX: 972-380-8913
E-mail: majestictrk@juno.com

	parts

See full listing in **Section One** under **Chevrolet**

Riverhill Truck Co
458 Wilde Rd
Jackson, TN 38301
901-988-5079

	parts

See full listing in **Section One** under **Chevrolet**

Roberts Motor Parts
17 Prospect St
West Newbury, MA 01985
978-363-5407; FAX: 978-363-2026
E-mail: sales@robertsmotorparts.com

	parts

See full listing in **Section One** under **Dodge**

Scotts Super Trucks
1972 Hwy 592 W
Penhold, AB Canada T0M 1R0
403-886-5572; FAX: 403-886-5577

	parts

See full listing in **Section One** under **Chevrolet**

Stainless Steel Brakes Corp
11470 Main Rd
Clarence, NY 14031
800-448-7722, 716-759-8666
FAX: 716-759-8688, 24 hr

	brake accessories
	disc conversion kits
	pads/fluid/rotors
	parking brake kits
	power steering parts

See full listing in **Section Two** under **brakes**

Tags Backeast
PO Box 581
Plainville, CT 06062
860-747-2942
E-mail: dataplt@snet.net

	data plates
	trim tags

See full listing in **Section Two** under **special services**

Tom's Classic Parts
5207 Sundew Terr
Tobyhanna, PA 18466
800-832-4073

	parts

See full listing in **Section One** under **Chevrolet**

Transgo Performance
2621 Merced Ave
El Monte, CA 91733
626-443-4953; FAX: 626-443-1079

	shift kits

See full listing in **Section Two** under **transmissions**

Trim Parts Inc | trim items
5161 Wolfpen Pleasant Hill
Milford, OH 45150
513-831-1472; FAX: 513-248-3402
E-mail: sales@trimparts.com

See full listing in **Section One** under **Chevrolet**

The Truck Shop | parts
PO Box 5035
104 W Marion Ave
Nashville, GA 31639
800-245-0556 orders
info: 912-686-3833, 912-686-3396
FAX: 912-686-3531

See full listing in **Section One** under **Chevrolet**

Ultimate Spray-On Truck Bedliner | bedliners
115 Garfield St
Sumas, WA 98295
800-989-9869; FAX: 604-864-0207
E-mail: info@ultimatelinings.com

See full listing in **Section Two** under **trucks & tractors**

Ultra Wheel Co | custom wheels
6300 Valley View Ave
Buena Park, CA 90620
714-994-1444; FAX: 714-994-0723

See full listing in **Section Two** under **wheels & wheelcovers**

George Zaha | FM conversions radio speakers
4900 Green Hollow Dr
Orion, MI 48359
248-393-1732 evenings

See full listing in **Section Two** under **radios**

Gordon Keeble

The Gordon Keeble Car Center | repairs restoration service
Westminster Rd
Brackley
Northants NN13 7EB
United Kingdom
01280-702311; FAX: 01280-702853

Specializing in Gordon Keeble cars 1964/1966 (only 100 were produced). Specialist in repairs, service and restoration. (Fiberglass body) Bertone styling, Corvette power.

Antique Motorcycle Restoration | restorations
14611 N Nebraska Ave
Tampa, FL 33613
813-979-9762; FAX: 813-979-9475

Restorations for Harley-Davidson 1936 Knuckleheads.

B & B Cylinder Head Inc | cylinder heads
320 Washington St
West Warwick, RI 02893
401-828-4900

See full listing in **Section Two** under **engine parts**

Bentley Publishers | books manuals
1734 Massachusetts Ave
Cambridge, MA 02138-1804
800-423-4595; FAX: 617-876-9235
E-mail: sales@rb.com

See full listing in **Section Four** under **books & publications**

Boyds Hot Rods & Collectable Cars | car dealer
8400 Cerritos Ave
Stanton, CA 90680
714-220-9870; FAX: 714-220-9877
E-mail: sales@boydshotrods.com

See full listing in **Section One** under **Chevrolet**

Francois Bruere | artwork
8 Avenue Olivier Heuze
LeMans 72000 France
(33) 02-4377-1877
FAX: (33) 02-4324-2038

See full listing in **Section Two** under **artwork**

California Jaguar | auto transport
29109 Triunfo Dr
Agoura, CA 91301
800-335-2482; FAX: 818-707-3062

See full listing in **Section Two** under **transport**

Charleston Custom Cycle | parts
211 Washington St
Charleston, IL 61920
217-345-2577

Mail order and open shop. Monday-Friday 10 am to 6 pm, Saturday 10 am to 3 pm. Specializing in NOS parts for Harley-Davidson motorcycles, snowmobiles, golf carts, 1948-1990.

Dale's Harley-Davidson of Mt Vernon | motorcycle dealership
12th St & Veterans Memorial Dr
Mt Vernon, IL 62864
618-244-4116; FAX: 618-244-5470
E-mail: daleshd@dales-hd.com

Mail order and open shop. Monday, Tuesday, Thursday, Friday 8 am to 5 pm, Saturday 8 am to 4 pm. Harley-Davidson dealership features Wheels Through Time vintage motorcycle museum, over 150 antique bikes on display. We ship UPS. Six time winner of *Dealernews* magazine's Top 100 program. Let us put you on the motorcycle of your dreams. Web site: www.dales-hd.com

Geeson Bros Motorcycle Museum & Workshop | museum
2-6 Water Ln
South Witham
Grantham Lincs NG33 5 PH
England
01572 767280, 01572 768195

See full listing in **Section Six** under **England**

H D Garage | artwork literature motorcycles
Barry Brown
Comp 8 Bedford Mills RR #2
Westport, ON Canada K0G 1X0
613-273-5036

See full listing in **Section Two** under **motorcycles**

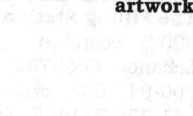

**Indian Joe Martin's Antique
Motorcycle Parts** | parts
PO Box 3156
Chattanooga, TN 37404
PH/FAX: 423-698-1787
E-mail: indianjo@bellsouth.net

See full listing in **Section Two** under **motorcycles**

JM Appraisal Co Inc | appraisals
1439 S Powerline Rd
Pompano Beach, FL 33069
954-969-0245; FAX: 954-969-0239
E-mail: jmarco1482@aol.com

See full listing in **Section Two** under **appraisals**

Kick-Start Motorcycle Parts Inc | parts
PO Box 9347
Wyoming, MI 49509
616-245-8991

Mail order only. Specializing in rebuilding, replacement and restoration parts for Harley-Davidson flathead and Knucklehead machines, 1929-1973. 272-page catalog, $5.

Luback & Co | parts
456 W 14th St 2B
Chicago Heights, IL 60411
708-481-9685; FAX: 708-481-5837
E-mail: lubackco@aol.com

Open Monday-Saturday 11 am to 4 pm. 1950-1975 Harley-Davidson OEM new genuine parts, accessories and tools.

Mid-America Auction Services | auctions
2277 W Hwy 36, Ste 214
St Paul, MN 55113
612-633-9655; FAX: 612-633-3212
E-mail: midauction@aol.com

See full listing in **Section Two** under **auctions & events**

Sammy Miller Motorcycle Museum | museum
Bashley Cross Rd
New Milton
Hampshire BH25 5SZ England
01425 620777; FAX: 01425 619696

See full listing in **Section Six** under **England**

Miracle of America Museum | museum
58176 Hwy 93
Polson, MT 59860
406-883-6804
E-mail: museum@cyberport.net

See full listing in **Section Six** under **Montana**

Moto Italia | parts
1060 Petaluma Blvd N
Petaluma, CA 94952
PH/FAX: 707-763-1982

Mail order and open shop. Monday-Friday 8 am to 6 pm, Saturday 9 am to 2 pm. Specializing in parts for Harley-Davidson motorcycles made in Italy from 1961-1978. Model Sprints and two-strokes from 50cc to 250cc. Web site: www.aa.net/~garage/motoital.html

Motorcycle Hall of Fame Museum | museum
13515 Yarmouth Dr
Pickerington, OH 43147
614-882-2782 info
614-856-1900 office
FAX: 614-856-1920
E-mail: afitch@ama-cycle.org

See full listing in **Section Six** under **Ohio**

Orpheograff | prints
BP33
72201 La Fleche Cedex France
(33) 243452629
FAX: (33) 243452512

See full listing in **Section Two** under **artwork**

Ottorich | restoration
619 Hammond St
Chestnut Hill, MA 02467
617-738-5488
E-mail: rdmfm@mediaone.net

See full listing in **Section One** under **Mercedes-Benz**

Guy R Palermo Auto Body | bodywork
241 Church Rd (rear) | custom paint
Wexford, PA 15090 | restoration
724-935-3790; FAX: 724-935-9121

See full listing in **Section Two** under **motorcycles**

The Ramsgate Motor Museum | museum
Westcliff Hall
Ramsgate, Kent England
01843 581948

See full listing in **Section Six** under **England**

TK Performance Inc | engine building
1508 N Harlan Ave | machine work
Evansville, IN 47711 | restoration
812-422-6820; FAX: 812-422-5282

Mail order and open shop. Monday-Friday 8 am to 5 pm, Saturday 9 am to 1 pm. Complete engine and chassis component building for Harley-Davidsons, all years, makes and models. Ground-up restorations, custom fabricating and machining of parts, complete fabrication of drag bikes and custom show pieces.

USAopoly Inc | Monopoly® game
565 Westlake St
Encinitas, CA 92024
760-634-5910; FAX: 760-634-5923
E-mail: allison@usaopoly.com

See full listing in **Section Two** under **models & toys**

Visby Bilmuseum | museum
Skogsholm
S-62190 Visby Sweden
0498-278161; FAX: 0498-203390

See full listing in **Section Six** under **Sweden**

J Wood & Co Auctioneers | auctions
RR 1 Box 316
Stockton Springs, ME 04981
207-567-4250; FAX: 207-567-4252
E-mail: jwoodandco@mindspring.com

See full listing in **Section Two** under **auctions & events**

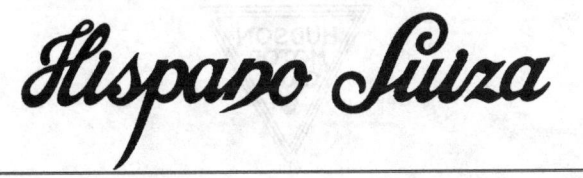

Blackhawk Collection | acquisitions
1092 Eagles Nest Pl | sales
Danville, CA 94506-3600
925-736-3444; FAX: 925-736-4375
E-mail: info@blackhawkcollection.com

See full listing in **Section One** under **Duesenberg**

600 Headquarters

	advice parts service

Miles Chappell
PO Box 1262
Felton, CA 95018
PH/FAX: 408-336-4600
E-mail: z600guru@ix.netcom.com

Mail order and weekend appointments only. Specializing in 1970-1972 Honda 600 sedan and coupe. New and used parts, engine rebuilding, reproduction parts, hydraulics specialist, free advice since 1981. Send $3 for latest catalog and parts list. No COD or credit cards accepted. Web site: www2.netcom.com/~z600guru/small.html

CSi

	parts

1100 S Raymond Ave, Suite H
Fullerton, CA 92831
714-879-7955; FAX: 714-879-7310
E-mail: csila@compuserve.com

See full listing in **Section One** under **BMW**

Sammy Miller Motorcycle Museum

	museum

Bashley Cross Rd
New Milton
Hampshire BH25 5SZ England
01425 620777; FAX: 01425 619696

See full listing in **Section Six** under **England**

Motorcycle Hall of Fame Museum

	museum

13515 Yarmouth Dr
Pickerington, OH 43147
614-882-2782 info
614-856-1900 office
FAX: 614-856-1920
E-mail: afitch@ama-cycle.org

See full listing in **Section Six** under **Ohio**

Vintage Auto LLC

	new/used parts service

605 Pine Knoll Dr
Greenville, SC 29609
864-292-8785; FAX: 864-967-0195
E-mail: vintagevw@aol.com

See full listing in **Section One** under **Volkswagen**

J Wood & Co Auctioneers

	auctions

RR 1 Box 316
Stockton Springs, ME 04981
207-567-4250; FAX: 207-567-4252
E-mail: jwoodandco@mindspring.com

See full listing in **Section Two** under **auctions & events**

Antique Radio Doctor

	radio repairs

Barry Dalton
196 Kilborn Dr
Grants Pass, OR 97526
541-474-2524 evenings

See full listing in **Section Two** under **radios**

Brasilia Press

	models

PO Box 2023
Elkhart, IN 46515
FAX: 219-262-8799

See full listing in **Section Two** under **models & toys**

Guild of Automotive Restorers

	restoration sales service

PO Box 1150
44 Bridge St
Bradford, ON Canada L3Z 2B5
905-775-0499; FAX: 905-775-0944
E-mail:
webmaster@guildautomotive.on.ca

See full listing in **Section Two** under **restoration shops**

Hudson Motor Car Co Memorabilia

	literature memorabilia novelties signs

Ken Poynter
19638 Huntington
Harper Woods, MI 48225
313-886-9292

Mail order only. Collector of anything pertaining to Hudsons, Essex, Terraplanes and Dovers. Trade and sell duplicates.

K-GAP

	repro parts

Automotive Parts
PO Box 3065
Santa Fe Springs, CA 90670
PH/FAX: 714-523-0403

Hudson, Essex, Terraplane authentic reproduction parts, made in the USA, featuring the products of Metro Moulded Parts. Weatherstrip, runningboard mats, lenses, accessories for 1929-1957. For catalog of parts available, send $2 (refundable with order).

NASHional Auto Parts & Cars

	cars parts

2412 Lincoln Ave
Alameda, CA 94501
510-522-2244; FAX: 510-864-8151

See full listing in **Section One** under **Nash**

Garth B Peterson

	accessories parts radios

122 N Conklin Rd
Veradale, WA 99037
509-926-4620 anytime

See full listing in **Section Two** under **comprehensive parts**

Don Robertson

	car dealer parts

2411 Gardner St
Elliston, VA 24087
540-268-2837

Hudson cars and parts.

Tom Taylor

	NOS parts

PO Box 129
Guinda, CA 95637
530-796-4106

See full listing in **Section One** under **Mopar**

Webb's Classic Auto Parts

	NOS parts reproduction parts service manuals used parts

5084 W State Rd 114
Huntington, IN 46750
219-344-1714; FAX: 219-344-1754

See full listing in **Section One** under **AMC**

Wenner's

	NOS parts

5449 Tannery Rd
Schnecksville, PA 18078
610-799-5419

See full listing in **Section One** under **AMC**

Charles Noe
64-1/2 Greenwood Ave
Bethel, CT 06801
PH/FAX: 203-748-4222
E-mail: mdchas@aol.com

broker
parts/auto purchases
parts/auto sales

See full listing in **Section Two** under **brokers**

Quality Tire Barn Inc
255 Twinsburg Rd
Northfield, OH 44067
330-467-1284

tires

See full listing in **Section Two** under **tires**

**Geeson Bros Motorcycle Museum
& Workshop**
2-6 Water Ln
South Witham
Grantham Lincs NG33 5 PH
England
01572 767280, 01572 768195

museum

See full listing in **Section Six** under **England**

H D Garage
Barry Brown
Comp 8 Bedford Mills RR #2
Westport, ON Canada K0G 1X0
613-273-5036

artwork
literature
motorcycles

See full listing in **Section Two** under **motorcycles**

**Indian Joe Martin's Antique
Motorcycle Parts**
PO Box 3156
Chattanooga, TN 37404
PH/FAX: 423-698-1787
E-mail: indianjo@bellsouth.net

parts

See full listing in **Section Two** under **motorcycles**

Kiwi Indian Parts
17399 Sage Ave
Riverside, CA 92504
909-780-5400; FAX: 909-780-7722
E-mail: indian@kiwi-indian.com

parts

Manufacturers of reproduction parts for Indian motorcycles.
Web site: www.kiwi-indian.com/

Sammy Miller Motorcycle Museum
Bashley Cross Rd
New Milton
Hampshire BH25 5SZ England
01425 620777; FAX: 01425 619696

museum

See full listing in **Section Six** under **England**

Motorcycle Hall of Fame Museum
13515 Yarmouth Dr
Pickerington, OH 43147
614-882-2782 info
614-856-1900 office
FAX: 614-856-1920
E-mail: afitch@ama-cycle.org

museum

See full listing in **Section Six** under **Ohio**

J Wood & Co Auctioneers
RR 1 Box 316
Stockton Springs, ME 04981
207-567-4250; FAX: 207-567-4252
E-mail: jwoodandco@mindspring.com

auctions

See full listing in **Section Two** under **auctions & events**

American-Foreign Auto Electric Inc
103 Main St
Souderton, PA 18964
215-723-4877

parts
rebuilding

See full listing in **Section Two** under **electrical systems**

Dick Ames Stainless Steel Exhaust
4850 Fallcrest Cir
Sarasota, FL 34233
941-923-8321; FAX: 941-923-9434
E-mail: dickamesfl@aol.com

exhaust systems

Mail order only. Specializing in stainless steel exhaust systems
made in England for Jaguar, Aston Martins and Morgans. See
monthly ads in Hemmings.

Antique & Classic Car Restoration
Hwy 107, Box 368
Magdalena, NM 87825

restoration

See full listing in **Section Two** under **restoration shops**

APA Industries
10505 San Fernando Rd
Pacoima, CA 91331
818-834-8473; FAX: 818-834-2795
E-mail: apaindustries@juno.com

accessories
parts

Specializing in parts, hoses and gaskets/seals for British cars;
also car covers, parts and accessories.

**Ashton Keynes Vintage
Restorations Ltd**
A Keith Bowley
Ashton Keynes, Swindon
Wilshire England
01285-861-288
FAX: 01285-860-604

coachbuilding
restoration

See full listing in **Section One** under **Rolls-Royce/Bentley**

Asom Electric
1204 McClellan Dr
Los Angeles, CA 90025
310-820-4457; FAX: 310-820-5908

electrical systems
rebuilding

See full listing in **Section Two** under **electrical systems**

Atlantic Enterprises | steering assemblies
221 Strand Industrial Dr
Little River, SC 29566
843-399-7565; FAX: 843-399-4600
E-mail: steering@atlantic-ent.com

See full listing in **Section Two** under **chassis parts**

The Auto Doctor Inc | mechanical parts
23125 Telegraph Rd | service repairs
Southfield, MI 48034
248-355-1505; FAX: 248-355-3460

See full listing in **Section One** under **BMW**

AutoMatch CARS | broker
(Computer Aided Referral Service) | car dealer network
2017 Blvd Napoleon | locator
Louisville, KY 40203
800-962-2771, 502-417-8793 mobile
502-452-1920 office; FAX: 502-479-6222
E-mail: amcars@aol.com or
aautomatch@aol.com

See full listing in **Section Two** under **car dealers**

Automotive Artistry | restoration
679 W Streetboro St
Hudson, OH 44236
330-650-1503
E-mail: dale@cmh.net

See full listing in **Section One** under **Triumph**

Automotive Artistry | restoration
4311 Mennonite Rd
Mantua, OH 44255
330-274-8699

See full listing in **Section One** under **Triumph**

G W Bartlett Co Inc | convertible tops
4301 Old & R3 N | interiors
Muncie, IN 47303 | rubber seals
800-338-8034 US/Canada
FAX: 765-282-4058
E-mail: osji@netdirect.net

For twenty years we have been manufacturers and suppliers of original specification Jaguar interiors, individual Jaguar interior components, rubber seals, convertible tops, top boots, tonneaus, top frame wood components and seat frame wood components. Our product line includes most post WW II Jaguars, from the XK 120s to the XJ6 SIII saloons. We use only the finest genuine leather, genuine Hardura, deep pile wood carpet, wool moquette and ICI vinyl along with well researched patterns to produce with confidence the most accurate original specification Jaguar interiors available anywhere. Web site: gwbartlett.com

BAS Ltd Jaguar Trim Specialist | interior parts
250 H St, Unit 8110
Blaine, WA 98231
800-661-5377; FAX: 640-990-9988
E-mail: basjag@helix.net

Mail order only. Specializing in interior products from the smallest seal to complete interior kits for all Jaguar motor cars, XK to XJ.

Bassett's Jaguar | parts
PO Box 245 | restoration
53 Stilson Rd | service
Wyoming, RI 02898 | upholstery
401-539-3010; FAX: 401-539-7861
E-mail: www.jagwillie@ids.net

Mail order and open shop. Monday-Friday 8 am to 5 pm. Specializing in parts, upholstery, restoration/service for Jaguars 1949-present. Also offer our services on other exotic types of cars.

BCP Sport & Classic Co | parts
10525 Airline Dr | service
Houston, TX 77037
281-448-4739; FAX: 281-448-0189

See full listing in **Section One** under **MG**

Best of Britain | car dealer
RR 1, Box 33 | restoration
South Ryegate, VT 05069
802-429-2266

Open daily 9 am to 5 pm. Licensed dealer, handling XKEs exclusively. Purchases, sales and complete restoration for XKE Series I, II, III.

BMC Classics Inc | parts
828 N Dixie Freeway | repair
New Smyrna Beach, FL 32168 | restoration
904-426-6405; FAX: 904-427-4570
E-mail: bmcar1@aol.com

See full listing in **Section Two** under **restoration shops**

BritBooks | books
PO Box 321
Otego, NY 13825
PH/FAX: 607-988-7956
E-mail: britbook@dmcom.net

See full listing in **Section Four** under **books & publications**

British Auto Parts Ltd | parts
93256 Holland Ln
Marcola, OR 97454
541-933-2880; FAX: 541-933-2302

See full listing in **Section One** under **Morris**

British Auto Shoppe | parts
1909 5th Ave | service
Moline, IL 61265
309-764-9513; FAX: 309-764-9576

See full listing in **Section One** under **MG**

British Auto/USA | parts
92 Londonderry Tpke | upholstery
Manchester, NH 03104
603-622-1050, 800-452-4787
FAX: 603-622-0849
E-mail: jaguar@britishautousa

Mail order and retail store. Monday-Friday 8 am to 5 pm, Saturday 8 am to 12 pm. Large selection of parts and upholstery for all post war Jaguars. Brake and suspension upgrades also. Part of the SNG Barratt Group. Web site: www.britishautousa.com

British Car Films | videos
PO Box 13862
London N4 3WB England
800-454-8341 toll-free
011 44181-3744850
FAX: 011 44181-3744852
E-mail: british.car@virgin.net

See full listing in **Section Two** under **videos**

British Car Keys | keys
Rt 144 Box 9957
Ellicott City, MD 21042-3647
410-750-2352
E-mail: britishcarkeys@hotmail.com

See full listing in **Section One** under **Austin-Healey**

British Car Magazine   periodical
343 Second St, Suite H
Los Altos, CA 94022-3639
650-949-9680; FAX: 650-949-9685
E-mail: britcarmag@aol.com

See full listing in **Section Four** under **periodicals**

British Car Service   restoration
2854 N Stone Ave   salvage yard
Tucson, AZ 85705
520-882-7026; FAX: 520-882-7053
E-mail: bcs@liveline.com

See full listing in **Section Five** under **Arizona**

British Car Specialists   parts
2060 N Wilson Way   repairs
Stockton, CA 95205   restoration
209-948-8767; FAX: 209-948-1030
E-mail: healeydoc@aol.com

See full listing in **Section One** under **Austin-Healey**

British Miles   accessories
9278 Old E Tyburn Rd   literature
Morrisville, PA 19067   parts
215-736-9300; FAX: 215-736-3089   restoration

See full listing in **Section One** under **MG**

British Motor Co   engine rebuilding
3825 W 11th Ave
Eugene, OR 97402
800-995-1895; FAX: 541-485-8544

Mail order and open shop. Monday-Friday 8 am to 5:30 pm.
Specializing in all Jaguar model engine rebuilding. At BMC we
understand your desire for the best workmanship available. We
use factory parts and commit the time and care necessary to do
a superior engine rebuild. Please call if you would like references
from some of our satisfied customers.

British Parts NW   parts
4105 SE Lafayette Hwy
Dayton, OR 97114
503-864-2001; FAX: 503-864-2081
E-mail: bpnw@onlinemac.com

See full listing in **Section One** under **Triumph**

British Racing Green   parts
30 Aleph Dr
Newark, DE 19702
302-368-1117; FAX: 302-368-5910
E-mail: info@brgparts.com

See full listing in **Section One** under **MG**

British Restorations   car dealer
4455 Paul St   restoration
Philadelphia, PA 19124
215-533-6696

Open shop only. Monday-Friday 8 am to 6 pm. Total restoration,
including body, mechanical, wood, interior, etc, of all sports and
classic cars. Specializing in Jaguars from 1948-1987. Also buys
and sells sports and classic cars.

British Wire Wheel   hubs
1650 Mansfield St   tires
Santa Cruz, CA 95062   wire wheels
831-479-4495; FAX: 831-462-1517

See full listing in **Section One** under **Austin-Healey**

British Wiring Inc   wiring accessories
20449 Ithaca Rd   wiring harnesses
Olympia Fields, IL 60461
PH/FAX: 708-481-9050

See full listing in **Section Two** under **electrical systems**

Francois Bruere   artwork
8 Avenue Olivier Heuze
LeMans 72000 France
(33) 02-4377-1877
FAX: (33) 02-4324-2038

See full listing in **Section Two** under **artwork**

California Wire Wheel   rechroming
6922 Turnbridge Way   tires
San Diego, CA 92119   tubes
619-698-8255; FAX: 619-589-9032   wheels

See full listing in **Section Two** under **wheels & wheelcovers**

Cambridge Motorsport   parts
Caxton Rd   race tuning
Great Gransden, NR Sandy
Beds SG19 3AH England
0044 1767 677969
FAX: 0044 1767 677026
E-mail:
cambridge.motorsport@dial.pipex.com

See full listing in **Section One** under **Triumph**

City Imports Ltd   bodywork
166 Penrod Ct   car sales
Glen Burnie, MD 21061   restorations
410-768-6660; FAX: 410-768-5955

Dealing in the following: Jaguar, MG, Triumph, Rolls-Royce,
Bentley, BMW, Mercedes-Benz, Saab, Range Rover. Bodywork,
restoration, car sales, regular maintenance. 21 years in the business. Experienced staff mechanics.

Classic Showcase   classic vehicles
913 Rancheros Dr   restorations
San Marcos, CA 92069
760-747-9947, 760-747-3188 sales
FAX: 760-747-4021
E-mail:
management@classicshowcase.com

See full listing in **Section Two** under **car dealers**

Collectors Choice LTD   parts
6400 Springfield-Lodi Rd   race preparation
Dane, WI 53529   restoration
608-849-9878; FAX: 608-849-9879   service

See full listing in **Section One** under **DeTomaso/Pantera**

Concours Cars of Colorado Ltd   accessories
2414 W Cucharras St   parts
Colorado Springs, CO 80904   service
719-473-6288; FAX: 719-473-9206

See full listing in **Section One** under **BMW**

Coventry West Inc   assemblies
5936-A Peachtree Rd   Jaguar parts
Atlanta, GA 30341
800-331-2193 toll-free
770-451-3839 Atlanta
FAX: 770-451-7561

Specializing in new, used, remanufactured parts and assemblies
for 1970s-current model Jaguars. We buy wrecked, burned
Jaguars to part out and recycle. Large selection of body panels
and components. Web site: www.coventrywest.com

Tom Crook Classic Cars
27611 42nd Ave S
Auburn, WA 98001
206-941-3454

car dealer

See full listing in **Section Two** under **car dealers**

Crow Engineering Jaguar Engines
433 Tremont St
Taunton, MA 02780
800-537-4146

engine rebuilding

Open seven days per week, 365 days per year, 24 hours per day. Jaguar from XKSS to XJ220. We rebuild your engine at your home or business. No need to mail your engine away or send your car out to be done. We do it all at your place.

Dashboards Plus
336 Cottonwood Ave
Hartland, WI 53029
800-221-8161; FAX: 414-367-9474

restoration parts
wood dash overlays

Exotic wood dash overlays and restoration parts. We offer genuine wood dash kits for over 600 different cars, trucks and motorcycles. All kits come with a limited lifetime warranty and are easily installed using the instructions provided with each kit. Web site: www.dashboardsplus.com

Dave's Auto Restoration
2285 Rt 307 E
Jefferson, OH 44047
PH/FAX: 216-858-2227
E-mail: davesauto@knownet.net

upholstery

See full listing in **Section Two** under **interiors & interior parts**

Deters Restorations
6205 Swiss Garden Rd
Temperance, MI 48182-1020
734-847-1820

restoration

See full listing in **Section Two** under **restoration shops**

Doc's Jags
125 Baker Rd
Lake Bluff, IL 60044
847-367-5247; FAX: 847-367-6363
E-mail: docsjags@worldnet.att.net

appraisals
interiors
restoration

Open Monday-Sunday by appointment. From January-May each year: Stoppp Trading Inc, 7777 N Pinesview Dr, Scottsdale, AZ 85258, PH: 602-607-0694; FAX: 602-607-0696. Largest classic Jaguar selection for sale in the world. All conditions, all models. Restore and maintain all Jaguars. Insurance appraisals are available as well as "expert witness" testimony. Also sell the finest Jaguar Connolly leather interiors in the world. We do NOT sell parts. Web site: www.docsjags.com/

Doctor Jaguar Inc
740 W 16th St
Costa Mesa, CA 92627
949-646-2816; FAX: 949-574-8097

restoration
service

Mail order and open shop. Monday-Friday 8:30 am to 5:30 pm PST. Service, restoration and used parts for all years Jaguar.

Doug's British Car Parts
2487 E Colorado Blvd
Pasadena, CA 91107
818-793-2494; FAX: 818-793-4339

accessories
parts

Mail order and open shop. Monday-Saturday 8:30 am to 6 pm. Specializing in new and used auto parts and accessories including Jaguar XK 120 and Mk VII through XKE, 3.8 Mk II, XJ6, 12, S; MG T Series through MGA to MGB, Midget, Triumph TR2-8, Spitfire, GT6, Austin-Healey 100-4/3000 Mk III BJ8; Rover 2000 TC, 3500S and 1980 3500, Sunbeam Alpine and Hillman.

East Coast Jaguar
802B Naaman's Rd
Wilmington, DE 19810
302-475-7200; FAX: 302-475-9258
E-mail: ecjaguar@aol.com

parts
service

Mail order and open shop. Monday-Friday 8:30 am to 5:30 pm. Specializing in parts and service for Jaguar XKs to XJs. Deal in remanufactured water pumps for Austin-Healey, BMW, Ferrari, Jaguar/Daimler, Maserati, MG, Mercedes, Morgan, Porsche, Rolls-Royce/Bentley, Rover and Triumph.

Eddie's Restorations
4725 Rt 30
Elwood, NJ 08217
609-965-2211

restoration

Shop open Monday-Friday 9 am to 5 pm. Restorations on classic imports, Jaguar XK 120, XK 140, XK 150 and XKE in particular, to factory new specifications, using new metal panels and new parts for rebuilding mechanical components.

The Fine Car Store
1105 Moana Dr
San Diego, CA 92107
619-223-7766; FAX: 619-223-6838

car dealer

See full listing in **Section One** under **Ferrari**

Finish Line
3593 SW 173rd Terr
Miramar, FL 33029
954-436-9101; FAX: 954-436-9102
E-mail: e.dlibrandi@worldnet.att.net

parts
supplies

See full listing in **Section One** under **Cobra**

Gran Turismo Jaguar
4285 Main St
Perry, OH 44081
440-259-5656; FAX: 440-259-5588
E-mail: sales@gtjaguar.com

engine rebuilding
performance parts
service

Mail order only. The world's largest Jaguar high-performance leader, with 35 years of success, featuring street and race performance parts and services for all Jaguar models from the 1940s-1990s including: 6-speed transmission kits; aluminum flywheels and clutches; suspension, brake and exhaust system upgrades; complete cylinder head and engine rebuilding; engine dynamometer testing; cams and cranks; air, fuel and oil system improvements; excellent customer service. Complete catalog and video available. Web site: www.gtjaguar.com

Grand Prix Classics Inc
7456 La Jolla Blvd
La Jolla, CA 92037
619-459-3500; FAX: 619-459-3512

racing cars
sports cars

See full listing in **Section Two** under **racing**

Pete Groh
9957 Frederick Rd
Ellicott City, MD 21042-3647
410-750-2352; FAX: 410-466-3566
E-mail: petegroh@yahoo.com

original British
keys

Mail order only. Specializing in original British keys for Austin-Healey, Austin, Hillman, Jaguar, Morris, MG, Singer, Triumph, Volvo, Vauxhall and Nash Metropolitan. Wilmot Breeden keys, FRN, FA, FP, FS and FT, $12 each, letters and number on side of key. Rubber headed key, WASO and British Leyland L swirl key, $14 each. Can cut by code based on number on ignition switch or three number on trunk stem. American key blank, cost $6 single sided key and $9 for double sided key. All inquiries include a SASE with your daytime telephone number. Web site: www.geocities.com/motorcity/flats/7843/

Harbor Auto Restoration 1504 SW 3rd St Pompano Beach, FL 33069 954-785-7887; FAX: 954-785-7388 E-mail: harbor@harbor-auto.com	restoration

See full listing in **Section Two** under **restoration shops**

Highway One Classic Automobiles and Highwayone.com Classic Classifieds 1035 California Dr Burlingame, CA 94010 650-342-7340; FAX: 650-343-0150 E-mail: djboscacci@msn.com	classic automobiles

See full listing in **Section One** under **Abarth**

Integrity Machine 383 Pipe Stave Hollow Rd Mount Sinai, NY 11766 888-446-9670; FAX: 516-476-9675	brake masters clutch masters wheel cylinders

See full listing in **Section Two** under **brakes**

Italy's Famous Exhaust 2711 183rd St Redondo Beach, CA 90278 310-793-5985 E-mail: famous@earthlink.net	exhaust systems wheels

See full listing in **Section Two** under **exhaust systems**

Jaguar Cars Archives 555 MacArthur Blvd Mahwah, NJ 07430 201-818-8144; FAX: 201-818-0281	research

See full listing in **Section Four** under **information sources**

Jaguar Daimler Heritage Trust Browns Ln Allesley, Coventry CV5 9DR England 0044 (0) 1203 402121 FAX: 0044 (0) 1203 405581	archive services photographic records

Mail order and open shop. Year round Monday-Friday 9 am to 4 pm. Archive services, photographic, research and vehicle hire and display for Jaguar 1922-1999, Lanchester and Daimler 1896-1999. Specializing in Jaguar, Daimler and Lanchester history. Membership available December 1998. Extensive archive and photographic records. Vehicle collection of 115.

Jaguar Heaven Auto Dismantler 1433 Tillie Lewis Dr Stockton, CA 95206 209-942-4524; FAX: 209-942-3670	parts

Mail order and open shop. Monday-Friday 8:30 am to 5 pm PST. Specializing in Jaguar parts (used, rebuilt and new) for Mark I, Mark II, Mark V, Mark VII, Mark VIII, Mark IX, Mark X, 420, 420G, E-type, XJ6 and XJS.

Jaguar of Puerto Rico Inc PO Box 13055 San Juan, PR 00908-3055 787-723-5177; FAX: 787-723-9488	car dealer parts service

Open shop only. Monday-Friday 8 am to 6 pm, Saturday 9 am to 4 pm. New Jaguar sales. Used Jaguar parts and service. Selected classic restorations. Sales of new Range Rovers.

The Jaguar Warehouse 5389 Ashleigh Rd Fairfax, VA 22030 PH/FAX: 703-968-3983 E-mail: jagware@erols.com	literature parts

Parts and literature for Jaguar XK 120, 140, 150 and 1948-1961 Jaguar XKs and sedans. Web site: www.erols.com/jagware/index2.html

Jahns Quality Pistons 1360 N Jefferson St Anaheim, CA 92807 714-579-3795, 800-225-0277 FAX: 714-524-6607	piston rings pistons

See full listing in **Section Two** under **engine parts**

John's Cars Inc 800 Jaguar Ln Dallas, TX 75226 800-866-JAGS (5247) parts orders only; 214-426-4100 FAX: 214-426-3116	conversion retrofits parts restoration service

Mail order and open shop. Monday-Friday 8 am to 6 pm. Jaguar XJ series, service, parts, restoration, V8 conversions and kits for DIY conversions XJ, E-type, TR7, Z car, etc. Rebuilt steering racks, water pumps, brake boosters, etc. GM transmission and alternator retrofits for Jaguars. Upgraded parts with lifetime warranties. Call for free information. Web site: www.johnscars.com

Kensington Motor Group Inc PO Box 2277 Sag Harbor, NY 11963 516-537-1868; FAX: 516-537-2641 E-mail: kenmotor@aol.com	consignment sales

See full listing in **Section One** under **Mercedes-Benz**

Chuck Konesky 110 Stolle Rd Elma, NY 14059 716-652-9638	parts

Mail order only. Call 24 hours a day, seven days a week. For XK 120s, 140s, 150s and E-types. New E-type parts available, but mostly parting out complete cars. Restorable Jaguars for sale.

Lake Oswego Restorations 19621 S Hazelhurst Ln West Linn, OR 97068 PH/FAX: 503-636-7503	restoration sales

See full listing in **Section One** under **Aston Martin**

Leatherique Leather Restoration Products PO Box 2678 Orange Park, FL 32065 904-272-0992; FAX: 904-272-1534 E-mail: lrpltd@aol.com	leather cleaning conditioning products

See full listing in **Section One** under **Rolls-Royce/Bentley**

Lindley Restorations Ltd 10 S Sanatoga Rd Pottstown, PA 19464 610-326-8484; FAX: 610-326-3845	parts sales service

Jaguar sales, service, restoration. Refinishing, frame straightening, engine and transmission overhaul, upholstery and structural wood fabrication, repair. Fully equipped to service pre-war to the latest model Jaguar. Over 30 years' experience. Many Jaguar Clubs of North America awards. 30 minutes west of Philadelphia. Pickup and delivery via enclosed trailer available.

LMARR Disk Ltd — wheel discs
PO Box 910
Glen Ellen, CA 95442-0910
707-938-9347; FAX: 707-938-3020
E-mail: lmarr@ibm.net

See full listing in **Section One** under **Rolls-Royce/Bentley**

Mac's Euro Motorcars & Transport — Alfa Romeos / parts / transport
1520 Burr Oak Rd
Homewood, IL 60430
708-799-3469

See full listing in **Section One** under **Alfa Romeo**

John A Meering Jaguar Hoses — hoses
6743 Newcastle Ct
Port Tobacco, MD 20677
301-609-8557

Mail order only. Jaguar hoses. Correct size and shape. Heater, radiator and carburetor hoses for XK 120, 140, 150 and Mark 7, 8, 9. Complete sets only. Send SASE for details. Hoses are new, not NOS, and are of modern construction. Also can have made hoses for most post-war British cars.

Mercedes-Benz Service by Angela & George/ABS Exotic Repair Inc — sales / service
700 N Andrews Ave
Fort Lauderdale, FL 33304
954-566-7785; FAX: 954-566-7271

See full listing in **Section One** under **Mercedes-Benz**

Mid-Jersey Motorama Inc — car dealer
1301 Asbury Ave
PO Box 1395
Asbury Park, NJ 07712
PH/FAX: 732-775-9885
beeper: 732-840-6111
E-mail: sjz1@aol.com

See full listing in **Section One** under **Cadillac/LaSalle**

Midbanc Financial Services — financing
PO Box 20402
Columbus, OH 43220
614-442-7701; FAX: 614-442-7704
E-mail: patricia@midbanc.com

See full listing in **Section Two** under **financing**

Moss Motors Ltd — accessories / parts
PO Box 847
440 Rutherford St
Goleta, CA 93117
800-235-6954; FAX: 805-692-2525

See full listing in **Section One** under **MG**

Motorcars Ltd — parts
8101 Hempstead
Houston, TX 77008
800-231-6563; FAX: 713-863-8238
E-mail: info@britishparts.com

Mail order. Monday-Friday 8 am to 6 pm CST. Specializing in Jaguar and Land Rover. New, used and remanufactured parts. Web site: www.britishparts.com

Muncie Imports & Classics — repair / restoration / upholstery
4401 St Rd 3 N
Muncie, IN 47303
800-462-4244; FAX: 317-287-9551
E-mail: mic@netdirect.net

Mail order and open shop. Monday-Friday 7:30 am to 5:30 pm, Saturday 9 am to 1 pm. Specializing in Jaguar and Corvette restoration, service, repair, paint and body. Upholstery for XK 120, 140, 150, Marks and E-types. OSJI factory authorized installer.

NOS Locators — parts
587 Pawtucket Ave
Pawtucket, RI 02860
401-725-5000

See full listing in **Section One** under **MG**

Omni Specialties — parts / restoration / service
10418 Lorain Ave
Cleveland, OH 44111
888-819-6464 (MGMG)
216-251-2269; FAX: 216-251-6083

See full listing in **Section One** under **MG**

Orpheograff — prints
BP33
72201 La Fleche Cedex France
(33) 243452629
FAX: (33) 243452512

See full listing in **Section Two** under **artwork**

Pacific International Auto — parts / sales / service
1118 Garnet Ave
San Diego, CA 92109
619-274-1920; FAX: 619-454-1815

British car specialists. Parts, sales, service, restorations. Hard-to-find parts for Jaguars, MGs, Triumphs. Jaguar XKEs, XK 120s, XK 140s, XK 150s, all sedans.

Paul's Discount Jaguar Parts — parts
1124 NW 134th Ave
Sunrise
Fort Lauderdale, FL 33323
954-846-7976; FAX: 954-846-9450
E-mail: paulsjag@ix.netcom.com

Mail order only. Phone hours 9 am to 7 pm EST. New and used parts for 1976-1991 Jaguar XJS, XJ-SC, convertibles; 1974-1987 Jaguar XJ6, XJ12, XJ6C and XJ12C models; especially rust-free body panels, new rubber paint kits, replacement authentic Jaguar wood kits, carpets, Connolly leather seat covers, armrest and console recovering service, new door panels, Euro headlamp conversions, new and used Jaguar alloy wheels. Knowledgeable staff, restoration advice, best prices.

Peninsula Imports — accessories / parts / trim
3749 Harlem Rd
Buffalo, NY 14215
800-999-1209; FAX: 905-847-3021
E-mail: imports@ican.net

See full listing in **Section One** under **BMW**

Precision Autoworks — restorations
2202 Federal Street
East Camden, NJ 08105
609-966-0080, NJ
FAX: 610-649-3577, PA

See full listing in **Section One** under **Mercedes-Benz**

Proper Jaguar — restoration
1806 S Alpine
Rockford, IL 61108
815-398-0303, 815-398-8664

Jaguar restoration, all years, by appointment. Also MGs and other sports and classic cars. Also restore and maintain vintage race cars. Have production and Formula 5000 experience.

Ragtops & Roadsters — bodywork/painting / British automobiles / engine rebuilding / vintage race prep
203 S 4th St
Perkasie, PA 18944
215-257-1202; FAX: 215-257-2688
E-mail: info@ragtops.com

See full listing in **Section Two** under **restoration shops**

Regal International Motor Cars Inc PO Box 6819 Hollywood, FL 33081 305-989-9777; FAX: 305-989-9778	**car dealer**

See full listing in **Section One** under **Rolls-Royce/Bentley**

Restoration Services 16049 W 4th Ave Golden, CO 80401 303-271-0356	**restoration**

See full listing in **Section One** under **Porsche**

Reward Service Inc 172 Overhill Rd Stormville, NY 12582 914-227-7647; FAX: 914-221-0293	**appraisals** **restoration** **transportation**

Automotive restoration and mechanical rebuilding of Jaguars and other British sports cars for 30 years. Appraisals, personalized transportation in the Northeast and consultation on restoration projects, by appointment. References. International Society of Appraisers guidelines adhered to.

RM Auto Restoration Ltd 9435 Horton Line Blenheim, ON Canada N0P 1A0 519-352-4575; FAX: 519-351-1337 E-mail: clark@rmcars.com	**panel fabrication** **parts** **restoration**

See full listing in **Section Two** under **restoration shops**

Rogers Motors 25 Leverett Rd Shutesbury, MA 01072 413-259-1722 E-mail: akor@ent.umass.edu	**used parts**

Specializing in used parts for MGA, MGB, Midget/Sprite, Jaguar Mk I, Mk II, S-type, 420 and Volvo Amazons.

Scarborough Faire Inc 1151 Main St Pawtucket, RI 02860 800-556-6300, 401-724-4200 FAX: 401-724-5392	**parts**

See full listing in **Section One** under **MG**

Smooth Line 2562 Riddle Run Rd Tarentum, PA 15084 724-274-6002; FAX: 724-274-6121	**body panels** **removable hardtops**

See full listing in **Section Two** under **tops**

Special Interest Car Parts 1340 Hartford Ave Johnston, RI 02919 800-556-7496; FAX: 401-831-7760	**parts**

Specializing in the distribution of British car parts worldwide for Jaguar 1948-on, MG and Midget, Triumph TR250, 6, 7, 8, Spitfire, GT6 and Range Rover.

Sports & Classics PO Box 1787 512 Boston Post Rd, Dept H Darien, CT 06820-1787	**parts**

See full listing in **Section Two** under **body parts**

Sports Car Haven 2-33 Flowerfield Industrial Pk St James, NY 11780 516-862-8058 E-mail: sch94@aol.com	**race prep** **restorations** **service**

See full listing in **Section One** under **Triumph**

Sports Car Haven 3414 Bloom Rd, Rt 11 Danville, PA 17821 570-275-5705	**parts** **restoration** **service**

See full listing in **Section One** under **MG**

Straight Six Jaguar 24321 Hatteras St Woodland Hills, CA 91367 PH/FAX: 818-716-1192	**parts** **service**

Specializing in parts and service for Jaguars 1936-1987.

Terry's Jaguar Parts Inc 117 E Smith ST Benton, IL 62812 800-851-9438; FAX: 618-438-2371 E-mail: terryjag@midwest.net	**parts**

Mail order and open shop. Specializing in Jaguar parts to present day. New, used and rebuilt parts. Catalog available. Web site: www.terrysjag.com

See our ad on this page

The Registry Pine Grove Stanley, VA 22851 540-778-3728; FAX: 540-778-2402 E-mail: britregstry@aol.com or oldwregistry@aol.com	**periodical**

See full listing in **Section Four** under **periodicals**

Thoroughbred Motors 3935 N US 301 Sarasota, FL 34234 941-359-2277; FAX: 941-359-2128	**car dealer** **parts**

Open Monday-Friday 9 am to 5 pm. Jaguar spare parts specialists, 1950-1998 models. Also new parts. Always buying and selling cars. 20 years' experience.

Tillack & Co Ltd
630 Mary Ann Dr
Redondo Beach, CA 90278
310-318-8760; FAX: 310-376-3392

parts
restoration

See full listing in **Section Two** under **restoration shops**

Vicarage Jaguar
5333 Collins Ave Suite 502
Miami Beach, FL 33140
305-866-9511; FAX: 305-866-5738
E-mail: vicarage@ix.netcom.com

parts
restoration

Mail order and open shop. Monday-Friday 8 am to 5 pm, Saturday 9 am to 1 pm. Specializing in restoration service, upgrades and parts for classic Jaguars. Web site: www.jagweb.com/vicarage

Victory Autoservices
Box 5060, RR 1
W Baldwin, ME 04091
207-625-4581

parts
restoration

See full listing in **Section One** under **Austin-Healey**

Vintage Jag Works
1390 W Hwy 26
Blackfoot, ID 83221
208-684-4767; FAX: 208-684-3386
E-mail: walt@vintagejag.com

consulting
how-to articles

Mail order and open shop. Monday-Friday 9 am to 5 pm MST and by appointment. Specializing in Jaguar, how-to articles, consulting on repair and restoration by phone and e-mail, parts and memorabilia for Jaguar cars, post WW II-present. Web site: www.vintagejag.com

Vintage Jaguar Spares
7804 Billington Ct
Fort Washington, MD 20744
301-248-6327; FAX: 301-248-5523
E-mail: brojag@erols.com

parts

Mail order only. "Mk IV", Mk V and SS-Jaguar. Price list free.

Vintage Restorations
The Old Bakery
Windmill Street, Tunbridge Wells
Kent, TN2 4UU England
UK 1892-525-899
FAX: UK 1892-525499

accessories
instruments

See full listing in **Section Two** under **instruments**

Von's Austin-Healey Restorations
10270 Barberville Rd
Fort Mill, SC 29715
803-548-4590; FAX: 803-548-4816
E-mail: vons@vnet.net

parts
repairs
restoration

See full listing in **Section One** under **Austin-Healey**

Voss Motors Inc
21849 Virginia Dr
Southfield, MI 48076
888-380-9277 toll-free
248-357-4750; FAX: 248-354-6577
E-mail: vossmotors@aol.com

service manuals

See full listing in **Section Two** under **literature dealers**

Welsh Enterprises Inc
223 N 5th St
PO Box 4130
Steubenville, OH 43952
800-875-5247; FAX: 888-477-5247
E-mail: contact@welshent.com

parts

Monday-Friday 9 am to 5 pm, Saturday 9 am to 1 pm. Over 50,000 square feet of new, used and rebuilt Jaguar spares. The largest independent retailer of Jaguar spares for restoration and service. Knowledgeable sales staff, worldwide shipping same day. Fast and reliable service at a competitive price. We stock the largest inventory of new, used and rebuilt Jaguar spares found anywhere. Call today for your catalog. Web site: www.welshent.com

Ed West CARS
1941 Jan Marie Pl
Tustin, CA 92780
714-832-2688; FAX: 714-832-9274

car dealer
parts

Mail order and open shop. Monday-Friday 9 am to 5 pm. For Jaguar XK 120s, 140s, 150s, Mk Is, IIs, VIIs, VIIIs and IXs. New, used and reproduction parts. Cars bought and sold. 27 years' experience. Send 2 stamps for SASE with model and year of Jaguar for parts list.

Western Jaguar
Cordell R Newby
1625 North Western
Wenatchee, WA 98801
509-662-7748; FAX: 509-662-7748

parts

Mail order only. Specializing in 1949-1951 Mark Vs with comprehensive inventory of new, NOS, reproduction and used parts for 1936-1989 models. Catalog, $3.

White Post Restorations
One Old Car Dr
White Post, VA 22663
540-837-1140; FAX: 540-837-2368

brakes
restoration

See full listing in **Section Two** under **brakes**

Wolf Steel
1 Ballerina
Frelighsburg, QC Canada J0J 1C0
450-298-5078; FAX: 450-298-5088
E-mail: allenhal@citenet.net

Alfa Romeo body
parts

Mail order and open shop by appointment. Manufacturer and distributor of Alfa Romeo body panels. Specializing in restoration of Jaguars and Alfa Romeos. Web site: www.alfaparts.net

World Upholstery & Trim
PO Box 2420
Camarillo, CA 93011
805-988-1848; FAX: 805-278-7886
E-mail: worlduph@mail.vcnet.com

carpet
tops
upholstery kits

See full listing in **Section Two** under **interiors & interior parts**

XKs Unlimited
850 Fiero Ln
San Luis Obispo, CA 93401
805-544-7864; FAX: 805-544-1664
E-mail: xksunltd@aol.com

instruments
parts
restorations

Mail order and open shop. Monday-Friday 8 am to 5 pm. Specializing in Jaguar parts and restoration, Range Rover parts, Smiths instruments and Stewart-Warner for Jaguar cars 1948-on, Range Rover, Land Rover Defender, Land Rover Discovery 1986-on. We also provide restoration services for most British marques and sports cars, Cobras, etc. Web site: www.xks.com

Delta Motorsports Inc	accessories
2724 E Bell Rd	catalog
Phoenix, AZ 85032	parts
602-265-8026; FAX: 602-971-8609	

Mail order and open shop. Monday-Friday 8 am to 5:30 pm MST. Factory authorized parts and accessories distributor for Jensen-Healey, Jensen Interceptor and Jensen GT.

JAE	parts
375 Pine #26	service
Goleta, CA 93117	tech info
805-967-5767; FAX: 805-967-6183	
E-mail: jefforjay@jaeparts.com	

See full listing in **Section One** under **Lotus**

Jensen Cars Ltd	parts
140 Franklin Ave	technical advice
Wyckoff, NJ 07481-3465	
201-847-8549, 8 pm to 10 pm, EST	
FAX: 201-847-8549, 9 am to 10 pm	

Jensen Interceptor parts for 1964-1976 Jensen CV8 and Interceptor.

K&D Enterprises	accessories
23117 E Echo Lake Rd	parts
Snohomish, WA 98296-5426	restorations
425-788-0507; FAX: 360-668-2003	
E-mail: tdb@halcyon.com	

Parts, services, restoration, accessories solely for the Jensen Interceptor saloon, convertible and coupe models, 1966 and later. Web site: http://interceptor.org

Von's Austin-Healey Restorations	parts
10270 Barberville Rd	repairs
Fort Mill, SC 29715	restoration
803-548-4590; FAX: 803-548-4816	
E-mail: vons@vnet.net	

See full listing in **Section One** under **Austin-Healey**

Dennis DuPont	automobilia
77 Island Pond Rd	literature
Derry, NH 03038	parts
603-434-9290	

See full listing in **Section One** under **Studebaker**

Eugene Gardner	license plates
10510 Rico Tatum Rd	
Palmetto, GA 30268	
770-463-4264	

See full listing in **Section Two** under **license plates**

K-F-D Services Inc	parts
HC 65, Box 49	restoration
Altonah, UT 84002	
801-454-3098; FAX: 801-454-3099	
E-mail: kfd-services@msn.com	

Mail order and open shop. Monday-Saturday 9 am to 4 pm MST. Specializing in restoration parts and service and customized cars for Kaiser, Frazer, Darrin, Henry J, all years.

John E Parker	plastic repros
4860 N Desert Tortoise Pl	rubber parts
Tucson, AZ 85745-9213	
520-743-3574	

Mail order and open shop. Monday-Saturday 8 am to 4 pm. Large inventory of new reproduction rubber parts and plastic reproductions. For Kaiser Frazers, Henry Js, Allstates and 1952-1955 Willys Aeros. Kaiser Frazer Owners' Club information available.

Waldron's Antique Exhaust Inc	exhaust systems
PO Box C	
25872 M-86	
Nottawa, MI 49075	
616-467-7185; FAX: 616-467-9041	

See full listing in **Section Two** under **exhaust systems**

Walker's Auto Pride Inc	cars
13115 Log Rd	parts
PO Box 134	
Peyton, CO 80831	
719-749-2668	

Open Monday-Thursday 7:30 am to 5:30 pm, Saturday by appointment. Kaiser Frazer cars and parts. 120 Kaiser Frazer cars. Specializing in Kaiser Frazer. Full line Kaiser Frazer parts. Parts sales for Kaiser Frazer cars including Henry J. 75 tons of new and used parts available.

Zeug's K-F Parts	parts
1435 Moreno Dr	
Simi Valley, CA 93063	
805-579-9445 weekends	

Mail order only. NOS and used Kaiser Frazer, Henry J and Kaiser Darrin parts. Send $2 for parts list.

Charles S Crail Automobiles	auto sales
36A Calle Cesar Chavez	
Santa Barbara, CA 93103	
805-568-1934; FAX: 805-568-1533	

See full listing in **Section One** under **Rolls-Royce/Bentley**

Rolls-Royce of Beverly Hills	parts
11401 West Pico Blvd	
Los Angeles, CA 90064	
800-321-9792, 310-477-4262	
FAX: 310-473-7498	
E-mail: smrr64@aol.com	

See full listing in **Section One** under **Rolls-Royce/Bentley**

Lamborghini

Drummond Coach and Paint
531 Raleigh Ave
El Cajon, CA 92020
619-579-7229; FAX: 619-579-2128

painting
restoration

See full listing in **Section One** under **Ferrari**

Exoticars USA
6 Washington St
Frenchtown, NJ 08825
908-996-4889; FAX: 908-996-6938

machine work
paint/bodywork
restoration/service
welding/fabrication

See full listing in **Section One** under **Ferrari**

Kreimeyer Co/Auto Legends Inc
3211 N Wilburn Ave
Bethany, OK 73008
405-789-9499; FAX: 405-789-7888

antennas/repair
glass/wholesale
parts/wholesale
radios/radio repair

See full listing in **Section One** under **Mercedes-Benz**

London Stainless Steel Exhaust Centre
249-253 Queenstown Rd
London, SW8 3NP England
011-44-171622-2120
FAX: 011-44-171627-0991
E-mail: 101445.341@compuserv.com

exhaust systems

See full listing in **Section Two** under **exhaust systems**

Motorcar Gallery Inc
715 N Federal Hwy
Fort Lauderdale, FL 33304
954-522-9900; FAX: 954-522-9966

car dealer

See full listing in **Section One** under **Ferrari**

Motorcars International
528 N Prince Ln
Springfield, MO 65802
417-831-9999; FAX: 417-831-8080
E-mail: sales@motorcars-intl.com

accessories
cars
services
tools

See full listing in **Section One** under **Ferrari**

Garry Roberts & Co
922 Sunset Dr
Costa Mesa, CA 92627
714-650-2690; FAX: 714-650-2730
E-mail: garryroberts@fea.net

cars
parts
service

See full listing in **Section One** under **Ferrari**

Rolls-Royce of Beverly Hills
11401 West Pico Blvd
Los Angeles, CA 90064
800-321-9792, 310-477-4262
FAX: 310-473-7498
E-mail: smrr64@aol.com

parts

See full listing in **Section One** under **Rolls-Royce/Bentley**

Tillack & Co Ltd
630 Mary Ann Dr
Redondo Beach, CA 90278
310-318-8760; FAX: 310-376-3392

parts
restoration

See full listing in **Section Two** under **restoration shops**

Vintage Motor Gaskets
W 604 19th
Spokane, WA 99203
509-747-9960, 509-747-0517
E-mail: dbrooke@ior.com

gaskets

See full listing in **Section Two** under **gaskets**

Auto Italia
3350 Woolsey Rd
Windsor, CA 95492
707-528-4825; FAX: 707-569-8717

parts

See full listing in **Section One** under **Fiat**

Bayless Inc
1111 Via Bayless
Marietta, GA 30066-2770
770-928-1446; FAX: 770-928-1342
800-241-1446, order line
(US & Canada)

accessories
parts

See full listing in **Section One** under **Fiat**

FAZA/Al Cosentino
Box 1917
Thousand Oaks, CA 91360
818-707-2301

books
information

See full listing in **Section One** under **Abarth**

International Auto Parts Inc
Rt 29 N
PO Box 9036
Charlottesville, VA 22906
800-788-4435, 804-973-0555
FAX: 804-973-2368

accessories
parts

See full listing in **Section One** under **Alfa Romeo**

C Obert & Co
2131-D Delaware Ave
Santa Cruz, CA 95060-5706
800-500-3428 orders
831-423-0218; FAX: 831-459-8128
E-mail: fiatplus@aol.com

parts
repairs

See full listing in **Section One** under **Fiat**

Doug Schellinger
13717 W Green Meadow Dr
New Berlin, WI 53151
414-786-8413
E-mail: dsac@execpc.com

automobilia
books
sales literature
toys

See full listing in **Section One** under **Fiat**

LINCOLN

Aabar's Cadillac & Lincoln Salvage & Parts	parts
9700 NE 23rd Oklahoma City, OK 73141 405-769-3318; FAX: 405-769-9542 E-mail: louanne1@juno.com	

See full listing in **Section One** under **Cadillac/LaSalle**

Antique Auto Electric	repro wiring
9109 (Rear) E Garvey Ave Rosemead, CA 91770 626-572-0938	

See full listing in **Section Two** under **electrical systems**

Antique & Classic Cars	car locator
1796 County Rd 7 Florence, AL 35633 205-760-0542	

See full listing in **Section One** under **Cadillac/LaSalle**

Auto Parts Exchange	NORS parts
PO Box 736 Reading, PA 19603 610-372-2813	NOS parts rebuilt parts used parts

Mail order and open shop. 7 am to 12 pm, 7 days. Open daily by appointment anytime. NOS, NORS and used parts for 1953-1979 Lincolns and 1958-1979 Thunderbirds. Parts tested before shipping if necessary. Rebuilding service for hydraulic top pumps, window motors. Brake and front end parts, etc. Remanufacturing parts for Lincolns. Worldwide shipping no problem.

Autowire Division	alternator
9109 (Rear) E. Garvey Avenue Rosemead, CA 91770 626-572-0938; FAX: 626-288-3311	conversions motors/relays switches

See full listing in **Section One** under **Ford 1954-up**

Baker's Auto-SRO Inc	parts
196 Providence Pike Putnam, CT 06260 860-928-7614, 800-962-9228 FAX: 860-928-0749	service

Mail order and open shop. Specializing in 1961-1979 Lincoln parts and services. 1961-1966 Thunderbird convertible top electrical repairs. Over 1.5 million parts in 30,000 square foot warehouse. Four full time mechanics specializing in convertible tops, power windows, heat, a/c, etc.

Bob's 36-48 Continental & Zephyr Parts	chrome service
10618 N Tee Ct Fountain Hills, AZ 85268-5723 602-837-0978; FAX: 602-837-0979	door sills instruments/parts water pumps

Mail order only. 1936-1948 Continental and Zephyr parts. Rebuilt water pumps, coils, dist, carburetors, NOS rotors, points, dist caps, hubcaps, scripts, stoplight assy, chroming show quality, dashboards, gauges, bumpers, aluminum door sills, stainless screw kits, restored medallions and thousands of other parts. Moved my 27 year collection of Lincoln Zephyr and Continental parts to my 6 car garage in sunny Arizona. Finally organized. Call or write for your needs.

Bob Burgess 1955-56 Ford Parts	parts
793 Alpha-Bellbrook Rd Bellbrook, OH 45305 937-426-8041	

See full listing in **Section One** under **Ford 1954-up**

California Continental & T-Bird Connection	consultant
PO Box 2281 Irwindale, CA 91706 818-962-6696 in CA	parts repairs

Mail order only. Specialty company handling repairs, parts and consultation of Lincoln Continentals and Marks 1961-1979, especially tops, windows and tricky electrical problems. Lincoln and T-Bird parts & service 1961-1979. Electrical specialty repairs, vacuum controls for a/c, etc. Convertible parts & service.

Cape Cod Classic Cars	car dealer
Pete Harvey PO Box 280 Cataumet, MA 02534 508-548-0660; FAX: 508-457-0660	

See full listing in **Section One** under **Cadillac/LaSalle**

John Cashman	convertible
8835 Purvis Rd Lithia, FL 33547-2604 813-737-5466 E-mail: jjlinc@ix.netcom.com	electrics new/used parts repairs

New, used and rebuilt parts for 1961-1979 Lincolns. Specializing in 1961-1967 convertibles. Have all electric, hydraulic and trim parts in stock from many parts cars and NOS stock. Also am doing mechanical and electrical work on these cars at my central FL shop. Call or write for details on how my 20 years' experience working on these cars can quickly fix your problems.

Chrome Masters	chrome plating
1109 W Orange Ave, Unit D Tallahassee, FL 32310 850-576-2100; FAX: 850-576-2772	pot metal restoration

See full listing in **Section Two** under **plating & polishing**

Classic Auto Air Mfg Co	air conditioning
2020 W Kennedy Blvd Tampa, FL 33606 813-251-2356, 813-251-4994	heating parts

See full listing in **Section One** under **Mustang**

Classic Car Works Ltd	restoration
3050 Upper Bethany Rd Jasper, GA 30143 770-735-3945	

See full listing in **Section Two** under **restoration shops**

Classic Ford Sales	salvage yard
PO Box 60 East Dixfield, ME 04227 207-562-4443; FAX: 207-562-4576 E-mail: classicford@quickconnect.com	

See full listing in **Section Five** under **Maine**

Classique Cars Unlimited	appraisals
7005 Turkey Bayou Rd PO Box 249 Lakeshore, MS 39558 800-543-8691, USA 228-467-9633; FAX: 228-467-9207 E-mail: parts@datasync.com	parts repairs restorations

Mail order/phone order. Monday-Friday 9 am to 6 pm, some Saturdays 9 am to 12 pm CST. 1958-1988 Lincoln and

Thunderbird new, used, reproduction parts. Three acres with three buildings full of parts for all your Lincoln and T-Bird needs. Shop work by appointment only. Appraisals for antique, classic, milestone, custom and special interest vehicles. Celebrating our 24th year! Home of the Karen A Williams Collection featuring cars of famous personalities. Catalogs available. Web site: www.classiquecars.com

Clean Sweep-Vacuum Windshield Wiper Motor Rebuilding 760 Knight Hill Rd Zillah, WA 98953 509-865-2481; FAX: 509-865-2189 E-mail: dkjaquith@prodigy.net	**motors** **repairs** **wiper parts**

See full listing in **Section Two** under **windshield wipers**

Color-Ite Refinishing Co Winning Colors 868 Carrington Rd, Rt 69 Bethany, CT 06524 203-393-0240; FAX: 203-393-0873 E-mail: colorite@ctinternet.com	**modern finishes** **restoration service**

See full listing in **Section Two** under **paints**

Bob Cook Classic Auto Parts Inc 2055 Van Cleave Rd, PO Box 600 Murray, KY 42071-0600 502-753-4000, 800-486-1137 FAX: 502-753-4600	**new parts** **NOS parts** **reproduced parts**

See full listing in **Section One** under **Ford 1954-up**

Buzz De Clerck 41760 Utica Rd Sterling Heights, MI 48313-3146 810-731-0765	**parts**

Mail order and open shop. All week 9 am to 9 pm. Specialize in

1969-1971 Lincoln Continental Mark III new and used parts. Can diagnose most problems with those cars over the phone or send to proper source for cure.

Don's Antique Auto Parts 37337 Niles Blvd Fremont, CA 94536 415-792-4390	**new parts** **used parts**

See full listing in **Section Two** under **comprehensive parts**

Edward W Drozd 84 Farm Hill Rd Wallingford, CT 06492 203-265-6638 E-mail: ewdrozd@snet.net	**grilles** **moldings**

See full listing in **Section One** under **Mercury**

Edgerton Classics Ltd 9215 St Rt 13 Camden, NY 13316-4933 315-245-3113	**restoration** **woodworking**

See full listing in **Section Two** under **restoration shops**

Egge Machine Company Inc 11707 Slauson Ave Santa Fe Springs, CA 90670 800-866-EGGE, 562-945-3419 FAX: 562-693-1635 E-mail: info@egge.com	**bearings** **pistons/rings** **timing components** **valve train**

See full listing in **Section Two** under **engine parts**

Jay M Fisher Acken Dr 4-B Clark, NJ 07066 732-388-6442	**mascots** **sidemount mirrors** **windwing brackets**

See full listing in **Section Two** under **accessories**

R O Hommel 933 Osage Rd Pittsburgh, PA 15243 412-279-8884	**body tags** **parts**

Mail order only. Used, NOS and reproduction parts for 1942-1948 Lincoln Continentals. Manufacture reproduction body tags for 1942-1948 Lincolns and Continentals. Glass parking light lenses reproduced; water pumps rebuilt; patent plates for firewall.

Horsepower Sales 130 Cardinal Dr Waynesville, NC 28786 516-532-7605 mobile, NY	**limousines**

See full listing in **Section Two** under **limousine rentals**

Bill Horton 5804 Jones Valley Dr Huntsville, AL 35802 256-881-6894	**vacuum motors**

See full listing in **Section One** under **Mercury**

Hot Rod & Custom Supply 1304 SE 10th St Cape Coral, FL 33990 941-574-7744; FAX: 941-574-8820	**custom parts** **engine parts** **speed parts**

See full listing in **Section One** under **Ford 1932-1953**

Jacks Wholesale Division 250 N Robertson Blvd, Ste 405 Beverly Hills, CA 90211-1793 310-839-9417; FAX: 310-839-1046	**limousines**

Lincoln and Cadillac limousines, Stutz Blackhawk, Rolls-Royce. Web site: www.jwdlimosales.com

Bob Johnson's Auto Literature 92 Blandin Ave Framingham, MA 01702 508-872-9173; FAX: 508-626-0991 E-mail: bjohnson@autopaper.com	**brochures literature manuals paint chips**

See full listing in **Section Two** under **literature dealers**

Keleen Leathers Inc 10526 W Cermak Rd Westchester, IL 60154 708-409-9800; FAX: 708-409-9801	**leather hides**

See full listing in **Section Two** under **interiors & interior parts**

Kenroy Ford Parts 2 Folwell Ln Mullica Hill, NJ 08062 609-478-2527 E-mail: duffieldm@aol.com	**NOS parts**

See full listing in **Section One** under **Ford 1954-up**

Lincoln Land Inc 1928 Sherwood St Clearwater, FL 34625 727-446-2193; FAX: 727-447-6179 E-mail: lincolnlandinc.com@worldnet.att.net	**cars parts service**

Phone orders and open shop. Monday-Friday 8 am to 5 pm. 1956-1992 Lincoln Continental cars, parts and service. Daily parts shipments worldwide. Web site: www.lincolnlandinc.com

Lincoln Old Parts Store Division of Mainly Convertibles 13805 W Hillsborough Ave Tampa, FL 33635 888-500-9717 orders 813-855-6869 tech FAX: 813-855-1376 E-mail: lincoln@llc.net	**parts repair restoration**

Mail order and open shop. Monday-Friday 9 am to 5 pm. New, reproduction, rebuilt and used parts. Rebuilding services, repairs and restorations for 1950s and 1960s Lincolns. Web site: www.lincolnoldparts.com

Lincoln Parts International 707 E 4th St, Bldg G Perris, CA 92570 800-382-1656, 909-657-5588 FAX: 909-657-4758 E-mail: lincprts@pe.net	**parts**

Mail order and open shop. Monday-Friday 8 am to 5 pm, Saturday 9 am to 2 pm. New, used and reproduction parts for 1961-1980s Lincolns, 1972-1979 Thunderbirds, 1974-1979 Cougars and 1971-1978 Mercury full-size. Quality guaranteed parts. Shipments daily worldwide. Visa, MasterCard, Discover and American Express. Free catalog of Lincoln parts. Web site: www.pe.net/~lincprts/

See our ad on this page

Lincoln Services Ltd Earle O Brown, Jr 229 Robinhood Ln McMurray, PA 15317 724-941-4567; FAX: 724-942-1940	**literature parts**

Mail order only. Parts bought, sold or traded for 1936-1948 Lincoln Zephyrs and Continentals, emphasis on HV-12 engine parts. Also Lincoln literature. Free catalog. Also information on membership in the Lincoln Continental Owners Club and/or the Lincoln Zephyr Owners Club.

Lincoln-Rubber Reproductions 9109 E Garvey Ave Rosemead, CA 91770 626-280-4546	**parts**

Mail order only. For 1940-1948 Continentals. Catalog, $4 USA.

Maffucci Sales Company Inc RD 1 Box 60, Rt 9 W Athens, NY 12015-9707 518-943-0100; FAX: 518-943-4534 E-mail: maffuccisales@mindspring.com	**literature parts**

Open by appointment only, Monday-Friday 9 am to 5 pm EST. Specializing in obsolete Lincoln, Mercury auto parts and literature for 1940s-early 1970s. Excellent inventory of new, reproduction and used auto parts and literature. Mostly mail order. Specialist in locating hard to find parts. Over 35 years' experience. Web site: lincolnmercuryparts.com

Mark II Enterprises 5225 Canyon Crest Dr Suite 71-217 Riverside, CA 92507 909-686-2752; FAX: 909-686-7245 E-mail: mark2@csi.com	**car covers parts**

See full listing in **Section Two** under **accessories**

Mercury & Ford Molded Rubber 12 Plymouth Ave Wilmington, MA 01887 978-658-8394	**parts**

See full listing in **Section One** under **Mercury**

Mid-Jersey Motorama Inc `car dealer`
1301 Asbury Ave
PO Box 1395
Asbury Park, NJ 07712
PH/FAX: 732-775-9885
beeper: 732-840-6111
E-mail: sjz1@aol.com

See full listing in **Section One** under **Cadillac/LaSalle**

Miller Obsolete Parts `locator service`
1329 Campus Dr `parts`
Vestal, NY 13850
607-722-5371; FAX: 607-770-9117
E-mail: fordpart@spectra.net

See full listing in **Section One** under **Ford 1954-up**

Max Nordeen's Wheels Museum `museum`
6400 N 400 Ave
Alpha, IL 61413
309-334-2589

See full listing in **Section Six** under **Illinois**

Oak Bows `top bows`
122 Ramsey Ave
Chambersburg, PA 17201
717-264-2602

See full listing in **Section Two** under **woodwork**

Regal International Motor Cars Inc `car dealer`
PO Box 6819
Hollywood, FL 33081
305-989-9777; FAX: 305-989-9778

See full listing in **Section One** under **Rolls-Royce/Bentley**

Rocky Mountain V8 Ford Parts `parts`
1124 Clark Cir
Colorado Springs, CO 80915
719-597-8375

See full listing in **Section One** under **Ford 1932-1953**

Tags Backeast `data plates`
PO Box 581 `trim tags`
Plainville, CT 06062
860-747-2942
E-mail: dataplt@snet.net

See full listing in **Section Two** under **special services**

Tom Taylor `NOS parts`
PO Box 129
Guinda, CA 95637
530-796-4106

See full listing in **Section One** under **Mopar**

Tech-Art Publications `books`
Jason Houston
Box 753
Ranchero Mirage, CA 92270
760-862-1979

See full listing in **Section Four** under **books & publications**

Pat Walsh Restorations `literature`
Box Q `rubber parts`
Wakefield, MA 01880
781-246-3266; FAX: 781-224-3311
E-mail: pwalshrest@aol.com

See full listing in **Section Two** under **rubber parts**

Wesley Obsolete Parts `parts`
116 Memory Ln
Liberty, KY 42539
606-787-5293; FAX: 606-787-7252

See full listing in **Section One** under **Ford 1954-up**

Westwind Limousine Sales `limousine sales`
2720 W National Rd
Dayton, OH 45414
937-898-9000; FAX: 937-898-9800

Specializing in limousine sales.

The Wixom Connection `parts`
2204 Steffanie Ct
Kissimmee, FL 34746
407-933-4030

Specializing in the supply of 1969-1971 Continental Mark III parts. Extensive collection of weatherstrip available for Mark III. Limited service work performed by appointment. Over 20 years of experience. Located near Walt Disney World, FL.

LOCOMOBILE

Errol's Steam Works `castings`
3123 Baird Rd `engines`
North Vancouver BC `parts`
Canada V7K 2G5
PH/FAX: 604-985-9494
E-mail: steamworks@idmail.com

Mail order and open shop by appointment. Early steam carriage parts. Castings and finished machined parts, pumps, steam automatics, etc. Dry-Land steam automobile engines, casting kits, machined kits and finished, ready to run engines. Also steam bicycle and tricycle engines, kits and finished ready to run sets with or without bicycle or tricycle.

International Towing & Recovery Museum `museum`
401 Broad St
Chattanooga, TN 37402
PH/FAX: 423-267-3132

See full listing in **Section Six** under **Tennessee**

Automotive Artistry `restoration`
4311 Mennonite Rd
Mantua, OH 44255
330-274-8699

See full listing in **Section One** under **Triumph**

Dave Bean Engineering `parts`
636 E St Charles St SR3H
San Andreas, CA 95249
209-754-5802; FAX: 209-754-5177
E-mail: admin@davebean.com

Specializing in parts for Lotus. Web site: www.davebean.com

Cockermouth Motor Museum
The Maltings
Brewery Ln
Cockermouth Cumbria England
01900 824448

museum

See full listing in **Section Six** under **England**

French Stuff
PO Box 39772
Glendale, CA 90039-0772
818-244-2498; FAX: 818-500-7628
E-mail: frenchap@gte.net

**accessories
engine rebuilding
parts
transaxle rebuild-
ing**

See full listing in **Section One** under **Renault**

JAE
375 Pine #26
Goleta, CA 93117
805-967-5767; FAX: 805-967-6183
E-mail: jefforjay@jaeparts.com

**parts
service
tech info**

Mail order and open shop. Monday-Friday 7:30 am to 5 pm,
Saturday by appointment. Parts, service and tech info for Lotus,
English Ford and English specialist cars (TVR, Elva, Jensen,
etc). Official Lotus Heritage parts dealer. Web site:
www.jaeparts.com

Kreimeyer Co/Auto Legends Inc
3211 N Wilburn Ave
Bethany, OK 73008
405-789-9499; FAX: 405-789-7888

**antennas/repair
glass/wholesale
parts/wholesale
radios/radio repair**

See full listing in **Section One** under **Mercedes-Benz**

Marcovicci-Wenz Engineering Inc
33 Comac Loop
Ronkonkoma, NY 11779
516-467-9040; FAX: 516-467-9041
E-mail: tedwenz@compuserve.com

Cosworth engines

See full listing in **Section Two** under **racing**

Omni Specialties
10418 Lorain Ave
Cleveland, OH 44111
888-819-6464 (MGMG)
216-251-2269; FAX: 216-251-6083

**parts
restoration
service**

See full listing in **Section One** under **MG**

Ragtops & Roadsters
203 S 4th St
Perkasie, PA 18944
215-257-1202; FAX: 215-257-2688
E-mail: info@ragtops.com

**bodywork/painting
British automobiles
engine rebuilding
vintage race prep**

See full listing in **Section Two** under **restoration shops**

RD Enterprises Ltd
290 Raub Rd
Quakertown, PA 18951
215-538-9323; FAX: 215-538-0158
E-mail: rdent@rdent.com

parts

Lotus owners: RD Enterprises has been supplying parts and
expert assistance for over 20 years. We have a large inventory of
original parts for Elan, Europa, Elite, Esprit and Turbo; engine,
suspension, drivetrain, electrics, hydraulics, body seals, badges
as well as aftermarket and accessory items; CarCapsules,
Double-S stainless exhausts, Panasport alloy wheels, Spax
adjustable shocks, accessories, books and scale models.
Visa/MasterCard accepted. Web site: www.rdent.com

Replicarz
99 State St
Rutland, VT 05701
802-747-7151
E-mail: replicarz@aol.com

**books
kits
models
videos**

See full listing in **Section Two** under **racing**

Rolls-Royce of Beverly Hills
11401 West Pico Blvd
Los Angeles, CA 90064
800-321-9792, 310-477-4262
FAX: 310-473-7498
E-mail: smrr64@aol.com

parts

See full listing in **Section One** under **Rolls-Royce/Bentley**

The Registry
Pine Grove
Stanley, VA 22851
540-778-3728; FAX: 540-778-2402
E-mail: britregstry@aol.com or
oldwregistry@aol.com

periodical

See full listing in **Section Four** under **periodicals**

Von's Austin-Healey Restorations
10270 Barberville Rd
Fort Mill, SC 29715
803-548-4590; FAX: 803-548-4816
E-mail: vons@vnet.net

**parts
repairs
restoration**

See full listing in **Section One** under **Austin-Healey**

Bassett's Jaguar
PO Box 245
53 Stilson Rd
Wyoming, RI 02898
401-539-3010; FAX: 401-539-7861
E-mail: www.jagwillie@ids.net

**parts
restoration
service
upholstery**

See full listing in **Section One** under **Jaguar**

BCP Sport & Classic Co
10525 Airline Dr
Houston, TX 77037
281-448-4739; FAX: 281-448-0189

**parts
service**

See full listing in **Section One** under **MG**

Collector Car Appraisers LLC
800 Waterford Dr
Frederick, MD 21702
301-473-8333; FAX: 301-698-4796
E-mail: gfmchugh@netstorm.net

appraisals

See full listing in **Section Two** under **appraisals**

Drummond Coach and Paint
531 Raleigh Ave
El Cajon, CA 92020
619-579-7229; FAX: 619-579-2128

**painting
restoration**

See full listing in **Section One** under **Ferrari**

Exoticars USA
6 Washington St
Frenchtown, NJ 08825
908-996-4889; FAX: 908-996-6938

**machine work
paint/bodywork
restoration/service
welding/fabrication**

See full listing in **Section One** under **Ferrari**

FAZA/Al Cosentino	**books**
Box 1917	**information**
Thousand Oaks, CA 91360	
818-707-2301	

See full listing in **Section One** under **Abarth**

The Fine Car Store	**car dealer**
1105 Moana Dr	
San Diego, CA 92107	
619-223-7766; FAX: 619-223-6838	

See full listing in **Section One** under **Ferrari**

The Italian Car Registry	**information source**
3305 Valley Vista Rd	
Walnut Creek, CA 94598-3943	
925-458-1163	

See full listing in **Section Four** under **information sources**

Kreimeyer Co/Auto Legends Inc	**antennas/repair**
3211 N Wilburn Ave	**glass/wholesale**
Bethany, OK 73008	**parts/wholesale**
405-789-9499; FAX: 405-789-7888	**radios/radio repair**

See full listing in **Section One** under **Mercedes-Benz**

London Stainless Steel Exhaust Centre	**exhaust systems**
249-253 Queenstown Rd	
London, SW8 3NP England	
011-44-171622-2120	
FAX: 011-44-171627- 0991	
E-mail: 101445.341@compuserv.com	

See full listing in **Section Two** under **exhaust systems**

MIE Corporation	**parts**
PO Box 1015	
Mercer Island, WA 98040	
425-455-4449; FAX: 425-688-1903	
E-mail: mie@maseratinet	

Maserati spare parts, $8,000,000 plus in new and used parts, over 30,000 line items in new parts alone. Knowledgeable personnel, computerized for easy ordering. Technical support. Web site: www.maseratinet.com

Motorcar Gallery Inc	**car dealer**
715 N Federal Hwy	
Fort Lauderdale, FL 33304	
954-522-9900; FAX: 954-522-9966	

See full listing in **Section One** under **Ferrari**

Garry Roberts & Co	**cars**
922 Sunset Dr	**parts**
Costa Mesa, CA 92627	**service**
714-650-2690; FAX: 714-650-2730	
E-mail: garryroberts@fea.net	

See full listing in **Section One** under **Ferrari**

Tillack & Co Ltd	**parts**
630 Mary Ann Dr	**restoration**
Redondo Beach, CA 90278	
310-318-8760; FAX: 310-376-3392	

See full listing in **Section Two** under **restoration shops**

Smooth Line	**body panels**
2562 Riddle Run Rd	**removable hardtops**
Tarentum, PA 15084	
724-274-6002; FAX: 724-274-6121	

See full listing in **Section Two** under **tops**

A&F Imported Parts Inc	**parts**
490 40th St	
Oakland, CA 94609	
888-263-7278; FAX: 707-256-0764	
E-mail: mmast64166@aol.com	

Mail order and open shop. Monday-Friday 7:30 am to 5 pm. Specializing in Mercedes-Benz and BMW parts for models from the 1950s-present. Web site: www.a-and-f.com

Aase Bros Inc	**salvage yard**
701 E Cypress St	
Anaheim, CA 92805	
714-956-2419; FAX: 714-956-2635	
E-mail: sales@aasebros.com	

See full listing in **Section Five** under **California**

Asom Electric	**electrical systems**
1204 McClellan Dr	**rebuilding**
Los Angeles, CA 90025	
310-820-4457; FAX: 310-820-5908	

See full listing in **Section Two** under **electrical systems**

ATVM	**literature**
97 Mt Royal Ave	**parts**
Aberdeen, MD 21001	
410-272-2252; FAX: 410-272-4940	

Mail order only. Mercedes-Benz parts and literature for 1934-1972 models.

Auto Craftsmen Restoration Inc	**appraisals**
27945 Elm Grove	**buyer/car locator**
San Antonio, TX 78261	**old M-B parts**
PH/FAX: 830-980-4027	**restoration**

See full listing in **Section Two** under **restoration shops**

Auto Enthusiasts	**seats**
200 Everett Ave	
Chelsea, MA 02150	
617-889-0606; FAX: 617-889-0847	

Mail order and open shop. Monday-Friday 8 am to 5 pm. Manufacturer and distributer of Mercedes-Benz SL rear seats (1972-1999) and station wagon third seats (1979-1996).

Autolux Inc	**Mercedes parts**
23242 Tasmania Cir	
Dana Point, CA 92629	
949-493-5578; FAX: 949-493-3710	

Mail order only. Mercedes-Benz replacement parts for Dure-lever heater and vent control levers, attach through vent openings in 20-30 minutes. Chassis #108, #109 and #113. Uni-di door lock diaphrams, Mercedes 1973-1980. AC-DI, repair air conditioning vacuum elements. Chassis #123 and #126. Seat adjustment handles, front and side, chassis #115, #116, #126. Gear replacements for sunroof, seat retractor arms and antenna.

AutoMatch CARS (Computer Aided Referral Service) 2017 Blvd Napoleon Louisville, KY 40205 800-962-2771, 502-417-8793 mobile 502-452-1920 office; FAX: 502-479-6222 E-mail: amcars@aol.com or aautomatch@aol.com	broker car dealer network locator

See full listing in **Section Two** under **car dealers**

Automobile Appraisal Service Steve Cram 1080 Eddy St #607 San Francisco, CA 94109 415-567-1087, 619-584-4678 FAX: 415-567-1245	appraisals

See full listing in **Section Two** under **appraisals**

Automotive Artistry 4311 Mennonite Rd Mantua, OH 44255 330-274-8699	restoration

See full listing in **Section One** under **Triumph**

Bassett's Jaguar PO Box 245 53 Stilson Rd Wyoming, RI 02898 401-539-3010; FAX: 401-539-7861 E-mail: www.jagwillie@ids.net	parts restoration service upholstery

See full listing in **Section One** under **Jaguar**

BCP Sport & Classic Co 10525 Airline Dr Houston, TX 77037 281-448-4739; FAX: 281-448-0189	parts service

See full listing in **Section One** under **MG**

Becker of North America Inc 16 Park Way Upper Saddle River, NJ 07458 888-423-3537; FAX: 201-327-2084 E-mail: info@beckerautosound.com	radio repair

Specializing in Mercedes-Benz radio repair. Web site: www.beckerautosound.com

JJ Best & Co 737 Main St PO Box 10 Chatham, MA 02633 508-945-6000; FAX: 508-945-6006	financing

See full listing in **Section Two** under **consultants**

Blackhawk Collection 1092 Eagles Nest Pl Danville, CA 94506-3600 925-736-3444; FAX: 925-736-4375 E-mail: info@blackhawkcollection.com	acquisitions sales

See full listing in **Section One** under **Duesenberg**

Blitzen Enterprises Inc 8341 E Evans Rd, Suite 104 Scottsdale, AZ 85260 888-254-8936 toll-free FAX: 602-991-6301 E-mail: mbparts@blitzen.com	parts

Mail order and open shop. Monday-Friday 8 am to 5:30 pm, Saturday 9 am to 12 pm. Mercedes-Benz parts for all 1950s-up. Specializing in fast moving service items and difficult to find items. Wholesale to the public. Web site: www.blitzen.com

BMC Classics Inc 828 N Dixie Freeway New Smyrna Beach, FL 32168 904-426-6405; FAX: 904-427-4570 E-mail: bmcar1@aol.com	parts repair restoration

See full listing in **Section Two** under **restoration shops**

British Restorations 4455 Paul St Philadelphia, PA 19124 215-533-6696	car dealer restoration

See full listing in **Section One** under **Jaguar**

Brooklyn Motoren Werke Inc 115 Market St Brooklyn, WI 53521 608-455-7441; FAX: 608-455-7442	appraisals parts restoration service

Open shop. Monday-Friday. Restoration, service and parts for post-war Mercedes-Benz. Innovative engineering. Specializing in 300 series.

Cabriolet Enterprises 2115 S Pontius Ave West Los Angeles, CA 90025 310-472-2062; FAX: 310-444-9976	consulting parts restoration services sales

Mail or fax orders, please. Workshop open by appointment. Specializing in Mercedes-Benz cabriolets of the 1950s (in order of interest): 220, 300S, 170S and 300. Providing a full range of restoration services. Sale of tops, headliners, boots and carpet sets, glass, NOS/used/rebuilt moldings, pot and sheetmetal and mechanical assemblies, luggage, 6/12 volt radios, original and reprinted literature. Provenance research, inspections, movie studio rentals and sale of Type 187 original, complete and authentic coupes and cabriolets from my personal forty-five year collection. Robert H I Silver, proprietor.

Celestial Mechanics 88 West 500 South Wellsville, UT 84339 435-245-4987 E-mail: volvox@cache.net	restoration

See full listing in **Section One** under **Volvo**

The Checkered Flag Collection Box 806 Millville, NJ 08332 609-327-1505	car dealer

See full listing in **Section One** under **Ferrari**

Dash Specialists 1910 Redbud Ln Medford, OR 97504 541-776-0040	interiors

See full listing in **Section One** under **Cadillac/LaSalle**

Dashboards Plus 336 Cottonwood Ave Hartland, WI 53029 800-221-8161; FAX: 414-367-9474	restoration parts wood dash overlays

See full listing in **Section One** under **Jaguar**

Dave's Auto Restoration 2285 Rt 307 E Jefferson, OH 44047 PH/FAX: 216-858-2227 E-mail: davesauto@knownet.net	**upholstery**

See full listing in **Section Two** under **interiors & interior parts**

Deutsches Museum Museumsinsel 1 D-80538 Munchen Germany 089 2179-1, 089 2179-260 089 2179-255; FAX: 089 2179-324	**museum**

See full listing in **Section Six** under **Germany**

DeVito Auto Restorations 470 Boston Post Rd Weston, MA 02493 781-893-4949 ext 142 FAX: 781-899-4900 E-mail: radjr@ix.netcom.com	**restorations** **rust repair**

See full listing in **Section Two** under **bodywork**

DTE Motorsports 242 South Rd Brentwood, NH 03833 PH/FAX: 603-642-3766 E-mail: ldnh49a@prodigy.com	**engines** **mechanical services** **race prep** **transportation**

Specializing in mechanical and component services, engines, transportation, race prep and support for Mercedes-Benz, Ferrari, Porsche, Bugatti and limited production marques. Aircraft mechanical licenses. 25 years' in classic car business.

EIS Engines Inc 215 SE Grand Ave Portland, OR 97214 800-547-0002, 503-232-5590 FAX: 503-232-5178 E-mail: edikeis@aol.com	**engines**

Replacement gas and diesel engines as well as engine parts for Mercedes-Benz vehicles from classic mid-1950s-current.

European Connection 313-1/2 Main St Falmouth, KY 41040 800-395-8636; FAX: 606-654-3700	**parts**

Mail order only. New and used parts. Over 700 wrecked Mercedes for parts. Lots of NOS. UPS and trucking. Visa, MasterCard and Discover accepted.

European Parts Specialists Ltd PO Box 6783 Santa Barbara, CA 93160 800-334-2749, 805-683-4020 FAX: 805-683-3689 E-mail: epsparts@impulse.net	**accessories** **parts**

Specializes in parts and accessories for Mercedes, BMW, Porsche, Volvo, Saab, Volkswagen and Audi. Web site: epsparts.com

EuroTech Services International 108 Milarepa Rd Azalea, OR 97410 541-837-3636; FAX: 541-837-3737 E-mail: jim@eurotech-services.com	**parts**

Mail order only. A German/American firm serving owners of Mercedes-Benz automobiles. Offers direct surface, air and 3 day courier procurement for "Germany-only" parts. Also uniquely specialized in sales, service and parts for exceptional Mercedes-Benz vehicles such as Unimog 4x4 trucks/tractors, off-road motorhomes and mobile workshops and auxiliary machinery in world-respected Unimog multi-implement technologies; 4x4 Gelaendewagen, 4x2 trucks, buses and motorhomes. Web site: www.eurotech-services.com

Bob Fatone's Mercedes Used Parts 166 W Main St Niantic, CT 06357 860-739-1923; FAX: 860-691-0669 E-mail: bobfatone@earthlink.net	**parts**

Mail order or open by appointment only. Specializing in most all used replacement parts, engine, body, chrome, interior, etc, for Mercedes highline chassis #111 coupe and convertible Models 220SE, 250SE, 280SE and some 4-door cars for years 1960-1971. 95% of orders are by mail.

Foreign Motors West 253 N Main St Natick, MA 01760 508-655-5350; FAX: 508-651-0178	**car sales**

See full listing in **Section One** under **Rolls-Royce/Bentley**

Paul Foulkes-Halbard Filching Wannock Eastbourne Polegate Sussex BN26 5QA England 011 441323 487838 011 441323 487124 FAX: 011 441323 486331	**brass age cars** **parts**

See full listing in **Section One** under **Bugatti**

Germany Direct 12325 West Ave San Antonio, TX 78216 888-588-4920; FAX: 210-341-8971	**parts**

Mail order and open shop. Monday-Friday 9 am to 12 noon and 1 pm to 5 pm. Specializing in parts for Mercedes-Benz 1960s and 1950s models.

Grand Prix Classics Inc 7456 La Jolla Blvd La Jolla, CA 92037 619-459-3500; FAX: 619-459-3512	**racing cars** **sports cars**

See full listing in **Section Two** under **racing**

Griot's Garage 3500-A 20th St E Tacoma, WA 98424 800-345-5789; FAX: 888-252-2252 E-mail: info@griotsgarage.com	**car care products** **paint** **tools**

See full listing in **Section Two** under **tools**

Hatch & Sons Automotive Inc 533 Boston Post Rd Wayland, MA 01778 508-358-3500; FAX: 508-358-3578	**detailing** **parts** **service** **wood refinishing**

Mail order and open shop. Monday-Saturday 8 am to 6 pm, Sunday 1 pm to 5 pm. Restoration, auto body, service, detailing, parts, leather work, wood refinishing, sales and consignment for Mercedes-Benz exclusively.

Highway One Classic Automobiles and Highwayone.com Classic Classifieds 1035 California Dr Burlingame, CA 94010 650-342-7340; FAX: 650-343-0150 E-mail: djboscacci@msn.com	**classic automobiles**

See full listing in **Section One** under **Abarth**

Hjeltness Restoration Inc 630 Alpine Way Escondido, CA 92029 760-746-9966; FAX: 760-746-7738	**restoration service**

See full listing in **Section Two** under **restoration shops**

Horst's Car Care 3160-1/2 N Woodford St Decatur, IL 62526 217-876-1112	**engine rebuilding**

Open shop only. Monday-Friday 8 am to 5 pm, Saturday 8 am to 12 noon. Mercedes-Benz engine rebuilding, 1950s-1990s.

House of Imports Inc 12203 W Colfax Ave Lakewood, CO 80215 303-232-2540; FAX: 303-232-3260	**car dealer**

Mail order and open shop. Monday-Saturday 9 am to 6 pm. Buys and sells used Mercedes-Benz.

Italy's Famous Exhaust 2711 183rd St Redondo Beach, CA 90278 310-793-5985 E-mail: famous@earthlink.net	**exhaust systems wheels**

See full listing in **Section Two** under **exhaust systems**

JAM Engineering Corp PO Box 2570 Monterey, CA 93942 800-JAM-CORP, 831-372-1787 E-mail: jam@redshift.com	**carburetors**

See full listing in **Section Two** under **carburetors**

Kensington Motor Group Inc PO Box 2277 Sag Harbor, NY 11963 516-537-1868; FAX: 516-537-2641 E-mail: kenmotor@aol.com	**consignment sales**

Consignment sales of vintage, classic, exotic, sports and luxury motor cars. Promoter of the Hamptons Auto Classic Collector Car Auction in May. Web site: www.kensingtonmotor.com

Kreimeyer Co/Auto Legends Inc 3211 N Wilburn Ave Bethany, OK 73008 405-789-9499; FAX: 405-789-7888	**antennas/repair glass/wholesale parts/wholesale radios/radio repair**

Specializing in auto glass for all vehicles: antique, classic, domestic, exotic and foreign at wholesale prices. Windshields and back glass for most models. Custom made glass and custom cutting available. Sales and repairs for Becker/Blaupunkt radios and Hirschmann antennas. Specializing in new Mercedes parts, 1950-1995, at wholesale prices. Specializing in 190SL and 300SL parts. Engine, fuel system and transmission service available. First class reproductions. 300SLR reproduction, 300SL sales/parts. Mercedes 1954 300SLR. High-performance 0-60 4.0 seconds! Own a piece of racing history. Photos available.

Leatherique Leather Restoration Products PO Box 2678 Orange Park, FL 32065 904-272-0992; FAX: 904-272-1534 E-mail: lrpltd@aol.com	**leather cleaning conditioning products**

See full listing in **Section One** under **Rolls-Royce/Bentley**

Lyco Engineering Inc 8645 N Territorial Rd Plymouth, MI 48170 734-459-7313; FAX: 734-459-2224	**machine work parts**

Mail order and open shop. Monday-Saturday 9 am to 6 pm. 30 years' experience with Mercedes-Benz 300SL cars, 1954-1964. Complete machine shop. Genuine and reproduction parts in stock. Engine, transmission, running gear, trim, tools, weatherstrips/seals, glass, all brake parts, wheels chromed. Many remanufactured parts on exchange basis. Also extensive inventory of parts for 1952-1962 300 Series coupes and sedans (formerly supplied by Chuck Brahms).

Machina Locksmith 3 Porter St Watertown, MA 02172-4145 PH/FAX: 617-923-1683	**car locks keys**

See full listing in **Section Two** under **locks & keys**

Marshall Antique & Classic Restorations 3714 Old Philadelphia Pike Bethlehem, PA 18015 610-868-7765; FAX: 610-868-7529	**coolant additives restoration services**

See full listing in **Section One** under **Rolls-Royce/Bentley**

Mercedes Auto Recycling 225C Salinas Rd Watsonville, CA 95076 800-264-2111, 831-786-0536 FAX: 831-786-0545 E-mail: admin@mercedesrecycling.com	**salvage yard**

See full listing in **Section Five** under **California**

Mercedes-Benz Service by Angela & George/ABS Exotic Repair Inc 700 N Andrews Ave Fort Lauderdale, FL 33304 954-566-7785; FAX: 954-522-0087	**sales service**

Open shop only. Monday-Friday 8:30 am to 7 pm, Saturday 8 am to 12 pm. Specialize in Mercedes-Benz, Jaguar and Rolls-Royce, all models, years. Mercedes-Benz and Jaguar service and parts. Classes for Mercedes-Benz and Jaguar owners, *Benz Smart* and *Jag Smart*, are held monthly. We offer 24 hour service, our pager number is 954-390-1993. We also sell our private collection of Mercedes-Benz.

Mercedes-Benz Visitor Center PO Box 100 Tuscaloosa, AL 35403-0100 888-2TOUR-MB, 205-507-2262 FAX: 205-507-2255	**museum**

Open year round. Monday-Friday 9 am to 5 pm, Saturday 10 am to 5 pm. Closed 2 weeks for Christmas and New Years and holidays. Houses the only Mercedes-Benz museum outside of Germany. Exhibits include corporate history, including a replica of the world's first motorized vehicle and motorcycle. Also featured are Mercedes-Benz safety developments, racing history and the Alabama-made M-class all activity vehicle. Several vintage vehicles are displayed, along with numerous audio-visual exhibits. Also housed in the Center is a retail boutique featuring apparel, collectibles and gift items. Exhibition cars of special note: 1956 300SL gullwing, 1907 Mercedes Simplex Spider, M-Class camouflage vehicle from Steven Spielberg's *Lost World*, 1886 Daimler Motorkutsche. Web site: www.mbusi.com

Michael's Auto Parts 5875 NW Kaiser Rd Portland, OR 97229 503-690-7750; FAX: 503-690-7735	**used Mercedes parts only**

See full listing in **Section Five** under **Oregon**

Michael's Classics Inc   **Unimogs**
954 Montauk Hwy
Bayport, NY 11705
516-363-4200; FAX: 516-363-9226
E-mail: info@unimognet.com

Specializing in sales and parts of Mercedes-Benz Unimogs, ex-military 4-wheel drive trucks for vintage 1957-1967. Web site: www.unimognet.com

Mid-Jersey Motorama Inc   **car dealer**
1301 Asbury Ave
PO Box 1395
Asbury Park, NJ 07712
PH/FAX: 732-775-9885
beeper: 732-840-6111
E-mail: sjz1@aol.com

See full listing in **Section One** under **Cadillac/LaSalle**

Millers Incorporated   **accessories**
7412 Count Circle   **parts**
Huntington Beach, CA 92647
714-375-6565; FAX: 714-847-6606
E-mail: sales@millermbz.com

Mail order and open shop. Monday-Friday 8 am to 5 pm. Specializing in parts and accessories for the classic Mercedes-Benz for 1950s, 1960s and 1970s. Especially Mercedes-Benz 190SLs; 230, 250, 280SLs, 450, 350, 500SL, SLCs; 220, 200 sedans; 250C, 300SD, TD, 380SEC. Web site: millermbz.com

Motorcars Ltd   **parts**
8101 Hempstead
Houston, TX 77008
800-231-6563; FAX: 713-863-8238
E-mail: info@britishparts.com

See full listing in **Section One** under **Jaguar**

Northern Motorsport Ltd   **repair**
PO Box 508, Rt 5   **restoration**
Wilder, VT 05088   **sales**
802-296-2099; FAX: 802-295-6599   **service**

See full listing in **Section Two** under **restoration shops**

The Old Carb Doctor   **carburetors**
Rt 3, Box 338   **fuel pumps**
Drucilla Church Rd
Nebo, NC 28761
800-945-CARB (2272)
704-659-1428

See full listing in **Section Two** under **carburetors**

Ottorich   **restoration**
619 Hammond St
Chestnut Hill, MA 02467
617-738-5488
E-mail: rdmfm@mediaone.net

Open shop by appointment only. Monday-Friday 7:30 am to 5 pm. Performs complete restoration of Mercedes-Benz, BMW and Harley-Davidson while also providing everyday technicals for these fine motor cars and bikes.

Paul Padget   **sales**
7641 Reinhold Dr
Cincinnati, OH 45237
513-821-2143

Best by appointment please. Specializing in sales of Mercedes and other specialty cars. Hemmings advertiser since 1962.

Paul's Autohaus Inc   **parts**
PO Box 978
Amherst, MA 01004
413-549-5081; FAX: 413-549-8018

Mail order only. Specializing in parts for antique/classic Mercedes-Benz, 170, 220, 300, 220S/SE, 190SL, 230SL, 250SL and 280SL.

Lyle Pearson Company   **accessories**
351 Auto Dr   **literature**
Boise, ID 83709   **parts**
208-377-3900; FAX: 208-375-0691

Mail order and open shop. Monday-Friday 7:30 am to 6 pm MST. Specializing in genuine parts, accessories and literature for Mercedes-Benz, Volvo, Land Rover/Range Rover and Acura.

Peninsula Imports   **accessories**
3749 Harlem Rd   **parts**
Buffalo, NY 14215   **trim**
800-999-1209; FAX: 905-847-3021
E-mail: imports@ican.net

See full listing in **Section One** under **BMW**

Performance Analysis Co   **climate control**
1345 Oak Ridge Tpke, Ste 258   **cruise control**
Oak Ridge, TN 37830
423-482-9175
E-mail:
george_murphy@compuserve.com

Mail order only. Specializing in climate control, cruise control, electronic modules and specialty parts for Mercedes-Benz automobiles.

John T Poulin   **car dealer**
Auto Sales/Star Service Center   **parts**
5th Ave & 111th St   **restoration service**
North Troy, NY 12182
518-235-8610

Mail order and open shop. Monday-Saturday 9 am to 6 pm. Specializing in sales of Mercedes-Benz and has a repair shop for all service and restoration of Mercedes with many used and new parts. Been in business of Mercedes-Benz for 45 years (complete car care). 1950s-1990s Mercedes and BMW used cars.

Precious Metal Automotive   **broker**
Restoration Co Inc   **restoration**
1601 College Ave SE
Grand Rapids, MI 49507
616-243-0220; FAX: 616-243-6646
E-mail: prshsmtl@pathwaynet.com

Full service 6,500 restoration and service facility devoted to the collectible Mercedes-Benz cars. More than 90 190SL restorations and many 230/250/280SLs, plus 220S/SE coupes and cabriolets and many other models. Cars bought, sold and brokered. Convenient midwest location. Web site: www.preciousauto.com

Precision Auto Designs   **accessories**
28 Railway Ave   **car covers**
Campbell, CA 95008   **restoration**
408-378-2332; FAX: 408-378-1301
E-mail: pad@precisionauto.com

Mail order only. Accessories for Mercedes-Benz and also exclusive manufacturer of Car Capsule, self inflating vehicle storage bubbles. Car covers, Mercedes-Benz restoration. Web site: precisionauto.com

Precision Autoworks 2202 Federal Street East Camden, NJ 08105 609-966-0080, NJ FAX: 610-649-3577, PA	restorations

Full or partial cosmetic and/or mechanical restorations for Mercedes-Benz, all models after WW II, both for show or drive.

Proper Motor Cars Inc 1811 11th Ave N St Petersburg, FL 33713-5794 727-821-8883; FAX: 727-821-0273 E-mail: propermotorcarsinc@email.msn.com	parts restoration service

See full listing in **Section One** under **Rolls-Royce/Bentley**

Regal International Motor Cars Inc PO Box 6819 Hollywood, FL 33081 305-989-9777; FAX: 305-989-9778	car dealer

See full listing in **Section One** under **Rolls-Royce/Bentley**

Restoration Services 16049 W 4th Ave Golden, CO 80401 303-271-0356	restoration

See full listing in **Section One** under **Porsche**

RM Auto Restoration Ltd 9435 Horton Line Blenheim, ON Canada N0P 1A0 519-352-4575; FAX: 519-351-1337 E-mail: clark@rmcars.com	panel fabrication parts restoration

See full listing in **Section Two** under **restoration shops**

Ron's Restorations Inc 2968-B Ask Kay Dr Smyrna, GA 30082 770-438-6102; FAX: 770-438-0037	interior trim restoration

Specializing in interior trim replacement, repair and total restorations for all Mercedes-Benz automobiles.

Royal Coach Works Ltd 2146 Lunceford Ln Lilburn, GA 30047 PH/FAX: 404-249-9040	appraisals

See full listing in **Section Two** under **appraisals**

Paul Russell & Company 106 Western Ave Essex, MA 01929 978-768-6919; FAX: 978-768-3523 E-mail: info@paulrussellandco.com	car dealer mechanical service parts restoration

See full listing in **Section Two** under **restoration shops**

Showroom Auto Sales 960 S Bascom Ave San Jose, CA 95128 408-279-0944; FAX: 408-279-0918	car dealer

Business hours: Monday-Friday 12 noon to 7 pm, Saturday 12 noon to 4 pm. Specializing in 1971 and older classic Mercedes-Benz convertibles. Also specializing in exotics and cars of distinction. Web site: www.showroomcars.com

Silver Star Restorations 116 Highway 19 Topton, NC 28781 704-321-4268 E-mail: silverstar@main.nc.us	parts restoration

Mail order and open shop. Monday-Friday 8 am to 5 pm. A full service restoration facility (paint, body, mechanical, electrical, woodwork, interiors) for coupes and convertibles and SL models. Pre-1972. Carry a complete line of original replacement parts. Also sell vintage Mercedes-Benz automobiles. Web site: www.silverstarrestorations.com

SL-Tech 230SL-250SL-280SL 1364 Portland Rd US Rt 1 Arundel/Kennebunkport, ME 04046 207-985-3001; FAX: 207-985-3011 E-mail: gernold@sltechw113.com	parts restoration service

Mail order and open shop. Monday-Friday 8 am to 12 pm, 2 pm to 6 pm, Saturday by appointment. Specializing in parts, service, restoration and convertible top frame repairs for 1963-1971 Mercedes-Benz W113 chassis, 230, 250, 280SL roadsters. Web site: www.sltechw113.com

Sports Leicht Restorations 16 Maple Street Topsfield, MA 01983 978-887-6644; FAX: 978-887-3889 E-mail: slr190sl@aol.com	restoration sales service

Restoration and service and sales. Specializing in Mercedes especially 190SL. Contact Alex Dearborn.

Star Classics Inc 7745 E Redfield #300 Scottsdale, AZ 85260 800-644-7827, 480-991-7495 FAX: 480-951-4096 E-mail: starcls@primenet.com	parts

Mail order and open shop. Monday-Friday 8 am to 5 pm. Parts for Mercedes-Benz of the 1950s. All the collectible models. Hood stars to tailpipe tip. anything made of rubber, chrome, etc. All lenses and trim items. Leather in all the original colors. Component restoration and exchange service available for same day shipping. All engine rebuild parts in stock for these models. Discount plan available. All credit cards accepted. Post-war to 1963. 170 sedan to the Gullwing and the 300S/Sc. Same day worldwide shipping. Web site: www.starclassics.com

Star Motors Neil Dubey 1694 Union Center Hwy Endicott, NY 13760 607-786-3918, 607-754-4272 FAX: 607-754-5112 E-mail: n300sel63@aol.com	parts restoration

Specializing in E service, restorations and parts, new, used and rebuilt for 300SEL, 300SEL 6.3, 450SEL, 450SEL 6.9, Grand 600 (all model years).

Star Quality 1 Alley Rd Lagrangeville, NY 12540 800-782-7199; FAX: 914-223-5394 E-mail: sq@mhv.net	parts

Mail order and open shop. Monday-Friday 8:30 am to 5:30 pm. Specializing in parts for Mercedes-Benz 190SL, 230/250/280SL, 350/450/380/560SL, 1955-1979.

Steve's Auto Restorations 4440 SE 174th Ave Portland, OR 97236 503-665-2222; FAX: 503-665-2225 E-mail: steve@realsteel.com	restoration

See full listing in **Section Two** under **restoration shops**

Stoddard Imported Cars Inc 38845 Mentor Ave Willoughby, OH 44094-0908 440-951-1040 in Ohio & overseas 800-342-1414; FAX: 440-946-9410 E-mail: sicars@ix.netcom.com	parts

See full listing in **Section One** under **Porsche**

Sweeney's Auto & Marine Upholstery Inc
dba Southampton Auto & Marine Upholstery
471 N Hwy, PO Box 1479
Southampton, NY 11969
516-283-2616; FAX: 516-283-2617

| carpets |
| interiors |
| tops |

Shop open Monday-Friday 8 am to 5 pm; Saturday 9 am to 2 pm. Convertible tops, vinyl tops, custom convertibles, carpeting and complete interiors for antique and classic cars. Specializing in Mercedes. Thirty-five years' experience.

Willow Automotive Service Inc
29870 Hwy 41
Lake Bluff, IL 60044
847-785-8080; FAX: 847-785-8106

| sales |
| service |

Open shop only. Monday-Friday 9 am to 5 pm, Saturday 9 am to 12 pm. Precision service, sales and purchase of Mercedes-Benz, Porsche and BMW.

Mercer Automobile Company
210 Davis Rd
Magnolia, NJ 08049
609-784-4044

| parts |
| service |

Open Monday-Friday 8 am to 4:30 pm. Parts and service for 1910-1922 Mercer automobiles.

AKH Wheels
1207 N A St
Ellensburg, WA 98926-2522
509-962-3390
E-mail: akhwheel@eburg.com

| Rallye wheels |
| styled steel wheels |
| vintage aluminum |

See full listing in **Section Two** under **wheels & wheelcovers**

AMK Products
18600 E 96th St
Broken Arrow, OK 74012
918-455-2651; FAX: 918-455-7441

| parts |

See full listing in **Section One** under **Mustang**

Antique Auto Electric
9109 (Rear) E Garvey Ave
Rosemead, CA 91770
626-572-0938

| repro wiring |

See full listing in **Section Two** under **electrical systems**

Auto Krafters Inc
PO Box 8
522 S Main St
Broadway, VA 22815
540-896-5910; FAX: 540-896-6412
E-mail: akraft@shentel.net

| parts |

See full listing in **Section One** under **Ford 1954-up**

Autowire Division
9109 (Rear) E. Garvey Avenue
Rosemead, CA 91770
626-572-0938; FAX: 626-288-3311

| alternator |
| conversions |
| motors/relays |
| switches |

See full listing in **Section One** under **Ford 1954-up**

Bob Burgess 1955-56 Ford Parts
793 Alpha-Bellbrook Rd
Bellbrook, OH 45305
937-426-8041

| parts |

See full listing in **Section One** under **Ford 1954-up**

Dennis Carpenter Ford Reproductions
PO Box 26398
Charlotte, NC 28221
704-786-8139; FAX: 704-786-8180

| parts |

See full listing in **Section One** under **Ford 1954-up**

Class-Tech Corp
62935 Layton Ave
Bend, OR 97701
800-874-9981

| wiring harnesses |

See full listing in **Section Two** under **electrical systems**

Classic Car Research
29508 Southfield Rd, Ste 106
Southfield, MI 48076
248-557-2880; FAX: 248-557-3511
E-mail: kawifreek@msn.com

| appraisals |
| consultant |
| part locating |

See full listing in **Section Two** under **appraisals**

Classic Ford Sales
PO Box 60
East Dixfield, ME 04227
207-562-4443; FAX: 207-562-4576
E-mail: classicford@quickconnect.com

| salvage yard |

See full listing in **Section Five** under **Maine**

Classic Mercury Parts
1393 Shippee Ln
Ojai, CA 93023
805-646-3345; FAX: 805-646-5386
E-mail: mfourez@aol.com

| parts |

Mail order only. Specializing in new, used, reproduction parts. Emblems, lenses, trunk liners, rubber parts, literature, manuals, stainless and chrome trim for 1949-1956 Mercury. Web site: classicmercury.com

Bob Cook Classic Auto Parts Inc
2055 Van Cleave Rd, PO Box 600
Murray, KY 42071-0600
502-753-4000, 800-486-1137
FAX: 502-753-4600

| new parts |
| NOS parts |
| reproduced parts |

See full listing in **Section One** under **Ford 1954-up**

Mike Dennis, Nebraska Mail Order
1845 S 48th St
Lincoln, NE 68506
402-489-3036; FAX: 402-489-1148

| parts |
| Trippe mounting |
| brackets/hardware |

See full listing in **Section One** under **Ford 1932-1953**

Edward W Drozd
84 Farm Hill Rd
Wallingford, CT 06492
203-265-6638
E-mail: ewdrozd@snet.net

| grilles |
| moldings |

Specializing in hard to find moldings including rockers, bezels for front and rear signal lights, backup housings, hood lip moldings, fender extension moldings, wheel lip moldings, truck moldings, complete grilles for 1969-1970, center grilles can be sold separately. 1969-1970 gas door assemblies and moldings pit-free. I have in stock NOS and show quality as well as driver parts that are in very nice shape. This is for the serious restorer as well as the hobbyist. I have parts for 1967-1973 but mostly for 1969-1970 cars. Web site: http://pages.cthome.net/cougar/

Egge Machine Company Inc	**bearings**
11707 Slauson Ave	**pistons/rings**
Santa Fe Springs, CA 90670	**timing components**
800-866-EGGE, 562-945-3419	**valve train**
FAX: 562-693-1635	
E-mail: info@egge.com	

See full listing in **Section Two** under **engine parts**

Engineering & Manufacturing Services	**sheetmetal**
Box 24362	
Cleveland, OH 44124-0362	
216-541-4585; FAX: 216-541-4989	

See full listing in **Section One** under **Ford 1932-1953**

Ford Powertrain Applications	**engines**
7702 E 96th St	
Puyallup, WA 98371	
PH/FAX: 253-848-9503	

See full listing in **Section One** under **Ford 1954-up**

Garton's Auto	**bicycles**
401 N 5th St (at 5th & Vine)	**Ford NOS parts**
Millville, NJ 08332-3129	**sales literature**
609-825-3618	

See full listing in **Section One** under **Ford 1932-1953**

Randy Goodling	**parts**
2046 Mill Rd	**parts locating**
Elizabethtown, PA 17022-9401	
717-367-6700	

Mail order and open shop by appointment only. Specializing in parts and information on 1967-1973 Mercury Cougars.

Green Valentine Inc	**car dealer**
5055 Covington Way	**woodies**
Memphis, TN 38134	
901-373-5555; FAX: 901-373-5568	

See full listing in **Section Two** under **car dealers**

Highway Classics	**parts**
949 N Cataract Ave, Unit J	
San Dimas, CA 91773	
909-592-8819; FAX: 909-592-4239	
E-mail: donnelson@earthlink.net	

See full listing in **Section One** under **Ford 1954-up**

Bill Horton	**vacuum motors**
5804 Jones Valley Dr	
Huntsville, AL 35802	
256-881-6894	

Mail order only. Rebuilder of headlight vacuum motors for 1967-1970 Mercury Cougar, 1967-1971 Thunderbird, 1969-1976 Lincoln, Lincoln Mk III/IV and 1970 Ford Torino. Mail order sales of 1967-1968 Cougar body parts including rechromed bumpers and restored grilles/taillight assemblies.

Hot Rod & Custom Supply	**custom parts**
1304 SE 10th St	**engine parts**
Cape Coral, FL 33990	**speed parts**
941-574-7744; FAX: 941-574-8820	

See full listing in **Section One** under **Ford 1932-1953**

Jerry's Automotive	**brake repair**
c/o Jerry Cinotti	
431 S Sierra Way	
San Bernadino, CA 92408	
909-884-6980; FAX: 909-884-7872	

See full listing in **Section Two** under **brakes**

Joe's Auto Sales	**parts**
5849-190th St E	
Hastings, MN 55033	
612-437-6787	

See full listing in **Section One** under **Ford 1954-up**

John's Classic Cougars	**accessories**
11522 E Lakewood Blvd	**parts**
Holland, MI 49424	
616-396-0390; FAX: 616-396-0366	
E-mail: jc-cougars@egl.net	

Mail order and open shop. Monday-Friday 9 am to 5 pm, Saturday by appointment. Specializing in new, good used and reproduction parts and accessories for 1967-1973 Mercury Cougars only. Complete Cougar catalog available for $4. "Cougars are our business...not a sideline!"

Ken's Cougars	**parts**
PO Box 5380	
Edmond, OK 73083	
405-340-1636; FAX: 405-340-5877	

Mail order and open shop. Monday-Friday 9 am to 5 pm CST. Specializing in 1967-1973 Mercury Cougar NOS, used and reproduction parts. We also offer complete restoration services. Web site: kenscougars.com

Kenroy Ford Parts	**NOS parts**
2 Folwell Ln	
Mullica Hill, NJ 08062	
609-478-2527	
E-mail: duffieldm@aol.com	

See full listing in **Section One** under **Ford 1954-up**

Lares Manufacturing	**power steering**
13517 Hwy 65 NE	**equipment**
Ham Lake, MN 55304	
800-334-5749; FAX: 612-754-2853	
E-mail: sales@larescorp.com	

See full listing in **Section One** under **Ford 1954-up**

LeBaron Bonney Co	**fabrics**
PO Box 6	**interior kits**
6 Chestnut St	**top kits**
Amesbury, MA 01913	
800-221-5408, 978-388-3811	
FAX: 978-388-1113	
E-mail: lbb-hc@greennet.net	

See full listing in **Section One** under **Ford 1932-1953**

Lincoln Parts International	**parts**
707 E 4th St, Bldg G	
Perris, CA 92570	
800-382-1656, 909-657-5588	
FAX: 909-657-4758	
E-mail: lincprts@pe.net	

See full listing in **Section One** under **Lincoln**

Ed Liukkonen	**accessories**
37 Cook Rd	**parts**
Templeton, MA 01468	
978-939-8126	

See full listing in **Section One** under **Ford 1954-up**

Maffucci Sales Company Inc
RD 1 Box 60, Rt 9 W
Athens, NY 12015
518-943-0100; FAX: 518-943-4534
E-mail:
maffuccisales@mindspring.com

literature
parts

See full listing in **Section One** under **Lincoln**

Mark's 1941-1948 Ford Parts
97 Hoodlum Hill Rd
Binghamton, NY 13905
607-729-1693

parts

See full listing in **Section One** under **Ford 1932-1953**

Mercury & Ford Molded Rubber
12 Plymouth Ave
Wilmington, MA 01887
978-658-8394

parts

Mail order and open shop. Specialize in Mercury rubber parts. Sell 1939-1956 Mercury and Ford molded rubber parts. Also some 1939-1948 Mercury used parts and 1939-1941 reproduced metal parts. Can also supply Ford and Ford pickup rubber parts, many years.

Mercury Research Co
639 Glanker St
Memphis, TN 38112
PH/FAX: 901-323-2195, recorder

new parts
shop manuals

Mail order only. New parts for 1949-1959 Mercury cars. Largest selection of Mercury parts. 65 page catalog, $4. In business over 20 years. Visa, MasterCard, personal checks accepted.

Mercury Restorations
Larry Adams
309 Seashore Dr
Swansboro, NC 28584
PH/FAX: 910-326-5852

dash plastic
restoration

Mail order only. 1941-1948 Mercury dash plastic restoration since 1978. Can restore broken or sunburned plastic to show car condition. No new parts or catalog.

Miller Obsolete Parts
1329 Campus Dr
Vestal, NY 13850
607-722-5371; FAX: 607-770-9117
E-mail: fordpart@spectra.net

locator service
parts

See full listing in **Section One** under **Ford 1954-up**

Northeast Ford
Box 66, Rt 9
East Sullivan, NH 03445
603-847-9956, 800-562-FORD
FAX: 603-847-9691

parts
restoration

See full listing in **Section One** under **Ford 1954-up**

Northwest Classic Falcons Inc
1964 NW Pettygrove St
Portland, OR 97209
503-241-9454; FAX: 503-241-1964
E-mail: ron@nwfalcon.com

parts

See full listing in **Section One** under **Ford 1954-up**

Obsolete Ford Parts Co
311 E Washington Ave
Nashville, GA 31639
912-686-2470, 912-686-5101
FAX: 912-686-7125

parts

See full listing in **Section One** under **Ford 1954-up**

Old Dominion Mustang/Camaro
509 S Washington Hwy, Rt 1
Ashland, VA 23005
804-798-3348; FAX: 804-798-5105

parts

See full listing in **Section One** under **Mustang**

Original Falcon, Comet, Ranchero, Fairlane Interiors
6343 Seaview Ave NW
Seattle, WA 98107-2664
206-781-5230; FAX: 206-781-5046
E-mail: falcons1@ix.netcom.com

interiors
weatherstripping

See full listing in **Section One** under **Ford 1954-up**

Patrick's Antique Cars & Trucks
PO Box 10648
Casa Grande, AZ 85230
520-836-1117; FAX: 520-836-1104
E-mail: patstrks@aol.com

parts

See full listing in **Section One** under **Chevrolet**

Greg Purdy's Mustang Supply
PO Box 784
Forest Hill, MD 21050
410-836-5991

parts

See full listing in **Section One** under **Mustang**

Rock Valley Antique Auto Parts
Box 352
Rt 72 and Rothwell Rd
Stillman Valley, IL 61084
815-645-2271; FAX: 815-645-2740

gas tanks

See full listing in **Section One** under **Ford 1932-1953**

Rocky Mountain V8 Ford Parts
1124 Clark Cir
Colorado Springs, CO 80915
719-597-8375

parts

See full listing in **Section One** under **Ford 1932-1953**

Sam's Vintage Ford Parts
5105 Washington
Denver, CO 80216
303-295-1709

parts

See full listing in **Section One** under **Ford 1954-up**

Special T's Unlimited Corp
PO Box 146
Prospect Heights, IL 60070
847-255-5494; FAX: 847-391-7666

general repair
parts
restoration
service

See full listing in **Section One** under **Mopar**

Stilwell's Obsolete Ford Parts
1617 Wedeking Ave
Evansville, IN 47711
812-425-4794

body parts
interiors
parts

See full listing in **Section One** under **Mustang**

Tags Backeast
PO Box 581
Plainville, CT 06062
860-747-2942
E-mail: dataplt@snet.net

data plates
trim tags

See full listing in **Section Two** under **special services**

Pat Walsh Restorations | literature
Box Q | rubber parts
Wakefield, MA 01880
781-246-3266; FAX: 781-224-3311
E-mail: pwalshrest@aol.com

See full listing in **Section Two** under **rubber parts**

Wesley Obsolete Parts | parts
116 Memory Ln
Liberty, KY 42539
606-787-5293; FAX: 606-787-7252

See full listing in **Section One** under **Ford 1954-up**

Wirth's Custom Automotive | custom accessories
PO Box 5 | fender skirts
505 Conner St | spinner hubcaps
Prairie du Rocher, IL 62277
618-284-3359
E-mail: roywirth@htc.net

See full listing in **Section Two** under **accessories**

Merkur

Rapido Group | accessories
80093 Dodson Rd | parts
Tygh Valley, OR 97063
541-544-3333

Mail order and open shop. Monday-Thursday 8 am to 5 pm, Friday 8 am to noon. Accessories and parts (OE, NOS, custom, high-performance) for Merkur XR4Ti and Scorpio, Turbo Thunderbird and SVO Mustang. Web site: www.rapidogroup.com

Messerschmidt

The Ramsgate Motor Museum | museum
Westcliff Hall
Ramsgate, Kent England
01843 581948

See full listing in **Section Six** under **England**

Classic American Parts Inc | parts
14213 Hereford Rd
Neosho, MO 64850
PH/FAX: 800-638-5461
E-mail: classam@clandjop.com

Specializing in auto parts for the Metropolitan 1954-1961. Mail order business specializing only in Metropolitan parts.

Pete Groh | original British
9957 Frederick Rd | keys
Ellicott City, MD 21042-3647
410-750-2352; FAX: 410-466-3566
E-mail: petegroh@yahoo.com

See full listing in **Section One** under **Jaguar**

Kip Motor Company Inc | literature
2127 Crown Rd | parts
Dallas, TX 75229 | restoration
972-243-0440; FAX: 972-243-2387
E-mail: kipmotor@aol.com

See full listing in **Section One** under **Austin**

Metro Motors | parts
Dale Cheney
1070 E Roland St
Carson City, NV 89701
702-883-7308
E-mail: cheney@reno.quik.com

Specializing in parts for Metropolitans. New, used and reconditioned. List available.

Metropolitan & British Triumph | British Leyland
9957 Frederick Rd | Lucas/Girling
Ellicott City, MD 21042-3647 | NOS British keys
410-750-2352 evenings | NOS British parts
E-mail: pete_groh@yahoo.com

Mail order only. Keys cut by code: single sided cut, $6; double sided cut, $9. Need number on face of the ignition switch or the three digit number on trunk handle stem. Wilmot Breeden keys; FA, FP, FS and FT original key, $12 each. WASO rubber headed key, $14 each. British Leyland, L swirl for TR7 and TR8, $14 each. With all orders include a SASE and your daytime telephone number. Photocopy of Lucas catalog, $12; Beck catalog, $14. Sample index page with the year/make of your car on request. Buy and sell NOS British parts. Web site: www.geocities.com/motorcity/flats/4796/

Metropolitan Pit Stop | literature
5324-26-28-30 Laurel Canyon Blvd | parts
North Hollywood, CA 91607 | restoration
800-PIT-STOP order toll-free
818-769-1515; FAX: 818-769-3500
E-mail: hi-valentine@webtv.net

Mail order and open store. Monday-Friday 10 am to 6 pm. Everything in Metropolitan parts. Repair shop. For 24 years, devoted exclusively to preservation, restoration and repair of Metropolitans. Buy Metropolitan parts and Metropolitan literature/memorabilia for permanent Metropolitan Historical Collection exhibition. Parts catalog free.

Treasure Chest Sales | parts
413 Montgomery
Jackson, MI 49202
517-787-1475

See full listing in **Section One** under **Nash**

Wenner's | NOS parts
5449 Tannery Rd
Schnecksville, PA 18078
610-799-5419

See full listing in **Section One** under **AMC**

Wymer Classic AMC | NOS parts
Mark & George Wymer | owner's manuals
340 N Justice St | repairs
Fremont, OH 43420 | service manuals
419-332-4291 | used parts
419-334-6945 after 5 pm

See full listing in **Section One** under **AMC**

1 CAAT Limited Co   restoration
1324 E Harper Ave
Maryville, TN 37804
423-983-7180
E-mail: jhenriks@icx.net

See full listing in **Section Two** under **restoration shops**

Abingdon Spares Ltd   parts
PO Box 37
South St
Walpole, NH 03608
603-756-4768
orders: 800-225-0251
FAX: 603-756-9614
E-mail: info@abingdonsparesltd.com

Mail order and open shop. Monday-Friday 9 am to 5 pm;
Saturday 9 am to 12 noon. Selling MGT series parts (TC, TD, TF
models) only. Web site: www.abingdonsparesltd.com

American-Foreign Auto Electric Inc   parts
103 Main St   rebuilding
Souderton, PA 18964
215-723-4877

See full listing in **Section Two** under **electrical systems**

Antique & Classic Car Restoration   restoration
Hwy 107, Box 368
Magdalena, NM 87825

See full listing in **Section Two** under **restoration shops**

APA Industries   accessories
10505 San Fernando Rd   parts
Pacoima, CA 91331
818-834-8473; FAX: 818-834-2795
E-mail: apaindustries@juno.com

See full listing in **Section One** under **Jaguar**

AutoMatch CARS   broker
(Computer Aided Referral Service)   car dealer network
2017 Blvd Napoleon   locator
Louisville, KY 40205
800-962-2771, 502-417-8793 mobile
502-452-1920 office; FAX: 502-479-6222
E-mail: amcars@aol.com
or aautomatch@aol.com

See full listing in **Section Two** under **car dealers**

Automotive Artistry   restoration
679 W Streetboro St
Hudson, OH 44236
330-650-1503
E-mail: dale@cmh.net

See full listing in **Section One** under **Triumph**

BCP Sport & Classic Co   parts
10525 Airline Dr   service
Houston, TX 77037
281-448-4739; FAX: 281-448-0189

Mail order and open shop. Specializing in British and German
parts and service for MG, Triumph, Jaguar, BMW, Mercedes-
Benz, Maserati from 1950-1998. Also buy antique electric fans.

Bentley Publishers   books
1734 Massachusetts Ave   manuals
Cambridge, MA 02138-1804
800-423-4595; FAX: 617-876-9235
E-mail: sales@rb.com

See full listing in **Section Four** under **books & publications**

Bonnets Up   restoration
5736 Spring St
Clinton, MD 20735
301-297-4759

See full listing in **Section Two** under **coachbuilders & designers**

BritBooks   books
PO Box 321
Otego, NY 13825
PH/FAX: 607-988-7956
E-mail: britbook@dmcom.net

See full listing in **Section Four** under **books & publications**

British Auto Parts Ltd   parts
93256 Holland Ln
Marcola, OR 97454
541-933-2880; FAX: 541-933-2302

See full listing in **Section One** under **Morris**

British Auto Shoppe   parts
1909 5th Ave   service
Moline, IL 61265
309-764-9513; FAX: 309-764-9576

Mail order and open shop. Monday-Friday 8:30 am to 5:30 pm,
Saturday by appointment. Parts (new and used) and service for
British cars. Engine rebuild, mechanical restoration and carb
rebuilding for MG, Triumph, Austin-Healey, Jaguar, Mini, Morris
and Austin.

British Car Films   videos
PO Box 13862
London N4 3WB England
800-454-8341 toll-free
011 44181-3744850
FAX: 011 44181-3744852
E-mail: british.car@virgin.net

See full listing in **Section Two** under **videos**

British Car Keys   keys
Rt 144 Box 9957
Ellicott City, MD 21042-3647
410-750-2352
E-mail: britishcarkeys@hotmail.com

See full listing in **Section One** under **Austin-Healey**

British Car Magazine   periodical
343 Second St, Suite H
Los Altos, CA 94022-3639
650-949-9680; FAX: 650-949-9685
E-mail: britcarmag@aol.com

See full listing in **Section Four** under **periodicals**

British Car Service   restoration
2854 N Stone Ave   salvage yard
Tucson, AZ 85705
520-882-7026; FAX: 520-882-7053
E-mail: bcs@liveline.com

See full listing in **Section Five** under **Arizona**

British Car Specialists
2060 N Wilson Way
Stockton, CA 95205
209-948-8767; FAX: 209-948-1030
E-mail: healeydoc@aol.com

	parts
	repairs
	restoration

See full listing in **Section One** under **Austin-Healey**

British Miles
9278 Old E Tyburn Rd
Morrisville, PA 19067
215-736-9300; FAX: 215-736-3089

	accessories
	literature
	parts
	restoration

Mail order and open shop. Monday-Friday 9 am to 6 pm. Specializing in new and used parts, restorations, repairs and bench rebuilding services for British sports cars, MG, Triumph, Austin-Healey and Jaguar. We also carry tech and workshop manuals, books and accessories. Deals in windshield wiper and lamp parts for kit cars.

See our ad on this page

British Parts NW
4105 SE Lafayette Hwy
Dayton, OR 97114
503-864-2001; FAX: 503-864-2081
E-mail: bpnw@onlinemac.com

| | parts |

See full listing in **Section One** under **Triumph**

British Racing Green
30 Aleph Dr
Newark, DE 19702
302-368-1117; FAX: 302-368-5910
E-mail: info@brgparts.com

	new parts
	rebuilt parts
	used parts

Full line of parts for cars made in England (MG, Triumph, Austin-Healey and Jaguar, etc), new, used and rebuilt. Over 35,000 part numbers stocked with 2 acre salvage yard. 23 years' experience. Web site: www.brgparts.com

British Restorations
4455 Paul St
Philadelphia, PA 19124
215-533-6696

| | car dealer |
| | restoration |

See full listing in **Section One** under **Jaguar**

British T Shop Inc
165 Rt 82
Oakdale, CT 06370
860-889-0178; FAX: 860-889-6096

	car/tractor dealer
	parts
	service

Mail order and open shop. Monday, Tuesday, Thursday and Friday 8 am to 4:30 pm, Wednesday and Saturday by appointment. Parts for MG and Triumph. Authorized dealer for Kioti, Long and Belarus compact tractors and farm implements including loaders, backhoes, mowers, rakes, tillers, posthole diggers, chippers, etc. Sales, service, parts.

British Wire Wheel
1650 Mansfield St
Santa Cruz, CA 95062
831-479-4495; FAX: 831-462-1517

	hubs
	tires
	wire wheels

See full listing in **Section One** under **Austin-Healey**

British Wiring Inc
20449 Ithaca Rd
Olympia Fields, IL 60461
PH/FAX: 708-481-9050

| | wiring accessories |
| | wiring harnesses |

See full listing in **Section Two** under **electrical systems**

California Wire Wheel
6922 Turnbridge Way
San Diego, CA 92119
619-698-8255; FAX: 619-589-9032

	rechroming
	tires
	tubes
	wheels

See full listing in **Section Two** under **wheels & wheelcovers**

Cambridge Motorsport
Caxton Rd
Great Gransden, NR Sandy
Beds SG19 3AH England
0044 1767 677969
FAX: 0044 1767 677026
E-mail: cambridge.motorsport@dial.pipex.com

| | parts |
| | race tuning |

See full listing in **Section One** under **Triumph**

Classic Showcase
913 Rancheros Dr
San Marcos, CA 92069
760-747-9947, 760-747-3188 sales
FAX: 760-747-4021
E-mail: management@classicshowcase.com

| | classic vehicles |
| | restorations |

See full listing in **Section Two** under **car dealers**

Classic Wood Mfg
1006 N Raleigh St
Greensboro, NC 27405
336-691-1344; FAX: 336-273-3074

| | wood kits |
| | wood replacement |

See full listing in **Section Two** under **woodwork**

Dashboards Plus
336 Cottonwood Ave
Hartland, WI 53029
800-221-8161; FAX: 414-367-9474

| | restoration parts |
| | wood dash overlays |

See full listing in **Section One** under **Jaguar**

Doug's British Car Parts 2487 E Colorado Blvd Pasadena, CA 91107 818-793-2494; FAX: 818-793-4339	**accessories** **parts**

See full listing in **Section One** under **Jaguar**

East Coast Jaguar 802B Naaman's Rd Wilmington, DE 19810 302-475-7200; FAX: 302-475-9258 E-mail: ecjaguar@aol.com	**parts** **service**

See full listing in **Section One** under **Jaguar**

Finish Line 3593 SW 173rd Terr Miramar, FL 33029 954-436-9101; FAX: 954-436-9102 E-mail: e.dlibrandi@worldnet.att.net	**parts** **supplies**

See full listing in **Section One** under **Cobra**

Don Flye 5 Doe Valley Rd Petersham, MA 01366 978-724-3318	**parts**

See full listing in **Section One** under **Austin-Healey**

Pete Groh 9957 Frederick Rd Ellicott City, MD 21042-3647 410-750-2352; FAX: 410-466-3566 E-mail: petegroh@yahoo.com	**original British** **keys**

See full listing in **Section One** under **Jaguar**

Heritage Motor Centre Banbury Rd Gaydon Warwichshire CV35 0BJ England 01926 641188; FAX: 01926 641555	**museum**

See full listing in **Section Six** under **England**

Heritage Upholstery and Trim 250 H St, Unit 8110 Blaine, WA 98231 604-990-0346; FAX: 604-990-9988	**interior kits** **trim** **upholstery**

See full listing in **Section One** under **Austin-Healey**

Kimble Engineering Ltd Unit 5 Old Mill Creek Dartmouth Devon TQ6 OHN England 0044 1803 835757 FAX: 0044 1803 834567	**aero screens** **steering wheels** **valve covers**

Mail order only. Specializing in MG, T-type, MGA, pre-war, 1935-1962. Deal in Brooklands aero screens, Brooklands steering wheels, aluminum valve covers.

Lake Oswego Restorations 19621 S Hazelhurst Ln West Linn, OR 97068 PH/FAX: 503-636-7503	**restoration** **sales**

See full listing in **Section One** under **Aston Martin**

M & G Vintage Auto 265 Rt 17, Box 226 Tuxedo Park, NY 10987 914-753-5900; FAX: 914-753-5613	**parts** **restoration** **service** **storage**

"The Source" for all your MG needs. Largest supplier of new and used MG parts to the trade. We buy, sell, trade cars and parts, 13 car showroom and full shop on premises. We run a full stocked MG TC/TD/TF, MGA, MGB mail order house. We can expertly rebuild your engine, transmission, carbs and gauges. Fully illustrated catalogs available upon request. Also offer vintage car storage.

McLean's Brit Bits 14 Sagamore Rd Rye, NH 03870 800-995-2487; FAX: 603-433-0009 E-mail: sam@britbits.com	**accessories** **parts** **sales** **service**

Mail order and open shop. Monday-Saturday 9 am to 6 pm, Sunday by appointment. Specializing in sales, service, new and used parts and accessories for MGs, Austin-Healeys, Triumphs, Sunbeams, Morris Minors, Jaguars, Lotus, Land Rovers and Hillman. Web site: www.britbits.com

MG Magazine Inc PO Box 85020 Fort Wayne, IN 46885-5020 888-870-4993, 616-375-4073, MI FAX: 219-485-0845 E-mail: mgmag2000@aol.com	**automobilia** **books** **magazine**

See full listing in **Section Four** under **books & publications**

MG Parts Centre (Barry Walker) Barley Leys Farm, Haselor Hill Temple Grafton NR Stratford-on-Avon B49 6NH England 0044 1789-400181 FAX: 0044 1789-400230	**parts**

Mail order and open shop. Daily 10 am to 7 pm. For MGs only, 1929-1953. M through TD parts. Many spares available.

Mini Mania 31 Winsor St Milpitas, CA 95035 408-942-5595; FAX: 408-942-5582 E-mail: info@minimania.com	**parts** **service**

See full listing in **Section One** under **Austin**

Mini Motors Classic Coachworks 2775 Cherry Ave NE Salem, OR 97303 503-362-3187; FAX: 503-375-9609 E-mail: 104306,114@compuserv	**parts** **restoration** **sales** **service**

See full listing in **Section One** under **Austin-Healey**

Moss Motors Ltd PO Box 847 440 Rutherford St Goleta, CA 93117 800-235-6954; FAX: 805-692-2525	**accessories** **parts**

Business hours are Monday-Friday 6 am to 7 pm, Saturday-Sunday 7 am to 4 pm PST. We're the oldest and largest supplier of quality parts and accessories for MG, Triumph, Austin-Healey and Jaguar. Free catalogs for MG TC-TD-TF, MGA, MGB, Sprite-Midget, Triumph TR2-4A, TR 250-6, TR7, Spitfire, Austin-Healey and Jaguar XK 120-150. Free quarterly newsletter with hundreds of sale items, tech articles, club news and events. Toll-free ordering with fast, dependable service and locations on both coasts. British Heritage approved supplier. Web site: www.mossmotors.com

Motorcars Ltd 8101 Hempstead Houston, TX 77008 800-231-6563; FAX: 713-863-8238 E-mail: info@britishparts.com	**parts**

See full listing in **Section One** under **Jaguar**

Motorhead Ltd
2811-B Old Lee Hwy
Fairfax, VA 22031
800-527-3140; FAX: 703-573-3195

parts
repairs

See full listing in **Section One** under **Austin-Healey**

Motormetrics
6369 Houston Rd
Macon, GA 31216
912-785-0275
E-mail:
fzampa@cennet.mc.peachnet.edu

used parts

See full listing in **Section One** under **Triumph**

Northwest Import Parts
10042 SW Balmer
Portland, OR 97219
503-245-3806; FAX: 503-245-9617

parts

Mail order and open shop. Specialize in new parts for MG cars. Mechanical, interior, rubber, electrical and restoration parts for MGs 1955-1980.

NOS Locators
587 Pawtucket Ave
Pawtucket, RI 02860
401-725-5000

parts

Limited range of deeply discounted overstocks, closeouts, bulk buyouts, etc, primarily for British sports cars, late 1950s on. Specific marques are: Austin-Healey, MG, Triumph, Jaguar.

O'Connor Classic Autos
2569 Scott Blvd
Santa Clara, CA 95050
888-FINE-MGS (346-3647)
FAX: 408-727-3987

car dealer
parts
restoration

Mail order and open shop. Monday-Friday 9 am to 5 pm. Restored and unrestored MG cars, including TC, TD, TF, MGA, MGB. Full line of parts and restoration sevices. Web site: www.oconnorclassics.com

---

Omni Specialties
10418 Lorain Ave
Cleveland, OH 44111
888-819-6464 (MGMG)
216-251-2269; FAX: 216-251-6083

parts
restoration
service

Mail order and open shop. Monday-Friday 9:30 am to 6:30 pm. Specializing in repair, service, parts, restoration for MG, Jaguar, Triumph, Austin-Healey, Lotus and other European classics including BMW, Porsche, VW and Audi. Service and repair for a price that's fair. 32 years' experience.

Pacific International Auto
1118 Garnet Ave
San Diego, CA 92109
619-274-1920; FAX: 619-454-1815

parts
sales
service

See full listing in **Section One** under **Jaguar**

Peninsula Imports
3749 Harlem Rd
Buffalo, NY 14215
800-999-1209; FAX: 905-847-3021
E-mail: imports@ican.net

accessories
parts
trim

See full listing in **Section One** under **BMW**

Ragtops & Roadsters
203 S 4th St
Perkasie, PA 18944
215-257-1202; FAX: 215-257-2688
E-mail: info@ragtops.com

bodywork/painting
British automobiles
engine rebuilding
vintage race prep

See full listing in **Section Two** under **restoration shops**

The Ramsgate Motor Museum
Westcliff Hall
Ramsgate, Kent England
01843 581948

museum

See full listing in **Section Six** under **England**

The Roadster Factory
328 Killen Rd
PO Box 332
Armagh, PA 15920
800-234-1104; FAX: 814-446-6729

accessories
parts

See full listing in **Section One** under **Triumph**

Rogers Motors
25 Leverett Rd
Shutesbury, MA 01072
413-259-1722
E-mail: akor@ent.umass.edu

used parts

See full listing in **Section One** under **Jaguar**

Scarborough Faire Inc
1151 Main St
Pawtucket, RI 02860
800-556-6300, 401-724-4200
FAX: 401-724-5392

parts

Manufacturer, worldwide wholesale distributor, importer/exporter of high quality spares for post WW II MGs and Austin-Healeys. Extensive range of proprietary manufactured products are supplied to all major British parts specialists and retailers throughout the world. During the past 30 years, thousands of MG owners have saved literally millions of dollars by choosing Scarborough's high quality products over its competitors.

Seven Enterprises Ltd
802 Bluecrab Rd, Ste 100
Newport News, VA 23606
800-992-7007; FAX: 800-296-3327

accessories
parts

See full listing in **Section One** under **Austin**

Shadetree Motors Ltd
3895 Mammoth Cave Ct
Pleasanton, CA 94588
PH/FAX: 925-846-1309
E-mail: kelsey@shadetreemotors.com

parts service

All aspects of MG parts. Authorized Moss Motors parts distributor. Specialize in TC, TD and TF parts. $500,000 inventory. Discount pricing. Web site: http://shadetreemotors.com

---

Smooth Line
2562 Riddle Run Rd
Tarentum, PA 15084
724-274-6002; FAX: 724-274-6121

body panels
removable hardtops

See full listing in **Section Two** under **tops**

Special Interest Car Parts
1340 Hartford Ave
Johnston, RI 02919
800-556-7496; FAX: 401-831-7760

parts

See full listing in **Section One** under **Jaguar**

Sports Car Haven
2-33 Flowerfield Industrial Pk
St James, NY 11780
516-862-8058
E-mail: sch94@aol.com

race prep
restorations
service

See full listing in **Section One** under **Triumph**

Sports Car Haven	parts
3414 Bloom Rd, Rt 11	restoration
Danville, PA 17821	service
570-275-5705	

Mail order and open shop. Monday-Friday 9 am to 5 pm,
Saturday 9 am to 11:30 am. Specializing in parts, new, used and
rebuilt. Also repairs, restoration, competition preparation for
Austin-Healey, MG, Triumph and Jaguar.

Sports Car Tours Inc	back road tours
PO Box 265	
Batesville, VA 22924	
804-823-4442	
E-mail: napol@rlc.net	

See full listing in **Section Two** under **special services**

Sports & Classics	parts
PO Box 1787	
512 Boston Post Rd, Dept H	
Darien, CT 06820-1787	

See full listing in **Section Two** under **body parts**

Texas MG	car locators
2290 W Hicks Rd, Unit 62	sales
Fort Worth, TX 76179	
817-439-3071	
E-mail: 71663.226@compuserve.com	

MG car search for all years. B parts, consignment sales for
1963-1980.

The Registry	periodical
Pine Grove	
Stanley, VA 22851	
540-778-3728; FAX: 540-778-2402	
E-mail: britregstry@aol.com or	
oldwregistry@aol.com	

See full listing in **Section Four** under **periodicals**

Thoroughbred Motors	parts
3935 N US 301	sales
Sarasota, FL 34234	service
941-359-2277; FAX: 941-359-2128	

See full listing in **Section One** under **Jaguar**

Triple C Motor Accessories	accessories
1900 Orange St	models
York, PA 17404	
717-854-4081; FAX: 717-854-6706	
E-mail: sales@triple-c.com	

Mail order and open shop. Monday-Friday 9 am to 5 pm.
Specializing in regalia, models and accessories for all British
marques. Web site: www.triple-c.com

University Motors Ltd	events
6490 E Fulton	line/bench service
Ada, MI 49301	restoration
616-682-0800; FAX: 616-682-0801	

Open Monday-Friday 9 am to 6 pm, Saturday 9 am to 1 pm,
summers only. Specializing in MG restoration, line and bench
service, technical support and events. NAMGBR and MGOC
approved workshop. MGCC trade member. British Motor Heritage
approved workshop. Web site: www.universitymotorsltd.com

V6 MGB	conversion plans
Box 741992	kits
Dallas, TX 75374	

Mail order only. Conversion plans and kits to install V6 in MGBs
only.

Hemmings' Vintage Auto Almanac©   Fourteenth Edition

Victoria British Ltd	accessories
Box 14991	parts
Lenexa, KS 66285-4991	
800-255-0088, 913-599-3299	

Mail order catalog. Monday-Friday 7 am to 9 pm, Saturday-
Sunday 9 am to 5 pm. One of the world's largest distributors of
parts and accessories for British sports cars. Offering the most
complete up-to-date information in our fully illustrated catalogs.
Stocks over 20,000 line items for MG, Triumph, Austin-Healey
and Sunbeam. Telephone orders are fast and easy with a reliable
on-line computer entry system. As a distributor for British Motor
Heritage in the US, the company is able to provide original
equipment and authentic reproduction parts. Great prices on
high-performance parts, accessories, upholstery, rubber and
chrome trim. Web site: victoriabritish.com

Victory Autoservices	parts
Box 5060, RR 1	restoration
W Baldwin, ME 04091	
207-625-4581	

See full listing in **Section One** under **Austin-Healey**

Vintage Restorations	accessories
The Old Bakery	instruments
Windmill Street, Tunbridge Wells	
Kent, TN2 4UU England	
UK 1892-525-899	
FAX: UK 1892-525499	

See full listing in **Section Two** under **instruments**

Von's Austin-Healey Restorations	parts
10270 Barberville Rd	repairs
Fort Mill, SC 29715	restoration
803-548-4590; FAX: 803-548-4816	
E-mail: vons@vnet.net	

See full listing in **Section One** under **Austin-Healey**

Voss Motors Inc	service manuals
21849 Virginia Dr	
Southfield, MI 48076	
888-380-9277 toll-free	
248-357-4750; FAX: 248-354-6577	
E-mail: vossmotors@aol.com	

See full listing in **Section Two** under **literature dealers**

Moon Registry	literature
Carl W Burst III	photographs
1600 N Woodlawn	
St Louis, MO 63124	
314-822-7807, 314-822-8688 recorder	

Specializing in all products of the Moon Motor Car Company:
Moon, Hol-Tan, Diana, Windsor and Ruxton. Restoration aid,
copies of factory photos, owner's manuals, tune-up data, parts
location assistance and names of other owners with similar models available at no charge. Please include phone number if writing.

MOTOR REPAIR

Mopar

Accurate Muffler Ltd
7125 Hwy 99 N
Roseburg, OR 97470
PH/FAX: 541-672-2661
E-mail: taswope@jeffnet.org

muffler products

Mail order and open shop. Monday-Friday 8 am to 4:30 pm.
Specializing in Mopar exhaust and muffler products. Web site:
www.learningplant.com/accurateltd

AKH Wheels
1207 N A St
Ellensburg, WA 98926-2522
509-962-3390
E-mail: akhwheel@eburg.com

**Rallye wheels
styled steel wheels
vintage aluminum**

See full listing in **Section Two** under **wheels & wheelcovers**

Alpha Omega Motorsport
15612 New Century Dr
Gardena, CA 90248
310-366-7993; FAX: 310-366-7499
E-mail: aomotor@pacbell.net

**parts
repairs
restorations**

See full listing in **Section One** under **Pontiac**

Antique Auto Fasteners
Guy C Close Jr & Son
13426 Valna Dr
Whittier, CA 90602
562-696-3307

**fasteners
hardware
hose clamps
molding clips**

See full listing in **Section Two** under **hardware**

Antique DeSoto-Plymouth
4206 Burnett Dr
Murrysville, PA 15668
724-733-1818 eves
FAX: 724-733-9884 or
412-243-4556 anytime
E-mail: parts4u@aol.com

Mopar parts

Mail order and open shop by appointment. Phone evenings. New
old stock 1938-1960 Chrysler, Plymouth, Dodge, DeSoto parts.
Hard-to-find Mopar parts: grilles, bumpers, chrome moldings,
etc. Send SASE with list of wants. Satisfaction guaranteed on all
we sell.

Antique Mopar Auto Sales
5758 McNicholl Dr
Hale, MI 48739-8984
517-257-3123

**cars
parts**

Mail order and open shop. Specializing in Mopar cars and parts
for 1936-1957 DeSoto, 1936-1969 Dodge, 1955-1964 Plymouth
and Barracuda.

Arizona Parts
320 E Pebble Beach
Tempe, AZ 85282
602-966-6683
800-328-8766, code 88602

**accessories
literature
parts**

Mail order only. For 1935-1998 Chrysler Corporation vehicles.
39,000 item computer inventory using Chrysler part numbers
with description and application available, (call for cost). New
and used parts, accessories and literature stocked. Send SASE
for current stock information.

Auto Decals Unlimited Inc
11259 E Via Linda, Ste 100-201
Scottsdale, AZ 85259
602-220-0800

**decals
stripe kits**

See full listing in **Section Two** under **decals**

Brewer's Performance Motor Parts
2580 S State Route 48
Ludlow Falls, OH 45339-9773
937-698-4259; FAX: 937-698-7109

parts

Specializing in four-speed conversions on 1962-1976 Mopar
muscle cars. Rebuilt Hurst shifters, A-833 rebuild kits, rebuilt
transmissions, restored pistol grips, new torque shafts, clutch
linkage, bellhousings, pedal assemblies, etc. From one small
part to complete conversions. Call the 4-speed specialists!

Bumper Boyz LLC
2435 E 54th St
Los Angeles, CA 90058
800-995-1703, 323-587-8976
FAX: 323-587-2013

**bumper repairs
reconditioning
sandblasting**

See full listing in **Section One** under **Chevrolet**

Christian Motorsports Illustrated
PO Box 129
Mansfield, PA 16933
570-549-2282; FAX: 570-549-3366

performance parts

Mail order and open shop. Monday-Friday 8 am to 5 pm.
Founded 1980. 3,700 members. 15 years of enthusiast informa-
tion and parts organization for Mopar enthusiasts, including
National Hemi Owners Association, Mopar Muscle Club,
Chrysler Performance Parts Association. Bi-monthly publication:
Chrysler Power Magazine, $19.75. Specializing in Chrysler and
Mopar performance parts for 1962-1978 Chrysler, Plymouth,
Dodge. Do not need to be a Mopar enthusiast. Dues: $40/year.

Classic and Muscle
Muscle Car Restoration Parts
PO Box 657
Elmsdale, NS Canada B0N 1M0
902-883-4489; FAX: 902-883-1392
E-mail: classicmuscle@sprint.ca

**reproduction parts
restoration parts**

See full listing in **Section One** under **Chevrolet**

Clester's Auto Rubber Seals Inc
PO Box 1113
Salisbury, NC 28145
704-637-9979; FAX: 704-636-7390

**gloveboxes
molded rubber
parts
weatherstripping**

See full listing in **Section Two** under **rubber parts**

**Coach Builders Muscle Car
Parts & Services**
PO Box 128
Baltimore, MD 21087-0128
410-426-5567

**interiors
parts
rust remover**

See full listing in **Section One** under **Chevrolet**

Dash Specialists
1910 Redbud Ln
Medford, OR 97504
541-776-0040

interiors

See full listing in **Section One** under **Cadillac/LaSalle**

Len Dawson
15541 Yokeko Dr
Anacortes, WA 98221
FAX: 360-293-1032

**chrome/trim items
electrical parts
mechanical parts**

Mail order only. One of the world's largest inventories of NOS parts
for 1935-1983 Chrysler products. Full line of mechanical and electrical parts, plus thousands of chrome and trim items. Send SASE
and Chrysler Corporation part numbers with inquiries.

Daniel N Dietrich RD 1 Kempton, PA 19529 215-756-6078	**restoration trim parts**

Mail order and open shop. Restores complete car bodies, 1941-1963 Mopar only, back to original factory finish. Also sells exterior chrome, stainless body moldings and trim.

Lee Ellison's MoreParts North PO Box 345 Orangeville, ON Canada L9W 2Z7 519-941-6331; FAX: 519-941-8903 E-mail: obsoleteparts@moreparts.com	**parts sheetmetal**

Mail order only. Specializing in obsolete and hard to find NOS for Chrysler, Plymouth and Dodge 1930s-1970s.

ETC Every Thing Cars 8727 Clarinda Pico Rivera, CA 90660 562-949-6981	**paint repairs restoration welding**

Shop open by phone appointment only. Monday-Friday 9 am to 6 pm. Deals in body, chassis, engine, trans, brakes, front ends, air conditoning, tune-ups, high-performance, carbs, ignition, detailing, frame-offs and partials. General auto restorations, 1960s-1975. References. R W Nash, owner, technician, craftsman. Reasonable rates. This business does not sell individual parts.

John Filiss 45 Kingston Ave Port Jervis, NY 12771 914-856-2942 E-mail: johnfiliss@hotmail.com	**appraisals**

See full listing in **Section Two** under **appraisals**

Jay M Fisher Acken Dr 4-B Clark, NJ 07066 732-388-6442	**mascots sidemount mirrors windwing brackets**

See full listing in **Section Two** under **accessories**

Grand Touring 2785 E Regal Park Dr Anaheim, CA 92806 714-630-0130; FAX: 714-630-6956	**engine rebuilding machine shop restoration suspension**

See full listing in **Section Two** under **restoration shops**

Jim Harris 16743 39th NE Seattle, WA 98155 206-364-6637	**cars parts**

Mail order and open shop. Cars and parts, Mopar 1927-1975. Specializes in sixties Imperials and Mopar muscle cars. In the hobby since 1974.

Mike Hershenfeld 3011 Susan Rd Bellmore, NY 11710 PH/FAX: 516-781-PART (7278) E-mail: mikesmopar@juno.com	**parts**

Mail order only. Specializing in Mopar NOS 1932-1970: engine, fuel, electrical, brakes, lenses, gauges, clutch, ignition, gaskets, cooling, suspension, chrome, literature.

Hidden Valley Auto Parts 21046 N Rio Bravo Maricopa, AZ 85239 602-252-2122, 602-252-6137 520-568-2945; FAX: 602-258-0951	**parts**

See full listing in **Section One** under **Chevrolet**

Imperial Motors Rt 3 Box 380 Campobello, SC 29322 864-895-3474; FAX: 864-895-1248	**parts**

See full listing in **Section One** under **Chrysler**

Jeff Johnson Motorsports PO Box 14327 Columbus, OH 43214 614-268-1181; FAX: 614-268-1141	**accessories literature parts**

Mail order only. Specializing in parts, literature and accessories for 1955-current Chrysler product cars and trucks.

Bob Johnson's Auto Literature 92 Blandin Ave Framingham, MA 01702 508-872-9173; FAX: 508-626-0991 E-mail: bjohnson@autopaper.com	**brochures literature manuals paint chips**

See full listing in **Section Two** under **literature dealers**

Kramer Automotive Specialties PO Box 5 Herman, PA 16039 724-285-5566; FAX: 724-285-8898	**body parts interiors sheetmetal**

Mail order only. Monday-Friday, noon to 6 pm. A, B, C and E-body parts, race Hemi, St Hemi, max wedge, body and engine restoration items. 1960s and early 1970s Dodge, Plymouth, Chrysler, with emphasis on factory race cars and muscle cars. Sheetmetal, interiors and chrome in NOS, good used and reproduction.

Lares Manufacturing 13517 Hwy 65 NE Ham Lake, MN 55304 800-334-5749; FAX: 612-754-2853 E-mail: sales@larescorp.com	**power steering equipment**

See full listing in **Section One** under **Ford 1954-up**

The Last Precinct Police Museum 15677 Hwy 62 W Eureka Springs, AR 72632 501-253-4948; FAX: 501-253-4949	**museum**

See full listing in **Section Six** under **Arkansas**

Leo R Lindquist 1851 US Hwy 14 Balaton, MN 56115-3200 PH/FAX: 507-734-2051	**1950s Hemi parts NORS parts NOS parts**

Mail order and shop open by appointment. Specializing in 241 to 392 Hemi engines and parts (mainly used); many small pieces available. No high-performance items. Also 1950s Chrysler Corporation vehicles and parts.

Long Road Productions 1663 Hewins St Ashley Falls, MA 01222 413-229-0474; FAX: 413-229-5903 E-mail: oldtrucks@longroadpro.com	**documentaries**

See full listing in **Section Two** under **videos**

Mike's Auto Parts Box 358 Ridgeland, MS 39158 601-856-7214	**ball/roller bearings engine parts wall calendars water pumps**

See full listing in **Section One** under **Chrysler**

MikeCo Antique, Kustom &	lenses
Obsolete Auto Parts	parts

**MikeCo Antique, Kustom &
Obsolete Auto Parts**
4053 Calle Tesoro, Unit C
Camarillo, CA 93012
805-482-1725; FAX: 805-987-8524

Mail order and open shop. Monday-Friday 3:30 pm to 7 pm,
Saturday 10 am to 5 pm PST, fax 24 hours. Specializing in lenses, stainless trim, tune-up and electrical, brake parts and
weatherstrip for Chrysler product vehicles 1930s-1975. Autolite
and Delco electrical parts and weatherstrip for American made
vehicles, 1915-1975. Heavy into Chrysler and General Motors
with stock of parts for independent makes.

Mopar Collector's Guide Magazine   magazine
10067 El Camino Ave
Baton Rouge, LA 70815
504-274-0609; FAX: 504-274-9033
E-mail: mcgpub@mcg-pub.com

Mail order only. *Mopar Collector's Guide* magazine is the world's
largest monthly Mopar only buy, sell, trade publication. Buy on
newsstand or subscribe. Subscribers always advertise free,
which pays for subscription. Four to six four color feature car
articles each month. Extensive price guide. All credit cards
accepted. Free current copy with your subscription when you
mention this ad. Subscription: $25/year (12 issues). Web site:
www.mcg-pub.com

Clayton T Nelson   NOS parts
Box 259
Warrenville, IL 60555
630-369-6589

See full listing in **Section One** under **Oldsmobile**

NS-One   NOS parts
PO Box 2459, Dept VA
Cedar Rapids, IA 52406
319-362-7717

See full listing in **Section One** under **Chrysler**

Obsolete Chrysler NOS Parts   literature
4206 Burnett Dr   parts
Murrysville, PA 15668
724-733-1818 eves
FAX: 724-733-9884 or
412-243-4556 anytime
E-mail: parts4u@aol.com

See full listing in **Section One** under **Chrysler**

Obsolete Parts of Iowa   NOS parts
PO Box 233
Earlville, IA 52041
E-mail: finsrus@mwci.net

Mail order only. Specializing in NOS Mopar parts for 1950s,
1960s, 1970s Chrysler, Plymouth, Dodge, DeSoto.

The Old Carb Doctor   carburetors
Rt 3, Box 338   fuel pumps
Drucilla Church Rd
Nebo, NC 28761
800-945-CARB (2272)
704-659-1428

See full listing in **Section Two** under **carburetors**

Older Car Restoration   repro parts
Martin Lum, Owner   restoration
304 S Main St, Box 428
Mont Alto, PA 17237
717-749-3383, 717-352-7701
E-mail: jlum@epix.net

Mail order and open shop. Monday-Friday 8 am to 5 pm. Partial
or total restorations on all kinds of cars. Offers a line of 1928-
1931 Mopar reproduction parts. Chrysler, Dodge, DeSoto,

Plymouth parts, service, mechanical and cosmetic restorations,
chrome plating and appraisals also available. Also reproduction
parts for 1950s DeSotos.

Original Auto Interiors   upholstery
7869 Trumble Rd
Columbus, MI 48063-3915
810-727-2486; FAX: 810-727-4344
E-mail: origauto@tir.com

See full listing in **Section Two** under **upholstery**

Plymouth, Dodge, Chrysler,   NOS parts for
DeSoto Parts   DeSoto
4206 Burnett Dr
Murrysville, PA 15668
724-733-1818 eves
FAX: 724-733-9884 or
412-243-4556 anytime
E-mail: parts4u@aol.com

See full listing in **Section One** under **DeSoto**

Power Play, Bob Walker   parts
276 Walkers Hollow Tr
Lowgap, NC 27024
336-352-4866; FAX: 336-789-8967
E-mail: rlwalker@infoave.net

See full listing in **Section One** under **Chrysler**

Sam Quinn Cadillac Parts   parts
Box 837
Estacada, OR 97023
503-637-3852

See full listing in **Section One** under **Cadillac/LaSalle**

R & R Fiberglass & Specialties | body parts
4850 Wilson Dr NW
Cleveland, TN 37312
423-476-2270; FAX: 423-473-9442
E-mail: rrfiberglass@wingnet.net

See full listing in **Section Two** under **fiberglass parts**

Rechrome Parts Ltd | bumpers
Box 62 (mail) | guards
96 E Main St (shipping)
Mendham, NJ 07945
800-516-7278; FAX: 973-543-4101
E-mail: rechrome@gti.net

Mail order and open shop. Daily 8 am to 7 pm. Specializing in Mopar bumpers and guards, all makes. Web site: www.old-ntime.com

See our ad on page 149

Reproduction Parts Marketing | parts
1920 Alberta Ave | restoration
Saskatoon, SK Canada S7K 1R9 | service
306-652-6668; FAX: 306-652-1123

See full listing in **Section One** under **Chevrolet**

Riddle's/Mr Plymouth | decals
20303 8th Ave NW | overdrives
Shoreline, WA 98177 | parts & info
206-285-6534 days | repro parts

Mail order only. Neil Riddle, proprietor. Parts 1940-1954. NOS, used and hard-to-find items a specialty. Send $2 for latest listing of products and reproductions. Technical advisor for Plymouth Owners Club, knowledgeable advice given. Also buy, sell, trade NOS parts. Old Mopar cars and parts locator service.

Sound Move Inc | radios
217 S Main St
Elkhart, IN 46516
800-901-0222, 219-294-5100
FAX: 219-293-4902

See full listing in **Section One** under **Chevrolet**

Special T's Unlimited Corp | general repair
PO Box 146 | parts
Prospect Heights, IL 60070 | restoration
847-255-5494; FAX: 847-391-7666 | service

Mail order and open shop. Shop address: 103 N Wheeling Rd, Prospect Heights, IL 60070. Mopar, specializing in 1956-1965 Plymouth/Dodge parts, repair, service, hi-performance. Repair of moldings, trim, anodizing, engine tuned (swirl pattern) for Sport Fury and Polara 500s. New headlight rings and restored grilles, etc. Engine and transmission changeovers and special detailing. Still service and repair Ford A and T, custom painting and detailing. Max wedge air cleaners, alum bumper brackets, repro Coronet 500 finish panels, chrome, die cast, bumper nameplates and more.

Ssnake-Oyl Products Inc | carpet underlay
Rt 2, Box 269-6 | firewall insulation
Hawkins, TX 75765 | seat belt restoration
800-284-7777; FAX: 903-769-4552

See full listing in **Section Two** under **interiors & interior parts**

Stainless Steel Brakes Corp | brake accessories
11470 Main Rd | disc conversion kits
Clarence, NY 14031 | pads/fluid/rotors
800-448-7722, 716-759-8666 | parking brake kits
FAX: 716-759-8688, 24 hr | power steering parts

See full listing in **Section Two** under **brakes**

Stencils & Stripes Unlimited Inc | NOS decals
1108 S Crescent Ave #21 | stripe kits
Park Ridge, IL 60068
847-692-6893; FAX: 847-692-6895

See full listing in **Section Two** under **decals**

Tags Backeast | data plates
PO Box 581 | trim tags
Plainville, CT 06062
860-747-2942
E-mail: dataplt@snet.net

See full listing in **Section Two** under **special services**

Tom Taylor | NOS parts
PO Box 129
Guinda, CA 95637
530-796-4106

Mail order only. Specializing in NOS antique auto parts for 1930-1960 domestic and orphan automobiles.

Totally Auto Inc | parts
337 Philmont Ave | restoration
Feasterville, PA 19053 | service
215-322-2277; FAX: 215-322-4755
E-mail: totalyauto@aol.com

Mail order and open shop by appointment. Monday-Friday 9 am to 4:30 pm. Chrysler only restoration parts, supplies and services. Offering a full line of restoration parts, clips and fastener kits, NOS and good used, as well as restoration correct spray paints. Our services include zinc and cadmium plating, powder and phosphate coating and component restoration. Why should you use our products and services? Doesn't it make sense to get your restoration parts from an established restoration shop that uses those parts to restore award winning Mopar muscle cars.

Vintage Power Wagons Inc | parts
302 S 7th St | trucks
Fairfield, IA 52556
515-472-4665; FAX: 515-472-4824

See full listing in **Section One** under **Dodge**

Pat Walsh Restorations | literature
Box Q | rubber parts
Wakefield, MA 01880
781-246-3266; FAX: 781-224-3311
E-mail: pwalshrest@aol.com

See full listing in **Section Two** under **rubber parts**

Weimann's Literature & Collectables | literature
16 Cottage Rd
Harwinton, CT 06791
860-485-0300
FAX: 860-485-1705, 24 hour

See full listing in **Section One** under **Plymouth**

Wheels & Spokes Inc | Mopar parts
383 Mopar Dr | restoration
Hays, KS 67601
785-628-6477; FAX: 785-628-6834

Mail order and open shop. Monday-Friday 8 am to 6 pm, Saturday 10 am to 5 pm CST. Specializing in auto restoration, complete used Mopar parts for Chrysler products 1955-1974.

Howard Whitelaw — fenders
29249 Bolingbrook Rd
Pepper Pike, OH 44124
216-721-6755 days
216-464-2159 evenings & weekends
FAX: 216-721-6758
E-mail: howardwhitelaw@prodigy.net

Mail order and open shop by appointment only. Specializing in Mopar from 1933-1974 (world's largest supply of Mopar fenders), but some Nash, Buick and Rambler fenders available. Send SASE with inquiry.

Wittenborn's Auto Service Inc — Mopar
133 Woodside Ave
Briarcliff Manor, NY 10510
914-941-2744

Open Monday-Friday 8:30 am to 5:45 pm, evenings and Saturday by appointment. Phone answering service. Repair and service on cars from twenties to present. Alignments, wheel balancing, steam cleaning. Emphasis on Plymouth Valiants and Dodge Darts. Used parts for slant 6 Valiants and Darts 1961-1980. "Everything from oil changes and tune-ups to major mechanical work. ASE certified mechanic."

Bonnets Up — restoration
5736 Spring St
Clinton, MD 20735
301-297-4759

See full listing in **Section Two** under **coachbuilders & designers**

The CM Booth Collection of Historic Vehicles — museum
Falstaff Antiques
63-67 High St
Rolvenden Kent TN17 4LP England
01580-241234

See full listing in **Section Six** under **England**

Geeson Bros Motorcycle Museum & Workshop — museum
2-6 Water Ln
South Witham
Grantham Lincs NG33 5 PH
England
01572 767280, 01572 768195

See full listing in **Section Six** under **England**

Isis Imports Ltd — cars, parts, restoration
PO Box 2290
Gateway Station
San Francisco, CA 94126
415-433-1344; FAX: 415-788-1850
E-mail: billfink@morgancars-usa.com

Mail order and open shop daily by appointment. Specializing in Morgan cars, parts, service and restoration.

Morgan Oasis Garage — restoration, service
PO Box 1010
N 51 Terrace Rd
Hoodsport, WA 98548
360-877-5160

Mail order and open shop. Monday-Friday 9 am to 6 pm PST. Specializing in service and restoration for Morgan 4-4, Plus 4, Plus 8.

Morgan Spares Ltd — car sales, consulting, obsolete parts, used parts
225 Simons Rd
Ancram, NY 12502
518-329-3877; FAX: 518-329-3892
E-mail: morganspares@taconic.net

Mail order and open shop. Monday-Friday 8 am to 5 pm, Saturday by appointment. Specializing in Morgan +4, 4/4, +8 from 1950-present. Complete body assemblies, sheetmetal, wood, interiors, weather equip, accessories, mechanical, electrical, stainless steel, race and performance items. 22 years of Morgan restoration, service and sales. Genuine Morgan factory parts. Lucas-Girling distributor. Obsolete, used and hard to find parts. Illustrated parts manual. Car sales and sales consulting service. Web site: www.morgan-spares.com

Olde World Restorations — parts, restoration
2727 Philmont Ave, Suite 350
Huntingdon Valley, PA 19006
215-947-8720; FAX: 215-947-8722

Mail order and open shop. Monday-Friday 9 am to 5:30 pm or by appointment. Morgan parts, repairs and restorations.

Ragtops & Roadsters — bodywork/painting, British automobiles, engine rebuilding, vintage race prep
203 S 4th St
Perkasie, PA 18944
215-257-1202; FAX: 215-257-2688
E-mail: info@ragtops.com

See full listing in **Section Two** under **restoration shops**

The Ramsgate Motor Museum — museum
Westcliff Hall
Ramsgate, Kent England
01843 581948

See full listing in **Section Six** under **England**

Sports Car Haven — race prep, restorations, service
2-33 Flowerfield Industrial Pk
St James, NY 11780
516-862-8058
E-mail: sch94@aol.com

See full listing in **Section One** under **Triumph**

Sports & Classics — parts
PO Box 1787
512 Boston Post Rd, Dept H
Darien, CT 06820-1787

See full listing in **Section Two** under **body parts**

Triple C Motor Accessories — accessories, models
1900 Orange St
York, PA 17404
717-854-4081
FAX: 717-854-6706
E-mail: sales@triple-c.com

See full listing in **Section One** under **MG**

XKs Unlimited — instruments, parts, restorations
850 Fiero Ln
San Luis Obispo, CA 93401
805-544-7864
FAX: 805-544-1664
E-mail: xksunltd@aol.com

See full listing in **Section One** under **Jaguar**

Gideon Booth
Rellandsgate, Kings Meaburn
Penrith
Cumbria CA10 3BT England
PH/FAX: 01931 714624

car collector
parts
restorations

Mail order and open shop. Daily 9 am to 8 pm. Specializing in Morris cars and trucks for all models 1913-1963. Car collector with 80 Morris vehicles. Reproduce fiberglass wings. Restorations. Many spare parts.

British Auto Parts Ltd
93256 Holland Ln
Marcola, OR 97454
541-933-2880; FAX: 541-933-2302

parts

Monday-Friday 8 am to 5 pm. Offering new, used and rebuilt parts for Morris Minor, MG, Triumph and Jaguar. 25 years' of exclusive British experience in supplying the common and hard-to-find for all British cars. Questions and problems welcomed. Daily shipping UPS, bank cards accepted.

British Auto Shoppe
1909 5th Ave
Moline, IL 61265
309-764-9513; FAX: 309-764-9576

parts
service

See full listing in **Section One** under **MG**

British Car Service
2854 N Stone Ave
Tucson, AZ 85705
520-882-7026; FAX: 520-882-7053
E-mail: bcs@liveline.com

restoration
salvage yard

See full listing in **Section Five** under **Arizona**

British Racing Green
30 Aleph Dr
Newark, DE 19702
302-368-1117; FAX: 302-368-5910
E-mail:info@brgparts.com

new parts
rebuilt parts
used parts

See full listing in **Section One** under **MG**

Pete Groh
9957 Frederick Rd
Ellicott City, MD 21042-3647
410-750-2352; FAX: 410-466-3566
E-mail: petegroh@yahoo.com

original British
keys

See full listing in **Section One** under **Jaguar**

Kip Motor Company Inc
2127 Crown Rd
Dallas, TX 75229
972-243-0440; FAX: 972-243-2387
E-mail: kipmotor@aol.com

literature
parts
restoration

See full listing in **Section One** under **Austin**

Lake Oswego Restorations
19621 S Hazelhurst Ln
West Linn, OR 97068
PH/FAX: 503-636-7503

restoration
sales

See full listing in **Section One** under **Aston Martin**

McLean's Brit Bits
14 Sagamore Rd
Rye, NH 03870
800-995-2487; FAX: 603-433-0009
E-mail: sam@britbits.com

accessories
parts
sales
service

See full listing in **Section One** under **MG**

Mini Mania
31 Winsor St
Milpitas, CA 95035
408-942-5595; FAX: 408-942-5582
E-mail: info@minimania.com

parts
service

See full listing in **Section One** under **Austin**

Mini Store
PO Box 7973
Van Nuys, CA 91409-7973
PH/FAX: 818-893-1421
E-mail: jorn@aol.com

cars
repairs
restorations

See full listing in **Section One** under **Austin**

Motormetrics
6369 Houston Rd
Macon, GA 31216
912-785-0275
E-mail:
fzampa@cennet.mc.peachnet.edu

used parts

See full listing in **Section One** under **Triumph**

Patton Orphan Spares
52 Nicole Pl
West Babylon, NY 11704
516-669-2598

parts

See full listing in **Section One** under **Renault**

Seven Enterprises Ltd
802 Bluecrab Rd, Ste 100
Newport News, VA 23606
800-992-7007; FAX: 800-296-3327

accessories
parts

See full listing in **Section One** under **Austin**

Sports Car Haven
3414 Bloom Rd, Rt 11
Danville, PA 17821
570-275-5705

parts
restoration
service

See full listing in **Section One** under **MG**

All American Rambler
11661 Martens River Cir #M
Fountain Valley, CA 92708
714-662-7200
E-mail: rambler411@aol.com

manuals
parts

See full listing in **Section One** under **AMC**

AMX Connection
David Simon
19641 Victory Blvd
Reseda, CA 91335-6621
818-344-4639

literature
parts

See full listing in **Section One** under **AMC**

Blaser's Auto, Nash, Rambler, AMC — NOS parts
3200 48th Ave
Moline, IL 61265-6453
309-764-3571; FAX: 309-764-1155
E-mail: blazauto@sprynet.com

See full listing in **Section One** under **AMC**

Charles Chambers Parts — parts
Box 60, HC 64
Goldthwaite, TX 76844
E-mail: gonzales@centex.net

Mail order only. Exclusively Nash parts. Good selection of items from ammeters to zerks. SASE required.

Doug Galvin Rambler Parts — parts
7559 Passalis Ln
Sacramento, CA 95829
916-689-3356

See full listing in **Section One** under **AMC**

Lucky Lee Lott (Author) — information / parts
800 E Diana St
Tampa, FL 33604
813-238-5408 (24 hours)

Mail order and open shop. Specializing in parts and information for Nash, Rambler, Ajax, Lafayette, 1902-1958. On I-275 North at Exit 31, Sligh Ave in Tampa. Here are Lucky Lee Lott Hell Drivers' cars of 1935-1955 on display from time to time with memorabilia of old time daredevils. and information or interviews. *Legend of Lucky Lee Lott Hell Drivers* autobiography now available with 150 pictures, turn-around, delivery, P/O, m/o, only $18.50 or send book of 10 stamps for autographed color photo only, p/p.

Metropolitan Pit Stop — literature / parts / restoration
5324-26-28-30 Laurel Canyon Blvd
North Hollywood, CA 91607
800-PIT-STOP order toll-free
818-769-1515; FAX: 818-769-3500
E-mail: hi-valentine@webtv.net

See full listing in **Section One** under **Metropolitan**

NASHional Auto Parts & Cars — cars / parts
2412 Lincoln Ave
Alameda, CA 94501
510-522-2244; FAX: 510-864-8151

Mail order only. Thursday-Saturday 10 am to 5 pm. Specializing in Nash, Rambler and AMC for 1902-1969. Reproduction rubber. Metro molded rubber dealer.

Garth B Peterson — accessories / parts / radios
122 N Conklin Rd
Veradale, WA 99037
509-926-4620 anytime

See full listing in **Section Two** under **comprehensive parts**

Treasure Chest Sales — parts
413 Montgomery
Jackson, MI 49202
517-787-1475

Mail order and open shop by appointment only. Retail mail order parts source for Nash, Metropolitan and AMC made automobiles, all years, NOS and used.

Webb's Classic Auto Parts — NOS parts / reproduction parts / service manuals / used parts
5084 W State Rd 114
Huntington, IN 46750
219-344-1714; FAX: 219-344-1754

See full listing in **Section One** under **AMC**

Wenner's — NOS parts
5449 Tannery Rd
Schnecksville, PA 18078
610-799-5419

See full listing in **Section One** under **AMC**

Howard Whitelaw — fenders
29249 Bolingbrook Rd
Pepper Pike, OH 44124
216-721-6755 days
216-464-2159 evenings & weekends
FAX: 216-721-6758
E-mail: howardwhitelaw@prodigy.net

See full listing in **Section One** under **Mopar**

Wymer Classic AMC — NOS parts / owner's manuals / repairs / service manuals / used parts
Mark & George Wymer
340 N Justice St
Fremont, OH 43420
419-332-4291
419-334-6945 after 5 pm

See full listing in **Section One** under **AMC**

NSU/USA Jim Sykes — literature / parts advice / restoration
717 N 68th St
Seattle, WA 98103
206-784-5084

Mail order and open shop. Monday-Saturday 1 pm to 7 pm. Any type NSU including motorcycles and Wankels. Restoration and parts advice free with SASE. Over 25 years' experience.

4-Speeds by Darrell — transmissions
PO Box 110
3 Water St
Vermilion, IL 61955
217-275-3743; FAX: 217-275-3515

See full listing in **Section Two** under **transmissions**

The 60 Oldsmobile Club — newsletter
Dick Major
10895 E Hibma Rd
Tustin, MI 49688
616-825-2891; FAX: 616-825-8324
E-mail: dmajor@netonecom.net

Information for 1960 Oldsmobiles. We are a newsletter.

A & M SoffSeal Inc — rubber parts / weatherstripping
104 May Dr
Harrison, OH 45030
800-426-0902
513-367-0028 service/info
FAX: 513-367-5506
E-mail: soffseal@soffseal.com

See full listing in **Section Two** under **rubber parts**

Anderson Automotive — cars, parts
1604 E Busch Blvd
Tampa, FL 33612
813-932-4611; FAX: 813-932-5025

Mail order and open shop. Monday-Friday 8 am to 5 pm. Parts and complete cars, used and new for 1968-1972 Olds 442, Cutlass only.

Antique & Classic Cars Inc — bodywork, machine work, painting, parts, service
328 S 3rd St
Hamilton, OH 45011
513-844-1146 in OH
800-798-3982 nationwide

See full listing in **Section One** under **Buick/McLaughlin**

Art's Antique & Classic Auto Services — restoration
1985 E 5th St #16
Tempe, AZ 85281
602-966-1195

See full listing in **Section One** under **Buick/McLaughlin**

Be Happy Automatic Transmission Parts — trans rebuild kits
414 Stivers Rd
Hillsboro, OH 45133
800-416-2862; FAX: 937-442-6133

See full listing in **Section Two** under **transmissions**

Bumper Boyz LLC — bumper repairs, reconditioning, sandblasting
2435 E 54th St
Los Angeles, CA 90058
800-995-1703, 323-587-8976
FAX: 323-587-2013

See full listing in **Section One** under **Chevrolet**

Chevrolet Parts Obsolete — accessories, parts
PO Box 0740
Murrieta, CA 92564-0740
909-279-2833; FAX: 909-279-4013
E-mail: spo@att.net

See full listing in **Section One** under **Chevrolet**

Chewning's Auto Literature — literature, manuals
2011 Elm Tree Terr
Buford, GA 30518
770-945-9795

See full listing in **Section Two** under **literature dealers**

Chief Service — parts, restoration
Herbert G Baschung
Brunnmatt, PO Box 155
CH-4914 Roggwil Switzerland
PH/FAX: 0041-62-9291777

See full listing in **Section Two** under **restoration shops**

Classic and Muscle — reproduction parts, restoration parts
Muscle Car Restoration Parts
PO Box 657
Elmsdale, NS Canada B0N 1M0
902-883-4489; FAX: 902-883-1392
E-mail: classicmuscle@sprint.ca

See full listing in **Section One** under **Chevrolet**

Coach Builders Muscle Car Parts & Services — interiors, parts, rust remover
PO Box 128
Baltimore, MD 21087-0128
410-426-5567

See full listing in **Section One** under **Chevrolet**

Coopers Vintage Auto Parts — parts
3087 N California St
Burbank, CA 91504
818-567-4140; FAX: 818-567-4101

See full listing in **Section One** under **Cadillac/LaSalle**

The Copper Cooling Works — radiators
2455 N 2550 E
Layton, UT 84040
801-544-9939

See full listing in **Section Two** under **radiators**

Dash Specialists — interiors
1910 Redbud Ln
Medford, OR 97504
541-776-0040

See full listing in **Section One** under **Cadillac/LaSalle**

Egge Machine Company Inc — bearings, pistons/rings, timing components, valve train
11707 Slauson Ave
Santa Fe Springs, CA 90670
800-866-EGGE, 562-945-3419
FAX: 562-693-1635
E-mail: info@egge.com

See full listing in **Section Two** under **engine parts**

Engineering & Manufacturing Services — sheetmetal
Box 24362
Cleveland, OH 44124-0362
216-541-4585; FAX: 216-541-4989

See full listing in **Section One** under **Ford 1932-1953**

John Filiss — appraisals
45 Kingston Ave
Port Jervis, NY 12771
914-856-2942
E-mail: johnfiliss@hotmail.com

See full listing in **Section Two** under **appraisals**

Fusick Automotive Products — restoration parts
22 Thompson Rd Box 655
East Windsor, CT 06088
860-623-1589; FAX: 860-623-3118
E-mail: dj442@ix.netcom.com

Mail order and open shop. Specializing in 1935-1977 Oldsmobile restoration parts. Separate catalogs available for 1935-1960 Oldsmobile, 1961-1977 Cutlass, 442, H/O and 1961-1976 88, 98, SF, Toronado. Catalogs $5 each.

Gardner Exhaust Systems — exhaust systems
2 Cedar Ln
Rhinebeck, NY 12572
PH/FAX: 914-876-8117
E-mail: gexhaust@aol.com

See full listing in **Section One** under **Chevelle/Camaro**

GM Obsolete — parts
909 W Magnolia St
Phoenix, AZ 85007
602-253-8081; FAX: 602-253-8411
E-mail: info@gmobsolete.com

See full listing in **Section One** under **Buick/McLaughlin**

Inline Tube
33783 Groes Beck Hwy
Fraser, MI 48026
800-385-9452 order
810-294-4093 tech
FAX: 810-294-7349
E-mail: kryta@aol.com

| brake lines/cables |
| choke tubes |
| flex brake hoses |
| fuel/vacuum lines |
| transmission lines |

See full listing in **Section Two** under **brakes**

Lares Manufacturing
13517 Hwy 65 NE
Ham Lake, MN 55304
800-334-5749; FAX: 612-754-2853
E-mail: sales@larescorp.com

**power steering
equipment**

See full listing in **Section One** under **Ford 1954-up**

Lectric Limited Inc
7322 S Archer Road
Justice, IL 60458
708-563-0400; FAX: 708-458-2662

parts

See full listing in **Section One** under **Corvette**

LES Auto Parts
Box 81
Dayton, NJ 08810
732-329-6128; FAX: 732-329-1036

parts

See full listing in **Section One** under **Chevrolet**

M & H Electric Fabricators Inc
13537 Alondra Blvd
Santa Fe Springs, CA 90670
562-926-9552; FAX: 562-926-9572
E-mail: sales@wiringharness.com

wiring harnesses

See full listing in **Section Two** under **electrical systems**

Clayton T Nelson
Box 259
Warrenville, IL 60555
630-369-6589

NOS parts

Mail order only. Specializing in NOS parts for Oldsmobile and Mopar, late 1940s-mid 1970s.

The Paddock® Inc
PO Box 30
221 W Main
Knightstown, IN 46148
800-428-4319; FAX: 800-286-4040
E-mail: paddock@indy.net

**accessories
parts**

See full listing in **Section One** under **Mustang**

M Parker Autoworks Inc
150 Heller Pl #17W
Dept HVAA99
Bellmawr, NJ 08031
609-933-0801; FAX: 609-933-0805
E-mail: facfit@erols.com

**battery cables
harnesses**

See full listing in **Section Two** under **electrical systems**

The Parts Place
217 Paul St
Elburn, IL 60119
PH/FAX: 630-365-1800
E-mail: pplace9594@aol.com

parts

See full listing in **Section One** under **Chevrolet**

Precision Rubber
Box 324
Didsbury, AB Canada T0M 0W0
403-335-9590; FAX: 403-335-8100

rubber parts

See full listing in **Section Two** under **rubber parts**

**Raine Automotive Springs
Warehouse**
425 Harding Hwy
Carney's Point, NJ 08069
609-299-9141; FAX: 609-299-9157

**springs
suspension parts**

See full listing in **Section Two** under **suspension parts**

REM Automotive Inc
2610 N Brandt Rd
Annville, PA 17003
717-838-4242; FAX: 717-838-5091

**interior parts
trunk lining**

See full listing in **Section Two** under **restoration aids**

**Robertson Bros & Sons
Restoration**
PO Box 5678
Sevierville, TN 37864-5678
423-970-1655; FAX: 423-908-6838
E-mail: classicbop@aol.com

**NOS parts
restoration parts
used parts**

Mail order only. Specializing in restoration parts, NOS and used parts for Buick 1950s-1960s, Rivieras and GS, Olds 1950s-1960s, Toronados and 442 (1964-1977), and Pontiac 1960s only, Grand Prix, GTO (1964-1972) and Firebirds (1967-1972). Restoration on automobilia signs.

Ross' Automotive Machine Co Inc
1763 N Main St
Niles, OH 44446
330-544-4466

**racing engines
rebuilding**

See full listing in **Section Two** under **engine rebuilding**

Harry Samuel
65 Wisner St
Pontiac, MI 48342-1066
248-335-1900
E-mail: hsamuel1@aol.com

**carpet
fabrics
interiors
upholstery covers**

See full listing in **Section Two** under **interiors & interior parts**

Special Auto Restoration
689 Fern Dr
Merritt Island, FL 32952
407-453-8343, 407-783-4758

restoration

See full listing in **Section One** under **Chevelle/Camaro**

Staley's Olds Parts
355 N Chestnut St
Monrovia, IN 46157
317-996-2215
E-mail: bstaley442@aol.com

NOS parts

NOS Oldsmobile parts, 1940s-1970s. Send $3 for list of parts for your year. 70 pages of Olds parts.

Stencils & Stripes Unlimited Inc
1108 S Crescent Ave #21
Park Ridge, IL 60068
847-692-6893; FAX: 847-692-6895

**NOS decals
stripe kits**

See full listing in **Section Two** under **decals**

Street-Wise Performance
Richie Mulligan
Box 105 Creek Rd
Tranquility, NJ 07879
973-786-6668 days
973-786-7133 evenings
FAX: 973-786-7861
E-mail: richie@goes.com

**differentials
parts
rebuild kits
transmissions**

See full listing in **Section Two** under **transmissions**

Supercars Unlimited — parts
8029 Unit A SW 17th
Portland, OR 97219-2857
503-244-8249; FAX: 503-244-9639
E-mail: supercars@transport.com

Mail order only. 9 am to 4 pm PST. Replacement parts and restoration items, mechanical parts (no chrome or sheetmetal) for 1964-1977 Oldsmobile Cutlass, 4-4-2 and Hurst/Olds. Cutlass/4-4-2 is all we do! Web site: www.supercarsunlimited.com

Tags Backeast — data plates / trim tags
PO Box 581
Plainville, CT 06062
860-747-2942
E-mail: dataplt@snet.net

See full listing in **Section Two** under **special services**

Tamraz's Parts Discount Warehouse — carpeting / upholstery / weatherstripping
10022 S Bode Rd
Plainfield, IL 60544
630-904-4500; FAX: 630-904-2329

See full listing in **Section One** under **Chevelle/Camaro**

Tanson Enterprises — performance parts / restoration parts
2508 J St, Dept HVA
Sacramento, CA 95816-4815
916-448-2950
FAX: 916-443-3269 *88
E-mail: tanson@pipeline.com

Performance and restoration parts for Oldsmobiles 1937-1970; specializing in the 1940s and 1950s. Heavy duty sway bars, early V8 conversions to late automatic transmissions, vibration dampers, gaskets, disc brake conversions, rubber parts, coil springs, electric wiper conversions.

Tom's Classic Parts — parts
5207 Sundew Terr
Tobyhanna, PA 18466
800-832-4073

See full listing in **Section One** under **Chevrolet**

Triangle Automotive — parts
PO Box 2293
Arcadia, CA 91077
626-357-2377

Mail order only. Specializing in original choice condition body and interior parts and optional equipment for 1965-1977 Olds Cutlass and 442. Also Pontiac GTO, LeMans and Firebird.

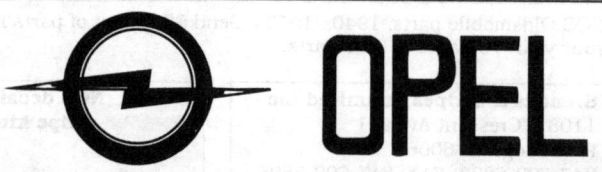

Opel GT Source — parts / technical info
18211 Zeni Ln
Tuolumne, CA 95379
209-928-1110; FAX: 209-928-3298
E-mail: opelgts@opelgtsource.com

Mail order. Monday-Friday 8 am to 12 pm, 1 pm to 5 pm PST. Opel parts, technical information, restoration, high-performance, custom body kits, race preparation, specializing in parts for 1968-1975 Opel parts. Offer the largest inventory of new Opel parts in North America. Also have a large selection of used Opel parts as well. Web site: www.opelgtsource.com/opel

Opel Oldtimer Service Denmark — literature / parts / parts locator
Landevejen 27
Toksvaerd
DK-4684 Holme-Olstrup Denmark
PH/FAX: +45-55-530100
best 11 am to 3 pm US Central time
E-mail: frank.kiessling@get2net.dk

Mail order only. Specializing in parts, parts location, parts rebuilding, parts catalogues, shop manuals and other literature for rear wheel drive Opel automobiles.

Opel Parts & Service Inc — parts / service
3961 S Military Hwy
Chesapeake, VA 23321
757-487-3851

Mail order and open shop. Monday-Friday 10 am to 5 pm. Specializing in Opels since 1970. 1957-1975 Opel NOS, rebuilt, reproduction and used parts. Major components service. Specializing in Rekord, Kadette, Manta and GT.

Opels Unlimited — parts / service
871 E Lambert Rd #C
La Habra, CA 90631
562-690-1051; FAX: 562-690-3352
E-mail: opelsunl@opelsunl.com

Evenings are best to call, also most Saturdays. The largest Opel parts company in the USA. Over 100 complete cars, service shops, showrooms, club specials, newsletters, videos, tech info, best prices and largest selection anywhere. Over 10,000 sq feet of rust-free sheetmetal, all models from 1955-1981. Life member club includes calendar girls, T-shirts, stickers and key chains. We beat any price on anything, parts, labor or services. Complete cars shipped anywhere in USA. Over 5,000 new original stock parts available. Take care and happy Opeling. Web site: www.opelsunl.com

Alpha Omega Motorsport — parts / repairs / restorations
15612 New Century Dr
Gardena, CA 90248
310-366-7993; FAX: 310-366-7499
E-mail: aomotor@pacbell.net

See full listing in **Section One** under **Pontiac**

Anderson Restoration — restorations
1235 Nash Ave
Kanawha, IA 50447
515-762-3528

See full listing in **Section Two** under **restoration shops**

Antique & Classic Cars — car locator
1796 County Rd 7
Florence, AL 35633
205-760-0542

See full listing in **Section One** under **Cadillac/LaSalle**

Antique & Classic Cars Inc — bodywork / machine work / painting / parts / service
328 S 3rd St
Hamilton, OH 45011
513-844-1146 in OH
800-798-3982 nationwide

See full listing in **Section One** under **Buick/McLaughlin**

Auto Europa	painting
221 Berrellesa St	restorations
Martinez, CA 94553	woodworking
925-229-3466; FAX: 925-313-0542	

See full listing in **Section Two** under **restoration shops**

Auto World Car Museum by Backer	museum
Business 54 N	
PO Box 135	
Fulton, MO 65251	
573-642-2080, 573-642-5344	
FAX: 573-642-0685	
E-mail: webacker@ktis.net	

See full listing in **Section Six** under **Missouri**

Be Happy Automatic Transmission Parts	trans rebuild kits
414 Stivers Rd	
Hillsboro, OH 45133	
800-416-2862; FAX: 937-442-6133	

See full listing in **Section Two** under **transmissions**

Blackhawk Collection	acquisitions
1092 Eagles Nest Pl	sales
Danville, CA 94506-3600	
925-736-3444; FAX: 925-736-4375	
E-mail: info@blackhawkcollection.com	

See full listing in **Section One** under **Duesenberg**

EJ Blend	literature
802 8th Ave	parts
Irwin, PA 15642-3702	
724-863-7624	

Mail order only. Monday-Friday 9 am to 5 pm. Specializing in Packard parts 1929-1942 and literature for 1933-1934 Twelves.

Bob's Radio & TV Service	radios
238 Ocean View	
Pismo Beach, CA 93449	
805-773-8200	

See full listing in **Section Two** under **radios**

Bill Boudway	restoration info
105 Deerfield Dr	
Canandaigua, NY 14424-2409	
716-394-6172	

Mail order only. Copies of restoration information, advertising material and parts lists for Packard Twin Six automobiles, 1916-1923. Hershey space #C2G-70.

Brasilia Press	models
PO Box 2023	
Elkhart, IN 46515	
FAX: 219-262-8799	

See full listing in **Section Two** under **models & toys**

Brinton's Antique Auto Parts	parts
6826 SW McVey Ave	
Redmond, OR 97756	
541-548-3483; FAX: 541-548-8022	

Mail order and open shop. Dismantle Packard cars and chassis and sell the parts taken off them. Sixes, Eights and Super 8s. Also 12-cylinders. Parts for 1920s-1958 Packards.

Cape Cod Classic Cars	car dealer
Pete Harvey	
PO Box 280	
Cataumet, MA 02534	
508-548-0660; FAX: 508-457-0660	

See full listing in **Section One** under **Cadillac/LaSalle**

Chrome Masters	chrome plating
1109 W Orange Ave, Unit D	pot metal restoration
Tallahassee, FL 32310	
850-576-2100; FAX: 850-576-2772	

See full listing in **Section Two** under **plating & polishing**

Classic Cars Inc	cars
52 Maple Terr	parts
Hibernia, NJ 07842	
973-627-1975; FAX: 973-627-3503	

Mail order only. Pre WW II Packard parts and Packard cars for 1928-1942. 4 page price sheet of new parts.

Classics 'n More Inc	repairs
1001 Ranck Mill Rd	restoration
Lancaster, PA 17602	
717-392-0599; FAX 717-392-2371	

See full listing in **Section Two** under **restoration shops**

Clean Air Performance Professionals (CAPP)	legislative watch
84 Hoy Ave	organization
Fords, NJ 08863	
732-738-7859; FAX: 732-738-7625	
E-mail: stellacapp@earthlink.net	

See full listing in **Section Three** under **legislative watch organizations**

Robert Connole	ignition coils
2525 E 32nd St	
Davenport, IA 52807	
319-355-6266	

Mail order only. Packard double coils, 1933-1934 eight-cylinder Northeast, 1934-1939 twelve-cylinder Autolite. All new coils, bases, wires and terminals. Autolite embossed on case for the new 12 coils. Ready to install.

Tom Crook Classic Cars	car dealer
27611 42nd Ave S	
Auburn, WA 98001	
206-941-3454	

See full listing in **Section Two** under **car dealers**

Dave's Auto Restoration	upholstery
2285 Rt 307 E	
Jefferson, OH 44047	
PH/FAX: 216-858-2227	
E-mail: davesauto@knownet.net	

See full listing in **Section Two** under **interiors & interior parts**

Deters Restorations	restoration
6205 Swiss Garden Rd	
Temperance, MI 48182-1020	
734-847-1820	

See full listing in **Section Two** under **restoration shops**

JB Donaldson Co	castings
2533 W Cypress	steering wheels
Phoenix, AZ 85009	wood parts
602-278-4505; FAX: 602-278-1112	

See full listing in **Section Two** under **steering wheels**

Durabuilt Automotive Hydraulics	hose assemblies
808 Meadows Ave	pumps
Canon City, CO 81212	top cylinders
PH/FAX: 719-275-1126	valves
E-mail: durabuilt@ris.net	

See full listing in **Section Two** under **tops**

Edgerton Classics Ltd
9215 St Rt 13
Camden, NY 13316-4933
315-245-3113

restoration
woodworking

See full listing in **Section Two** under **restoration shops**

Egge Machine Company Inc
11707 Slauson Ave
Santa Fe Springs, CA 90670
800-866-EGGE, 562-945-3419
FAX: 562-693-1635
E-mail: info@egge.com

bearings
pistons/rings
timing components
valve train

See full listing in **Section Two** under **engine parts**

Jay M Fisher
Acken Dr 4-B
Clark, NJ 07066
732-388-6442

mascots
sidemount mirrors
windwing brackets

See full listing in **Section Two** under **accessories**

From Rust To Riches
16643 Rt 144
Mt Airy, MD 21771
301-854-5900, 410-442-3637
301-854-5956; FAX: 301-854-5957
E-mail: tatrabill@aol.com

appraisals
car dealer
repairs
restoration

See full listing in **Section Two** under **restoration shops**

Green Valentine Inc
5055 Covington Way
Memphis, TN 38134
901-373-5555; FAX: 901-373-5568

car dealer
woodies

See full listing in **Section Two** under **car dealers**

Guild of Automotive Restorers
PO Box 1150
44 Bridge St
Bradford, ON Canada L3Z 2B5
905-775-0499; FAX: 905-775-0944
E-mail:
webmaster@guildautomotive.on.ca

restoration
sales
service

See full listing in **Section Two** under **restoration shops**

Hagerty Classic Insurance
PO Box 87
Traverse City, MI 49685
800-922-4050; FAX: 616-941-8227

insurance

See full listing in **Section Two** under **insurance**

James Hill
Box 547-V
Goodwell, OK 73939
580-349-2736 evenings/weekends

ignition parts
source list

Mail order only from above address during school year (summers at 1107 Washington, Emporia, KS 66801). Packard only supplying publication: 1999 edition, *Sources of Packard Parts and Services* with 30 pages of source information, 8 pages of name/address listings and 4 pages of fax numbers. Cost is $5 postpaid in USA and Canada, $7 US funds airmail to other countries with perfect value guarantee. New edition is planned for summer of 2000.

Interesting Parts Inc
Paul TerHorst
27526 N Owens Rd
Mundelein, IL 60060
PH/FAX: 847-949-1030

appraisals
gaskets
parts
storage
transport

See full listing in **Section Two** under **comprehensive parts**

JECC Inc
PO Box 616
West Paterson, NJ 07424
973-890-9682; FAX: 973-812-2724

chassis parts
gaskets
transmissions

See full listing in **Section One** under **Buick/McLaughlin**

Jerry's Automotive
c/o Jerry Cinotti
431 S Sierra Way
San Bernadino, CA 92408
909-884-6980; FAX: 909-884-7872

brake repair

See full listing in **Section Two** under **brakes**

Jesser's Classic Keys
26 West St, Dept HVA
Akron, OH 44303-2344
330-376-8181; FAX: 330-384-9129

automobilia
keys

See full listing in **Section Two** under **locks & keys**

Keleen Leathers Inc
10526 W Cermak Rd
Westchester, IL 60154
708-409-9800; FAX: 708-409-9801

leather hides

See full listing in **Section Two** under **interiors & interior parts**

L & L Antique Auto Trim
403 Spruce, Box 177
Pierce City, MO 65723
417-476-2871

runningboard
moldings

See full listing in **Section Two** under **special services**

Gerald J Lettieri
132 Old Main St
Rocky Hill, CT 06067
860-529-7177; FAX: 860-257-3621

gaskets
parts

See full listing in **Section Two** under **gaskets**

Lincoln Highway Packards
Main St
PO Box 94
Schellsburg, PA 15559
814-733-4356; FAX: 814-839-4276

engine rebuilding
restoration

Open Monday-Friday 8 am to 4 pm, other times by appointment. Specializing in restoration on Packards and Cords. We do auto restoration, engine, transmission, differential overhaul, carburetor rebuilding, starter, generator, regulator repair, rewiring.

Max Merritt Auto Parts
PO Box 10
Franklin, IN 46131
317-736-6233; FAX: 317-736-6235

accessories
parts

Specializing in NOS, NORS, reproduction and used parts and accessories for Packard automobiles 1930-1956. Stainless steel molding for runningboard trim, hood moldings, and misc other applications for Buick, Cadillac, Chrysler, Dodge, Lincoln, Packard, Pierce-Arrow and others.

Motor Foundry & Tooling Inc
7382 Doniphan Dr
Canutillo, TX 79835-6601
915-877-3343; FAX: 915-877-7071

brake drums
castings
exhaust manifolds
water pumps

Mail order and open shop. Monday-Friday 8 am to 5 pm. Specializing in Chrysler, Cord, Auburn, Cadillac, Packard, Buick, Duesenberg, Rolls-Royce, Pierce-Arrow, Peerless, Stutz, trucks and tractors. Deals in exhaust manifolds, cylinder heads, blocks, water pumps, light brackets, step plates, window frames, door/window handles, gear cases, brake drums. Wax investment, plaster, dry/green sand castings. Alloys: aluminum, zinc-3, bronze, cast iron, stainless steel and steel.

Northeast Classic Car Museum — museum
NYS Rt 23
24 Rexford St
Norwich, NY 13815
607-334-AUTO (334-2886)
FAX: 607-336-6745
E-mail: neccm@ascent.net

See full listing in **Section Six** under **New York**

Oak Bows — top bows
122 Ramsey Ave
Chambersburg, PA 17201
717-264-2602

See full listing in **Section Two** under **woodwork**

ORF Corp — ring and pinion gears
Phil Bray
8858 Ferry Rd
Grosse Ile, MI 48138
734-676-5520; FAX: 734-676-9438
E-mail: carolbray@yahoo.com

See full listing in **Section Two** under **special services**

Packard Archives — accessories / artwork / automobilia
918 W Co Rd C-2
St Paul, MN 55113-1942
651-484-1184
E-mail: estatecars@earthlink.net

Highest prices paid for Packard automobile dealership and factory memorabilia/collectibles. Cash for dealer giveaways, lapel pins, signs, NOS parts, literature, clocks, filmstrips and movies. Original artwork, accessories, Packard jewelry, rings, watches, awards, pin backs, buttons, advertising promotional items, master salesman awards, metal tin cans and bottles, etc, anything Packard.

Packard Farm — parts
97 N 150 W
Greenfield, IN 46140
317-462-3124
800-922-1957 orders only
FAX: 317-462-8891

Mail order and open shop. Monday-Friday 8:30 am to 5 pm. Saturday 8:30 am to 12 noon by appointment. Mostly Chevrolets and Studebakers.

Packard Store — parts
9 Hall Hill Rd
Sterling, CT 06377
860-564-5345
E-mail:
george.simone@worldnet.att.net
or dexterrule@aol.com

Mail order or visit old barn full of Packard parts. A one stop place for 1940 Packards. We have a huge selection of sheetmetal, trim, interior and driveline parts for all models. Glass for gauges with letters and numbers. We have the paint for gauges and interior. Flock is available for all Packards, 1930s-1950s.

Packards & Collector Cars — conversion kits
425 E Laurel
Sierra Madre, CA 91024
626-355-4023, 714-539-8579
FAX: 626-355-4072

Mail order only. The Ultra-Torc II, a transmission conversion kit to convert Packards to the Chrysler Torqueflite 727 transmission. The kits are for 1951-1954 and 1955-1956 Packards.

Patrician Industries Inc — parts
22644 Nona
Dearborn, MI 48124
313-565-3573
E-mail: packards1@aol.com

Mail order and open shop by appointment only. Handles a full line of new, used and reproduction Packard parts for Packards 1940-56.

Potomac Packard — wiring harnesses
PO Box 117
Tiger, GA 30576
800-859-9532 orders, 706-782-2345
FAX: 706-782-2344

Manufactures and supplies electrical wiring harnesses and equipment for Packards, 1916-1956. Our products are made to exacting standards, using Packard engineering drawings or original wiring harnesses as patterns. All harnesses are made using the correct gauge wire and color code then loomed or overbraided as original. Each wire is identified for easy installation. Our harnesses are 100 point in both appearance and service and satisfaction is assured or money refunded. Send $2 for 36 page catalog, includes a $5 coupon.

Precision Rubber — rubber parts
Box 324
Didsbury, AB Canada T0M 0W0
403-335-9590; FAX: 403-335-8100

See full listing in **Section Two** under **rubber parts**

R-Mac Publications Inc — magazine
5439 SW US Hwy 41
Jasper, FL 32052
904-792-2480; FAX: 904-792-3230
E-mail: rbm@r-mac.com

See full listing in **Section Four** under **books & publications**

The Ramsgate Motor Museum — museum
Westcliff Hall
Ramsgate, Kent England
01843 581948

See full listing in **Section Six** under **England**

Restorations Unlimited II Inc — restoration
304 Jandus Rd
Cary, IL 60013
847-639-5818

See full listing in **Section Two** under **restoration shops**

RM Auto Restoration Ltd — panel fabrication / parts / restoration
9435 Horton Line
Blenheim, ON Canada N0P 1A0
519-352-4575; FAX: 519-351-1337
E-mail: clark@rmcars.com

See full listing in **Section Two** under **restoration shops**

Don Rook — parts
184 Raspberry Ln
Mena, AR 71953
501-394-7555

See full listing in **Section One** under **Chrysler**

SMS Auto Fabrics — upholstery
2325 SE 10th Ave
Portland, OR 97214
503-234-1175; FAX: 503-234-0651

See full listing in **Section Two** under **interiors & interior parts**

Steve's Studebaker-Packard
PO Box 6914
Napa, CA 94581
707-255-8945

car dealer
parts
suspension repairs

Mail order and open shop. Evenings and weekends. Appointment suggested. Specialized Packard services, such as torsion-level suspension and tele-touch electric shift repairs and rebuilding. Specializing in parts for 1951-1956 Packards and 1953-1966 Studebakers. Packard and Studebaker vehicle sales.

Supreme Metal Polishing
84A Rickenbacker Cir
Livermore, CA 94550
925-449-3490; FAX: 925-449-1475
E-mail: supremet@home.com

metal working
parts restoration
plating services
polishing

See full listing in **Section Two** under **plating & polishing**

Tom Taylor
PO Box 129
Guinda, CA 95637
530-796-4106

NOS parts

See full listing in **Section One** under **Mopar**

John Ulrich
450 Silver Ave
San Francisco, CA 94112
PH/FAX: 510-223-9587 days

parts

Mail order and open shop by appointment only. Monday-Friday 9 am to 5 pm. Packard parts from 1928-1956. Approximately 20% of the inventory is NOS, the balance is from parted out cars. Strongest part of inventory is 1938-1941 Junior and Senior Series. I buy inventories. I have available sheetmetal, fenders, hoods, wheels, drums, trim, engines, transmissions, differentials, engine parts, switches, dash parts, gauges and 1,000s more parts. I also offer a no hassle guarantee, if not satisfied return within 60 days for refund or exchange.

Tom Vagnini
58 Anthony Rd, RR 3
Pittsfield, MA 01201
413-698-2526

used parts

Mail order and open shop. Monday-Saturday by appointment. 10 am to 4 pm. Specializing in used parts for Packards 1923-1931.

Viking Worldwise Inc
190 Doe Run Rd
Manheim, PA 17545
800-842-9198; FAX: 717-664-5556
E-mail: gkurien@success.net

leather jackets

See full listing in **Section Two** under **apparel**

Wallace Walmsley
4732 Bancroft St, #7
San Diego, CA 92116
619-283-3063

parts

Mail order and open shop 6 days by appointment. Specializing in Packard parts, 1935-1942. Sunvisors for GM cars, 1934-1939 convertibles.

Yesterday's Radio
7759 Edgewood Ln
Seven Hills, OH 44131-5902
PH/FAX: 216-524-2018
E-mail: jerry@yesterdaysradio.com

interior plastic
radio parts

Interior plastic: gearshift knobs, window crank knobs, dash knobs, antenna mounts and knobs, escutcheons and some dash plastic. Chromed die cast door escutcheons. Specializing in radio parts, knobs, push-buttons, push-button caps, escutcheons and related items. A Packard catalog can be downloaded from the web site or mailed upon request. Web site: www.yesterdaysradio.com

Tom Crook Classic Cars
27611 42nd Ave S
Auburn, WA 98001
206-941-3454

car dealer

See full listing in **Section Two** under **car dealers**

Foreign Motors West
253 N Main St
Natick, MA 01760
508-655-5350; FAX: 508-651-0178

car sales

See full listing in **Section One** under **Rolls-Royce/Bentley**

Paul Foulkes-Halbard
Filching Wannock Eastbourne
Polegate
Sussex BN26 5QA England
011 441323 487838
011 441323 487124
FAX: 011 441323 486331

brass age cars
parts

See full listing in **Section One** under **Bugatti**

Mercedes-Benz Service by Angela & George/ABS Exotic Repair Inc
700 N Andrews Ave
Fort Lauderdale, FL 33304
954-566-7785; FAX: 954-566-7271

sales
service

See full listing in **Section One** under **Mercedes-Benz**

Rayce Inc
4656 SW 75th Ave
Miami, FL 33155
800-426-2221, 305-261-3355
FAX: 305-261-3615

parts

See full listing in **Section One** under **Alfa Romeo**

Voss Motors Inc
21849 Virginia Dr
Southfield, MI 48076
888-380-9277 toll-free
248-357-4750; FAX: 248-354-6577
E-mail: vossmotors@aol.com

service manuals

See full listing in **Section Two** under **literature dealers**

PIERCE-ARROW

The Brassworks
289 Prado Rd
San Louis Obispo, CA 93401
800-342-6759; FAX: 805-544-5615

radiators

See full listing in **Section Two** under **radiators**

L & L Antique Auto Trim
403 Spruce, Box 177
Pierce City, MO 65723
417-476-2871

runningboard
moldings

See full listing in **Section Two** under **special services**

Section One
Marque Specialists

Motor Foundry & Tooling Inc | brake drums
7382 Doniphan Dr | castings
Canutillo, TX 79835-6601 | exhaust manifolds
915-877-3343; FAX: 915-877-7071 | water pumps

See full listing in **Section One** under **Packard**

Space Farms Zoo & Museum | museum
218 Rt 519 | zoo
Sussex, NJ 07461
973-875-3223; FAX: 973-875-9397
E-mail: fpspace@warwick.net

See full listing in **Section Six** under **New Jersey**

AKH Wheels | Rallye wheels
1207 N A St | styled steel wheels
Ellensburg, WA 98926-2522 | vintage aluminum
509-962-3390
E-mail: akhwheel@eburg.com

See full listing in **Section Two** under **wheels & wheelcovers**

Antique DeSoto-Plymouth | Mopar parts
4206 Burnett Dr
Murrysville, PA 15668
724-733-1818 eves
FAX: 724-733-9884 or
412-243-4556 anytime
E-mail: parts4u@aol.com

See full listing in **Section One** under **Mopar**

Antique Mopar Auto Sales | cars
5758 McNicholl Dr | parts
Hale, MI 48739-8984
517-257-3123

See full listing in **Section One** under **Mopar**

Bill's Speed Shop | body parts
13951 Millersburg Rd
Navarre, OH 44662
330-832-9403; FAX: 330-832-2098

See full listing in **Section One** under **Chevrolet**

Brewer's Performance Motor Parts | parts
2560 S State Route 48
Ludlow Falls, OH 45339-9773
937-698-4259; FAX: 937-698-7109

See full listing in **Section One** under **Mopar**

Convertible Service | convertible parts
5126-HA Walnut Grove Ave | manufacture/service
San Gabriel, CA 91776 | top mechanism
800-333-1140, 626-285-2255
FAX: 626-285-9004

See full listing in **Section Two** under **tops**

Dynatech Engineering | motor mounts
PO Box 1446
Alta Loma, CA 91701-8446
805-492-6134
E-mail:
dynatechengineering@yahoo.com

See full listing in **Section Two** under **engine parts**

Egge Machine Company Inc | bearings
11707 Slauson Ave | pistons/rings
Santa Fe Springs, CA 90670 | timing components
800-866-EGGE, 562-945-3419 | valve train
FAX: 562-693-1635
E-mail: info@egge.com

See full listing in **Section Two** under **engine parts**

ETC Every Thing Cars | paint
8727 Clarinda | repairs
Pico Rivera, CA 90660 | restoration
562-949-6981 | welding

See full listing in **Section One** under **Mopar**

Halpin Used Auto & Truck Parts | NOS auto/truck
1093 Rt 123 | parts
Mayfield, NY 12117 | used auto/truck
518-863-4906 | parts
E-mail: junkyard2064@webtv.net

See full listing in **Section Five** under **New York**

Historic Video Archives | videotapes
PO Box 189-VA
Cedar Knolls, NJ 07927-0189

See full listing in **Section Two** under **automobilia**

Imperial Motors | parts
Rt 3 Box 380
Campobello, SC 29322
864-895-3474; FAX: 864-895-1248

See full listing in **Section One** under **Chrysler**

Jeff Johnson Motorsports | accessories
4421 Aldrich Pl | literature
Columbus, OH 43214 | parts
614-268-1181; FAX: 614-268-1141

See full listing in **Section One** under **Mopar**

Rudy R Koch | manuals
PO Box 291
Chester Heights, PA 19017
PH/FAX: 610-558-5699

Mail order only. For 1957 Plymouths, manuals, moldings, etc.

Kramer Automotive Specialties | body parts
PO Box 5 | interiors
Herman, PA 16039 | sheetmetal
724-285-5566; FAX: 724-285-8898

See full listing in **Section One** under **Mopar**

Legendary Auto Interiors Ltd | soft trim
121 W Shore Blvd
Newark, NY 14513
800-363-8804
FAX: 800-SEAT-UPH (732-8874)

See full listing in **Section One** under **Chrysler**

Lloyd's Literature | literature
PO Box 491
Newbury, OH 44065
800-292-2665, 440-338-1527
FAX: 440-338-2222

See full listing in **Section Two** under **literature dealers**

Mike's Auto Parts | ball/roller bearings
Box 358 | engine parts
Ridgeland, MS 39158 | wall calendars
601-856-7214 | water pumps

See full listing in **Section One** under **Chrysler**

**MikeCo Antique, Kustom &
Obsolete Auto Parts** — lenses / parts
4053 Calle Tesoro, Unit C
Camarillo, CA 93012
805-482-1725; FAX: 805-987-8524

See full listing in **Section One** under **Mopar**

Clayton T Nelson — NOS parts
Box 259
Warrenville, IL 60555
630-369-6589

See full listing in **Section One** under **Oldsmobile**

NS-One — NOS parts
PO Box 2459, Dept VA
Cedar Rapids, IA 52406
319-362-7717

See full listing in **Section One** under **Chrysler**

Obsolete Chrysler NOS Parts — literature / parts
4206 Burnett Dr
Murrysville, PA 15668
724-733-1818 eves
FAX: 724-733-9884 or
412-243-4556 anytime
E-mail: parts4u@aol.com

See full listing in **Section One** under **Chrysler**

Obsolete Parts of Iowa — NOS parts
PO Box 233
Earlville, IA 52041
E-mail: finsrus@mwci.net

See full listing in **Section One** under **Mopar**

**Plymouth, Dodge, Chrysler,
DeSoto Parts** — NOS parts for DeSoto
4206 Burnett Dr
Murrysville, PA 15668
724-733-1818 eves
FAX: 724-733-9884 or
412-243-4556 anytime
E-mail: parts4u@aol.com

See full listing in **Section One** under **DeSoto**

R & R Fiberglass & Specialties — body parts
4850 Wilson Dr NW
Cleveland, TN 37312
423-476-2270; FAX: 423-473-9442
E-mail: rrfiberglass@wingnet.net

See full listing in **Section Two** under **fiberglass parts**

Restorations By Julius — restoration
10101-1/2 Canoga Ave
Chatsworth, CA 91311
818-882-2825; FAX: 818-882-2855
E-mail: julius@cyberweb1.com

Open Tuesday-Friday 8 am to 5 pm. Restoration, repair and
sales of 1962-1971 Chrysler, Plymouth and Dodge products.
Web site: www.cyberweb1.com/julius

Riddle's/Mr Plymouth — decals / overdrives / parts & info / repro parts
20303 8th Ave NW
Shoreline, WA 98177
206-285-6534 days

See full listing in **Section One** under **Mopar**

Roberts Motor Parts — parts
17 Prospect St
West Newbury, MA 01985
978-363-5407; FAX: 978-363-2026
E-mail: sales@robertsmotorparts.com

See full listing in **Section One** under **Dodge**

Sherman & Associates Inc — body panels / body parts / fenders/floors / quarter panels
61166 Van Dyke Rd
Washington, MI 48094
810-677-6800; FAX: 810-677-6801

See full listing in **Section Two** under **body parts**

Paul Slater Auto Parts — parts
9496 85th St N
Stillwater, MN 55082
612-429-4235

See full listing in **Section One** under **Dodge**

Sound Move Inc — radios
217 S Main St
Elkhart, IN 46516
800-901-0222, 219-294-5100
FAX: 219-293-4902

See full listing in **Section One** under **Chevrolet**

Tags Backeast — data plates / trim tags
PO Box 581
Plainville, CT 06062
860-747-2942
E-mail: dataplt@snet.net

See full listing in **Section Two** under **special services**

Texas Viper Hotline — Prowlers / Vipers
5405 Montclair
Colleyville, TX 76034
817-267-1299; FAX: 972-986-1519

See full listing in **Section One** under **Dodge**

Totally Auto Inc — parts / restoration / service
337 Philmont Ave
Feasterville, PA 19053
215-322-2277; FAX: 215-322-4755
E-mail: totalyauto@aol.com

See full listing in **Section One** under **Mopar**

**Weimann's Literature &
Collectables** — literature
16 Cottage Rd
Harwinton, CT 06791
860-485-0300
FAX: 860-485-1705, 24 hour

Mail order or appointment only. Plymouth, Dodge/Dodge truck,
DeSoto, Chrysler, Imperial literature. We carry most 1928 to date
showroom catalogs, folders, data/trim books, service/shop, parts
listing books, plus tech service/sales records/filmstrips, etc.
Owner's manuals, accessories, books. Almost anything paper.
Color and b&w copying service for Plymouth. We buy, sell, trade.
Please send stamped addressed envelope with inquiries.

Bob West Muscle Cars — muscle cars
637 Sellmeyer Ln
Lewisville, TX 75067
972-317-5525; FAX: 972-317-5528

Specializing in 1969-1970 B-body and 1970-1971 E-body only.

Wheels & Spokes Inc — Mopar parts / restoration
383 Mopar Dr
Hays, KS 67601
785-628-6477; FAX: 785-628-6834

See full listing in **Section One** under **Mopar**

PONTIAC®

4-Speeds by Darrell PO Box 110 3 Water St Vermilion, IL 61955 217-275-3743; FAX: 217-275-3515	transmissions

See full listing in **Section Two** under **transmissions**

A & M SoffSeal Inc 104 May Dr Harrison, OH 45030 800-426-0902 513-367-0028 service/info FAX: 513-367-5506 E-mail: soffseal@soffseal.com	rubber parts weatherstripping

See full listing in **Section Two** under **rubber parts**

Alpha Omega Motorsport 15612 New Century Dr Gardena, CA 90248 310-366-7993; FAX: 310-366-7499 E-mail: aomotor@pacbell.net	parts repairs restorations

Mail order and open shop. Monday-Friday 10 am to 6 pm PST. Specialize in Packard, Pontiac, Chrysler, Plymouth, Dodge, Cadillac, Pierce-Arrow, Ford and Oldsmobile, 1910s-1970. Parts, repairs and restorations. Web site: http://home.pacbell.net/aomotor

American Classics Unlimited Inc PO Box 192-V Oak Lawn, IL 60454-0192 PH/FAX: 708-424-9223	automobilia models and toys

See full listing in **Section Two** under **models & toys**

Art's Antique & Classic Auto Services 1985 E 5th St #16 Tempe, AZ 85281 602-966-1195	restoration

See full listing in **Section One** under **Buick/McLaughlin**

Auto Decals Unlimited Inc 11259 E Via Linda, Ste 100-201 Scottsdale, AZ 85259 602-220-0800	decals stripe kits

See full listing in **Section Two** under **decals**

Boneyard Stan's Stanley Jones 218 N 69th Ave Phoenix, AZ 85043 PH/FAX: 623-936-8045	cars parts

Mail order and open shop. Daily, call first. Specializing in 1950-1980s Pontiac cars and parts. Also have many other types of cars and will locate cars and parts. Shipping anywhere, US, Canada, overseas.

Bumper Boyz LLC 2435 E 54th St Los Angeles, CA 90058 800-995-1703, 323-587-8976 FAX: 323-587-2013	bumper repairs reconditioning sandblasting

See full listing in **Section One** under **Chevrolet**

Camaro Specialties 112 Elm St East Aurora, NY 14052 716-652-7086; FAX: 716-652-2279 E-mail: dunlop@wzrd.com	parts restoration

See full listing in **Section One** under **Chevelle/Camaro**

Chevrolet Parts Obsolete PO Box 0740 Murrieta, CA 92564-0740 909-279-2833; FAX: 909-279-4013 E-mail: spo@att.net	accessories parts

See full listing in **Section One** under **Chevrolet**

Chief Service Herbert G Baschung Brunnmatt, PO Box 155 CH-4914 Roggwil Switzerland PH/FAX: 0041-62-9291777	parts restoration

See full listing in **Section Two** under **restoration shops**

Dick Choler Cars & Service Inc 640 E Jackson Blvd Elkhart, IN 46516 219-522-8281; FAX: 219-294-5350	car dealer literature model cars

Mail order and open shop. Car dealer, literature, posters, car pictures and model cars of all years. Specializing in Pontiacs for 49 years, big, small or just Pontiacs. We counsel on all years to your satisfaction.

Classic and Muscle Muscle Car Restoration Parts PO Box 657 Elmsdale, NS Canada B0N 1M0 902-883-4489; FAX: 902-883-1392 E-mail: classicmuscle@sprint.ca	reproduction parts restoration parts

See full listing in **Section One** under **Chevrolet**

Classic Industries Inc Firebird Parts and Accessories Catalog 17832 Gothard St Huntington Beach, CA 92647 800-854-1280 parts/info FAX: 800-300-3081 toll-free E-mail: info@classicindustries.com	accessories parts

Largest selection of Firebird/Trans Am parts and accessories ever assembled in one catalog. Well over 400 full color pages of the finest quality restoration products and late model accessories. Only $5, refunded on first order. Call our 24-hour toll-free catalog hotline, 888-GM-CATALOG, and receive the industry's most comprehensive parts catalog from the undisputed leader in the industry, Classic Industries. Web site: www.classicindustries.com

See our ad inside the front cover

Coach Builders Muscle Car Parts & Services PO Box 128 Baltimore, MD 21087-0128 410-426-5567	interiors parts rust remover

See full listing in **Section One** under **Chevrolet**

Competitive Automotive Inc 2095 W Shore Rd (Rt 117) Warwick, RI 02886 401-739-6262, 401-739-6288 FAX: 401-739-1497	parts restoration

See full listing in **Section One** under **Chevelle/Camaro**

Coopers Vintage Auto Parts 3087 N California St Burbank, CA 91504 818-567-4140; FAX: 818-567-4101	**parts**

See full listing in **Section One** under **Cadillac/LaSalle**

CPR 431 S Sierra Way San Bernardino, CA 92408 909-884-6980; FAX: 909-884-7872	**new parts** **reproduction parts** **used parts**

All mechanical, brake, rubber, trim, suspension, new, used and reproduction parts for Pontiac 1927-present. Parts lists are available, phone or mail request.

Custom Classic Cars 2046 E 12B Road Bourbon, IN 46504 219-342-5007; FAX: 219-342-0399 E-mail: customclassiccars@waveone.net	**parts** **restoration**

See full listing in **Section One** under **Chevrolet**

Dynatech Engineering PO Box 1446 Alta Loma, CA 91701-8446 805-492-6134 E-mail: dynatechengineering@yahoo.com	**motor mounts**

See full listing in **Section Two** under **engine parts**

East West Auto Parts Inc 4605 Dawson Rd Tulsa, OK 74115 800-447-2886; FAX: 918-832-7900	**GM parts** **European import** **parts**

See full listing in **Section Five** under **Oklahoma**

Egge Machine Company Inc 11707 Slauson Ave Santa Fe Springs, CA 90670 800-866-EGGE, 562-945-3419 FAX: 562-693-1635 E-mail: info@egge.com	**bearings** **pistons/rings** **timing components** **valve train**

See full listing in **Section Two** under **engine parts**

Engineering & Manufacturing Services Box 24362 Cleveland, OH 44124-0362 216-541-4585; FAX: 216-541-4989	**sheetmetal**

See full listing in **Section One** under **Ford 1932-1953**

ETC Every Thing Cars 8727 Clarinda Pico Rivera, CA 90660 562-949-6981	**paint** **repairs** **restoration** **welding**

See full listing in **Section One** under **Mopar**

John Filiss 45 Kingston Ave Port Jervis, NY 12771 914-856-2942 E-mail: johnfiliss@hotmail.com	**appraisals**

See full listing in **Section Two** under **appraisals**

Fire-Aro Restoration Parts Supply Co 9251 Yonge St Unit 8, Ste 108 Richmand, Hill ON Canada L4C 9T3 888-249-4939 toll-free 905-881-7337; FAX: 905-881-2445	**accessories** **parts**

See full listing in **Section One** under **Chevelle/Camaro**

Fowlkes Realty & Auction 500 Hale St Newman Grove, NE 68758 800-275-5522; FAX: 402-447-6000	**appraisals** **auctions**

See full listing in **Section One** under **Chevrolet**

Gardner Exhaust Systems 2 Cedar Ln Rhinebeck, NY 12572 PH/FAX: 914-876-8117 E-mail: gexhaust@aol.com	**exhaust systems**

See full listing in **Section One** under **Chevelle/Camaro**

Green's Obsolete Parts 2 Lomar Park Dr Unit #3 Pepperell, MA 01463 978-433-9363; FAX: 978-433-8746	**NOS parts** **used parts**

Mail order and open shop. Monday-Friday 9 am to 6 pm, Saturday 9 am to 1 pm EST. Specializing in NOS and some used parts for all 1936-1986 Pontiacs. We have a large inventory of mostly NOS parts for most restorations. We can also answer most questions with our extensive library of Pontiac literature. Free computer parts lists available for specified years and models of Pontiacs.

Hamel's Automotive Inc RR 2 Box 61 Wingdale, NY 12594 914-832-9454 E-mail: startnagan@aol.com	**restorations**

See full listing in **Section Two** under **restoration shops**

Hjeltness Restoration Inc 630 Alpine Way Escondido, CA 92029 760-746-9966; FAX: 760-746-7738	**restoration** **service**

See full listing in **Section Two** under **restoration shops**

Indian Adventures Inc 121 South St PO Box 206 Foxboro, MA 02035 508-359-4660; FAX: 508-359-5435	**parts**

See full listing in **Section Two** under **comprehensive parts**

Inline Tube 33783 Groes Beck Hwy Fraser, MI 48026 800-385-9452 order 810-294-4093 tech FAX: 810-294-7349 E-mail: kryta@aol.com	**brake lines/cables** **choke tubes** **flex brake hoses** **fuel/vacuum lines** **transmission lines**

See full listing in **Section Two** under **brakes**

Jerry's Automotive c/o Jerry Cinotti 431 S Sierra Way San Bernardino, CA 92408 909-884-6980; FAX: 909-884-7872	**brake repair**

See full listing in **Section Two** under **brakes**

The Judge's Chambers 114 Prince George Dr Hampton, VA 23669 757-838-2059 evenings	**automobilia** **parts**

Mail order only. Parts for 1969-1971 Pontiac GTO Judge, including stripe kits/decals, spoilers, glovebox emblems, hood tachometers, Ram Air systems, GTO and Judge memorabilia and videos. Also appraisals and services.

Dave Kauzlarich
60442 N Tranquility Rd
Lacombe, LA 70445
504-882-3000
E-mail: fierog97j@aol.com

literature
memorabilia

See full listing in **Section Two** under **literature dealers**

Kurt Kelsey
Antique Pontiac Parts
14083 P Ave
Iowa Falls, IA 50126
PH/FAX: 515-648-9086

parts dealer

Mail order and open shop. Call ahead for directions. Also usually several Pontiacs for sale. Large stock of antique and obsolete Pontiac parts. Fast, personalized service.

Lectric Limited Inc
7322 S Archer Road
Justice, IL 60458
708-563-0400; FAX: 708-458-2662

parts

See full listing in **Section One** under **Corvette**

LES Auto Parts
Box 81
Dayton, NJ 08810
732-329-6128; FAX: 732-329-1036

parts

See full listing in **Section One** under **Chevrolet**

M & H Electric Fabricators Inc
13537 Alondra Blvd
Santa Fe Springs, CA 90670
562-926-9552; FAX: 562-926-9572
E-mail: sales@wiringharness.com

wiring harnesses

See full listing in **Section Two** under **electrical systems**

Only Yesterday Classic Autos Inc
24 Valley Rd
Port Washington, NY 11050
516-767-3477; FAX: 516-767-8964

cars

See full listing in **Section One** under **Chevrolet**

Original Auto Interiors
7869 Trumble Rd
Columbus, MI 48063-3915
810-727-2486; FAX: 810-727-4344
E-mail: origauto@tir.com

upholstery

See full listing in **Section Two** under **upholstery**

Original Parts Group Inc
17892 Gothard St
Huntington Beach, CA 92647
800-243-8355 US/Canada
714-841-5363; FAX: 714-847-8159

accessories
parts

Mail order and open shop. Monday-Friday 7:30 am to 5 pm, Saturday 10 am to 3 pm PST. Manufacturer and distributor of original and reproduction 1964-1973 GTO, Tempest, LeMans, 1964-1987 Chevelle, El Camino and 1970-1987 Monte Carlo parts and accessories: emblems, interior trim, moldings, sheetmetal, electrical, engine parts, dash pads, door panels, seat upholstery, chrome trim parts, weatherstripping, gaskets, body seals, underbody bushings and much more, along with an extensive line of obsolete GM items.

The Paddock® Inc
PO Box 30
221 W Main
Knightstown, IN 46148
800-428-4319; FAX: 800-286-4040
E-mail: paddock@indy.net

accessories
parts

See full listing in **Section One** under **Mustang**

M Parker Autoworks Inc
150 Heller Pl #17W
Dept HVAA99
Bellmawr, NJ 08031
609-933-0801; FAX: 609-933-0805
E-mail: facfit@erols.com

battery cables
harnesses

See full listing in **Section Two** under **electrical systems**

The Parts Place
217 Paul St
Elburn, IL 60119
PH/FAX: 630-365-1800
E-mail: pplace9594@aol.com

parts

See full listing in **Section One** under **Chevrolet**

Parts Unlimited Inc
Todd Bidwell
12101 Westport Rd
Louisville, KY 40245-1789
502-425-3766; FAX: 502-425-0055

interiors
weatherstrips

See full listing in **Section One** under **Chevrolet**

Performance Years Pontiac
2880 Bergey Rd, Unit O
Hatfield, PA 19440
215-712-7400; FAX: 215-712-9968
E-mail: perfyrs@netreach.net

parts

Mail order only. Pontiac parts for GTO, Tempest, LeMans, Firebird, Trans Am, Grand Prix, Catalina, Bonneville, 1955-1977. Web site: http://1pontiac.com

Phoenix Graphix Inc
5861 S Kyrene Rd #10
Tempe, AZ 85283
800-941-4550

decals
stripe kits

See full listing in **Section Two** under **decals**

PMD Specialties
20498 82nd Ave
Langley, BC Canada V2Y 2A9
604-888-4100; FAX: 604-513-1188

component restoration
OEM/used/NOS parts
restoration specialist
verification/appraisals

Our expertise lies mainly in the GTO (1964-1974), Grand Prix (1962, 1969-1972), Trans Am (1970-1973), American and Canadian full-size Pontiacs (1962), engine parts for 1960-1981. Some NOS GM parts. Tri-power, Ram Air specialist. Body, chassis, driveline parts. Complete, partial, component restorations. Specific cars/parts search. Usually available for consultation on Monday 9 am to 4 pm, Thursdays 9 am to 5 pm, Saturdays 1 pm to 5 pm PST, please call/fax needs/wants prior to consultation. We appreciate your patience as we try to fill your needs.

Ponti-Action Racing
PO Box 354
Medfield, MA 02052
888-RAM-AIRS; FAX: 508-359-5435
E-mail: gtogeezer@aol.com

engine builders

Pontiac engine builders.

Pontiac Engines Custom Built
Box 2422
Longmont, CO 80502
303-776-0877
E-mail: pontiacgregg@earthlink.net

custom built
engines

Mail order and open shop. Monday-Saturday 9 am to 5 pm, call first. Specializing in custom built Pontiac engines ready to drop in for 1960-1999 Pontiac cars. Call for other make motors. Engines custom built or yours custom rebuilt, street or strip, ported heads, balanced to 1/2 gram, etc, all engines dialed in, short blocks and heads available. Free catalog. Web site: www.pontiacengines.net

Precision Pontiac
2719 Columbus Ave
Columbus, OH 43209
614-258-3500; FAX: 614-258-0060
E-mail: peter.serio@gte.net

	parts
	repairs

Mail order only. Specializing in engine detail, shifters rebuilt and rechromed, 1965-1967 rally gauges, factory options, used small parts. Original Pontiac vacuum gauges restored and for sale. Catalog $2. Web site: www.precisionpontiac.com

Precision Rubber
Box 324
Didsbury, AB Canada T0M 0W0
403-335-9590; FAX: 403-335-8100

rubber parts

See full listing in **Section Two** under **rubber parts**

Raine Automotive Springs Warehouse
425 Harding Hwy
Carney's Point, NJ 08069
609-299-9141; FAX: 609-299-9157

springs
suspension parts

See full listing in **Section Two** under **suspension parts**

Redden's Relics
PO Box 300
Boiling Springs, PA 17007
717-258-8142; FAX: 717-258-4861
E-mail: reddeng@pa.net

NOS parts

Mail order only. For Pontiacs, NOS Firebirds, Tempests/GTOs, Grand Prixs and big Pontiacs. Send year, body style and $2 for computer list of NOS parts available. Web site: www.oldntime.com/relics/

Robertson Bros & Sons Restoration
PO Box 5678
Sevierville, TN 37864-5678
423-970-1655; FAX: 423-908-6838
E-mail: classicbop@aol.com

NOS parts
restoration parts
used parts

See full listing in **Section One** under **Oldsmobile**

Harry Samuel
65 Wisner St
Pontiac, MI 48342-1066
248-335-1900
E-mail: hsamuel1@aol.com

carpet
fabrics
interiors
upholstery covers

See full listing in **Section Two** under **interiors & interior parts**

Sherman & Associates Inc
61166 Van Dyke Rd
Washington, MI 48094
810-677-6800; FAX: 810-677-6801

body panels
body parts
fenders/floors
quarter panels

See full listing in **Section Two** under **body parts**

Sound Move Inc
217 S Main St
Elkhart, IN 46516
800-901-0222, 219-294-5100
FAX: 219-293-4902

radios

See full listing in **Section One** under **Chevrolet**

Ssnake-Oyl Products Inc
Rt 2, Box 269-6
Hawkins, TX 75765
800-284-7777; FAX: 903-769-4552

carpet underlay
firewall insulation
seat belt restoration

See full listing in **Section Two** under **interiors & interior parts**

Hemmings' Vintage Auto Almanac©   Fourteenth Edition

Stencils & Stripes Unlimited Inc
1108 S Crescent Ave #21
Park Ridge, IL 60068
847-692-6893; FAX: 847-692-6895

NOS decals
stripe kits

See full listing in **Section Two** under **decals**

Tags Backeast
PO Box 581
Plainville, CT 06062
860-747-2942
E-mail: dataplt@snet.net

data plates
trim tags

See full listing in **Section Two** under **special services**

Tom's Classic Parts
5207 Sundew Terr
Tobyhanna, PA 18466
800-832-4073

parts

See full listing in **Section One** under **Chevrolet**

Vintage Parts 411
4909 Ruffner St
San Diego, CA 92111
800-MOTORHEAD
FAX: 619-467-0777
E-mail: cars@vintageparts.com

books

See full listing in **Section Four** under **information sources**

Waldron's Antique Exhaust Inc
PO Box C
25872 M-86
Nottawa, MI 49075
616-467-7185; FAX: 616-467-9041

exhaust systems

See full listing in **Section Two** under **exhaust systems**

356 Enterprises
Vic & Barbara Skirmants
27244 Ryan Rd
Warren, MI 48092
810-575-9544; FAX: 810-558-3616

parts

Mail order and open shop. Specializing in Porsche 356s made from 1948-1965. Engines, transmissions, suspension, brakes, all mechanical parts. Specializing in vintage racing and performance parts and services, including close ratio gear sets and transmission modifications for racing.

Aase Bros Inc
701 E Cypress St
Anaheim, CA 92805
714-956-2419; FAX: 714-956-2635
E-mail: sales@aasebros.com

salvage yard

See full listing in **Section Five** under **California**

AM Racing Inc
PO Box 451
Danvers, MA 01923
PH/FAX: 978-774-4613

race prep
sales
vintage racing

See full listing in **Section Two** under **racing**

The Auto Doctor Inc	mechanical parts
23125 Telegraph Rd
Southfield, MI 48034
248-355-1505; FAX: 248-355-3460

service repairs

See full listing in **Section One** under **BMW**

Auto Quest Investment Cars Inc	car dealer
710 W 7th St
PO Box 22
Tifton, GA 31793
912-382-4750; FAX: 912-382-4752
E-mail: info@auto-quest.com

See full listing in **Section Two** under **car dealers**

AutoMatch CARS	broker
(Computer Aided Referral Service)
2017 Blvd Napoleon
Louisville, KY 40205
800-962-2771, 502-417-8793 mobile
502-452-1920 office
FAX: 502-479-6222
E-mail: amcars@aol.com or aau-
tomatch@aol.com

car dealer network
locator

See full listing in **Section Two** under **car dealers**

Automotive Artistry	restoration
679 W Streetboro St
Hudson, OH 44236
330-650-1503
E-mail: dale@cmh.net

See full listing in **Section One** under **Triumph**

Bassett's Jaguar	parts
PO Box 245
53 Stilson Rd
Wyoming, RI 02898
401-539-3010; FAX: 401-539-7861
E-mail: jagwillie@ids.net

restoration
service
upholstery

See full listing in **Section One** under **Jaguar**

Best Deal	accessories
8171 Monroe St
Stanton, CA 90680
800-354-9202; FAX: 714-995-5918
E-mail: bestdeal@deltnet.com

parts

Open shop. Monday-Friday 9 am to 5 pm, Saturday 9 am to 3 pm. Catalog of new and used Porsche parts and accessories available. 20 years in the business of selling new and used parts for 356, 911, 914, 924 and 944. Web site: http://users.deltanet.com/~bestdeal

Blitzen Enterprises Inc	parts
8341 E Evans Rd, Suite 104
Scottsdale, AZ 85260
888-254-8936 toll-free
FAX: 602-991-6301
E-mail: mbparts@blitzen.com

See full listing in **Section One** under **Mercedes-Benz**

BMC Classics Inc	parts
828 N Dixie Freeway
New Smyrna Beach, FL 32168
904-426-6405; FAX: 904-427-4570
E-mail: bmcar1@aol.com

repair
restoration

See full listing in **Section Two** under **restoration shops**

Classic Coachworks	bodywork
735 Frenchtown Rd
Milford, NJ 08848
908-996-3400; FAX: 908-996-0204

painting
restoration

See full listing in **Section Two** under **restoration shops**

Classic Showcase	classic vehicles
913 Rancheros Dr
San Marcos, CA 92069
760-747-9947, 760-747-3188 sales
FAX: 760-747-4021
E-mail: management@classicshowcase.com

restorations

See full listing in **Section Two** under **car dealers**

Collector Car Appraisers LLC	appraisals
800 Waterford Dr
Frederick, MD 21702
301-473-8333; FAX: 301-698-4796
E-mail: gfmchugh@netstorm.net

See full listing in **Section Two** under **appraisals**

Dave's Auto Restoration	upholstery
2285 Rt 307 E
Jefferson, OH 44047
PH/FAX: 216-858-2227
E-mail: davesauto@knownet.net

See full listing in **Section Two** under **interiors & interior parts**

Doc & Cy's Restoration Parts	parts
1427 S Meridian St
Indianapolis, IN 46225-1525
800-950-0356; FAX: 317-634-5662

Mail order and open shop. Monday-Friday 9 am to 5 pm. Specializing in restoration sheetmetal, rubber, trim, interior and mechanical parts for Porsche 356, 911/912, 914 and 924/944. New and used parts available. Web site: www.docncys.com

Driven By Design	information
225 Crossroad Blvd
Carmel, CA 93923
831-625-1393, 800-366-1393
FAX: 831-625-9342
E-mail: drbydesign@earthlink.net

products
services

Mail order and open shop. Monday-Friday 9:30 am to 6 pm. Specializing in Porsche information products and services, videos/books for all years. Inspection videos for the 356, 911, 930, $39.95. Produce and distribute a video *How To Buy a Better Used Car*. Publish *The Directory*, a resource book for Porsche parts suppliers (worldwide), $26.95.

DTE Motorsports	engines
242 South Rd
Brentwood, NH 03833
PH/FAX: 603-642-3766
E-mail: ldnh49a@prodigy.com

mechanical services
race prep
transportation

See full listing in **Section One** under **Mercedes-Benz**

European Parts Specialists Ltd	accessories
PO Box 6783
Santa Barbara, CA 93160
800-334-2749, 805-683-4020
FAX: 805-683-3689
E-mail: epsparts@impulse.net

parts

See full listing in **Section One** under **Mercedes-Benz**

Excellence Magazine	magazine
42 Digital Dr #5
Novato, CA 94949
415-382-0580; FAX: 415-382-0587

See full listing in **Section Four** under **periodicals**

Grand Prix Classics Inc	racing cars
7456 La Jolla Blvd
La Jolla, CA 92037
619-459-3500; FAX: 619-459-3512

sports cars

See full listing in **Section Two** under **racing**

Griot's Garage
3500-A 20th St E
Tacoma, WA 98424
800-345-5789; FAX: 888-252-2252
E-mail: info@griotsgarage.com

| car care products |
| paint |
| tools |

See full listing in **Section Two** under **tools**

Hjeltness Restoration Inc
630 Alpine Way
Escondido, CA 92029
760-746-9966; FAX: 760-746-7738

| restoration |
| service |

See full listing in **Section Two** under **restoration shops**

International Mercantile
PO Box 2818
Del Mar, CA 92014-2818
800-356-0012, 760-438-2205
FAX: 760-438-1428

| rubber parts |

Since 1971. Full service in-house design, machine shop and fabricating facility dedicated to the 356, 912 and early 911. All products are made in the US, of the highest quality. All products equal OEM or excede original specifications. New products monthly. Please write or call for latest brochure. Web site: im356-911.com

Mac's Euro Motorcars & Transport
1520 Burr Oak Rd
Homewood, IL 60430
708-799-3469

| Alfa Romeos |
| parts |
| transport |

See full listing in **Section One** under **Alfa Romeo**

Machina Locksmith
3 Porter St
Watertown, MA 02172-4145
PH/FAX: 617-923-1683

| car locks |
| keys |

See full listing in **Section Two** under **locks & keys**

Motorcars International
528 N Prince Ln
Springfield, MO 65802
417-831-9999; FAX: 417-831-8080
E-mail: sales@motorcars-intl.com

| accessories |
| cars |
| services |
| tools |

See full listing in **Section One** under **Ferrari**

Muncie Imports & Classics
4401 St Rd 3 N
Muncie, IN 47303
800-462-4244; FAX: 317-287-9551
E-mail: mic@netdirect.net

| repair |
| restoration |
| upholstery |

See full listing in **Section One** under **Jaguar**

PAR Porsche Specialists
310 Main St
New Rochelle, NY 10801
914-637-8800, 800-367-7270
FAX: 914-637-6078
E-mail: parcars@bestweb.net

| accessories |
| car dealer |
| parts |

Mail order and open shop. Monday-Friday 8:30 am to 5:30 pm; Saturday 9 am to 1 pm. Porsche specialist in both new and used parts and accessories. Pre-owned Porsches, 1950-present, 356, 911, 928, 944 and Boxster. Sold on consignment. Over 100 cars available at any one time. Distributor of Recaro automotive seats and office chairs. Web site: www.parcars.com

Paul's Select Cars & Parts for Porsche®
2280 Gail Dr
Riverside, CA 92509
909-685-9340; FAX: 909-685-9342
E-mail: pauls356-s90@webtv.net

| cars |
| parts |

Dry California, rust-free experience parts for most air cooled

Porsches. Call us last for that hard-to-find part. Good prices as always.

Perfect Panels of America
1690 Thomas Paine Pkwy
Centerville, OH 45459
937-435-4543; FAX: 937-435-4548
E-mail: porshfreek@aol.com

| body panels |

Mail order and open shop. Monday-Friday 7:30 am to 6 pm, Saturday 9:30 am to 12 pm. Manufacturer of replacement body panels for Porsche 914 and 911. 914: hinge plate, hinge bolts, left and right lower door patches, left and right roll panels, complete right suspension consoles, left and right door steps, battery tray, battery tray support, battery hold clamp, jack tubes, jack supports, left and right inner rockers. 911: left and right outer rockers, left and right inner rockers, jack tubes, jack plates. Web site: http://members.aol.com/porshfreek/homepage.html

Pony Parts of America
1690 Thomas Paine Pkwy
Centerville, OH 45459
937-435-4543; FAX: 937-435-4548
E-mail: porshfreek@aol.com

| floor boards |
| frame rails |

See full listing in **Section One** under **Mustang**

Precision Autoworks
2202 Federal Street
East Camden, NJ 08105
609-966-0080, NJ
FAX: 610-649-3577, PA

| restorations |

See full listing in **Section One** under **Mercedes-Benz**

Replicarz
99 State St
Rutland, VT 05701
802-747-7151
E-mail: replicarz@aol.com

| books |
| kits |
| models |
| videos |

See full listing in **Section Two** under **racing**

Restoration Services
16049 W 4th Ave
Golden, CO 80401
303-271-0356

| restoration |

Mail order and open shop. Monday-Friday 8 am to 5 pm. An automotive oriented shop, specializing since 1972 in Porsche, Mercedes-Benz and vintage race cars and other exotics. Metal replacement, fabrication, sandblasting, lead work, mig welding, gas welding, complete paint, spot paint, detailing, upholstery rebuilds, top rebuilds, trim repair, trim polishing, glass replacement, electrical repair, rewiring, mechanical overhauls, suspension overhauls, wheel refinishing, tire sales, auto locating services, appraisals, Porsche and Mercedes parts.

Paul Russell & Company
106 Western Ave
Essex, MA 01929
978-768-6919; FAX: 978-768-3523
E-mail: info@paulrussellandco.com

| car dealer |
| mechanical service |
| parts |
| restoration |

See full listing in **Section Two** under **restoration shops**

Showroom Auto Sales
960 S Bascom Ave
San Jose, CA 95128
408-279-0944; FAX: 408-279-0918

| car dealer |

See full listing in **Section One** under **Mercedes-Benz**

Spyder Enterprises Inc
RFD 1682
Laurel Hollow, NY 11791-9644
516-367-1616; FAX: 516-367-3260
E-mail: singer356@aol.com

| accessories |
| artwork |
| automobilia |
| books |

Mail and telephone order only. Vintage Porsche (356 and Spyder) cars, parts, accessories, memorabilia, and literature. Active buyer and seller of original authentic posters, photos and memorabilia relating to the vintage Porsche, Ferrari, Formula One and sports-racers of the 1950s-1960s. Publishes for sale and/or trade list; SASE 2 oz. Publisher of fine quality automotive books and limited edition artwork. Manufacturer of embroidered items and leather accessories for the Porsche 356 and Ferrari California Spyder.

Stoddard Imported Cars Inc	**parts**
38845 Mentor Ave	
Willoughby, OH 44094-0908	
440-951-1040 in Ohio & overseas	
800-342-1414; FAX: 440-946-9410	
E-mail: sicars@ix.netcom.com	

International Porsche and Mercedes parts mail order. Extensive inventory for all model Porsches with emphasis on vintage Porsche 356, 911, 914 and Mercedes 190SL, 230SL, 250SL, 280SL restoration. Catalogs available for 190SL-280SL Mercedes and all model Porsches. For more information visit our web site: www.stoddard.com

Stormin Norman's Bug Shop	**repair**
201 Commerce Dr #3	**restoration**
Fort Collins, CO 80524	
970-493-5873	

See full listing in **Section One** under **Volkswagen**

Stuttgart Automotive Inc	**parts**
1690 Thomas Paine Pkwy	**service**
Centerville, OH 45459	
937-435-4543; FAX: 937-435-4548	
E-mail: porshfreek@aol.com	

Mail order and open shop. For 1955-1999 Porsches. Complete service. Many obsolete parts in stock for 356 Series. Also manufacturer of replacement body panels for 911, 914 and Mustang. Web site: http://members.aol.com/porshfreek/homepage.html

Translog Motorsports	**car dealer**
619-635 W Poplar St	**parts**
York, PA 17404	**restoration**
PH/FAX: 717-846-1885	

Mail order and open shop. Monday-Saturday 9 am to 6 pm. Engine, transmission and body modifications to your specifications. Specializing in restoring Porsches. Large inventory of used and new Porsche parts. Custom-built Porsches. Specializing in 914-6 GT replicas, parts duplicated from the Sunoco 914-6 GT.

Willhoit Auto Restoration	**engine rebuilding**
1360 Gladys Ave	**restoration**
Long Beach, CA 90804	
562-439-3333; FAX: 562-439-3956	

Mail order and open shop. Monday-Friday 8 am to 5 pm. Complete in-house restoration services for all models of Porsche 356 (including 4 cam). Including: show quality painting, metalwork and rust repair, engine and transaxle rebuilding, interior installation, car appraisals and pre-purchase inspections. Also a very large used parts inventory.

Willow Automotive Service Inc	**sales**
29870 Hwy 41	**service**
Lake Bluff, IL 60044	
847-785-8080; FAX: 847-785-8106	

See full listing in **Section One** under **Mercedes-Benz**

Zim's Autotechnik	**parts**
1804 Reliance Pkwy	**service**
Bedford, TX 76021	
800-356-2964; FAX: 817-545-2002	
E-mail: zimips@allzim.com	

Mail order and open shop. Monday-Friday 8 am to 5:30 pm, Saturday 9 am to 1 pm CST. Porsche (only) service and parts. We specialize in the maintenance and repair of Porsche automobiles. Zim's has a large inventory of parts including hard to find

parts for older vehicles. We have been in business for over 25 years. Web site: www.allzim.com

4-CV Service	**accessories**
3301 Shetland Rd	**parts**
Beavercreek, OH 45434	
E-mail: mike7353@aol.com	

Mail order only. NOS and used parts, accessories and information for restorers of Renault 4-CVs and related vehicles. Some Dauphine mechanical parts. Thirty-plus years' experience with all models of 1948-1961 4-CVs. For information, contact Michael Self at above address or e-mail.

French Stuff	**accessories**
PO Box 39772	**engine rebuilding**
Glendale, CA 90039-0772	**parts**
818-244-2498; FAX: 818-500-7628	**transaxle rebuilding**
E-mail: frenchap@gte.net	

Wholesale and mail order 24 hrs, phone and fax. Will call counter 4-8 PST for local pickups. Direct importers, office in Paris. Established in 1958. Stock and high-performance parts and accessories for all models Renault, Peugeot, Alpine, Matra, Panhard, Deutsch-Bonnet. Technical literature. Lotus Europas S1/S2: engines, transaxles, stock and high-performance parts. V6 PRV engines and 5-speed transaxles for DeLorean & Peugeot. Engines and transaxle rebuilding all Renault models. Specialized R5 Turbo, Alpine, Gordini, V6.

Jacques Rear Engine Renault Parts	**parts**
13839 Hwy 8 Business	
El Cajon, CA 92021	
619-561-6687; FAX: 619-561-6123	

Mail order and open shop. Monday-Saturday, some Sundays, home business. Renaults from the late 1940s, 1950s, 1960s and early 1970s. In stock parts, 4CV, Dauphine, Caravelle, R8, R10, even the smallest parts.

Patton Orphan Spares	**parts**
52 Nicole Pl	
West Babylon, NY 11704	
516-669-2598	

Mail order only. Sell spare parts for orphan makes such as Renault Dauphines, Austin A40s and Morris Minor 1000s. Spares are mechanical parts primarily, new and used. Factory shop and parts manuals for same automobiles for sale. Also Renault Alliances and Encores, 1983-1987.

Cockermouth Motor Museum	**museum**
The Maltings	
Brewery Ln	
Cockermouth Cumbria England	
01900 824448	

See full listing in **Section Six** under **England**

Vintage Restorations
The Old Bakery
Windmill Street, Tunbridge Wells
Kent, TN2 4UU England
UK 1892-525-899
FAX: UK 1892-525499

accessories
instruments

See full listing in **Section Two** under **instruments**

Albers Rolls-Royce
360 S First St
Zionsville, IN 46077
317-873-2360, 317-873-2560
FAX: 317-873-6860

car dealer
parts

Monday-Friday 8 am to 5 pm. America's oldest exclusive authorized Rolls-Royce/Bentley dealer. New and pre-owned motor cars available. Largest stock of parts in North America from pre-war to current series. We are now in our 4th decade of service "where total commitment to the product does make a difference". Please supply your chassis/identification number when ordering parts.

Ashton Keynes Vintage Restorations Ltd
A Keith Bowley
Ashton Keynes, Swindon
Wilshire England
01285-861-288
FAX: 01285-860-604

coachbuilding
restoration

Coachbuilders and restorers of vintage and classic cars. Panel work, painting and electrical and mechanical restorations. Specializing in Rolls-Royce, Bentley, Jaguar and all classic marques. Engine reconditioning, white metaling and line boring, specialist machining.

Asom Electric
1204 McClellan Dr
Los Angeles, CA 90025
310-820-4457; FAX: 310-820-5908

electrical systems
rebuilding

See full listing in **Section Two** under **electrical systems**

Atlantic Enterprises
221 Strand Industrial Dr
Little River, SC 29566
843-399-7565; FAX: 843-399-4600
E-mail: steering@atlantic-ent.com

steering assemblies

See full listing in **Section Two** under **chassis parts**

Auto Craftsmen Restoration Inc
27945 Elm Grove
San Antonio, TX 78261
PH/FAX: 830-980-4027

appraisals
buyer/car locator
old M-B parts
restoration

See full listing in **Section Two** under **restoration shops**

Automobile Appraisal Service
Steve Cram
1080 Eddy St #607
San Francisco, CA 94109
415-567-1087, 619-584-4678
FAX: 415-567-1245

appraisals

See full listing in **Section Two** under **appraisals**

Bassett Classic Restoration
2616 Sharon St, Suite D
Kenner, LA 70062
PH/FAX: 504-469-2982
(have auto switching device)

parts
plating
restoration
service

Mail order and open shop. Monday-Saturday 9 am to 6 pm. Upholstery, woodworking, reveneering and mechanical restorations. Parts, sales and service. Also paint, bodywork and cadmium plating. In business since 1973. We have restored RROC National First Place and Senior Award winning motor cars. We work on Rolls-Royce and Bentley motorcars exclusively. We do complete restorations, woodwork refinishing and interiors are our specialty. Celebrating 26 years of meticulous, affordable craftsmanship.

Bassett's Jaguar
PO Box 245
53 Stilson Rd
Wyoming, RI 02898
401-539-3010; FAX: 401-539-7861
E-mail: www.jagwillie@ids.net

parts
restoration
service
upholstery

See full listing in **Section One** under **Jaguar**

Be Happy Automatic Transmission Parts
414 Stivers Rd
Hillsboro, OH 45133
800-416-2862; FAX: 937-442-6133

trans rebuild kits

See full listing in **Section Two** under **transmissions**

bentleydriversclub.com
23238 Erwin St
Woodland Hills, CA 91367
818-887-6557; FAX: 818-346-3627
E-mail: glwales@aol.com

car dealer
collectibles

Mail order only. Rolls-Royce, Bentley automobiles and unusual collectibles for all years and models. Web site: bentleydriversclub.com

Blackhawk Collection
1092 Eagles Nest Pl
Danville, CA 94506-3600
925-736-3444; FAX: 925-736-4375
E-mail: info@blackhawkcollection.com

acquisitions
sales

See full listing in **Section One** under **Duesenberg**

The Brassworks
289 Prado Rd
San Louis Obispo, CA 93401
800-342-6759; FAX: 805-544-5615

radiators

See full listing in **Section Two** under **radiators**

British Auto/USA
92 Londonderry Tpke
Manchester, NH 03104
603-622-1050, 800-452-4787
FAX: 603-622-0849
E-mail: jaguar@britishautousa

parts
upholstery

See full listing in **Section One** under **Jaguar**

British Restorations
4455 Paul St
Philadelphia, PA 19124
215-533-6696

car dealer
restoration

See full listing in **Section One** under **Jaguar**

Michael Chapman
Priorsleigh, Mill Lane
Cleeve Prior
Worcestershire, WR115JZ
England
0044-1789-773897
FAX: 0044-1789-773588

automobilia

See full listing in **Section Two** under **automobilia**

Classic Auto Restoration
15445 Ventura Blvd #60
Sherman Oaks, CA 91413
818-905-6267; FAX: 818-906-1249
E-mail: rollsroyce1@earthlink.net

acquisitions
restoration
sales

Open by appointment only. Rolls-Royce, Bentley and fine classic automobile restoration, appraisals, acquisitions and sales. Picture vehicle rental services. Specializing in classic and exotic automobiles. Custom fabrication and preparation of all makes and models to the motion picture and television industry.

Coachbuilt Motors
907 E Hudson St
Columbus, OH 43211
614-261-1541

repairs

Mail order and open shop. Tuesday-Friday 8 am to 5:30 pm, Saturday by appointment. Rolls-Royce mail order and repair service shop.

Collectors Choice LTD
6400 Springfield-Lodi Rd
Dane, WI 53529
608-849-9878; FAX: 608-849-9879

parts
race preparation
restoration
service

See full listing in **Section One** under **DeTomaso/Pantera**

Charles S Crail Automobiles
36A Calle Cesar Chavez
Santa Barbara, CA 93103
805-568-1934; FAX: 805-568-1533

auto sales

Auto sales for pre and post war classic European marques such as Rolls-Royce, Bentley, Delahaye, Delage, Aston Martin, etc.

Dave's Auto Restoration
2285 Rt 307 E
Jefferson, OH 44047
PH/FAX: 216-858-2227
E-mail: davesauto@knownet.net

upholstery

See full listing in **Section Two** under **interiors & interior parts**

Deters Restorations
6205 Swiss Garden Rd
Temperance, MI 48182-1020
734-847-1820

restoration

See full listing in **Section Two** under **restoration shops**

Durabuilt Automotive Hydraulics
808 Meadows Ave
Canon City, CO 81212
PH/FAX: 719-275-1126
E-mail: durabuilt@ris.net

hose assemblies
pumps
top cylinders
valves

See full listing in **Section Two** under **tops**

East Coast Jaguar
802B Naaman's Rd
Wilmington, DE 19810
302-475-7200; FAX: 302-475-9258
E-mail: ecjaguar@aol.com

parts
service

See full listing in **Section One** under **Jaguar**

Enfield Auto Restoration Inc
4 Print Shop Rd
Enfield, CT 06082
860-749-7917; FAX: 860-749-2836

panel beating
restorations
Rolls-Royce parts
woodworking

See full listing in **Section Two** under **restoration shops**

The Enthusiasts Shop
John Parnell
PO Box 80471
Baton Rouge, LA 70898
225-928-7456; FAX: 225-928-7665

cars
pre-war parts
transportation

Mail order only. Specializing in Rolls-Royce and Bentley cars and pre-war parts. Buying, selling literature for pre-1966 Rolls-Royce and Bentleys. Also do inspections and transportation. Will purchase cars in any condition or location. Finder's fees paid. Pre-war abandoned restoration projects and incomplete cars wanted. References gladly furnished.

Foreign Motors West
253 N Main St
Natick, MA 01760
508-655-5350; FAX: 508-651-0178

car sales

Mail order and open shop. Monday-Friday 8 am to 6 pm, Saturday 8 am to noon. Specializing in Rolls-Royce/Bentley, Mercedes-Benz, BMW, Land Rover, Peugeot for all years and models.

Paul Foulkes-Halbard
Filching Wannock Eastbourne
Polegate
Sussex BN26 5QA England
011 441323 487838
011 441323 487124
FAX: 011 441323 486331

brass age cars
parts

See full listing in **Section One** under **Bugatti**

From Rust To Riches
16643 Rt 144
Mt Airy, MD 21771
301-854-5900, 410-442-3637
301-854-5956; FAX: 301-854-5957
E-mail: tatrabill@aol.com

appraisals
car dealer
repairs
restoration

See full listing in **Section Two** under **restoration shops**

Glazier Pattern & Coachworks
3720 Loramie-Washington Rd
Houston, OH 45333
937-492-7355; FAX: 937-492-9987
E-mail: s.glazier.fam@juno.com

coachwork
interior woodwork
restoration of wood
bodied cars

See full listing in **Section One** under **Chrysler**

Guild of Automotive Restorers
PO Box 1150
44 Bridge St
Bradford, ON Canada L3Z 2B5
905-775-0499; FAX: 905-775-0944
E-mail:
webmaster@guildautomotive.on.ca

restoration
sales
service

See full listing in **Section Two** under **restoration shops**

Tony Handler Inc
2028 Cotner Ave
Los Angeles, CA 90025
310-473-7773; FAX: 310-479-1197

parts

Mail order and open shop. Monday-Friday 8 am to 6 pm, Saturday-Sunday by appointment. World's largest stock of used parts for post-war Rolls-Royce and Bentley cars. Technical advice and personalized service. Restoration candidates and rebuildable Rolls-Royce and Bentleys. Web site: www.rollsfix.com

Peter Harper	car dealer
Stretton House, Northwich Road	
Lower Stretton	
Nr Warrington, WA4 4PF England	
01925 730411; FAX: 01925 730224	

Call for appointment. Near M6 motorway. Car collector with 15-20 cars including some London to Brighton and brass age cars, prewar-1965 Rolls-Royces and Bentleys. Usually a few prewar sports cars and open touring cars. Also pre-1930 motorcycles, usually around 15 flat tank machines, eg Norton, AJS, Indian, FN (4), etc. No parts.

Heritage Upholstery and Trim	interior kits
250 H St, Unit 8110	trim
Blaine, WA 98231	upholstery
604-990-0346; FAX: 604-990-9988	

See full listing in **Section One** under **Austin-Healey**

Jacks Wholesale Division	limousines
250 N Robertson Blvd, Ste 405	
Beverly Hills, CA 90211-1793	
310-839-9417; FAX: 310-839-1046	

See full listing in **Section One** under **Lincoln**

Jersey Motor Museum	museum
St Peter's Village	
Jersey JE3 7AG Channel Islands	
01534-482966	

See full listing in **Section Six** under **Channel Islands**

David M King, Automotive Books	literature
5 Brouwer Ln	
Rockville Centre, NY 11570	
516-766-1561; FAX: 516-766-7502	

Mail order only. Automotive books. Buyer and seller of books on all makes plus racing, biographies, auto travel and annuals. Specializing in literature, books, catalogs, ads, manuals, etc, for Rolls-Royces and Bentleys. Publishers of the *Rolls-Royce Review, The Journal of Rolls-Royce and Bentley Book and Literature Collecting.*

Kreimeyer Co/Auto Legends Inc	antennas/repair
3211 N Wilburn Ave	radios
Bethany, OK 73008	radio repair service
405-789-9499; FAX: 405-789-7888	wholesale glass/parts

See full listing in **Section One** under **Mercedes-Benz**

Leatherique Leather Restoration Products	leather cleaning
PO Box 2678	conditioning
Orange Park, FL 32065	products
904-272-0992; FAX: 904-272-1534	
E-mail: lrpltd@aol.com	

Mail order only. Leather restoration and preservation products for Rolls-Royce, Bentley, Jaguar (English Connolly leather), MG, Mercedes-Benz, Lincoln Continental, Lexus, BMW. Leather conditioning and cleaning. Named simply the best by Rolls-Royce car owners club since 1968. Also, custom color, matched leather dye, which is water based making it soft and natural, not brittle like lacquer dyes.

LMARR Disk Ltd	wheel discs
PO Box 910	
Glen Ellen, CA 95442-0910	
707-938-9347; FAX: 707-938-3020	
E-mail: lmarr@ibm.net	

Mail order only. Specializing in wheel discs for prewar Rolls-Royce, PI, PII, PIII, Wraith, 20/25, 25/30, Bentley 3-1/2, 4-1/4, Speed 6, 8 litre, Bentley rear wheelcover, Alfa, Bugatti, Delage D8, Lagonda, Jaguar Mk IV, Hispano-Suiza, Lincoln, Voisin.

Marshall Antique & Classic Restorations	coolant additives
3714 Old Philadelphia Pike	restoration services
Bethlehem, PA 18015	
610-868-7765; FAX: 610-868-7529	

Specialize in restoration services for Rolls-Royce, Bentley, Mercedes-Benz. Distributor of No-Rosion™ products.

McLellan's Automotive History	books
Robert and Sharon McLellan	factory literature
9111 Longstaff Dr	magazines
Houston, TX 77031-2711	memorabilia
713-772-3285; FAX: 713-772-3287	press kits/programs
E-mail: mclellans@worldnet.att.net	sales literature

See full listing in **Section Two** under **literature dealers**

Mercedes-Benz Service by Angela & George/ABS Exotic Repair Inc	sales
700 N Andrews Ave	service
Fort Lauderdale, FL 33304	
954-566-7785; FAX: 954-566-7271	

See full listing in **Section One** under **Mercedes-Benz**

Mid-Jersey Motorama Inc	car dealer
1301 Asbury Ave	
PO Box 1395	
Asbury Park, NJ 07712	
PH/FAX: 732-775-9885	
beeper: 732-840-6111	
E-mail: sjz1@aol.com	

See full listing in **Section One** under **Cadillac/LaSalle**

Midbanc Financial Services	financing
PO Box 20402	
Columbus, OH 43220	
614-442-7701; FAX: 614-442-7704	
E-mail: patricia@midbanc.com	

See full listing in **Section Two** under **financing**

Motorcar Gallery Inc	car dealer
715 N Federal Hwy	
Fort Lauderdale, FL 33304	
954-522-9900; FAX: 954-522-9966	

See full listing in **Section One** under **Ferrari**

The Museum of Science & Industry in Manchester	museum
Liverpool Rd	
Castlefield	
Manchester M34FP England	
+44 (0) 161-832-2244	
FAX: +44 (0) 161-834-5135	
E-mail: curatorial@mussci.u-net.com	

See full listing in **Section Six** under **England**

Northern Motorsport Ltd	repair
PO Box 508, Rt 5	restoration
Wilder, VT 05088	sales
802-296-2099; FAX: 802-295-6599	service

See full listing in **Section Two** under **restoration shops**

Omega Automobile Appraisals | appraisals
115 18 Ave SE
St Petersburg, FL 33705
727-894-5690

Open shop only. Monday-Saturday at customer's convenience. Specializing in Rolls-Royce and Bentley. Appraises all makes, models and years of autos and trucks. Member of and schooled by International Society of Appraisers since 1982. Appraisals for insurance coverage, pre or post purchase, marriage or business dissolution, loan valuation, probate, bankruptcy, value disputes, donations for tax deductions, restoration, diminished value.

Oregon Crewe Cutters Inc | parts
1665 Redwood Ave
Grants Pass, OR 97527
541-479-5663; FAX: 541-479-6339

Mail order and open shop. Monday-Friday 8 am to 5 pm. World's largest stock of used parts for post-war Rolls-Royce and Bentley cars. Technical advice and personalized service. Web site: www.rollsfix.com

Powers Parts Inc | literature
425 Pine Ave | parts
PO Box 796
Anna Maria, FL 34216
941-778-7270; FAX: 941-778-0289
E-mail: powersinc@aol.com

Mail order and open shop. Monday-Friday 9 am to 4 pm. New and used parts and literature for 1933-1939 Bentleys, Rolls-Royces and WW II small horsepower Rolls-Royces.

Precision Autoworks | restorations
2202 Federal Street
East Camden, NJ 08105
609-966-0080, NJ
FAX: 610-649-3577, PA

See full listing in **Section One** under **Mercedes-Benz**

Proper Motor Cars Inc | parts
1811 11th Ave N | restoration
St Petersburg, FL 33713-5794 | service
727-821-8883; FAX: 727-821-0273
E-mail:
propermotorcarsinc@email.msn.com

Mail order only and open shop. Monday-Friday 8 am to 4:30 pm. Restoration and maintenance of Rolls-Royces and Bentleys. Also restoration and maintenance of vintage sports and racing cars. All types of restoration. Mercedes-Benz, Ferrari and other European cars serviced and restored. Largest stock of Rolls-Royce new and used parts in the Southeast. Bosch authorized service.

Regal International Motor Cars Inc | car dealer
PO Box 6819
Hollywood, FL 33081
305-989-9777; FAX: 305-989-9778

Deals in Rolls-Royce, Mercedes, Jaguar, Avanti, special interest cars.

RM Auto Restoration Ltd | panel fabrication
9435 Horton Line | parts
Blenheim, ON Canada N0P 1A0 | restoration
519-352-4575; FAX: 519-351-1337
E-mail: clark@rmcars.com

See full listing in **Section Two** under **restoration shops**

Rolls-Royce of Beverly Hills | parts
11401 West Pico Blvd
Los Angeles, CA 90064
800-321-9792, 310-477-4262
FAX: 310-473-7498
E-mail: smrr64@aol.com

Mail order and open shop. Monday-Friday 8 am to 5:30 pm.

Specializing in Rolls-Royce and Bentley parts of all years. We have recently started handling parts for pre WW II models too. Web site: www.rollsroycebeverlyhills.com

Royal Coach Works Ltd | appraisals
2146 Lunceford Ln
Lilburn, GA 30047
PH/FAX: 404-249-9040

See full listing in **Section Two** under **appraisals**

Sandringham House Museum & Grounds | museum
Sandringham
Nr King's Lynn
Norfolk PE356EN England
01553-772675; FAX: 01485-541571

See full listing in **Section Six** under **England**

Supreme Metal Polishing | metal working
84A Rickenbacker Cir | parts restoration
Livermore, CA 94550 | plating services
925-449-3490; FAX: 925-449-1475 | polishing
E-mail: supremet@home.com

See full listing in **Section Two** under **plating & polishing**

Teddy's Garage | parts
8530 Louise Ave | restoration
Northridge, CA 91325 | service
818-341-0505

Mail order and open shop. Monday-Friday 8 am to 6 pm. Restores, services and repairs Rolls-Royces, Bentleys, Jaguars, MGs and other fine British automobiles. We have a large stock of parts for pre-1966 Rolls and Bentley cars. If we don't have it, we will get it. Finest workmanship for finest cars.

Thoroughbred Motors | parts
3935 N US 301 | sales
Sarasota, FL 34234 | service
941-359-2277; FAX: 941-359-2128

See full listing in **Section One** under **Jaguar**

Vantage Motorworks Inc | restoration
1898 NE 151 St | sales
N Miami, FL 33162 | service
305-940-1161; FAX: 305-949-7481

Open shop only. Monday-Saturday 8 am to 5 pm. Rolls-Royce/Bentley sales, service, restoration for postwar Rolls-Royce and Bentleys, particular emphasis on S/Cloud series, 1956-1967.

Viking Worldwise Inc | leather jackets
190 Doe Run Rd
Manheim, PA 17545
800-842-9198; FAX: 717-664-5556
E-mail: gkurien@success.net

See full listing in **Section Two** under **apparel**

Vintage Restorations | accessories
The Old Bakery | instruments
Windmill Street, Tunbridge Wells
Kent, TN2 4UU England
UK 1892-525-899
FAX: UK 1892-525499

See full listing in **Section Two** under **instruments**

White Post Restorations | brakes
One Old Car Dr | restoration
White Post, VA 22663
540-837-1140; FAX: 540-837-2368

See full listing in **Section Two** under **brakes**

Wolfson Engineering
512 Pkwy W
Las Vegas, NV 89106
PH/FAX: 702-384-4196

mech engineering

See full listing in **Section Two** under **special services**

 **RANGE ROVER**

Atlantic British Ltd
Halfmoon Light Industrial Park
6 Badertscher Dr
Clifton Park, NY 12065
800-533-2210; FAX: 518-664-6641
E-mail: ab@roverparts.com

accessories
parts

North America's largest independent mail order Rover parts and accessories distributor. Free catalog available for Land Rover, Range Rover, Discovery, Defender and Sterling vehicles. Web site: www.roverparts.com

Atlantic Enterprises
221 Strand Industrial Dr
Little River, SC 29566
843-399-7565; FAX: 843-399-4600
E-mail: steering@atlantic-ent.com

steering assemblies

See full listing in **Section Two** under **chassis parts**

British Auto Parts Ltd
93256 Holland Ln
Marcola, OR 97454
541-933-2880; FAX: 541-933-2302

parts

See full listing in **Section One** under **Morris**

British Bulldog Spares Ltd
394 Kilburn St
Fall River, MA 02724
888-874-3888; FAX: 508-674-5025
E-mail: bulldog@meganet.net

accessories
parts
service

Specializing in parts, accessories and service for Land Rover, Range Rover, Discovery and Defender. Web site: www.britishbulldog.com

British Car Films
PO Box 13862
London N4 3WB England
800-454-8341 toll-free
011 44181-3744850
FAX: 011 44181-3744852
E-mail: british.car@virgin.net

videos

See full listing in **Section Two** under **videos**

British Car Service
2854 N Stone Ave
Tucson, AZ 85705
520-882-7026; FAX: 520-882-7053
E-mail: bcs@liveline.com

restoration
salvage yard

See full listing in **Section Five** under **Arizona**

British Motor Co
3825 W 11th Ave
Eugene, OR 97402
800-995-1895; FAX: 541-485-8544

engine rebuilding

See full listing in **Section One** under **Jaguar**

British Pacific Ltd
3317 Burton Ave
Burbank, CA 91504
818-841-8945; FAX: 818-841-3825
E-mail: britpac@aol.com

parts

Mail order and retail counter. Monday-Friday 9 am to 5 pm. Exclusively Land Rover parts 1958-1997. Catalogs available for Series II, IIA, III; Defender, Discovery, Range Rover. Genuine, OEM and aftermarket parts and accessories.

Doug's British Car Parts
2487 E Colorado Blvd
Pasadena, CA 91107
818-793-2494; FAX: 818-793-4339

accessories
parts

See full listing in **Section One** under **Jaguar**

Foreign Motors West
253 N Main St
Natick, MA 01760
508-655-5350; FAX: 508-651-0178

car sales

See full listing in **Section One** under **Rolls-Royce/Bentley**

Heritage Motor Centre
Banbury Rd
Gaydon
Warwichshire CV35 0BJ England
01926 641188; FAX: 01926 641555

museum

See full listing in **Section Six** under **England**

Jaguar of Puerto Rico Inc
PO Box 13055
San Juan, PR 00908-3055
787-723-5177; FAX: 787-723-9488

car dealer
parts
service

See full listing in **Section One** under **Jaguar**

London Stainless Steel Exhaust Centre
249-253 Queenstown Rd
London, SW8 3NP England
011-44-171622-2120
FAX: 011-44-171627-0991
E-mail: 101445.341@compuserv.com

exhaust systems

See full listing in **Section Two** under **exhaust systems**

Mid-Jersey Motorama Inc
1301 Asbury Ave
PO Box 1395
Asbury Park, NJ 07712
PH/FAX: 732-775-9885
beeper: 732-840-6111
E-mail: sjz1@aol.com

car dealer

See full listing in **Section One** under **Cadillac/LaSalle**

Motorcars Ltd
8101 Hempstead
Houston, TX 77008
800-231-6563; FAX: 713-863-8238
E-mail: info@britishparts.com

parts

See full listing in **Section One** under **Jaguar**

Lyle Pearson Company
351 Auto Dr
Boise, ID 83709
208-377-3900; FAX: 208-375-0691

accessories
literature
parts

See full listing in **Section One** under **Mercedes-Benz**

Rovers West
1815 E 19th St Unit 2
Tucson, AZ 85719
520-670-9377; FAX: 520-670-9080
E-mail: rover@azstarnet.com

accessories
parts

Mail/phone order. Monday-Friday 10 am to 6 pm, weekends by appointment. Specializing in new and used parts, high-performance parts, off-road accessories and optional equipment for Land Rover, Range Rovers, Rover 2000, 3500S, SD-1 Rovers. Web site: www.roverswest.com

Sandringham House Museum & Grounds
Sandringham
Nr King's Lynn
Norfolk PE356EN England
01553-772675; FAX: 01485-541571

museum

See full listing in **Section Six** under **England**

Spectral Kinetics
17 Church St
Garnerville, NY 10923
914-947-3126; FAX: 914-429-6041
E-mail: harve86@ibm.net

parts
restoration

Mail order and open shop by appointment. Specializes in the sale of new and used Rover sedan parts, particularly the 2000, 3500S and SD1 models. Also specializes in early Range Rovers. Rebuilding and restoration services. "We sell parts for what we drive."

Vintage Motor Gaskets
W 604 19th
Spokane, WA 99203
509-747-9960, 509-747-0517
E-mail: dbrooke@ior.com

gaskets

See full listing in **Section Two** under **gaskets**

XKs Unlimited
850 Fiero Ln
San Luis Obispo, CA 93401
805-544-7864; FAX: 805-544-1664
E-mail: xksunltd@aol.com

instruments
parts
restorations

See full listing in **Section One** under **Jaguar**

SAAB

The Auto Doctor Inc
23125 Telegraph Rd
Southfield, MI 48034
248-355-1505; FAX: 248-355-3460

mechanical parts
service repairs

See full listing in **Section One** under **BMW**

Chicago Classic Imports
6948 N Western Ave
Chicago, IL 60645
773-381-2600; FAX: 773-381-2616
E-mail: saab@chicagoclassicimports.com

parts
service

Mail order and open shop. Monday-Friday 9 am to 6 pm. Specializing in service and parts for Saab and Volvo, 1967-up. Web site: www.chicagoclassicimports.com

East West Auto Parts Inc
4605 Dawson Rd
Tulsa, OK 74115
800-447-2886; FAX: 918-832-7900

GM parts
European import
parts

See full listing in **Section Five** under **Oklahoma**

European Parts Specialists Ltd
PO Box 6783
Santa Barbara, CA 93160
800-334-2749, 805-683-4020
FAX: 805-683-3689
E-mail: epsparts@impulse.net

accessories
parts

See full listing in **Section One** under **Mercedes-Benz**

Irving Galis
357 Atlantic Ave
Marblehead, MA 01945

books
dealer items
literature

Mail order only. 1) Out-of-print automobile books; 2) Saab literature, books and dealer items list. Send SASE (each list).

Italy's Famous Exhaust
2711 183rd St
Redondo Beach, CA 90278
310-793-5985
E-mail: famous@earthlink.net

exhaust systems
wheels

See full listing in **Section Two** under **exhaust systems**

Rayce Inc
4656 SW 75th Ave
Miami, FL 33155
800-426-2221, 305-261-3355
FAX: 305-261-3615

parts

See full listing in **Section One** under **Alfa Romeo**

Miller Energy Inc
3200 South Clinton Ave
S Plainfield, NJ 07080
908-755-6700; FAX: 908-755-0312
E-mail allyon@aol.com

engine parts

Mail order only. Level gauge, sight glass for Stanley steam engine.

Stanley Museum
School St
Kingfield, ME 04947
207-265-2729; FAX: 207-265-4700
E-mail: stanleym@somtel.org

museum

See full listing in **Section Six** under **Maine**

Vintage Steam Products
396 North Rd
Chester, NJ 07930-2327
973-584-3319
E-mail: arthart@bell-labs.com

parts
supplies

Mail order only. Specializing in reproduction parts and supplies for Stanleys and other early steam powered automobiles.

Stearns-Knight

Arthur W Aseltine
18215 Challenge Cut-Off Rd
Forbestown, CA 95941
530-675-2773

| parts |
| research |
| restoration |

Mail order and open shop. Monday-Friday 8 am to 5:30 pm; Saturday and Sunday by appointment. Total or partial restoration of Stearns, Stearns-Knight, Daimler, Minerva and other sleeve-valve motorcars. 40 years' experience with sleeve-valve motors. All work guaranteed.

1956 Studebaker Golden Hawk Owners Register
31700 Wekiva River Rd
Sorrento, FL 32776-9233
E-mail: 56sghor@prodigy.net

| information |
| exchange |

Information exchange through a periodic newsletter called *56J Only* for 1956 Studebaker Golden Hawks. Owners only.

Bumper Boyz LLC
2435 E 54th St
Los Angeles, CA 90058
800-995-1703, 323-587-8976
FAX: 323-587-2013

| bumper repairs |
| reconditioning |
| sandblasting |

See full listing in **Section One** under **Chevrolet**.

Classic Enterprises
Box 92
Barron, WI 54812
715-537-5422

| sheetmetal |

Manufacturer of top quality sheetmetal restoration reproductions. Specializes in restoration reproductions (sheetmetal) for Studebakers and 1946-1986 Willys Jeeps. Floor pans for 1957-1958 Fords. We either meet or exceed all metal gauge requirements. All products are backed by a 30-day satisfaction guarantee.

Dakota Studebaker Parts
RR 1, Box 103A
Armour, SD 57313
605-724-2527

| parts |

Mail order only. Specializes in parts for Studebaker trucks, pickups and cars 1936-1964.

Dennis DuPont
77 Island Pond Rd
Derry, NH 03038
603-434-9290

| automobilia |
| literature |
| parts |

Mail order only. Sell NOS and used parts for Studebaker from mid 1930s-1966. Also have Studebaker literature, ads and automobilia. Buy Studebaker NOS parts, literature and automobilia. If it says Studebaker we are interested.

Egge Machine Company Inc
11707 Slauson Ave
Santa Fe Springs, CA 90670
800-866-EGGE, 562-945-3419
FAX: 562-693-1635
E-mail: info@egge.com

| bearings |
| pistons/rings |
| timing components |
| valve train |

See full listing in **Section Two** under **engine parts**

Eugene Gardner
10510 Rico Tatum Rd
Palmetto, GA 30268
770-463-4264

| license plates |

See full listing in **Section Two** under **license plates**

Garton's Auto
401 N 5th St (at 5th & Vine)
Millville, NJ 08332-3129
609-825-3618

| bicycles |
| Ford NOS parts |
| sales literature |

See full listing in **Section One** under **Ford 1932-1953**

Kelley's Korner
22 14th St
Bristol, TN 37620
423-968-5583

| parts |
| repair |

Mail order and open shop. Monday-Saturday 9 am to 5 pm. Studebaker repair, parts for Studebaker cars and trucks 1925-1966. Engine rebuilds, brake overhauls, front end work, electrical work and wiring harnesses.

L & L Antique Auto Trim
403 Spruce, Box 177
Pierce City, MO 65723
417-476-2871

| runningboard |
| moldings |

See full listing in **Section Two** under **special services**

Loga Enterprises
5399 Old Town Hall Rd
Eau Claire, WI 54701
715-832-7302

| convertible tops |
| interior parts |

Mail order only. Specializing in Studebaker 1937-1966 for interior panels, firewall liners, headliners, kick pads, truck headliners, trunk mats, carpets, convertible tops, gloveboxes. Also door boards, firewall pads, hood pads, door clips, custom interior panels.

Phil's Studebaker
11250 Harrison Rd
Osceola, IN 46561-9375
219-674-0084

| NOS parts |
| used parts |

Mail order. For 1947-1966 Studebakers. NOS, reproduction and excellent used Studebaker parts and accessories. NOS door panels.

Royal Gorge Studebaker
109 W Front St
Florence, CO 81226
719-784-4169 shop
719-275-3289 home

| parts |
| restoration |

Mail order and open shop. Monday-Saturday 9 am to 6 pm. Specializing in restoration and parts for Studebakers, all years to 1966.

Charles Schnetlage
22136 Roscoe Blvd
Canoga Park, CA 91304
818-347-0334; FAX: 818-347-0868

| books |
| engine paint |
| rubber products |

Mail order only. For Studebakers, books, rubber products, brake and mechanical parts, 1928-1957 engine paint.

Steve's Studebaker-Packard
PO Box 6914
Napa, CA 94581
707-255-8945

| | car dealer
parts
suspension repairs |

See full listing in **Section One** under **Packard**

Studebaker of California
1400 Santa Fe Ave
Long Beach, CA 90813
562-435-0157; FAX: 562-436-3074

| | **parts** |

Open shop. Monday-Friday 8 am to 4:30 pm. Reproduction and NOS for postwar Studebaker and Avanti automobiles.

Studebaker Parts & Locations
228 Marquiss Cir
Clinton, TN 37716
615-457-3002
E-mail: studebaker_joe@msn.com

| | **parts**
parts locator |

Mail order only. Specializing in parts, new and used, for 1939-1966 Studebakers, Avanti, Avanti II. Web site: http://homestead.dejanews.com/user.stude/studebaker.html

Studebakers West
335A Convention Way
Redwood City, CA 94063
650-366-8787

| | **mechanical**
rebuilding
transmission parts
wiring harnesses |

Mail order and open shop. Monday-Friday 9 am to 12 noon and 1 pm to 5 pm; Saturday 9 am to 12 noon. Mechanical, chassis, engine, transmission and new wiring harnesses. Over 13,000 part numbers in stock. "Studebakers are our business, our only business."

Tom Taylor
PO Box 129
Guinda, CA 95637
530-796-4106

| | **NOS parts** |

See full listing in **Section One** under **Mopar**

Pat Walsh Restorations
Box Q
Wakefield, MA 01880
781-246-3266; FAX: 781-224-3311
E-mail: pwalshrest@aol.com

| | **literature**
rubber parts |

See full listing in **Section Two** under **rubber parts**

Grand Touring
2785 E Regal Park Dr
Anaheim, CA 92806
714-630-0130; FAX: 714-630-6956

| | **engine rebuilding**
machine shop
restoration
suspension |

See full listing in **Section Two** under **restoration shops**

Jacks Wholesale Division
250 N Robertson Blvd, Ste 405
Beverly Hills, CA 90211-1793
310-839-9417; FAX: 310-839-1046

| | **limousines** |

See full listing in **Section One** under **Lincoln**

Ernie Toth
8153 Cloveridge Rd
Chagrin Falls, OH 44022
440-338-3565

| | **brake fluid** |

Mail order only. Dot 5 silicone brake fluid, gallons/quarts.

Vintage Motor Gaskets
W 604 19th
Spokane, WA 99203
509-747-9960, 509-747-0517
E-mail: dbrooke@ior.com

| | **gaskets** |

See full listing in **Section Two** under **gaskets**

Visby Bilmuseum
Skogsholm
S-62190 Visby Sweden
0498-278161; FAX: 0498-203390

| | **museum** |

See full listing in **Section Six** under **Sweden**

1 CAAT Limited Co
1324 E Harper Ave
Maryville, TN 37804
423-983-7180
E-mail: jhenriks@icx.net

| | **restoration** |

See full listing in **Section Two** under **restoration shops**

American-Foreign Auto Electric Inc
103 Main St
Souderton, PA 18964
215-723-4877

| | **parts**
rebuilding |

See full listing in **Section Two** under **electrical systems**

British Racing Green
30 Aleph Dr
Newark, DE 19702
302-368-1117; FAX: 302-368-5910
E-mail: info@brgparts.com

| | **new parts**
rebuilt parts
used parts |

See full listing in **Section Two** under **electrical systems**

Classic Sunbeam Auto Parts Inc
2 Tavano Rd
Ossining, NY 10562
800-24-SUNBEAM
E-mail: classicsun@aol.com

| | **body parts**
carpets
electrical parts
upholstery |

Mail order only. Phone hours: Monday-Saturday 10 am to 10 pm. New OEM quality reproductions of running parts, trim, upholstery, carpets, tops, electrical and body parts for 1959-1967 Alpines and Tigers. 24 page catalog. Web site: www.classicsunbeam.com

Doug's British Car Parts
2487 E Colorado Blvd
Pasadena, CA 91107
818-793-2494; FAX: 818-793-4339

| | **accessories**
parts |

See full listing in **Section One** under **Jaguar**

Geeson Bros Motorcycle Museum & Workshop
2-6 Water Ln
South Witham
Grantham Lincs NG33 5 PH
England
01572 767280, 01572 768195

| | **museum** |

See full listing in **Section Six** under **England**

McLean's Brit Bits
14 Sagamore Rd
Rye, NH 03870
800-995-2487; FAX: 603-433-0009
E-mail: sam@britbits.com

accessories
parts
sales
service

See full listing in **Section One** under **MG**

Sports Car Haven
2-33 Flowerfield Industrial Pk
St James, NY 11780
516-862-8058
E-mail: sch94@aol.com

race prep
restorations
service

See full listing in **Section One** under **Triumph**

Sunbeam Specialties
PO Box 771
Los Gatos, CA 95031
408-371-1642; FAX: 408-371-8070
E-mail: sunsp19@idt.net

parts
restoration supplies

Mail order and open shop. Monday-Friday 8 am to 5 pm. Carries an extensive supply of mechanical, hydraulic and soft trim and restoration supplies for Sunbeam Alpine and Tiger cars. Will ship overseas. Fast service.

Tiger Tom's
RD 2 Box 600
Blacks Bridge Rd
Annville, PA 17003
PH/FAX: 717-832-1116
E-mail: tigertoms@aol.com

service

Mail order and open shop. Monday-Friday 8 am to 5 pm. Restoration service of all components for Sunbeam Alpine and Tiger.

Victoria British Ltd
Box 14991
Lenexa, KS 66285-4991
800-255-0088, 913-599-3299

accessories
parts

See full listing in **Section One** under **MG**

TALBOT

Auto Europa
221 Berrellesa St
Martinez, CA 94553
925-229-3466; FAX: 925-313-0542

painting
restorations
woodworking

See full listing in **Section Two** under **restoration shops**

Charles S Crail Automobiles
36A Calle Cesar Chavez
Santa Barbara, CA 93103
805-568-1934; FAX: 805-568-1533

auto sales

See full listing in **Section One** under **Rolls-Royce/Bentley**

Paul Foulkes-Halbard
Filching Wannock Eastbourne
Polegate
Sussex BN26 5QA England
011 441323 487838, 011 441323 487124
FAX: 011 441323 486331

brass age cars
parts

See full listing in **Section One** under **Bugatti**

TERRAPLANE

Hudson Motor Car Co Memorabilia
Ken Poynter
19638 Huntington
Harper Woods, MI 48225
313-886-9292

literature
memorabilia
novelties
signs

See full listing in **Section One** under **Hudson**

K-GAP
Automotive Parts
PO Box 3065
Santa Fe Springs, CA 90670
PH/FAX: 714-523-0403

repro parts

See full listing in **Section One** under **Hudson**

TOYOTA

CSi
1100 S Raymond Ave, Suite H
Fullerton, CA 92831
714-879-7955; FAX: 714-879-7310
E-mail: csila@compuserve.com

parts

See full listing in **Section One** under **BMW**

KATO USA Inc
100 Remington Rd
Schaumburg, IL 60173
847-781-9500; FAX: 847-781-9570

models

1/43 scale automobile models of Nissan 300ZX and Toyota Supra. Available through hobby dealers or direct order. Web site: www.katousa.com

Keiser Motors
1169 Dell Ave #A
Campbell, CA 95008
408-374-7303

Land Cruisers

Specializing in Toyota Land Cruisers, FJ40, FJ55, FJ60, FJ80.

Land Cruiser Solutions Inc
20 Thornell Rd
Newton, NH 03858
603-382-3555; FAX: 603-378-0431
E-mail: twbii@aol.com

accessories
services

Mail order and open shop. Monday-Saturday 9 am to 5 pm EST and by appointment. Specialize in OEM parts and aftermarket accessories, and provides services for the Toyota Land Cruiser, FJ40, FJ45, FJ60 and the new FJ80 models. LCS is the nation's original supplier of the revolutionary aluminum body tub for both the FJ40 and FJ45 Land Cruiser. Web site: landcruisersolutions.com

Specter Off-Road Inc
21600 Nordhoff St, Dept HM
Chatsworth, CA 91311
818-882-1238; FAX: 818-882-7144
E-mail: sor@sor.com

accessories
parts

Mail order and open shop. Monday-Friday 9 am to 6 pm EST;

1st and 3rd Saturday 10 am to 2 pm. Toyota Land Cruiser parts and accessories only. World's most complete line top quality new and used, unique and hard to find Land Cruiser items. 30,000 sq ft warehouse, largest collection of rare non-USA Land Cruisers on display in the world. We invite you to visit our showroom. We ship worldwide. Annual 500 page catalog with price list available, $5 USA, $15 foreign. Web site: www.sor.com

TRIUMPH

1 CAAT Limited Co	restoration
1324 E Harper Ave	
Maryville, TN 37804	
423-983-7180	
E-mail: jhenriks@icx.net	

See full listing in **Section Two** under **restoration shops**

American-Foreign Auto Electric Inc	parts
103 Main St	rebuilding
Souderton, PA 18964	
215-723-4877	

See full listing in **Section Two** under **electrical systems**

APA Industries	accessories
10505 San Fernando Rd	parts
Pacoima, CA 91331	
818-834-8473; FAX: 818-834-2795	
E-mail: apaindustries@juno.com	

See full listing in **Section One** under **Jaguar**

Asom Electric	electrical systems
1204 McClellan Dr	rebuilding
Los Angeles, CA 90025	
310-820-4457; FAX: 310-820-5908	

See full listing in **Section Two** under **electrical systems**

Atlantic Enterprises	steering assemblies
221 Strand Industrial Dr	
Little River, SC 29566	
843-399-7565; FAX: 843-399-4600	
E-mail: steering@atlantic-ent.com	

See full listing in **Section Two** under **chassis parts**

Automotive Artistry	restoration
679 W Streetboro St	
Hudson, OH 44236	
330-650-1503	
E-mail: dale@cmh.net	

Open shop only. Monday-Friday 8 am to 5 pm. Restoration of sports cars, all years and makes. Partial or body-off. Complete services offered, mechanical, body, upholstery and painting.

Automotive Artistry	restoration
4311 Mennonite Rd	
Mantua, OH 44255	
330-274-8699	

Open Monday-Friday 9 am to 6 pm, Saturday by appointment. Post-war European, Austin-Healey, Jaguar, MG, Triumph, Lotus, Fiat, Ferrari. Maintenance to bare bones. Mechanical, electrical, carburetion, body, paint.

BCP Sport & Classic Co	parts
10525 Airline Dr	service
Houston, TX 77037	
281-448-4739; FAX: 281-448-0189	

See full listing in **Section One** under **MG**

BritBooks	books
PO Box 321	
Otego, NY 13825	
PH/FAX: 607-988-7956	
E-mail: britbook@dmcom.net	

See full listing in **Section Four** under **books & publications**

British Auto Parts Ltd	parts
93256 Holland Ln	
Marcola, OR 97454	
541-933-2880; FAX: 541-933-2302	

See full listing in **Section One** under **Morris**

British Auto Shoppe	parts
1909 5th Ave	service
Moline, IL 61265	
309-764-9513; FAX: 309-764-9576	

See full listing in **Section One** under **MG**

British Car Keys	keys
Rt 144 Box 9957	
Ellicott City, MD 21042-3647	
410-750-2352	
E-mail: britishcarkeys@hotmail.com	

See full listing in **Section One** under **Austin-Healey**

British Car Magazine	periodical
343 Second St, Suite H	
Los Altos, CA 94022-3639	
650-949-9680; FAX: 650-949-9685	
E-mail: britcarmag@aol.com	

See full listing in **Section Four** under **periodicals**

British Car Service	restoration
2854 N Stone Ave	salvage yard
Tucson, AZ 85705	
520-882-7026; FAX: 520-882-7053	
E-mail: bcs@liveline.com	

See full listing in **Section Five** under **Arizona**

British Car Specialists	parts
2060 N Wilson Way	repairs
Stockton, CA 95205	restoration
209-948-8767; FAX: 209-948-1030	
E-mail: healeydoc@aol.com	

See full listing in **Section One** under **Austin-Healey**

British Miles	accessories
9278 Old E Tyburn Rd	literature
Morrisville, PA 19067	parts
215-736-9300; FAX: 215-736-3089	restoration

See full listing in **Section One** under **MG**

British Parts NW	parts
4105 SE Lafayette Hwy	
Dayton, OR 97114	
503-864-2001; FAX: 503-864-2081	
E-mail: bpnw@onlinemac.com	

Mail/phone orders only. Monday-Friday 8 am to 5 pm. Direct importer for Triumph, Jaguar, MGA, B (engine parts only) and Austin-Healey 100-4 through 3000 (engine parts only). Carry a full line of polyurethane bushings for TR4A-6, Spitfire, GT6 and TR7, 8. High-performance engine parts for all Triumph engines plus MG are also available. Web site: www.bpnorthwest.com

British Racing Green — new parts / rebuilt parts / used parts
30 Aleph Dr
Newark, DE 19702
302-368-1117; FAX: 302-368-5910
E-mail: info@brgparts.com

See full listing in **Section Two** under **electrical systems**

British Restorations — car dealer / restoration
4455 Paul St
Philadelphia, PA 19124
215-533-6696

See full listing in **Section One** under **Jaguar**

British T Shop Inc — car/tractor dealer / parts / service
165 Rt 82
Oakdale, CT 06370
860-889-0178; FAX: 860-889-6096

See full listing in **Section One** under **MG**

British Wire Wheel — hubs / tires / wire wheels
1650 Mansfield St
Santa Cruz, CA 95062
831-479-4495; FAX: 831-462-1517

See full listing in **Section One** under **Austin-Healey**

British Wiring Inc — wiring accessories / wiring harnesses
20449 Ithaca Rd
Olympia Fields, IL 60461
PH/FAX: 708-481-9050

See full listing in **Section Two** under **electrical systems**

Cambridge Motorsport — parts / race tuning
Caxton Rd
Great Gransden, NR Sandy
Beds SG19 3AH England
0044 1767 677969
FAX: 0044 1767 677026
E-mail:
cambridge.motorsport@dial.pipex.com

Triumph TR2-6 and MGB race tuning specialists for engine components and ancillaries. Aluminum sumps, radiators, roller rockers, pistons, crankshafts, flywheels.

Doug's British Car Parts — accessories / parts
2487 E Colorado Blvd
Pasadena, CA 91107
818-793-2494; FAX: 818-793-4339

See full listing in **Section One** under **Jaguar**

East Coast Jaguar — parts / service
802B Naaman's Rd
Wilmington, DE 19810
302-475-7200; FAX: 302-475-9258
E-mail: ecjaguar@aol.com

See full listing in **Section One** under **Jaguar**

Eightparts — accessories / parts
1815 E 19th St Unit 2
Tucson, AZ 85719
520-670-9377; FAX: 520-670-9080
E-mail: rover@azstarnet.com

Mail/phone order. Monday-Friday 10 am to 6 pm, weekends by appointment. Specializing in new and used parts, high-performance, accessories and optional equipment for TR8 and Stag. Also Triumph TR7 parts. Web site: www.roverswest.com

Don Flye — parts
5 Doe Valley Rd
Petersham, MA 01366
978-724-3318

See full listing in **Section One** under **Austin-Healey**

Golden Gulf Classics Inc — repairs / restorations
PO Box 490
22530 Hwy 49
Saucier, MS 39574
228-831-2650; FAX: 228-831-1513
E-mail: gudhowdy@datasync.com

Mail order and open shop. Monday-Friday 7 am to 5 pm. Classic automobile restoration, British and American. In-house sheet-metal, rust repair, paint, mechanical and electrical. Web site: www2.datasync.com/goldengulfclassics/

Heritage Motor Centre — museum
Banbury Rd
Gaydon
Warwichshire CV35 0BJ England
01926 641188; FAX: 01926 641555

See full listing in **Section Six** under **England**

Heritage Upholstery and Trim — interior kits / trim / upholstery
250 H St, Unit 8110
Blaine, WA 98231
604-990-0346; FAX: 604-990-9988

See full listing in **Section One** under **Austin-Healey**

John's Cars Inc — conversion retrofits / parts / restoration / service
800 Jaguar Ln
Dallas, TX 75226
800-866-JAGS (5247) parts orders only
214-426-4100; FAX: 214-426-3116

See full listing in **Section One** under **Jaguar**

Lake Oswego Restorations — restoration / sales
19621 S Hazelhurst Ln
West Linn, OR 97068
PH/FAX: 503-636-7503

See full listing in **Section One** under **Aston Martin**

McLean's Brit Bits — accessories / parts / sales / service
14 Sagamore Rd
Rye, NH 03870
800-995-2487; FAX: 603-433-0009
E-mail: sam@britbits.com

See full listing in **Section One** under **MG**

Sammy Miller Motorcycle Museum — museum
Bashley Cross Rd
New Milton
Hampshire BH25 5SZ England
01425 620777; FAX: 01425 619696

See full listing in **Section Six** under **England**

Mini Mania — parts / service
31 Winsor St
Milpitas, CA 95035
408-942-5595; FAX: 408-942-5582
E-mail: info@minimania.com

See full listing in **Section One** under **Austin**

Morgan Spares Ltd — car sales / consulting / obsolete parts / used parts
225 Simons Rd
Ancram, NY 12502
518-329-3877; FAX: 518-329-3892
E-mail: morganspares@taconic.net

See full listing in **Section One** under **Morgan**

Moss Motors Ltd — accessories / parts
PO Box 847
440 Rutherford St
Goleta, CA 93117
800-235-6954; FAX: 805-692-2525

See full listing in **Section One** under **MG**

Motorcars Ltd 8101 Hempstead Houston, TX 77008 800-231-6563; FAX: 713-863-8238 E-mail: info@britishparts.com	parts

See full listing in **Section One** under **Jaguar**

Motorhead Ltd 2811-B Old Lee Hwy Fairfax, VA 22031 800-527-3140; FAX: 703-573-3195	parts repairs

See full listing in **Section One** under **Austin-Healey**

Motormetrics 6369 Houston Rd Macon, GA 31216 912-785-0275 E-mail: fzampa@cennet.mc.peachnet.edu	used parts

Mail order. TR3, Morris Minor, MG Midget, MGA, Austin Seven, Alfa Romeo and Fiat X-19 used parts. Free price list with SASE.

NOS Locators 587 Pawtucket Ave Pawtucket, RI 02860 401-725-5000	parts

See full listing in **Section One** under **MG**

Omni Specialties 10418 Lorain Ave Cleveland, OH 44111 888-819-6464 (MGMG) 216-251-2269; FAX: 216-251-6083	parts restoration service

See full listing in **Section One** under **MG**

Pacific International Auto 1118 Garnet Ave San Diego, CA 92109 619-274-1920; FAX: 619-454-1815	parts sales service

See full listing in **Section One** under **Jaguar**

Peninsula Imports 3749 Harlem Rd Buffalo, NY 14215 800-999-1209; FAX: 905-847-3021 E-mail: imports@ican.net	accessories parts trim

See full listing in **Section One** under **BMW**

Ragtops & Roadsters 203 S 4th St Perkasie, PA 18944 215-257-1202; FAX: 215-257-2688 E-mail: info@ragtops.com	bodywork/painting British automobiles engine rebuilding vintage race prep

See full listing in **Section Two** under **restoration shops**

The Roadster Factory 328 Killen Rd PO Box 332 Armagh, PA 15920 800-234-1104; FAX: 814-446-6729	accessories parts

Telephone orders Monday-Thursday 8 am to 9 pm; Friday-Saturday 8 am to 6 pm EST; counter sales Monday-Saturday 8 am to 6 pm. Original components and accessories for Triumph TR2 through TR8, Spitfire, GT6 and MGB. Manufacturer of high quality replacement parts. Minor components to rebuilt units and nuts and bolts to body shells. Company owned and operated by Triumph and MGB enthusiasts since 1978. Free catalogs. Web site: www.the-roadster-factory.com

Smooth Line 2562 Riddle Run Rd Tarentum, PA 15084 724-274-6002; FAX: 724-274-6121	body panels removable hardtops

See full listing in **Section Two** under **tops**

Special Interest Car Parts 1340 Hartford Ave Johnston, RI 02919 800-556-7496; FAX: 401-831-7760	parts

See full listing in **Section One** under **Jaguar**

Sports Car Haven 2-33 Flowerfield Industrial Pk St James, NY 11780 516-862-8058 E-mail: sch94@aol.com	race prep restorations service

Mail order and open shop. Monday-Friday 9 am to 6 pm, Saturday 9 am to 2 pm. Over 30 years' experience in service, restorations, race prep and parts for British and other sports cars. SCCA and vintage race cars prepped. Triumph engine thrust washer problems solved. Authorized Moss distributor.

Sports Car Haven 3414 Bloom Rd, Rt 11 Danville, PA 17821 570-275-5705	parts restoration service

See full listing in **Section One** under **MG**

Sports Car Tours Inc PO Box 265 Batesville, VA 22924 804-823-4442 E-mail: napol@rlc.net	back road tours

See full listing in **Section Two** under **special services**

Sports & Classics PO Box 1787 512 Boston Post Rd, Dept H Darien, CT 06820-1787	parts

See full listing in **Section Two** under **body parts**

The Registry Pine Grove Stanley, VA 22851 540-778-3728; FAX: 540-778-2402 E-mail: britregstry@aol.com or oldwregistry@aol.com	periodical

See full listing in **Section Four** under **periodicals**

Thoroughbred Motors 3935 N US 301 Sarasota, FL 34234 941-359-2277; FAX: 941-359-2128	parts sales service

See full listing in **Section One** under **Jaguar**

Triple C Motor Accessories 1900 Orange St York, PA 17404 717-854-4081; FAX: 717-854-6706 E-mail: sales@triple-c.com	accessories models

See full listing in **Section One** under **MG**

Triumph World Magazine PO Box 75 Tadworth Surrey KT20 7XF England 01737 814311; FAX: 01737 814591 E-mail: triumphworld@chp.ltd.uk	periodical

Triumph World magazine is a bi-monthly, top quality magazine devoted entirely to the ever-popular classic cars produced under the Triumph banner, such famous sports car models that carry the marque name to the four corners of the globe. The TR range, Spitfire and Stag plus those other unique models that epitomize the best of British styling and engineering. Subscription: $37/year (6 issues). Web site: www.chp.ltd.uk

Victoria British Ltd
Box 14991
Lenexa, KS 66285-4991
800-255-0088, 913-599-3299

accessories
parts

See full listing in **Section One** under **MG**

Victory Autoservices
Box 5060, RR 1
W Baldwin, ME 04091
207-625-4581

parts
restoration

See full listing in **Section One** under **Austin-Healey**

Von's Austin-Healey Restorations
10270 Barberville Rd
Fort Mill, SC 29715
803-548-4590; FAX: 803-548-4816
E-mail: vons@vnet.net

parts
repairs
restoration

See full listing in **Section One** under **Austin-Healey**

J Wood & Co Auctioneers
RR 1 Box 316
Stockton Springs, ME 04981
207-567-4250; FAX: 207-567-4252
E-mail: jwoodandco@mindspring.com

auctions

See full listing in **Section Two** under **auctions & events**

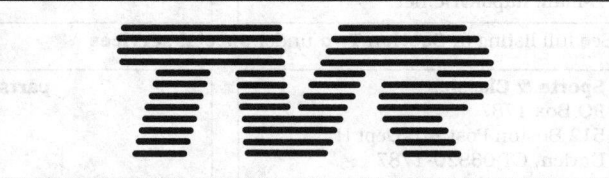

Cambridge Motorsport
Caxton Rd
Great Gransden, NR Sandy
Beds SG19 3AH England
0044 1767 677969
FAX: 0044 1767 677026
E-mail:
cambridge.motorsport@dial.pipex.com

parts
race tuning

See full listing in **Section One** under **Triumph**

Classic Motor Works
100 Station St
Johnstown, PA 15905
814-288-6911; FAX: 814-288-4455
E-mail: birdcmw@aol.com

parts

New and used parts for TVR sports cars from Grantura to 280i.

JAE
375 Pine #26
Goleta, CA 93117
805-967-5767; FAX: 805-967-6183
E-mail: jefforjay@jaeparts.com

parts
service
tech info

See full listing in **Section One** under **Lotus**

Sports Car Haven
3414 Bloom Rd, Rt 11
Danville, PA 17821
570-275-5705

parts
restoration
service

See full listing in **Section One** under **MG**

Triple C Motor Accessories
1900 Orange St
York, PA 17404
717-854-4081; FAX: 717-854-6706
E-mail: sales@triple-c.com

accessories
models

See full listing in **Section One** under **MG**

UK Spares/TVR Sports Cars
609 Highland St
Wethersfield, CT 06109-3979
PH/FAX: 860-563-1647
FAX: 860-529-3479
E-mail: tvr.sports.cars@juno.com

accessories
car covers
convertible tops
ignition parts
suspension parts

Mail order only. Specializing in TVR parts, service, restoration for all years/models TVR. Also supply parts for all other British cars. US importer. Lucas/Girling, Spax, Centerforce clutches, Lumenition ignition, MSD ignition, K&N filters, Bel-Ray synthetic lubricants, Hayden fans, Deves piston rings, Gunson's (UK) specialty tools including Colortune, polyurethane bushings, cross-drilled/vented rotors, best custom-fit car covers/floor mats, convertible tops, replaceable bulb headlamps/aux lighting, OEM seatbelts, lug nuts, aluminum valve covers, door mirrors, books/manuals, accessories, giftware, authentic English picnic baskets.

Vanden Plas

From Rust To Riches
16643 Rt 144
Mt Airy, MD 21771
301-854-5900, 410-442-3637
301-854-5956; FAX: 301-854-5957
E-mail: tatrabill@aol.com

appraisals
car dealer
repairs
restoration

See full listing in **Section Two** under **restoration shops**

Kip Motor Company Inc
2127 Crown Rd
Dallas, TX 75229
972-243-0440; FAX: 972-243-2387
E-mail: kipmotor@aol.com

literature
parts
restoration

See full listing in **Section One** under **Austin**

4 ever 4
Rt 10
Marlow, NH 03456
877-4EVER4-VW, 603-446-7820

car dealer
parts
service

Mail order and open shop. Monday-Friday 9 am to 6 pm, Thursday 9 am to 9 pm, weekends by prior appointment only. Specializing in Volkswagen parts and services for air cooled vehicles. Purchases and sells vehicles, toys, parts and literature, full service shop, many NOS parts and thousands of tagged and tested used parts, UPS daily. Involved with VW since 1967. A friendly, one man business. No catalog. We love all Vanagons. Web site: www.4evr4-vw-aircl-allvans.com

The Auto Doctor Inc | mechanical parts
23125 Telegraph Rd | service repairs
Southfield, MI 48034
248-355-1505; FAX: 248-355-3460

See full listing in **Section One** under **BMW**

Bentley Publishers | books
1734 Massachusetts Ave | manuals
Cambridge, MA 02138-1804
800-423-4595; FAX: 617-876-9235
E-mail: sales@rb.com

See full listing in **Section Four** under **books & publications**

Discount Auto Parts | salvage yard
4703 Broadway SE
Albuquerque, NM 87105
505-877-6782

See full listing in **Section Five** under **New Mexico**

European Parts Specialists Ltd | accessories
PO Box 6783 | parts
Santa Barbara, CA 93160
800-334-2749, 805-683-4020
FAX: 805-683-3689
E-mail: epsparts@impulse.net

See full listing in **Section One** under **Mercedes-Benz**

John's Car Corner | body parts
Rt 5, PO Box 85 | car dealer
Westminster, VT 05158 | mechanical parts
802-722-3180; FAX: 802-722-3181 | restoration service
E-mail: johnscc@sover.net

Mail order and open shop. Monday-Friday 8 am to 5 pm, Saturday 9 am to 12 pm. Millions of new and used parts for Volkswagen and Audi, all years and all models. Over 30 years in business.

Karmann Ghia Parts & Restoration | parts
PO Box 997
Ventura, CA 93002
800-927-2787; FAX: 805-641-3333
E-mail: info@karmannghia.com

Mail order. Wholesale/retail. Parts, new and used for Volkswagen Karmann Ghias, all years. Manufacturers and importers for all parts (except engine and transmission) for all years of Karmann Ghias. Web site: karmannghia.com

Last Chance Repair & Restoration | repairs
PO Box 362A | restoration
Myers Rd
Shaftsbury, VT 05262

See full listing in **Section Two** under **restoration shops**

People Kars | models/more
290 Third Ave Ext | VW toys
Rensselaer, NY 12144
518-465-0477; FAX: 518-465-0614
E-mail: peoplekars@aol.com

Mail order and shows. Specializing in toys, models and collectibles for all types and years of Volkswagens. People Kars feature VW models from Vitesse, Solido, Mini Champs, Shabak, Siku and more plus an extensive collection of older discontinued models, toys and promotional pieces, all with the VW enthusiast in mind. Please contact for current catalog/list.

The Real Source | accessories
PO Box 1248 | parts
Effingham, IL 62401
800-LUV-BUGG (588-2844), dept VS9
FAX: 217-347-2952
E-mail: madbug@madvet.com

The Real Source™ of parts and accessories for your Volkswagen!

From VW's claim to fame, the Bug, to Karmann Ghia, Bus, Type 3 and Thing, this free full-color catalog is geared to your air-cooled 1950-1979 and New Beetle. Highlights restoration, performance and custom components, as well as accessories, apparel, collectibles and much more.

Stormin Norman's Bug Shop | repair
201 Commerce Dr #3 | restoration
Fort Collins, CO 80524
970-493-5873

Open Tuesday-Friday 8 am to 5:30 pm. Repair and complete restoration services for Volkswagen Beetles.

Tabco Inc | body parts
11655 Chillicothe Rd
Chesterland, OH 44026-1994
216-921-5850; FAX: 216-921-5862

See full listing in **Section Two** under **sheetmetal**

TMI Products Inc | classic car
191 Granite St | interiors
Corona, CA 91719
800-624-7960, 909-272-1996
FAX: 909-272-1584
E-mail: tmiprods@aol.com

The largest manufacturer of quality replacement upholstery trim products for classic cars. Specializing in Volkswagen models from 1949-1993 and Mustang from 1964-1/2 to 1973. TMI offers the finest trim products available today. Featuring all the correct colors, grains and patterns that are guaranteed to fit. Best of all the Mustang upholstery is MCA approved. Call or write today for your free catalog and local distributor. Please specify model of car. Web site: www.tmiproducts.com

Vintage Auto LLC | new/used parts
605 Pine Knoll Dr | service
Greenville, SC 29609
864-292-8785; FAX: 864-967-0195
E-mail: vintagevw@aol.com

Mail order and open shop. Monday-Friday 8 am to 6 pm, Saturday 9 am to 1 pm. Volkswagen and Honda service, new and used parts, preowned cars. All years and models. We offer all stock and custom parts for VWs, both air and water cooled. Service all Hondas. Have 50+ parts cars to sell used parts off of. 20+ preowned VWs and Hondas. Web site: vintageonline.com

Volkswagen Collectors | literature
c/o Jerry Jess | memorabilia
3121 E Yucca St | toys
Phoenix, AZ 85028-2616
PH/FAX: 602-867-7672
E-mail: vwstuff@uswest.net

Mail order only. Collectors of Volkswagen. Toys, literature, memorabilia, cars and accessories. Buy, sell and trade VWs and have been for 20+ years. Also locate or sell your VW for free. Send $1 for illustrated catalog. Web site: www.mindspring.com/~deasterw/jess/jess.html

West Coast Metric Inc | apparel
24002 Frampton Ave | carpets
Harbor City, CA 90710 | plastic parts
310-325-0005; FAX: 310-325-9733 | rubber parts
E-mail: wcm@westcoastmetric.com

Mail order and open shop. Monday-Friday 7 am to 5 pm PST. Specializing in quality rubber and plastic restoration parts for 1946-1999 Volkswagens, including Bugs, buses, Ghias, Type IIIs, Vanagons, Things and new Beetles. VW apparel, upholstery, carpets, grille emblems, badges, mirrors, lenses, hardware, car covers and more. Web site: www.westcoastmetric.com

Section One
Marque Specialists

VOLVO

Dick Ames Stainless Steel Exhaust | **exhaust systems**
4850 Fallcrest Cir
Sarasota, FL 34233
941-923-8321; FAX: 941-923-9434
E-mail: dickamesfl@aol.com

See full listing in **Section One** under **Jaguar**

Brasilia Press | **models**
PO Box 2023
Elkhart, IN 46515
FAX: 219-262-8799

See full listing in **Section Two** under **models & toys**

Celestial Mechanics | **restoration**
88 West 500 South
Wellsville, UT 84339
435-245-4987
E-mail: volvox@cache.net

Mail order and open shop. Weekends 7 am to 7 pm. Small shop where we average one loving restoration per year. No detail is too small. Projects begin in spring and are completed in the fall. Minor projects welcomed anytime. We are expensive but will barter. Specializing in Volvo 1800 models 1961-1969 and Mercedes-Benz 1960s.

Chicago Classic Imports | **parts** **service**
6948 N Western Ave
Chicago, IL 60645
773-381-2600; FAX: 773-381-2616
E-mail:
saab@chicagoclassicimports.com

See full listing in **Section One** under **Saab**

Concours Cars of Colorado Ltd | **accessories** **parts** **service**
2414 W Cucharras St
Colorado Springs, CO 80904
719-473-6288; FAX: 719-473-9206

See full listing in **Section One** under **BMW**

Dan's Volvo Service | **restoration**
6615 S MacDill Ave
Tampa, FL 33611
813-831-1616

Open Monday-Friday 9 am to 5 pm. Complete repair and restoration service on all vintage PV544, 122-S, 1800-S Volvos, parts.

European Parts Specialists Ltd | **accessories** **parts**
PO Box 6783
Santa Barbara, CA 93160
800-334-2749, 805-683-4020
FAX: 805-683-3689
E-mail: epsparts@impulse.net

See full listing in **Section One** under **Mercedes-Benz**

Foreign Autotech | **parts**
3235 C Sunset Ln
Hatboro, PA 19040
215-441-4421; FAX: 215-441-4490
E-mail: fap1800@aol.com

Specializing in new, reproduction and used parts for Volvo P1800, P, S, E and ES Models 1961-1973. As the world's largest supplier of P1800 parts we are continually developing reproduc-tion parts that have long been out of production. Our engineering skills (proven by our domination of the 1997 and 1998 Volvo Historics Vintage Racing Championships) enable us to exceed the quality of OEM parts. In addition to vast stocks of new parts, we have used parts from over 150 donor cars. Web site: www.foreignautotech.com

Pete Groh | **original British** **keys**
9957 Frederick Rd
Ellicott City, MD 21042-3647
410-750-2352; FAX: 410-466-3566
E-mail: petegroh@yahoo.com

See full listing in **Section One** under **Jaguar**

David Hueppchen | **parts** **service**
N 6808 Hwy OJ
PO Box 540
Plymouth, WI 53073
920-893-2531; FAX: 920-893-6800
E-mail: ojrallye@excel.net

Mail order and open shop. Monday-Friday 9 am to 12 pm, 2 pm to 6 pm. New and used parts, service by appointment for Volvo 122, 140, 1800, 240 and 262C Bertone coupe. Over 40 driver and parts cars on hand. Restoration, vintage race preparation also done. Importer of high tech Swedish headers, cams and much more for Volvo ohv and sohc motors. Web site: www.vclassics.com/ojrallye.htm

Italy's Famous Exhaust | **exhaust systems** **wheels**
2711 183rd St
Redondo Beach, CA 90278
310-793-5985
E-mail: famous@earthlink.net

See full listing in **Section Two** under **exhaust systems**

London Stainless Steel Exhaust Centre | **exhaust systems**
249-253 Queenstown Rd
London, SW8 3NP England
011-44-171622-2120
FAX: 011-44-171627-0991
E-mail: 101445.341@compuserv.com

See full listing in **Section Two** under **exhaust systems**

Paul Padget | **sales**
7641 Reinhold Dr
Cincinnati, OH 45237
513-821-2143

See full listing in **Section One** under **Mercedes-Benz**

Lyle Pearson Company | **accessories** **literature** **parts**
351 Auto Dr
Boise, ID 83709
208-377-3900; FAX: 208-375-0691

See full listing in **Section One** under **Mercedes-Benz**

R E Pierce | **parts** **restoration**
47 Stone Rd
Wendell Depot, MA 01380
978-544-7442; FAX: 978-544-2978
E-mail: robin@billsgate.com

Tires to roofrack restorations on 122s, P-1800s and 140s. 18 years' of collecting and restoring classic Volvos. 78 parts cars and stock piles of used parts. Free estimates, reasonable prices. Located in northcentral MA, near Orange/Athol. Call for an appointment.

Rayce Inc | **parts**
4656 SW 75th Ave
Miami, FL 33155
800-426-2221, 305-261-3355
FAX: 305-261-3615

See full listing in **Section One** under **Alfa Romeo**

Rogers Motors
25 Leverett Rd
Shutesbury, MA 01072
413-259-1722
E-mail: akor@ent.umass.edu

used parts

See full listing in **Section One** under **Jaguar**

Swedish Classics Inc
PO Box 557
Oxford, MD 21654
800-258-4422; FAX: 410-226-5543

parts

Restoration and repair parts for vintage and new Volvos. Web site: swedishclassics.com

Voluparts Inc
751 Trabert Ave NW
Atlanta, GA 30318
404-352-3402; FAX: 404-352-1077
E-mail: voluparts@mindspring.com

parts

Mail order and open shop. Monday-Friday 9 am to 6 pm. 18,000 square foot warehouse. New, used and rebuilt Volvo parts. Web site: voluparts.com

Volvo Shop Inc
5220 New Milford Rd
Ravenna, OH 44266
330-297-1297
E-mail: volvocarl@aol.com

**parts
restoration**

Volvos from mid 1950s-1990s. Have new and used parts for P1800, 544, 122, 140, 240, 700, 900 Series, also complete cars for parts or restoration.

Antiques Warehouse
Michael J Welch
3700 Rt 6
Eastham, MA 02642
508-255-1437; FAX: 508-247-9166
E-mail: miketoys1@aol.com

**automobilia
bikes
toy trucks**

See full listing in **Section Two** under **models & toys**

Garton's Auto
401 N 5th St (at 5th & Vine)
Millville, NJ 08332-3129
609-825-3618

**bicycles
Ford NOS parts
sales literature**

See full listing in **Section One** under **Ford 1932-1953**

Marky D's Bikes & Pedal Goods
7047 Springridge Rd
West Bloomfield, MI 48322
810-737-1657; FAX: 810-398-2581

**bicycles
mopeds
motorbikes
pedal goods**

See full listing in **Section Two** under **bicycles**

Brian's 4wd Parts LLC
428 N Harbor St
Branford, CT 06405
PH/FAX: 203-481-5873
E-mail: willysgp@aol.com

**literature
parts**

Mail order and open shop. Monday-Friday 9 am to 5 pm, weekends by chance or appointment. Parts and literature for Jeep vehicles produced by Willys, Kaiser and AMC. New, used, rebuilt and NOS parts available. Full or partial restoration services available for any year or make Jeep vehicle. Single component or full rebuild to your satisfaction. Active buyers of Jeep literature, vehicles and collectibles. New Jeep enthusiasts always welcome.

Classic Enterprises
Box 92
Barron, WI 54812
715-537-5422

sheetmetal

See full listing in **Section One** under **Studebaker**

Cockermouth Motor Museum
The Maltings
Brewery Ln
Cockermouth Cumbria England
01900 824448

museum

See full listing in **Section Six** under **England**

**Commonwealth Automotive
Restorations**
1725 Hewins St
Ashley Falls, MA 01222
413-229-3196

**body rebuilding
parts
restoration**

See full listing in **Section Two** under **military vehicles**

The Jeepster Man
238 Ramtown Greenville Rd
Howell, NJ 07731
732-458-3966; FAX: 732-458-9289

**literature
parts**

Mail order and open shop. Monday-Friday 9 am to 5 pm; Saturday 9 am to 12 noon. Large selection of Jeep and Jeepster parts. Send 75¢ SASE and model designation for free list. Shop manuals for all Willys vehicles. Contact The Jeepster Man for all hard to find parts. New items, horn rings, car covers, sunvisors, choke cables, o/s mirrors.

Mike's Auto Parts
Box 358
Ridgeland, MS 39158
601-856-7214

**ball/roller bearings
engine parts
wall calendars
water pumps**

See full listing in **Section One** under **Chrysler**

Obsolete Jeep® & Willys® Parts
Division of Florida 4 Wheel Drive &
Truck Parts
6110 17th St E
Bradenton, FL 34203
941-756-7844
PH/FAX: 941-756-7757

**literature
parts**

Mail order and open shop. Monday-Friday 11 am to 6 pm. Jeep/Willys parts. New, used, rebuilt, NOS, hard-to-find, manuals. Bought out many dealers, dismantled many vehicles. Shipping nationwide daily. Try us! Web site: www.hotbyte.com/fl4wd/

| **John E Parker**
4860 N Desert Tortoise Pl
Tucson, AZ 85745-9213
520-743-3574 | **plastic repros
rubber parts** |

See full listing in **Section One** under **Kaiser Frazer**

| **Quality Tire Barn Inc**
255 Twinsburg Rd
Northfield, OH 44067
330-467-1284 | **tires** |

See full listing in **Section Two** under **tires**

| **Space Farms Zoo & Museum**
218 Rt 519
Sussex, NJ 07461
973-875-3223; FAX: 973-875-9397
E-mail: fpspace@warwick.net | **museum
zoo** |

See full listing in **Section Six** under **New Jersey**

| **Whippet Resource Center**
John Olson
1241 23000 Rd
Parsons, KS 67357
316-421-0643 | **literature
memorabilia** |

Specializing in literature, information, memorabilia for Whippet cars and trucks, all years, 1926-1931. Providing information about Whippets, buying literature and memorabilia about Whippets.

| **Willys America**
PO Box 538
Cazadero, CA 95421
707-632-5258 | **parts
restoration** |

Monday-Saturday by appointment. Parts, restoration and repow-er conversions for 1946-1964 Willys trucks, wagons, Jeepster and Delivery. Many restored vehicles on display. Web site: www.willysamerica.com

| **The Willys Man**
Ron Ladley
1850 Valley Forge Rd
Lansdale, PA 19446
610-584-1665; FAX: 610-584-8537 | **literature
parts
vehicles** |

Mail order and open shop. Weeknights and weekends. Supplier and adviser of 1933-1942 Willys cars, trucks, parts and literature for over 35 years (no post-war Willys Jeep parts or fwd parts).

| **Willys Wood**
35336 Chaucer Dr
North Ridgeville, OH 44039
440-327-2916 | **wood parts** |

Mail order only. Replacement body wood for 1933/1936, 1940/1941 Willys coupes, sedan deliveries and pickups, steel or fiberglass, stock or chopped. Kits or individual pieces available. Call or write for illustrated price list.

| **Willys Works Inc**
1933 W Gardner Ln
Tucson, AZ 85705
520-888-5082 | **car dealer
parts
restoration
service** |

Mail order and open shop. Tuesday-Friday 10 am to 6 pm, Saturday 9 am to 4 pm. Primarily mechanical parts and Jeep universal, utility wagon and pickup, vintage and modern.

Zimmer

| **Zimmer Neo-Classic Motor Car Co**
1415 W Genesee St
Syracuse, NY 13204
315-422-7011 ext 125
FAX: 315-422-1721
E-mail: newtimes@rway.com | **manufacturing** |

Mail order and open shop. Monday-Friday 9 am to 5 pm. Specializing in Zimmer Golden Spirit vintage autos for 1979-1998 Zimmers. Manufacturing 1997-1998 Zimmer Golden Spirit motor cars. Deals in Zimmer Golden Spirit and Zimmer Quicksilver. Web site: www.nyautos.com

See our ad on this page

Tourguide:
Marque Specialists

Planning a trip? Or perhaps you would just like to know what old-car resources are in your home territory. In either case, the tourguide to Section One will help.

This tourguide offers you an alphabetical listing of marque specialists with open shops by state and foreign country. Simply turn to the page number indicated for complete information on the object of your visit, including hours of operation, complete address, and phone number.

Alabama

- 82   Good Old Days Garage Inc, Birmingham
- 135   Mercedes-Benz Visitor Center, Tuscaloosa

Arizona

- 25   Art's Antique & Classic Auto Services, Tempe
- 133   Blitzen Enterprises Inc, Scottsdale
- 58   Cn'V Corvette Sales, Tempe
- 125   Delta Motorsports Inc, Phoenix
- 53   Desert Muscle Cars, Tucson
- 43   Fred's Truck Parts, Tucson
- 101   Gemini Racing Systems Inc, Chandler
- 27   GM Obsolete, Phoenix
- 16   Heinze Enterprise, Scottsdale
- 43   Hidden Valley Auto Parts, Maricopa
- 125   John E Parker, Tucson
- 48   Patrick's Antique Cars & Trucks, Casa Grande
- 62   Performance Chevy, Phoenix
- 98   Sanderson Ford, Glendale
- 22   Southwest Avanti Sales & Service, Phoenix
- 137   Star Classics Inc, Scottsdale
- 111   T-Bird Specialists, Tucson
- 111   Thunderbird, Falcon & Fairlane Connections, Phoenix
- 99   Vintage Ford & Chevrolet Parts of Arizona Inc, Phoenix
- 186   Willys Works Inc, Tucson

Arkansas

- 95   Jerry's Classic Cars & Parts Inc, Springdale
- 67   Dan Rook, Mena

California

- 132   A&F Imported Parts Inc, Oakland
- 15   All American Rambler, Fountain Valley
- 163   Alpha Omega Motorsport, Gardena
- 176   Arthur W Aseltine, Forbestown
- 91   Autowire Division, Rosemead
- 167   Best Deal, Stanton
- 37   Boyds Hot Rods & Collectable Cars, Stanton
- 174   British Pacific Ltd, Burbank
- 20   British Wire Wheel, Santa Cruz
- 26   Buick Bonery, Sacramento
- 37   Bumper Boyz LLC, Los Angeles
- 85   C & G Early Ford Parts, Escondido
- 30   California Collectors' Classics (CCC), Irwindale
- 85   Car Controls Div, Rosemead
- 79   Caribou Imports Inc, Lake Forest
- 52   Chevyland Parts & Accessories, Rancho Cordova
- 30   Ed Cholakian Enterprises Inc, Sylmar
- 26   Classic Buicks Inc, Chino
- 31   Coopers Vintage Auto Parts, Burbank
- 58   Corvette Mike, Anaheim
- 58   Corvette Pacifica, Atascadero
- 23   CSi, Fullerton
- 40   Custom Autosound Mfg, Anaheim
- 40   Danchuk Mfg, Santa Ana
- 71   DeLorean One, Chatsworth
- 120   Doctor Jaguar Inc, Costa Mesa
- 120   Doug's British Car Parts, Pasadena
- 59   Doug's Corvette Service, North Hollywood
- 167   Driven By Design, Carmel
- 77   Drummond Coach and Paint, El Cajon
- 59   EC Products Design Inc, Atascadero
- 53   The El Camino Store, Goleta
- 81   Ford Obsolete, Rosemead
- 17   Gordon Imports Inc, Santa Fe Springs
- 60   Guldstrand Engineering Inc, Culver City
- 73   Hall Pantera, Paramount
- 171   Tony Handler Inc, Los Angeles
- 94   Highway Classics, San Dimas
- 13   Highway One Classic Automobiles and Highwayone.com Classic Classifieds, Burlingame
- 169   Jacques Rear Engine Renault Parts, El Cajon
- 131   JAE, Goleta
- 121   Jaguar Heaven Auto Dismantler, Stockton
- 108   Larry's Thunderbird and Mustang Parts Inc, Fullerton
- 129   Lincoln Parts International, Perris
- 141   Metropolitan Pit Stop, North Hollywood
- 46   Mike's Chevy Parts, Canoga Park
- 149   MikeCo Antique, Kustom & Obsolete Auto Parts, Camarillo
- 136   Millers Incorporated, Huntington Beach
- 19   Mini Mania, Milpitas
- 144   Moss Motors Ltd, Goleta
- 115   Moto Italia, Petaluma
- 71   Motorsport Auto, Orange
- 103   Mustang Service Center, North Hollywood
- 104   Mustangs & More, Ventura
- 80   C Obert & Co, Santa Cruz
- 145   O'Connor Classic Autos, Santa Clara
- 47   Old Chevy Parts Store, San Marcos
- 165   Original Parts Group Inc, Huntington Beach
- 73   Pantera Parts Connection, Mountain View
- 33   Piru Cads, Piru
- 109   Prestige Thunderbird Inc, Santa Fe Springs
- 89   Red's Headers & Early Ford Speed Equipment, Fort Bragg
- 49   Restoration Specialties, Lompoc
- 162   Restorations By Julius, Chatsworth
- 173   Rolls-Royce of Beverly Hills, Los Angeles
- 89   Sacramento Vintage Ford Parts, Rancho Cordova
- 137   Showroom Auto Sales, San Jose
- 98   SoCal Pickups Inc, Buena Park
- 56   The Source Inc, Del Mar
- 178   Specter Off-Road Inc, Chatsworth
- 54   Steve's Camaros, San Bruno
- 177   Studebaker of California, Long Beach
- 177   Studebakers West, Redwood City
- 178   Sunbeam Specialties, Los Gatos
- 22   Ed Swart Motors Inc, Torrance
- 111   T-Birds By Nick, Panorama City
- 173   Teddy's Garage, Northridge
- 111   Thunderbird Headquarters, Concord
- 105   TMC (Traction Master Co), Los Angeles
- 55   True Connections, Riverside
- 84   Vintage Speed Parts, Rosemead
- 124   Ed West CARS, Tustin
- 183   West Coast Metric Inc, Harbor City
- 169   Willhoit Auto Restoration, Long Beach
- 124   XKs Unlimited, San Luis Obispo

Colorado

- 14   Centerline Products, Boulder
- 135   House of Imports Inc, Lakewood
- 103   Mustang Classics, Denver

Section One
Marque Specialists

73 Pantera Performance Center, Castle Rock
168 Restoration Services, Golden
176 Royal Gorge Studebaker, Florence
98 Sam's Vintage Ford Parts, Denver
183 Stormin Norman's Bug Shop, Fort Collins
125 Walker's Auto Pride Inc, Peyton

Connecticut

14 Alfas Unlimited Inc, Norfolk
127 Baker's Auto-SRO Inc, Putnam
185 Brian's 4wd Parts LLC, Branford
143 British T Shop Inc, Oakdale
81 CT Model A Parts & Service, West Hartford
154 Fusick Automotive Products, East Windsor
82 Joe Lagana, Canterbury
103 Mostly Mustangs Inc, Hamden
104 Mustangs Unlimited, Manchester
159 Packard Store, Sterling
49 PRO Antique Auto Parts, Windsor Locks

Delaware

120 East Coast Jaguar, Wilmington

Florida

15 American Performance Products, Cocoa
154 Anderson Automotive, Tampa
37 Bow Tie Chevy Association, Orlando
101 Classic Auto Air Mfg Co, Tampa
39 Classic Chevy International, Orlando
101 Classic Creations of Central Florida, Lakeland
184 Dan's Volvo Service, Tampa
108 Hollywood Classic Motorcars Inc, Hallandale
129 Lincoln Land Inc, Clearwater
129 Lincoln Old Parts Store, Tampa
80 Linearossa International Inc, Ft Lauderdale
153 Lucky Lee Lott (Author), Tampa
135 Mercedes-Benz Service by Angela & George/ABS Exotic Repair Inc, Fort Lauderdale
78 Motorcar Gallery Inc, Fort Lauderdale
185 Obsolete Jeep® & Willys® Parts, Bradenton
173 Omega Automobile Appraisals, St Petersburg
173 Powers Parts Inc, Anna Maria
173 Proper Motor Cars Inc, St Petersburg
63 Rogers Corvette Center, Maitland
123 Thoroughbred Motors, Sarasota
173 Vantage Motorworks Inc, North Miami
124 Vicarage Jaguar, Miami Beach

Georgia

79 Bayless Inc, Marietta
68 Cobra Restorers Ltd, Kennesaw
82 Hancock's Engine Rebuilders and Balancing Service, Athens
96 Melvin's Classic Ford Parts Inc, Lithonia
46 Monroe Motorsports Inc, Lithonia
47 Obsolete Chevrolet Parts Co, Nashville
97 Obsolete Ford Parts Co, Nashville
54 Rick's First Generation Camaro Parts & Accessories, Athens
90 Joe Smith Ford & Hot Rod Parts, Marietta
50 The Truck Shop, Nashville
185 Voluparts Inc, Atlanta

Idaho

136 Lyle Pearson Company, Boise
124 Vintage Jag Works, Blackfoot

Illinois

80 Bob's Antique Auto Parts Inc, Rockford
142 British Auto Shoppe, Moline
114 Charleston Custom Cycle, Charleston
175 Chicago Classic Imports, Chicago

58 Chicago Corvette Supply, Justice
59 D&M Corvette Specialists Ltd, Downers Grove
114 Dale's Harley-Davidson of Mt Vernon, Mt Vernon
135 Horst's Car Care, Decatur
44 Kessler's Antique Cars & Body Shop, Olney
115 Luback & Co, Chicago Heights
150 Special T's Unlimited Corp, Prospect Heights
123 Terry's Jaguar Parts Inc, Benton
138 Willow Automotive Service Inc, Lake Bluff

Indiana

170 Albers Rolls-Royce, Zionsville
91 Blint Equipment Inc, LaPorte
163 Dick Choler Cars & Service Inc, Elkhart
40 Custom Classic Cars, Bourbon
167 Doc & Cy's Restoration Parts, Indianapolis
122 Muncie Imports & Classics, Muncie
159 Packard Farm, Greenfield
104 The Paddock® Inc, Knightstown
63 Jack Podell Fuel Injection Spec, South Bend
50 Sound Move Inc, Elkhart
115 TK Performance Inc, Evansville
16 Webb's Classic Auto Parts, Huntington

Iowa

165 Kurt Kelsey, Iowa Falls
46 Merv's Classic Chevy Parts, Iowa Falls
75 Vintage Power Wagons Inc, Fairfield

Kansas

150 Wheels & Spokes Inc, Hays

Kentucky

50 Strader Classics, Elizabethtown

Louisiana

170 Bassett Classic Restoration, Kenner

Maine

80 Bryant's Antique Auto Parts, Hampden
137 SL-Tech 230SL-250SL-280SL, Arundel/Kennebunkport
22 Victory Autoservices, West Baldwin

Maryland

57 Andover Automotive Inc, Laurel
71 Banzai Motorworks, Beltsville
59 Corvette Specialties of MD Inc, Eldersburg
31 Driving Passion Ltd USA, Clarksville
20 Healey Surgeons Inc, Takoma Park
83 Myers Model A Ford Parts, Mustang & Car Trailers, Williamsport

Massachusetts

18 Austin Works East, Sandwich
132 Auto Enthusiasts, Chelsea
120 Crow Engineering Jaguar Engines, Taunton
171 Foreign Motors West, Natick
81 Freeman's Garage, Norton
113 GMC Solutions, Franklin
164 Green's Obsolete Parts, Pepperell
134 Hatch & Sons Automotive Inc, Wayland
44 J & K Old Chevy Stuff, Plymouth
82 Lang's Old Car Parts Inc, Winchendon
140 Mercury & Ford Molded Rubber, Wilmington
83 PV Antique & Classic Ford, Tewksbury
65 Wild Bill's Corvette & Hi-Performance Center Inc, Wrentham

Michigan

166 356 Enterprises, Warren
147 Antique Mopar Auto Sales, Hale
22 The Auto Doctor Inc, Southfield

38 CARS Inc, Berkley
55 Classic Car Care, Ionia
59 Corvette Rubber Company, Cadillac
128 Buzz De Clerck, Sterling Heights
86 Fairlane Automotive Specialties, St Johns
139 John's Classic Cougars, Holland
135 Lyco Engineering Inc, Plymouth
62 Michigan Corvette Recyclers, Riga
22 Nostalgic Motor Cars, Wixom
62 Paragon Reproductions Inc, Swartz Creek
111 Thunderbird Center, Hazel Park
146 University Motors Ltd, Ada

Minnesota
81 Classtique Upholstery & Top Co, Isanti
95 Joe's Auto Sales, Hastings
95 Lares Manufacturing, Ham Lake
46 National Chevy Assoc, St Paul

Mississippi
180 Golden Gulf Classics Inc, Saucier

Missouri
38 Chevy Duty Pickup Parts, Kansas City
95 L B Repair, Savannah
78 Motorcars International, Springfield

Nevada
107 Concours Parts & Accessories, Carson City

New Hampshire
182 4 ever 4, Marlow
142 Abingdon Spares Ltd, Walpole
22 Bavarian Autosport, Portsmouth
118 British Auto/USA, Manchester
86 Early Ford Engines, Claremont
74 Fitzgerald Motorsports, Laconia
178 Land Cruiser Solutions Inc, Newton
144 McLean's Brit Bits, Rye
96 Northeast Ford, East Sullivan

New Jersey
57 Antique Cars, Parts & Trains, Millville
120 Eddie's Restorations, Elwood
42 Fifties Forever, Garfield
87 Half Ton Fun, Jackson
185 The Jeepster Man, Howell
45 LES Auto Parts, Dayton
138 Mercer Automobile Company, Magnolia
48 Passenger Car Supply, Swedesboro
150 Rechrome Parts Ltd, Mendham
110 Sunyaks, Bound Brook
111 Pat Wilson's Thunderbird Parts, New Milford

New Mexico
99 Valley Motor Supply, Roswell

New York
107 Custom Autocraft Inc, St James
42 Dave's Auto Machine & Parts, Ischua
86 Early Ford V8 Sales Inc, Ballston Spa
81 Ford Parts Specialists, Queens Village
87 Joblot Automotive Inc, Queens Village
60 Long Island Corvette Supply Inc, Copiague
102 Long Island Mustang Restoration Parts, Islandia
82 Mac's Antique Auto Parts, Lockport
151 Morgan Spares Ltd, Ancram
70 Norm's Custom Shop, Bath
168 PAR Porsche Specialists, New Rochelle
24 Peninsula Imports, Buffalo
136 John T Poulin Auto Sales/Star Service Center, North Troy

89 S & S Antique Auto, Deposit
90 Dick Spadaro, Altamont
181 Sports Car Haven, St James
137 Star Quality, Lagrangeville
138 Sweeney's Auto & Marine Upholstery Inc, Southampton
151 Wittenborn's Auto Service Inc, Briarcliff Manor
186 Zimmer Neo-Classic Motor Car Co, Syracuse

North Carolina
35 60 Chev Sam, Hamptonville
92 Carolina Classics, Durham
70 Dennis Carpenter Cushman Reproductions, Charlotte
92 Dennis Carpenter Ford Reproductions, Charlotte
107 Classic Sheetmetal Inc, Charlotte
108 Jim's T-Bird Parts & Service, Winston-Salem
137 Silver Star Restorations, Topton

Ohio
15 American Parts Depot, West Manchester
25 Antique & Classic Cars Inc, Hamilton
179 Automotive Artistry, Hudson
179 Automotive Artistry, Mantua
26 Bicknell Engine Company, Enon
37 Bill's Speed Shop, Navarre
107 Classic Auto Supply Company Inc, Coshocton
171 Coachbuilt Motors, Columbus
82 Gaslight Auto Parts Inc, Urbana
16 Kennedy American Inc, West Jefferson
33 Mahoning Auto, North Jackson
145 Omni Specialties, Cleveland
168 Perfect Panels of America, Centerville
104 Pony Parts of America, Centerville
105 Rode's Restoration, Galion
84 Snyder's Antique Auto Parts Inc, New Springfield
169 Stuttgart Automotive Inc, Centerville
50 Trim Parts Inc, Milford
124 Welsh Enterprises Inc, Steubenville
51 Ted Williams Enterprises, Lisbon
16 Wymer Classic AMC, Fremont

Oklahoma
29 Aabar's Cadillac & Lincoln Salvage & Parts, Oklahoma City
139 Ken's Cougars, Edmond
97 Obsolete Ford Parts Inc, Oklahoma City

Oregon
147 Accurate Muffler Ltd, Roseburg
106 Bird Nest, Portland
157 Brinton's Antique Auto Parts, Redmond
152 British Auto Parts Ltd, Marcola
119 British Motor Co, Eugene
40 Cliff's Classic Chevrolet Parts Co, Portland
86 Bob Drake Reproductions Inc, Grants Pass
42 The Filling Station, Lebanon
15 For Ramblers Only, Portland
53 Gold Eagle Classics, Aloha
21 Mini Motors Classic Coachworks, Salem
145 Northwest Import Parts, Portland
47 Old Car Parts, Portland
173 Oregon Crewe Cutters Inc, Grants Pass
141 Rapido Group, Tygh Valley
110 T-Bird Sanctuary, Tualatin
90 Wescott's Auto Restyling, Boring

Pennsylvania
72 Avanti Auto Service, Glen Mills
80 Bill's Model Acres Ford Farm, Watsontown
106 Bob's Bird House, Chadds Ford
100 Tony D Branda Performance, Altoona
143 British Miles, Morrisville
119 British Restorations, Philadelphia

37 C & P Chevy Parts, Kulpsville
147 Christian Motorsports Illustrated, Mansfield
101 CJ Pony Parts Inc, Harrisburg
56 Corvair Ranch Inc, Gettysburg
59 Corvette World, Greensburg
59 County Corvette, Lionville
148 Daniel N Dietrich, Kempton
59 Dobbins Restoration Publishing, Hatboro
42 Mike Drago Chevy Parts, Easton
42 East Coast Chevy Inc, Doylestown
102 Glazier's Mustang Barn Inc, Souderton
20 Healey Coop, Exeter
32 Holcombe Cadillac Parts, Bensalem
158 Lincoln Highway Packards, Schellsburg
45 Lutty's Chevy Warehouse, Cheswick
45 Martz Classic Chevy Parts, Thomasville
67 Obsolete Chrysler NOS Parts, Murrysville
151 Olde World Restorations, Huntingdon Valley
149 Older Car Restoration, Mont Alto
109 William H Randel, Hatboro
181 The Roadster Factory, Armagh
64 Bob Sottile's Hobby Car Auto Sales Inc, Martinsburg
146 Sports Car Haven, Danville
18 Steelwings, Ivyland
64 Stoudt Auto Sales, Reading
50 Stringbean's Pickup Parts, Johnstown
99 Tee-Bird Products Inc, Exton
111 Thunderbirds East, Chadds Ford
178 Tiger Tom's, Annville
169 Translog Motorsports, York
146 Triple C Motor Accessories, York
186 The Willys Man, Lansdale

Puerto Rico

121 Jaguar of Puerto Rico Inc, San Juan

Rhode Island

118 Bassett's Jaguar, Wyoming
52 Competitive Automotive Inc, Warwick

South Carolina

84 Smith & Jones Distributing Company Inc, West Columbia
183 Vintage Auto LLC, Greenville
22 Von's Austin-Healey Restorations, Fort Mill

Tennessee

99 A&A Mustang Parts & Mfg Co, Oak Ridge
85 Classic Carriages, Athens
86 Early Ford Parts, Memphis
176 Kelley's Korner, Bristol
51 Volunteer State Chevy Parts, Greenbrier

Texas

142 BCP Sport & Classic Co, Houston
39 Classic Auto Restoration Service Inc, Rockwall
76 Edsel Associates, Fort Worth
134 Germany Direct, San Antonio
32 Honest John's Caddy Corner, Justin
82 Howell's Sheetmetal Co, Nederland
121 John's Cars Inc, Dallas
82 Kid Stuff, Porter
19 Kip Motor Company Inc, Dallas
44 Al Knoch Interiors, El Paso
62 Marcel's Corvette Parts, Humble
158 Motor Foundry & Tooling Inc, Canutillo
62 Old Air Products, Fort Worth
14 Orion Motors European Parts Inc, Houston
169 Zim's Autotechnik, Bedford

Utah

184 Celestial Mechanics, Wellsville
125 K-F-D Services Inc, Altonah

Vermont

118 Best of Britain, South Ryegate
56 Bill Cotrofeld Automotive Inc, East Arlington
183 John's Car Corner, Westminster

Virginia

91 Auto Krafters Inc, Broadway
30 Cadillac Crazy, Winchester
104 Old Dominion Mustang/Camaro, Ashland
156 Opel Parts & Service Inc, Chesapeake
19 Seven Enterprises Ltd, Newport News
64 Still Cruisin' Corvettes, Haymarket
84 Vintage Ford Center Inc, Leesburg
106 Virginia Classic Mustang Inc, Broadway
65 Virginia Vettes Parts & Sales, Williamsburg
65 Zip Products, Mechanicsville

Washington

100 Andy's Classic Mustangs, Greenacres
26 Buick Specialists, Kent
58 Corvette & High-Performance, Olympia
94 Ford Powertrain Applications, Puyallup
148 Jim Harris, Seattle
151 Morgan Oasis Garage, Hoodsport
153 NSU/USA Jim Sykes, Seattle
88 Old Ford Parts, Algona
97 Original Falcon, Comet, Ranchero, Fairlane Interiors, Seattle
48 Pick-ups Northwest, Snohomish
56 Safari O-Rings, Renton

West Virginia

103 Mean Mustang Supply Inc, South Charleston

Wisconsin

13 Alfa Heaven Inc, Aniwa
133 Brooklyn Motoren Werke Inc, Brooklyn
37 Butch's Trim, Big Bend
73 Collectors Choice LTD, Dane
40 CPX-RTS Auto Parts, Milwaukee
20 Fourintune Garage Inc, Cedarburg
184 David Hueppchen, Plymouth
45 Lee's Classic Chevy Sales, Glenbeulah
95 Loyal Ford Mercury Inc, New Holstein
110 Regal Roadsters Ltd, Madison
76 Brooks Stevens Auto Collection Inc, Mequon

Canada

36 All Chevy/Canadian Impala, Parksville BC
57 B & B Restorations, Elmvale ON
39 Classic and Muscle, Elmsdale NS
83 The Old Car Centre, Langley BC
49 Reproduction Parts Marketing, Saskatoon SK
49 Scotts Super Trucks, Penhold AB

England

152 Gideon Booth, Cumbria CA10 3BT
121 Jaguar Daimler Heritage Trust, Allesley, Coventry CV5 9DR
144 MG Parts Centre (Barry Walker), NR Stratford-on-Avon B49 6NH
84 Saturn Industries, Gloucestershire GL 16 8AN
70 Barry Thorne, Surrey RH5 5FU

Sweden

17 S-E Autoparts, 78193 Borlange
34 TA Motor AB, Lulea S 97347
64 Lars Tidblom Automobil, Sundbyberg 17231

Section Two:
Generalists

4,047 listings

In this section, vendors who offer parts, literature, services or other items for a variety of makes and models are listed under general categories. As in Section One, if a vendor provides several services or products, an abbreviated subsidiary listing will appear in all of the appropriate sections with a cross reference to the main listing located in the category with the greatest concentration of the vendor's business.

The taglines located in the right-hand box of each listing provide a quick guide to what the vendor primarily offers.

This section of the Almanac is intended to serve owners of virtually every car make being collected. Restorers or collectors interested in parts or services for specific car marques should check Section One also, which presents vendor listings by marque specialty.

**Section Two
Generalists**

---

accessories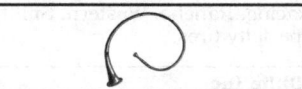

A-1 Street Rods
631 E Las Vegas St
Colorado Springs, CO 80903
719-632-4920, 719-577-4588
FAX: 719-634-6577

parts

See full listing in **Section Two** under **street rods**

Aardvark International
PO Box 509
Whittier, CA 90608
562-699-8887; FAX: 562-699-2288
E-mail: usa@talbotco.com

*CIBIE lights
mirrors*

Mail order only. Specializing in Talbot™ sport mirrors for Alfa Romeo, Aston Martin, Austin-Healey, BMW, Cobra, Cooper, DeTomaso, Facel Vega, Ferrari, Fiat, Jaguar, Lamborghini, Lancia, Lotus, Maserati, Mercedes-Benz, MG, NSU, Opel, Porsche, Sunbeam, Triumph, TVR, Volkswagen, Iso, McLaren, Brabham and various race cars. Many models in chrome finish or aluminum. Housings are handspun to perfection. Three different mounting systems are available. Mirror elements are flat or convex "first surface" glass. Talbot™ mirrors are the finest money can buy and are stamped with the correct Talbot™ markings. CIBIE headlights and auxilliary lights, USA distributor.

AC Enterprises
13387 Gladstone Ave
Sylmar, CA 91342
818-367-8337

gloveboxes

Gloveboxes for most cars and trucks. Will work to sketch for custom application. SASE please.

Accessoryland Truckin' Supplies
10723 Rt 61 S
Dubuque, IA 52003
319-556-5482; FAX: 319-556-9087

*accessories
foglights/spotlights
mounting brackets
parts*

See full listing in **Section One** under **Chevrolet**

Action Performance Inc
1619 Lakeland Ave
Bohemia, NY 11716
516-244-7100; FAX: 516-244-7172

accessories

Mail order and open shop. Monday-Friday 9:30 am to 7:30 pm, Saturday 9 am to 5:30 pm, Sunday 10 am to 3 pm. High-performance auto accessories for street, drag racing, oval track, pro-street.

Addison Generator Inc
21 W Main St Rear
Freehold, NJ 07728
732-431-2438; FAX: 732-431-4503

*auto parts
repairs
supplies*

See full listing in **Section Two** under **electrical systems**

American Performance Products
675 S Industry Rd
Cocoa, FL 32926
407-632-8299; FAX: 407-632-5119
E-mail: amc@oldcarparts.com

parts

See full listing in **Section One** under **AMC**

Anderson's Car Door Monograms
32700 Coastsite #102
Rancho Palos Verdes, CA 90275
800-881-9049, 310-377-1007
FAX: 310-377-0169

car door monograms

Mail order only. Car door monograms, three initials pre-spaced for foolproof installation. Die cut from 3-M cast vinyl. Looks just like hand lettered enamel. Available in script, block, old English or in a circle. Colors: gold, silver, black, white, blue, red. Set of two three-letter monograms, $27.50 prepaid. To order, put three initials on a piece of paper, underline initial of last name which will appear in the center. Free literature. Unconditional money back guarantee.

Antique Auto Battery
2320 Old Mill Rd
Hudson, OH 44236
800-426-7580, 330-425-2395
FAX: 330-425-4642
E-mail: sales@antiqueautobattery.com

*batteries
battery cables*

See full listing in **Section Two** under **batteries**

Antique Radio Service
12 Shawmut Ave
Wayland, MA 01778
800-201-2635; FAX: 508-653-2418

radio service

See full listing in **Section Two** under **radios**

APA Industries
10505 San Fernando Rd
Pacoima, CA 91331
818-834-8473; FAX: 818-834-2795
E-mail: apaindustries@juno.com

*accessories
parts*

See full listing in **Section One** under **Jaguar**

Hemmings' Vintage Auto Almanac© Fourteenth Edition

Aremco Products Inc | **compound**
707-B Executive Blvd
Valley Cottage, NY 10989
914-268-0039; FAX: 914-268-0041
E-mail: aremco@aremco.com

Mail order only. Aremco's new Pyromax line features high temperature sealers, adhesives and paints for repairing and coating pits, holes and cracks in engine blocks, cylinder heads, manifolds, headers and other exhaust components. Product trade names include Pyro-Putty, Pyro-Paint, Pyro-Weld and Pyro-Seal. Web site: www.aremco.com

Atlantic British Ltd | **accessories**
Halfmoon Light Industrial Park | **parts**
6 Badertscher Dr
Clifton Park, NY 12065
800-533-2210; FAX: 518-664-6641
E-mail: ab@roverparts.com

See full listing in **Section One** under **Rover/Land Rover**

Auto-Mat Co | **accessories**
69 Hazel St | **carpet sets**
Hicksville, NY 11801 | **interiors**
800-645-7258 orders
516-938-7373; FAX: 516-931-8438
E-mail: browner5@ix.netcom.com

See full listing in **Section Two** under **interiors & interior parts**

Backyard Buddy Corp | **automotive lift**
1818 N Main St
PO Box 5104
Niles, OH 44446
800-837-9353, 330-544-9372
FAX: 330-544-9311

Mail order and display area. Manufacture a complete line of

automotive lifts, 4-post and 2-post. The 4-post, 6,000 lb is ideal for the home hobbiest, used for storage and service. Convenience options including drip pans, casters and jack platforms, all American made in our own plants. Worldwide shipping. Check our web site or calling our 800 number puts you in direct contact with our manufacturing facility. Web site: www.backyard-buddy.com

See our ad on this page

Bay Ridges Classic Chevy | **accessories**
1550 Bayly St #38A | **parts**
Pickering, ON Canada L1W 3W1
905-839-6169; FAX: 905-420-6613

See full listing in **Section One** under **Chevrolet**

Big Boys Toys | **accessories**
Richard Boutin | **bodywork**
Rt 67A Box 174A | **tires**
North Bennington, VT 05257 | **wheels**
800-286-1721; FAX: 802-447-0962

Automotive specialty store, customizing trucks and cars. Specialty wheels, bodywork. Lund, Dee Zee, Deflecta, American Racing, Rancho, Western, Smitty built, Holley, Cooper tires and specialty tires.

Billie Inc | **garage diaper**
PO Box 1161 | **mats**
Ashburn, VA 20146-1161
800-878-6328; FAX: 703-858-0102

See full listing in **Section Two** under **car care products**

Bob's Classic Auto Glass | **glass**
21170 Hwy 36
Blachly, OR 97412
800-624-2130

See full listing in **Section Two** under **glass**

Bonneville Sports Inc | **accessories**
3544 Enterprise Dr | **clothing**
Amaheim, CA 92807
888-999-7258, 714-666-1966
FAX: 714-666-1955
E-mail: bonspeed@aol.com

See full listing in **Section Two** under **apparel**

Buick Bonery | **parts**
6970 Stamper Way
Sacramento, CA 95828
916-381-5271; FAX: 916-381-0702

See full listing in **Section One** under **Buick/McLaughlin**

Caddytown™/Pawl Engineering Co | **memorabilia**
4960 Arrowhead | **parts**
PO Box 240105 | **toys**
West Bloomfield, MI 48324
PH/FAX: 248-682-2007
E-mail: pawl@earthlink.net

See full listing in **Section One** under **Cadillac/LaSalle**

Canadian Mustang | **parts**
20529 62 Ave
Langley, BC Canada V3A 8R4
604-534-6424; FAX: 604-534-6694
E-mail: parts@canadianmustang.com

See full listing in **Section One** under **Mustang**

CBS Performance Automotive | **ignition systems**
2605-A W Colorado Ave | **performance products**
Colorado Springs, CO 80904
800-685-1492; FAX: 719-578-9485

See full listing in **Section Two** under **ignition parts**

Michael Chapman
Priorsleigh, Mill Lane
Cleeve Prior
Worcestershire, WR115JZ England
0044-1789-773897
FAX: 0044-1789-773588

automobilia

See full listing in **Section Two** under **automobilia**

Chev's of the 40's
2027 B St, Dept HVA
Washougal, WA 98671
800-999-CHEV (2438)
FAX: 360-835-7988

parts

See full listing in **Section One** under **Chevrolet**

Ed Cholakian Enterprises Inc
dba All Cadillacs of the 40's and 50's
12811 Foothill Blvd
Sylmar, CA 91342
800-808-1147, 818-361-1147
FAX: 818-361-9738

museum
parts

See full listing in **Section One** under **Cadillac/LaSalle**

Classic Aire Car Coolers
J & M Engineering Inc
PO Box 739
Camas, WA 98607
PH/FAX: 360-834-5227

car cooler

Mail order only. Dealing in the modern version of the classic window mounted evaporative car cooler. Web site: www.classicaire.com

Classic Car Part Art
207 S Mt Carmel
Wichita, KS 67213
316-945-6865

artwork

See full listing in **Section Two** under **artwork**

Classic Chevy International
PO Box 607188
Orlando, FL 32860-7188
800-456-1957, 407-299-1957
FAX: 407-299-3341
E-mail: cciworld@aol.com

modified parts
repro parts
used parts

See full listing in **Section One** under **Chevrolet**

Classic Motors
PO Box 1011
San Mateo, CA 94403
650-342-4117; FAX: 650-340-9473
E-mail: tonyleo@pacbell.net

appraisals
locator service
movie rentals
parts/restoration

See full listing in **Section Two** under **restoration shops**

Cobra Restorers Ltd
3099 Carter Dr
Kennesaw, GA 30144
770-427-0020; FAX: 770-427-8658

parts
restoration
service

See full listing in **Section One** under **Cobra**

Comet Products
Cherry Parke 101-B
Cherry Hill, NJ 08002
609-795-4810; FAX: 609-354-6313

accessories
emblems

See full listing in **Section Two** under **grille emblem badges**

**Comfy/Inter-American
Sheepskins Inc**
1346 Centinela Ave
West Los Angeles, CA 90025-1901
800-521-4014; FAX: 310-442-6080
E-mail: sales@comfysheep.com

floor mats
seat covers

See full listing in **Section Two** under **interiors & interior parts**

Concours Cars of Colorado Ltd
2414 W Cucharras St
Colorado Springs, CO 80904
719-473-6288; FAX: 719-473-9206

accessories
parts
service

See full listing in **Section One** under **BMW**

Convertible Service
5126-HA Walnut Grove Ave
San Gabriel, CA 91776
800-333-1140, 626-285-2255
FAX: 626-285-9004

convertible parts
manufacture/service
top mechanism

See full listing in **Section Two** under **tops**

Corvette & High-Performance
Division of Classic & High-
Performance Inc
2840 Black Lake Blvd SW #D
Olympia, WA 98512
360-754-7890

accessories
parts

See full listing in **Section One** under **Corvette**

Corvette America
PO Box 324
Rt 322
Boalsburg, PA 16827
800-458-3475
foreign: 814-364-2141
FAX: 814-364-9615, 24 hours
E-mail: vettebox@corvetteamerica.com

accessories
fiberglass
interiors
leisure items
parts

See full listing in **Section One** under **Corvette**

Corvette Specialties of MD Inc
1912 Liberty Rd
Eldersburg, MD 21784
410-795-3180; FAX: 410-795-3247

parts
restoration
service

See full listing in **Section One** under **Corvette**

Crossfire Manufacturing
166-B N Mercer Ave
PO Box 263
Sharpsville, PA 16150
800-458-3478
PH/FAX: 724-962-4639
E-mail: xfire@nauticom.net

accessories

See full listing in **Section Two** under **ignition parts**

Crutchfield Corp
1 Crutchfield Park
Charlottesville, VA 22911
800-955-9009; FAX: 804-817-1010

car stereos

See full listing in **Section Two** under **radios**

CT Model A Parts & Service
75 Prospect Ave
West Hartford, CT 06106
860-233-1928; FAX: 860-233-1926
E-mail: ctmap@aol.com

parts
restorations
service

See full listing in **Section One** under **Ford 1903-1931**

Richard Culleton	**accessories**
4318 SW 19th Pl	
Cape Coral, FL 33914	
800-931-7836 voice mail	
315-685-7414 (home)	
941-542-8640	

Mail order and car shows only. Wholesale and retail. 1950s nostalgic accessories. Moon products, shift knobs, specialty valve caps, door locks, etc.

Damper Dudes	**balancers**
5509 Cedar Rd #2	**chrome**
Redding, CA 96001	**paint**
800-413-2673, 530-244-7225	
FAX: 530-244-2690	
E-mail: rliddell@snowcrest.net	

See full listing in **Section Two** under **engine parts**

Dare Classics	**leather handles**
PO Box 1834	**leather straps**
Elk Grove, CA 95759	**luggage**
916-212-6018; FAX: 916-686-6112	**trunks**

Mail order only. Reproduce or design custom luggage and trunks for antique and classic automobiles. Repair and restore original luggage and trunks. Manufacture custom leather handles and straps per customer specifications.

Dashhugger	**dashboard covers**
PO Box 933	
Clovis, CA 93613	
559-298-4529; FAX: 559-298-3428	
E-mail: sales@dashhugger.com	

See full listing in **Section Two** under **interiors & interior parts**

Dashlite/LHI Inc	**rechargeable**
PO Box 9280	**flashlight**
1280 B Huff Ln	
Jackson Hole, WY 83002-9280	
800-328-9069, 307-733-1495	
FAX: 307-733-5927	
E-mail: info@dashlite.com	

Rechargeable flashlights for the car. Our flashlight fits in the cigarette lighter or accessory outlet and recharges as you drive. "Dashlight Flashlight" fits all cigarette outlets in all makes and models. Web site: www.dashlite.com

Davies Corvette	**accessories**
7141 US Hwy 19	**parts**
New Port Richey, FL 34653	
800-236-2383, 727-842-8000	
FAX: 727-846-8216	
E-mail: davies@corvetteparts.com	

See full listing in **Section One** under **Corvette**

Buzz De Clerck	**parts**
41760 Utica Rd	
Sterling Heights, MI 48313-3146	
810-731-0765	

See full listing in **Section One** under **Lincoln**

DeLorean One	**bodywork**
20229 Nordhoff St	**parts**
Chatsworth, CA 91311	**service**
818-341-1796; FAX: 818-998-6381	

See full listing in **Section One** under **DeLorean**

Development Associates	**electrical parts**
12791-G Newport Ave	
Tustin, CA 92780	
714-730-6843; FAX: 714-730-6863	
E-mail: devassoc@yahoo.com	

See full listing in **Section Two** under **electrical systems**

Diamond Liners Inc	**bedliners**
5430 Tweedy Blvd	
South Gate, CA 90280	
800-543-1212 CA only	
323-567-1032	
FAX: 323-566-2271	
E-mail: jhbender@diamondliners.com	

Specially formulated, sprayed-on polyurethane coating that provides a permanent textured surface. The coating protects against rust, corrosion and harsh chemicals. The liner is durable and resistant to impact or abrasions, EPA-safe and solvent-free. Diamond Liner fits every curve of your truck, equipment or restoration vehicle. Web site: diamondliners.com

Direct Wholesale	**alarms**
6135 Country Rd 58	**remote starters**
Bergholz, OH 43908	
800-659-0764	

See full listing in **Section Two** under **anti-theft**

Bob Drake Reproductions Inc	**repro parts**
1819 NW Washington Blvd	
Grants Pass, OR 97526	
800-221-3673; FAX: 541-474-0099	
E-mail: bobdrake@bobdrake.com	

See full listing in **Section One** under **Ford 1932-1953**

Eckler's Quality Parts &	**accessories**
Accessories for Corvettes	**parts**
PO Box 5637	
Titusville, FL 32783	
800-327-4868; FAX: 407-383-2059	
E-mail: ecklers@ecklers.com	

See full listing in **Section One** under **Corvette**

Lee Ellison's MoreParts North	**parts**
PO Box 345	**sheetmetal**
Orangeville, ON Canada L9W 2Z7	
519-941-6331; FAX: 519-941-8903	
E-mail: obsoleteparts@moreparts.com	

See full listing in **Section One** under **Mopar**

Enthusiast's Specialties	**automobilia**
350 Old Connecticut Path	
Framingham, MA 01701	
800-718-3999; FAX: 508-872-4914	
E-mail: alvis1934@aol.com	

See full listing in **Section Two** under **automobilia**

The Enthusiasts Shop	**cars**
John Parnell	**pre-war parts**
PO Box 80471	**transportation**
Baton Rouge, LA 70898	
225-928-7456; FAX: 225-928-7665	

See full listing in **Section One** under **Rolls-Royce/Bentley**

Eurosport Daytona Inc	**license plates**
355 Tomoka Ave	
Ormond Beach, FL 32174-6222	
800-874-8044, 904-672-7199	
FAX: 904-673-0821	

See full listing in **Section Two** under **license plates**

Jay M Fisher
Acken Dr 4-B
Clark, NJ 07066
732-388-6442

mascots
sidemount mirrors
windwing brackets

Mail order only. Manufacturer of sidemount mirrors, 1900-1970, inside mirror restoration, windwing brackets, radiator caps, mascots, small parts fabrication, leather straps, restoration of any mirrors. Catalog, $2 cash plus 55¢ SASE.

For Ramblers Only
2324 SE 34th Ave
Portland, OR 97214
503-232-0497
E-mail: ramblers@teleport.com

accessories
parts

See full listing in **Section One** under **AMC**

Gaslight Auto Parts Inc
PO Box 291
Urbana, OH 43078
937-652-2145; FAX: 937-652-2147

accessories
parts

See full listing in **Section One** under **Ford 1903-1931**

Gasoline Alley LLC
1700E Iron Ave
PO Box 737
Salina, KS 67402
800-326-8372, 785-822-1003
FAX: 785-827-9337
E-mail: morrison@midusa.net

drip pans

Mail order only. Manufacture Perma-Pan drip pans which feature a DuPont Tedlar® top surface making the easiest cleaning pan on the market. Also sell Coustasheet, a vibration damping and sound barrier material that can make cars 10-15 dB quieter. Web site: www.gasolinealleyllc.com

Gold Plated Emblems & Auto Accessories
2095 Pine Ridge Rd
Naples, FL 34109
800-231-7765, 941-592-5552
FAX: 941-597-0768
E-mail: sales@goldplated.com

plating equipment
wood dash kits

See full listing in **Section Two** under **plating & polishing**

Griot's Garage
3500-A 20th St E
Tacoma, WA 98424
800-345-5789; FAX: 888-252-2252
E-mail: info@griotsgarage.com

car care products
paint
tools

See full listing in **Section Two** under **tools**

Hale's Products
906 19th St
Wheatland, WY 82201
800-333-0989
E-mail: phale@wyoming.com

license plates

See full listing in **Section Two** under **license plates**

Halpin Used Auto & Truck Parts
1093 Rt 123
Mayfield, NY 12117
518-863-4906
E-mail: junkyard2064@webtv.net

NOS auto/truck
parts
used auto/truck
parts

See full listing in **Section Five** under **New York**

Haneline Products Co
PO Box 430
Morongo Valley, CA 92256
760-363-6597; FAX: 760-363-7321

electrical/gauges
instrument panels
power windows
stainless parts

Mail order only. Manufacture bolt-in retro instrument panels. Engine turned stainless steel accessories. Cars and trucks

1920s-1980s. Trim parts, door sills, firewalls, distributor-Teleflex, Westach, Classic, S-W, VDO, Auto Meter, Dakota Digital gauges, electric life power windows, door locks, keyless entry. Wire Works, Ididit, Le Carra, Vintage Air, Old Air and others.

Ned R Healy & Company Inc
17602 Griffin Ln
PO Box 2120
Huntington Beach, CA 92647
714-848-2251; FAX: 714-848-7251

accessories
parts

Sell parts, accessories, supplies and die cast toy cars to new car dealers. Web site: http://users.deltanet.com/~healyinc/

Hooker Headers
1024 W Brooks St
Ontario, CA 91762
909-983-5871; FAX: 909-986-9860

exhaust systems

See full listing in **Section Two** under **exhaust systems**

International E-Z UP Inc
1601 Iowa Ave
Riverside, CA 92507
909-781-0843; FAX: 909-781-0586
E-mail: info@ezup.com

awnings
canopies

E-Z UP Instant Shelters set up in less than 60 seconds with no ropes, poles or assembly required. The patented double-truss design is fully self-contained, perfect for race pits, car shows, sales booths and sun protection. Heavy duty fabric tops available in a variety of colors and custom silk-screening for high visibility. E-Z UPs range in sizes from 8x8 to 10x20 feet. Web site: www.ezup.com

Jim's T-Bird Parts & Service
710 Barney Ave
Winston-Salem, NC 27107
PH/FAX: 336-784-9363
E-mail: tbirdjims@aol.com

parts
restoration
service

See full listing in **Section One** under **Thunderbird**

K&S Industries
1801 Union Center Hwy
Endicott, NY 13760
PH/FAX: 888-PICK-KNS
E-mail: pleximan@888pickkns.com

display cases

See full listing in **Section Two** under **models & toys**

Karl's Collectibles
28 Bates St
Lewiston, ME 04240
800-636-0457, 207-784-0098
FAX: 207-786-4576
E-mail: slalemand@exploremaine.com

banks
collectibles
logo design

See full listing in **Section Two** under **models & toys**

Lee's Kustom Auto & Street Rods
RR 3 Box 3061A
Rome, PA 18837
570-247-2326
E-mail: lka41@epix.net

accessories
parts
restoration

See full listing in **Section Two** under **street rods**

Lord Byron Inc
420 Sackett Point Rd
North Haven, CT 06473
203-287-9881; FAX: 203-288-9456

fender covers

See full listing in **Section Two** under **car covers**

M & R Products | hardware
1940 SW Blvd | tie-downs
Vineland, NJ 08360
800-524-2560, 609-696-9450
FAX: 609-696-4999
E-mail: mrproducts@mrproducts.com

Tie-downs: automotive, motorcycle and utility. Related hardware (D-rings, track systems) and racing safety equipment (harnesses, window net and collars). Web site: mrproducts.com

Larry Machacek | decals
PO Box 515 | license plates
Porter, TX 77365 | novelties
281-429-2505

See full listing in **Section Two** under **automobilia**

Madera Concepts | restoration
606 Olive St | woodwork
Santa Barbara, CA 93101 | woodwork repair
800-800-1579, 805-962-1579
FAX: 805-962-7359
E-mail: jwayco@west.net

See full listing in **Section Two** under **woodwork**

Marcel's Corvette Parts | parts
15100 Lee Rd #101
Humble, TX 77396
800-546-2111 order line
281-441-2111 info line
FAX: 281-441-3057

See full listing in **Section One** under **Corvette**

Mark II Enterprises | car covers
5225 Canyon Crest Dr | parts
Suite 71-217
Riverside, CA 92507
909-686-2752; FAX: 909-686-7245
E-mail: mark2@csi.com

1956-1957 Continental Mark II parts. Large inventory of NOS, NORS, used and rebuilt parts for Mark II and 1956-1957 Lincoln autos. Covers: car cover closeout, 100s below cost, $50-$125, 8 fabrics, special orders, guaranteed lowest price, custom tailored by world's largest manufacturer, 45,000 patterns. Located in Riverside, at same address since 1956. 45+ cars for parts. Major credit cards accepted. Web site: www.markii.com

Max Neon Design Group | custom face logos
19807 Sussex Dr | glass light-up
St Clair Shores, MI 48081-3257 | clocks
810-773-5000; FAX: 810-772-6224 | neon clocks

See full listing in **Section Two** under **automobilia**

McLean's Brit Bits | accessories
14 Sagamore Rd | parts
Rye, NH 03870 | sales
800-995-2487; FAX: 603-433-0009 | service
E-mail: sam@britbits.com

See full listing in **Section One** under **MG**

Meguiar's Inc | cleaners
17991 Mitchell S | polishes
Irvine, CA 92614 | waxes
949-752-8000; FAX: 949-752-6659

Meguiar's has been creating brilliant surface care products since 1901. Specialize in producing waxes, polishes, cleaners and other product accessories for the automotive, marine and furniture markets. You will find Meguiar's in all major retail and professional stores across the nation or you can order direct by calling our customer care department at 800-347-5700. Web site: www.meguiars.com

Millers Incorporated | accessories
7412 Count Circle | parts
Huntington Beach, CA 92647
714-375-6565; FAX: 714-847-6606
E-mail: sales@millermbz.com

See full listing in **Section One** under **Mercedes-Benz**

Mint Condition Auto Upholstery | convertible tops
PO Box 134 | interiors
Silverdale New Zealand | spring-gaiters
PH/FAX: 64-9-424 2257 | wheelcovers
E-mail: mint.condition@xtra.co.nz

See full listing in **Section Two** under **special services**

Moss Motors Ltd | accessories
PO Box 847 | parts
440 Rutherford St
Goleta, CA 93117
800-235-6954; FAX: 805-692-2525

See full listing in **Section One** under **MG**

Motorsport Auto | parts
1139 W Collins Ave
Orange, CA 92667
800-633-6331, 714-639-2620
FAX: 714-639-7460
E-mail: motorsport@worldnet.att.net

See full listing in **Section One** under **Datsun**

MotorWeek | TV program
11767 Owings Mills Blvd
Owings Mills, MD 21117
410-356-5600; FAX: 410-581-4113
E-mail: motorweek@mpt.org

See full listing in **Section Four** under **information sources**

Murphy's Motoring Accessories Inc | car covers
PO Box 618
Greendale, WI 53129-0618
800-529-8315, 414-529-8333

See full listing in **Section Two** under **car covers**

National Parts Depot | accessories
3101 SW 40th Blvd | restoration parts
Gainesville, FL 32608
800-874-7595 toll-free 24 hours
352-378-2473 local

See full listing in **Section Two** under **comprehensive parts**

NMW Products | dollies
35 Orlando Dr
Raritan, NJ 08869
908-256-3800

Mail order and open shop. Monday-Friday 8 am to 4:30 pm. Manufacturer of car dollies/engine shop dollies.

O'Brien Truckers | accessories
5 Perry Hill | belt buckles
North Grafton, MA 01536-1532 | plaques
508-839-3033; FAX: 508-839-9490 | valve covers
E-mail: obt@ziplink.net

See full listing in **Section Two** under **plaques**

OJ Rallye Automotive | accessories
PO Box 540 | car care products
N 6808 Hwy OJ | lighting parts
Plymouth, WI 53073
920-893-2531; FAX: 920-893-6800
E-mail: ojrallye@excel.net

See full listing in **Section Two** under **lighting equipment**

Operations Plus
PO Box 26347
Santa Ana, CA 92799
PH/FAX: 714-962-2776
E-mail: aquacel@aquacel.com

accessories
parts

See full listing in **Section One** under **Cobra**

Paul's Select Cars & Parts for Porsche®
2280 Gail Dr
Riverside, CA 92509
909-685-9340; FAX: 909-685-9342
E-mail: pauls356-s90@webtv.net

cars
parts

See full listing in **Section One** under **Porsche**

PE/Snappin Turtle Tie-Down Straps
803 Petersburg Rd
Carlisle, PA 17013
800-TIE-DOWN; FAX: 717-258-1348

locks
tie-down straps
winches

See full listing in **Section Two** under **trailers**

People Kars
290 Third Ave Ext
Rensselaer, NY 12144
518-465-0477; FAX: 518-465-0614
E-mail: peoplekars@aol.com

models/more
VW toys

See full listing in **Section One** under **Volkswagen**

Performance Automotive Inc
1696 New London Tpke
PO Box 10
Glastonbury, CT 06033
860-633-7868; FAX: 860-657-9110

accessories
car care

See full listing in **Section Two** under **car care products**

The Plateman
Jim Estrup
269 Webber Hill Rd
Kennebunk, ME 04043
207-985-4800; FAX: 207-985-TAGS

license plates

See full listing in **Section Two** under **license plates**

Precision Auto Designs
28 Railway Ave
Campbell, CA 95008
408-378-2332; FAX: 408-378-1301
E-mail: pad@precisionauto.com

accessories
car covers
restoration

See full listing in **Section One** under **Mercedes-Benz**

Prostripe
Division of Spartan International Inc
1845 Cedar St
Holt, MI 48842
800-248-7800; FAX: 517-694-7952
E-mail: information@spartanintl.com

graphics
molding
pinstriping

See full listing in **Section Two** under **striping**

Pulfer & Williams
213 Forest Rd
PO Box 67
Hancock, NH 03449-0067
603-525-3532; FAX: 603-525-4293

mascots
nameplates
radiator emblems

See full listing in **Section Two** under **radiator emblems & mascots**

Quik-Shelter
PO Box 1123
Orange, CT 06477
800-211-3730; FAX: 203-937-8897
E-mail: info@quikshelter.com

temporary garages

See full listing in **Section Two** under **car covers**

The Rampman
PO Box 718
New Kingstown, PA 17072
800-717-0326, 717-241-5474
FAX: 717-258-9009
E-mail: therampman@aol.com

ramps

Mail order and open shop by appointment. Sunday-Saturday. Aluminum ramps/ramps for car trailers, lawn and garden, motorcycles and disability ramps. Drive on ramps to service vehicle.

Re-Flex Border Marker
138 Grant St
Lexington, MA 02173
781-862-1343

border markers
posts

See full listing in **Section Two** under **hardware**

Rick's First Generation Camaro Parts & Accessories
420 Athena Dr
Athens, GA 30601
800-359-7717; FAX: 706-548-8581
E-mail: firstgen@negia.net

accessories
parts

See full listing in **Section One** under **Chevelle/Camaro**

Robertson Bros & Sons Restoration
PO Box 5678
Sevierville, TN 37864-5678
423-970-1655; FAX: 423-908-6838
E-mail: classicbop@aol.com

NOS parts
restoration parts
used parts

See full listing in **Section One** under **Oldsmobile**

RodDoors
PO Box 2110
Chico, CA 95927
530-896-1513; FAX: 530-896-1518
E-mail: roddoors@juno.com

door panels
interior accessories

See full listing in **Section Two** under **street rods**

Ron's Restorations Inc
2968-B Ask Kay Dr
Smyrna, GA 30082
770-438-6102; FAX: 770-438-0037

interior trim
restoration

See full listing in **Section One** under **Mercedes-Benz**

Scotts Manufacturing
25520 Ave Stanford #304
Valencia, CA 91355
800-544-5596; FAX: 805-295-9342

electric fans
fan electronics

See full listing in **Section Two** under **electrical systems**

Scotts Super Trucks
1972 Hwy 592 W
Penhold, AB Canada T0M 1R0
403-886-5572; FAX: 403-886-5577

parts

See full listing in **Section One** under **Chevrolet**

Sea-Tac Specialties
Don Guilbault
6714-247 St Ct E
Graham, WA 98338
253-847-8545; FAX: 253-847-6455

hat pins
key chains

Wholesale stock pins for pin vendors. Custom orders for clubs, events, promoters, miscellaneous organizations. Catalog, $3, refunded with first order.

Smith & Jones Distributing Company Inc
1 Biloxi Square
West Columbia, SC 29170
803-822-8500; FAX: 803-822-8477

| | parts |

See full listing in **Section One** under **Ford 1903-1931**

SoCal Pickups Inc
6321 Manchester Blvd
Buena Park, CA 90621
800-SOCAL-49; FAX: 714-994-2584

| | parts |

See full listing in **Section One** under **Ford 1954-up**

Southern Autotronics Inc
3300 Norfolk St
Richmond, VA 23230
804-353-5400, 800-446-2880
FAX: 804-358-3216
E-mail: ecs@carradio.com

| | radio restorations |
| | repairs |

See full listing in **Section Two** under **radios**

Southern Rods & Parts Inc
2125 Airport Rd
Gleer, SC 29651
864-848-0601; FAX: 864-801-0601

	accessories
	headlights
	power windows
	radiators

See full listing in **Section Two** under **street rods**

Specter Off-Road Inc
21600 Nordhoff St, Dept HM
Chatsworth, CA 91311
818-882-1238; FAX: 818-882-7144
E-mail: sor@sor.com

| | accessories |
| | parts |

See full listing in **Section One** under **Toyota**

Sterling Specialties
42 Ponderosa Lane
Monroe, NY 10950
914-782-7614

| | car care products |

See full listing in **Section Two** under **car care products**

Stinger by Axe
Hwy 177 N
PO Box 296
Council Grove, KS 66846
800-854-4850; FAX: 316-767-5040
E-mail: axeeqip@midusa.net

| | lifts |

See full listing in **Section Two** under **storage care products**

Strader Classics
Bill Strader
2849 Locust Grove Rd
Elizabethtown, KY 42701
502-737-5294

| | parts |

See full listing in **Section One** under **Chevrolet**

Straw Church Speed Shop
602 Passaic St
Phillipsburg, NJ 08865
908-454-7487
E-mail: strawchurch_ss@hotmail.com

	accessories
	engine swaps
	parts

See full listing in **Section Two** under **car & parts locators**

Street Player
PO Box 1262
Elverta, CA 95626

	fender skirts
	hydraulics/moldings
	tires/wire spoke rims

Car club helping low-riders get their car accessories and hydraulics so they will be able to cruise and look good. Club discount, car for sale, low-riding videos. Accessories, fender skirts, hydraulics, moldings, tires, wire spoke rims, aircraft dumps. Catalog, $5, cash/money order only.

Superior Equipment
703 W 53rd St N
Wichita, KS 67204
800-526-9992; FAX: 316-831-0154
E-mail: mail@superlifts.com

| | auto lifts |
| | shop tools |

See full listing in **Section Two** under **tools**

Te Puke Vintage Auto Barn
26 Young Rd
Te Puke New Zealand
PH/FAX: 07 5736547

	parts
	restoration
	sales

See full listing in **Section Two** under **restoration shops**

Tuxedo Turntables by Tuxedo Enterprises
4914 Gassner Rd
Brookshire, TX 77423
888-TUXEDO-T

| | display turntables |

Mail order and open shop by appointment only. Specializing in display turntables for show cars and other items (manufacture and sales), cars, motorcycles, etc. Web site: www.tuxedoenterprises.com

UK Spares/TVR Sports Cars
609 Highland St
Wethersfield, CT 06109-3979
PH/FAX: 860-563-1647
FAX: 860-529-3479
E-mail: tvr.sports.cars@juno.com

	accessories
	car covers
	convertible tops
	ignition parts
	suspension parts

See full listing in **Section One** under **TVR**

Ultimate Appearance Ltd
113 Arabian Trail
Smithfield, VA 23430
888-446-3078; FAX: 757-255-2620

	cleaners
	detailing products
	detailing services
	polish/wax

See full listing in **Section Two** under **car care products**

The V8 Store
3010 NE 49th St
Vancouver, WA 98663
360-693-7468
360-694-7853 nights
FAX: 360-693-0982

	accessories
	parts
	service

See full listing in **Section Two** under **street rods**

Valco Cincinnati Consumer Products Inc
411 Circle Freeway Dr
Cincinnati, OH 45246
513-874-6550; FAX: 513-874-3612

	adhesives
	detailing products
	sealants
	tools

See full listing in **Section Two** under **tools**

Vintage Ford Center Inc
19437 Harmony Church Rd
Leesburg, VA 20175
888-813-FORD (3673)
FAX: 703-777-3738
E-mail: mdla@masinc.com

| | accessories |
| | parts |

See full listing in **Section One** under **Ford 1903-1931**

Volkswagen Collectors
c/o Jerry Jess
3121 E Yucca St
Phoenix, AZ 85028-2616
PH/FAX: 602-867-7672
E-mail: vwstuff@juno.com

	literature
	memorabilia
	toys

See full listing in **Section One** under **Volkswagen**

Volunteer State Chevy Parts
Hwy 41 S
PO Box 10
Greenbrier, TN 37073
615-643-4583; FAX: 615-643-5100

accessories
parts

See full listing in **Section One** under **Chevrolet**

Wallace Walmsley
4732 Bancroft St, #7
San Diego, CA 92116
619-283-3063

parts

See full listing in **Section One** under **Packard**

Wirth's Custom Automotive
PO Box 5
505 Conner St
Prairie du Rocher, IL 62277
618-284-3359
E-mail: roywirth@htc.net

custom accessories
fender skirts
spinner hubcaps

Mail order only. 1940s, 1950s and 1960s custom accessories, Lake pipes, dummy spotlights, Smithy mufflers, spinner hub-caps, fender skirts, dice and skull items and much more. Web site: www.wirthscustomauto.com

air conditioning

Ace Antique Auto Restoration
65 S Service Rd
Plainview, NY 11803
516-752-6065; FAX: 516-752-1484

air conditioning
body rebuilding
restoration
wiring harnesses

See full listing in **Section Two** under **restoration shops**

Cal West Auto Air & Radiators Inc
24309 Creekside Rd #119
Valencia, CA 91355
800-535-2034; FAX: 805-254-6120
E-mail: mike@calwest-radiators.com

a/c condensers
fan shrouds
gas tanks
heaters
radiators

See full listing in **Section Two** under **radiators**

Gas Tank and Radiator Rebuilders
20123 Hwy 362
Waller, TX 77484
800-723-3759
E-mail: donhart@donhart.com

abrasive blasting
gas tank rebuilding
heaters
radiator repair

See full listing in **Section Two** under **fuel system parts**

K C Obsolete Parts
3343 N 61
Kansas City, KS 66104
913-334-9479; FAX: 913-788-2795

parts

See full listing in **Section One** under **Ford 1954-up**

National Parts Depot
3101 SW 40th Blvd
Gainesville, FL 32608
800-874-7595 toll-free 24 hours
352-378-2473 local

accessories
restoration parts

See full listing in **Section Two** under **comprehensive parts**

Performance Analysis Co
1345 Oak Ridge Tpke, Ste 258
Oak Ridge, TN 37830
423-482-9175
E-mail:
george_murphy@compuserve.com

climate control
cruise control

See full listing in **Section One** under **Mercedes-Benz**

Skip's Auto Parts
Skip Bollinger
1500 Northaven Dr
Gladstone, MO 64118
816-455-2337; FAX: 816-459-7547
E-mail: carpartman@aol.com

chassis parts
ignition parts
water pumps

See full listing in **Section Two** under **water pumps**

Pat Wilson's Thunderbird Parts
235 River Rd
New Milford, NJ 07646-1721
888-262-1153; FAX: 201-634-1916

parts

See full listing in **Section One** under **Thunderbird**

anti-theft

Bathurst Company
6875 Oakland Rd
Loveland, OH 45140
513-683-3122; FAX: 513-683-4701

auto accessories
battery accessories

See full listing in **Section Two** under **electrical systems**

Direct Wholesale
6135 Country Rd 58
Bergholz, OH 43908
800-659-0764

alarms
remote starters

Mail order only. Wholesale distributor. Do-it-yourself alarms, Pro-Series alarms, keyless entries, remote starters for all makes, models and years of vehicles. Web site: www.directwholesale.net

ISG
7100 Monache Mtn Blvd
Inyokern, CA 93527
760-377-5013; FAX: 760-377-5073
E-mail: isg@isg-web.com

security devices

Mail order and open shop. Monday-Friday 10 am to 4 pm. State of the art security devices. Manufacturer of a satellite controlled vehicle immobilizer and various surveillance devices. Web site: isg-web.com

Jacobs Electronics
500 N Baird St
Midland, TX 79701
915-685-3345, 800-627-8800
FAX: 915-687-5951
E-mail: retsales@marshill.com

ignition systems

See full listing in **Section Two** under **ignition parts**

Miltronics Mfg Inc
95 Krif Rd
Keene, NH 03431
603-352-3333 business line
800-NH-ALERT or
800-828-9089 order lines

detection system

Driveway Alert enhances your living by monitoring driveways, entryways, back yards, pool areas, etc. Use this wireless, monitoring and detection system to safeguard your world. Be alerted when someone enters your property. The basic system is made up of an infra-red sensor transmitter which detects and/or senses the activity and a receiver which receives the transmission and alerts the household. The systems can be built up with more than 1 sensor or receiver for complete detection and reception throughout home and property. Call the manufacturer. Web site: www.miltronics1.com

apparel

Bonneville Sports Inc
3544 Enterprise Dr
Amaheim, CA 92807
888-999-7258, 714-666-1966
FAX: 714-666-1955
E-mail: bonspeed@aol.com

accessories
clothing

Color catalog packed with custom clothing and cool car stuff for you, your car and your garage. Not only do we create the finest automotive apparel in the world, we manufacture and source the best in garage goodies and automobilia. Now have Tony Nancy vintage drag racing, Posie and Troy Trepanier t-shirts and more. Also have a great catalog showroom in Anaheim, just 15 minutes from Disneyland. Web site: www.bonnevillesports.com

California Car Cover Co
21125 Superior St
Chatsworth, CA 91311
800-423-5525; FAX: 818-998-2442

accessories
apparel
car covers
tools

See full listing in **Section Two** under **car covers**

Classic Motorcar Investments
3755 Terra Loma Dr
Bullhead City, AZ 86442
520-763-5869
E-mail: classic@mohaveaz.com

apparel

Deal in 1950s fashions, class jackets, poodle skirts, Elvis and Marilyn items and fabulous 1950s fads.

Hooker Headers
1024 W Brooks St
Ontario, CA 91762
909-983-5871; FAX: 909-986-9860

exhaust systems

See full listing in **Section Two** under **exhaust systems**

Mercedes-Benz Visitor Center
PO Box 100
Tuscaloosa, AL 35403-0100
888-2TOUR-MB, 205-507-2262
FAX: 205-507-2255

museum

See full listing in **Section One** under **Mercedes-Benz**

Motorcars International
528 N Prince Ln
Springfield, MO 65802
417-831-9999; FAX: 417-831-8080
E-mail: sales@motorcars-intl.com

accessories
cars
services
tools

See full listing in **Section One** under **Ferrari**

Motorsports Racing
914 S Santa Fe #101
Vista, CA 92084
760-630-0547; FAX: 760-630-3085

accessories
apparel
art

Mail order only. Your exclusive source for Mr Norm's genuine accessories, memorabilia and vehicle documentation, and Yenko Motorsports apparel and accessories, featuring The One and Only On The Planet 68 Yenko COPO Camaro. Also, a huge selection of automotive apparel for all enthusiasts, including the Match Race Madness line of nostalgia drag racing apparel, plus posters and more for street rods, customs, 1950s cars, muscle cars, Camaros, Mustangs, Vettes, Harleys, and race cars.

National Road-Zane Grey Museum
8850 East Pike
Norwich, OH 43767
800-752-2602; FAX: 740-872-3510

museum

See full listing in **Section Six** under **Ohio**

O'Brien Truckers
5 Perry Hill
North Grafton, MA 01536-1532
508-839-3033; FAX: 508-839-9490
E-mail: obt@ziplink.net

accessories
belt buckles
plaques
valve covers

See full listing in **Section Two** under **plaques**

People's Choice & Lost in the 50s
28170 Ave Crocker #209
Valencia, CA 91355
800-722-1965, 661-295-1965
FAX: 661-295-1931

1950s clothing
1950s memorabilia
automobilia items
celebrity items

See full listing in **Section Two** under **automobilia**

Top Dead Center Apparel
PO Box 753
18 Main St
Wells River, VT 05081
802-757-2553; FAX: 802-757-3312
E-mail:
greenmtmonogram@connriver.net

apparel

Mail order and open shop. Daily 9 am to 5 pm. Screen printed apparel for the automotive trade.

Viking Worldwise Inc
190 Doe Run Rd
Manheim, PA 17545
800-842-9198; FAX: 717-664-5556
E-mail: gkurien@success.net

leather jackets

Mail order and open shop. Monday-Friday 9 am to 6 pm, Saturday by appointment/chance EST. Apparel custom leather jackets. Top quality custom leather jackets made of lambskin, fully lined, with your logo, design, car, hobby, inlaid in full color leather. No minimums. Quantities from 1 to 1,000. Imagine your club logo, car etc inlaid in leather on a custom leather jacket made just for you. Prices range from $325-$450 on average, depending on design. Racing teams and corporate orders our specialty. Web site: www.vikingworldwise.com

Vintage Shop Coats 40 Fourth St #106 Petaluma, CA 94952 925-837-7869; FAX: 707-762-7901	shop coats

Classic shop coats. Web site: www.vintageshopcoats.com

See our ad on page 200

West Coast Metric Inc 24002 Frampton Ave Harbor City, CA 90710 310-325-0005; FAX: 310-325-9733 E-mail: wcmi@earthlink.net	apparel carpets plastic parts rubber parts

See full listing in **Section One** under **Volkswagen**

appraisals

A-One Auto Appraisals 19 Hope Ln Narragansett, RI 02882 401-783-7701, RI; 407-668-9610, FL	appraisals

Auto appraisals on all types antique, street rods, customs and special interest. License #472. New England area and Florida.

AAAC-Antique Automobile **Appraisal & Consulting** PO Box 700153 Plymouth, MI 48170 PH/FAX: 734-453-7644 E-mail: aaac@ameritech.net	appraisals Cadillac parts consulting

See full listing in **Section One** under **Cadillac/LaSalle**

AAG-Auto Appraisal Group Inc PO Box 7034 Charlottesville, VA 22906 800-848-2886, 804-295-1722 FAX: 804-295-7918 E-mail: aag@autoappraisal.com	appraisals

Classic and collectible auto value specialists. Nationwide comprehensive professional service. Pre-purchase inspections, insurance documentation, estate tax matters, property settlements. IRS forms. Inspections by AAG certified examiners. Locations: California, Connecticut, Florida, Massachusetts, New Jersey, New York, North Carolina, Pennsylvania, Texas, Utah, Vermont, Virginia, Washington, Wisconsin. Extensive information gathering, originality and historical research, current market comparable analysis, factual reporting. Web site: www.autoappraisal.com

Accurate Auto Appraisers 1362 Hopkins St Berkeley, CA 94702 800-733-4937, 510-528-9377 FAX: 510-527-7803 E-mail: autoappraisal@usa.net	appraisals

Qualifications include: ten years as owner-manager of automotive leasing and rental business, including responsibility for determining resale value and depreciation; fifteen years as owner-operator of complete automotive service facility, including estimations; forty years as a craftsman in metal finishing and paint restoration; experience as buyer and seller at automotive auctions; thirty years as licensed automotive dealer in California; International Automotive Appraisers Association certified, member #5105289377. Web site: www.accuratevalue.com

Akorn Automotive Appraisals Inc 4634 Old Princess Anne Rd Virginia Beach, VA 23462-6453 757-467-4391 E-mail: akorna@aol.com	appraisals consulting

Mail order and open shop by appointment only. Value appraisals, pre-purchase inspections, restoration consulting. IAAA member, #1003051995.

AMC Classic Appraisers 7963 Depew St Arvada, CO 80003 303-428-8760; FAX: 303-428-1070	appraisals

Mail order and open shop. Monday-Saturday 10 am to 7 pm. Collector car appraisals and on site evaluations. All cars 1900-present, includes stock, custom, modified cars, trucks, motorcycles, all makes and models. Certified Master Appraiser, IAAA member, #1006050095.

John Analla's Auto Appraisal Service 8952 Geraldine Ave San Diego, CA 92123-2915 619-278-4084; FAX: 619-278-7435 E-mail: ja.analla@excite.com	appraisals

Open shop only. Five days a week. Appraisals for foreign and domestic with special emphasis on classics and collectibles. Exotics, limousines, motorhomes, motorcycles, boats, Senior Certified member of the American Society of Appraisers, member of International Automobile Appraisers Association (member #1006100097), California business license #80061238.

Antique & Classic Auto Appraisal Robert F Keefe 18812 Monteverde Dr Springhill, FL 34610 727-856-5168	appraisals consultant

Appraiser and consultant for antique, classic and special interest vehicles. 30 years' involvement in the old car field. Associate member of the International Society of Appraisers. Pre-purchase and travel available.

Antique & Special Interest Car **Appraisals** 22 Shipman Rd Andover, MA 01810-1716 978-475-7707 evenings	appraisals

Open shop only. Antique and special interest cars only, full condition reports, history, narrative and candid report with actual value survey by comparisons. 25 years' experience.

Appraisal Express PO Box 925 Torrance, CA 90508-0925 310-782-2300; FAX: 310-782-2380	appraisals

Value appraisals, damage repair estimates, total loss evaluations on collisions, recovered and unrecovered thefts. Value disputes and expert testimony. Licensed insurance adjusters. Founded by Bruce Summers in 1975. Heavy insurance carrier account base. Over 300 vehicles inspected each month. Servicing southern California. Six full-time appraisers. 48 hour turnaround. Web site: appraisalexpress.com

Archer & Associates 1807 East Ave Hayward, CA 94541 510-581-4911; FAX: 510-537-7864	appraisals consultant promotion sales/purchasing

Shop open Monday-Saturday 9 am to 10 pm. Automotive historian/collector. Maximum qualifications. Nationwide service.

Section Two Generalists

Walt Armstrong
74 Montsweag Rd
Woolwich, ME 04579
207-442-7450

> **inspections**

Mail order and on-site visits. On-site inspections of cars in the Maine area for prospective buyers in other parts of the country. For antique and sports vehicles, specifically British cars. You can save time and money by having your prospective purchase inspected by me before you make your trip or I'll accompany you for advice.

ARS, Automotive Research Services
Division of Auto Search International
1702 W Camelback #301
Phoenix, AZ 85015
602-230-7111; FAX: 602-230-7282

> **appraisals**
> **research**

Mail order and open shop. Daily 10 am to 10 pm PST, central Phoenix location. Appraisals and research. Free phone consultation. Don't sell, settle, donate or buy until you verify. All years cars, light trucks, street rods and customs too. NADA Advisory Board member, 11 years' full-time vehicle research experience. No conflicts of interest. Excellent reference library. Data packages prepared. Affordable rates. Can travel. From pre-purchase inspections to qualified expert witness testimony. Our detailed reports and substantiated comprehensive appraisals stand tall under any circumstance, including total loss insurance claim mediation, fires and unrecovered thefts. Also available as neutral umpire for disputed claims. Collectible vehicle specialists since 1987.

Auto Advisors
14 Dudley Rd
Billerica, MA 01821
978-667-0075

> **appraisals**

Licensed appraiser for cars, trucks and motorcycles. Specializing in appraisals for antique and classic cars of all types and models. Also work with court approved divorces and estates.

Auto Appraisal Service
2208 N Leg Rd
Augusta, GA 30909
706-736-7070; FAX: 706-736-7080

> **appraisals**

Mail order and open shop. Monday-Friday 10 am to 6 pm. Auto and truck appraisals. IAAA member, #1005130097.

Auto Consultants & Appraisal Service
Charles J Kozelka
PO Box 111
Macedonia, OH 44056
330-467-0748; FAX: 330-467-3725

> **appraisals**

Professional appraisals for antique, classic, special interest and late model vehicles. Video appraisals at extra charge. Certified automobile accident and vehicle theft investigator. Expert witness and court testimony. Pre-purchase inspections or liquidation evaluations our specialty. Technical assistance on vehicle transactions, restorations or any auto related service. Consultant for commercial advertising, promotions, entertainment, special events, etc. Vehicle locator and broker service available.

Auto Evaluators
5062 S 108th St, Ste 225
Omaha, NE 68137
402-681-2968; FAX: 402-331-0638

> **appraisals**

Mail order and open shop by appointment. Appraise late model, classic, antique, street rods and custom cars. Stated value insurance appraisals our specialty. Mail appraisals nationwide. Automotive legal consultant, court tested expert witness, any legality. Bankruptcy, divorce, tax issues, estates, quality of repair or diminution of value issues. 20 years' of automotive experience. Calls returned anywhere. 24-hour phone. We can help.

Auto-Line Enterprises Inc
2 Lyons Rd
Armonk, NY 10504
914-681-1757; FAX: 914-273-5159
E-mail: garfconect@aol.com

> **appraisals**
> **broker services**

Mail and telephone orders. Appraisal and broker services provided by an experienced dealer with over 28 years in the business. All types of classics, antiques and special interest autos included. Purchase and sale consulting services available.

Auto Nostalgia Enr
332 St Joseph
Mont St Gregoire, QC Canada J0J 1K0
PH/FAX: 450-346-3644
E-mail: autonostalgia@vif.com

> **literature**
> **manuals**
> **models**
> **tractor decals**

See full listing in **Section Two** under **literature dealers**

Auto Quest Investment Cars Inc
710 W 7th St
PO Box 22
Tifton, GA 31793
912-382-4750; FAX: 912-382-4752
E-mail: info@auto-quest.com

> **car dealer**

See full listing in **Section Two** under **car dealers**

Auto World Sales
2245 Q St
Lincoln, NE 68503
402-435-7111; FAX: 402-435-7131
E-mail: autowwka@navix.net

> **appraisals**
> **sales**

Monday-Saturday 9 am to 6 pm. Sale of older rust-free pickups, 1970-1990. Hand picked from the Southwest, out of the "rust belt". Offer professional appraisals on classic and collectible cars and pickups, in a four state area. Member of the International Auto Appraisers Association since 1995, member #1006030095. Web site: www.carseekers.com

Automobile Appraisal Service
Steve Cram
1080 Eddy St #607
San Francisco, CA 94109
415-567-1087, 619-584-4678
FAX: 415-567-1245

> **appraisals**

Deal in all automobiles, appraiser, historian, author. Totally independent, does not broker cars; hence, no conflict of interests. Free phone consultations. San Francisco to San Diego.

Automobilia Auctions Inc
132 Old Main St
Rocky Hill, CT 06067
860-529-7177; FAX: 860-257-3621

> **appraisals**
> **auctions**

See full listing in **Section Two** under **auctions & events**

Automotive Legal Service Inc
PO Box 626
Dresher, PA 19025
800-487-4947, 215-659-4947
FAX: 215-657-5843
E-mail: autolegal@aol.com

> **appraisals**

State licensed automotive appraisal specialists. Antique, classic, exotic, kit, muscle car, pro street, street rod, cars, vans, trucks, original, restored, modified, incomplete, hard to value, insurance claims and restoration disputes, arbitration, litigation our specialty. Member Collector Car and Truck, NADA, OCPG Advisory Panels, National Muscle Car Association Regional director, qualified expert witness 129 times, also current model Accident Investigation/Reconstruction Lemon Law. Quality references, maximum credibility, reasonable rates, travel USA. Free consultation. Web site: www.automotivelegal.com

AV Auto Appraisals
137 Niagara St
St Catharines, ON Canada L2R 4L4
905-687-9066; FAX: 905-687-7381

appraisals

Automobile appraisals for vintage, classic, antique, muscle cars for all makes, models and years. Will travel in Canada to appraise and do prepurchase inspections for parties south of the border. IAAA member (#1002100198).

Donald Avise
2944 Hwy F48 W
Newton, IA 50208
515-792-4131; FAX: 515-792-8042

appraisals

Automotive appraisal for antique, collector, custom autos. IAAA member (#100191294).

AVM Automotive Consulting
Box 338
Montvale, NJ 07645-0338
201-391-5194; FAX: 201-782-0663
E-mail: avmtony@aol.com

appraisals
consultant

Open 9 am to 9 pm weekdays. Specializing in appraisals, pre-purchase inspections and consulting for antique, classic and custom vehicles and equipment. Will travel or by mail. Writing appraisals for over twenty years for legal and estate settlements. Automotive products and business consulting with 30 years' experience. Services are available for individuals, attorneys and corporations. Member of the International Automotive Appraisers Association (member #1000071994) makes prompt inspections possible worldwide.

Bastian Automotive Restoration
4170 Finch Ave
Fairfield, OH 45014
PH/FAX: 513-738-4268

appraisals
restoration

See full listing in **Section Two** under **restoration shops**

Dave Bayowski
3686 Niles Carver Rd
Mineral Ridge, OH 44440
PH/FAX: 330-544-0242

appraisals

Auto appraisals for antique, classic, custom and street rod. ISA, IAAA (member #1002180098). 30 years' experience in restoration, consulting and appraising.

Bill's Collector Cars
6478 County Rd #1
South Point, OH 45680
740-894-5175

appraisals
car dealer

See full listing in **Section Two** under **car dealers**

Blair Collectors & Consultants
2821 SW 167th Pl
Seattle, WA 98166
206-242-6745, 206-246-1305

appraisals
consultant
literature

Mail order and open shop. Monday-Friday 9 am to 10 pm PST. Collector car appraisals, cars and parts locating service, technical and restoration/customizing advice, car importing advice and assistance, data packages for all cars, buy/sell literature. Covers vintage, classic, muscle, street rods and imports. Professional engineer with over 40 years' experience.

Brookside Classics
189 S Spencer Rd
Spencer, MA 01562
PH/FAX: 508-885-2017
E-mail: brooksideclassics@juno.com

appraisals

Appraisals for antique, classic and special interest vehicles. Excellent for insurance, estate, market value, loans. IAAA member (#1003060099).

Bryant's Antique Auto Parts
851 Western Ave
Hampden, ME 04444
207-862-4019

appraisals
chassis/engine
parts/sheetmetal
wiring harnesses

See full listing in **Section One** under **Ford 1903-1931**

CALSPECC Restorations
20818 E Weldon
Tivy Valley, CA 93657-9107
209-787-1000; FAX: 209-787-1100
E-mail: meckhaus@aol.com

appraisals
car dealer

By appointment only. All phases of restorations on British sports cars. Partial to body-off restorations. MG TC/TD/TF, MGA, Triumph, Austin-Healey, Morgan, Jaguars, etc. Specializing in driving restorations. We go through cars for driveability, new paint, chrome, rubber, etc.

Car Critic
202 Woodshire Ln
Naples, FL 34105
941-435-1157; FAX: 941-261-4864
E-mail: puppys4u@aol.com

appraisals
inspections

Mail order and open shop. Daily 8 am to 8 pm. Perform nationwide pre-purchase inspections, certified appraisals, mechanical failure analysis, off lease inspections prior to or immediately after lease termination, physical damage appraisals for insurance companies, diminution (loss) of value, automobile fire investigations, accident scene inspections, investigations and photographs and civil expert testimonial. This work is performed on automobiles, trucks, motorcycles, boats and watercraft. Perform repair facility fraud investigations as well as local evaluations for attorneys, banks and consumers. Member of IAAA, A&N, ASE.

Chicago Car Exchange
1 Collector Car Dr
Box 530
Lake Bluff, IL 60044
847-680-1950; FAX: 847-680-1961
E-mail: oldtoys@wwa.com

appraisals
car dealer
car locator
financing
storage

See full listing in **Section Two** under **car dealers**

Charles W Clarke
Automotive Consultant/Appraiser
17 Saddle Ridge Dr
West Simsbury, CT 06092-2118
PH/FAX: 860-658-2714

appraiser
car dealer
consultant

See full listing in **Section Two** under **consultants**

Classic Auto Appraisals
3497 Simpson Rd SE
Rochester, MN 55904
507-289-7111

appraisals

Appraisals for special interest, antique, milestones, muscle and classic cars. Our specialty: 1950s, 1960s rods and customs. For insurance coverage, estates, loan valuation, charitable contributions, marriage, business/settlements, pre-sale, pre-purchase inspections.

Classic Auto Restoration
15445 Ventura Blvd #60
Sherman Oaks, CA 91413
818-905-6267; FAX: 818-906-1249
E-mail: rollsroyce1@earthlink.net

acquisitions
restoration
sales

See full listing in **Section One** under **Rolls-Royce/Bentley**

Classic Auto Restoration
437 Greene St
Buffalo, NY 14212
716-896-6663

appraisals
plating
polishing
restoration

See full listing in **Section Two** under **restoration shops**

Section Two
Generalists

Classic Car Appraisals
37 Wyndwood Rd
West Hartford, CT 06107
PH/FAX: 860-236-0125

> appraisals

Open shop only. Flexible days and hours. Complete and thorough appraisal of your automobile, exterior, interior, engine compartment and undercarriage. Photos included. Welcomed by insurance agencies and law firms. Also available: a magazine type write-up of your car, called an "auto biography", complete with photos, historical background on the model and your personal history with the car. Also available: personal plaque of your car complete with photo, owner information and a listing of awards won.

Classic Car Research
29508 Southfield Rd, Ste 106
Southfield, MI 48076
248-557-2880; FAX: 248-557-3511
E-mail: kawifreek@msn.com

> appraisals
> consultant
> part locating

Appraisals, parts locating, consulting, new and used muscle car parts. Entering our 13th year in business. IAAA member (#1001070097). Web site: http://adcomm.com/jmkclassiccars

Classic Motors
PO Box 1321
Shirley, MA 01464
978-425-4614

> appraisals
> car dealer
> consulting

See full listing in **Section Two** under **car dealers**

Classique Cars Unlimited
7005 Turkey Bayou Rd
PO Box 249
Lakeshore, MS 39558
800-543-8691, USA
228-467-9633; FAX: 228-467-9207
E-mail: parts@datasync.com

> appraisals
> parts
> repairs
> restorations

See full listing in **Section One** under **Lincoln**

Collector Car Appraisers LLC
800 Waterford Dr
Frederick, MD 21702
301-473-8333; FAX: 301-698-4796
E-mail: gfmchugh@netstorm.net

> appraisals

Telephone orders only. Seven days 8 am to 8 pm. Appraisals: Maryland, Virginia, Delaware, District of Columbia and southern Pennsylvania. 38 years' experience. Expert witness, consultant, broker.

Collector Car & Truck Market Guide
41 N Main St
North Grafton, MA 01536
508-839-6707; FAX: 508-839-6266
E-mail: vmr@vmrintl.com

> price guide

See full listing in **Section Four** under **periodicals**

Collector's Carousel
84 Warren Ave
Westbrook, ME 04092
207-854-0343; FAX: 207-856-6913

> appraisals
> sales
> service

See full listing in **Section Two** under **car dealers**

Lance S Coren, CAA, CMA
20545 Eastwood Ave
Torrance, CA 90503-3611
310-370-4114; FAX: 310-371-4120

> appraisals

Mail order and open by appointment only. The only FIA and ORDINEX Certified Automotive Appraiser in the western United States. Material damage appraisals, actual cash evaluations. Exotic, classic and race cars. American Bar Association and IRS qualified. Insurance, bank, charity, museum, court evaluations. Expert witness testimony. Arbitration and mediation. Auto manufacturer and United Nations acknowledged expert. Celebrity

clientele. 20 years' experience. Servicing the United States, Europe and Japan. Senior member: Society of Automotive Appraisers, International Automotive Appraisers Guild, Automotive Arbitration Council.

Corvette Enterprise Brokerage
The Power Broker
52 Van Houten Ave
Passaic Park, NJ 07055
973-472-7021

> appraisals
> broker
> car locator
> investment planning

See full listing in **Section One** under **Corvette**

Creative Automotive Consultants
PO Box 2221
San Rafael, CA 94912-2221
707-824-9004; FAX: 707-824-9002
E-mail: cars4cac@earthlink.net

> appraisals
> car locator
> promotion

See full listing in **Section Two** under **consultants**

Customs & Classics
PO Box 737
Clayton, CA 94517
PH/FAX: 925-672-7230
E-mail: japolk@jps.net

> appraisals

Appraisal services for antique, collectible and modern automobiles. Web site: customsclassics.com

Davies Valuations
18 Club Ct
Wasaga Beach, ON Canada L0L 2P0
705-429-7682, 416-219-7660
E-mail: edavies@interhop.net

> appraisals

By appointment. We come to your location. Value appraisals on all makes and models of collector or special interest automobiles. IAAA member, #1007010097.

The Davis Registry
4073 Ruby
Ypsilanti, MI 48197-9317
734-434-5581, 313-662-1001
E-mail: kfnut@umich.edu

> periodical
> quarterly bulletin

See full listing in **Section Four** under **books & publications**

Dearborn Automobile Co
16 Maple St (at Rt 1)
Topsfield, MA 01983
978-887-6644; FAX: 978-887-3889
E-mail: slr190sl@aol.com

> appraisals
> car dealer

Open Monday-Friday 9 am to 5 pm, Saturday 9 am to 12 noon. All types of rare Mercedes bought, sold and brokered, appraisals. Specializing in Mercedes 1949-1971. Appraiser for estates and insurance.

Robert DeMars Ltd Auto Appraisers/Historians
2222 Lakeview Ave, Ste 160/256
West Palm Beach, FL 33401
561-832-0171; FAX: 561-738-7632
E-mail: carapraisr@aol.com

> appraisals
> auto historians
> car locator
> research library
> resto consultants

Appraiser/Historians: telephone consultation worldwide for fast information and recommendations! Available in person, by mail, e-mail and fax. We're the 30 year pioneers of the field of collector car appraisal, traveling the world. Low mileage, Antique, Classic, Sports, Musclecar, Racecar, Pebble Beach Concours and prototype "Dream Cars" a specialty. Clients and inspectors thru US, Europe, Japan, South America. As historians and performance/race drivers with a large research library, we appreciate fine machinery and monitor the "Now Market" for trends and values. Pebble Beach, CA/Palm Beach, FL. Please note new main office and phone. Web site: www.varoom.com/add2.html

Russ Dentico's Sales & Auto Appraisal Consulting
PO Box 566
Trenton, MI 48183
734-675-3306; FAX: 734-675-8908

appraisals

Open Tuesday-Friday 11 am to 5 pm. Appraisal service for attorney estate service, Corvette and special interest vehicles, salvage appraisal service (licensed salvage and used car dealer). IAAA member (#1005020095).

Doc's Jags
125 Baker Rd
Lake Bluff, IL 60044
847-367-5247; FAX: 847-367-6363
E-mail: docsjags@worldnet.att.net

appraisals
interiors
restoration

See full listing in **Section One** under **Jaguar**

Drosten Automotive Appraisal Co
569-B Constitution Ave
Camarillo, CA 93010
805-482-4661; FAX: 805-484-4720
E-mail: fredd@isle.net

appraisals

Open Monday-Friday 9 am to 6 pm. Appraiser of conventional, classic, antique, custom and street rod cars and trucks. Certified Master Automotive Appraiser by International Automotive Appraisers Association (member #100021495) and Appraisal Institute.

Eckhaus Appraisal Service
20818 E Weldon
Tivy Valley, CA 93657-9107
209-787-1000; FAX: 209-787-1100
E-mail: meckhaus@aol.com

appraisals

Established 1968. Inspection and appraisals for insurance coverage, lending institutions, estates, etc. Member International Society of Appraisers. Pre-purchase inspections anywhere in the world. One car or large collections. Absolute confidentiality assured.

Richard H Feibusch
211 Dimmick Ave
Venice, CA 90291
310-392-6605; FAX: 310-396-1933
E-mail: rfeibusch@loop.com

appraisals

Appraiser and automotive journalist. Recognized by the IRS, Probate Court and all major insurance companies. Antiques, classics, special interest, foreign, rods, customs and kit/home-built cars. Los Angeles area only. Web site: www.englishcars.com

FEN Enterprises of New York Inc
PO Box 1559
1324 Rt 376
Wappingers Falls, NY 12590
914-462-5959, 914-462-5094
FAX: 914-462-8450

parts
restoration

See full listing in **Section One** under **Cadillac/LaSalle**

FIAInspectors.com
PO Box 1308
Largo, FL 33779
727-588-0331; FAX: 727-588-0580
E-mail: bills@fiainspectors.com

appraisals

Appraisals nationwide. IAAA member, #1008010096.

Fiesta's Classic Car Center
3901 N Kings Hwy
St Louis, MO 63115
314-385-4567

appraisals
consignment sales
storage

See full listing in **Section Two** under **storage**

John Filiss
45 Kingston Ave
Port Jervis, NY 12771
914-856-2942
E-mail: johnfiliss@hotmail.com

appraisals

Mail order and open shop by appointment. Specialize in low-cost, professional appraisals for insurance purposes, also divorces and estate settlements. Nationwide service. Web site: www.motionalmemories.com

Florida Inspection Associates
PO Box 1308
Largo, FL 33770
727-588-0331; FAX: 727-588-0580
E-mail: bills@fiainspectors.com

appraisals

FIA has provided certified appraisals and inspections since 1987. Offer nationwide service on all makes, models and years of motor vehicles, recreation or motorcycles. IAAA certified master appraiser Bill Schultz. 450 locations nationwide. Web site: www.fiainspectors.com

From Rust To Riches
16643 Rt 144
Mt Airy, MD 21771
301-854-5900, 410-442-3637
301-854-5956; FAX: 301-854-5957
E-mail: tatrabill@aol.com

appraisals
car dealer
repairs
restoration

See full listing in **Section Two** under **restoration shops**

Green Mountain Vintage Auto
20 Bramley Way
Bellows Falls, VT 05101
PH/FAX: 802-463-3141
E-mail: vintauto@sover.net

damage appraisals
ignition parts
vehicle evaluations

Mail order only. Call or e-mail your needs. Specializing in vehicle evaluations and damage appraisals for all models. Also deal in ignition parts for late 1930s-1960s vehicles.

The Gullwing Garage Ltd
Bricklin SVI Specialists
5 Cimorelli Dr
New Windsor, NY 12553-6201
914-561-0019 anytime

appraisals
literature
parts
service

See full listing in **Section One** under **Bricklin**

Hand's Elderly Auto Care
2000 Galveston St
Grand Prairie, TX 75051
PH/FAX: 972-642-4288

repair
restoration

See full listing in **Section Two** under **restoration shops**

John H Heldreth & Associates
919 W Main St, Ste L-4
Lakeview Plaza
Hendersonville, TN 37075
615-824-5994; FAX: 615-822-4919

appraisals

Open Monday-Friday 8:30 am to 5 pm, outside appointments by phone. Appraisals for all makes and models. IAAA member, #1006010095.

Don Hoelscher, Auto Appraiser
52 Waynesboro Ct
St Charles, MO 63304
314-939-9667
E-mail: dhoelsch@mail.win.org

appraisals

By appointment only. Appraisals of classic, antique, special interest/collector cars, trucks and other vehicles, all years and models.

Hubbard and Associates
Appraisers of Collectible Autos
80 W Bellevue Dr #200
Pasadena, CA 91105
626-568-0122; FAX: 626-568-1510

appraisals

Office hours Monday-Friday 9 am to 5 pm by appointment only. Appraisals for insurance, probate, marriage dissolution and pre-purchase inspections. Licensed, Board certified, Senior member American Society of Appraisers. Professional resume and references upon request. Twenty years' experience. Expert witness, arbitration and litigation.

**International Automotive
Appraisers Assoc**
Box 338
Montvale, NJ 07645
201-391-3251; FAX: 201-782-0663
E-mail: avmtony@aol.com

appraisals

Incorporated in New Jersey on September 1, 1994. Publications, organizations and the courts recognize and approve its policies. Recognized professional automotive appraisers from Australia, Canada, Europe and the US including Puerto Rico and Hawaii comprise the membership. *The Auto Appraiser News* is the official newsletter of the IAAA. It devotes total content to automotive appraisers, appraisals and the industry that they serve. A roster that lists members, their expertise and their geographic locations is available to organizations and insurers. Goals include educating and training appraisers and promoting professionalism amongst them. The IAAA is in the process of documenting standards and practices of automotive appraisers.

Jesser's Auto Clinic
26 West St
Akron, OH 44303
330-376-8181; FAX: 330-384-9129

appraisals

Open shop. Monday-Friday 10 am to 4 pm. By appointment and on-site appraisals. Bonded and insured, over 15 years' experience. Personal, professional, certified appraisals and pre-purchase inspections, all portfolios done in triplicate with full color photographs. For all domestic and foreign models. Stated insurance values, loan appraisals, appraisals for any purpose. Insurance arbitrator, expert witness. Member, advisor, board member NADA Exotics and Collectibles. Member International Automotive Appraisers Association (member #100231294). Active memberships in AACA, CCCA, VMCCA, MCS, BCA, MCA, OCA, WPC, PAC, PIMCC, CTC, CLC, CCI, POCI, LCOC, HOG and twenty others. Up-to-date, well maintained reference library. Web site: www.jessersclassickeys.com

JM Appraisal Co Inc
1439 S Powerline Rd
Pompano Beach, FL 33069
954-969-0245; FAX: 954-969-0239
E-mail: jmarco1482@aol.com

appraisals

Auto, truck, marine and property appraisals for all needs. Specializing in custom and classic automobiles and Harley-Davidson motorcycles. IAAA member, #1004140097.

K & K Vintage Motorcars LC
9848 SW Frwy
Houston, TX 77074
713-541-2281; FAX: 713-541-2286

**restoration
sales
service**

See full listing in **Section Two** under **restoration shops**

Ken's Cougars
PO Box 5380
Edmond, OK 73083
405-340-1636; FAX: 405-340-5877

parts

See full listing in **Section One** under **Mercury**

J A Kennedy Inc
1727 Hartford Tpke
North Haven, CT 06473
203-239-2227

appraisals

Specializing in appraisals of both damage and value for antique, classic and special interest cars.

Laigle Motorsporte Ltd
5707 Schumacher Ln
Houston, TX 77057
713-781-6900; FAX: 713-781-6556
E-mail: laigle@usa.net

appraisals

Certified appraiser for special interest automobiles. Member IAAA (#100171294), board member NADA Galleria area, Houston, TX. Insurance appraisals. Expert witness, legal consultant

Landry Classic MotorCars
34 Goodhue Ave
Chicopee, MA 01020
413-592-2746; FAX: 413-594-8378

appraisals

Open 7 days by appointment only. Specializing in all types of professional appraisals including stated value, pre-purchase inspections for all collector cars and trucks. Licensed and certified in several states. Member of 13 national clubs.

Col Glenn Larson
4423-A Canyon Dr
Amarillo, TX 79110
806-358-9797; FAX: 806-467-0280
E-mail: colonel@arn.net

**appraisals
auctioneer**

Certified appraisals for collector cars. Collector car auctioneer. Over 10 years' experience. References available. IAAA member, #1010010097.

Larson Motor Co
Russell Larson
4423-A Canyon Dr
Amarillo, TX 79110
806-358-9797

**appraisals
restoration
sales**

See full listing in **Section Two** under **car dealers**

**Legacy Antique Vehicle
Appraisal Service**
PO Box 691
Middletown, MD 21769
301-371-7654
E-mail: legacyappraisal@juno.com

**appraisals
pre-purchase
inspections**

Appraisals, pre-purchase inspections for antique, collector, special interest vehicles including street rods. Serving Washington/Baltimore metro areas, central and western Maryland and northern Virginia. Call for appointment. IAAA member, #1001010096.

Bob Lichty
1330 Fulton Rd NW
Canton, OH 44703
330-456-7869; FAX: 330-455-0363
E-mail: rrubin@neo.rr.com

**appraisals
consultant
promoter**

Appraisals, pre-purchase inspections, estates, insurance. Consultant to publishers, museums, event promotion. Donation placement assistance. F&F cereal car collector. Author *AACA History.*

M & L Automobile Appraisal
2662 Palm Terr
Deland, FL 32720
904-734-1761

appraisals

Open daily by appointment. Florida licensed to appraise antique, classic, special interest, custom/altered automobiles, motorcycles, custom trailers and toys for insurance coverage, loan valuation, estate settlements or disputes.

M & M Automobile Appraisers Inc
584 Broomspun St
Henderson, NV 89015
702-568-5120; FAX: 702-568-5158

appraisals
broker
consultant

Appraise special interest, collectible and antique automobiles for insurance coverage, loan valuation, marriage or business dissolutions and value disputes. Expert witness insurance arbitration and investment consultation.

Randall Marcus Vintage Automobiles
706 Hanshaw Rd
Ithaca, NY 14850
607-257-5939; FAX: 607-272-8806

broker
car locator
consultant

See full listing in **Section Two** under **brokers**

Gerry Martel & Classic Carriages
173 Main St
Fitchburg, MA 01420
978-343-6382; FAX: 978-342-1939

appraisals

Appraisals for all collector cars. IAAA member (#1005050095). 20 years' experience.

Bill McCoskey
16643 Rt 144
Mt Airy, MD 21771
301-854-5900, 410-442-3637
FAX: 301-854-5957
E-mail: tatrabill@aol.com

appraisals
repairs

Certified value appraisals, diminution in value claims, insurance claim arbitration service and effective expert witness court testimony. Pre-claim value reconstruction and appraisal-by-mail service available. Over 25 years in the antique and classic car business and hobby, rare European cars a specialty. Well-equipped restoration shop on premises, offering top quality repairs to all antique and classic cars at below market prices. High quality repairs available worldwide, "have tools will travel".

McIntyre Auctions
PO Box 60
East Dixfield, ME 04227
800-894-4300, 207-562-4443
FAX: 207-562-4576
E-mail: classicford@quickconnect.com

auctions
automobilia
literature
petroliana

See full listing in **Section Two** under **auctions & events**

Memory Lane Motors
562 County Rd 121
Fenelon Falls, ON Canada K0M 1N0
705-887-CARS; FAX: 705-887-4028

car dealer
restoration
service

See full listing in **Section Two** under **restoration shops**

Memory Lane Motors Inc
1231 Rt 176
Lake Bluff, IL 60044
847-362-4600

appraisals
car dealer
storage

See full listing in **Section Two** under **car dealers**

Dennis Mitosinka's Classic Cars and Appraisals Service
619 E Fourth St
Santa Ana, CA 92701
714-953-5303; FAX: 714-953-1810

appraisals
books

Appraisals of all types of autos. For the most professional service, for disputes in value, litigation, insurance, donations, diminished value purchases or sales. Call for cost estimates. Certified appraiser with over 29 years' experience. Also large selection of auto books, mostly out of print.

NorCal Auto
615D Saint John St
Pleasanton, CA 94566
888-224-6005; FAX: 925-426-8845
E-mail: mwjohn@hotmail.com

appraisals

Open shop only. Monday-Friday 8 am to 5 pm PST. Auto appraisals for any year vehicle. Pre-purchase appraisals. Classics, street rods, etc. Fast, friendly service. Multiple car discounts. Video and e-mail service. Call toll-free.

Old Car Co
Rich House
3112 Eaglewood Pl
St Charles, MO 63303
314-926-2789

appraisals

Appraisal service for classic cars, hot rods, antique cars and collector cars. Reliable, experienced and up to date. We come to you. IAAA member, #1011120097.

Omega Automobile Appraisals
115 18 Ave SE
St Petersburg, FL 33705
PH/FAX: 727-894-5690

appraisals

See full listing in **Section One** under **Rolls-Royce/Bentley**

Paradise Classic Auto Appraisal
5894 Cornell
Taylor, MI 48180
313-291-2758

appraisals
transport

Auto appraisal and transporting. IAAA member, #1008010095.

CT Peters Inc Appraisers
2A W Front St
Red Bank, NJ 07701
732-747-9450 Red Bank
732-528-9451 Brielle

appraisals

Mail order and open shop. Monday-Friday 9 am to 5 pm. Antique, classic and vintage motor cars appraised throughout the tri-state area since 1976. For insurance, fair market and estate values. Appointments at your premises available or send photographs for appraisal by mail. References available. Also offer fast, effective, discreet methods of selling investment quality automobiles through our exclusive tri-state area computer client mailing list.

Prairie Auto
Jeremiah Larson
7087 Orchid Ln
Maple Grove, MN 55311
612-420-8600; FAX: 612-420-8637
E-mail: jer4cars@aol.com

appraisals
car dealers

See full listing in **Section Two** under **car dealers**

Precision Autoworks
2202 Federal Street
East Camden, NJ 08105
609-966-0080, NJ
FAX: 610-649-3577, PA

restorations

See full listing in **Section One** under **Mercedes-Benz**

Prestige Thunderbird Inc
10215 Greenleaf Ave
Santa Fe Springs, CA 90670
800-423-4751, 562-944-6237
FAX: 562-941-8677
E-mail:
tbirds@prestigethunderbird.com

appraisals
radios
repairs
restorations
tires

See full listing in **Section One** under **Thunderbird**

Rader's Relics — appraisals / car dealer
2601 W Fairbanks Ave
Winter Park, FL 32789
407-647-1940; FAX: 407-647-1930
E-mail: therelic@bellsouth.net

See full listing in **Section Two** under **car dealers**

William H Randel — appraisals / car locators
PO Box 173
Hatboro, PA 19040
215-675-8969; FAX: 215-441-0960
E-mail: tbrdnut@bellatlantic.net

See full listing in **Section One** under **Thunderbird**

The Rappa Group — appraisals
174 Brady Ave
Hawthorne, NY 10532
914-747-7010; FAX: 914-747-7013
E-mail: djrappa@rappa.com

Antique, classic, custom, street rod and exotic vehicle insurance and appraisals. IAAA member, #1000241294. Web site: www.rappa.com

Reinholds Restorations — appraisals / repairs / restoration
c/o Rick Reinhold
PO Box 178, 255 N Ridge Rd
Reinholds, PA 17569-0178
717-336-5617; FAX: 717-336-7050

See full listing in **Section Two** under **restoration shops**

Reward Service Inc — appraisals / restoration / transportation
172 Overhill Rd
Stormville, NY 12582
914-227-7647; FAX: 914-221-0293

See full listing in **Section One** under **Jaguar**

Route 66 Collectible Cars and Antiques — consignment sales
1933 Del Monte Blvd
Seaside, CA 93955
831-393-9329; FAX: 831-393-9391
E-mail: cars@route66.com

See full listing in **Section Two** under **car dealers**

Royal Coach Works Ltd — appraisals
2146 Lunceford Ln
Lilburn, GA 30047
PH/FAX: 404-249-9040

Restorations by appointment. Appraisals for pre-purchase and insurance. IAAA member (#1005140098). Restorations, woodwork, maintenance, parts for Rolls-Royce to 1985, Aston to 1992, Mercedes 600 to 1975.

Richard C Ryder — appraisals
828 Prow Ct
Sacramento, CA 95822
916-442-3424 anytime
916-600-4825 mobile
FAX: 916-442-4939
E-mail: rydvntrzcwnet.com

Collector car evaluations for individuals, insurance, lenders, legal or government agencies.

James T Sandoro — appraisals / consultant
24 Myrtle Ave
Buffalo, NY 14204
716-855-1931

Confidential automotive consultant, appraiser, expert witness, trial consultant. 33 years' full time experience. Unique qualifications. Retained by the largest collections, museums, government agencies, restoration shops. I can give you an overview and act as an expert in your behalf as well as a trial consultant regarding collector vehicles, motorcycles, memorabilia, etc. I only testify in cases I believe in. My referrals are from other appraisers, dealers and restorers. Available anywhere in the world.

Sequence Appraisals — appraisals
PO Box 322
Springfield, NJ 07081
PH/FAX: 800-376-0076
E-mail: sequence90@aol.com

Specializing in vehicle value appraisals for classic, custom and antique vehicles. Web site: www.sequenceauto.com

Bernard A Siegal, ASA — appraisals
Automotive Restoration Services
PO Box 140722
Dallas, TX 75214
214-827-2678; FAX: 214-826-0000

Monday-Saturday 9 am to 6 pm CST. Appraisals for all marques and all years. Valuation for insurance, pre-purchase inspection, physical damage appraisals, loss of value, divorces, estate settlements. One of ten Senior members of the American Society of Appraisers accredited and tested in this field. Eight areas of certification by Automotive Service Excellence. Licensed Texas adjuster. All valuation reports conform to USPAP standards.

RL Smith Sales Inc — appraisals
Gregory S Smith, President
466 Hays Rd
Rensselaer, NY 12144-4701
518-449-4240; FAX: 518-463-1288
E-mail: gsmith9215@aol.com

Mail order and open shop. Monday-Saturday 9 am to 7 pm EST. Appraisals, Albany, NY, area. Estates, collector, insurance and donation, expert witness, all types of vehicles. IAAA certified member (#1002050098). Realistic work, fairly priced.

Sotheby's Motor Cars — auction company
1334 York Ave
New York, NY 10021
212-606-7920; FAX: 212-606-7886

See full listing in **Section Two** under **auctions & events**

Steele's Appraisal — appraisals
Shore Dr, Box 276
Maynard, MA 01754
978-897-8984

Mail order and open shop. 7 days 5 pm to 8 pm. Travel the New England area to view and appraise antique and special interest autos to prevent sight-unseen purchases by out-of-the-area buyers.

Sterling Restorations Inc — appraisals / restorations
1705 Eastwood Dr
Sterling, IL 61081
815-625-2260; FAX: 815-625-0799

Open shop only. Monday-Friday 8 am to 4:30 pm, Saturday by appointment. Restoration of antique and classic autos. Appraisal service, member of International Automotive Appraisers Association (#1002040099).

Still Cruisin' Corvettes — appraisals / repairs / restoration
5759 Benford Dr
Haymarket, VA 20169
703-754-1960; FAX: 703-754-1222

See full listing in **Section One** under **Corvette**

Timeless Masterpieces — appraisals / consultant
221 Freeport Dr
Bloomingdale, IL 60108
630-893-1058 evenings

Appraisals, consulting, research, historian of pre-1975 antique, classic, vintage automobiles. Auction/agent representation. Write or call for information. Established 1976.

Titus & Gibson Auto Appraisal Service | appraisals
215 E Comanche St
Ponca City, OK 74604
800-672-3157, 580-718-0553

Appraise cars from 1900-1970. IAAA member (#1002250199).

Sol W Toder | appraisals
PO Box 186
Houston, PA 15342
724-745-1300; FAX: 724-745-7406

Appraisals of inventory and equipment of salvage yards. Also experienced court qualified expert witness in matters regarding the auto salvage industry. IAAA member, #1007190096.

Top Hat John | appraisals
PO Box 46024
Mt Clemens, MI 48046-6024
810-465-1933

Appraisal service by Top Hat John, automotive historian, custom classic, special interest. Prior to purchase or sale, insurance coverage, settlement, investment portfolio. References. Local or travel. Able to identify, negotiate and close sale if necessary. Detail oriented. Member Society of Automotive Historians.

Lou Trepanier, Appraiser #1 | appraisals consultant
250 Highland St
Taunton, MA 02780
508-823-6512; FAX: 508-285-4841

Stated value appraisals, antique, classic, customs and exotics. Consultant to hobbyists and businesses, licensed and appointed and sworn arbitrator for insurance, financial or legals. 40 years in automotive services. Guaranteed neutral umpire service for disputed claims.

USA of Yesterday | appraisals indoor storage sales vehicle consignment
455 St Helens Ave
Tacoma, WA 98402
253-627-1052; FAX: 253-627-3424
E-mail: uofy@collectorcar.com

Monday-Saturday 10 am to 5:30 pm. Sales of vintage and special interest vehicles, vehicle consignment, short and long term indoor storage and vehicle appraisals. Focus is on American cars, 1930-1975. IAAA member, #1006010096. Web site: www.collectorcar.com

USAppraisal | appraisals
754 Walker Rd
PO Box 472
Great Falls, VA 22066-0472
703-759-9100; FAX: 703-759-9099
E-mail: dhkinney@usappraisal.com

Open 7 days by appointment. Appraisals for all makes and models of automobiles and trucks of all years. Available nationwide. 25 years' collector car experience. All appraisals and record keeping conform to USPAP standards. David H Kinney, ASA, accredited Senior member, American Society of Appraisers. For further information visit our web site: www.usappraisal.com

Valenti Classics Inc | collectibles restoration sales service
355 S Hwy 41
Caledonia, WI 53108
414-835-2070; FAX: 414-835-2575
E-mail: vci@valenticlassics.com

See full listing in **Section Two** under **car dealers**

Vehicle Appraisers Inc | appraisals
59 Wheeler Ave
Milford, CT 06460
203-877-1066
E-mail: vehicle@snet.net

Appointment only. Licensed since 1975 in all 50 states to do appraisals of both value and damage. Have performed over 8,000 appraisals. One of the largest private automotive libraries in the eastern United States with crash books as far back as 1947. Answer any questions at no charge. Write, phone or e-mail. Private and commercial accepted.

Vehicle Preservation Society | appraisals
PO Box 9800
San Diego, CA 92169
619-449-1010; FAX: 619-449-6388
E-mail: director@vehicles.cc

Established 1989. Formed to provide all services promoting the hobby and supported by an international membership. Services offered include certified appraisals and condition reports on any vehicle worldwide. VPS is qualified by the IRS, USPAP and the American Bar Association to perform all classic and special interest vehicle valuations. VPS represents vehicle owners for insurance, umpire and arbitration disputes. Vehicle insurance, bank, charity, museum and court valuations since 1967. Our member services are unlimited and have been published in *Hemmings Motor News*, February 1999. Private lifetime memberships are only $95. Ask for free fax info. Web site (due for 1999): www.vehiclesociety.com

Vintage Auto Ent | appraisals auctioneer
PO Box 2183
Manchester Center, VT 05255
PH/FAX: 802-362-4719
E-mail: savage1951@aol.com

All makes and years. Will travel internationally. Collections a specialty. Serving individuals, banks, insurance companies, institutions for over 25 years. Experienced in cars and fine automobilia.

Vintage Vehicles Co Inc | detail restoration
8190 20th Dr
Wautoma, WI 54982
920-787-2656

See full listing in **Section Two** under **restoration shops**

Clenton R Wells | appraisals
1220 Redwood Ln
Selma, CA 93662
559-896-2607; FAX: 559-896-1243

Appraisals for 1949-1957 Chevrolets. Member of IAAA, #1004020099.

West Coast Auto Appraisals | appraisals
930 Venice Blvd Suite 209
Venice, CA 90291
PH/FAX: 310-827-8400
E-mail: wcaa@msn.com

Auto appraisals for all types of vehicles, experienced with insurance, tax donation, estate settlements, pre-purchase and expert witness. Phone advice is free. Based in southern California, can travel. IAAA member, #1006160097. Web site: www.wcaa.com

Johnny Williams Services | appraisals car/parts locator consultant lighting systems design
2613 Copeland Rd
Tyler, TX 75701
800-937-0900, 903-597-3687
voice mail #7225

Mail order and open shop. Monday-Friday 4 pm to 10 pm CST. Active hobbyist who assists others on a one to one basis. Over 30 years' experience in most aspects of the old car field. Professional lighting consultant specializing in industrial and

Section Two
Generalists

commercial installations. Special interest and street rod appraisals. Locates cars and parts. Offers sales consultation.

James Wood	**appraisals**
1102 E Jefferson St	
Mishawaka, IN 46545	
219-256-0239; FAX: 219-254-2722	

Specializing in street rods, muscle cars, Corvettes, 1932-1948 Fords. Certified appraisals for automobiles. IAAA (member #1004270097), ASA, ISA, NIAPA, IIADA.

Yesterday's Auto Sales	**appraisals**
2800 Lyndale Ave S	**car dealer**
Minneapolis, MN 55408	
612-872-9733; FAX: 612-872-1386	
E-mail: al-hagan@msn.com	

See full listing in **Section Two** under **car dealers**

artwork

Anderson's Car Door Monograms	**car door monograms**
32700 Coastsite #102	
Rancho Palos Verdes, CA 90275	
800-881-9049, 310-377-1007	
FAX: 310-377-0169	

See full listing in **Section Two** under **accessories**

Antique Car Paintings	**color prints**
6889 Fairwood	**ink drawings**
Dearborn Heights, MI 48127	**original illustrations**
313-274-7774	

Mail order and open shop. Monday-Saturday 9 am to 5 pm. Retired Ford Motor Co artist with 49 years' experience. Have painted 1,193 original paintings of old cars. Also full color prints of 1932 Fords, 1936 Fords, Model As and 40 Fords, 1932 Duesenberg roadster, 1930 Cadillac roadster, 1934 Packard touring, 1930 Rolls-Royce touring.

Auto Art by Paul G McLaughlin	**artwork**
2720 Tennessee NE	**toys**
Albuquerque, NM 87110	
505-296-2554	

Mail order only. Automotive art in pen and ink, pencil, oil and watercolor. Photographs, toys and other auto memorabilia.

AutoFashions Restoration & Creations	**auto parts**
2209-B Hamlets Chapel Rd	**auto sales**
Pittsboro, NC 27312	**handcrafts**
PH/FAX: 919-542-5566	**restoration**
send automatically	**rubber ink stamps**
E-mail: autofashions@mindspring.com	

See full listing in **Section Two** under **restoration shops**

Automobilia Auctions Inc	**appraisals**
132 Old Main St	**auctions**
Rocky Hill, CT 06067	
860-529-7177; FAX: 860-257-3621	

See full listing in **Section Two** under **auctions & events**

Automotive Art Specialties	**drawings**
Dan McCrary	**paintings**
PO Box 18795	**prints**
Charlotte, NC 28218	
704-372-2899; FAX: 704-375-8686	
E-mail: mccrarydan@aol.com	

Anyday by appointment. Original water color paintings, drawings and limited edition prints on a wide variety of automotive subjects.

Automotive Fine Art	**artwork**
37986 Tralee Trail	
Northville, MI 48167	
248-476-9529	

Mail order and studio open by appointment only. Specializing in original, dramatic works of automotive art in permanent medium. Signed and numbered print editions of classic automobiles by artist Tom Hale. Variety of automotive posters available.

bentleydriversclub.com	**car dealer**
23238 Erwin St	**collectibles**
Woodland Hills, CA 91367	
818-887-6557; FAX: 818-346-3627	
E-mail: glwales@aol.com	

See full listing in **Section One** under **Rolls-Royce/Bentley**

Blackhawk Editions	**automotive prints**
1092 Eagles Nest Pl	
Danville, CA 94506	
925-736-3444; FAX: 925-736-4375	
E-mail: auto@blackhawkart.com	

Publishers of limited edition automotive canvas and paper prints of historic motor racing scenes. Web site: www.blackhawkart.com

Blast From the Past	**neon clocks**
1824 M St, Ste 1	**neon signs**
Lincoln, NE 68028	
402-332-5050	
E-mail: blast2past@aol.com	

See full listing in **Section Two** under **automobilia**

John E Boehm	**artwork**
T/A Boehm Design Ltd	
PO Box 9096	
Silver Spring, MD 20916	
301-649-6449	

Automotive art renderings of antique, classic, special interest and other historic and modern day automobiles. Artist drawings of buildings (both residential and commercial with or without cars). Also original automotive styling, designs for individual need or for corporations and art illustrations for publicity or promotional uses.

Francois Bruere	**artwork**
8 Avenue Olivier Heuze	
LeMans 72000 France	
(33) 02-4377-1877	
FAX: (33) 02-4324-2038	

Specializing in artwork, hyperrealism paintings, limited editions for Harley-Davidson, Ferrari, Jaguar, American cars and ACO. Official painter for the 24 hours of LeMans races (exhibitions in Europe, USA, Japan, ask for dates and catalogues).

Car Collectables	**banks**
32 White Birch Rd	**Christmas cards**
Madison, CT 06443	**note cards**
PH/FAX: 203-245-2242	

Mail order only. Company geared specifically to meet the interests of collectors, restorers and all those who appreciate vintage automobiles. Offer holiday greeting cards, beautifully illustrated in full color, as well as note cards, metal car coin banks and many other fine gift items, all with antique car motifs.

Ceramicar	**auto-related**
679 Lapla Rd	**ceramics**
Kingston, NY 12401	
PH/FAX: 914-338-2199	

See full listing in **Section Two** under **novelties**

Classic Car Appraisals
37 Wyndwood Rd
West Hartford, CT 06107
PH/FAX: 860-236-0125

appraisals

See full listing in **Section Two** under **appraisals**

Classic Car Part Art
207 S Mt Carmel
Wichita, KS 67213
316-945-6865

artwork

Mail order only. Automotive artwork by nationally known artist Dan Welty. Dan uses car parts to create original and custom made pieces of art and decor items. These items range from functional pieces like clocks and lamps to outrageously fun pieces, like his latest creations, "Fish-n-liecense", you've got to see it.

Classic Transportation
3667 Mahoning Ave
Youngstown, OH 44515
330-793-3026; FAX: 330-793-9729

automobilia

See full listing in **Section Two** under **automobilia**

Creative Wood Sculptures
W W Fayette
1372 W Axton Rd
Ferndale, WA 98248
360-312-1700

wood carvings

Mail order and open shop. Monday-Friday 8 am to 5 pm. Wood carvings of old cars in original colors and woodgrain. Will do any car from a photograph. Each carving one of a kind. For serious collectors only. Extremely rare 3 dimensional balsa wood replicas of classic automobiles. Mr Fayette devotes 400-600 hours on each piece. Perfect for shop or business. Color models start at $10,000, woodgrain $2,200. Send $1 for photo showing completed artwork.

Dash Graining by Mel Erikson
31 Meadow Rd
Kings Park, NY 11754
PH/FAX: 516-544-1102 days
516-360-7789 nights

dashboard restoration

See full listing in **Section Two** under **woodgraining**

Chris Davis
The Old Vicarage
49 Yates Hay Rd, Malvern Link
Worcestershire, WR14 1LH England
PH/FAX: 01684-560410

bronzes

Foundry bronze automotive sculptures including Aston Martin, Bentley, Bugatti, Ferrari, Invicta, Jaguar, Porsche and MG. Commissioned trophies a specialty.

Driven By Desire
300 N Fraley St
Kane, PA 16735
814-837-7590; FAX: 814-837-6850
E-mail: driven@penn.com

automobilia
car dealer
models

See full listing in **Section Two** under **car dealers**

Gaylord Sales
Frank Ranghelli
125 Dugan Ln
Toms River, NJ 08753
732-349-9213; FAX: 732-341-5353

automobilia
automotive art
mascots

See full listing in **Section Two** under **radiator emblems & mascots**

Guenther Graphics
PO Box 266
LeClaire, IA 52753
PH/FAX: 319-289-9010
E-mail: fanzter@aol.com

artwork

Mail order and open shop. Monday-Saturday 8 am to 8 pm CST. Hand-rendered full color artwork of your vehicle, unframed and framed. Computer rendered artwork of your vehicle with specific sponsor logos and colors for sponsor presentation proposals. Brochures, flyers, business cards, newsletters, logos, posters and T-shirt designs for individuals and clubs. Cars, trucks, motorcycles, boats, planes, trailers, pitcarts, buildings, homes, products and more can be illustrated. Call Douglas Guenther for quotes. To view samples visit our web site: www.fanzter.com

Wayne Huffaker, Automobilia Artist
925 S Mason Rd, Dept 168
Katy, TX 77450
281-579-8516

artwork

Mail order only. Automobilia art, limited edition prints and commission auto art. Specialize in period service station, diner, restaurant scenes highlighting cars and trucks of the 1930s-1950s. Also have car-airplane art series.

Jack Juratovic
819 Absequami Trail
Lake Orion, MI 48362
PH/FAX: 248-814-0627

artwork
magazine

Mail order only. Fine art, limited edition auto art, corporate and private commissions. Publish *Automotive Art* magazine, *AFAS Journal*.

Kaiser Illustration
133 Troy-Schenectady Rd
Watervliet, NY 12189
PH/FAX: 518-272-0754

automotive art
design
illustration

Mail order only. Kaiser Illustration offers limited edition automotive art prints by artist Bruce Kaiser. Also specialize in automotive commerical advertising, design, illustration and commissioned art.

Karl's Collectibles
28 Bates St
Lewiston, ME 04240
800-636-0457, 207-784-0098
FAX: 207-786-4576
E-mail: slalemand@exploremaine.com

banks
collectibles
logo design

See full listing in **Section Two** under **models & toys**

Dale Klee
25322 Eureka Ave
Wyoming, MN 55092
651-464-2200; FAX: 651-464-7688
E-mail: daleklee@oldcarart.com

fine art prints

Limited edition fine art prints with a rustic old car theme. Color brochures available. Prices range from $45-$75 per print. Web site: www.oldcarart.com

LA Ltd Design Graphics
822A S McDuffie St
Anderson, SC 29624
PH/FAX: 864-231-7715

artwork
design
greeting cards

See full listing in **Section Two** under **automobilia**

David Lawrence Gallery
PO Box 3702
Beverly Hills, CA 90212
310-278-0882; FAX: 310-278-0883

artwork
drawings
photography

Mail order and open shop by appointment only. Posters, photography, paintings, drawings and trophies. Mostly dealing in racing. Formula One memorabilia, Italian and American coachbuilder drawings. All works date from 1900-1979.

Legendary Motorcars	model cars
1 Wayside Village #350	
Marmora, NJ 08223	
800-926-3950; FAX: 609-399-2512	

See full listing in **Section Two** under **models & toys**

Max Neon Design Group	custom face logos
19807 Sussex Dr	glass light-up
St Clair Shores, MI 48081-3257	clocks
810-773-5000; FAX: 810-772-6224	neon clocks

See full listing in **Section Two** under **automobilia**

McIntyre Auctions	auctions
PO Box 60	automobilia
East Dixfield, ME 04227	literature
800-894-4300, 207-562-4443	petroliana
FAX: 207-562-4576	
E-mail: classicford@quickconnect.com	

See full listing in **Section Two** under **auctions & events**

Thom Montanari, Automotive Artist	car portraits
51 Lamb-Hope Rd	fine art
Hopewell, NJ 08525	illustrations
609-466-7753; FAX: 609-466-7939	
E-mail: tmontanari@aol.com	

Deal in automotive illustration, fine art, car portraits, corporate and private commissions, original paintings, posters, limited edition prints. Visit the online gallery for comprehensive sales information. Web site: www.avantimotorsports.com

Motorhead Art & Collectibles	automotive art
4311 45th Ave NE	die cast cars
Tacoma, WA 98422	
800-859-0164 orders, 253-924-0776	
FAX: 253-924-0788	
E-mail: autartman@aol.com	

Automotive subject art, books and die cast cars for sale. Domestic subjects only.

Motorsports Racing	accessories
914 S Santa Fe #101	apparel
Vista, CA 92084	art
760-630-0547; FAX: 760-630-3085	

See full listing in **Section Two** under **apparel**

Museum of Transportation	museum
15 Newton St	
Brookline, MA 02445	
617-522-6547; FAX: 617-524-0170	

See full listing in **Section Six** under **Massachusetts**

National Road-Zane Grey Museum	museum
8850 East Pike	
Norwich, OH 43767	
800-752-2602; FAX: 740-872-3510	

See full listing in **Section Six** under **Ohio**

Orpheograff	prints
BP33	
72201 La Fleche Cedex France	
(33) 243452629	
FAX: (33) 243452512	

Mail order only. Specializing in art editions (limited editions, prints, etc) for any automotive subject (car, bike, train, plane, etc). Citroen official license, 24 Heures Du Mans official license, American Le Mans Series official license.

Owen Prints	art prints
13838 Hwy 94 S-15	
Jamul, CA 91935	
619-669-3679; FAX: 619-464-5230	

Mail order only. Limited and open edition art prints of life along Route 66 in the 1920s, 1930s and 1940s.

Packard Archives	accessories
918 W Co Rd C-2	artwork
St Paul, MN 55113-1942	automobilia
651-484-1184	
E-mail: estatecars@earthlink.net	

See full listing in **Section One** under **Packard**

Paragon Models & Art	artwork
1431-B SE 10th St	models
Cape Coral, FL 33990	
941-458-0024; FAX: 941-574-4329	
E-mail:	
paragonmodels-art@worldnet.att.net	

See full listing in **Section Two** under **models & toys**

Pelham Prints	drawings
2819 N 3rd St	note cards
Clinton, IA 52732-1717	
319-242-0280	

Mail order only. Antique or classic autos illustrated for note cards. Also pen and ink and scratchboard drawings of antique and classic autos. Write for free information.

Photo Plaque Design	car show plaques
16508 McKinley St	dash plaques
Belton, MO 64012	
PH/FAX: 816-331-4073	
E-mail: photodezin@aol.com	

See full listing in **Section Two** under **plaques**

Hugo Prado Limited Edition	fine art prints
Corvette Art Prints	
PO Box 18437	
Chicago, IL 60618-0437	
PH/FAX: 800-583-7627	
E-mail: vetteart@aol.com	

See full listing in **Section One** under **Corvette**

RB's Prototype/Classic Expressions	automotive artwork
PO Box 16774	furniture
Stamford, CT 06905	
203-329-2715; FAX: 203-329-8029	
E-mail: rbproto@aol.com	

See full listing in **Section Two** under **automobilia**

Red Lion Racing	photographs
8318 Avenida Castro	posters
Cucamonga, CA 91730	
909-987-9818; FAX: 909-987-6538	
E-mail: rlracing@cris.com	

Mail order and open shop anytime. Deal in reproduction auto, air and boat racing posters from the past. Also vintage auto racing photographs, 1912-1935. Poster catalog available for $3, refundable with your first order. Vintage auto racing photo catalog, *Ironmen/Ironcars* is $10, also refundable with order. Web site: www.visref.com/redlion

Frank Riley Automotive Art	automotive prints
PO Box 95	
Hawthorne, NJ 07506	
800-848-9459	

Mail order only. Limited edition automotive prints by award winning artist. Museum quality printing on the best acid-free paper

available. A beautiful investment, available framed or unframed. Brochure of all prints available upon request.

| **Jack Schmitt Studio**
PO Box 1761
San Juan Capistrano, CA 92693 | **paintings**
prints |

Gasoline classics: over 80 limited edition and open edition prints of carefully and accurately detailed paintings of vintage gasoline stations and classic cars from the 1930s-1960s. Catalog, $2, refundable on first purchase.

| **St Louis Car Museum & Sales**
1575 Woodson Rd
St Louis, MO 63114
314-993-1330; FAX: 314-993-1540 | **museum** |

See full listing in **Section Six** under **Missouri**

| **Jay Texter**
417 Haines Mill Rd
Allentown, PA 18104
610-821-0963
E-mail: jaytexter@ot.com | **photography** |

See full listing in **Section Two** under **photography**

| **Top Dead Center Apparel**
PO Box 753
18 Main St
Wells River, VT 05081
802-757-2553; FAX: 802-757-3312
E-mail:
greenmtmonogram@connriver.net | **apparel** |

See full listing in **Section Two** under **apparel**

| **Transport Books at DRB Motors Inc**
16 Elrose Ave
Toronto, ON Canada M9M 2H6
800-665-2665, 416-744-7675
FAX: 416-744-7696
E-mail: info@transportbooks.com | **books**
manuals
periodicals
videos |

See full listing in **Section Four** under **books & publications**

| **Peter Tytla Artist**
PO Box 43
East Lyme, CT 06333-0043
860-739-7105 | **photographic collages** |

Both mail order and open shop. Every day 9 am to 9 pm. Artwork/automotive art. Specializing in humorous photographic collages of rusty cars from the 1920s and 1930s. It takes 200 to 400 separate original photographs to create 1 image. 39 images available in 4 sizes, starting at $25. Framing (museum quality) approximately 25% below retail. Also specialize in personalization. I can put you, your family, car and dog, etc, in one of the images and it will appear that you are in it (only an additional $20).

| **Walneck's Inc**
7923 Janes Ave
Woodridge, IL 60517
630-985-4995; FAX: 630-985-2750 | **motorcycles**
murals
posters |

Posters and many size wall murals, up to 10' in length of many classic motorcycles and Corvette cars. Some color posters. Penetrating oil. Call, fax or write for our free catalog of products.

| **Brady Ward-Scale Autoworks**
313 Bridge St #4
Manchester, NH 03104-5045
603-623-5925
FAX: 603-623-5925 ext 66
E-mail: bradyward@mediaone.net | **models** |

See full listing in **Section Two** under **models & toys**

| **Weber's Nostalgia Supermarket**
6611 Anglin Dr
Fort Worth, TX 76119
817-534-6611; FAX: 817-534-3316 | **collectibles**
gas pump supplies
old photos
signs |

See full listing in **Section Two** under **novelties**

| **Danny Whitfield, Automotive Artist**
11 N Plaza Blvd
Rochester Hills, MI 48307
248-299-3755; FAX: 248-299-4131
E-mail: autovision@thewing.com | **artwork** |

Mail order and open shop. Automotive fine art, auto design, graphic and technical illustrations, auto art commissions. Automotive limited edition prints and posters. Web site: www.dannywhitfield.com

auctions and events

| **Amherst Antique Auto Show**
157 Hollis Rd
Amherst, NH 03031
603-883-0605, NH
FAX: 617-641-0647, MA | **swap meets** |

Antique swap and sell meets. Last Sunday of each month, April-October (7 shows), open 6 am, since 1960. Largest in New Hampshire. 505 dealers, 150 show car spaces. Free admission, $5 site parking. Good food, beautiful grounds. Come have fun.

| **"The Auction"-Las Vegas**
3535 Las Vegas Blvd S
Las Vegas, NV 89109
702-794-3174; FAX: 702-369-7430
E-mail: info@vegasauction.com | **auction**
dealer
events
expo
sales |

Antique, classic and collector car auction and exposition sale, held at the Imperial Palace Hotel and Casino in Las Vegas, Nevada. For more information, contact Rob Williams, General Manager of The Auction. Web site: www.vegasauction.com

| **Auto Transport Services**
5367 Fargo Rd
Avoca, MI 48006
810-324-2598; FAX: 810-324-6094 | **transport** |

See full listing in **Section Two** under **transport**

| **Automobilia Auctions Inc**
132 Old Main St
Rocky Hill, CT 06067
860-529-7177; FAX: 860-257-3621 | **appraisals**
auctions |

Mail order and open shop by appointment. No-reserve consignment auctions of automobilia, literature, petroliana, mascots, signs and other quality vintage auto collector's items from 1900-1970. Estates and appraisals a specialty.

| **Autotron**
PO Box 142 (Graafsebaan 133)
A 50 Motorway 's-Hertogenbosch-Nijmegen
Rosmalen 5240 AC (56248 NL)
Netherlands
0031-73-5233300
FAX: 0031-73-5216795
E-mail: info@autotron.nl | **museum** |

See full listing in **Section Six** under **Netherlands**

**Section Two
Generalists**

Barrett-Jackson Auction Co LLC | auctions
5530 E Washington St
Phoenix, AZ 85034
602-273-0791; FAX: 602-244-1538
E-mail: info@barrett-jackson.com

Barrett-Jackson Auction is more than an auction, it is an automotive event. The world's greatest classic car auction which is held annually in January. The dates set for 2000 are January 20-23. Featuring classic, collectible, sports muscle, antique, fifties and sixties automobiles. Exposition of rare collectible cars are also shown. Web site: www.barrett-jackson.com

Bloomington Gold® Corvettes USA | Corvette show
PO Box 457
Marengo, IL 60152
815-568-1960; FAX: 815-568-8650
E-mail: bginfo@bloomingtongold.com

See full listing in **Section One** under **Corvette**

British Invasion Inc | shows
433 Mountain Rd
Stowe, VT 05672
802-253-5320; FAX: 802-253-8944
E-mail: englandinn@aol.com

Specializing in British classic and sports car shows for all cars manufactured in Great Britain. Web site: britishinvasion.com

Carlisle Productions | auctions
1000 Bryn Mawr Rd | car shows
Carlisle, PA 17013-1588 | flea markets
717-243-7855; FAX: 717-243-0255
E-mail: cp@epix.net

2000 Carlisle collector car events, held at the Carlisle Pennsylvania Fairgrounds: Spring Carlisle, April 27-30; Import-Kit/Replicar Nationals, May 19-21; Custom Compact Power Jam, May 19-21; All-Ford Nationals, June 2-4; All-Truck Nationals, June 23-25; Chryslers at Carlisle, July 14-16; Summer Carlisle, July 28-30; Corvettes at Carlisle, August 25-27; Fall Carlisle, September 28-October 1. Call, fax, write or e-mail for a free event brochure. For a complete listing of all Carlisle events: www.carsatcarlisle.com

See our ad on this page

Coys of Kensington | auctions
2-4 Queen's Gate Mews
London SW7 5QJ England
0171-584-7444
FAX: 0171-584-2733
E-mail:
auctions@coys-of-kensington.co.uk
or events@coys-of-kensington.co.uk

Founded in 1919, one of England's oldest and best known specialists in the sale of historic motor cars. In addition to our many international auctions held annually, Coys' London showrooms always have a vast selection of both pre and post-war collectors motor cars. Will travel anywhere in the world to obtain a classic motor car. For further information, please do not hesitate to contact us. Web site: www.coys-of-kensington.co.uk

George Cross & Sons Inc | car show
PO Box 3923 | swap meet
Tustin, CA 92781
714-538-7091; FAX: 714-538-7080
E-mail: pomonasm@pacbell.net

George Cross & Sons Inc promotes The West Coast's Largest Antique Auto, Corvette, Porsche, Street Rod and Volkswagen Car Show and Swap Meet, 8 times a year, at Farplex in Pomona, California.

Glenn Curtiss Museum | museum
8419 St Rt 54
Hammondsport, NY 14840
607-569-2160; FAX: 607-569-2040

See full listing in **Section Six** under **New York**

Henry Ford Museum & | museum
Greenfield Village
20900 Oakwood Blvd
Dearborn, MI 48121-1970
313-271-1620; FAX: 313-982-6247

See full listing in **Section Six** under **Michigan**

Grapevine Convention & | car shows
Visitors Bureau | conventions
1 Liberty Park Plaza | meetings
Grapevine, TX 76051
800-457-6338; FAX: 817-410-3038
E-mail: gvtexas1@aol.com

Grapevine, Texas, located between Dallas and Fort Worth, offers the ideal location for car shows and car club conventions. The DFW Hilton and Hyatt Regency DFW have extensive experience in providing accommodations for car lovers. Ample parking, rural roads and a secure setting are just a few of the reasons why car clubs love Grapevine. Call for more information and a guide.

Harley Rendezvous Classic | motorcycle events
1142 Batter St
Pattersonville, NY 12137
518-864-5659; FAX: 518-864-5917
E-mail: frank@harleyrendezvous.com

See full listing in **Section Two** under **motorcycles**

Hershey in the Spring | car corral
PO Box 234 | car show
Annville, PA 17003 | flea market
717-867-4810, 6 to 9 pm

Automotive flea market, car corral and car show. Located in

Chocolatetown USA, Hershey, PA (White Field). For more information, send SASE to HITS.

International Classic Auctions	auctions
1265 S Gilbert Rd	
Gilbert, AZ 85296	
800-243-1957; FAX: 602-963-1277	

Iowa Gas Swap Meet	auction
1739 E Grand Ave	swap meet
Des Moines, IA 50316	
515-276-2099, 515-251-8811	
FAX: 515-265-5170	
E-mail: iowagasjon@aol.com	

Founded 1986. Largest oil, gas and auto related advertising collectibles show, swap meet and auctions. Held annually in August in Des Moines. Annual publication mailed following each year's event. Registration fee: $18/year. Web site: www.iowagas.com

The Josey's Heaven Hill Farm	swap meets
1839 NW C-138	
Branford, FL 32008	
904-935-0348	

Automotive, antique and collectible swap meets in February, May and November for all automotive related items, new and used. May show is restricted to 1948 and older vehicles, original or restored, no customized.

Kensington Motor Group Inc	consignment sales
PO Box 2277	
Sag Harbor, NY 11963	
516-537-1868; FAX: 516-537-2641	
E-mail: kenmotor@aol.com	

See full listing in **Section One** under **Mercedes-Benz**

G Potter King Inc	auction
5 W Taunton Ave	flea market
Berlin, NJ 08009	show
609-768-6900, 800-227-3868	
FAX: 609-768-1383	

Atlantic City Classic Car Auction/Antique Show/Flea Market. New dates and one additional day added to the weekend event, February 24-27, 2000. Presented by G Potter King Inc.

Klassic Kolor Auctions	auction "color"
PO Box 55243	broadcaster
Hayward, CA 94545-0243	master of ceremonies
510-795-2776	
FAX: available upon request	
E-mail: voodoowear@hotmail.com	

Michael Ben-Edward is a broadcaster, actor and the voice of *Easyriders Video Tapes* (Gentle Ben). Specializing in auction ring "color" of vintage and classic motorcycles, automobiles and airplanes.

Col Glenn Larson	appraisals
4423-A Canyon Dr	auctioneer
Amarillo, TX 79110	
806-358-9797; FAX: 806-467-0280	
E-mail: colonel@arn.net	

See full listing in **Section Two** under **appraisals**

M & S Enterprises	auction
PO Box 2055	
Valparaiso, IN 46384-2055	
219-464-9918	

Held in August (2 weeks before Labor Day). Annual Midwest Corvette and Chevy show, swap and auction. Big swap meet, 42 class Chevy show, giant foodfest, beer garden and more. Call for free brochure.

McIntyre Auctions	auctions
PO Box 60	automobilia
East Dixfield, ME 04227	literature
800-894-4300, 207-562-4443	petroliana
FAX: 207-562-4576	
E-mail: classicford@quickconnect.com	

Mail order and open shop. Monday-Friday 9 am to 5 pm, closed Saturday. Established January 15, 1976. Specializing in automobilia, toys, literature and petroliana. Host a large auto auction each Memorial Day in Maine. Call for details. Web site: www.classicford.com

Dana Mecum Auctions Inc	auctions
Box 422	
Marengo, IL 60152	
815-568-8888; FAX: 815-568-6615	

Mail order and open shop. Monday-Friday 9 am to 5 pm, Saturday by appointment. Approximately 20 events per year.

Michigan Antique Festivals	auto show
2156 Rudy Ct	swap meet
Midland, MI 48642	
517-687-9001; FAX: 517-687-7116	

Write or call for information. Monday-Friday 7 pm to 9 pm. Special interest auto show, sales lot and swap meet. Held at Midland, Michigan, fairgrounds, 1999 dates: September 25-26; 2000 dates: June 3-4, July 22-23, September 23-24; 2001 dates: June 2-3, July 21-22, September 22-23. Featuring Michigan's largest special interest auto sales lot. For sale (and show) autos register at gate. Swap spaces by advance only.

Mid-America Auction Services	auctions
2277 W Hwy 36, Ste 214	
St Paul, MN 55113	
612-633-9655; FAX: 612-633-3212	
E-mail: midauction@aol.com	

Classic, collector and special interest automobile auctions. Motorcycle auctions, automobile and motorcycle appraisals. *Motorcycle Price Guide* is an antique, classic and special interest motorcycle price guide, for motorcycles 1905-1985. Includes special section devoted to auction results of 1,000 rare or low production makes and models. Cost: $20/year.

Museum of Transportation	museum
15 Newton St	
Brookline, MA 02445	
617-522-6547; FAX: 617-524-0170	

See full listing in **Section Six** under **Massachusetts**

Niagara CHT Productions Inc	swap meets
PO Box 112	
Akron, NY 14001	
716-542-2585	

"Niagara" auto swap meet and car shows, June 24, 25, 2000, Lockport, New York, Niagara County fairgrounds.

Nostalgia Productions Inc	shows
268 Hillcrest Blvd	swap meets
St Ignace, MI 49781	
906-643-8087; FAX: 906-643-9784	
E-mail: edreavie@nostalgia-prod.com	

Production of auto, truck, toy shows, swap meets and cruise nights. From pedal cars to 18 wheelers. Web sites: www.nostalgia-prod.com or www.auto-shows.com

Old Bridge Township Raceway Park	shows
230 Pension Rd	swap meets
Englishtown, NJ 07726	
732-446-7800; FAX: 732-446-1373	
E-mail: etownrcwy@aol.com	

A facility that presents auto shows and swap meets. Web site: www.etownraceway.com

Oldtimer Galerie International — auctions
Guerbestrasse 1
Toffen 3125 Switzerland
++41-31-8196161
FAX: ++41-31-8193747
E-mail: oldtimergalerie@bluewin.ch

Open Tuesday-Sunday 10 am to 6 pm. Specializing in all kinds of antique and classic cars as well as motorbikes. Auctioneers. Web site: www.oldtimergalerie.ch

Palm Springs Exotic Car Auctions — auctions
602 E Sunny Dunes Rd
Palm Springs, CA 92264
760-320-3290; FAX: 760-323-7031

Sale of 300 antique, classic and special interest autos. Held at the Palm Springs Convention Center, last weekend in February and end of October each year. Web site: www.classic-carauction.com

Pate Swap Meet — swap meet
Registrar
7751 Oak Vista
Houston, TX 77087
713-649-0922

Third largest swap meet in US. Held every April at the Texas Motor Speedway in Fort Worth, TX.

Phoenix Classic Car Swap — swap meet
3801 E Washington St
Phoenix, AZ 85034
602-273-9638; FAX: 602-273-7375
E-mail: ppns0010@aol.com

Swap meet with a wide variety of parts, services and show vehicles. Web site: www.americanparknswap.com

Pikes Peak Auto Hill Climb Educational Museum — museum
135 Manitou Ave
Manitou Springs, CO 80829
719-685-4400; FAX: 719-685-5885
E-mail: ppihc@ppihc.com

See full listing in **Section Six** under **Colorado**

Lloyd Ralston Gallery — toys
400 Long Beach Blvd
Stratford, CT 06615
203-386-9399; FAX: 203-386-9519
E-mail: lrgallery@aol.com

See full listing in **Section Two** under **models & toys**

Red Baron's Antiques — auctions
6450 Roswell Rd
Atlanta, GA 30328
404-252-3770; FAX: 404-257-0268
rbaron1@bellsouth.net

Open Monday-Friday 9 am to 6 pm, Saturday 9 am to 4 pm. Retail store with exciting auctions thrice yearly. Each auction is no minimum, no reserve, featuring over 50 vintage automobiles, automobilia, as well as over 2,500 lots of important architectural antiques, decorative arts and collectibles, including chandeliers, fine furniture, sculpture, stained glass and much more. For a free color catalog, please call or write. Web site: www.redbaronsantiques.com

Garry Roberts & Co — cars / parts / service
922 Sunset Dr
Costa Mesa, CA 92627
714-650-2690; FAX: 714-650-2730
E-mail: garryroberts@fea.net

See full listing in **Section One** under **Ferrari**

Sedgwick Fall Festival — rod run
509 Harrison
Sedgwick, KS 67135
316-772-5675

Founded 1992. 10 members. Group formed to put on a rod run during the city's Fall Festival. It is held the third Saturday of September from 8:30 am to 5 pm. Awards for top 3 in 23 classes. Lots of door prizes along with motel room for long distance. September 18, 1999, we will be giving away a complete street rod for someone entered in the show. All money given to various charities in this area.

Sotheby's — auctions
34-35 New Bond Street
London W1A 2AA England
44-171-293-6469
FAX: 44-171-293-5958
E-mail: jessica.percival@sothebys.com

Regular international auctions of collector's motor vehicles, motorcycles and automobilia are held throughout the year. For advice on buying, selling or valuation please contact Sotheby's car department. Web site: www.sothebys.com

Sotheby's Motor Cars — auction sales
1334 York Ave
New York, NY 10021
212-606-7920; FAX: 212-606-7886

International auction sales of vintage, classic, sports and racing automobiles. World auction records achieved for Duesenberg, Packard, Rolls-Royce, Bentley and Ferrari. All inquiries welcome. Web site: sothebys.com

Sparrow Auction Company — auction company
59 Wheeler Ave
Milford, CT 06460
203-877-1066
E-mail: vehicle@snet.net

Both mail order and open shop by appointment. Full service auction company specializing in the auction of anything for and related to automobiles including automobiles, models, parts, literature and salvage. Will travel anywhere or you may consign items to our local auctions. Experience in the auction of insurance salvage and the auction of salvage yards.

Springfield 99 Swap Meet & Car Show — swap meet
492 W Second St, Ste 204
Xenia, OH 45385
937-376-0111; FAX: 937-372-1171

Calendar of events: fall show, September 10-12, 1999; winter show, November 13-14, 1999; spring show, May 26-28, 2000. Cars and Parts Springfield 99 swap meet and car show at Clark County Fairgrounds, I-70 Exit 59, Springfield, OH. Hundreds of vendors, cars for sale and show cars. Ohio's largest event of its type. Call or write to the above address for info and/or free brochure.

Start/Finish Productions — swap meets
PO Box 2124
Vernon, CT 06066-5124
860-871-6376

Autoparts Swap n' Sell. All automotive swap meet, 300 vendors, one million parts, 12x15 ft space. Antique, classic, special interest. January 15-16, 2000, Eastern States Expo, indoors, Springfield, MA, 30,000 attend.

Trunzo's Antique Cars — antique cars / auctions / restorations
4213 Ohio River Blvd
Pittsburgh, PA 15202
412-734-0717

Auctions and events. Complete and partial restorations. Antique cars bought and sold.

Webster Auto Swap Meet
6250 Tennessee Ave
New Port Richey, FL 34653
800-438-8559, 813-848-7171
FAX: 813-846-8922

auction
car show
swap meet

Automotive, antique, swap meet, auction, car and truck show, car corral, 1st Sunday of each month except for July/August. Also a 3 day show February 18-20, 2000. Visit us at our web site: www.websterautoswap.com

Tom Williams Auction Co
3311-C Lapeer Rd
Auburn Hills, MI 48326
248-373-8555; FAX: 248-373-9299

auctions

Our company has been producing car auctions across the country for 19 years. Some of these events have swap meets, car shows and other activities in conjunction with the auction.

J Wood & Co Auctioneers
RR 1 Box 316
Stockton Springs, ME 04981
207-567-4250; FAX: 207-567-4252
E-mail: jwoodandco@mindspring.com

auctions

Between October 16-April 14: PH: 352-795-8895, FAX: 352-795-9328, FL. Special events. Office open weekdays. Vintage motorcycle auctions, antique and classic motorcycle auctions and events. Also, liquidating motorcycle shops and estate collections. March in Daytona; July in Ohio.

Zephyrhills Festivals and Auction Inc
PO Box 848
Odessa, FL 33556
office: 813-920-7206
FAX: 813-920-8512
Park: 813-782-0835
FAX: 813-780-7863

auction
swap meet

Giant automotive, antique and collectibles swap meet, collector car auction, flywheel engine exhibit, antique auto exhibition racing and live music. Spaces are 10' wide x 30' deep. Held twice a year. Fall show, November, weekend before Thanksgiving (15th year in 1999); winter show, weekend after President's Day in February (26th year in 2000). Four day show, Thursday-Sunday. Call for information on selling cars or becoming a bidder.

automobilia

American Classics Unlimited Inc
PO Box 192-V
Oak Lawn, IL 60454-0192
PH/FAX: 708-424-9223

automobilia
models
toys

See full listing in **Section Two** under **models & toys**

Amherst Antique Auto Show
157 Hollis Rd
Amherst, NH 03031
603-883-0605, NH
FAX: 617-641-0647, MA

swap meets

See full listing in **Section Two** under **auctions & events**

Antiques Warehouse
Michael J Welch
3700 Rt 6
Eastham, MA 02642
508-255-1437; FAX: 508-247-9166
E-mail: miketoys1@aol.com

automobilia
bikes
toy trucks

See full listing in **Section Two** under **models & toys**

Aquarius Antiques
Jim & Nancy Schaut
7147 W Angela Dr
Glendale, AZ 85308
602-878-4293
E-mail: jnschaut@aol.com

memorabilia
toys

Mail order only. Buy and sell antique toys, automobilia and advertising, especially auto and motorcycle memorabilia. Web site: members.aol.com/jr1955/web.html

Auto Art by Paul G McLaughlin
2720 Tennessee NE
Albuquerque, NM 87110
505-296-2554

artwork
toys

See full listing in **Section Two** under **artwork**

Auto Nostalgia Enr
332 St Joseph
Mont St Gregoire, QC Canada J0J 1K0
PH/FAX: 450-346-3644

literature
manuals
models
tractor decals

See full listing in **Section Two** under **literature dealers**

Auto Zone
33202 Woodward Ave
Birmingham, MI 48009
800-647-7288; FAX: 248-646-5381
E-mail: info@azautozone.com

books
magazines
models
videos

See full listing in **Section Two** under **models & toys**

Automobilia
Division of Lustron Industries
18 Windgate Dr
New City, NY 10956
PH/FAX: 914-639-6806
E-mail: lustron@worldnet.att.net

models

See full listing in **Section Two** under **models & toys**

Automobilia Auctions Inc
132 Old Main St
Rocky Hill, CT 06067
860-529-7177; FAX: 860-257-3621

appraisals
auctions

See full listing in **Section Two** under **auctions & events**

Automotive Art Specialties
Dan McCrary
PO Box 18795
Charlotte, NC 28218
704-372-2899; FAX: 704-375-8686
E-mail: mccrarydan@aol.com

drawings
paintings
prints

See full listing in **Section Two** under **artwork**

Berliner Classic Motorcars Inc
1975 Stirling Rd
Dania, FL 33004
954-923-7271; FAX: 954-926-3306
E-mail: sales@motorcars.com

automobilia
car dealer
motorcycles

See full listing in **Section Two** under **car dealers**

Blast From the Past
21006 Cornhusker Rd
Gretna, NE 68028
402-332-5050
E-mail: blast2past@aol.com

neon clocks
neon signs

Mail order and open shop. Monday-Friday 9 am to 5 pm. Custom neon signs and clocks are our specialty. Manufacture and distribute nostalgic neons of all types, todays highest quality with the look of yesterday. Satisfaction guaranteed. Great for garage, office, showroom, etc. Many old auto themes. Also custom restoration services for old soda machines, gas pumps, pedal cars, etc. Original advertising signs (auto dealership neon and non-neon, soda, gas/oil) also bought, sold, traded. Your one stop nostalgic shop. Web site: http://pmadt.com/blastpast

Gideon Booth Rellandsgate, Kings Meaburn Penrith Cumbria CA10 3BT England PH/FAX: 01931 714624	**car collector** **parts** **restorations**

See full listing in **Section One** under **Morris**

Bright Displays 1314 Lakemont Dr Pittsburgh, PA 15243 PH/FAX: 412-279-7037	**molded auto logos** **neon signs**

Mail order and open shop. Carlisle and Hershey flea markets. Antique auto and dealer's neon signs and molded auto logos.

British Only Motorcycles and Parts Inc 32451 Park Ln Garden City, MI 48135 734-421-0303; FAX: 734-422-9253 E-mail: info@british-only.com	**literature** **memorabilia** **motorcycles** **parts**

See full listing in **Section Two** under **motorcycles**

Caddytown™/Pawl Engineering Co 4960 Arrowhead PO Box 240105 West Bloomfield, MI 48324 PH/FAX: 248-682-2007 E-mail: pawl@earthlink.net	**memorabilia** **parts** **toys**

See full listing in **Section One** under **Cadillac/LaSalle**

California Car Cover Co 21125 Superior St Chatsworth, CA 91311 800-423-5525; FAX: 818-998-2442	**accessories** **apparel** **car covers** **tools**

See full listing in **Section Two** under **car covers**

Ceramicar 679 Lapla Rd Kingston, NY 12401 PH/FAX: 914-338-2199	**auto-related** **ceramics**

See full listing in **Section Two** under **novelties**

Michael Chapman Priorsleigh, Mill Lane Cleeve Prior Worcestershire, WR115JZ England 0044-1789-773897 FAX: 0044-1789-773588	**automobilia**

Mail order and open shop by prior appointment only. Specialize in Rolls-Royce/Bentley, Hispano and quality vehicle parts. Finest selection veteran, Edwardian, vintage lamps, horns, emblems, instruments, books, badges, tools, mascots, etc, all makes, 1890-1960. The finest selection in Europe. No inquiry is too large or too small. Also high-wheeler bicycles and cycling memorabilia sometimes available.

"Check The Oil!" Magazine PO Box 937 Powell, OH 43065-0937 614-848-5038; FAX: 614-436-4760	**magazine**

See full listing in **Section Two** under **petroliana**

Chewning's Auto Literature 2011 Elm Tree Terr Buford, GA 30518 770-945-9795	**literature** **manuals**

See full listing in **Section Two** under **literature dealers**

Classic Car Part Art 207 S Mt Carmel Wichita, KS 67213 316-945-6865	**artwork**

See full listing in **Section Two** under **artwork**

Classic Mercury Parts 1393 Shippee Ln Ojai, CA 93023 805-646-3345; FAX: 805-646-5386 E-mail: mfourez@aol.com	**parts**

See full listing in **Section One** under **Mercury**

The Classic Motorist PO Box 363 Rotterdam Junction, NY 12150-0363	**automotive books** **literature** **motoring accessories**

Mail order only. British and American automotive books, art, literature, periodicals, club publications, and motoring accessories. Specializing in custom coachwork and formal car memorabilia. Early auto radio literature and signs. Collector of Classic Era Danbury and Franklin Mint models. Packard enthusiast desiring club, marque and CCCA publications. Please send 4 stamps for descriptive catalog.

Classic Transportation 3667 Mahoning Ave Youngstown, OH 44515 330-793-3026; FAX: 330-793-9729	**automobilia**

Deal in automobilia and nostalgia including pedal car parts, gas pump restoration items, neon clocks, 1950s clothing, repro signs and automotive art prints.

Coker Tire 1317 Chestnut St Chattanooga, TN 37402 800-251-6336 toll-free 423-265-6368 local & international FAX: 423-756-5607	**tires**

See full listing in **Section Two** under **tires**

The Collector's Guild 41 Counter St Kingston, ON Canada K7K 6C7 800-653-0251; FAX: 613-536-5211 E-mail: cars@collectorsguild.on.ca	**models** **toys**

See full listing in **Section Two** under **models & toys**

Cotswold Motor Museum & Toy Collection The Old Mill Bourton on the Water Gloucestershire GL542BY England 1451-821255	**museum**

See full listing in **Section Six** under **England**

Creative Products of Minnesota Inc 400 N Seeley Ave Dunnell, MN 56127 507-695-2301; FAX: 507-695-2302 E-mail: crprod@beucomm.net	**mailbox**

Mail order only. Fiberglass mailbox of a 1930s style coupe car and 1930s style coupe pickup.

Buzz De Clerck 41760 Utica Rd Sterling Heights, MI 48313-3146 810-731-0765	**parts**

See full listing in **Section One** under **Lincoln**

DeLorean Literature 3116 Welsh Rd Philadelphia, PA 19136-1810 215-338-6142 E-mail: delorean.literature@excite.com	collectibles **literature**

See full listing in **Section One** under **DeLorean**

Driven By Desire 300 N Fraley St Kane, PA 16735 814-837-7590; FAX: 814-837-6850 E-mail: driven@penn.com	automobilia car dealer **models**

See full listing in **Section Two** under **car dealers**

Eastwood Automobilia Box 296 Malvern, PA 19355-0714 800-343-9353; FAX: 610-644-0560	collectibles scale models **transportation**

Daily 8 am to 9 pm EST. Free transportation collectables catalog. You'll discover an interesting assortment of exclusive limited edition scale models, along with hard-to-find nostalgic items from many different areas of transportation history, cars and planes, tractors and trains. 30 day money back guarantee on all Eastwood products. Catalog free. Web site: www.ewab.com

The Eastwood Company-Tools Box 296 Malvern, PA 19355-0714 800-345-1178 FAX: 610-644-0560	paints plating & polishing powder coating restoration aids **rustproofing**

See full listing in **Section Two** under **tools**

Emblemagic Co PO Box 420 Grand River, OH 44045-0420 440-209-0792 E-mail: arborhil@aol.com	decorative emblems plastic insert **emblems**

See full listing in **Section Two** under **grille emblem badges**

Enthusiast's Specialties 350 Old Connecticut Path Framingham, MA 01701 800-718-3999; FAX: 508-872-4914 E-mail: alvis1934@aol.com	**automobilia**

Mail order only. Import fine English hampers (picnic baskets). Also supply logo cap tire valves, vintage motorsport photography, grille badges, lapel pins and "country of origin" magnetic plates. Single issues and complete years of *Road & Track* and *Car & Driver* as well as back issues of *Autocar* (England). Specializing in European marques, European manfacturer inquiries invited. Web site: www.classic-sportscar.com

Eurosport Daytona Inc 355 Tomoka Ave Ormond Beach, FL 32174-6222 800-874-8044, 904-672-7199 FAX: 904-673-0821	**license plates**

See full listing in **Section Two** under **license plates**

EWA & Miniature Cars USA Inc 205 US Hwy 22 Green Brook, NJ 08812-1909 732-424-7811; FAX: 732-424-7814 E-mail: ewa@ewacars.com	books models subscriptions **videos**

See full listing in **Section Two** under **models & toys**

Fantasy Models PO Box 570 Wright City, MO 63390 888-745-8254; FAX: 800-745-8254 E-mail: scale43@inlink.com	**models**

See full listing in **Section Two** under **models & toys**

Fill Er Up Brian Steiner 2613 Old Philadelphia Pike PO Box 406 Bird In Hand, PA 17505 717-397-2519	automobilia **petroliana**

Mail order and open shop. Wednesday-Saturday 10 am to 5 pm. Automobilia, petroliana, new and old collectables. Located in center of Amish farmlands. Books, gas pumps, signs, clocks, automotive art and antiques.

Galaxie Ltd Box 655 Butler, WI 53007 414-673-6386, 414-790-9922 FAX: 414-673-6366	kits **model trailers**

See full listing in **Section Two** under **models & toys**

Gateway Global USA 10485 NW 28th St Miami, FL 33172-2152 305-500-9641; FAX: 305-500-9642 E-mail: gatautousa@aol.com	**models**

See full listing in **Section Two** under **models & toys**

Gaylord Sales Frank Ranghelli 125 Dugan Ln Toms River, NJ 08753 732-349-9213; FAX: 732-341-5353	automobilia automotive art **mascots**

See full listing in **Section Two** under **radiator emblems & mascots**

Get It On Paper Gary Weickart, President 185 Maple St Islip, NY 11751 516-581-3897	automobilia literature **toys**

Mail order and open shop. Every Saturday and Sunday 12 noon to 5 pm. Offer sales brochures, original ads, shop manuals and owner's manuals for your old cars and trucks. Also a nice selection of automotive books and magazines, models, toys, license plates, old advertising signs and the occasional old car. We need to acquire your model kit collection (either built or unbuilt). Call or send your list with prices for an immediate answer.

Jerry Goldsmith Promos 4634 Cleveland Heights Lakeland, FL 33813 941-644-7013, 941-646-8490 PH/FAX: 941-644-5013 E-mail: shirley.goldsmith@gte.net	**models**

Mail order and open shop. Tuesday-Saturday 10 am to 6 pm. Corvette and Chevrolet promotional models from 1953-present. Also other automobilia. Same day shipping. Price list available upon request. Visa/MC.

Grandpa's Attic 112 E Washington Goshen, IN 46528 219-534-2778	**toys**

See full listing in **Section Two** under **models & toys**

Grey Motor Co 18845 Van Buren Blvd 10-A Riverside, CA 92508 800-343-5496; FAX: 909-789-9751	display cabinets

Mail order only. Display cabinets for collectibles, die cast models.

The Gullwing Garage Ltd Bricklin SVI Specialists 5 Cimorelli Dr New Windsor, NY 12553-6201 914-561-0019 anytime	appraisals literature parts service

See full listing in **Section One** under **Bricklin**

Hale's Products 906 19th St Wheatland, WY 82201 800-333-0989 E-mail: phale@wyoming.com	license plates

See full listing in **Section Two** under **license plates**

Richard Hamilton 28 E 46th St Indianapolis, IN 46205 317-283-1902	sales literature

See full listing in **Section Two** under **literature dealers**

Historic Video Archives PO Box 189-VA Cedar Knolls, NJ 07927-0189	videotapes

Mail order only. The greatest (often the only) source of original TV commercials and promo films on video for antique and classic cars 1935-1970. Tremendous selection, choose from over 1,000 titles! Auto racing, vintage TV shows, movies, documentaries, cartoons, newsreels, all kinds of rare footage. Tapes that cannot

be found at local video stores, at prices the public can afford. Send $3 for our big illustrated catalog.

Hot Rod Nostalgia™ PO Box 249 West Point, CA 95255-0249 209-754-3697; FAX: 209-754-5521 E-mail: hvaa@hotrodnostalgia.com	"magalog"

See full listing in **Section Four** under **books & publications**

Hotchkiss Mfg/Clear Case PO Box 810 Merlin, OR 97532 800-444-5005; FAX: 541-476-0268 E-mail: hotchkiss@chatlink.com	display cases

See full listing in **Section Two** under **models & toys**

Wayne Huffaker, Automobilia Artist 925 S Mason Rd, Dept 168 Katy, TX 77450 281-579-8516	artwork

See full listing in **Section Two** under **artwork**

Imperial Palace Auto Collection 3535 Las Vegas Blvd S Las Vegas, NV 89109 702-794-3174; FAX: 702-369-7430 E-mail: ipauto@ipautocollection.com	museum

See full listing in **Section Six** under **Nevada**

Steve Jelf-14 Box 200 Rt 5 Arkansas City, KS 67005 316-442-1626	signs

Mail order and open shop by appointment. Large reproductions of antique auto, oil and other advertising signs, including several available nowhere else. Dozens available. Send SASE for details and free photos.
See our ad on page 221

Jesser's Classic Keys 26 West St, Dept HVA Akron, OH 44303-2344 330-376-8181; FAX: 330-384-9129	automobilia keys

See full listing in **Section Two** under **locks & keys**

The Josey's Heaven Hill Farm 1839 NW C-138 Branford, FL 32008 904-935-0348	swap meets

See full listing in **Section Two** under **auctions & events**

Jack Juratovic 819 Absequami Trail Lake Orion, MI 48362 PH/FAX: 248-814-0627	artwork magazine

See full listing in **Section Two** under **artwork**

K&S Industries 1801 Union Center Hwy Endicott, NY 13760 PH/FAX: 888-PICK-KNS E-mail: pleximan@888pickkns.com	display cases

See full listing in **Section Two** under **models & toys**

Karl's Collectibles 28 Bates St Lewiston, ME 04240 800-636-0457, 207-784-0098 FAX: 207-786-4576 E-mail: slalemand@exploremaine.com	banks collectibles logo design

See full listing in **Section Two** under **models & toys**

The Klemantaski Collection
65 High Ridge Rd, Suite 219
Stamford, CT 06905
PH/FAX: 203-968-2970
E-mail: klemcoll@aol.com

books
photography

See full listing in **Section Two** under **photography**

Harold Kloss
PO Box 37
Humboldt, AZ 86329-0037
602-632-7684

wood models

See full listing in **Section Two** under **models & toys**

l'art et l'automobile
Red Horse Plaza
74 Montauk Hwy
East Hampton, NY 11937
516-329-8580; FAX: 516-329-8589
E-mail: jvautoart@aol.com

artwork
memorabilia

Retail store and mail order. Specializing in automotive paintings, lithos, posters, models, toys, objects, sculptures, new and old books and memorabilia from the beginning of the automotive era to present. A unique place for the automotive enthusiast. Web site: arteauto.com

LA Ltd Design Graphics
822A S McDuffie St
Anderson, SC 29624
PH/FAX: 864-231-7715

artwork
design
greeting cards

Christmas and all-occasion greeting cards featuring scenes with 1/43 scale die cast miniature cars and trucks, realistic detail. Also design old car event logos, produce newsletters and flyers, etc.

David Lawrence Gallery
PO Box 3702
Beverly Hills, CA 90212
310-278-0882; FAX: 310-278-0883

artwork
drawings
photography

See full listing in **Section Two** under **artwork**

Legendary Motorcars
1 Wayside Village #350
Marmora, NJ 08223
800-926-3950; FAX: 609-399-2512

model cars

See full listing in **Section Two** under **models & toys**

Dave Lincoln
Box 331
Yorklyn, DE 19736
610-444-4144, PA
E-mail: tagbarn@msn.com

license plates

See full listing in **Section Two** under **license plates**

Lone Wolf
9375 Bearwalk Path
Brooksville, FL 34613
352-596-9949
E-mail: lonewolfwhistle@bigfoot.com

wolf whistles

Wolf whistles-they're back! Only better than ever, polished stainless steel or bronze, also 3 new powder coat colors: candy red, blue, purple. This is the whistle made in the USA. Each whistle comes with a universal mount and lots of fun. Getting the chicks or guys is up to you. 30 day satisfaction guaranteed. Repair kits also available for original Hollywood whistles. Thanks for buying American made Lone Wolf. Web site: www.lonewolfwhistle.com

George & Denise Long
915 E Court St
Marion, NC 28752
828-652-9229 (24 hrs w/recorder)

automobilia

Mail order only. Broad range of automobilia, all makes, general to obscure. Emphasis in cars with promotional model cars, also other toy vehicle replicas, tin, rubber, die cast, plastic, ranging from Matchbox to pedal cars and large variety discontinued

model kits. Vast assortment with majority old and very little new items. Huge stock of automobile dealership/service station premiums such as procelain signs, jewelry, banks, key chains, ashtrays, rulers, literature, trinkets, giveaway novelties, etc.

Larry Machacek
PO Box 515
Porter, TX 77365
281-429-2505

decals
license plates
novelties

Sell self-adhesive vinyl decal reproductions of 1951-1975 Texas safety inspection stickers ($20 each), plus original Texas license plates (1917-1975) at various prices. Also sell reproduction WW II gasoline windshield ration stickers and posters from era photographs of cars.

Main Attractions
PO Box 4923
Chatsworth, CA 91311
818-709-9855; FAX: 818-998-0906

posters
videos

See full listing in **Section Four** under **information sources**

Manchester Motor Car Co
319 Main St
Manchester, CT 06040
860-643-5874; FAX: 860-643-6190
E-mail: mmcollc@aol.com

automobilia
parts
petroliana
restorations

See full listing in **Section Two** under **comprehensive parts**

Max Neon Design Group
19807 Sussex Dr
St Clair Shores, MI 48081-3257
810-773-5000; FAX: 810-772-6224

custom face logos
glass light-up
clocks
neon clocks

Mail order only. Designer, manufacturer, distributor of replica neon and glass light-up clocks depicting automotive, petro, motorcycle, etc, face logos. Custom face logos for individual or corporate clients also available.

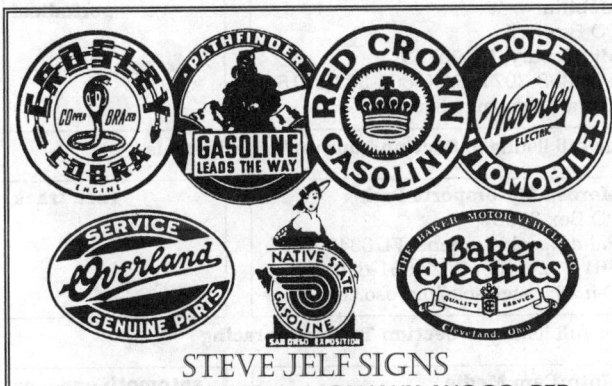

McIntyre Auctions
PO Box 60
East Dixfield, ME 04227
800-894-4300, 207-562-4443
FAX: 207-562-4576
E-mail: classicford@quickconnect.com

auctions
automobilia
literature
petroliana

See full listing in **Section Two** under **auctions & events**

Mike's Auto Parts
Box 358
Ridgeland, MS 39158
601-856-7214

ball/roller bearings
engine parts
wall calendars
water pumps

See full listing in **Section One** under **Chrysler**

Milestone Motorcars
Mark Tyra
3317 Nevel Meade Dr
Prospect, KY 40059
502-228-5945 am, 502-447-9475 pm
FAX: 502-228-1856
E-mail: mmotorcar@aol.com

die cast cars

Die cast cars and trucks, over 700 to select from. 1:18th scale is our specialty but we stock from 1:43rd scale and up to 1:12th scale. Check us out for limited editions and discontinued pieces. Visit our web site: http://members.aol.com/mmotorcars/catalog.htm

---

MITCHCO
1922 N Los Robles Ave
Pasadena, CA 91104-1105
626-401-4303

rubber stamps

Mail order only. If you can't put the classic in your garage, you can put it on your business cards, checks or note cards with Cool Car Stamps by MITCHCO. Automobile rubber stamps of classic and vintage cars. Catalogue of images, $2 (refundable with first order). Wholesale and custom inquiries welcome.

Mobilia
PO Box 575
Middlebury, VT 05753
802-388-3071; FAX: 802-388-2215
E-mail: info@mobilia.com

periodical

See full listing in **Section Four** under **periodicals**

Moroso Motorsports Park
PO Box 31907
Palm Beach Gardens, FL 33420
561-622-1400; FAX: 561-626-2053
E-mail: racetrack@moroso.com

race track

See full listing in **Section Two** under **racing**

MotorCam Media
138 N Alling Rd
Tallmadge, OH 44278
800-240-1777; FAX: 330-633-3249
E-mail: carvideo@motorcam.com

automotive videos

See full listing in **Section Two** under **videos**

Motorhead Art & Collectibles
4311 45th Ave NE
Tacoma, WA 98422
800-859-0164 orders, 253-924-0776
FAX: 253-924-0788
E-mail: autartman@aol.com

automotive art
die cast cars

See full listing in **Section Two** under **artwork**

Motorsports Racing
914 S Santa Fe #101
Vista, CA 92084
760-630-0547; FAX: 760-630-3085

accessories
apparel
art

See full listing in **Section Two** under **apparel**

MotorWeek
11767 Owings Mills Blvd
Owings Mills, MD 21117
410-356-5600; FAX: 410-581-4113
E-mail: motorweek@mpt.org

TV program

See full listing in **Section Four** under **information sources**

Museum of Transportation
15 Newton St
Brookline, MA 02445
617-522-6547; FAX: 617-524-0170

museum

See full listing in **Section Six** under **Massachusetts**

Dave Newell's Chevrobilia
PO Box 588
Orinda, CA 94563
510-223-4725

literature
memorabilia

See full listing in **Section One** under **Chevrolet**

Max Nordeen's Wheels Museum
6400 N 400 Ave
Alpha, IL 61413
309-334-2589

museum

See full listing in **Section Six** under **Illinois**

North Yorkshire Motor Museum
D T Mathewson
Roxby Garage, Pickering Rd
Thornton-le-Dale, North Yorkshire
England
01751 474455; FAX: 01944 758188

museum

See full listing in **Section Six** under **England**

Nostalgic Images Inc (formerly NEO)
631 Harrison St
Defiance, OH 43512
419-784-1728; FAX: 419-782-9459
E-mail: questions@nostalgicimages.com

collectibles
memorabilia
signs

Over 300 styles of collector metal signs. Approx size 12"x17". Most signs $6 or less. Quantity pricing available. Harley-Davidson, Ford, Chevy, Coca-Cola, Elvis and more. Ship USA and overseas. Please visit our web site for collector close-outs also. Web site: www.nostalgicimages.com

---

O'Brien Truckers
5 Perry Hill
North Grafton, MA 01536-1532
508-839-3033; FAX: 508-839-9490
E-mail: obt@ziplink.net

accessories
belt buckles
plaques
valve covers

See full listing in **Section Two** under **plaques**

Ohio Jukebox Co
6211 Cubbison Rd
Cumberland, OH 43732
740-638-5059

jukeboxes

See full listing in **Section Two** under **novelties**

Oil Company Collectibles Inc
PO Box 556
LaGrange, OH 44050
440-355-6608; FAX: 440-355-4955
E-mail: scottpcm@aol.com

books
gasoline globes
signs

Largest supplier and buyer of original gasoline pump globes in the world. Original gasoline globes, signs, etc. Buy and sell original gasoline globes, signs and related collectibles. We carry related books on same subject too. Web site: www.oilcollectibles.com

On Mark International Inc	replicas

On Mark International Inc
8923 S 43rd W Ave
Tulsa, OK 74132
918-446-7906; FAX: 918-445-1514
E-mail: onmark@ix.netcom.com

See full listing in **Section Two** under **models & toys**

Packard Archives — accessories / artwork / automobilia
918 W Co Rd C-2
St Paul, MN 55113-1942
651-484-1184
E-mail: estatecars@earthlink.net

See full listing in **Section One** under **Packard**

Past Gas Company — automobilia / gas pumps
308 Willard St
Cocoa, FL 32922
407-636-0449; FAX: 407-636-1006

Restored gas pumps, Coke machines, neon clocks, etc. Eco Tireflator parts, Fry visible parts. Complete gas pump restoration catalog, $2.

People's Choice & Lost in the 50s — 1950s clothing / 1950s memorabilia / automobilia items / celebrity items
28170 Ave Crocker #209
Valencia, CA 91355
800-722-1965, 661-295-1965
FAX: 661-295-1931

World's largest variety of 1950s stuff. Over 800 nostalgia products including bobbin' head dogs, shrunken heads, poodle and 1950s clothes, Kustom Kemp car stuff, car hop trays and accessories, dice and 8 ball items, neon clocks, spinner knobs, magnets, Elvis, Marilyn, James Dean, Betty Boop, Felix, Oscar Meyer, Coca Cola, Route 66, Coop, Von Dutch, Big Boy, wolf whistles, hula dolls, drag strip items and much, much more. Current catalog, $4.

The Plateman — license plates
Jim Estrup
269 Webber Hill Rd
Kennebunk, ME 04043
207-985-4800; FAX: 207-985-TAGS

See full listing in **Section Two** under **license plates**

Hugo Prado Limited Edition Corvette Art Prints — fine art prints
PO Box 18437
Chicago, IL 60618-0437
PH/FAX: 800-583-7627
E-mail: vetteart@aol.com

See full listing in **Section One** under **Corvette**

Promotionals 1934-1983 Dealership Vehicles in Miniature — price guide
2696 Brookmar
York, PA 17404
PH/FAX: 717-792-4936

Promotionals 1934-1983, Dealership Vehicles in Miniature is a guide for annual promotional cars and trucks with values for three levels of condition and 250 color photos. $19.95 plus $3 shipping.

Lloyd Ralston Gallery — toys
400 Long Beach Blvd
Stratford, CT 06615
203-386-9399; FAX: 203-386-9519
E-mail: lrgallery@aol.com

See full listing in **Section Two** under **models & toys**

RB's Prototype/Classic Expressions — automotive artwork / furniture
PO Box 16774
Stamford, CT 06905
203-329-2715; FAX: 203-329-8029
E-mail: rbproto@aol.com

Custom design and fabrication of automotive artwork, furniture, etc. The Car Bar, an automotive liquor cabinet. Refer to the aol site for details. Web site: http://members.aol.com/rbproto

Red Crown Automobilia — automobilia / literature / petroliana
1720 Rupert NE
Grand Rapids, MI 49505
616-361-9887

See full listing in **Section Two** under **petroliana**

Red Lion Racing — photographs / posters
8318 Avenida Castro
Cucamonga, CA 91730
909-987-9818; FAX: 909-987-6538
E-mail: rlracing@cris.com

See full listing in **Section Two** under **artwork**

The Reflected Image — mirror reproduction / mirror resilvering
21 W Wind Dr
Northford, CT 06472
PH/FAX: 203-484-0760
E-mail: scott@reflectedimage.com

See full listing in **Section Two** under **special services**

Frank Riley Automotive Art — automotive prints
PO Box 95
Hawthorne, NJ 07506
800-848-9459

See full listing in **Section Two** under **artwork**

Robertson Bros & Sons Restoration — NOS parts / restoration parts / used parts
PO Box 5678
Sevierville, TN 37864-5678
423-970-1655; FAX: 423-908-6838
E-mail: classicbop@aol.com

See full listing in **Section One** under **Oldsmobile**

Route 66 Collectible Cars and Antiques — consignment sales
1933 Del Monte Blvd
Seaside, CA 93955
831-393-9329; FAX: 831-393-9391
E-mail: cars@route66.com

See full listing in **Section Two** under **car dealers**

San Remo Hobby and Toy — models / trading cards
93 Beaver Dr
Kings Park, NY 11754-2209
PH/FAX: 516-724-5722

See full listing in **Section Two** under **models & toys**

Scale Collectors USA — garage dioramas
8353 NW 54th St
Miami, FL 33166
305-592-9920; FAX: 305-592-9421
E-mail: mreavia@bellsouth.net

Open Monday-Friday 9 am to 5 pm. Handcrafted car garages and car repair shops. Dioramas suitable for 1:18 scale models with all the tools and accessories included as a real garage has them. 3-dimensional picture frames with real 1/2 a car in 1:18 scale mounted onto the frame ready to hang up on the wall. Color catalog available, $5.

Doug Schellinger
13717 W Green Meadow Dr
New Berlin, WI 53151
414-786-8413
E-mail: dsac@execpc.com

automobilia
books
sales literature
toys

See full listing in **Section One** under **Fiat**

Jack Schmitt Studio
PO Box 1761
San Juan Capistrano, CA 92693

paintings
prints

See full listing in **Section Two** under **artwork**

Ron Scobie Enterprises
7676 120th St N
Hugo, MN 55038
651-653-6503
E-mail: rscobie@gaspump.com

gas pump parts

See full listing in **Section Two** under **petroliana**

Scott Signal Co
8368 W Farm Rd 84
Willard, MO 65781
417-742-5040

stoplights

Mail order and open shop. Daily 8 am to 8 pm. Stoplights, walk/don't walk, parking meters, sequencer kits, poles. 2 page color brochure, $3. Web site: www.trafficlights.com

Sea-Tac Specialties
Don Guilbault
6714-247 St Ct E
Graham, WA 98338
253-847-8545; FAX: 253-847-6455

hat pins
key chains

See full listing in **Section Two** under **accessories**

Silver Image Photographics
3102 Vestal Pkwy E
Vestal, NY 13850
607-797-8795

business cards
photo car cards
photofinishing

Mail order and open shop. Monday-Friday 9 am to 6 pm. Custom photo color lab. Makes custom photo car cards, color business cards with your car, your name and address, make and year of car. Enlargements and poster prints of your car.

Henri Simar J R
Rue du College, BP 172
B-4800 Verviers Belgium
32-87335501; FAX: 32-87335122

books
literature

See full listing in **Section Two** under **literature dealers**

Skopos Motor Museum
Alexandra Hills, Alexandra Rd
Batley
West Yorkshire WA7 6JA England
01924-444423

museum

See full listing in **Section Six** under **England**

Robert H Snyder
PO Drawer 821
Yonkers, NY 10702
914-476-8500
FAX: 914-476-8573, 24 hours
E-mail: cohascodpc@earthlink.net

literature
parts

See full listing in **Section One** under **Cadillac/LaSalle**

Sparrow Auction Company
59 Wheeler Ave
Milford, CT 06460
203-877-1066
E-mail: vehicle@snet.net

auction company

See full listing in **Section Two** under **auctions & events**

Spirit Enterprises
4325 Sunset Dr
Lockport, NY 14094
716-434-9938 showroom
716-434-0077 warehouse

automobilia
stereo systems

Mail order and open shop. Daily 8 am to 8 pm. Hard-to-find car kits from 1950s-1970s, plus new releases. Specializing in stereo systems for high-performance, American made cars. Over 4,000 model cars and die cast in stock at all times.

St Louis Car Museum & Sales
1575 Woodson Rd
St Louis, MO 63114
314-993-1330; FAX: 314-993-1540

museum

See full listing in **Section Six** under **Missouri**

Supercar Collectibles Ltd
7311-75th Circle N
Minneapolis, MN 55428
612-425-6020; FAX: 612-425-3357

muscle car replicas

See full listing in **Section Two** under **models & toys**

TCMB Models & Stuff
8207 Clinton Ave S
Bloomington, MN 55420-2315
612-884-3997; FAX: 612-884-2827
E-mail: tcmb@gte.net

models

See full listing in **Section Two** under **models & toys**

Jay Texter
417 Haines Mill Rd
Allentown, PA 18104
610-821-0963
E-mail: jaytexter@ot.com

photography

See full listing in **Section Two** under **photography**

**Edward Tilley Automotive
Collectibles**
PO Box 4233
Cary, NC 27519-4233
919-460-8262
E-mail: edandsusan@aol.com

automobilia
literature
parts

Mail order only. Buy and sell promotional models, out of print books, automobilia, literature, auto related toys and vintage racing collectibles. Since 1979. See our online catalog at http://members.aol.com/edandsusan/automobilia.html

Town & Country Toys
227 Midvale Dr
PO Box 574
Marshall, WI 53559
608-655-4961
E-mail: dejaeger@itis.com

banks
Ertl cars
mini license plates

See full listing in **Section Two** under **models & toys**

Peter Tytla Artist
PO Box 43
East Lyme, CT 06333-0043
860-739-7105

photographic
collages

See full listing in **Section Two** under **artwork**

Valenti Classics Inc
355 S Hwy 41
Caledonia, WI 53108
414-835-2070; FAX: 414-835-2575
E-mail: vci@valenticlassics.com

collectibles
restoration
sales
service

See full listing in **Section Two** under **car dealers**

Vic's Place Inc | restoration parts
124 N 2nd St
Guthrie, OK 73044
405-282-5586; FAX: 405-282-6850
E-mail: vics@telepath.com

See full listing in **Section Two** under **petroliana**

Vintage Jag Works | consulting
1390 W Hwy 26 | how-to articles
Blackfoot, ID 83221
208-684-4767; FAX: 208-684-3386
E-mail: walt@vintagejag.com

See full listing in **Section One** under **Jaguar**

Vintage Shop Coats | shop coats
40 Fourth St #106
Petaluma, CA 94952
925-837-7869; FAX: 707-762-7901

See full listing in **Section Two** under **apparel**

Volkswagen Collectors | literature
c/o Jerry Jess | memorabilia
3121 E Yucca St | toys
Phoenix, AZ 85028-2616
PH/FAX: 602-867-7672
E-mail: vwstuff@juno.com

See full listing in **Section One** under **Volkswagen**

Brady Ward-Scale Autoworks | models
313 Bridge St #4
Manchester, NH 03104-5045
603-623-5925
FAX: 603-623-5925 ext 66
E-mail: bradyward@mediaone.net

See full listing in **Section Two** under **models & toys**

Webster Auto Swap Meet | auction
6250 Tennessee Ave | car show
New Port Richey, FL 34653 | swap meet
800-438-8559, 813-848-7171
FAX: 813-846-8922

See full listing in **Section Two** under **auctions & events**

West Michigan Die-Cast Cars | die cast cars
2523 W Kinney Rd
Ludington, MI 49431
616-843-4278

See full listing in **Section Two** under **models & toys**

Kirk F White | models
PO Box 999 | tin toys
New Smyrna Beach, FL 32170
904-427-6660; FAX: 904-427-7801

See full listing in **Section Two** under **models & toys**

Zephyrhills Festivals and | auction
Auction Inc | swap meet
PO Box 848
Odessa, FL 33556
813-920-7206; FAX: 813-920-8512
Park: 813-782-0835
FAX: 813-780-7863

See full listing in **Section Two** under **auctions & events**

babbitting

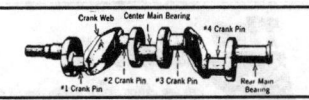

The Babbitt Pot | bearing boring
Zigmont G Billus | engine rebuilding
1693 St Rt 4 | rebabbitting
Fort Edward, NY 12828
518-747-4277

Mail order and open shop. Monday-Friday 9 am to 5 pm,
Saturday by appointment. Babbitt bearing specialist and antique
engine rebuilder for 25 years, using the best materials and best
effort.

Car Collectables | banks
32 White Birch Rd | Christmas cards
Madison, CT 06443 | note cards
PH/FAX: 203-245-2242

See full listing in **Section Two** under **artwork**

Harkin Machine Shop | engine rebuilding
903 43rd St NE | rebabbitting
Watertown, SD 57201
605-886-7880

See full listing in **Section Two** under **engine rebuilding**

Northwestern Auto Supply Inc | parts
1101 S Division
Grand Rapids, MI 49507
800-704-1078, 616-241-1714
FAX: 616-241-0924

See full listing in **Section Two** under **engine parts**

Paul's Rod & Bearing Ltd | babbitting
PO Box 29098
Parkville, MO 64152-0398
816-587-4747; FAX: 816-587-4312

Mail order and open shop. Monday-Thursday 6 am to 4:30 pm,
closed Friday. Babbitting of rods and main bearings for antique
cars.

Precision Babbitt Service | babbitting
4681 Lincoln Ave | engine rebuilding
Beamsville, ON Canada L0R 1B3
905-563-4364
E-mail: tkoudys@sprint.ca

Mail order and open shop. Evenings and Saturday. Complete
custom engine rebuilding. Babbitt bearings poured and
machined for any application, using certified tin-base alloy.
Specializes in, but not limited to, Model T, A, B and V8. All work
done in shop.

Vintage Motor and Machine | auto components
Gene French | fixtures
1513 Webster Ct | industrial
Ft Collins, CO 80524 | components
970-498-9224

See full listing in **Section Two** under **machine work**

batteries

Addison Generator Inc | auto parts
21 W Main St Rear | repairs
Freehold, NJ 07728 | supplies
732-431-2438; FAX: 732-431-4503

See full listing in **Section Two** under **electrical systems**

The Collector Car Battery

NEW CASTLE BATTERY MFG. CO.

Antique Auto Battery
2320 Old Mill Rd
Hudson, OH 44236
800-426-7580, 330-425-2395
FAX: 330-425-4642
E-mail: info@antiqueautobattery.com

batteries
battery cables

The world's only manufacturer of hard rubber raised letter Antique Batteries licensed by The Big Three that offers complete coverage of accurate reproduction batteries for all models. All with hard rubber script cases, correct caps and the tar tops have our famous nonsticky Poly Tar®. No damp dry rebuilds, blems or seconds. Finest quality dry charged factory fresh batteries available for your cars and trucks. Complete line of cables. MasterCard, Visa, American Express, Discover or COD. Web site: www.antiqueautobattery.com

Battery Ignition Co Inc
91 Meadow St
Hartford, CT 06114
860-296-4215; FAX: 860-947-3259
E-mail: biscokid@aol.com

parts
rebuilding
rebushing

See full listing in **Section Two** under **carburetors**

Cole's Ign & Mfg
52 Legionaire Dr
Rochester, NY 14617
PH/FAX: 716-342-9613

battery cables
ignition wire sets

See full listing in **Section Two** under **ignition parts**

Collector's Auto Supply
528 Appian Way
Coquitlam, BC Canada V3J 2A5
888-772-7848; FAX: 604-931-4450
E-mail: car@bc.sympatico.ca

parts

See full listing in **Section Two** under **comprehensive parts**

Deltran Corporation
801 US Hwy 92 E
Deland, FL 32724
904-736-7900; FAX: 904-736-9984

battery chargers

Mail order and open shop. Monday-Friday 7 am to 5:30 pm. Specialty battery chargers with the collector car enthusiast in mind. Specifically, the Super Smart Battery Tender® designed for batteries that are used infrequently. Temperature, voltage and amperage controlled for safety and reliability.

See our ad on this page

Bruce Falk
1105 Nichilson
Joliet, IL 60435
815-726-6455
E-mail: bbfalk@aol.com

parts

See full listing in **Section One** under **Chevrolet**

National Parts Depot
3101 SW 40th Blvd
Gainesville, FL 32608
800-874-7595 toll-free 24 hours
352-378-2473 local

accessories
restoration parts

See full listing in **Section Two** under **comprehensive parts**

New Castle Battery Mfg Co
3601 Wilmington Rd
PO Box 5040
New Castle, PA 16105-0040
724-658-5501; FAX: 724-658-5559

batteries

Mail order and open shop. Monday-Friday 8 am to 5 pm. Antique and classic car reproduction batteries for Chevy, Chrysler, Ford and Mustang automobiles and small pickups.

See our ad on this page

Thunderbolt Traders Inc	battery cables
6900 N Dixie Dr	
Dayton, OH 45414-3297	
513-890-3344; FAX: 513-890-9403	

See full listing in **Section One** under **Edsel**

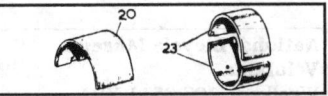

AAdvanced Transmissions	rear axle service
15 Parker St	restoration
Worcester, MA 01610	ring/pinion
508-752-9674, 508-752-9679	trans parts/sales/
FAX: 508-842-0191	rebuilding/service

See full listing in **Section Two** under **transmissions**

Allied Bearing Sales	bearings
8962 Ellis Ave	seals
Los Angeles, CA 90034	
310-837-0752	
800-421-3658 nationwide	
FAX: 310-837-0755	

Mail order and open shop. Monday-Friday 8 am to 4 pm. Supply all types of bearings for automotive applications, except engine bearings. Ball, cylindrical roller and tapered roller bearings and seals. Many part numbers are for obsolete or classic cars. Foreign and domestic. Many obsolete seals also in stock.

Daytona Turbo Action Camshafts	camshafts
1109 US #1	engine parts
PO Box 5094	
Ormond Beach, FL 32175	
888-RARE-CAM, 800-505-CAMS	
904-676-7478; FAX: 904-258-1582	
E-mail: info@camshafts.com	

Phone and mail order. Monday-Friday 9 am to 9 pm. Specializing in obsolete engine parts and custom ground camshafts for post-war US cars and trucks. Visa, MC, Discover. Web site: www.camshafts.com

Horst's Car Care	engine rebuilding
3160-1/2 N Woodford St	
Decatur, IL 62526	
217-876-1112	

See full listing in **Section One** under **Mercedes-Benz**

National Parts Depot	accessories
3101 SW 40th Blvd	restoration parts
Gainesville, FL 32608	
800-874-7595 toll-free 24 hours	
352-378-2473 local	

See full listing in **Section Two** under **comprehensive parts**

Northwestern Auto Supply Inc	parts
1101 S Division	
Grand Rapids, MI 49507	
800-704-1078, 616-241-1714	
FAX: 616-241-0924	

See full listing in **Section Two** under **engine parts**

OlCar Bearing Co	bearings
135 James Creek Rd	seals
Southern Pines, NC 28387	
910-693-3324; FAX: 910-693-1943	
E-mail: brgdr@gohp.net	

Mail order only. Bearings and seals for: axles, clutch, differential, pinion, transmission, steering knuckle and wheels. All years, most model cars and trucks.

Paul's Rod & Bearing Ltd	babbitting
PO Box 29098	
Parkville, MO 64152-0398	
816-587-4747; FAX: 816-587-4312	

See full listing in **Section Two** under **babbitting**

Rochester Clutch & Brake Co	brakes
35 Niagara St	clutches
Rochester, NY 14605	
716-232-2579; FAX: 716-232-3279	

See full listing in **Section Two** under **brakes**

Taylor Auto Parts	bearings
PO Box 650	brakes
Esparto, CA 95627	gaskets
530-787-1929	seals

See full listing in **Section Two** under **comprehensive parts**

Total Seal Inc	piston rings
11202 N 24th Ave, Ste 101	
Phoenix, AZ 85029	
602-678-4977; FAX: 602-678-4991	
E-mail: totseal@amug.org	

See full listing in **Section Two** under **engine parts**

Section Two
Generalists

West Amity Auto Parts 5685 Merrick Rd Massapequa, NY 11758 516-795-4610; FAX: 516-795-4117 E-mail: crein69929@erols.com	**custom machining engine rebuilding**

See full listing in **Section Two** under **engine rebuilding**

bicycles

Antiques Warehouse Michael J Welch 3700 Rt 6 Eastham, MA 02642 508-255-1437; FAX: 508-247-9166 E-mail: miketoys1@aol.com	**automobilia bikes toy trucks**

See full listing in **Section Two** under **models & toys**

Britbikes Box 2183 Manchester Center, VT 05255 PH/FAX: 802-362-4719 E-mail: savage1951@aol.com	**vintage bicycles**

Mail order only. Vintage English bicycles, 1900-1960 including Raleigh, Rudge, Dunelt, BSA, Humber, Triumph, Phillips, Dursley-Pedersen et al. Parts, accessories, dealer displays, literature and memorabilia bought, sold and traded.

British Cycling Museum The Old Station Camelford Cornwall PL32 9TZ England PH/FAX: 01840-212811	**museum**

See full listing in **Section Six** under **England**

Coker Tire 1317 Chestnut St Chattanooga, TN 37402 800-251-6336 toll-free 423-265-6368 local & international FAX: 423-756-5607	**tires**

See full listing in **Section Two** under **tires**

Das osterr. Motorradmuseum Museumgasse 6 A-3730 Eggenburg Austria 43 2984 2151; FAX: 43 2984 2119	**museum**

See full listing in **Section Six** under **Austria**

Henry Ford Museum & Greenfield Village 20900 Oakwood Blvd Dearborn, MI 48121-1970 313-271-1620; FAX: 313-982-6247	**museum**

See full listing in **Section Six** under **Michigan**

Gaylord Sales Frank Ranghelli 125 Dugan Ln Toms River, NJ 08753 732-349-9213; FAX: 732-341-5353	**automobilia automotive art mascots**

See full listing in **Section Two** under **radiator emblems & mascots**

Marky D's Bikes & Pedal Goods 7047 Springridge Rd West Bloomfield, MI 48322 810-737-1657; FAX: 810-398-2581	**bicycles mopeds motorbikes pedal goods**

Buying and selling old/classic bicycles, mopeds, motorbikes and unusual pedal goods.

National Bicycle Museum Velorama Waalkade 107 6511 XR Nijmegen Netherlands 024-3225851; FAX: 024-3607177	**museum**

See full listing in **Section Six** under **Netherlands**

National Cycle Exhibition The Automobile Palace Temple St Llandrindod Wells Powys Mid Wales LD1 5DL Wales 01597-825531	**museum**

See full listing in **Section Six** under **Wales**

Skopos Motor Museum Alexandra Hills, Alexandra Rd Batley West Yorkshire WA7 6JA England 01924-444423	**museum**

See full listing in **Section Six** under **England**

Steve's Antiques/POR-15 Steve Verhoeven 5609 S 4300 W Hooper, UT 84315 888-817-6715 toll-free, 801-985-4835 E-mail: steve@stevesantiques.com	**bicycles POR-15 distributor**

See full listing in **Section Two** under **rustproofing**

body parts

5362 Corvette Place 4602 Kenbridge Dr Greensboro, NC 27410 336-852-1011; FAX: 336-852-6107	**Corvette parts**

See full listing in **Section One** under **Corvette**

60 Chev Sam 2912 Wright Rd Hamptonville, NC 27020 336-468-1745	**parts**

See full listing in **Section One** under **Chevrolet**

ADP Hollander 14800 28th Ave N #190 Plymouth, MN 55447 800-761-9266; FAX: 800-825-1124 E-mail: hollander@autonet.net	**interchange info manuals**

See full listing in **Section Two** under **car & parts locators**

American Performance Products 675 S Industry Rd Cocoa, FL 32926 407-632-8299; FAX: 407-632-5119 E-mail: amc@oldcarparts.com	**parts**

See full listing in **Section One** under **AMC**

Amherst Antique Auto Show	swap meets
157 Hollis Rd	
Amherst, NH 03031	
603-883-0605, NH	
FAX: 617-641-0647, MA	

See full listing in **Section Two** under **auctions & events**

Anderson Automotive	cars
1604 E Busch Blvd	parts
Tampa, FL 33612	
813-932-4611; FAX: 813-932-5025	

See full listing in **Section One** under **Oldsmobile**

Andy's Classic Mustangs	parts
18502 E Sprague	service
Greenacres, WA 99016	
509-924-9824	

See full listing in **Section One** under **Mustang**

Auto Body Specialties Inc	accessories
Rt 66	body parts
Middlefield, CT 06455	
888-277-1960 toll-free orders only	
860-346-4989; FAX: 860-346-4987	

Mail order and open shop. Monday, Tuesday 9 am to 6 pm; Wednesday, Friday 9 am to 5 pm; Thursday 9 am to 7 pm; Saturday 9 am to 3 pm. Body parts and accessories, Reproduction, original and used for GM, Ford, Chrysler 1950-present cars, pickups and vans. Web site: www.autobodyspecialt.com

B & T Truck Parts	pickup parts
906 E Main St	
PO Box 799	
Siloam Springs, AR 72761	
501-524-5959; FAX: 501-524-5559	

See full listing in **Section Two** under **trucks & tractors**

Bay Ridges Classic Chevy	accessories
1550 Bayly St #38A	parts
Pickering, ON Canada L1W 3W1	
905-839-6169; FAX: 905-420-6613	

See full listing in **Section One** under **Chevrolet**

Big Boys Toys	accessories
Richard Boutin	bodywork
Rt 67A Box 174A	tires
North Bennington, VT 05257	wheels
800-286-1721; FAX: 802-447-0962	

See full listing in **Section Two** under **accessories**

Bill's Speed Shop	body parts
13951 Millersburg Rd	
Navarre, OH 44662	
330-832-9403; FAX: 330-832-2098	

See full listing in **Section One** under **Chevrolet**

Bob's Brickyard Inc	parts
1030 N Hickory Ridge Tr	
Milford, MI 48380	
248-685-9508; FAX: 248-685-8662	
E-mail: bobsbrick@aol.com	

See full listing in **Section One** under **Bricklin**

Bob's Bird House	parts
124 Watkin Ave	
Chadds Ford, PA 19317	
610-358-3420; FAX: 610-558-0729	

See full listing in **Section One** under **Thunderbird**

Gideon Booth	car collector
Rellandsgate, Kings Meaburn	parts
Penrith	restorations
Cumbria CA10 3BT England	
PH/FAX: 01931 714624	

See full listing in **Section One** under **Morris**

The Buckle Man	buckles
Douglas D Drake	
28 Monroe Ave	
Pittsford, NY 14534	
716-381-4604	

See full listing in **Section Two** under **hardware**

Caddy Central	cars
11117 Tippett Rd	locating service
Clinton, MD 20735	parts
301-234-0135; FAX: 301-234-0140	
E-mail: cadlocator@aol.com	

See full listing in **Section One** under **Cadillac/LaSalle**

California Pony Cars	parts
1906 Quaker Ridge Pl	
Ontario, CA 91761	
909-923-2804; FAX: 909-947-8593	
E-mail: 105232.3362@compuserve.com	

See full listing in **Section One** under **Mustang**

Canadian Mustang	parts
20529 62 Ave	
Langley, BC Canada V3A 8R4	
604-534-6424; FAX: 604-534-6694	
E-mail: parts@canadianmustang.com	

See full listing in **Section One** under **Mustang**

CARS Inc	interior
1964 W 11 Mile Rd	
Berkley, MI 48072	
248-398-7100; FAX: 248-398-7078	
E-mail: carsinc@worldnet.att.net	

See full listing in **Section One** under **Chevrolet**

Jim Carter's Antique Truck Parts	truck parts
1508 E Alton	
Independence, MO 64055	
800-336-1913; FAX: 800-262-3749	
E-mail: jimcartertruck.parts@worldnet.att.net	

See full listing in **Section One** under **Chevrolet**

Cheyenne Pickup Parts	body panels
Box 959	bumpers
Noble, OK 73068	carpet
405-872-3399; FAX: 405-872-0385	weatherstripping

See full listing in **Section Two** under **trucks & tractors**

Ed Cholakian Enterprises Inc	museum
dba All Cadillacs of the 40's and 50's	parts
12811 Foothill Blvd	
Sylmar, CA 91342	
800-808-1147, 818-361-1147	
FAX: 818-361-9738	

See full listing in **Section One** under **Cadillac/LaSalle**

Classic Auto	restoration
251 SW 5th Ct	
Pompano Beach, FL 33060	
PH/FAX: 954-786-1687	

See full listing in **Section Two** under **restoration shops**

Classic Chevy International | modified parts / repro parts / used parts
PO Box 607188
Orlando, FL 32860-7188
800-456-1957, 407-299-1957
FAX: 407-299-3341
E-mail: cciworld@aol.com

See full listing in **Section One** under **Chevrolet**

Classic Ford Sales | salvage yard
PO Box 60
East Dixfield, ME 04227
207-562-4443; FAX: 207-562-4576
E-mail: classicford@quickconnect.com

See full listing in **Section Five** under **Maine**

Classic Sheetmetal Inc | body panels / sheetmetal
4010 A Hartley St
Charlotte, NC 28206
800-776-4040, 704-596-5186
FAX: 704-596-3895

See full listing in **Section One** under **Thunderbird**

Coopers Vintage Auto Parts | parts
3087 N California St
Burbank, CA 91504
818-567-4140; FAX: 818-567-4101

See full listing in **Section One** under **Cadillac/LaSalle**

Custom Classic Cars | parts / restoration
2046 E 12B Road
Bourbon, IN 46504
219-342-5007; FAX: 219-342-0399
E-mail: customclassiccars@waveone.net

See full listing in **Section One** under **Chevrolet**

Dakota Studebaker Parts | parts
RR 1, Box 103A
Armour, SD 57313
605-724-2527

See full listing in **Section One** under **Studebaker**

DeLorean One | bodywork / parts / service
20229 Nordhoff St
Chatsworth, CA 91311
818-341-1796; FAX: 818-998-6381

See full listing in **Section One** under **DeLorean**

Dependable RV & Auto Service | parts / restoration / service
2619 Rt 11 N
Lafayette, NY 13084
315-677-5336; FAX: 315-677-5258

See full listing in **Section Two** under **service shops**

Desert Dog Auto Parts Inc | body parts
1316 S Boeger Ave
Westchester, IL 60154-3404
708-409-1040; FAX: 708-409-8232
E-mail: ddog@desertdogautoparts.com

Mail order and open shop. Monday-Friday 8 am to 5 pm.
Anything American, 1950-1980s. Specializing in rust-free sheet-metal, pit-free chrome, bumper restoration program. Accept
Visa, MasterCard and ship worldwide. Web site:
www.desertdogautoparts.com

Hemmings' Vintage Auto Almanac©   Fourteenth Edition

Desert Valley Auto Parts | cars / parts
22500 N 21st Ave
Phoenix, AZ 85027
800-905-8024, 602-780-8024
FAX: 602-582-9141
E-mail: rust-free-parts@worldnet.att.net

See full listing in **Section Five** under **Arizona**

Mike Drago Chevy Parts | Chevrolet parts
141 E St Joseph St
Easton, PA 18042
PH/FAX: 610-252-5701
E-mail: dragomdcp@aol.com

See full listing in **Section One** under **Chevrolet**

Driving Passion Ltd USA | cars / parts / salvage yard
Marc Tuwiner
7132 Chilton Ct
Clarksville, MD 21029
PH/FAX: 301-596-9078
E-mail: mt.tees@erols.com

See full listing in **Section One** under **Cadillac/LaSalle**

East West Auto Parts Inc | European import / parts / GM parts
4605 Dawson Rd
Tulsa, OK 74115
800-447-2886; FAX: 918-832-7900

See full listing in **Section Five** under **Oklahoma**

Eckler's Quality Parts & Accessories for Corvettes | accessories / parts
PO Box 5637
Titusville, FL 32783
800-327-4868; FAX: 407-383-2059
E-mail: ecklers@ecklers.com

See full listing in **Section One** under **Corvette**

The El Camino Store | parts
57 B Depot Rd
Goleta, CA 93117
805-681-8164; FAX: 805-681-8166
E-mail: ec@elcaminostore.com

See full listing in **Section One** under **Chevelle/Camaro**

Lee Ellison's MoreParts North | parts / sheetmetal
PO Box 345
Orangeville, ON Canada L9W 2Z7
519-941-6331; FAX: 519-941-8903
E-mail: obsoleteparts@moreparts.com

See full listing in **Section One** under **Mopar**

Fairlane Automotive Specialties | fiberglass bodies / parts
210 E Walker St
St Johns, MI 48879
517-224-6460

See full listing in **Section One** under **Ford 1932-1953**

For Ramblers Only | accessories / parts
2324 SE 34th Ave
Portland, OR 97214
503-232-0497
E-mail: ramblers@teleport.com

See full listing in **Section One** under **AMC**

Freddie Beach Restoration | accessories / restoration parts
1834 Woodstock Rd
Fredericton, NB Canada E3C 1L4
506-450-9074; FAX: 506-459-0708
E-mail: vallise@city.fredericton.nb.ca

See full listing in **Section Two** under **car & parts locators**

J Giles Automotive | car & parts locator / exporter
703 Morgan Ave
Pascagoula, MS 39567-2116
228-769-1012; FAX: 228-769-8904
E-mail: jgauto@datasync.com

See full listing in **Section Two** under **car & parts locators**

Halpin Used Auto & Truck Parts | NOS auto/truck parts / used auto/truck parts
1093 Rt 123
Mayfield, NY 12117
518-863-4906
E-mail: junkyard2064@webtv.net

See full listing in **Section Five** under **New York**

Hoffman Automotive Distributor | parts
US Hwy #1, Box 818
Hilliard, FL 32046
904-845-4421

Mail order and open shop. Monday-Friday 9 am to 5 pm, Saturday 9 am to 2 pm. Started business in 1969. Sell NOS and reproduction parts, 1955-1972 Chevy parts and are currently branching out to Mustang parts, 1968-1972.

Holcombe Cadillac Parts | parts
2933 Century Ln
Bensalem, PA 19020
215-245-4560; FAX: 215-633-9916

See full listing in **Section One** under **Cadillac/LaSalle**

Hollywood Classic Motorcars Inc | cars / parts
363 Ansin Blvd
Hallandale, FL 33009
800-235-2444, 954-454-4641
FAX: 954-457-3801
E-mail: hcm@tbird.net

See full listing in **Section One** under **Thunderbird**

Bruce Horkey's Wood & Parts | pickup parts
Rt 4 Box 188
Windom, MN 56101
507-831-5625; FAX: 507-831-0280

See full listing in **Section Two** under **trucks & tractors**

Bill Horton | vacuum motors
5804 Jones Valley Dr
Huntsville, AL 35802
256-881-6894

See full listing in **Section One** under **Mercury**

Howell's Sheetmetal Co | body panels / sheetmetal
PO Box 792
Nederland, TX 77627
800-375-6663, 409-727-1999
FAX: 409-727-7127
E-mail: dhowell@fordor.com

See full listing in **Section One** under **Ford 1903-1931**

Impala Bob's Inc | restoration parts
4753 E Falcon Dr
Dept HVAA14
Mesa, AZ 85215
800-IMPALAS orders
480-924-4800 retail store
480-981-1600 office
FAX: 800-716-6237, 480-981-1675
E-mail: info@impalas.com

See full listing in **Section One** under **Chevrolet**

Imperial Motors | parts
Rt 3 Box 380
Campobello, SC 29322
864-895-3474; FAX: 864-895-1248

See full listing in **Section One** under **Chrysler**

Jefferis Autobody | windshield glass kit
269 Tank Farm Rd
San Luis Obispo, CA 93401
800-807-1937; FAX: 805-543-4757

See full listing in **Section Two** under **glass**

K&D Enterprises | accessories / parts / restorations
23117 E Echo Lake Rd
Snohomish, WA 98296-5426
425-788-0507; FAX: 360-668-2003
E-mail: tdb@halcyon.com

See full listing in **Section One** under **Jensen**

K&W Kollectibles | parts / repair / restoration
220 Industrial Pkwy S #6
Aurora, ON Canada L4G 3V6
416-410-7741; FAX: 905-727-5771
E-mail: kwkoll@sympatico.ca

See full listing in **Section One** under **Buick/McLaughlin**

K-F-D Services Inc | parts / restoration
HC 65, Box 49
Altonah, UT 84002
801-454-3098; FAX: 801-454-3099
E-mail: kfd-services@msn.com

See full listing in **Section One** under **Kaiser Frazer**

KopyKatz Restoration Parts | bumpers / fenders / hoods / panels / truck beds
2536 N Sheridan Blvd
Denver, CO 80214
303-458-5332; FAX: 303-477-1496
E-mail: kopykatz@earthlink.net

Open Monday-Friday 8 am to 5 pm. Specializing in new after-market body parts: hoods, fenders, rust repair panels, weather-strip, trim, interior items. American muscle and domestic trucks 1960s-1970s.

L & L Antique Auto Trim | runningboard / moldings
403 Spruce, Box 177
Pierce City, MO 65723
417-476-2871

See full listing in **Section Two** under **special services**

Land Cruiser Solutions Inc | accessories / services
20 Thornell Rd
Newton, NH 03858
603-382-3555; FAX: 603-378-0431
E-mail: twbii@aol.com

See full listing in **Section One** under **Toyota**

Marcel's Corvette Parts 15100 Lee Rd #101 Humble, TX 77396 800-546-2111 order line 281-441-2111 info line FAX: 281-441-3057	**parts**

See full listing in **Section One** under **Corvette**

David Martin Box 61 Roosevelt, TX 76874 915-446-4439	**parts**

See full listing in **Section One** under **Chrysler**

McDonald Obsolete Parts Company RR 3, Box 94 Rockport, IN 47635 812-359-4965; FAX: 812-359-5555 E-mail: mcdonald@psci.net	**body parts chassis parts**

See full listing in **Section One** under **Ford 1954-up**

Merv's Classic Chevy Parts 1330 Washington Iowa Falls, IA 50126 515-648-3168, 515-648-9675	**parts**

See full listing in **Section One** under **Chevrolet**

Michael's Auto Parts 5875 NW Kaiser Rd Portland, OR 97229 503-690-7750; FAX: 503-690-7735	**used Mercedes parts only**

See full listing in **Section Five** under **Oregon**

Mill Supply Inc PO Box 28400 Cleveland, OH 44128 800-888-5072; FAX: 888-781-2700 E-mail: info@millsupply.com	**clips fasteners panels**

See full listing in **Section Two** under **sheetmetal**

Motorsport Auto 1139 W Collins Ave Orange, CA 92667 800-633-6331, 714-639-2620 FAX: 714-639-7460 E-mail: motorsport@worldnet.att.net	**parts**

See full listing in **Section One** under **Datsun**

National Parts Depot 3101 SW 40th Blvd Gainesville, FL 32608 800-874-7595 toll-free 24 hours 352-378-2473 local	**accessories restoration parts**

See full listing in **Section Two** under **comprehensive parts**

Northwest Classic Falcons Inc 1964 NW Pettygrove St Portland, OR 97209 503-241-9454; FAX: 503-241-1964 E-mail: ron@nwfalcon.com	**parts**

See full listing in **Section One** under **Ford 1954-up**

Paragon Reproductions Inc 8040 S Jennings Rd Swartz Creek, MI 48473 810-655-4641; FAX: 810-655-6667 E-mail: www.info@corvette-paragon.com	**Corvette repro parts**

See full listing in **Section One** under **Corvette**

The Parts Scout® Bodo Repenn Diagonalstrasse 18A D-20537 Hamburg Germany *49-40-21980130 FAX: *49-40-21980132	**parts parts locator**

See full listing in **Section Two** under **comprehensive parts**

Paul's Discount Jaguar Parts 1124 NW 134th Ave Sunrise Fort Lauderdale, FL 33323 954-846-7976; FAX: 954-846-9450 E-mail: paulsjag@ix.netcom.com	**parts**

See full listing in **Section One** under **Jaguar**

Paul's Select Cars & Parts for Porsche® 2280 Gail Dr Riverside, CA 92509 909-685-9340; FAX: 909-685-9342 E-mail: pauls356-s90@webtv.net	**cars parts**

See full listing in **Section One** under **Porsche**

Perfect Panels of America 1690 Thomas Paine Pkwy Centerville, OH 45459 937-435-4543; FAX: 937-435-4548 E-mail: porshfreek@aol.com	**body panels**

See full listing in **Section One** under **Porsche**

Pony Parts of America 1690 Thomas Paine Pkwy Centerville, OH 45459 937-435-4543; FAX: 937-435-4548 E-mail: porshfreek@aol.com	**floor boards frame rails**

See full listing in **Section One** under **Mustang**

R J & L Automotive Fasteners 58 Bristol Ave Rochester, NY 14617-2702 PH/FAX: 716-467-7421	**fasteners**

See full listing in **Section Two** under **hardware**

Raybuck Autobody Parts RD 4, Box 170 Punxsutawney, PA 15767 814-938-5248; FAX: 814-938-4250	**body parts**

Mail order and open shop. Monday-Friday 8 am to 5 pm. New high quality reproduction body parts for pickups, vans and jeeps.

The Real Source PO Box 1248 Effingham, IL 62401 800-LUV-BUGG (588-2844), dept VS9 FAX: 217-347-2952 E-mail: madbug@madvet.com	**accessories parts**

See full listing in **Section One** under **Volkswagen**

Recks & Relics Ford Trucks 2675 Hamilton Mason Rd Hamilton, OH 45011 513-868-3489 E-mail: truck@choice.net	**truck parts**

See full listing in **Section One** under **Ford 1932-1953**

Regal Roadsters Ltd 301 W Beltline Hwy Madison, WI 53713 PH/FAX: 608-273-4141	replicars restoration

See full listing in **Section One** under **Thunderbird**

Replica Plastics 210 W Washington St Box 1147 Dothan, AL 36301 800-873-5871; FAX: 334-792-1175 E-mail: stone@mail.ala.net	fiberglass parts

See full listing in **Section Two** under **fiberglass parts**

Rocker King 804 Chicago Ave Waukesha, WI 53188-3511 414-549-9583; FAX: 414-549-9643 E-mail: sonoma@execpc.com	body parts sheetmetal parts

See full listing in **Section Two** under **sheetmetal**

Rolling Steel Body Parts 7320 Martingale Dr Chesterland, OH 44026-2007 888-765-5460; FAX: 440-729-7658 E-mail: rollingsteel@hotmail.com	body parts

Dealing in body parts and panels. Steel repair body panels that fit 1947-up cars and trucks. Featuring made in USA parts. Web site: rollingsteel.net

See our ad on page 436

S & S Antique Auto Pine St Deposit, NY 13754 607-467-2929; FAX: 607-467-2109	parts

See full listing in **Section One** under **Ford 1932-1953**

Sherman & Associates Inc 61166 Van Dyke Rd Washington, MI 48094 810-677-6800; FAX: 810-677-6801	body panels/parts fenders floors quarter panels

Mail order and open shop. Monday-Friday 8:30 am to 5 pm, Saturday 10 am to 1 pm EST. Specialize in restoration body parts and panels for Ford, GM, Chrysler, imports and light trucks, 1949-up. Have complete fenders, quarters and hoods plus patch panels for spot repair of damaged or rusted areas. Our product line includes components for vintage restorations and late model crash repairs, plus general maintenance and customization items including heater cores, radiators, running-boards, fender flares, trim rings, rear spoilers, step-type truck bumpers and other add-on accessories. To assure prompt service we have moved to a new 110,000 sq ft facility to house all our products under one roof. Web site: www.shermanparts.com

Paul Slater Auto Parts 9496 85th St N Stillwater, MN 55082 612-429-4235	parts

See full listing in **Section One** under **Dodge**

Smith & Jones Distributing Company Inc 1 Biloxi Square West Columbia, SC 29170 803-822-8500; FAX: 803-822-8477	parts

See full listing in **Section One** under **Ford 1903-1931**

Smooth Line 2562 Riddle Run Rd Tarentum, PA 15084 724-274-6002; FAX: 724-274-6121	body panels removable hardtops

See full listing in **Section Two** under **tops**

Sports & Classics PO Box 1787 512 Boston Post Rd, Dept H Darien, CT 06820-1787	parts

Mail order and open shop. Monday-Friday 9 am to 5 pm, Saturday 10 am to 1 pm. Fiberglass and steel body panels, wiring harnesses, convertible tops, leather upholstery, exhaust, trimmings, large stock of original factory parts, plus club discounts with proof of membership, etc. Manufacture replacement parts. Dealer inquiries invited. Parts for Austin-Healey, Lotus, MG, Morgan, Jaguar and Triumph. 350 page catalog, $10.

Star Quality 1 Alley Rd Lagrangeville, NY 12540 800-782-7199; FAX: 914-223-5394 E-mail: sq@mhv.net	parts

See full listing in **Section One** under **Mercedes-Benz**

Stilwell's Obsolete Car Parts 1617 Wedeking Ave Evansville, IN 47711 812-425-4794	body parts interiors parts

See full listing in **Section One** under **Mustang**

Strader Classics Bill Strader 2849 Locust Grove Rd Elizabethtown, KY 42701 502-737-5294	parts

See full listing in **Section One** under **Chevrolet**

Stringbean's Pickup Parts 985 Cushon St Johnstown, PA 15902 PH/FAX: 814-539-6440 E-mail: s-bean@surfshop.net	parts service

See full listing in **Section One** under **Chevrolet**

Tabco Inc 11655 Chillicothe Rd Chesterland, OH 44026-1994 216-921-5850; FAX: 216-921-5862	body parts

See full listing in **Section Two** under **sheetmetal**

Tamraz's Parts Discount Warehouse 10022 S Bode Rd Plainfield, IL 60544 630-904-4500; FAX: 630-904-2329	carpeting upholstery weatherstripping

See full listing in **Section One** under **Chevelle/Camaro**

Thompson Hill Metalcraft 23 Thompson Hill Rd Berwick, ME 03901 207-698-5756 E-mail: wpeach@thompsonhill.com	metal forming panel beating welding

See full listing in **Section Two** under **sheetmetal**

Bill Thomsen 1118 Wooded Acres Ln Moneta, VA 24121 540-297-1200	salvage yard

See full listing in **Section Five** under **Virginia**

John Ulrich
450 Silver Ave
San Francisco, CA 94112
PH/FAX: 510-223-9587 days

parts

See full listing in **Section One** under **Packard**

Tom Vagnini
58 Anthony Rd, RR 3
Pittsfield, MA 01201
413-698-2526

used parts

See full listing in **Section One** under **Packard**

Vintage Car Corral
1401 NW 53rd Ave
PO Box 384
Gainesville, FL 32602
PH/FAX: 352-376-0660

parts
toys

See full listing in **Section Two** under **comprehensive parts**

Volvo Shop Inc
5220 New Milford Rd
Ravenna, OH 44266
330-297-1297
E-mail: volvocarl@aol.com

parts
restoration

See full listing in **Section One** under **Volvo**

Wales Antique Chevy Truck Parts
143 Center
Carleton, MI 48117
734-654-8836

parts

See full listing in **Section One** under **Chevrolet**

Wallace Walmsley
4732 Bancroft St, #7
San Diego, CA 92116
619-283-3063

parts

See full listing in **Section One** under **Packard**

West Coast Sheetmetal
Lawrence M Camuso
219 S 20th St
San Jose, CA 95116
408-286-6537

body parts

Mail order only. Monday-Friday 9 am to 5 pm. Rust-free body parts for all late 1950s-1980s American cars. Parts for all different body styles including doors, fenders, quarter panels, trunk lids, hoods, fuel tanks, etc. Specializing in Oldsmobiles.

Pat Wilson's Thunderbird Parts
235 River Rd
New Milford, NJ 07646-1721
888-262-1153; FAX: 201-634-1916

parts

See full listing in **Section One** under **Thunderbird**

Zephyrhills Festivals and Auction Inc
PO Box 848
Odessa, FL 33556
813-920-7206; FAX: 813-920-8512
Park: 813-782-0835
FAX: 813-780-7863

auction
swap meet

See full listing in **Section Two** under **auctions & events**

bodywork

Ace Antique Auto Restoration
65 S Service Rd
Plainview, NY 11803
516-752-6065; FAX: 516-752-1484

air conditioning
body rebuilding
restoration
wiring harnesses

See full listing in **Section Two** under **restoration shops**

ACE Automotive Cleaning Equipment Co
897 S Washington Suite 232
Holland, MI 49423
616-772-3260; FAX: 616-772-3261

sandblasting
equipment

See full listing in **Section Two** under **rust removal & stripping**

Adler's Antique Autos Inc
801 NY Rt 43
Stephentown, NY 12168
518-733-5749
E-mail: advdesign1@aol.com

auto preservation
Chevrolet knowledge
parts
repair
restoration

See full listing in **Section Two** under **restoration shops**

Antique & Classic Cars Inc
328 S 3rd St
Hamilton, OH 45011
513-844-1146 in OH
800-798-3982 nationwide

bodywork
machine work
painting
parts
service

See full listing in **Section One** under **Buick/McLaughlin**

Auto Restoration by William R Hahn
Palermo Auto Body
241 Church Rd (rear)
Wexford, PA 15090
724-935-3790 shop, 412-367-2538 home
FAX: 724-935-9121

custom work
restoration

See full listing in **Section Two** under **restoration shops**

Bassett Classic Restoration
2616 Sharon St, Suite D
Kenner, LA 70062
PH/FAX: 504-469-2982
(have auto switching device)

parts
plating
restoration
service

See full listing in **Section One** under **Rolls-Royce/Bentley**

Bay Area Industrial Dry Stripping
151 11th St
Richmond, CA 94801-3523
510-412-9890, 510-805-1887

blasting
paint removal

See full listing in **Section Two** under **rust removal & stripping**

Berkshire Auto's Time Was
Box 347, 10 Front Street
Collinsville, CT 06022
860-693-2332

restoration

See full listing in **Section Two** under **restoration shops**

Big Boys Toys
Richard Boutin
Rt 67A Box 174A
North Bennington, VT 05257
800-286-1721; FAX: 802-447-0962

accessories
bodywork
tires
wheels

See full listing in **Section Two** under **accessories**

Bob's Brickyard Inc
1030 N Hickory Ridge Tr
Milford, MI 48380
248-685-9508; FAX: 248-685-8662
E-mail: bobsbrick@aol.com

parts

See full listing in **Section One** under **Bricklin**

City Imports Ltd
166 Penrod Ct
Glen Burnie, MD 21061
410-768-6660; FAX: 410-768-5955

bodywork
car sales
restorations

See full listing in **Section One** under **Jaguar**

Classic Sheetmetal Inc
4010 A Hartley St
Charlotte, NC 28206
800-776-4040, 704-596-5186
FAX: 704-596-3895

body panels
sheetmetal

See full listing in **Section One** under **Thunderbird**

Classics Plus LTD
N7306 Lakeshore Dr
N Fond du Lac, WI 54937
888-923-1007

restoration

See full listing in **Section Two** under **steering wheels**

Commonwealth Automotive Restorations
1725 Hewins St
Ashley Falls, MA 01222
413-229-3196

body rebuilding
parts
restoration

See full listing in **Section Two** under **military vehicles**

County Corvette
PO Box 258
Lionville, PA 19353
610-363-0872, 610-363-7670 sales
FAX: 610-363-5325

restoration
sales
service

See full listing in **Section One** under **Corvette**

Cover-It
17 Wood St
West Haven, CT 06516-3843
800-932-9344; FAX: 203-931-4754
E-mail: coverit@ct1.nai.net

all-weather shelters

See full listing in **Section Two** under **car covers**

D&M Corvette Specialists Ltd
1804 Ogden Ave
Downers Grove, IL 60515
630-968-0031; FAX: 630-968-0465

parts
restoration
sales
service

See full listing in **Section One** under **Corvette**

Dan's Restorations
PO Box 144
Snake Hill Rd
Sand Lake, NY 12153
518-674-2061

woodgraining

See full listing in **Section Two** under **woodgraining**

DeLorean One
20229 Nordhoff St
Chatsworth, CA 91311
818-341-1796; FAX: 818-998-6381

bodywork
parts
service

See full listing in **Section One** under **DeLorean**

DeVito Auto Restorations
470 Boston Post Rd
Weston, MA 02493
781-893-4949 ext 142
FAX: 781-899-4900
E-mail: radjr@ix.netcom.com

restorations
rust repair

Open shop. Monday-Friday 8:30 am to 5 pm. Complete or partial restoration of Mercedes-Benz, Jaguars, Fiats, Ferraris, most makes of cars. Specialize in heavy rust repair, top quality paint, complete mechanical work for all makes. Web site: www.pnpco.com

East Coast Chevy Inc
Ol '55 Chevy Parts
4154A Skyron Dr
Doylestown, PA 18938
215-348-5568; FAX: 215-348-0560

custom work
parts
restoration

See full listing in **Section One** under **Chevrolet**

Foreign Autotech
3235 C Sunset Ln
Hatboro, PA 19040
215-441-4421; FAX: 215-441-4490
E-mail: fap1800@aol.com

parts

See full listing in **Section One** under **Volvo**

Fuller's Restoration Inc
Old Airport Rd
Manchester Center, VT 05255
802-362-3643; FAX: 802-362-3360
E-mail: chevy@vermontel.com

repairs
restoration

See full listing in **Section Two** under **restoration shops**

Grey Hills Auto Restoration
PO Box 630
51 Vail Rd
Blairstown, NJ 07825
908-362-8232; FAX: 908-362-6796

restoration
service

See full listing in **Section Two** under **restoration shops**

Hatfield Restorations
PO Box 846
Canton, TX 75103
903-567-6742; FAX: 903-567-0645
E-mail: pathat@vzinet.com

restoration

See full listing in **Section Two** under **restoration shops**

Hyde Auto Body
44-1/2 S Squirrel Rd
Auburn Hills, MI 48326
PH/FAX: 248-852-7832
E-mail: bodyman8@juno.com

refinishing
restoration

See full listing in **Section Two** under **restoration shops**

JCM Industries
2 Westwood Dr
Danbury, CT 06811
800-752-0245

wax hardener

See full listing in **Section Two** under **car care products**

Jefferis Autobody
269 Tank Farm Rd
San Luis Obispo, CA 93401
800-807-1937; FAX: 805-543-4757

windshield glass kit

See full listing in **Section Two** under **glass**

Keilen's Auto Restoring | restoration
580 Kelley Blvd (R)
North Attleboro, MA 02760
508-699-7768

See full listing in **Section Two** under **restoration shops**

Kwik Poly T Distributing Inc | restoration aids
24 St Henry Ct
St Charles, MO 63301
314-724-1065

See full listing in **Section Two** under **restoration aids**

L & N Olde Car Co | restoration
9992 Kinsman Rd
PO Box 378
Newbury, OH 44065
440-564-7204; FAX: 440-564-8187

See full listing in **Section Two** under **restoration shops**

Libbey's Classic Car Restoration Center | bodywork, restoration, service
137 N Quinsigamond Ave
Shrewsbury, MA 01545
PH/FAX: 508-792-1560

See full listing in **Section Two** under **restoration shops**

Lyme Pond Restorations | restoration
PO Box 202
Barnard, VT 05031
802-457-4657

See full listing in **Section Two** under **restoration shops**

Mastermind Inc | new/used parts, restoration
32155 Joshua Dr
Wildomar, CA 92595
PH/FAX: 909-674-0509
E-mail: mike@mastermindinc.net

See full listing in **Section One** under **Cadillac/LaSalle**

McCann Auto Restoration | custom work, restoration, sandblasting
US Rt 1, PO Box 1025
Houlton, ME 04730
207-532-2206

See full listing in **Section Two** under **restoration shops**

Memory Lane Motors | car dealer, restoration, service
562 County Rd 121
Fenelon Falls, ON Canada K0M 1N0
705-887-CARS; FAX: 705-887-4028

See full listing in **Section Two** under **restoration shops**

Mill Supply Inc | clips, fasteners, panels
PO Box 28400
Cleveland, OH 44128
800-888-5072; FAX: 888-781-2700
E-mail: info@millsupply.com

See full listing in **Section Two** under **sheetmetal**

Mustang Classics | parts, restoration, sales, service
3814 Walnut St
Denver, CO 80205
303-295-3140

See full listing in **Section One** under **Mustang**

New Era Motors | restoration
11611 NE 50th Ave, Unit 6
Vancouver, WA 98686
360-573-8788

See full listing in **Section Two** under **woodwork**

R E Pierce | parts, restoration
47 Stone Rd
Wendell Depot, MA 01380
978-544-7442; FAX: 978-544-2978
E-mail: robin@billsgate.com

See full listing in **Section One** under **Volvo**

Pilgrim's Auto Restorations | bodywork, metal fabrication, paint, restoration
3888 Hill Rd
Lakeport, CA 95453
707-262-1062; FAX: 707-263-6956
E-mail: pilgrims@pacific.net

See full listing in **Section Two** under **restoration shops**

Restorations Unlimited II Inc | restoration
304 Jandus Rd
Cary, IL 60013
847-639-5818

See full listing in **Section Two** under **restoration shops**

Rick's Relics | bodywork, painting, restoration
Wheeler Rd
Pittsburg, NH 03592
603-538-6612

See full listing in **Section Two** under **restoration shops**

Rod-1 Shop | street rods
210 Clinton Ave
Pitman, NJ 08071
609-228-7631; FAX: 609-582-5770

See full listing in **Section Two** under **street rods**

Ed Rouze | painting guide book
406 Sheila Blvd
Prattville, AL 36066
334-365-2381

See full listing in **Section Two** under **painting**

T Schmidt | rust removers
827 N Vernon
Dearborn, MI 48128-1542
313-562-7161

See full listing in **Section Two** under **rust removal & stripping**

Silver Star Restorations | parts, restoration
116 Highway 19
Topton, NC 28781
704-321-4268
E-mail: silverstar@main.nc.us

See full listing in **Section One** under **Mercedes-Benz**

Steck Manufacturing Co Inc | tools
1115 S Broadway
Dayton, OH 45408
800-227-8325; FAX: 937-222-6666

See full listing in **Section Two** under **tools**

Stone Barn Inc | restoration
202 Rt 46, Box 117
Vienna, NJ 07880
908-637-4444; FAX: 908-637-4290

See full listing in **Section Two** under **restoration shops**

Strange Motion Inc | customizing, design, fabrication
14696 N 350th Ave
Cambridge, IL 61238
PH/FAX: 309-927-3346
E-mail: strange@netins.net

See full listing in **Section Two** under **street rods**

Sunchaser Tools
3202 E Foothill Blvd
Pasadena, CA 91107
626-795-1588; FAX: 626-795-6494

**metal-finishing kit
video**

See full listing in **Section Two** under **restoration aids**

Tower Paint Co Inc
Box 2345
Oshkosh, WI 54903
920-235-6520; FAX: 920-235-6521
E-mail: tpi@towerpaint.com

paint

See full listing in **Section Two** under **paints**

Vampire Products
50 Four Coins Dr
Canonsburg, PA 15317
800-866-7260; FAX: 724-745-6040
E-mail: vampire@hanseninc.com

**air dryers
filters**

See full listing in **Section Two** under **restoration shops**

Willhoit Auto Restoration
1360 Gladys Ave
Long Beach, CA 90804
562-439-3333; FAX: 562-439-3956

**engine rebuilding
restoration**

See full listing in **Section One** under **Porsche**

Willow Automotive Service
Box 4640 Rt 212
Willow, NY 12495
914-679-4679

**bodywork
painting
restoration**

See full listing in **Section Two** under **restoration shops**

brakes

60 Chev Sam
2912 Wright Rd
Hamptonville, NC 27020
336-468-1745

parts

See full listing in **Section One** under **Chevrolet**

A&F Imported Parts Inc
490 40th St
Oakland, CA 94609
888-263-7278; FAX: 707-256-0764
E-mail: mmast64166@aol.com

parts

See full listing in **Section One** under **Mercedes-Benz**

Ace Antique Auto Restoration
65 S Service Rd
Plainview, NY 11803
516-752-6065; FAX: 516-752-1484

**air conditioning
body rebuilding
restoration
wiring harnesses**

See full listing in **Section Two** under **restoration shops**

All British Car Parts Inc
2847 Moores Rd
Baldwin, MD 21013
410-692-9572; FAX: 410-692-5654

parts

See full listing in **Section Two** under **electrical systems**

Allied Power Brake Co
8730 Michigan Ave
Detroit, MI 48210
313-584-8208

brakes

Mail order and open shop. Monday-Friday 8 am to 5 pm. Power brake specialists.

Angeli Machine Co
417 N Varney St
Burbank, CA 91502
818-846-5359
E-mail: angelimach@aol.com

machine work

See full listing in **Section Two** under **machine work**

Antique Auto Parts Cellar
PO Box 3
6 Chauncy St
South Weymouth, MA 02190
781-335-1579; FAX: 781-335-1925

**brake/chassis/
engine parts
fuel pumps/kits
gaskets
water pumps**

See full listing in **Section Two** under **comprehensive parts**

Authentic Automotive
529 Buttercup Trail
Mesquite, TX 75149
972-289-6373; FAX: 972-289-4303

**power brakes
power steering**

See full listing in **Section One** under **Chevrolet**

Automotive Friction
4621 SE 27th Ave
Portland, OR 97202
503-234-0606; FAX: 503-234-1026

**brakes
clutches
water pumps**

See full listing in **Section Two** under **clutches**

Bronx Automotive
501 Tiffany St
Bronx, NY 10474
718-589-2979

parts

See full listing in **Section Two** under **ignition parts**

California Pony Cars
1906 Quaker Ridge Pl
Ontario, CA 91761
909-923-2804; FAX: 909-947-8593
E-mail:
105232.3362@compuserve.com

parts

See full listing in **Section One** under **Mustang**

Canadian Mustang
20529 62 Ave
Langley, BC Canada V3A 8R4
604-534-6424; FAX: 604-534-6694
E-mail:
parts@canadianmustang.com

parts

See full listing in **Section One** under **Mustang**

Carson's Antique Auto Parts
235 Shawfarm Rd
Holliston, MA 01746
508-429-2269; FAX: 508-429-0761
E-mail: w1066@gis.net

parts

See full listing in **Section Two** under **engine parts**

Chassis Engineering Inc
119 N 2nd St, Box 70
West Branch, IA 52358
319-643-2645; FAX: 319-643-2801

**brakes
chassis parts
suspension parts**

See full listing in **Section Two** under **chassis parts**

Section Two
Generalists

| Chicago Classic Imports
6948 N Western Ave
Chicago, IL 60645
773-381-2600; FAX: 773-381-2616
E-mail:
saab@chicagoclassicimports.com | **parts**
service |

See full listing in **Section One** under **Saab**

| Classic Tube
Division of Classic & Performance
Spec Inc
80 Rotech Dr
Lancaster, NY 14086
800-TUBES-11 (882-3711)
716-759-1800; FAX: 716-759-1014 | **brake lines**
choke tubes
fuel lines
transmission lines
vacuum lines |

Pre-bent brake, fuel, transmission, choke, vacuum lines manufactured in stainless or OE steel with stainless (an exclusive) or OE steel fittings. All lines are manufactured on computerized CNC state-of-the-art tube benders for 100% accuracy. Applications, for domestic or foreign cars and trucks, available from stock or made to your custom specifications. We lead the industry in the most accurate and largest selection of lines. Make your car or truck safer. Web site: www.classictube.com

| Collector's Auto Supply
528 Appian Way
Coquitlam, BC Canada V3J 2A5
888-772-7848; FAX: 604-931-4450
E-mail: car@bc.sympatico.ca | **parts** |

See full listing in **Section Two** under **comprehensive parts**

| CPR
431 S Sierra Way
San Bernardino, CA 92408
909-884-6980; FAX: 909-884-7872 | **new parts**
reproduction parts
used parts |

See full listing in **Section One** under **Pontiac**

| Florida Caliper Manufacturers Inc
1450 SW 10th St #3
Delray Beach, FL 33444
561-272-5238 | **brake systems**
chassis parts
suspension parts |

See full listing in **Section One** under **Corvette**

| George Frechette
14 Cedar Dr
Granby, MA 01033
800-528-5235 | **brake cylinder**
sleeving |

Sleeving of brake cylinders with stainless steel for most makes and models of older cars and motorcycles.

| Mike Hershenfeld
3011 Susan Rd
Bellmore, NY 11710
PH/FAX: 516-781-PART (7278)
E-mail: mikesmopar@juno.com | **parts** |

See full listing in **Section One** under **Mopar**

| Holcombe Cadillac Parts
2933 Century Ln
Bensalem, PA 19020
215-245-4560; FAX: 215-633-9916 | **parts** |

See full listing in **Section One** under **Cadillac/LaSalle**

| Inline Tube
33783 Groes Beck Hwy
Fraser, MI 48026
800-385-9452 order
810-294-4093 tech
FAX: 810-294-7349
E-mail: kryta@aol.com | **brake lines/cables**
choke tubes
flex brake hoses
fuel/vacuum lines
transmission lines |

Mail order and open shop. Monday-Friday 9 am to 6 pm. Manufacture prebent brake lines, fuel lines, vacuum and transmission lines for any American auto. Also manufacturer of stainless parking brake cables for any American auto. All cables are available in aircraft quality stainless steel and are manufactured identical to the factory original, in appearance application and fit. Custom applications welcome. Web site: www.inlinetube.com

| Integrity Machine
383 Pipe Stave Hollow Rd
Mount Sinai, NY 11766
888-446-9670; FAX: 516-476-9675 | **brake masters**
clutch masters
wheel cylinders |

Mail order and open shop. Monday-Friday 8 am to 5 pm. Deal in brake masters, clutch masters, wheel cylinders, clutch slave cylinders, sleeved with brass to original sizes. Complete rebuilding also available. Caliper rebuilding available. Visa, M/C.

| Jerry's Automotive
c/o Jerry Cinotti
431 S Sierra Way
San Bernadino, CA 92408
909-884-6980; FAX: 909-884-7872 | **brake repair** |

Mail order and open shop. Monday-Friday 8 am to 5 pm. Brakes: Bendix, Treadle-Vac and Delco Moraine power units rebuilt, 1953-1960, all units are complete, disassembled, parts cleaned and inspected, all units are pressure tested and vacuum tested to ensure total quality, all work guaranteed.

| Kanter Auto Products
76 Monroe St
Boonton, NJ 07005
800-526-1096, 201-334-9575
FAX: 201-334-5423 | **car cover**
carpets
parts |

See full listing in **Section Two** under **comprehensive parts**

| Last Chance Repair & Restoration
PO Box 362A
Myers Rd
Shaftsbury, VT 05262 | **repairs**
restoration |

See full listing in **Section Two** under **restoration shops**

| Muskegon Brake & Dist Co
848 E Broadway
Muskegon, MI 49444
616-733-0874; FAX: 616-733-0635 | **brakes**
springs
suspensions |

Mail order and open shop. Monday-Friday 7:30 am to 5:30 pm, Saturday 9 am to 12 pm. Retail/wholesale service. Dealers welcome. Brakes, suspension and springs for most vehicles. Specializing in these parts and services for Corvettes. Sleeving of all brake cylinders. Manufacture leaf springs for all makes and models. Located in Muskegon, MI, since 1945. Accept all major credit cards. Can ship almost anywhere. Web site: www.muskegonbrake.com

| National Parts Depot
3101 SW 40th Blvd
Gainesville, FL 32608
800-874-7595 toll-free 24 hours
352-378-2473 local | **accessories**
restoration parts |

See full listing in **Section Two** under **comprehensive parts**

| Northwestern Auto Supply Inc
1101 S Division
Grand Rapids, MI 49507
800-704-1078, 616-241-1714
FAX: 616-241-0924 | **parts** |

See full listing in **Section Two** under **engine parts**

The Plasmeter Corporation | **brake drums**
173 Queen Ave SE
Albany, OR 97321
541-928-3233; FAX: 541-928-0596

See full listing in **Section One** under **Ford 1903-1931**

Power Brake Booster Exchange Inc | **brake boosters**
4533 SE Division St
Portland, OR 97206
503-238-8882

Mail order and open shop. Monday-Friday 9 am to 5 pm. Power brake booster rebuilder, 1959-1990. Plating available, 1 year warranty. Power brake booster only without master cylinder, call "Booster" Dewey.

Power Brake X-Change Inc | **parts**
336 Lamont Pl
Pittsburgh, PA 15232
800-580-5729, 412-441-5729
FAX: 412-441-9333

Mail order and open shop. Monday-Friday 8 am to 4 pm. Remanufacturer of power manual gearboxes, pumps, control valves, cylinders with new chrome shafts, rack and pinions. Brake boosters, Hydro Vacs, Treadle-Vacs, Hydro Boosts, vacuum pumps and antilocks.

Rochester Clutch & Brake Co | **brakes** **clutches**
35 Niagara St
Rochester, NY 14605
716-232-2579; FAX: 716-232-3279

Mail order and open shop. Monday-Friday 7:30 am to 4 pm. Specializing in clutch and brake remanufacturing, all vehicles and machines. All antiques and vintage racing. Special materials. Custom applications. 60 years' experience.

Sierra Specialty Auto | **cylinder rebuilding**
3494 Chandler Rd
Quincy, CA 95971
800-4-BRASS-1; FAX: 530-283-4845
E-mail: joe@restoresource.com

Mail order only. Brake and clutch cylinders sleeved with brass. Cars, trucks, tractors, motorcycles. Complete rebuilding available for most cylinders. Guaranteed. Also one-wire conversions and rebuild kits for Delco 10DN, 10SI and 12SI alternators. Web site: restoresource.com

---

SoCal Pickups Inc | **parts**
6321 Manchester Blvd
Buena Park, CA 90621
800-SOCAL-49; FAX: 714-994-2584

See full listing in **Section One** under **Ford 1954-up**

Stainless Steel Brakes Corp | **brake accessories** **disc conversion kits** **pads/fluid/rotors** **parking brake kits** **power steering parts**
11470 Main Road
Clarence, NY 14031
800-448-7722, 716-759-8666
FAX: 716-759-8688, 24 hr

Mail order, jobbers and w/ds welcome. Drum to disc brake "bolt-on", front or rear axle conversion kits for Ford, GM muscle cars, SUVs, pickups and Jeeps. New power steering control valves, cylinders for 1963-1982 Corvettes. Stainless steel sleeved calipers, master cylinders and accessories for Mustang, Corvette, GM muscle cars, upscale imports, Mopars and AMC. New Corvette caliper housings, master cylinders and rear disc brake calipers with integral parking brakes. Stainless steel sleeves and pistons. Custom caliper and cylinder rebuilding. Web site: www.stainlesssteelbrakes.com (site has 5 sub-sites)

Straight Six Jaguar | **parts** **service**
24321 Hatteras St
Woodland Hills, CA 91367
PH/FAX: 818-716-1192

See full listing in **Section One** under **Jaguar**

Ed Strain Inc | **power brakes**
6555 44th St #2006
Pinellas Park, FL 33781
800-266-1623

Open Monday-Friday 8 am to 2 pm. Rebuilder of power brake units for 1953-1960 Bendix, Treadle-Vac and Moraine. We also wind coils.

Studebaker Parts & Locations | **parts** **parts locator**
228 Marquiss Cir
Clinton, TN 37716
615-457-3002
E-mail: studebaker_joe@msn.com

See full listing in **Section One** under **Studebaker**

Tanson Enterprises | **performance parts** **restoration parts**
2508 J St, Dept HVA
Sacramento, CA 95816-4815
916-448-2950
FAX: 916-443-3269 *88
E-mail: tanson@pipeline.com

See full listing in **Section One** under **Oldsmobile**

Taylor Auto Parts | **bearings** **brakes** **gaskets** **seals**
PO Box 650
Esparto, CA 95627
530-787-1929

See full listing in **Section Two** under **comprehensive parts**

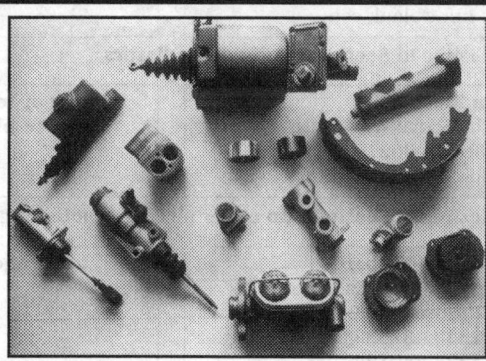

Ernie Toth   brake fluid
8153 Cloveridge Rd
Chagrin Falls, OH 44022
440-338-3565

See full listing in **Section One** under **Stutz**

Wallace Walmsley   parts
4732 Bancroft St, #7
San Diego, CA 92116
619-283-3063

See full listing in **Section One** under **Packard**

White Post Restorations   brakes
One Old Car Dr   restoration
PO Drawer D
White Post, VA 22663
540-837-1140; FAX: 540-837-2368

Brakes sleeved and completely rebuilt. Shoes relined and booster
rebuilds. Quick service. Lifetime written warranty. Better than
new. For the ultimate solution to your brake cylinder problems,
call us now. All of our work is fully guaranteed. Web site:
www.whitepost.com
See our ad on page 239

Zip Products   accessories
8067 Fast Ln   parts
Mechanicsville, VA 23111
804-746-2290, 800-962-9632
FAX: 804-730-7043
E-mail: zipvette@erols.com

See full listing in **Section One** under **Corvette**

brass cars/parts

Blaak Radiateurenbedryf   radiators
Blaaksedyk oost 19
Heinenoord 3274LA Netherlands
31-186-601732; FAX: 31-186-603044
E-mail: info@blaak.com

See full listing in **Section Two** under **radiators**

Custom Plating   bumper specialist
3030 Alta Ridge Way   chrome plating
Snellville, GA 30278   parts
770-736-1118

See full listing in **Section Two** under **plating & polishing**

Paul Foulkes-Halbard   brass age cars
Filching Wannock Eastbourne   parts
Polegate, Sussex BN26 5QA England
011 441323 487838
011 441323 487124
FAX: 011 441323 486331

See full listing in **Section One** under **Bugatti**

Lang's Old Car Parts Inc   parts
202 School St
Winchendon, MA 01475
800-TPARTS-1, 978-297-1919
FAX: 978-297-2126

See full listing in **Section One** under **Ford 1903-1931**

Ben McAdam   electrical parts
500 Clover Ln
Wheeling, WV 26003
304-242-3388

See full listing in **Section Two** under **ignition parts**

Zephyrhills Festivals   auction
and Auction Inc   swap meet
PO Box 848
Odessa, FL 33556
813-920-7206; FAX: 813-920-8512
Park: 813-782-0835
FAX: 813-780-7863

See full listing in **Section Two** under **auctions & events**

brokers

AM Racing Inc   race prep
PO Box 451   sales
Danvers, MA 01923   vintage racing
PH/FAX: 978-774-4613

See full listing in **Section Two** under **racing**

Auto Consultants   appraisals
& Appraisal Service
Charles J Kozelka
PO Box 111
Macedonia, OH 44056
330-467-0748; FAX: 330-467-3725

See full listing in **Section Two** under **appraisals**

Auto-Line Enterprises Inc   appraisals
2 Lyons Rd   broker services
Armonk, NY 10504
914-681-1757; FAX: 914-273-5159
E-mail: garfconect@aol.com

See full listing in **Section Two** under **appraisals**

Charles W Clarke   appraisals
Automotive Consultant/Appraiser   car dealer
17 Saddle Ridge Dr   consultant
West Simsbury, CT 06092-2118
PH/FAX: 860-658-2714

See full listing in **Section Two** under **consultants**

Classic Auto Brokers   broker
18812 Monteverde Dr
Springhill, FL 34610
727-856-5168

Brokering only top quality vehicles. Specializing in Mustang,
Shelby and Thunderbird.

Classic Auto Restoration   acquisitions
15445 Ventura Blvd #60   restoration
Sherman Oaks, CA 91413   sales
818-905-6267; FAX: 818-906-1249
E-mail: rollsroyce1@earthlink.net

See full listing in **Section One** under **Rolls-Royce/Bentley**

Collector Car & Truck Market Guide   price guide
41 N Main St
North Grafton, MA 01536
508-839-6707; FAX: 508-839-6266
E-mail: vmr@vmrintl.com

See full listing in **Section Four** under **periodicals**

Corvette Enterprise Brokerage   appraisals
The Power Broker   broker
52 Van Houten Ave   car locator
Passaic Park, NJ 07055   investment planning
973-472-7021

See full listing in **Section One** under **Corvette**

Freeman's Garage
29 Ford Rd
Norton, MA 02766
508-285-6500; FAX: 508-285-6566

parts
restoration
sales
service

See full listing in **Section One** under **Ford 1903-1931**

Mark Gillett
PO Box 9177
Dallas, TX 75209
PH/FAX: 214-902-9258
011-525-559-6240 Mexico City, Mexico
E-mail: autonet@onramp.net

car locator
sales

See full listing in **Section Two** under **car dealers**

The Gullwing Garage Ltd
Bricklin SVI Specialists
5 Cimorelli Dr
New Windsor, NY 12553-6201
914-561-0019 anytime

appraisals
literature
parts
service

See full listing in **Section One** under **Bricklin**

Hall of Fame & Classic Car Museum, DIRT
PO Box 240
1 Speedway Dr
Weedsport, NY 13166
315-834-6606; FAX: 315-834-9734

car dealer

See full listing in **Section Six** under **New York**

Kensington Motor Group Inc
PO Box 2277
Sag Harbor, NY 11963
516-537-1868; FAX: 516-537-2641
E-mail: kenmotor@aol.com

consignment sales

See full listing in **Section One** under **Mercedes-Benz**

M & M Automobile Appraisers Inc
584 Broomspun St
Henderson, NV 89015
702-568-5120; FAX: 702-568-5158

appraiser
broker
consultant

See full listing in **Section Two** under **appraisals**

Randall Marcus Vintage Automobiles
706 Hanshaw Rd
Ithaca, NY 14850
607-257-5939; FAX: 607-272-8806

broker
car locator
consultant

Sale and purchase of fine vintage automobiles arranged worldwide. Consultation provided on acquisition and liquidation of collections. Pre-purchase inspections and valuation gladly performed. Specializing in all pre-1940 automobiles as well as 1930s-1960s vintage British sports and touring cars.

Bill McCoskey
16643 Rt 144
Mt Airy, MD 21771
301-854-5900, 410-442-3637
FAX: 301-854-5957
E-mail: tatrabill@aol.com

appraisals
repairs

See full listing in **Section Two** under **appraisals**

Memory Lane Motors Inc
1231 Rt 176
Lake Bluff, IL 60044
847-362-4600

appraisals
car dealer
storage

See full listing in **Section Two** under **car dealers**

Charles Noe
64-1/2 Greenwood Ave
Bethel, CT 06801
PH/FAX: 203-748-4222
E-mail: mdchas@aol.com

broker
parts/auto purchases
parts/auto sales

Specialize in 1932-1933 Chevrolet and Hupmobiles, parts and cars. Listing service for all automobile makes. Always looking for quality cars and car parts. Also pedal car, pedal car parts, vintage toys and trains.

Precious Metal Automotive Restoration Co Inc
1601 College Ave SE
Grand Rapids, MI 49507
616-243-0220; FAX: 616-243-6646
E-mail: prshsmtl@pathwaynet.com

broker
restoration

See full listing in **Section One** under **Mercedes-Benz**

camshafts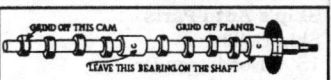

Air Flow Research
10490 Ilex Ave
Pacoima, CA 91331
818-890-0616; FAX: 818-890-0490

cylinder heads

See full listing in **Section One** under **Chevrolet**

Atlas Engine Rebuilding Co Inc
8631 S Avalon Blvd
Los Angeles, CA 90003
323-778-3497; FAX: 323-778-4556

engine rebuilding
machine work

See full listing in **Section Two** under **engine rebuilding**

Cam-Pro
1417 1st Ave SW
Great Falls, MT 59404
800-525-2581, 406-453-9989

camshaft repair
engine parts

Mail order and open shop. Monday-Saturday 10 am to 5 pm. Camshaft grinding and repair. Lifter resurfacing. New cams, lifters and other engine parts.

Crane Cams Inc
530 Fentress Blvd
Daytona Beach, FL 32114
904-258-6174; FAX: 904-258-6167

camshafts

Mail order and open shop. Monday-Friday 8 am to 5 pm. Precision manufactured camshafts, valve train components, camshaft regrinding for antique vehicles, classic vehicles, muscle cars. Breakerless ignition conversion kits for US and imported vehicles. Web site: www.cranecams.com

Daytona Turbo Action Camshafts
1109 N US #1
PO Box 5094
Ormond Beach, FL 32175
888-RARE-CAM, 800-505-CAMS
904-676-7478; FAX: 904-258-1582
E-mail: info@camshafts.com

camshafts
engine parts

See full listing in **Section Two** under **bearings**

Gromm Racing Heads
664-J Stockton Ave
San Jose, CA 95126
408-287-1301

cylinder heads
racing parts

See full listing in **Section Two** under **racing**

Section Two Generalists

| **Horst's Car Care**
3160-1/2 N Woodford St
Decatur, IL 62526
217-876-1112 | **engine rebuilding** |

See full listing in **Section One** under **Mercedes-Benz**

| **Maximum Torque Specialties**
PO Box 925
Delavan, WI 53115
414-740-1118; FAX: 414-740-1161 | **high-perf parts**
restoration parts |

See full listing in **Section One** under **Cadillac/LaSalle**

| **Performance Chevy**
2995 W Whitton
Phoenix, AZ 85017
800-203-6621; FAX: 602-254-1094 | **engine parts**
restoration |

See full listing in **Section One** under **Corvette**

| **Skip's Auto Parts**
Skip Bollinger
1500 Northaven Dr
Gladstone, MO 64118
816-455-2337; FAX: 816-459-7547
E-mail: carpartman@aol.com | **chassis parts**
ignition parts
water pumps |

See full listing in **Section Two** under **water pumps**

| **Tatom Vintage Vendors**
PO Box 2504
Mt Vernon, WA 98273
360-424-8314; FAX: 360-424-6717
E-mail: flatheads@tatom.com | **engine rebuilding**
machine shop |

See full listing in **Section Two** under **engine rebuilding**

| **West Amity Auto Parts**
5685 Merrick Rd
Massapequa, NY 11758
516-795-4610; FAX: 516-795-4117
E-mail: crein69929@erols.com | **custom machining**
engine rebuilding |

See full listing in **Section Two** under **engine rebuilding**

car & parts locators

| **A-1 Street Rods**
631 E Las Vegas St
Colorado Springs, CO 80903
719-632-4920, 719-577-4588
FAX: 719-634-6577 | **parts** |

See full listing in **Section Two** under **street rods**

| **AAAC-Antique Automobile Appraisal & Consulting**
PO Box 700153
Plymouth, MI 48170
PH/FAX: 734-453-7644
E-mail: aaac@ameritech.net | **appraisals**
Cadillac parts
consulting |

See full listing in **Section One** under **Cadillac/LaSalle**

| **ADP Hollander**
14800 28th Ave N #190
Plymouth, MN 55447
800-761-9266; FAX: 800-825-1124
E-mail: hollander@autonet.net | **interchange info**
manuals |

Looking for parts for your classic car? Increase your search possibilities with *Hollander Interchange Classic Search Manuals* from ADP Hollander, the most complete and accurate source for indexing interchangeable parts among vehicles. Trusted by automotive professionals for more than 60 years, *Hollander Interchange Classic Search Manuals* are perfect for classic car

enthusiasts and do-it-yourself mechanics. Web site: www.hollander-auto-parts.com

| **All British Car Parts Inc**
2847 Moores Rd
Baldwin, MD 21013
410-692-9572; FAX: 410-692-5654 | **parts** |

See full listing in **Section Two** under **electrical systems**

| **Amherst Antique Auto Show**
157 Hollis Rd
Amherst, NH 03031
603-883-0605, NH
FAX: 617-641-0647, MA | **swap meets** |

See full listing in **Section Two** under **auctions & events**

| **Anderson Automotive**
1604 E Busch Blvd
Tampa, FL 33612
813-932-4611; FAX: 813-932-5025 | **cars**
parts |

See full listing in **Section One** under **Oldsmobile**

| **ARS, Automotive Research Services**
Division of Auto Search International
1702 W Camelback #301
Phoenix, AZ 85015
602-230-7111; FAX: 602-230-7282 | **appraisals**
research |

See full listing in **Section Two** under **appraisals**

| **Auto Body Specialties Inc**
Rt 66
Middlefield, CT 06455
888-277-1960 toll-free orders only
860-346-4989; FAX: 860-346-4987 | **accessories**
body parts |

See full listing in **Section Two** under **body parts**

| **AutoMatch CARS**
(Computer Aided Referral Service)
2017 Blvd
Napoleon Louisville, KY 40205
800-962-2771, 502-417-8793 mobile
502-452-1920 office; FAX: 502-479-6222
E-mail: amcars@aol.com or
aautomatch@aol.com | **broker**
car dealer network
locator |

See full listing in **Section Two** under **car dealers**

| **The Autoworks Ltd**
90 Center Ave
Westwood, NJ 07675
201-358-0200; FAX: 201-358-0442 | **restoration**
sales
service |

See full listing in **Section Two** under **service shops**

| **AVM Automotive Consulting**
Box 338, Montvale, NJ 07645-0338
201-391-5194; FAX: 201-782-0663
E-mail: avmtony@aol.com | **appraisals**
consultant |

See full listing in **Section Two** under **appraisals**

| **bentleydriversclub.com**
23238 Erwin St
Woodland Hills, CA 91367
818-887-6557; FAX: 818-346-3627
E-mail: glwales@aol.com | **car dealer**
collectibles |

See full listing in **Section One** under **Rolls-Royce/Bentley**

| **Caddy Central**
11117 Tippett Rd
Clinton, MD 20735
301-234-0135; FAX: 301-234-0140
E-mail: cadlocator@aol.com | **cars**
locating service
parts |

See full listing in **Section One** under **Cadillac/LaSalle**

Checker Motors	cars
1314 Rollins Rd	**parts**
Burlingame, CA 94010	**rentals**
650-340-8669; FAX: 650-340-9473	

See full listing in **Section One** under **Checker**

Chev's of the 40's	parts
2027 B St, Dept HVA	
Washougal, WA 98671	
800-999-CHEV (2438)	
FAX: 360-835-7988	

See full listing in **Section One** under **Chevrolet**

Chicago Car Exchange	appraisals
1 Collector Car Dr	**car dealer**
Box 530	**car locator**
Lake Bluff, IL 60044	**financing**
847-680-1950; FAX: 847-680-1961	**storage**
E-mail: oldtoys@wwa.com	

See full listing in **Section Two** under **car dealers**

Chief Service	parts
Herbert G Baschung	**restoration**
Brunnmatt, PO Box 155	
CH-4914 Roggwil Switzerland	
PH/FAX: 0041-62-9291777	

See full listing in **Section Two** under **restoration shops**

Classic Car Research	appraisals
29508 Southfield Rd, Ste 106	**consultant**
Southfield, MI 48076	**part locating**
248-557-2880; FAX: 248-557-3511	
E-mail: kawifreek@msn.com	

See full listing in **Section Two** under **appraisals**

Coffey's Classic Transmissions	transmissions
2290 W Hicks Rd, Unit 42	
Hanger 30-1	
Ft Worth, TX 76111	
817-439-1611	

See full listing in **Section Two** under **transmissions**

Collector Car & Truck Market Guide	price guide
41 N Main St	
North Grafton, MA 01536	
508-839-6707; FAX: 508-839-6266	
E-mail: vmr@vmrintl.com	

See full listing in **Section Four** under **periodicals**

Corvette Enterprise Brokerage	appraisals
The Power Broker	**broker**
52 Van Houten Ave	**consultant**
Passaic Park, NJ 07055	**investment**
973-472-7021	**planning**

See full listing in **Section One** under **Corvette**

Corvette Mike	accessories
1133 N Tustin Ave	**parts**
Anaheim, CA 92807	**sales**
800-327-8388, 714-630-0700	**service**
FAX: 714-630-0777	
E-mail: cvtmike@deltanet.com	

See full listing in **Section One** under **Corvette**

Buzz De Clerck	parts
41760 Utica Rd	
Sterling Heights, MI 48313-3146	
810-731-0765	

See full listing in **Section One** under **Lincoln**

DeLorean One	bodywork
20229 Nordhoff St	**parts**
Chatsworth, CA 91311	**service**
818-341-1796; FAX: 818-998-6381	

See full listing in **Section One** under **DeLorean**

Desert Valley Auto Parts	cars
22500 N 21st Ave	**parts**
Phoenix, AZ 85027	
800-905-8024, 602-780-8024	
FAX: 602-582-9141	
E-mail:	
rust-free-parts@worldnet.att.net	

See full listing in **Section Five** under **Arizona**

Driving Passion Ltd USA	cars
Marc Tuwiner	**parts**
7132 Chilton Ct	**salvage yard**
Clarksville, MD 21029	
PH/FAX: 301-596-9078	
E-mail: mt.tees@erols.com	

See full listing in **Section One** under **Cadillac/LaSalle**

David Elliott	auto transport
11796 Franklin	**car locator**
Minocqua, WI 54548	
715-356-1335	

See full listing in **Section Two** under **transport**

Richard H Feibusch	appraisals
211 Dimmick Ave	
Venice, CA 90291	
310-392-6605; FAX: 310-396-1933	
E-mail: rfeibusch@loop.com	

See full listing in **Section Two** under **appraisals**

Finders Service	parts finders
454-458 W Lincoln Hwy	
Chicago Heights, IL 60411-2463	
708-481-9685; FAX: 708-481-5837	
E-mail: findersvc@aol.com	

Mail order only. Offer free information and order form packet sent by USPS mail if given complete name, address, city, state, country and mailing code. OEM new and used genuine parts, accessories, literature, service manuals, catalogs, tools, keys and locks, American and European all years and makes 1900-1995 including government surplus parts. Research Service Department hours: Monday-Friday 11 am to 4 pm. Web site: www.usaworks@com.findersvc

Fort Wayne Clutch & Driveline	axles
2424 Goshen Rd	**axleshafts**
Fort Wayne, IN 46808	**clutches**
219-484-8505; FAX: 219-484-8605	**driveshafts**
E-mail: coca@mail.fwi.com	

See full listing in **Section Two** under **clutches**

Freddie Beach Restoration	accessories
1834 Woodstock Rd	**restoration parts**
Fredericton, NB Canada E3C 1L4	
506-450-9074; FAX: 506-459-0708	
E-mail: vallise@city.fredericton.nb.ca	

Quality restoration parts and accessories for cars and trucks. I can supply high-performance parts as well. Authorized dealer for Year One Inc, Legendary Auto Interiors, Cross Canada Auto Parts, Coker Tire, ACC Carpets, SoffSeal Weatherstripping and Detail Rubber Products, The Paddock Inc. Have assisted in automotive restorations since 1994.

J Giles Automotive | car & parts locator
703 Morgan Ave | exporter
Pascagoula, MS 39567-2116
228-769-1012; FAX: 228-769-8904
E-mail: jgauto@datasync.com

Arrange shipment of all vehicles to any port. For foreign clients, locate, inspect, purchase and ship all types of vehicles. Full spares support for all years, makes and models for foreign and domestic clients. Worldwide references.

Mark Gillett | car locator
PO Box 9177 | sales
Dallas, TX 75209
PH/FAX: 214-902-9258
011-525-559-6240 Mexico City, Mexico
E-mail: autonet@onramp.net

See full listing in **Section Two** under **car dealers**

GMC Solutions | literature
Robert English | parts
PO Box 675
Franklin, MA 02038-0675
508-520-3900; FAX: 508-520-7861
E-mail: oldcarkook@aol.com

See full listing in **Section One** under **GMC**

The Gullwing Garage Ltd | appraisals
Bricklin SVI Specialists | literature
5 Cimorelli Dr | parts
New Windsor, NY 12553-6201 | service
914-561-0019 anytime

See full listing in **Section One** under **Bricklin**

Halpin Used Auto & Truck Parts | NOS auto/truck
1093 Rt 123 | parts
Mayfield, NY 12117 | used auto/truck
518-863-4906 | parts
E-mail: junkyard2064@webtv.net

See full listing in **Section Five** under **New York**

Happy Daze Classic Cars | car dealer
257 Morris Ct
Fond Du Lac, WI 54935
920-922-8450

See full listing in **Section Two** under **car dealers**

Hollywood Classic Motorcars Inc | cars
363 Ansin Blvd | parts
Hallandale, FL 33009
800-235-2444, 954-454-4641
FAX: 954-457-3801
E-mail: hcm@tbird.net

See full listing in **Section One** under **Thunderbird**

Jacques Rear Engine Renault Parts | parts
13839 Hwy 8 Business
El Cajon, CA 92021
619-561-6687; FAX: 619-561-6123

See full listing in **Section One** under **Renault**

Jim's T-Bird Parts & Service | parts
710 Barney Ave | restoration
Winston-Salem, NC 27107 | service
PH/FAX: 336-784-9363
E-mail: tbirdjims@aol.com

See full listing in **Section One** under **Thunderbird**

K & K Vintage Motorcars LC | restoration
9848 SW Frwy | sales
Houston, TX 77074 | service
713-541-2281; FAX: 713-541-2286

See full listing in **Section Two** under **restoration shops**

K-F-D Services Inc | parts
HC 65, Box 49 | restoration
Altonah, UT 84002
801-454-3098; FAX: 801-454-3099
E-mail: kfd-services@msn.com

See full listing in **Section One** under **Kaiser Frazer**

Landry Classic MotorCars | appraisals
34 Goodhue Ave
Chicopee, MA 01020
413-592-2746; FAX: 413-594-8378

See full listing in **Section Two** under **appraisals**

Dave Lincoln | license plates
Box 331
Yorklyn, DE 19736
610-444-4144, PA
E-mail: tagbarn@msn.com

See full listing in **Section Two** under **license plates**

Manchester Motor Car Co | automobilia
319 Main St | parts
Manchester, CT 06040 | petroliana
860-643-5874; FAX: 860-643-6190 | restorations
E-mail: mmcollc@aol.com

See full listing in **Section Two** under **comprehensive parts**

Randall Marcus Vintage Automobiles | broker
706 Hanshaw Rd | car locator
Ithaca, NY 14850 | consultant
607-257-5939; FAX: 607-272-8806

See full listing in **Section Two** under **brokers**

Memory Lane Motors Inc | appraisals
1231 Rt 176 | car dealer
Lake Bluff, IL 60044 | storage
847-362-4600

See full listing in **Section Two** under **car dealers**

National Parts Locator Service | parts locator
636 East 6th St # 81
Ogden, UT 84404-2415
801-627-7210

Mail order only. Locate parts, accessories, literature, services, novelties, interior, upholstery, memorabilia for automobiles, trucks and motorcycles, foreign and domestic, from 1895-present. Looking for an automobile, truck or a motorcycle? National and international locator directory. How to buy a used automobile? Auctions? Anything automotive, challenge us.

Old Tin Australia | salvage yard
PO Box 26
Wendouree Victoria 3355 Australia
03 5336 FORD; FAX: 03 5339 9900

See full listing in **Section Five** under **Australia**

Opel Oldtimer Service Denmark | literature
Landevejen 27 | parts
Toksvaerd | parts locator
DK-4684 Holme-Olstrup Denmark
PH/FAX: +45-55-530100
best 11 am to 3 pm US Central time
E-mail: frank.kiessling@get2net.dk

See full listing in **Section One** under **Opel**

The Parts Scout® | parts
Bodo Repenn | parts locator
Diagonalstrasse 18A
D-20537 Hamburg Germany
*49-40-21980130
FAX: *49-40-21980132

See full listing in **Section Two** under **comprehensive parts**

R E Pierce | parts
47 Stone Rd | restoration
Wendell Depot, MA 01380
978-544-7442; FAX: 978-544-2978
E-mail: robin@billsgate.com

See full listing in **Section One** under **Volvo**

John T Poulin | car dealer
Auto Sales/Star Service Center | parts
5th Avenue & 111th St | restoration service
North Troy, NY 12182
518-235-8610

See full listing in **Section One** under **Mercedes-Benz**

Precious Metal Automotive | broker
Restoration Co Inc | restoration
1601 College Ave SE
Grand Rapids, MI 49507
616-243-0220; FAX: 616-243-6646
E-mail: prshsmtl@pathwaynet.com

See full listing in **Section One** under **Mercedes-Benz**

William H Randel | appraisals
PO Box 173 | car locators
Hatboro, PA 19040
215-675-8969; FAX: 215-441-0960
E-mail: tbrdnut@bellatlantic.net

See full listing in **Section One** under **Thunderbird**

RARE Corvettes | cars
Joe Calcagno | parts
Box 1080
Soquel, CA 95073
831-475-4442; FAX: 831-475-1115

See full listing in **Section One** under **Corvette**

Special Interest Car Parts | parts
1340 Hartford Ave
Johnston, RI 02919
800-556-7496; FAX: 401-831-7760

See full listing in **Section One** under **Jaguar**

Stone Barn Inc | restoration
202 Rt 46, Box 117
Vienna, NJ 07880
908-637-4444; FAX: 908-637-4290

See full listing in **Section Two** under **restoration shops**

Straw Church Speed Shop | accessories
602 Passaic St | engine swaps
Phillipsburg, NJ 08865 | parts
908-454-7487
E-mail:
strawchurch_ss@hotmail.com

Mail order and open shop. Monday-Sunday 11 am to 10 pm. Speed shop and hot rod shop, high-performance accessories, truck, street, import, race, circle, sprint cars. Specialize in Corvette engine swaps, small block to big block conversion kits, 1963-1982, complete kit. Rebuild carburetors, ring and pinion installation. Also any wheels made. We have or can get custom engine kit designed for your needs, stock to race, all big name parts, mix and match. Nitrous oxide to supercharged custom built engines to fit your needs. Dedicated to your service and racing success. If you need a part and can't find it, give us a call, we can get any part you want. Web site: www.strawchurch.qpg.com

T-Bird Sanctuary | parts
9997 SW Avery
Tualatin, OR 97062
503-692-9848; FAX: 503-692-9849

See full listing in **Section One** under **Thunderbird**

Timeless Masterpieces | appraisals
221 Freeport Dr | consultant
Bloomingdale, IL 60108
630-893-1058 evenings

See full listing in **Section Two** under **appraisals**

U S Oldies & Classics | car dealer
Vunt 3 | parts
Holsbeek 3220 Belgium
3216446611; FAX: 3216446520

See full listing in **Section Two** under **car dealers**

Johnny Williams Services | appraisals
2613 Copeland Rd | car & parts locator
Tyler, TX 75701 | consultant
903-597-3687, 800-937-0900 | lighting systems
voice mail #7225 | design

See full listing in **Section Two** under **appraisals**

car care products

ACE Automotive Cleaning | sandblasting
Equipment Co | equipment
897 S Washington Suite 232
Holland, MI 49423
616-772-3260; FAX: 616-772-3261

See full listing in **Section Two** under **rust removal & stripping**

Addison Generator Inc | auto parts
21 W Main St Rear | repairs
Freehold, NJ 07728 | supplies
732-431-2438; FAX: 732-431-4503

See full listing in **Section Two** under **electrical systems**

Amsoil | car care products
9 Claremont Dr | lubricants
Flat Rock, NC 28731 | undercoating
704-696-8500

See full listing in **Section Two** under **lubricants**

Section Two Generalists

Section Two
Generalists

Backyard Buddy Corp
1818 N Main St
PO Box 5104
Niles, OH 44446
800-837-9353, 330-544-9372
FAX: 330-544-9311

automotive lift

See full listing in **Section Two** under **accessories**

Bill & Brad's Tropical Formula
1141 Pierce St
Clearwater, FL 33756
800-FUN-WAXX, 727-442-6711
FAX: 727-443-3415

car wash
cheater spray
paste wax

Mail order and open shop. Professional detailer making special car care products. Make and use these products at our shop in Clearwater, Florida. Premium #1 Carnauba paste wax ($25); paint food (pre-wax); coconut car wash ($15); tire concentrate (dressing); cheater spray ($12). Also buy and sell special cars, example 57 Chev FI conv. All first class cars, no projects.

Billie Inc
PO Box 1161
Ashburn, VA 20146-1161
800-878-6328; FAX: 703-858-0102

garage diaper
mats

Mail and phone orders. 24 hours, 7 days a week. Non-leak super absorbent under-the-car mat. Sold as individual mats and economical 30 foot rolls.

Leon Blackledge Sales Co
156 N School Ln
Souderton, PA 18964-1153
800-525-7515, 215-734-4270
FAX: 215-723-7004

polish

Markets Wonder Tool, the only dual headed orbital polisher-sander. Complete line of Duragloss® and Wax Shop® polishes and cleaners. "Mr. Moly" (0.05 micron particle size molybdenum disulphide) engine treatment, "you will feel the difference", Becker automotive audio systems. German engineering at its finest.

The Blaster Chemical Companies
8500 Sweet Valley Dr
Valley View, OH 44125
800-858-6605; FAX: 216-901-5801

cleaners
degreasers
penetrants

See full listing in **Section Two** under **lubricants**

Brisson Enterprises
PO Box 1595
Dearborn, MI 48121-1595
313-584-3577

lead

Mail order only. Monday-Friday 10 am to 6 pm EST. Real leaded fuel stops engine knock, pinging, valve damage in classic engines. LS-130 makes real leaded fuel with genuine tetraethyl lead. Boosts octane, restores horsepower, superior to all substitutes on the market. Safe, easy to use, instructions provided. $26.95/gallon plus s&h. Credit cards accepted.

Buenger Enterprises/GoldenRod
Dehumidifier
3600 S Harbor Blvd
Oxnard, CA 93035
800-451-6797; FAX: 805-985-1534

dehumidifiers

Mail order only. The GoldenRod dehumidifier protects your prized auto from dampness, rust and mildew. It is easy to install, maintenance free and operates for pennies a day. Our product is UL listed, made in the USA and guaranteed for ten years. You've spent so much time restoring your old car, why not protect it with the GoldenRod?

Buffalo Milke Automotive
Polishing Products Inc
PO Box 1955
Pleasanton, CA 94566
888-GO-BUFFALO
FAX: 925-417-7445
E-mail:
buffalomilke@buffalomilke.com

spray wax

Buffalo Milke® instant spray wax. Three products in one: cleaner, detailer and wax. Cleans and protects both paint and chrome surfaces. Leaves no white residue or powder on rubber, textured or grainy trim parts. No harsh abrasives, cover large areas quickly, excellent on clear coat, any painted surface as well as chrome, glass and plexi-glass. Lasts through several washings, hides minor spider webbing and scratches. Money back guarantee. Proudly made in the USA. Web site: www.buffalomilke.com

Caladium Chemical Co
657 S Lakeview Rd
Lake Placid, FL 33852
941-465-6345; FAX: 941-465-9734

hand cleaner
polishes
waxes

Mail order only. Formula 111 waterless hand cleaner, waxes and polishes, cleaners and protectants.

California Car Cover Co
21125 Superior St
Chatsworth, CA 91311
800-423-5525; FAX: 818-998-2442

accessories
apparel
car covers
tools

See full listing in **Section Two** under **car covers**

Capt Lee's Spra' Strip
PO Box 203
Hermitage, TN 37076
800-421-9498; FAX: 615-889-1798

paint remover

See full listing in **Section Two** under **rust removal & stripping**

Color-Plus Leather Restoration
System
106 Harrier Ct, 3767 Sunrise Lake
Milford, PA 18337-9315
570-686-3158; FAX: 570-686-4161
E-mail: jpcolorplus@pikeonline.net

leather conditioning
leather dye

See full listing in **Section Two** under **leather restoration**

Comfy/Inter-American
Sheepskins Inc
1346 Centinela Ave
West Los Angeles, CA 90025-1901
800-521-4014; FAX: 310-442-6080
E-mail: sales@comfysheep.com

floor mats
seat covers

See full listing in **Section Two** under **interiors & interior parts**

Cover-It
17 Wood St
West Haven, CT 06516-3843
800-932-9344; FAX: 203-931-4754
E-mail: coverit@ct1.nai.net

all-weather shelters

See full listing in **Section Two** under **car covers**

Cover-Up Enterprises
Division of Trans International
Group Ltd
1444 Manor Ln
Blue Bell, PA 19422
800-268-3757; FAX: 215-654-9252

car covers

See full listing in **Section Two** under **car covers**

Cyclo Industries LLC
10190 Riverside Dr
Palm Beach Gardens, FL 33410
800-843-7813, 561-775-9600
FAX: 561-622-1055
E-mail: cyclo@cyclo.com

cleaners
lubricants

Offer a complete line of professionally formulated, time tested cleaners, lubricants and additives in dynamic packages. Products designed for the complete maintenance and enhanced performance of motor vehicles, marine, home and industrial applications. For almost 40 years the Cyclo brand of products have been tested and preferred by professional mechanics to maintain and extend the use and performance of cars, trucks, plane and industrial machinery. Offering a full line of service chemicals including a variety of cleaners, lubricants and additives. Call or write for more information. Web site: www.cyclo.com

D-A Lubricant Co
1340 W 29th St
Indianapolis, IN 46208
800-232-4503; FAX: 317-926-8132

lubricants

See full listing in **Section Two** under **lubricants**

Dashhugger
PO Box 933
Clovis, CA 93613
559-298-4529; FAX: 559-298-3428
E-mail: sales@dashhugger.com

dashboard covers

See full listing in **Section Two** under **interiors & interior parts**

Deltran Corporation
801 US Hwy 92 E
Deland, FL 32724
904-736-7900; FAX: 904-736-9984

battery chargers

See full listing in **Section Two** under **batteries**

Dr Vinyl and Assoc Ltd
9501 E 350 Hwy
Raytown, MO 64133
816-356-3312; FAX: 816-356-9049
E-mail: tbuckley@drvinyl.com

dent repair
interior repair
paint touch-up

Mail order and open shop. Monday-Friday 8 am to 5 pm. Interior repair and recoloring, paintless dent repair, minor exterior paint touch-up, vinyl and leather cleaning and conditioning kit. Web site: www.drvinyl.com

Dri-Wash 'n Guard
Independent Distributor
PO Box 1331
Palm Desert, CA 92261
800-428-1883, 760-346-1984
FAX: 760-568-6354

automotive care
products
boat care products

Cleans and protects virtually everything you own without using water; Enviro-tech International's waterless and water saving technologies make it simple, efficient and economical. Dri-Wash 'n Guard cleans, seals, protects and polishes without scratching any non-porous surface, fine automobiles, RVs, boats, airplanes and equipment. A full line of carpet, fabric and upholstery, leather and vinyl, metal polish and home products are also available. Don't overlook the health care and body product lines now available. Monthly publication, *InfoGram.*

Emgee/Clean Tools
10 Plaza Dr
Westmont, IL 60559
630-887-7707; FAX: 630-887-1347

drying product

The Absorber, an all purpose drying product that is compact and reusable. The Absorber dries faster and absorbs 50% more water than other drying products. A safe, non-abrasive, lintless material that is resistant to grease, oil and most chemicals. The Absorber is machine washable and will last for years.

Fast Lane Products
PO Box 7000-50
Palos Verdes Peninsula, CA 90274
800-327-8669; FAX: 310-541-2235
E-mail: info@fastlaneproducts.com

chamois
drain tubs
hand wringers

Mail order only. Monday-Friday 9 am to 5 pm PST. Commercial quality hand wringers, drain tubs and premium synthetic chamois for easy maintenance of cars, trucks, airplanes and boats. Web site: www.fastlaneproducts.com

The Finished Look
PO Box 191413
Sacramento, CA 95819-1413
800-827-6715; FAX: 916-451-3984
E-mail: info@thefinishedlook.com

POR-15 products

See full listing in **Section Two** under **rustproofing**

Gasoline Alley LLC
1700E Iron Ave
PO Box 737
Salina, KS 67402
800-326-8372, 785-822-1003
FAX: 785-827-9337
E-mail: morrison@midusa.net

drip pans

See full listing in **Section Two** under **accessories**

Griot's Garage
3500-A 20th St E
Tacoma, WA 98424
800-345-5789; FAX: 888-252-2252
E-mail: info@griotsgarage.com

car care products
paint
tools

See full listing in **Section Two** under **tools**

Iverson Automotive
14704 Karyl Dr
Minnetonka, MN 55345
800-325-0480; FAX: 612-938-5707

polishes
pot metal
restoration

See full listing in **Section Two** under **plating & polishing**

JCM Industries
2 Westwood Dr
Danbury, CT 06811
800-752-0245

wax hardener

Mail order only. Offering a hardener for car waxes. Makes car finishes hard as a rock. It's like putting two coats of wax on a car or truck.

Koala International
PO Box 255
Uwchland, PA 19480
610-458-8395; FAX: 610-458-8735

convertible
maintenance
products

Convertible top maintenance products used for cleaning, protecting and maintaining simulated and genuine convertible tops made vinyl. Also a plastic polish for removing scratches and haze from rear windows, lenses and bezels, permanently. Dealer inquiries are welcomed.

KozaK® Auto Drywash® Inc
6 S Lyon St
Batavia, NY 14020
800-237-9927, 716-343-8111
FAX: 716-343-3732
E-mail: info@kozak.com

cloths

Mail order and open shop. Manufacturer of KozaK® Drywash® brand cleaning cloths for cars and furniture. Also new printing services available with mailing services (i.e. Cheshire® labeling and inserting). You'll never drive a dirty car again. KozaK® safely cleans and polishes your car without water. Sold and guaranteed since 1926. Call Ed Harding, President, for info. Web site: www.kozak.com

Leatherique Leather Restoration Products PO Box 2678 Orange Park, FL 32065 904-272-0992; FAX: 904-272-1534 E-mail: lrpltd@aol.com	leather cleaning conditioning products

See full listing in **Section One** under **Rolls-Royce/Bentley**

Liquid Glass Enterprises Inc PO Box 1170 Teaneck, NJ 07666 201-387-6755; FAX: 201-387-2168 E-mail: lheywang@ix.netcom.com	car care products

Car care products. Manufacturer of the Liquid Glass Total Appearance System. This includes Liquid Glass polish, car wash and pre-cleaner. Also Connoisseur's choice line of protectants and cleaners. Web site: www.liquidglass.com

M & R Products 1940 SW Blvd Vineland, NJ 08360 800-524-2560, 609-696-9450 FAX: 609-696-4999 E-mail: mrproducts@mrproducts.com	hardware tie-downs

See full listing in **Section Two** under **accessories**

Mac's Custom Tie-Downs 105 Sanderson Rd Chehalis, WA 98532 800-666-1586 orders 360-748-1180; FAX: 360-748-1185	automotive tie-downs

See full listing in **Section Two** under **trailers**

Maintenance Specialties Company 21 Valley Forge Rd PO Box 251 New Castle, DE 19720 800-777-6715; FAX: 302-328-2315	rustproofing paints

See full listing in **Section Two** under **rustproofing**

Malm Chem Corp PO Box 300, Dept HVA Pound Ridge, NY 10576 914-764-5775; FAX: 914-764-5785 E-mail: jkolin@cloud9.net	polish wax

Dealing in auto wax, polishes and tools for their application. Website: www.malms.com

Marshall Antique & Classic Restorations 3714 Old Philadelphia Pike Bethlehem, PA 18015 610-868-7765; FAX: 610-868-7529	coolant additives restoration services

See full listing in **Section One** under **Rolls-Royce/Bentley**

Motorcars International 528 N Prince Ln Springfield, MO 65802 417-831-9999; FAX: 417-831-8080 E-mail: sales@motorcars-intl.com	accessories cars services tools

See full listing in **Section One** under **Ferrari**

Murphy's Motoring Accessories Inc PO Box 618 Greendale, WI 53129-0618 800-529-8315, 414-529-8333	car covers

See full listing in **Section Two** under **car covers**

Northern Tool & Equipment PO Box 1219 Burnsville, MN 55337-0219 800-533-5545	engines generators hydraulics

See full listing in **Section Two** under **tools**

OJ Rallye Automotive PO Box 540 N 6808 Hwy OJ Plymouth, WI 53073 920-893-2531; FAX: 920-893-6800 E-mail: ojrallye@excel.net	accessories car care products lighting parts

See full listing in **Section Two** under **lighting equipment**

Performance Automotive Inc 1696 New London Tpke PO Box 10 Glastonbury, CT 06033 860-633-7868; FAX: 860-657-9110	accessories car care

Dealing in accessories and car care products, retail/wholesale, detailing and concours preparation. Enthusiasts serving enthusiasts, providing total car care. Web site: www.perfauto.com

Preserve Inc 1430 E 1800 N Hamilton, IL 62341 217-746-2411; FAX: 217-746-2231	storage containers

See full listing in **Section Two** under **storage care products**

Protective Products Corp Box 246 Johnston, IA 50131 888-772-1277; FAX: 515-999-2708 E-mail: ppc1@aol.com	chemical products

See full listing in **Section Two** under **restoration aids**

T Schmidt 827 N Vernon Dearborn, MI 48128-1542 313-562-7161	rust removers

See full listing in **Section Two** under **rust removal & stripping**

Showtime Auto Acc 899 N Market St Selinsgrove, PA 17870 800-232-8861; FAX: 570-374-5775 E-mail: showtime@sunlink.net	fasteners

Mail order and open shop. Monday-Friday 9 am to 5 pm. Specialize in car care products and stainless fasteners. Give us a call or stop in and visit our shop. Web site: showtimeauto.com

Silver Image Photographics 3102 Vestal Pkwy E Vestal, NY 13850 607-797-8795	business cards photo car cards photofinishing

See full listing in **Section Two** under **automobilia**

Standard Abrasives **Motorsports Division** 4201 Guardian St Simi Valley, CA 93063 800-383-6001, 805-520-5800 ext 371 FAX: 805-577-7398	abrasives

See full listing in **Section Two** under **restoration aids**

Sterling Specialties
42 Ponderosa Lane
Monroe, NY 10950
914-782-7614

car care products

Mail and phone orders. Oil drain valves by Fumoto, Kozak cloths, AMS/oil synthetic lubricants, Semichrome. Free brochure.

Stoner Inc
1070 Robert Fulton Hwy
Quarryville, PA 17566
717-786-7355; FAX: 717-786-9088
E-mail: stoner1@epix.net

**cleaners
lubricants**

Mail order and open shop. Phone Monday-Friday 8 am to 8 pm. Specialty auto detailing cleaners, lubricants and appearance dressing for auto enthusiasts and detailers. More Shine Less Time™ detail dressing for tires, plastic, vinyl, rubber and trim. Web site: www.stonersolutions.com

Superior Equipment
703 W 53rd St N
Wichita, KS 67204
800-526-9992; FAX: 316-831-0154
E-mail: mail@superlifts.com

**auto lifts
shop tools**

See full listing in **Section Two** under **tools**

Thermax Inc
5385 Alpha Ave
Reno, NV 89506
800-247-7177; FAX: 702-972-4809

interior detailing

Since 1971, Thermax has pioneered the cleaning industry as it is known today. The Therminator models are manufactured for fast, easy cleaning of vehicle interiors. Improve the quality of your interior, save time by using Thermax and make more money in the process. The Thermax distributor can show you the advantage of the Therminator line. Call today and receive a free demonstration which allows you to see the latest in cleaning technology. Web site: www.thermaxvac.com

Tower Paint Co Inc
Box 2345
Oshkosh, WI 54903
920-235-6520; FAX: 920-235-6521
E-mail: tpi@towerpaint.com

paint

See full listing in **Section Two** under **paints**

Ultimate Appearance Ltd
113 Arabian Tr
Smithfield, VA 23430
888-446-3078; FAX: 757-255-2620

**cleaners
detailing products
detailing services
polish/wax**

Mail order and open shop. Stocking exclusive detailing products. IBIZ world class products, Novus plastic polish line, Stoner professional, PZIs, Lexol, Sprayway, 303 products, Wenol, Clay Magic, brushes and mitts, car covers, floor mats and Pinnacle. Detailing seminars by appointment. Auto detailing services provided. Catalog available. MasterCard, Visa, Discover and American Express accepted.

Valco Cincinnati Consumer Products Inc
411 Circle Freeway Dr
Cincinnati, OH 45246
513-874-6550; FAX: 513-874-3612

**adhesives
detailing products
sealants
tools**

See full listing in **Section Two** under **tools**

Vintage Ford Center Inc
19437 Harmony Church Rd
Leesburg, VA 20175
888-813-FORD (3673)
FAX: 703-777-3738
E-mail: mdla@masinc.com

**accessories
parts**

See full listing in **Section One** under **Ford 1903-1931**

The Wax Shop
PO Box 10226
Bakersfield, CA 93389-0226
800-323-9192, 661-397-5274
FAX: 661-397-6817
E-mail: dbonin@accelnet.com

**cleaners
polishes
waxes**

Mail order and open shop. Monday-Friday 8 am to 5 pm PST. Specialize in premium quality car care products that are the overwhelming choice among top restorers, detailers and collectors worldwide. Founded in 1980, The Wax Shop created and manufactures its entire line of products. There are over 20 specialty products that range from waxes, polishes, cleaners and dressings. Each product is specifically designed for ease-of-use and unmatched results. Gallon sizes are available. Web site: the-waxshop.com

Ziebart/Tidy Car
803 Mt Royal Blvd
Pittsburgh, PA 15223
412-486-4711

**accessories
detailing
rustproofing**

See full listing in **Section Two** under **rustproofing**

car covers

Keeps Out Dust Damp and Light — THE GILBERT AUTO COVER

APA Industries
10505 San Fernando Rd
Pacoima, CA 91331
818-834-8473; FAX: 818-834-2795
E-mail: apaindustries@juno.com

**accessories
parts**

See full listing in **Section One** under **Jaguar**

Auto-Mat Co
69 Hazel St
Hicksville, NY 11801
800-645-7258 orders
516-938-7373; FAX: 516-931-8438
E-mail: browner5@ix.netcom.com

**accessories
carpet sets
interiors**

See full listing in **Section Two** under **interiors & interior parts**

California Car Cover Co
9525 DeSoto
Chatsworth, CA 91311
800-423-5525; FAX: 818-998-2442

**accessories
apparel
car covers
tools**

Specialize in protecting your valuable automotive investments. Offer covers made from six different materials to ensure your getting the best possible cover for your application and we have nearly 30,000 precision master patterns from which to build a custom fit cover from. Other items in our line include specialty tools and accessories for your garage, a wide assortment of car care products, novelty items and apparel. Catalog free for the asking.

Car Cover Company
146 W Pomona Ave
Monrovia, CA 91016
626-357-7718

car covers

Mail order and open shop. Monday-Friday 9 am to 5 pm. Manufacturer of custom car covers for muscle cars and classics. Specializing in selling wholesale to mail order houses. Can make or get any car cover pattern for any car, provided our customers can use these patterns on an ongoing basis.

Classic Motoring Accessories
146 W Pomona Ave
Monrovia, CA 91016
800-327-3045, 626-357-8264

accessories
car covers

Mail order and open shop. Monday-Friday 9 am to 5 pm. Manufacture own custom car covers for muscle cars and classics. Our retail prices are lower than our competitors. Also have thousands of chrome goodies, silver and gold jewelry with diamonds, fans, overheating equipment, Heartbeat of America jackets, valve covers, and much more. Please send for our free 64-page catalog.

Cover-It
17 Wood St
West Haven, CT 06516-3843
800-932-9344; FAX: 203-931-4754
E-mail: coverit@ct1.nai.net

all-weather shelters

Mail order and open shop. Monday-Friday 8 am to 6 pm, Saturday 8 am to 4 pm. Our all-weather shelters provide protection for cars, boats, trucks, RVs, motorcycles, docks, pools, paint booths, sandblasting, workshops, industrial contracts, greenhouses and more! Shelters withstand wind, rain, snow, sap and sun. From 4' to 60' wide, any length made with heavy duty galvanized steel frame with a waterproof UV treated "Rip-Stop" cover. Portable, assemble quickly and easily. The perfect solution for covering anything and everything year-round, economically and securely.

Cover-Up Enterprises
Division of Trans International
Group Ltd
1444 Manor Ln
Blue Bell, PA 19422
800-268-3757; FAX: 215-654-9252

car covers

Mail order and auto shows. High quality car covers, lowest prices (from $59.95) for all cars, trucks, vans, cycles and limos (all years).

Kanter Auto Products
76 Monroe St
Boonton, NJ 07005
800-526-1096, 201-334-9575
FAX: 201-334-5423

car cover
carpets
parts

See full listing in **Section Two** under **comprehensive parts**

Lord Byron Inc
420 Sackett Point Rd
North Haven, CT 06473
203-287-9881; FAX: 203-288-9456

fender covers

Specializing in official GM licensed auto fender covers. Manufacture custom printed auto fender covers and can manufacture covers with custom logos for specialty car clubs and parts suppliers. In addition, we market our own line of official licensed GM fender covers.

Mark II Enterprises
5225 Canyon Crest Dr
Suite 71-217
Riverside, CA 92507
909-686-2752; FAX: 909-686-7245
E-mail: mark2@csi.com

car covers
parts

See full listing in **Section Two** under **accessories**

Motorcars International
528 N Prince Ln
Springfield, MO 65802
417-831-9999; FAX: 417-831-8080
E-mail: sales@motorcars-intl.com

accessories
cars
services
tools

See full listing in **Section One** under **Ferrari**

Murphy's Motoring Accessories Inc
PO Box 618
Greendale, WI 53129-0618
800-529-8315, 414-529-8333

car covers

Specialist in custom-fit covers for cars, trucks, vans and SUVs from 1900-1998 models. Eight fabrics including EVOLUTION® 4 Fabric, NOAH™ Barrier Fabric and DUSTOP™ Soft-As-Flannel Fabric from Kimberly-Clark's First Family of Car Cover Fabrics. More than 35,000 custom-fit patterns available. Also have simple procedure for making one-of-a-kind covers from your photos and measurements. Product lines include tonneau covers, dash savers, fender covers, front end masks and other car care and protection products.

National Parts Depot
3101 SW 40th Blvd
Gainesville, FL 32608
800-874-7595 toll-free 24 hours
352-378-2473 local

accessories
restoration parts

See full listing in **Section Two** under **comprehensive parts**

OJ Rallye Automotive
PO Box 540
N 6808 Hwy OJ
Plymouth, WI 53073
920-893-2531; FAX: 920-893-6800
E-mail: ojrallye@excel.net

accessories
car care products
lighting parts

See full listing in **Section Two** under **lighting equipment**

Performance Automotive Inc
1696 New London Tpke
PO Box 10
Glastonbury, CT 06033
860-633-7868; FAX: 860-657-9110

accessories
car care

See full listing in **Section Two** under **car care products**

Precision Auto Designs
28 Railway Ave
Campbell, CA 95008
408-378-2332; FAX: 408-378-1301
E-mail: pad@precisionauto.com

accessories
car covers
restoration

See full listing in **Section One** under **Mercedes-Benz**

Preserve Inc
1430 E 1800 N
Hamilton, IL 62341
217-746-2411; FAX: 217-746-2231

storage containers

See full listing in **Section Two** under **storage care products**

Quik-Shelter
PO Box 1123
Orange, CT 06477
800-211-3730; FAX: 203-937-8897
E-mail: info@quikshelter.com

temporary garages

Manufacturer of all purpose garages, screen houses and greenhouses; made of heavy duty galvanized metal tubing with a rip scrim fabric cover. Any size available. Many styles to choose from. Easy assembly, all bolt together. Dealers and exporters welcome (sell these diversified money making products). Web site: www.quikshelter.com

S & S Manufacturing Inc
217 W 26th St
South Sioux City, NE 68776
800-397-1159, 402-494-4498
FAX: 402-494-4757
E-mail: wsteve1023@aol.com

canopies

Mail order and open shop. Monday-Friday 8:30 am to 5 pm. Canopies for car shows and car ports.

Sailorette's Nautical Nook 451 Davy Ln Wilmington, IL 60481 815-476-1644; FAX: 815-476-2524	covers **interiors**

See full listing in **Section Two** under **upholstery**

Samson Technology Corporation 2280 SW 70th Ave #3 Davie, FL 33317 PH/FAX: 954-916-9322 E-mail: samson@icanect.net	anodizing car cover **chrome plating** **electroplating** **systems**

See full listing in **Section Two** under **plating & polishing**

UK Spares/TVR Sports Cars 609 Highland St Wethersfield, CT 06109-3979 PH/FAX: 860-563-1647 FAX: 860-529-3479 E-mail: tvr.sports.cars@juno.com	accessories car covers **convertible tops** **ignition parts** **suspension parts**

See full listing in **Section One** under **TVR**

West Coast Metric Inc 24002 Frampton Ave Harbor City, CA 90710 310-325-0005; FAX: 310-325-9733 E-mail: wcmi@earthlink.net	apparel carpets **plastic parts** **rubber parts**

See full listing in **Section One** under **Volkswagen**

car dealers

Ace Antique Automotive Since 1963 PO Box 81021 San Diego, CA 92138 619-702-9084; FAX: 619-702-9178	consignments **estates**

Open shop by appointment. Classic car sales, estate liquidation, over 35 years' experience, large selection of cars: antiques, classics, exotics.

Albers Rolls-Royce 190 W Sycamore Zionsville, IN 46077 317-873-2360, 317-873-2560 FAX: 317-873-6860	car dealer **parts**

See full listing in **Section One** under **Rolls-Royce/Bentley**

Alfas Unlimited Inc 89 Greenwoods Rd W, Rt 44 Norfolk, CT 06058 860-542-5351; FAX: 860-542-5993 E-mail: alfasun@esslink.com	engine rebuilding parts **restoration** **service**

See full listing in **Section One** under **Alfa Romeo**

AM Racing Inc PO Box 451 Danvers, MA 01923 PH/FAX: 978-774-4613	race prep sales **vintage racing**

See full listing in **Section Two** under **racing**

Antique & Classic Cars Inc 328 S 3rd St Hamilton, OH 45011 513-844-1146 in OH 800-798-3982 nationwide	bodywork machine work **painting** **parts** **service**

See full listing in **Section One** under **Buick/McLaughlin**

Appleton Garage PO Box B West Rockport, ME 04865 207-594-2062	car dealer parts **wheelcovers**

See full listing in **Section Two** under **wheels & wheelcovers**

Auto Quest Investment Cars Inc 710 W 7th St PO Box 22 Tifton, GA 31793 912-382-4750; FAX: 912-382-4752 E-mail: info@auto-quest.com	car dealer

Open Monday-Friday 8:30 am to 5 pm. Dealer since 1932 of domestic and foreign classic and exotic vehicles. 90 plus vehicles on display at the dealership. Worldwide shipping available. The extensive web site has prices and color photos of every vehicle in stock and is updated every business day. Dealership and gift shop is located 600 yards east of Exit 18 on I-75, US 319, US 82 and GA 520 at Tifton, GA. Web site: www.auto-quest.com

Auto Transport Services 5367 Fargo Rd Avoca, MI 48006 810-324-2598; FAX: 810-324-6094	transport

See full listing in **Section Two** under **transport**

Auto World Sales 2245 Q St Lincoln, NE 68503 402-435-7111; FAX: 402-435-7131 E-mail: autowwka@nevix.net	appraisals **sales**

See full listing in **Section Two** under **appraisals**

Auto-Line Enterprises Inc 2 Lyons Rd Armonk, NY 10504 914-681-1757; FAX: 914-273-5159 E-mail: garfconect@aol.com	appraisals **broker services**

See full listing in **Section Two** under **appraisals**

AutoMatch CARS (Computer Aided Referral Service) 2017 Blvd Napoleon Louisville, KY 40205 800-962-2771, 502-417-8793 mobile 502-452-1920 office; FAX: 502-479-6222 E-mail: amcars@aol.com or aautomatch@aol.com	broker car dealer network **locator**

Buy, sell, trade, locate and consign all makes. Specializing in exotic and special interest. Over 1,000 representatives around the world help you save.
Web site: www.freeyellow.com/members3/automatch

Jerry Bensinger 1197 Trails Edge Dr Hubbard, OH 44425-3353 330-759-5224; FAX: 330-759-5225	car dealer

Monday-Friday 9 am to 5 pm. Sale of very nice or restorable Ferraris, Maseratis, Jaguars, Astons, Austin-Healeys, etc. International shipping, references, 20 years in business with regularly satisfied customers.

bentleydriversclub.com 23238 Erwin St Woodland Hills, CA 91367 818-887-6557; FAX: 818-346-3627 E-mail: glwales@aol.com	car dealer **collectibles**

See full listing in **Section One** under **Rolls-Royce/Bentley**

Berliner Classic Motorcars Inc	automobilia
1975 Stirling Rd	car dealer
Dania, FL 33004	motorcycles
954-923-7271; FAX: 954-926-3306	
E-mail: sales@motorcars.com	

Mail order and open showroom. Monday-Friday 9 am to 5 pm, most Saturdays 10 am to 1 pm. Licensed dealer that buys and sells classic and antique automobiles, classic motorcycles and a wide variety of memorabilia. 15,000 square foot showroom located in south Fort Lauderdale, Florida, minutes from the airport and interstate. We have it all, drivers to #1 judged show condition cars, American and European, jukeboxes, Coca-Cola items, gas pumps, music boxes, etc. Accept items on consignment and for storage. Experienced in exporting. Party and special events facility. Web site: www.motorcars.com

Bill's Collector Cars	appraisals
6478 County Rd #1	car dealer
South Point, OH 45680	
740-894-5175	

Open Monday-Saturday 10 am to 6 pm, evenings and Sundays by appointment. Appraisals for estates, banks and individuals. Over 35 years' experience. Honesty and integrity in all our dealings with the old car hobby.

Bright Displays	molded auto logos
1314 Lakemont Dr	neon signs
Pittsburgh, PA 15243	
PH/FAX: 412-279-7037	

See full listing in **Section Two** under **automobilia**

Cars of Distinction	antique cars
3358 F St	classic cars
San Diego, CA 92102	
619-544-0063	

Buy and sell antique and classic cars.

Central Valley Classics	consignment sales
4810 N Blackstone Ave	
Fresno, CA 93726	
559-222-8691; FAX: 559-222-8693	
E-mail: cvc@psnw.com	

Largest indoor consignment store in central California. Have over 100 special interest and classic cars for sale in our 30,000 sq ft showroom in Fresno, CA. Non-commission store so you never pay more than the owner's asking price. Check out our current inventory on our web site, updated daily. IAAA member, #1003070097. Web site: classicshowroom.com

Checker Motors	cars
1314 Rollins Rd	parts
Burlingame, CA 94010	rentals
650-340-8669; FAX: 650-340-9473	

See full listing in **Section One** under **Checker**

Chicago Car Exchange	appraisals
1 Collector Car Dr	car dealer
Box 530	car locator
Lake Bluff, IL 60044	financing
847-680-1950; FAX: 847-680-1961	storage
E-mail: oldtoys@wwa.com	

Open shop. Monday-Friday 10 am to 6 pm, Saturday 10 am to 5 pm. 20,000 square foot showroom with over 150 collectable cars. Buy, sell, consign, appraise, locate, detail and store collector cars. Strive to give accurate representations of cars to long distance buyers. Establishes long-standing, working relationships with clients. Specialties are pre-war, vintage, muscle, Mercedes, Cadillac, Pontiac and Hudson. Financing available. Worldwide shipping. Phone/fax for current inventory list. Web site: www.chicagocarexchange.com

Dick Choler Cars & Service Inc	car dealer
640 E Jackson Blvd	literature
Elkhart, IN 46516	model cars
219-522-8281; FAX: 219-294-5350	

See full listing in **Section One** under **Pontiac**

City Imports Ltd	bodywork
166 Penrod Ct	car sales
Glen Burnie, MD 21061	restorations
410-768-6660; FAX: 410-768-5955	

See full listing in **Section One** under **Jaguar**

Charles W Clarke	appraiser
Automotive Consultant/Appraiser	car dealer
17 Saddle Ridge Dr	consultant
West Simsbury, CT 06092-2118	
PH/FAX: 860-658-2714	

See full listing in **Section Two** under **consultants**

Classic Cars Inc	cars
52 Maple Terr	parts
Hibernia, NJ 07842	
973-627-1975; FAX: 973-627-3503	

See full listing in **Section One** under **Packard**

Classic Cars & Parts	car dealer
Division of AKV Auto	parts
Mike Chmilarski	
622 Rt 109	
Lindenhurst, NY 11757	
516-888-3914	

Mail order and open shop. Buy, sell and trade General Motors cars and parts. Specializing in 1959-1972. Also late model special interest vehicles for sale, all marques.

Classic Motors	appraisals
PO Box 1321	car dealer
Shirley, MA 01464	consulting
978-425-4614	

Open by appointment only. Antique, classic and special interest vehicles. Specialize in the sale of brass-era cars. Also, we do appraisals and pre-purchase inspection on all makes, models and years.

Classic Showcase	classic vehicles
913 Rancheros Dr	restorations
San Marcos, CA 92069	
760-747-9947, 760-747-3188 sales	
FAX: 760-747-4021	
E-mail:	
management@classicshowcase.com	

Mail order and open shop. Monday-Friday 9 am to 5 pm by appointment. Restoration facility address above, showroom address: 955 Rancheros Dr, San Marcos, CA 92069. Specializing in restoration of British, German and Italian classic vehicles that we sell. Restorations are taken to show level or daily driver. Specialize in Jaguar, Austin-Healey, MG, Triumph, Mercedes, Porsche, BMW, Ferrari, Alfa Romeo, Fiat and microcars. References available upon request. Worldwide shipping available as well. Web site: www.classicshowcase.com

Cn'V Corvette Sales	parts
2166 E University Dr	sales
Tempe, AZ 85281	service
602-994-8388; FAX: 602-423-0407	
E-mail: sales@cnv-corvettes.com	

See full listing in **Section One** under **Corvette**

| Coach Builders Limited Inc
1410 S Main St
PO Box 1978
High Springs, FL 32655
904-454-2060; FAX: 904-454-4080 | **car dealer**
conv conversion |

See full listing in **Section Two** under **restoration shops**

| Collector Car & Truck Market Guide
41 N Main St
North Grafton, MA 01536
508-839-6707; FAX: 508-839-6266
E-mail: vmr@vmrintl.com | **price guide** |

See full listing in **Section Four** under **periodicals**

| Collector's Carousel
84 Warren Ave
Westbrook, ME 04092
207-854-0343; FAX: 207-856-6913 | **appraisals**
sales
service |

Antique auto sales, service and appraisals.

| Contemporary and Investment
Automobiles
2700 Peachtree Square
Doraville, GA 30360
770-455-1200; FAX: 770-455-0023
E-mail: georjarex@aol.com | **buy/sell/trade**
mechanical work
memorabilia |

Buy, sell, trade antique, classic, muscle, sport, kit, street rod, custom, race, any type of special interest cars, trucks and motorcycles. Over 120 cars in our enclosed facility in a northern suburb of Atlanta, GA. Also have a good selection of memorabilia. Do mechanical work on cars, build street rods in our Alabama facility. Web site: www.c-it.com/cia

| Corvette Mike
1133 N Tustin Ave
Anaheim, CA 92807
800-327-8388, 714-630-0700
FAX: 714-630-0777
E-mail: cvtmike@deltanet.com | **accessories**
parts
sales
service |

See full listing in **Section One** under **Corvette**

| County Corvette
PO Box 258
Lionville, PA 19353
610-363-0872, 610-363-7670 sales
FAX: 610-363-5325 | **restoration**
sales
service |

See full listing in **Section One** under **Corvette**

| Tom Crook Classic Cars
27611 42nd Ave S
Auburn, WA 98001
206-941-3454 | **car dealer** |

Specializing in classic car sales for Packards, Cadillacs, Duesenberg, Jaguar, Ford and all classics 1925-1948.

| D&M Corvette Specialists Ltd
1804 Ogden Ave
Downers Grove, IL 60515
630-968-0031; FAX: 630-968-0465 | **parts**
restoration
sales
service |

See full listing in **Section One** under **Corvette**

| Davies Corvette
7141 US Hwy 19
New Port Richey, FL 34653
800-236-2383, 727-842-8000
FAX: 727-846-8216
E-mail: davies@corvetteparts.com | **accessories**
parts |

See full listing in **Section One** under **Corvette**

| Desert Valley Auto Parts
22500 N 21st Ave
Phoenix, AZ 85027
800-905-8024, 602-780-8024
FAX: 602-582-9141
E-mail:
rust-free-parts@worldnet.att.net | **cars**
parts |

See full listing in **Section Five** under **Arizona**

| Driven By Desire
300 N Fraley St
Kane, PA 16735
814-837-7590; FAX: 814-837-6850
E-mail: driven@penn.com | **automobilia**
car dealer
models |

Mail order and open shop. Monday-Thursday 1 pm to 6 pm, Friday 1 pm to 9 pm, Saturday 12 pm to 5 pm. Collector car sales, mostly 1960s. The area's largest selection of foreign and domestic model car and truck kits, paint, supplies, etc. Die cast metal models, specializing in 1/18 scale, books, posters, auto related T-shirts, marque jackets and general automobilia. Stock car racing items: jackets, T-shirts, fan flags and more. Web site: users.penn.com/~driven/dxd.html

| Duffy's Collectible Cars
250 Classic Car Ct SW
Cedar Rapids, IA 52404
319-364-7000; FAX: 319-364-4036
E-mail: duluth@aol.com | **car dealer** |

Mail order and open shop. Monday-Friday 8:30 am to 5 pm, Saturday 8:30 am to 4:30 pm, closed Sundays. Gift shop and tours. Collector car sales and service. Specializing in cars from 1930-1970. Fully restored hardtops and convertibles. 100 car showroom. Sales, finance, storage, delivery and appraisals. Celebrating our 58th year. Web site: www.duffys.com

| Eckhaus Motor Company
20818 E Weldon
Tivy Valley, CA 93657-9107
559-787-1000; FAX: 559-787-1100 | **car dealer**
restoration shop |

By appointment only. Sale and restoration of British vehicles. Established 1968. Purchase all British cars. Prompt payment. Confidentiality assured.

| The Fine Car Store
1105 Moana Dr
San Diego, CA 92107
619-223-7766; FAX: 619-223-6838 | **cars** |

See full listing in **Section One** under **Ferrari**

| Freeman's Garage
29 Ford Rd
Norton, MA 02766
508-285-6500; FAX: 508-285-6566 | **parts**
restoration
sales
service |

See full listing in **Section One** under **Ford 1903-1931**

| Freman's Auto
138 Kountz Rd
Whitehall, MT 59759
406-287-5436; FAX: 406-287-9103 | **car dealer**
salvage yard |

Mail order only. Sell parts for all makes and models. 1950-1980, over 25,000 cars. Worldwide shipping. Some complete cars available.

| George's Auto & Tractor Sales Inc
1450 N Warren Rd
North Jackson, OH 44451
330-538-3020; FAX: 330-538-3033 | **Blue Dots/car dealer**
Dri-Wash metal polish
upholstery cleaner
New Castle batteries |

Mail order and open shop. Monday-Friday 9 am to 5 pm. Blue Dots, New Castle batteries, special interest autos. Dri-wash leather and vinyl treatment, Dri-Wash 'n Guard waterless car wash and protective glaze. Fluid film rust and corrosion preventative.

Leo Gephart Classic Cars
7360 E Acoma Dr, Ste 14
Scottsdale, AZ 85260
602-948-2286, 602-998-8263
FAX: 602-948-2390

car dealer
parts

Mail order and open shop. Monday-Friday 9 am to 5 pm, Saturday by appointment only. Antique and classic cars, exotic sports cars, historical race cars, Duesenbergs and early Ford V8s. Also Duesenberg parts: superchargers, bumpers, gas tanks, script sidemount mirrors and chassis parts. Over 50 years' experience dealing with high-performance cars of all eras. 1941 Cadillac parts. In the specialized car business over 52 years, continuous service, 20 years at this same address. Web site: www.traderonline.com

Mark Gillett
PO Box 9177
Dallas, TX 75209
PH/FAX: 214-902-9258
011-525-559-6240 Mexico City, Mexico
E-mail: autonet@onramp.net

car locator
sales

Open by appointment only. Sales and locating of specialty cars and vintage race cars. Specializing in finding old, dead race cars. Extensive contacts in Latin America.

Green Valentine Inc
5055 Covington Way
Memphis, TN 38134
901-373-5555; FAX: 901-373-5568

car dealer
woodies

Specializing in wood station wagons, wood convertibles for any brand.

Happy Daze Classic Cars
257 Morris Ct
Fond Du Lac, WI 54935
920-922-8450

car dealer

Mail order and open shop. Cars shown by appointment only. Buy, sell and trade outstanding collectible cars from the 1930s-early 1970s. All cars are displayed in our indoor, heated, sales facility. Specializing in rust-free, low mileage originals and cars which have undergone frame-off restorations.

J & K Old Chevy Stuff
Ship Pond Rd
Plymouth, MA 02360
508-224-7616

car dealer
parts
sheetmetal

See full listing in **Section One** under **Chevrolet**

K & K Vintage Motorcars LC
9848 SW Frwy
Houston, TX 77074
713-541-2281; FAX: 713-541-2286

restoration
sales
service

See full listing in **Section Two** under **restoration shops**

Larson Motor Co
Russell Larson
4423 A Canyon Dr
Amarillo, TX 79110
806-358-9797

appraisals
restoration
sales

Mail order and open shop. Monday-Friday 9 am to 4 pm. Sales, service and restoration of collector cars. Certified appraisals. Over 40 years' experience. IAAA member, #1002110097.

Manchester Motor Car Co
319 Main St
Manchester, CT 06040
860-643-5874; FAX: 860-643-6190
E-mail: mmcollc@aol.com

automobilia
parts
petroliana
restorations

See full listing in **Section Two** under **comprehensive parts**

W L Wally Mansfield
214 N 13th St
Wymore, NE 68466-1640
402-645-3546

cars
parts
trucks

See full listing in **Section Two** under **comprehensive parts**

Bill McCoskey
16643 Rt 144
Mt Airy, MD 21771
301-854-5900, 410-442-3637
FAX: 301-854-5957
E-mail: tatrabill@aol.com

appraisals
repairs

See full listing in **Section Two** under **appraisals**

Medicine Bow Motors Inc
343 One Horse Creek Rd
Florence, MT 59833
406-273-0002

car dealer

Specializing in 1946-1951 Ford car parts. Handle 1950s custom goodies. Builders of street rods, customs and quality restorations.

Memory Lane Motors
562 County Rd 121
Fenelon Falls, ON Canada K0M 1N0
705-887-CARS; FAX: 705-887-4028

car dealer
restoration
service

See full listing in **Section Two** under **restoration shops**

Memory Lane Motors Inc
1231 Rt 176
Lake Bluff, IL 60044
847-362-4600

appraisals
car dealer
storage

Open shop only, Monday-Saturday 9 am to 5 pm. Buy, sell, trade and consign antique and classic cars. Also do vehicle appraisals and provide storage for automobiles. Web site: www.memorylanemotors.com

Motorcar Gallery Inc
715 N Federal Hwy
Fort Lauderdale, FL 33304
954-522-9900; FAX: 954-522-9966

car dealer

See full listing in **Section One** under **Ferrari**

Ohio Limo and Coach Sales
PO Box 681
Bellefontaine, OH 43311
937-592-3746; FAX: 937-593-3299
E-mail: ohiolimo@ohiolimo.com

car dealer

Open by appointment. Dealer of specialty vehicles including limousines, convertibles and sports cars. Web site: www.ohiolimo.com

John T Poulin Auto Sales
Star Service Center
5th Ave & 111th St
North Troy, NY 12182
518-235-8610

car dealer
parts
restoration service

See full listing in **Section One** under **Mercedes-Benz**

Prairie Auto
Jeremiah Larson
7087 Orchid Ln
Maple Grove, MN 55311
612-420-8600; FAX: 612-420-8637
E-mail: jer4cars@aol.com

appraisals
car dealers

Antique and collectible autos, 1930-1972. Also late model sales and appraisals on all aspects automotive related: diminished value, arbitration, insurance purposes. IAAA member, #100201294.

Prestige Motors | car dealer
120 N Bessie Rd
Spokane, WA 99212
PH/FAX: 509-926-3611

Investment quality, special interest car retailer. Handle antiques, muscle cars, street rods, sports cars and classics.

Proteam Corvette Sales Inc | car collection
PO Box 606 | car dealer
Napoleon, OH 43545-0606
888-592-5086, 419-592-5086
FAX: 419-592-4242
E-mail:
proteam@proteam-corvette.com

See full listing in **Section One** under **Corvette**

Rader's Relics | appraisals
2601 W Fairbanks Ave | car dealer
Winter Park, FL 32789
407-647-1940; FAX: 407-647-1930
E-mail: therelic@bellsouth.net

Mail order and open shop. Monday-Friday 9 am to 4:30 pm, Saturday 9 am to 12 pm. 19 years in business at 1-4 and Fairbanks. Home of the two year buy-back warranty. Consider our greatest asset a good reputation locally and internationally. A 10% deposit holds any car for 30 days and is fully refundable if you come see the car and don't like it for any reason. Buying, selling and appraising antiques and classics. Keeping an inventory of about 40 cars at all times.

William H Randel | appraisals
PO Box 173 | car locators
Hatboro, PA 19040
215-675-8969; FAX: 215-441-0960
E-mail: tbrdnut@bellatlantic.net

See full listing in **Section One** under **Thunderbird**

RARE Corvettes | cars
Joe Calcagno | parts
Box 1080
Soquel, CA 95073
831-475-4442; FAX: 831-475-1115

See full listing in **Section One** under **Corvette**

Regal International Motor Cars Inc | car dealer
PO Box 6819
Hollywood, FL 33081
305-989-9777; FAX: 305-989-9778

See full listing in **Section One** under **Rolls-Royce/Bentley**

Retrospect Automotive | accessories
970-980 E Jericho Tpk | car sales
Huntington Station, NY 11746 | parts
516-421-0255; FAX: 516-421-0473

Mail order and open shop. Monday-Saturday 8 am to 6 pm. Parts and accessories, classic car sales of domestic cars, muscle cars of the 1950s-1972.

Rogers Corvette Center | car dealer
8675 N Orlando Ave
Maitland, FL 32751
407-628-8300; FAX: 407-628-8388
E-mail: sales@rogerscorvette.com

See full listing in **Section One** under **Corvette**

Route 66 Collectible Cars and Antiques | consignment sales
1933 Del Monte Blvd
Seaside, CA 93955
831-393-9329; FAX: 831-393-9391
E-mail: cars@route66.com

Monterey County's only indoor classic car showroom. A great place to find original, well kept American and European collectible cars. Consignment sales of cars, trucks, motorcycles and other antiques. Web site: www.route66cars.com

St Louis Car Museum & Sales | museum
1575 Woodson Rd
St Louis, MO 63114
314-993-1330; FAX: 314-993-1540

See full listing in **Section Six** under **Missouri**

Brooks Stevens Auto Collection Inc | parts
10325 N Port Washington Rd | restoration
Mequon, WI 53092 | service
414-241-4185; FAX: 414-241-4166
E-mail: apjb@prodigy.net

See full listing in **Section One** under **Excalibur**

Thoroughbred Motors | car dealer
3935 N US 301 | parts
Sarasota, FL 34234
941-359-2277; FAX: 941-359-2128

See full listing in **Section One** under **Jaguar**

U S Oldies & Classics | car dealer
Vunt 3 | parts
Holsbeek 3220 Belgium
3216446611; FAX: 3216446520

Open by appointment only. Specializing in classic American made automobiles, 1930-1972, especially Cadillac, Lincoln, Packard, Corvette, in very good to perfect condition. Supply parts on order for the European market: Cadillac, T-Bird, Mustang, Corvette, Packard and Lincoln.

USA of Yesterday | appraisals
455 St Helens Ave | indoor storage
Tacoma, WA 98402 | sales
253-627-1052; FAX: 253-627-3424 | vehicle consignment
E-mail: uofy@collectorcar.com

See full listing in **Section Two** under **appraisals**

Valenti Classics Inc | collectibles
355 S Hwy 41 | restoration
Caledonia, WI 53108 | sales
414-835-2070; FAX: 414-835-2575 | service
E-mail: vci@valenticlassics.com

Mail order and open shop. Monday-Saturday 8 am to 6 pm. Sales, service and restoration of classic and collectible automobiles. Also sell gas related signs, pumps and collectibles. Business is family owned and operated. Antique mall also at same location. Web site: www.valenticlassics.com

Vintage Auto Parts | car dealer
PO Box 323 | new/used parts
Temple, PA 19560-0323
610-939-9593, answering machine

See full listing in **Section One** under **BMW**

Volo Antique Auto Museum | museum
27582 Volo Village Rd
Volo, IL 60073
815-385-3644; FAX: 815-385-0703

See full listing in **Section Six** under **Illinois**

Westchester Vintage Coach Inc Box 252 Yonkers, NY 10705 914-693-1624	**car dealer**

Antique car sales. Appraisals only.

Willhoit Auto Restoration 1360 Gladys Ave Long Beach, CA 90804 562-439-3333; FAX: 562-439-3956	**engine rebuilding** **restoration**

See full listing in **Section One** under **Porsche**.

Wiseman Motor Co Inc Bill Wiseman, Owner PO Box 848 Marion, NC 28752 828-724-9313	**car dealer**

Buying and selling antique and classic cars. Model A Fords and early V8s a specialty. Our 35th year.

Yesterday's Auto Sales 2800 Lyndale Ave S Minneapolis, MN 55408 612-872-9733; FAX: 612-872-1386 E-mail: al-hagan@msn.com	**appraisals** **car dealer**

Open Monday-Friday 10 am to 4 pm, Saturday 10 am to 2 pm. Since 1983, have been a full-time collector car dealer. Inventory includes cars foreign and domestic, from the 1960s back to the 1920s. Located in an historic two story building near downtown Minneapolis. Web site: www.yesterdaysauto.com

carburetors

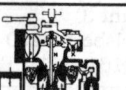

Andy's Classic Mustangs 18502 E Sprague Greenacres, WA 99016 509-924-9824	**parts** **service**

See full listing in **Section One** under **Mustang**.

Apple Hydraulics Inc 1610 Middle Rd Calverton, NY 11933-1419 800-882-7753, 516-369-9515 FAX: 516-369-9516	**brake rebuilding** **shock rebuilding**

See full listing in **Section Two** under **suspension parts**.

Arch Carburetor 583 Central Ave Newark, NJ 07107 973-482-2755 E-mail: mmfried1@aol.com	**carburetors**

Mail order and open shop. Monday-Friday 7:30 am to 3 pm, Saturday 8 am to 12 pm. Rebuilding and restoration of carburetors. Web site: www.archcarburetor.com

Battery Ignition Co Inc 91 Meadow St Hartford, CT 06114 860-296-4215; FAX: 860-947-3259 E-mail: biscokid@aol.com	**parts** **rebuilding** **rebushing**

Mail order and open shop. Monday-Friday 8:30 am to 5 pm, Thursday until 8 pm. Since 1926 offering parts, rebuilding and rebushing services for most domestic carburetors, including automotive, marine, industrial and antique applications. Also available, search services for hard to find fuel system and electrical parts. Web site: www.users.neca.com/biscokid

Carbs Unlimited 53996 Luzerne Macomb, MI 48042 810-786-0253; FAX: 810-786-6360 E-mail: weatherly@teleweb.net	**carb rebuilding** **carb replating**

Carburetor rebuilding. Rebuild, recolor and replate all American carburetors. 1 and 2-bbl, $140; 4-bbl, $190; plus 10% shipping.

Carburetor Engineering 3324 E Colorado Pasadena, CA 91107 626-795-3221	**carburetor rebuilding** **distributor rebuilding** **fuel pump rebuilding**

Mail order and open shop. Monday-Friday 8:30 am to 5 pm. Established in 1942. Custom rebuild antique and classic carburetors, fuel pumps and distributors, recolor carburetors, and fuel pumps as original.

The Carburetor Refactory 815 Harbour Way S #5 Richmond, CA 94804 510-237-1277; FAX: 510-237-2092	**parts** **rebuilding** **rebushing**

Mail order (UPS) and open shop. Monday-Thursday 7:30 am to 5:30 pm. Rebuild and rebush American, Japanese and European carburetors. Also sell parts for those carburetors including throttle shafts, butterflies, rebuild kits, TPS, Varajet, pull-offs, etc. Web site: www.carbkits.com

The Carburetor Shop 204 E 15th St Eldon, MO 65026 573-392-7378 FAX: 573-392-7176 (24 hours, 7 days)	**carburetors** **carburetor kits** **carburetor repair** **carburetor restoration**

Open shop. Phone hours: Monday-Thursday 8 am to 5 pm. Over 150,000 carburetors on hand 1900-1974. Rebuilding, restoration available. We guarantee our work. Manufacturer of rebuilding kits with following coverage: 1974-1925, 99.9%; 1924-1912, 80%; 1911-1904, 25%. Other carburetors parts available with purchase of repair kit. Also huge library of original carburetor literature for sale. MasterCard and Visa accepted (no fee). Web site: www.thecarburetorshop.com

Carl's Ford Parts 23219 South St, Box 38 Homeworth, OH 44634 PH/FAX: 330-525-7291	**muscle parts**

See full listing in **Section One** under **Mustang**.

Carson's Antique Auto Parts 235 Shawfarm Rd Holliston, MA 01746 508-429-2269; FAX: 508-429-0761 E-mail: w1066@gis.net	**parts**

See full listing in **Section Two** under **engine parts**.

Chicago Corvette Supply 7322 S Archer Rd Justice, IL 60458 708-458-2500; FAX: 708-458-2662	**parts**

See full listing in **Section One** under **Corvette**.

Classic Preservation Coalition PO Box 262 Taborton Rd Sand Lake, NY 12153-0262 518-674-2445; FAX: 518-674-3732 E-mail: houghton@empireone.net	**restoration**

Mail order only. Retail and wholesale restoration of carburetors and fuel pumps for 34 years for classic cars and boats. Sale of new production carburetor kits 1932-1980 and new production fuel pump rebuilding kits. Parts located and sold for all parts categories. MasterCard, Visa, AmEx gladly accepted for all retail transactions. Sale to wholesale only of new production water pump rebuilding kits and new production water pumps; inquire. We love what we do and it shows. Web site: http://members.xoom.com/c_p_c

---

Corvair Underground
PO Box 339
Dundee, OR 97115
800-825-8247, 503-434-1648
FAX: 503-434-1626

parts

See full listing in **Section One** under **Corvair**

Joe Curto Inc
22-09 126th St
College Point, NY 11356
718-762-SUSU
FAX: 718-762-6287 (h)

English carburetors
English parts
repairs

See full listing in **Section Two** under **comprehensive parts**

Ferris Auto Electric Ltd
106 Lakeshore Dr
North Bay, ON Canada P1A 2A6
705-474-4560; FAX: 705-474-9453

parts
service

See full listing in **Section Two** under **electrical systems**

For Ramblers Only
2324 SE 34th Ave
Portland, OR 97214
503-232-0497
E-mail: ramblers@teleport.com

accessories
parts

See full listing in **Section One** under **AMC**

Ignition Distributor Service
19042 SE 161st
Renton, WA 98058
425-255-8052

rebuilding carbs

Mail order only. Limited open shop. Complete rebuilding service for Rochester Q-Jets (4-bbl), 1966 and newer. Work includes the following modifications: secondary and main wells sealed better than factory new, idle tubes (Jets) made removeable for easy recalibration, primary throttle shaft bushed, plus all gaskets, needle and seat, and float replaced. Price is $150 for non-electronic models, call for these prices. Plating is not included. Add shipping and sales tax. Many cores available.

J & C's Parts
7127 Ward Rd
North Tonawanda, NY 14120
716-693-4090; FAX: 716-695-7144

parts

See full listing in **Section One** under **Buick/McLaughlin**

JAM Engineering Corp
PO Box 2570
Monterey, CA 93942
800-JAM-CORP, 831-372-1787
E-mail: jam@redshift.com

carburetors

Mail order only. Design and manufacture of 50 State Legal Weber and Holley carburetor replacement packages. Kits include linkage, air cleaner adapters, hardware and more. Specializing in BMW and Mercedes-Benz. Web site: www.jameng.com

---

Ken's Carburetors
2301 Barnum Ave
Stratford, CT 06615
203-375-9340

carburetors
distributors
parts

See full listing in **Section One** under **Ford 1932-1953**

Midel Pty Ltd
4 Frazer Street
Lakemba, NSW 2195 Australia
61-2-97595598; FAX: 61-2-97581155
E-mail: info@sumidel.com

carburetor parts

Mail order and open shop. Monday-Friday 9 am to 5 pm. Wholesale and retail spare parts sales of SU carburetors and fuel pumps and component parts for vehicles from the thirties to current models. Manufacturer of sand cast 2" SU carburetors and components. Restorer of carburetors and pumps. New carburetors for MG J, P, K3, L, TC, TD, TF. Web site: www.sumidel.com

---

Millers Incorporated
7412 Count Circle
Huntington Beach, CA 92647
714-375-6565; FAX: 714-847-6606
E-mail: sales@millermbz.com

accessories
parts

See full listing in **Section One** under **Mercedes-Benz**

National Parts Depot
3101 SW 40th Blvd
Gainesville, FL 32608
800-874-7595 toll-free 24 hours
352-378-2473 local

accessories
restoration parts

See full listing in **Section Two** under **comprehensive parts**

Nationwide Auto Restoration
1038 Watt St
Jeffersonville, IN 47130
812-280-0165; FAX: 812-280-8961
E-mail: restore@unidial.com

bodywork
paint
upholstery

See full listing in **Section Two** under **restoration shops**

The Old Carb Doctor
Rt 3, Box 338
Drucilla Church Rd
Nebo, NC 28761
800-945-CARB (2272)
704-659-1428

carburetors
fuel pumps

Mail order and open shop. Monday-Saturday 8 am to 7 pm. Carburetors completely restored from core supplied by customer. Castings resurfaced and repaired, shafts rebushed and resealed, rust removal, steel and brass refinished, guaranteed full service restoration at reasonable rates, 1900-1980. Mechanical screw together fuel pumps of the same vintage also restored.

Precision Carburetor
289C Skidmore Rd
Deer Park, NY 11729
516-667-3854; FAX: 516-595-1059

carburetor
rebuilding

Carburetor rebuilding, 1920s-present. 50 years' experience. 2,000+ units in stock. Specializing in high quality rebuilding for domestic, foreign, industrial and marine. Complete fabrication facility, computer listing and identification service, major club references. UPS service.

Rick's Carburetor Repair
PO Box 46
Blissville Rd
Hydeville, VT 05750
802-265-3006
E-mail: robinric@sover.net

carburetor
rebuilding

Mail order and open shop. Monday-Friday 8 am to 5 pm, Saturday 8 am to 12 pm; mail order calls anytime. Dealing in carburetor rebuilding, classic cars through present day. Guaranteed quality workmanship, 25 years' experience, competitive prices, fast turnaround via UPS service or US postal service.

Straight Six Jaguar
24321 Hatteras St
Woodland Hills, CA 91367
PH/FAX: 818-716-1192

parts
service

See full listing in **Section One** under **Jaguar**

Section Two
Generalists

Straw Church Speed Shop
602 Passaic St
Phillipsburg, NJ 08865
908-454-7487
E-mail:
strawchurch_ss@hotmail.com

accessories
engine swaps
parts

See full listing in **Section Two** under **car & parts locators**

Sugarbush Products Inc
117 Bristol Rd
Chalfont, PA 18914
215-822-1495; FAX: 215-997-2519
E-mail: wechsler@voicenet.com

carburetors

Mail order and open shop. Monday-Friday 8 am to 5 pm. NOS and used carburetors bought and sold. Deal in vintage carburetors only.

carpets

All Seams Fine
23 Union St
Waterbury, VT 05676
800-244-7326 (SEAM)
802-244-8843

interior
restorations

See full listing in **Section Two** under **upholstery**

Custom Interiors
PO Box 51174
Indian Orchard, MA 01151
800-423-6053; FAX: 413-589-9178

carpets
headliners
upholstery

See full listing in **Section Two** under **upholstery**

Firewall Insulators & Quiet Ride Solutions
6333 Pacific Ave, Ste 523
Stockton, CA 95207
209-477-4840; FAX: 209-477-0918
E-mail: timcox@gotnet.net

auto insulation
firewall insulators
gloveboxes
sound deadening

See full listing in **Section Two** under **upholstery**

Highway Classics
949 N Cataract Ave, Unit J
San Dimas, CA 91773
909-592-8819; FAX: 909-592-4239
E-mail: donnelson@earthlink.net

parts

See full listing in **Section One** under **Ford 1954-up**

Dave Knittel Upholstery
850 E Teton #7
Tucson, AZ 85706
PH/FAX: 520-746-1588

interiors
tops
upholstery

See full listing in **Section Two** under **upholstery**

Land Cruiser Solutions Inc
20 Thornell Rd
Newton, NH 03858
603-382-3555; FAX: 603-378-0431
E-mail: twbii@aol.com

accessories
services

See full listing in **Section One** under **Toyota**

Linearossa International Inc
3931 SW 47th Ave
Ft Lauderdale, FL 33314
954-327-9888; FAX: 954-791-6555

parts

See full listing in **Section One** under **Fiat**

Nanco Marketing Agency Inc
PO Box 97
Leominster, MA 01453
800-545-8547; FAX: 508-534-0677

automotive
carpeting

Automotive carpeting, preformed automotive carpeting, most models, many colors. Also carpeting sold by the yard, Rt 66 apparel, tote bags, pocket books, pillows, etc.

National Parts Depot
3101 SW 40th Blvd
Gainesville, FL 32608
800-874-7595 toll-free 24 hours
352-378-2473 local

accessories
restoration parts

See full listing in **Section Two** under **comprehensive parts**

Newport Upholstery Source
250 H St, Unit 8110
Blaine, WA 98231
604-990-0346; FAX: 604-990-9988

carpets
tops
upholstery

See full listing in **Section Two** under **upholstery**

Performance Automotive Inc
1696 New London Tpke
PO Box 10
Glastonbury, CT 06033
860-633-7868; FAX: 860-657-9110

accessories
car care

See full listing in **Section Two** under **car care products**

Raybuck Autobody Parts
RD 4, Box 170
Punxsutawney, PA 15767
814-938-5248; FAX: 814-938-4250

body parts

See full listing in **Section Two** under **body parts**

Sailorette's Nautical Nook
451 Davy Ln
Wilmington, IL 60481
815-476-1644; FAX: 815-476-2524

covers
interiors

See full listing in **Section Two** under **upholstery**

Tamraz's Parts Discount Warehouse
10022 S Bode Rd
Plainfield, IL 60544
630-904-4500; FAX: 630-904-2329

carpeting
upholstery
weatherstripping

See full listing in **Section One** under **Chevelle/Camaro**

Thermax Inc
5385 Alpha Ave
Reno, NV 89506
800-247-7177; FAX: 702-972-4809

interior detailing

See full listing in **Section Two** under **car care products**

John J Waluk
31 Squirrel Ln
Levittown, NY 11756
516-796-2984; FAX: 516-796-5423
E-mail: bb70@msn.com

flocking

See full listing in **Section Two** under **special services**

castings

Air Flow Research
10490 Ilex Ave
Pacoima, CA 91331
818-890-0616; FAX: 818-890-0490

cylinder heads

See full listing in **Section One** under **Chevrolet**

Alamillo Patterns
RR 2, Box 98 G
Rio Grande City, TX 78582
956-488-1021; FAX: 956-488-2161

castings
machining
patterns

Both mail order and open shop. Monday-Saturday 7 am to 7 pm. Castings, patterns and machining. Alamillo Patterns has the manpower and technology necessary to meet your requirements on almost any kind of casting up to 500# on the following alloys: cast iron, ductile iron, aluminum, bronze and steel. Also have complete support of our pattern shop insuring a high quality product.

ASC&P International
PO Box 255
Uwchland, PA 19480
610-458-8395; FAX: 610-458-8735

custom molding
fiberglass
plastic

See full listing in **Section Two** under **fiberglass parts**

Dwight H Bennett
1330 Ximeno Ave
Long Beach, CA 90804
PH/FAX: 562-498-6488

emblem repair
hardware repair
mascot repair
plaque repair

See full listing in **Section Two** under **radiator emblems & mascots**

Cast Aluminum Repair
1520 Marshall Ln
Conyers, GA 30094
770-929-1363
E-mail: heliarctig@aol.com

repair

Mail order and open shop. Tuesday-Friday 7 pm to 10 pm, Saturday 9 am to 5 pm. Cast aluminum repair.

Casting Salvage Technologies
26 Potomac Creek Dr
Falmouth, VA 22405
800-833-8814; FAX: 540-659-9453

repairs

Mail order and open shop. Monday-Saturday 8 am to 5 pm. Repairing castings, motor blocks and cylinder heads.

Chevi Shop Custom Casting
338 Main Ave
Box 75
Milledgeville, IL 61051
815-225-7565; FAX: 815-225-7616

custom castings
parts

See full listing in **Section One** under **Chevrolet**

Emblemagic Co
PO Box 420
Grand River, OH 44045-0420
440-209-0792
E-mail: arborhil@aol.com

decorative
emblems
plastic insert
emblems

See full listing in **Section Two** under **grille emblem badges**

Errol's Steam Works
3123 Baird Rd
North Vancouver, BC Canada V7K 2G5
PH/FAX: 604-985-9494
E-mail: steamworks@idmail.com

castings
engines
parts

See full listing in **Section One** under **Locomobile**

Excelsweld USA/Cylinder Head Specialist
1231 16th Ave
Oakland, CA 94606
800-743-4323; FAX: 510-534-1107

welding

See full listing in **Section Two** under **machine work**

Fini-Finish Metal Finishing
24657 Mound Rd
Warren, MI 48091
810-758-0050; FAX: 810-758-0054

plating
polishing
pot metal repair

See full listing in **Section Two** under **plating & polishing**

Harter Industries Inc
PO Box 502
Holmdel, NJ 07733
732-566-7055; FAX: 732-566-6977
E-mail: harter101@aol.com

parts
restoration

See full listing in **Section Two** under **comprehensive parts**

Model Engineering
Gene or Jeff Sanders
3284 S Main St
Akron, OH 44329
330-644-3450; FAX: 330-644-0088

new parts casting

Casting new parts from drawings or the original part. Aluminum, bronze, iron. Machine shop and pattern shop services.

Motor Foundry & Tooling Inc
7382 Doniphan Dr
Canutillo, TX 79835-6601
915-877-3343; FAX: 915-877-7071

brake drums
castings
exhaust manifolds
water pumps

See full listing in **Section One** under **Packard**

North GA Patterns
Rt 2 Box 2154
Oak Valley Rd
Toccoa, GA 30577
706-886-0183; FAX: 706-886-5483

castings
patterns

Broken or beyond repair? Engine blocks, heads, manifolds, brake drums, any cast part large or small. Can make patterns for parts and get new castings in any type metal.

O'Brien Truckers
5 Perry Hill
North Grafton, MA 01536-1532
508-839-3033; FAX: 508-839-9490
E-mail: obt@ziplink.net

accessories
belt buckles
plaques
valve covers

See full listing in **Section Two** under **plaques**

Richardson Restorations
1861 W Woodward Ave
Tulare, CA 93274
559-688-5002

custom work
repairs
restoration

See full listing in **Section Two** under **restoration shops**

chassis parts

60 Chev Sam
2912 Wright Rd
Hamptonville, NC 27020
336-468-1745

parts

See full listing in **Section One** under **Chevrolet**

Ace Antique Auto Restoration
65 S Service Rd
Plainview, NY 11803
516-752-6065; FAX: 516-752-1484

air conditioning
body rebuilding
restoration
wiring harnesses

See full listing in **Section Two** under **restoration shops**

Action Performance Inc — accessories
1619 Lakeland Ave
Bohemia, NY 11716
516-244-7100; FAX: 516-244-7172

See full listing in **Section Two** under **accessories**

Anderson Automotive — cars / parts
1604 E Busch Blvd
Tampa, FL 33612
813-932-4611; FAX: 813-932-5025

See full listing in **Section One** under **Oldsmobile**

Antique Auto Parts Cellar — brake/chassis/engine parts / fuel pumps/kits / gaskets / water pumps
PO Box 3
6 Chauncy St
South Weymouth, MA 02190
781-335-1579; FAX: 781-335-1925

See full listing in **Section Two** under **comprehensive parts**

Atlantic Enterprises — steering assemblies
221 Strand Industrial Dr
Little River, SC 29566
843-399-7565; FAX: 843-399-4600
E-mail: steering@atlantic-ent.com

Mail order and open shop. Monday-Friday 8 am to 5 pm. Specializing in rebuilt rack and pinion steering assemblies for Jaguar, Aston Martin, Jensen, Triumph, Rover, Rolls-Royce, Bentley. Web site: atlantic-ent.com

Authentic Automotive — power brakes / power steering
529 Buttercup Trail
Mesquite, TX 75149
972-289-6373; FAX: 972-289-4303

See full listing in **Section One** under **Chevrolet**

Briz Bumpers — bumpers
8002 NE Hwy 99, #260
Vancouver, WA 98665
360-573-8628

Mail order only. Manufacture, retail, wholesale ribbed alloy bumpers for street rods, customs and trucks. Also bumper brackets, license plate guards, air scoops for brake backing plates and hubcaps for Kelsey-Hayes wheels.

Bronx Automotive — parts
501 Tiffany St
Bronx, NY 10474
718-589-2979

See full listing in **Section Two** under **ignition parts**

Bryant's Antique Auto Parts — appraisals / chassis/engine parts / sheetmetal / wiring harnesses
851 Western Ave
Hampden, ME 04444
207-862-4019

See full listing in **Section One** under **Ford 1903-1931**

Car-Line Manufacturing & Distribution Inc — chassis parts / engine parts / sheetmetal
1250 Gulf St, PO Box 1192
Beaumont, TX 77701
409-833-9757; FAX: 409-835-2468

See full listing in **Section Two** under **sheetmetal**

Chassis Engineering Inc — brakes / chassis parts / suspension parts
119 N 2nd St, Box 70
West Branch, IA 52358
319-643-2645; FAX: 319-643-2801

Mail order only. Monday-Friday 8 am to 4:30 pm. Chassis Engineering Inc has manufactured chassis components for street rods for over 30 years. Suspensions, brakes, engine and transmission mounting kits. Frames, springs and many related

chassis parts for 1928-1948 Fords, 1935-1954 Chevrolets, 1933-1934 Dodge and Plymouths.

Collector's Auto Supply — parts
528 Appian Way
Coquitlam, BC Canada V3J 2A5
888-772-7848; FAX: 604-931-4450
E-mail: car@bc.sympatico.ca

See full listing in **Section Two** under **comprehensive parts**

CPR — new parts / reproduction parts / used parts
431 S Sierra Way
San Bernardino, CA 92408
909-884-6980; FAX: 909-884-7872

See full listing in **Section One** under **Pontiac**

CT Model A Parts & Service — parts / restorations / service
75 Prospect Ave
West Hartford, CT 06106
860-233-1928; FAX: 860-233-1926
E-mail: ctmap@aol.com

See full listing in **Section One** under **Ford 1903-1931**

Dakota Studebaker Parts — parts
RR 1, Box 103A
Armour, SD 57313
605-724-2527

See full listing in **Section One** under **Studebaker**

Dependable RV & Auto Service — parts / restoration / service
2619 Rt 11 N
Lafayette, NY 13084
315-677-5336; FAX: 315-677-5258

See full listing in **Section Two** under **service shops**

Early Ford V8 Sales Inc — parts
Curtis Industrial Park, Bldg 37
831 Rt 67
Ballston Spa, NY 12020
518-884-2825; FAX: 518-884-2633
E-mail: earlyford@prodigy.net

See full listing in **Section One** under **Ford 1932-1953**

Eckler's Quality Parts & Accessories for Corvettes — accessories / parts
PO Box 5637
Titusville, FL 32783
800-327-4868; FAX: 407-383-2059
E-mail: ecklers@ecklers.com

See full listing in **Section One** under **Corvette**

Florida Caliper Manufacturers Inc — brake systems / chassis parts / suspension parts
1450 SW 10th St #3
Delray Beach, FL 33444
561-272-5238

See full listing in **Section One** under **Corvette**

Guldstrand Engineering Inc — parts
11924 W Jefferson Blvd
Culver City, CA 90230
310-391-7108; FAX: 310-391-7424
E-mail: gss@guldstrand.com

See full listing in **Section One** under **Corvette**

Harter Industries Inc — parts / restoration
PO Box 502
Holmdel, NJ 07733
732-566-7055; FAX: 732-566-6977
E-mail: harter101@aol.com

See full listing in **Section Two** under **comprehensive parts**

Mike Hershenfeld
3011 Susan Rd
Bellmore, NY 11710
PH/FAX: 516-781-PART (7278)
E-mail: mikesmopar@juno.com

parts

See full listing in **Section One** under **Mopar**

Hoffman Automotive Distributor
US Hwy #1, Box 818
Hilliard, FL 32046
904-845-4421

parts

See full listing in **Section Two** under **body parts**

Holcombe Cadillac Parts
2933 Century Ln
Bensalem, PA 19020
215-245-4560; FAX: 215-633-9916

parts

See full listing in **Section One** under **Cadillac/LaSalle**

Jackson's Oldtime Parts
4502 Grand Ave
Duluth, MN 55807
218-624-5791, 888-399-7278
E-mail: sales@oldtimeparts.com

parts

See full listing in **Section Two** under **engine parts**

JECC Inc
PO Box 616
West Paterson, NJ 07424
973-890-9682; FAX: 973-812-2724

chassis parts
gaskets
transmissions

See full listing in **Section One** under **Buick/McLaughlin**

K&W Kollectibles
220 Industrial Pkwy S #6
Aurora, ON Canada L4G 3V6
416-410-7741; FAX: 905-727-5771
E-mail: kwkoll@sympatico.ca

parts
repair
restoration

See full listing in **Section One** under **Buick/McLaughlin**

Kenask Spring Co
307 Manhattan Ave
Jersey City, NJ 07307
201-653-4589

springs

See full listing in **Section Two** under **suspension parts**

Roger Kraus Racing
2896 Grove Way
Castro Valley, CA 94546
510-582-5031; FAX: 510-886-5605

shocks
tires
wheels

See full listing in **Section Two** under **tires**

Marcel's Corvette Parts
15100 Lee Rd #101
Humble, TX 77396
800-546-2111 order line
281-441-2111 info line
FAX: 281-441-3057

parts

See full listing in **Section One** under **Corvette**

David Martin
Box 61
Roosevelt, TX 76874
915-446-4439

parts

See full listing in **Section One** under **Chrysler**

McDonald Obsolete Parts Company
RR 3, Box 94
Rockport, IN 47635
812-359-4965; FAX: 812-359-5555
E-mail: mcdonald@psci.net

body parts
chassis parts

See full listing in **Section One** under **Ford 1954-up**

Donald McKinsey
PO Box 94H
Wilkinson, IN 46186
765-785-6284

fuel pumps
ignition parts
literature
spark plugs

See full listing in **Section Two** under **ignition parts**

Michael's Auto Parts
5875 NW Kaiser Rd
Portland, OR 97229
503-690-7750; FAX: 503-690-7735

used Mercedes
parts only

See full listing in **Section Five** under **Oregon**

MRL Automotive
PO Box 117230
Carrollton, TX 75011-7230
972-394-3489; FAX: 800-210-0200

rubber lubricants

See full listing in **Section Two** under **lubricants**

National Parts Depot
3101 SW 40th Blvd
Gainesville, FL 32608
800-874-7595 toll-free 24 hours
352-378-2473 local

accessories
restoration parts

See full listing in **Section Two** under **comprehensive parts**

Northern Auto Parts Warehouse Inc
PO Box 3147
Sioux City, IA 51102
800-831-0884; FAX: 712-258-0088

parts

See full listing in **Section Two** under **engine parts**

Northwestern Auto Supply Inc
1101 S Division
Grand Rapids, MI 49507
616-241-1714, 800-704-1078
FAX: 616-241-0924

parts

See full listing in **Section Two** under **engine parts**

Performance Coatings
9768 Feagin Rd
Jonesboro, GA 30236
770-478-2775; FAX: 770-478-1926

ceramic coatings
engine parts
suspension parts

See full listing in **Section Two** under **exhaust systems**

Power Steering Services Inc
2347 E Kearney St
Springfield, MO 65803
417-864-6676; FAX: 417-864-7103
E-mail: cwoyner@aol.com

pumps
rack & pinion
steering gearboxes

See full listing in **Section Two** under **special services**

Hemmings' Vintage Auto Almanac©   Fourteenth Edition

Section Two
Generalists

Quanta Restoration and Performance Products	fan belts gas tanks
743 Telegraph Rd Rising Sun, MD 21911-1810 800-235-8788, 410-658-5700 FAX: 410-658-5758 E-mail: quanta@quantaproducts.com	

Mail order and retail store. Exact reproduction Corvette gas tanks including OL Anderson logo, new gas tanks for 1955 and newer vehicles, gas tank straps, AC Delco sending units, GM licensed restoration fan belts, body panels, OE style wheels, steel and aluminum radiators, Holley carburetors and performance products, fuel pumps, chassis detailing products, specialty paints, frame stencils, Holley carburetor restoration, driveshaft and halfshaft restoration and more. Call or visit our showroom. Web site: www.quantaproducts.com

RARE Corvettes	cars parts
Joe Calcagno Box 1080 Soquel, CA 95073 831-475-4442; FAX: 831-475-1115	

See full listing in **Section One** under **Corvette**

William H Robenolt	front suspension parts
5121 S Bridget Point Floral City, FL 34436 352-344-2007	

See full listing in **Section Two** under **suspension parts**

Rochester Clutch & Brake Co	brakes clutches
35 Niagara St Rochester, NY 14605 716-232-2579; FAX: 716-232-3279	

See full listing in **Section Two** under **brakes**

Rolling Steel Body Parts	body parts
7320 Martingale Dr Chesterland, OH 44026-2007 888-765-5460; FAX: 440-729-7658 E-mail: rollingsteel@hotmail.com	

See full listing in **Section Two** under **body parts**

Joe Smith Ford & Hot Rod Parts	parts service
2140 Canton Rd, Unit C Marietta, GA 30066 800-235-4013, 770-426-9850 FAX: 770-426-9854 E-mail: hank@joesmithauto.com	

See full listing in **Section One** under **Ford 1932-1953**

Smith & Jones Distributing Company Inc	parts
1 Biloxi Square West Columbia, SC 29170 803-822-8500; FAX: 803-822-8477	

See full listing in **Section One** under **Ford 1903-1931**

Star Quality	parts
1 Alley Rd La Grangeville, NY 12540 800-782-7199; FAX: 914-223-5394 E-mail: sq@mhv.net	

See full listing in **Section One** under **Mercedes-Benz**

Bill Thomsen	salvage yard
1118 Wooded Acres Ln Moneta, VA 24121 540-297-1200	

See full listing in **Section Five** under **Virginia**

Tom Vagnini	used parts
58 Anthony Rd, RR 3 Pittsfield, MA 01201 413-698-2526	

See full listing in **Section One** under **Packard**

Vehicle Spring Service	springs suspensions
7582 Industrial Way Stanton, CA 90680 714-379-8077; FAX: 714-897-1892	

See full listing in **Section Two** under **suspension parts**

Vintage Car Corral	parts toys
1401 NW 53rd Ave PO Box 384 Gainesville, FL 32602 PH/FAX: 352-376-0660	

See full listing in **Section Two** under **comprehensive parts**

Wallace Walmsley	parts
4732 Bancroft St, #7 San Diego, CA 92116 619-283-3063	

See full listing in **Section One** under **Packard**

Wild Bill's Corvette & Hi-Performance Center Inc	parts rebuilding service
446 Dedham St Wrentham, MA 02093 508-384-7373; FAX: 508-384-9366 E-mail: wildbillscorvette@worldnet.att.net	

See full listing in **Section One** under **Corvette**

clutches

Automotive Friction	brakes clutches water pumps
4621 SE 27th Ave Portland, OR 97202 503-234-0606; FAX: 503-234-1026	

Mail order and open shop. Monday-Friday 8 am to 5 pm PST. Rebuilding clutches, brakes and water pumps.

Automotive Restorations Inc	clutch rebuilding mechanical services restorations
Stephen Babinsky 4 Center St Bernardsville, NJ 07924 908-766-6688; FAX: 908-766-6684 E-mail: autorestnj@aol.com	

See full listing in **Section Two** under **restoration shops**

Dave Bean Engineering	parts
636 E St Charles St SR3H San Andreas, CA 95249 209-754-5802; FAX: 209-754-5177 E-mail: admin@davebean.com	

See full listing in **Section One** under **Lotus**

Fort Wayne Clutch & Driveline	axles axleshafts clutches driveshafts
2424 Goshen Rd Fort Wayne, IN 46808 219-484-8505; FAX: 219-484-8605 E-mail: coca@mail.fwi.com	

Mail order and open shop. Monday-Friday 8 am to 5 pm, Saturday 8:30 am to 12:30 pm. Wide variety of clutches, clutch parts, driveshafts, driveshaft parts, axleshafts and axleshaft parts. Specialize in antiques, obsolete, foreign and just plain hard to find parts. Carry a wide stock of parts for everything from lawn mowers to earth movers. A staff of professionals with over 100 years' experience. Large portion of our business is done through mail order. Ship worldwide. If we do not stock the part you are looking for, we can usually make it. Web site: www.fortwayneclutch.com

National Parts Depot	accessories restoration parts
3101 SW 40th Blvd Gainesville, FL 32608 800-874-7595 toll-free 24 hours 352-378-2473 local	

See full listing in **Section Two** under **comprehensive parts**

Orion Motors European Parts Inc	parts
10722 Jones Rd Houston, TX 77065 800-736-6410, 281-894-1982 FAX: 281-849-1997 E-mail: orion-yugo@yugoparts.com	

See full listing in **Section One** under **Alfa Romeo**

coachbuilders & designers

Ashton Keynes Vintage Restorations Ltd	coachbuilding restoration
A Keith Bowley Ashton Keynes, Swindon Wilshire England 01285-861-288; FAX: 01285-860-604	

See full listing in **Section One** under **Rolls-Royce/Bentley**

AutoFashions Restoration & Creations	auto parts auto sales handcrafts restoration rubber ink stamps
2209-B Hamlets Chapel Rd Pittsboro, NC 27312 PH/FAX: 919-542-5566 send automatically E-mail: autofashions@mindspring.com	

See full listing in **Section Two** under **restoration shops**

Automotive Restorations Inc	body fabrication mechanical painting restorations upholstery woodwork
Kent S Bain 1785 Barnum Ave Stratford, CT 06614 203-377-6745; FAX: 203-386-0486 E-mail: carbain@compuserve.com	

See full listing in **Section Two** under **restoration shops**

Backyard Buddy Corp	automotive lift
1818 N Main St PO Box 5104 Niles, OH 44446 800-837-9353, 330-544-9372 FAX: 330-544-9311	

See full listing in **Section Two** under **accessories**

Bonnets Up	restoration
5736 Spring St Clinton, MD 20735 301-297-4759	

Mail order and open shop by appointment only. Monday-Saturday 7 am to 3 pm. Ron Naida, owner, in business over 20 years. Provide numerous services, SU carb rebuilding to ground-up restorations on British, German and Italian marques. Our facilities consist of custom metal fabrication, woodworking equipment, specialized assembly jigs. Full bodywork and paint facilities, and the latest in welding technology for accomplishing difficult jobs. Handle any form of servicing to your specs. Wood frame construction to factory specs, sheetmetal replacement

panels and complete frame reskinning, fabrication of firewalls, toolboxes, fender valances, quarter/rear panels, doors/louvers. Mechanical services, complete engine rebuilding.

The Classic Motorist	automotive books literature motoring accessories
PO Box 363 Rotterdam Junction, NY 12150-0363	

See full listing in **Section Two** under **automobilia**

Deters Restorations	restoration
6205 Swiss Garden Rd Temperance, MI 48182-1020 734-847-1820	

See full listing in **Section Two** under **restoration shops**

Fairlane Automotive Specialties	fiberglass bodies parts
210 E Walker St St Johns, MI 48879 517-224-6460	

See full listing in **Section One** under **Ford 1932-1953**

Jack Juratovic	artwork magazine
819 Absequami Trail Lake Orion, MI 48362 PH/FAX: 248-814-0627	

See full listing in **Section Two** under **artwork**

Marshall Antique & Classic Restorations	coolant additives restoration services
3714 Old Philadelphia Pike Bethlehem, PA 18015 610-868-7765; FAX: 610-868-7529	

See full listing in **Section One** under **Rolls-Royce/Bentley**

New Era Motors	restoration
11611 NE 50th Ave, Unit 6 Vancouver, WA 98686 360-573-8788	

See full listing in **Section Two** under **woodwork**

Odyssey Restorations Inc	parts restoration
8080 Central Ave NE Spring Lake Park, MN 55432 612-786-1518; FAX: 612-786-1524	

See full listing in **Section Two** under **restoration shops**

Ray's Upholstering	partial/total restoration
600 N St Frances Cabrini Ave Scranton, PA 18504 800-296-RAYS; FAX: 717-963-0415	

See full listing in **Section Two** under **restoration shops**

Specialty Power Window	power window kits windshield wiper kit
2087 Collier Rd, Forsyth, GA 31029 800-634-9801; FAX: 912-994-3124	

See full listing in **Section Two** under **street rods**

Thompson Hill Metalcraft	metal forming panel beating welding
23 Thompson Hill Rd Berwick, ME 03901 207-698-5756 E-mail: wpeach@thompsonhill.com	

See full listing in **Section Two** under **sheetmetal**

The Woodie Works	woodworking
245 VT Rt 7A Arlington, VT 05250 PH/FAX: 802-375-9305 E-mail: dkwoodie@vermontel.com	

See full listing in **Section Two** under **woodwork**

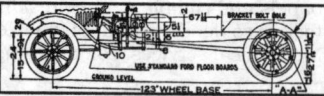

comprehensive parts

Accessoryland Truckin' Supplies
10723 Rt 61 S
Dubuque, IA 52003
319-556-5482; FAX: 319-556-9087

accessories foglights/spotlights mounting brackets parts

See full listing in **Section One** under **Chevrolet**

ADP Hollander
14800 28th Ave N #190
Plymouth, MN 55447
800-761-9266; FAX: 800-825-1124
E-mail: hollander@autonet.net

interchange info manuals

See full listing in **Section Two** under **car & parts locators**

All British Car Parts Inc
2847 Moores Rd
Baldwin, MD 21013
410-692-9572; FAX: 410-692-5654

parts

See full listing in **Section Two** under **electrical systems**

American Performance Products
675 S Industry Rd
Cocoa, FL 32926
407-632-8299; FAX: 407-632-5119
E-mail: amc@oldcarparts.com

parts

See full listing in **Section One** under **AMC**

Antique Auto Parts
PO Box 64
60 View Dr
Elkview, WV 25071
304-965-1821

parts parts cars

Mail order and open shop. Monday-Friday 9 am to dusk, Saturday 9 am to 5 pm. Antique parts for all makes and models, plus 120 parts cars from 1935-1972. Parting out 100 cars and trucks from 1935-1972. Over 25 years in business.

Antique Auto Parts Cellar
PO Box 3
6 Chauncy St
South Weymouth, MA 02190
781-335-1579; FAX: 781-335-1925

brake/chassis/ engine parts fuel pumps/kits gaskets water pumps

Mail order and open shop. Monday-Friday 9 am to 5 pm. Supply new, new old stock and our own reproduction quality mechanical parts for US cars and trucks from 1910-1991. Revulcanizing motor mounts (100+ different ones, plus thousands of NOS), fuel pumps and kits, water pumps, motor parts: pistons, rings, valves, guides, tappets, timing components (more than 20 of our own manufacture), gaskets (more than 200 cut on our own dies); bearings and seals; brake and suspension parts; rebuilding services on starters, generators, tank senders, distributors, vacuum advances, clutches. Providing the hobby with guaranteed parts and services since 1975.

See our ad on this page

Atlantic British Ltd
Halfmoon Light Industrial Park
6 Badertscher Dr
Clifton Park, NY 12065
800-533-2210; FAX: 518-664-6641
E-mail: ab@roverparts.com

accessories parts

See full listing in **Section One** under **Rover/Land Rover**

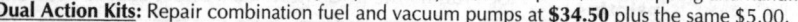

Auto Parts Exchange PO Box 736 Reading, PA 19603 610-372-2813	**NORS parts NOS parts rebuilt parts used parts**

See full listing in **Section One** under **Lincoln**

Blaser's Auto, Nash, Rambler, AMC 3200 48th Ave Moline, IL 61265-6453 309-764-3571; FAX: 309-764-1155 E-mail: blazauto@sprynet.com	**NOS parts**

See full listing in **Section One** under **AMC**

Cheyenne Pickup Parts Box 959 Noble, OK 73068 405-872-3399; FAX: 405-872-0385	**body panels bumpers carpet weatherstripping**

See full listing in **Section Two** under **trucks & tractors**

Chris' Parts Cars 1409 Rt 179 Lambertville, NJ 08530-3413 609-397-9045	**cars parts**

Cars seen by appointment only. Complete cars from 1940s, 1950s and 1960s, many are restorable, over 200 parts cars. Would rather sell complete cars, not parts, on most. Prices range from $75-$475. I am retired, these are cars collected through my auto body repair business of thirty-five years. It is very hard to reach me by phone, better to write and SASE for an answer.

Classic Cars & Parts Division of AKV Auto Mike Chmilarski 622 Rt 109 Lindenhurst, NY 11757 516-888-3914	**car dealer parts**

See full listing in **Section Two** under **car dealers**

Classic Chevy International PO Box 607188 Orlando, FL 32860-7188 800-456-1957, 407-299-1957 FAX: 407-299-3341 E-mail: cciworld@aol.com	**modified parts repro parts used parts**

See full listing in **Section One** under **Chevrolet**

Collector's Auto Supply 528 Appian Way Coquitlam, BC Canada V3J 2A5 888-772-7848; FAX: 604-931-4450 E-mail: car@bc.sympatico.ca	**parts**

New and used mechanical, braking, chassis, body and rubber parts for vehicles to 1909. Electrical and tune-up items a specialty. Free all makes illustrated tune-up parts catalogues for 1974 and earlier by mail or fax. Specify ignition system manufacturer: Asian (to 1960); Autolite (to mid-1920s); Delco-Remy (to mid-1920s); Bosch (to mid-1950s); Ducellier (to mid-1950s); Lucas (to mid-1930s); Marelli (to mid-1950s); SEV (to mid-1950s) and Ford (to 1909). No retail display. Second location: 1733 H St #330-793, Blaine, WA 98230-5107. Web site: www3.bc.sympatico.ca/car/

Corvette Specialties of MD Inc 1912 Liberty Rd Eldersburg, MD 21784 410-795-3180; FAX: 410-795-3247	**parts restoration service**

See full listing in **Section One** under **Corvette**

Coventry West Inc 5936-A Peachtree Rd Atlanta, GA 30341 800-331-2193 toll-free 770-451-3839 Atlanta FAX: 770-451-7561	**assemblies Jaguar parts**

See full listing in **Section One** under **Jaguar**

Joe Curto Inc 22-09 126th St College Point, NY 11356 718-762-SUSU FAX: 718-762-6287 (h)	**English carburetors English parts repairs**

Mail order and open shop. Monday-Friday 9 am to 6:30 pm EST. Large stocks of SU and British Stromberg parts, new and used. Comprehensive rebuilding service, as well as a knowledgeable staff to serve you. 25 years' in the British car trade, well versed in the ins and outs of Lucas, Girling and Lockheed systems. Offer full rebuilding of water pumps, starters, generators, wiper motors, calipers, servos. Also do repairs and restorations on your vehicle.

D&M Corvette Specialists Ltd 1804 Ogden Ave Downers Grove, IL 60515 630-968-0031; FAX: 630-968-0465	**parts restoration sales service**

See full listing in **Section One** under **Corvette**

Davies Corvette 7141 US Hwy 19 New Port Richey, FL 34653 727-842-8000, 800-236-2383 FAX: 727-846-8216 E-mail: davies@corvetteparts.com	**accessories parts**

See full listing in **Section One** under **Corvette**

Daytona Turbo Action Camshafts 1109 N US #1 PO Box 5094 Ormond Beach, FL 32175 888-RARE-CAM, 800-505-CAMS 904-676-7478; FAX: 904-258-1582 E-mail: info@camshafts.com	**camshafts engine parts**

See full listing in **Section Two** under **bearings**

Don's Antique Auto Parts 37337 Niles Blvd Fremont, CA 94536 415-792-4390	**new parts used parts**

Mail order and open shop. Monday-Saturday 9:30 am to 6 pm. Deal in American parts up to 1954 for most cars and trucks. Specialize in 1936-1948 Lincoln Zephyrs and Continentals. New, used and rebuilt parts.

Bob Drake Reproductions Inc 1819 NW Washington Blvd Grants Pass, OR 97526 800-221-3673; FAX: 541-474-0099 E-mail: bobdrake@bobdrake.com	**repro parts**

See full listing in **Section One** under **Ford 1932-1953**

Eckler's Quality Parts & Accessories for Corvettes PO Box 5637 Titusville, FL 32783 800-327-4868; FAX: 407-383-2059 E-mail: ecklers@ecklers.com	**accessories parts**

See full listing in **Section One** under **Corvette**

**Section Two
Generalists**

Fire-Aro Restoration Parts Supply Co
9251 Yonge St Unit 8, Ste 108
Richmond Hill, ON Canada L4C 9T3
888-249-4939 toll-free
905-881-7337; FAX: 905-881-2445

accessories
parts

See full listing in **Section One** under **Chevelle/Camaro**

For Ramblers Only
2324 SE 34th Ave
Portland, OR 97214
503-232-0497
E-mail: ramblers@teleport.com

accessories
parts

See full listing in **Section One** under **AMC**

J Giles Automotive
703 Morgan Ave
Pascagoula, MS 39567-2116
228-769-1012; FAX: 228-769-8904
E-mail: jgauto@datasync.com

car & parts locator
exporter

See full listing in **Section Two** under **car & parts locators**

Gowen Auto Parts
Rt 2, PO Box 249
Coffeyville, KS 67337
316-251-4237

parts

Mail order and open shop. Antique and classic parts, 1910s-1970s. Mostly engine, brake and suspension parts. Also classic rebuilt short blocks.

Harter Industries Inc
PO Box 502
Holmdel, NJ 07733
732-566-7055; FAX: 732-566-6977
E-mail: harter101@aol.com

parts
restoration

Mail order and shop open by appointment only. Restoration and replacement of almost any cast, machined, small formed sheetmetal or wood part for antique and classic cars. "We work from your old part, a borrowed part or a carefully dimensioned sketch or photograph." Service for car owners and restorers. Call or write to help solve hard-to-find parts problems.

Wayne Hood
228 Revell Rd
Grenada, MS 38901
601-227-8426

NORS parts
NOS parts

Mail order and open shop. Monday-Saturday 8 am to 6 pm. NOS, NORS parts for cars and trucks, 1930s-1960s. Specialize in fair prices and quick service. Have mostly mechanical parts and some lenses for all makes, 1930s-1960s.

IMCADO Manufacturing Co
50 Winthrop Ave
PO Box 87
Umatilla, FL 32784-0087
352-669-3308

leather equipment

Mail order and open shop. Monday-Friday 9 am to 5 pm. Complete line of leather equipment for any motorcar ever built from 1896-on. Hood belts, top straps, crank holsters, fan belts, axle straps, gaiters, joint boots, etc. Original replacement authenticated and approved, prime grade cowhide with select hardware. 12-month warranty.

Indian Adventures Inc
121 South St
PO Box 206
Foxboro, MA 02035
508-359-4660; FAX: 508-359-5435

parts

Authorized retailers only. Specialty and reproduction parts for 1960s and 1970s Pontiacs including engine cradles, throttle shafts, license pockets, frame repair kits, rear end dollies, carburetor rebuild kits and other restoration helpers.

Interesting Parts Inc
Paul TerHorst
27526 N Owens Rd
Mundelein, IL 60060
PH/FAX: 847-949-1030

appraisals
gaskets
parts
storage
transport

Mail order and open shop by appointment only. Local transportation and storage service. Classic parts especially for Packard, Cadillac, Auburn, etc. Also reproduction gaskets and appraisal services.

Jess Auto Supply Co
119 Market
Wilmington, DE 19801
302-654-6021

parts

Mail order and open shop. Monday-Friday 9 am to 6 pm, Saturday 9 am to 3 pm, Sunday 12 noon to 3 pm. Auto parts store since 1919. Parts for cars covering 1940-1990. No body parts.

Joyce's Model A & T Parts
PO Box 70
Manchaca, TX 78652-0070
512-282-1196

new parts
NOS parts
rebuilt parts

See full listing in **Section One** under **Ford 1903-1931**

Kanter Auto Products
76 Monroe St
Boonton, NJ 07005
800-526-1096, 201-334-9575
FAX: 201-334-5423

car cover
carpets
parts

Monday-Friday 8:30 am to 8 pm, Saturday 9 am to 2 pm. Helping you keep fun on the American road since 1960. New 76 page catalog, featuring front end kits, brakes, engine parts, interior/exterior trim, carpet sets, exhaust, fuel and water pumps, suspension parts, weatherstripping, electrical parts, books and manuals, transmission parts, carburetors and more for 1930-1990 domestic cars and trucks. Web site: www.kanter.com

Lee's Kustom Auto & Street Rods
RR 3 Box 3061A
Rome, PA 18837
570-247-2326
E-mail: lka41@epix.net

accessories
parts
restoration

See full listing in **Section Two** under **street rods**

Leo R Lindquist
1851 US Hwy 14
Balaton, MN 56115-3200
PH/FAX: 507-734-2051

1950s Hemi parts
NORS parts
NOS parts

See full listing in **Section One** under **Mopar**

M & T Manufacturing Co
30 Hopkins Lane
Peace Dale, RI 02883
401-789-0472; FAX: 401-789-5650
E-mail: sales@mtmfg.com

convertible
hold-down cables
wooden top bows

See full listing in **Section Two** under **woodwork**

Manchester Motor Car Co
319 Main St
Manchester, CT 06040
860-643-5874; FAX: 860-643-6190
E-mail: mmcollc@aol.com

automobilia
parts
petroliana
restorations

Mail order and open shop. Monday-Wednesday and Friday 9 am to 5 pm, Thursday 9 am to 9 pm, Saturday 9 am to 3 pm. Operate as a dealership for antique, classic and muscle American cars and light trucks. Supply NOS, NORS, used, new and reproduction parts, automobilia and petroliana, antique tools and toys and literature and manuals. Complete restoration facility, doing body and mechanical work as well as interior, tops and detailing. Also offer an extensive parts locator and vehicle locator service. Car clubs are invited to have meetings in our vintage shop. Web site: www.manchestermotorcarco.com

W L Wally Mansfield 214 N 13th St Wymore, NE 68466-1640 402-645-3546	**cars** **parts** **trucks**

Mail order and open shop by appointment only. Pre-war cars, trucks and parts. Specializing in Model T and A, NOS and good used parts. Also 1925-1948 Chevrolet, 1914-1948 Ford and 1920-1926 Dodge, all makes to 1950.

Mark Auto Co Inc Layton, NJ 07851 973-948-4157; FAX: 973-948-5458	**parts** **restoration** **supplies**

See full listing in **Section One** under **Ford 1903-1931**

The Maverick Connection 137 Valley Dr Ripley, WV 25271 PH/FAX: 304-372-7825	**literature** **parts**

See full listing in **Section One** under **Ford 1954-up**

Monroe Motorsports Inc 7138 Maddox Rd Lithonia, GA 30058 770-482-9219; FAX: 770-482-6690	**new/used parts** **rechroming**

See full listing in **Section One** under **Chevrolet**

Mustang Classics 3814 Walnut St Denver, CO 80205 303-295-3140	**parts** **restoration** **sales** **service**

See full listing in **Section One** under **Mustang**

National Chevy Assoc 947 Arcade Street St Paul, MN 55106 612-778-9522; FAX: 800-785-5354	**parts**

See full listing in **Section One** under **Chevrolet**

National Parts Depot 3101 SW 40th Blvd Gainesville, FL 32608 800-874-7595 toll-free 24 hours 352-378-2473 local	**accessories** **restoration parts**

Mail order and walk-in. 24 hours, 7 days per week, toll-free order lines. Walk-in hours: Monday-Friday 8 am to 9 pm, Saturday-Sunday 8 am to 5 pm. Additional locations: 12784 Currie Ct, Livonia, MI 48150, PH: 800-521-6104; 2330 Tipton Dr #800, Charlotte, NC 28206, PH: 800-368-6451; 1376 Walter St #1, Ventura, CA 93003, PH: 800-235-3445. Specializing in restoration parts and accessories for 1965-1973 Mustang, 1967-1981 Camaro, 1964-1972 Chevelle, El Camino, Malibu, 1955-1957 Thunderbird. Concours correct restoration parts. World's largest and fastest supplier. Following catalogs are available, free to restorers: 1964-1972 Chevelle, 1967-1981 Camaro, 1965-1973 Mustang, 1955-1957 T-Bird. For free catalog, call 352-378-9000, 24 hours, or visit our web site: www.npdlink.com

National Parts Locator Service 636 East 6th St # 81 Ogden, UT 84404-2415 801-627-7210	**parts locator**

See full listing in **Section Two** under **car & parts locators**

Obsolete Auto Parts Co PO Box 5, 143 Comleroy Rd Kurrajong, NSW 2758 Australia 61-2-45-731424 FAX: 61-2-45-732106	**parts** **parts locating** **service**

Mail order and open shop. Monday-Saturday 9 am to 5 pm. AJ Noonan, owner. 1900-1960s new and used parts for English, European and American vehicles. Largest varied range of items in southern hemisphere. Parts locating service. Many rare items in stock. Fast, efficient international service provided. Information sheet, $1 US.

Old Ford Parts 35 4th Ave N Algona, WA 98001 253-833-8494; FAX: 253-833-2190	**parts**

See full listing in **Section One** under **Ford 1932-1953**

Original Parts Group Inc 17892 Gothard St Huntington Beach, CA 92647 800-243-8355 US/Canada 714-841-5363; FAX: 714-847-8159	**accessories** **parts**

See full listing in **Section One** under **Pontiac**

Parts House 2912 Hunter St Fort Worth, TX 76112 817-451-2708 E-mail: theparts@flash.net	**accessories** **parts**

Mail, e-mail, telephone orders and open shop. Cars and light trucks: 1920-1975 suspension/steering; engine valves, valve train, lifters, pistons, gaskets, bearings, starters, generators, fuel pumps, water pumps; brake parts, drivetrain bearings and seals, 1949-1963 floor mats, trunk mats, car and truck seat covers; 1949-1961 reproduction and NOS sheetmetal, lenses. Auto and pickup parts, new and rebuilt. Specializing in Chevrolet pickup 1941-1946, 1947-1953, 1954, 1955-1959, 1960-1966 and 1967-1972 fenders, runningboards, grilles, beds, cabs, hoods, doors, other related sheetmetal.

The Parts Scout® Bodo Repenn Diagonalstrasse 18A D-20537 Hamburg Germany *49-40-21980130 FAX: *49-40-21980132	**parts** **parts locator**

Mail order only. Parts locator, worldwide supply of quality spare parts and accessories. Specializing in luxury and sports cars of all makes from 1920-1975, fast international service, 24 hour fax line.

Garth B Peterson 122 N Conklin Rd Veradale, WA 99037 509-926-4620 anytime	**accessories** **parts** **radios**

Tremendous supply of NOS/used Hudson, Essex, Terraplane, Dover, Nash, Rambler, Metropolitan, AMC parts, accessories and sheetmetal. Modern generation not hep to all manufacturers or their various cars. Also new/used parts and accessories for all 1930-1970 cars. Original car radios and hood ornaments for all cars. We try to do the impossible for you. SASE please.

Phelan Antique Auto Parts 73 Hillview St Hamilton Guelph, ON Canada L8S 2Z3 905-527-0002; FAX: 905-527-5929 E-mail: phelanantiqueauto@hwcn.org	**parts**

See full listing in **Section One** under **Ford 1903-1931**

R E Pierce — parts, restoration
47 Stone Rd
Wendell Depot, MA 01380
978-544-7442; FAX: 978-544-2978
E-mail: robin@billsgate.com

See full listing in **Section One** under **Volvo**

J Pinto — electric motors/relays/switches/solenoids repair
31 Spruce
HC 1, Box F7
Swiftwater, PA 18370
570-839-3441
E-mail: lectri@yahoo.com

See full listing in **Section Two** under **electrical systems**

Pre-Sixties Cars and Parts Ltd — appraisals, auto sales/locator, body repairs, parts
75 Victoria Rd
South Guelph, ON Canada N1E 5P7
800-364-7710; FAX: 519-766-4497

Mail order and open shop. Monday-Saturday 9 am to 6 pm. Central source for parts to fit North American cars, 1920s-1970s. Established 20 years. Auto locator service, flatbed service, auto appraisals, inspections, auto body repairs and refinishing, mechanical repairs and auto sales. Large and varied stock of parts. Buy and sell job lots of new or rebuilt parts.

Pro Motorcar Products Inc — car care products, gauges, paint thickness, sanding block, screw saver
22025 US 19 N
Clearwater, FL 33765
800-323-1090, 813-726-9225
FAX: 813-726-6587

New gauges for inspecting body and paint of collector cars. Manufacturer of innovative products for paint and body. Spot Rot® autobody gauge finds filler, hidden rust, collision damage, complete with used vehicle buying guide, $14.95. Pro Gauge® accurately measures paint thickness, avoid problems, $49. Multi-purpose PrepPen Glass Fiber Brush cleans rust, electrical contacts, guns, etc, $6.95. ChipKit™ complete easy do-it-yourself fix for paint chips, scratches, includes PrepPen, $16.95. Liquid Torque® removes stripped screws, $5.95. Microbrush lint free minibrush for quick touch up in hard to reach areas, $6.95. Pro Block professional final finish sanding block, $11.95. Web site: www.promotorcar.com

Sam Quinn Cadillac Parts — parts
Box 837
Estacada, OR 97023
503-637-3852

See full listing in **Section One** under **Cadillac/LaSalle**

R-D-T Plans and Parts — car parts, trailer plans
PO Box 2272
Merced, CA 95344-0272
209-383-4441

See full listing in **Section Two** under **trailers**

RB's Obsolete Automotive — parts
7711 Lake Ballinger Way
Edmonds, WA 98026-9163
425-670-6739; FAX: 425-670-9151
E-mail: rbobsole@gte.net

Mail order and open shop. Monday-Thursday 10 am to 5:30 pm, Friday 10 am to 5 pm, Saturday 10 am to 3 pm. Deal in aftermarket products for street rods, classics, antiques and special interest vehicles. Specializing in Chevrolet and Ford cars and trucks. Visit us at various NSRA and Goodguys events across the country. Web site: rbsobsolete.com

Reproduction Parts Marketing — parts, restoration, service
1920 Alberta Ave
Saskatoon, SK Canada S7K 1R9
306-652-6668; FAX: 306-652-1123

See full listing in **Section One** under **Chevrolet**

Restoration Specialties and Supply Inc — parts
PO Box 328, 148 Minnow Creek Ln
Windber, PA 15963
814-467-9842; FAX: 814-467-5323
E-mail: restspec@surfshop.net

Mail order and open shop. Monday-Friday 9 am to 5 pm. Weatherstripping, clips, fasteners, mattings, screws and bolts. Family owned corporation with each order receiving the prompt attention it deserves. 75% of all orders are shipped the same day as received. Illustrated catalog available, $3.50 US and Canada, $6 overseas. Web site: www.surfshop.net/users/restspec/index.htm

Restoration Supply Company — accessories, restoration, supplies
2060 Palisade Dr
Reno, NV 89509
775-825-5663; FAX: 775-825-9330
E-mail: restoration@rsc.reno.nv.us

See full listing in **Section Two** under **restoration aids**

Roaring Twenties Antiques — automobilia, gasoline collectibles, parts, signs
Rt 1 Box 104-D
Madison, VA 22727
703-948-3744, 703-948-6290
FAX: 703-948-3744
E-mail: roaringtwnties@ns.gemlink.com

Open Thursday-Monday 10 am to 5 pm, Sunday 12 pm to 5 pm. Automobilia, car parts, signs, service station and gasoline collectibles, collectible toy cars and trucks, interesting and unique memorabilia for sale. Rt 29 N, 2 miles south of scenic Madison, Virginia. In the foothills of the Blue Ridge, 26 miles north of Charlottesville, 90 miles south of Washington, DC. Web site: http://maxpages.com/madisonvavisit

Scarborough Faire Inc — parts
1151 Main St
Pawtucket, RI 02860
800-556-6300, 401-724-4200
FAX: 401-724-5392

See full listing in **Section One** under **MG**

Donald E Schneider — parts
Marinette & Menominee
RR 1, N7340 Miles Rd
Porterfield, WI 54159
715-732-4958

Mail order and open shop by appointment only. NOS parts for 1930-1969 cars and trucks. No body parts. Club parts being sold to finance club library.

Joe Smith Ford & Hot Rod Parts — parts, service
2140 Canton Rd, Unit C
Marietta, GA 30066
800-235-4013, 770-426-9850
FAX: 770-426-9854
E-mail: hank@joesmithauto.com

See full listing in **Section One** under **Ford 1932-1953**

Special Interest Cars — manuals, parts
451 Woody Rd
Oakville, ON Canada L6K 2Y2
905-844-8063; FAX: 905-338-8063

Mail order and open shop. Monday-Friday 8 am to 5:30 pm. Canada's largest obsolete automotive warehouse specializing in hard to find steering and brake parts. Currently supply 50-60 dealers. Large stock of import brake, ignition, water pumps, clutches, suspension, etc by Lucas, Quinton Hazel and other makes for sale enbloc or will break up for quantity sales wholesale. Also an obsolete Ford warehouse, inquire for all your needs. Lots of NOS sales literature, shop and owner's manuals.

Speed & Spares America (IPM Group) 16117 Runnymede St, Unit H Van Nuys, CA 91406-2913 818-781-1711; FAX: 818-781-8842 E-mail: jaydalton@earthlink.net	parts racing equipment

Mail order and open shop. Monday-Friday 8 am to 4 pm. Supplies parts and racing equipment to businesses overseas. NOS and replacement parts and racing equipment for 1950-present GMCs, Fords, Chryslers and AMC/Jeeps. Also warehouse in England: Speed & Spares America, Unit 4, Epsom Business Park, Kiln Ln, Epsom, Surrey KT17 1JF, England, PH: 01372-745-747; FAX: 01372-728-485. Web site: speedandspares.co.uk

Speedway Motors Inc 300 Speedway Cir Lincoln, NE 68502 402-474-4411; FAX: 402-477-7476	parts

Mail order and open shop. Monday-Friday 8 am to 6 pm, Saturday 9 am to 1 pm. Over 22,000 unique parts for the restorer and street rodder are available through our 350 page annual catalog. Specialize in hard to find parts including an extensive selection of flathead Ford parts. Offer 100s of fiberglass replacement body parts from our own factory. Affordable street rod kits and so much more.

Star Classics Inc 7745 E Redfield #300 Scottsdale, AZ 85260 800-644-7827, 480-991-7495 FAX: 480-951-4096 E-mail: starcls@primenet.com	parts

See full listing in **Section One** under **Mercedes-Benz**

Straight Six Jaguar 24321 Hatteras St Woodland Hills, CA 91367 PH/FAX: 818-716-1192	parts service

See full listing in **Section One** under **Jaguar**

Superior Pump Exchange Co 12901 Crenshaw Blvd Hawthorne, CA 90250-5511 310-676-4995 E-mail: autoh20@aol.com	water pumps

See full listing in **Section Two** under **water pumps**

Taylor Auto Parts PO Box 650 Esparto, CA 95627 530-787-1929; FAX: 530-787-1921	bearings brakes gaskets seals

Mail order and open shop. Monday-Saturday 9 am to 5 pm. Specializing in NOS mechanical parts for domestic vehicles, 1920s-1970s. Large inventory of ignition, brakes, bearings, seals, fuel and water pumps, electrical, chassis, engine parts and gaskets.

Thunderbird Headquarters 1080 Detroit Ave Concord, CA 94518 800-227-2174, US FAX: 925-689-1771, 800-964-1957 E-mail: tbirdhq@tbirdhq.com	accessories literature parts upholstery

See full listing in **Section One** under **Thunderbird**

TMC Publications 5817 Park Heights Ave Baltimore, MD 21215 410-367-4490; FAX: 410-466-3566	literature Mercedes parts

See full listing in **Section Two** under **literature dealers**

Jim Tucker "The Heater Valve Guy" 29597 Paso Robles Rd Valley Center, CA 92082 760-749-3488	carburetors heater valves trans gears U-joints

Mail order and open shop by appointment. Specializing in new Ranco and Harrison thermostatically controlled heater control valves. Also rebuild your original heater valve, 1949-1963, all makes. Vacuum and mechanical valves for cars 1963-1975 also on hand. Carburetors for all makes 1946-1970 (rebuilt) in stock. Transmission gears and U-joints also on hand, for 1948-1963 cars. In business full time for 18 years. Advertising in *Hemmings Motor News*.

Vintage Auto Parts PO Box 323 Temple, PA 19560-0323 610-939-9593 answering machine	car dealer new/used parts

See full listing in **Section One** under **BMW**

Vintage Auto Parts Inc 24300 Hwy 9 Woodinville, WA 98072 800-426-5911, 425-486-0777 FAX: 425-486-0778 E-mail: erics@vapinc.com	cars parts

Mail order and open shop. Monday-Friday 8 am to 5 pm PST. 10,000 sq ft warehouse filled with the world's most complete stock of new old stock parts for 1916-1970 American cars and trucks plus ten acres of cars and trucks for parts. All of our catalogs are now on our web site: www.vapinc.com

Vintage Car Corral 905 NW 53 Ave C-2 PO Box 384 Gainesville, FL 32602 PH/FAX: 352-376-0660	parts toys

Mail order and open shop. Monday-Friday 11 am to 3:30 pm. Specializing in parts and toys, Ertl, spec cast for 1930s-1970s.

Wild Bill's Corvette & Hi-Performance Center Inc 446 Dedham St Wrentham, MA 02093 508-384-7373; FAX: 508-384-9366 E-mail: wildbillscorvette@worldnet.att.net	parts rebuilding service

See full listing in **Section One** under **Corvette**

R Donald Williams 2642 Brotherton Rd Berlin, PA 15530-7318 814-267-3250	parts

Mail order and open shop. Monday-Saturday, phone after 3 pm. Miscellaneous antique auto parts, gaskets, ignition and engines.

Section Two Generalists

Wizzy's Collector Car Parts
1801 S 2nd St
Milwaukee, WI 53204
800-328-6554; FAX: 414-645-5457
E-mail: sales@wizzys.com

| engine |
| ignition |
| mechanical |
| suspension |
| transmission |

Mechanical parts specialists since 1914. Emphasis on tune-up kits, engine parts, suspension, transmission gears, U-joints, bearings ball and taper, seals, flywheel ring gears, valves, pistons and rings, copper head gaskets, bulbs, distributors and advances, wiper motors, arms, blades and much more for US cars and trucks, 1920-1979. Clean stock, reasonable prices and personal service for our customers and vendors. Contact us for your parts or free brochure. Web site: www.wizzys.com

Zim's Autotechnik
1804 Reliance Pkwy
Bedford, TX 76021
800-356-2964; FAX: 817-545-2002
E-mail: zimips@allzim.com

| parts |
| service |

See full listing in **Section One** under **Porsche**

consultants

AAAC-Antique Automobile Appraisal & Consulting
PO Box 700153
Plymouth, MI 48170
PH/FAX: 734-453-7644
E-mail: aaac@ameritech.net

| appraisals |
| Cadillac parts |
| consulting |

See full listing in **Section One** under **Cadillac/LaSalle**

AAG-Auto Appraisal Group Inc
PO Box 7034
Charlottesville, VA 22906
800-848-2886; FAX: 804-295-7918
E-mail: aag@autoappraisal.com

| appraisals |

See full listing in **Section Two** under **appraisals**

AM Racing Inc
PO Box 451
Danvers, MA 01923
PH/FAX: 978-774-4613

| race prep |
| sales |
| vintage racing |

See full listing in **Section Two** under **racing**

ARS, Automotive Research Services
Division of Auto Search International
1702 W Camelback #301
Phoenix, AZ 85015
602-230-7111; FAX: 602-230-7282

| appraisals |
| research |

See full listing in **Section Two** under **appraisals**

Auto Consultants & Appraisal Service
Charles J Kozelka
PO Box 111
Macedonia, OH 44056
330-467-0748; FAX: 330-467-3725

| appraisals |

See full listing in **Section Two** under **appraisals**

Auto-Line Enterprises Inc
2 Lyons Rd
Armonk, NY 10504
914-681-1757; FAX: 914-273-5159
E-mail: garfconect@aol.com

| appraisals |
| broker services |

See full listing in **Section Two** under **appraisals**

Automotive Legal Service Inc
PO Box 626
Dresher, PA 19025
800-487-4947, 215-659-4947
FAX: 215-657-5843
E-mail: autolegal@aol.com

| appraisals |

See full listing in **Section Two** under **appraisals**

The Autoworks Ltd
90 Center Ave
Westwood, NJ 07675
201-358-0200; FAX: 201-358-0442

| restoration |
| sales |
| service |

See full listing in **Section Two** under **service shops**

JJ Best & Co
737 Main St
PO Box 10
Chatham, MA 02633
508-945-6000; FAX: 508-945-6006

| financing |

Open Monday-Friday 8 am to 9 pm, Saturday 10 am to 4 pm EST. Specializing in financing antique, collectible, sports, rods, exotic and fine automobiles. Great rates and long terms, 5-12 years. Will take an application on the phone and usually let a customer know within 10 minutes of approval or denial. Very familiar with most cars from 1901-1990 and we offer financing up to 90% of market value. Web site: jjbest.com

AVM Automotive Consulting
Box 338
Montvale, NJ 07645-0338
201-391-5194; FAX: 201-782-0663
E-mail: avmtony@aol.com

| appraisals |
| consultant |

See full listing in **Section Two** under **appraisals**

Big Time Productions
780 Munras Ave
Monterey, CA 93940
831-655-0409; FAX: 831-375-9102
E-mail: bigtime@redshift.com

| video production |

See full listing in **Section Two** under **videos**

Blair Collectors & Consultants
2821 SW 167th Pl
Seattle, WA 98166
206-242-6745, 206-246-1305

| appraisals |
| consultant |
| literature |

See full listing in **Section Two** under **appraisals**

Car Critic
202 Woodshire Ln
Naples, FL 34105
941-435-1157; FAX: 941-261-4864
E-mail: puppys4u@aol.com

| appraisals |
| inspections |

See full listing in **Section Two** under **appraisals**

**Charles W Clarke
Automotive Consultant/Appraiser**
17 Saddle Ridge Dr
West Simsbury, CT 06092-2118
PH/FAX: 860-658-2714

| appraisals |
| car dealer |
| consultant |

Appraisals, consulting. Connecticut, Hartford area based, can travel. Personal service and fees tailored to your needs. 40 years' automotive experience, appraisals, brokering, locating, etc. Connecticut licensed appraiser.

Classic Auto Restoration
15445 Ventura Blvd #60
Sherman Oaks, CA 91413
818-905-6267; FAX: 818-906-1249
E-mail: rollsroyce1@earthlink.net

| acquisitions |
| restoration |
| sales |

See full listing in **Section One** under **Rolls-Royce/Bentley**

Classic Car Appraisals
37 Wyndwood Rd
West Hartford, CT 06107
PH/FAX: 860-236-0125

appraisals

See full listing in **Section Two** under **appraisals**

Classic Car Research
29508 Southfield Rd, Ste 106
Southfield, MI 48076
248-557-2880; FAX: 248-557-3511
E-mail: kawifreek@msn.com

appraisals
consultant
part locating

See full listing in **Section Two** under **appraisals**

**Clean Air Performance
Professionals (CAPP)**
84 Hoy Ave
Fords, NJ 08863
732-738-7859; FAX: 732-738-7625
E-mail: stellacapp@earthlink.net

legislative watch
organization

See full listing in **Section Three** under **legislative watch organizations**

Lance S Coren, CAA, CMA
20545 Eastwood Ave
Torrance, CA 90503-3611
310-370-4114; FAX: 310-371-4120

appraisals

See full listing in **Section Two** under **appraisals**

Corvette Enterprise Brokerage
The Power Broker
52 Van Houten Ave
Passaic Park, NJ 07055
973-472-7021

appraisals
broker
consultant
investment
planning

See full listing in **Section One** under **Corvette**

Creative Automotive Consultants
PO Box 2221
San Rafael, CA 94912-2221
707-824-9004; FAX: 707-824-9002
E-mail: cars4cac@earthlink.net

appraisals
car locator
promotion

All hours by appointment. Appraisals for all collector vehicles. Auto location service, worldwide. Period vehicles for the visual arts industry and special events. We need listings of all age and type vehicles. All periods (1900's-1990's). Auction coordination and support. Vehicle investment/purchase consultation. 21 years' experience. Cars for films. Expert witness testimony. Web site: www.creativeautomotive.com

Development Associates
12791-G Newport Ave
Tustin, CA 92780
714-730-6843; FAX: 714-730-6863
E-mail: devassoc@yahoo.com

electrical parts

See full listing in **Section Two** under **electrical systems**

Driving Passion Ltd USA
Marc Tuwiner
7132 Chilton Ct
Clarksville, MD 21029
PH/FAX: 301-596-9078
E-mail: mt.tees@erols.com

cars
parts
salvage yard

See full listing in **Section One** under **Cadillac/LaSalle**

Freeman's Garage
29 Ford Rd
Norton, MA 02766
508-285-6500; FAX: 508-285-6566

parts
restoration
sales
service

See full listing in **Section One** under **Ford 1903-1931**

Mark Gillett
PO Box 9177
Dallas, TX 75209
PH/FAX: 214-902-9258
011-525-559-6240 Mexico City, Mexico
E-mail: autonet@onramp.net

car locator
sales

See full listing in **Section Two** under **car dealers**

Hank Hoiler Olde Car Shoppe
431 Portzer Rd
Quakertown, PA 18951
215-536-1334

consultant
light maintenance

Open by appointment only. Light maintenance and problem solving. Consulting. Actively in the automotive restoration business 55 years, now continue with consulting. Only American manufactured vehicles.

ISG
7100 Monache Mtn Blvd
Inyokern, CA 93527
760-377-5013; FAX: 760-377-5073
E-mail: isg@isg-web.com

security devices

See full listing in **Section Two** under **anti-theft**

Eliot James Enterprises Inc
PO Box 3986
Dana Point, CA 92629-8986
949-661-0889; FAX: 949-661-1901

development info

See full listing in **Section Four** under **books & publications**

Jesser's Auto Clinic
26 West St
Akron, OH 44303
330-376-8181; FAX: 330-384-9129

appraisals

See full listing in **Section Two** under **appraisals**

LA Ltd Design Graphics
822A S McDuffie St
Anderson, SC 29624
PH/FAX: 864-231-7715

artwork
design
greeting cards

See full listing in **Section Two** under **automobilia**

Landry Classic MotorCars
34 Goodhue Ave
Chicopee, MA 01020
413-592-2746; FAX: 413-594-8378

appraisals

See full listing in **Section Two** under **appraisals**

M & L Automobile Appraisal
2662 Palm Terr
Deland, FL 32720
904-734-1761

appraisals

See full listing in **Section Two** under **appraisals**

M & M Automobile Appraisers Inc
584 Broomspun St
Henderson, NV 89015
702-568-5120; FAX: 702-568-5158

appraisals
broker
consultant

See full listing in **Section Two** under **appraisals**

Randall Marcus Vintage Automobiles
706 Hanshaw Rd
Ithaca, NY 14850
607-257-5939; FAX: 607-272-8806

broker
car locator
consultant

See full listing in **Section Two** under **brokers**

Marshall Antique & Classic Restorations
3714 Old Philadelphia Pike
Bethlehem, PA 18015
610-868-7765; FAX: 610-868-7529

coolant additives
restoration services

See full listing in **Section One** under **Rolls-Royce/Bentley**

Bill McCoskey
16643 Rt 144
Mt Airy, MD 21771
301-854-5900, 410-442-3637
FAX: 301-854-5957
E-mail: tatrabill@aol.com

appraisals
repairs

See full listing in **Section Two** under **appraisals**

Memory Lane Motors Inc
1231 Rt 176
Lake Bluff, IL 60044
847-362-4600

appraisals
car dealer
storage

See full listing in **Section Two** under **car dealers**

Morgan Spares Ltd
225 Simons Rd
Ancram, NY 12502
518-329-3877; FAX: 518-329-3892
E-mail: morganspares@taconic.net

car sales
consulting
obsolete parts
used parts

See full listing in **Section One** under **Morgan**

NorCal Auto
615D Saint John St
Pleasanton, CA 94566
888-224-6005; FAX: 925-426-8845
E-mail: mwjohn@hotmail.com

appraisals

See full listing in **Section Two** under **appraisals**

Performance Analysis Co
1345 Oak Ridge Tpke, Ste 258
Oak Ridge, TN 37830
423-482-9175
E-mail:
george_murphy@compuserve.com

climate control
cruise control

See full listing in **Section One** under **Mercedes-Benz**

Reward Service Inc
172 Overhill Rd
Stormville, NY 12582
914-227-7647; FAX: 914-221-0293

appraisals
restoration
transportation

See full listing in **Section One** under **Jaguar**

Still Cruisin' Corvettes
5759 Benford Dr
Haymarket, VA 20169
703-754-1960; FAX: 703-754-1222

appraisals
repairs
restoration

See full listing in **Section One** under **Corvette**

Stone Barn Inc
202 Rt 46, Box 117
Vienna, NJ 07880
908-637-4444; FAX: 908-637-4290

restoration

See full listing in **Section Two** under **restoration shops**

Timeless Masterpieces
221 Freeport Dr
Bloomingdale, IL 60108
630-893-1058 evenings

appraisals
consultant

See full listing in **Section Two** under **appraisals**

USAppraisal
754 Walker Rd
PO Box 472
Great Falls, VA 22066-0472
703-759-9100; FAX: 703-759-9099
E-mail: dhkinney@usappraisal.com

appraisals

See full listing in **Section Two** under **appraisals**

Valco Cincinnati Consumer Products Inc
411 Circle Freeway Dr
Cincinnati, OH 45246
513-874-6550; FAX: 513-874-3612

adhesives
detailing products
sealants
tools

See full listing in **Section Two** under **tools**

Vintage Jag Works
1390 W Hwy 26
Blackfoot, ID 83221
208-684-4767; FAX: 208-684-3386
E-mail: walt@vintagejag.com

consulting
how-to articles

See full listing in **Section One** under **Jaguar**

Johnny Williams Services
2613 Copeland Road
Tyler, TX 75701
903-597-3687, 800-937-0900
voice mail #7225

appraisals
car/parts locator
consultant
lighting systems
design

See full listing in **Section Two** under **appraisals**

Wolfson Engineering
512 Parkway W
Las Vegas, NV 89106
PH/FAX: 702-384-4196

mech engineering

See full listing in **Section Two** under **special services**

custom cars

Ace Antique Auto Restoration
65 S Service Rd
Plainview, NY 11803
516-752-6065; FAX: 516-752-1484

air conditioning
body rebuilding
restoration
wiring harnesses

See full listing in **Section Two** under **restoration shops**

American Autowire Systems Inc
150 Heller Pl #17W
Dept HVAA99
Bellmawr, NJ 08031
800-482-9473; FAX: 609-933-0805
E-mail: facfit@erols.com

battery cables
electrical systems
switches/components

See full listing in **Section Two** under **street rods**

Amherst Antique Auto Show
157 Hollis Rd
Amherst, NH 03031
603-883-0605, NH
FAX: 617-641-0647, MA

swap meets

See full listing in **Section Two** under **auctions & events**

Antique & Classic Car Restorations
4716 Monkey Hill Rd
Oak Harbor, WA 98227
360-240-0909

painting
restorations
woodwork

See full listing in **Section Two** under **restoration shops**

ARS, Automotive Research Services — appraisals / research
Division of Auto Search International
1702 W Camelback #301
Phoenix, AZ 85015
602-230-7111; FAX: 602-230-7282

See full listing in **Section Two** under **appraisals**

Bob's Classic Auto Glass — glass
21170 Hwy 36
Blachly, OR 97412
800-624-2130

See full listing in **Section Two** under **glass**

Boop Photography — photography
2347 Derry St
Harrisburg, PA 17104-2728
717-564-8533
E-mail: msboop@paonline.com

See full listing in **Section Two** under **photography**

Briz Bumpers — bumpers
8002 NE Hwy 99, #260
Vancouver, WA 98665
360-573-8628

See full listing in **Section Two** under **chassis parts**

Coffey's Classic Transmissions — transmissions
2290 W Hicks Rd, Unit 42
Hanger 30-1
Ft Worth, TX 76111
817-439-1611

See full listing in **Section Two** under **transmissions**

Contemporary and Investment Automobiles — buy/sell/trade / mechanical work / memorabilia
2700 Peachtree Square
Doraville, GA 30360
770-455-1200; FAX: 770-455-0023
E-mail: georjarex@aol.com

See full listing in **Section Two** under **car dealers**

Crossfire Manufacturing — accessories
166-B N Mercer Ave, PO Box 263
Sharpsville, PA 16150
800-458-3478
PH/FAX: 724-962-4639
E-mail: xfire@nauticom.net

See full listing in **Section Two** under **ignition parts**

Custom Plating — bumper specialist / chrome plating / parts
3030 Alta Ridge Way
Snellville, GA 30278
770-736-1118

See full listing in **Section Two** under **plating & polishing**

Early Wheel Co Inc — steel wheels
Box 1438
Santa Ynez, CA 93460
805-688-1187; FAX: 805-688-0257

See full listing in **Section Two** under **wheels & wheelcovers**

Guldstrand Engineering Inc — parts
11924 W Jefferson Blvd
Culver City, CA 90230
310-391-7108; FAX: 310-391-7424
E-mail: gss@guldstrand.com

See full listing in **Section One** under **Corvette**

K-F-D Services Inc — parts / restoration
HC 65, Box 49
Altonah, UT 84002
801-454-3098; FAX: 801-454-3099
E-mail: kfd-services@msn.com

See full listing in **Section One** under **Kaiser Frazer**

Dave Knittel Upholstery — interiors / tops / upholstery
850 E Teton #7
Tucson, AZ 85706
PH/FAX: 520-746-1588

See full listing in **Section Two** under **upholstery**

Land Cruiser Solutions Inc — accessories / services
20 Thornell Rd
Newton, NH 03858
603-382-3555; FAX: 603-378-0431
E-mail: twbii@aol.com

See full listing in **Section One** under **Toyota**

Lokar Inc — performance parts
10924 Murdock Dr
Knoxville, TN 37932
423-966-2269; FAX: 423-671-1999
E-mail: lokarinc@aol.com

See full listing in **Section Two** under **street rods**

Lone Wolf — wolf whistles
9375 Bearwalk Path
Brooksville, FL 34613
352-596-9949
E-mail: lonewolfwhistle@bigfoot.com

See full listing in **Section Two** under **automobilia**

Memoryville USA Inc — restoration
1008 W 12th St
Rolla, MO 65401
573-364-1810

See full listing in **Section Two** under **restoration shops**

Old Coach Works Restoration Inc — appraisals / restoration
1206 Badger St
Yorkville, IL 60560-1701
630-553-0414; FAX: 630-553-1053
oldcoachworks@msn.com

See full listing in **Section Two** under **restoration shops**

Pilgrim's Auto Restorations — bodywork / metal fabrication / paint / restoration
3888 Hill Rd
Lakeport, CA 95453
707-262-1062; FAX: 707-263-6956
E-mail: pilgrims@pacific.net

See full listing in **Section Two** under **restoration shops**

Power Effects® — exhaust systems
1800H Industrial Park Dr
Grand Haven, MI 49417
877-3POWRFX toll-free
616-847-4200
FAX: 616-847-4210

See full listing in **Section Two** under **exhaust systems**

Prestige Motors — car dealer
120 N Bessie Rd
Spokane, WA 99212
PH/FAX: 509-926-3611

See full listing in **Section Two** under **car dealers**

Section Two
Generalists

Quik-Shelter | temporary garages
PO Box 1123
Orange, CT 06477
800-211-3730; FAX: 203-937-8897
E-mail: info@quikshelter.com

See full listing in **Section Two** under **car covers**

Ray's Upholstering | partial/total restoration
600 N St Frances Cabrini Ave
Scranton, PA 18504
800-296-RAYS; FAX: 717-963-0415

See full listing in **Section Two** under **restoration shops**

RB's Prototype Model & Machine Co | machine work
44 Marva Ln
Stamford, CT 06903
203-329-2715; FAX: 203-329-8029

See full listing in **Section Two** under **service shops**

Ridgefield Auto Upholstery | interiors tops
34 Bailey Ave
Ridgefield, CT 06877
203-438-7583; FAX: 203-438-2666

See full listing in **Section Two** under **interiors & interior parts**

Rod-1 Shop | street rods
210 Clinton Ave
Pitman, NJ 08071
609-228-7631; FAX: 609-582-5770

See full listing in **Section Two** under **street rods**

RodDoors | door panels interior accessories
PO Box 2110
Chico, CA 95927
530-896-1513; FAX: 530-896-1518
E-mail: roddoors@juno.com

See full listing in **Section Two** under **street rods**

Rodster Inc | conversion kits
128 Center St #B
El Segundo, CA 90245
310-322-2767; FAX: 310-322-2761

See full listing in **Section Two** under **street rods**

Brooks Stevens Auto Collection Inc | parts restoration service
10325 N Port Washington Rd
Mequon, WI 53092
414-241-4185; FAX: 414-241-4166
E-mail: apjb@prodigy.net

See full listing in **Section One** under **Excalibur**

Strange Motion Inc | customizing design fabrication
14696 N 350th Ave
Cambridge, IL 61238
PH/FAX: 309-927-3346
E-mail: strange@netins.net

See full listing in **Section Two** under **street rods**

decals

Anderson's Car Door Monograms | car door monograms
32700 Coastsite #102
Rancho Palos Verdes, CA 90275
310-377-1007, 800-881-9049
FAX: 310-377-0169

See full listing in **Section Two** under **accessories**

Auto Decals Unlimited Inc | decals stripe kits
11259 E Via Linda, Ste 100-201
Scottsdale, AZ 85259
602-220-0800

Mail order only. Automotive decals and stripe kits for all muscle cars, all years, makes and models.

Auto Nostalgia Enr | literature manuals models tractor decals
332 St Joseph
Mont St Gregoire, QC Canada J0J 1K0
PH/FAX: 450-346-3644
E-mail: autonostalgia@vif.com

See full listing in **Section Two** under **literature dealers**

Bright Displays | molded auto logos neon signs
1314 Lakemont Dr
Pittsburgh, PA 15243
PH/FAX: 412-279-7037

See full listing in **Section Two** under **automobilia**

Caddytown™/Pawl Engineering Co | memorabilia parts toys
4960 Arrowhead
PO Box 240105
West Bloomfield, MI 48324
PH/FAX: 248-682-2007
E-mail: pawl@earthlink.net

See full listing in **Section One** under **Cadillac/LaSalle**

Del's Decals | decals
6150 Baldwin St
Hudsonville, MI 49426

Mail order only. Engine compartment decals for the air cleaner, oil filter, valve cover, etc. SASE for free list, please state make.

Eurosport Daytona Inc | license plates
355 Tomoka Ave
Ormond Beach, FL 32174-6222
800-874-8044, 904-672-7199
FAX: 904-673-0821

See full listing in **Section Two** under **license plates**

Freddie Beach Restoration | accessories restoration parts
1834 Woodstock Rd
Fredericton, NB Canada E3C 1L4
506-450-9074; FAX: 506-459-0708
E-mail: vallise@city.fredericton.nb.ca

See full listing in **Section Two** under **car & parts locators**

Hemmings Motor News | free HMN windshield decal
Free Decal Request
PO Box 256
Bennington, VT 05201

Free, full-color window decal for *Hemmings Motor News* readers who want to share their enthusiasm for vintage vehicles. Please send self-addressed stamped envelope and specify the quantity (one-five), that you can use.

Larry Machacek | decals license plates novelties
PO Box 515
Porter, TX 77365
281-429-2505

See full listing in **Section Two** under **automobilia**

National Parts Depot | accessories restoration parts
3101 SW 40th Blvd
Gainesville, FL 32608
800-874-7595 toll-free 24 hours
352-378-2473 local

See full listing in **Section Two** under **comprehensive parts**

Operations Plus PO Box 26347 Santa Ana, CA 92799 PH/FAX: 714-962-2776 E-mail: aquacel@aquacel.com	**accessories** **parts**

See full listing in **Section One** under **Cobra**

Jim Osborn Reproductions Inc 101 Ridgecrest Dr Lawrenceville, GA 30245 770-962-7556; FAX: 770-962-5881	**decals** **manuals**

Mail order and open shop. Monday-Friday 8 am to 5 pm. Largest selection of restoration decals, owner's and shop manuals. All new catalog, $5. Web site: www.osborn-reproduction.com

People Kars 290 Third Ave Ext Rensselaer, NY 12144 518-465-0477; FAX: 518-465-0614 E-mail: peoplekars@aol.com	**models/more** **VW toys**

See full listing in **Section One** under **Volkswagen**

Phoenix Graphix Inc 5861 S Kyrene Rd #10 Tempe, AZ 85283 800-941-4550	**decals** **stripe kits**

Mail order only. "Any decal, any car, any year!" Specialists in 1964-1991 Trans-Am, Z-28, Mustang, Plymouth and Dodge decals. Carry all lines, including Turbo and Special Edition packages. Affordable. High quality and original appearance. GM licensed manufacturer. Established 1985.

Prostripe Division of Spartan International Inc 1845 Cedar St Holt, MI 48842 800-248-7800; FAX: 517-694-7952 E-mail: information@spartanintl.com	**graphics** **molding** **pinstriping**

See full listing in **Section Two** under **striping**

Star Classics Inc 7745 E Redfield #300 Scottsdale, AZ 85260 800-644-7827, 480-991-7495 FAX: 480-951-4096 E-mail: starcls@primenet.com	**parts**

See full listing in **Section One** under **Mercedes-Benz**

Stencils & Stripes Unlimited Inc 1108 S Crescent Ave #21 Park Ridge, IL 60068 847-692-6893; FAX: 847-692-6895	**NOS decals** **stripe kits**

Mail order only. Offer reproduction paint and stripe kits along with NOS decals and stripes. Kits are available for Camaro, Chevelle, El Camino, Corvette, Nova, Olds 442, Dodge, Plymouth, Pontiac T/A, GTO and H/O models, AMC plus Ford. All reproduction kits use special high-performance vinyls. Specializing in reproduction paint stencil, decals and stripes for 1967-up GM, Ford, Chrysler and GMC. Licensed by GM.

electrical systems

Ace Antique Auto Restoration 65 S Service Rd Plainview, NY 11803 516-752-6065; FAX: 516-752-1484	**air conditioning** **body rebuilding** **restoration** **wiring harnesses**

See full listing in **Section Two** under **restoration shops**

Addison Generator Inc 21 W Main St Rear Freehold, NJ 07728 732-431-2438; FAX: 732-431-4503	**auto parts** **repairs** **supplies**

Mail order and open shop. Monday-Friday 8 am to 5 pm. Rebuild or repair of: starters, generators, alternators for all makes and models, cars, trucks and tractors. One wire alternators and a complete line of auto parts and supplies.

All British Car Parts Inc 2847 Moores Rd Baldwin, MD 21013 410-692-9572; FAX: 410-692-5654	**parts**

Buy and sell new and new old stock Lucas, Girling, Lockheed. Current, discontinued, NLA, supersessions, hard to find items. Lamps, lenses, switches, ignition, starters, alternators, brake hydraulics and components, virtually anything Lucas, Girling, Lockheed, post 1950-today. Fax your obsolete Lucas/Girling list for offer.

American Autowire Systems Inc 150 Heller Pl #17W Dept HVAA99 Bellmawr, NJ 08031 800-482-9473; FAX: 609-933-0805 E-mail: facfit@erols.com	**battery cables** **electrical systems** **switches/components**

See full listing in **Section Two** under **street rods**

American-Foreign Auto Electric Inc 103 Main Street Souderton, PA 18964 215-723-4877	**parts** **rebuilding**

Monday-Friday 8 am to 5 pm, Saturday by appointment. Authorized Lucas service station. Parts and expertise to rebuild vintage starters and generators as well as late style alternators and starters.

Antique Auto Battery 2320 Old Mill Rd, Hudson, OH 44236 800-426-7580, 330-425-2395 FAX: 330-425-4642 E-mail: sales@antiqueautobattery.com	**batteries** **battery cables**

See full listing in **Section Two** under **batteries**

Antique Auto Electric 9109 (Rear) E Garvey Ave Rosemead, CA 91770 626-572-0938	**repro wiring**

Open Monday-Friday 9 am to 5 pm. For all years and models. Specializing in 1908-1948 Fords, Mercurys and Lincolns, SASE required for catalog and information. New alternator conversion catalogs for As and V8s, $6. Specify catalog desired.

Antique Radio Service 12 Shawmut Ave Wayland, MA 01778 800-201-2635; FAX: 508-653-2418	**radio service**

See full listing in **Section Two** under **radios**

Asom Electric 1204 McClellan Dr Los Angeles, CA 90025 310-820-4457; FAX: 310-820-5908	**electrical systems** **rebuilding**

Auto electrical rebuilding for all Bosch, Lucas, Delco, French Motorola. Deal in Jaguar, Rolls-Royce, BMW, Range Rover, Mercedes-Benz.

Barnett & Small Inc 151E Industry Ct Deer Park, NY 11729 516-242-2100; FAX: 516-242-2101	**electrical parts**

Antique auto parts, all NOS. Also generators, voltage regulators, starters, speedometers, carburetors and electric wiper motors. 47 years in business. Auto parts dealers.

Bathurst Company 6875 Oakland Rd Loveland, OH 45140 513-683-3122; FAX: 513-683-4701	**auto accessories** **battery accessories**

Mail and phone orders. The battery disconnect switches (4 models available) are for the protection of the mechanic when working on a vehicle. Fire and theft protection to your auto, tractor, boat and RV. Also, the switches help keep your battery from discharging. Visa and MasterCard welcome. Dealer inquiries.

Robert D Bliss 2 Delmar Pl Edison, NJ 08837 732-549-0977	**electrical parts** **ignition parts**

Mail order and open shop. Monday-Friday after 6 pm, Saturday and Sunday all day. New distributor caps, rotors, points, condensers, voltage regulators, headlight, ignition, starter, stoplight switches; horn relays; generator and starter parts from 1920-1970; headlight relays; headlight bulbs; ignition wire sets.

British Only Motorcycles and Parts Inc 32451 Park Ln Garden City, MI 48135 734-421-0303; FAX: 734-422-9253 E-mail: info@british-only.com	**literature** **memorabilia** **motorcycles** **parts**

See full listing in **Section Two** under **motorcycles**

British Wiring Inc 20449 Ithaca Rd Olympia Fields, IL 60461 PH/FAX: 708-481-9050	**wiring accessories** **wiring harnesses**

Specializing in wiring harnesses and wiring accessories for British classic cars and motorcycles. The US representative for the largest British harness manufacturer. Stock a large selection of harnesses, terminals, grommets, connectors, etc, along with bulk wire. Harnesses for pre-war models are available. Harness price lists are available free of charge (specify marque) and our accessory catalog is $2, refundable with purchase.

Bryant's Antique Auto Parts 851 Western Ave Hampden, ME 04444 207-862-4019	**appraisals** **chassis/engine** **parts/sheetmetal** **wiring harnesses**

See full listing in **Section One** under **Ford 1903-1931**

Certified Auto Electric Inc 25057 Broadway Ave Oakwood Village, OH 44146 440-439-1100; FAX: 440-439-2163 E-mail: earli@apk.net	**generators** **parts** **rebuilding service** **starters**

Mail order and open shop. Monday-Friday 8 am to 5 pm EST, Saturday 9 am to 12 pm EST. Rebuilding electrical parts for all makes and models, ie generators, starters, alternators. Generator to alternator conversions, 6-volt, 8-volt, 12-volt and 24-volt. Chrome units available. Web site: www.mall-express.com/cert-auto-elect

Chicago Corvette Supply 7322 S Archer Rd Justice, IL 60458 708-458-2500; FAX: 708-458-2662	**parts**

See full listing in **Section One** under **Corvette**

Class-Tech Corp 62935 Layton Ave Bend, OR 97701 800-874-9981	**wiring harnesses**

Mail order only. Authentic reproduction Ford wiring harnesses through the 1950s, this includes Mercury, pickups, and 1955-1957 T-Birds. Dealer inquiries welcome.

Classic Car Club of Southern California PO Box 3742 Orange, CA 92857	**generators** **starters**

Mail order only. Deal in tags, decals for use on starters, generators and oil filters, plus special items for certain makes, 1925-1948. SASE for free illustrated list.

Robert Connole 2525 E 32nd St Davenport, IA 52807 319-355-6266	**ignition coils**

See full listing in **Section One** under **Packard**

Dakota Studebaker Parts RR 1, Box 103A Armour, SD 57313 605-724-2527	**parts**

See full listing in **Section One** under **Studebaker**

Development Associates 12791-G Newport Ave Tustin, CA 92780 714-730-6843; FAX: 714-730-6863 E-mail: devassoc@yahoo.com	**electrical parts**

Mail order. Monday-Friday 9 am to 6 pm. Retail and wholesale advanced electronic sequencers for 1965-1968 Thunderbirds and 1967-1968 Cougars. These units replace the original electro-mechanical motor and cam switch assembly no longer available from Ford. These improved units are compatible in form and fit and offer substantial ownership benefits in terms of performance, reliability and installation ease. This company, with over 28 years of hardware/software and systems experience, also offers its services for development of custom automotive electronics. Web site: www.michinoku.or.jp/~viper/da/

Early Ford V8 Sales Inc Curtis Industrial Park, Bldg 37 831 Rt 67 Ballston Spa, NY 12020 518-884-2825; FAX: 518-884-2633 E-mail: earlyford@prodigy.net	**parts**

See full listing in **Section One** under **Ford 1932-1953**

Ferris Auto Electric Ltd 106 Lakeshore Dr North Bay, ON Canada P1A 2A6 705-474-4560; FAX: 705-474-9453	**parts** **service**

Mail order and open shop. Monday-Friday 8 am to 5:30 pm. For your antique vehicle requirements, specializing in custom wiring harness, either braided or plastic wire, rebuilding of generators, starters, alternators, carburetors, distributors or magnetos and speedometers. Speedometer cables and casings made to order.

Fifth Avenue Graphics Fifth Avenue Antique Auto Parts 415 Court St Clay Center, KS 67432 785-632-3450; FAX: 785-632-6154 E-mail: fifthave@kansas.net	**cooling systems** **electrical systems** **fuel systems**

Mail order and open shop. Monday-Friday 9 am to 5:30 pm, Saturday 9 am to noon. Fifth Avenue specializes in electrical, cooling and fuel systems for all types of antique and classic vehicles. They have successfully prepared cars entered in the Great

American Race since 1989. They have also completed numerous projects for the Hollywood movie studios, the most recent was for the movie "LA Confidential". Send $3 for current catalog.

Ron Francis' Wire Works	**fuel injection**
167 Keystone Rd	**harnesses**
Chester, PA 19013	**wiring accessories**
800-292-1940 orders, 610-485-1937	**wiring kits**
E-mail: rfwwx@aol.com	

See full listing in **Section Two** under **wiring harnesses**

Fun Projects Inc	**electrical parts**
37 W 222 Rt 64, Ste 164	**mechanical parts**
St Charles, IL 60175	
630-584-1471	
E-mail: piewagon@funprojects.com	

Mail order only. Design and manufacture of electrical parts for vintage cars. Make voltage regulators for Ford cars, 1919-1939 and other cars on special order. Early brass era Model T Ford parts. Pinion bearings, Model T horns.
Web site: www.funprojects.com

Green Mountain Vintage Auto	**damage appraisals**
20 Bramley Way	**ignition parts**
Bellows Falls, VT 05101	**vehicle evaluations**
PH/FAX: 802-463-3141	
E-mail: vintauto@sover.net	

See full listing in **Section Two** under **appraisals**

Haneline Products Co	**gauges**
PO Box 430	**instrument panels**
Morongo Valley, CA 92256	**stainless parts**
760-363-6597; FAX: 760-363-7321	**trim parts**

See full listing in **Section Two** under **accessories**

Harnesses Unlimited	**wiring harnesses**
PO Box 435	**wiring supplies**
Wayne, PA 19087	
610-688-3998	

Mail order only. USA manufacturer of wiring harness systems that use cloth braided and lacquered wire. Each system comes with installation instructions and wiring schematics. All makes except Ford, Lincoln and Mercury. Also offering wiring supplies and harness braiding service. Catalog or information, $5. If calling by phone, leave message, all calls are returned.

Mike Hershenfeld	**parts**
3011 Susan Rd	
Bellmore, NY 11710	
PH/FAX: 516-781-PART (7278)	
E-mail: mikesmopar@juno.com	

See full listing in **Section One** under **Mopar**

J & C's Parts	**parts**
7127 Ward Rd	
North Tonawanda, NY 14120	
716-693-4090; FAX: 716-695-7144	

See full listing in **Section One** under **Buick/McLaughlin**

Jim's T-Bird Parts & Service	**parts**
710 Barney Ave	**restoration**
Winston-Salem, NC 27107	**service**
PH/FAX: 336-784-9363	
E-mail: tbirdjims@aol.com	

See full listing in **Section One** under **Thunderbird**

Keilen's Auto Restoring	**restoration**
580 Kelley Blvd (R)	
North Attleboro, MA 02760	
508-699-7768	

See full listing in **Section Two** under **restoration shops**

L & N Olde Car Co	**restoration**
9992 Kinsman Rd	
PO Box 378	
Newbury, OH 44065	
440-564-7204; FAX: 440-564-8187	

See full listing in **Section Two** under **restoration shops**

Last Chance Repair & Restoration	**repairs**
PO Box 362A	**restoration**
Myers Rd	
Shaftsbury, VT 05262	

See full listing in **Section Two** under **restoration shops**

Lincoln Highway Packards	**engine rebuilding**
Main St	**restoration**
PO Box 94	
Schellsburg, PA 15559	
814-733-4356; FAX: 814-839-4276	

See full listing in **Section One** under **Packard**

M & H Electric Fabricators Inc	**wiring harnesses**
13537 Alondra Blvd	
Santa Fe Springs, CA 90670	
562-926-9552; FAX: 562-926-9572	
E-mail: sales@wiringharness.com	

Mail order and open shop. Monday-Friday 8 am to 4:30 pm. Deal in the manufacturing of exact reproduction wiring harnesses for most GM vehicles from 1955-1976. Call for applications and pricing. Web site: www.wiringharness.com

Jack Marcheski	**12/6-volt**
100 Dry Creek Rd	**converters**
Hollister, CA 95023	**rebuilding**
831-637-3453	**repair**

Mail order and open shop. Daily 8 am to 5 pm. Gas gauge sending unit repair, rebuilding; also 12/6-volt converters.

Ben McAdam	**electrical parts**
500 Clover Ln	
Wheeling, WV 26003	
304-242-3388	

See full listing in **Section Two** under **ignition parts**

Michael's Auto Parts	**used Mercedes**
5875 NW Kaiser Rd	**parts only**
Portland, OR 97229	
503-690-7750; FAX: 503-690-7735	

See full listing in **Section Five** under **Oregon**

Morgan Oasis Garage	**restoration**
PO Box 1010	**service**
N 51 Terrace Rd	
Hoodsport, WA 98548	
360-877-5160	

See full listing in **Section One** under **Morgan**

Motorsport Auto	**parts**
1139 W Collins Ave	
Orange, CA 92667	
800-633-6331, 714-639-2620	
FAX: 714-639-7460	
E-mail: motorsport@worldnet.att.net	

See full listing in **Section One** under **Datsun**

National Parts Depot	**accessories**
3101 SW 40th Blvd	**restoration parts**
Gainesville, FL 32608	
800-874-7595 toll-free 24 hours	
352-378-2473 local	

See full listing in **Section Two** under **comprehensive parts**

M Parker Autoworks Inc	**battery cables**
150 Heller Pl #17W	**harnesses**
Dept HVAA99	
Bellmawr, NJ 08031	
609-933-0801; FAX: 609-933-0805	
E-mail: facfit@erols.com	

Mail order and open shop. Monday-Friday 8 am to 5 pm. Largest manufacturer of replacement wiring harnesses, battery cables, etc, for 1955-1982 GM cars and trucks. All factory-fit harnesses are built to original GM specifications with emphasis on quality and originality using original GM components and specs. High-performance alternator and HEI modifications are available. Factory-fit harnesses are supported by a knowledgeable technical support staff and backed by a money back guarantee. Visa, MC, COD accepted. Catalog, $4. Dealer inquiries welcome. Web site: www.factoryfit.com

See our ad on page 445

Performance Analysis Co	**climate control**
1345 Oak Ridge Tpke, Ste 258	**cruise control**
Oak Ridge, TN 37830	
423-482-9175	
E-mail:	
george_murphy@compuserve.com	

See full listing in **Section One** under **Mercedes-Benz**

J Pinto	**electric motors/**
31 Spruce	**relays/switches/**
HC 1, Box F7	**solenoids repair**
Swiftwater, PA 18370	
570-839-3441	
E-mail: lectri@yahoo.com	

Electric motors and all switches, relays, solenoids (including overdrive) restored, 6 and 12 volt. Stay original. OEM specs or better. "We can when others can't™". 50+ years' experience: w/wiper, w/washer, headlight, fan, blower, conv top, horns, power window, locks, seat, antenna. No charge if unrestorable. Free 3 day shipping West, Midwest. Send to: J Pinto at above address. Web site: http://mars.spaceports.com/~lectri

Dennis Portka	**horns**
4326 Beetow Dr	**knock-off wheels**
Hamburg, NY 14075	
716-649-0921	

See full listing in **Section One** under **Corvette**

Potomac Packard	**wiring harnesses**
PO Box 117	
Tiger, GA 30576	
800-859-9532 orders, 706-782-2345	
FAX: 706-782-2344	

See full listing in **Section One** under **Packard**

Rhode Island Wiring Services Inc	**wiring harnesses**
567 Liberty Ln, Box 434	
W Kingston, RI 02892	
401-789-1955; FAX: 401-783-0091	
E-mail: riwire@brainiac.com	

Mail order and open shop. Monday-Friday 9 am to 5 pm. Exact reproduction wiring harnesses using braided or plastic wire, depending on original. Web site: www.brainiac.com/riwire

Rockland Auto Electric	**electrical parts**
88 S Main St	
Pearl River, NY 10965	
914-735-3362, 914-735-3372	

Mail order and open shop. Monday-Friday 8 am to 5:30 pm, Saturday 8 am to 5 pm. Rebuild starters, generators and alternators for all years and makes of automobiles and other motor vehicles. Full line of voltage regulators and solenoids; chrome starters and alternators also available.

Scotts Manufacturing	**electric fans**
25520 Ave Stanford #304	**fan electronics**
Valencia, CA 91355	
800-544-5596; FAX: 805-295-9342	

Deal in custom built electric cooling fans, 7" to 16" radiator cooling fans in 6, 12 and 24-volt. Also transmission and engine oil coolers with electric fans. Fan electronics, low profile 2" mini fans. Replacement parts for electric fans. Web site: http://home.earthlink.net/~scottsfans

Sierra Specialty Auto	**cylinder rebuilding**
3494 Chandler Rd	
Quincy, CA 95971	
800-4-BRASS-1; FAX: 530-283-4845	
E-mail: joe@restoresource.com	

See full listing in **Section Two** under **brakes**

Silicone Wire Systems	**ignition wire sets**
3462 Kirkwood Dr	
San Jose, CA 95117-1549	
E-mail: sethracer@aol.com	

See full listing in **Section One** under **Corvair**

Southern Autotronics Inc	**radio restorations**
3300 Norfolk St	**repairs**
Richmond, VA 23230	
804-353-5400, 800-446-2880	
FAX: 804-358-3216	
E-mail: ecs@carradio.com	

See full listing in **Section Two** under **radios**

Ed Strain Inc	**magnetos**
6555 44th St #2006	
Pinellas Park, FL 33781	
800-266-1623	

Open Monday-Friday 8 am to 2 pm. Magnetos rebuilt, restored, repaired, coil winding. Home of obsolete technology.

Sunburst Technology	**electronic**
PO Box 598	**technical**
Lithia Springs, GA 30122	**consultant**
770-949-2979; FAX: 770-942-6091	
E-mail: sunburst2000@juno.com	

See full listing in **Section Four** under **information sources**

Tanson Enterprises	**performance parts**
2508 J St, Dept HVA	**restoration parts**
Sacramento, CA 95816-4815	
916-448-2950	
FAX: 916-443-3269 *88	
E-mail: tanson@pipeline.com	

See full listing in **Section One** under **Oldsmobile**

Thunderbolt Traders Inc	**battery cables**
6900 N Dixie Dr	
Dayton, OH 45414-3297	
513-890-3344; FAX: 513-890-9403	

See full listing in **Section One** under **Edsel**

Vintage Ford Center Inc	**accessories**
19437 Harmony Church Rd	**parts**
Leesburg, VA 20175	
888-813-FORD (3673)	
FAX: 703-777-3738	
E-mail: mdla@masinc.com	

See full listing in **Section One** under **Ford 1903-1931**

YnZ's Yesterdays Parts | **wiring harnesses**
333 E Stuart Ave A, Dept AA
Redlands, CA 92374
909-798-1498; FAX: 909-335-6237

Mail order only. For over 2,000 different makes and models. Copies of original wiring harnesses using lacquer coated, braided wire. Simplified number coded instructions. Satisfaction guaranteed. Catalog, $2.

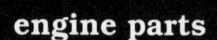 **engine parts**

60 Chev Sam | **parts**
2912 Wright Rd
Hamptonville, NC 27020
336-468-1745

See full listing in **Section One** under **Chevrolet**

A&F Imported Parts Inc | **parts**
490 40th St
Oakland, CA 94609
888-263-7278; FAX: 707-256-0764
E-mail: mmast64166@aol.com

See full listing in **Section One** under **Mercedes-Benz**

Action Performance Inc | **accessories**
1619 Lakeland Ave
Bohemia, NY 11716
516-244-7100; FAX: 516-244-7172

See full listing in **Section Two** under **accessories**

Advanced Maintenance Technologies Inc | **filters** / **lubricants**
Box 250, Mountain Rd
Stowe, VT 05672
802-253-7385; FAX: 802-253-7815
E-mail:
info@advancedmaintenance.com

Mail order and open shop. Monday-Friday 8 am to 6 pm. Filters, lubricants and fittings designed to reduce maintenance costs and extend engine life. Web site: www.advancedmaintenance.com

Atlas Engine Rebuilding Co Inc | **engine rebuilding** / **machine work**
8631 S Avalon Blvd
Los Angeles, CA 90003
323-778-3497; FAX: 323-778-4556

See full listing in **Section Two** under **engine rebuilding**

B & B Cylinder Head Inc | **cylinder heads**
320 Washington St
West Warwick, RI 02893
401-828-4900

Mail order and open shop. Monday-Friday 8 am to 4:30 pm. Cylinder heads, restoration, fabrication, high-performance, no-lead conversions. Antique, obsolete to late model high tech. Custom engines built completely. Motorcycles, trucks, etc.

Bayless Inc | **accessories** / **parts**
1111 Via Bayless
Marietta, GA 30066-2770
770-928-1446; FAX: 770-928-1342
800-241-1446, order line (US & Canada)

See full listing in **Section One** under **Fiat**

Dave Bean Engineering | **parts**
636 E St Charles St SR3H
San Andreas, CA 95249
209-754-5802; FAX: 209-754-5177
E-mail: admin@davebean.com

See full listing in **Section One** under **Lotus**

Bob's Bird House | **parts**
124 Watkin Ave
Chadds Ford, PA 19317
610-358-3420; FAX: 610-558-0729

See full listing in **Section One** under **Thunderbird**

Brisson Enterprises | **lead**
PO Box 1595
Dearborn, MI 48121-1595
313-584-3577

See full listing in **Section Two** under **car care products**

Bronx Automotive | **parts**
501 Tiffany St
Bronx, NY 10474
718-589-2979

See full listing in **Section Two** under **ignition parts**

Bryant's Antique Auto Parts | **appraisals** / **chassis/engine parts** / **sheetmetal** / **wiring harnesses**
851 Western Ave
Hampden, ME 04444
207-862-4019

See full listing in **Section One** under **Ford 1903-1931**

Cam-Pro | **camshaft repair** / **engine parts**
1417 1st Ave SW
Great Falls, MT 59404
800-525-2581, 406-453-9989

See full listing in **Section Two** under **camshafts**

Car-Line Manufacturing & Distribution Inc | **chassis parts** / **engine parts** / **sheetmetal**
1250 Gulf St, PO Box 1192
Beaumont, TX 77701
409-833-9757; FAX: 409-835-2468

See full listing in **Section Two** under **sheetmetal**

Carl's Ford Parts | **muscle parts**
23219 South St, Box 38
Homeworth, OH 44634
PH/FAX: 330-525-7291

See full listing in **Section One** under **Mustang**

Carson's Antique Auto Parts | **parts**
235 Shawfarm Rd
Holliston, MA 01746
508-429-2269; FAX: 508-429-0761
E-mail: w1066@gis.net

Mail order only. Monday-Saturday 9 am to 6 pm EST. Specializing in Auburn, Buick, Cadillac, Chevrolet, Chrysler, Cord, DeSoto, Dodge, Essex, Graham, Graham-Paige, Hudson, Hupmobile, International, Oldsmobile, Overland, Plymouth, Pontiac, Studebaker, Whippet mechanical, ignition, brake, headlight parts, lenses, runningboard moldings, seals, gaskets and transmission gears. Web site: www.webmerchants.com/carson

Casting Salvage Technologies | **repairs**
26 Potomac Creek Dr
Falmouth, VA 22405
800-833-8814; FAX: 540-659-9453

See full listing in **Section Two** under **castings**

Stan Chernoff | **mechanical parts** / **restoration parts** / **technical info** / **trim parts**
1215 Greenwood Ave
Torrance, CA 90503
310-320-4554; FAX: 310-328-7867
E-mail: az589@lafn.org

See full listing in **Section One** under **Datsun**

Ed Cholakian Enterprises Inc | museum parts
dba All Cadillacs of the 40's and 50's
12811 Foothill Blvd
Sylmar, CA 91342
800-808-1147, 818-361-1147
FAX: 818-361-9738

See full listing in **Section One** under **Cadillac/LaSalle**

Collector's Auto Supply | parts
528 Appian Way
Coquitlam, BC Canada V3J 2A5
888-772-7848; FAX: 604-931-4450
E-mail: car@bc.sympatico.ca

See full listing in **Section Two** under **comprehensive parts**

Concours Parts & Accessories | parts
3493 Arrowhead Dr
Carson City, NV 89706
800-722-0009; FAX: 800-725-8644

See full listing in **Section One** under **Thunderbird**

Corvair Underground | parts
PO Box 339
Dundee, OR 97115
800-825-8247, 503-434-1648
FAX: 503-434-1626

See full listing in **Section One** under **Corvair**

CPR | new parts reproduction parts used parts
431 S Sierra Way
San Bernardino, CA 92408
909-884-6980; FAX: 909-884-7872

See full listing in **Section One** under **Pontiac**

Crane Cams Inc | camshafts
530 Fentress Blvd
Daytona Beach, FL 32114
904-258-6174; FAX: 904-258-6167

See full listing in **Section Two** under **camshafts**

Crossfire Manufacturing | accessories
166-B N Mercer Ave, PO Box 263
Sharpsville, PA 16150
800-458-3478
PH/FAX: 724-962-4639
E-mail: xfire@nauticom.net

See full listing in **Section Two** under **ignition parts**

Custom Plating | bumper specialist chrome plating parts
3030 Alta Ridge Way
Snellville, GA 30278
770-736-1118

See full listing in **Section Two** under **plating & polishing**

Dakota Studebaker Parts | parts
RR 1, Box 103A
Armour, SD 57313
605-724-2527

See full listing in **Section One** under **Studebaker**

Damper Dudes | balancers chrome paint
5509 Cedar Rd #2
Redding, CA 96001
800-413-2673, 530-244-7225
FAX: 530-244-2690
E-mail: rliddell@snowcrest.net

Deal in harmonic balancers for all makes and models, new and remanufactured. Special finishes, powder paint, chrome available. Balancing and custom degree work also. Since 1993.

Daytona Turbo Action Camshafts | camshafts engine parts
1109 US #1
PO Box 5094
Ormond Beach, FL 32175
888-RARE-CAM, 800-505-CAMS
904-676-7478; FAX: 904-258-1582
E-mail: info@camshafts.com

See full listing in **Section Two** under **bearings**

Dynatech Engineering | motor mounts
PO Box 1446
Alta Loma, CA 91701-8446
805-492-6134
E-mail: dynatechengineering@yahoo.com

Mail order only. Leading provider of muscle car motor mounts. Dynatech's patented "lock up" design. Allows the engine to float on the insulators during normal driving then lock-up during hard acceleration. These mounts improve launch characteristics and eliminate the need for harsh solid mounts. When installed they look like standard OEM mounts. Call or write for a free *Mitymounts* catalog.

Early Ford V8 Sales Inc | parts
Curtis Industrial Park, Bldg 37
831 Rt 67
Ballston Spa, NY 12020
518-884-2825; FAX: 518-884-2633
E-mail: earlyford@prodigy.net

See full listing in **Section One** under **Ford 1932-1953**

Eckler's Quality Parts & Accessories for Corvettes | accessories parts
PO Box 5637
Titusville, FL 32783
800-327-4868; FAX: 407-383-2059
E-mail: ecklers@ecklers.com

See full listing in **Section One** under **Corvette**

Egge Machine Company Inc | bearings pistons/rings timing components valve train
11707 Slauson Ave
Santa Fe Springs, CA 90670
800-866-EGGE, 562-945-3419
FAX: 562-693-1635
E-mail: info@egge.com

Sales desk open Monday-Friday 7:30 am to 4 pm PST. "The World's Source for Old Car Parts". Specializing in engine parts for domestic cars and light trucks. 1900s-1970s. Call for catalog. Web site: www.egge.com
See our ad inside the back cover

EIS Engines Inc | engines
215 SE Grand Ave
Portland, OR 97214
800-547-0002, 503-232-5590
FAX: 503-232-5178
E-mail: edikeis@aol.com

See full listing in **Section One** under **Mercedes-Benz**

Errol's Steam Works | castings engines parts
3123 Baird Rd
North Vancouver, BC Canada V7K 2G5
PH/FAX: 604-985-9494
E-mail: steamworks@idmail.com

See full listing in **Section One** under **Locomobile**

Ford Powertrain Applications | engines
7702 E 96th St
Puyallup, WA 98371
PH/FAX: 253-848-9503

See full listing in **Section One** under **Ford 1954-up**

Foreign Autotech
3235 C Sunset Ln
Hatboro, PA 19040
215-441-4421; FAX: 215-441-4490
E-mail: fap1800@aol.com

parts

See full listing in **Section One** under **Volvo**

Gaslight Auto Parts Inc
PO Box 291
Urbana, OH 43078
937-652-2145; FAX: 937-652-2147

accessories
parts

See full listing in **Section One** under **Ford 1903-1931**

J Giles Automotive
703 Morgan Ave
Pascagoula, MS 39567-2116
228-769-1012; FAX: 228-769-8904
E-mail: jgauto@datasync.com

car & parts locator
exporter

See full listing in **Section Two** under **car & parts locators**

Good Old Days Garage Inc
2341 Farley Pl
Birmingham, AL 35226
205-822-4569; FAX: 205-823-1944

engine building
Firestone tires
parts
service

See full listing in **Section One** under **Ford 1903-1931**

Gromm Racing Heads
664-J Stockton Ave
San Jose, CA 95126
408-287-1301

cylinder heads
racing parts

See full listing in **Section Two** under **racing**

Halpin Used Auto & Truck Parts
1093 Rt 123
Mayfield, NY 12117
518-863-4906
E-mail: junkyard2064@webtv.net

NOS auto/truck
parts
used auto/truck
parts

See full listing in **Section Five** under **New York**

Mike Hershenfeld
3011 Susan Rd
Bellmore, NY 11710
PH/FAX: 516-781-PART (7278)
E-mail: mikesmopar@juno.com

parts

See full listing in **Section One** under **Mopar**

James Hill
Box 547-V
Goodwell, OK 73939
580-349-2736 evenings/weekends

ignition parts
source list

See full listing in **Section One** under **Packard**

Hollywood Classic Motorcars Inc
363 Ansin Blvd
Hallandale, FL 33009
800-235-2444, 954-454-4641
FAX: 954-457-3801
E-mail: hcm@tbird.net

cars
parts

See full listing in **Section One** under **Thunderbird**

Horst's Car Care
3160-1/2 N Woodford St
Decatur, IL 62526
217-876-1112

engine rebuilding

See full listing in **Section One** under **Mercedes-Benz**

Jackson's Oldtime Parts
4502 Grand Ave
Duluth, MN 55807
218-624-5791, 888-399-7278
E-mail: sales@oldtimeparts.com

parts

Mail order and open shop. Monday-Friday 8 am to 5:30 pm, Saturday 8 am to 1 pm. Large automotive parts store which purchases the older automotive parts from other automotive parts stores, warehouse distributors and aftermarket manufacturers. Sell the parts that an automotive parts store considers obsolete as it is no longer listed in current catalogs. Sell NOS engine, chassis, brake and drivetrain parts which are old, obsolete or no longer in production from 1930-1979. Web site: oldtimeparts.com

Jahns Quality Pistons
1360 N Jefferson St
Anaheim, CA 92807
714-579-3795, 800-225-0277
FAX: 714-524-6607

piston rings
pistons

Specializing in pistons, pins and piston rings for all applications and years from 1-3/4 to 10 inch bores. Antiques, imports, industrial, tractors, trucks and experimental.

Joyce's Model A & T Parts
PO Box 70
Manchaca, TX 78652-0070
512-282-1196

new parts
NOS parts
rebuilt parts

See full listing in **Section One** under **Ford 1903-1931**

Kanter Auto Products
76 Monroe St
Boonton, NJ 07005
800-526-1096, 201-334-9575
FAX: 201-334-5423

car cover
carpets
parts

See full listing in **Section Two** under **comprehensive parts**

Ken's Carburetors
2301 Barnum Ave
Stratford, CT 06615
203-375-9340

carburetors
distributors
parts

See full listing in **Section One** under **Ford 1932-1953**

Lindskog Balancing
1170 Massachusetts Ave
Boxborough, MA 01719-1415
978-263-2040; FAX: 978-263-4035

engine balancing

See full listing in **Section Two** under **engine rebuilding**

Linearossa International Inc
3931 SW 47th Ave
Ft Lauderdale, FL 33314
954-327-9888; FAX: 954-791-6555

parts

See full listing in **Section One** under **Fiat**

David Martin
Box 61
Roosevelt, TX 76874
915-446-4439

parts

See full listing in **Section One** under **Chrysler**

Maximum Torque Specialties
PO Box 925
Delavan, WI 53115
414-740-1118; FAX: 414-740-1161

high-perf parts
restoration parts

See full listing in **Section One** under **Cadillac/LaSalle**

Michigan Corvette Recyclers
11995 US 223
Riga, MI 49276
800-533-4650; FAX: 517-486-4124

Corvette parts
new/used parts

See full listing in **Section One** under **Corvette**

Miller Energy Inc
3200 South Clinton Ave
S Plainfield, NJ 07080
908-755-6700; FAX: 908-755-0312
E-mail allyon@aol.com

engine parts

See full listing in **Section One** under **Stanley**

Millers Incorporated
7412 Count Circle
Huntington Beach, CA 92647
714-375-6565; FAX: 714-847-6606
E-mail: sales@millermbz.com

accessories
parts

See full listing in **Section One** under **Mercedes-Benz**

Moline Engine Service Inc
3227 23rd Ave
Moline, IL 61265
309-764-9735

parts
rebuilding

Open Monday-Friday 9 am to 5 pm. Complete auto machine shop stocking crankshafts, cylinder heads, connecting rods, etc. for cars from 1950-date. Engine rebuilding, balancing, crankshaft exchange. Internal engine parts all US. 48 years in business.

Mooney's Antique Chevrolet Parts
HC 01, Box 645C
Goodrich, TX 77335
409-365-2899, 9 am to 6 pm
409-685-4577, 6 pm to 9 pm
orders only
FAX: 409-685-4711

engine parts
rubber parts

See full listing in **Section One** under **Chevrolet**

Northern Auto Parts Warehouse Inc
PO Box 3147
Sioux City, IA 51102
800-831-0884; FAX: 712-258-0088

parts

Hundreds of engine rebuild kits available. Plus carbs, manifolds, oil pumps, etc from stock to performance. You have the vehicle, we have the parts. Web site: www.naparts.com

Northwestern Auto Supply Inc
1101 S Division
Grand Rapids, MI 49507
616-241-1714, 800-704-1078
FAX: 616-241-0924

parts

Mail order and retail store. Monday-Friday 8 am to 5:30 pm, Saturday by appointment. An old time parts store that enjoys servicing the old, classic and current car enthusiast. Deal in mechanical parts such as engine, brake, ignition, chassis and drivetrain. When ordering ask for Sam.

Obsolete Chevrolet Parts Co
524 Hazel Ave
PO Box 68
Nashville, GA 31639-0068
800-248-8785; FAX: 912-686-3056
E-mail: obschevy@surfsouth.com

engine parts
radiators
rubber parts
transmissions

See full listing in **Section One** under **Chevrolet**

Obsolete Jeep® & Willys® Parts
Division of Florida 4 Wheel Drive &
Truck Parts
6110 17th St E
Bradenton, FL 34203
941-756-7844
PH/FAX: 941-756-7757

literature
parts

See full listing in **Section One** under **Willys**

Opel Oldtimer Service Denmark
Landevejen 27
Toksvaerd
DK-4684 Holme-Olstrup Denmark
PH/FAX: +45-55-530100
best 11 am to 3 pm US Central time
E-mail: frank.kiessling@get2net.dk

literature
parts
parts locator

See full listing in **Section One** under **Opel**

Operations Plus
PO Box 26347
Santa Ana, CA 92799
PH/FAX: 714-962-2776
E-mail: aquacel@aquacel.com

accessories
parts

See full listing in **Section One** under **Cobra**

Paragon Reproductions Inc
8040 S Jennings Rd
Swartz Creek, MI 48473
810-655-4641; FAX: 810-655-6667
E-mail:
www.info@corvette-paragon.com

Corvette repro
parts

See full listing in **Section One** under **Corvette**

Parts House
2912 Hunter St
Fort Worth, TX 76112
817-451-2708
E-mail: theparts@flash.net

accessories
parts

See full listing in **Section Two** under **comprehensive parts**

The Parts Scout®
Bodo Repenn
Diagonalstrasse 18A
D-20537 Hamburg Germany
*49-40-21980130
FAX: *49-40-21980132

parts
parts locator

See full listing in **Section Two** under **comprehensive parts**

Partwerks of Chicago
718 S Prairie Rd
New Lenox, IL 60451
815-462-3000; FAX: 815-462-3006
E-mail: partwerks9@aol.com

parts
service

Mail order and open shop. Monday-Saturday 8 am to 6 pm. Parts and services for all German autos.

Paul's Select Cars & Parts for Porsche®
2280 Gail Dr
Riverside, CA 92509
909-685-9340; FAX: 909-685-9342
E-mail: pauls356-s90@webtv.net

cars
parts

See full listing in **Section One** under **Porsche**

Performance Chevy
2995 W Whitton
Phoenix, AZ 85017
800-203-6621; FAX: 602-254-1094

engine parts
restoration

See full listing in **Section One** under **Corvette**

| Performance Coatings
9768 Feagin Rd
Jonesboro, GA 30236
770-478-2775; FAX: 770-478-1926 | **ceramic coatings**
engine parts
suspension parts |

See full listing in **Section Two** under **exhaust systems**

| Power Play, Bob Walker
276 Walkers Hollow Tr
Lowgap, NC 27024
336-352-4866; FAX: 336-789-8967
E-mail: rlwalker@infoave.net | **parts** |

See full listing in **Section One** under **Chrysler**

| Red Bird Racing
6640 Valley St
Coeur d'Alene, ID 83815
208-762-5305 | **parts** |

See full listing in **Section One** under **Chevrolet**

| Red's Headers & Early Ford Speed
Equipment
22950 Bednar Ln
Fort Bragg, CA 95437-8411
707-964-7733; FAX: 707-964-5434
E-mail: red@reds-headers.com | **headers**
mechanical parts |

See full listing in **Section One** under **Ford 1932-1953**

| Rochester Clutch & Brake Co
35 Niagara St
Rochester, NY 14605
716-232-2579; FAX: 716-232-3279 | **brakes**
clutches |

See full listing in **Section Two** under **brakes**

| SC Automotive
Rt 3 Box 9
New Ulm, MN 56073
800-62-SS-409 (627-7409)
507-354-1958 info
FAX: 800-6477-FAX (647-7329) | **parts**
restoration |

See full listing in **Section One** under **Chevrolet**

| Scotts Manufacturing
25520 Ave Stanford #304
Valencia, CA 91355
800-544-5596; FAX: 805-295-9342 | **electric fans**
fan electronics |

See full listing in **Section Two** under **electrical systems**

| Joe Smith Ford & Hot Rod Parts
2140 Canton Rd, Unit C
Marietta, GA 30066
800-235-4013, 770-426-9850
FAX: 770-426-9854
E-mail: hank@joesmithauto.com | **parts**
service |

See full listing in **Section One** under **Ford 1932-1953**

| Smith & Jones Distributing
Company Inc
1 Biloxi Square
West Columbia, SC 29170
803-822-8500; FAX: 803-822-8477 | **parts** |

See full listing in **Section One** under **Ford 1903-1931**

| Special Interest Car Parts
1340 Hartford Ave
Johnston, RI 02919
800-556-7496; FAX: 401-831-7760 | **parts** |

See full listing in **Section One** under **Jaguar**

| Star Quality
1 Alley Rd
Lagrangeville, NY 12540
800-782-7199; FAX: 914-223-5394
E-mail: sq@mhv.net | **parts** |

See full listing in **Section One** under **Mercedes-Benz**

| Straight Six Jaguar
24321 Hatteras St
Woodland Hills, CA 91367
PH/FAX: 818-716-1192 | **parts**
service |

See full listing in **Section One** under **Jaguar**

| Straw Church Speed Shop
602 Passaic St
Phillipsburg, NJ 08865
908-454-7487
E-mail: strawchurch_ss@hotmail.com | **accessories**
engine swaps
parts |

See full listing in **Section Two** under **car & parts locators**

| Studebaker Parts & Locations
228 Marquiss Cir
Clinton, TN 37716
615-457-3002
E-mail: studebaker_joe@msn.com | **parts**
parts locator |

See full listing in **Section One** under **Studebaker**

| Superior Pump Exchange Co
12901 Crenshaw Blvd
Hawthorne, CA 90250-5511
310-676-4995
E-mail: autoh20@aol.com | **water pumps** |

See full listing in **Section Two** under **water pumps**

| Swedish Classics Inc
PO Box 557
Oxford, MD 21654
800-258-4422; FAX: 410-226-5543 | **parts** |

See full listing in **Section One** under **Volvo**

| T-Bird Sanctuary
9997 SW Avery
Tualatin, OR 97062
503-692-9848; FAX: 503-692-9849 | **parts** |

See full listing in **Section One** under **Thunderbird**

| TA Motor AB
Torpslingan 21
Lulea S 97347 Sweden
+46-920-18888
FAX: +46-920-18821 | **accessories**
parts |

See full listing in **Section One** under **Cadillac/LaSalle**

| Tatom Vintage Vendors
PO Box 2504
Mt Vernon, WA 98273
360-424-8314; FAX: 360-424-6717
E-mail: flatheads@tatom.com | **engine rebuilding**
machine shop |

See full listing in **Section Two** under **engine rebuilding**

Total Seal Inc 11202 N 24th Ave, Ste 101 Phoenix, AZ 85029 602-678-4977; FAX: 602-678-4991 E-mail: totseal@amug.org	**piston rings**

Total Seal, in its 31st year, is the manufacturer of Total Seal gapless piston rings that are currently used extensively in the performance market. Using gapless technology, Offer a more efficient ring that will cut engine leakdown to 2% or less. By cutting the blow-by, your engine will have cleaner oil, improved bearing life, more power and run more efficiently. Stock many hard to find applications. Web site: www.totalseal.com

Vibratech Inc (Fluidampr) 11980 Walden Ave Alden, NY 14004 716-937-3603; FAX: 716-937-4692	**performance parts**

Manufacture Fluidamprs-performance harmonic dampers, used in high-performance street and race applications.

Vintage Ford Center Inc 19437 Harmony Church Rd Leesburg, VA 20175 888-813-FORD (3673) FAX: 703-777-3738 E-mail: mdla@masinc.com	**accessories** **parts**

See full listing in **Section One** under **Ford 1903-1931**

Vintage Motor Gaskets W 604 19th Spokane, WA 99203 509-747-9960, 509-747-0517 E-mail: dbrooke@ior.com	**gaskets**

See full listing in **Section Two** under **gaskets**

Paul Weaver's Garage 680 Sylvan Way Bremerton, WA 98310 360-373-7870	**rings**

Piston rings for cars, trucks and tractors through 1980. Please specify oversize, quantity and widths.

Winslow Mfg Co 5700 Dean Ave Raleigh, NC 27604 919-790-9713	**parts rebuilding**

Mail order only. Proprietorship specializing in the rebuilding and reconstruction of worn machinery and automobile parts with original rubber bushings. New material is high strength silicone. Harmonic balancer and flexible coupling rebuilding.

Zip Products 8067 Fast Ln Mechanicsville, VA 23111 804-746-2290, 800-962-9632 FAX: 804-730-7043 E-mail: zipvette@erols.com	**accessories** **parts**

See full listing in **Section One** under **Corvette**

engine rebuilding

356 Enterprises Vic & Barbara Skirmants 27244 Ryan Rd Warren, MI 48092 810-575-9544; FAX: 810-558-3616	**parts**

See full listing in **Section One** under **Porsche**

Ace Antique Auto Restoration 65 S Service Rd Plainview, NY 11803 516-752-6065; FAX: 516-752-1484	**air conditioning** **body rebuilding** **restoration** **wiring harnesses**

See full listing in **Section Two** under **restoration shops**

Action Performance Inc 1619 Lakeland Ave Bohemia, NY 11716 516-244-7100; FAX: 516-244-7172	**accessories**

See full listing in **Section Two** under **accessories**

Aldrich Auto Supply Inc 95 Prospect St Hatfield, MA 01038 800-533-2306, 413-247-0230	**engine rebuilding**

Mail order and open shop. Monday-Friday 8 am to 5:30 pm. Auto engine rebuilding shop specializing in unleaded gas conversions and complete overhauls of classic, vintage and hi-performance engines. Also repair of cracked aluminum and cast iron engine components.

Andy's Classic Mustangs 18502 E Sprague Greenacres, WA 99016 509-924-9824	**parts** **service**

See full listing in **Section One** under **Mustang**

Atlas Engine Rebuilding Co Inc 8631 S Avalon Blvd Los Angeles, CA 90003 323-778-3497; FAX: 323-778-4556	**engine rebuilding** **machine work**

Open shop only. Monday-Friday 8 am to 5 pm. In business for over 35 years. Complete engine rebuilding and machine shop. Crankshaft grinding and camshaft grinding. All internal engine parts.

Austin Works East PO Box 1997 Sandwich, MA 02563 PH/FAX: 508-833-3109 E-mail: austnworks@aol.com	**parts** **service**

See full listing in **Section One** under **Austin**

Automotive Restorations Inc Stephen Babinsky 4 Center St Bernardsville, NJ 07924 908-766-6688; FAX: 908-766-6684 E-mail: autorestnj@aol.com	**clutch rebuilding** **mechanical** **services** **restorations**

See full listing in **Section Two** under **restoration shops**

B & B Cylinder Head Inc 320 Washington St West Warwick, RI 02893 401-828-4900	**cylinder heads**

See full listing in **Section Two** under **engine parts**

Bicknell Engine Company 7055 Dayton Rd Enon, OH 45323 937-864-5224	**parts** **repair** **restoration**

See full listing in **Section One** under **Buick/McLaughlin**

BPE Racing Heads 702 Dunn Way Placentia, CA 92870 714-572-6072; FAX: 714-572-6073 E-mail: steve@bpeheads.com	**cylinder heads**

See full listing in **Section Two** under **machine work**

Cam-Pro
1417 1st Ave SW
Great Falls, MT 59404
800-525-2581, 406-453-9989

camshaft repair
engine parts

See full listing in **Section Two** under **camshafts**

Classic Carriages
267 County Rd 420
Athens, TN 37303
PH/FAX: 423-744-7496

repair
restoration

See full listing in **Section One** under **Ford 1932-1953**

Corvette Mike
1133 N Tustin Ave
Anaheim, CA 92807
800-327-8388, 714-630-0700
FAX: 714-630-0777
E-mail: cvtmike@deltanet.com

accessories
parts
sales
service

See full listing in **Section One** under **Corvette**

County Corvette
PO Box 258
Lionville, PA 19353
610-363-0872, 610-363-7670 sales
FAX: 610-363-5325

restoration
sales
service

See full listing in **Section One** under **Corvette**

Crow Engineering Jaguar Engines
433 Tremont St
Taunton, MA 02780
800-537-4146

engine rebuilding

See full listing in **Section One** under **Jaguar**

Damper Dudes
5509 Cedar Rd #2
Redding, CA 96001
800-413-2673, 530-244-7225
FAX: 530-244-2690
E-mail: rliddell@snowcrest.net

balancers
chrome
paint

See full listing in **Section Two** under **engine parts**

Done Right Engine & Machine Inc
12955 York Delta Unit J
North Royalton, OH 44133
440-582-1366; FAX: 440-582-2005

engine rebuilding
machine shop

Complete engine rebuilding and machine shop services, specializing in antique and classic engines. Complete turn key engines along with removal and installation service. Custom built engines to meet customer's needs.

EIS Engines Inc
215 SE Grand Ave
Portland, OR 97214
800-547-0002, 503-232-5590
FAX: 503-232-5178
E-mail: edikeis@aol.com

engines

See full listing in **Section One** under **Mercedes-Benz**

Errol's Steam Works
3123 Baird Rd
North Vancouver, BC Canada V7K 2G5
PH/FAX: 604-985-9494
E-mail: steamworks@idmail.com

castings
engines
parts

See full listing in **Section One** under **Locomobile**

Excelsweld USA/Cylinder Head Specialist
1231 16th Ave
Oakland, CA 94606
800-743-4323; FAX: 510-534-1107

welding

See full listing in **Section Two** under **machine work**

Ford Powertrain Applications
7702 E 96th St
Puyallup, WA 98371
PH/FAX: 253-848-9503

engines

See full listing in **Section One** under **Ford 1954-up**

Grand Touring
2785 E Regal Park Dr
Anaheim, CA 92806
714-630-0130; FAX: 714-630-6956

engine rebuilding
machine shop
restoration
suspension

See full listing in **Section Two** under **restoration shops**

Grey Hills Auto Restoration
PO Box 630
51 Vail Rd
Blairstown, NJ 07825
908-362-8232; FAX: 908-362-6796

restoration
service

See full listing in **Section Two** under **restoration shops**

Harkin Machine Shop
903 43rd St NE
Watertown, SD 57201
605-886-7880

engine rebuilding
rebabbitting

Mail order and open shop. Monday-Friday 8 am to 6 pm. Rebabbitting engine bearings and complete rebuilding of antique car engines.

Horst's Car Care
3160-1/2 N Woodford St
Decatur, IL 62526
217-876-1112

engine rebuilding

See full listing in **Section One** under **Mercedes-Benz**

K&W Kollectibles
220 Industrial Pkwy S #6
Aurora, ON Canada L4G 3V6
416-410-7741; FAX: 905-727-5771
E-mail: kwkoll@sympatico.ca

parts
repair
restoration

See full listing in **Section One** under **Buick/McLaughlin**

Knight Automotive Engineering Inc
Kettle Cove Industrial Park
743 Western Ave, Rt 127
Gloucester, MA 01930
978-525-3491

engine rebuilding

Mail order and open shop. Monday-Friday 8 am to 5 pm, Saturday by appointment. Complete automotive machine shop including babbitting and align boring. Custom rebuilding of all makes of engines. Specializing in rebuilding Ford engines from Model Ts to present. Providing the automotive hobby with quality engine rebuilding for over 20 years. Visitors always welcome. Stop by or call.

Koffel's Place II
740 River Rd
Huron, OH 44839
419-433-4410; FAX: 419-433-2166

engine rebuilding
machine shop

Mail order and open shop. Monday-Friday 8 am to 6 pm, Wednesday 8 am to 9 pm. Two locations providing quality service and parts. Engine building for racing, collector cars, street rods, antique cars and boats. Complete in-house machine shop services and dyno testing.

Krem Engineering
10204 Perry Hwy
Meadville, PA 16335
814-724-4806; FAX: 814-337-2992
E-mail: info@krem-enterprises.com

engine rebuilding
repairs
restoration

See full listing in **Section Two** under **restoration shops**

L & N Olde Car Co | restoration
9992 Kinsman Rd
PO Box 378
Newbury, OH 44065
440-564-7204; FAX: 440-564-8187

See full listing in **Section Two** under **restoration shops**

Last Chance Repair & Restoration | repairs restoration
PO Box 362A
Myers Rd
Shaftsbury, VT 05262

See full listing in **Section Two** under **restoration shops**

Libbey's Classic Car Restoration Center | bodywork restoration service
137 N Quinsigamond Ave
Shrewsbury, MA 01545
PH/FAX: 508-792-1560

See full listing in **Section Two** under **restoration shops**

Lincoln Highway Packards | engine rebuilding restoration
Main St
PO Box 94
Schellsburg, PA 15559
814-733-4356; FAX: 814-839-4276

See full listing in **Section One** under **Packard**

Lindley Restorations Ltd | parts sales service
10 S Sanatoga Rd
Pottstown, PA 19464
610-326-8484; FAX: 610-326-3845

See full listing in **Section One** under **Jaguar**

Lindskog Balancing | engine balancing
1170 Massachusetts Ave
Boxborough, MA 01719-1415
978-263-2040; FAX: 978-263-4035

Complete engine balancing and individual engine component balancing. Antique work is our specialty.

Moline Engine Service Inc | parts rebuilding
3227 23rd Ave
Moline, IL 61265
309-764-9735

See full listing in **Section Two** under **engine parts**

Morgan Oasis Garage | restoration service
PO Box 1010
N 51 Terrace Rd
Hoodsport, WA 98548
360-877-5160

See full listing in **Section One** under **Morgan**

Motorworks Inc | remanufactured engines
4210 Salem St
Philadelphia, PA 19124
800-327-9905; FAX: 215-533-4112
E-mail:
motorworks@motorworksinc.com

Motorworks and Dr Motorworx remanufactured engine installation centers. Specializing in remanufactured engines for cars, trucks, vans, boats, RVs. 54 centers nationwide. Franchise opportunities are available. Web site: www.motorworksinc.com

Nationwide Auto Restoration | bodywork paint upholstery
1038 Watt St
Jeffersonville, IN 47130
812-280-0165; FAX: 812-280-8961
E-mail: restore@unidial.com

See full listing in **Section Two** under **restoration shops**

Northern Auto Parts Warehouse Inc | parts
PO Box 3147
Sioux City, IA 51102
800-831-0884; FAX: 712-258-0088

See full listing in **Section Two** under **engine parts**

Odyssey Restorations Inc | parts restoration
8080 Central Ave NE
Spring Lake Park, MN 55432
612-786-1518; FAX: 612-786-1524

See full listing in **Section Two** under **restoration shops**

Partwerks of Chicago | parts service
718 S Prairie Rd
New Lenox, IL 60451
815-462-3000; FAX: 815-462-3006
E-mail: partwerks9@aol.com

See full listing in **Section Two** under **engine parts**

Performance Chevy | engine parts restoration
2995 W Whitton
Phoenix, AZ 85017
800-203-6621; FAX: 602-254-1094

See full listing in **Section One** under **Corvette**

Pitcher's Auto Restoration | engine repair parts restoration
54 Metaterraine Ave
Perryville, RI 02879
401-783-4392

See full listing in **Section Two** under **restoration shops**

Ponti-Action Racing | engine builders
PO Box 354
Medfield, MA 02052
888-RAM-AIRS; FAX: 508-359-5435
E-mail: gtogeezer@aol.com

See full listing in **Section One** under **Pontiac**

Pontiac Engines Custom Built | custom built engines
Box 2422
Longmont, CO 80502
303-776-0877
E-mail: pontiacgregg@earthlink.net

See full listing in **Section One** under **Pontiac**

Power Play, Bob Walker | parts
276 Walkers Hollow Tr
Lowgap, NC 27024
336-352-4866; FAX: 336-789-8967
E-mail: rlwalker@infoave.net

See full listing in **Section One** under **Chrysler**

R & L Engines Inc | engine rebuilding restorations
308 Durham Rd
Dover, NH 03820
603-742-8812; FAX: 603-742-8137

Mail order and open shop. Monday-Friday 8 am to 5 pm, Saturday 8 am to 12 noon. Deal in specialty engine rebuilding, antique restoration, classic, street rod, high-performance and marine. Web site: rlengines.com

Roadrunner Tire & Auto | restoration speedometer repair
4850 Hwy 377 S
Fort Worth, TX 76116
817-244-4924

See full listing in **Section Two** under **restoration shops**

Ross' Automotive Machine Co Inc 1763 N Main St Niles, OH 44446 330-544-4466	**racing engines rebuilding**

Mail order and open shop. Specializing in 1949-1964 Olds motors. Deal in 1949-1970 Chev, Olds, Buick, Pontiac. Stock rebuilds, unleaded conversions, racing engines, balancing, dyno testing, etc. A 6 man racing engine shop with the most modern equipment including dyno and ultrasonic testing. Capable of very close tolerance machining as we build NASCAR motors and are especially interested in 1949-1964 Olds motors.

Scotts Manufacturing 25520 Ave Stanford #304 Valencia, CA 91355 800-544-5596; FAX: 805-295-9342	**electric fans fan electronics**

See full listing in **Section Two** under **electrical systems**

Shepard's Automotive Div of Fine Ride Industries 4131 S Main St Akron, OH 44319 330-644-2000; FAX: 330-644-6522	**appraisals engine remanufacturing**

Specialist/remanufacturing antique motors. Rebuilding standard/performance engines. Known worldwide for our remanufactured Cadillac-Hemis-Packards, max wedge motors and long list of many others. Specialist 1920s-1970s power plants. Work performed in-house with 2 hi-tech machine shops. Motors are show quality and pre-run on test stand to assure guarantee. 48 years of engine building. "Best on the block". Web site: www.enterit.com/shepards2000.htm

Silver Star Restorations 116 Highway 19 Topton, NC 28781 704-321-4268 E-mail: silverstar@main.nc.us	**parts restoration**

See full listing in **Section One** under **Mercedes-Benz**

Joe Smith Ford & Hot Rod Parts 2140 Canton Rd, Unit C Marietta, GA 30066 800-235-4013, 770-426-9850 FAX: 770-426-9854 E-mail: hank@joesmithauto.com	**parts service**

See full listing in **Section One** under **Ford 1932-1953**

Brooks Stevens Auto Collection Inc 10325 N Port Washington Rd Mequon, WI 53092 414-241-4185; FAX: 414-241-4166 E-mail: apjb@prodigy.net	**parts restoration service**

See full listing in **Section One** under **Excalibur**

Stone Barn Inc 202 Rt 46, Box 117 Vienna, NJ 07880 908-637-4444; FAX: 908-637-4290	**restoration**

See full listing in **Section Two** under **restoration shops**

Straight Six Jaguar 24321 Hatteras St Woodland Hills, CA 91367 PH/FAX: 818-716-1192	**parts service**

See full listing in **Section One** under **Jaguar**

Tatom Vintage Vendors PO Box 2504 Mt Vernon, WA 98273 360-424-8314; FAX: 360-424-6717 E-mail: flatheads@tatom.com	**engine rebuilding machine shop**

In business for over 10 years. Engine restoration and the construction of vintage, specialty, hi-performance and race engines. Full service machine shop including cast iron repair. Substantial number of major brand speed equipment parts available. Call for catalog. Web site: tatom.com

See our ad on this page

Teddy's Garage 8530 Louise Ave Northridge, CA 91325 818-341-0505	**parts restoration service**

See full listing in **Section One** under **Rolls-Royce/Bentley**

Thul Auto Parts Inc 225 Roosevelt Ave Plainfield, NJ 07060 800-276-8485, 908-754-3333 FAX: 908-756-0239 E-mail: thulauto@juno.com	**boring machine work rebabbitting vintage auto parts**

Open Monday-Friday 8 am to 5:30 pm. Rebabbitting, crankshaft grinding and build up, align boring, resleeving, reboring, large general machine shop. Some old engines and parts, cracked blocks and heads repaired. Resleeving, reboring, crack repairs, large general machine shop. Web site: www.thulautoparts.com

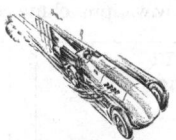

Section Two
Generalists

Total Seal Inc
11202 N 24th Ave, Ste 101
Phoenix, AZ 85029
602-678-4977; FAX: 602-678-4991
E-mail: totseal@amug.org

piston rings

See full listing in **Section Two** under **engine parts**

Vintage Motor and Machine
Gene French
1513 Webster Ct
Ft Collins, CO 80524
970-498-9224

auto components
fixtures
industrial
components

See full listing in **Section Two** under **machine work**

Vintage Racing Services
1785 Barnum Ave
Stratford, CT 06497
203-386-1736; FAX: 203-386-0486
E-mail:
vrs@vintageracingservices.com

storage
track support
transportation

See full listing in **Section Two** under **racing**

West Amity Auto Parts
5685 Merrick Rd
Massapequa, NY 11758
516-795-4610; FAX: 516-795-4117
E-mail: crein69929@erols.com

custom machining
engine rebuilding

Specializing in engine rebuilding for flathead Fords. Antique engine rebuilding, high-performance engines and custom machining. Web site: www.waapmachine.com

Wild Bill's Corvette & Hi-Performance Center Inc
446 Dedham St
Wrentham, MA 02093
508-384-7373; FAX: 508-384-9366
E-mail:
wildbillscorvette@worldnet.att.net

parts
rebuilding
service

See full listing in **Section One** under **Corvette**

Willow Automotive Service
Box 4640 Rt 212
Willow, NY 12495
914-679-4679

bodywork
painting
restoration

See full listing in **Section Two** under **restoration shops**

Zim's Autotechnik
1804 Reliance Pkwy
Bedford, TX 76021
800-356-2964; FAX: 817-545-2002
E-mail: zimips@allzim.com

parts
service

See full listing in **Section One** under **Porsche**

exhaust systems

5362 Corvette Place
4602 Kenbridge Dr
Greensboro, NC 27410
336-852-1011; FAX: 336-852-6107

Corvette parts

See full listing in **Section One** under **Corvette**

A&A Mustang Parts & Mfg Co
105 Fordham Rd
Oak Ridge, TN 37830
423-482-9445

exhaust systems
parts
restorations

See full listing in **Section One** under **Mustang**

Accurate Muffler Ltd
7125 Hwy 99 N
Roseburg, OR 97470
PH/FAX: 541-672-2661
E-mail: taswope@jeffnet.org

muffler products

See full listing in **Section One** under **Mopar**

Aremco Products Inc
707-B Executive Blvd
Valley Cottage, NY 10989
914-268-0039; FAX: 914-268-0041
E-mail: aremco@aremco.com

compound

See full listing in **Section Two** under **accessories**

Gideon Booth
Rellandsgate, Kings Meaburn
Penrith
Cumbria CA10 3BT England
PH/FAX: 01931 714624

car collector
parts
restorations

See full listing in **Section One** under **Morris**

Tony D Branda Performance
Shelby and Mustang Parts
1434 E Pleasant Valley Blvd
Altoona, PA 16602
814-942-1869; FAX: 814-944-0801
E-mail: cobranda@aol.com

accessories
decals
emblems
sheetmetal
wheels

See full listing in **Section One** under **Mustang**

Cars of the Past
11180 Kinsman Rd
Newbury, OH 44065
440-564-2277

restoration

See full listing in **Section Two** under **restoration shops**

Chev's of the 40's
2027 B St, Dept HVA
Washougal, WA 98671
800-999-CHEV (2438)
FAX: 360-835-7988

parts

See full listing in **Section One** under **Chevrolet**

Double S Exhausts Ltd
Station Rd
Cullompton, Devon EX15 1BW
England
0044-1884-33454
FAX: 0044-1884-32829

exhausts

Mail order and open shop. Monday-Friday 9 am to 5 pm. Specializing in stainless steel exhaust and later pipes. Check out our catalog on the internet. Web site: stainlesssteelexhausts.com

Ford Powertrain Applications
7702 E 96th St
Puyallup, WA 98371
PH/FAX: 253-848-9503

engines

See full listing in **Section One** under **Ford 1954-up**

Jim Fortin
95 Weston St
Brockton, MA 02301-3334
508-586-4855
E-mail: het1@aol.com

exhaust systems

Mail order and open shop by appointment only. Phone hours: Monday-Friday noon to midnight; weekends by chance. Prefer e-mail or telephone calls, however, all letters with SASE answered. Exhaust systems manufactured for most cars and light trucks from 1909-muscle car era. Pipes manufactured in heavy steel, inquire for aluminized or stainless steel. Most mufflers aluminized. Have large amount of NORS mufflers available from mid 1950s-late 1960s. We also have carburetor heat tubes for 1920s, 1930s Buicks. Lower radiator water connector tubes available for Mopar, GM, Ford, Hudson, Packard. Guaranteed satisfaction on all parts sold. Established 1967. At 53, I've been exhausting myself for over 33 years.

Gardner Exhaust Systems 2 Cedar Ln Rhinebeck, NY 12572 PH/FAX: 914-876-8117 E-mail: gexhaust@aol.com	exhaust systems

See full listing in **Section One** under **Chevelle/Camaro**

High Performance Coatings 550 W 3615 S Salt Lake City, UT 84115 800-456-4721, 801-262-6807 FAX: 801-262-6307 E-mail: hpcsales@hpcoatings.com	coatings

Mail order and open shop. Monday-Friday 8 am to 5 pm. Specializing in all cars and motorcycles exhaust system coatings, thermal barrier coatings, dry film lubricative coatings, corrosion resistant coatings. Web site: www.hpcoatings.com

Hooker Headers 1024 W Brooks St Ontario, CA 91762 909-983-5871; FAX: 909-986-9860	exhaust systems

Manufacturer of the world's best headers, performance mufflers, cat-back and dual exhaust kits. Hooker tips and car bars. Hooker also offers metallic, ceramic thermal barrier coating services.

Italy's Famous Exhaust 2711 183rd St Redondo Beach, CA 90278 310-793-5985 E-mail: famous@earthlink.net	exhaust systems wheels

Mail order only. 24 hours. Dealing in Daytona free flow exhaust systems and Campagnolo wheels. Exclusive global distributor for FAZA. Web site: www.famousexhaust.com

London Stainless Steel Exhaust Centre 249-253 Queenstown Rd London, SW8 3NP England 011-44-171622-2120 FAX: 011-44-171627- 0991 E-mail: 101445.341@compuserv.com	exhaust systems

Mail order and open shop. Monday-Saturday 8:30 am to 5:30 pm. The widest range of stainless steel exhausts anywhere, fast UPS delivery.

Marcel's Corvette Parts 15100 Lee Rd #101 Humble, TX 77396 800-546-2111 order line 281-441-2111 info line FAX: 281-441-3057	parts

See full listing in **Section One** under **Corvette**

National Parts Depot 3101 SW 40th Blvd Gainesville, FL 32608 800-874-7595 toll-free 24 hours 352-378-2473 local	accessories restoration parts

See full listing in **Section Two** under **comprehensive parts**

Pace Setter Performance Products 2841 W Clarendon Ave Phoenix, AZ 85017 602-266-1964; FAX: 602-650-1136	exhaust systems fluid transfer hose intake tubes shifters

Manufacture and open shop. Monday-Friday 8 am to 4:30 pm

MST. Exhaust systems for import cars and trucks, including Triumph, Austin-Healey, MG, VW, Nissan and Honda. Web site: www.pacesetterexhaust.com

Performance Coatings 9768 Feagin Rd Jonesboro, GA 30236 770-478-2775; FAX: 770-478-1926	ceramic coatings engine parts suspension parts

Deal in metallic ceramic coatings for exhaust components. Powder coatings for chassis, suspension and engine components.

Porcelain Patch & Glaze Co Inc 966 86th Ave Oakland, CA 94621 510-635-2188	porcelain enameling

Open Monday-Friday 9 am to 3 pm. Specializing in porcelain enameling of intake and exhaust manifolds. Welding and repairs available. UPS orders.

Power Effects® 1800H Industrial Park Dr Grand Haven, MI 49417 877-3POWRFX toll-free 616-847-4200 FAX: 616-847-4210	exhaust systems

Power Effects® performance components and engineered systems are designed for cars, sport trucks, sport utility vehicles and street rods. Flange mounted cast aluminum exhaust components and mandrel bent tubing provide maximum flexibility and ease of installation. Aluminum tuneable Power Capsules™ replace conventional mufflers offering superior air flow and a deep, rich-sounding exhaust. Aluminum Power Tips™ finish off the tailpipe end and are available to fit 2-1/4, 2-1/2, 2-3/4 and 3 inch tubing using our flanges. Web site: www.powereffects.com

Section Two Generalists

Section Two Generalists

RD Enterprises Ltd   **parts**
290 Raub Rd
Quakertown, PA 18951
215-538-9323; FAX: 215-538-0158
E-mail: rdent@rdent.com

See full listing in **Section One** under **Lotus**

Red Bird Racing   **parts**
6640 Valley St
Coeur d'Alene, ID 83815
208-762-5305

See full listing in **Section One** under **Chevrolet**

Red's Headers & Early Ford Speed   **headers**
Equipment   **mechanical parts**
22950 Bednar Ln
Fort Bragg, CA 95437-8411
707-964-7733; FAX: 707-964-5434
E-mail: red@reds-headers.com

See full listing in **Section One** under **Ford 1932-1953**

SC Automotive   **parts**
Rt 3 Box 9   **restoration**
New Ulm, MN 56073
800-62-SS-409 (627-7409)
507-354-1958 info
FAX: 800-6477-FAX (647-7329)

See full listing in **Section One** under **Chevrolet**

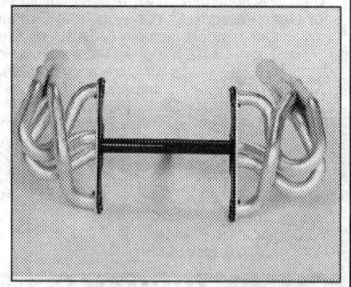

Stahl Headers Inc   **exhaust systems**
1515 Mount Rose Ave
York, PA 17403
717-846-1632; FAX: 717-854-9486
E-mail: judys@stahlheaders.com

Mail order only. Manufacturer of high-performance exhaust systems (headers). Exhaust parts and accessories. Web site: www.stahlheaders.com
              See our ad on this page

Waldron's Antique Exhaust Inc   **exhaust systems**
PO Box C
25872 M-86
Nottawa, MI 49075
800-503-9428, 616-467-7185
FAX: 616-467-9041

Mail order and open shop. Monday-Friday 9 am to 5 pm. New exhaust systems for 1920s-1980s cars. Oldest and most complete old car exhaust system supplier in the USA.

Zip Products   **accessories**
8067 Fast Ln   **parts**
Mechanicsville, VA 23111
804-746-2290, 800-962-9632
FAX: 804-730-7043
E-mail: zipvette@erols.com

See full listing in **Section One** under **Corvette**

fans

Flex-a-lite   **fans**
PO Box 580
Milton, WA 98354
253-922-2700; FAX: 253-922-0226
E-mail: flex@flex-a-lite.com

Dealing in high-performance cooling fans, both electric and belt-driven. Transmission and engine oil coolers.
Web site: www.flex-a-lite.com

J Pinto   **electric motors,**
31 Spruce   **relays, switches,**
HC 1, Box F7   **solenoids repair**
Swiftwater, PA 18370
570-839-3441
E-mail: lectri@yahoo.com

See full listing in **Section Two** under **electrical systems**

Southern Rods & Parts Inc   **accessories**
2125 Airport Rd   **headlights**
Gleer, SC 29651   **power windows**
864-848-0601; FAX: 864-801-0601   **radiators**

See full listing in **Section Two** under **street rods**

fiberglass parts

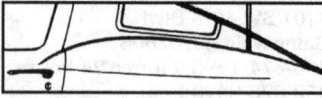

American Performance Products   **parts**
675 S Industry Rd
Cocoa, FL 32926
407-632-8299; FAX: 407-632-5119
E-mail: amc@oldcarparts.com

See full listing in **Section One** under **AMC**

ASC&P International PO Box 255 Uwchland, PA 19480 610-458-8395; FAX: 610-458-8735	**custom molding** **fiberglass** **plastic**

Injection molded plastic reproduction. Also compression molded fiberglass from original parts. Short run production is our specialty. In-house mold making to insure quality. Casting services of plastics also available. Hardness ranges from floppy (rubber) to rigid. Will repair original bakelite parts as well as other old styles of plastic.

Auto Body Specialties Inc Rt 66 Middlefield, CT 06455 888-277-1960 toll-free orders only 860-346-4989; FAX: 860-346-4987	**accessories** **body parts**

See full listing in **Section Two** under **body parts**

Bob's Brickyard Inc 1030 N Hickory Ridge Tr Milford, MI 48380 248-685-9508; FAX: 248-685-8662 E-mail: bobsbrick@aol.com	**parts**

See full listing in **Section One** under **Bricklin**

Tony D Branda Performance Shelby and Mustang Parts 1434 E Pleasant Valley Blvd Altoona, PA 16602 814-942-1869; FAX: 814-944-0801 E-mail: cobranda@aol.com	**accessories** **decals** **emblems** **sheetmetal** **wheels**

See full listing in **Section One** under **Mustang**

Cn'V Corvette Sales 2166 E University Dr Tempe, AZ 85281 602-994-8388; FAX: 602-423-0407 E-mail: sales@cnv-corvettes.com	**parts** **sales** **service**

See full listing in **Section One** under **Corvette**

Corvette America PO Box 324, Rt 322 Boalsburg, PA 16827 800-458-3475 foreign: 814-364-2141 FAX: 814-364-9615, 24 hours E-mail: vettebox@corvetteamerica.com	**accessories** **fiberglass** **interiors** **leisure items** **parts**

See full listing in **Section One** under **Corvette**

D & D Plastic Chrome Plating Jim & Marty Price 4534 S Detroit Ave Toledo, OH 43614 419-389-1748	**chroming** **plating**

See full listing in **Section Two** under **plating & polishing**

Fairlane Automotive Specialties 210 E Walker St St Johns, MI 48879 517-224-6460	**fiberglass bodies** **parts**

See full listing in **Section One** under **Ford 1932-1953**

Grossmueller's Classic Corvette 55 Sitgreaves St Phillipsburg, NJ 08865 610-258-2028 FAX: 610-258-7013, PA E-mail: wfg@gccorvettes.com	**NOS parts** **used parts**

See full listing in **Section One** under **Corvette**

Bruce Horkey's Wood & Parts Rt 4 Box 188 Windom, MN 56101 507-831-5625; FAX: 507-831-0280	**pickup parts**

See full listing in **Section Two** under **trucks & tractors**

Kwik Poly T Distributing Inc 24 St Henry Ct St Charles, MO 63301 314-724-1065	**restoration aids**

See full listing in **Section Two** under **restoration aids**

Marcel's Corvette Parts 15100 Lee Rd #101 Humble, TX 77396 800-546-2111 order line 281-441-2111 info line FAX: 281-441-3057	**parts**

See full listing in **Section One** under **Corvette**

The Maverick Connection 137 Valley Dr Ripley, WV 25271 PH/FAX: 304-372-7825	**literature** **parts**

See full listing in **Section One** under **Ford 1954-up**

Michigan Corvette Recyclers 11995 US 223 Riga, MI 49276 800-533-4650; FAX: 517-486-4124	**Corvette parts** **new/used parts**

See full listing in **Section One** under **Corvette**

R & R Fiberglass & Specialties 4850 Wilson Dr NW Cleveland, TN 37312 423-476-2270; FAX: 423-473-9442 E-mail: rrfiberglass@wingnet.net	**body parts**

Dealing in fiberglass, fenders, runningboards, grille shells and misc fiberglass body parts for Ford, Chevy, Plymouth, Dodge, Ford 1923-1948 car/1928-1956 truck, Chevy 1931-1950 car/1933-1966 truck, Plymouth and Dodge 1931-1948 car/1933-1985 truck. Also aluminum grille insert for Plymouth and Dodge 1932-1936 car and 1933-1938 Dodge truck. Web site: www.wingnet.net/~rrfiberglass

Recks & Relics Ford Trucks 2675 Hamilton Mason Rd Hamilton, OH 45011 513-868-3489 E-mail: truck@choice.net	**truck parts**

See full listing in **Section One** under **Ford 1932-1953**

Regal Roadsters Ltd 301 W Beltline Hwy Madison, WI 53713 PH/FAX: 608-273-4141	**replicars** **restoration**

See full listing in **Section One** under **Thunderbird**

Replica Plastics 210 W Washington St Box 1147 Dothan, AL 36302 800-873-5871; FAX: 334-792-1175 E-mail: stone@mail.ala.net	**fiberglass parts**

Mail order and open shop. Monday-Friday 7 am to 6 pm. Dealing in fiberglass quarter panel extensions. Furnish over 400 fiberglass replacement panels for all GM cars. Ship worldwide, same day. Web site: www.replica-plastics.com

Section Two
Generalists

Smooth Line
2562 Riddle Run Rd
Tarentum, PA 15084
724-274-6002; FAX: 724-274-6121

body panels
removable hardtops

See full listing in **Section Two** under **tops**

Speedway Motors Inc
300 Speedway Cir
Lincoln, NE 68502
402-474-4411; FAX: 402-477-7476

parts

See full listing in **Section Two** under **comprehensive parts**

Brooks Stevens Auto Collection Inc
10325 N Port Washington Rd
Mequon, WI 53092
414-241-4185; FAX: 414-241-4166
E-mail: apjb@prodigy.net

parts
restoration
service

See full listing in **Section One** under **Excalibur**

Stringbean's Pickup Parts
985 Cushon St
Johnstown, PA 15902
PH/FAX: 814-539-6440
E-mail: s-bean@surfshop.net

parts
service

See full listing in **Section One** under **Chevrolet**

Wescott's Auto Restyling
19701 SE Hwy 212
Boring, OR 97009
800-523-6279; FAX: 503-658-2938
E-mail: marykarl@gte.net

body parts

See full listing in **Section One** under **Ford 1932-1953**

financing

Blueprint Auto Insurance Agency
100 Corporate Pl
Peabody, MA 01960
800-530-5305; FAX: 978-535-3759
E-mail: bluprntins@aol.com

insurance

See full listing in **Section Two** under **insurance**

Cn'V Corvette Sales
2166 E University Dr
Tempe, AZ 85281
602-994-8388; FAX: 602-423-0407
E-mail: sales@cnv-corvettes.com

parts
sales
service

See full listing in **Section One** under **Corvette**

First National Bank of Sumner
101-N Christy Ave
Sumner, IL 62466
618-936-2396; FAX: 618-936-9079
E-mail: hobbes@wworld.com

financing

Offering simple interest loan financing for the purchase of antique and collector automobiles. Web site: fnbsumner.com

Midbanc Financial Services
PO Box 20402
Columbus, OH 43220
614-442-7701; FAX: 614-442-7704
E-mail: patricia@midbanc.com

financing

Financing for collectible automobiles. Web site: www.midbanc.com

fire engines

Bob's Speedometer Service
32411 Grand River Ave
Farmington, MI 48336
800-592-9673; FAX: 248-473-5517

gauges
speedometers
tachometers

See full listing in **Section Two** under **instruments**

Carburetor Engineering
3324 E Colorado
Pasadena, CA 91107
626-795-3221

carburetor rebuilding
distributor rebuilding
fuel pump rebuilding

See full listing in **Section Two** under **carburetors**

Ceramicar
679 Lapla Rd
Kingston, NY 12401
PH/FAX: 914-338-2199

auto-related
ceramics

See full listing in **Section Two** under **novelties**

Connecticut Fire Museum
PO Box 297
Warehouse Point, CT 06088
860-623-4732

museum

See full listing in **Section Six** under **Connecticut**

Darrell's Automotive and Restorations
2639 N Tripp Ave
Odessa, TX 79763
915-381-7713

repairs
restorations

Mail order and open shop. Monday-Friday 9 am to 5 pm. Automotive repairs and restorations. Specialize in all Fords and fire apparatus. Buy, sell and restore fire apparatus. Also buy and sell antique cars, trucks and parts. Front end alignment and tire balance.

Lyme Pond Restorations
PO Box 202
Barnard, VT 05031
802-457-4657

restoration

See full listing in **Section Two** under **restoration shops**

Ben McAdam
500 Clover Ln
Wheeling, WV 26003
304-242-3388

electrical parts

See full listing in **Section Two** under **ignition parts**

R-Mac Publications Inc
5439 SW US Hwy 41
Jasper, FL 32052
904-792-2480; FAX: 904-792-3230
E-mail: rbm@r-mac.com

magazine

See full listing in **Section Four** under **books & publications**

Reinholds Restorations
c/o Rick Reinhold
PO Box 178, 255 N Ridge Rd
Reinholds, PA 17569-0178
717-336-5617; FAX: 717-336-7050

appraisals
repairs
restoration

See full listing in **Section Two** under **restoration shops**

fuel system parts

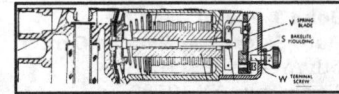

5362 Corvette Place — Corvette parts
4602 Kenbridge Dr
Greensboro, NC 27410
336-852-1011; FAX: 336-852-6107

See full listing in **Section One** under **Corvette**

Antique Auto Parts Cellar — brake/chassis/ engine parts / fuel pumps/kits / gaskets / water pumps
PO Box 3
6 Chauncy St
South Weymouth, MA 02190
781-335-1579; FAX: 781-335-1925

See full listing in **Section Two** under **comprehensive parts**

Brisson Enterprises — lead
PO Box 1595
Dearborn, MI 48121-1595
313-584-3577

See full listing in **Section Two** under **car care products**

Bronx Automotive — parts
501 Tiffany St
Bronx, NY 10474
718-589-2979

See full listing in **Section Two** under **ignition parts**

Chicago Corvette Supply — parts
7322 S Archer Rd
Justice, IL 60458
708-458-2500; FAX: 708-458-2662

See full listing in **Section One** under **Corvette**

Classic Preservation Coalition — restoration
PO Box 262
Taborton Rd
Sand Lake, NY 12153-0262
518-674-2445; FAX: 518-674-3732
E-mail: houghton@empireone.net

See full listing in **Section Two** under **carburetors**

Classic Tube — brake lines / choke tubes / fuel lines / transmission lines / vacuum lines
Division of Classic & Performance
Spec Inc
80 Rotech Dr, Lancaster, NY 14086
800-TUBES-11 (882-3711)
716-759-1800; FAX: 716-759-1014

See full listing in **Section Two** under **brakes**

Concours Parts & Accessories — parts
3493 Arrowhead Dr
Carson City, NV 89706
800-722-0009; FAX: 800-725-8644

See full listing in **Section One** under **Thunderbird**

Lee Ellison's MoreParts North — parts / sheetmetal
PO Box 345
Orangeville, ON Canada L9W 2Z7
519-941-6331; FAX: 519-941-8903
E-mail:
obsoleteparts@moreparts.com

See full listing in **Section One** under **Mopar**

Ferris Auto Electric Ltd — parts / service
106 Lakeshore Dr
North Bay, ON Canada P1A 2A6
705-474-4560; FAX: 705-474-9453

See full listing in **Section Two** under **electrical systems**

Ron Francis' Wire Works — fuel injection / harnesses / wiring accessories / wiring kits
167 Keystone Rd
Chester, PA 19013
800-292-1940 orders, 610-485-1937
E-mail: rfwwx@aol.com

See full listing in **Section Two** under **wiring harnesses**

Gas Tank and Radiator Rebuilders — abrasive blasting / gas tank rebuilding / heaters / radiator repair
20123 Hwy 362
Waller, TX 77484
800-723-3759
E-mail: donhart@donhart.com

Gas tank rebuilding and restoration, radiator, heater, air conditioning condenser and heat exchanger repair, rebuilding and restoration. New gas tanks, radiators, heaters and air conditioning condensers and evaporators. Oil pan and transmission pan repair and restoration. Abrasive blasting and rust removal. Antique and vintage specialists. Professional service, environmentally conscious and fully insured. Three locations to serve you: Rockville, MD; Houston, TX; Stockton, CA. Web site: www.vintagevehicle.com/loopersc.htm

Gas Tank Renu — gas tank rebuilding
3329 Auburn St
Rockford, IL 61101
800-407-0525; FAX: 815-962-4516
E-mail: info@butitta.com

Mail order and open shop. Monday-Friday 7 am to 5 pm. Specializing in gas tank rebuilding for antiques, cars, trucks, tractors, snowmobiles and motorcycles. Web site: www.butitta.com/gastank

Gas Tank Renu USA — fuel tank repair
12727 Greenfield
Detroit, MI 48227
800-997-3688; FAX: 313-273-4759
E-mail: danrenu@aol.com

Repair of fuel tanks for automotive and marine industries. Lifetime warranty on any vehicle less than 3/4 ton. Web site: gastankrenu.com

Arthur Gould — fuel pumps / water pumps
6 Dolores Ln
Fort Salonga, NY 11768
516-754-5010; FAX: 516-754-0212

Largest stock of fuel pumps and water pumps in the US. Fastest turnaround on rebuilding. One year guarantee on all work.

Hotchkiss Vacuum Tank Service — repair kits / restoration
2102 S Brentwood Pl
Essexville, MI 48732-1489
517-894-2073

Mail order only. Restoration of the vacuum fuel feed system tank, repair kits, gaskets and parts.

Instrument Services Inc — clocks / gauges / instruments
11765 Main St
Roscoe, IL 61073
800-558-2674; FAX: 815-623-6416

See full listing in **Section Two** under **instruments**

Kanter Auto Products
76 Monroe St
Boonton, NJ 07005
800-526-1096, 201-334-9575
FAX: 201-334-5423

car cover
carpets
parts

See full listing in **Section Two** under **comprehensive parts**

Ken's Carburetors
2301 Barnum Ave
Stratford, CT 06615
203-375-9340

carburetors
distributors
parts

See full listing in **Section One** under **Ford 1932-1953**

**Mac's Radiator Service &
Gas Tank Renu LA**
9681 Alondra Blvd
Bellflower, CA 90706
562-920-1871; FAX: 562-920-8491
E-mail: bruce@macs-radiator.com

gas tanks
radiators

See full listing in **Section Two** under **radiators**

Jack Marcheski
100 Dry Creek Rd
Hollister, CA 95023
831-637-3453

12/6-volt
converters
rebuilding
repair

See full listing in **Section Two** under **electrical systems**

Donald McKinsey
PO Box 94H
Wilkinson, IN 46186
765-785-6284

fuel pumps
ignition parts
literature
spark plugs

See full listing in **Section Two** under **ignition parts**

Montclair Radiator Service
10598 Rose Ave
Montclair, CA 91763
909-621-9531

fuel tanks
radiators

See full listing in**Section Two** under **radiators**

National Parts Depot
3101 SW 40th Blvd
Gainesville, FL 32608
800-874-7595 toll-free 24 hours
352-378-2473 local

accessories
restoration parts

See full listing in **Section Two** under **comprehensive parts**

Partwerks of Chicago
718 S Prairie Rd
New Lenox, IL 60451
815-462-3000; FAX: 815-462-3006
E-mail: partwerks9@aol.com

parts
service

See full listing in **Section Two** under **engine parts**

**Paul's Select Cars & Parts for
Porsche®**
2280 Gail Dr
Riverside, CA 92509
909-685-9340; FAX: 909-685-9342
E-mail: pauls356-s90@webtv.net

cars
parts

See full listing in **Section One** under **Porsche**

Jack Podell Fuel Injection Spec
106 Wakewa Ave
South Bend, IN 46617
219-232-6430; FAX: 219-234-8632

fuel system parts
fuel system
rebuilding

See full listing in **Section One** under **Corvette**

**John T Poulin
Auto Sales/Star Service Center**
5th Avenue & 111th St
North Troy, NY 12182
518-235-8610

car dealer
parts
restoration service

See full listing in **Section One** under **Mercedes-Benz**

**Quanta Restoration and
Performance Products**
743 Telegraph Rd
Rising Sun, MD 21911-1810
800-235-8788, 410-658-5700
FAX: 410-658-5758
E-mail:
quanta@quantaproducts.com

fan belts
gas tanks

See full listing in **Section Two** under **chassis parts**

Renner's Corner
10320 E Austin
Manchester, MI 48158
734-428-8424; FAX: 734-428-1090

bushings/hardware
carb/pump kits
gauges/gaskets
rebuild service

See full listing in **Section One** under **Ford 1932-1953**

Skip's Auto Parts
Skip Bollinger
1500 Northaven Dr
Gladstone, MO 64118
816-455-2337; FAX: 816-459-7547
E-mail: carpartman@aol.com

chassis parts
ignition parts
water pumps

See full listing in **Section Two** under **water pumps**

Taylor Auto Parts
PO Box 650
Esparto, CA 95627
530-787-1929

bearings
brakes
gaskets
seals

See full listing in **Section Two** under **comprehensive parts**

Zim's Autotechnik
1804 Reliance Pkwy
Bedford, TX 76021
800-356-2964; FAX: 817-545-2002
E-mail: zimips@allzim.com

parts
service

See full listing in **Section One** under **Porsche**

gaskets

Antique Auto Parts Cellar
PO Box 3
6 Chauncy St
South Weymouth, MA 02190
781-335-1579; FAX: 781-335-1925

brake/chassis/
engine parts
fuel pumps/kits
gaskets
water pumps

See full listing in **Section Two** under **comprehensive parts**

APA Industries
10505 San Fernando Rd
Pacoima, CA 91331
818-834-8473; FAX: 818-834-2795
E-mail: apaindustries@juno.com

accessories
parts

See full listing in **Section One** under **Jaguar**

Aremco Products Inc
707-B Executive Blvd
Valley Cottage, NY 10989
914-268-0039; FAX: 914-268-0041
E-mail: aremco@aremco.com

compound

See full listing in **Section Two** under **accessories**

Be Happy Automatic Transmission Parts — *trans rebuild kits*
414 Stivers Rd
Hillsboro, OH 45133
800-416-2862; FAX: 937-442-6133

See full listing in **Section Two** under **transmissions**

Best Gasket-Custom Shop — *gaskets*
Division of Best Gasket
519 W 156th St
Gardena, CA 90248
310-329-1157

Copper head gaskets expertly handcrafted for unique automobile and industrial engines. Retail orders welcome.

Best Gasket Inc — *gaskets*
11558 Washington Blvd Unit F
Whittier, CA 90606
888-333-BEST, 562-699-6631
FAX: 562-699-5034
E-mail: sales@bestgasket.com or best1@inreach.com

Mail order and open shop. Monday-Friday 8 am to 4 pm PST. Manufacturer of gaskets for domestic automotive and light duty truck engines from the Model T to the V8s of the 1960s. Sell wholesale only. $500 initial stock order required to buy direct. Also do custom work.

Gideon Booth — *car collector / parts / restorations*
Rellandsgate, Kings Meaburn
Penrith
Cumbria CA10 3BT England
PH/FAX: 01931 714624

See full listing in **Section One** under **Morris**

Carson's Antique Auto Parts — *parts*
235 Shawfarm Rd
Holliston, MA 01746
508-429-2269; FAX: 508-429-0761
E-mail: w1066@gis.net

See full listing in **Section Two** under **engine parts**

Jim Carter's Antique Truck Parts — *truck parts*
1508 E Alton
Independence, MO 64055
800-336-1913; FAX: 800-262-3749
E-mail: jimcartertruck.parts@worldnet.att.ne

See full listing in **Section One** under **Chevrolet**

Clean Seal Inc — *rubber seals*
PO Box 2919
South Bend, IN 46680-2919
800-366-3682; FAX: 219-299-8044
E-mail: cleanseal@cleanseal.com

Dealing in extruded rubber seals. Web site: www.cleanseal.com

Clester's Auto Rubber Seals Inc — *gloveboxes / molded rubber / parts / weatherstripping*
PO Box 1113
Salisbury, NC 28145
704-637-9979; FAX: 704-636-7390

See full listing in **Section Two** under **rubber parts**

Corvair Underground — *parts*
PO Box 339
Dundee, OR 97115
800-825-8247, 503-434-1648
FAX: 503-434-1626

See full listing in **Section One** under **Corvair**

JECC Inc — *chassis parts / gaskets / transmissions*
PO Box 616
West Paterson, NJ 07424
973-890-9682; FAX: 973-812-2724

See full listing in **Section One** under **Buick/McLaughlin**

Gerald J Lettieri — *gaskets / parts*
132 Old Main St
Rocky Hill, CT 06067
860-529-7177; FAX: 860-257-3621

Gaskets, head, manifold, oil pan, full engine sets, copper O-rings. Large NOS inventory. Over 30 years of satisfied service.

Molina Gaskets — *head gaskets*
23126 Mariposa Ave
Torrance, CA 90502
310-539-1883; FAX: 310-539-3886

Specializing in copper and asbestos head gaskets, custom made for any car, tractor or marine engine.

Northern Auto Parts Warehouse Inc — *parts*
PO Box 3147
Sioux City, IA 51102
800-831-0884; FAX: 712-258-0088

See full listing in **Section Two** under **engine parts**

Olson's Gaskets — *gaskets*
3059 Opdal Rd E
Port Orchard, WA 98366
PH/FAX: 360-871-1207
24 hr machine
E-mail: olsongasket@sincom.com

Mail and phone orders. Monday-Saturday. Engine gaskets, NOS, new production, handmaking service. Full sets, head gaskets, manifolds, etc, for cars, trucks, tractors, etc. Visa/MasterCard. Web site: www.sinclair.net/~olsongaskets

Orion Motors European Parts Inc — *parts*
10722 Jones Rd
Houston, TX 77065
800-736-6410, 281-894-1982
FAX: 281-849-1997
E-mail: orion-yugo@yugoparts.com

See full listing in **Section One** under **Alfa Romeo**

Powers Parts Co — *gaskets*
Roy F Powers
1354 Ridge Rd
Fabius, NY 13063
315-683-5376

Mail order and open shop. 6 days by chance, call first. NOS gaskets, car, truck, tractor, industrial. Light on classics.

Standard Abrasives Motorsports Division — *abrasives*
4201 Guardian St
Simi Valley, CA 93063
800-383-6001
805-520-5800 ext 371
FAX: 805-577-7398

See full listing in **Section Two** under **restoration aids**

Studebaker Parts & Locations — *parts / parts locator*
228 Marquiss Cir
Clinton, TN 37716
615-457-3002
E-mail: studebaker_joe@msn.com

See full listing in **Section One** under **Studebaker**

| Taylor Auto Parts
PO Box 650
Esparto, CA 95627
530-787-1929 | bearings
brakes
gaskets
seals |

See full listing in **Section Two** under **comprehensive parts**

| Total Seal Inc
11202 N 24th Ave, Ste 101
Phoenix, AZ 85029
602-678-4977; FAX: 602-678-4991
E-mail: totseal@amug.org | piston rings |

See full listing in **Section Two** under **engine parts**

| John Ulrich
450 Silver Ave
San Francisco, CA 94112
PH/FAX: 510-223-9587 days | parts |

See full listing in **Section One** under **Packard**

| Vintage Motor Gaskets
W 604 19th
Spokane, WA 99203
509-747-9960, 509-747-0517
E-mail: dbrooke@ior.com | gaskets |

Mail order only. Gaskets made to order. High quality accurate reproductions from your pattern. Head and manifold gaskets available in copper, steel, stainless or composite materials. Small production runs on other gaskets. Friendly service, competitive rates. Visa, MasterCard welcome.

| R Donald Williams
2642 Brotherton Rd
Berlin, PA 15530-7318
814-267-3250 | parts |

See full listing in **Section Two** under **comprehensive parts**

glass

| Airplane Plastics
9785 Julie Ct
Tipp City, OH 45371
937-669-2677; FAX: 937-669-2777 | plastic
transparencies |

Open shop. Monday-Friday 8 am to 5 pm EST. Dealing in custom plastic transparencies. Windshields, headlamp shields, aircraft canopies. Restorations: customs, street rods, aircrafts and boats.

| American Restorations Unlimited TA
14 Meakin Ave
PO Box 34
Rochelle Park, NJ 07662
201-843-3567; FAX: 201-843-3238
E-mail: amerrest@earthlink.net | restoration parts |

Mail order and open shop. Monday-Saturday 8 am to 8 pm. Going on our 20th year keeping legends on the road. Represent over 175 manufacturers of restorations parts from 1928-1980s. Specialize in the following categories: glass-flat glass, curved for all American cars and trucks, T-tops for all years, we even can supply flat dash glass; transmission parts-parts and kits for automatic transmissions, 1940-1965 and up, also standard transmission parts starting with 1935, we now can rebuild your automatic or standard transmission; engine parts and rebuilding as well as complete gas tank restoration.

| Bob's Classic Auto Glass
21170 Hwy 36
Blachly, OR 97412
800-624-2130 | glass |

Mail order only. Daily 9 am to 9 pm. Antique auto glass for all

makes and models, 1920-1960. No foreign. Reproduced in clear, green, grey and bronze.

| Bob Fatone's Mercedes Used Parts
166 W Main St
Niantic, CT 06357
860-739-1923; FAX: 860-691-0669
E-mail: bobfatone@earthlink.net | parts |

See full listing in **Section One** under **Mercedes-Benz**

| Gold Plated Emblems & Auto
Accessories
2095 Pine Ridge Rd
Naples, FL 34109
800-231-7765, 941-592-5552
FAX: 941-597-0768
E-mail: sales@goldplated.com | plating equipment
wood dash kits |

See full listing in **Section Two** under **plating & polishing**

| Jefferis Autobody
269 Tank Farm Rd
San Luis Obispo, CA 93401
800-807-1937; FAX: 805-543-4757 | windshield glass kit |

Monday-Friday 8 am to 5 pm PST. Glass: vintage or street rod, clear, green, gray or bronze tint. Safet laminated DOT approved, complete kits or pieces. Home of the V-Butt® windshield. Ship UPS, special packing, fully insured. Visa, MasterCard, Discover.

| JLM
PO Box 1348
Maud Rd
Palmer, AK 99645
907-745-4670; FAX: 907-745-5510
E-mail: jlmob@alaska.net | power window lifts |

Mail order only. Power window lifts for all cars with flat glass. 12v conversion units. Web site: www.alaska.net/~jlmob

| Michigan Corvette Recyclers
11995 US 223
Riga, MI 49276
800-533-4650; FAX: 517-486-4124 | Corvette parts
new/used parts |

See full listing in **Section One** under **Corvette**

| N/C Ind Antique Auto Parts
301 S Thomas Ave
PO Box 254
Sayre, PA 18840
570-888-6216; FAX: 570-888-1821
E-mail: kdb@cyber-quest.com | windshield frames |

Mail order and open shop. Monday-Friday 8 am to 5 pm. Specializing in windshield frames for almost all makes and models cars and trucks. 1933-1934 Plymouth and Dodge parts.

| NOS Locators
587 Pawtucket Ave
Pawtucket, RI 02860
401-725-5000 | parts |

See full listing in **Section One** under **MG**

| OEM Glass Inc
Rt 9 E
PO Box 362
Bloomington, IL 61702
309-662-2122; FAX: 309-663-7474 | auto glass |

Mail order only. Auto and truck glass for 1920-1976 cars and trucks. Specializing in original logos and date codes for show cars.

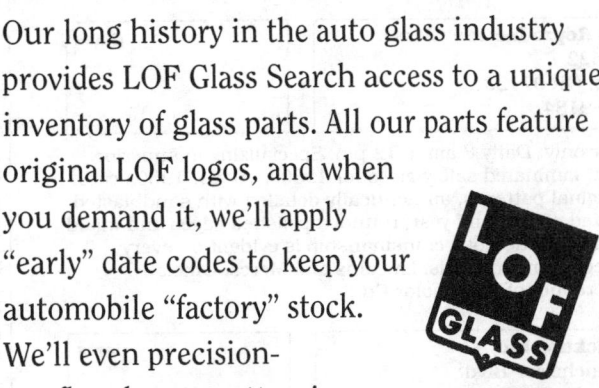

Section Two Generalists

Redden's Auto Glass Engraving
7219 W 75 S
Lafayette, IN 47905-9263
765-572-2293

engraving

Open by appointment only. Engrave any automobile, boat, truck, RV glass (excluding windshields) using a high speed drill. Equipment is portable so work can be done at customer's residence. Can engrave any design that can be photocopied.

The Reflected Image
21 W Wind Dr
Northford, CT 06472
PH/FAX: 203-484-0760
E-mail: scott@reflectedimage.com

mirror
reproduction
mirror resilvering

See full listing in **Section Two** under **special services**

Rick's Relics
Wheeler Rd
Pittsburg, NH 03592
603-538-6612

bodywork
painting
restoration

See full listing in **Section Two** under **restoration shops**

Sanders Reproduction Glass
PO Box 522
Hillsboro, OR 97123
503-648-9184

glass

Mail order only. Daily 8 am to 12 pm. Specializing in superior quality flat laminated safety glass for 1930s, 1940s, 1950s cars. Cut to original patterns, authentically detailed with sandblasted script, dated month and year, rounded polished edges and inlaid black edging. Meticulous craftsmanship is evident on every piece. Specializing in Fords, Lincolns and Mercs. Officially licensed product of Ford Motor Co.

SoCal Pickups Inc
6321 Manchester Blvd
Buena Park, CA 90621
800-SOCAL-49; FAX: 714-994-2584

parts

See full listing in **Section One** under **Ford 1954-up**

Specialty Power Window
2087 Collier Rd
Forsyth, GA 31029
800-634-9801; FAX: 912-994-3124

power window kits
windshield wiper
kit

See full listing in **Section Two** under **street rods**

Bill Thomsen
1118 Wooded Acres Ln
Moneta, VA 24121
540-297-1200

salvage yard

See full listing in **Section Five** under **Virginia**

Vintage Glass USA
PO Box 336
326 S River Rd
Tolland, CT 06084
800-889-3826, 860-872-0018

auto glass

Mail order and open shop. Monday-Friday 9 am to 5 pm EST. Auto glass, flat and curved for American cars and trucks, 1915-1970.

Volvo Shop Inc
5220 New Milford Rd
Ravenna, OH 44266
330-297-1297
E-mail: volvocarl@aol.com

parts
restoration

See full listing in **Section One** under **Volvo**

grille emblem badges

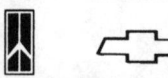 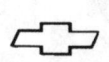

bentleydriversclub.com
23238 Erwin St
Woodland Hills, CA 91367
818-887-6557; FAX: 818-346-3627
E-mail: glwales@aol.com

car dealer
collectibles

See full listing in **Section One** under **Rolls-Royce/Bentley**

Comet Products
Cherry Parke 101-B
Cherry Hill, NJ 08002
609-795-4810; FAX: 609-354-6313

accessories
emblems

Mail order only. Manufacture car emblem badges for the front car grille. Over 500 types are available: countries, states, autos, auto clubs, military, fraternal organizations, etc. Also makes lapel pins, belt buckles, key chains, key fobs, decals, patches, magnetic country of origin ovals. Catalog, $3. Dept HV.

D&D Automobilia
813 Ragers Hill Rd
South Fork, PA 15956
814-539-5653

plastic parts
steering wheels

See full listing in **Section Two** under **steering wheels**

The El Camino Store
57 B Depot Rd
Goleta, CA 93117
805-681-8164; FAX: 805-681-8166
E-mail: ec@elcaminostore.com

parts

See full listing in **Section One** under **Chevelle/Camaro**

Emblemagic Co
PO Box 420
Grand River, OH 44045-0420
440-209-0792
E-mail: arborhil@aol.com

decorative
emblems
plastic insert
emblems

Sell, restore, reproduce clear top plastic insert emblems used on grille, trunk, interior and exterior, wheel hubs, etc. Also sell and restore cloisonne, enamel radiator badges or decorative emblems.

Enthusiast's Specialties
350 Old Connecticut Path
Framingham, MA 01701
800-718-3999; FAX: 508-872-4914
E-mail: alvis1934@aol.com

automobilia

See full listing in **Section Two** under **automobilia**

Eurosport Daytona Inc
355 Tomoka Ave
Ormond Beach, FL 32174-6222
800-874-8044, 904-672-7199
FAX: 904-673-0821

license plates

See full listing in **Section Two** under **license plates**

**Gold Plated Emblems &
Auto Accessories**
2095 Pine Ridge Rd
Naples, FL 34109
800-231-7765, 941-592-5552
FAX: 941-597-0768
E-mail: sales@goldplated.com

plating equipment
wood dash kits

See full listing in **Section Two** under **plating & polishing**

Iverson Automotive
14704 Karyl Dr
Minnetonka, MN 55345
800-325-0480; FAX: 612-938-5707

polishes
pot metal
restoration

See full listing in **Section Two** under **plating & polishing**

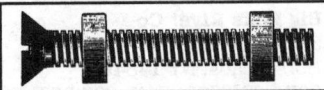

hardware

Karmann Ghia Parts & Restoration
PO Box 997
Ventura, CA 93002
800-927-2787; FAX: 805-641-3333
E-mail: info@karmannghia.com

parts

See full listing in **Section One** under **Volkswagen**

National Parts Depot
3101 SW 40th Blvd
Gainesville, FL 32608
800-874-7595 toll-free 24 hours
352-378-2473 local

accessories
restoration parts

See full listing in **Section Two** under **comprehensive parts**

SoCal Pickups Inc
6321 Manchester Blvd
Buena Park, CA 90621
800-SOCAL-49; FAX: 714-994-2584

parts

See full listing in **Section One** under **Ford 1954-up**

Swedish Classics Inc
PO Box 557
Oxford, MD 21654
800-258-4422; FAX: 410-226-5543

parts

See full listing in **Section One** under **Volvo**

West Coast Metric Inc
24002 Frampton Ave
Harbor City, CA 90710
310-325-0005; FAX: 310-325-9733
E-mail: wcmi@earthlink.net

apparel
carpets
plastic parts
rubber parts

See full listing in **Section One** under **Volkswagen**

Antique Auto Fasteners
Guy C Close Jr & Son
13426 Valna Dr
Whittier, CA 90602
562-696-3307

fasteners
hardware
hose clamps
molding clips

Mail order and open shop. Fasteners for upholstery and cloth tops. Molding trim clips and bolts. Match samples for most cars thru 1965. Stainless capped bumper bolts. Brass Sherman hose clamps. NOS Swiss and Ferro lock mechanisms for 1935-1936 Mopar, 1935-1949 Ford closed cars; miscellaneous springs; 1934-1955 inside door handles; 1939-1947 GM trunk handles. Striker plates, special screws and bolts, trim hardware, speed nuts, hinge pins, door checkstraps, pedal pads, assist straps and robe ropes. Illustrated catalog, $4. SASE.

See our ad on this page

Auto Hardware Specialties
3123 McKinley Ave
Sheldon, IA 51201
712-324-2091; FAX: 712-324-2480
E-mail: rweber@rconnect.com

hardware fasteners

See full listing in **Section One** under **Chevrolet**

Dwight H Bennett
1330 Ximeno Ave
Long Beach, CA 90804
PH/FAX: 562-498-6488

emblem repair
hardware repair
mascot repair
plaque repair

See full listing in **Section Two** under **radiator emblems & mascots**

Big Flats Rivet Co — rivets / tools
35 Sunny Dell Cir
Horseheads, NY 14845
607-562-3501; FAX: 607-562-3711
E-mail: bfrivet@ibm.net

Mail order only. Rivets and installation tools for all makes of antique autos. Round tire valve nuts (brass) for Fords and other early cars.

The Buckle Man — buckles
Douglas D Drake
28 Monroe Ave
Pittsford, NY 14534
716-381-4604

Strap buckles for all types of needs (I do not sell leather straps, only the buckles for your straps). These are NOS buckles, brass, nickel and black for all your restoration needs: sidemount and mirror tie downs, top and windshield strap buckles, trunk strap buckles, spring cover buckles, trunk and luggage strap buckles, etc. Whether it is for a brass era car or a classic, try The Buckle Man. Over 125 buckle styles, 10,000 in stock. Send Xerox copy of your needs and I will match to my stock.

East Coast Chevy Inc — custom work / parts / restoration
Ol '55 Chevy Parts
4154A Skyron Dr
Doylestown, PA 18938
215-348-5568; FAX: 215-348-0560

See full listing in **Section One** under **Chevrolet**

The Enthusiasts Shop — cars / pre-war parts / transportation
John Parnell
PO Box 80471
Baton Rouge, LA 70898
225-928-7456; FAX: 225-928-7665

See full listing in **Section One** under **Rolls-Royce/Bentley**

Fast Lane Products — chamois / drain tubs / hand wringers
PO Box 7000-50
Palos Verdes Peninsula, CA 90274
800-327-8669; FAX: 310-541-2235
E-mail: info@fastlaneproducts.com

See full listing in **Section Two** under **car care products**

Harter Industries Inc — parts / restoration
PO Box 502
Holmdel, NJ 07733
732-566-7055; FAX: 732-566-6977
E-mail: harter101@aol.com

See full listing in **Section Two** under **comprehensive parts**

JLM — power window lifts
PO Box 1348
Maud Rd
Palmer, AK 99645
907-745-4670; FAX: 907-745-5510
E-mail: jlmob@alaska.net

See full listing in **Section Two** under **glass**

M & R Products — hardware / tie-downs
1940 SW Blvd
Vineland, NJ 08360
800-524-2560, 609-696-9450
FAX: 609-696-4999
E-mail: mrproducts@mrproducts.com

See full listing in **Section Two** under **accessories**

Mr G's Enterprises — fasteners / screw kits
5613 Elliott Reeder Rd
Fort Worth, TX 76117
817-831-3501; FAX: 817-831-0638
E-mail: mrgs@earthlink.net

Mail order and open shop. Monday-Friday 9 am to 5 pm. Specializing in fasteners, screw kits and rechrome plastic for all makes and models. Web site: mrgusa.com
See our ad on this page

National Parts Depot — accessories / restoration parts
3101 SW 40th Blvd
Gainesville, FL 32608
800-874-7595 toll-free 24 hours
352-378-2473 local

See full listing in **Section Two** under **comprehensive parts**

Old Ford Parts — parts
35 4th Ave N
Algona, WA 98001
253-833-8494; FAX: 253-833-2190

See full listing in **Section One** under **Ford 1932-1953**

Pennsylvania Metal Cleaning — derusting / stainless fasteners / stripping
200 17th St
Monaca, PA 15061-1969
724-728-5535

See full listing in **Section Two** under **rust removal & stripping**

R J & L Automotive Fasteners — fasteners
58 Bristol Ave
Rochester, NY 14617-2702
PH/FAX: 716-467-7421

Monday-Friday 4 pm to 9 pm, fax 24 hours. Specializing in manufacturing obsolete or those hard-to-find fasteners. Also carry 1,000s of original style clips and fasteners. Samples are required for a proper match. Illustrated catalog, $6 US, $10 international. Dealers inquire.

RB's Prototype Model & Machine Co | machine work
44 Marva Ln
Stamford, CT 06903
203-329-2715; FAX: 203-329-8029

See full listing in **Section Two** under **service shops**

Re-Flex Border Marker | border markers posts
138 Grant St
Lexington, MA 02173
781-862-1343

Mail order only. Flexible border markers and posts for marking driveways, parking areas, work areas or anywhere that must be made more visible.

Restoration Supply Company | accessories restoration supplies
2060 Palisade Dr
Reno, NV 89509
775-825-5663; FAX: 775-825-9330
E-mail: restoration@rsc.reno.nv.us

See full listing in **Section Two** under **restoration aids**

Specialty Fasteners | fasteners
183 Blanchard Way
Tecumseh, ON Canada N8N 2L9
519-727-4848; FAX: 519-727-4844
E-mail: lancastr@wincom.net

Specializing in chrome and polished stainless fasteners. Engine kits for classics made to order. Manufacturer and distributor, all sizes and materials. Short runs, one-offs, CNC capable. No catalogs. Motorcycle fasteners available. Specialize in Harley-Davidson.

Totally Stainless | stainless hardware
PO Box 3249
Gettysburg, PA 17325
717-677-8811; FAX: 717-677-4525
E-mail: info@totallystainless.com

Mail order only. Stainless steel bolts, screws, nuts, washers, clamps and more. Offer the largest selection of US and metric fasteners available. Over 5,000 ready to install assembly kits are available. Web site: totallystainless.com

Tom Vagnini | used parts
58 Anthony Rd, RR 3
Pittsfield, MA 01201
413-698-2526

See full listing in **Section One** under **Packard**

heaters

Autolux Inc | Mercedes parts
23242 Tasmania Cir
Dana Point, CA 92629
949-493-5578; FAX: 949-493-3710

See full listing in **Section One** under **Mercedes-Benz**

Blaak Radiateurenbedryf | radiators
Blaaksedyk oost 19
Heinenoord 3274LA Netherlands
31-186-601732
FAX: 31-186-603044
E-mail: info@blaak.com

See full listing in **Section Two** under **radiators**

Gas Tank and Radiator Rebuilders | abrasive blasting gas tank rebuilding heaters radiator repair
20123 Hwy 362
Waller, TX 77484
800-723-3759
E-mail: donhart@donhart.com

See full listing in **Section Two** under **fuel system parts**

National Parts Depot | accessories restoration parts
3101 SW 40th Blvd
Gainesville, FL 32608
800-874-7595 toll-free 24 hours
352-378-2473 local

See full listing in **Section Two** under **comprehensive parts**

Performance Analysis Co | climate control cruise control
1345 Oak Ridge Tpke, Ste 258
Oak Ridge, TN 37830
423-482-9175
E-mail:
george_murphy@compuserve.com

See full listing in **Section One** under **Mercedes-Benz**

J Pinto | electric motors/ relays/switches/ solenoids repair
31 Spruce
HC 1, Box F7
Swiftwater, PA 18370
570-839-3441
E-mail: lectri@yahoo.com

See full listing in **Section Two** under **electrical systems**

hubcaps

Big Boys Toys | accessories bodywork tires wheels
Richard Boutin
Rt 67A Box 174A
North Bennington, VT 05257
800-286-1721; FAX: 802-447-0962

See full listing in **Section Two** under **accessories**

Burr Nyberg Screw-on Hubcaps | hubcaps
198 Union Blvd #200
Denver, CO 80228
804-951-3294 days, VA
FAX: 303-988-7145
E-mail: e_burrnyberg@yahoo.com

Original screw-on hubcaps reproduced: many cars of the teens, 1920s and early 1930s had screw-on hubcaps that through the ages became dented or lost. Now able to reproduce exact copies of original hubcaps made by a craftsman to the highest quality standard. Any screw-on hubcap can be made following your original sample or pattern. Current prices are given upon request. Delivery time is usually 12-16 weeks.

California Classic Mustang | steel wheels
1102 Industrial Ave
Escondido, CA 92128
888-320-8929, 760-746-6580
FAX: 760-746-6581
E-mail: mmatt1965@aol.com

See full listing in **Section One** under **Mustang**

Iverson Automotive | polishes pot metal restoration
14704 Karyl Dr
Minnetonka, MN 55345
800-325-0480; FAX: 612-938-5707

See full listing in **Section Two** under **plating & polishing**

National Parts Depot
3101 SW 40th Blvd
Gainesville, FL 32608
800-874-7595 toll-free 24 hours
352-378-2473 local

| accessories restoration parts |

See full listing in **Section Two** under **comprehensive parts**

ignition parts

A&F Imported Parts Inc
490 40th St
Oakland, CA 94609
888-263-7278; FAX: 707-256-0764
E-mail: mmast64166@aol.com

| parts |

See full listing in **Section One** under **Mercedes-Benz**

Battery Ignition Co Inc
91 Meadow St
Hartford, CT 06114
860-296-4215; FAX: 860-947-3259
E-mail: biscokid@aol.com

| parts rebuilding rebushing |

See full listing in **Section Two** under **carburetors**

Dave Bean Engineering
636 E St Charles St SR3H
San Andreas, CA 95249
209-754-5802; FAX: 209-754-5177
E-mail: admin@davebean.com

| parts |

See full listing in **Section One** under **Lotus**

Robert D Bliss
2 Delmar Pl
Edison, NJ 08837
732-549-0977

| electrical parts ignition parts |

See full listing in **Section Two** under **electrical systems**

Bronx Automotive
501 Tiffany St
Bronx, NY 10474
718-589-2979

| parts |

Mail order only. Mostly parts for 1930-1970. Taillight lenses, ignition parts, fuel pumps, brakes, suspension parts, engine parts, other assorted parts. Carb kits, brake wheel cylinders and kits. Early high-performance manifolds, cams, carbs, valve covers, etc.

CBS Performance Automotive
2605-A W Colorado Ave
Colorado Springs, CO 80904
800-685-1492; FAX: 719-578-9485

| ignition systems performance products |

Mail order and open shop. Monday-Saturday 8 am to 6 pm. Never change points again! CBS Performance is your supplier for the Ignitor by Pertronix. The Ignitor replaces your points and condenser with an electronic ignition system that fits neatly inside your stock distributor cap. The Ignitor is available for most vehicles between 1956 and 1974 and is only $79. Call for more information. Web site: www.cbsperformance.com

Cole's Ign & Mfg
52 Legionaire Dr
Rochester, NY 14617
PH/FAX: 716-342-9613

| battery cables ignition wire sets |

Ignition wire sets, custom made battery cables and ground straps, light wire supplies, brass hose clamps, Rajah terminals, air cleaner elements (dry type), auto loom, magneto ends, armored cab and more.

Collector's Auto Supply
528 Appian Way
Coquitlam, BC Canada V3J 2A5
888-772-7848; FAX: 604-931-4450
E-mail: car@bc.sympatico.ca

| parts |

See full listing in **Section Two** under **comprehensive parts**

Robert Connole
2525 E 32nd St
Davenport, IA 52807
319-355-6266

| ignition coils |

See full listing in **Section One** under **Packard**

Crane Cams Inc
530 Fentress Blvd
Daytona Beach, FL 32114
904-258-6174; FAX: 904-258-6167

| camshafts |

See full listing in **Section Two** under **camshafts**

Crossfire Manufacturing
166-B N Mercer Ave, PO Box 263
Sharpsville, PA 16150
800-458-3478
PH/FAX: 724-962-4639
E-mail: xfire@nauticom.net

| accessories |

Manufacturer of specialty distributor caps that send plug wires from the cap to cylinders in perfect order. Also offer a new HEI distributor for Chevrolet 8-cylinder engines.

CT Model A Parts & Service
75 Prospect Ave
West Hartford, CT 06106
860-233-1928; FAX: 860-233-1926
E-mail: ctmap@aol.com

| parts restorations service |

See full listing in **Section One** under **Ford 1903-1931**

Ferris Auto Electric Ltd
106 Lakeshore Dr
North Bay ON Canada P1A 2A6
705-474-4560; FAX: 705-474-9453

| parts service |

See full listing in **Section Two** under **electrical systems**

Ficken Wiper Service
Box 11
132 Calvert Ave
West Babylon, NY 11702
516-587-3332; FAX: 516-661-9125
E-mail: wiperman@aol.com

| ignition parts wiper parts |

See full listing in **Section Two** under **windshield wipers**

Gaslight Auto Parts Inc
PO Box 291
Urbana, OH 43078
937-652-2145; FAX: 937-652-2147

| accessories parts |

See full listing in **Section One** under **Ford 1903-1931**

Green Mountain Vintage Auto
20 Bramley Way
Bellows Falls, VT 05101
PH/FAX: 802-463-3141
E-mail: vintauto@sover.net

| damage appraisals ignition parts vehicle evaluations |

See full listing in **Section Two** under **appraisals**

J & C's Parts
7127 Ward Rd
North Tonawanda, NY 14120
716-693-4090; FAX: 716-695-7144

| parts |

See full listing in **Section One** under **Buick/McLaughlin**

Jacobs Electronics   ignition systems
500 N Baird St
Midland, TX 79701
915-685-3345, 800-627-8800
FAX: 915-687-5951
E-mail: jacobssales@caprok.net

Mail order, international and dosmetic dealers. High-performance ignition systems, including timing controls, anti-theft and nitrous safety systems. Web site: www.jacobselectronics.com

Ken's Carburetors   carburetors
2301 Barnum Ave   distributors
Stratford, CT 06615   parts
203-375-9340

See full listing in **Section One** under **Ford 1932-1953**

Ben McAdam   electrical parts
500 Clover Ln
Wheeling, WV 26003
304-242-3388

Mail and phone order anytime. Open shop by appointment. Ignition parts 1913-1965. Electrical parts and points, distributor caps, rotors, condensers, generator and starter brushes. Abbot thru Wolsey.

Donald McKinsey   fuel pumps
PO Box 94H   ignition parts
Wilkinson, IN 46186   literature
765-785-6284   spark plugs

Mail order only. 6-volt electronic fuel pumps, spark plugs (obsolete), shock absorbers, misc items and some literature.

MikeCo Antique, Kustom &   lenses
Obsolete Auto Parts   parts
4053 Calle Tesoro, Unit C
Camarillo, CA 93012
805-482-1725; FAX: 805-987-8524

See full listing in **Section One** under **Mopar**

MSD Ignition   ignition parts
1490 Henry Brennan Dr
El Paso, TX 79936
915-857-5200; FAX: 915-857-3344
E-mail: msdign@msdignition.com

Manufacturer of high-performance ignition systems and accessories. Web site: www.msdignition.com

National Parts Depot   accessories
3101 SW 40th Blvd   restoration parts
Gainesville, FL 32608
800-874-7595 toll-free 24 hours
352-378-2473 local

See full listing in **Section Two** under **comprehensive parts**

PerTronix Inc   ignition systems
440 E Arrow Hwy
San Dimas, CA 91773-3340
909-599-5955; FAX: 909-599-6424

Leading manufacturer of solid-state electronic ignition systems. The Ignitor is a retro-fit replacement for points and fits entirely inside the distributor. Applications include automotive, truck, bus, industrial, agricultural and marine engines. Offer our Flame-Thrower high-performance 40,000 volt coils (chrome and black oil filled and epoxy) and spark plug wires (choose from 8.0mm custom-look in blue, red or black and stock-look 7.0mm black). Web site: www.pertronix.com

Restoration Supply Company   accessories
2060 Palisade Dr   restoration supplies
Reno, NV 89509
775-825-5663; FAX: 775-825-9330
E-mail: restoration@rsc.reno.nv.us

See full listing in **Section Two** under **restoration aids**

Silicone Wire Systems   ignition wire sets
3462 Kirkwood Dr
San Jose, CA 95117-1549
E-mail: sethracer@aol.com

See full listing in **Section One** under **Corvair**

Skip's Auto Parts   chassis parts
Skip Bollinger   ignition parts
1500 Northaven Dr   water pumps
Gladstone, MO 64118
816-455-2337; FAX: 816-459-7547
E-mail: carpartman@aol.com

See full listing in **Section Two** under **water pumps**

Sunburst Technology   electronic technical
PO Box 598   consultant
Lithia Springs, GA 30122
770-949-2979; FAX: 770-942-6091
E-mail: sunburst2000@juno.com

See full listing in **Section Four** under **information sources**

Taylor Auto Parts   bearings
PO Box 650   brakes
Esparto, CA 95627   gaskets
530-787-1929   seals

See full listing in **Section Two** under **comprehensive parts**

UK Spares/TVR Sports Cars   accessories
609 Highland St   car covers
Wethersfield, CT 06109-3979   convertible tops
PH/FAX: 860-563-1647   ignition parts
FAX: 860-529-3479   suspension parts
E-mail: tvr.sports.cars@juno.com

See full listing in **Section One** under **TVR**

John Ulrich   parts
450 Silver Ave
San Francisco, CA 94112
PH/FAX: 510-223-9587 days

See full listing in **Section One** under **Packard**

Wizzy's Collector Car Parts   engine
1801 S 2nd St   ignition
Milwaukee, WI 53204   mechanical
800-328-6554; FAX: 414-645-5457   suspension
E-mail: sales@wizzys.com   transmission

See full listing in **Section Two** under **comprehensive parts**

Zim's Autotechnik   parts
1804 Reliance Pkwy   service
Bedford, TX 76021
800-356-2964; FAX: 817-545-2002
E-mail: zimips@allzim.com

See full listing in **Section One** under **Porsche**

instruments

Ace Antique Auto Restoration
65 S Service Rd
Plainview, NY 11803
516-752-6065; FAX: 516-752-1484

| air conditioning
body rebuilding
restoration
wiring harnesses |

See full listing in **Section Two** under **restoration shops**

Albrico Auto & Truck Parts
PO Box 3179
Camarillo, CA 93010
805-482-9792; FAX: 805-383-1013

| lamp assemblies
lenses |

See full listing in **Section Two** under **lighting equipment**

Bill's Speedometer Shop
109 Twinbrook Pl
Sidney, OH 45365
937-492-7800
E-mail: speedo@bright.net

| repairs
restoration |

Repair and restoration of speedometers for all cars 1932-1972. Cables and ratio drives to correct readings. Many NOS parts to make your speedometer look and feel great.

Bob's Speedometer Service
32411 Grand River Ave
Farmington, MI 48336
800-592-9673; FAX: 248-473-5517

| gauges
speedometers
tachometers |

Mail order and open shop. Monday-Friday 8 am to 5 pm EST. Speedometers, tachometers, clocks, gauges, clusters, gas tank sending units, GM cruise controls, cables and castings, ratio boxes for automobiles, trucks, customs, hot rods, boats, mili-

tary, fire engines, motorcycles, bicycles, complete repair, restoration and customizing, 1883-1999.

See our ad on this page

The Clockworks
1745 Meta Lake Ln
Eagle River, WI 54521
800-398-3040; FAX: 715-479-5759
E-mail: clockworks@juno.com

| clock service |

Automobile clock service and quartz conversions. All makes and models, 1930s-1980s, serviced from $39.95. Quartz conversions from $59.95. Most service completed within 24 hours. MasterCard and Visa welcome. Over 12,000 serviced since 1988.

Corvette Specialties of MD Inc
1912 Liberty Rd
Eldersburg, MD 21784
410-795-3180; FAX: 410-795-3247

| parts
restoration
service |

See full listing in **Section One** under **Corvette**

Dakota Ultrasonics
155A DuBois St
Santa Cruz, CA 95060
831-427-4402; FAX: 831-427-4403

| gauges
sonic testers |

See full listing in **Section Two** under **tools**

Development Associates
12791-G Newport Ave
Tustin, CA 92780
714-730-6843; FAX: 714-730-6863
E-mail: devassoc@yahoo.com

| electrical parts |

See full listing in **Section Two** under **electrical systems**

Ferris Auto Electric Ltd
106 Lakeshore Dr
North Bay, ON Canada P1A 2A6
705-474-4560; FAX: 705-474-9453

| parts
service |

See full listing in **Section Two** under **electrical systems**

Fifth Avenue Graphics
Fifth Avenue Antique Auto Parts
415 Court St
Clay Center, KS 67432
785-632-3450; FAX: 785-632-6154
E-mail: fifthave@kansas.net

| cooling systems
electrical systems
fuel systems |

See full listing in **Section Two** under **electrical systems**

Grossmueller's Classic Corvette
55 Sitgreaves St
Phillipsburg, NJ 08865
610-258-2028; FAX: 610-258-7013, PA
E-mail: wfg@gccorvettes.com

| NOS parts
used parts |

See full listing in **Section One** under **Corvette**

Haneline Products Co
PO Box 430
Morongo Valley, CA 92256
760-363-6597; FAX: 760-363-7321

| gauges
instrument panels
stainless parts
trim parts |

See full listing in **Section Two** under **accessories**

Harter Industries Inc
PO Box 502
Holmdel, NJ 07733
732-566-7055; FAX: 732-566-6977
E-mail: harter101@aol.com

| parts
restoration |

See full listing in **Section Two** under **comprehensive parts**

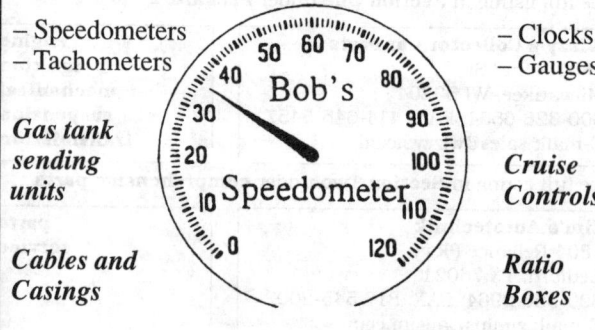

Instrument Services Inc
11765 Main St
Roscoe, IL 61073
800-558-2674; FAX: 815-623-2993

clocks
gauges
instruments

Mail order and open shop. Monday-Friday 8 am to 4:30 pm. Restore and service all makes and models of foreign and domestic clocks, speedos, tachs, clusters, gas tank sending units and GM cruise controls. Car, truck, motorcycle, tractor and marine. Do-it-yourself original electric and quartz conversion kits with free how-to video. Complete Corvette clocks, 1968-1982. Thousands of NOS clocks in stock. Free catalog.

See our ad on this page

International Speedometer
9540 W Ogden Ave
Brookfield, IL 60513
708-387-0606; FAX: 708-387-0240

sales
service

Mail order and open shop. Monday-Saturday 8 am to 5 pm. Service for all years and makes speedometers, tachometers and clocks.

David Lindquist
Automobile Clock Repair
12427 Penn St
Whittier, CA 90602
562-698-4445

clock repair

Mail order and open shop. Monday-Friday 1 pm to 7 pm PST. Automobile clock repair services and automobile clock sales. Quartz conversions on most 1956-up domestic automobile clocks.

Jack Marcheski
100 Dry Creek Rd
Hollister, CA 95023
831-637-3453

12/6-volt
converters
rebuilding
repair

See full listing in **Section Two** under **electrical systems**

Carlton Marsden Co
403 High St
Wild Rose, WI 54984
920-622-3473

car clocks

Repair and restoration of all car clocks up to 1975.

J Pinto
31 Spruce
HC 1, Box F7
Swiftwater, PA 18370
570-839-3441
E-mail: lectri@yahoo.com

electric motors/
relays/switches/
solenoids repair

See full listing in **Section Two** under **electrical systems**

Reynolds Speedometer Repair
4 Lobao Dr
Danvers, MA 01923
978-774-6848

repair
restoration
sales

Mail order and open shop. Quality repair and restoration of American and European speedometers, tachometers, cables, gauges, dial and glass refinishing, plating. NOS and restored units for sale.

Roadrunner Tire & Auto
4850 Hwy 377 S
Fort Worth, TX 76116
817-244-4924

restoration
speedometer repair

See full listing in **Section Two** under **restoration shops**

Southern Autotronics Inc
3300 Norfolk St
Richmond, VA 23230
804-353-5400, 800-446-2880
FAX: 804-358-3216
E-mail: ecs@carradio.com

radio restorations
repairs

See full listing in **Section Two** under **radios**

Speed-o-Tac
3328 Silver Spur Ct
Thousand Oaks, CA 91360
805-492-6600

repairs
restoration

Mail order and open shop. 6 days 9 am to 5 pm. Dealing in repair, service and restoration of vintage and classic mechanical speedometers and tachometers, including the following: Stewart-Warner, SS White, Waltham, AC Delco, GM, King Seeley, Ford, Chrysler, Motometer US, Motometer European; all VDO instruments: Porsche, M-B, BMW, VW, etc. Cables and ratio boxes made to order (to correct cable input to the speedometer). SASE for free data sheet to determine ratio needs. Call before shipping instrument for repair

The Temperature Gauge Guy
521 Wood St
Dunedin, FL 34698
727-733-6716

gauges repaired

Mail order. Summer address: 45 Prospect St, Essex Junction, VT 05452, PH: 802-878-2811. Repair of temperature gauges and of some King-Seeley gas gauges. No electric instrument or radiator cap motometer repair.

Section Two
Generalists

Tom Vagnini
58 Anthony Rd, RR 3
Pittsfield, MA 01201
413-698-2526

used parts

See full listing in **Section One** under **Packard**

Vintage Restorations
The Old Bakery
Windmill Street, Tunbridge Wells
Kent, TN2 4UU England
UK 1892-525-899
FAX: UK 1892-525499

accessories instruments

Mail order and open shop by appointment only. Specializing in the complete restoration, supply and fabrication of instruments and dashboard accessories, mostly for European sports and exotic cars such as Alfa Romeo, Alvis, Aston Martin, Bentley, Bugatti, Ferrari, Maserati, MG, Rolls-Royce and Riley. MasterCard and Visa accepted. Send for leaflet or look us up on the web site: www.mgcars.org.uk/vr/

Westberg Manufacturing Inc
3400 Westach Way
Sonoma, CA 95476
800-400-7024, 707-938-2121
FAX: 707-938-4968
E-mail: westach@juno.com

gauges instruments tachometers

Mail order and open shop. Dual 2-1/16 gauges available. In business 54 years. Web site: westach.com

XKs Unlimited
850 Fiero Ln
San Luis Obispo, CA 93401
805-544-7864; FAX: 805-544-1664
E-mail: xksunltd@aol.com

instruments parts restorations

See full listing in **Section One** under **Jaguar**

Scott Young
332 Devon Dr
San Rafael, CA 94903
415-472-5126

instruments

Mail order only. Furnishing dash glass and metal instrument dial restoration for over 18 years. Dash glass silkscreened (numbers on glass) for speedometers, clocks and radios. In-stock dash glass for over 200 cars in the 1930s, 1940s and early 1950s. Authentic metal dial restoration (numbers on metal). Our process is appropriate for show cars or cars of value.

insurance

American Collectors Insurance Inc
498 Kings Hwy North
PO Box 8343
Cherry Hill, NJ 08002
800-360-2277; FAX: 609-779-7289

insurance

Since 1976, have been dedicated to taking the hassle and expense out of insuring collector vehicles. Today thousands of collectors from coast to coast rely on American Collectors for exceptional coverage, pricing and service. For an instant rate quote on your classic car, truck, motorcycle or street rod, please visit our web site or call us toll-free. Web site: www.americancollectorsins.com

ARS, Automotive Research Services
Division of Auto Search International
1702 W Camelback #301
Phoenix, AZ 85015
602-230-7111; FAX: 602-230-7282

appraisals research

See full listing in **Section Two** under **appraisals**

Automotive Legal Service Inc
PO Box 626
Dresher, PA 19025
800-487-4947, 215-659-4947
FAX: 215-657-5843
E-mail: autolegal@aol.com

appraisals

See full listing in **Section Two** under **appraisals**

Blueprint Auto Insurance Agency
100 Corporate Pl
Peabody, MA 01960
800-530-5305; FAX: 978-535-3759
E-mail: bluprntins@aol.com

insurance

Antique and collector car insurance available in most states. Including street rods and exotics.

Classic Car Lobby
Henri Simar Jr
Rue Des Combattants, 81
4800 Verviers Belgium
32-87335501; FAX: 32-87335122

insurance

Mail order and open shop. Monday-Saturday 9 am to 12 pm, 2 pm to 6 pm, closed Sunday. Specialist for classic car insurance and insurance broker.

Collector Car Insurance Inc
PO Box 414
Leo, IN 46765
219-627-3355, 800-787-7637
FAX: 219-627-6317

insurance

Insurance for street rods, customs, antiques, exotics, collectible Corvettes, automobiles.

Condon & Skelly Collectible Vehicle Insurance
121 E Kings Hwy, Ste 203
Maple Shade, NJ 08052
800-257-9496

insurance

Have been the insurance of the collector car hobby since 1974. Offer complete coverage for your authentic antique, classic or special interest autos, trucks or motorcycles. Insurance for vintage farm tractors, military vehicles, street rods, customs, modifieds, kits and replicas is also available. Underwritten by A+ rated St Paul Mercury Insurance Company. Call for a quote. Web site: www.condonskelly.com
See our ad on page 307

Denmark Insurance Services
Collector's Choice Classic & Custom
Car Insurance Program
23230 Chagrin Blvd, Ste 950
Beachwood, OH 44122
800-284-5867, 216-765-1688 ext 1704
FAX: 216-765-7101

insurance

Mail order and open shop. 8:30 am to 5 pm EST, 24 hour fax. Classic and antique auto insurances including vintage motorcycles, street rods and custom vehicles. Based on availability, certain states may be excluded. Agency also offers all lines of insurance. In business for over 50 years.

Great American Insurance
Classic Collectors Program
PO Box 429569
Cincinnati, OH 45242-9569
800-252-5233; FAX: 513-530-8405
E-mail: classiccollectors@yahoo.com

insurance

Collectible auto insurance for antiques, classics, exotics, street rods, replicas, military vehicles and antique fire engines. Web site: www.classiccollectors.com
See our ad on page 308

J.C. Taylor Antique Auto Insurance Information Sheet

Underwritten by Maryland Casualty (A member of the worldwide <u>Zurich Insurance Group</u>)
with offices and claim facilities in principal U.S. cities.

1 (800) 345-8290   (610) 853-1300

Applicant _____ Date of Birth _____ Occupation _____

Address _____ Zip _____

Phone Number ( ) _____

1. Operator License Number _____ Number of Antique Autos owned _____

2. List all losses in past three years and moving violations – antique and modern cars. (Date-Cause-Payment.) _____
_____

3. Total Annual Mileage: Club Functions _____ Other Purposes _____

4. Name of antique or car club to which you belong _____

5. List modern cars used by daily transportation (owned) _____ (or company cars) _____

6. Where are cars garaged? Under one roof? Construction of garage–brick-frame-fire resistive _____
_____

7. Has rated horsepower or other specifications been changed? Yes _____ No _____ If yes, explain: _____
_____

8. The following coverages are available. Indicate those desired by placing "X" in proper boxes.

❑ Liability ($100,000 single limit) Bodily Injury and Property Damage. Annual Rates: 1st car $15.00, 2nd $10.00, 3rd $5.00

❑ Uninsured/Underinsured Motorist – Rates as required by your State. Car 1 _____ $_____ Car 2 $_____ Car 3 $_____
_____

❑ Liability ($300,000 single limit) Bodily Injury and Property Damage. Annual Rates: 1st car $20.00, 2nd $14.00, 3rd $8.00

❑ Medical Payments of $1,000: 1st car $4.00, 2nd car $3.00, 3rd car $2.00. Units in excess of 3, NO CHARGE

Physical Damage

❑ Physical Damage (Comprehensive Includes Fire and Theft) – Annual Rates – $0.35 per $100 of insurance for each vehicle.
NO DEDUCTIBLE. 25 years or older.

❑ Physical Damage (Collision) – Annual Rate – $0.35 per $100 of insurance for each vehicle. NO DEDUCTIBLE. 25 years or older.

(Note – Collision is not written as a singular coverage but is available with Comprehensive)

❑ Physical Damage (Comprehensive Includes Fire and Theft) – $0.70 per $100 of insurance for each vehicle. Less than 25 years.

❑ Physical Damage (Collision) – $0.70 per $100 of amount of insurance for each vehicle. Less than 25 years.

9. Date this coverage is to be effective _____ **Policy Minimum Premium $50.00**.

ANTIQUE AUTOS TO BE INSURED

We Require: 1. PHOTO of all vehicles listed 2. APPRAISAL for each vehicle valued at $20,000 or over

Year	Make	Body Type Series or Model	V.I.N. (Vehicle I.D. Number) Serial or Motor Number	Present Valuation (Amount of Insurance)
1.				
2.				
3.				
4.				

Use separate sheet for additional cars to be insured.
An application may be forwarded to you for additional information.

My vehicle(s) will be used mainly in exhibitions, club activities, parades and other functions of public interest and will not be used primarily for the transportation of passenger goods.

If you are a resident of FL, PA, or NJ, send copy of regular car policy.

NOT AVAILABLE IN ALL STATES

Signature: _____ Date: _____

NOTE: Your insurance will become effective upon payment of the entire premium, acceptance of the risk and compliance with all state specific laws and regulations. Please sign and forward with your remittance, payable to:

J.C. TAYLOR ANTIQUE AUTO INSURANCE AGENCY, INC.

320 South 69th Street
Upper Darby, Pennsylvania 19082

1 (800) 345-8290   (610) 853-1300

Grundy Worldwide
PO Box 1209
Glenside, PA 19038
800-338-4005; FAX: 215-887-5017

insurance

Collector vehicle insurance for collectible automobiles with no model, year limitation, no mileage limitation. Underwritten by A++ rated carrier, finest industry standards set and maintained. Call today. Web site: www.grundy.com

Hagerty Classic Insurance
PO Box 87
Traverse City, MI 49685
800-922-4050; FAX: 616-941-8227

insurance

Mail order only. Provides agreed value coverage, superior service and exceptionally competitive rates for antique, classic, limited edition and special interest vehicles. Offers flexible mileage, usage and underwriting guidelines and a variety of appropriate liability packages to meet your needs. The program is underwritten by Greenwich Insurance Company which is rated A (excellent) by A M Best. Trust your classic to nothing less than Hagerty Classic Insurance. Call or write for a no-obligation quote. Web site: www.hagerty.com

Jesser's Auto Clinic
26 West St
Akron, OH 44303
330-376-8181; FAX: 330-384-9129

appraisals

See full listing in **Section Two** under **appraisals**

Pete Reinthaler Insurance
PO Box 2004
Bellaire, TX 77402-2004
713-669-1127; FAX: 713-864-2068
E-mail: par2004@aol.com

insurance

Mail order and open shop. Monday-Friday 8:30 am to 5 pm. Antique auto insurance for all types of cars.

Sparrow Auction Company
59 Wheeler Ave
Milford, CT 06460
203-877-1066
E-mail: vehicle@snet.net

auction company

See full listing in **Section Two** under **auctions & events**

Zehr Insurance Brokers Ltd
65 Huron St
New Hamburg, ON Canada N0B 2G0
519-662-1710; FAX: 519-662-2025

insurance

Mail order and open shop. Monday-Friday 9 am to 5 pm. Special rated auto insurance for antique, classic, special interest automobiles plus all lines of general insurance in Ontario.

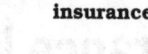
interiors & interior parts

AAC Restorations
Rt 1 Box 409
Mount Clare, WV 26408
304-622-2849

seat springs

See full listing in **Section Two** under **upholstery**

Ace Antique Auto Restoration
65 S Service Rd
Plainview, NY 11803
516-752-6065; FAX: 516-752-1484

air conditioning
body rebuilding
restoration
wiring harnesses

See full listing in **Section Two** under **restoration shops**

All Seams Fine
23 Union St
Waterbury, VT 05676
800-244-7326 (SEAM)
802-244-8843

interior
restorations

See full listing in **Section Two** under **upholstery**

Andover Automotive Inc
PO Box 3143
Laurel, MD 20709
410-381-6700; FAX: 410-381-6703
E-mail: andoauto@clark.net

parts
seat belts

See full listing in **Section One** under **Corvette**

Arrow Fastener Co Inc
271 Mayhill St
Saddle Brook, NJ 07663

nail guns
rivet tools
staple guns

See full listing in **Section Two** under **tools**

Auto Custom Carpet Inc
Jeff Moses
PO Box 1350, 1429 Noble St
Anniston, AL 36201
800-633-2358, 205-236-1118
FAX: 800-516-8274
E-mail: info@accmats.net

carpets
floor mats

See full listing in **Section One** under **Chevrolet**

Auto-Mat Co
69 Hazel St
Hicksville, NY 11801
800-645-7258 orders
516-938-7373; FAX: 516-931-8438
E-mail: browner5@ix.netcom.com

accessories
carpet sets
interiors

Mail order and open shop. Monday-Friday 8 am to 5 pm, Saturday 8 am to 1 pm. Specializing in auto interior restorations and accessories for all years and models, foreign and domestic, cars and trucks. Work can be done on cars or just seats in our large installation department or ready made products can be shipped for do-it-yourself installation. Carpet sets, upholstery kits, seat covers, tops, headliners, trunk mats, rubber mats, personalized carpet mats, steering wheels, sheepskins, car covers, Recaro seats and more. Send $1 for catalog or visit our showroom. Web site: www.autointeriors.net

Auto Upholstery Unlimited
36 Glenmoor Dr
East Haven, CT 06512
203-467-6433

convertible tops
upholstery supplies

Mail order only. Supplying original equipment NOS seat fabrics and vinyls, snaps and fasteners. Send sample of material needed and SASE for free match. Yardage available. Carpeting and convertible tops.

B & T Truck Parts 906 E Main St PO Box 799 Siloam Springs, AR 72761 501-524-5959; FAX: 501-524-5559	**pickup parts**

See full listing in **Section Two** under **trucks & tractors**

G W Bartlett Co Inc 4301 Old & R3 N Muncie, IN 47303 800-338-8034 US/Canada FAX: 765-282-4058 E-mail: osji@netdirect.net	**convertible tops** **interiors** **rubber seals**

See full listing in **Section One** under **Jaguar**

BAS Ltd Jaguar Trim Specialist 250 H St, Unit 8110 Blaine, WA 98231 800-661-5377; FAX: 640-990-9988 E-mail: basjag@helix.net	**interior parts**

See full listing in **Section One** under **Jaguar**

Bob's Bird House 124 Watkin Ave Chadds Ford, PA 19317 610-358-3420; FAX: 610-558-0729	**parts**

See full listing in **Section One** under **Thunderbird**

Buenger Enterprises/GoldenRod Dehumidifier 3600 S Harbor Blvd Oxnard, CA 93035 800-451-6797; FAX: 805-985-1534	**dehumidifiers**

See full listing in **Section Two** under **car care products**

Canadian Mustang 20529 62 Ave Langley, BC Canada V3A 8R4 604-534-6424; FAX: 604-534-6694 E-mail: parts@canadianmustang.com	**parts**

See full listing in **Section One** under **Mustang**

CARS Inc 1964 W 11 Mile Rd Berkley, MI 48072 248-398-7100; FAX: 248-398-7078 E-mail: carsinc@worldnet.att.net	**interior**

See full listing in **Section One** under **Chevrolet**

Stan Chernoff 1215 Greenwood Ave Torrance, CA 90503 310-320-4554; FAX: 310-328-7867 E-mail: az589@lafn.org	**mechanical parts** **restoration parts** **technical info** **trim parts**

See full listing in **Section One** under **Datsun**

Chicago Corvette Supply 7322 S Archer Rd Justice, IL 60458 708-458-2500; FAX: 708-458-2662	**parts**

See full listing in **Section One** under **Corvette**

Classic Chevy International PO Box 607188 Orlando, FL 32860-7188 800-456-1957, 407-299-1957 FAX: 407-299-3341 E-mail: cciworld@aol.com	**modified parts** **repro parts** **used parts**

See full listing in **Section One** under **Chevrolet**

Classic Creations of Central Florida 3620 Hwy 92E Lakeland, FL 33801 941-665-2322; FAX: 941-666-5348 E-mail: flclassics@aol.com	**parts** **restoration** **service**

See full listing in **Section One** under **Mustang**

Classtique Upholstery Supply PO Box 278-HMN Isanti, MN 55040 612-444-3768, 612-444-4025 FAX: 612-444-9980	**carpet sets** **headliners**

Mail order and store sales. Dealing in ready to install carpet sets, headliners, convertible tops and many related parts for most American cars 1950s-1970s. All GM, Ford, Chrysler, etc cars. Advise year and body style of car, send samples if possible for match. Established 1959. Catalog, $3, refunded with order.

Classtique Upholstery & Top Co PO Box 278 HK Isanti, MN 55040 612-444-4025; FAX: 612-444-9980	**top kits** **upholstery kits**

See full listing in **Section One** under **Ford 1903-1931**

Cn'V Corvette Sales 2166 E University Dr Tempe, AZ 85281 602-994-8388; FAX: 602-423-0407 E-mail: sales@cnv-corvettes.com	**parts** **sales** **service**

See full listing in **Section One** under **Corvette**

Color-Plus Leather Restoration System 106 Harrier Ct,3767 Sunrise Lake Milford, PA 18337-9315 570-686-3158; FAX: 570-686-4161 E-mail: jpcolorplus@pikeonline.net	**leather** **conditioning** **leather dye**

See full listing in **Section Two** under **leather restoration**

Comfy/Inter-American Sheepskins Inc 1346 Centinela Ave West Los Angeles, CA 90025-1901 800-521-4014; FAX: 310-442-6080 E-mail: sales@comfysheep.com	**floor mats** **seat covers**

Mail order and open shop. Monday-Friday 7:30 am to 5 pm, Saturday 10 am to 4 pm. Specializing in sheepskin seat covers and sheepskin floor mats for most all automobiles and airplanes. Also offer sheepskin accessories: heel pads, seat belt covers, steering wheel covers, wash mitts. Web site: www.comfysheep.com

Concours Parts & Accessories 3493 Arrowhead Dr Carson City, NV 89706 800-722-0009; FAX: 800-725-8644	**parts**

See full listing in **Section One** under **Thunderbird**

Corbeau Seats 9503 South 560 West Sandy, UT 84070 801-255-3737; FAX: 801-255-3222 E-mail: info@corbeau.com	**bucket seats**

Custom bucket seats for street, race and off-road vehicles. Available in cloth, leather and vinyl. Web site: www.corbeau.com

Dom Corey Upholstery & Antique Auto
1 Arsene Way
Fairhaven Business Park
Fairhaven, MA 02719
508-997-6555

carpets/conv tops
dash covers
door panels
headliners
seats
upholstery

Mail order and open shop. Monday-Friday 8:30 am to 5 pm EST. Specializing in vehicle interiors, both new and old (1902-1998). Custom design interiors and redo originals as needed. Mostly car show and muscle cars as well as 1920s-1950s. Seats, carpets, door panels, headliners, convertible tops, dash covers, tonneau covers, motorcycles, trucks, Land Rovers, boat tops, etc.

Corvair Ranch Inc
1079 Bon-Ox Rd
Gettysburg, PA 17325
717-624-2805; FAX: 717-624-1196

auto sales
parts
restoration
service

See full listing in **Section One** under **Corvair**

Corvair Underground
PO Box 339
Dundee, OR 97115
800-825-8247, 503-434-1648
FAX: 503-434-1626

parts

See full listing in **Section One** under **Corvair**

Corvette America
PO Box 324, Rt 322
Boalsburg, PA 16827
800-458-3475; foreign: 814-364-2141
FAX: 814-364-9615, 24 hours
E-mail: vettebox@corvetteamerica.com

accessories
fiberglass
interiors
leisure items
parts

See full listing in **Section One** under **Corvette**

Corvette Specialties of MD Inc
1912 Liberty Rd
Eldersburg, MD 21784
410-795-3180; FAX: 410-795-3247

parts
restoration
service

See full listing in **Section One** under **Corvette**

Coventry West Inc
5936-A Peachtree Rd
Atlanta, GA 30341
800-331-2193 toll-free
770-451-3839 Atlanta
FAX: 770-451-7561

assemblies
Jaguar parts

See full listing in **Section One** under **Jaguar**

Custom Interiors
PO Box 51174
Indian Orchard, MA 01151
800-423-6053; FAX: 413-589-9178

carpets
headliners
upholstery

See full listing in **Section Two** under **upholstery**

D&D Automobilia
813 Ragers Hill Rd
South Fork, PA 15956
814-539-5653

plastic parts
steering wheels

See full listing in **Section Two** under **steering wheels**

Dash Graining by Mel Erikson
31 Meadow Rd
Kings Park, NY 11754
PH/FAX: 516-544-1102 days
360-7789 nights

dashboard
restoration

See full listing in **Section Two** under **woodgraining**

Dash Specialists
1910 Redbud Ln
Medford, OR 97504
541-776-0040

interiors

See full listing in **Section One** under **Cadillac/LaSalle**

Dashhugger
PO Box 933
Clovis, CA 93613
559-298-4529; FAX: 559-298-3428
E-mail: sales@dashhugger.com

dashboard covers

Mail order only. High quality dashboard covers for all makes and models of cars, trucks and vans. Web site: www.dashhugger.com

Dave's Auto Restoration
2285 Rt 307 E
Jefferson, OH 44047
PH/FAX: 216-858-2227
E-mail: davesauto@knownet.net

upholstery

Open shop. Monday-Friday 8:30 am to 5:30 pm. Specializing in automotive upholstery for all makes and models, Porsche, Jaguar, Mercedes, Rolls-Royce, Bentley, Packard, Ferrari, Pierce-Arrow, Duesenberg and Auburn Cord, 1900-present. Reconditioned Porsche Targa tops by mail order.

Doc's Jags
125 Baker Rd
Lake Bluff, IL 60044
847-367-5247; FAX: 847-367-6363
E-mail: docsjags@worldnet.att.net

appraisals
interiors
restoration

See full listing in **Section One** under **Jaguar**

Douglass Interior Products
2000 124th Ave NE
Bellevue, WA 98005
800-722-7272, 425-455-2120
FAX: 425-451-4779
E-mail: rbd@dipi.com

leather hides
vinyl

Deal in genuine leather hides, wide selection of colors in stock. All top selection European cowhide. Average size 55 sq ft. Also carry trim weight leather in selected colors. Vinyl, carpet and sheepskin, all in stock. Natural wool headliner fabrics and synthetic headliner material in a range of colors. Web site: www.dipi.com
See our ad on page 313

Mike Drago Chevy Parts
141 E St Joseph St
Easton, PA 18042
PH/FAX: 610-252-5701
E-mail: dragomdcp@aol.com

Chevrolet parts

See full listing in **Section One** under **Chevrolet**

East Coast Chevy Inc
Ol '55 Chevy Parts
4154A Skyron Dr
Doylestown, PA 18938
215-348-5568; FAX: 215-348-0560

custom work
parts
restoration

See full listing in **Section One** under **Chevrolet**

The El Camino Store
57 B Depot Rd
Goleta, CA 93117
805-681-8164; FAX: 805-681-8166
E-mail: ec@elcaminostore.com

parts

See full listing in **Section One** under **Chevelle/Camaro**

The Enthusiasts Shop
John Parnell
PO Box 80471
Baton Rouge, LA 70898
225-928-7456; FAX: 225-928-7665

cars
pre-war parts
transportation

See full listing in **Section One** under **Rolls-Royce/Bentley**

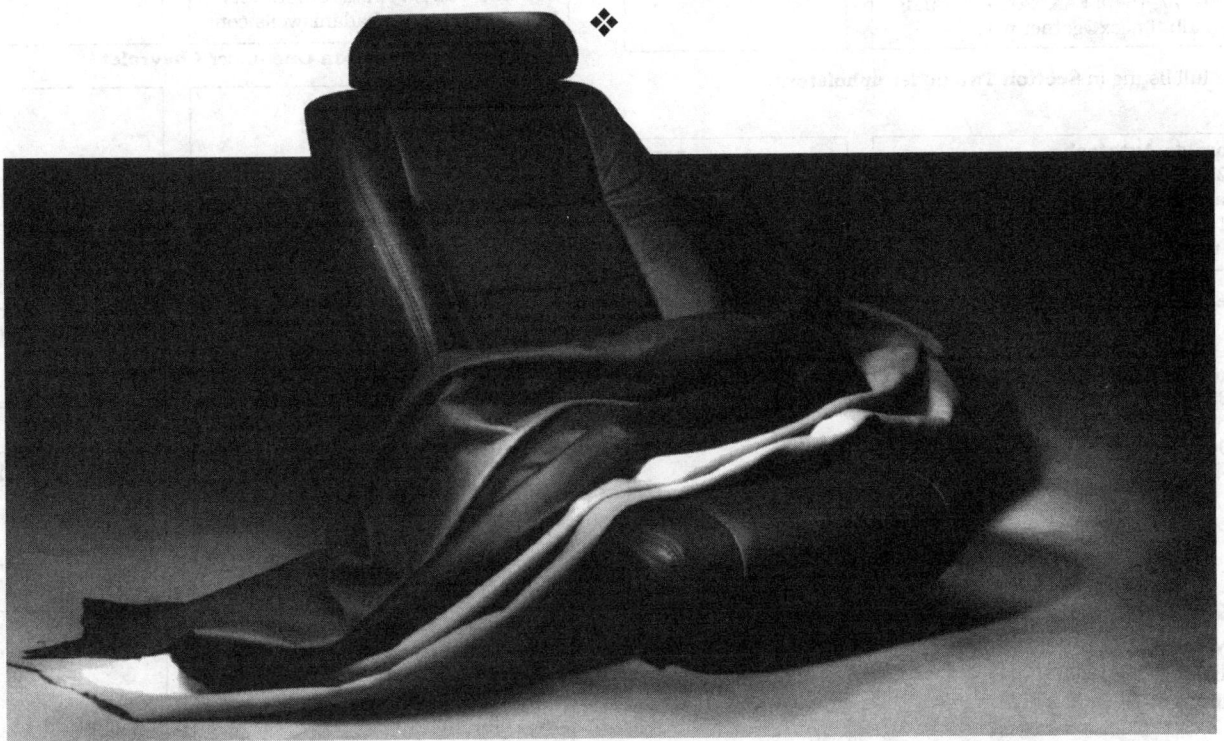

Bob Fatone's Mercedes Used Parts
166 W Main St
Niantic, CT 06357
860-739-1923; FAX: 860-691-0669
E-mail: bobfatone@earthlink.net

parts

See full listing in **Section One** under **Mercedes-Benz**

Firewall Insulators & Quiet Ride Solutions
6333 Pacific Ave, Ste 523
Stockton, CA 95207
209-477-4840; FAX: 209-477-0918
E-mail: timcox@gotnet.net

auto insulation
firewall insulators
gloveboxes
sound deadening

See full listing in **Section Two** under **upholstery**

Foreign Autotech
3235 C Sunset Ln
Hatboro, PA 19040
215-441-4421; FAX: 215-441-4490
E-mail: fap1800@aol.com

parts

See full listing in **Section One** under **Volvo**

Freddie Beach Restoration
1834 Woodstock Rd
Fredericton, NB Canada E3C 1L4
506-450-9074; FAX: 506-459-0708
E-mail: vallise@city.fredericton.nb.ca

accessories
restoration parts

See full listing in **Section Two** under **car & parts locators**

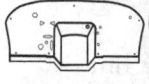
Hampton Coach Inc
6 Chestnut St, PO Box 6
Amesbury, MA 01913
888-388-8726, 978-388-8047
FAX: 978-388-1113
E-mail: lbb-hc@greennet.net

fabrics
top kits
upholstery kits

See full listing in **Section One** under **Chevrolet**

Harmon's Incorporated
Hwy 27 N
PO Box 6C
Geneva, IN 46740
219-368-7221; FAX: 219-368-9396
E-mail: harmons1@adamswells.com

interiors
parts

See full listing in **Section One** under **Chevrolet**

Highway Classics
949 N Cataract Ave, Unit J
San Dimas, CA 91773
909-592-8819; FAX: 909-592-4239
E-mail: donnelson@earthlink.net

parts

See full listing in **Section One** under **Ford 1954-up**

Bill Hirsch Auto Parts
396 Littleton Ave
Newark, NJ 07103
973-642-2404; FAX: 973-642-6161
E-mail: hirschauto@aol.com

enamel lacquer
hubcaps
top material

See full listing in **Section Two** under **paints**

Hoffman Automotive Distributor
US Hwy #1, Box 818
Hilliard, FL 32046
904-845-4421

parts

See full listing in **Section Two** under **body parts**

Hollywood Classic Motorcars Inc
363 Ansin Blvd
Hallandale, FL 33009
800-235-2444, 954-454-4641
FAX: 954-457-3801
E-mail: hcm@tbird.net

cars
parts

See full listing in **Section One** under **Thunderbird**

Impala Bob's Inc
4753 E Falcon Dr
Dept HVAA14
Mesa, AZ 85215
800-IMPALAS orders
480-924-4800 retail store
480-981-1600 office
FAX: 800-716-6237, 480-981-1675
E-mail: info@impalas.com

restoration parts

See full listing in **Section One** under **Chevrolet**

Infinite Rainbows Auto Upholstery
PO Box 408
North San Juan, CA 95960
530-292-3106

interiors
tops

Upholsterer of two consecutive Antique Automobile Club of America Grand National Prize winning automobiles. Complete handcrafted interiors and tops in one man shop. Guarantee absolute attention to detail. Close to Sacramento, CA and Reno, NV. No kits or yardage.

Jerry's Classic Cars & Parts Inc
4097 McRay Ave
Springdale, AR 72764
800-828-4584; FAX: 501-750-1682
E-mail: jcc@jerrysclassiccars.com

parts
restoration

See full listing in **Section One** under **Ford 1954-up**

Just Dashes Inc 5941 Lemona Ave Van Nuys, CA 91411 800-247-DASH, 818-780-9005 FAX: 818-780-9014	armrests dash pads door panels headrests

Worldwide mail order and open shop. Monday-Friday 8:30 am to 5:30 pm. Manufacture and restore dash pads, door panels, armrests and consoles using OEM materials and an exclusive thermo-forming process. Also available: reproduction, OEM, NOS and used dash pads. Specializing in vehicles 1954 and up. All work guaranteed. Web site: www.justdashes.com

K&D Enterprises 23117 E Echo Lake Rd Snohomish, WA 98296-5426 425-788-0507; FAX: 360-668-2003 E-mail: tdb@halcyon.com	accessories parts restorations

See full listing in **Section One** under **Jensen**

K&W Kollectibles 220 Industrial Pkwy S #6 Aurora, ON Canada L4G 3V6 416-410-7741; FAX: 905-727-5771 E-mail: kwkoll@sympatico.ca	parts repair restoration

See full listing in **Section One** under **Buick/McLaughlin**

Keleen Leathers Inc 10526 W Cermak Rd Westchester, IL 60154 708-409-9800; FAX: 708-409-9801 E-mail: keleenlea@aol.com	leather hides

Leather hides from automotive leather specialists. Have been serving automobile restorers for twenty years with top quality hides at the most competitive prices. Call us with your questions, whether you want to custom tan an exact match of your original leather or select from our hundreds of stock colors. *See our ad on page 627*

Dave Knittel Upholstery 850 E Teton #7 Tucson, AZ 85706 PH/FAX: 520-746-1588	interiors tops upholstery

See full listing in **Section Two** under **upholstery**

Al Knoch Interiors 130 Montoya Rd El Paso, TX 79932 800-880-8080; FAX: 915-581-1545 E-mail: alknoch@flash.net	carpets interiors tooling services tops

See full listing in **Section One** under **Chevrolet**

Koolmat 26258 Cranage Rd Olmsted Falls, OH 44138 440-427-1888; FAX: 440-427-1889 E-mail: koolmat1@gte.net	insulators

See full listing in **Section Two** under **restoration aids**

Kwik Poly T Distributing Inc 24 St Henry Ct St Charles, MO 63301 314-724-1065	restoration aids

See full listing in **Section Two** under **restoration aids**

LeBaron Bonney Co PO Box 6 6 Chestnut St Amesbury, MA 01913 800-221-5408, 978-388-3811 FAX: 978-388-1113 E-mail: lbb-hc@greennet.net	fabrics interior kits top kits

See full listing in **Section One** under **Ford 1932-1953**

Legendary Auto Interiors Ltd 121 W Shore Blvd Newark, NY 14513 800-363-8804 FAX: 800-SEAT-UPH (732-8874)	soft trim

See full listing in **Section One** under **Chrysler**

Loga Enterprises 5399 Old Town Hall Rd Eau Claire, WI 54701 715-832-7302	convertible tops interior parts

See full listing in **Section One** under **Studebaker**

Lokar Inc 10924 Murdock Dr Knoxville, TN 37932 423-966-2269; FAX: 423-671-1999 E-mail: lokarinc@aol.com	performance parts

See full listing in **Section Two** under **street rods**

Lyme Pond Restorations PO Box 202 Barnard, VT 05031 802-457-4657	restoration

See full listing in **Section Two** under **restoration shops**

Madera Concepts 606 Olive St Santa Barbara, CA 93101 800-800-1579, 805-962-1579 FAX: 805-962-7359 E-mail: jwayco@west.net	restoration woodwork woodwork repair

See full listing in **Section Two** under **woodwork**

Majestic Truck Parts 17726 Dickerson Dallas, TX 75252 972-248-6245; FAX: 972-380-8913 E-mail: majestictrk@juno.com	parts

See full listing in **Section One** under **Chevrolet**

Merv's Classic Chevy Parts 1330 Washington Iowa Falls, IA 50126 515-648-3168, 515-648-9675	parts

See full listing in **Section One** under **Chevrolet**

Mint Condition Auto Upholstery PO Box 134 Silverdale New Zealand PH/FAX: 64-9-424 2257 E-mail: mint.condition@xtra.co.nz	convertible tops interiors spring-gaiters wheelcovers

See full listing in **Section Two** under **special services**

Motorsport Auto 1139 W Collins Ave Orange, CA 92667 800-633-6331, 714-639-2620 FAX: 714-639-7460 E-mail: motorsport@worldnet.att.net	parts

See full listing in **Section One** under **Datsun**

Muncie Imports & Classics 4401 St Rd 3 N Muncie, IN 47303 800-462-4244; FAX: 317-287-9551 E-mail: mic@netdirect.net	repair restoration upholstery

See full listing in **Section One** under **Jaguar**

National Parts Depot
3101 SW 40th Blvd
Gainesville, FL 32608
800-874-7595 toll-free 24 hours
352-378-2473 local

accessories
restoration parts

See full listing in **Section Two** under **comprehensive parts**

Newport Upholstery Source
250 H St, Unit 8110
Blaine, WA 98231
604-990-0346; FAX: 604-990-9988

carpets
tops
upholstery

See full listing in **Section Two** under **upholstery**

Norm's Custom Shop
6897 E William St Ext
Bath, NY 14810
PH/FAX: 607-776-2357

interiors
tops

See full listing in **Section One** under **Cord**

Original Parts Group Inc
17892 Gothard St
Huntington Beach, CA 92647
800-243-8355 US/Canada
714-841-5363; FAX: 714-847-8159

accessories
parts

See full listing in **Section One** under **Pontiac**

Parts House
2912 Hunter St
Fort Worth, TX 76112
817-451-2708
E-mail: theparts@flash.net

accessories
parts

See full listing in **Section Two** under **comprehensive parts**

Parts Unlimited Inc
Todd Bidwell
12101 Westport Rd
Louisville, KY 40245-1789
502-425-3766; FAX: 502-425-0055

interiors
weatherstrips

See full listing in **Section One** under **Chevrolet**

Partwerks of Chicago
718 S Prairie Rd
New Lenox, IL 60451
815-462-3000; FAX: 815-462-3006
E-mail: partwerks9@aol.com

parts
service

See full listing in **Section Two** under **engine parts**

Passenger Car Supply
102 Cloverdale Rd
Swedesboro, NJ 08085
609-467-7966

parts

See full listing in **Section One** under **Chevrolet**

Paul's Discount Jaguar Parts
1124 NW 134th Ave
Sunrise
Fort Lauderdale, FL 33323
954-846-7976; FAX: 954-846-9450
E-mail: paulsjag@ix.netcom.com

parts

See full listing in **Section One** under **Jaguar**

Precision Auto Designs
28 Railway Ave
Campbell, CA 95008
408-378-2332; FAX: 408-378-1301
E-mail: pad@precisionauto.com

accessories
car covers
restoration

See full listing in **Section One** under **Mercedes-Benz**

RARE Corvettes
Joe Calcagno
Box 1080
Soquel, CA 95073
831-475-4442; FAX: 831-475-1115

cars
parts

See full listing in **Section One** under **Corvette**

Ray's Upholstering
600 N St Frances Cabrini Ave
Scranton, PA 18504
800-296-RAYS; FAX: 717-963-0415

partial/total
restoration

See full listing in **Section Two** under **restoration shops**

The Real Source
PO Box 1248
Effingham, IL 62401
800-LUV-BUGG (588-2844), dept VS9
FAX: 217-347-2952
E-mail: madbug@madvet.com

accessories
parts

See full listing in **Section One** under **Volkswagen**

The Reflected Image
21 W Wind Dr
Northford, CT 06472
PH/FAX: 203-484-0760
E-mail: scott@reflectedimage.com

mirror reproduction
mirror resilvering

See full listing in **Section Two** under **special services**

REM Automotive Inc
2610 N Brandt Rd
Annville, PA 17003
717-838-4242; FAX: 717-838-5091

interior parts
trunk lining

See full listing in **Section Two** under **restoration aids**

Restoration Specialties
John Sarena
124 North F St
Lompoc, CA 93436
805-736-2627

interiors
restoration

See full listing in **Section One** under **Chevrolet**

Ridgefield Auto Upholstery
34 Bailey Ave
Ridgefield, CT 06877
203-438-7583; FAX: 203-438-2666

interiors
tops

Mail order and open shop. Monday-Friday 8 am to 6 pm,
Saturday 8 am to noon. Foreign and domestic, antique to present, complete or partial interior replacement or restoration, convertible top, repair and replacement, custom made and ready
made. One man shop assures strict attention to quality and
detail. Custom work a speciality.

RodDoors
PO Box 2110
Chico, CA 95927
530-896-1513; FAX: 530-896-1518
E-mail: roddoors@juno.com

door panels
interior accessories

See full listing in **Section Two** under **street rods**

Ron's Restorations Inc
2968-B Ask Kay Dr
Smyrna, GA 30082
770-438-6102; FAX: 770-438-0037

interior trim
restoration

See full listing in **Section One** under **Mercedes-Benz**

Sailorette's Nautical Nook
451 Davy Ln
Wilmington, IL 60481
815-476-1644; FAX: 815-476-2524

covers
interiors

See full listing in **Section Two** under **upholstery**

Harry Samuel 65 Wisner St Pontiac, MI 48342-1066 248-335-1900 E-mail: hsamuel1@aol.com	**carpet fabrics interiors upholstery covers**

Mail and phone orders. Soft trim for 1950-1977 Buick, Cadillac, Chevrolet, Ford, Lincoln, Mercury, Mopar, Oldsmobile and (specializing in) Pontiac. Cut, sewn and molded carpets for above cars plus NOS factory original carpets for 1961-1964 Buicks, Oldsmobiles and Pontiacs. Original seat upholstery covers for 1960-1965 Bonneville, Catalina Ventura, 2+2 and Grand Prix. Headliners, package trays, hood pads, trunk kits, vinyl and cloth yardage and more for all GM cars, some Chrysler and Ford cars.

Scarborough Faire Inc 1151 Main St Pawtucket, RI 02860 800-556-6300, 401-724-4200 FAX: 401-724-5392	**parts**

See full listing in **Section One** under **MG**

Silver Star Restorations 116 Highway 19 Topton, NC 28781 704-321-4268 E-mail: silverstar@main.nc.us	**parts restoration**

See full listing in **Section One** under **Mercedes-Benz**

Paul Slater Auto Parts 9496 85th St N Stillwater, MN 55082 612-429-4235	**parts**

See full listing in **Section One** under **Dodge**

Smith & Jones Distributing Company Inc 1 Biloxi Square West Columbia, SC 29170 803-822-8500; FAX: 803-822-8477	**parts**

See full listing in **Section One** under **Ford 1903-1931**

SMS Auto Fabrics 2325 SE 10th Ave Portland, OR 97214 503-234-1175; FAX: 503-234-0651	**upholstery**

Mail order and open shop. Monday-Friday 8:30 am to 5 pm. Upholstery, including cloth, vinyl and leather, for all makes and models of American cars, from 1940s-1980s. Also make exact reproduction door panels for 1950s and 1960s cars.

Robert H Snyder PO Drawer 821 Yonkers, NY 10702 914-476-8500 FAX: 914-476-8573, 24 hours E-mail: cohascodpc@earthlink.net	**literature parts**

See full listing in **Section One** under **Cadillac/LaSalle**

SoCal Pickups Inc 6321 Manchester Blvd Buena Park, CA 90621 800-SOCAL-49; FAX: 714-994-2584	**parts**

See full listing in **Section One** under **Ford 1954-up**

Ssnake-Oyl Products Inc Rt 2, Box 269-6 Hawkins, TX 75765 800-284-7777; FAX: 903-769-4552	**carpet underlay firewall insulation seat belt restoration**

Seat belts restored to show quality condition. NOS seat belts, automotive insulation systems underlayment, water shields and firewall insulation. Specializing in seat belt restoration for 1950s, 1960s and 1970s. Visit our web site: www.ssnake-oyl.com

Sta-Dri Pouches **Beach Filler Products Inc** RD 1, Box 105 Glen Rock, PA 17327 800-BEACH85; FAX: 717-235-4858 E-mail: beachfilters@hotmail.com	**corrosion protection mildew protection moisture protection**

See full listing in **Section Two** under **storage care products**

Star Quality 1 Alley Rd Lagrangeville, NY 12540 800-782-7199; FAX: 914-223-5394 E-mail: sq@mhv.net	**parts**

See full listing in **Section One** under **Mercedes-Benz**

Stilwell's Obsolete Car Parts 1617 Wedeking Ave Evansville, IN 47711 812-425-4794	**body parts interiors parts**

See full listing in **Section One** under **Mustang**

Swedish Classics Inc PO Box 557 Oxford, MD 21654 800-258-4422; FAX: 410-226-5543	**parts**

See full listing in **Section One** under **Volvo**

Sweeney's Auto & Marine Upholstery Inc dba Southampton Auto & Marine Upholstery 471 N Hwy, PO Box 1479 Southampton, NY 11969 516-283-2616; FAX: 516-283-2617	**carpets interiors tops**

See full listing in **Section One** under **Mercedes-Benz**

T-Bird Sanctuary 9997 SW Avery Tualatin, OR 97062 503-692-9848; FAX: 503-692-9849	**parts**

See full listing in **Section One** under **Thunderbird**

Thermax Inc 5385 Alpha Ave Reno, NV 89506 800-247-7177; FAX: 702-972-4809	**interior detailing**

See full listing in **Section Two** under **car care products**

Bill Thomsen 1118 Wooded Acres Ln Moneta, VA 24121 540-297-1200	**salvage yard**

See full listing in **Section Five** under **Virginia**

Thunderbird Headquarters 1080 Detroit Ave Concord, CA 94518 800-227-2174, US FAX: 925-689-1771, 800-964-1957 E-mail: tbirdhq@tbirdhq.com	**accessories literature parts upholstery**

See full listing in **Section One** under **Thunderbird**

TMI Products Inc — classic car interiors
191 Granite St
Corona, CA 91719
800-624-7960, 909-272-1996
FAX: 909-272-1584
E-mail: tmiprods@aol.com

See full listing in **Section One** under **Volkswagen**

Town Auto Top Co — convertible repairs interiors
111 Clinton Rd
Fairfield, NJ 07004
973-575-9333; FAX: 973-808-8366

See full listing in **Section Two** under **restoration shops**

Ultimate Upholstery — interiors top restoration upholstery
14610 W Futura Dr
Sun City West, AZ 85375
602-975-4366

See full listing in **Section Two** under **restoration shops**

Vicarage Jaguar — parts restoration
5333 Collins Ave Suite 502
Miami Beach, FL 33140
305-866-9511; FAX: 305-866-5738
E-mail: vicarage@ix.netcom.com

See full listing in **Section One** under **Jaguar**

Victoria British Ltd — accessories parts
Box 14991
Lenexa, KS 66285-4991
800-255-0088, 913-599-3299

See full listing in **Section One** under **MG**

Volunteer State Chevy Parts — accessories parts
Hwy 41 S
PO Box 10
Greenbrier, TN 37073
615-643-4583; FAX: 615-643-5100

See full listing in **Section One** under **Chevrolet**

Wales Antique Chevy Truck Parts — parts
143 Center
Carleton, MI 48117
734-654-8836

See full listing in **Section One** under **Chevrolet**

John J Waluk — flocking
31 Squirrel Ln
Levittown, NY 11756
516-796-2984; FAX: 516-796-5423
E-mail: bb70@msn.com

See full listing in **Section Two** under **special services**

Pat Wilson's Thunderbird Parts — parts
235 River Rd
New Milford, NJ 07646-1721
888-262-1153; FAX: 201-634-1916

See full listing in **Section One** under **Thunderbird**

Woolies (I&C Woolstenholmes Ltd) — accessories trim upholstery
Whitley Way, Northfields Ind Estate
Market Deeping
Nr Peterborough, PE6 8LD England
0044-1778-347347
FAX: 0044-1778-341847
E-mail: info@woolies-trim.co.uk

Mail order and open shop. Monday-Friday 8:30 am to 5 pm, other times by appointment. Woolies trim, wing pipings, window channels, headlinings, leather/cloth and vinyls, duck and mohair hoodings, moquettes, carpets, felt and Hardura off-the-roll, Bedford cords, rubber and sponge extrusions, fasteners and draught excluders. Also extruded aluminum sections, leather renovation kits and black/polished pressed aluminum number plates, 3-1/2 inch and 3-1/8 inch digit size and goggles. Catalog, $3 (in bills). Web site: www.woolies-trim.co.uk

World Upholstery & Trim — carpet tops upholstery kits
PO Box 2420
Camarillo, CA 93011
805-988-1848; FAX: 805-278-7886
E-mail: worlduph@mail.vcnet.com

Mail order and kit installation shop. Monday-Friday 7 am to 5 pm, Saturday 8 am to 12 pm. Specializing in authentic reproduction seat upholstery kits, carpet, headliners, convertible tops, related items for Alfa, BMW, Jaguar, Mercedes, Porsche, Saab, VW and Fiat. Web site: www.worlduph.com
See our ad on page 440

Zip Products — accessories parts
8067 Fast Ln
Mechanicsville, VA 23111
804-746-2290, 800-962-9632
FAX: 804-730-7043
E-mail: zipvette@erols.com

See full listing in **Section One** under **Corvette**

kit cars & replicars

Automotive Legal Service Inc — appraisals
PO Box 626
Dresher, PA 19025
800-487-4947, 215-659-4947
FAX: 215-657-5843
E-mail: autolegal@aol.com

See full listing in **Section Two** under **appraisals**

Backyard Buddy Corp — automotive lift
1818 N Main St
PO Box 5104
Niles, OH 44446
800-837-9353, 330-544-9372
FAX: 330-544-9311

See full listing in **Section Two** under **accessories**

EVA Sports Cars — kit cars
RR 1
Vankleek Hill, ON Canada K0B 1R0
613-678-3377; FAX: 613-678-6110

Open five days a week, Saturday by appointment. Cobra 427 replicar, space frame chassis, custom twin A-arm front suspension, NASCAR 4-bar rear set-up with pan hard rod. Partially assembled cars for $10,000. The Diva, 1950s style roadster, fiberglass body and tube steel space frame. In-house A-arm top and lower front suspension, 5-link rear, uses Chevy 350 cu in small block motor and vintage style model with Aero screens now available.

Fairlane Automotive Specialties — fiberglass bodies parts
210 E Walker St
St Johns, MI 48879
517-224-6460

See full listing in **Section One** under **Ford 1932-1953**

Finish Line — parts supplies
3593 SW 173rd Terr
Miramar, FL 33029
954-436-9101; FAX: 954-436-9102
E-mail: e.dlibrandi@worldnet.att.net

See full listing in **Section One** under **Cobra**

Koolmat 26258 Cranage Rd Olmsted Falls, OH 44138 440-427-1888; FAX: 440-427-1889 E-mail: koolmat1@gte.net	insulators

See full listing in **Section Two** under **restoration aids**

Lee's Kustom Auto & Street Rods RR 3 Box 3061A Rome, PA 18837 570-247-2326 E-mail: lka41@epix.net	accessories parts restoration

See full listing in **Section Two** under **street rods**

Little Old Cars 3410 Fulton Dr NW Canton, OH 44718 216-455-4685	model cars

See full listing in **Section Two** under **models & toys**

Lokar Inc 10924 Murdock Dr Knoxville, TN 37932 423-966-2269; FAX: 423-671-1999 E-mail: lokarinc@aol.com	performance parts

See full listing in **Section Two** under **street rods**

Memory Lane Motors 562 County Rd 121 Fenelon Falls, ON Canada K0M 1N0 705-887-CARS; FAX: 705-887-4028	car dealer restoration service

See full listing in **Section Two** under **restoration shops**

Norm's Custom Shop 6897 E William St Ext Bath, NY 14810 PH/FAX: 607-776-2357	interiors tops

See full listing in **Section One** under **Cord**

Old Coach Works Restoration Inc 1206 Badger St Yorkville, IL 60560-1701 630-553-0414; FAX: 630-553-1053 E-mail: oldcoachworks@msn.com	appraisals restoration

See full listing in **Section Two** under **restoration shops**

Operations Plus PO Box 26347 Santa Ana, CA 92799 PH/FAX: 714-962-2776 E-mail: aquacel@aquacel.com	accessories parts

See full listing in **Section One** under **Cobra**

Power Effects® 1800H Industrial Park Dr Grand Haven, MI 49417 877-3POWRFX toll-free 616-847-4200 FAX: 616-847-4210	exhaust systems

See full listing in **Section Two** under **exhaust systems**

The Real Source PO Box 1248 Effingham, IL 62401 800-LUV-BUGG (588-2844), dept VS9 FAX: 217-347-2952 E-mail: madbug@madvet.com	accessories parts

See full listing in **Section One** under **Volkswagen**

Regal Roadsters Ltd 301 W Beltline Hwy Madison, WI 53713 PH/FAX: 608-273-4141	replicars restoration

See full listing in **Section One** under **Thunderbird**

RodDoors PO Box 2110 Chico, CA 95927 530-896-1513; FAX: 530-896-1518 E-mail: roddoors@juno.com	door panels interior accessories

See full listing in **Section Two** under **street rods**

Rodster Inc 128 Center St #B El Segundo, CA 90245 310-322-2767; FAX: 310-322-2761	conversion kits

See full listing in **Section Two** under **street rods**

Saturn Industries 10-14 Newland St, Coleford Royal Forest of Dean Gloucestershire GL 16 8AN England 01594 834321; FAX: 01594 835456	axles/instruments literature nostalgic bits repro parts street rods

See full listing in **Section One** under **Ford 1903-1931**

Specialty Power Window 2087 Collier Rd Forsyth, GA 31029 800-634-9801; FAX: 912-994-3124	power window kits windshield wiper kit

See full listing in **Section Two** under **street rods**

Wheel-A-Dapters 9103 E Garvey Ave Rosemead, CA 91770 626-288-2290	replicar kits

Mail order and open shop. Monday-Friday 12 pm to 5 pm, Saturday 9 am to 3 pm. For replicar kits using wire Ford wheels. Also Ford, Pinto, Chevrolet and Volkswagen. Most 4/5/6 lug combinations. Adapter catalog $4, refundable.

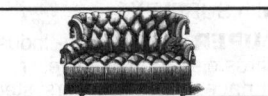

leather restoration

All Seams Fine 23 Union St Waterbury, VT 05676 800-244-7326 (SEAM), 802-244-8843	interior restorations

See full listing in **Section Two** under **upholstery**

Section Two / Generalists

**Color-Plus Leather
Restoration System**
106 Harrier Ct
3767 Sunrise Lake
Milford, PA 18337-9315
570-686-3158; FAX: 570-686-4161
E-mail: jpcolorplus@pikeonline.net

*leather
conditioning
leather dye*

Mail order only. Leather and vinyl restoration products and colorants. SOFFENER™, complete leather conditioner, restores old leather to glove-like softness. Maintains and preserves new leather. SURFLEX™, water-base colorant for leather and vinyl, user-friendly. Achieve professional results. Custom color matching is our specialty. Call for free 18-page booklet. Complete how-to, product descriptions and price list. Web site: www.colorplus.com

See our ad on this page

Dr Vinyl and Assoc Ltd
9501 E 350 Hwy
Raytown, MO 64133
816-356-3312; FAX: 816-356-9049
E-mail: tbuckley@drvinyl.com

*dent repair
interior repair
paint touch-up*

See full listing in **Section Two** under **car care products**

Keleen Leathers Inc
10526 W Cermak Rd
Westchester, IL 60154
708-409-9800; FAX: 708-409-9801

leather hides

See full listing in **Section Two** under **interiors & interior parts**

**Leatherique Leather
Restoration Products**
PO Box 2678
Orange Park, FL 32065
904-272-0992; FAX: 904-272-1534
E-mail: lrpltd@aol.com

*leather cleaning
conditioning
products*

See full listing in **Section One** under **Rolls-Royce/Bentley**

license plates   `13589 N Y`

American Classics Unlimited Inc
PO Box 192-V
Oak Lawn, IL 60454-0192
PH/FAX: 708-424-9223

*automobilia
models and toys*

See full listing in **Section Two** under **models & toys**

Classic Car Part Art
207 S Mt Carmel
Wichita, KS 67213
316-945-6865

artwork

See full listing in **Section Two** under **artwork**

Norman D'Amico
44 Middle Rd
Clarksburg, MA 01247
413-663-6886

license plates

Mail order and open shop. License plates of all states, years, types and countries. Also driving licenses, registrations, plate color and data information charts, etc. Miscellaneous license plate frames.

Darryl's
266 Main St
Duryea, PA 18642
PH/FAX: 717-451-1600

restoration

Mail order only. Show quality license plate restoration with all damage, dents, tears, holes, rust, etc, repaired to new condition and painted in original colors, numbers will duplicate originals not brush painted or taped off. This is the finest restoration available. Car, truck, motorcycle, bicycle, reflective number, plates and duplications. Our plates have an automotive quality hand polished and waxed finish. Call or write for more information.

Eurosign Metalwerke Inc
PO Box 93-6331
Margate, FL 33093
954-979-1448; FAX: 954-970-0430

license plates

Mail order only. Leading manufacturer of antique license plates from the United States and around the world featuring: Euro rectangular and oval plates, USA plates from 1900s-on and a wide variety of license plate frames and plate holders. Our antique replica plates are stamped in metal and look so good that thousands of *Hemmings'* readers have been satisfied customers. Our plates are also used in Hollywood movies, TV shows and commercials. Web site: www.euro-sign.com

See our ad on page 321

Eurosport Daytona Inc
355 Tomoka Ave
Ormond Beach, FL 32174-6222
800-874-8044, 904-672-7199
FAX: 904-673-0821

license plates

The manufacturer of classic and vanity license plates, frames and accessories. Specializing in laser cut Lazer-Tags™, stainless steel and authentic Euro plates. The largest selection of license plates available in the USA.

Eugene Gardner	license plates
10510 Rico Tatum Rd	
Palmetto, GA 30268	
770-463-4264	

Mail order and open shop by appointment only. Phone hours: 7 am to 8 pm. License plates bought, sold and traded. Discounts on large orders. Send SASE for the License Plate Club information.

Get It On Paper	automobilia
Gary Weickart, President	literature
185 Maple St	toys
Islip, NY 11751	
516-581-3897	

See full listing in **Section Two** under **automobilia**

Hale's Products	license plates
906 19th St	
Wheatland, WY 82201	
800-333-0989	
E-mail: phale@wyoming.com	

Mail order only. Specializing in 1960s Wyoming license plates (car and truck). Cars: 1967 red/white, 1968 brown/gold and extras. "Real cowboy plates", plain $7; mounted with barbed wire, $16.

Howard Hinz	license plates
Box 216	
Vero Beach, FL 32961	
561-567-9121; FAX: 561-567-0986	
E-mail: flp8s@webtv.net	

Sell Florida license plates only, 1913-1980.

Richard Hurlburt	license plates
27 West St	parts
Greenfield, MA 01301	toys
413-773-3235	

Mail order and open shop. Auto related collectibles and toys. New and used parts for 1972-1979 Datsun model 620 pickup trucks. Also antique, classic, aircraft-related items, advertising signs, vehicle literature. Large stock of 1903-1980 USA, Canada, and foreign license plates. Send wants with SASE.

Dave Lincoln	license plates
Box 331	
Yorklyn, DE 19736	
610-444-4144, PA	
E-mail: tagbarn@msn.com	

Mail order and open shop by appointment. License plates, USA/foreign. All years and types. Buy, sell, swap. Thousands available. Porcelains a specialty. Recent plates sold in bulk. YOM, birth year, etc. SASE with specific requests. Collections, accumulations wanted. Will travel.

George & Denise Long	automobilia
915 E Court St	
Marion, NC 28752	
828-652-9229 (24 hrs w/recorder)	

See full listing in **Section Two** under **automobilia**

Larry Machacek	decals
PO Box 515	license plates
Porter, TX 77365	novelties
281-429-2505	

See full listing in **Section Two** under **automobilia**

O'Brien Truckers	accessories
5 Perry Hill	belt buckles
North Grafton, MA 01536-1532	plaques
508-839-3033; FAX: 508-839-9490	valve covers
E-mail: obt@ziplink.net	

See full listing in **Section Two** under **plaques**

The Plateman	license plates
Jim Estrup	
269 Webber Hill Rd	
Kennebunk, ME 04043	
207-985-4800; FAX: 207-985-TAGS	

Mail order only. Hundreds of license plates available to display on your vintage vehicle or on your garage wall. Most states available. Car, motorcycle, commercial, low numbers, foreign and various other desirable types. Singles and pairs. Many years available up to the 1990s. Receive a free genuine license plate when you request my license plate sales list. Want lists and special requests cheerfully accepted. Fast and friendly service. Plates also bought and traded.

Skimino Enterprises	body parts
129 Skimino Rd	license plates
Williamsburg, VA 23188-2229	mechanical parts
757-565-1422	

Mail order and open shop. Daily 9 am to 1 pm. Specializing in miscellaneous parts for any car and Virginia license plates. Mechanical parts and body parts. Update parts weekly.

Town & Country Toys	banks
227 Midvale Dr	Ertl cars
PO Box 574	mini license plates
Marshall, WI 53559	
608-655-4961	
E-mail: dejaeger@itis.com	

See full listing in **Section Two** under **models & toys**

Al Trommers-Rare Auto Literature	hubcaps/wheelcovers
614 Vanburenville Rd	license plates
Middletown, NY 10940	literature/records

See full listing in **Section Two** under **literature dealers**

lighting equipment

Accessoryland Truckin' Supplies	accessories
10723 Rt 61 S	foglights/spotlights
Dubuque, IA 52003	mounting brackets
319-556-5482; FAX: 319-556-9087	parts

See full listing in **Section One** under **Chevrolet**

Albrico Auto & Truck Parts	lamp assemblies
PO Box 3179	lenses
Camarillo, CA 93010	
805-482-9792; FAX: 805-383-1013	

Mail order only. Dealing in lenses, lamp assemblies, lamp bezels and housings, speedometers, dash instruments, clocks, door handles and window cranks.

All British Car Parts Inc	parts
2847 Moores Rd	
Baldwin, MD 21013	
410-692-9572; FAX: 410-692-5654	

See full listing in **Section Two** under **electrical systems**

Robert D Bliss	electrical parts
2 Delmar Pl	ignition parts
Edison, NJ 08837	
732-549-0977	

See full listing in **Section Two** under **electrical systems**

Carson's Antique Auto Parts	parts
235 Shawfarm Rd	
Holliston, MA 01746	
508-429-2269; FAX: 508-429-0761	
E-mail: w1066@gis.net	

See full listing in **Section Two** under **engine parts**

Chicago Classic Imports	parts
6948 N Western Ave	service
Chicago, IL 60645	
773-381-2600; FAX: 773-381-2616	
E-mail:	
saab@chicagoclassicimports.com	

See full listing in **Section One** under **Saab**

Collins Metal Spinning	headlight rims
6371 W 100 S	
New Palestine, IN 46163	
317-894-3008	

Mail order and open shop. Monday-Saturday 8:30 am to 4:30 pm; other times by appointment. Anything round in brass, copper, aluminum and steel.

Mike Dennis, Nebraska Mail Order	parts
1845 S 48th St	Trippe mounting
Lincoln, NE 68506	brackets/hardware
402-489-3036; FAX: 402-489-1148	

See full listing in **Section One** under **Ford 1932-1953**

Development Associates	electrical parts
12791-G Newport Ave	
Tustin, CA 92780	
714-730-6843; FAX: 714-730-6863	
E-mail: devassoc@yahoo.com	

See full listing in **Section Two** under **electrical systems**

The Enthusiasts Shop	cars
John Parnell	pre-war parts
PO Box 80471	transportation
Baton Rouge, LA 70898	
225-928-7456; FAX: 225-928-7665	

See full listing in **Section One** under **Rolls-Royce/Bentley**

Bruce Falk	parts
1105 Nichilson	
Joliet, IL 60435	
815-726-6455	
E-mail: bbfalk@aol.com	

See full listing in **Section One** under **Chevrolet**

George's Auto & Tractor Sales Inc	Blue Dots/car dealer
1450 N Warren Rd	Dri-Wash metal polish
North Jackson, OH 44451	upholstery cleaner
330-538-3020; FAX: 330-538-3033	New Castle batteries

See full listing in **Section Two** under **car dealers**

W F Harris Lighting	work lights
PO Box 5023	
Monroe, NC 28111-5023	
704-283-7477; FAX: 704-283-6880	

Mail order only. Automotive work lights. Underhood and underdash task lights, larger work lights with accessories including rolling light/tool tray and rolling light cart that can be propped up for work on sides of vehicles.

Headlight Headquarters | lights
Donald I Axelrod | parts
35 Timson St |
Lynn, MA 01902 |
781-598-0523 |

Mail order and open shop by appointment only. Headlights and headlight parts for 1914-1939 automobiles. No Ford. SASE required.

Joyce's Model A & T Parts | new parts
PO Box 70 | NOS parts
Manchaca, TX 78652-0070 | rebuilt parts
512-282-1196 |

See full listing in **Section One** under **Ford 1903-1931**

Leigh & Sharon Knudson Truck | stoplights
Light Sales | truck lights
719 Ohms Way | turn signals
Costa Mesa, CA 92627 |
949-645-5938; FAX: 949-646-6820 |
E-mail: catruckman@aol.com |

Restoration and re-marketing of glass era truck lights. Amber arrow turn signals, stoplights and glass lensed marker lights a specialty. No electric headlights available from us.

MikeCo Antique, Kustom & | lenses
Obsolete Auto Parts | parts
4053 Calle Tesoro, Unit C |
Camarillo, CA 93012 |
805-482-1725; FAX: 805-987-8524 |

See full listing in **Section One** under **Mopar**

National Parts Depot | accessories
3101 SW 40th Blvd | restoration parts
Gainesville, FL 32608 |
800-874-7595 toll-free 24 hours |
352-378-2473 local |

See full listing in **Section Two** under **comprehensive parts**

OJ Rallye Automotive | accessories
PO Box 540 | car care products
N 6808 Hwy OJ | lighting parts
Plymouth, WI 53073 |
920-893-2531; FAX: 920-893-6800 |
E-mail: ojrallye@excel.net |

Mail order and open shop. Monday-Friday, 9 am to 12 pm, 2 pm to 6 pm. World's largest assortment of European lighting part numbers in stock. Carello, Cibie, Hella, Lucas, Marchal and other pre-war to current high tech fog, driving and headlight parts, bulbs and kits available in 6, 12 and 24-volt. Restoration of lamps is also offered. Other quality accessories and car care products sold, retail and wholesale. Web site: www.vclassics.com/ojrallye.htm

UK Spares/TVR Sports Cars | accessories
609 Highland St | car covers
Wethersfield, CT 06109-3979 | convertible tops
PH/FAX: 860-563-1647 | ignition parts
FAX: 860-529-3479 | suspension parts
E-mail: tvr.sports.cars@juno.com |

See full listing in **Section One** under **TVR**

Johnny Williams Services | appraisals
2613 Copeland Road | car/parts locator
Tyler, TX 75701 | consultant
903-597-3687, 800-937-0900 | lighting systems
voice mail #7225 | design

See full listing in **Section Two** under **appraisals**

limousine rentals

Horsepower Sales | limousines
130 Cardinal Dr |
Waynesville, NC 28786 |
516-532-7605 mobile, NY |

Specializing in limousine sales.

Jacks Wholesale Division | limousines
250 N Robertson Blvd, Ste 405 |
Beverly Hills, CA 90211-1793 |
310-839-9417; FAX: 310-839-1046 |

See full listing in **Section One** under **Lincoln**

Westwind Limousine Sales | limousine sales
2720 W National Rd |
Dayton, OH 45414 |
937-898-9000; FAX: 937-898-9800 |

See full listing in **Section One** under **Lincoln**

literature dealers

American Classics Unlimited Inc | automobilia
PO Box 192-V | models
Oak Lawn, IL 60454-0192 | toys
PH/FAX: 708-424-9223 |

See full listing in **Section Two** under **models & toys**

Antique Auto Keys | keys
Douglas Vogel |
PO Box 335 |
Dexter, MI 48130 |
734-424-9336; FAX: 734-424-9337 |

Mail order only. Original keys and locks for 1900-1975 cars, keys cut from code or original lock. Large inventory of old locks and cylinders.

The Auto Buff, Books & | books
Collectibles | literature
13809 Ventura Blvd | manuals
Sherman Oaks, CA 91423 |
E-mail: simona@aol.com |

Mail order only. Automotive literature including out-of-print books, owner's manuals, shop manuals and sales literature covering antique and modern cars from racing to restoration.

Auto Nostalgia Enr | literature
332 St Joseph | manuals
Mont St Gregoire, QC Canada J0J 1K0 | models
PH/FAX: 450-346-3644 | tractor decals
E-mail: autonostalgia@vif.com |

Mail order and open shop. Monday-Saturday 9 am to 8 pm, closed Sundays. Automotive literature, shop manuals, parts lists, car books, tractor manuals, owner's manuals, sales catalogs, new and used. Also models, plastic, die cast, all makes, white metal. Hobby shop for collectors of real vehicles and models. New and old toys and literature. Buy, sell, trade. Credit cards ok. Web site: www.vif.com/users/autonostalgia/

Auto World Books | literature
Box 562 | magazines
Camarillo, CA 93011 | research service
805-987-5570 |

Mail order only. Car and truck literature, manuals and magazines, US and foreign. Free research service.

Auto-West Advertising Gary Hinkle PO Box 3875 Modesto, CA 95352 209-524-9541, 209-522-4777	sales literature

Mail order and open shop by appointment only. Specialize in all US and foreign postwar literature, postcards and owner's manuals.

Automotive Bookstore 1830 12th Ave Seattle, WA 98122	books manuals

Mail order and open shop. Monday-Friday 10 am to 4 pm. Out of print bookstore specializing in original factory shop manuals for domestic, Asian and European cars, trucks and motorcycles. Thousands of auto related magazines, too. Stock a large selection of aftermarket manuals of all kinds and also have books on the building trades, antique electronics, woodworking, metalworking and boats. Located on Seattle's Capitol Hill at the corner of Twelfth Ave and E Denny Way.

Irv Bishko Literature 14550 Watt Rd Novelty, OH 44072 440-338-4811	literature

Authentic original shop manuals, parts books, sales brochures, owner's manuals, dealer albums, color/upholstery and data books, etc. Wide selection of domestic and foreign literature for cars and trucks, 1900-present. SASE or phone.

Blair Collectors & Consultants 2821 SW 167th Pl Seattle, WA 98166 206-242-6745, 206-246-1305	appraisals consultant literature

See full listing in **Section Two** under **appraisals**

EJ Blend 802 8th Ave Irwin, PA 15642-3702 724-863-7624	literature parts

See full listing in **Section One** under **Packard**

M K Boatright 629 Santa Monica Corpus Christi, TX 78411 361-852-6639; FAX: 361-853-7168	books literature models

Mail order only. 1930s-1980s. Sales albums, model cars, library books and other miscellaneous literature for US and foreign cars and trucks

BritBooks PO Box 321 Otego, NY 13825 PH/FAX: 607-988-7956 E-mail: britbook@dmcom.net	books

See full listing in **Section Four** under **books & publications**

British Only Motorcycles and Parts Inc 32451 Park Ln Garden City, MI 48135 734-421-0303; FAX: 734-422-9253 E-mail: info@british-only.com	literature memorabilia motorcycles parts

See full listing in **Section Two** under **motorcycles**

California Auto Literature PO Box 2552 Palm Springs, CA 92263 888-806-3620; FAX: 760-329-3398	literature manuals

Mail order, open shop and warehouse. Monday-Saturday 9 am to 5 pm. Interstate 10 at Indian Ave exit, behind Harley-Davidson, Palm Springs, CA. Huge selection of domestic service manuals, owner's manuals, parts books, paint chips, sales literature, dealer albums, etc. Library inquiries invited. Credit cards accepted.

Chewning's Auto Literature 2011 Elm Tree Terr Buford, GA 30518 770-945-9795	literature manuals

Mail order only. Specializing in literature for all makes and models. Shop manuals, owner's manuals, sales catalogs, parts books, etc. Also buy automotive literature. Send list or call for a prompt, courteous reply.

Dick Choler Cars & Service Inc 640 E Jackson Blvd Elkhart, IN 46516 219-522-8281; FAX: 219-294-5350	car dealer literature model cars

See full listing in **Section One** under **Pontiac**

Colleccio d'Automobils de Salvador Claret 17410 Sils Girona Spain 972-853036; FAX: 972-853502 E-mail: sclaret@logiccontrol.es	books catalogs literature photos

Open year round. 7 days a week. Specializing in literature, catalogs, photos for Hispano Suiza, Elizalde, Abadal, Ricart, Pegaso, Nacional Pescara (Spanish cars). Publish *Edicious Benzina*, 4 books a year, monographic books about popular Spanish automobiles. Also publish *Guia del Vehiculo Antique Y Clasico 98*. Web sites: www.museuautomobilsclaret.com or www.edicionsbenzina.com

Crank'en Hope Publications 401 Sloan Alley Blairsville, PA 15717-1481 724-459-8853; FAX: 724-459-8860 E-mail: cranken@nb.net	assembly manuals body manuals parts books shop manuals

Mail order and open shop. Monday-Friday 9 am to 9 pm EST. Shop manuals, parts books, body manuals, Chevrolet assembly manuals and more. Retail and wholesale. If visiting our shop, please phone ahead for hours. Accept Visa and MasterCard. For our most recent catalog please include 3 first class stamps or $1 cash to cover postage. Extend discounts to clubs, libraries and organizations.

The Davis Registry 4073 Ruby Ypsilanti, MI 48197-9317 734-434-5581, 313-662-1001 E-mail: kfnut@umich.edu	periodical quarterly bulletin

See full listing in **Section Four** under **books & publications**

Buzz De Clerck 41760 Utica Rd Sterling Heights, MI 48313-3146 810-731-0765	parts

See full listing in **Section One** under **Lincoln**

DeLorean Literature 3116 Welsh Rd Philadelphia, PA 19136-1810 215-338-6142 E-mail: delorean.literature@excite.com	collectibles literature

See full listing in **Section One** under **DeLorean**

Driven By Desire 300 N Fraley St Kane, PA 16735 814-837-7590; FAX: 814-837-6850 E-mail: driven@penn.com	automobilia car dealer models

See full listing in **Section Two** under **car dealers**

| **Faxon Auto Literature** | **literature** |
| 3901 Carter Ave | **manuals** |

Faxon Auto Literature
3901 Carter Ave
Riverside, CA 92501
800-458-2734; FAX: 909-786-4166

Open Monday-Friday 6 am to 6 pm, Saturday 8 am to 4 pm. Find all of your manuals and literature with one free call. You can own the best manuals and literature for your vehicle. Familiar with every manual and most of the literature that exists and will match the correct book to your needs from the most complete inventory in the world. Money back guarantee. Inquiries use 909-786-4177. Visa, MasterCard, American Express and Discover welcome; also CODs or money order.

Fill Er Up — automobilia, petroliana
Brian Steiner
2613 Old Philadelphia Pike
PO Box 406
Bird In Hand, PA 17505
717-397-2519

See full listing in **Section Two** under **automobilia**

Get It On Paper — automobilia, literature, toys
Gary Weickart, President
185 Maple St
Islip, NY 11751
516-581-3897

See full listing in **Section Two** under **automobilia**

Giorgio Nada Editore — motoring books
Via Treves 15/17
Vimodrone (Milan) 20090 Italy
++39-02-27301126
FAX: ++39-02-27301454
E-mail: nadamail@sii.it

Office open Monday-Friday 9 am to 6 pm. Publisher of various titles on motoring and of the official *Ferrari Factory Anniversary* book. Catalog on request. Shipment everywhere in the world. Web site: www.giorgionadaeditore.it

GMC Solutions — literature, parts
Robert English
PO Box 675
Franklin, MA 02038-0675
508-520-3900; FAX: 508-520-7861
E-mail: oldcarkook@aol.com

See full listing in **Section One** under **GMC**

Richard Hamilton — sales literature
28 E 46th St
Indianapolis, IN 46205
317-283-1902

Mail order only. Dealing in sales literature for Australian, British, Canadian, French, Indian, Mexican, Japanese and US cars. Also offer books, press kits, ads, models and magazines. Have Ferrari and other exotic literature (Bitter, Excalibur, etc).

Justin Hartley — reprinted literature
17 Fox Meadow Ln
West Hartford, CT 06107-1216
860-523-0056
860-604-9950 cellular
FAX: 860-233-8840

See full listing in **Section One** under **Cadillac/LaSalle**

James Hill — ignition parts, source list
Box 547-V
Goodwell, OK 73939
580-349-2736 evenings/weekends

See full listing in **Section One** under **Packard**

Historic Video Archives — videotapes
PO Box 189-VA
Cedar Knolls, NJ 07927-0189

See full listing in **Section Two** under **automobilia**

Homer's Mechanical Books — farm tractors, marine, motorcycles, repair manuals
409 Hampton Creek Ct
Columbia, SC 29209
888-5HOMERS toll-free
803-783-8873 nights
E-mail: homers@cyberstate.infi.net

Mail order. Repair manuals for farm tractors (antique and modern). Also have manuals for cars, trucks, motorcycles, marine engines, ATVs, jet skis, outdoor power equipment, snowmobiles, cars and trucks. We discount how-to videos, restoration guides and histories. Call for a free list. Buy repair manuals of all types and are especially interested in buying farm tractor repair manuals, parts catalogues and sales literature. Web site: www.homersbooks.com

Hosking Cycle Works — books, manuals, motorcycle parts, reprints
136 Hosking Ln
Accord, NY 12404
914-626-4231; FAX: 914-626-3245
E-mail: cycle@ulster.net

Mail order only. Shop manuals, parts books, marque histories, reprints and new computer back issue magazine service; now have world's largest collection of enamel lapel pins (hat pins) for all motorcycles in addition to our books. Catalog listing over 1,000 motorcycle books, free via third class; $1 first class mail. ROKON RT and MX 340 motorcycle parts. Service and parts books. Anything for vintage racing or show restorations of ROKON motorcycles. Web site: www.hoskingcycle.com

Import Car Parts Marketing — books
Steve Fields
1021 Laguna St #4
Santa Barbara, CA 93101
805-965-3280; FAX: 805-965-5680
E-mail: jsfields@earthlink.net

Mail order and open shop by appointment. Specializing in out-of-print automotive history books. Racing, sports cars, import and exotic cars. Also race programs and race posters.

International Automobile Archives — sales literature
Kai Jacobsen
Wiesenweg 3b
85757 Karlsfeld Germany
011-49-8131-93158
FAX: 011-49-8131-505973

Mail order and open shop. Automotive sales literature of the postwar period from all countries of the world. Also technical data available for nearly every car from 1947 until today. Specialize in sports and exotic cars. Comprehensive list, $5 airmail.

International Ford History Project — newsletter
PO Box 11415
Olympia, WA 98508
360-754-9585
E-mail: ifhp@aol.com

See full listing in **Section Four** under **newsletters**

Jeff Johnson Motorsports — accessories, literature, parts
4421 Aldrich Pl
Columbus, OH 43214
614-268-1181; FAX: 614-268-1141

See full listing in **Section One** under **Mopar**

Bob Johnson's Auto Literature | brochures
92 Blandin Ave | literature
Framingham, MA 01702 | manuals
508-872-9173; FAX: 508-626-0991 | paint chips
E-mail: bjohnson@autopaper.com |

Most complete selection of sales brochures, owner's manuals, repair manuals, parts books, showroom albums, color and upholstery books, paint chips for auto, truck, farm, construction. Buy collections or single items. Web site: www.autopaper.com

See our ad on this page

The Josey's Heaven Hill Farm | swap meets
1839 NW C-138 |
Branford, FL 32008 |
904-935-0348 |

See full listing in **Section Two** under **auctions & events**

Dave Kauzlarich | literature
60442 N Tranquility Rd | memorabilia
Lacombe, LA 70445 |
504-882-3000 |
E-mail: fierog97j@aol.com |

Mail order only. Buying, selling and trading 1984-1988 Pontiac and Fiero literature and memorabilia.

David M King, Automotive Books | literature
5 Brouwer Ln |
Rockville Centre, NY 11570 |
516-766-1561; FAX: 516-766-7502 |

See full listing in **Section One** under **Rolls-Royce/Bentley**

Shepard Kinsman | sales literature
909 Eastridge |
Miami, FL 33157 |
305-255-7067 |
E-mail: autolitk@dc.seflin.org |

Large 1931-1980. Domestic and foreign collection being sold. Marque lists available.

Dan Kirchner | owner's manuals
404 N Franklin | sales literature
Dearborn, MI 48128 | shop manuals
313-277-7187 |
FAX: 313-277-7187 *51 |

Mail order only. Automotive literature, shop manuals, owner's manuals, sales literature, dealer books, 1900-present. SASE with wants.

Kosters Motorboghandel | owner's manuals
Ostergade 9 | shop manuals
8900 Randers Denmark |
45-86-42-6613; FAX: 45-86-42-0813 |

Mail order and open shop. Specialize in European shop manuals and owner's manuals for cars and motorcycles, from turn-of-the-century onwards.

David Lawrence Gallery | artwork
PO Box 3702 | drawings
Beverly Hills, CA 90212 | photography
310-278-0882; FAX: 310-278-0883 |

See full listing in **Section Two** under **artwork**

Libreria Dell'Automobile | car books
International Motoring Book Shop | motorcycle books
Corso Venezia 43 |
Milan 20121 Italy |
++39-02-76006624 |
FAX: ++39-02-27301454 |
E-mail: nadamail@sii.it |

Mail order and open shop. Monday-Saturday 9:30 am to 12:30 pm, 2:30 pm to 7 pm. More than 10,000 titles on cars and motorcycles always available. Specialist on Ferrari publications. Catalogue on request. Shipment everywhere in the world.

Lloyd's Literature | literature
PO Box 491 |
Newbury, OH 44065 |
800-292-2665, 440-338-1527 |
FAX: 440-338-2222 |

Mail order only. Shop manuals, owner's manuals, sales literature, parts books, dealer albums. Specialize in automobile literature for all US and foreign cars and trucks 1915-1995. SASE with all inquiries. Fast dependable service.

George & Denise Long | automobilia
915 E Court St |
Marion, NC 28752 |
828-652-9229 (24 hrs w/recorder) |

See full listing in **Section Two** under **automobilia**

Gwyn Machacek | literature
PO Box 515 |
Porter, TX 77365 |
281-429-2505 |

See full listing in **Section One** under **Ford 1903-1931**

Ron Magnuson | owner's manuals
PO Box 448 | sales literature
North Plains, OR 97133 | shop manuals
503-647-2353 |

Mail order only. Original auto literature for most makes and years; shop and owner's manuals, sales brochures and more. Pre-war a specialty.

The Maverick Connection 137 Valley Dr Ripley, WV 25271 PH/FAX: 304-372-7825	literature **parts**

See full listing in **Section One** under **Ford 1954-up**

McCoy's Memorabilia 35583 N 1830 E Rossville, IL 60963-7175 PH/FAX: 217-748-6513 E-mail: indy500@soltec.net	memorabilia **racing literature**

Mail order. Buying and selling Indy 500 and other auto race literature, memorabilia and vintage auto magazines, will do computer search for information on auto races, race cars, race car drivers, vintage autos, tech info.

Ken McGee Auto Literature 36 Newgate St Goderich, ON Canada N7A 1P1 888-275-2666 orders, toll-free 519-524-5821; FAX: 519-524-9679 E-mail: kenmcgeebooks@odyssey.on.ca.	literature

Largest stock of original North American car and truck literature in Canada. Specializing in pre-war. Car and truck original literature from 1897-1997. Sales brochures, parts and shop manuals, owner's manuals, data books, dealer albums, etc. Major credit cards accepted. Next day shipping. If selling your collection, please write us, thank you. Web site: www.kenmcgeeautobooks.com

McIntyre Auctions PO Box 60 East Dixfield, ME 04227 800-894-4300, 207-562-4443 FAX: 207-562-4576 E-mail: classicford@quickconnect.com	auctions **automobilia** **literature** **petroliana**

See full listing in **Section Two** under **auctions & events**

Donald McKinsey PO Box 94H Wilkinson, IN 46186 765-785-6284	fuel pumps **ignition parts** **literature** **spark plugs**

See full listing in **Section Two** under **ignition parts**

McLellan's Automotive History Robert and Sharon McLellan 9111 Longstaff Dr Houston, TX 77031-2711 713-772-3285; FAX: 713-772-3287 E-mail: mclellans@worldnet.att.net	books **factory literature** **magazines/** **memorabilia** **press kits/programs** **sales literature**

Mail order only. High quality rare books, sales literature, press kits, magazines, programs, factory literature, dealer literature and memorabilia bought and sold. Domestic and foreign. 1900-present. Racing, classics, antiques, sports cars, commercial, professional and recreational vehicles. Guaranteed original and in excellent condition. Free catalog or diskette of inventory. World's largest web site for automotive literature. Source of information for over 40 years. Free shipping. Web site: www.mclellansautomotive.com

Walter Miller 6710 Brooklawn Pkwy Syracuse, NY 13211 315-432-8282; FAX: 315-432-8256	literature

Mail order only. Over two million pieces of original literature in stock. World's largest selection of original US and foreign automobile, truck, motorcycle sales brochures, repair manuals, owner's manuals, parts books and showroom items. I am a serious buyer and travel to purchase literature. Web site: www.autolit.com

Mobey's 318 Burkhart Ln, PO Box 535 Gallipolis, OH 45631 614-446-9700	literature **memorabilia**

Mail order only. Also buy HET memorabilia and literature.

MotoMedia PO Box 489 Lansdowne, PA 19050 PH/FAX: 610-623-6930	books **magazines**

Mail order and flea market sales. More than 20,000 carefully selected issues and 300 books in stock. General interest and racing a specialty. Visa and MasterCard accepted. $2.50 for current lists.

Motorama 2000 Studio 3 The Old Brewery Centre High Street Hastings East Sussex, TN34 3ER England PH/FAX: 01424-440100	press kits **sales literature**

Mail order only. Sales brochures and press kits available from all the European and Detroit auto shows. Also carry large stock of postwar brochures from most makes. Worldwide mail order service, prompt, friendly attention given. Especially enjoy dealing with Americans.

MotorCam Media 138 N Alling Rd Tallmadge, OH 44278 800-240-1777; FAX: 330-633-3249 E-mail: carvideo@motorcam.com	automotive videos

See full listing in **Section Two** under **videos**

Dave Newell's Chevrobilia PO Box 588 Orinda, CA 94563 510-223-4725	literature **memorabilia**

See full listing in **Section One** under **Chevrolet**

Obsolete Jeep® & Willys® Parts Division of Florida 4 Wheel Drive & Truck Parts 6110 17th St E Bradenton, FL 34203 941-756-7844 PH/FAX: 941-756-7757	literature **parts**

See full listing in **Section One** under **Willys**

Opel Oldtimer Service Denmark Landevejen 27 Toksvaerd DK-4684 Holme-Olstrup Denmark PH/FAX: +45-55-530100 best 11 am to 3 pm US Central time E-mail: frank.kiessling@get2net.dk	literature **parts** **parts locator**

See full listing in **Section One** under **Opel**

Original Ford Motor Co Literature PO Box 7-AA Hudson, KY 40145-0007 502-257-8642; FAX: 502-257-8643 E-mail: whiteb@bellsouth.net	collectibles **literature**

See full listing in **Section One** under **Ford 1932-1953**

Jim Osborn Reproductions Inc 101 Ridgecrest Dr Lawrenceville, GA 30245 770-962-7556; FAX: 770-962-5881	decals **manuals**

See full listing in **Section Two** under **decals**

Packard Archives — accessories / artwork / automobilia
918 W Co Rd C-2
St Paul, MN 55113-1942
651-484-1184
E-mail: estatecars@earthlink.net

See full listing in **Section One** under **Packard**

Parts of the Past — literature
PO Box 602
Waukesha, WI 53187
414-679-4212

Shop manuals, owner's manuals, sales literature for most 1930s-1990s American cars, trucks. Call or send SASE with needs for quote. Visa/MasterCard accepted.

Paul Politis — manuals / sales literature
Box 335, HC 75
McConnellsburg, PA 17233
717-987-3702; FAX: 717-987-4284

Mail order only. Over 100,000 reasonably priced shop manuals, owner manuals, sales literature, paint chip sets, etc for US and import cars and trucks, 1910-present. Serving the hobby since 1974.

J Preikschat — literature / parts
PO Box 310
White City SK Canada S0G 5B0
E-mail: bigjohn@sk.sympatico.ca

Mail order only. Canadian and American automotive literature and aftermarket parts manuals. NOS and used GM parts from 1935-1975 and used AMC parts from the 1960s and 1970s.

Bert Provisor — body/owner/shop manuals / data/facts books / showroom albums
930 S Holt Ave
Los Angeles, CA 90035
310-652-0518

Shop, body, parts and owner's manuals, showroom albums, data/facts books, wiring diagrams, service bulletins, color chips, accessories, warranties. *National Service Data, Motors*, and some sales literature. Largest selection of original manuals west of the Mississippi. SASE only.

Doug Schellinger — automobilia / books / sales literature / toys
13717 W Green Meadow Dr
New Berlin, WI 53151
414-786-8413
E-mail: dsac@execpc.com

See full listing in **Section One** under **Fiat**

Schiff European Automotive Literature Inc — literature
505 Atwood Ave
Cranston, RI 02920
401-946-4711; FAX: 401-946-5785
E-mail: seal11@aol.com

Mail order, phone and fax orders, in store. Monday-Friday 8 am to 3 pm, Saturday 8 am to 11 am. Barry Schiff, owner. Owner's manuals, parts catalogs and workshop manuals for all foreign cars.

Henri Simar J R — books / literature
Rue du College, BP 172
B-4800 Verviers Belgium
32-87335501; FAX: 32-87335122

Mail order. Deal in sales literature, handbooks, workshop manuals, books, posters, magazines. I am collecting all MG, Mini, Lotus, John Player Special, James Bond items.

Robert H Snyder — literature / parts
PO Drawer 821
Yonkers, NY 10702
914-476-8500
FAX: 914-476-8573, 24 hours
E-mail: cohascodpc@earthlink.net

See full listing in **Section One** under **Cadillac/LaSalle**

Sparrow Auction Company — auction company
59 Wheeler Ave
Milford, CT 06460
203-877-1066
E-mail: vehicle@snet.net

See full listing in **Section Two** under **auctions & events**

Thunderbird Headquarters — accessories / literature / parts / upholstery
1080 Detroit Ave
Concord, CA 94518
800-227-2174, US
FAX: 925-689-1771, 800-964-1957
E-mail: tbirdhq@tbirdhq.com

See full listing in **Section One** under **Thunderbird**

Edward Tilley Automotive Collectibles — automobilia / literature / parts
PO Box 4233
Cary, NC 27519-4233
919-460-8262
E-mail: edandsusan@aol.com

See full listing in **Section Two** under **automobilia**

TMC Publications — literature / manuals
5817 Park Heights Ave
Baltimore, MD 21215
410-367-4490; FAX: 410-466-3566

Mail order and open shop. Monday-Saturday 9 am to 6 pm. Specializing in workshop manuals for Mercedes-Benz cars produced from 1946-1993, also owner's manuals, wiring diagrams, parts books, literature, etc. Carry BMW, Jaguar, Audi, Porsche, Peugeot, Subaru, Mitsubishi, Saab, Volvo, Lexus and Mazda. Web site: www.tmcpubl.com

Transport Books at DRB Motors Inc — books / manuals / periodicals / videos
16 Elrose Ave
Toronto, ON Canada M9M 2H6
800-665-2665, 416-744-7675
FAX: 416-744-7696
E-mail: info@transportbooks.com

See full listing in **Section Four** under **books & publications**

Al Trommers-Rare Auto Literature — hubcaps/wheelcovers / license plates / literature/records
614 Vanburenville Rd
Middletown, NY 10940

Mail order only. Shop open by written request only, include SASE. Specializing in thousands of hard and soft cover auto books, tons of old auto magazines and club publications. Lots of Chilton Motors' repair manuals, lots of NOS original literature, brochures, shop manuals, owner's manuals, postcards, license plates, hubcaps, wheelcovers, music, records and tapes from when your car was new, doo whops, rock and roll, jazz, etc. Originals and reissues, plus much more.

Vintage Books — books / literature
6613 E Mill Plain
Vancouver, WA 98661
360-694-9519; FAX: 360-694-7644
E-mail: vintageb@teleport.com

Mail order and open shop. Monday-Saturday 10 am to 6 pm. General stock bookstore specializing in automotive literature. We have a large selection of books (general and marque history, restoration, etc), plus shop manuals, owner's manuals, sales literature, ads and magazines. Web site: www.vintage-books.com

Voss Motors Inc
21849 Virginia Dr
Southfield, MI 48076
888-380-9277 toll-free
248-357-4750; FAX: 248-354-6577
E-mail: vossmotors@aol.com

service manuals

Mail order and open shop. Monday-Friday and Sunday 9 am to 9 pm. Service manuals for all automobiles and light trucks, both domestic and import, including obscure and hard-to-find. Reasonable prices with excellent personalized service. Web site: www.books4cars.com

Ted Weems
PO Box 810665
Dallas, TX 75381-0665
972-247-8169
E-mail: tedweems@flash.net

**parts catalogs
sales brochures
shop/owner's
manuals**

Mail order only. Shop manuals, owner's manuals, parts catalogs and sales brochures. Buy, sell and trade. A leading dealer in the Southwest in literature and promotional items for 32 years. Web site: www.flash.net/~tedweems

Weimann's Literature & Collectables
16 Cottage Rd
Harwinton, CT 06791
860-485-0300
FAX: 860-485-1705, 24 hour

literature

See full listing in **Section One** under **Plymouth**

White Auto Literature Mart
PO Box 7-AA
Hudson, KY 40145-0007
502-257-8642; FAX: 502-257-8643
E-mail: whiteb@bellsouth.net

literature

Original sales literature for most cars and trucks. One half million piece inventory, SASE with your needs.

Colonel Bill White
Auto Literature Sales
PO Box 7-AA
Hudson, KY 40145-0007
502-257-8642; FAX: 502-257-8643
E-mail: whiteb@bellsouth.net

literature

Automobile and truck sales literature, owner's manuals.

John W Wimble
1407 Stoneycreek Dr
Richmond, VA 23233

sales literature

Mail order only. Post-war sales literature. Extensive list available, $5 appreciated but not necessary. Prompt, professional service, low prices, satisfaction guaranteed. Also buying.

Zephyrhills Festivals and Auction Inc
PO Box 848
Odessa, FL 33556
office: 813-920-7206
FAX: 813-920-8512
Park: 813-782-0835
FAX: 813-780-7863

**auction
swap meet**

See full listing in **Section Two** under **auctions & events**

locks & keys

AUTOTEC
12915 Eastbrook Pl
Brookfield, WI 53005-6520
414-797-9988

lock work

Mail order and open shop by appointment. Best time to call is 8 pm to 10 pm CST. Foreign and domestic vehicle lock work exclusively. Repairs, recoding, making keys. This is a full-time occupation. In business since 1982. Large inventory.

Jarvis Old Car Keys & Locks
Box 2245
Alderwood Manor, WA 98036
PH/FAX: 425-776-2804

**keys
locks**

Mail order only. Local swap meets. Locks and keys for old cars. Have cylinders and some handles for cars of the 1930s and 1940s. Codes changed and keys cut to code.

Jesser's Classic Keys
26 West St, Dept HVA
Akron, OH 44303-2344
330-376-8181; FAX: 330-384-9129

**automobilia
keys**

Mail order, car shows and open shop: 10 am to 4 pm five days; mail order: 9 am to 9 pm EST seven days. Complete line of NOS keys and gold plated keys for all American cars and trucks from 1900-date. Keys stamped and cut by code. Have many of those hard-to-find keys and lock cylinders, please inquire and include year, make and model. Also carry automobilia, key rings, grille badges, belt buckles, pins, money clips and more. Visa, MasterCard, AmEx, Discover. Web site: www.jessersclassickeys.com

Machina Locksmith
3 Porter St
Watertown, MA 02172-4145
PH/FAX: 617-923-1683

**car locks
keys**

All vehicle lockwork, car locks in stock. Hi-security keys and by code.

McGard Inc
3875 California Rd
Orchard Park, NY 14127
716-662-8980; FAX: 716-662-8985
E-mail: jmondo@mcgard.com

**lug nuts
wheel locks**

Deal in original equipment wheel locks and aftermarket wheel locks and lug nuts. Web site: www.mcgard.com

Metropolitan & British Triumph
9957 Frederick Rd
Ellicott City, MD 21042-3647
410-750-2352 evenings
E-mail: pete_groh@yahoo.com

**British Leyland
original British
keys
WASO
Wilmot Breeden**

See full listing in **Section One** under **Metropolitan**

NATC Inc
2880 Bergey Rd, Unit 01
Hatfield, PA 19440
215-712-9980; FAX: 215-712-9968
E-mail: perfyrs@netreach.net

**keys
locks**

NATC has a full line trailer accessories catalog with every option and upgrade you can image for your trailer. From basic replacement parts to special kits to add unique features like mobile work stations, car lifts, 110-volt power and lighting, living quarters and the most sophisticated tie-down systems available. Call today for a free catalog.

National Parts Depot | accessories
3101 SW 40th Blvd | restoration parts
Gainesville, FL 32608
800-874-7595 toll-free 24 hours
352-378-2473 local

See full listing in **Section Two** under **comprehensive parts**

Uhlenhopp Lock | lock restoration
29983 Superior Rd | NOS locks
Clarksville, IA 50619 | rebuilding
319-278-4355 | rekeying

Mail order and open shop.

Douglas J Vogel | keys
4779 Meadow Lark Ln | locks
Dexter, MI 48130
734-424-9336; FAX: 734-424-9337

Mail order only. Keys and locks for antique cars and trucks. Original locks from 1920-1995. Keys cut from codes, original key blanks 1910-1999.

lubricants

Advanced Maintenance | filters
Technologies Inc | lubricants
Box 250, Mountain Rd
Stowe, VT 05672
802-253-7385; FAX: 802-253-7815
E-mail:
info@advancedmaintenance.com

See full listing in **Section Two** under **engine parts**

Amsoil | car care products
9 Claremont Dr | lubricants
Flat Rock, NC 28731 | undercoating
704-696-8500

Mail order only. Dealing in synthetic oils and lubricants, undercoating, fuel additives, filters and car care products.

Billie Inc | garage diaper
PO Box 1161 | mats
Ashburn, VA 20146-1161
800-878-6328; FAX: 703-858-0102

See full listing in **Section Two** under **car care products**

The Blaster Chemical Companies | cleaners
8500 Sweet Valley Dr | degreasers
Valley View, OH 44125 | penetrants
800-858-6605; FAX: 216-901-5801

Mail order or available through NAPA stores. The manufacturer of the legendary PB Blaster Penetrating Catalyst, quite possibly the world's best penetrant and an auto restorer's most versatile tool. Also offer cleaners, degreasers, polish, fuel and oil additives and more. Web site: www.pbblaster.com

Brisson Enterprises | lead
PO Box 1595
Dearborn, MI 48121-1595
313-584-3577

See full listing in **Section Two** under **car care products**

D-A Lubricant Co | lubricants
1340 W 29th St
Indianapolis, IN 46208
800-232-4503; FAX: 317-926-8132

Mail order and through distributors. Manufacturer of premium lubricant products for more than 75 years. Products are formu-

lated to protect classic, vintage and special interest autos. Dealer inquiries welcome. Web site: www.dalube.com

High Performance Coatings | coatings
550 W 3615 S
Salt Lake City, UT 84115
800-456-4721, 801-262-6807
FAX: 801-262-6307
E-mail: hpcsales@hpcoatings.com

See full listing in **Section Two** under **exhaust systems**

JCM Industries | wax hardener
2 Westwood Dr
Danbury, CT 06811
800-752-0245

See full listing in **Section Two** under **car care products**

MRL Automotive | rubber lubricants
PO Box 117230
Carrollton, TX 75011-7230
972-394-3489; FAX: 800-210-0200

Mail order only. Specializing in rubber lubricants specific to undercarriage chassis rubber parts for autos, trucks, SUVs and 4x4s.

Nationwide Auto Restoration | bodywork
1038 Watt St | paint
Jeffersonville, IN 47130 | upholstery
812-280-0165; FAX: 812-280-8961
E-mail: restore@unidial.com

See full listing in **Section Two** under **restoration shops**

Sterling Specialties | car care products
42 Ponderosa Lane
Monroe, NY 10950
914-782-7614

See full listing in **Section Two** under **car care products**

Stoner Inc | cleaners
1070 Robert Fulton Hwy | lubricants
Quarryville, PA 17566
717-786-7355; FAX: 717-786-9088
E-mail: stoner1@epix.net

See full listing in **Section Two** under **car care products**

VACO Inc | lubricators
PO Box 6
Florence, MA 01062
413-586-0978

Mail order only. Upper cylinder lubricators.

Valco Cincinnati Consumer | adhesives
Products Inc | detailing products
411 Circle Freeway Dr | sealants
Cincinnati, OH 45246 | tools
513-874-6550; FAX: 513-874-3612

See full listing in **Section Two** under **tools**

machine work

AAdvanced Transmissions | rear axle service
15 Parker St | restoration
Worcester, MA 01610 | ring/pinion
508-752-9674, 508-752-9679 | trans parts/sales/
FAX: 508-842-0191 | rebuilding/service

See full listing in **Section Two** under **transmissions**

Ace Antique Auto Restoration
65 S Service Rd
Plainview, NY 11803
516-752-6065; FAX: 516-752-1484

air conditioning
body rebuilding
restoration
wiring harnesses

See full listing in **Section Two** under **restoration shops**

Angeli Machine Co
417 N Varney St
Burbank, CA 91502
818-846-5359
E-mail: angelimach@aol.com

machine work

Monday-Friday 9 am to 5 pm. Master and wheel cylinder resleeving with stainless steel and other machine shop services.

Antique & Classic Cars Inc
328 S 3rd St
Hamilton, OH 45011
513-844-1146 in OH
800-798-3982 nationwide

bodywork
machine work
painting
parts
service

See full listing in **Section One** under **Buick/McLaughlin**

Atlas Engine Rebuilding Co Inc
8631 S Avalon Blvd
Los Angeles, CA 90003
323-778-3497; FAX: 323-778-4556

engine rebuilding
machine work

See full listing in **Section Two** under **engine rebuilding**

Automotive Restorations Inc
Stephen Babinsky
4 Center St
Bernardsville, NJ 07924
908-766-6688; FAX: 908-766-6684
E-mail: autorestnj@aol.com

clutch rebuilding
mechanical
services
restorations

See full listing in **Section Two** under **restoration shops**

B & B Cylinder Head Inc
320 Washington St
West Warwick, RI 02893
401-828-4900

cylinder heads

See full listing in **Section Two** under **engine parts**

Bob's Automotive Machine
30 Harrison Ave
Harrison, NJ 07029
973-483-0059; FAX: 973-483-6092

engine parts
machine shop

Mail order and open shop. Monday-Friday 9 am to 6 pm, Saturday 9 am to 12 noon. Specializing in early 1960s Ford engine parts. Area's most complete machine shop service from boring to balancing, to complete engine dynamometer analysis.

BPE Racing Heads
702 Dunn Way
Placentia, CA 92870
714-572-6072; FAX: 714-572-6073
E-mail: steve@bpeheads.com

cylinder heads

Mail order and open shop. Monday-Friday 9 am to 6 pm. Cylinder head and manifold porting and polishing: automotive, motorcycle, 2-valve, multi-valve, aluminum, cast iron, stock, aftermarket, domestic, import. Cylinder head restoration: seats and guides installed, welding, thread restoration. Air flow testing: heads, manifolds, mufflers, intercoolers, air cleaners, etc. Can build fixtures for your project. Cast aluminum manifold restoration and fabrication: cut, splice, weld, install injector bosses. Problem specialists: emergency repairs, tight deadlines, special projects, tough challenges and limited runs. Web site: bpeheads.com

---

Cam-Pro
1417 1st Ave SW
Great Falls, MT 59404
800-525-2581, 406-453-9989

camshaft repair
engine parts

See full listing in **Section Two** under **camshafts**

Done Right Engine & Machine Inc
12955 York Delta Unit J
North Royalton, OH 44133
440-582-1366; FAX: 440-582-2005

engine rebuilding
machine shop

See full listing in **Section Two** under **engine rebuilding**

EIS Engines Inc
215 SE Grand Ave
Portland, OR 97214
800-547-0002, 503-232-5590
FAX: 503-232-5178
E-mail: edikeis@aol.com

engines

See full listing in **Section One** under **Mercedes-Benz**

Errol's Steam Works
3123 Baird Rd
North Vancouver, BC Canada V7K 2G5
PH/FAX: 604-985-9494
E-mail: steamworks@idmail.com

castings
engines
parts

See full listing in **Section One** under **Locomobile**

Excelsweld USA/Cylinder Head Specialist
1231 16th Ave
Oakland, CA 94606
800-743-4323; FAX: 510-534-1107

welding

Mail order and open shop. Monday-Friday 7 am to 5 pm. Cylinder head specialist, cast iron and aluminum welding and repair of cylinder heads, blocks, housings, manifolds, pressure testing and sealing of castings. Machine shop specializing in crack repair.

George Frechette
14 Cedar Dr
Granby, MA 01033
800-528-5235

brake cylinder
sleeving

See full listing in **Section Two** under **brakes**

George's Speed Shop
716 Brantly Ave
Dayton, OH 45404
937-233-0353; FAX: 937-236-3501

machine shop
race engine building
race engine parts

See full listing in **Section Two** under **racing**

Gromm Racing Heads
664-J Stockton Ave
San Jose, CA 95126
408-287-1301

cylinder heads
racing parts

See full listing in **Section Two** under **racing**

Harter Industries Inc
PO Box 502
Holmdel, NJ 07733
732-566-7055; FAX: 732-566-6977
E-mail: harter101@aol.com

parts
restoration

See full listing in **Section Two** under **comprehensive parts**

Horst's Car Care
3160-1/2 N Woodford St
Decatur, IL 62526
217-876-1112

engine rebuilding

See full listing in **Section One** under **Mercedes-Benz**

Section Two Generalists

Koffel's Place II
740 River Rd
Huron, OH 44839
419-433-4410; FAX: 419-433-2166

| engine rebuilding |
| machine shop |

See full listing in **Section Two** under **engine rebuilding**

Krem Engineering
10204 Perry Hwy
Meadville, PA 16335
814-724-4806; FAX: 814-337-2992
E-mail: info@krem-enterprises.com

| engine rebuilding |
| repairs |
| restoration |

See full listing in **Section Two** under **restoration shops**

Lindskog Balancing
1170 Massachusetts Ave
Boxborough, MA 01719-1415
978-263-2040; FAX: 978-263-4035

| engine balancing |

See full listing in **Section Two** under **engine rebuilding**

Maximum Torque Specialties
PO Box 925
Delavan, WI 53115
414-740-1118; FAX: 414-740-1161

| high-perf parts |
| restoration parts |

See full listing in **Section One** under **Cadillac/LaSalle**

McGee Motorsports Group
29127 Arnold Dr
Sonoma, CA 95476
707-996-1112; FAX: 707-996-9148

| race prep |
| restoration |

See full listing in **Section Two** under **racing**

Mid Valley Engineering
16637 N 21st St
Phoenix, AZ 85022
602-482-1251; FAX: 602-788-0812

| machine work |
| parts |
| restoration |

See full listing in **Section Two** under **transmissions**

R & L Engines Inc
308 Durham Rd
Dover, NH 03820
603-742-8812; FAX: 603-742-8137

| engine rebuilding |
| restorations |

See full listing in **Section Two** under **engine rebuilding**

RB's Prototype Model & Machine Co
44 Marva Ln
Stamford, CT 06903
203-329-2715; FAX: 203-329-8029

| machine work |

See full listing in **Section Two** under **service shops**

Red's Headers & Early Ford Speed Equipment
22950 Bednar Ln
Fort Bragg, CA 95437-8411
707-964-7733; FAX: 707-964-5434
E-mail: red@reds-headers.com

| headers |
| mechanical parts |

See full listing in **Section One** under **Ford 1932-1953**

Rochester Clutch & Brake Co
35 Niagara St
Rochester, NY 14605
716-232-2579; FAX: 716-232-3279

| brakes |
| clutches |

See full listing in **Section Two** under **brakes**

William G Shearman
PO Box 547
Jamestown, NY 14702-0547
716-484-0940

| windshield frame |
| tubing |

See full listing in **Section One** under **Ford 1903-1931**

Simons Balancing & Machine Inc
1987 Ashley River Rd
Charleston, SC 29407
843-766-3911; FAX: 843-766-9003

| machine work |

Balancing, boring, crank grinding, flywheel work, line boring, rod work, valve work.

Tatom Vintage Vendors
PO Box 2504
Mt Vernon, WA 98273
360-424-8314; FAX: 360-424-6717
E-mail: flatheads@tatom.com

| engine rebuilding |
| machine shop |

See full listing in **Section Two** under **engine rebuilding**

Thul Auto Parts Inc
PO Box 446
Plainfield, NJ 07060
800-276-8485, 908-754-3333
FAX: 908-756-0239
E-mail: thulauto@juno.com

| boring |
| machine work |
| rebabbitting |
| vintage auto parts |

See full listing in **Section Two** under **engine rebuilding**

Vintage Motor and Machine
Gene French
1513 Webster Ct
Ft Collins, CO 80524
970-498-9224

| auto components |
| fixtures |
| industrial |
| components |

Mail order and open shop. Monday-Friday 7:30 am to 5 pm, Saturday 8 am to 12 pm. Manufacture babbitt bearing molds and fixtures for Model A and T Fords as well as other vehicles. Perform rebabbitting for most automotive and light industrial applications and general machine shop services including lathe, mill surface grinding and electric discharge machining. Design and building of injection and compression molds and short run production of industrial and automotive components.

West Amity Auto Parts
5685 Merrick Rd
Massapequa, NY 11758
516-795-4610; FAX: 516-795-4117
E-mail: crein69929@erols.com

| custom machining |
| engine rebuilding |

See full listing in **Section Two** under **engine rebuilding**

Willow Automotive Service
Box 4640 Rt 212
Willow, NY 12495
914-679-4679

| bodywork |
| painting |
| restoration |

See full listing in **Section Two** under **restoration shops**

manufacturing

A&A Mustang Parts & Mfg Co
105 Fordham Rd
Oak Ridge, TN 37830
423-482-9445

| exhaust systems |
| parts |
| restorations |

See full listing in **Section One** under **Mustang**

Alum-Line Inc
PO Box 59
US Hwy 9 W
Cresco, IA 52136
319-547-3247; FAX: 319-547-5366
E-mail: alumline@sbtek.net.com

| fabrication |
| manufacturing |

See full listing in **Section Two** under **trailers**

Angeli Machine Co
417 N Varney St
Burbank, CA 91502
818-846-5359
E-mail: angelimach@aol.com

machine work

See full listing in **Section Two** under **machine work**

Blast From the Past
1824 M St, Ste 1
Lincoln, NE 68028
402-332-5050
E-mail: blast2past@aol.com

neon clocks
neon signs

See full listing in **Section Two** under **automobilia**

Bonk's Automotive Inc
4480 Lazelda Dr
Milan, MI 48160
800-207-6906; FAX: 734-434-0845
E-mail: bonkers@bonkauto.com

automotive tools

See full listing in **Section Two** under **tools**

Chassis Engineering Inc
119 N 2nd St, Box 70
West Branch, IA 52358
319-643-2645; FAX: 319-643-2801

brakes
chassis parts
suspension parts

See full listing in **Section Two** under **chassis parts**

Clark & Clark Specialty Products Inc
568 Central Ave
Holland, MI 49423
616-396-4157; FAX: 616-396-0983
E-mail: obertro@macatawa.org

manufacturing

Open 9 am to 5 pm EST. Specializing in the development and manufacturing of short-run (100-5,000 annual volume) products. Supply about 65 automotive parts and accessories to catalog sellers and retail shops. From polyethylene transmission covers to brass logo tire valve caps. Plastics, metals, composites, wood, upholstered goods. Rotational molding, injection molding, thermoforming, casting, stamping, laser cutting, weldments, CNC routing and machining, screw machine turnings, etc. Wholesale only. Always looking for product ideas, automotive or otherwise.

Cobra Trailers
PO Box 18105
Savannah, GA 31418
800-262-7286; FAX: 912-233-2937

rollback trailers

See full listing in **Section Two** under **trailers**

Damper Dudes
5509 Cedar Rd #2
Redding, CA 96001
800-413-2673, 530-244-7225
FAX: 530-244-2690
E-mail: rliddell@snowcrest.net

balancers
chrome
paint

See full listing in **Section Two** under **engine parts**

Danchuk Mfg
3201 S Standard Ave
Santa Ana, CA 92705
714-751-1957; FAX: 714-850-1957
E-mail: info@danchuk.com

accessories
parts
restoration

See full listing in **Section One** under **Chevrolet**

Golden Mile Sales Inc
J DeAngelo
2439 S Bradford St
Allentown, PA 18103-5821
PH/FAX: 610-791-4497, 24 hours

NORS parts
NOS parts
sheetmetal

See full listing in **Section One** under **American Austin/Bantam**

Hillsboro Trailers
220 Industrial Rd
Hillsboro, KS 67063
800-835-0209
E-mail: hii@gplains.com

trailers

See full listing in **Section Two** under **trailers**

Imtek Environmental Corporation
PO Box 2066
Alpharetta, GA 30023
770-667-8621; FAX: 770-667-8683
E-mail: imtek@no-odor.com

ammonia removal products
odor control products

Manufacturer of environmentally friendly odor and pollution control products for consumer and commercial applications. Over 100 types of unique environmentally friendly products such as: odor control products, ammonia removal products, water softeners. Web site: www.no-odor.com

Karmann Ghia Parts & Restoration
PO Box 997
Ventura, CA 93002
800-927-2787; FAX: 805-641-3333
E-mail: info@karmannghia.com

parts

See full listing in **Section One** under **Volkswagen**

Motorworks Inc
4210 Salem St
Philadelphia, PA 19124
800-327-9905; FAX: 215-533-4112
E-mail: motorworks@motorworksinc.com

remanufactured engines

See full listing in **Section Two** under **engine rebuilding**

P-Ayr Products
719 Delaware St
Leavenworth, KS 66048
913-651-5543; FAX: 913-651-2084
E-mail: sales@payr.com

replicas

See full listing in **Section One** under **Chevrolet**

PK Lindsay Co Inc
63 Nottingham Rd
Deerfield, NH 03037
800-258-3576; FAX: 800-843-2974

paint removal
rust removal

See full listing in **Section Two** under **rust removal & stripping**

Power Steering Services Inc
2347 E Kearney St
Springfield, MO 65803
417-864-6676; FAX: 417-864-7103
E-mail: cwoyner@aol.com

pumps
rack & pinion
steering gearboxes

See full listing in **Section Two** under **special services**

Rolling Steel Body Parts
7320 Martingale Dr
Chesterland, OH 44026-2007
888-765-5460; FAX: 440-729-7658
E-mail: rollingsteel@hotmail.com

body parts

See full listing in **Section Two** under **body parts**

William G Shearman
PO Box 547
Jamestown, NY 14702-0547
716-484-0940

windshield frame
tubing

See full listing in **Section One** under **Ford 1903-1931**

Zimmer Neo-Classic Motor Car Co   manufacturing
1415 W Genesee St
Syracuse, NY 13204
315-422-7011 ext 125
FAX: 315-422-1721
E-mail: newtimes@rway.com

See full listing in **Section One** under **Zimmer**

military vehicles

Automobilia   models
Division of Lustron Industries
18 Windgate Dr
New City, NY 10956
PH/FAX: 914-639-6806
E-mail: lustron@worldnet.att.net

See full listing in **Section Two** under **models & toys**

The Beachwood Canvas Works   canvas covers
PO Box 137   parts
Island Heights, NJ 08732   tops
732-929-3168; FAX: 732-929-3479   upholstery
E-mail: beachwood@adelphia.net

Research and reproduction of canvas tops, seat cushions, enclo-
sures, decals, wiring harnesses, top bows and other antique
four-wheel drive products to original manfacturers' specifications. Supply antique military and civilian Jeep and truck parts
and canvas. Web site: www.beachwoodcanvas.com

Cobbaton Combat Collection   museum
Chittlehampton
Umberleigh
N Devon EX37 9RZ England
PH/FAX: 01769-540740
E-mail: cobbaton_combat@yahoo.com

See full listing in **Section Six** under **England**

Commonwealth Automotive   body rebuilding
Restorations   parts
1725 Hewins St   restoration
Ashley Falls, MA 01222
413-229-3196

Mail order and open shop. Monday-Saturday 8 am to 8 pm,
Sunday by appointment. Specializing in complete body, mechanical work, turnkey vehicles built to order, civilian, military, parts
and supplies. Jeep body rebuilding service one of many specialties.

The Davis Registry   periodical
4073 Ruby   quarterly bulletin
Ypsilanti, MI 48197-9317
734-434-5581, 313-662-1001
E-mail: kfnut@umich.edu

See full listing in **Section Four** under **books & publications**

Dusty Memories and Faded Glory   rentals
118 Oxford Hgts Rd
Somerset, PA 15501-1134
814-443-2393; FAX: 814-443-9452

Rental of military vehicles, trucks and tractors for veterans'
organizations, movies, commercials and shows.

Historical Military Armor Museum   museum
2330 Crystal St
Anderson, IN 46012
765-649-TANK; FAX: 765-642-0262

See full listing in **Section Six** under **Indiana**

Kick-Start Motorcycle Parts Inc   parts
PO Box 9347
Wyoming, MI 49509
616-245-8991

See full listing in **Section One** under **Harley-Davidson**

Koolmat   insulators
26258 Cranage Rd
Olmsted Falls, OH 44138
440-427-1888; FAX: 440-427-1889
E-mail: koolmat1@gte.net

See full listing in **Section Two** under **restoration aids**

Miracle of America Museum   museum
58176 Hwy 93
Polson, MT 59860
406-883-6804
E-mail: museum@cyberport.net

See full listing in **Section Six** under **Montana**

Museum of the Spa-   museum
Francorchamps Track
Old Abbey
4970 Stavelot Belgium
PH/FAX: 080-8627-06

See full listing in **Section Six** under **Belgium**

Nelson's Surplus Jeeps and Parts   car dealer
1024 E Park Ave   parts
Columbiana, OH 44408   tires
330-482-5191

Phone hours: Monday-Friday 9 am to 12 noon; shop hours:
Saturday 10:30 am to 3 pm; other times by appointment.
Specializing in military Jeeps, parts and all sizes of US military
tread tires.

Old Coach Works Restoration Inc   appraisals
1206 Badger St   restoration
Yorkville, IL 60560-1701
630-553-0414; FAX: 630-553-1053
E-mail: oldcoachworks@msn.com

See full listing in **Section Two** under **restoration shops**

Paragon Models & Art   artwork
1431-B SE 10th St   models
Cape Coral, FL 33990
941-458-0024; FAX: 941-574-4329
E-mail:
paragonmodels-art@worldnet.att.net

See full listing in **Section Two** under **models & toys**

Redi-Strip Company   abrasive media
100 W Central Ave   baking soda blasting
Roselle, IL 60172   paint removal
630-529-2442; FAX: 630-529-3626   rust removal

See full listing in **Section Two** under **rust removal & stripping**

Richardson Restorations   custom work
1861 W Woodward Ave   repairs
Tulare, CA 93274   restoration
559-688-5002

See full listing in **Section Two** under **restoration shops**

Skopos Motor Museum   museum
Alexandra Hills, Alexandra Rd
Batley
West Yorkshire WA7 6JA England
01924-444423

See full listing in **Section Six** under **England**

Specialty Power Window 2087 Collier Rd Forsyth, GA 31029 800-634-9801; FAX: 912-994-3124	power window kits windshield wiper kit

See full listing in **Section Two** under **street rods**

This Old Truck Magazine PO Box 500 Missouri City, TX 77459 800-310-7047 subscriptions 937-767-1433 publishing office FAX: 937-767-2726 E-mail: antique@antiquepower.com	magazine

See full listing in **Section Four** under **periodicals**

Wallace W Wade Specialty Tires PO Box 560906 530 Regal Row Dallas, TX 75356 800-666-TYRE, 214-688-0091 FAX: 214-634-8465	tires

See full listing in **Section Two** under **tires**

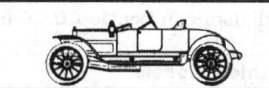

models & toys

American Classics Unlimited Inc PO Box 192-V Oak Lawn, IL 60454-0192 PH/FAX: 708-424-9223	automobilia models toys

Mail order and car shows. Collectible transportation models include all makes of current and older dealer promotional model cars, promotional model trucks/banks, die cast model cars, model kits and accessories. 1/87th-1/12th scales are carried along with current boxed Matchbox #1-75 issues. Current stock listing, $2.

Antiques Warehouse Michael J Welch 3700 Rt 6 Eastham, MA 02642 508-255-1437; FAX: 508-247-9166 E-mail: miketoys1@aol.com	automobilia bikes toy trucks

Mail order and open shop. May-October daily, November-April by appointment. Antique toys, buy, sell, trade, pressed steel, pedal cars, balloon tire bikes, automobilia, petroliana, nostalgia and much, much more. Now open at Atlantic Oaks Camp, at above address. Web site: http://members.ebay.com/aboutme/mike4toys/

Aquarius Antiques Jim & Nancy Schaut 7147 W Angela Dr Glendale, AZ 85308 602-878-4293 E-mail: jnschaut@aol.com	memorabilia toys

See full listing in **Section Two** under **automobilia**

Arrow Fastener Co Inc 271 Mayhill St Saddle Brook, NJ 07663	nail guns rivet tools staple guns

See full listing in **Section Two** under **tools**

Asheville DieCast 1434 Brevard Rd Asheville, NC 28806-9560 800-343-4685, 888-343-4685 704-667-9690; FAX: 704-667-1110 E-mail: sales@asheville-diecast.com	banks models

Mail order and open shop. Monday-Friday 9 am to 5:30 pm, Saturday 9 am to 5 pm. Check out the large selection of collectible banks, replica signs and vehicle replicas. Brand name products such as: Brooklin, Corgi, Eagle Race, Ertl, First Gear, Gearbox, Hartoy, Liberty Classics (SpecCast), Lledo Days Gone, Lledo Vanguard Series, Maisto, Old Style gas pump replicas (7.5" tall), Desktop wood airplane replicas, plastic gas station promotionals, Revell, Road Champs, Andy Rooney porcelain sign replicas, Solido & Yat Ming (Road Tough & Road Legends). Web site: http://asheville-diecast.com

Astro Models 13856 Roxanne Rd Sterling Heights, MI 48312-5673 810-268-3479 E-mail: paully@home.com	accessories parts

Mail order only. Deal in model car parts and hand cast accessories, model car wired distributors, model car license plates, drag truck support decals. 1/24, 1/25 scale only.

Auto Muzeuma Haris (Bross) Testverek 1117 Budapest XI, Moricz Zsigmond Korter 12 Hungary 01 (1) 3656893	museum

See full listing in **Section Six** under **Hungary**

Auto Nostalgia Enr 332 St Joseph Mont St Gregoire, QC Canada J0J 1K0 PH/FAX: 450-346-3644 E-mail: autonostalgia@vif.com	literature manuals models tractor decals

See full listing in **Section Two** under **literature dealers**

Auto Zone 33202 Woodward Ave Birmingham, MI 48009 800-647-7288; FAX: 248-646-5381 E-mail: info@azautozone.com	books magazines models videos

Mail order and open shop. Monday-Friday 10 am to 8 pm, Saturday 10 am to 7 pm, closed Sundays. Metro Detroit's largest selection of automobilia including a large selection of books covering all makes and subjects. More than 120 different magazines from around the world. Die cast models from 1:87th scale to 1:12th scale including Brooklin, Minichamps, Brumm, Best/Bang and Kyosho as well as plastic kits, promos, videos, clothing and collectibles. The store for the auto enthusiast.

Automobilia Division of Lustron Industries 18 Windgate Dr New City, NY 10956 PH/FAX: 914-639-6806 E-mail: lustron@worldnet.att.net	models

Mail order only. 1/43 scale die cast models of classic and historic European cars with emphasis on race cars. These are models of cars from the turn of the century through the 1980s. Also offer convenience of automatic shipments and extra savings to club members.

Autotron   **museum**
PO Box 142 (Graafsebaan 133)
A 50 Motorway 's-Hertogenbosch-
Nijmegen
Rosmalen 5240 AC (56248 NL)
Netherlands
0031-73-5233300
FAX: 0031-73-5216795
E-mail: info@autotron.nl

See full listing in **Section Six** under **Netherlands**

Berliner Classic Motorcars Inc   **automobilia**
1975 Stirling Rd   **car dealer**
Dania, FL 33004   **motorcycles**
954-923-7271; FAX: 954-926-3306
E-mail: sales@motorcars.com

See full listing in **Section Two** under **car dealers**

Bonneville Sports Inc   **accessories**
3544 Enterprise Dr   **clothing**
Amaheim, CA 92807
888-999-7258, 714-666-1966
FAX: 714-666-1955
E-mail: bonspeed@aol.com

See full listing in **Section Two** under **apparel**

Brasilia Press   **models**
PO Box 2023
Elkhart, IN 46515
FAX: 219-262-8799

Dealing in Brooklin, US Model Mint, Goldvarg, Robeddie,
Lansdowne and Somerville handmade miniature automobiles.
Model car price guides, paperback and on CD-ROM for PCs. As
importers, we will furnish dealer listing.

British Only Motorcycles and   **literature**
Parts Inc   **memorabilia**
32451 Park Ln   **motorcycles**
Garden City, MI 48135   **parts**
734-421-0303; FAX: 734-422-9253
E-mail: info@british-only.com

See full listing in **Section Two** under **motorcycles**

Caddytown™/Pawl Engineering Co   **memorabilia**
4960 Arrowhead   **parts**
PO Box 240105   **toys**
West Bloomfield, MI 48324
PH/FAX: 248-682-2007
E-mail: pawl@earthlink.net

See full listing in **Section One** under **Cadillac/LaSalle**

Car Collectables   **banks**
32 White Birch Rd   **Christmas cards**
Madison, CT 06443   **note cards**
PH/FAX: 203-245-2242

See full listing in **Section Two** under **artwork**

Car Toy Collectibles Magazine   **magazine**
7950 Deering Ave
Canoga Park, CA 91304-5063
818-887-0550; FAX: 818-884-1343
E-mail: mail@challengeweb.com

See full listing in **Section Four** under **periodicals**

Ceramicar   **auto-related**
679 Lapla Rd   **ceramics**
Kingston, NY 12401
PH/FAX: 914-338-2199

See full listing in **Section Two** under **novelties**

Classic Transportation   **automobilia**
3667 Mahoning Ave
Youngstown, OH 44515
330-793-3026; FAX: 330-793-9729

See full listing in **Section Two** under **automobilia**

The Collector's Guild   **models**
41 Counter St   **toys**
Kingston, ON Canada K7K 6C7
800-653-0251; FAX: 613-536-5211
E-mail: cars@collectorsguild.on.ca

Mail order and open shop/showroom. Monday-Friday 8 am to 6
pm, Saturday 10 am to 5 pm. Specializing in die cast metal
model cars and trucks, mainly 1/18th scale cars, 1/24th and
1/64th scale trucks. Over 500 different models in stock. Call
613-536-5209 for free catalog. Web site:
www.collectorsguild.on.ca.

DeLorean Literature   **collectibles**
3116 Welsh Rd   **literature**
Philadelphia, PA 19136-1810
215-338-6142
E-mail:
delorean.literature@excite.com

See full listing in **Section One** under **DeLorean**

Dominion Models   **models**
PO Box 515
Salem, VA 24153
PH/FAX: 540-375-3750

Mail order only. Specialize in 1/43rd scale die cast and white
metal models of American cars. Free illustrated brochure
available.

Driven By Desire   **automobilia**
300 N Fraley St   **car dealer**
Kane, PA 16735   **models**
814-837-7590; FAX: 814-837-6850
E-mail: driven@penn.com

See full listing in **Section Two** under **car dealers**

Dual Connection   **models**
Box 569   **toys**
Gibsonia, PA 15044
724-898-9660; FAX: 724-898-9680
E-mail: rich@dualconnection.com

Mail order only. Deal in toys and models of all types of cars and
motorcycles, old and new. Exclusive importer for the Vitesse
Group, Onyx, Quart 70, City and Victoria. Wholesale retail. Web
site: www.dualconnection.com

Eastwood Automobilia   **collectibles**
Box 296   **scale models**
Malvern, PA 19355-0714   **transportation**
800-343-9353
FAX: 610-644-0560

See full listing in **Section Two** under **automobilia**

EWA & Miniature Cars USA Inc   **books**
205 US Hwy 22   **models**
Green Brook, NJ 08812-1909   **subscriptions**
732-424-7811; FAX: 732-424-7814   **videos**
E-mail: ewa@ewacars.com

Mail order and showroom. Publish *Classic & Sportscar*, monthly
publication filled with timely news, previews of upcoming events,
auction news & event information. Includes huge classified section. Published in England. Featuring 8,000 different scale models from 400 manufacturers. Subscription: $59/year. Also avail-
able are subscriptions for 36 foreign automobile magazines,
including back issues and 3,000 different auto books. Also 600

auto videos. Almost 10,000 different products. Huge 100-page color catalog, $4. Web site: www.ewacars.com

---

Fantasy Models
PO Box 570
Wright City, MO 63390
888-745-8254; FAX: 800-745-8254
E-mail: scale43@inlink.com

models

Mail order only. Deal in 1/43rd scale models of US cars, sports cars, Formula I and other race cars.

Fill Er Up
Brian Steiner
2613 Old Philadelphia Pike
PO Box 406
Bird In Hand, PA 17505
717-397-2519

automobilia
petroliana

See full listing in **Section Two** under **automobilia**

Galaxie Ltd
Box 655
Butler, WI 53007
414-673-6386, 414-790-9922
FAX: 414-673-6366

kits
model trailers

Mail order only. Manufacturer, distributor and mail order business selling our own Galaxie brand kits. 1/25 scale model trailer kits, vintage slingshot dragster model kits. 1/25 scale styrene plastic, 1948 Chevy Aerosedan kits, 1948 Chevy sedan delivery kits. These kits can be built stock, vintage custom or vintage racing. Parts are included to build 1946, 1947 or 1948 years.

Gateway Global USA
10485 NW 28th St
Miami, FL 33172-2152
305-500-9641; FAX: 305-500-9642
E-mail: gatautousa@aol.com

models

Deal in die cast models. Authentic, accurate, many scales, collectables.

Get It On Paper
Gary Weickart, President
185 Maple St
Islip, NY 11751
516-581-3897

automobilia
literature
toys

See full listing in **Section Two** under **automobilia**

Jerry Goldsmith Promos
4634 Cleveland Heights
Lakeland, FL 33813
941-644-7013, 941-646-8490
PH/FAX: 941-644-5013
E-mail: shirley.goldsmith@gtc.net

models

See full listing in **Section Two** under **automobilia**

Good Old Days Vintage Motorcar Museum
Main St, PO Box 311
Hardy, AR 72542
870-856-4884; FAX: 870-856-4885

museum

See full listing in **Section Six** under **Arkansas**

Grandpa's Attic
112 E Washington
Goshen, IN 46528
219-534-2778

toys

Mail order and open shop. Monday-Friday 9:30 am to 5 pm, Saturday until 3 pm. Specializing in die cast collector toys.

Grey Motor Co
18845 Van Buren Blvd 10-A
Riverside, CA 92508
800-343-5496; FAX: 909-789-9751

display cabinets

See full listing in **Section Two** under **automobilia**

H D Garage
Barry Brown
Comp 8 Bedford Mills RR #2
Westport, ON Canada K0G 1X0
613-273-5036

artwork
literature
motorcycles

See full listing in **Section Two** under **motorcycles**

Richard Hamilton
28 E 46th St
Indianapolis, IN 46205
317-283-1902

sales literature

See full listing in **Section Two** under **literature dealers**

Hotchkiss Mfg/Clear Case
PO Box 810
Merlin, OR 97532
800-444-5005; FAX: 541-476-0268
E-mail: hotchkiss@chatlink.com

display cases

Quality wood and acrylic display cases for collector cars, trains, ships and dolls. Web site: www.chatlink.com/~hotchkiss

---

International House of Toys
16582 Jamesville Rd
Muskego, WI 53150
414-422-9505; FAX: 414-422-9507

toys

Mail order and open shop. Monday-Friday 10 am to 6 pm, Saturday 10 am to 4 pm. Specializing in die cast toys.

The Josey's Heaven Hill Farm
1839 NW C-138
Branford, FL 32008
904-935-0348

swap meets

See full listing in **Section Two** under **auctions & events**

Jack Juratovic
819 Absequami Trail
Lake Orion, MI 48362
PH/FAX: 248-814-0627

artwork
magazine

See full listing in **Section Two** under **artwork**

K&S Industries
1801 Union Center Hwy
Endicott, NY 13760
PH/FAX: 888-PICK-KNS
E-mail: pleximan@888pickkns.com

display cases

Mail order only. Monday-Friday 9 am to 5 pm EST. Acrylic display cases for model cars. Web site: www.888pickkns.com

---

Karl's Collectibles
28 Bates St
Lewiston, ME 04240
800-636-0457, 207-784-0098
FAX: 207-786-4576
E-mail:
slalemand@exploremaine.com

banks
collectibles
logo design

Mail order and open shop. Monday-Friday 9 am to 5 pm. Die cast banks and collectibles, as well as custom logo and printing needs. Design, market and broker collectibles, specializing in the motorcycle trade but not exclusive. Design logos for new companies as well as companies looking for that new look. Web site: www.exploremaine.com/~lalemand/karlscollectibles

Harold Kloss PO Box 37 Humboldt, AZ 86329-0037 520-632-7684	**wood models**

Mail order only. Build one of a kind wood models for any make or model. Custom orders. All handcrafted.

LA Ltd Design Graphics 822A S McDuffie St Anderson, SC 29624 PH/FAX: 864-231-7715	**artwork** **design** **greeting cards**

See full listing in **Section Two** under **automobilia**

The Last Precinct Police Museum 15677 Hwy 62 W Eureka Springs, AR 72632 501-253-4948; FAX: 501-253-4949	**museum**

See full listing in **Section Six** under **Arkansas**

Legendary Motorcars 1 Wayside Village #350 Marmora, NJ 08223 FAX: 609-399-2512	**model cars**

Producer of handbuilt model cars for the connoisseur collector. Very limited production. 1/43rd scale, resin cast, retail price $325 and up. First issue is a 1960 Lincoln Continental Mark V coupe and convertible. Second issue is a 1956 Continental Mark II coupe and convertible. Write or fax for more information.

Little Old Cars 3410 Fulton Dr NW Canton, OH 44718 216-455-4685	**model cars**

Mail order and open shop. Monday-Friday 4 pm to 10 pm, Saturday-Sunday 8 am to 10 pm. Specializing in promotional model cars, 1950s-up. Also unbuilt kits. Buy, sell and trade. All correspondences welcome. No catalog available. Please include SASE for immediate response.

George & Denise Long 915 E Court St Marion, NC 28752 828-652-9229 (24 hrs w/recorder)	**automobilia**

See full listing in **Section Two** under **automobilia**

Marky D's Bikes & Pedal Goods 7047 Springridge Rd West Bloomfield, MI 48322 810-737-1657; FAX: 810-398-2581	**bicycles** **mopeds** **motorbikes** **pedal goods**

See full listing in **Section Two** under **bicycles**

Mercedes-Benz Visitor Center PO Box 100 Tuscaloosa, AL 35403-0100 888-2TOUR-MB, 205-507-2262 FAX: 205-507-2255	**museum**

See full listing in **Section One** under **Mercedes-Benz**

Midwestern Industries LLC 67742 CR 23 New Paris, IN 46553 219-831-5200; FAX: 219-831-5210 E-mail: kdarcy@midwesternindllc.com	**model cars**

80 different models and body styles of mini cars. Prowlers, Vipers, 1957 Chevy, 1957 Thunderbird, NASCARS, Dodge Dakota and Ram, Kenworth Peterbuilt, Model Ts, Model As. Web site: www.midwesternindllc.com

Model Engineering Gene or Jeff Sanders 3284 S Main St Akron, OH 44329 330-644-3450; FAX: 330-644-0088	**new parts casting**

See full listing in **Section Two** under **castings**

Motorhead Art & Collectibles 4311 45th Ave NE Tacoma, WA 98422 800-859-0164 orders, 253-924-0776 FAX: 253-924-0788 E-mail: autartman@aol.com	**automotive art** **die cast cars**

See full listing in **Section Two** under **artwork**

Museum of the Spa- **Francorchamps Track** Old Abbey 4970 Stavelot Belgium PH/FAX: 080-8627-06	**museum**

See full listing in **Section Six** under **Belgium**

On Mark International Inc 8923 S 43rd W Ave Tulsa, OK 74132 918-446-7906; FAX: 918-445-1514 E-mail: onmark@ix.netcom.com	**replicas**

Producer of die cast replica trucks and planes. Web site: www.onmarkint.com

Paragon Models & Art 1431-B SE 10th St Cape Coral, FL 33990 941-458-0024; FAX: 941-574-4329 E-mail: paragonmodels-art@worldnet.att.net	**artwork** **models**

Mail order and open shop. Monday-Friday 9 am to 5 pm. Automotive collectibles, cool stuff. Web site: www.paragonmodelsandart.com

People Kars 290 Third Ave Ext Rensselaer, NY 12144 518-465-0477; FAX: 518-465-0614 E-mail: peoplekars@aol.com	**models/more** **VW toys**

See full listing in **Section One** under **Volkswagen**

Pikes Peak Auto Hill Climb **Educational Museum** 135 Manitou Ave Manitou Springs, CO 80829 719-685-4400; FAX: 719-685-5885 E-mail: ppihc@ppihc.com	**museum**

See full listing in **Section Six** under **Colorado**

PM Research Inc 4110 Niles Hill Rd Wellsville, NY 14895 716-593-3169; FAX: 716-593-5637 E-mail: pmrgang@pmresearchinc.com	**books** **models**

Mail order only. Model steam engines, model pipe and miniature pipe fittings. Offer two model boilers and seven model machine shop tools that really work. Also have a line of Stirling hot air engines and accessories and carry a large selection of books relating to the above subjects. Catalogs are available, $3. Web site: www.pmresearchinc.com

**Hugo Prado Limited Edition
Corvette Art Prints**
PO Box 18437
Chicago, IL 60618-0437
PH/FAX: 800-583-7627
E-mail: vetteart@aol.com

fine art prints

See full listing in **Section One** under **Corvette**

**Promotionals 1934-1983
Dealership Vehicles in Miniature**
2696 Brookmar
York, PA 17404
PH/FAX: 717-792-4936

price guide

See full listing in **Section Two** under **automobilia**

Lloyd Ralston Gallery
400 Long Beach Blvd
Stratford, CT 06615
203-386-9399; FAX: 203-386-9519
E-mail: lrgallery@aol.com

toys

Mail order and open shop. Monday-Friday 10 am to 4 pm. Deal in vintage die cast toys, Corgi, Dinky, Matchbox, Tootsie Toy. We buy and sell them plus we hold 4 catalogued auctions a year.

Rideable Antique Bicycle Replicas
2329 Eagle Ave
Alameda, CA 94501
510-769-0980; FAX: 510-521-7145
E-mail: mbarron@barrongroup.com

*bicycles
tires*

See full listing in **Section Two** under **motorcycles**

Sammy's Street Strollers
2725 Chinook Ct
Union City, CA 94587
510-489-3502; FAX: 510-489-2994
E-mail: sammy@slipnet.com

baby stroller

See full listing in **Section One** under **Ford 1932-1953**

San Remo Hobby and Toy
93 Beaver Dr
Kings Park, NY 11754-2209
PH/FAX: 516-724-5722

*models
trading cards*

Full line Johnny Lightning and Polar lights kits. Promotional model cars. Model car kits. Send SASE for list.

Scott Signal Co
8368 W Farm Rd 84
Willard, MO 65781
417-742-5040

stoplights

See full listing in **Section Two** under **automobilia**

Shines Unlimited
11709 Oakland
Schoolcraft, MI 49087
616-679-4002

*car buckles
toys*

Mail order only. 1/18, 1/24 Ertl toys, Maisto, Burago, Racing Champions, Road Champs, all makes and models. Also car buckles, car necklaces, car earrings and all types of plastic model kits. Hot Wheels, Matchbox cars, old and new, loose and in packages. Send want list or for request list. Send LSASE (2 oz) for list of inventory cars. Allow 2 weeks for shipping.

Skopos Motor Museum
Alexandra Hills, Alexandra Rd
Batley
West Yorkshire WA7 6JA England
01924-444423

museum

See full listing in **Section Six** under **England**

Space Farms Zoo & Museum
218 Rt 519
Sussex, NJ 07461
973-875-3223; FAX: 973-875-9397
E-mail: fpspace@warwick.net

*museum
zoo*

See full listing in **Section Six** under **New Jersey**

Sparrow Auction Company
59 Wheeler Ave
Milford, CT 06460
203-877-1066
E-mail: vehicle@snet.net

auction company

See full listing in **Section Two** under **auctions & events**

Spec Cast
428 6th Ave NW
Box 368
Dyersville, IA 52040-0368
319-875-8706; FAX: 319-875-8056

models

Leading manufacturer of quality die cast and pewter collectibles. Including vehicles and airplane banks, 1/16 tractors, belt buckles and pewter replicas.

St Louis Car Museum & Sales
1575 Woodson Rd
St Louis, MO 63114
314-993-1330; FAX: 314-993-1540

museum

See full listing in **Section Six** under **Missouri**

Supercar Collectibles Ltd
7311-75th Circle N
Minneapolis, MN 55428
612-425-6020; FAX: 612-425-3357

muscle car replicas

Deal in die cast metal 1/18th scale replicas of American muscle cars. Very collectible, detailed, limited editions, that have been received very well by collectors. Call to get on our mailing list, 6 mailings per year.

TCMB Models & Stuff
8207 Clinton Ave S
Bloomington, MN 55420-2315
612-884-3997; FAX: 612-884-2827
E-mail: tcmb@gte.net

models

Mail order only. Metal model kits, 1/25 scale vehicle banks and 1/43rd scale vehicles. Accept Visa, MasterCard, American Express and Discover cards. Web site: http://home1.gte.net/tcmb

---

Tech-Art Publications
Jason Houston
Box 753
Ranchero Mirage, CA 92270
760-862-1979

books

See full listing in **Section Four** under **books & publications**

**Edward Tilley Automotive
Collectibles**
PO Box 4233
Cary, NC 27519-4233
919-460-8262
E-mail: edandsusan@aol.com

*automobilia
literature
parts*

See full listing in **Section Two** under **automobilia**

Town & Country Toys
227 Midvale Dr
PO Box 574
Marshall, WI 53559
608-655-4961
E-mail: dejaeger@itis.com

| banks |
| Ertl cars |
| mini license plates |

Mail order and open shop. Tuesday and Thursday 7 pm to 9 pm, Saturday afternoons. Dealing in 1/18th scale die cast Ertl cars. Originator and supplier of Ertl's Mach 1s. Farm toys, truck and airplane banks, engraved miniature license plates. Send for list, specify interest.

Toys For Collectors
PO Box 1406
Attleboro Falls, MA 02763
508-695-0588; FAX: 508-699-8649

| models |

Mail order and showroom open by appointment. Scale models of automobiles, fire trucks, construction equipment, military, etc, in various scales. Carry one of the largest selections of metal models, factory and handbuilt, ready to display, no kits. Color catalog available for $8.

USAopoly Inc
565 Westlake St
Encinitas, CA 92024
760-634-5910; FAX: 760-634-5923
E-mail: allison@usaopoly.com

| Monopoly® game |

Mail order only. Special editions of the Monopoly® game: Corvette, Harley-Davidson, NASCAR and Mustang. Web site: usaopoly.com

Vintage Car Corral
1401 NW 53rd Ave
PO Box 384
Gainesville, FL 32602
PH/FAX: 352-376-0660

| parts |
| toys |

See full listing in **Section Two** under **comprehensive parts**

Volkswagen Collectors
c/o Jerry Jess
3121 E Yucca St
Phoenix, AZ 85028-2616
PH/FAX: 602-867-7672
E-mail: vwstuff@juno.com

| literature |
| memorabilia |
| toys |

See full listing in **Section One** under **Volkswagen**

Brady Ward-Scale Autoworks
313 Bridge St #4
Manchester, NH 03104-5045
603-623-5925
FAX: 603-623-5925 ext 66
E-mail: bradyward@mediaone.net

| models |

Mail order and open shop by appointment only. Professional builder of Pocher Classic 1/8 scale models, specializing in Bugatti and Alfa Romeo. All models are built to the customers specifications and include real leather and wood interiors, automotive quality paint and added engine details, wiring and linkages. Custom paint and coachwork are available, including mahogany skiff bodied cars. Also the exclusive source for Randy Owens' Classic Formula One art prints, featuring Gilles Villeneuve, Monaco, Long Beach, etc. Web site: http://people.ne.mediaone.net/bradyward

West Michigan Die-Cast Cars
2523 W Kinney Rd
Ludington, MI 49431
616-843-4278

| die cast cars |

Deal in 1/18th scale die cast cars, airplanes, 1/64th scale semis.

Kirk F White
PO Box 999
New Smyrna Beach, FL 32170
904-427-6660; FAX: 904-427-7801

| models |
| tin toys |

Mail order and open shop by appointment only. Early gas engined racing cars of all types. Early historied hot rods, racing memorabilia, fine large scale racing models. All types of early European transportation tin toys.

Yankee Candle Car Museum
Yankee Candle Co Rt 5
South Deerfield, MA 01373
413-665-2020; FAX: 413-665-2399

| museum |

See full listing in **Section Six** under **Massachusetts**

Clarence Young Autohobby
302 Reems Creek
Weaverville, NC 28787
828-645-3444
PH/FAX: 828-645-5243
E-mail: cya@carhobby.com

| antique toy vehicles |
| dealer promos |
| exclusive metal cars |
| exclusive resin cars |
| promo price guide |

Mail order and open shop by appointment. Obsolete dealer promotionals, model kits and antique toy vehicles. Manufacturer of 1/25th metal cars and resin cars. Showroom sales materials. Web site: www.carhobby.com

motorcycles

AMC Classic Appraisers
7963 Depew St
Arvada, CO 80003
303-428-8760; FAX: 303-428-1070

| appraisals |

See full listing in **Section Two** under **appraisals**

Auto Muzeuma Haris (Bross) Testverek
1117 Budapest
XI, Moricz Zsigmond Korter 12
Hungary
01 (1) 3656893

| museum |

See full listing in **Section Six** under **Hungary**

Berliner Classic Motorcars Inc
1975 Stirling Rd
Dania, FL 33004
954-923-7271; FAX: 954-926-3306
E-mail: sales@motorcars.com

| automobilia |
| car dealer |
| motorcycles |

See full listing in **Section Two** under **car dealers**

Bimmer Magazine
42 Digital Dr #5
Novato, CA 94949
415-382-0580; FAX: 415-382-0587

| magazine |

See full listing in **Section Four** under **periodicals**

BPE Racing Heads
702 Dunn Way
Placentia, CA 92870
714-572-6072; FAX: 714-572-6073
E-mail: steve@bpeheads.com

| cylinder heads |

See full listing in **Section Two** under **machine work**

**British Only Motorcycles and
Parts Inc**
32451 Park Ln
Garden City, MI 48135
734-421-0303; FAX: 734-422-9253
E-mail: info@british-only.com

	literature
	memorabilia
	motorcycles
	parts

Mail order and open shop. Monday-Friday 10 am to 6 pm.
Dealing in British motorcylces and parts. Literature and memorabilia for all motorcycles. Online auction site at:
gearheadauction.com Web site: british-only.com

Francois Bruere
8 Avenue Olivier Heuze
LeMans 72000 France
(33) 02-4377-1877
FAX: (33) 02-4324-2038

artwork

See full listing in **Section Two** under **artwork**

California Triples
5928 Laird Ave
Oakland, CA 94605
510-569-9430; FAX: 510-569-4236
E-mail: jkovace829@aol.com

sales

Specializing in all brands of motorcycles, 20 ft and 40 ft contain-
er loads only. Vintage Kawasaki parts specialist. Ship worldwide.
Come visit us in San Francisco Bay area.

Coker Tire
1317 Chestnut St
Chattanooga, TN 37402
800-251-6336 toll-free
423-265-6368 local & international
FAX: 423-756-5607

tires

See full listing in **Section Two** under **tires**

Glenn Curtiss Museum
8419 St Rt 54
Hammondsport, NY 14840
607-569-2160; FAX: 607-569-2040

museum

See full listing in **Section Six** under **New York**

Dale's Harley-Davidson of Mt Vernon
12th St & Veterans Memorial Dr
Mt Vernon, IL 62864
618-244-4116; FAX: 618-244-5470
E-mail: daleshd@dales-hd.com

	motorcycle
	dealership

See full listing in **Section One** under **Harley-Davidson**

Das osterr. Motorradmuseum
Museumgasse 6
A-3730 Eggenburg Austria
43 2984 2151; FAX: 43 2984 2119

museum

See full listing in **Section Six** under **Austria**

Dual Connection
Box 569
Gibsonia, PA 15044
724-898-9660; FAX: 724-898-9680
E-mail: rich@dualconnection.com

	models
	toys

See full listing in **Section Two** under **models & toys**

Finders Service
454-458 W Lincoln Hwy
Chicago Heights, IL 60411-2463
708-481-9685; FAX: 708-481-5837
E-mail: findersvc@aol.com

parts finders

See full listing in **Section Two** under **car & parts locators**

Florida Caliper Manufacturers Inc
1450 SW 10th St #3
Delray Beach, FL 33444
561-272-5238

	brake systems
	chassis parts
	suspension parts

See full listing in **Section One** under **Corvette**

**Henry Ford Museum &
Greenfield Village**
20900 Oakwood Blvd
Dearborn, MI 48121-1970
313-271-1620; FAX: 313-982-6247

museum

See full listing in **Section Six** under **Michigan**

George Frechette
14 Cedar Dr
Granby, MA 01033
800-528-5235

	brake cylinder
	sleeving

See full listing in **Section Two** under **brakes**

J Giles Automotive
703 Morgan Ave
Pascagoula, MS 39567-2116
228-769-1012; FAX: 228-769-8904
E-mail: jgauto@datasync.com

	car & parts locator
	exporter

See full listing in **Section Two** under **car & parts locators**

H D Garage
Barry Brown
Comp 8 Bedford Mills RR #2
Westport, ON Canada K0G 1X0
613-273-5036

	artwork
	literature
	motorcycles

Rare pre-WW II motorcycles and related literature and artworks
(bronzes, paintings, miniatures, etc), Brough-Superior, Crocker,
early Harley (especially racers) and American 4-cylinder specialist. Parts information and restoration and location services for
these and others. OHC Norton collector and specialist.
Continental European racing bikes, etc sought, top dollar paid
and finder's fee.

Harley Rendezvous Classic
1142 Batter St
Pattersonville, NY 12137
518-864-5659; FAX: 518-864-5917
E-mail: frank@harleyrendezvous.com

motorcycle events

Specializing in motorcycle events and swap meets.

Harper's Moto Guzzi
32401 Stringtown Rd
Greenwood, MO 64034
800-752-9735, 816-697-3411
FAX: 816-566-3413

	accessories
	bikes
	parts

Mail order and open shop. Monday-Friday 9 am to 5 pm,
Saturday 9 am to 1 pm, closed Sundays and all holidays. We are
exploding with lots of stock. New, used and hard-to-find Moto
Guzzi bikes and parts. Lots of NOS too. Aftermarket accessories
for the Moto Guzzi motorcycle, only $3 for aftermarket catalog
USA; foreign airmail, $5 US. Bike flyer available, listing most of
the bikes we have for sale. Ship bikes and parts worldwide. Visa,
MasterCard, American Express or cash. Web site: www.harper-
motoguzzi.com

Hooker Headers
1024 W Brooks St
Ontario, CA 91762
909-983-5871; FAX: 909-986-9860

exhaust systems

See full listing in **Section Two** under **exhaust systems**

Hosking Cycle Works
136 Hosking Ln
Accord, NY 12404
914-626-4231; FAX: 914-626-3245
E-mail: cycle@ulster.net

| books |
| manuals |
| motorcycle parts |
| reprints |

See full listing in **Section Two** under **literature dealers**

Indian Joe Martin's Antique Motorcycle Parts
PO Box 3156
Chattanooga, TN 37404
PH/FAX: 423-698-1787
E-mail: indianjo@bellsouth.net

| parts |

Mail order only. Indian and Harley-Davidson motorcycle business offering NOS military surplus and quality reproduction parts for Indian and pre-1973 Harley-Davidson motorcycles, shipped worldwide. Parts catalog available, $3 USA and Canada, $5 foreign airmail.

Iverson Automotive
14704 Karyl Dr
Minnetonka, MN 55345
800-325-0480; FAX: 612-938-5707

| polishes |
| pot metal |
| restoration |

See full listing in **Section Two** under **plating & polishing**

Jesser's Auto Clinic
26 West St
Akron, OH 44303
330-376-8181; FAX: 330-384-9129

| appraisals |

See full listing in **Section Two** under **appraisals**

Karl's Collectibles
28 Bates St
Lewiston, ME 04240
800-636-0457, 207-784-0098
FAX: 207-786-4576
E-mail:
slalemand@exploremaine.com

| banks |
| collectibles |
| logo design |

See full listing in **Section Two** under **models & toys**

Kick-Start Motorcycle Parts Inc
PO Box 9347
Wyoming, MI 49509
616-245-8991

| parts |

See full listing in **Section One** under **Harley-Davidson**

Lindskog Balancing
1170 Massachusetts Ave
Boxborough, MA 01719-1415
978-263-2040; FAX: 978-263-4035

| engine balancing |

See full listing in **Section Two** under **engine rebuilding**

Luback & Co
456 W 14th St 2B
Chicago Heights, IL 60411
708-481-9685; FAX: 708-481-5837
E-mail: lubackco@aol.com

| parts |

See full listing in **Section One** under **Harley-Davidson**

M & R Products
1940 SW Blvd
Vineland, NJ 08360
800-524-2560, 609-696-9450
FAX: 609-696-4999
E-mail:
mrproducts@mrproducts.com

| hardware |
| tie-downs |

See full listing in **Section Two** under **accessories**

Main Attractions
PO Box 4923
Chatsworth, CA 91311
818-709-9855; FAX: 818-998-0906

| posters |
| videos |

See full listing in **Section Four** under **information sources**

Marky D's Bikes & Pedal Goods
7047 Springridge Rd
West Bloomfield, MI 48322
810-737-1657; FAX: 810-398-2581

| bicycles |
| mopeds |
| motorbikes |
| pedal goods |

See full listing in **Section Two** under **bicycles**

Mid-America Auction Services
2277 W Hwy 36, Ste 214
St Paul, MN 55113
612-633-9655; FAX: 612-633-3212
E-mail: midauction@aol.com

| auctions |

See full listing in **Section Two** under **auctions & events**

Sammy Miller Motorcycle Museum
Bashley Cross Rd
New Milton
Hampshire BH25 5SZ England
01425 620777; FAX: 01425 619696

| museum |

See full listing in **Section Six** under **England**

Miracle of America Museum
58176 Hwy 93
Polson, MT 59860
406-883-6804
E-mail: museum@cyberport.net

| museum |

See full listing in **Section Six** under **Montana**

Moores Cycle Supply
49 Custer St
West Hartford, CT 06110
860-953-1689; FAX: 860-953-4366

| motorcycles |
| parts |

Mail order and open shop. Monday-Friday 12 noon to 8 pm, Saturday 2 pm to 5 pm. Deal in motorcycles, parts for Triumphs, BSA, Norton motorcycles.

Motorcycle Hall of Fame Museum
13515 Yarmouth Dr
Pickerington, OH 43147
614-882-2782 info
614-856-1900 office
FAX: 614-856-1920
E-mail: afitch@ama-cycle.org

| museum |

See full listing in **Section Six** under **Ohio**

Motorcycle Museum
(Motorrad Museum)
Lengericher Str
49479 Ibbenburen Germany
05451-6454

| museum |

See full listing in **Section Six** under **Germany**

Motorsports Racing
914 S Santa Fe #101
Vista, CA 92084
760-630-0547; FAX: 760-630-3085

| accessories |
| apparel |
| art |

See full listing in **Section Two** under **apparel**

Museum of the Spa-Francorchamps Track
Old Abbey
4970 Stavelot Belgium
PH/FAX: 080-8627-06

| museum |

See full listing in **Section Six** under **Belgium**

National Parts Locator Service 636 East 6th St # 81 Ogden, UT 84404-2415 801-627-7210	parts locator

See full listing in **Section Two** under **car & parts locators**

North Yorkshire Motor Museum D T Mathewson Roxby Garage, Pickering Rd Thornton-le-Dale, North Yorkshire England 01751 474455; FAX: 01944 758188	museum

See full listing in **Section Six** under **England**

Old Coach Works Restoration Inc 1206 Badger St Yorkville, IL 60560-1701 630-553-0414; FAX: 630-553-1053 E-mail: oldcoachworks@msn.com	appraisals restoration

See full listing in **Section Two** under **restoration shops**

Guy R Palermo Auto Body 241 Church Rd (rear) Wexford, PA 15090 724-935-3790; FAX: 724-935-9121	bodywork custom paint restoration

Open Monday-Friday 8 am to 5 pm, evenings and Saturdays by appointment. Full or partial restoration, collision and custom work on all years, domestic and foreign, automobiles, trucks and motorcycles. Specializing in Harley-Davidson factory correct paint schemes and color matching. Also award winning custom paint and custom designed hot rod motorcycles.

Paragon Models & Art 1431-B SE 10th St Cape Coral, FL 33990 941-458-0024; FAX: 941-574-4329 E-mail: paragonmodels-art@worldnet.att.net	artwork models

See full listing in **Section Two** under **models & toys**

Performance Coatings 9768 Feagin Rd Jonesboro, GA 30236 770-478-2775; FAX: 770-478-1926	ceramic coatings engine parts suspension parts

See full listing in **Section Two** under **exhaust systems**

The Plateman Jim Estrup 269 Webber Hill Rd Kennebunk, ME 04043 207-985-4800; FAX: 207-985-TAGS	license plates

See full listing in **Section Two** under **license plates**

Redi-Strip Company 100 W Central Ave Roselle, IL 60172 630-529-2442; FAX: 630-529-3626	abrasive media baking soda blasting paint removal rust removal

See full listing in **Section Two** under **rust removal & stripping**

Reinholds Restorations c/o Rick Reinhold PO Box 178, 255 N Ridge Rd Reinholds, PA 17569-0178 717-336-5617; FAX: 717-336-7050	appraisals repairs restoration

See full listing in **Section Two** under **restoration shops**

Rideable Antique Bicycle Replicas 2329 Eagle Ave Alameda, CA 94501 510-769-0980; FAX: 510-521-7145 E-mail: mbarron@barrongroup.com	bicycles tires

Mail order only. Specializing in 1880 full-size antique high wheel bicycles, 15 different models from 1870-1895. Solid rubber tires for pedal cars, tea carts, buggy wheel, gasoline cart. 1880 replica catalogs. Bicycle oil lamps; 1950s replica bicycles, parts, wheels, whitewall tires. Schwinn Stingray replica parts, spring forks, frames, etc. Spokes, any size, motorcycle, antique bicycle. Web site: www.hiwheel.com

Route 66 Collectible Cars and Antiques 1933 Del Monte Blvd Seaside, CA 93955 831-393-9329; FAX: 831-393-9391 E-mail: cars@route66.com	consignment sales

See full listing in **Section Two** under **car dealers**

Sanders Antique Auto Restoration 1120 22nd St Rockford, IL 61108 815-226-0535	restoration

See full listing in **Section Two** under **restoration shops**

Skopos Motor Museum Alexandra Hills, Alexandra Rd Batley West Yorkshire WA7 6JA England 01924-444423	museum

See full listing in **Section Six** under **England**

Space Farms Zoo & Museum 218 Rt 519 Sussex, NJ 07461 973-875-3223; FAX: 973-875-9397 E-mail: fpspace@warwick.net	museum zoo

See full listing in **Section Six** under **New Jersey**

Standard Abrasives Motorsports Division 4201 Guardian St Simi Valley, CA 93063 800-383-6001 805-520-5800 ext 371 FAX: 805-577-7398	abrasives

See full listing in **Section Two** under **restoration aids**

TK Performance Inc 1508 N Harlan Ave Evansville, IN 47711 812-422-6820; FAX: 812-422-5282	engine building machine work restoration

See full listing in **Section One** under **Harley-Davidson**

Toys n' Such 437 Dawson St Sault Sainte Marie, MI 49783 906-635-0356 E-mail: rtraut@portup.com	parts

Mail order only. For English cycles, 1940s-1960s, some German and Italian parts from same years, along with dealer brochures. Also buying toy motorcycles and race cars. Mopar parts for sale, NOS, 1940s-1960s; also dealer brochures for sale. US and European, including Canadian.

Walneck's Classic Cycle Trader PO Box 2576 Norfolk, VA 23501 757-640-4000; FAX: 757-314-2508	magazine

See full listing in **Section Four** under **periodicals**

Walneck's Inc 7923 Janes Ave Woodridge, IL 60517 630-985-4995; FAX: 630-985-2750	**motorcycles** **murals** **posters**

See full listing in **Section Two** under **artwork**

Wheels Through Time Museum Rt 1 Mt Vernon, IL 62864 PH/FAX: 618-244-5470 E-mail: daleshd@dales-hd.com	**museum**

See full listing in **Section Six** under **Illinois**

Xanders' Britbikes 1280 Stringtown Rd Grove City, OH 43123 614-871-9001 E-mail: norton@earthling.net	**motorcycle parts**

Mail order service. Specialists in parts, accessories and machine work for Norton Twins and unit Triumph and BSA. Bikes and parts bought and sold. Parts quotes gladly given by e-mail.

novelties

American Arrow Corp 105 Kinross Clawson, MI 48017 248-435-6115; FAX: 248-435-4670 E-mail: dsommer@greatid.com	**mascots** **wire wheel** **rebuilding**

Manufacturer of classic era parts since 1966. Pilot Ray turning lights, stainless steel mascots, metal edge windwings, tonneau windshields, new and rebuilt wire wheels and much more. Also fired porcelain license plates, art quality trophies and awards, fine art transportation collectibles and lighted Lalique mascots. Call or send for catalog. Web site: www.donsommer.com

Anderson's Car Door Monograms 32700 Coastsite #102 Rancho Palos Verdes, CA 90275 310-377-1007, 800-881-9049 FAX: 310-377-0169	**car door** **monograms**

See full listing in **Section Two** under **accessories**

Blast From the Past 1824 M St, Ste 1 Lincoln, NE 68028 402-332-5050 E-mail: blast2past@aol.com	**neon clocks** **neon signs**

See full listing in **Section Two** under **automobilia**

Bonneville Sports Inc 3544 Enterprise Dr Amaheim, CA 92807 888-999-7258, 714-666-1966 FAX: 714-666-1955 E-mail: bonspeed@aol.com	**accessories** **clothing**

See full listing in **Section Two** under **apparel**

Caddytown™/Pawl Engineering Co 4960 Arrowhead PO Box 240105 West Bloomfield, MI 48324 PH/FAX: 248-682-2007 E-mail: pawl@earthlink.net	**memorabilia** **parts** **toys**

See full listing in **Section One** under **Cadillac/LaSalle**

Car Toy Collectibles Magazine 7950 Deering Ave Canoga Park, CA 91304-5063 818-887-0550; FAX: 818-884-1343 E-mail: mail@challengeweb.com	**magazine**

See full listing in **Section Four** under **periodicals**

Ceramicar 679 Lapla Rd Kingston, NY 12401 PH/FAX: 914-338-2199	**auto-related** **ceramics**

Manufacture ceramic automobile cookie jars. Handmade in the USA. Signed and dated in limited editions of 200. Body styles are not model or year specific. They are fantasy cars that combine typical design elements of the 1930s, 1940s and 1950s. Styles include taxis, police and fire chief's cars, convertibles, ice cream, pick-up and delivery trucks. Big, (14"x9"x9"), colorful and chromy, prices average around $300. Personalization available. Please call or write for a price list and dazzling photo.

Classic Car Appraisals 37 Wyndwood Rd West Hartford, CT 06107 PH/FAX: 860-236-0125	**appraisals**

See full listing in **Section Two** under **appraisals**

Classic Car Part Art 207 S Mt Carmel Wichita, KS 67213 316-945-6865	**artwork**

See full listing in **Section Two** under **artwork**

Classic Motorcar Investments 3755 Terra Loma Dr Bullhead City, AZ 86442 520-763-5869 E-mail: classic@mohaveaz.com	**apparel**

See full listing in **Section Two** under **apparel**

Classic Transportation 3667 Mahoning Ave Youngstown, OH 44515 330-793-3026; FAX: 330-793-9729	**automobilia**

See full listing in **Section Two** under **automobilia**

Coin-Op Classics 17844 Toiyabe St Fountain Valley, CA 92708 714-968-3020; FAX: 714-963-1716 E-mail: pmovsesian@aol.com	**coin-op books** **coin-op machines**

See full listing in **Section Four** under **books & publications**

Collectibles For You 6001 Canyon Rd Harrisburg, PA 17111 717-558-2653; FAX: 717-558-7325 E-mail: cllect4you@aol.com	**memorabilia**

Mail order only. Porcelain reproduction auto signs, copper automotive printers' blocks, auto pins and jewelry. Coca-Cola, Pepsi and 1950s collectibles.

The Collector's Guild 41 Counter St Kingston, ON Canada K7K 6C7 800-653-0251; FAX: 613-536-5211 E-mail: cars@collectorsguild.on.ca	**models** **toys**

See full listing in **Section Two** under **models & toys**

Crutchfield Corp   car stereos
1 Crutchfield Park
Charlottesville, VA 22911
800-955-9009; FAX: 804-817-1010

See full listing in **Section Two** under **radios**

Richard Culleton   accessories
4318 SW 19th Pl
Cape Coral, FL 33914
800-931-7836 voice mail
315-685-7414 (home)
941-542-8640

See full listing in **Section Two** under **accessories**

Driven By Desire   automobilia
300 N Fraley St   car dealer
Kane, PA 16735   models
814-837-7590; FAX: 814-837-6850
E-mail: driven@penn.com

See full listing in **Section Two** under **car dealers**

Eurosport Daytona Inc   license plates
355 Tomoka Ave
Ormond Beach, FL 32174-6222
800-874-8044, 904-672-7199
FAX: 904-673-0821

See full listing in **Section Two** under **license plates**

Excitement Inc   decor items
1203 5th Ave
Rock Island, IL 61201
309-794-3022

Import and distribute handmade statuary (life size or jumbo).
Example: cigar store Indians, suits of armour, etc, etc. Over 75
different items.

Galaxie Ltd   kits
Box 655   model trailers
Butler, WI 53007
414-673-6386, 414-790-9922
FAX: 414-673-6366

See full listing in **Section Two** under **models & toys**

Gateway Global USA   models
10485 NW 28th St
Miami, FL 33172-2152
305-500-9641; FAX: 305-500-9642
E-mail: gatautousa@aol.com

See full listing in **Section Two** under **models & toys**

Grey Motor Co   display cabinets
18845 Van Buren Blvd 10-A
Riverside, CA 92508
800-343-5496; FAX: 909-789-9751

See full listing in **Section Two** under **automobilia**

Hale's Products   license plates
906 19th St
Wheatland, WY 82201
800-333-0989
E-mail: phale@wyoming.com

See full listing in **Section Two** under **license plates**

Historic Video Archives   videotapes
PO Box 189-VA
Cedar Knolls, NJ 07927-0189

See full listing in **Section Two** under **automobilia**

Hot Rod Cafe   gourmet coffee
1314 Rollins Rd
Burlingame, CA 94010
650-340-8669; FAX: 650-340-9473
E-mail: tonyleo@pacbell.net

Start your day with Hot Rod coffee, gourmet roasted coffee for
car collectors and hot rodders. We blend our coffee in 3 grades:
unleaded (decaffeinated), regular (our special blend) and hi-test
(our dark roast).

Hot Rod Nostalgia™   "magalog"
PO Box 249
West Point, CA 95255-0249
209-754-3697; FAX: 209-754-5521
E-mail: hvaa@hotrodnostalgia.com

See full listing in **Section Four** under **books & publications**

Hotchkiss Mfg/Clear Case   display cases
PO Box 810
Merlin, OR 97532
800-444-5005; FAX: 541-476-0268
E-mail: hotchkiss@chatlink.com

See full listing in **Section Two** under **models & toys**

Steve Jelf-14   signs
Box 200 Rt 5
Arkansas City, KS 67005
316-442-1626

See full listing in **Section Two** under **automobilia**

K&S Industries   display cases
1801 Union Center Hwy
Endicott, NY 13760
PH/FAX: 888-PICK-KNS
E-mail: pleximan@888pickkns.com

See full listing in **Section Two** under **models & toys**

Karl's Collectibles   banks
28 Bates St   collectibles
Lewiston, ME 04240   logo design
800-636-0457, 207-784-0098
FAX: 207-786-4576
E-mail:
slalemand@exploremaine.com

See full listing in **Section Two** under **models & toys**

LA Ltd Design Graphics   artwork
822A S McDuffie St   design
Anderson, SC 29624   greeting cards
PH/FAX: 864-231-7715

See full listing in **Section Two** under **automobilia**

Lone Wolf   wolf whistles
9375 Bearwalk Path
Brooksville, FL 34613
352-596-9949
E-mail: lonewolfwhistle@bigfoot.com

See full listing in **Section Two** under **automobilia**

George & Denise Long   automobilia
915 E Court St
Marion, NC 28752
828-652-9229 (24 hrs w/recorder)

See full listing in **Section Two** under **automobilia**

Larry Machacek   decals
PO Box 515   license plates
Porter, TX 77365   novelties
281-429-2505

See full listing in **Section Two** under **automobilia**

Section Two Generalists

Mercedes-Benz Visitor Center | museum
PO Box 100
Tuscaloosa, AL 35403-0100
888-2TOUR-MB, 205-507-2262
FAX: 205-507-2255

See full listing in **Section One** under **Mercedes-Benz**

MITCHCO | rubber stamps
1922 N Los Robles Ave
Pasadena, CA 91104-1105
626-401-4303

See full listing in **Section Two** under **automobilia**

MotorWeek | TV program
11767 Owings Mills Blvd
Owings Mills, MD 21117
410-356-5600; FAX: 410-581-4113
E-mail: motorweek@mpt.org

See full listing in **Section Four** under **information sources**

National Road-Zane Grey Museum | museum
8850 East Pike
Norwich, OH 43767
800-752-2602; FAX: 740-872-3510

See full listing in **Section Six** under **Ohio**

Ohio Jukebox Co | jukeboxes
6211 Cubbison Rd
Cumberland, OH 43732
740-638-5059

Mail order and open shop. Monday-Friday 9 am to 5 pm CST.
Specialize in 1950 jukeboxes. Buy, sell, repair. 5-year warranty.

Original Ford Motor Co Literature | collectibles literature
PO Box 7-AA
Hudson, KY 40145-0007
502-257-8642; FAX: 502-257-8643
E-mail: whiteb@bellsouth.net

See full listing in **Section One** under **Ford 1932-1953**

Park Avenue China Inc | ceramic mugs glassware plates
645 Evergreen Dr
East Palestine, OH 44413
330-426-3328

Mail order and open shop. Monday-Friday 9 am to 5 pm,
Saturday until 12 noon. Dealing in coffee mugs and tankards,
glazed ivory porcelain with color decal, 7 oz and 9 oz. Several
designs available. All US made. No set-up charge for custom
decal work. No minimum order. Custom auto design logo on 8-
1/2" porcelain plates available. Custom glassware also available.
Satisfaction assured. Quantity discounts, 10% discount on
orders $100 or over. All prices plus UPS. Also optional gold band
at rim. Call for details.

Past Patterns | clothing patterns
PO Box 2446
Richmond, IN 47375-2446
317-962-3333; FAX: 317-962-3773
E-mail: pastpat@thepoint.net

Mail order only. Each multi-sized pattern is a fascinating view
into the past. Victorian and Edwardian catalog, covering the
years 1830-1939, $4.

People Kars | models/more VW toys
290 Third Ave Ext
Rensselaer, NY 12144
518-465-0477; FAX: 518-465-0614
E-mail: peoplekars@aol.com

See full listing in **Section One** under **Volkswagen**

People's Choice & Lost in the 50s | 1950s clothing 1950s memorabilia automobilia items celebrity items
28170 Ave Crocker #209
Valencia, CA 91355
800-722-1965, 661-295-1965
FAX: 661-295-1931

See full listing in **Section Two** under **automobilia**

RB's Prototype/Classic Expressions | automotive artwork furniture
PO Box 16774
Stamford, CT 06905
203-329-2715; FAX: 203-329-8029
E-mail: rbproto@aol.com

See full listing in **Section Two** under **automobilia**

Re-Flex Border Marker | border markers posts
138 Grant St
Lexington, MA 02173
781-862-1343

See full listing in **Section Two** under **hardware**

Rideable Antique Bicycle Replicas | bicycles tires
2329 Eagle Ave
Alameda, CA 94501
510-769-0980; FAX: 510-521-7145
E-mail: mbarron@barrongroup.com

See full listing in **Section Two** under **motorcycles**

Joseph Russell | accessories collectibles memorabilia
455 Ollie
Cottage Grove, WI 53527
608-839-4736
E-mail: jrussell@mailbag.com

Auto memorabilia, unusual old spark plugs, collectibles,
motometers, glass swirl gearshift knobs, Ford plant badges,
license plate attachments. Model T keys, watch fobs and accessories bought and sold.

Sammy's Street Strollers | baby stroller
2725 Chinook Ct
Union City, CA 94587
510-489-3502; FAX: 510-489-2994
E-mail: sammy@slipnet.com

See full listing in **Section One** under **Ford 1932-1953**

Saturn Industries | axles/instruments literature nostalgic bits repro parts street rods
10-14 Newland St, Coleford
Royal Forest of Dean
Gloucestershire GL 16 8AN England
01594 834321; FAX: 01594 835456

See full listing in **Section One** under **Ford 1903-1931**

Scott Signal Co | stoplights
8368 W Farm Rd 84
Willard, MO 65781
417-742-5040

See full listing in **Section Two** under **automobilia**

Shines Unlimited | car buckles toys
11709 Oakland
Schoolcraft, MI 49087
616-679-4002

See full listing in **Section Two** under **models & toys**

Silver Image Photographics | business cards photo car cards photofinishing
3102 Vestal Pkwy E
Vestal, NY 13850
607-797-8795

See full listing in **Section Two** under **automobilia**

Sky Signs Balloons Ltd | balloons
Box 887
Valley Forge, PA 19481
800-582-4095, 610-933-6952
FAX: 610-935-7808
E-mail: skysigns@netreach.net

Phone and fax orders. Monday-Friday 8:30 am to 5 pm. Stand out from the crowd. Giant blimps and balloons. Use indoors or outdoors. Advertise your name, logo or product line. Make product replicas, animals, character shapes, seasonal decorations and banners. Web site: www.skysignsballoons.com

Supercar Collectibles Ltd | muscle car replicas
7311-75th Circle N
Minneapolis, MN 55428
612-425-6020; FAX: 612-425-3357

See full listing in **Section Two** under **models & toys**

Peter Tytla Artist | photographic collages
PO Box 43
East Lyme, CT 06333-0043
860-739-7105

See full listing in **Section Two** under **artwork**

Weber's Nostalgia Supermarket | collectibles
6611 Anglin Dr | gas pump supplies
Fort Worth, TX 76119 | old photos
817-534-6611; FAX: 817-534-3316 | signs

Mail order and open shop. Monday-Friday 9 am to 5 pm. Specializing in gas pump restoration, supplies, ie: globes, signs, decals, hoses, nozzles, glass, rubber, etc. Also large selection of gameroom decor and old photos. Ship immediately, worldwide. Dealer inquiries welcome. Catalog free with order or $4, refundable.

Yankee Candle Car Museum | museum
Yankee Candle Co Rt 5
South Deerfield, MA 01373
413-665-2020; FAX: 413-665-2399

See full listing in **Section Six** under **Massachusetts**

painting

Ace Antique Auto Restoration | air conditioning
65 S Service Rd | body rebuilding
Plainview, NY 11803 | restoration
516-752-6065; FAX: 516-752-1484 | wiring harnesses

See full listing in **Section Two** under **restoration shops**

Auto Restoration by William R Hahn | custom work
Palermo Auto Body | restoration
241 Church Rd (rear)
Wexford, PA 15090
724-935-3790 shop
412-367-2538 home
FAX: 724-935-9121

See full listing in **Section Two** under **restoration shops**

Automotive Restorations Inc | body fabrication
Kent S Bain | mechanical
1785 Barnum Ave | painting
Stratford, CT 06614 | restorations
203-377-6745; FAX: 203-386-0486 | upholstery
E-mail: carbain@compuserve.com | woodwork

See full listing in **Section Two** under **restoration shops**

Bay Area Industrial Dry Stripping | blasting
151 11th St | paint removal
Richmond, CA 94801-3523
510-412-9890, 510-805-1887

See full listing in **Section Two** under **rust removal & stripping**

Cars of the Past | restoration
11180 Kinsman Rd
Newbury, OH 44065
440-564-2277

See full listing in **Section Two** under **restoration shops**

CJ Spray Inc | painting equipment
370 Airport Rd
South St Paul, MN 55075
800-328-4827 ext 1240
FAX: 651-450-5671

Mail order and open shop. Monday-Friday 8 am to 5 pm CST. Spray painting equipment.

Classic Auto | restoration
251 SW 5th Ct
Pompano Beach, FL 33060
PH/FAX: 954-786-1687

See full listing in **Section Two** under **restoration shops**

Classic Auto Rebuilders/CAR | painting/plating
Box 9796 | restoration
Fargo, ND 58106 | woodwork

See full listing in **Section Two** under **restoration shops**

Classic Auto Restoration | acquisitions
15445 Ventura Blvd #60 | restoration
Sherman Oaks, CA 91413 | sales
818-905-6267; FAX: 818-906-1249
E-mail: rollsroyce1@earthlink.net

See full listing in **Section One** under **Rolls-Royce/Bentley**

Classics Plus LTD | restoration
N7306 Lakeshore Dr
N Fond du Lac, WI 54937
888-923-1007

See full listing in **Section Two** under **steering wheels**

County Auto Restoration | bodywork
6 Gavin Rd | brakes
Mt Vernon, NH 03057 | restoration
603-673-4840 | woodwork

See full listing in **Section Two** under **restoration shops**

Dan's Restorations | woodgraining
PO Box 144
Snake Hill Rd
Sand Lake, NY 12153
518-674-2061

See full listing in **Section Two** under **woodgraining**

Davies Corvette | accessories
7141 US Hwy 19 | parts
New Port Richey, FL 34653
727-842-8000, 800-236-2383
FAX: 727-846-8216
E-mail: davies@corvetteparts.com

See full listing in **Section One** under **Corvette**

The Eastwood Company-Tools | plating & polishing
Box 296 | powder coating
Malvern, PA 19355-0714 | restoration aids
800-345-1178 | rustproofing
FAX: 610-644-0560 | sandblasters/welders

See full listing in **Section Two** under **tools**

Grey Hills Auto Restoration PO Box 630 51 Vail Rd Blairstown, NJ 07825 908-362-8232; FAX: 908-362-6796	**restoration service**

See full listing in **Section Two** under **restoration shops**

Hatfield Restorations PO Box 846 Canton, TX 75103 903-567-6742; FAX: 903-567-0645 E-mail: pathat@vzinet.com	**restoration**

See full listing in **Section Two** under **restoration shops**

High Performance Coatings 550 W 3615 S Salt Lake City, UT 84115 800-456-4721, 801-262-6807 FAX: 801-262-6307 E-mail: hpcsales@hpcoatings.com	**coatings**

See full listing in **Section Two** under **exhaust systems**

Hjeltness Restoration Inc 630 Alpine Way Escondido, CA 92029 760-746-9966; FAX: 760-746-7738	**restoration service**

See full listing in **Section Two** under **restoration shops**

Hyde Auto Body 44-1/2 S Squirrel Rd Auburn Hills, MI 48326 PH/FAX: 248-852-7832 E-mail: bodyman8@juno.com	**refinishing restoration**

See full listing in **Section Two** under **restoration shops**

L & N Olde Car Co 9992 Kinsman Rd PO Box 378 Newbury, OH 44065 440-564-7204; FAX: 440-564-8187	**restoration**

See full listing in **Section Two** under **restoration shops**

Lake Buchanan Industries Inc Rt 1, Box 184-C Buchanan Dam, TX 78609 888-552-5278 toll-free 512-793-2867; FAX: 512-793-2869 E-mail: lbi:@tstar.net	**blasting cabinet**

See full listing in **Section Two** under **tools**

Libbey's Classic Car Restoration Center 137 N Quinsigamond Ave Shrewsbury, MA 01545 PH/FAX: 508-792-1560	**bodywork restoration service**

See full listing in **Section Two** under **restoration shops**

Nationwide Auto Restoration 1038 Watt St Jeffersonville, IN 47130 812-280-0165; FAX: 812-280-8961 E-mail: restore@unidial.com	**bodywork paint upholstery**

See full listing in **Section Two** under **restoration shops**

Old Coach Works Restoration Inc 1206 Badger St Yorkville, IL 60560-1701 630-553-0414; FAX: 630-553-1053 E-mail: oldcoachworks@msn.com	**appraisals restoration**

See full listing in **Section Two** under **restoration shops**

Pilgrim's Auto Restorations 3888 Hill Rd Lakeport, CA 95453 707-262-1062; FAX: 707-263-6956 E-mail: pilgrims@pacific.net	**bodywork metal fabrication paint restoration**

See full listing in **Section Two** under **restoration shops**

PK Lindsay Co Inc 63 Nottingham Rd Deerfield, NH 03037 800-258-3576; FAX: 800-843-2974	**paint removal rust removal**

See full listing in **Section Two** under **rust removal & stripping**

Pro-Strip 2415 W State Blvd Fort Wayne, IN 46808 219-436-2828; FAX: 219-432-1941 E-mail: prostrip@tk7.net	**paint removal rust removal**

See full listing in **Section Two** under **rust removal & stripping**

Redi-Strip Company 100 W Central Ave Roselle, IL 60172 630-529-2442; FAX: 630-529-3626	**abrasive media baking soda blasting paint removal rust removal**

See full listing in **Section Two** under **rust removal & stripping**

Restorations Unlimited II Inc 304 Jandus Rd Cary, IL 60013 847-639-5818	**restoration**

See full listing in **Section Two** under **restoration shops**

Rick's Relics Wheeler Rd Pittsburg, NH 03592 603-538-6612	**bodywork painting restoration**

See full listing in **Section Two** under **restoration shops**

Riverbend Abrasive Blasting 44308 St Rt 36 W Coshocton, OH 43812-9741 614-622-0867	**blasting painting polishing restoration**

See full listing in **Section Two** under **rust removal & stripping**

Ed Rouze 406 Sheila Blvd Prattville, AL 36066 334-365-2381	**painting guide book**

Mail order only. Author of comprehensive how-to automobile painting guide, *Paint Your Car Like A Pro*. Details every step from start to finish, written in easy to understand language. Also author of *555 Restoration, Performance & Appearance Tips*, a compilation of 555 restoration tips in a 120-page book using the same easy to read format, covers everything from air compressors to welding.

T Schmidt 827 N Vernon Dearborn, MI 48128-1542 313-562-7161	**rust removers**

See full listing in **Section Two** under **rust removal & stripping**

Steck Manufacturing Co Inc 1115 S Broadway Dayton, OH 45408 800-227-8325; FAX: 937-222-6666	**tools**

See full listing in **Section Two** under **tools**

Stone Barn Inc
202 Rt 46, Box 117
Vienna, NJ 07880
908-637-4444; FAX: 908-637-4290

restoration

See full listing in **Section Two** under **restoration shops**

TiP Tools & Equipment
7075 Route 446, PO Box 649
Canfield, OH 44406
330-533-3384 local
800-321-9260 US/Canada
FAX: 330-533-2876

abrasive blasters
air compressors
tools

See full listing in **Section Two** under **restoration aids**

Vampire Products
50 Four Coins Dr
Canonsburg, PA 15317
800-866-7260; FAX: 724-745-6040
E-mail: vampire@hanseninc.com

air dryers
filters

See full listing in **Section Two** under **restoration shops**

Verne's Chrome Plating Inc
1559 W El Segundo Blvd
Gardena, CA 90249
323-754-4126; FAX: 323-754-3873

chrome plating
polishing
powder coating

See full listing in **Section Two** under **plating & polishing**

Willhoit Auto Restoration
1360 Gladys Ave
Long Beach, CA 90804
562-439-3333; FAX: 562-439-3956

engine rebuilding
restoration

See full listing in **Section One** under **Porsche**

paints

Automotive Paints Unlimited
4585 Semora Rd
Roxboro, NC 27573
336-599-5155

acrylic enamels
acrylic lacquers
paints
polyurethanes

Mail order and open shop. Monday-Friday 9 am to 5 pm. Supplier of paints for vehicles, 1904-present. In business since 1976. The paint place.

Color-Ite Refinishing Co
Winning Colors
868 Carrington Rd, Rt 69
Bethany, CT 06524
203-393-0240; FAX: 203-393-0873
E-mail: colorite@ctinternet.com

modern finishes
restoration service

Mail order and open shop. Monday-Friday 9 am to 5 pm, Saturday 9 am to 2 pm. Original paint colors in modern finishes. Restorations and sales of original 1940-1948 Lincoln Continentals, full or partial restorations, specializing in early Lincolns. Also, master chip booklets for selected models. Focus has changed from restorations to the paint and leather finishes. Manufacturers are Sherwin-Williams for the paint and SEM for the leather/vinyl colorants. Web site: www.color-ite.com

The Finished Look
PO Box 191413
Sacramento, CA 95819-1413
800-827-6715; FAX: 916-451-3984
E-mail: info@thefinishedlook.com

POR-15 products

See full listing in **Section Two** under **rustproofing**

Hibernia Auto Restorations Inc
52 Maple Terr
Hibernia, NJ 07842
973-627-1882; FAX: 973-627-3503

lacquer
restoration

See full listing in **Section Two** under **restoration shops**

Bill Hirsch Auto Parts
396 Littleton Ave
Newark, NJ 07103
973-642-2404; FAX: 973-642-6161
E-mail: hirschauto@aol.com

enamel lacquer
hubcaps
top material

Mail order and open shop. Monday-Friday 8 am to 4 pm. Manufacturer of hubcaps for Cadillac, Chevrolet, Buick, Packard, Ford, Pierce-Arrow. Engine enamels for most American cars, exhaust and manifold paints, gas tank sealer, gas preservative, miracle rustproof paint, leather, broadcloth, Bedford cloth, top material, carpet, carpet sets, car covers, convertible tops, much more. Web site: www.hirschauto.com

Imperial Restoration Inc
308 Lockport St
Lemont, IL 60439
630-257-5822
FAX: 630-257-5892

chassis coatings
engine enamels
gas tank sealer
paint/rust remover
rust preventives

See full listing in **Section Two** under **restoration aids**

JCM Industries
2 Westwood Dr
Danbury, CT 06811
800-752-0245

wax hardener

See full listing in **Section Two** under **car care products**

Magnet Paint
1701 Utica Ave
Brooklyn, NY 11234
800-922-9981; FAX: 718-253-4430
E-mail: magneter@ix.netcom.com

clear coats
paints
primers

Deal in high-performance automotive refinish and industrial maintenance paints, primers, clear coats and specialty products. Finishes include acrylic urethanes, acrylic enamels and synthetics. Web site: www.magnetpaint.com

Maintenance Specialties Company
21 Valley Forge Rd
PO Box 251
New Castle, DE 19720
800-777-6715; FAX: 302-328-2315

rustproofing paints

See full listing in **Section Two** under **rustproofing**

OEM Paints Inc
PO Box 461736
Escondido, CA 92046-1736
760-747-2100

custom
aerosol colors

Offer unique, innovative and Ecoformulated™ custom aerosols that meet highest standards of quality and performance. These are the latest and hottest upscale finishes for those who demand authenticity. Experience popular original equipment colors manufactured with todays technology. Best of all they are made in the USA and licensed by major automotive manufacturers. Web site: oempaints.com

Quanta Restoration and Performance Products
743 Telegraph Rd
Rising Sun, MD 21911-1810
800-235-8788, 410-658-5700
FAX: 410-658-5758
E-mail: quanta@quantaproducts.com

fan belts
gas tanks

See full listing in **Section Two** under **chassis parts**

Ed Rouze
406 Sheila Blvd
Prattville, AL 36066
334-365-2381

painting guide book

See full listing in **Section Two** under **painting**

Tar Heel Parts Inc
PO Box 2604
Matthews, NC 28106-2604
800-322-1957, 704-753-9114 (local)
FAX: 704-753-9117

buffing supplies

See full listing in **Section Two** under **plating & polishing**

Tower Paint Co Inc
Box 2345
Oshkosh, WI 54903
920-235-6520; FAX: 920-235-6521
E-mail: tpi@towerpaint.com

paint

Paint and custom spray cans for 1930-present for auto's engine, frame, interior and exterior. Web site: www.towerpaint.com

petroliana

GA$OLINE

Antiques Warehouse
Michael J Welch
3700 Rt 6
Eastham, MA 02642
508-255-1437; FAX: 508-247-9166
E-mail: miketoys1@aol.com

automobilia
bikes
toy trucks

See full listing in **Section Two** under **models & toys**

Asheville DieCast
1434 Brevard Rd
Asheville, NC 28806-9560
800-343-4685, 888-343-4685
704-667-9690; FAX: 704-667-1110
E-mail: sales@asheville-diecast.com

banks
models

See full listing in **Section Two** under **models & toys**

Automobilia Auctions Inc
132 Old Main St
Rocky Hill, CT 06067
860-529-7177; FAX: 860-257-3621

appraisals
auctions

See full listing in **Section Two** under **auctions & events**

Berliner Classic Motorcars Inc
1975 Stirling Rd
Dania, FL 33004
954-923-7271; FAX: 954-926-3306
E-mail: sales@motorcars.com

automobilia
car dealer
motorcycles

See full listing in **Section Two** under **car dealers**

Blast From the Past
1824 M St, Ste 1
Lincoln, NE 68028
402-332-5050
E-mail: blast2past@aol.com

neon clocks
neon signs

See full listing in **Section Two** under **automobilia**

Brisson Enterprises
PO Box 1595
Dearborn, MI 48121-1595
313-584-3577

lead

See full listing in **Section Two** under **car care products**

"Check The Oil!" Magazine
PO Box 937
Powell, OH 43065-0937
614-848-5038; FAX: 614-436-4760

magazine

Bi-monthly publication for enthusiasts and collectors of the memorabilia and history of the petroleum industry. Anything associated with the oil and gas business of days gone by, eg: gas pumps, globes, signs, maps, oil bottles, etc. Subscription: $21.95/year US, $30/year Canada, $37/year overseas.

Classic Transportation
3667 Mahoning Ave
Youngstown, OH 44515
330-793-3026; FAX: 330-793-9729

automobilia

See full listing in **Section Two** under **automobilia**

Fantasy Models
PO Box 570
Wright City, MO 63390
888-745-8254; FAX: 800-745-8254
E-mail: scale43@inlink.com

models

See full listing in **Section Two** under **models & toys**

Fill Er Up
Brian Steiner
2613 Old Philadelphia Pike
PO Box 406
Bird In Hand, PA 17505
717-397-2519

automobilia
petroliana

See full listing in **Section Two** under **automobilia**

Steve Jelf-14
Box 200 Rt 5
Arkansas City, KS 67005
316-442-1626

signs

See full listing in **Section Two** under **automobilia**

Dave Lincoln
Box 331
Yorklyn, DE 19736
610-444-4144, PA
E-mail: tagbarn@msn.com

license plates

See full listing in **Section Two** under **license plates**

George & Denise Long
915 E Court St
Marion, NC 28752
828-652-9229 (24 hrs w/recorder)

automobilia

See full listing in **Section Two** under **automobilia**

Manchester Motor Car Co
319 Main St
Manchester, CT 06040
860-643-5874; FAX: 860-643-6190
E-mail: mmcollc@aol.com

automobilia
parts
petroliana
restorations

See full listing in **Section Two** under **comprehensive parts**

Max Neon Design Group
19807 Sussex Dr
St Clair Shores, MI 48081-3257
810-773-5000; FAX: 810-772-6224

custom face logos
glass light-up
clocks
neon clocks

See full listing in **Section Two** under **automobilia**

McIntyre Auctions
PO Box 60
East Dixfield, ME 04227
800-894-4300, 207-562-4443
FAX: 207-562-4576
E-mail:
classicford@quickconnect.com

auctions
automobilia
literature
petroliana

See full listing in **Section Two** under **auctions & events**

Miracle of America Museum 58176 Hwy 93 Polson, MT 59860 406-883-6804 E-mail: museum@cyberport.net	**museum**

See full listing in **Section Six** under **Montana**

Petro Classics 8829 W Camino De Oro Peoria, AZ 85382 602-825-9070; FAX: 602-825-7030 E-mail: bj@petroclassics.com	**collectibles** **restoration**

Mail order and open shop. Monday-Friday 9 am to 5 pm. Deal in petroliana restoration, Pepsi-Cola collectibles, amusement rides and pedal cars. Web site: www.petroclassics.com

The Plateman Jim Estrup 269 Webber Hill Rd Kennebunk, ME 04043 207-985-4800; FAX: 207-985-TAGS	**license plates**

See full listing in **Section Two** under **license plates**

Red Crown Automobilia 1720 Rupert NE Grand Rapids, MI 49505 616-361-9887	**automobilia** **petroliana**

Mail order, swap meets. Specializing in petroliana, automotive memorabilia, auto promotional items, dealer giveaways and oil company collectibles.

Red Lion Racing 8318 Avenida Castro Cucamonga, CA 91730 909-987-9818; FAX: 909-987-6538 E-mail: rlracing@cris.com	**photographs** **posters**

See full listing in **Section Two** under **artwork**

Jack Schmitt Studio PO Box 1761 San Juan Capistrano, CA 92693	**paintings** **prints**

See full listing in **Section Two** under **artwork**

Ron Scobie Enterprises 7676 120th St N Hugo, MN 55038 651-653-6503 E-mail: rscobie@gaspump.com	**gas pump parts**

Manufacturing parts for antique gasoline pumps and air meters. Also make "Master" oil bottle spouts from the original machines. Web site: www.gaspump.com

Scott Signal Co 8368 W Farm Rd 84 Willard, MO 65781 417-742-5040	**stoplights**

See full listing in **Section Two** under **automobilia**

Town & Country Toys 227 Midvale Dr PO Box 574 Marshall, WI 53559 608-655-4961 E-mail: dejaeger@itis.com	**banks** **Ertl cars** **mini license plates**

See full listing in **Section Two** under **models & toys**

Valenti Classics Inc 355 S Hwy 41 Caledonia, WI 53108 414-835-2070; FAX: 414-835-2575 E-mail: vci@valenticlassics.com	**collectibles** **restoration** **sales** **service**

See full listing in **Section Two** under **car dealers**

Vic's Place Inc 124 N 2nd St Guthrie, OK 73044 405-282-5586; FAX: 405-282-6850 E-mail: vics@telepath.com	**restoration parts**

Shop open Monday-Saturday 8 am to 5 pm. Restoration parts for all makes of gas pumps. 40 page color catalog available. Restoration and original pumps available. 5,000 square foot shop.

Vintage Shop Coats 40 Fourth St #106 Petaluma, CA 94952 925-837-7869; FAX: 707-762-7901	**shop coats**

See full listing in **Section Two** under **apparel**

Zephyrhills Festivals and Auction Inc PO Box 848 Odessa, FL 33556 office: 813-920-7206 FAX: 813-920-8512 Park: 813-782-0835 FAX: 813-780-7863	**auction** **swap meet**

See full listing in **Section Two** under **auctions & events**

photography

Big Time Productions 780 Munras Ave Monterey, CA 93940 831-655-0409; FAX: 831-375-9102 E-mail: bigtime@redshift.com	**video production**

See full listing in **Section Two** under **videos**

Boop Photography 2347 Derry St Harrisburg, PA 17104-2728 717-564-8533 E-mail: msboop@paonline.com	**photography**

Mail order and open shop. Sunday-Saturday 9 am to 9 pm EST. Automotive photography, drag racing, classics, street rods. Former car club photographer. Nikon equipment. 7 years' experience. Degree in photography.

Gerry Cappel Photographic 5340 Stonehaven Dr Yorba Linda, CA 92887 714-779-5180; FAX: 714-779-2740 E-mail: gcappel@csi.com	**photography**

Deal in photography of classic and collector automobiles.

Car Critic 202 Woodshire Ln Naples, FL 34105 941-435-1157; FAX: 941-261-4864 E-mail: puppys4u@aol.com	**appraisals** **inspections**

See full listing in **Section Two** under **appraisals**

Larry Couzens Photography
16 E 17th St
New York, NY 10003
212-620-9790; FAX: 212-620-9791

photography

Custom photography of automobiles for individuals, car clubs and businesses. Highly experienced in all camera formats and film sizes. Still photography and video services available. Local and out of town assignments accepted.

Richard Hamilton
28 E 46th St
Indianapolis, IN 46205
317-283-1902

sales literature

See full listing in **Section Two** under **literature dealers**

Hot Rod Nostalgia™
PO Box 249
West Point, CA 95255-0249
209-754-3697; FAX: 209-754-5521
E-mail: hvaa@hotrodnostalgia.com

"magalog"

See full listing in **Section Four** under **books & publications**

The Klemantaski Collection
65 High Ridge Rd, Suite 219
Stamford, CT 06905
PH/FAX: 203-968-2970
E-mail: klemcoll@aol.com

books
photography

Mail order only. Motor racing photography by Louis Klemantaski, Nigel Snowdon, Robert Daley, Alan R Smith, Colin Waldeck and Edward Eves. Also publish books of our photographs. Supply enthusiasts, collectors, authors and publishers worldwide.

LA Ltd Design Graphics
822A S McDuffie St
Anderson, SC 29624
PH/FAX: 864-231-7715

artwork
design
greeting cards

See full listing in **Section Two** under **automobilia**

The Last Precinct Police Museum
15677 Hwy 62 W
Eureka Springs, AR 72632
501-253-4948; FAX: 501-253-4949

museum

See full listing in **Section Six** under **Arkansas**

David Lawrence Gallery
PO Box 3702
Beverly Hills, CA 90212
310-278-0882; FAX: 310-278-0883

artwork
drawings
photography

See full listing in **Section Two** under **artwork**

Photographs on Canvas by Tom Bork
PO Box 1121
Grants Pass, OR 97528
541-474-0854
E-mail: bork@cdsnet.net

photo alteration
photography

Mail order only. Take your photograph and print it on canvas suitable for framing. Can also alter photographs (remove people from car picture) or put your car on a different background.

Practical Images
PO Box 245
Haddam, CT 06438-0245
860-704-0525
E-mail: practimages@snet.net

int'l VHS video
conversions
photo scanning
photography

Mail order only. Digital photo scanning (photos, slides, negatives, artwork), International VHS video conversions, freelance photography (for advertisements, personal, legal, insurance, etc). Please write for more information. Web site: www.practimages.com

Red Lion Racing
8318 Avenida Castro
Cucamonga, CA 91730
909-987-9818; FAX: 909-987-6538
E-mail: rlracing@cris.com

photographs
posters

See full listing in **Section Two** under **artwork**

Silver Image Photographics
3102 Vestal Pkwy E
Vestal, NY 13850
607-797-8795

business cards
photo car cards
photofinishing

See full listing in **Section Two** under **automobilia**

Richard Spiegelman Productions Inc
19 Guild Hall Dr
Scarborough, ON Canada M1R 3Z7
416-759-1644
E-mail: carphoto@interlog.com or
carphoto@yahoo.com

photography
slides

See full listing in **Section Four** under **information sources**

Sunflower Studios
8 Scottsdale Rd
South Burlington, VT 05403
802-862-3768
E-mail:
sunflowerstudios@worldnet.att.net

photography

Fine art automobile photography on location. Specialists in car show photography.

Jay Texter
417 Haines Mill Rd
Allentown, PA 18104
610-821-0963
E-mail: jaytexter@ot.com

photography

Automotive and motorsport photography, editorial, advertising or private commissions. Traditional or electronic output. Immortalize your vehicle or mobilia collection with a sense of style. Quality and craftsmanship guaranteed. Web site: www.jaytexter.com

Peter Tytla Artist
PO Box 43
East Lyme, CT 06333-0043
860-739-7105

photographic
collages

See full listing in **Section Two** under **artwork**

plaques

Bright Displays
1314 Lakemont Dr
Pittsburgh, PA 15243
PH/FAX: 412-279-7037

molded auto logos
neon signs

See full listing in **Section Two** under **automobilia**

Classic Car Appraisals
37 Wyndwood Rd
West Hartford, CT 06107
PH/FAX: 860-236-0125

appraisals

See full listing in **Section Two** under **appraisals**

Nostalgic Reflections
PO Box 350
Veradale, WA 99037
PH/FAX: 509-226-3522

custom etched plates
dash glass/decals
porcelain radiator
medallions/scripts

Mail order and open shop. Monday-Saturday 8 am to 6 pm. Reproduction serial plates, decals, door sill plates, porcelain medallions, instrument faces, dash glass, special castings and plating, radiator scripts.

O'Brien Truckers	**accessories**
5 Perry Hill	**belt buckles**
North Grafton, MA 01536-1532	**plaques**
508-839-3033; FAX: 508-839-9490	**valve covers**
E-mail: obt@ziplink.net	

Mail order only. Cast aluminum car club plaques, belt buckles and key chains. Air cleaners and nostalgic engine accessories. Complete line of No Club Lone Wolf items, license plate toppers, valley covers, Hemi valve covers, lake pipe caps and many other nostalgic accessories.

Photo Plaque Design	**car show plaques**
16508 McKinley St	**dash plaques**
Belton, MO 64012	
PH/FAX: 816-331-4073	
E-mail: photodezin@aol.com	

Specializing in custom engraved car event awards and participant dash plaques. Your cars and ideas can be captured on a one of a kind photo engraved plaque to commemorate your event. Our photo engraving has the highest resolution available today for remarkable, finely detailed, engraved images. New process, 4-color digital printed plaques now available. Send SASE for catalogue and sample. Web site: http://members.aol.com/PHOTODEZIN/Plaques.html

plastic parts

Autolux Inc	**Mercedes parts**
23242 Tasmania Cir	
Dana Point, CA 92629	
949-493-5578; FAX: 949-493-3710	

See full listing in **Section One** under **Mercedes-Benz**

The Bumper Doctor	**bumpers**
9188 E San Salvador #101	**parts**
Scottsdale, AZ 85258	
602-314-1349; FAX: 602-314-3717	
E-mail: bumperdoc@aol.com	

We train individuals to repair all automotive plastic parts. Bumpers are our main business, we recycle all urethane and plastic bumpers to as-new condition.

D&D Automobilia	**plastic parts**
813 Ragers Hill Rd	**steering wheels**
South Fork, PA 15956	
814-539-5653	

See full listing in **Section Two** under **steering wheels**

Emblemagic Co	**decorative**
PO Box 420	**emblems**
Grand River, OH 44045-0420	**plastic insert**
440-209-0792	**emblems**
E-mail: arborhil@aol.com	

See full listing in **Section Two** under **grille emblem badges**

Karmann Ghia Parts & Restoration	**parts**
PO Box 997	
Ventura, CA 93002	
800-927-2787; FAX: 805-641-3333	
E-mail: info@karmannghia.com	

See full listing in **Section One** under **Volkswagen**

National Parts Depot	**accessories**
3101 SW 40th Blvd	**restoration parts**
Gainesville, FL 32608	
800-874-7595 toll-free 24 hours	
352-378-2473 local	

See full listing in **Section Two** under **comprehensive parts**

Yesterday's Radio	**interior plastic**
7759 Edgewood Ln	**radio parts**
Seven Hills, OH 44131-5902	
PH/FAX: 216-524-2018	
E-mail: jerry@yesterdaysradio.com	

See full listing in **Section One** under **Packard**

plating & polishing

A & A Plating Inc	**plating**
9400 E Wilson Rd	**polishing**
Independence, MO 64053	
816-833-0045; FAX: 816-254-1517	

Mail order and open shop. Monday-Friday 7 am to 6 pm, Saturday 8 am to 12 pm. Chrome, nickel and copper plating for steel, aluminum, die cast and brass, cast iron, pot metal. Polishing of stainless steel, brass, aluminum, copper, nickel and silver.

See our ad on this page

ACPlating | **plating**
Division of SUM Inc
317 Mt Vernon
Bakersfield, CA 93307
661-324-5454; FAX: 661-324-5381

Mail order and open shop. Monday-Friday 8 am to 4:30 pm PST. Founded in 1975, ACPlating has focused on providing the professional and amateur auto restorer the avenue to return all their brightwork to better than new condition. Stainless steel, pot metal, steel bumpers and brass parts are all meticulously stripped, straightened, hand polished, copper plated, copper buffed, pitfilled, then nickel and chrome plated. For all your high quality needs in metal finishing visit ACPlating. Web site: ac-plating.com

Advanced Plating & Powder Coating | **accessories chrome parts polishing**
955 E Trinity Ln
Nashville, TN 37207
800-588-6686, 615-227-6900
FAX: 615-262-7935

Mail order and open shop. Monday-Friday 8 am to 4:30 pm, Saturday 8 am to 12 noon. Custom polishing, chrome, nickel, copper, acid copper, black chrome, 24 kt gold, powder coating. Specialize in the restoration and repair of pot metal, grilles, bumpers and aluminum. Complete restoration service, all work guaranteed. Chrome parts and accessories for GM. Web site: www.advancedplating.com

See our ad on this page

Ano-Brite Inc | **anodizing polishing restoration welding**
6945 Farmdale Ave
North Hollywood, CA 91605
818-982-0997; FAX: 818-982-0804
E-mail: ano-brite@hotmail.com

Mail order and open shop. Monday-Friday 8:30 am to 4:30 pm. Deal in aluminum and stainless steel trim restoration, anodizing, straightening, polishing and welding. Web site: www.anobrite.com

Bassett Classic Restoration | **parts plating restoration service**
2616 Sharon St, Suite D
Kenner, LA 70062
PH/FAX: 504-469-2982
(have auto switching device)

See full listing in **Section One** under **Rolls-Royce/Bentley**

Caswell Electroplating in Miniature | **plating kits**
4336 Rt 31
Palmyra, NY 14522
315-597-5140, 315-597-6378
FAX: 315-597-1457
E-mail: sales@caswellplating.com

Professional quality plating kits for chrome, nickel, black oxide, anodizing, zinc and chromating, silver and gold, copper, cadmium, brass. Tanks, heaters, chemicals and manuals. Complete line of professional buffing and polishing tools and supplies. Web site: www.caswellplating.com

Chevi Shop Custom Casting | **custom castings parts**
338 Main Ave
Box 75
Milledgeville, IL 61051
815-225-7565; FAX: 815-225-7616

See full listing in **Section One** under **Chevrolet**

Chrome Masters | **chrome plating pot metal restoration**
4509 Wimbleton Ct
Tallahassee, FL 32310
850-576-2100; FAX: 850-576-2772

Mail order and open shop. Monday-Saturday 8 am to 6 pm. Restoration of pitted pot metal and chrome plating for all vintage, antique car buffs.

Circle N Stainless | **stainless steel trim restoration**
1517 NW 33rd
Lawton, OK 73505
580-355-9366
E-mail: neald@juno.com

See full listing in **Section Two** under **special services**

Classic Auto Rebuilders/CAR | **painting/plating restoration woodwork**
Box 9796
Fargo, ND 58106

See full listing in **Section Two** under **restoration shops**

Classic Auto Restoration | **appraisals plating/polishing restoration**
437 Greene St
Buffalo, NY 14212
716-896-6663

See full listing in **Section Two** under **restoration shops**

Classics Plus LTD | **restoration**
N7306 Lakeshore Dr
N Fond du Lac, WI 54937
888-923-1007

See full listing in **Section Two** under **steering wheels**

County Auto Restoration	bodywork
6 Gavin Rd	brakes
Mt Vernon, NH 03057	restoration
603-673-4840	woodwork

See full listing in **Section Two** under **restoration shops**

Custom Plating	bumper specialist
3030 Alta Ridge Way	chrome plating
Snellville, GA 30278	parts
770-736-1118	

Chrome plating of bumpers, engine parts, suspension parts, interior and exterior parts, pot metal. Polishing and straightening of aluminum and stainless trim. 39 years' experience.

CustomChrome Plating Inc	electroplating
963 Mechanic St	plating
PO Box 125	polishing
Grafton, OH 44044	
440-926-3116	

Mail order and open shop. Monday-Thursday 8 am to 5 pm, Friday 8 am to 4 pm. Polishing, buffing and electroplating. Chrome, nickel, copper plating on customer's parts.

D & D Plastic Chrome Plating	chroming
Jim & Marty Price	plating
4534 S Detroit Ave	
Toledo, OH 43614	
419-389-1748	

Monday-Saturday. Rechrome your plastic or fiberglass parts such as dash bezels, armrests, etc. Put the interior of your collector car back to the original finish. 3 week turnaround.

Dalmar	electroplating
11759 S Cleveland Ave, Suite 28	plating supplies
Ft Myers, FL 33907	
941-275-6540; FAX: 941-275-1731	
E-mail: dalmar@peganet.com	

Electroplating and electroforming equipment, chemicals, supplies and kits. Featuring chrome, nickel, gold, copper, silver, brass, bronze and cadmium plating. Our kits will plate on metallic and non-metallic surfaces. Manufacture both brush and tank plating kits. Free catalog. Complete catalog and prices on our web site: www.dalmarplating.com

Mike Drago Chevy Parts	Chevrolet parts
141 E St Joseph St	
Easton, PA 18042	
PH/FAX: 610-252-5701	
E-mail: dragomdcp@aol.com	

See full listing in **Section One** under **Chevrolet**

Fini-Finish Metal Finishing	plating
24657 Mound Rd	polishing
Warren, MI 48091	pot metal repair
810-758-0050; FAX: 810-758-0054	

Polishing and buffing on all metals. Copper, nickel, chrome and cadmium plating on all metals. Repair work on pot metal (zinc die cast) our specialty.

Gold Plated Emblems & Auto Accessories	plating equipment
2095 Pine Ridge Rd	wood dash kits
Naples, FL 34109	
800-231-7765, 941-592-5552	
FAX: 941-597-0768	
E-mail: sales@goldplated.com	

Mail order and open shop. Manufacturing of gold plating equipment chemicals, wood dash kits, pre-gold plated car emblem kits, windshield repair kits for most American and imported autos. Web site: goldplated.com

Hanlon Plating Co Inc	plating
925 E 4th St	
Richmond, VA 23224	
804-233-2021	

Replating of old car, boat, cycle parts, etc. Repairing damaged or bent bumpers.

Impala Bob's Inc	restoration parts
4753 E Falcon Dr	
Dept HVAA14	
Mesa, AZ 85215	
800-IMPALAS orders	
480-924-4800 retail store	
480-981-1600 office	
FAX: 800-716-6237, 480-981-1675	
E-mail: info@impalas.com	

See full listing in **Section One** under **Chevrolet**

Iverson Automotive	polishes
14704 Karyl Dr	pot metal
Minnetonka, MN 55345	restoration
800-325-0480; FAX: 612-938-5707	

Mail order and open shop. Monday-Saturday 8:30 am to 6:30 pm. Stainless, pot metal and aluminum trim restoration. Have developed a 10-step state of the art process to put the life and luster back into dented, scratched and deteriorated auto trim. There is a critical difference between polishing auto trim and restoring auto trim, anyone can polish. Also manufacture stainless, aluminum and chrome polishes called "Iverson Automotive Secret Sauce". Do all the work myself and guarantee your satisfaction.

Lake Buchanan Industries Inc	blasting cabinet
Rt 1, Box 184-C	
Buchanan Dam, TX 78609	
888-552-5278 toll-free	
512-793-2867; FAX: 512-793-2869	
E-mail: lbi:@tstar.net	

See full listing in **Section Two** under **tools**

Martin's of Philadelphia	buffing
7327 State Rd	copper plating
Philadelphia, PA 19136	metal grinding
215-331-5565; FAX: 215-331-7113	

Specialize in copper plating, nickel and chrome, metal grinding buffing of antique, classic auto parts, also boats, barber chairs, etc. Any collectible for refinishing of all auto parts for all years, makes and models. Have been offering the finest quality chrome for 38 years and our work is guaranteed.

Master Plating	plating
2109 Newton Ave	restoration
San Diego, CA 92113	
619-232-3092; FAX: 619-232-3094	

Repair/restoration of plated parts of all makes and models. Replate with copper, nickel, chrome, to show quality (100 point or very close).

Paul's Chrome Plating Inc
90 Pattison St
Evans City, PA 16033
800-245-8679, 724-538-3367
FAX: 724-538-3403
E-mail: pcp@fyi.net

repair
restoration

Mail order and open shop. Monday-Friday 8 am to 5 pm, Wednesday evening 7 pm to 8:30 pm, Saturday by appointment only. Triple plate rechroming, repair and restoration of all metal parts, including pot metal (zinc die cast).

Pot Metal Restorations
4794 C Woodlane Cir
Tallahassee, FL 32303
850-562-3847; FAX: 850-562-0538

pot metal restoring/
rechroming

Mail order and open shop. Monday-Friday 8 am to 5 pm. Pitted pot metal restoration and rechroming.

Precision Pot Metal/Bussie Restoration Inc
1008 Loring Ave #28
Orange Park, FL 32073
904-269-8788

pot metal
restoration

Open Monday-Friday 8 am to 5 pm. Pot metal repair and chroming, plastic parts rechromed, full auto restoration or partial restorations and painting.

Qual Krom-Great Lakes Plant
4725-A Iroquois Ave
Erie, PA 16511
800-673-2427; FAX: 814-899-8632

plating
repairs
restoration

Mail order and open shop. Monday-Friday 8 am to 5 pm, Saturday by appointment. Custom restoration plating of your parts, guaranteed show quality only. Do all repairs necessary to restore your steel, zinc die castings and stainless steel parts.

The Reflected Image
21 W Wind Dr
Northford, CT 06472
PH/FAX: 203-484-0760
E-mail: scott@reflectedimage.com

mirror
reproduction
mirror resilvering

See full listing in **Section Two** under **special services**

Riverbend Abrasive Blasting
44308 St Rt 36 W
Coshocton, OH 43812-9741
614-622-0867

blasting
painting/polishing
restoration

See full listing in **Section Two** under **rust removal & stripping**

Samson Technology Corporation
2280 SW 70th Ave #3
Davie, FL 33317
PH/FAX: 954-916-9322
E-mail: samson@icanect.net

anodizing
car cover
chrome plating
electroplating
systems

Mail order and open shop. Manufacturer of portable and tank electroplating systems as well as the JetCover, the retractable car cover. Also offer a complete line of electroplating and buffing supplies. Portable anodizing and heavy chrome plating systems. Web site: samson24k.com

Standard Abrasives Motorsports Division
4201 Guardian St
Simi Valley, CA 93063
800-383-6001
805-520-5800 ext 371
FAX: 805-577-7398

abrasives

See full listing in **Section Two** under **restoration aids**

Star Chrome
4009 Ogden Ave
Chicago, IL 60623
312-521-9000

plating
polishing

Mail order and open shop. Monday-Saturday 6 am to 12 noon. Chrome, gold, and nickel plating and polishing for antique and classic cars, street rods and motorcycles. Specializing in pot metal repair and restoration of the highest quality. Work taken only in the morning. All work show quality and guaranteed. In business since 1970.

Supreme Metal Polishing
84A Rickenbacker Cir
Livermore, CA 94550
925-449-3490; FAX: 925-449-1475
E-mail: supremet@home.com

metal working
parts restoration
plating services
polishing

Priceless parts finished to impeccable standards. Special attention to reflective clarity and trueness of linear reflections. Delicate finishing of precision machined parts. 28 years of show winners ranging from "America's most beautiful roadster" to 1998 Pebble Beach Best of Show. Serving both private and professional restorers and enthusiasts. References available upon request.

See our ad on this page

Tar Heel Parts Inc
PO Box 2604
Matthews, NC 28106-2604
800-322-1957, 704-753-9114 (local)
FAX: 704-753-9117

buffing supplies

Mail order only. Buffing specialty and auto restoration supply company. Offer Baldor buffers, buffing supplies, arbors and mandrels, abrasives, flanging pliers, Seymour paints, sandblasters, bead blast cabinets, and more. Please call for more information and a complimentary catalog.

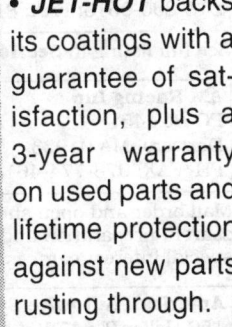

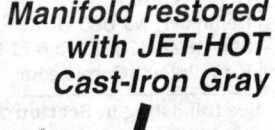
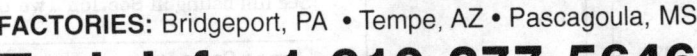

TiP Tools & Equipment
7075 Route 446, PO Box 649
Canfield, OH 44406
330-533-3384 local
800-321-9260 US/Canada
FAX: 330-533-2876

abrasive blasters
air compressors
tools

See full listing in **Section Two** under **restoration aids**

Verne's Chrome Plating Inc
1559 W El Segundo Blvd
Gardena, CA 90249
323-754-4126; FAX: 323-754-3873

chrome plating
polishing
powder coating

Restoration quality polishing and chrome plating. We are not a big bumper outfit or production shop, we are a small restoration shop. In business since 1959.

racing

356 Enterprises
Vic & Barbara Skirmants
27244 Ryan Rd
Warren, MI 48092
810-575-9544; FAX: 810-558-3616

parts

See full listing in **Section One** under **Porsche**

Action Performance Inc
1619 Lakeland Ave
Bohemia, NY 11716
516-244-7100; FAX: 516-244-7172

accessories

See full listing in **Section Two** under **accessories**

Air Flow Research
10490 Ilex Ave
Pacoima, CA 91331
818-890-0616; FAX: 818-890-0490

cylinder heads

See full listing in **Section One** under **Chevrolet**

AM Racing Inc
PO Box 451
Danvers, MA 01923
PH/FAX: 978-774-4613

race prep
sales
vintage racing

Mail order and open shop. Monday-Friday 8 am to 5 pm. Sales, search, preparation and showing of vintage, historic, classic and special interest cars, especially racing, 1940s-1960s.

American Autowire Systems Inc
150 Heller Pl #17W
Dept HVAA99
Bellmawr, NJ 08031
800-482-9473; FAX: 609-933-0805
E-mail: facfit@erols.com

battery cables
electrical systems
switches/components

See full listing in **Section Two** under **street rods**

Andy's Classic Mustangs
18502 E Sprague
Greenacres, WA 99016
509-924-9824

parts
service

See full listing in **Section One** under **Mustang**

Skip Barber Racing School
29 Brook St
Lakeville, CT 06039
800-221-1131; FAX: 860-435-1321
E-mail: speed@skipbarber.com

racing school

The Skip Barber Racing School, the world's largest, offers on-track racing programs for experienced vintage competitors and aspiring racers alike, ranging from the 3 hour *Introduction to*

Racing (sm) to the industry standard *Three Day Racing School (sm)*. Classes are taught in open-wheel Formula Dodge race cars and are available nationwide. Also offer advanced street driving schools, teaching street-based defensive driving techniques. Call for details. Web site: www.skipbarber.com

Bonk's Automotive Inc
4480 Lazelda Dr
Milan, MI 48160
800-207-6906; FAX: 734-434-0845
E-mail: bonkers@bonkauto.com

automotive tools

See full listing in **Section Two** under **tools**

Bonneville Sports Inc
3544 Enterprise Dr
Amaheim, CA 92807
888-999-7258, 714-666-1966
FAX: 714-666-1955
E-mail: bonspeed@aol.com

accessories
clothing

See full listing in **Section Two** under **apparel**

Boop Photography
2347 Derry St
Harrisburg, PA 17104-2728
717-564-8533
E-mail: msboop@paonline.com

photography

See full listing in **Section Two** under **photography**

BPE Racing Heads
702 Dunn Way
Placentia, CA 92870
714-572-6072; FAX: 714-572-6073
E-mail: steve@bpeheads.com

cylinder heads

See full listing in **Section Two** under **machine work**

British Only Motorcycles and Parts Inc
32451 Park Ln
Garden City, MI 48135
734-421-0303; FAX: 734-422-9253
E-mail: info@british-only.com

literature
memorabilia
motorcycles
parts

See full listing in **Section Two** under **motorcycles**

Classic Carriages
267 County Rd 420
Athens, TN 37303
PH/FAX: 423-744-7496

repair
restoration

See full listing in **Section One** under **Ford 1932-1953**

Cobra Restorers Ltd
3099 Carter Dr
Kennesaw, GA 30144
770-427-0020; FAX: 770-427-8658

parts
restoration
service

See full listing in **Section One** under **Cobra**

Coffey's Classic Transmissions
2290 W Hicks Rd, Unit 42
Hanger 30-1
Ft Worth, TX 76111
817-439-1611

transmissions

See full listing in **Section Two** under **transmissions**

Crane Cams Inc
530 Fentress Blvd
Daytona Beach, FL 32114
904-258-6174; FAX: 904-258-6167

camshafts

See full listing in **Section Two** under **camshafts**

Doug's Corvette Service | race prep
11634 Vanowen St | repairs
North Hollywood, CA 91605
818-765-9117

See full listing in **Section One** under **Corvette**

DTE Motorsports | engines
242 South Rd | mechanical
Brentwood, NH 03833 | services
PH/FAX: 603-642-3766 | race prep
E-mail: ldnh49a@prodigy.com | transportation

See full listing in **Section One** under **Mercedes-Benz**

Dual Connection | models
Box 569 | toys
Gibsonia, PA 15044
724-898-9660; FAX: 724-898-9680
E-mail: rich@dualconnection.com

See full listing in **Section Two** under **models & toys**

Freddie Beach Restoration | accessories
1834 Woodstock Rd | restoration parts
Fredericton, NB Canada E3C 1L4
506-450-9074; FAX: 506-459-0708
E-mail: vallise@city.fredericton.nb.ca

See full listing in **Section Two** under **car & parts locators**

George's Speed Shop | machine shop
716 Brantly Ave | race engine building
Dayton, OH 45404 | race engine parts
937-233-0353; FAX: 937-236-3501

Open shop only. Stock to full race engine parts and building. Full machine shop service. Two in-house dyno cells.

Grand Prix Classics Inc | racing cars
7456 La Jolla Blvd | sports cars
La Jolla, CA 92037
619-459-3500; FAX: 619-459-3512

In business for twenty years and specialize in the buying and sellling of historic sports cars and racing cars. On display in our facility you will find 10-15 historically significant cars. Active participants in historic racing events worldwide. If you have a car to sell or are looking for a special car to buy, feel free to contact us. Learn more about us by looking at our web page. Web site: www.grandprixclassics.com

Gromm Racing Heads | cylinder heads
664-J Stockton Ave | racing parts
San Jose, CA 95126
408-287-1301

Open Monday-Friday 8:30 am to 5:30 pm. Specializing in hi-performance (racing, RV and vintage) cylinder heads and racing parts sales.

Historic Video Archives | videotapes
PO Box 189-VA
Cedar Knolls, NJ 07927-0189

See full listing in **Section Two** under **automobilia**

Hooker Headers | exhaust systems
1024 W Brooks St
Ontario, CA 91762
909-983-5871; FAX: 909-986-9860

See full listing in **Section Two** under **exhaust systems**

Hot Rod Nostalgia™ | "magalog"
PO Box 249
West Point, CA 95255-0249
209-754-3697; FAX: 209-754-5521
E-mail: hvaa@hotrodnostalgia.com

See full listing in **Section Four** under **books & publications**

J & C's Parts | parts
7127 Ward Rd
North Tonawanda, NY 14120
716-693-4090; FAX: 716-695-7144

See full listing in **Section One** under **Buick/McLaughlin**

Koffel's Place II | engine rebuilding
740 River Rd | machine shop
Huron, OH 44839
419-433-4410; FAX: 419-433-2166

See full listing in **Section Two** under **engine rebuilding**

Krem Engineering | engine rebuilding
10204 Perry Hwy | repairs
Meadville, PA 16335 | restoration
814-724-4806; FAX: 814-337-2992
E-mail: info@krem-enterprises.com

See full listing in **Section Two** under **restoration shops**

Lindskog Balancing | engine balancing
1170 Massachusetts Ave
Boxborough, MA 01719-1415
978-263-2040; FAX: 978-263-4035

See full listing in **Section Two** under **engine rebuilding**

M & R Products | hardware
1940 SW Blvd | tie-downs
Vineland, NJ 08360
800-524-2560, 609-696-9450
FAX: 609-696-4999
E-mail: mrproducts@mrproducts.com

See full listing in **Section Two** under **accessories**

Main Attractions | posters
PO Box 4923 | videos
Chatsworth, CA 91311
818-709-9855; FAX: 818-998-0906

See full listing in **Section Four** under **information sources**

Marcovicci-Wenz Engineering Inc | Cosworth engines
33 Comac Loop
Ronkonkoma, NY 11779
516-467-9040; FAX: 516-467-9041
E-mail: tedwenz@compuserve.com

Mail order and open shop. Monday-Saturday 8 am to 6 pm. Specializing in engine parts and services for road racing motors of the 1960s, 1970s and 1980s. Also Cosworth and Ferrari.

McGee Motorsports Group | race prep
29127 Arnold Dr | restoration
Sonoma, CA 95476
707-996-1112; FAX: 707-996-9148

Open Monday-Friday 8:30 am to 6 pm, often weekends. Located at Sears Point International Raceway. Modern and vintage race car preparation, fabrication, restoration. Car and driver on-track development and training. Custom modifications or authentic restorations. Modification, fabrication and development for current race cars.

Mid Valley Engineering 16637 N 21st St Phoenix, AZ 85022 602-482-1251; FAX: 602-788-0812	**machine work** **parts** **restoration**

See full listing in **Section Two** under **transmissions**

Moroso Motorsports Park PO Box 31907 Palm Beach Gardens, FL 33420 561-622-1400; FAX: 561-626-2053 E-mail: racetrack@moroso.com	**race track**

Daily 9 am to 5 pm. Multi-purpose year round race track with a 2.25 mile road course and 1/4 mile NHRA drag strip. Weekly races Wednesday, Friday and Saturday and special events monthly that feature car shows, swap meets and restoration market place. Exhibition cars include Jet Funny cars, dragsters, trucks, top fuel, pro mods. Web site: goracing.com/moroso

MotorCam Media 138 N Alling Rd Tallmadge, OH 44278 800-240-1777; FAX: 330-633-3249 E-mail: carvideo@motorcam.com	**automotive videos**

See full listing in **Section Two** under **videos**

Motorsports Racing 914 S Santa Fe #101 Vista, CA 92084 760-630-0547; FAX: 760-630-3085	**accessories** **apparel** **art**

See full listing in **Section Two** under **apparel**

Museum of the Spa-Francorchamps Track Old Abbey 4970 Stavelot Belgium PH/FAX: 080-8627-06	**museum**

See full listing in **Section Six** under **Belgium**

OJ Rallye Automotive PO Box 540 N 6808 Hwy OJ Plymouth, WI 53073 920-893-2531; FAX: 920-893-6800 E-mail: ojrallye@excel.net	**accessories** **car care products** **lighting parts**

See full listing in **Section Two** under **lighting equipment**

Pikes Peak Auto Hill Climb Educational Museum 135 Manitou Ave Manitou Springs, CO 80829 719-685-4400; FAX: 719-685-4400 E-mail: ppihc@ppihc.com	**museum**

See full listing in **Section Six** under **Colorado**

Power Effects® 1800H Industrial Park Dr Grand Haven, MI 49417 877-3POWRFX toll-free 616-847-4200 FAX: 616-847-4210	**exhaust systems**

See full listing in **Section Two** under **exhaust systems**

R & L Engines Inc 308 Durham Rd Dover, NH 03820 603-742-8812; FAX: 603-742-8137	**engine rebuilding** **restorations**

See full listing in **Section Two** under **engine rebuilding**

RD Enterprises Ltd 290 Raub Rd Quakertown, PA 18951 215-538-9323; FAX: 215-538-0158 E-mail: rdent@rdent.com	**parts**

See full listing in **Section One** under **Lotus**

Red Lion Racing 8318 Avenida Castro Cucamonga, CA 91730 909-987-9818; FAX: 909-987-6538 E-mail: rlracing@cris.com	**photographs** **posters**

See full listing in **Section Two** under **artwork**

Replicarz 99 State St Rutland, VT 05701 802-747-7151 E-mail: replicarz@aol.com	**books** **kits** **models** **videos**

Mail order only. Die cast miniature models, plastic model kits, books, videos. Specialize in racing, current and Vintage Formula 1, Indy, DTM, WSC, LeMans and more.

Garry Roberts & Co 922 Sunset Dr Costa Mesa, CA 92627 714-650-2690; FAX: 714-650-2730 E-mail: garryroberts@fea.net	**cars** **parts** **service**

See full listing in **Section One** under **Ferrari**

Ross' Automotive Machine Co Inc 1763 N Main St Niles, OH 44446 330-544-4466	**racing engines** **rebuilding**

See full listing in **Section Two** under **engine rebuilding**

RPM Catalog PO Box 12031 Kansas City, KS 66109 913-788-3219; FAX: 913-788-9682 E-mail: dale@dalewilch.com	**parts** **speed equipment**

Catalog listing of used race cars and hot rod cars, parts and equipment. Subscription: $20/year. Web site: www.dalewilch.com

Doug Schellinger 13717 W Green Meadow Dr New Berlin, WI 53151 414-786-8413 E-mail: dsac@execpc.com	**automobilia** **books** **sales literature** **toys**

See full listing in **Section One** under **Fiat**

Simons Balancing & Machine Inc 1987 Ashley River Rd Charleston, SC 29407 843-766-3911; FAX: 843-766-9003	**machine work**

See full listing in **Section Two** under **machine work**

Speed & Spares America (IPM Group) 16117 Runnymede St, Unit H Van Nuys, CA 91406-2913 818-781-1711; FAX: 818-781-8842 E-mail: jaydalton@earthlink.net	**parts** **racing equipment**

See full listing in **Section Two** under **comprehensive parts**

Ed Swart Motors Inc — cars / parts / restoration
2675 Skypark Dr, Unit 104
Torrance, CA 90505
310-530-9715; FAX: 310-530-9786

See full listing in **Section One** under **Bitter**

Tatom Vintage Vendors — engine rebuilding / machine shop
PO Box 2504
Mt Vernon, WA 98273
360-424-8314; FAX: 360-424-6717
E-mail: flatheads@tatom.com

See full listing in **Section Two** under **engine rebuilding**

Thompson Hill Metalcraft — metal forming / panel beating / welding
23 Thompson Hill Rd
Berwick, ME 03901
207-698-5756
E-mail: wpeach@thompsonhill.com

See full listing in **Section Two** under **sheetmetal**

Edward Tilley Automotive Collectibles — automobilia / literature / parts
PO Box 4233
Cary, NC 27519-4233
919-460-8262
E-mail: edandsusan@aol.com

See full listing in **Section Two** under **automobilia**

Total Seal Inc — piston rings
11202 N 24th Ave, Ste 101
Phoenix, AZ 85029
602-678-4977; FAX: 602-678-4991
E-mail: totseal@amug.org

See full listing in **Section Two** under **engine parts**

Valco Cincinnati Consumer Products Inc — adhesives / detailing products / sealants / tools
411 Circle Freeway Dr
Cincinnati, OH 45246
513-874-6550; FAX: 513-874-3612

See full listing in **Section Two** under **tools**

Vicarage Jaguar — parts / restoration
5333 Collins Ave Suite 502
Miami Beach, FL 33140
305-866-9511; FAX: 305-866-5738
E-mail: vicarage@ix.netcom.com

See full listing in **Section One** under **Jaguar**

Vintage Racing Services — storage / track support / transportation
1785 Barnum Ave
Stratford, CT 06497
203-386-1736; FAX: 203-386-0486
E-mail: vrs@vintageracingservices.com

Open Monday-Friday 9 am to 6 pm, Saturday by appointment. Shop address: 305 Sniffens Ln, Stratford, CT 06497; office located at above address. Vintage race car restoration, preparation and track support. Transport to and attend over 25 US and international events each year. US agents for Elva cars. Specialize in Elva, Lotus, Chevron and other post war British purpose built race cars in addition to Porsche, BMW, Datsun and other production vehicles. Web site: www.vintageracingservices.com

Kirk F White — models / tin toys
PO Box 999
New Smyrna Beach, FL 32170
904-427-6660; FAX: 904-427-7801

See full listing in **Section Two** under **models & toys**

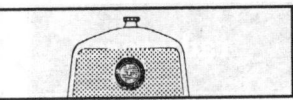

radiator emblems & mascots

Dwight H Bennett — emblem repair / hardware repair / mascot repair / plaque repair
1330 Ximeno Ave
Long Beach, CA 90804
PH/FAX: 562-498-6488

Mail order and open shop by arrangement, 7 days. Deal in repair, restoration and reproduction of metal cast and/or fabricated objects that other people say are irreparable such as: emblems, enameled emblems, chrome strips, trim, mascots, hardware, photo etched plaques, silkscreen plaques, white metal repair, door handles, knobs, etc. Also do prototyping and custom one-off pieces.

bentleydriversclub.com — car dealer / collectibles
23238 Erwin St
Woodland Hills, CA 91367
818-887-6557; FAX: 818-346-3627
E-mail: glwales@aol.com

See full listing in **Section One** under **Rolls-Royce/Bentley**

Brass Script — brass script
Arthur Evans
32 Richmond-Belvidere Rd
Bangor, PA 18013-9544
610-588-7541

Brass script for antique car radiators. Over 800 original scripts. SASE required for pencil rub and price.

Emblemagic Co — decorative emblems / plastic insert emblems
PO Box 420
Grand River, OH 44045-0420
440-209-0792
E-mail: arborhil@aol.com

See full listing in **Section Two** under **grille emblem badges**

Jay M Fisher — mascots / sidemount mirrors / windwing brackets
Acken Dr 4-B
Clark, NJ 07066
732-388-6442

See full listing in **Section Two** under **accessories**

Gaylord Sales — automobilia / automotive art / mascots
Frank Ranghelli
125 Dugan Ln
Toms River, NJ 08753
732-349-9213; FAX: 732-341-5353

Mail order, car shows (mostly the big ones, Carlisle, Hershey, Auburn, etc). Mascots, automotive art: paintings, bronzes, collector posters, all forms of automobilia. Have been doing the above for 23 years. Always interested in purchasing items.

Pulfer & Williams — mascots / nameplates / radiator emblems
213 Forest Rd
PO Box 67
Hancock, NH 03449-0067
603-525-3532; FAX: 603-525-4293

Mail order only. Manufacture emblems, nameplates, handles reproduction mascots.

Section Two Generalists

radiators

American Honeycomb Radiator Mfg Co — manufacturing, repairs
Neil Thomas
171 Hwy 34
Holmdel, NJ 07733
718-948-7772 days
732-946-8743 eves

Mail order and open shop. Monday-Friday 9 am to 4 pm EST. Manufacturer of cartridge type and cellular antique radiators. Also manufacture odd one-of-a-kind radiators and refurbish antique radiators. Exhibited in national and private airplane and automobile museums. Send for free color brochure.
See our ad on this page

Blaak Radiateurenbedryf — radiators
Blaaksedyk oost 19
Heinenoord 3274LA Netherlands
31-186-601732; FAX: 31-186-603044
E-mail: info@blaak.com

Mail order and open shop. Monday-Friday 8:30 am to 5:30 pm. Specializing in pre-1940 radiators. All types of cellular and cartridge honeycomb cores. Web site: www.blaak.com

The Brassworks — radiators
289 Prado Rd
San Louis Obispo, CA 93401
800-342-6759; FAX: 805-544-5615

Mail order and open shop. Monday-Friday 8 am to 5 pm. Manufacture all foreign and domestic radiators, 1890s-up. Model T to Rolls-Royce and everything in between. All work guaranteed. Ship worldwide.

Cal West Auto Air & Radiators Inc — a/c condensers, fan shrouds, gas tanks, heaters, radiators
24309 Creekside Rd #119
Valencia, CA 91355
800-535-2034; FAX: 805-254-6120
E-mail: mike@calwest-radiators.com

Mail order and open shop. Monday-Saturday; open 24 hrs/7 days for emergencies. Radiators (new, recored and custom), air conditioning condensers and heaters. 1955-1957 Chevy, Camaro, Corvette, Mustang and T-Bird radiators. Antique radiators available. Custom catalog available. Automotive products online. Web site: www.calwestauto.com

The Copper Cooling Works — radiators
2455 N 2550 E
Layton, UT 84040
801-544-9939

Mail order only. Build new, exact copies of the disc and tube radiators used on the early chain drive cars. Started in 1966 and have had many new radiators on top winning cars throughout the world. Specializing in Cadillac and Oldsmobile.

Gano Filter — coolant filters
1205 Sandalwood Ln
Los Altos, CA 94024
650-968-7017

Mail order only. In-line coolant filter, prevents radiator clogging. Permanent, easily cleaned accessory, available in brass or transparent, durable thermoplastic. Kits include necessary clamps and instructions for proper installation. Plastic kits $25 each or 2/$46; brass kits $32 or 2/$60. Also available: heater core filter in brass, $15 each. All prices include shipping. Satisfaction guaranteed or money back. Free information and wholesale prices on request.

Gas Tank and Radiator Rebuilders — abrasive blasting, gas tank rebuilding, heaters, radiator repair
20123 Hwy 362
Waller, TX 77484
800-723-3759
E-mail: donhart@donhart.com

See full listing in **Section Two** under **fuel system parts**

Highland Radiator Inc — parts, service
Rt 9 W
Highland, NY 12528
914-691-7020; FAX: 914-691-2489

Mail order and open shop. Monday-Friday 8 am to 5 pm. Complete auto radiator repair and services facility. Specializing in antique, classic, special interest and all types of automotive radiators. Expertly repaired, restored, rebuilt or recored, quality craftsmanship. Honeycomb cores available. 40 years' experience.

Mac's Radiator Service & Gas Tank Renu LA — gas tanks, radiators
9681 Alondra Blvd
Bellflower, CA 90706
562-920-1871; FAX: 562-920-8491
E-mail: bruce@macs-radiator.com

Mail order and open shop. Monday-Saturday 8 am to 5 pm. New gas tanks, gas tank restoration, extra capacity gas tanks for trucks and vans, Griffin all aluminum racing radiators, copper/brass radiators, plastic tank radiators, motorcycle trank restoration, gas tank sending units rebuilding. Web site: www.macs-radiator.com

Montclair Radiator Service — fuel tanks, radiators
10598 Rose Ave
Montclair, CA 91763
909-621-9531

Shop open Monday-Friday 7 am to 5 pm, Saturday 7 am to 12 noon. Modification of radiators. Work on all types of cars including desert cool, cellular, heavy duty and CL cores. Specializing in antique car radiators. Also restored fuel tanks. Twenty-three years' experience.

| National Parts Depot
3101 SW 40th Blvd
Gainesville, FL 32608
800-874-7595 toll-free 24 hours
352-378-2473 local | **accessories**
restoration parts |

See full listing in **Section Two** under **comprehensive parts**

| Obsolete Chevrolet Parts Co
524 Hazel Ave
PO Box 68
Nashville, GA 31639-0068
800-248-8785; FAX: 912-686-3056
E-mail: obschevy@surfsouth.com | **engine parts**
radiators
rubber parts
transmissions |

See full listing in **Section One** under **Chevrolet**

| Phelan Antique Auto Parts
73 Hillview St
Hamilton
Guelph, ON Canada L8S 2Z3
905-527-0002; FAX: 905-527-5929
E-mail: phelanantiqueauto@hwcn.org | **parts** |

See full listing in **Section One** under **Ford 1903-1931**

| Powell Radiator Service
1277 W Main St, Box 427
Wilmington, OH 45177
937-382-2096 | **restoration** |

Mail order and open shop. Monday-Friday 8 am to 5 pm EST. Show quality restorations on any type or year of radiator (except aluminum). Some old radiators in stock needing restoration but available for sale or restoration.

| Glen Ray Radiators Inc
2105 Sixth St
Wausau, WI 54401
800-537-3775 | **rebuilding**
recoring |

Mail order and open shop. Monday-Friday 7 am to 5:30 pm. Radiator rebuilding and recoring.

| Raybuck Autobody Parts
RD 4, Box 170
Punxsutawney, PA 15767
814-938-5248; FAX: 814-938-4250 | **body parts** |

See full listing in **Section Two** under **body parts**

| RB's Obsolete Automotive
7711 Lake Ballinger Way
Edmonds, WA 98026-9163
425-670-6739; FAX: 425-670-9151
E-mail: rbobsole@gte.net | **parts** |

See full listing in **Section Two** under **comprehensive parts**

| S & S Antique Auto
Pine St
Deposit, NY 13754
607-467-2929; FAX: 607-467-2109 | **parts** |

See full listing in **Section One** under **Ford 1932-1953**

| Southern Rods & Parts Inc
2125 Airport Rd
Gleer, SC 29651
864-848-0601; FAX: 864-801-0601 | **accessories**
headlights
power windows
radiators |

See full listing in **Section Two** under **street rods**

| Vintage Wings and Radiators
Lord North St
Miles Platting
Manchester M40 8H7   England
PH/FAX: 0161 202 6247 | **body panels**
radiator cores |

Suppliers of wings and other body panels in steel and aluminum, radiator cores (tubular and film type) in brass, gilled tubes and dummy honeycombs.

radios

| Antique Automobile Radio Inc
700 Tampa Rd
Palm Harbor, FL 34683
800-933-4926, 727-785-8733
FAX: 727-789-0283
E-mail:
sales@antiqueautomobileradio.com | **radio accessories**
radio parts
stereo conversions |

Mail order and open shop. Monday-Friday 8 am to 4:30 pm EST. Manufacture over 60 types of radio vibrators, power inverters (to operate 12-volt accessories on 6-volt systems) and FM conversion kits. Stocks speakers, tubes, transformers, antennas, dial glass. 3,500+ radios in inventory. Visa, MasterCard, Discover. Free catalog. Dealer inquiries invited. Web site: antiqueautomobileradio.com

| Antique Radio Doctor
Barry Dalton
196 Kilborn Dr
Grants Pass, OR 97526
541-474-2524 evenings | **radio repairs** |

Mail order only. Deal in the repair of vintage auto radios, 1930-1965, GM, Ford, Mopar. Free estimate of repairs. Rapid turnaround. Please, no tape decks. Specializing in vacuum tube gear.

| Antique Radio Service
12 Shawmut Ave
Wayland, MA 01778
800-201-2635; FAX: 508-653-2418 | **radio service** |

Mail order and open shop. Monday-Friday 8:30 am to 5:30 pm by appointment. Radios bought, sold, traded, restored, rebuilt; speaker repair, vibrators; FM conversions, stereo conversions, power inverters and boosters.

| Bob's Radio & TV Service
238 Ocean View
Pismo Beach, CA 93449
805-773-8200 | **radios** |

Mail order and open shop with radio museum. Monday-Friday and most Saturdays 8 am to 5:30 pm. Vintage car radio restorations and FM additions, 1932-1970, most models, American only. Flat rates to repair/overhaul. Vintage home radios are also welcome. No parts for sale. Visa and MasterCard accepted. Web site: www.netceptions.com/bobs

| Classic Car Radio Service®
25 Maple Rd
PO Box 764
Woodacre, CA 94973
415-488-4596; FAX: 415-488-1512
E-mail: healy@classicradio.com | **radio repair**
radio restoration |

Radio repair and restoration. Five year, parts and labor, written transferrable guarantee. The only true bargain is quality. Don't spoil the "pride of your car", insist on authentic restoration maintaining the value and integrity of your classic automobile. The best sound, the best performance. MasterCard and Visa accepted. The original Classic Car Radio Service®. Web site: www.classicradio.com/

| The Classic Motorist
PO Box 363
Rotterdam Junction, NY 12150-0363 | automotive books
literature
motoring accessories |

See full listing in **Section Two** under **automobilia**

| Crutchfield Corp
1 Crutchfield Park
Charlottesville, VA 22911
800-955-9009; FAX: 804-817-1010 | car stereos |

Car stereo components and systems, home theater and home audio, video, car security products, telephones, extensive technical support available on 800 line for customers. Free catalog. Web site: www.crutchfield.com

| Custom Autosound Mfg
808 W Vermont Ave
Anaheim, CA 92805
800-888-8637; FAX: 714-533-0361
E-mail: info@custom-autosound.com | CD players
custom radios
speaker upgrades |

See full listing in **Section One** under **Chevrolet**

| Elliott's Car Radio
313 Linfield Rd
Parkerford, PA 19457
610-495-6360; FAX: 610-495-7723 | radio repairs
speaker kits |

Mail order and open shop. Monday-Friday 9 am to 5 pm. Specializing in the repair of car radios and tape decks. Repair and sales of car radios 1958-1990. Speaker kits for Chevelle 1965-1972, speaker kits for GM cars 1965-1980. Radio and speaker wiring for GM 1960-1990.

Radio Pushbuttons Above Control   6 disc CD Player ▲   Model USA-05 shown in a '55 Chevrolet

New! AM-FM Cassette, CD Controller Radio to Fit Classic Vehicles!
100 watt, full feature, including Compact Disc Player controls from radio pushbuttons. Optional 6-Disc Player for a complete modern audio system. Available for all classic applications.

New! SECRETAUDIO Hidden AM/FM Compact Disc Audio System!
Secretaudio is a computer modem sized unit for easy installation under dash, seat or glove box. A great solution for any vehicle. Features AM/FM stereo - 100 Watts CD changer controller. Wireless remote. Controls all functions of radio. Remote sensor has hinged mount to swivel under dash when not in use. Available for all classic applications.

CALL FOR A LOCAL DEALER REFERENCE - FREE CATALOG
1-800-88-TUNES

http://www.custom-autosound.com
808 WEST VERMONT AVE. ANAHEIM, CA 92805

| Jim Gensch
1810 Juliet
St Paul, MN 55105
612-690-2029 | radios
repair
vibrators |

Mail order and open shop by appointment only. Vintage car and home radio repair, 1920s-1960. Hundreds of restored car radios in stock through the 1970s.

| Grossmueller's Classic Corvette
55 Sitgreaves St
Phillipsburg, NJ 08865
610-258-2028; FAX: 610-258-7013, PA
E-mail: wfg@gccorvettes.com | NOS parts
used parts |

See full listing in **Section One** under **Corvette**

| William Hulbert Jr
PO Box 151
13683 Rt 11
Adams Center, NY 13606
315-583-5765 | radios |

Radios, pre-1959. Restored sets for sale or restore yours. Dead sets taken on trade. One year guarantee after you've installed it in your car and are using it. Will also trade for parts for my own cars and trucks.

| Jukebox Friday Night
1114 Robert Dr
Cochran, GA 31014
912-934-8866 | parts
repairs
restoration |

Mail order only. Repair, restore, parts for home and car radios. Repair, parts for juke boxes. Electronic parts: tubes, vibrators, transformers.

| Marquette Radio
7852 W Sycamore Dr
Orland Park, IL 60462
708-633-0545
E-mail: alsvir@ameritech.net | radios
tape players |

Mail order and open shop. Original 1963-1985 factory AM-FM radios and tape players.

| Michigan Corvette Recyclers
11995 US 223
Riga, MI 49276
800-533-4650; FAX: 517-486-4124 | Corvette parts
new/used parts |

See full listing in **Section One** under **Corvette**

| National Parts Depot
3101 SW 40th Blvd
Gainesville, FL 32608
800-874-7595 toll-free 24 hours
352-378-2473 local | accessories
restoration parts |

See full listing in **Section Two** under **comprehensive parts**

| Normans' Classic Auto Radio
7651 Park Blvd
Pinellas Park, FL 33781
888-222-3433, 727-546-1788 | custom sales |

Mail order and open by appointment. Radio sales of custom AM/FM cassette radios that fit and fill original dash openings without modifications. Prices start at $159. Also CD changers and FM converters. No repairs or conversions.

| Passenger Car Supply
102 Cloverdale Rd
Swedesboro, NJ 08085
609-467-7966 | parts |

See full listing in **Section One** under **Chevrolet**

Prestige Thunderbird Inc
10215 Greenleaf Ave
Santa Fe Springs, CA 90670
800-423-4751, 562-944-6237
FAX: 562-941-8677
E-mail:
tbirds@prestigethunderbird.com

	appraisals
	radios
	repairs
	restorations
	tires

See full listing in **Section One** under **Thunderbird**

Southern Autotronics Inc
3300 Norfolk St
Richmond, VA 23230
804-353-5400, 800-446-2880
FAX: 804-358-3216
E-mail: ecs@carradio.com

	radio restorations
	repairs
	speedometers

Mail order and open shop. Monday-Saturday 8 am to 5:30 pm. Automobile radio restorations, 1940-up. Vacuum tube, transistor and digital. Wonderbar, 8-tracks, cassette and CD players rebuilt. Factory authorized Ford, GM-Delco and Blaupunkt, Pioneer, Sony Clarion car audio. Custom installations at our 6 Virginia and North Carolina stores. Repair over 1,000 units nationwide a week. Warrant the entire unit not just the parts we use. Factory authorized repair for GM-Delco analog and digital speedometers, tachometers and instrument clusters. Exchange units available for nationwide next day air delivery. MasterCard, Visa and American Express. Web site: www.carradio.com

---

Spirit Enterprises
4325 Sunset Dr
Lockport, NY 14094
716-434-9938 showroom
716-434-0077 warehouse

	automobilia
	stereo systems

See full listing in **Section Two** under **automobilia**

Vintage Radio Shop
Wilford Wilkes Sr
101 Swoope St, Box 103
Brisbin, PA 16620
814-378-8526; FAX: 814-378-6149

	parts
	radios
	repairs

Mail order or open by appointment. Exclusively European auto radios, 1940s-1970. Tube or transistor. Blaupunkt, Becker, Telefunken, Radiomobile, etc. The only shop catering to these specialized auto radios exclusively. Repairs, restoration. Stocking new dial faces, knobs, push-buttons, etc. Visa/MC. All work done myself personally.

Yesterday's Radio
7759 Edgewood Ln
Seven Hills, OH 44131-5902
PH/FAX: 216-524-2018
E-mail: jerry@yesterdaysradio.com

	interior plastic
	radio parts

See full listing in **Section One** under **Packard**

George Zaha
4900 Green Hollow Dr
Orion, MI 48359
248-393-1732 evenings

	FM conversions
	radios
	speakers

Radios repaired, sold and purchased since 1934. Over 50 years of service guarantees you the best quality at the best prices. FM conversions, vibrators, speaker reconing, massive stock of radios and NOS parts inventory. Complete sales and service facility. All work fully guaranteed one year.

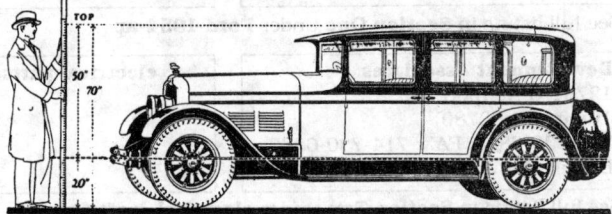

ACE Automotive Cleaning Equipment Co
897 S Washington Suite 232
Holland, MI 49423
616-772-3260; FAX: 616-772-3261

	sandblasting
	equipment

See full listing in **Section Two** under **rust removal & stripping**

ADP Hollander
14800 28th Ave N #190
Plymouth, MN 55447
800-761-9266; FAX: 800-825-1124
E-mail: hollander@autonet.net

	interchange info
	manuals

See full listing in **Section Two** under **car & parts locators**

Albrico Auto & Truck Parts
PO Box 3179
Camarillo, CA 93010
805-482-9792; FAX: 805-383-1013

	lamp assemblies
	lenses

See full listing in **Section Two** under **lighting equipment**

Amherst Antique Auto Show
157 Hollis Rd
Amherst, NH 03031
603-883-0605, NH
FAX: 617-641-0647, MA

	swap meets

See full listing in **Section Two** under **auctions & events**

Antique Radio Service
12 Shawmut Ave
Wayland, MA 01778
800-201-2635; FAX: 508-653-2418

	radio service

See full listing in **Section Two** under **radios**

Aremco Products Inc
707-B Executive Blvd
Valley Cottage, NY 10989
914-268-0039; FAX: 914-268-0041
E-mail: aremco@aremco.com

	compound

See full listing in **Section Two** under **accessories**

Atlantic British Ltd
Halfmoon Light Industrial Park
6 Badertscher Dr
Clifton Park, NY 12065
800-533-2210; FAX: 518-664-6641
E-mail: ab@roverparts.com

	accessories
	parts

See full listing in **Section One** under **Rover/Land Rover**

Bay Area Industrial Dry Stripping
151 11th St
Richmond, CA 94801-3523
510-412-9890, 510-805-1887

	blasting
	paint removal

See full listing in **Section Two** under **rust removal & stripping**

Bob's Brickyard Inc
1030 N Hickory Ridge Tr
Milford, MI 48380
248-685-9508; FAX: 248-685-8662
E-mail: bobsbrick@aol.com

	parts

See full listing in **Section One** under **Bricklin**

Bob's Classic Auto Glass   **glass**
21170 Hwy 36
Blachly, OR 97412
800-624-2130

See full listing in **Section Two** under **glass**

Bob's Bird House   **parts**
124 Watkin Ave
Chadds Ford, PA 19317
610-358-3420; FAX: 610-558-0729

See full listing in **Section One** under **Thunderbird**

Bonk's Automotive Inc   **automotive tools**
4480 Lazelda Dr
Milan, MI 48160
800-207-6906; FAX: 734-434-0845
E-mail: bonkers@bonkauto.com

See full listing in **Section Two** under **tools**

Brisson Enterprises   **lead**
PO Box 1595
Dearborn, MI 48121-1595
313-584-3577

See full listing in **Section Two** under **car care products**

The Buckle Man   **buckles**
Douglas D Drake
28 Monroe Ave
Pittsford, NY 14534
716-381-4604

See full listing in **Section Two** under **hardware**

Buenger Enterprises/GoldenRod   **dehumidifiers**
Dehumidifier
3600 S Harbor Blvd
Oxnard, CA 93035
800-451-6797; FAX: 805-985-1534

See full listing in **Section Two** under **car care products**

C & P Chevy Parts   **parts**
50 Schoolhouse Rd   **restoration**
PO Box 348VA   **supplies**
Kulpsville, PA 19443
215-721-4300, 800-235-2475
FAX: 215-721-4539

See full listing in **Section One** under **Chevrolet**

Capt Lee's Spra' Strip   **paint remover**
PO Box 203
Hermitage, TN 37076
800-421-9498; FAX: 615-889-1798

See full listing in **Section Two** under **rust removal & stripping**

CARS Inc   **interior**
1964 W 11 Mile Rd
Berkley, MI 48072
248-398-7100; FAX: 248-398-7078
E-mail: carsinc@worldnet.att.net

See full listing in **Section One** under **Chevrolet**

Cast Aluminum Repair   **repair**
1520 Marshall Ln
Conyers, GA 30094
770-929-1363
E-mail: heliarctig@aol.com

See full listing in **Section Two** under **castings**

Caswell Electroplating in Miniature   **plating kits**
4336 Rt 31
Palmyra, NY 14522
315-597-5140, 315-597-6378
FAX: 315-597-1457
E-mail: sales@caswellplating.com

See full listing in **Section Two** under **plating & polishing**

Stan Chernoff   **mechanical parts**
1215 Greenwood Ave   **restoration parts**
Torrance, CA 90503   **technical info**
310-320-4554; FAX: 310-328-7867   **trim parts**
E-mail: az589@lafn.org

See full listing in **Section One** under **Datsun**

Classic Mercury Parts   **parts**
1393 Shippee Ln
Ojai, CA 93023
805-646-3345; FAX: 805-646-5386
E-mail: mfourez@aol.com

See full listing in **Section One** under **Mercury**

Color-Plus Leather   **leather**
Restoration System   **conditioning**
106 Harrier Ct, 3767 Sunrise Lake   **leather dye**
Milford, PA 18337-9315
570-686-3158; FAX: 570-686-4161
E-mail: jpcolorplus@pikeonline.net

See full listing in **Section Two** under **leather restoration**

Cover-It   **all-weather shelters**
17 Wood St
West Haven, CT 06516-3843
800-932-9344; FAX: 203-931-4754
E-mail: coverit@ct1.nai.net

See full listing in **Section Two** under **car covers**

Dalmar   **electroplating**
11759 S Cleveland Ave, Suite 28   **plating supplies**
Ft Myers, FL 33907
941-275-6540; FAX: 941-275-1731
E-mail: dalmar@peganet.com

See full listing in **Section Two** under **plating & polishing**

Damper Dudes   **balancers**
5509 Cedar Rd #2   **chrome**
Redding, CA 96001   **paint**
800-413-2673, 530-244-7225
FAX: 530-244-2690
E-mail: rliddell@snowcrest.net

See full listing in **Section Two** under **engine parts**

Daytona MIG   **welders and plasma**
1821 Holsonback Dr   **cutters**
Daytona Beach, FL 32117
800-331-9353; FAX: 904-274-1237

See full listing in **Section Two** under **tools**

Dearborn Classics   **accessories**
PO Box 7649   **restoration parts**
Bend, OR 97708-7649
800-252-7427; FAX: 800-500-7886

See full listing in **Section One** under **Ford 1954-up**

Development Associates   **electrical parts**
12791-G Newport Ave
Tustin, CA 92780
714-730-6843; FAX: 714-730-6863
E-mail: devassoc@yahoo.com

See full listing in **Section Two** under **electrical systems**

Dr Vinyl and Assoc Ltd 9501 E 350 Hwy Raytown, MO 64133 816-356-3312; FAX: 816-356-9049 E-mail: tbuckley@drvinyl.com	dent repair interior repair paint touch-up

See full listing in **Section Two** under **car care products**

Bob Drake Reproductions Inc 1819 NW Washington Blvd Grants Pass, OR 97526 800-221-3673; FAX: 541-474-0099 E-mail: bobdrake@bobdrake.com	repro parts

See full listing in **Section One** under **Ford 1932-1953**

Dri-Wash 'n Guard Independent Distributor PO Box 1331 Palm Desert, CA 92261 800-428-1883, 760-346-1984 FAX: 760-568-6354	automotive care products boat care products

See full listing in **Section Two** under **car care products**

Early Wheel Co Inc Box 1438 Santa Ynez, CA 93460 805-688-1187; FAX: 805-688-0257	steel wheels

See full listing in **Section Two** under **wheels & wheelcovers**

The Eastwood Company-Tools Box 296 Malvern, PA 19355-0714 800-345-1178 FAX: 610-644-0560	plating & polishing powder coating restoration aids rustproofing sandblasters/welders

See full listing in **Section Two** under **tools**

Ecoclean 2000 100 N Meadows Rd Medfield, MA 02052 888-399-2600, 508-359-9675 FAX: 508-359-7311 E-mail: rusteco1x@aol.com	rust dissolver

See full listing in **Section Two** under **rust removal & stripping**

The Enthusiasts Shop John Parnell PO Box 80471 Baton Rouge, LA 70898 225-928-7456; FAX: 225-928-7665	cars pre-war parts transportation

See full listing in **Section One** under **Rolls-Royce/Bentley**

Excelsweld USA/Cylinder Head Specialist 1231 16th Ave Oakland, CA 94606 800-743-4323; FAX: 510-534-1107	welding

See full listing in **Section Two** under **machine work**

The Finished Look PO Box 191413 Sacramento, CA 95819-1413 800-827-6715; FAX: 916-451-3984 E-mail: info@thefinishedlook.com	POR-15 products

See full listing in **Section Two** under **rustproofing**

Firewall Insulators & Quiet Ride Solutions 6333 Pacific Ave, Ste 523 Stockton, CA 95207 209-477-4840; FAX: 209-477-0918 E-mail: timcox@gotnet.net	auto insulation firewall insulators gloveboxes sound deadening

See full listing in **Section Two** under **upholstery**

Fred's Truck Parts 4811 S Palant Tucson, AZ 85735 520-883-7151	parts

See full listing in **Section One** under **Chevrolet**

Gasoline Alley LLC 1700E Iron Ave PO Box 737 Salina, KS 67402 800-326-8372, 785-822-1003 FAX: 785-827-9337 E-mail: morrison@midusa.net	drip pans

See full listing in **Section Two** under **accessories**

Golden Mile Sales Inc J DeAngelo 2439 S Bradford St Allentown, PA 18103-5821 PH/FAX: 610-791-4497, 24 hours	NORS parts NOS parts sheetmetal

See full listing in **Section One** under **American Austin/Bantam**

Hoffman Automotive Distributor US Hwy #1, Box 818 Hilliard, FL 32046 904-845-4421	parts

See full listing in **Section Two** under **body parts**

Imperial Restoration Inc 308 Lockport St Lemont, IL 60439 630-257-5822 FAX: 630-257-5892	chassis coatings engine enamels gas tank sealer paint/rust remover rust preventives

Mail order only. POR-15 restoration products which include POR-15 rust preventive paint (applied directly over rust to seal it permanently), gas tank sealer, high temp coatings, engine enamels (matching factory colors), paint remover/stripper, metal ready rust remover, epoxy putty and more.

Independence Porcelain Enamel 703 S Cottage Independence, MO 64050 816-252-8180; FAX: 816-252-8181	manifolds

Mail order and open shop. Monday-Friday 8 am to 4 pm. Porcelain coating automobile manifolds.

Instrument Services Inc 11765 Main St Roscoe, IL 61073 800-558-2674; FAX: 815-623-6416	clocks gauges instruments

See full listing in **Section Two** under **instruments**

J & G Auto Parts 3050 Wild Run Rd Pennsburg, PA 18073 215-679-4683 after 5 pm	clips fasteners weatherstripping

Supply clips, fasteners and weatherstripping for restorations. Attend all major car shows and flea markets.

**Section Two
Generalists**

J & K Old Chevy Stuff
Ship Pond Rd
Plymouth, MA 02360
508-224-7616

car dealer
parts
sheetmetal

See full listing in **Section One** under **Chevrolet**

JCM Industries
2 Westwood Dr
Danbury, CT 06811
800-752-0245

wax hardener

See full listing in **Section Two** under **car care products**

Ken's Cougars
PO Box 5380
Edmond, OK 73083
405-340-1636; FAX: 405-340-5877

parts

See full listing in **Section One** under **Mercury**

Kenask Spring Co
307 Manhattan Ave
Jersey City, NJ 07307
201-653-4589

springs

See full listing in **Section Two** under **suspension parts**

Al Knoch Interiors
130 Montoya Rd
El Paso, TX 79932
800-880-8080; FAX: 915-581-1545
E-mail: alknoch@flash.net

carpets
interiors
tooling services
tops

See full listing in **Section One** under **Chevrolet**

Koolmat
26258 Cranage Rd
Olmsted Falls, OH 44138
440-427-1888; FAX: 440-427-1889
E-mail: koolmat1@gte.net

insulators

Manufacturer of high temp weather-resistant 1100 degree cured
composite insulation, also lowers sound by 23 decibels. Plus
abrasion resistant great for restoration jobs. Web site:
www.koolmat.com

Kwik Poly T Distributing Inc
24 St Henry Ct
St Charles, MO 63301
314-724-1065

restoration aids

Mail order only. Kwik Poly is used in all types of wood problems
and reconstructuring, plus dozens of other restoration repairs,
including fuel tanks, oil tanks, steering wheels, fiberglass, rusted sheetmetal, electrical, engine, pitted surface repairs, molding.

Lake Buchanan Industries Inc
Rt 1, Box 184-C
Buchanan Dam, TX 78609
888-552-5278 toll-free
512-793-2867; FAX: 512-793-2869
E-mail: lbi:@tstar.net

blasting cabinet

See full listing in **Section Two** under **tools**

**Leatherique Leather
Restoration Products**
PO Box 2678
Orange Park, FL 32065
904-272-0992; FAX: 904-272-1534
E-mail: lrpltd@aol.com

leather cleaning
conditioning
products

See full listing in **Section One** under **Rolls-Royce/Bentley**

Loga Enterprises
5399 Old Town Hall Rd
Eau Claire, WI 54701
715-832-7302

convertible tops
interior parts

See full listing in **Section One** under **Studebaker**

Madera Concepts
606 Olive St
Santa Barbara, CA 93101
800-800-1579, 805-962-1579
FAX: 805-962-7359
E-mail: jwayco@west.net

restoration
woodwork
woodwork repair

See full listing in **Section Two** under **woodwork**

Maintenance Specialties Company
21 Valley Forge Rd
PO Box 251
New Castle, DE 19720
800-777-6715; FAX: 302-328-2315

rustproofing paints

See full listing in **Section Two** under **rustproofing**

Malm Chem Corp
PO Box 300, Dept HVA
Pound Ridge, NY 10576
914-764-5775; FAX: 914-764-5785
E-mail: jkolin@cloud9.net

polish
wax

See full listing in **Section Two** under **car care products**

The Masters Company
30 Willow Dr Suite A
Fort Thomas, KY 41075-2035
800-385-5811; FAX: 606-441-6765
E-mail: badger@cinternet.net

parts
tools

See full listing in **Section Two** under **tools**

Mint Condition Auto Upholstery
PO Box 134
Silverdale New Zealand
PH/FAX: 64-9-424 2257
E-mail: mint.condition@xtra.co.nz

convertible tops
interiors
spring-gaiters
wheelcovers

See full listing in **Section Two** under **special services**

Moroso Motorsports Park
PO Box 31907
Palm Beach Gardens, FL 33420
561-622-1400; FAX: 561-626-2053
E-mail: racetrack@moroso.com

race track

See full listing in **Section Two** under **racing**

Muscle Express
509 Commerce Way W #3
Jupiter, FL 33458
800-323-3043 order line
561-744-3043 tech line

parts

See full listing in **Section One** under **Chevelle/Camaro**

OEM Glass Inc
Rt 9 E
PO Box 362
Bloomington, IL 61702
309-662-2122; FAX: 309-663-7474

auto glass

See full listing in **Section Two** under **glass**

Original Parts Group Inc
17892 Gothard St
Huntington Beach, CA 92647
800-243-8355 US/Canada
714-841-5363; FAX: 714-847-8159

accessories
parts

See full listing in **Section One** under **Pontiac**

P-Ayr Products   replicas
719 Delaware St
Leavenworth, KS 66048
913-651-5543; FAX: 913-651-2084
E-mail: sales@payr.com

See full listing in **Section One** under **Chevrolet**

Pennsylvania Metal Cleaning   derusting
200 17th St   stainless fasteners
Monaca, PA 15061-1969   stripping
724-728-5535

See full listing in **Section Two** under **rust removal & stripping**

People's Choice & Lost in the 50s   1950s clothing
28170 Ave Crocker #209   1950s memorabilia
Valencia, CA 91355   automobilia items
800-722-1965, 661-295-1965   celebrity items
FAX: 661-295-1931

See full listing in **Section Two** under **automobilia**

Bill Peters   steering wheel
41 Vassar Pl   restoration
Rockville Centre, NY 11570
516-766-8397

See full listing in **Section Two** under **steering wheels**

PK Lindsay Co Inc   paint removal
63 Nottingham Rd   rust removal
Deerfield, NH 03037
800-258-3576; FAX: 800-843-2974

See full listing in **Section Two** under **rust removal & stripping**

Pollard Co   parts
Joe Pollard
9331 Johnell Rd
Chatsworth, CA 91311
PH/FAX: 818-999-1485

See full listing in **Section One** under **Checker**

Poly All Fast Set International Inc   sealants
PO Box 1150   wood care products
44 Bridge St
Bradford, ON Canada L3Z 2B5
905-778-9010; FAX: 905-778-9011
E-mail: polyall@on.aibn.com

A new product, Poly All 2000, repairs rotten wood, use on fiber-glass, use on metal to seal. Web site: www.headwaters.com/

Preserve Inc   storage containers
1430 E 1800 N
Hamilton, IL 62341
217-746-2411; FAX: 217-746-2231

See full listing in **Section Two** under **storage care products**

Protective Products Corp   chemical products
Box 246
Johnston, IA 50131
888-772-1277; FAX: 515-999-2708
E-mail: ppc1@aol.com

Unique chemical products which greatly reduce the labor time in restoration and surface care products which produce prize winning results. PPC products are currently used by many of the national leading shops and nationally recognized show car winners.

Quanta Restoration and   fan belts
Performance Products   gas tanks
743 Telegraph Rd
Rising Sun, MD 21911-1810
800-235-8788, 410-658-5700
FAX: 410-658-5758
E-mail: quanta@quantaproducts.com

See full listing in **Section Two** under **chassis parts**

R J & L Automotive Fasteners   fasteners
58 Bristol Ave
Rochester, NY 14617-2702
PH/FAX: 716-467-7421

See full listing in **Section Two** under **hardware**

RB's Obsolete Automotive   parts
7711 Lake Ballinger Way
Edmonds, WA 98026-9163
425-670-6739; FAX: 425-670-9151
E-mail: rbobsole@gte.net

See full listing in **Section Two** under **comprehensive parts**

REM Automotive Inc   interior parts
2610 N Brandt Rd   trunk lining
Annville, PA 17003
717-838-4242; FAX: 717-838-5091

Supply manufactured soft good parts throughout the United States and Canada. Parts are die-cut for precision fit for most all domestic cars. Production, warehousing and shipping is all done in our facility. Renowned for our ability to fabricate, in-house, nearly everything we sell, as well as develop customer generated special projects. At REM, the emphasis is on quality, products and delivery to the customer.

Restoration Supply Company   accessories
2060 Palisade Dr   restoration
Reno, NV 89509   supplies
775-825-5663; FAX: 775-825-9330
E-mail: restoration@rsc.reno.nv.us

Mail order only. Deal in authentic hard to find restoration supplies and accessories for the automobile and marine enthusiast.

RodDoors   door panels
PO Box 2110   interior accessories
Chico, CA 95927
530-896-1513; FAX: 530-896-1518
E-mail: roddoors@juno.com

See full listing in **Section Two** under **street rods**

T Schmidt   rust removers
827 N Vernon
Dearborn, MI 48128-1542
313-562-7161

See full listing in **Section Two** under **rust removal & stripping**

Ron Scobie Enterprises   gas pump parts
7676 120th St N
Hugo, MN 55038
651-653-6503
E-mail: rscobie@gaspump.com

See full listing in **Section Two** under **petroliana**

William G Shearman   windshield frame
PO Box 547   tubing
Jamestown, NY 14702-0547
716-484-0940

See full listing in **Section One** under **Ford 1903-1931**

Paul Slater Auto Parts 9496 85th St N Stillwater, MN 55082 612-429-4235	**parts**

See full listing in **Section One** under **Dodge**

Sta-Dri Pouches **Beach Filler Products Inc** RD 1, Box 105 Glen Rock, PA 17327 800-BEACH85; FAX: 717-235-4858 E-mail: beachfilters@hotmail.com	**corrosion protection** **mildew protection** **moisture protection**

See full listing in **Section Two** under **storage care products**

Standard Abrasives **Motorsports Division** 4201 Guardian St Simi Valley, CA 93063 800-383-6001, 805-520-5800 ext 371 FAX: 805-577-7398	**abrasives**

Mail order only. Monday-Friday 8 am to 5 pm PST. Specialty abrasives and surface conditioning products to make work easier, cleaner and more productive on a variety of restoration and customization applications including frame work, bodywork, wheels and trim. Product kits available. Call for free catalog. Web site: www.sa-motorsports.com

Sunchaser Tools 3202 E Foothill Blvd Pasadena, CA 91107 626-795-1588; FAX: 626-795-6494	**metal-finishing kit** **video**

Mail order and open shop. Monday-Friday 9 am to 6 pm. Autobody tools, hand, air and electric tools. This tool company has been written about in over 35 magazine articles because of their unique new method of dent repair where no bondo is needed. It's called the "Friction System", by using their 9" stainless amazing shrinking disc, it accurately heat shrinks the stretched part in dents so it will return to its original shape. This system will work on all sheetmetal whether on a Honda hood or a Model A fender. This system actually anneals the once damaged panel so it will return to the same workability as if never hit. 100% guarantee to work for anyone who gets properly trained through their complete 3.5 hour training video course and must purchase the "Friction System" kit.

Tar Heel Parts Inc PO Box 2604 Matthews, NC 28106-2604 800-322-1957, 704-753-9114 (local) FAX: 704-753-9117	**buffing supplies**

See full listing in **Section Two** under **plating & polishing**

This Old Truck Magazine PO Box 500 Missouri City, TX 77459 800-310-7047 subscriptions 937-767-1433 publishing office FAX: 937-767-2726 E-mail: antique@antiquepower.com	**magazine**

See full listing in **Section Four** under **periodicals**

TiP Tools & Equipment 7075 Route 446, PO Box 649 Canfield, OH 44406 330-533-3384 local 800-321-9260 US/Canada FAX: 330-533-2876	**abrasive blasters** **air compressors** **tools**

Mail order and open shop. Monday-Friday 9 am to 6 pm, Saturday 9 am to 1:30 pm. Manufacturer/supplier of abrasive blasters, glass bead cabinets, parts and supplies. Plus Quincy, Campbell Hausfeld and Coleman air compressors, TiP and Binks HVLP paint systems, Baldor Buffers and buffing supplies,

Lincoln Welders, Chicago Pneumatic air tools and other related restoration equipment. Free 104 page catalog. Over 29 years' experience. Web site: www.tiptools.com
See our ad on page 422

TMI Products Inc 191 Granite St Corona, CA 91719 800-624-7960, 909-272-1996 FAX: 909-272-1584 E-mail: tmiprods@aol.com	**classic car** **interiors**

See full listing in **Section One** under **Volkswagen**

Tower Paint Co Inc Box 2345 Oshkosh, WI 54903 920-235-6520; FAX: 920-235-6521 E-mail: tpi@towerpaint.com	**paint**

See full listing in **Section Two** under **paints**

Ultimate Appearance Ltd 113 Arabian Trail Smithfield, VA 23430 888-446-3078; FAX: 757-255-2620	**cleaners** **detailing products** **detailing services** **polish/wax**

See full listing in **Section Two** under **car care products**

Vampire Products 50 Four Coins Dr Canonsburg, PA 15317 800-866-7260; FAX: 724-745-6040 E-mail: vampire@hanseninc.com	**air dryers** **filters**

See full listing in **Section Two** under **restoration shops**

Vintage Glass USA PO Box 336 326 S River Rd Tolland, CT 06084 800-889-3826, 860-872-0018	**auto glass**

See full listing in **Section Two** under **glass**

Vintage Parts 411 4909 Ruffner St San Diego, CA 92111 800-MOTORHEAD FAX: 619-467-0777 E-mail: cars@vintageparts.com	**books**

See full listing in **Section Four** under **information sources**

Voss Motors Inc 21849 Virginia Dr Southfield, MI 48076 888-380-9277 toll-free 248-357-4750; FAX: 248-354-6577 E-mail: vossmotors@aol.com	**service manuals**

See full listing in **Section Two** under **literature dealers**

John J Waluk 31 Squirrel Ln Levittown, NY 11756 516-796-2984; FAX: 516-796-5423 E-mail: bb70@msn.com	**flocking**

See full listing in **Section Two** under **special services**

White Post Restorations One Old Car Dr White Post, VA 22663 540-837-1140; FAX: 540-837-2368	**brakes** **restoration**

See full listing in **Section Two** under **brakes**

Williams Lowbuck Tools Inc 4175 California Ave Norco, CA 91760 909-735-7848; FAX: 909-735-1210 E-mail: wlowbuck@aol.com	**tools**

See full listing in **Section Two** under **tools**

World Upholstery & Trim PO Box 2420 Camarillo, CA 93011 805-988-1848; FAX: 805-278-7886 E-mail: worlduph@mail.vcnet.com	**carpet** **tops** **upholstery kits**

See full listing in **Section Two** under **interiors & interior parts**

Wymer Classic AMC Mark & George Wymer 340 N Justice St Fremont, OH 43420 419-332-4291, 419-334-6945 after 5 pm	**NOS parts** **owner's manuals** **repairs** **service manuals** **used parts**

See full listing in **Section One** under **AMC**

restoration shops

1 CAAT Limited Co 1324 E Harper Ave Maryville, TN 37804 423-983-7180 E-mail: jhenriks@icx.net	**restoration**

Maintenance and restoration for classic British motorcars. "1 Car at a Time".

A&A Mustang Parts & Mfg Co 105 Fordham Rd Oak Ridge, TN 37830 423-482-9445	**exhaust systems** **parts** **restorations**

See full listing in **Section One** under **Mustang**

Absolutely British II 1720 S Grove Ave, Unit A Ontario, CA 91761 PH/FAX: 909-947-0200	**restoration** **service**

Shop open Monday-Friday 7 am to 4:30 pm. Restoration, service and parts for all Austin-Healey, MG and Triumph TR2-6 sports cars.

Ace Antique Auto Restoration 65 S Service Rd Plainview, NY 11803 516-752-6065; FAX: 516-752-1484	**air conditioning** **body rebuilding** **restoration** **wiring harnesses**

Mail order and open shop. Monday-Friday 8 am to 5 pm. Partial and complete restoration services. Fabrication, body rebuilding, paint, powertrain rebuilding, glass interior and chrome plating, air conditioning installation, wiring harnesses. Web site: aceautobody.com

See our ad on this page

Adams Custom Engines Inc 806 Glendale Ave Sparks, NV 89431-5720 775-358-8070; FAX: 775-358-8040	**restorations**

Mail order and open shop. Monday-Friday 8 am to 5 pm. Full and partial restorations of antique and classic automobiles. 30 years' experience. Specializing in woodgraining. Quality work for the most discriminating, national award winning work. 344 body-off restorations since 1965.

Section Two Generalists

Adler's Antique Autos Inc
801 NY Rt 43
Stephentown, NY 12168
518-733-5749
E-mail: advdesign1@aol.com

| auto preservation |
| Chevrolet knowledge |
| parts |
| repair |
| restoration |

Open Monday-Friday 9 am to 5 pm; other hours and days by appointment. Chevrolet car and truck specialist. Specialize in factory authentic restoration, both body and mechanical. MIG welding, panel fabrication, sandblasting and painting are done to factory or the owner's specifications. Over 600 GM vehicles in stock for parts salvage as well as potential restoration projects, dating back to 1934. Dealer for Chevrolet truck reproduction parts. Expert on Chevrolet Advance Design trucks, 1947-1955. See work we've done 27 years ago still going strong. All parts and work guaranteed. Author and historian.

Alfas Unlimited Inc
89 Greenwoods Rd W, Rt 44
Norfolk, CT 06058
860-542-5351; FAX: 860-542-5993
E-mail: alfasun@esslink.com

| engine rebuilding |
| parts |
| restoration |
| service |

See full listing in **Section One** under **Alfa Romeo**

All Seams Fine
23 Union St
Waterbury, VT 05676
800-244-7326 (SEAM), 802-244-8843

| interior |
| restorations |

See full listing in **Section Two** under **upholstery**

American International Transmissions
7145 E Earll Dr
Scottsdale, AZ 85251
602-946-5391

| differentials |
| restoration |

See full listing in **Section Two** under **transmissions**

The Antique Auto Shop
603 Lytle Avenue
Elsmere, KY 41018
(606) 342-8363

THE ANTIQUE AUTO SHOP

Excellence in Restoration

Let us transform your special car to its original elegance!

Full or Partial Restoration of your Classic, Special Interest or Sports Car

- PRIDE IN WORKMANSHIP
- METAL FINISHING & LEAD WORK
- COMPLETE MECHANICAL SERVICE
- SHOW-WINNING PAINT

20 minutes south of Cincinnati, Ohio

ANC Restoration
Chris Palmerie
254 New Haven Ave
Waterbury, CT 06708
203-574-2249
E-mail: cpwp2@javanet.com

| restorations |

Mail order and open shop. Monday-Saturday, answering service available 24 hours. Antique auto restoration, buffing, dent removal, stainless steel and aluminum for antique vehicles, all makes and models, preferably before 1970s.

Anderson Restoration
1235 Nash Ave
Kanawha, IA 50447
515-762-3528

| restorations |

Open shop only. Monday-Saturday 5:30 am to 4:30 pm. Complete or partial restorations to show quality of antique and classic automobiles. References available. 1928 and 1932 Packards, two 1911s, 1914, 1916, 1956 and 1965 Fords, 1904 Sandusky Courier, all AACA Silver Platter winners.

Antique & Classic Car Restoration
Hwy 107, Box 368
Magdalena, NM 87825

| restoration |

Shop open by appointment only. Specializing in complete frame-up restorations for MG, Paige, Reo and Jaguar.

Antique & Classic Car Restorations
4716 Monkey Hill Rd
Oak Harbor, WA 98227
360-240-0909

| painting |
| restorations |
| woodwork |

Open shop only. Monday-Friday 8 am to 5 pm, Saturday 8 am to 4 pm. Small shop specializing in total frame-up restorations, sheetmetal fabrications, painting and woodwork. 32 years' experience.

Antique Auto Restoration
Randy Reed, Owner
1975 Del Monte Blvd
Seaside, CA 93955
408-393-9411; FAX: 408-393-1041

| restoration |

Full or partial restorations or service. Experienced in British, German, Italian and American makes. Visit us when on the Monterey Peninsula for golfing, racing or the Concours. Web site: antiqueautorestoration.com

The Antique Auto Shop
603 Lytle Ave
Elsmere, KY 41018
606-342-8363; FAX: 606-342-9076
E-mail: antaut@aol.com

| mechanical service |
| restoration |

Open Monday-Friday 6 am to 4:30 pm. Full or partial restoration on antique, classic and sport cars from body-off the frame show cars to partial and component restoration. Paint, body and mechanical service. Same location 25 years. Appraisals by appointment. Custom car covers. Web site: www.antiqueautoshop.com

See our ad on this page

Art's Antique & Classic Auto Services
1985 E 5th St #16
Tempe, AZ 85281
602-966-1195

| restoration |

See full listing in **Section One** under **Buick/McLaughlin**

Auto Craftsmen Restoration Inc
27945 Elm Grove
San Antonio, TX 78261
PH/FAX: 830-980-4027

| appraisals |
| buyer/car locator |
| old M-B parts |
| restoration |

Mail order and open shop. Monday-Friday 8 am to 5 pm. Specializing in Mercedes-Benz and Rolls-Royce, Mustang convertibles, others considered. Top winning show cars have been restored by this shop.

Auto Europa	**painting**
221 Berrellesa St	**restorations**
Martinez, CA 94553	**woodworking**
925-229-3466; FAX: 925-313-0542	

Mail order and open shop. Monday-Friday 8 am to 5 pm. Complete restoration services, 5-man shop dedicated to all phases of restoration, in-house machine shop, sheetmetal, panel fabrication, woodworking, painting. Marques restored: Alfa, Bugatti, Cord, Duesenberg, Ferrari, Jaguar, Lola, Lamborghini, Lincoln, LaSalle, Mercedes, Packard, Pierce-Arrow, Plymouth, Rolls-Royce, Talbot-Lago. Many First Place winners, including Best of Show at Pebble Beach twice.

Auto Restoration	**transmission**
8150 S CR 1250 W	**conversion kits**
Albany, IN 47320	
PH/FAX: 765-789-4037	

See full listing in **Section One** under **Ford 1903-1931**

Auto Restoration by William R Hahn	**custom work**
Palermo Auto Body	**restoration**
241 Church Rd (rear)	
Wexford, PA 15090	
724-935-3790 shop, 412-367-2538 home	
FAX: 724-935-9121	

Open Monday-Friday 8 am to 5 pm, Saturday and evenings by appointment. Ground-up or partial restorations on all years, domestic and foreign vehicles. Will hand build the dream car you deserve, to your choice of concours quality, points correct or driver. Every level includes show quality with exceptional roadability. All are built to last long enough to become a family heirloom. Qualifications include national award winners. Over twenty years specializing in restoration. Detail oriented.

AutoFashions Restoration & Creations	**auto parts**
	auto sales
2209-B Hamlets Chapel Rd	**handcrafts**
Pittsboro, NC 27312	**restoration**
PH/FAX: 919-542-5566	**rubber ink stamps**
send automatically	
E-mail: autofashions@mindspring.com	

New and used auto parts, auto sales, handcrafts and rubber ink stamps. Catalogs, $1.50. Currently not accepting new restoration projects. Send inquiries by e-mail or snail mail. Web site: www.autofashions.com

Automotive Restorations Inc	**body fabrication**
Kent S Bain	**mechanical**
1785 Barnum Ave	**painting**
Stratford, CT 06614	**restorations**
203-377-6745; FAX: 203-386-0486	**upholstery**
E-mail: carbain@compuserve.com	**woodwork**

Mail order and open shop. Monday-Friday 10 am to 5 pm, Saturday 9 am to 12 pm. Specializing in steel and aluminum body panels for all coachbuilt cars for Rolls-Royce, Bentley, Aston Martin, Ferrari, Maserati, AC, Jaguar and so on. Restoration services, including all mechanical repairs and component rebuilding, collector car maintenance/storage program, panel beating and body fabrication, upholstery, painting, woodwork. 22 person shop, established 1977. Web site: www.automotiverestorations.com
See our ad on this page

Automotive Restorations Inc	**clutch rebuilding**
Stephen Babinsky	**mechanical**
4 Center St	**services**
Bernardsville, NJ 07924	**restorations**
908-766-6688; FAX: 908-766-6684	
E-mail: autorestnj@aol.com	

Mail order and open shop. Monday-Saturday 8 am to 6 pm, closed Sundays. Partial and full restorations. Specializing in

1930s classic cars and specialized services, ie: cast iron welding, repair of manifolds, heads, blocks, etc, and clutch rebuilding and relining, radiator core manufacture and repair, full mechanical services, etc.

The Autoworks Ltd	**restoration**
90 Center Ave	**sales**
Westwood, NJ 07675	**service**
201-358-0200; FAX: 201-358-0442	

See full listing in **Section Two** under **service shops**

B & B Restorations	**parts**
Box 591	**restoration**
Elmvale, ON Canada L0L 1P0	**service**
705-322-2455	
E-mail: bbrestoration@georgian.net	

See full listing in **Section One** under **Corvette**

B & L Body Shop	**restoration**
20 O'Shea Ln	
Waynesville, NC 28786-4524	
828-456-8277	

Complete restoration of antique autos. Call first for confirmation. Established in 1968.

Back-In-Time Automotive Restorations	**restoration**
57 Cannonball Rd	
Pompton Lakes, NJ 07442	
PH/FAX: 973-616-6300	

Open Monday-Friday 8 am to 6 pm, Saturday by appointment. Body and mechanical restoration, metal fabrication, show paint, upholstery and electrical, machine shop on premises, problem solvers. In-house babbitt work.

RL Bailey Co 27902 45th Ave S Auburn, WA 98001 PH/FAX: 253-854-5247 E-mail: rbailey2@gte.net	restorations steering wheels woodgraining

See full listing in **Section Two** under **woodgraining**

Banzai Motorworks 6735 Midcities Ave Beltsville, MD 20705 PH/FAX: 301-937-5746 E-mail: zspert@erols.com	pre-purchase insp/consultation parts repairs/restoration service

See full listing in **Section One** under **Datsun**

Bassett Classic Restoration 2616 Sharon St, Suite D Kenner, LA 70062 PH/FAX: 504-469-2982 (have auto switching device)	parts plating restoration service

See full listing in **Section One** under **Rolls-Royce/Bentley**

Bastian Automotive Restoration 4170 Finch Ave Fairfield, OH 45014 PH/FAX: 513-738-4268	appraisals restoration

Open Monday-Friday 8 am to 5 pm, Saturday 9 am to 1 pm. Certified appraisers available by appointment. National show winning restoration of classic, antique, muscle and vintage race automobiles. Vintage automobile repair and authentic rewiring. National show preparation available. Our work has won National, AACA and CCCA awards, as well as Best of Class at National Concours d'Elegance. International Automobile Appraisers Association, member #1003160096.

Bay Area Industrial Dry Stripping 151 11th St Richmond, CA 94801-3523 510-412-9890, 510-805-1887	blasting paint removal

See full listing in **Section Two** under **rust removal & stripping**

Bayliss Automobile Restorations 2/15 Bon Mace Close, Berkeley Vale Via Gosford NSW 2261 Australia 61-2-43885253 FAX: 61-2-43893152	repainting repairs sheetmetal work

Repairing, rebodying and repainting of vintage, thoroughbred and classic cars. Body panels and sheetmetal work fabricated to your specifications (or to original) in steel or aluminum. All mechanical and upholstery work can also be undertaken.

Berkshire Auto's Time Was Box 347, 10 Front Street Collinsville, CT 06022 860-693-2332	restoration

Specializing in repair of street rods, custom or classic cars including insurance claim work. Our frame-work is second to none. Can custom mix any color in urethane paint. Motto: "Repair, not total, your old car". Also full body-off or partial restoratio

Bicknell Engine Company 7055 Dayton Rd Enon, OH 45323 937-864-5224	parts repair restoration

See full listing in **Section One** under **Buick/McLaughlin**

Bill's Model Acres Ford Farm RD 1 Box 283, 8th St Rd Watsontown, PA 17777 570-538-3200, PA 908-479-4479, NJ	parts restoration

See full listing in **Section One** under **Ford 1903-1931**

Billie Inc PO Box 1161 Ashburn, VA 20146-1161 800-878-6328; FAX: 703-858-0102	garage diaper mats

See full listing in **Section Two** under **car care products**

Blackheart Enterprises Ltd 305-12 Knickerbocker Ave Bohemia, NY 11716 516-752-6065; FAX: 516-694-1078	parts restoration

See full listing in **Section One** under **Checker**

Blint Equipment Inc 2204 E Lincolnway LaPorte, IN 46350 219-362-7021	parts tractor rebuilding

See full listing in **Section One** under **Ford 1954-up**

BMC Classics Inc 828 N Dixie Freeway New Smyrna Beach, FL 32168 904-426-6405; FAX: 904-427-4570 E-mail: bmcar1@aol.com	parts repair restoration

Open shop. Monday-Friday 8 am to 5:30 pm, Saturday 8 am to 12 pm. Restorations, repairs, service, parts. Specializing in Jaguar, Austin-Healey, Triumph, Mercedes, Porsche from 1950s-1980s. Web site: www.dreamsonwheels.com

Bob's Speedometer Service 32411 Grand River Ave Farmington, MI 48336 800-592-9673; FAX: 248-473-5517	gauges speedometers tachometers

See full listing in **Section Two** under **instruments**

Bonnet to Boot 7217 Geyser Ave Reseda, CA 91335 818-757-7050; FAX: 818-340-8674	restoration

Mail order and open shop. Restoration shop. Service and parts for Bentley, Jaguar and Rolls-Royce. Original British license plates. Color-Tune tool dealer. Web site: bonnettoboot

Bonnets Up 5736 Spring St Clinton, MD 20735 301-297-4759	restoration

See full listing in **Section Two** under **coachbuilders & designers**

J D Booth Ltd RR 2 Box 2390 Spring Grove, PA 17362-9644 717-229-0805 E-mail: thebooths@netrax.net	restoration

Open shop only. Monday-Friday 8 am to 5:30 pm EST, Saturday by appointment. Restoration, maintenance and modification. Specializing in Triumph TR2 and 3, experienced with many other British and Italian vehicles. Feel free to call for information.

Bright Displays 1314 Lakemont Dr Pittsburgh, PA 15243 PH/FAX: 412-279-7037	molded auto logos neon signs

See full listing in **Section Two** under **automobilia**

British Auto/USA
92 Londonderry Tpke
Manchester, NH 03104
603-622-1050, 800-452-4787
FAX: 603-622-0849
E-mail: jaguar@britishautousa

parts
upholstery

See full listing in **Section One** under **Jaguar**

British Car Specialists
2060 N Wilson Way
Stockton, CA 95205
209-948-8767; FAX: 209-948-1030
E-mail: healeydoc@aol.com

parts
repairs
restoration

See full listing in **Section One** under **Austin-Healey**

British Miles
9278 Old E Tyburn Rd
Morrisville, PA 19067
215-736-9300; FAX: 215-736-3089

accessories
literature
parts
restoration

See full listing in **Section One** under **MG**

Bryant's Antique Auto Parts
851 Western Ave
Hampden, ME 04444
207-862-4019

appraisals
chassis/engine/parts
sheetmetal
wiring harnesses

See full listing in **Section One** under **Ford 1903-1931**

Cars of the Past
11180 Kinsman Rd
Newbury, OH 44065
440-564-2277

restoration

Shop open Monday-Friday 8 am to 5:30 pm, Saturday 8:30 am to 12 noon. Complete or partial restorations on antiques, classics, special interest, exotics and trucks. Custom painting and graphics, custom pipe bending on all types of exhaust, including stainless steel. 1955-1957 Chevys, Corvettes, 1955-1957 T-Birds and trucks are our specialties.

Celestial Mechanics
88 West 500 South
Wellsville, UT 84339
435-245-4987
E-mail: volvox@cache.net

restoration

See full listing in **Section One** under **Volvo**

Central Alabama Restorations
Ed Rouze, Owner
1665 McQueen Smith Rd S
Prattville, AL 36066
334-361-7433

appraisals
restoration

Complete restoration work. Full-time, 5-man shop. New, modern building. Partials or complete restorations. Rust fabrication, welding, painting, blasting, bodywork, interiors, appraisals. Reliable and honest. Quality workmanship, fair rates. Many National winners. Restorations are our only business.

Chief Service
Herbert G Baschung
Brunnmatt, PO Box 155
CH-4914 Roggwil Switzerland
PH/FAX: 0041-62-9291777

parts
restoration

Mail order and open shop by appointment only. Specializing in restoration, full or partial, plus parts, new and used for pre-1960 Oldsmobile, Pontiac and Buick. Complete or partial restoration for all pre-1960 US makes to period perfect condition. Buy, trade, sell cars, parts, literature and memorabilia, 1930-1960. Can locate your dream car.

City Imports Ltd
166 Penrod Ct
Glen Burnie, MD 21061
410-768-6660; FAX: 410-768-5955

bodywork
car sales
restorations

See full listing in **Section One** under **Jaguar**

Classic Auto
251 SW 5th Ct
Pompano Beach, FL 33060
PH/FAX: 954-786-1687

restoration

Restoration of autos, specializing in Ford products, Mustangs and T-Birds. Also street rods, custom cars, custom painting.

Classic Auto Rebuilders/CAR
Box 9796
Fargo, ND 58106

painting/plating
restoration
woodwork

Mail order and open shop by appointment only. Complete and partial restorations, plating, castings, welding, painting, convertible conversions, trim work, woodwork, customizing and metal work and parts fabrication. Complete coach and limousine building.

Classic Auto Restoration
15445 Ventura Blvd #60
Sherman Oaks, CA 91413
818-905-6267; FAX: 818-906-1249
E-mail: rollsroyce1@earthlink.net

acquisitions
restoration
sales

See full listing in **Section One** under **Rolls-Royce/Bentley**

Classic Auto Restoration
437 Greene St
Buffalo, NY 14212
716-896-6663

appraisals
plating
polishing
restoration

Mail order. Chrome plating, pot metal repair, stainless steel repair and polishing, aluminum polishing, top show quality for over 25 years by United Custom Plating Ltd, 905-791-0990. Also do appraisals.

Classic Auto Restoration
Service Inc
381 National Dr
Rockwall, TX 75032-6556
972-722-9663

restoration

See full listing in **Section One** under **Chevrolet**

Classic Car Radio Service®
25 Maple Rd
PO Box 764
Woodacre, CA 94973
415-488-4596; FAX: 415-488-1512
E-mail: healy@classicradio.com

radio repair
radio restoration

See full listing in **Section Two** under **radios**

Classic Car Works Ltd
3050 Upper Bethany Rd
Jasper, GA 30143
770-735-3945

restoration

Monday-Saturday 8 am to 6 pm. Service and restoration of all antique, classic and sports cars, American and foreign. Specialize in Buicks and all English cars for all years and models. Electrical and mechanical problems solved. Expert paint, body and interior work. All convertible tops repaired and replaced.

Classic Carriages
267 County Rd 420
Athens, TN 37303
PH/FAX: 423-744-7496

repair
restoration

See full listing in **Section One** under **Ford 1932-1953**

Classic Coachworks 735 Frenchtown Rd Milford, NJ 08848 908-996-3400; FAX: 908-996-0204	**bodywork** **painting** **restoration**

Open Monday-Saturday by appointment only. Restoration and restyling facility specializing in cars from 1950-present. All work performed by certified craftsmen and supervised by a certified master craftsman. ASE certified and I-Car certified master repair/refinish technicians. I-Car Gold Class repair facility. Bodywork, painting and restorations for 1950s-present Corvette, Mustang, T-Bird, Mercedes, Rolls-Royce and Porsche. Collision work to all years, makes and models. Web site: www.classiccoachworks.com

Classic Coachworks 4209 Misty Ridge Dr Haymarket, VA 20169 703-754-9366; FAX: 703-754-4933	**restoration**

The art of restoration. Body and frame restoration and refinishing. MGB, Midgets. Reasonable prices. Over 30 years' experience with MG.

Classic Creations of Central Florida 3620 Hwy 92E Lakeland, FL 33801 941-665-2322; FAX: 941-666-5348 E-mail: flclassics@aol.com	**parts** **restoration** **service**

See full listing in **Section One** under **Mustang**

Classic Motors PO Box 1011 San Mateo, CA 94403 650-342-4117; FAX: 650-340-9473 E-mail: tonyleo@pacbell.net	**appraisals** **locator service** **movie rentals** **parts/restoration**

Mail order and open shop. Monday-Friday 9 am to 6 pm. Automotive restoration. Specializing in convertibles and collector cars. Appraisals, service and parts for convertibles and collector cars. Corvette parts locator service. Collectable car and truck locator service. Movie car and prop rental service specializing in convertibles, sports cars and Corvettes.

Classic Showcase 913 Rancheros Dr San Marcos, CA 92069 760-747-9947, 760-747-3188 sales FAX: 760-747-4021 E-mail: management@classicshowcase.com	**classic vehicles** **restorations**

See full listing in **Section Two** under **car dealers**

Classics and Customs 6414 123rd Ave N Largo, FL 33773 888-221-1847 toll-free 813-536-8372	**appraisals** **guide** **painting** **restoration** **rust repairs**

Open Monday-Friday 8 am to 6 pm, Saturday by appointment. Partial and complete frame-up restorations. Specializing in 1950s-1960s GM products including traditional sheetmetal fabricating, metal finishing and welding. Award winning body and finish work. Show quality detailing. Also publish the most comprehensive tip and technique book ever written covering all aspects of antique auto restoration, *Secrets of the Pros*. Because of the limited printing, supply going fast. Call now.

Classics 'n More Inc 1001 Ranck Mill Rd Lancaster, PA 17602 717-392-0599; FAX 717-392-2371	**repairs** **restoration**

Shop open Monday-Friday 8:00 am to 4:30 pm. Restoration shop, classics, antiques, Corvettes, T-Birds, Mustangs, Triumphs, VWs and others. Specialize in automotive restoration.

for cars of the twenties to cars and trucks of the nineties. Deal in all phases of automotive repair, frame-up restoration to everyday driver cars.

Classics Plus LTD N7306 Lakeshore Dr N Fond du Lac, WI 54937 888-923-1007	**restoration**

See full listing in **Section Two** under **steering wheels**

Coach Builders Limited Inc 1410 S Main St PO Box 1978 High Springs, FL 32655 904-454-2060; FAX: 904-454-4080	**car dealer** **conv conversion**

Monday-Friday 8 am to 5 pm. Convertible conversions of Cadillac Eldorado.

Cobra Restorers Ltd 3099 Carter Dr Kennesaw, GA 30144 770-427-0020; FAX: 770-427-8658	**parts** **restoration** **service**

See full listing in **Section One** under **Cobra**

Collector's Carousel 84 Warren Ave Westbrook, ME 04092 207-854-0343; FAX: 207-856-6913	**appraisals** **sales** **service**

See full listing in **Section Two** under **car dealers**

Color-Ite Refinishing Co Winning Colors 868 Carrington Rd, Rt 69 Bethany, CT 06524 203-393-0240; FAX: 203-393-0873 E-mail: colorite@ctinternet.com	**modern finishes** **restoration service**

See full listing in **Section Two** under **paints**

Commonwealth Automotive Restorations 1725 Hewins St Ashley Falls, MA 01222 413-229-3196	**body rebuilding** **parts** **restoration**

See full listing in **Section Two** under **military vehicles**

Concours Quality Auto Restoration 32535 Pipeline Rd Gresham, OR 97080 503-663-4335; FAX: 503-663-3435	**pot metal** **restoration** **repro gloveboxes**

Mail order and open shop. Monday-Saturday 8 am to 6 pm or leave message. Specializing in pot metal welding, repair and restoration. Also glovebox reproduction, all cars with original style and color interior flocking.

Corvette Specialties of MD Inc 1912 Liberty Rd Eldersburg, MD 21784 410-795-3180; FAX: 410-795-3247	**parts** **restoration** **service**

See full listing in **Section One** under **Corvette**

County Auto Restoration 6 Gavin Rd Mt Vernon, NH 03057 603-673-4840	**bodywork** **brakes** **restoration** **woodwork**

Open shop. Monday-Friday 8 am to 5 pm, Saturday by appointment. Small shop specializing in total frame-up or partial restoration on antique cars and trucks, foreign or domestic. Sheetmetal panel and part fabrication, painting, woodwork, woodgraining, and upholstering. Also service antique vehicles. Over 40 years' experience. References upon request.

CT Model A Parts & Service 75 Prospect Ave West Hartford, CT 06106 860-233-1928; FAX: 860-233-1926 E-mail: ctmap@aol.com	parts restorations service

See full listing in **Section One** under **Ford 1903-1931**

Custom Classic Cars 2046 E 12B Road Bourbon, IN 46504 219-342-5007; FAX: 219-342-0399 E-mail: customclassiccars@waveone.net	parts restoration

See full listing in **Section One** under **Chevrolet**

D&M Corvette Specialists Ltd 1804 Ogden Ave Downers Grove, IL 60515 630-968-0031; FAX: 630-968-0465	parts restoration sales service

See full listing in **Section One** under **Corvette**

Dan's Restorations PO Box 144 Snake Hill Rd Sand Lake, NY 12153 518-674-2061	woodgraining

See full listing in **Section Two** under **woodgraining**

Dan's Volvo Service 6615 S MacDill Ave Tampa, FL 33611 813-831-1616	restoration

See full listing in **Section One** under **Volvo**

Dash Graining by Mel Erikson 31 Meadow Rd Kings Park, NY 11754 PH/FAX: 516-544-1102 days 516-360-7789 nights	dashboard restoration

See full listing in **Section Two** under **woodgraining**

Davies Corvette 7141 US Hwy 19 New Port Richey, FL 34653 727-842-8000, 800-236-2383 FAX: 727-846-8216 E-mail: davies@corvetteparts.com	accessories parts

See full listing in **Section One** under **Corvette**

DeLorean One 20229 Nordhoff St Chatsworth, CA 91311 818-341-1796; FAX: 818-998-6381	bodywork parts service

See full listing in **Section One** under **DeLorean**

Dependable RV & Auto Service 2619 Rt 11 N Lafayette, NY 13084 315-677-5336; FAX: 315-677-5258	parts restoration service

See full listing in **Section Two** under **service shops**

Deters Restorations 6205 Swiss Garden Rd Temperance, MI 48182-1020 734-847-1820	restoration

Mail order and open shop. Monday-Friday 7 am to 5 pm, Saturday 9 am to 2 pm. Antique, special interest and street rod restorations complete and partial. Sheetmetal fabrication.

DeVito Auto Restorations 470 Boston Post Rd Weston, MA 02493 781-893-4949 ext 142 FAX: 781-899-4900 E-mail: radjr@ix.netcom.com	restorations rust repair

See full listing in **Section Two** under **bodywork**

DiSchiavi Enterprises Inc 1248 Yardville Allentown Rd Allentown, NJ 08501 609-259-0787	restoration

Complete and partial restoration of antique, classic, sports and exotic automobiles. Specializing in 1953-1999 Chevrolet Corvettes. Restore to NCRS, NCCC and Bloomington Gold standards. Excellence in custom painting and coachwork. 30 year reputation for unsurpassed quality at an affordable price.

Dobbins Restoration Publishing 16 E Montgomery Avenue Hatboro, PA 19040 215-443-0779	literature parts restoration

See full listing in **Section One** under **Corvette**

Doc's Jags 125 Baker Rd Lake Bluff, IL 60044 847-367-5247; FAX: 847-367-6363 E-mail: docsjags@worldnet.att.net	appraisals interiors restoration

See full listing in **Section One** under **Jaguar**

Doctor Jaguar Inc 740 W 16th St Costa Mesa, CA 92627 949-646-2816; FAX: 949-574-8097	restoration service

See full listing in **Section One** under **Jaguar**

Greg Donahue Collector Car Restorations Inc 12900 S Betty Pt Floral City, FL 34436 352-344-4329; FAX: 352-344-0015	parts restoration

See full listing in **Section One** under **Ford 1954-up**

Done Right Engine & Machine Inc 12955 York Delta Unit J North Royalton, OH 44133 440-582-1366; FAX: 440-582-2005	engine rebuilding machine shop

See full listing in **Section Two** under **engine rebuilding**

DTE Motorsports 242 South Rd Brentwood, NH 03833 PH/FAX: 603-642-3766 E-mail: ldnh49a@prodigy.com	engines mechanical services race prep transportation

See full listing in **Section One** under **Mercedes-Benz**

East Coast Chevy Inc Ol '55 Chevy Parts 4154A Skyron Dr Doylestown, PA 18938 215-348-5568; FAX: 215-348-0560	custom work parts restoration

See full listing in **Section One** under **Chevrolet**

Eckhaus Motor Company 20818 E Weldon Tivy Valley, CA 93657-9107 559-787-1000; FAX: 559-787-1100	car dealer restoration shop

See full listing in **Section Two** under **car dealers**

Ecoclean 2000	rust dissolver
100 N Meadows Rd Medfield, MA 02052 888-399-2600, 508-359-9675 FAX: 508-359-7311 E-mail: rusteco1x@aol.com	

See full listing in **Section Two** under **rust removal & stripping**

Eddie's Restorations	restoration
4725 Rt 30 Elwood, NJ 08217 609-965-2211	

See full listing in **Section One** under **Jaguar**

Edgerton Classics Ltd	restoration woodworking
9215 St Rt 13 Camden, NY 13316-4933 315-245-3113	

Open Monday-Friday 9 am to 5 pm or by appointment. Classic auto restoration. Twenty years' experience utilizing the most technologically advanced materials combined with old fashioned craftsmanship to produce high point, show-winning restorations of full classics. The finest metal working, fabrication, woodworking and mechanical work available. Absolutely the highest attention to detail and originality. Full or partial projects considered. Investment quality automobiles available.

Enfield Auto Restoration Inc	panel beating restorations Rolls-Royce parts woodworking
4 Print Shop Rd Enfield, CT 06082 860-749-7917; FAX: 860-749-2836	

Mail order and open shop. Monday-Friday 8 am to 5:30 pm. Full service. Restoration, panel beating, fabrication services, woodworking, bodywork and paint, maintenance sales and services, wire-on leather service and coach building. Springfield Rolls-Royce parts.

ETC Every Thing Cars	paint repairs restoration welding
8727 Clarinda Pico Rivera, CA 90660 562-949-6981	

See full listing in **Section One** under **Mopar**

FEN Enterprises of New York Inc	parts restoration
PO Box 1559 1324 Rt 376 Wappingers Falls, NY 12590 914-462-5959, 914-462-5094 FAX: 914-462-8450	

See full listing in **Section One** under **Cadillac/LaSalle**

Flatlander's Hot Rod	parts restoration street rods
1005 W 45th St Norfolk, VA 23508 757-440-1932; FAX: 757-423-8601	

See full listing in **Section Two** under **street rods**

Fourintune Garage Inc	restoration
W63 N147 Washington Ave Cedarburg, WI 53012 414-375-0876; FAX: 414-675-2874	

See full listing in **Section One** under **Austin-Healey**

George Frechette	brake cylinder sleeving
14 Cedar Dr Granby, MA 01033 800-528-5235	

See full listing in **Section Two** under **brakes**

Freeman's Garage	parts restoration sales service
29 Ford Rd Norton, MA 02766 508-285-6500; FAX: 508-285-6566	

See full listing in **Section One** under **Ford 1903-1931**

Freman's Auto	car dealer salvage yard
138 Kountz Rd Whitehall, MT 59759 406-287-5436; FAX: 406-287-9103	

See full listing in **Section Two** under **car dealers**

From Rust To Riches	appraisals car dealer repairs restoration
16643 Rt 144 Mt Airy, MD 21771 301-854-5900, 410-442-3637 301-854-5956; FAX: 301-854-5957 E-mail: tatrabill@aol.com	

Mail order and open shop. Largest old car facility in the Washington DC, Baltimore, Frederick and northern Virginia areas. Full service, repairs, parts and award winning restorations of most cars and trucks through the early 1970s. Specialists in American and European cars including Packard, Cadillac, Rolls-Royce, Bentley, Studebaker and more. Obscure European cars welcome. Expert certified appraiser on-site. 15,000 square foot facility located just minutes from I-70. Over 30 years in the old car hobby and business.

Fuller's Restoration Inc	repairs restoration
Old Airport Rd Manchester Center, VT 05255 802-362-3643; FAX: 802-362-3360 E-mail: chevy@vermontel.com	

Open shop only. Monday-Friday 8 am to 5 pm. Rust, collision and restoration, all makes and models, free estimates.

Gas Tank and Radiator Rebuilders	abrasive blasting gas tank rebuilding heaters radiator repair
20123 Hwy 362 Waller, TX 77484 800-723-3759 E-mail: donhart@donhart.com	

See full listing in **Section Two** under **fuel system parts**

Golden Gulf Classics Inc	repairs restorations
PO Box 490 22530 Hwy 49 Saucier, MS 39574 228-831-2650; FAX: 228-831-1513 E-mail: gudhowdy@datasync.com	

See full listing in **Section One** under **Triumph**

Golden Mile Sales Inc	NORS parts NOS parts sheetmetal
J DeAngelo 2439 S Bradford St Allentown, PA 18103-5821 PH/FAX: 610-791-4497, 24 hours	

See full listing in **Section One** under **American Austin/Bantam**

Grand Touring	engine rebuilding machine shop restoration suspension
2785 E Regal Park Dr Anaheim, CA 92806 714-630-0130; FAX: 714-630-6956	

Parts mail order and open shop. Monday-Saturday 8 am to 5 pm. Complete in-house restoration facilities offering paint, interior, plating, machine shop, engine building/dyno services. Custom design and fabrication of body panels, suspension, interior and engine parts. Specializing in 1900-1970 automobiles and motorcycles, including GM, Ford, Duesenberg, Mopar, Packard, Stutz, vintage race cars, plus British, Japanese and European bikes. From body-off restorations to simple repairs, we provide the best craftsmanship available. Our restorations have been featured in every major auto and motorcycle publication and have won every major concours event including Pebble Beach.

Grey Hills Auto Restoration	restoration
PO Box 630	service
51 Vail Rd	
Blairstown, NJ 07825	
908-362-8232; FAX: 908-362-6796	

Offering services for all makes and models, antique, classic, collector, muscle cars and street rods.

Guild of Automotive Restorers	restoration
PO Box 1150, 44 Bridge St	sales
Bradford ON Canada L3Z 2B5	service
905-775-0499; FAX: 905-775-0944	
E-mail:	
webmaster@guildautomotive.on.ca	

Dedicated to the restoration and sale of the world's great cars. Services include true coachbuilding, ash framing, panel beating, mechanical and trim parts fabrication, engine rebuilding, paint and upholstering. Restore and service automobiles with an emphasis on the full classics of the 1920s and 1930s. From complete frame-off restorations to small repairs and service. The Guild offers fine quality workmanship. Service a wide variety of cars including Bugatti, Rolls-Royce, Bentley, Packard, Pierce-Arrow, GM, Ford and many more. Web site: www.guildautomotive.on.ca

Hamel's Automotive Inc	restorations
RR 2 Box 61	
Wingdale, NY 12594	
914-832-9454	
E-mail: startnagan@aol.com	

Specializing in restoration of antique automobiles. Professional quality service for over 20 years. Full frame-off or partial restoration. Call Doug at above phone number.

Hand's Elderly Auto Care	repair
2000 Galveston St	restoration
Grand Prairie, TX 75051	
PH/FAX: 972-642-4288	

Mail order and open shop. Monday-Friday 8 am to 5 pm. Maintaining, repairing and restoring antique automobiles, turn of the century to the 1950s. Specializing in Cadillac and Chevrolet.

Harbor Auto Restoration	restoration
1504 SW 3rd St	
Pompano Beach, FL 33069	
954-785-7887; FAX: 954-785-7388	
E-mail: harbor@harbor-auto.com	

Open Monday-Friday 7 am to 4 pm, Saturday by appointment only. A family owned and operated state of the art facility. Specializing in total or partial restoration of foreign, domestic, classic, street rod and muscle vehicles with hundreds of nationally acclaimed competition victories to our credit. Web site: www.harbor-auto.com

See our ad on this page

Hatfield Restorations	restoration
PO Box 846	
Canton, TX 75103	
903-567-6742; FAX: 903-567-0645	
E-mail: pathat@vzinet.com	

Open shop only. Monday-Friday 8 am to 5 pm. Complete or partial restorations. Street rod design and construction. Woodwork and metal fabrication. Quality workmanship and attention to detail. We invite you to come by and visit the shop. Also do interior work.

Hibernia Auto Restorations Inc	lacquer
52 Maple Terr	restoration
Hibernia, NJ 07842	
973-627-1882; FAX: 973-627-3503	

Open Monday-Friday 7 am to 5 pm. Restoration of any collectible car, full or partial restoration. Nitrocellulose and acrylic lacquer for sale.

Hjeltness Restoration Inc	restoration
630 Alpine Way	service
Escondido, CA 92029	
760-746-9966; FAX: 760-746-7738	

Specializing in the restoration, service and repair of Mercedes 300SL and other classic automobiles. Internationally recognized for our attention to authenticity and detail.

Hollywood Classic Motorcars Inc	cars
363 Ansin Blvd	parts
Hallandale, FL 33009	
800-235-2444, 954-454-4641	
FAX: 954-457-3801	
E-mail: hcm@tbird.net	

See full listing in **Section One** under **Thunderbird**

The Horn Shop	horn restoration
7129 Oriskany Rd	
Rome, NY 13440	

Mail order only. Rebuild the motor section of your antique auto, motorcycle or boat horn. Mechanical and electrical repairs, includes the rewinding of the field coils and armature. If your horn is damaged beyond repair or missing completely, we will try to locate the correct horn for your marque's year and model. For inspection and written estimate of repairs, send the horn motor section, $10 and a SASE.

Hyde Auto Body
44-1/2 S Squirrel Rd
Auburn Hills, MI 48326
PH/FAX: 248-852-7832
E-mail: bodyman8@juno.com

refinishing
restoration

Open shop only. Monday-Friday 9 am to 6 pm, Saturday 9 am to 1 pm. Classic auto restoration and refinishing. Web site: http://members.xoom.com/hydeautobody/

Jerry's Classic Cars & Parts Inc
4097 McRay Ave
Springdale, AR 72764
800-828-4584; FAX: 501-750-1682
E-mail: jcc@jerrysclassiccars.com

parts
restoration

See full listing in **Section One** under **Ford 1954-up**

Jim's T-Bird Parts & Service
710 Barney Ave
Winston-Salem, NC 27107
PH/FAX: 336-784-9363
E-mail: tbirdjims@aol.com

parts
restoration
service

See full listing in **Section One** under **Thunderbird**

John's Car Corner
Rt 5, PO Box 85
Westminster, VT 05158
802-722-3180; FAX: 802-722-3181

body parts
car dealer
mechanical parts
restoration service

See full listing in **Section One** under **Volkswagen**

JWF Restorations Inc
11955 SW Faircrest St
Portland, OR 97225-4615
503-643-3225; FAX: 503-646-4009

restoration

See full listing in **Section One** under **AC**

SINCE 1976 we have been providing the finest in complete and partial restoration of Classic and Antique automobiles. Our 24 years of experience will guarantee satisfaction for your next 100 point show car or tour vehicle.

L & N OLDE CAR CO.

9992 Kinsman Road, Box 378
Newbury, OH 44065
(440) 564-7204

K & K Vintage Motorcars LC
9848 SW Frwy
Houston, TX 77074
713-541-2281; FAX: 713-541-2286

restoration
sales
service

Open Monday-Friday 9 am to 5 pm, Saturday by appointment. Sales, service and restoration of classic and exotic cars. Specializing in Maserati, Jaguar, MGs, Fords and all other makes of domestic and foreign pre or post-war. Over 20 years' experience. Worldwide references upon request.

K&D Enterprises
23117 E Echo Lake Rd
Snohomish, WA 98296-5426
425-788-0507; FAX: 360-668-2003
E-mail: tdb@halcyon.com

accessories
parts
restorations

See full listing in **Section One** under **Jensen**

K-F-D Services Inc
HC 65, Box 49
Altonah, UT 84002
801-454-3098; FAX: 801-454-3099
E-mail: kfd-services@msn.com

parts
restoration

See full listing in **Section One** under **Kaiser Frazer**

Keilen's Auto Restoring
580 Kelley Blvd (R)
North Attleboro, MA 02760
508-699-7768

restoration

Open shop only. Monday-Friday 8 am to 5 pm, Saturday 8 am to 12 noon. Restoring all years and makes of cars and trucks, all types of painting and customizing, street rods and mechanical repairs.

Kelley's Korner
22 14th St
Bristol, TN 37620
423-968-5583

parts
repair

See full listing in **Section One** under **Studebaker**

Ken's Cougars
PO Box 5380
Edmond, OK 73083
405-340-1636; FAX: 405-340-5877

parts

See full listing in **Section One** under **Mercury**

Ken's Klassics
20803 State Hwy 60
Muscoda, WI 53573-5466
608-739-4242; FAX: 608-739-4241

car sales
restoration

Shop open Monday-Friday 8 am to 5 pm, Saturday by appointment. Established in 1981. A complement of eight experienced craftsmen specializing in complete and partial restorations of classic, collectible and special interest vehicles. Meticulous workmanship performed at reasonable rates and honest billings. Certified PPG show quality paint and refinishing services. National show and pleasure car restorations. References gladly given. Please visit our beautiful facility anytime.

Kip Motor Company Inc
2127 Crown Rd
Dallas, TX 75229
972-243-0440; FAX: 972-243-2387
E-mail: kipmotor@aol.com

literature
parts
restoration

See full listing in **Section One** under **Austin**

Krem Engineering 10204 Perry Hwy Meadville, PA 16335 814-724-4806; FAX: 814-337-2992 E-mail: info@krem-enterprises.com	**engine rebuilding** **repairs** **restoration**

Mail order and open shop. Monday-Friday 8 am to 5 pm. Restoration problems are what we do best, the stuff no one else can or wants to do. Can make or repair the uncommon, non-existent or difficult components. Also do problem engine and driveline rebuilds. Use original manufacturing practices and procedures whenever possible. Twenty-eight years' experience. Automobile, airplane, train, boat, tractor or machine. Web site: www.krem-enterprises.com

L & N Olde Car Co 9992 Kinsman Rd PO Box 378 Newbury, OH 44065 440-564-7204; FAX: 440-564-8187	**restoration**

Complete or partial restoration. Specializing in collector and show automobiles. Concours or to custom specifications, show quality paint and finish, sheetmetal and aluminum fabrication. Wood fabrication and coachwork, mechanical, electrical, lead work. Machine work and parts fabrication. Maintenance work and repairs. Serving our customers since 1976.
See our ad on page 380

Larson Motor Co Russell Larson 4423 A Canyon Dr Amarillo, TX 79110 806-358-9797	**appraisals** **restoration** **sales**

See full listing in **Section Two** under **car dealers**

Last Chance Repair & Restoration PO Box 362A Myers Rd Shaftsbury, VT 05262	**repairs** **restoration**

Mail order and open shop. Monday-Friday 7 am to 3:30 pm. Chassis preparations and restoration. Special interest in Ford pickups and old VW Beetles. Parts and vehicles for sale or located. Five years' Great American Race experience. Emphasis on reliability.

LaVine Restorations Inc 1349 Beech Rd Nappanee, IN 46550 219-773-7561; FAX: 219-773-7595	**restoration**

Shop open Monday-Friday 8 am to 5 pm, Saturday by appointment. Specializing in professional national show restorations and pleasure car restorations. Antique, classic, special interest and street rod.

L B Repair 1308 W Benten Savannah, MO 64485-1549 816-324-3913	**restoration**

See full listing in **Section One** under **Ford 1954-up**

Lee's Kustom Auto & Street Rods RR 3 Box 3061A Rome, PA 18837 570-247-2326 E-mail: lka41@epix.net	**accessories** **parts** **restoration**

See full listing in **Section Two** under **street rods**

Libbey's Classic Car Restoration Center 137 N Quinsigamond Ave Shrewsbury, MA 01545 PH/FAX: 508-792-1560	**bodywork** **restoration** **service**

Open shop. Monday-Friday 9 am to 6 pm, some Saturdays 9 am to 12 noon. Complete and partial restoration, service, problem

solving, mechanical, electrical and bodywork for all types of classic and special interest cars and antiques. Have done restorations on several Duesenbergs (two CCAC 100 pt cars), as well as Stanley Steamers, Packards, T-Birds, Mustangs and Cadillacs.

Jeff Lilly Restoration Inc 11125 FM 1560 San Antonio, TX 78254 PH/FAX: 210-695-5151	**classic car** **restoration** **street rod building**

Classic cars and custom street rods built on an hourly basis. Separate buildings for mechanical, body, painting, upholstery, assembly, creates organization, efficiency and a cleaner finished product of highest quality. Organized disassembly process to find all the parts needed for your classic. 3/16 gaps between body panels with stunning paint will complement your cars physique. Our work appears monthly in national magazines for your review in choosing us as your restoration company. Visit our web site for a complete shop tour. Web site: www.jefflilly.com

Lincoln Highway Packards Main St PO Box 94 Schellsburg, PA 15559 814-733-4356; FAX: 814-839-4276	**engine rebuilding** **restoration**

See full listing in **Section One** under **Packard**

Lindley Restorations Ltd 10 S Sanatoga Rd Pottstown, PA 19464 610-326-8484; FAX: 610-326-3845	**parts** **sales** **service**

See full listing in **Section One** under **Jaguar**

Lindskog Balancing 1170 Massachusetts Ave Boxborough, MA 01719-1415 978-263-2040; FAX: 978-263-4035	**engine balancing**

See full listing in **Section Two** under **engine rebuilding**

Lyme Pond Restorations PO Box 202 Barnard, VT 05031 802-457-4657	**restoration**

Open shop only. Monday-Friday 8 am to 5 pm. A small shop offering complete restoration services, mechanical, bodywork, upholstery. Rust repairs, convertible tops, British cars our specialty. All makes and models of automobiles, trucks and motorcycles.

Madera Concepts 606 Olive St Santa Barbara, CA 93101 800-800-1579, 805-962-1579 FAX: 805-962-7359 E-mail: jwayco@west.net	**restoration** **woodwork** **woodwork repair**

See full listing in **Section Two** under **woodwork**

Manchester Motor Car Co 319 Main St Manchester, CT 06040 860-643-5874; FAX: 860-643-6190 E-mail: mmcollc@aol.com	**automobilia** **parts** **petroliana** **restorations**

See full listing in **Section Two** under **comprehensive parts**

Marshall Antique & Classic Restorations 3714 Old Philadelphia Pike Bethlehem, PA 18015 610-868-7765; FAX: 610-868-7529	**coolant additives** **restoration services**

See full listing in **Section One** under **Rolls-Royce/Bentley**

Master Plating 2109 Newton Ave San Diego, CA 92113 619-232-3092; FAX: 619-232-3094	plating restoration

See full listing in **Section Two** under **plating & polishing**

Mastermind Inc 32155 Joshua Dr Wildomar, CA 92595 PH/FAX: 909-674-0509 E-mail: mike@mastermindinc.net	new/used parts restoration

See full listing in **Section One** under **Cadillac/LaSalle**

The Masters Company 30 Willow Dr Suite A Fort Thomas, KY 41075-2035 800-385-5811; FAX: 606-441-6765 E-mail: badger@cinternet.net	parts tools

See full listing in **Section Two** under **tools**

McCann Auto Restoration US Rt 1, PO Box 1025 Houlton, ME 04730 207-532-2206	custom work restoration sandblasting

Open shop only. Monday-Friday 8 am to 5 pm. Complete or partial restoration of classic, antique or special interest cars and trucks. Also sandblasting and custom work.

McGee Motorsports Group 29127 Arnold Dr Sonoma, CA 95476 707-996-1112; FAX: 707-996-9148	race prep restoration

See full listing in **Section Two** under **racing**

Memory Lane Motors 562 County Rd 121 Fenelon Falls, ON Canada K0M 1N0 705-887-CARS; FAX: 705-887-4028	car dealer restoration service

Mail order and open shop. Monday-Friday 8 am to 5 pm, Saturday 8:30 am to noon usually. Interesting older autos, talked about enthusiastically. Bought, sold, serviced, recreated. Restore antique and classic vehicles, mechanical and body repair, Krown rust control center, float vehicles on a ramp truck. Used motor vehicles for sale.

Memoryville USA Inc 1008 W 12th St Rolla, MO 65401 573-364-1810	restoration

Mail order and open shop. Monday-Friday 8 am to 4:30 pm. Can restore any automobile, partial or complete, either for driving or to show quality, in one of the largest established restoration shops in the United States. Restoration is done in our shop by highly skilled craftsmen, with over 25 years' experience, who specialize in all phases of restoration work including mechanical, woodworking, painting, upholstering, pinstriping, woodgraining and parts fabrication. For more information, write or call for our free brochure.

Alan Mest Early Model Auto Repair 17212 Gramercy Pl Gardena, CA 90247 310-532-8657, 310-372-1039 FAX: 310-376-6009	mechanical repair restoration

Shop open six days 9 am to 6 pm. Repair and restoration of all pre-1955 American made autos.

Mid Valley Engineering 16637 N 21st St Phoenix, AZ 85022 602-482-1251; FAX: 602-788-0812	machine work parts restoration

See full listing in **Section Two** under **transmissions**

Morgan Oasis Garage PO Box 1010 N 51 Terrace Rd Hoodsport, WA 98548 360-877-5160	restoration service

See full listing in **Section One** under **Morgan**

Morgan Spares Ltd 225 Simons Rd Ancram, NY 12502 518-329-3877; FAX: 518-329-3892 E-mail: morganspares@taconic.net	car sales consulting obsolete parts used parts

See full listing in **Section One** under **Morgan**

Muncie Imports & Classics 4401 St Rd 3 N Muncie, IN 47303 800-462-4244; FAX: 317-287-9551 E-mail: mic@netdirect.net	repair restoration upholstery

See full listing in **Section One** under **Jaguar**

Muscle Express 509 Commerce Way W #3 Jupiter, FL 33458 800-323-3043 order line 561-744-3043 tech line	parts

See full listing in **Section One** under **Chevelle/Camaro**

Mustang Classics 3814 Walnut St Denver, CO 80205 303-295-3140	parts restoration sales service

See full listing in **Section One** under **Mustang**

Mustangs & More 2065 Sperry Ave #C Ventura, CA 93003 800-356-6573; FAX: 805-642-6468 E-mail: mustmore@aol.com	parts restoration

See full listing in **Section One** under **Mustang**

Nationwide Auto Restoration 1038 Watt St Jeffersonville, IN 47130 812-280-0165; FAX: 812-280-8961 E-mail: restore@unidial.com	bodywork paint upholstery

Mail order and open shop. Monday-Friday 9 am to 4 pm, Saturday 9 am to 12 noon. Dealing in Austin-Healey, MG, Triumph, Morgan, Jaguar, Porsche. Full and partial restorations, bodywork, upholstery, paint, mechanical. National award winning work. Nationally recognized in national auto magazines.

NCA Automotive 4532 W Palm Ln Phoenix, AZ 85035 602-272-9009 E-mail: nca@primenet.com	restoration

Stainless steel restoration, straightening and polishing. Also aluminum.

New Era Motors 11611 NE 50th Ave, Unit 6 Vancouver, WA 98686 360-573-8788	**restoration**

See full listing in **Section Two** under **woodwork**

Norm's Custom Shop 6897 E William St Ext Bath, NY 14810 PH/FAX: 607-776-2357	**interiors** **tops**

See full listing in **Section One** under **Cord**

Northern Motorsport Ltd PO Box 508, Rt 5 Wilder, VT 05088 802-296-2099; FAX: 802-295-6599	**repair** **restoration** **sales** **service**

Open shop. Monday-Friday 8 am to 6 pm. Specialize in service, repair and mechanical restoration of pre-1970s Rolls-Royces, Bentleys, Mercedes, Bugattis and Packards. Full service shop providing service and repairs to current model year European automobiles as well as our beloved antiques. With machine tools on premises, we can fabricate some parts. References and pictures upon request. Contact: Mike Zack. Also sell European and antique automobiles.

Odyssey Restorations Inc 8080 Central Ave NE Spring Lake Park, MN 55432 612-786-1518; FAX: 612-786-1524	**parts** **restoration**

Mail order and open shop. Monday-Friday 8 am to 5 pm, Saturday by appointment. Specializing in concours restorations of brass and CCCA Classic cars, exotic engine and driveline restorations and major tour prep. Difficult, rare, early projects a specialty. Consistent major Concours winners and worldwide tour participants. Parts and services for Franklin automobiles 1902-1934.

Old Coach Works Restoration Inc 1206 Badger St Yorkville, IL 60560-1701 630-553-0414; FAX: 630-553-1053 E-mail oldcoachworks@msn.com	**appraisals** **restoration**

Open shop only. Monday-Friday 7 am to 5 pm, Saturday by appointment. Specializing in complete or partial restoration service on all antique, classic or special interest automobiles. Also enjoy sports cars, street rods and an occasional motorcycle. 25 years at the same location. Nationwide pickup and delivery available. Call for a free brochure. Appraisal service also available. Web site: www.oldcoachworks.com

Older Car Restoration Martin Lum, Owner 304 S Main St, Box 428 Mont Alto, PA 17237 717-749-3383, 717-352-7701 E-mail: jlum@epix.net	**repro parts** **restoration**

See full listing in **Section One** under **Mopar**

Bob Ore Restorations 4725 Iroquois Ave Erie, PA 16511 814-898-3933; FAX: 814-899-8632	**chemical stripping** **chrome plating** **restoration**

Open Monday-Friday 8 am to 5 pm, Saturday 8 am to 11:30 am. Specializing in complete or partial restoration, service and maintenance of all automobiles. In-house chemical stripping and show quality chrome plating. Enclosed transport, references available. 25 years' experience.

Ottorich 619 Hammond St Chestnut Hill, MA 02467 617-738-5488 E-mail: rdmfm@mediaone.net	**restoration**

See full listing in **Section One** under **Mercedes-Benz**

Bill Peters 41 Vassar Pl Rockville Centre, NY 11570 516-766-8397	**steering wheel** **restoration**

See full listing in **Section Two** under **steering wheels**

A Petrik 504 Edmonds Ave NE Renton, WA 98056 425-255-4852 E-mail: rnrserv@hotmail.com	**heater control** **valve rebuilding**

Mail order only. Rebuilding service for all Ranco and Harrison heater control valves, 1930s-1960s. Established 1972. Web site: www.heatercontrolvalve.com

R E Pierce 47 Stone Rd Wendell Depot, MA 01380 978-544-7442; FAX: 978-544-2978 E-mail: robin@billsgate.com	**parts** **restoration**

See full listing in **Section One** under **Volvo**

Pilgrim's Auto Restorations 3888 Hill Rd Lakeport, CA 95453 707-262-1062; FAX: 707-263-6956 E-mail: pilgrims@pacific.net	**bodywork** **metal fabrication** **paint** **restoration**

Shop open Monday-Friday 8 am to 5 pm, Saturday 8 am to 12 noon. Offer restoration, metal fabrication, body and paint. Web site: www.autorestore.com

Pitcher's Auto Restoration 54 Metaterraine Ave Perryville, RI 02879 401-783-4392 E-mail: pep@edgenet.net	**engine repair** **parts** **restoration**

Mail order and open shop. Monday-Friday 8 am to 5 pm, Saturday by appointment. Complete or partial restorations for all vehicles. Also babbitt bearing service and complete engine service for early cars. Mechanical repairs and fabrications for hard-to-find parts.

Precious Metal Automotive Restoration Co Inc 1601 College Ave SE Grand Rapids, MI 49507 616-243-0220; FAX: 616-243-6646 E-mail: prshsmtl@pathwaynet.com	**broker** **restoration**

See full listing in **Section One** under **Mercedes-Benz**

Precision Auto Designs 28 Railway Ave Campbell, CA 95008 408-378-2332; FAX: 408-378-1301 E-mail: pad@precisionauto.com	**accessories** **car covers** **restoration**

See full listing in **Section One** under **Mercedes-Benz**

Precision Pot Metal/Bussie Restoration Inc 1008 Loring Ave #28 Orange Park, FL 32073 904-269-8788	**pot metal** **restoration**

See full listing in **Section Two** under **plating & polishing**

Section Two
Generalists

Proper Jaguar 1806 S Alpine Rockford, IL 61108 815-398-0303, 815-398-8664	restoration

See full listing in **Section One** under **Jaguar**

Al Prueitt & Sons Inc 8 Winter Ave, PO Box 158 Glen Rock, PA 17327 717-428-1305, 800-766-0035 FAX: 717-235-4428	restoration upholstery woodwork

Shop open Monday-Friday 8 am to 4:30 pm. Complete restorations, upholstery, wood refinishing for antique and classic cars. Expert paint and bodywork, all types of mechanical work. Rolls-Royce service. Family run business with over thirty years' experience restoring cars of all makes. Please visit our shop anytime.

R & L Engines Inc 308 Durham Rd Dover, NH 03820 603-742-8812; FAX: 603-742-8137	engine rebuilding restorations

See full listing in **Section Two** under **engine rebuilding**

Ragtops & Roadsters 203 S 4th St Perkasie, PA 18944 215-257-1202; FAX: 215-257-2688 E-mail: info@ragtops.com	bodywork/painting British automobiles engine rebuilding vintage race prep

Open shop only. Monday-Friday 9 am to 5 pm, evenings and Saturday by appointment. Minor repairs to full concours restorations of all British and special interest automobiles. Vintage race car prep and restoration. The more unusual the car the more we enjoy it. Mechanical, engine rebuilds, interior trimming, body and paint refinishing, fabrication. Web site: www.ragtops.com

Ray's Upholstering 600 N St Frances Cabrini Ave Scranton, PA 18504 800-296-RAYS; FAX: 717-963-0415	partial/total restoration

Open Monday-Friday 8 am to 5 pm. Restore antique, classic and specialized automobiles. Partial or total restorations. Our specialty are custom interiors for street rods in leather and imitation suede.

RB's Prototype Model & Machine Co 44 Marva Ln Stamford, CT 06903 203-329-2715; FAX: 203-329-8029	machine work

See full listing in **Section Two** under **service shops**

Realistic Auto Restorations Inc 2519 6th Ave S St Petersburg, FL 33712 727-327-5162; FAX: 727-327-1877 E-mail: jsamu58686@aol.com	restoration

Complete or partial restorations on antique, special interest, foreign and domestic autos. Specialists in sheetmetal fabrication, paint and body, mechanics, upholstery, woodwork, wiring and stainless steel repair, etc. Family owned and operated since 1978. Many Concours and National trophy winners. No job too small.

Redding Corp Box 477 George's Mills, NH 03751 603-763-2566; FAX: 603-763-5682	restoration

Open Monday-Friday 8 am to 4 pm. Offering general restoration ranging from dependable drivers to show. Any make. Estimates cheerfully provided, references available too.

Regal Roadsters Ltd 301 W Beltline Hwy Madison, WI 53713 PH/FAX: 608-273-4141	replicars restoration

See full listing in **Section One** under **Thunderbird**

Reinholds Restorations c/o Rick Reinhold PO Box 178, 255 N Ridge Rd Reinholds, PA 17569-0178 717-336-5617; FAX: 717-336-7050	appraisals repairs restoration

Open shop only. Monday-Friday 8 am to 5 pm, Saturdays and evenings by appointment. Complete quality restorations, repairs, service, appraisals, cars, trucks, fire engines, motorcycles. Anything, wood working, engine rebuilding, gas tank tumble cleaning, woodgraining.

Reproduction Parts Marketing 1920 Alberta Ave Saskatoon, SK Canada S7K 1R9 306-652-6668; FAX: 306-652-1123	parts restoration service

See full listing in **Section One** under **Chevrolet**

Restoration Specialties John Sarena 124 North F St Lompoc, CA 93436 805-736-2627	interiors restoration

See full listing in **Section One** under **Chevrolet**

Restorations Unlimited II Inc 304 Jandus Rd Cary, IL 60013 847-639-5818	restoration

Open shop only. Monday-Friday 7 am to 5 pm, Saturday by appointment. A full service restoration center performing all phases in-house. Paint, upholstery, panel forming. Concours preparation. Restorations of foreign and domestic, aluminum, steel and glass. Have a history of winning cars at Pebble Beach, Meadowbrook, LCOC, AACA. Call us for that special project. Celebrating our 29th year in the restoration business. Web site: www.dwinc.com/ruii

Richard's Auto Restoration RD 3, Box 83A Wyoming, PA 18644 717-333-4191	restoration

Mail order and open shop. Monday-Friday 7:30 am to 3:30 pm. Sandblasting and glass bead work done.

Richardson Restorations 1861 W Woodward Ave Tulare, CA 93274 559-688-5002	custom work repairs restoration

Restoration of antique and classic autos. Fabrication of custom rods, subframing, top chops and restyling. Sand casting of small parts.

Rick's Relics Wheeler Rd Pittsburg, NH 03592 603-538-6612	bodywork painting restoration

Shop open Monday-Saturday 8 am to 5 pm. Complete and partial restorations for antique, classic and special interest cars. Painting, glass work, wiring, bodywork with lead. All makes, foreign and domestic. 36 years' experience in the trade.

Riverbend Abrasive Blasting 44308 St Rt 36 W Coshocton, OH 43812-9741 614-622-0867	blasting painting/polishing restoration

See full listing in **Section Two** under **rust removal & stripping**

RM Auto Restoration Ltd 9435 Horton Line Blenheim, ON Canada N0P 1A0 519-352-4575; FAX: 519-351-1337 E-mail: clark@rmcars.com	**panel fabrication** **parts** **restoration**

Open Monday-Friday 9 am to 5 pm, Saturday by appointment. Complete award-winning or partial restorations of Cadillac, Packard, Jaguar, Rolls-Royce, Stutz, Ferrari and Mercedes-Benz. All work done in-house to the highest quality. Located 45 minutes east of Detroit. Web site: www.rmcars.com

Roadrunner Tire & Auto 4850 Hwy 377 S Fort Worth, TX 76116 817-244-4924	**restoration** **speedometer repair**

Mail order and open shop. Monday-Friday 7:30 am to 5:30 pm CST. Mechanical restoration, engine rebuilding, suspension, brakes. Also mail order speedometer repair. Have had 12 Great Race entries, all finished.

Robertson Bros & Sons Restoration PO Box 5678 Sevierville, TN 37864-5678 423-970-1655; FAX: 423-908-6838 E-mail: classicbop@aol.com	**NOS parts** **restoration parts** **used parts**

See full listing in **Section One** under **Oldsmobile**

Rod-1 Shop 210 Clinton Ave Pitman, NJ 08071 609-228-7631; FAX: 609-582-5770	**street rods**

See full listing in **Section Two** under **street rods**

Rode's Restoration 1406 Lohr Rd Galion, OH 44833 419-468-5182; FAX: 419-462-1753 E-mail: rodes@bright.net	**parts** **restoration**

See full listing in **Section One** under **Mustang**

Ron's Restorations Inc 2968-B Ask Kay Dr Smyrna, GA 30082 770-438-6102; FAX: 770-438-0037	**interior trim** **restoration**

See full listing in **Section One** under **Mercedes-Benz**

RPM Catalog PO Box 12031 Kansas City, KS 66109 913-788-3219; FAX: 913-788-9682 E-mail: dale@dalewilch.com	**parts** **speed equipment**

See full listing in **Section Two** under **racing**

Paul Russell & Company 106 Western Ave Essex, MA 01929 978-768-6919; FAX: 978-768-3523 E-mail: info@paulrussellandco.com	**car dealer** **mechanical service** **parts** **restoration**

Open Monday-Thursday 8 am to 6 pm. Our restoration craftsmen offer mechanical, upholstery, parts, bodywork and paint, panel beating and coachbuilding services on all 1950s and pre-war European classics such as Mercedes-Benz, Bugatti, Porsche and BMW. Sales, consignment, purchasing of all classic automobiles. Web site: www.paulrussellandco.com

Sanders Antique Auto Restoration 1120 22nd St Rockford, IL 61108 815-226-0535	**restoration**

Open Monday-Friday 8 am to 4:30 pm. Partial and complete restorations plus some repair. Most of our work is antique and classic cars, but we enjoy special interest and sports cars, street rods and motorcycles.

SC Automotive Rt 3 Box 9 New Ulm, MN 56073 800-62-SS-409 (627-7409) 507-354-1958 info FAX: 800-6477-FAX (647-7329)	**parts** **restoration**

See full listing in **Section One** under **Chevrolet**

Schaeffer & Long 210 Davis Rd Magnolia, NJ 08049 609-784-4044	**restoration**

Open Monday-Friday 8 am to 4:30 pm. Restorations, complete or partial. In business since 1968.

Sheldon Classic Auto Restoration Inc 1245 N 3rd, Space G Lawrence, KS 66044 785-843-6776	**restoration**

Over twenty years' experience, over ten years in business. Vintage American and European. Many show winners.

Silver Star Restorations 116 Highway 19 Topton, NC 28781 704-321-4268 E-mail: silverstar@main.nc.us	**parts** **restoration**

See full listing in **Section One** under **Mercedes-Benz**

SL-Tech 230SL-250SL-280SL 1364 Portland Rd US Rt 1 Arundel/Kennebunkport, ME 04046 207-985-3001; FAX: 207-985-3011 E-mail: gernold@sltechw113.com	**parts** **restoration** **service**

See full listing in **Section One** under **Mercedes-Benz**

Chris Smith's Creative Workshop Motorcar Restoration 118 NW Park St Dania, FL 33004 954-920-3303; FAX: 954-920-9950 E-mail: restor1st@aol.com	**parts** **restoration** **service**

Mail order and open shop. Monday-Friday 9 am to 5 pm. First quality ground-up, frame-off restorations. Parts, wood, steel and aluminum fabrication. Upholstery and trim. Complete in-house service specializing in Mercedes, Ferrari, Porsche, Lamborghini, antiques and special interest autos. Immersion paint and rust removal. Sandblasting parts, fabrication, detail, race car prep. Also large reference library.

Special Auto Restoration 689 Fern Dr Merritt Island, FL 32952 407-453-8343, 407-783-4758	**restoration**

See full listing in **Section One** under **Chevelle/Camaro**

Sterling Restorations Inc 1705 Eastwood Dr Sterling, IL 61081 815-625-2260; FAX: 815-625-0799	**appraisals** **restorations**

See full listing in **Section Two** under **appraisals**

Steve's Auto Restorations
4440 SE 174th Ave
Portland, OR 97236
503-665-2222; FAX: 503-665-2225
E-mail: steve@realsteel.com

restoration

Mail order and open shop. Monday-Friday 7 am to 4:30 pm.
Complete ground-up show quality restorations on antiques and
classics, specializing in 300SL Mercedes, pre-war Mercedes, one-
off and production run classics. Street rod design and construction. Mechanical, bodywork, paint, wiring, upholstery, metal fabrication. Resilvering of headlight reflectors. Complete light
restoration, Halogen conversions, headlight lens, bulb and gasket sales. New "real steel" 33-34 roadster and cabriolet bodies,
sheetmetal also available. Web sites: www.realsteel.com or
www.stevesautorestorations.com

Still Cruisin' Corvettes
5759 Benford Dr
Haymarket, VA 20169
703-754-1960; FAX: 703-754-1222

appraisals
repairs
restoration

See full listing in **Section One** under **Corvette**.

Stockton Wheel Service
648 W Fremont St
Stockton, CA 95203
209-464-7771, 800-395-9433
FAX: 209-464-4725
E-mail: sales@stocktonwheel.com

wheel repair

See full listing in **Section Two** under **wheels & wheelcovers**.

Stone Barn Inc
202 Rt 46, Box 117
Vienna, NJ 07880
908-637-4444; FAX: 908-637-4290

restoration

Restore antique, classic, exotic and special interest automobiles.

Stormin Norman's Bug Shop
201 Commerce Dr #3
Fort Collins, CO 80524
970-493-5873

repair
restoration

See full listing in **Section One** under **Volkswagen**.

Stringbean's Pickup Parts
985 Cushon St
Johnstown, PA 15902
PH/FAX: 814-539-6440
E-mail: s-bean@surfshop.net

parts
service

See full listing in **Section One** under **Chevrolet**.

Supreme Metal Polishing
84A Rickenbacker Cir
Livermore, CA 94550
925-449-3490; FAX: 925-449-1475
E-mail: supremet@home.com

metal working
parts restoration
plating services
polishing

See full listing in **Section Two** under **plating & polishing**.

Te Puke Vintage Auto Barn
26 Young Rd
Te Puke New Zealand
PH/FAX: 07 5736547

parts
restoration
sales

Mail order and open shop. Daily 9 am to 5 pm. Car display,
restoration and sales of old cars. Specialize in cars from the
1920s-1970s. Have parts and restore any make, do not have a
preference.

Teddy's Garage
8530 Louise Ave
Northridge, CA 91325
818-341-0505

parts
restoration
service

See full listing in **Section One** under **Rolls-Royce/Bentley**.

Thermax Inc
5385 Alpha Ave
Reno, NV 89506
800-247-7177; FAX: 702-972-4809

interior detailing

See full listing in **Section Two** under **car care products**

Thunderbirds East
Andy Lovelace
140 Wilmington W Chester Pike
Chadds Ford, PA 19317
610-358-1021; FAX: 610-558-9615

parts
restoration

See full listing in **Section One** under **Thunderbird**

Tillack & Co Ltd
630 Mary Ann Dr
Redondo Beach, CA 90278
310-318-8760; FAX: 310-376-3392

parts
restoration

Est 1979 as full service restoration shop. Specializing in Italian
and English exotics, Ferrari, Jaguar, Porsche, 356, Cisitalia,
Lamborghini, Maserati. Fully licensed auto dealership. Full
restoration, parts, custom welding, machining and fabrication,
race prep. Tax deferred exchanges and collection management.

Town Auto Top Co
111 Clinton Rd
Fairfield, NJ 07004
973-575-9333; FAX: 973-808-8366

convertible repairs
interiors

Shop open Monday-Friday 8:30 am to 5:30 pm. All types of
hands-on custom work. Interior restorations of all types, especially leather restoring. Some scissor frame convertible parts.
Also 1971-1976 GM available. Interior parts and engines for
these cars also available. Convertibles our specialties. Complete
restoration of classic autos, quality oriented support network of
shops and mechanics, upholstery, engine, chrome and body. You
always get what you pay for, plus special attention to the details
for over 30 years.

Trunzo's Antique Cars
4213 Ohio River Blvd
Pittsburgh, PA 15202
412-734-0717

antique cars
auctions
restorations

See full listing in **Section Two** under **auctions & events**

Ultimate Upholstery
14610 W Futura Dr
Sun City West, AZ 85375
602-975-4366

interiors
top restoration
upholstery

Shop open by appointment only. Emphasis on finely crafted interior and top restoration. Exclusively for antique and classic cars
from 1900-1948 and exotic cars. Bill Podsedly, owner.

Valenti Classics Inc
355 S Hwy 41
Caledonia, WI 53108
414-835-2070; FAX: 414-835-2575
E-mail: vci@valenticlassics.com

collectibles
restoration
sales
service

See full listing in **Section Two** under **car dealers**

Vampire Products
50 Four Coins Dr
Canonsburg, PA 15317
800-866-7260; FAX: 724-745-6040
E-mail: vampire@hanseninc.com

air dryers
filters

Manufacturer of compressed air dryers, filters, auto drains.

**Glenn Vaughn Restoration
Services Inc**
550 N Greenferry
Post Falls, ID 83854
208-773-3525; FAX: 208-773-3526

restoration

Automobile restoration: complete or partial, show car or driver
restorations. Located in a low overhead area, so our labor rates

are very competitive, while our focus is on efficiency, quality and integrity.

Vehicle Spring Service 7582 Industrial Way Stanton, CA 90680 714-379-8077; FAX: 714-897-1892	**springs** **suspensions**

See full listing in **Section Two** under **suspension parts**

Verne's Chrome Plating Inc 1559 W El Segundo Blvd Gardena, CA 90249 323-754-4126; FAX: 323-754-3873	**chrome plating** **polishing** **powder coating**

See full listing in **Section Two** under **plating & polishing**

Vintage Vehicles Co Inc N 1940 20th Dr Wautoma, WI 54982 920-787-2656	**detail** **restoration**

Open Monday-Friday 8:30 am to 5:30 pm. Many years' experience restoring classic, antique, sports and special interest cars. Also weld, remove dents and polish to factory finish: aluminum and stainless moldings, grilles, shells, hubcaps and beauty rings. Nationally recognized, complete or partial restorations. Complete facilities for all aspects of restoration. Strong on classics and foreigns. Motorcycle case repair, machining and polishing. Cycle fenders too.

Vintage Wings and Radiators Lord North St Miles Platting Manchester M40 8H7 England PH/FAX: 0161 202 6247	**body panels** **radiator cores**

See full listing in **Section Two** under **radiators**

Volvo Shop Inc 5220 New Milford Rd Ravenna, OH 44266 330-297-1297 E-mail: volvocarl@aol.com	**parts** **restoration**

See full listing in **Section One** under **Volvo**

John J Waluk 31 Squirrel Ln Levittown, NY 11756 516-796-2984; FAX: 516-796-5423 E-mail: bb70@msn.com	**flocking**

See full listing in **Section Two** under **special services**

Pete Watson Enterprises PO Box 488 Epworth, GA 30541 706-632-7675	**car dealer** **restoration**

Shop open by appointment only. Specializing in Fords.

West Coast Classics Inc 795 W San Jose Ave Claremont, CA 91711 909-624-7156	**car sales**

Car sales and antique and collector car toys for sale. Also fender skirts, hubcaps, parts and motors.

Wheels & Spokes Inc 383 Mopar Dr Hays, KS 67601 785-628-6477; FAX: 785-628-6834	**Mopar parts** **restoration**

See full listing in **Section One** under **Mopar**

White Post Restorations One Old Car Dr, PO Drawer D White Post, VA 22663 540-837-1140; FAX: 540-837-2368 E-mail: info@whitepost.com	**restoration**

Complete or partial for all automobiles older than 25 years. One of the largest, modern, fully equipped with the best and most experienced employees in the world. Call us if you want a good driver or national show winner. Web site: www.whitepost.com
See our ad on this page

Widmann's Garage 1801 Liberty St Hamilton, NJ 08629 609-392-1553; FAX: 609-392-1709	**repairs** **restorations**

Open Monday-Saturday 9 am to 5:30 pm. Deal in repairs and restorations of antiques, classics, customs and street rods. Specializing in trucks of all types.

Wild Bill's Corvette & Hi-Performance Center Inc 446 Dedham St Wrentham, MA 02093 508-384-7373; FAX: 508-384-9366 E-mail: wildbillscorvette@worldnet.att.net	**parts** **rebuilding** **service**

See full listing in **Section One** under **Corvette**

Willhoit Auto Restoration 1360 Gladys Ave Long Beach, CA 90804 562-439-3333; FAX: 562-439-3956	**engine rebuilding** **restoration**

See full listing in **Section One** under **Porsche**

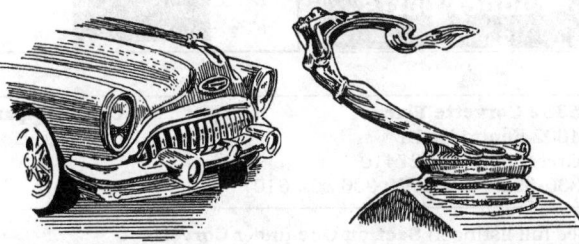
Section Two Generalists

Willow Automotive Service	bodywork
Box 4640 Rt 212	painting
Willow, NY 12495	restoration
914-679-4679	

Open shop Monday-Saturday by appointment. Antique, classic, muscle, exotic and foreign. Scheduled maintenance to ground-up restoration. Bodywork, metal fabrication, painting, in-house machine shop, woodwork service available, full mechanical shop. One-man shop assures attention to detail, call Arthur for services.

Willys America	parts
PO Box 538	restoration
Cazadero, CA 95421	
707-632-5258	

See full listing in **Section One** under **Willys**

Wilson's Classic Auto	restoration
417 Kaufman Rt 150	
PO Box 58	
Congerville, IL 61729	
309-448-2408; FAX: 309-448-2409	

Open shop only. Monday-Friday 8 am to 5 pm, Saturday 8 am to 12 pm. Award winning restorations, total or partial. We care more about quality than low price. Give us a call.

WTH Service and Restorations Inc	restorations
6561 Commerce Ct	
Warrenton, VA 20187-2300	
540-349-3034; FAX: 540-349-9652	
E-mail:	
wthauto@wthrestorations.com	

Open Monday-Thursday 7 am to 5 pm EST. High quality restorations, antique and classic automobiles, tractors and aircraft. E-mail us today and receive our newsletter via the internet.

WW Motor Cars & Parts Inc	restoration
132 N Main Street	
PO Box 667	
Broadway, VA 22815	
540-896-8243; FAX: 540-896-8244	

Open Monday-Thursday 7 am to 5:30 pm, Friday and Saturday by appointment. Complete or partial restorations of antique and classic automobiles and trucks. Our goal is to perform restoration work of national award winning caliber, whether for a trailer only show car or just a good driver. Top quality work, guaranteed. Also offer consignment sales, powder coating and cast iron welding.

XKs Unlimited	instruments
850 Fiero Ln	parts
San Luis Obispo, CA 93401	restorations
805-544-7864; FAX: 805-544-1664	
E-mail: xksunltd@aol.com	

See full listing in **Section One** under **Jaguar**

rubber parts

5362 Corvette Place	Corvette parts
4602 Kenbridge Dr	
Greensboro, NC 27410	
336-852-1011; FAX: 336-852-6107	

See full listing in **Section One** under **Corvette**

A & M SoffSeal Inc	rubber parts
104 May Dr	weatherstripping
Harrison, OH 45030	
513-367-0028	
800-426-0902 service/info	
FAX: 513-367-5506	
E-mail: soffseal@soffseal.com	

Manufacture the highest quality weatherstripping and rubber detail. Product line includes weatherstripping for GM cars, GM, GMC, Ford and Dodge trucks, A, B and E-body performance Chrysler plus an unlimited selection for street rods and customs. SoffSeal's USA made weatherstripping, pedal pads, extrusions, gasket materials are engineered with sun and ozone resistant materials and backed by our 100% lifetime satisfaction guarantee and can be purchased directly from SoffSeal or from one of our worldwide distributors. Web site: www.soffseal.com

A-1 Street Rods	parts
631 E Las Vegas St	
Colorado Springs, CO 80903	
719-632-4920, 719-577-4588	
FAX: 719-634-6577	

See full listing in **Section Two** under **street rods**

Accessoryland Truckin' Supplies	accessories
10723 Rt 61 S	foglights/spotlights
Dubuque, IA 52003	mounting brackets
319-556-5482; FAX: 319-556-9087	parts

See full listing in **Section One** under **Chevrolet**

American Performance Products	parts
675 S Industry Rd	
Cocoa, FL 32926	
407-632-8299; FAX: 407-632-5119	
E-mail: amc@oldcarparts.com	

See full listing in **Section One** under **AMC**

Autolux Inc	Mercedes parts
23242 Tasmania Cir	
Dana Point, CA 92629	
949-493-5578; FAX: 949-493-3710	

See full listing in **Section One** under **Mercedes-Benz**

Bay Ridges Classic Chevy	accessories
1550 Bayly St #38A	parts
Pickering, ON Canada L1W 3W1	
905-839-6169; FAX: 905-420-6613	

See full listing in **Section One** under **Chevrolet**

Brothers Truck Parts	accessories
4375 Prado Rd #105	parts
Corona, CA 91720	
800-977-2767; FAX: 909-808-9788	
E-mail: sales@brotherstrucks.com	

See full listing in **Section Two** under **trucks & tractors**

Stan Chernoff	mechanical parts
1215 Greenwood Ave	restoration parts
Torrance, CA 90503	technical info
310-320-4554; FAX: 310-328-7867	trim parts
E-mail: az589@lafn.org	

See full listing in **Section One** under **Datsun**

Chev's of the 40's	parts
2027 B St, Dept HVA	
Washougal, WA 98671	
800-999-CHEV (2438)	
FAX: 360-835-7988	

See full listing in **Section One** under **Chevrolet**

Classic Mercury Parts 1393 Shippee Ln Ojai, CA 93023 805-646-3345; FAX: 805-646-5386 E-mail: mfourez@aol.com	**parts**

See full listing in **Section One** under **Mercury**

Clester's Auto Rubber Seals Inc PO Box 1113 Salisbury, NC 28145 704-637-9979; FAX: 704-636-7390	**gloveboxes** **molded rubber** **parts** **weatherstripping**

Mail order and open shop. Monday-Friday 8:30 am to 5 pm. Manufacture rubber weatherstripping (ie: windshield seals, door seals, trunk seals), molded rubber parts and other products for Chevrolet, Ford and Mopar cars and trucks. Also International Harvester pickups and Travelalls, Studebaker cars and trucks. Web site: www.clestersauto.com

Convertible Service 5126-HA Walnut Grove Ave San Gabriel, CA 91776 800-333-1140, 626-285-2255 FAX: 626-285-9004	**convertible parts** **manufacture** **service** **top mechanism**

See full listing in **Section Two** under **tops**

Corvette Rubber Company H-10640 W Cadillac Rd Cadillac, MI 49601 888-216-9412 toll-free 616-779-2888; FAX: 616-779-9833	**rubber products** **weatherstripping**

See full listing in **Section One** under **Corvette**

CPR 431 S Sierra Way San Bernardino, CA 92408 909-884-6980; FAX: 909-884-7872	**new parts** **reproduction parts** **used parts**

See full listing in **Section One** under **Pontiac**

The El Camino Store 57 B Depot Rd Goleta, CA 93117 805-681-8164; FAX: 805-681-8166 E-mail: ec@elcaminostore.com	**parts**

See full listing in **Section One** under **Chevelle/Camaro**

Foreign Autotech 3235 C Sunset Ln Hatboro, PA 19040 215-441-4421; FAX: 215-441-4490 E-mail: fap1800@aol.com	**parts**

See full listing in **Section One** under **Volvo**

Freddie Beach Restoration 1834 Woodstock Rd Fredericton, NB Canada E3C 1L4 506-450-9074; FAX: 506-459-0708 E-mail: vallise@city.fredericton.nb.ca	**accessories** **restoration parts**

See full listing in **Section Two** under **car & parts locators**

Highway Classics 949 N Cataract Ave, Unit J San Dimas, CA 91773 909-592-8819; FAX: 909-592-4239 E-mail: donnelson@earthlink.net	**parts**

See full listing in **Section One** under **Ford 1954-up**

Hoffman Automotive Distributor US Hwy #1, Box 818 Hilliard, FL 32046 904-845-4421	**parts**

See full listing in **Section Two** under **body parts**

Impala Bob's Inc 4753 E Falcon Dr Dept HVAA14 Mesa, AZ 85215 800-IMPALAS orders 480-924-4800 retail store 480-981-1600 office FAX: 800-716-6237, 480-981-1675 E-mail: info@impalas.com	**restoration parts**

See full listing in **Section One** under **Chevrolet**

International Mercantile PO Box 2818 Del Mar, CA 92014-2818 800-356-0012, 760-438-2205 FAX: 760-438-1428	**rubber parts**

See full listing in **Section One** under **Porsche**

J & G Auto Parts 3050 Wild Run Rd Pennsburg, PA 18073 215-679-4683 after 5 pm	**clips** **fasteners** **weatherstripping**

See full listing in **Section Two** under **restoration aids**

Jerry's Classic Cars & Parts Inc 4097 McRay Ave Springdale, AR 72764 800-828-4584; FAX: 501-750-1682 E-mail: jcc@jerrysclassiccars.com	**parts** **restoration**

See full listing in **Section One** under **Ford 1954-up**

Karmann Ghia Parts & Restoration PO Box 997 Ventura, CA 93002 800-927-2787; FAX: 805-641-3333 E-mail: info@karmannghia.com	**parts**

See full listing in **Section One** under **Volkswagen**

Karr Rubber Manufacturing 133 Lomita St El Segundo, CA 90245 800-955-5277, 310-322-1993 FAX: 310-640-6872	**rubber parts**

Manufacturer of thousands of extrusion shapes. Can custom make almost any molded parts based upon customer samples, including door seals, roof rails, vent window seals, shift boots, grommets, etc. Web site: www.karrubber.com

K C Obsolete Parts 3343 N 61 Kansas City, KS 66104 913-334-9479; FAX: 913-788-2795	**parts**

See full listing in **Section One** under **Ford 1954-up**

KopyKatz Restoration Parts 2536 N Sheridan Blvd Denver, CO 80214 303-458-5332; FAX: 303-477-1496 E-mail: kopykatz@earthlink.net	**bumpers** **fenders** **hoods** **panels** **truck beds**

See full listing in **Section Two** under **body parts**

Legendary Auto Interiors Ltd   soft trim
121 W Shore Blvd
Newark, NY 14513
800-363-8804
FAX: 800-SEAT-UPH (732-8874)

See full listing in **Section One** under **Chrysler**

The Maverick Connection   literature
137 Valley Dr   parts
Ripley, WV 25271
PH/FAX: 304-372-7825

See full listing in **Section One** under **Ford 1954-up**

Mercury & Ford Molded Rubber   parts
12 Plymouth Ave
Wilmington, MA 01887
978-658-8394

See full listing in **Section One** under **Mercury**

Merv's Classic Chevy Parts   parts
1330 Washington
Iowa Falls, IA 50126
515-648-3168, 515-648-9675

See full listing in **Section One** under **Chevrolet**

MikeCo Antique, Kustom &   lenses
Obsolete Auto Parts   parts
4053 Calle Tesoro, Unit C
Camarillo, CA 93012
805-482-1725; FAX: 805-987-8524

See full listing in **Section One** under **Mopar**

Millers Incorporated   accessories
7412 Count Circle   parts
Huntington Beach, CA 92647
714-375-6565; FAX: 714-847-6606
E-mail: sales@millermbz.com

See full listing in **Section One** under **Mercedes-Benz**

Mooney's Antique Chevrolet Parts   engine parts
HC 01, Box 645C   rubber parts
Goodrich, TX 77335
409-365-2899, 9 am to 6 pm
409-685-4577, 6 pm to 9 pm
orders only
FAX: 409-685-4711

See full listing in **Section One** under **Chevrolet**

Motorsport Auto   parts
1139 W Collins Ave
Orange, CA 92667
800-633-6331, 714-639-2620
FAX: 714-639-7460
E-mail: motorsport@worldnet.att.net

See full listing in **Section One** under **Datsun**

MRL Automotive   rubber lubricants
PO Box 117230
Carrollton, TX 75011-7230
972-394-3489; FAX: 800-210-0200

See full listing in **Section Two** under **lubricants**

National Parts Depot
3101 SW 40th Blvd
Gainesville, FL 32608
800-874-7595 toll-free 24 hours
352-378-2473 local

accessories
restoration parts

See full listing in **Section Two** under **comprehensive parts**

Obsolete Chevrolet Parts Co
524 Hazel Ave
PO Box 68
Nashville, GA 31639-0068
800-248-8785; FAX: 912-686-3056
E-mail: obschevy@surfsouth.com

engine parts
radiators
rubber parts
transmissions

See full listing in **Section One** under **Chevrolet**

Obsolete Jeep® & Willys® Parts
Division of Florida 4 Wheel Drive &
Truck Parts
6110 17th St E
Bradenton, FL 34203
941-756-7844
PH/FAX: 941-756-7757

literature
parts

See full listing in **Section One** under **Willys**

Old Auto Rubber Company
4/4 Appin Place
PO Box 328, St. Mary's 2760
Dunheved, Sydney Australia
61 (2) 9623-5333
FAX: 61 (2) 9833-1041, 24 hrs

parts

Mail order and open shop. Monday-Friday 8:30 am to 5 pm.
Specializing in mail order. Extrusions, molded rubber parts,
door and screen seals, body hardware, engine and suspension
mounts. Also sheetmetal body panels and rust repair sections.
In-house rubber moldings, small run specialists. Post samples,
fax drawings. Prompt quotations. Vintage to mid-1980s for all
Australian Holden and Ford. Major British, many Japanese and
American models. When in Sydney, come and visit. Catalog #19,
$20/ US airmail.

Original Parts Group Inc
17892 Gothard St
Huntington Beach, CA 92647
800-243-8355 US/Canada
714-841-5363; FAX: 714-847-8159

accessories
parts

See full listing in **Section One** under **Pontiac**

Phelan Antique Auto Parts
73 Hillview St
Hamilton
Guelph, ON Canada L8S 2Z3
905-527-0002; FAX: 905-527-5929
E-mail: phelanantiqueauto@hwcn.org

parts

See full listing in **Section One** under **Ford 1903-1931**

Pollard Co
Joe Pollard
9331 Johnell Rd
Chatsworth, CA 91311
PH/FAX: 818-999-1485

parts

See full listing in **Section One** under **Checker**

Precision Auto Designs
28 Railway Ave
Campbell, CA 95008
408-378-2332; FAX: 408-378-1301
E-mail: pad@precisionauto.com

accessories
car covers
restoration

See full listing in **Section One** under **Mercedes-Benz**

Precision Rubber
Box 324
Didsbury, AB Canada T0M 0W0
403-335-9590; FAX: 403-335-8100

rubber parts

Specializing in the reproduction of runningboard mats for all
vintage vehicles (as original). Street rod mats can be custom
designed and color coordinated to match your vehicle. Also specialize in runningboard metal repair and mat installation.

**Quanta Restoration and
Performance Products**
743 Telegraph Rd
Rising Sun, MD 21911-1810
800-235-8788, 410-658-5700
FAX: 410-658-5758
E-mail: quanta@quantaproducts.com

fan belts
gas tanks

See full listing in **Section Two** under **chassis parts**

Raybuck Autobody Parts
RD 4, Box 170
Punxsutawney, PA 15767
814-938-5248; FAX: 814-938-4250

body parts

See full listing in **Section Two** under **body parts**

RB's Obsolete Automotive
7711 Lake Ballinger Way
Edmonds, WA 98026-9163
425-670-6739; FAX: 425-670-9151
E-mail: rbobsole@gte.net

parts

See full listing in **Section Two** under **comprehensive parts**

The Real Source
PO Box 1248
Effingham, IL 62401
800-LUV-BUGG (588-2844), dept VS9
FAX: 217-347-2952
E-mail: madbug@madvet.com

accessories
parts

See full listing in **Section One** under **Volkswagen**

Star Quality
1 Alley Rd
Lagrangeville, NY 12540
800-782-7199; FAX: 914-223-5394
E-mail: sq@mhv.net

parts

See full listing in **Section One** under **Mercedes-Benz**

Swedish Classics Inc
PO Box 557
Oxford, MD 21654
800-258-4422; FAX: 410-226-5543

parts

See full listing in **Section One** under **Volvo**

Tamraz's Parts Discount Warehouse
10022 S Bode Rd
Plainfield, IL 60544
630-904-4500; FAX: 630-904-2329

carpeting
upholstery
weatherstripping

See full listing in **Section One** under **Chevelle/Camaro**

Tanson Enterprises
2508 J St, Dept HVA
Sacramento, CA 95816-4815
916-448-2950
FAX: 916-443-3269 *88
E-mail: tanson@pipeline.com

performance parts
restoration parts

See full listing in **Section One** under **Oldsmobile**

Section Two
Generalists

Thunderbird Headquarters
1080 Detroit Ave
Concord, CA 94518
800-227-2174, US
FAX: 925-689-1771, 800-964-1957
E-mail: tbirdhq@tbirdhq.com

accessories
literature
parts
upholstery

See full listing in **Section One** under **Thunderbird**

Wales Antique Chevy Truck Parts
143 Center
Carleton, MI 48117
734-654-8836

parts

See full listing in **Section One** under **Chevrolet**

Pat Walsh Restorations
Box Q
Wakefield, MA 01880
781-246-3266; FAX: 781-224-3311
E-mail: pwalshrest@aol.com

literature
rubber parts

Mail order only. Monday-Friday 8 am to 5 pm. Specializing in weatherseals, floor mats, NOS, rubber, service manuals, parts books, trunk mats, interiors, carpets, trunk interiors, window seals, glass runs and settings, other restoration items, 1900s-1980s.

Wefco Rubber Manufacturing Company Inc
21000 Osborne St, Ste 2
Canoga Park, CA 91304-1758
818-886-8872; FAX: 818-886-8875

rubber extrusions

Mail order and open shop. Monday-Friday 7 am to 4 pm. Extrusions: rubber and soft sponge, die cuts, windshield rubber splicing. Send sample or drawing of molded parts needed and 1/2-inch sample or drawing of extrusion needed. "No job too big or too small." Catalog, $10.

West Coast Metric Inc
24002 Frampton Ave
Harbor City, CA 90710
310-325-0005; FAX: 310-325-9733
E-mail: wcmi@earthlink.net

apparel
carpets
plastic parts
rubber parts

See full listing in **Section One** under **Volkswagen**

The Wixom Connection
2204 Steffanie Ct
Kissimmee, FL 34746
407-933-4030

parts

See full listing in **Section One** under **Lincoln**

World Upholstery & Trim
PO Box 2420
Camarillo, CA 93011
805-988-1848; FAX: 805-278-7886
E-mail: worlduph@mail.vcnet.com

carpet
tops
upholstery kits

See full listing in **Section Two** under **interiors & interior parts**

rust removal & stripping

ACE Automotive Cleaning Equipment Co
897 S Washington, Suite 232
Holland, MI 49423
616-772-3260; FAX: 616-772-3261

sandblasting
equipment

Mail order only. Sandblasting equipment and parts cleaners.

ACPlating
Division of SUM Inc
317 Mt Vernon
Bakersfield, CA 93307
661-324-5454; FAX: 661-324-5381

plating

See full listing in **Section Two** under **plating & polishing**

Bay Area Industrial Dry Stripping
151 11th St
Richmond, CA 94801-3523
510-412-9890, 510-805-1887

blasting
paint removal

Open Monday-Friday 9:30 am to 6:30 pm, Saturday-Sunday by appointment. Utilize plastic media in the removal of automotive paint and coatings. Far superior to conventional stripping methods, no chemicals, no residue, far less abrasive than sandblasting, there's no pitting or warping. Specializing in the stripping of automotive fiberglass as well as carbon fiber. For gentle and safe removal of rust, we now offer garnet blasting as well. Safe, reliable service, years of experience. Inquiries welcome.

Capt Lee's Spra' Strip
PO Box 203
Hermitage, TN 37076
800-421-9498; FAX: 615-889-1798

paint remover

Mail order and open shop. Monday-Friday 12 pm to 4:30 pm CST. Dealing in Auto Spra' Strip Paint Remover, Capt Lee's Rust-Away and Metal Prep and Conditioner.

County Auto Restoration
6 Gavin Rd
Mt Vernon, NH 03057
603-673-4840

bodywork
brakes
restoration
woodwork

See full listing in **Section Two** under **restoration shops**

DeVito Auto Restorations
470 Boston Post Rd
Weston, MA 02493
781-893-4949 ext 142
FAX: 781-899-4900
E-mail: radjr@ix.netcom.com

restorations
rust repair

See full listing in **Section Two** under **bodywork**

Ecoclean 2000
100 N Meadows Rd
Medfield, MA 02052
888-399-2600, 508-359-9675
FAX: 508-359-7311
E-mail: rusteco1x@aol.com

rust dissolver

Open Monday-Friday 9 am to 7 pm EST. The only warehouse distributor of RUSTECO. Rust dissolver-environmentally safe. Nontoxic, vegetable based, biodegradable liquid that deoxidizes rust and dissolves it away. There is no chemical reaction with metal, paint or chrome, no handling or disposal restrictions and no comparative product as safe. Reusable and recyclable as well. Call or write for more information.

Fini-Finish Metal Finishing
24657 Mound Rd
Warren, MI 48091
810-758-0050; FAX: 810-758-0054

plating
polishing
pot metal repair

See full listing in **Section Two** under **plating & polishing**

The Finished Look
PO Box 191413
Sacramento, CA 95819-1413
800-827-6715; FAX: 916-451-3984
E-mail: info@thefinishedlook.com

POR-15 products

See full listing in **Section Two** under **rustproofing**

Gas Tank and Radiator Rebuilders 20123 Hwy 362 Waller, TX 77484 800-723-3759 E-mail: donhart@donhart.com	**abrasive blasting** **gas tank rebuilding** **heaters** **radiator repair**

See full listing in **Section Two** under **fuel system parts**

Guyson Corp of USA W J Grande Industrial Park Saratoga Springs, NY 12866-9044 518-587-7894; FAX: 518-587-7840 E-mail: jetsinfo@guyson.com	**restoration aids**

Manufacturer of blast cleaning and surface finishing cabinets, both manually operated and automatic.

Imperial Restoration Inc 308 Lockport St Lemont, IL 60439 630-257-5822 FAX: 630-257-5892	**chassis coatings** **engine enamels** **gas tank sealer** **paint/rust remover** **rust preventives**

See full listing in **Section Two** under **restoration aids**

Lake Buchanan Industries Inc Rt 1, Box 184-C Buchanan Dam, TX 78609 888-552-5278 toll-free 512-793-2867; FAX: 512-793-2869 E-mail: lbi:@tstar.net	**blasting cabinet**

See full listing in **Section Two** under **tools**

Maintenance Specialties Company 21 Valley Forge Rd PO Box 251 New Castle, DE 19720 800-777-6715; FAX: 302-328-2315	**rustproofing paints**

See full listing in **Section Two** under **rustproofing**

Nor-Cal Metal Stripping 10010 Old Redwood Hwy Windsor, CA 95492 800-698-9470	**rust removal**

Shop open Monday-Friday 9 am to 5 pm; Saturday 9 am to 12 noon. Paint and rust removal by chemical immersion process. Eighteen foot tanks with car body and frame capacity.

Painting & Stripping Corp 10051 Greenleaf Ave Santa Fe Springs, CA 90670 562-946-1521; FAX: 562-946-8039	**powder coating** **stripping**

Open shop only. Monday-Friday 7 am to 3:30 pm. All cars and trucks. Service only. Motorcycles. Any metal parts. Stripping and powder coating.

Paul's Chrome Plating Inc 90 Pattison St Evans City, PA 16033 800-245-8679, 724-538-3367 FAX: 724-538-3403 E-mail: pcp@fyi.net	**repair** **restoration**

See full listing in **Section Two** under **plating & polishing**

Pennsylvania Metal Cleaning 200 17th St Monaca, PA 15061-1969 724-728-5535	**derusting** **stainless fasteners** **stripping**

Mail order and open shop. Monday-Friday 8 am to 5 pm, Saturday 8 am to 12 noon. Opened in 1978. Can strip and derust anything from a bolt to a body, using non-destructive alkaline system. Tanks are 20 feet in length. Individuals, commercial or industrial. Extensive selection of stainless steel nuts, bolts, washers, screws, cotter pins, wood screws and nails.

Specialty items include exhaust system clamps. Model A bumper end bolts and door hinge screws in stainless steel.

PK Lindsay Co Inc 63 Nottingham Rd Deerfield, NH 03037 800-258-3576; FAX: 800-843-2974	**paint removal** **rust removal**

Mail order only. Manufacturer of portable abrasive blasters used in the automobile restoration industry. Commonly used to remove rust/corrosion from frames or paint from fenders. Also manufacture portable air compressors.

Pro-Strip 2415 W State Blvd Fort Wayne, IN 46808 219-436-2828; FAX: 219-432-1941 E-mail: prostrip@tk7.net	**paint removal** **rust removal**

Mail order and open shop. Monday-Friday 7 am to 5 pm, Saturday 8 am to 12 noon. Providing service since 1985. Offer complete rust and paint removal from individual parts to complete automobiles. State of the art methods of paint and rust removal. Can also custom powder coat your part in a wide variety of colors, wrinkle finishes and textures, also buffing and polishing on metal. Powder coating items up to 13' long. Cast iron repair, blocks, heads, manifolds. Web site: www.prostrip.com

Raybuck Autobody Parts RD 4, Box 170 Punxsutawney, PA 15767 814-938-5248; FAX: 814-938-4250	**body parts**

See full listing in **Section Two** under **body parts**

Redi-Strip Company Box 72199 Roselle, IL 60172 630-529-2442; FAX: 630-529-3626	**abrasive media** **baking soda blasting** **paint removal** **rust removal**

Mail order and open shop. Monday-Friday 8 am to 5 pm, Saturday 8:30 am to 11:30 am. Non-destructive chemical paint and alkaline electrolytic immersion process rust removal. Also non-abrasive blasting removes paint and coatings from delicate substrates. Abrasive blasting removes rust and etch and texturize surfaces. Baking soda safely removes paints from fiberglass, aluminum and steel.

Richard's Auto Restoration RD 3, Box 83A Wyoming, PA 18644 717-333-4191	**restoration**

See full listing in **Section Two** under **restoration shops**

Riverbend Abrasive Blasting 44308 St Rt 36 W Coshocton, OH 43812-9741 614-622-0867	**blasting** **painting** **polishing** **restoration**

Mail order and open shop. Monday-Friday 9 am to 5 pm, Saturday by appointment. Multi-media abrasive blasting, stainless steel trim restoration, metal buffing and polishing, vehicle restoration, painting and powdercoating. Emphasis on fine unhurried workmanship.

T Schmidt 827 N Vernon Dearborn, MI 48128-1542 313-562-7161	**rust removers**

Mail order only. Deal in Oxisolv rust removers, metal preps, degreasers, wire wheel cleaners and parts washers.

Tar Heel Parts Inc	**buffing supplies**
PO Box 2604
Matthews, NC 28106-2604
800-322-1957, 704-753-9114 (local)
FAX: 704-753-9117

See full listing in **Section Two** under **plating & polishing**

TiP Tools & Equipment	**abrasive blasters**
7075 Route 446, PO Box 649
Canfield, OH 44406
330-533-3384 local
800-321-9260 US/Canada
FAX: 330-533-2876

air compressors
tools

See full listing in **Section Two** under **restoration aids**

Tri-State Metal Cleaning	**cleaning**
4725 Iroquois Ave
Erie, PA 16511
814-898-3933
FAX: 814-899-8632 after 3:30 pm

rust removal
stripping

Mail order and open shop. Monday-Friday 8 am to 5 pm. Large capacity tanks, 18' long x 8' wide x 6' deep, to remove many years of accumulated grime, paint and rust from bodies, engines and frames. When we do the dirty work, hundreds of labor hours of hand cleaning and stripping are eliminated.

Ziebart/Tidy Car	**accessories**
803 Mt Royal Blvd
Pittsburgh, PA 15223
412-486-4711

detailing
rustproofing

See full listing in **Section Two** under **rustproofing**

rustproofing

Amsoil	**car care products**
9 Claremont Dr
Flat Rock, NC 28731
704-696-8500

lubricants
undercoating

See full listing in **Section Two** under **lubricants**

The Finished Look	**POR-15 products**
PO Box 191413
Sacramento, CA 95819-1413
800-827-6715; FAX: 916-451-3984
E-mail: info@thefinishedlook.com

West Coast distributor of POR-15 restoration products. Stop rust, rust preventive coatings, gas tank sealer, heat paints, engine enamels, cleaners/degreaser and rust remover. Web site: www.thefinishedlook.com

High Performance Coatings	**coatings**
550 W 3615 S
Salt Lake City, UT 84115
800-456-4721, 801-262-6807
FAX: 801-262-6307
E-mail: hpcsales@hpcoatings.com

See full listing in **Section Two** under **exhaust systems**

Imperial Restoration Inc	**chassis coatings**
308 Lockport St
Lemont, IL 60439
630-257-5822
FAX: 630-257-5892

engine enamels
gas tank sealer
paint/rust remover
rust preventives

See full listing in **Section Two** under **restoration aids**

Maintenance Specialties Company	**rustproofing paints**
21 Valley Forge Rd
PO Box 251
New Castle, DE 19720
800-777-6715; FAX: 302-328-2315

Mail order only. 24 hour order line. Sell the complete POR-15 line of rustproofing paints and chemicals. Free shipping.

Memory Lane Motors	**car dealer**
562 County Rd 121
Fenelon Falls, ON Canada K0M 1N0
705-887-CARS; FAX: 705-887-4028

restoration service

See full listing in **Section Two** under **restoration shops**

Preserve Inc	**storage containers**
1430 E 1800 N
Hamilton, IL 62341
217-746-2411; FAX: 217-746-2231

See full listing in **Section Two** under **storage care products**

Steve's Antiques/POR-15	**bicycles**
Steve Verhoeven
5609 S 4300 W
Hooper, UT 84315
888-817-6715 toll-free
801-985-4835
E-mail: steve@stevesantiques.com

POR-15 distributor

Stop rust permanently. Distributor POR-15 products. Rust Inhibitor coatings, engine parts, degreasers, gas tank sealers, fuel preservatives, exhaust coatings, epoxy putties, much more. Also gas pumps and parts. Original and reproduction antique advertising signs. 1950s and 1960s Schwinns, specializing in Schwinn Stingrays. Call for a free catalog.

Ziebart/Tidy Car	**accessories**
803 Mt Royal Blvd
Pittsburgh, PA 15223
412-486-4711

detailing
rustproofing

Open Monday-Friday 8 am to 5 pm, Saturday 9 am to 12 noon. Treat rusted metal with rust inhibitors then rust protect the entire vehicle. Also detail restored and unrestored cars and trucks along with custom accessories.

service shops

AAdvanced Transmissions	**rear axle service**
15 Parker St
Worcester, MA 01610
508-752-9674, 508-752-9679
FAX: 508-842-0191

restoration
ring/pinion
trans parts/sales/
rebuilding/service

See full listing in **Section Two** under **transmissions**

Advanced Maintenance Technologies Inc	**filters**
Box 250, Mountain Rd
Stowe, VT 05672
802-253-7385; FAX: 802-253-7815
E-mail: info@advancedmaintenance.com

lubricants

See full listing in **Section Two** under **engine parts**

Antique Radio Service	**radio service**
12 Shawmut Ave
Wayland, MA 01778
800-201-2635; FAX: 508-653-2418

See full listing in **Section Two** under **radios**

Arch Carburetor	carburetors

583 Central Ave
Newark, NJ 07107
973-482-2755
E-mail: mmfried1@aol.com

See full listing in **Section Two** under **carburetors**

The Autoworks Ltd	restoration sales service

90 Center Ave
Westwood, NJ 07675
201-358-0200; FAX: 201-358-0442

Open shop. Monday-Friday 6:30 am to 5 pm, Saturday by
appointment. Deal in service, consignment sales, partial or complete restoration on classic, vintage and collector British marques, any year, any model.

RL Bailey Co	restorations steering wheels woodgraining

27902 45th Ave S
Auburn, WA 98001
PH/FAX: 253-854-5247
E-mail: rbailey2@gte.net

See full listing in **Section Two** under **woodgraining**

Banzai Motorworks	pre-purchase insp/consultation parts repairs/restoration service

6735 Midcities Ave
Beltsville, MD 20705
PH/FAX: 301-937-5746
E-mail: zspert@erols.com

See full listing in **Section One** under **Datsun**

Bicknell Engine Company	parts repair restoration

7055 Dayton Rd
Enon, OH 45323
937-864-5224

See full listing in **Section One** under **Buick/McLaughlin**

Billie Inc	garage diaper mats

PO Box 1161
Ashburn, VA 20146-1161
800-878-6328; FAX: 703-858-0102

See full listing in **Section Two** under **car care products**

Blint Equipment Inc	parts tractor rebuilding

2204 E Lincolnway
LaPorte, IN 46350
219-362-7021

See full listing in **Section One** under **Ford 1954-up**

Bob's Speedometer Service	gauges speedometers tachometers

32411 Grand River Ave
Farmington, MI 48336
800-592-9673; FAX: 248-473-5517

See full listing in **Section Two** under **instruments**

Bob's Bird House	parts

124 Watkin Ave
Chadds Ford, PA 19317
610-358-3420; FAX: 610-558-0729

See full listing in **Section One** under **Thunderbird**

Bright Displays	molded auto logos neon signs

1314 Lakemont Dr
Pittsburgh, PA 15243
PH/FAX: 412-279-7037

See full listing in **Section Two** under **automobilia**

British Car Specialists	parts repairs restoration

2060 N Wilson Way
Stockton, CA 95205
209-948-8767; FAX: 209-948-1030
E-mail: healeydoc@aol.com

See full listing in **Section One** under **Austin-Healey**

Classic Car Works Ltd	restoration

3050 Upper Bethany Rd
Jasper, GA 30143
770-735-3945

See full listing in **Section Two** under **restoration shops**

Classic Carriages	repair restoration

267 County Rd 420
Athens, TN 37303
PH/FAX: 423-744-7496

See full listing in **Section One** under **Ford 1932-1953**

Classic Creations of Central Florida	parts restoration service

3620 Hwy 92E
Lakeland, FL 33801
941-665-2322; FAX: 941-666-5348
E-mail: flclassics@aol.com

See full listing in **Section One** under **Mustang**

Coffey's Classic Transmissions	transmissions

2290 W Hicks Rd, Unit 42
Hanger 30-1
Ft Worth, TX 76111
817-439-1611

See full listing in **Section Two** under **transmissions**

Corvette Mike	accessories parts sales service

1133 N Tustin Ave
Anaheim, CA 92807
800-327-8388, 714-630-0700
FAX: 714-630-0777
E-mail: cvtmike@deltanet.com

See full listing in **Section One** under **Corvette**

Coventry West Inc	assemblies Jaguar parts

5936-A Peachtree Rd
Atlanta, GA 30341
800-331-2193 toll-free
770-451-3839 Atlanta
FAX: 770-451-7561

See full listing in **Section One** under **Jaguar**

CT Model A Parts & Service	parts restorations service

75 Prospect Ave
West Hartford, CT 06106
860-233-1928; FAX: 860-233-1926
E-mail: ctmap@aol.com

See full listing in **Section One** under **Ford 1903-1931**

D&M Corvette Specialists Ltd	parts restoration sales service

1804 Ogden Ave
Downers Grove, IL 60515
630-968-0031; FAX: 630-968-0465

See full listing in **Section One** under **Corvette**

Damper Dudes	balancers chrome paint

5509 Cedar Rd #2
Redding, CA 96001
800-413-2673, 530-244-7225
FAX: 530-244-2690
E-mail: rliddell@snowcrest.net

See full listing in **Section Two** under **engine parts**

Section Two Generalists

Dependable RV & Auto Service | parts restoration service
2619 Rt 11 N
Lafayette, NY 13084
315-677-5336; FAX: 315-677-5258

Mail order and open shop. Monday-Friday 9 am to 5 pm or by appointment. Deal in recreational vehicle and general auto/truck repair, but have acquired a large and diverse collection of early Ford V8 and also engage in restoration and street rod fabrication.

Doc's Jags | appraisals interiors restoration
125 Baker Rd
Lake Bluff, IL 60044
847-367-5247; FAX: 847-367-6363
E-mail: docsjags@worldnet.att.net

See full listing in **Section One** under **Jaguar**

Done Right Engine & Machine Inc | engine rebuilding machine shop
12955 York Delta, Unit J
North Royalton, OH 44133
440-582-1366; FAX: 440-582-2005

See full listing in **Section Two** under **engine rebuilding**

DTE Motorsports | engines mechanical services race prep transportation
242 South Rd
Brentwood, NH 03833
PH/FAX: 603-642-3766
E-mail: ldnh49a@prodigy.com

See full listing in **Section One** under **Mercedes-Benz**

Freeman's Garage | parts restoration sales service
29 Ford Rd
Norton, MA 02766
508-285-6500; FAX: 508-285-6566

See full listing in **Section One** under **Ford 1903-1931**

Golden Gulf Classics Inc | repairs restorations
PO Box 490
22530 Hwy 49
Saucier, MS 39574
228-831-2650; FAX: 228-831-1513
E-mail: gudhowdy@datasync.com

See full listing in **Section One** under **Triumph**

Hyde Auto Body | refinishing restoration
44-1/2 S Squirrel Rd
Auburn Hills, MI 48326
PH/FAX: 248-852-7832
E-mail: bodyman8@juno.com

See full listing in **Section Two** under **restoration shops**

Ignition Distributor Service | rebuilding carbs
19042 SE 161st
Renton, WA 98058
425-255-8052

See full listing in **Section Two** under **carburetors**

K&W Kollectibles | parts repair restoration
220 Industrial Pkwy S #6
Aurora, ON Canada L4G 3V6
416-410-7741; FAX: 905-727-5771
E-mail: kwkoll@sympatico.ca

See full listing in **Section One** under **Buick/McLaughlin**

Kelley's Korner | parts repair
22 14th St
Bristol, TN 37620
423-968-5583

See full listing in **Section One** under **Studebaker**

Kenask Spring Co | springs
307 Manhattan Ave
Jersey City, NJ 07307
201-653-4589

See full listing in **Section Two** under **suspension parts**

Memoryville USA Inc | restoration
1008 W 12th St
Rolla, MO 65401
573-364-1810

See full listing in **Section Two** under **restoration shops**

Model Engineering | new parts casting
Gene or Jeff Sanders
3284 S Main St
Akron, OH 44329
330-644-3450; FAX: 330-644-0088

See full listing in **Section Two** under **castings**

Morgan Oasis Garage | restoration service
PO Box 1010
N 51 Terrace Rd
Hoodsport, WA 98548
360-877-5160

See full listing in **Section One** under **Morgan**

Mustang Classics | parts restoration sales service
3814 Walnut St
Denver, CO 80205
303-295-3140

See full listing in **Section One** under **Mustang**

Northern Motorsport Ltd | repair restoration sales service
PO Box 508, Rt 5
Wilder, VT 05088
802-296-2099; FAX: 802-295-6599

See full listing in **Section Two** under **restoration shops**

The Old Carb Doctor | carburetors fuel pumps
Rt 3, Box 338
Drucilla Church Rd
Nebo, NC 28761
800-945-CARB (2272)
704-659-1428

See full listing in **Section Two** under **carburetors**

Opel Oldtimer Service Denmark | literature parts parts locator
Landevejen 27
Toksvaerd
DK-4684 Holme-Olstrup Denmark
PH/FAX: +45-55-530100
best 11 am to 3 pm US Central time
E-mail: frank.kiessling@get2net.dk

See full listing in **Section One** under **Opel**

Bill Peters | steering wheel restoration
41 Vassar Pl
Rockville Centre, NY 11570
516-766-8397

See full listing in **Section Two** under **steering wheels**

John T Poulin | car dealer parts restoration service
Auto Sales/Star Service Center
5th Avenue & 111th St
North Troy, NY 12182
518-235-8610

See full listing in **Section One** under **Mercedes-Benz**

R & L Engines Inc
308 Durham Rd
Dover, NH 03820
603-742-8812; FAX: 603-742-8137

engine rebuilding
restorations

See full listing in **Section Two** under **engine rebuilding**

RB's Prototype Model & Machine Co
44 Marva Ln
Stamford, CT 06903
203-329-2715; FAX: 203-329-8029

machine work

Mail order and open shop. Monday-Friday 8 am to 6 pm EST. Fabricating or machining parts to rebuild parts for automobiles. Custom machine work (no engine internals). Duplicating small parts for cars (radio knobs, handles, springs, bushings, plastic parts, etc). Billet aluminum work. Dashes, air cleaners, valve covers, etc. One of a kind work. No job too small or large.

Reinholds Restorations
c/o Rick Reinhold
PO Box 178, 255 N Ridge Rd
Reinholds, PA 17569-0178
717-336-5617; FAX: 717-336-7050

appraisals
repairs
restoration

See full listing in **Section Two** under **restoration shops**

Rochester Clutch & Brake Co
35 Niagara St
Rochester, NY 14605
716-232-2579; FAX: 716-232-3279

brakes
clutches

See full listing in **Section Two** under **brakes**

Ron's Restorations Inc
2968-B Ask Kay Dr
Smyrna, GA 30082
770-438-6102; FAX: 770-438-0037

interior trim
restoration

See full listing in **Section One** under **Mercedes-Benz**

Simons Balancing & Machine Inc
1987 Ashley River Rd
Charleston, SC 29407
843-766-3911; FAX: 843-766-9003

machine work

See full listing in **Section Two** under **machine work**

Still Cruisin' Corvettes
5759 Benford Dr
Haymarket, VA 20169
703-754-1960; FAX: 703-754-1222

appraisals
repairs
restoration

See full listing in **Section One** under **Corvette**

Teddy's Garage
8530 Louise Ave
Northridge, CA 91325
818-341-0505

parts
restoration
service

See full listing in **Section One** under **Rolls-Royce/Bentley**

Thermax Inc
5385 Alpha Ave
Reno, NV 89506
800-247-7177; FAX: 702-972-4809

interior detailing

See full listing in **Section Two** under **car care products**

Valenti Classics Inc
355 S Hwy 41
Caledonia, WI 53108
414-835-2070; FAX: 414-835-2575
E-mail: vci@valenticlassics.com

collectibles
restoration
sales
service

See full listing in **Section Two** under **car dealers**

Vampire Products
50 Four Coins Dr
Canonsburg, PA 15317
800-866-7260; FAX: 724-745-6040
E-mail: vampire@hanseninc.com

air dryers
filters

See full listing in **Section Two** under **restoration shops**

Vehicle Spring Service
7582 Industrial Way
Stanton, CA 90680
714-379-8077; FAX: 714-897-1892

springs
suspensions

See full listing in **Section Two** under **suspension parts**

Vintage Glass USA
PO Box 336
326 S River Rd
Tolland, CT 06084
800-889-3826, 860-872-0018

auto glass

See full listing in **Section Two** under **glass**

Volvo Shop Inc
5220 New Milford Rd
Ravenna, OH 44266
330-297-1297
E-mail: volvocarl@aol.com

parts
restoration

See full listing in **Section One** under **Volvo**

John J Waluk
31 Squirrel Ln
Levittown, NY 11756
516-796-2984; FAX: 516-796-5423
E-mail: bb70@msn.com

flocking

See full listing in **Section Two** under **special services**

White Post Restorations
One Old Car Dr
White Post, VA 22663
540-837-1140; FAX: 540-837-2368

brakes
restoration

See full listing in **Section Two** under **brakes**

Widmann's Garage
1801 Liberty St
Hamilton, NJ 08629
609-392-1553; FAX: 609-392-1709

repairs
restorations

See full listing in **Section Two** under **restoration shops**

Wild Bill's Corvette & Hi-Performance Center Inc
446 Dedham St
Wrentham, MA 02093
508-384-7373; FAX: 508-384-9366
E-mail: wildbillscorvette@worldnet.att.net

parts
rebuilding
service

See full listing in **Section One** under **Corvette**

Willys America
PO Box 538
Cazadero, CA 95421
707-632-5258

parts
restoration

See full listing in **Section One** under **Willys**

Wittenborn's Auto Service Inc
133 Woodside Ave
Briarcliff Manor, NY 10510
914-941-2744

Mopar

See full listing in **Section One** under **Mopar**

Wymer Classic AMC
Mark & George Wymer
340 N Justice St
Fremont, OH 43420
419-332-4291
419-334-6945 after 5 pm

| NOS parts |
| owner's manuals |
| **repairs** |
| service manuals |
| **used parts** |

See full listing in **Section One** under **AMC**

sheetmetal

Accessoryland Truckin' Supplies
10723 Rt 61 S
Dubuque, IA 52003
319-556-5482; FAX: 319-556-9087

| **accessories** |
| **foglights/spotlights** |
| **mounting brackets** |
| **parts** |

See full listing in **Section One** under **Chevrolet**

ACE Automotive Cleaning Equipment Co
897 S Washington, Suite 232
Holland, MI 49423
616-772-3260; FAX: 616-772-3261

| **sandblasting** |
| **equipment** |

See full listing in **Section Two** under **rust removal & stripping**

American Restorations Unlimited TA
14 Meakin Ave
PO Box 34
Rochelle Park, NJ 07662
201-843-3567; FAX: 201-843-3238
E-mail: amerrest@earthlink.net

| **restoration parts** |

See full listing in **Section Two** under **glass**

Antique & Classic Car Restorations
4716 Monkey Hill Rd
Oak Harbor, WA 98227
360-240-0909

| **painting** |
| **restorations** |
| **woodwork** |

See full listing in **Section Two** under **restoration shops**

Auto Body Specialties Inc
Rt 66
Middlefield, CT 06455
888-277-1960 toll-free orders only
860-346-4989; FAX: 860-346-4987

| **accessories** |
| **body parts** |

See full listing in **Section Two** under **body parts**

Automotive Restorations Inc
Stephen Babinsky
4 Center St
Bernardsville, NJ 07924
908-766-6688; FAX: 908-766-6684
E-mail: autorestnj@aol.com

| **clutch rebuilding** |
| **mechanical** |
| **services** |
| **restorations** |

See full listing in **Section Two** under **restoration shops**

B & T Truck Parts
906 E Main St
PO Box 799
Siloam Springs, AR 72761
501-524-5959; FAX: 501-524-5559

| **pickup parts** |

See full listing in **Section Two** under **trucks & tractors**

Bay Ridges Classic Chevy
1550 Bayly St #38A
Pickering, ON Canada L1W 3W1
905-839-6169; FAX: 905-420-6613

| **accessories** |
| **parts** |

See full listing in **Section One** under **Chevrolet**

Bonnets Up
5736 Spring St
Clinton, MD 20735
301-297-4759

| **restoration** |

See full listing in **Section Two** under **coachbuilders & designers**

Tony D Branda Performance
Shelby and Mustang Parts
1434 E Pleasant Valley Blvd
Altoona, PA 16602
814-942-1869; FAX: 814-944-0801
E-mail: cobranda@aol.com

| **accessories** |
| **decals** |
| **emblems** |
| **sheetmetal** |
| **wheels** |

See full listing in **Section One** under **Mustang**

Brothers Truck Parts
4375 Prado Rd #105
Corona, CA 91720
800-977-2767; FAX: 909-808-9788
E-mail: sales@brotherstrucks.com

| **accessories** |
| **parts** |

See full listing in **Section Two** under **trucks & tractors**

Car-Line Manufacturing & Distribution Inc
1250 Gulf St
PO Box 1192
Beaumont, TX 77701
409-833-9757; FAX: 409-835-2468

| **chassis parts** |
| **engine parts** |
| **sheetmetal** |

Mail order and open shop. Monday-Friday 8 am to 5 pm.
Manufacturing USA sheetmetal, wood and seat springs for Model
T and A Fords, 1909-1931. Carry a full line of engine and chassis parts. Some V8 parts (metal, seat springs). Catalog available.

CARS Inc
1964 W 11 Mile Rd
Berkley, MI 48072
248-398-7100; FAX: 248-398-7078
E-mail: carsinc@worldnet.att.net

| **interior** |

See full listing in **Section One** under **Chevrolet**

Jim Carter's Antique Truck Parts
1508 E Alton
Independence, MO 64055
800-336-1913; FAX: 800-262-3749
E-mail:
jimcartertruck.parts@worldnet.att.net

| **truck parts** |

See full listing in **Section One** under **Chevrolet**

Classic Enterprises
Box 92
Barron, WI 54812
715-537-5422

| **sheetmetal** |

See full listing in **Section One** under **Studebaker**

Classic Sheetmetal Inc
4010 A Hartley St
Charlotte, NC 28206
800-776-4040, 704-596-5186
FAX: 704-596-3895

| **body panels** |
| **sheetmetal** |

See full listing in **Section One** under **Thunderbird**

County Auto Restoration
6 Gavin Rd
Mt Vernon, NH 03057
603-673-4840

| **bodywork** |
| **brakes** |
| **restoration** |
| **woodwork** |

See full listing in **Section Two** under **restoration shops**

Danchuk Mfg
3201 S Standard Ave
Santa Ana, CA 92705
714-751-1957; FAX: 714-850-1957
E-mail: info@danchuk.com

accessories
parts
restoration

See full listing in **Section One** under **Chevrolet**

Desert Valley Auto Parts
22500 N 21st Ave
Phoenix, AZ 85027
800-905-8024, 602-780-8024
FAX: 602-582-9141
E-mail: rust-free-parts@worldnet.att.net

cars
parts

See full listing in **Section Five** under **Arizona**

Driving Passion Ltd USA
Marc Tuwiner
7132 Chilton Ct
Clarksville, MD 21029
PH/FAX: 301-596-9078
E-mail: mt.tees@erols.com

cars
parts
salvage yard

See full listing in **Section One** under **Cadillac/LaSalle**

Early Ford V8 Sales Inc
Curtis Industrial Park, Bldg 37
831 Rt 67
Ballston Spa, NY 12020
518-884-2825; FAX: 518-884-2633
E-mail: earlyford@prodigy.net

parts

See full listing in **Section One** under **Ford 1932-1953**

East West Auto Parts Inc
4605 Dawson Rd
Tulsa, OK 74115
800-447-2886; FAX: 918-832-7900

European import
parts
GM parts

See full listing in **Section Five** under **Oklahoma**

**Engineering & Manufacturing
Services**
Box 24362
Cleveland, OH 44124-0362
216-541-4585; FAX: 216-541-4989

sheetmetal

See full listing in **Section One** under **Ford 1932-1953**

FEN Enterprises of New York Inc
PO Box 1559
1324 Rt 376
Wappingers Falls, NY 12590
914-462-5959, 914-462-5094
FAX: 914-462-8450

parts
restoration

See full listing in **Section One** under **Cadillac/LaSalle**

Foreign Autotech
3235 C Sunset Ln
Hatboro, PA 19040
215-441-4421; FAX: 215-441-4490
E-mail: fap1800@aol.com

parts

See full listing in **Section One** under **Volvo**

Gaslight Auto Parts Inc
PO Box 291
Urbana, OH 43078
937-652-2145; FAX: 937-652-2147

accessories
parts

See full listing in **Section One** under **Ford 1903-1931**

Howell's Sheetmetal Co
PO Box 792
Nederland, TX 77627
800-375-6663, 409-727-1999
FAX: 409-727-7127
E-mail: dhowell@fordor.com

body panels
sheetmetal

See full listing in **Section One** under **Ford 1903-1931**

Imperial Motors
Rt 3 Box 380
Campobello, SC 29322
864-895-3474; FAX: 864-895-1248

parts

See full listing in **Section One** under **Chrysler**

J & K Old Chevy Stuff
Ship Pond Rd
Plymouth, MA 02360
508-224-7616

car dealer
parts
sheetmetal

See full listing in **Section One** under **Chevrolet**

KopyKatz Restoration Parts
2536 N Sheridan Blvd
Denver, CO 80214
303-458-5332; FAX: 303-477-1496
E-mail: kopykatz@earthlink.net

bumpers
fenders
hoods
panels
truck beds

See full listing in **Section Two** under **body parts**

Kwik Poly T Distributing Inc
24 St Henry Ct
St Charles, MO 63301
314-724-1065

restoration aids

See full listing in **Section Two** under **restoration aids**

L & N Olde Car Co
9992 Kinsman Rd
PO Box 378
Newbury, OH 44065
440-564-7204; FAX: 440-564-8187

restoration

See full listing in **Section Two** under **restoration shops**

Lake Buchanan Industries Inc
Rt 1, Box 184-C
Buchanan Dam, TX 78609
888-552-5278 toll-free
512-793-2867; FAX: 512-793-2869
E-mail: lbi:@tstar.net

blasting cabinet

See full listing in **Section Two** under **tools**

Linearossa International Inc
3931 SW 47th Ave
Ft Lauderdale, FL 33314
954-327-9888; FAX: 954-791-6555

parts

See full listing in **Section One** under **Fiat**

Bob Marriott
497 Delaware Ave
Delmar, NY 12054

sheetmetal parts
shop manuals

See full listing in **Section One** under **Thunderbird**

The Maverick Connection
137 Valley Dr
Ripley, WV 25271
PH/FAX: 304-372-7825

literature
parts

See full listing in **Section One** under **Ford 1954-up**

McCann Auto Restoration
US Rt 1, PO Box 1025
Houlton, ME 04730
207-532-2206

custom work
restoration
sandblasting

See full listing in **Section Two** under **restoration shops**

Merv's Classic Chevy Parts   parts
1330 Washington
Iowa Falls, IA 50126
515-648-3168, 515-648-9675

See full listing in **Section One** under **Chevrolet**

Mill Supply Inc   clips
PO Box 28400   fasteners
Cleveland, OH 44128   panels
800-888-5072; FAX: 888-781-2700
E-mail: info@millsupply.com

Replacement panels and supplies for collision and rust repair.
Mill Supply carries the widest selection of replacement panels
for your car, truck or van. Plus, a variety of fasteners, clips and
body shop supplies. Call or write for specific information.
Complete 192 page catalog, $4. Web site: www.millsupply.com

Millers Incorporated   accessories
7412 Count Circle   parts
Huntington Beach, CA 92647
714-375-6565; FAX: 714-847-6606
E-mail: sales@millermbz.com

See full listing in **Section One** under **Mercedes-Benz**

National Parts Depot   accessories
3101 SW 40th Blvd   restoration parts
Gainesville, FL 32608
800-874-7595 toll-free 24 hours
352-378-2473 local

See full listing in **Section Two** under **comprehensive parts**

PANELBEATING

Fabrication – Repair – Restoration
of sheetmetal panels
and components
for antiques and street rods

Thompson Hill
METALCRAFT

23 Thompson Hill Rd.
Berwick, ME 03901

(207) 698-5756

www.thompsonhill.com

e-mail: wpeach@thompsonhill.com

Obsolete Jeep® & Willys® Parts   literature
Division of Florida 4 Wheel Drive &   parts
Truck Parts
6110 17th St E
Bradenton, FL 34203
941-756-7844
PH/FAX: 941-756-7757

See full listing in **Section One** under **Willys**

Parts House   accessories
2912 Hunter St   parts
Fort Worth, TX 76112
817-451-2708
E-mail: theparts@flash.net

See full listing in **Section Two** under **comprehensive parts**

Passenger Car Supply   parts
102 Cloverdale Rd
Swedesboro, NJ 08085
609-467-7966

See full listing in **Section One** under **Chevrolet**

Pilgrim's Auto Restorations   bodywork
3888 Hill Rd   metal fabrication
Lakeport, CA 95453   paint
707-262-1062; FAX: 707-263-6956   restoration
E-mail: pilgrims@pacific.net

See full listing in **Section Two** under **restoration shops**

Raybuck Autobody Parts   body parts
RD 4, Box 170
Punxsutawney, PA 15767
814-938-5248; FAX: 814-938-4250

See full listing in **Section Two** under **body parts**

The Real Source   accessories
PO Box 1248   parts
Effingham, IL 62401
800-LUV-BUGG (588-2844), dept VS9
FAX: 217-347-2952
E-mail: madbug@madvet.com

See full listing in **Section One** under **Volkswagen**

Rocker King   body parts
804 Chicago Ave   sheetmetal parts
Waukesha, WI 53188-3511
414-549-9583; FAX: 414-549-9643
E-mail: sonoma@execpc.com

Phone sales seven days a week, 9 am to 9 pm. Mail order
inquiries include SASE. Sell reproduction rocker panels, dog
legs, door skins, quarter panel and fender sections for cars made
from 1935-1964 and trucks from 1946-1985. Web site:
www.execpc.com/~sonoma/

Rolling Steel Body Parts   body parts
7320 Martingale Dr
Chesterland, OH 44026-2007
888-765-5460; FAX: 440-729-7658
E-mail: rollingsteel@hotmail.com

See full listing in **Section Two** under **body parts**

Royals' Garage   NOS parts
16-24 Calhoun St   used parts
Torrington, CT 06790
860-489-4500

See full listing in **Section One** under **Corvette**

S & S Antique Auto   **parts**
Pine St
Deposit, NY 13754
607-467-2929; FAX: 607-467-2109

See full listing in **Section One** under **Ford 1932-1953**

Strader Classics   **parts**
Bill Strader
2849 Locust Grove Rd
Elizabethtown, KY 42701
502-737-5294

See full listing in **Section One** under **Chevrolet**

Strange Motion Inc   **customizing**
14696 N 350th Ave   **design**
Cambridge, IL 61238   **fabrication**
PH/FAX: 309-927-3346
E-mail: strange@netins.net

See full listing in **Section Two** under **street rods**

Stringbean's Pickup Parts   **parts**
985 Cushon St   **service**
Johnstown, PA 15902
PH/FAX: 814-539-6440
E-mail: s-bean@surfshop.net

See full listing in **Section One** under **Chevrolet**

Tabco Inc   **body parts**
11655 Chillicothe Rd
Chesterland, OH 44026-1994
216-921-5850; FAX: 216-921-5862

Mail order and open shop. Monday-Friday 8:30 am to 5 pm.
Manufacture and distribute steel rust repair parts for cars,
trucks and vans, both domestic and foreign.

Thompson Hill Metalcraft   **metal forming**
23 Thompson Hill Rd   **panel beating**
Berwick, ME 03901   **welding**
207-698-5756
E-mail: wpeach@thompsonhill.com

Open shop only. Monday-Friday 9 am to 5 pm. Panel beating,
metal forming, metal finishing and welding. Aluminum and steel.
Hand-builts, customs and antiques. Web site:
www.thompsonhill.com
See our ad on page 400

John Ulrich   **parts**
450 Silver Ave
San Francisco, CA 94112
PH/FAX: 510-223-9587 days

See full listing in **Section One** under **Packard**

Pat Wilson's Thunderbird Parts   **parts**
235 River Rd
New Milford, NJ 07646-1721
888-262-1153; FAX: 201-634-1916

See full listing in **Section One** under **Thunderbird**

special services

A AAAdvantage Auto Transport Inc   **transport**
8920 S Hardy
Tempe, AZ 85284
800-233-4875
E-mail: webinfo@aaaadv.com

See full listing in **Section Two** under **transport**

AAAC-Antique Automobile   **appraisals**
Appraisal & Consulting   **Cadillac parts**
PO Box 700153   **consulting**
Plymouth, MI 48170
PH/FAX: 734-453-7644
E-mail: aaac@ameritech.net

See full listing in **Section One** under **Cadillac/LaSalle**

AIS Gator Exports Inc   **export**
201 Springsong Rd
Lithia, FL 33547
813-689-2790; FAX: 813-685-1222

Shipping of various vehicles worldwide.

ANC Restoration   **restorations**
Chris Palmerie
254 New Haven Ave
Waterbury, CT 06708
203-574-2249
E-mail: cpwpa@javanet.com

See full listing in **Section Two** under **restoration shops**

Ano-Brite Inc   **anodizing**
6945 Farmdale Ave   **polishing**
North Hollywood, CA 91605   **restoration**
818-982-0997; FAX: 818-982-0804   **welding**
E-mail: ano-brite@hotmail.com

See full listing in **Section Two** under **plating & polishing**

Antique Radio Service   **radio service**
12 Shawmut Ave
Wayland, MA 01778
800-201-2635; FAX: 508-653-2418

See full listing in **Section Two** under **radios**

Arch Carburetor   **carburetors**
583 Central Ave
Newark, NJ 07107
973-482-2755
E-mail: mmfried1@aol.com

See full listing in **Section Two** under **carburetors**

Authentic Automotive   **power brakes**
529 Buttercup Trail   **power steering**
Mesquite, TX 75149
972-289-6373; FAX: 972-289-4303

See full listing in **Section One** under **Chevrolet**

Auto Transport Services   **transport**
5367 Fargo Rd
Avoca, MI 48006
810-324-2598; FAX: 810-324-6094

See full listing in **Section Two** under **transport**

Automotive Art Specialties   **drawings**
Dan McCrary   **paintings**
PO Box 18795   **prints**
Charlotte, NC 28218
704-372-2899; FAX: 704-375-8686
E-mail: mccrarydan@aol.com

See full listing in **Section Two** under **artwork**

Automotive Legal Service Inc   **appraisals**
PO Box 626
Dresher, PA 19025
800-487-4947, 215-659-4947
FAX: 215-657-5843
E-mail: autolegal@aol.com

See full listing in **Section Two** under **appraisals**

Automotive Restorations Inc
Kent S Bain
1785 Barnum Ave
Stratford, CT 06614
203-377-6745; FAX: 203-386-0486
E-mail: carbain@compuserve.com

body fabrication
mechanical
painting
restorations
upholstery
woodwork

See full listing in **Section Two** under **restoration shops**

The Autoworks Ltd
90 Center Ave
Westwood, NJ 07675
201-358-0200; FAX: 201-358-0442

restoration
sales
service

See full listing in **Section Two** under **service shops**

Skip Barber Racing School
29 Brook St
Lakeville, CT 06039
800-221-1131; FAX: 860-435-1321
E-mail: speed@skipbarber.com

racing school

See full listing in **Section Two** under **racing**

Big Time Productions
780 Munras Ave
Monterey, CA 93940
831-655-0409; FAX: 831-375-9102
E-mail: bigtime@redshift.com

video production

See full listing in **Section Two** under **videos**

Blueprint Auto Insurance Agency
100 Corporate Pl
Peabody, MA 01960
800-530-5305; FAX: 978-535-3759
E-mail: bluprntins@aol.com

insurance

See full listing in **Section Two** under **insurance**

Bob's Classic Auto Glass
21170 Hwy 36
Blachly, OR 97412
800-624-2130

glass

See full listing in **Section Two** under **glass**

Bob's Speedometer Service
32411 Grand River Ave
Farmington, MI 48336
800-592-9673; FAX: 248-473-5517

gauges
speedometers
tachometers

See full listing in **Section Two** under **instruments**

Bristol Classics Ltd
2511 State Hwy 7
Excelsior, MN 55331
612-470-7851; FAX: 612-474-9609
E-mail:
stoddwarr.er@bristol-classics-ltd.com

wooden boat
restoration

Wooden boat restoration, sales (we buy classic boats), service.
Financing available. Transportation worldwide. Appraisal consulting, expert finishing. Established 1975. Large inventory of the finest selection of custom runabouts, utilities and launches.
Web site: www.bristol-classics.ltd.com

Car Critic
202 Woodshire Ln
Naples, FL 34105
941-435-1157; FAX: 941-261-4864
E-mail: puppys4u@aol.com

appraisals
inspections

See full listing in **Section Two** under **appraisals**

Carburetor Engineering
3324 E Colorado
Pasadena, CA 91107
626-795-3221

carburetor rebuilding
distributor rebuilding
fuel pump rebuilding

See full listing in **Section Two** under **carburetors**

Cast Aluminum Repair
1520 Marshall Ln
Conyers, GA 30094
770-929-1363
E-mail: heliarctig@aol.com

repair

See full listing in **Section Two** under **castings**

Circle N Stainless
1517 NW 33rd
Lawton, OK 73505
580-355-9366
E-mail: neald@juno.com

stainless steel
trim restoration

Mail order and open shop. Monday-Saturday 7 am to 8 pm.
Restoration of stainless steel trim, no heavy buffer lines, all smoothing is done by hand sanding. No payment due until parts are returned and inspected.

City Imports Ltd
166 Penrod Ct
Glen Burnie, MD 21061
410-768-6660; FAX: 410-768-5955

bodywork
car sales
restorations

See full listing in **Section One** under **Jaguar**

Classic Car Appraisals
37 Wyndwood Rd
West Hartford, CT 06107
PH/FAX: 860-236-0125

appraisals

See full listing in **Section Two** under **appraisals**

Cobra Trailers
PO Box 18105
Savannah, GA 31418
800-262-7286; FAX: 912-233-2937

rollback trailers

See full listing in **Section Two** under **trailers**

Larry Couzens Photography
16 E 17th St
New York, NY 10003
212-620-9790; FAX: 212-620-9791

photography

See full listing in **Section Two** under **photography**

Dan's Restorations
PO Box 144
Snake Hill Rd
Sand Lake, NY 12153
518-674-2061

woodgraining

See full listing in **Section Two** under **woodgraining**

Dash Graining by Mel Erikson
31 Meadow Rd
Kings Park, NY 11754
PH/FAX: 516-544-1102 days
516-360-7789 nights

dashboard
restoration

See full listing in **Section Two** under **woodgraining**

Dashhugger
PO Box 933
Clovis, CA 93613
559-298-4529; FAX: 559-298-3428
E-mail: sales@dashhugger.com

dashboard covers

See full listing in **Section Two** under **interiors & interior parts**

Dusty Memories and Faded Glory
118 Oxford Hgts Rd
Somerset, PA 15501-1134
814-443-2393; FAX: 814-443-9452

rentals

See full listing in **Section Two** under **military vehicles**

Emblemagic Co
PO Box 420
Grand River, OH 44045-0420
440-209-0792
E-mail: arborhil@aol.com

decorative emblems plastic insert emblems

See full listing in **Section Two** under **grille emblem badges**

Excelsweld USA/Cylinder Head Specialist
1231 16th Ave
Oakland, CA 94606
800-743-4323; FAX: 510-534-1107

welding

See full listing in **Section Two** under **machine work**

Exotic Car Transport Inc
PO Box 91
Ocoee, FL 34761
800-766-8797; FAX: 407-654-9951
E-mail: info@exoticcartransport.com

transport

See full listing in **Section Two** under **transport**

Ferris Auto Electric Ltd
106 Lakeshore Dr
North Bay, ON Canada P1A 2A6
705-474-4560; FAX: 705-474-9453

parts service

See full listing in **Section Two** under **electrical systems**

First National Bank of Sumner
PO Box 145
Sumner, IL 62466
618-936-2396; FAX: 618-936-9079
E-mail: hobbes@wworld.com

financing

See full listing in **Section Two** under **financing**

The Generation Gap
123 Peachtree Park
Byron, GA 31008
912-956-2678; FAX: 912-956-2608

antiques sales

Open Monday-Saturday 9 am to 7 pm, Sunday 12 noon to 6 pm. Specializing in sales of antique, classic and special interest autos for the past 28 years. Now located in our new 15,000 sq ft showroom on I-75 at Exit 46 under the big peach in Byron, GA. Offering quality antiques and great prices on Wells Cargo trailers. Be sure and visit our coffee shop, The Daily Grind, and sip your coffee in a 1900s San Francisco trolley car. Web site: www.automotiveventures.com

Guenther Graphics
PO Box 266
LeClaire, IA 52753
PH/FAX: 319-289-9010
E-mail: fanzter@aol.com

artwork

See full listing in **Section Two** under **artwork**

Guldstrand Engineering Inc
11924 W Jefferson Blvd
Culver City, CA 90230
310-391-7108; FAX: 310-391-7424
E-mail: gss@guldstrand.com

parts

See full listing in **Section One** under **Corvette**

Hyde Auto Body
44-1/2 S Squirrel Rd
Auburn Hills, MI 48326
PH/FAX: 248-852-7832
E-mail: bodyman8@juno.com

refinishing restoration

See full listing in **Section Two** under **restoration shops**

Imtek Environmental Corporation
PO Box 2066
Alpharetta, GA 30023
770-667-8621; FAX: 770-667-8683
E-mail: imtek@no-odor.com

ammonia removal products odor control products

See full listing in **Section Two** under **manufacturing**

Instrument Services Inc
11765 Main St
Roscoe, IL 61073
800-558-2674; FAX: 815-623-6416

clocks gauges instruments

See full listing in **Section Two** under **instruments**

J & C's Parts
7127 Ward Rd
North Tonawanda, NY 14120
716-693-4090; FAX: 716-695-7144

parts

See full listing in **Section One** under **Buick/McLaughlin**

Jaguar Daimler Heritage Trust
Browns Ln
Allesley, Coventry CV5 9DR England
0044 (0) 1203 402121
FAX: 0044 (0) 1203 405581

archive services photographic records

See full listing in **Section One** under **Jaguar**

Jerry's Classic Cars & Parts Inc
4097 McRay Ave
Springdale, AR 72764
800-828-4584; FAX: 501-750-1682
E-mail: jcc@jerrysclassiccars.com

parts restoration

See full listing in **Section One** under **Ford 1954-up**

Jesser's Auto Clinic
26 West St
Akron, OH 44303
330-376-8181; FAX: 330-384-9129

appraisals

See full listing in **Section Two** under **appraisals**

Katen and Associates Inc
405 Greenbriar Rd
Lexington, KY 40503-2637
PH/FAX: 606-278-0758
E-mail: kainc@juno.com

welding

Mail order and open shop. Monday-Friday 8 am to 5 pm and by appointment. Micro-tig welding of small ferrous and stainless steel components.

Kenask Spring Co
307 Manhattan Ave
Jersey City, NJ 07307
201-653-4589

springs

See full listing in **Section Two** under **suspension parts**

Klassic Kolor Auctions
PO Box 55243
Hayward, CA 94545-0243
510-795-2776
FAX: available upon request
E-mail: voodoowear@hotmail.com

auction "color" broadcaster master of ceremonies

See full listing in **Section Two** under **auctions & events**

Krem Engineering 10204 Perry Hwy Meadville, PA 16335 814-724-4806; FAX: 814-337-2992 E-mail: info@krem-enterprises.com	**engine rebuilding** **repairs** **restoration**

See full listing in **Section Two** under **restoration shops**

L & L Antique Auto Trim 403 Spruce, Box 177 Pierce City, MO 65723 417-476-2871	**runningboard** **moldings**

Mail order only. Dealing in runningboard moldings.

Lee's Kustom Auto & Street Rods RR 3 Box 3061A Rome, PA 18837 570-247-2326 E-mail: lka41@epix.net	**accessories** **parts** **restoration**

See full listing in **Section Two** under **street rods**

M & L Automobile Appraisal 2662 Palm Terr Deland, FL 32720 904-734-1761	**appraiser**

See full listing in **Section Two** under **appraisals**

Mar-Ke Woodgraining 1102 Hilltop Dr Loveland, CO 80537 970-663-7803; FAX: 970-663-1138	**woodgraining**

See full listing in **Section Two** under **woodgraining**

STEERING GEARBOXES & PUMPS....

POWER STEERING SERVICES INC.

REBUILT TO FACTORY SPECS WITH THE HIGHEST QUALITY PARTS.

••••

BOTH MANUAL & POWER GEARBOXES AVAILABLE FOR CARS AND TRUCKS.

••••

ALSO, QUICK-RATIO STEERING GEARBOX CONVERSIONS FOR 60'S & 70'S CARS. "BORGESON" UNIVERSAL STEERING SHAFTS FOR ANY APPLICATION.

••••

We ship everywhere!
Call Chip for quotes and availability.

(417) 864-6676

2347 E. Kearney St. • Springfield, MO 65803

www.powersteering.com

Bill McCoskey 16643 Rt 144 Mt Airy, MD 21771 301-854-5900, 410-442-3637 FAX: 301-854-5957 E-mail: tatrabill@aol.com	**appraisals** **repairs**

See full listing in **Section Two** under **appraisals**

Memoryville USA Inc 1008 W 12th St Rolla, MO 65401 573-364-1810	**restoration**

See full listing in **Section Two** under **restoration shops**

Mint Condition Auto Upholstery PO Box 134 Silverdale New Zealand PH/FAX: 64-9-424 2257 E-mail: mint.condition@xtra.co.nz	**convertible tops** **interiors** **spring-gaiters** **wheelcovers**

Mail order and open shop. Monday-Friday 8 am to 5 pm. Deal in coach-trimming classic and vintage cars, manufacture spring-gaiters (handmade leather-gaiters), interiors, convertible tops, wheelcovers, etc.

NorCal Auto 615D Saint John St Pleasanton, CA 94566 888-224-6005; FAX: 925-426-8845 E-mail: mwjohn@hotmail.com	**appraisals**

See full listing in **Section Two** under **appraisals**

ORF Corp Phil Bray 8858 Ferry Rd Grosse Ile, MI 48138 734-676-5520; FAX: 734-676-9438 E-mail: carolbray@yahoo.com	**ring and pinion** **gears**

High speed ring and pinion gears for Packards, Cadillacs, Duesenberg and other makes. Custom manufacture a gear set for your vehicle. Also produce Packard wire center cowl lacing and hood check straps.

The Parts Scout® Bodo Repenn Diagonalstrasse 18A D-20537 Hamburg Germany *49-40-21980130 FAX: *49-40-21980132	**parts** **parts locator**

See full listing in **Section Two** under **comprehensive parts**

Performance Analysis Co 1345 Oak Ridge Tpke, Ste 258 Oak Ridge, TN 37830 423-482-9175 E-mail: george_murphy@compuserve.com	**climate control** **cruise control**

See full listing in **Section One** under **Mercedes-Benz**

Dennis Portka 4326 Beetow Dr Hamburg, NY 14075 716-649-0921	**horns** **knock-off wheels**

See full listing in **Section One** under **Corvette**

Power Steering Services Inc 2347 E Kearney St Springfield, MO 65803 417-864-6676; FAX: 417-864-7103 E-mail: cwoyner@aol.com	**pumps** **rack & pinion** **steering gearboxes**

Rebuilt and new steering gearboxes for cars and trucks. Both power and manual steering gears available. Also quick ratio

steering gear conversions for GM power steering gearboxes. New Borgeson steering universal joints and shafts. Power steering pumps. Ship everywhere. Web site: www.powersteering.com
See our ad on page 404

| **Practical Images**
PO Box 245
Haddam, CT 06438-0245
860-704-0525
E-mail: practimages@snet.net | **int'l VHS video conversions photo scanning photography** |

See full listing in **Section Two** under **photography**

| **Precision Pot Metal/Bussie Restoration Inc**
1008 Loring Ave #28
Orange Park, FL 32073
904-269-8788 | **pot metal restoration** |

See full listing in **Section Two** under **plating & polishing**

| **RB's Prototype Model & Machine Co**
44 Marva Ln
Stamford, CT 06903
203-329-2715; FAX: 203-329-8029 | **machine work** |

See full listing in **Section Two** under **service shops**

| **Redi-Strip Company**
100 W Central Ave
Roselle, IL 60172
630-529-2442; FAX: 630-529-3626 | **abrasive media baking soda blasting paint removal rust removal** |

See full listing in **Section Two** under **rust removal & stripping**

| **The Reflected Image**
21 W Wind Dr
Northford, CT 06472
PH/FAX: 203-484-0760
E-mail: scott@reflectedimage.com | **mirror reproduction mirror resilvering** |

Mail order only. Mirror resilvering, dial gauge restoration, coin-op mirror reproduction, glass and mirror sand carving and personalization products. Web site: www.reflectedimage.com

| **T Schmidt**
827 N Vernon
Dearborn, MI 48128-1542
313-562-7161 | **rust removers** |

See full listing in **Section Two** under **rust removal & stripping**

| **William G Shearman**
PO Box 547
Jamestown, NY 14702-0547
716-484-0940 | **windshield frame tubing** |

See full listing in **Section One** under **Ford 1903-1931**

| **Silver Image Photographics**
3102 Vestal Pkwy E
Vestal, NY 13850
607-797-8795 | **business cards photo car cards photofinishing** |

See full listing in **Section Two** under **automobilia**

| **Special T's Unlimited Corp**
PO Box 146
Prospect Heights, IL 60070
847-255-5494; FAX: 847-391-7666 | **general repair parts restoration service** |

See full listing in **Section One** under **Mopar**

| **Sports Car Tours Inc**
PO Box 265
Batesville, VA 22924
804-823-4442
E-mail: napol@rlc.net | **back road tours** |

Mail order and open shop. Open 24 hours, 7 days a week. Offer 3 day/2 night back road tours of scenic and historic Virginia, using 9 different classic sports cars where tourers drive 2 different cars each day and spend evenings in Virginia's best inns and hotels. Vehicles include: Porsche 356, Triumph TR3, TR8 and TR6, MGA and MGB, Alfa, Fiat 2000, Miata and Austin Healey. Web site: www.sportscartours.com

| **Stockton Wheel Service**
648 W Fremont St
Stockton, CA 95203
209-464-7771, 800-395-9433
FAX: 209-464-4725
E-mail: sales@stocktonwheel.com | **wheel repair** |

See full listing in **Section Two** under **wheels & wheelcovers**

| **Ed Strain Inc**
6555 44th St #2006
Pinellas Park, FL 33781
800-266-1623 | **power brakes** |

See full listing in **Section Two** under **brakes**

| **Tags Backeast**
PO Box 581
Plainville, CT 06062
860-747-2942
E-mail: dataplt@snet.net | **data plates trim tags** |

Mail order only. Restoration of data plates, trim tags for 1952-1969 Ford family; 1960-1974 Mopars; 1930s-1970s GM family. Legitimate authentic cars only. Web site: www.vtxpress.com/data-plate

| **Toronto Vintage Vehicles**
536 Pefferlaw Rd
Pefferlaw, ON Canada L0E 1N0
705-437-3817; FAX: 705-437-2722
E-mail: havebus@ils.net | **vehicles for movies** |

We supply picture vehicles to the film industry (commercials, movies, TV series, etc). Our vehicles are predominently hero cars and all privately owned. Over 500 vintage and collector vehicles. Web site: www.havebus.com

| **Valley Wire Wheel Service**
14731 Lull St
Van Nuys, CA 91405
818-785-7237; FAX: 818-994-2042 | **wheel restoration wheels** |

See full listing in **Section Two** under **wheels & wheelcovers**

| **Vintage Racing Services**
1785 Barnum Ave
Stratford, CT 06497
203-386-1736; FAX: 203-386-0486
E-mail: vrs@vintageracingservices.com | **storage track support transportation** |

See full listing in **Section Two** under **racing**

| **Vod Varka Springs**
US Rt 30, PO Box 170
Clinton, PA 15026
412-859-6897 home
PH/FAX: 724-695-3268 work | **anything of wire wire forms wire springs** |

Mail order only. Manufacturer of custom wire springs, wire forms and anything made of wire. No job too big or too small. Clubs and dealers welcome.

| **John J Waluk**
31 Squirrel Ln
Levittown, NY 11756
516-796-2984; FAX: 516-796-5423
E-mail: bb70@msn.com | **flocking** |

Mail order only. "Flocking of parts" service: a black velvet like finish that is applied to gloveboxes, weatherstripping, center consoles and other areas depending on type of car or truck.

White Post Restorations
One Old Car Dr
White Post, VA 22663
540-837-1140; FAX: 540-837-2368

brakes
restoration

See full listing in **Section Two** under **brakes**

Wild About Wheels
274 Great Rd
Acton, MA 01720-4702
978-264-9921
800-538-0539 (orders)
FAX: 978-264-9547
E-mail: globaltv@tiac.net

video tapes

Mail order and via the web. Wild About Wheels TV and Video produces award winning automotive television and video programming including *Wild About Wheels, Motortrend Television* and *Wheels*. Web store has over 100 automotive videos, most produced by Wild About Wheels. Automotive corporate services are also a large part of our business including event coverage, marketing and training videos. Web site: wildaboutwheels.com

Winslow Mfg Co
5700 Dean Ave
Raleigh, NC 27604
919-790-9713

parts rebuilding

See full listing in **Section Two** under **engine parts**

Wolfson Engineering
512 Parkway W
Las Vegas, NV 89106
PH/FAX: 702-384-4196

mech engineering

Mail order and open shop by appointment. Major and minor mechanical engineering projects, modifications, research and development, designs, welding, fabrication. Difficult new and used parts secured. Specialist in Rolls-Royce and American muscle cars. Member SAE, Society of Automotive Engineers and 30 year member RROC. Not accepting assignments with Asian cars or computer related electronics.

steering wheels

Automotive Specialties
11240 E Sligh Ave
Seffner, FL 33584
800-676-1928

restoration

Steering wheel restoration, woodgrain dash and molding restoration.

RL Bailey Co
27902 45th Ave S
Auburn, WA 98001
PH/FAX: 253-854-5247
E-mail: rbailey2@gte.net

restorations
steering wheels
woodgraining

See full listing in **Section Two** under **woodgraining**

Budnik Wheels Inc
7412 Prince Dr
Huntington Beach, CA 92647
714-848-1996; FAX: 714-848-5051

aluminum wheels
steering wheels

See full listing in **Section Two** under **wheels & wheelcovers**

Classics Plus LTD
N7306 Lakeshore Dr
N Fond du Lac, WI 54937
888-923-1007

restoration

Specializing in the restoration of stock, modified or street rod automobiles. Also complete restoration of steering wheels, plus a variety of woodgrainings.

**Comfy/Inter-American
Sheepskins Inc**
1346 Centinela Ave
West Los Angeles, CA 90025-1901
800-521-4014; FAX: 310-442-6080
E-mail: sales@comfysheep.com

floor mats
seat covers

See full listing in **Section Two** under **interiors & interior parts**

D&D Automobilia
813 Ragers Hill Rd
South Fork, PA 15956
814-539-5653

plastic parts
steering wheels

Mail order and open shop. Monday-Friday 8 am to 5 pm. Recasting steering wheels, dash and gearshift knobs and other plastic parts. All colors, clear, transparents, woodgrain, marbles and new speckled marble.

JB Donaldson Co
2533 W Cypress
Phoenix, AZ 85009
602-278-4505; FAX: 602-278-1112

castings
steering wheels
wood parts

Mail order only. Show quality plastic steering wheel recastings for Cadillac, Buick, Packard and other makes steering wheels. Woody parts, complete kits and complete restorations for GM, Buicks and Packards 1937-1953.

Finish Line
3593 SW 173rd Terr
Miramar, FL 33029
954-436-9101; FAX: 954-436-9102
E-mail: e.dlibrandi@worldnet.att.net

parts
supplies

See full listing in **Section One** under **Cobra**

Gary's Steering Wheel Restoration
2677 Ritner Hwy
Carlisle, PA 17013
717-243-5646; FAX: 717-243-5072
E-mail: wheelrest@aol.com

repairs

Mail order and open shop. Monday-Friday 9 am to 6 pm, Saturday by appointment. Repair all types of plastic steering wheels. Specialize in woodgrain wheels, Corvette, GTO, AMX, Roadrunner, Challenger, also inlay type wheels, Cadillac, Oldsmobile, T-Bird and Ford. Repair cracks using an acrylic plastic and then primer and seal, then top coated with four coats of acrylic urethane paint. Show quality work. Free estimates. Your satisfaction guaranteed. Since 1981, see us at Carlisle Spring, Summer, and Fall meets at space K-189, Ford H-126, Mopar H-56, Corvette D-129. Web site: www.dealonwheels.com/parts/garys/

Grant Products Inc
700 Allen Ave
Glendale, CA 91201
818-247-2910; FAX: 818-241-4683

steering wheels

Manufacturer of a complete line of custom steering wheels. Sell wholesale only.

Kimble Engineering Ltd
Unit 5 Old Mill Creek
Dartmouth
Devon TQ6 0HN England
0044 1803 835757
FAX: 0044 1803 834567

aero screens
steering wheels
valve covers

See full listing in **Section One** under **MG**

Koch's
26943 Ruether Ave, Unit M
Canyon Country, CA 91351
661-252-9264; FAX: 661-252-2834
E-mail: kochsvw@earthlink.net

restoration

Mail order and open shop. Monday-Friday 8 am to 5 pm. Steering wheel restorations. Web site: www.kochs.com

Performance Automotive Inc — accessories / car care
1696 New London Tpke
PO Box 10
Glastonbury, CT 06033
860-633-7868; FAX: 860-657-9110

See full listing in **Section Two** under **car care products**

Bill Peters — steering wheel restoration
41 Vassar Pl
Rockville Centre, NY 11570
516-766-8397

Mail order and open shop. Monday-Saturday reasonable hours. Steering wheel restoration, recasting, color and clear. For Auburn, Cord, Chrysler, Cadillac V16-V8, Chevrolet, Willys, Pontiac, Packard, Rolls/Bentley, Studebaker, Mercedes-Benz, Lincoln. All wheels, A-Z, Concours quality, domestic, imports. Woodgrain, modern, custom fabrication, truck, marine, aircraft.

Power Steering Services Inc — pumps / rack & pinion / steering gearboxes
2347 E Kearney St
Springfield, MO 65803
417-864-6676; FAX: 417-864-7103
E-mail: cwoyner@aol.com

See full listing in **Section Two** under **special services**

storage

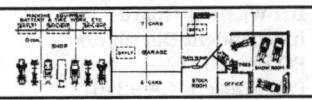

Automotive Restorations Inc — body fabrication / mechanical / painting / restorations / upholstery / woodwork
Kent S Bain
1785 Barnum Ave
Stratford, CT 06614
203-377-6745; FAX: 203-386-0486
E-mail: carbain@compuserve.com

See full listing in **Section Two** under **restoration shops**

The Autoworks Ltd — restoration / sales / service
90 Center Ave
Westwood, NJ 07675
201-358-0200; FAX: 201-358-0442

See full listing in **Section Two** under **service shops**

Berliner Classic Motorcars Inc — automobilia / car dealer / motorcycles
1975 Stirling Rd
Dania, FL 33004
954-923-7271; FAX: 954-926-3306
E-mail: sales@motorcars.com

See full listing in **Section Two** under **car dealers**

Chicago Car Exchange — appraisals / car dealer / car locator / financing / storage
1 Collector Car Dr
Box 530
Lake Bluff, IL 60044
847-680-1950; FAX: 847-680-1961
E-mail: oldtoys@wwa.com

See full listing in **Section Two** under **car dealers**

Collector's Carousel — appraisals / sales / service
84 Warren Ave
Westbrook, ME 04092
207-854-0343; FAX: 207-856-6913

See full listing in **Section Two** under **car dealers**

Deltran Corporation — battery chargers
801 US Hwy 92 E
Deland, FL 32724
904-736-7900; FAX: 904-736-9984

See full listing in **Section Two** under **batteries**

Exotic Car Transport Inc — transport
PO Box 91
Ocoee, FL 34761
800-766-8797; FAX: 407-654-9951
E-mail: info@exoticcartransport.com

See full listing in **Section Two** under **transport**

Family Sports Storage Inc — storage
4400 Killarney Park Dr
Burton, MI 48529
810-743-5670

Open by appointment only. Either heated inside storage or outside storage.

Fiesta's Classic Car Center — appraisals / consignment sales / storage
3901 N Kings Hwy
St Louis, MO 63115
314-385-4567

Open daily except holidays. Specializing in clean, secure storage. Your classic is protected by a 24 hour state-of-the-art security system. Conveniently located in the center of the USA. Can assist in preparation and transportation to car shows and auctions. Consignment sales showroom available. Will build to suit multi-car garages per your specifications. Base rate for 1999 is $50 per month per vehicle.

Interesting Parts Inc — appraisals / gaskets / parts / storage / transport
Paul TerHorst
27526 N Owens Rd
Mundelein, IL 60060
PH/FAX: 847-949-1030

See full listing in **Section Two** under **comprehensive parts**

K&S Industries — display cases
1801 Union Center Hwy
Endicott, NY 13760
PH/FAX: 888-PICK-KNS
E-mail: pleximan@888pickkns.com

See full listing in **Section Two** under **models & toys**

Memory Lane Motors Inc — appraisals / car dealer / storage
1231 Rt 176
Lake Bluff, IL 60044
847-362-4600

See full listing in **Section Two** under **car dealers**

Miracle Steel Structures — steel buildings
505 N Hwy 169 Suite 500
Minneapolis, MN 55441-6420
800-521-0386, 612-593-1000
FAX: 612-544-1835
E-mail: buildings@miracletruss.com

Pre-engineered, construct yourself steel buildings for people to build their own garage, repair/workshop, storage, etc. Web site: www.miracletruss.com

Preserve Inc — storage containers
1430 E 1800 N
Hamilton, IL 62341
217-746-2411; FAX: 217-746-2231

See full listing in **Section Two** under **storage care products**

Quik-Shelter
PO Box 1123
Orange, CT 06477
800-211-3730; FAX: 203-937-8897
E-mail: info@quikshelter.com

temporary garages

See full listing in **Section Two** under **car covers**

St Louis Car Museum & Sales
1575 Woodson Rd
St Louis, MO 63114
314-993-1330; FAX: 314-993-1540

museum

See full listing in **Section Six** under **Missouri**

Superior Equipment
703 W 53rd St N
Wichita, KS 67204
800-526-9992; FAX: 316-831-0154
E-mail: mail@superlifts.com

auto lifts
shop tools

See full listing in **Section Two** under **tools**

USA of Yesterday
455 St Helens Ave
Tacoma, WA 98402
253-627-1052; FAX: 253-627-3424
E-mail: uofy@collectorcar.com

appraisals
indoor storage
sales
vehicle consignment

See full listing in **Section Two** under **appraisals**

storage care products

Amsoil
9 Claremont Dr
Flat Rock, NC 28731
704-696-8500

car care products
lubricants
undercoating

See full listing in **Section Two** under **lubricants**

Archway Press Inc
19 W 44th St
New York, NY 10036
800-374-4766; FAX: 212-869-5215
E-mail: archway@mindspring.com

garage blueprints

See full listing in **Section Four** under **books & publications**

Billie Inc
PO Box 1161
Ashburn, VA 20146-1161
800-878-6328; FAX: 703-858-0102

garage diaper
mats

See full listing in **Section Two** under **car care products**

Buenger Enterprises/GoldenRod Dehumidifier
3600 S Harbor Blvd
Oxnard, CA 93035
800-451-6797; FAX: 805-985-1534

dehumidifiers

See full listing in **Section Two** under **car care products**

Cover-Up Enterprises
Division of Trans International
Group Ltd
1444 Manor Ln
Blue Bell, PA 19422
800-268-3757; FAX: 215-654-9252

car covers

See full listing in **Section Two** under **car covers**

Cytech Double Park Lifts
6352 N Hillside
Wichita, KS 67219
800-754-8786, 800-433-6720
FAX: 316-744-9221
E-mail: lewis216@southwind.net

service lifts

Manufacturer of 4-post automotive storage and/or service lifts. Lift is portable with caster kit option. Web site: www.kars.com/cytech

D-A Lubricant Co
1340 W 29th St
Indianapolis, IN 46208
800-232-4503; FAX: 317-926-8132

lubricants

See full listing in **Section Two** under **lubricants**

Deltran Corporation
801 US Hwy 92 E
Deland, FL 32724
904-736-7900; FAX: 904-736-9984

battery chargers

See full listing in **Section Two** under **batteries**

Dri-Wash 'n Guard
Independent Distributor
PO Box 1331
Palm Desert, CA 92261
800-428-1883, 760-346-1984
FAX: 760-568-6354

automotive care
products
boat care products

See full listing in **Section Two** under **car care products**

Murphy's Motoring Accessories Inc
PO Box 618
Greendale, WI 53129-0618
800-529-8315, 414-529-8333

car covers

See full listing in **Section Two** under **car covers**

Preserve Inc
1430 E 1800 N
Hamilton, IL 62341
217-746-2411; FAX: 217-746-2231
E-mail: preserve@adams.net

storage containers

Mail order and open shop. Monday-Sunday 24 hours. Manufacture environmentally controlled storage containers for collector cars and motorcycles. First storage system that preserves cars or motorcycles in dust-free atmosphere and stops corrosion.

Quik-Shelter
PO Box 1123
Orange, CT 06477
800-211-3730; FAX: 203-937-8897
E-mail: info@quikshelter.com

temporary garages

See full listing in **Section Two** under **car covers**

Sta-Dri Pouches
Beach Filler Products Inc
RD 1, Box 105
Glen Rock, PA 17327
800-BEACH85; FAX: 717-235-4858
E-mail: beachfilters@hotmail.com

corrosion protection
mildew protection
moisture protection

Mail order only. Sta-Dri Pouches: protect your investment from moisture, mildew and corrosion. Rust, mildew and corrosion can damage your auto's interior, especially while storing put Sta-Dri Pouches on the seats, dashboard and engine compartment. Can be regenerated. Web site: www.beachfilters.com

Stinger by Axe — lifts
Hwy 177 N
PO Box 296
Council Grove, KS 66846
800-854-4850; FAX: 316-767-5040
E-mail: axeeqip@midusa.net

Manufacturer of a complete line of classic and race car storage systems. Residential and trailer auto lifts designed for the discriminating restorer/collector/racer. Line of residential lifts includes three different models. Trailer lifts are custom made to accommodate any trailer needs. All lifts are electric over hydraulic and are powder coat painted for a lifetime of use. Structure of lifts have a lifetime warranty. Showcase your vehicle(s) on a Stinger by Axe Lift. Web site: www.axeequipment.com

street rods

A-1 Street Rods — parts
631 E Las Vegas St
Colorado Springs, CO 80903
719-632-4920, 719-577-4588
FAX: 719-634-6577

Mail order and open shop. Monday-Friday 9:30 am to 5:30 pm, Saturday 9:30 am to 1 pm. Specialize in Chevrolet 1937-1957 and Ford 1928-1948 parts. Sell antique and classic car parts, street rod parts, accessories, rubber parts, chassis parts and cars.

A-One Auto Appraisals — appraisals
19 Hope Ln
Narragansett, RI 02882
401-783-7701, RI; 407-668-9610, FL

See full listing in **Section Two** under **appraisals**

Ace Antique Auto Restoration — air conditioning / body rebuilding / restoration / wiring harnesses
65 S Service Rd
Plainview, NY 11803
516-752-6065; FAX: 516-752-1484

See full listing in **Section Two** under **restoration shops**

All Seams Fine — interior restorations
23 Union St
Waterbury, VT 05676
800-244-7326 (SEAM), 802-244-8843

See full listing in **Section Two** under **upholstery**

American Autowire Systems Inc — battery cables / electrical systems / switches/components
150 Heller Pl #17W
Dept HVAA99
Bellmawr, NJ 08031
800-482-9473; FAX: 609-933-0805
E-mail: facfit@erols.com

Premier manufacturer of cutting edge automotive electrical systems covering street rods, street machines, race cars, custom cars and original equipment segments of the car market. Primary emphasis is on technically superior complete panel systems incorporating late model innovations in the easiest to install system on the market. Full line of accessory wiring kits and related components. Technical support and money back guarantee. Visa and MasterCard accepted. Dealer inquiries welcome. Web site: www.americanautowire.com

ARS, Automotive Research Services — appraisals / research
Division of Auto Search International
1702 W Camelback #301
Phoenix, AZ 85015
602-230-7111; FAX: 602-230-7282

See full listing in **Section Two** under **appraisals**

Auto Transport Services — transport
5367 Fargo Rd
Avoca, MI 48006
810-324-2598; FAX: 810-324-6094

See full listing in **Section Two** under **transport**

Automotive Legal Service Inc — appraisals
PO Box 626
Dresher, PA 19025
800-487-4947, 215-659-4947
FAX: 215-657-5843
E-mail: autolegal@aol.com

See full listing in **Section Two** under **appraisals**

Bob's Classic Auto Glass — glass
21170 Hwy 36
Blachly, OR 97412
800-624-2130

See full listing in **Section Two** under **glass**

Bonneville Sports Inc — accessories / clothing
3544 Enterprise Dr
Amaheim, CA 92807
888-999-7258, 714-666-1966
FAX: 714-666-1955
E-mail: bonspeed@aol.com

See full listing in **Section Two** under **apparel**

Boop Photography — photography
2347 Derry St
Harrisburg, PA 17104-2728
717-564-8533
E-mail: msboop@paonline.com

See full listing in **Section Two** under **photography**

BPE Racing Heads — cylinder heads
702 Dunn Way
Placentia, CA 92870
714-572-6072; FAX: 714-572-6073
E-mail: steve@bpeheads.com

See full listing in **Section Two** under **machine work**

Briz Bumpers — bumpers
8002 NE Hwy 99, #260
Vancouver, WA 98665
360-573-8628

See full listing in **Section Two** under **chassis parts**

Budnik Wheels Inc — aluminum wheels / steering wheels
7412 Prince Dr
Huntington Beach, CA 92647
714-848-1996; FAX: 714-848-5051

See full listing in **Section Two** under **wheels & wheelcovers**

CBS Performance Automotive — ignition systems / performance products
2605-A W Colorado Ave
Colorado Springs, CO 80904
800-685-1492; FAX: 719-578-9485

See full listing in **Section Two** under **ignition parts**

Classic Carriages — repair / restoration
267 County Rd 420
Athens, TN 37303
PH/FAX: 423-744-7496

See full listing in **Section One** under **Ford 1932-1953**

Coffey's Classic Transmissions 2290 W Hicks Rd, Unit 42 Hanger 30-1 Ft Worth, TX 76111 817-439-1611	transmissions

See full listing in **Section Two** under **transmissions**

Collector's Carousel 84 Warren Ave Westbrook, ME 04092 207-854-0343; FAX: 207-856-6913	appraisals sales service

See full listing in **Section Two** under **car dealers**

Contemporary and Investment Automobiles 2700 Peachtree Square Doraville, GA 30360 770-455-1200; FAX: 770-455-0023 E-mail: georjarex@aol.com	buy/sell/trade mechanical work memorabilia

See full listing in **Section Two** under **car dealers**

Crossfire Manufacturing 166-B N Mercer Ave PO Box 263 Sharpsville, PA 16150 800-458-3478 PH/FAX: 724-962-4639 E-mail: xfire@nauticom.net	accessories

See full listing in **Section Two** under **ignition parts**

Richard Culleton 4318 SW 19th Pl Cape Coral, FL 33914 800-931-7836 voice mail 315-685-7414 (home) 941-542-8640	accessories

See full listing in **Section Two** under **accessories**

Custom Plating 3030 Alta Ridge Way Snellville, GA 30278 770-736-1118	bumper specialist chrome plating parts

See full listing in **Section Two** under **plating & polishing**

Dan's Restorations PO Box 144 Snake Hill Rd Sand Lake, NY 12153 518-674-2061	woodgraining

See full listing in **Section Two** under **woodgraining**

Dependable RV & Auto Service 2619 Rt 11 N Lafayette, NY 13084 315-677-5336; FAX: 315-677-5258	parts restoration service

See full listing in **Section Two** under **service shops**

Deters Restorations 6205 Swiss Garden Rd Temperance, MI 48182-1020 734-847-1820	restoration

See full listing in **Section Two** under **restoration shops**

Bob Drake Reproductions Inc 1819 NW Washington Blvd Grants Pass, OR 97526 800-221-3673; FAX: 541-474-0099 E-mail: bobdrake@bobdrake.com	repro parts

See full listing in **Section One** under **Ford 1932-1953**

Dual Connection Box 569 Gibsonia, PA 15044 724-898-9660; FAX: 724-898-9680 E-mail: rich@dualconnection.com	models toys

See full listing in **Section Two** under **models & toys**

Early Wheel Co Inc Box 1438 Santa Ynez, CA 93460 805-688-1187; FAX: 805-688-0257	steel wheels

See full listing in **Section Two** under **wheels & wheelcovers**

Fairlane Automotive Specialties 210 E Walker St St Johns, MI 48879 517-224-6460	fiberglass bodies parts

See full listing in **Section One** under **Ford 1932-1953**

Flatlander's Hot Rods 1005 W 45th St Norfolk, VA 23508 757-440-1932; FAX: 757-423-8601	chassis manufacturing parts street rods

Open daily. Traditional and nostalgic hot rod parts. Manufacturer of 1932 Ford 5-w coupe and roadster bodies as well as complete chassis for 1928-1934 Ford cars and trucks. Also manufacture hot rod tubular axles and many related components for street rods 1928-1948. MasterCard, Visa, worldwide shipping. Our 20th year. Catalog, $3. Web site: www.hotrodsworldwide.com/catalogs/flatland.htm

Fort Wayne Clutch & Driveline 2424 Goshen Rd Fort Wayne, IN 46808 219-484-8505; FAX: 219-484-8605 E-mail: coca@mail.fwi.com	axles axleshafts clutches driveshafts

See full listing in **Section Two** under **clutches**

Ron Francis' Wire Works 167 Keystone Rd Chester, PA 19013 800-292-1940 orders, 610-485-1937 E-mail: rfwwx@aol.com	fuel injection harnesses wiring accessories wiring kits

See full listing in **Section Two** under **wiring harnesses**

Golden Mile Sales Inc J DeAngelo 2439 S Bradford St Allentown, PA 18103-5821 PH/FAX: 610-791-4497, 24 hours	NORS parts NOS parts sheetmetal

See full listing in **Section One** under **American Austin/Bantam**

Grey Hills Auto Restoration PO Box 630 51 Vail Rd Blairstown, NJ 07825 908-362-8232; FAX: 908-362-6796	restoration service

See full listing in **Section Two** under **restoration shops**

Gromm Racing Heads 664-J Stockton Ave San Jose, CA 95126 408-287-1301	cylinder heads racing parts

See full listing in **Section Two** under **racing**

Haneline Products Co PO Box 430 Morongo Valley, CA 92256 760-363-6597; FAX: 760-363-7321	gauges instrument panels stainless parts trim parts

See full listing in **Section Two** under **accessories**

Hatfield Restorations | restoration
PO Box 846
Canton, TX 75103
903-567-6742; FAX: 903-567-0645
E-mail: pathat@vzinet.com

See full listing in **Section Two** under **restoration shops**

High Performance Coatings | coatings
550 W 3615 S
Salt Lake City, UT 84115
800-456-4721, 801-262-6807
FAX: 801-262-6307
E-mail: hpcsales@hpcoatings.com

See full listing in **Section Two** under **exhaust systems**

The Hot Rod Shop | car dealer chassis conversion
16741 State Rd 1
Spencerville, IN 46788
219-627-5474; FAX: 219-627-6317

Street rod and collector car dealer. 1941-1948 Ford to GM chassis conversion kit.

Howell's Sheetmetal Co | body panels sheetmetal
PO Box 792
Nederland, TX 77627
800-375-6663, 409-727-1999
FAX: 409-727-7127
E-mail: dhowell@fordor.com

See full listing in **Section One** under **Ford 1903-1931**

Jefferis Autobody | windshield glass kit
269 Tank Farm Rd
San Luis Obispo, CA 93401
800-807-1937; FAX: 805-543-4757

See full listing in **Section Two** under **glass**

Dave Knittel Upholstery | interiors tops upholstery
850 E Teton #7
Tucson, AZ 85706
PH/FAX: 520-746-1588

See full listing in **Section Two** under **upholstery**

Koffel's Place II | engine rebuilding machine shop
740 River Rd
Huron, OH 44839
419-433-4410; FAX: 419-433-2166

See full listing in **Section Two** under **engine rebuilding**

Koolmat | insulators
26258 Cranage Rd
Olmsted Falls, OH 44138
440-427-1888; FAX: 440-427-1889
E-mail: koolmat1@gte.net

See full listing in **Section Two** under **restoration aids**

Lee's Kustom Auto & Street Rods | accessories parts restoration
RR 3 Box 3061A
Rome, PA 18837
570-247-2326
E-mail: lka41@epix.net

Mail order and open shop. Monday-Friday 8 am to 5 pm, Saturday 8 am to 12 pm. Complete shop for street rods, kit cars, race cars and total restorations on antique and classic autos. A one stop shop for parts, upholstery, engine, speed equipment, etc and accessories. Autos bought and sold.

Lokar Inc | performance parts
10924 Murdock Dr
Knoxville, TN 37932
423-966-2269; FAX: 423-671-1999
E-mail: lokarinc@aol.com

Mail order only. Manufacturer of US quality made performance products. Shifters, emergency hand brakes and brake cables. Throttle cables, kick-down kits, component mounting brackets and flexible transmission dipsticks. Other products include flexible engine dipstick, throttle pedal assemblies, hood and trunk release kits, back-up light switch/neutral safety switch kits, cut-to-fit speedometer cables, etc. Applications available for all transmission applications, including new LT-1 engines.

Lone Wolf | wolf whistles
9375 Bearwalk Path
Brooksville, FL 34613
352-596-9949
E-mail: lonewolfwhistle@bigfoot.com

See full listing in **Section Two** under **automobilia**

M & R Products | hardware tie-downs
1940 SW Blvd
Vineland, NJ 08360
800-524-2560, 609-696-9450
FAX: 609-696-4999
E-mail: mrproducts@mrproducts.com

See full listing in **Section Two** under **accessories**

Main Attractions | posters videos
PO Box 4923
Chatsworth, CA 91311
818-709-9855; FAX: 818-998-0906

See full listing in **Section Four** under **information sources**

The Masters Company | parts tools
30 Willow Dr, Suite A
Fort Thomas, KY 41075-2035
800-385-5811; FAX: 606-441-6765
E-mail: badger@cinternet.net

See full listing in **Section Two** under **tools**

MotorCam Media | automotive videos
138 N Alling Rd
Tallmadge, OH 44278
800-240-1777; FAX: 330-633-3249
E-mail: carvideo@motorcam.com

See full listing in **Section Two** under **videos**

Motorsports Racing | accessories apparel art
914 S Santa Fe #101
Vista, CA 92084
760-630-0547; FAX: 760-630-3085

See full listing in **Section Two** under **apparel**

Murphy's Motoring Accessories Inc | car covers
PO Box 618
Greendale, WI 53129-0618
800-529-8315, 414-529-8333

See full listing in **Section Two** under **car covers**

Norm's Custom Shop | interiors tops
6897 E William St Ext
Bath, NY 14810
PH/FAX: 607-776-2357

See full listing in **Section One** under **Cord**

Nostalgia Productions Inc
268 Hillcrest Blvd
St Ignace, MI 49781
906-643-8087; FAX: 906-643-9784
E-mail: edreavie@nostalgia-prod.com

shows
swap meets

See full listing in **Section Two** under **auctions & events**

Obsolete Ford Parts Inc
8701 S I-35
Oklahoma City, OK 73149
405-631-3933; FAX: 405-634-6815

parts

See full listing in **Section One** under **Ford 1954-up**

Paintwerks by Jeff Tischler
PO Box 488
Tranquility, NJ 07879
PH/FAX: 973-579-9619
E-mail: paintwerks@webtv.net

pinstriping

See full listing in **Section Two** under **striping**

People's Choice & Lost in the 50s
28170 Ave Crocker #209
Valencia, CA 91355
800-722-1965, 661-295-1965
FAX: 661-295-1931

1950s clothing
1950s memorabilia
automobilia items
celebrity items

See full listing in **Section Two** under **automobilia**

Performance Coatings
9768 Feagin Rd
Jonesboro, GA 30236
770-478-2775; FAX: 770-478-1926

ceramic coatings
engine parts
suspension parts

See full listing in **Section Two** under **exhaust systems**

Pick-ups Northwest
1430 Bickford Ave
Snohomish, WA 98290
360-568-9166; FAX: 360-568-1233

parts
trim

See full listing in **Section One** under **Chevrolet**

Jack Podell Fuel Injection Spec
106 Wakewa Ave
South Bend, IN 46617
219-232-6430; FAX: 219-234-8632

fuel system parts
fuel system
rebuilding

See full listing in **Section One** under **Corvette**

Power Effects®
1800H Industrial Park Dr
Grand Haven, MI 49417
877-3POWRFX toll-free
616-847-4200; FAX: 616-847-4210

exhaust systems

See full listing in **Section Two** under **exhaust systems**

Power Steering Services Inc
2347 E Kearney St
Springfield, MO 65803
417-864-6676; FAX: 417-864-7103
E-mail: cwoyner@aol.com

pumps
rack & pinion
steering gearboxes

See full listing in **Section Two** under **special services**

Prestige Motors
120 N Bessie Rd
Spokane, WA 99212
PH/FAX: 509-926-3611

car dealer

See full listing in **Section Two** under **car dealers**

R & L Engines Inc
308 Durham Rd
Dover, NH 03820
603-742-8812; FAX: 603-742-8137

engine rebuilding
restorations

See full listing in **Section Two** under **engine rebuilding**

RB's Obsolete Automotive
7711 Lake Ballinger Way
Edmonds, WA 98026-9163
425-670-6739; FAX: 425-670-9151
E-mail: rbobsole@gte.net

parts

See full listing in **Section Two** under **comprehensive parts**

**Red's Headers & Early Ford Speed
Equipment**
22950 Bednar Ln
Fort Bragg, CA 95437-8411
707-964-7733; FAX: 707-964-5434
E-mail: red@reds-headers.com

headers
mechanical parts

See full listing in **Section One** under **Ford 1932-1953**

Restorations Unlimited II Inc
304 Jandus Rd
Cary, IL 60013
847-639-5818

restoration

See full listing in **Section Two** under **restoration shops**

Rock Valley Antique Auto Parts
Box 352
Rt 72 and Rothwell Rd
Stillman Valley, IL 61084
815-645-2271; FAX: 815-645-2740

gas tanks

See full listing in **Section One** under **Ford 1932-1953**

Rod-1 Shop
210 Clinton Ave
Pitman, NJ 08071
609-228-7631; FAX: 609-582-5770

street rods

Open shop only. Monday-Friday 7 am to 5 pm, weekends by appointment. Street rods, restorations of 1930, 1940, 1950 and 1960 cars, original or customs and muscle cars, turnkey or partial. Welding, wiring, performance, chassis modifications, front end installations, sheetmetal work and bodywork.

RodDoors
PO Box 2110
Chico, CA 95927
530-896-1513; FAX: 530-896-1518
E-mail: roddoors@juno.com

door panels
interior accessories

Mail order only. Designer of door panels and interior accessories that allow the street rodder/restorer to do much of the upholstery work themselves, without sewing, drilling or the use of screws or clips. Thom Taylor, Taylor Designs and other designers have produced a series of thirty-eight (38) custom designs. In addition to door panels, a complete line of cowl panels, quarter panels, package trays, trunk kits, rear cab covers, door pulls, under dash covers, armrests and speaker templates are available.

Rodster Inc
128 Center St #B
El Segundo, CA 90245
310-322-2767; FAX: 310-322-2761

conversion kits

A rodster is an easy cruisin' street rod you build on an 1983-1994 Chevy S-10 Blazer. Easy build conversion kits from $3,995-$6,995. Web site: www.rodster.com

Sammy's Street Strollers	baby stroller
2725 Chinook Ct	
Union City, CA 94587	
510-489-3502; FAX: 510-489-2994	
E-mail: sammy@slipnet.com	

See full listing in **Section One** under **Ford 1932-1953**

Sanders Antique Auto Restoration	restoration
1120 22nd St	
Rockford, IL 61108	
815-226-0535	

See full listing in **Section Two** under **restoration shops**

Saturn Industries	axles/instruments
10-14 Newland St, Coleford	literature
Royal Forest of Dean	nostalgic bits
Gloucestershire GL 16 8AN England	repro parts
01594 834321; FAX: 01594 835456	street rods

See full listing in **Section One** under **Ford 1903-1931**

Sedgwick Fall Festival	rod run
509 Harrison	
Sedgwick, KS 67135	
316-772-5675	

See full listing in **Section Two** under **auctions & events**

Joe Smith Ford & Hot Rod Parts	parts
2140 Canton Rd, Unit C	service
Marietta, GA 30066	
800-235-4013, 770-426-9850	
FAX: 770-426-9854	
E-mail: hank@joesmithauto.com	

See full listing in **Section One** under **Ford 1932-1953**

Southern Rods & Parts Inc	accessories
2125 Airport Rd	headlights
Gleer, SC 29651	power windows
864-848-0601; FAX: 864-801-0601	radiators

Mail order and open shop. Monday-Friday 8:30 am to 5:30 pm, Saturday 9 am to 1 pm. Sale of street rod parts and accessories, ranging from a/c kits to headers, wheels, headlights, radiators and power windows. Warehouse prices to the public.

Sparrow Auction Company	auction company
59 Wheeler Ave	
Milford, CT 06460	
203-877-1066	
E-mail: vehicle@snet.net	

See full listing in **Section Two** under **auctions & events**

Specialty Power Window	power window kits
2087 Collier Rd	windshield wiper
Forsyth, GA 31029	kit
800-634-9801; FAX: 912-994-3124	

Mail order and open shop. Monday-Friday 8 am to 5 pm EST. Complete power window kits and windshield wiper kits for street rods, cars, trucks and kit cars. Web site: www.specialtypowerwindows.com

Speedway Motors Inc	parts
300 Speedway Cir	
Lincoln, NE 68502	
402-474-4411; FAX: 402-477-7476	

See full listing in **Section Two** under **comprehensive parts**

Steve's Auto Restorations	restoration
4440 SE 174th Ave	
Portland, OR 97236	
503-665-2222; FAX: 503-665-2225	
E-mail: steve@realsteel.com	

See full listing in **Section Two** under **restoration shops**

Stockton Wheel Service	wheel repair
648 W Fremont St	
Stockton, CA 95203	
209-464-7771, 800-395-9433	
FAX: 209-464-4725	
E-mail: sales@stocktonwheel.com	

See full listing in **Section Two** under **wheels & wheelcovers**

Strange Motion Inc	customizing
14696 N 350th Ave	design
Cambridge, IL 61238	fabrication
PH/FAX: 309-927-3346	
E-mail: strange@netins.net	

Award winning street rod and custom design, fabrication, concepts, paint, body, interiors (Harleys also). Full custom twin rail tubular chassis work has been featured in over 30 magazines worldwide. Web site: www.geocities.com/motorcity/lane/7386/strangemotion.html

Supreme Metal Polishing	metal working
84A Rickenbacker Cir	parts restoration
Livermore, CA 94550	plating services
925-449-3490; FAX: 925-449-1475	polishing
E-mail: supremet@home.com	

See full listing in **Section Two** under **plating & polishing**

Tanson Enterprises	performance parts
2508 J St, Dept HVA	restoration parts
Sacramento, CA 95816-4815	
916-448-2950	
FAX: 916-443-3269 *88	
E-mail: tanson@pipeline.com	

See full listing in **Section One** under **Oldsmobile**

Tatom Vintage Vendors	engine rebuilding
PO Box 2504	machine shop
Mt Vernon, WA 98273	
360-424-8314; FAX: 360-424-6717	
E-mail: flatheads@tatom.com	

See full listing in **Section Two** under **engine rebuilding**

Thompson Hill Metalcraft	metal forming
23 Thompson Hill Rd	panel beating
Berwick, ME 03901	welding
207-698-5756	
E-mail: wpeach@thompsonhill.com	

See full listing in **Section Two** under **sheetmetal**

The V8 Store	accessories
3010 NE 49th St	parts
Vancouver, WA 98663	service
360-693-7468	
360-694-7853 nights	
FAX: 360-693-0982	

Mail order and open shop. Monday-Friday 7:30 am to 5 pm, nights and Saturday by appointment. Rod and custom supply store specializing in authentic fifties accessories. Also have both used and NOS engine, drivetrain, body parts, flathead speed equipment. Have added the complete line of Offenhauser performance products.

Section Two
Generalists

Vintage Glass USA — auto glass
PO Box 336
326 S River Rd
Tolland, CT 06084
800-889-3826, 860-872-0018

See full listing in **Section Two** under **glass**

Wescott's Auto Restyling — body parts
19701 SE Hwy 212
Boring, OR 97009
800-523-6279; FAX: 503-658-2938
E-mail: marykarl@gte.net

See full listing in **Section One** under **Ford 1932-1953**

West Amity Auto Parts — custom machining / engine rebuilding
5685 Merrick Rd
Massapequa, NY 11758
516-795-4610; FAX: 516-795-4117
E-mail: crein69929@erols.com

See full listing in **Section Two** under **engine rebuilding**

Kirk F White — models / tin toys
PO Box 999
New Smyrna Beach, FL 32170
904-427-6660; FAX: 904-427-7801

See full listing in **Section Two** under **models & toys**

Johnny Williams Services — appraisals / car & parts locator / consultant / lighting systems / design
2613 Copeland Road
Tyler, TX 75701
903-597-3687, 800-937-0900
voice mail #7225

See full listing in **Section Two** under **appraisals**

 striping

Auto Decals Unlimited Inc — decals / stripe kits
11259 E Via Linda, Ste 100-201
Scottsdale, AZ 85259
602-220-0800

See full listing in **Section Two** under **decals**

Dr Vinyl and Assoc Ltd — dent repair / interior repair / paint touch-up
9501 E 350 Hwy
Raytown, MO 64133
816-356-3312; FAX: 816-356-9049
E-mail: tbuckley@drvinyl.com

See full listing in **Section Two** under **car care products**

National Parts Depot — accessories / restoration parts
3101 SW 40th Blvd
Gainesville, FL 32608
800-874-7595 toll-free 24 hours
352-378-2473 local

See full listing in **Section Two** under **comprehensive parts**

Paintwerks by Jeff Tischler — pinstriping
PO Box 488
Tranquility, NJ 07879
PH/FAX: 973-579-9619
E-mail: paintwerks@webtv.net

Shop open by appointment only. Custom hand-painted pinstriping and monogramming. Specializing in street rods, kustoms, classic automobiles and motorcycles. Some traveling possible. Located in Newton, NJ, area. 28 years' experience.

The Pinstriper — pinstriping
19 Hope Ln
Narragansett, RI 02882
401-783-7701, RI; 407-668-9610, FL

Mail order and open shop. Saturday 10 am to 6 pm. Specialist in hand painted pinstripes, scroll or straight line. Your place or mine. 30+ years' experience; FL, RI, CT, MA.

Prostripe — graphics / molding / pinstriping
Division of Spartan International Inc
1845 Cedar St
Holt, MI 48842
800-248-7800; FAX: 517-694-7952
E-mail: information@spartanintl.com

Manufacturer of automotive striping, graphics, molding, accessories, limo tint brand window films and utility self-adhesive products. Web site: www.spartanintl.com

 suspension parts

356 Enterprises — parts
Vic & Barbara Skirmants
27244 Ryan Rd
Warren, MI 48092
810-575-9544; FAX: 810-558-3616

See full listing in **Section One** under **Porsche**

A&F Imported Parts Inc — parts
490 40th St
Oakland, CA 94609
888-263-7278; FAX: 707-256-0764
E-mail: mmast64166@aol.com

See full listing in **Section One** under **Mercedes-Benz**

A-1 Shock Absorber Co — shocks / sway bars
Shockfinders Division
PO Box 2028
Silverthorne, CO 80498
800-344-1966; FAX: 970-513-8283

Mail order and open shop. Monday-Friday 8 am to 5 pm. Hard-to-find shock specialists. Tube type shocks for cars and trucks 1928-1979 in stock. Gas or hydraulic, 1-3/16" or 1-3/8" piston size. Also spring assist and air shocks. Lever shocks rebuilt for domestic and foreign applications. No struts, hydraulics or low riders. Want the best shocks available? Our gas charged extra heavy duty shocks have a 50% larger piston, twice the oil capacity and heavier gauge metal compared to a heavy duty.
See our ad on page 648

Action Performance Inc — accessories
1619 Lakeland Ave
Bohemia, NY 11716
516-244-7100; FAX: 516-244-7172

See full listing in **Section Two** under **accessories**

Antique Auto Parts Cellar — brake/chassis/ engine parts / fuel pumps/kits / gaskets / water pumps
PO Box 3
6 Chauncy St
South Weymouth, MA 02190
781-335-1579; FAX: 781-335-1925

See full listing in **Section Two** under **comprehensive parts**

Apple Hydraulics Inc 1610 Middle Rd Calverton, NY 11933-1419 516-369-9515, 800-882-7753 FAX: 516-369-9516	**brake rebuilding** **shock rebuilding**

Mail order and open shop. Monday-Friday 8 am to 4:30 pm. Shock absorbers rebuilt, knee action and lever type. Largest USA rebuilder of Delco, Armstrong, Girling, Houdaille, American, British and other vintage shocks 1915-1974. Brake cylinders sleeved and completely rebuilt, service includes brake masters, boosters, servos, wheel cylinders, calipers and rebuild kits. Fast service. Fast service, Visa, MasterCard, COD orders welcome. Free catalog.

Atlantic Enterprises 221 Strand Industrial Dr Little River, SC 29566 843-399-7565; FAX: 843-399-4600 E-mail: steering@atlantic-ent.com	**steering assemblies**

See full listing in **Section Two** under **chassis parts**

Authentic Automotive 529 Buttercup Trail Mesquite, TX 75149 972-289-6373; FAX: 972-289-4303	**power brakes** **power steering**

See full listing in **Section One** under **Chevrolet**

Dave Bean Engineering 636 E St Charles St SR3H San Andreas, CA 95249 209-754-5802; FAX: 209-754-5177 E-mail: admin@davebean.com	**parts**

See full listing in **Section One** under **Lotus**

Bonk's Automotive Inc 4480 Lazelda Dr Milan, MI 48160 800-207-6906; FAX: 734-434-0845 E-mail: bonkers@bonkauto.com	**automotive tools**

See full listing in **Section Two** under **tools**

California Pony Cars 1906 Quaker Ridge Pl Ontario, CA 91761 909-923-2804; FAX: 909-947-8593 E-mail: 105232.3362@compuserve.com	**parts**

See full listing in **Section One** under **Mustang**

Canadian Mustang 20529 62 Ave Langley, BC Canada V3A 8R4 604-534-6424; FAX: 604-534-6694 E-mail: parts@canadianmustang.com	**parts**

See full listing in **Section One** under **Mustang**

Chassis Engineering Inc 119 N 2nd St, Box 70 West Branch, IA 52358 319-643-2645; FAX: 319-643-2801	**brakes** **chassis parts** **suspension parts**

See full listing in **Section Two** under **chassis parts**

Stan Chernoff 1215 Greenwood Ave Torrance, CA 90503 310-320-4554; FAX: 310-328-7867 E-mail: az589@lafn.org	**mechanical parts** **restoration parts** **technical info** **trim parts**

See full listing in **Section One** under **Datsun**

Chicago Corvette Supply 7322 S Archer Rd Justice, IL 60458 708-458-2500; FAX: 708-458-2662	**parts**

See full listing in **Section One** under **Corvette**

Classic Chevy International PO Box 607188 Orlando, FL 32860-7188 800-456-1957, 407-299-1957 FAX: 407-299-3341 E-mail: cciworld@aol.com	**modified parts** **repro parts** **used parts**

See full listing in **Section One** under **Chevrolet**

Classic Creations of Central Florida 3620 Hwy 92E Lakeland, FL 33801 941-665-2322; FAX: 941-666-5348 E-mail: flclassics@aol.com	**parts** **restoration** **service**

See full listing in **Section One** under **Mustang**

Coil Spring Specialties 632 W Bertrand St Mary's, KS 66536 785-437-2025; FAX: 785-437-2266 E-mail: info@coilsprings.com	**custom coil springs**

Mail order only. Deal in custom coil springs for all makes and models. Specializing in classic and muscle car applications. 100% calibrate to factory specifications so you get the right spring the first time. Can also custom make springs for any special application you may require. Web site: www.coilsprings.com

See our ad on this page

Concours Parts & Accessories
3493 Arrowhead Dr
Carson City, NV 89706
800-722-0009; FAX: 800-725-8644

parts

See full listing in **Section One** under **Thunderbird**

Corvair Underground
PO Box 339
Dundee, OR 97115
800-825-8247, 503-434-1648
FAX: 503-434-1626

parts

See full listing in **Section One** under **Corvair**

Corvette America
PO Box 324, Rt 322
Boalsburg, PA 16827
800-458-3475, foreign: 814-364-2141
FAX: 814-364-9615, 24 hours
E-mail:
vettebox@corvetteamerica.com

accessories
fiberglass
interiors
leisure items
parts

See full listing in **Section One** under **Corvette**

Coventry West Inc
5936-A Peachtree Rd
Atlanta, GA 30341
800-331-2193 toll-free
770-451-3839 Atlanta
FAX: 770-451-7561

assemblies
Jaguar parts

See full listing in **Section One** under **Jaguar**

CPR
431 S Sierra Way
San Bernardino, CA 92408
909-884-6980; FAX: 909-884-7872

new parts
reproduction parts
used parts

See full listing in **Section One** under **Pontiac**

Custom Plating
3030 Alta Ridge Way
Snellville, GA 30278
770-736-1118

bumper specialist
chrome plating
parts

See full listing in **Section Two** under **plating & polishing**

Mike Drago Chevy Parts
141 E St Joseph St
Easton, PA 18042
PH/FAX: 610-252-5701
E-mail: dragomdcp@aol.com

Chevrolet parts

See full listing in **Section One** under **Chevrolet**

Eaton Detroit Spring Service Co
1555 Michigan Ave
Detroit, MI 48216
313-963-3839; FAX: 313-963-7047
E-mail: ken@eatonsprings.com

bushings
coil springs
leaf springs
shackles
U-bolts

Mail order and open shop. Monday-Friday 8 am to 5:30 pm. Supply any leaf or coil spring for American cars and trucks from the 1902 curved dash Oldsmobile to present. With a library of over 17,000 OEM blueprints, can manufacture to OEM specs or custom make to your specs. Complete line of shackles, bushings and U-bolts. Licensed by both Ford Motor and GM restoration parts programs which guarantees the quality and authenticity of our springs and components. Web Site: www.eatonsprings.com

See our ad on this page

FEN Enterprises of New York Inc
PO Box 1559
1324 Rt 376
Wappingers Falls, NY 12590
914-462-5959, 914-462-5094
FAX: 914-462-8450

parts
restoration

See full listing in **Section One** under **Cadillac/LaSalle**

Five Points Classic Auto Shocks
2911 A S Main
Santa Ana, CA 92707
714-979-0451; FAX: 714-241-3454

shock absorbers

Mail order and open shop. Monday-Friday 9 am to 5 pm. Deal in shock absorbers. Rebuild lever type shocks for all makes and models. Rebuild certain tubular shocks.

Florida Caliper Manufacturers Inc
1450 SW 10th St #3
Delray Beach, FL 33444
561-272-5238

brake systems
chassis parts
suspension parts

See full listing in **Section One** under **Corvette**

For Ramblers Only
2324 SE 34th Ave
Portland, OR 97214
503-232-0497
E-mail: ramblers@teleport.com

accessories
parts

See full listing in **Section One** under **AMC**

Guldstrand Engineering Inc
11924 W Jefferson Blvd
Culver City, CA 90230
310-391-7108; FAX: 310-391-7424
E-mail: gss@guldstrand.com

parts

See full listing in **Section One** under **Corvette**

Mike Hershenfeld
3011 Susan Rd
Bellmore, NY 11710
PH/FAX: 516-781-PART (7278)
E-mail: mikesmopar@juno.com

parts

See full listing in **Section One** under **Mopar**

Holcombe Cadillac Parts 2933 Century Ln Bensalem, PA 19020 215-245-4560; FAX: 215-633-9916	parts

See full listing in **Section One** under **Cadillac/LaSalle**

K&D Enterprises 23117 E Echo Lake Rd Snohomish, WA 98296-5426 425-788-0507; FAX: 360-668-2003 E-mail: tdb@halcyon.com	accessories parts restorations

See full listing in **Section One** under **Jensen**

Kanter Auto Products 76 Monroe St Boonton, NJ 07005 800-526-1096, 201-334-9575 FAX: 201-334-5423	car cover carpets parts

See full listing in **Section Two** under **comprehensive parts**

K C Obsolete Parts 3343 N 61 Kansas City, KS 66104 913-334-9479; FAX: 913-788-2795	parts

See full listing in **Section One** under **Ford 1954-up**

Kenask Spring Co 307 Manhattan Ave Jersey City, NJ 07307 201-653-4589	springs

Mail order and open shop. Monday-Saturday 9 am to 4 pm. Dealing in auto and truck leaf springs and coil springs, also all parts related to springs. Rubbers, bushings, U-bolts, shackles, hangers, pins, bolts, insulators, etc. Also install what we sell.

Roger Kraus Racing 2896 Grove Way Castro Valley, CA 94546 510-582-5031; FAX: 510-886-5605	shocks tires wheels

See full listing in **Section Two** under **tires**

L B Repair 1308 W Benten Savannah, MO 64485-1549 816-324-3913	restoration

See full listing in **Section One** under **Ford 1954-up**

Linearossa International Inc 3931 SW 47th Ave Ft Lauderdale, FL 33314 954-327-9888; FAX: 954-791-6555	parts

See full listing in **Section One** under **Fiat**

Mint Condition Auto Upholstery PO Box 134 Silverdale New Zealand PH/FAX: 64-9-424 2257 E-mail: mint.condition@xtra.co.nz	convertible tops interiors spring-gaiters wheelcovers

See full listing in **Section Two** under **special services**

MRL Automotive PO Box 117230 Carrollton, TX 75011-7230 972-394-3489; FAX: 800-210-0200	rubber lubricants

See full listing in **Section Two** under **lubricants**

Muskegon Brake & Dist Co 848 E Broadway Muskegon, MI 49444 616-733-0874; FAX: 616-733-0635	brakes springs suspensions

See full listing in **Section Two** under **brakes**

National Parts Depot 3101 SW 40th Blvd Gainesville, FL 32608 800-874-7595 toll-free 24 hours 352-378-2473 local	accessories restoration parts

See full listing in **Section Two** under **comprehensive parts**

Northern Auto Parts Warehouse Inc PO Box 3147 Sioux City, IA 51102 800-831-0884; FAX: 712-258-0088	parts

See full listing in **Section Two** under **engine parts**

Northwest Classic Falcons Inc 1964 NW Pettygrove St Portland, OR 97209 503-241-9454; FAX: 503-241-1964 E-mail: ron@nwfalcon.com	parts

See full listing in **Section One** under **Ford 1954-up**

Northwestern Auto Supply Inc 1101 S Division Grand Rapids, MI 49507 616-241-1714, 800-704-1078 FAX: 616-241-0924	parts

See full listing in **Section Two** under **engine parts**

Obsolete Jeep® & Willys® Parts Division of Florida 4 Wheel Drive & Truck Parts 6110 17th St E Bradenton, FL 34203 941-756-7844 PH/FAX: 941-756-7757	literature parts

See full listing in **Section One** under **Willys**

The Parts Scout® Bodo Repenn Diagonalstrasse 18A D-20537 Hamburg Germany *49-40-21980130 FAX: *49-40-21980132	parts parts locator

See full listing in **Section Two** under **comprehensive parts**

Performance Coatings 9768 Feagin Rd Jonesboro, GA 30236 770-478-2775; FAX: 770-478-1926	ceramic coatings engine parts suspension parts

See full listing in **Section Two** under **exhaust systems**

Pollard Co Joe Pollard 9331 Johnell Rd Chatsworth, CA 91311 PH/FAX: 818-999-1485	parts

See full listing in **Section One** under **Checker**

Hemmings' Vintage Auto Almanac© Fourteenth Edition

Power Steering Services Inc | pumps
2347 E Kearney St | rack & pinion
Springfield, MO 65803 | steering gearboxes
417-864-6676; FAX: 417-864-7103
E-mail: cwoyner@aol.com

See full listing in **Section Two** under **special services**

Raine Automotive Springs | springs
Warehouse | suspension parts
425 Harding Hwy
Carney's Point, NJ 08069
609-299-9141; FAX: 609-299-9157

Mail order only. New replacement coil springs, 1934-1984; also leaf springs and suspension parts. Specialty custom raised or lowered coil springs.

RARE Corvettes | cars
Joe Calcagno | parts
Box 1080
Soquel, CA 95073
831-475-4442; FAX: 831-475-1115

See full listing in **Section One** under **Corvette**

Rare Parts Inc | suspension parts
621 Wilshire Ave
Stockton, CA 95203
209-948-6005; FAX: 209-948-2851
E-mail: rparts@rareparts.com

Mail order and open shop. Five days a week 8 am to 5 pm. Purchase and manufacture suspension parts for vehicles from 1930-1994. Distribute through all W/D, jobbers and auto repair/restoration businesses. Yes, we can manufacture! Give us your needs.

Fine Tires for Collector Vehicles!

Coker Tire

1317 Chestnut Street, Chattanooga, TN 37402
Local & Int'l (423)265-6368 Fax (423)756-5607
www.coker.com
Call for a FREE Catalog!
1-800-251-6336
C177HMA0

RB's Obsolete Automotive | parts
7711 Lake Ballinger Way
Edmonds, WA 98026-9163
425-670-6739; FAX: 425-670-9151
E-mail: rbobsole@gte.net

See full listing in **Section Two** under **comprehensive parts**

RD Enterprises Ltd | parts
290 Raub Rd
Quakertown, PA 18951
215-538-9323; FAX: 215-538-0158
E-mail: rdent@rdent.com

See full listing in **Section One** under **Lotus**

Red Bird Racing | parts
6640 Valley St
Coeur d'Alene, ID 83815
208-762-5305

See full listing in **Section One** under **Chevrolet**

Rick's First Generation Camaro | accessories
Parts & Accessories | parts
420 Athena Dr
Athens, GA 30601
800-359-7717; FAX: 706-548-8581
E-mail: firstgen@negia.net

See full listing in **Section One** under **Chevelle/Camaro**

William H Robenolt | front suspension
5121 S Bridget Point | parts
Floral City, FL 34436
352-344-2007

Mail order and open shop by appointment only. Obsolete NOS/NORS front suspension parts. Mid 1930s-1970s. Write for availability and quote, fair prices and prompt service.

Star Classics Inc | parts
7745 E Redfield #300
Scottsdale, AZ 85260
800-644-7827, 480-991-7495
FAX: 480-951-4096
E-mail: starcls@primenet.com

See full listing in **Section One** under **Mercedes-Benz**

Studebaker Parts & Locations | parts
228 Marquiss Cir | parts locator
Clinton, TN 37716
615-457-3002
E-mail: studebaker_joe@msn.com

See full listing in **Section One** under **Studebaker**

Swedish Classics Inc | parts
PO Box 557
Oxford, MD 21654
800-258-4422; FAX: 410-226-5543

See full listing in **Section One** under **Volvo**

T-Bird Sanctuary | parts
9997 SW Avery
Tualatin, OR 97062
503-692-9848; FAX: 503-692-9849

See full listing in **Section One** under **Thunderbird**

TA Motor AB | accessories
Torpslingan 21 | parts
Lulea S 97347 Sweden
+46-920-18888
FAX: +46-920-18821

See full listing in **Section One** under **Cadillac/LaSalle**

Thunderbird Headquarters
1080 Detroit Ave
Concord, CA 94518
800-227-2174, US
FAX: 925-689-1771, 800-964-1957
E-mail: tbirdhq@tbirdhq.com

accessories
literature
parts
upholstery

See full listing in **Section One** under **Thunderbird**

TMC (Traction Master Co)
2917 W Olympic Blvd
Los Angeles, CA 90006
213-382-1131
E-mail: tmcgroup@aol.com

suspensions

See full listing in **Section One** under **Mustang**

Vehicle Spring Service
7582 Industrial Way
Stanton, CA 90680
714-379-8077; FAX: 714-897-1892

springs
suspensions

Both mail order and open shop. Monday-Friday 8 am to 5 pm,
Saturday 8 am to 12 pm. Complete spring shop facility. Sell and
rebuild springs. New leaf springs and coils for all vehicles.
Custom rearching and rebuilding of leaf springs. Custom air
suspension conversions for RV and work vehicles.

Zip Products
8067 Fast Ln
Mechanicsville, VA 23111
804-746-2290, 800-962-9632
FAX: 804-730-7043
E-mail: zipvette@erols.com

accessories
parts

See full listing in **Section One** under **Corvette**

tires

Big Boys Toys
Richard Boutin
Rt 67A Box 174A
North Bennington, VT 05257
800-286-1721; FAX: 802-447-0962

accessories
bodywork
tires
wheels

See full listing in **Section Two** under **accessories**

Coker Tire
1317 Chestnut St
Chattanooga, TN 37402
800-251-6336 toll-free
423-265-6368 local & international
FAX: 423-756-5607

tires

Call for a free catalog featuring authentic, original equipment
tires, tubes and flaps for Model Ts to muscle cars. Vintage
brands such as Firestone, Firestone Wide Oval, BF Goodrich
Silvertowns, Vintage Michelin and US Royal. Also available, the
world's first true wide whitewall radial tire as well as muscle car
and street rod wheels. Helpful sales staff, toll-free number and
major credit cards accepted. Web site: www.coker.com
See our ad on page 418

Kelsey Tire Inc
PO Box 564
Camdenton, MO 65020
800-325-0091; FAX: 800-845-7581
E-mail: kelsey@kelseytire.com

auto tires

Specializing in Goodyear and General vintage auto tires. Web
site: www.kelseytire.com

Section Two
Generalists

Roger Kraus Racing
2896 Grove Way
Castro Valley, CA 94546
510-582-5031; FAX: 510-886-5605

shocks
tires
wheels

Specialize in vintage race tires. Dunlop vintage, Goodyear vintage, Englebert, Michelin, Avon, Hoosier and BFG G-force. Wheels by American, PS Engineering, Panasport, Jongbloed. Web site: www.rogerkrausracing.com

Lucas Automotive
2850 Temple Ave
Long Beach, CA 90806
800-952-4333; FAX: 562-595-0381

tires

Mail order and open shop. Monday-Friday 9 am to 5 pm (8 pm EST). Antique and classic tires.

Phelan Antique Auto Parts
73 Hillview St
Hamilton
Guelph, ON Canada L8S 2Z3
905-527-0002; FAX: 905-527-5929
E-mail: phelanantiqueauto@hwcn.org

parts

See full listing in **Section One** under **Ford 1903-1931**

Prestige Thunderbird Inc
10215 Greenleaf Ave
Santa Fe Springs, CA 90670
800-423-4751, 562-944-6237
FAX: 562-941-8677
E-mail:
tbirds@prestigethunderbird.com

appraisals
radios
repairs
restorations
tires

See full listing in **Section One** under **Thunderbird**

Quality Tire Barn Inc
255 Twinsburg Rd
Northfield, OH 44067
330-467-1284

tires

Specializing in hard-to-get antique auto and truck tires from 1930-1960, 30 Sayors and Schoville 4-door vans, 30 Jordan 4-door, 29 Chrysler 4-door, 31 Hupmobile and electric Volkswagens.

Rideable Antique Bicycle Replicas
2329 Eagle Ave
Alameda, CA 94501
510-769-0980; FAX: 510-521-7145
E-mail: mbarron@barrongroup.com

bicycles
tires

See full listing in **Section Two** under **motorcycles**

O B Smith Chevy Parts
PO Box 11703
990 New Circle Rd NW
Lexington, KY 40577
606-253-1957; FAX: 606-233-3129

parts
tires

See full listing in **Section One** under **Chevrolet**

Stockton Wheel Service
648 W Fremont St
Stockton, CA 95203
209-464-7771, 800-395-9433
FAX: 209-464-4725
E-mail: sales@stocktonwheel.com

wheel repair

See full listing in **Section Two** under **wheels & wheelcovers**

Universal Vintage Tire Co
2994 Elizabethtown Rd
Hershey, PA 17033
800-233-3827; FAX: 717-534-0719

tires

Mail order and open shop. Monday-Friday 8 am to 5 pm. Established 1968. Knowledgeable sales staff. Tires for vintage and classic automobiles. Also tubes with metal valve stems,

authentic hardware and brass runningboard trim. Web site: www.universaltire.com

Wallace W Wade Specialty Tires
PO Box 560906
530 Regal Row
Dallas, TX 75356
800-666-TYRE, 214-688-0091
FAX: 214-634-8465

tires

Mail order and open shop. Monday-Friday 8:30 am to 5:30 pm, most Saturdays, appointments preferred. Antique, vintage and classic auto tires in many brands, plus obsolete Michelin tires, military ND tires. Tire chains, repair materials for tires, metal valve caps and brass valve stem covers, patches, boots. Antique truck tires, vintage tractor tires, tires for cannons, pedal car tires, turf and lawn tires, vintage racing tires. Checker flags and pennants, race track flags, car club pennants. Flags for all countries. Web site: www.wallacewade.com

Willies Antique Tires
5257 W Diversey Ave
Chicago, IL 60639
773-622-4037, 800-742-6226
FAX: 773-622-0623

tires
wire wheels

Open shop. Monday-Friday 8:30 am to 5:30 pm, Saturday 9 am to 2 pm. New tires for antique, classic and muscle cars. BF Goodrich, Firestone, US Royals, Cadillac and Thunderbird chrome wire wheels and more. Mounting and balancing available. Fast service.

tools

A & I Supply
401 Radio City Dr
N Pekin, IL 61554
800-260-2647; FAX: 309-382-1420

tools

Mail order and open shop. Monday-Friday 8 am to 5 pm, Saturday 9 am to 1 pm. Stock your shop with 15,000 different tools and equipment. Name brand hand tools, body shop tools, air tools, power tools, air compressors, abrasives specialty tools, sheetmetal equipment and all type of shop equipment.

Addison Generator Inc
21 W Main St Rear
Freehold, NJ 07728
732-431-2438; FAX: 732-431-4503

auto parts
repairs
supplies

See full listing in **Section Two** under **electrical systems**

American IMC Inc
1623 Cedar Line Dr
Rockhill, SC 29730
803-980-6570; FAX: 803-980-5751

air compressors

Air compressors.

Arrow Fastener Co Inc
271 Mayhill St
Saddle Brook, NJ 07663

nail guns
rivet tools
staple guns

Deal in the manufacture and sale of precision built staplers, rivet tools, staple and nail guns, hot melt glue guns, staples, nails, adhesives and rivets. Web site: www.arrowfastener.com

Backyard Buddy Corp
1818 N Main St
PO Box 5104
Niles, OH 44446
800-837-9353, 330-544-9372
FAX: 330-544-9311

automotive lift

See full listing in **Section Two** under **accessories**

Bonk's Automotive Inc   automotive tools
4480 Lazelda Dr
Milan, MI 48160
800-207-6906; FAX: 734-434-0845
E-mail: bonkers@bonkauto.com

Universal automotive work stand, power lift transmission stand and specialty automotive tools. Web site: www.bonkauto.com

California Car Cover Co   accessories
21125 Superior St   apparel
Chatsworth, CA 91311   car covers
800-423-5525; FAX: 818-998-2442   tools

See full listing in **Section Two** under **car covers**

Custom Bandsaw Blades   bandsaw blades
103 N High St
Muncie, IN 47308-0543
800-378-0761; FAX: 317-289-2889

Mail order and open shop. Monday-Friday 8 am to 4 pm EST. Bandsaw blades made to custom lengths to fit any machine. Large selection of blade material in stock.

Dakota Ultrasonics   gauges
155A DuBois St   sonic testers
Santa Cruz, CA 95060
831-427-4402; FAX: 831-427-4403

Ultrasonic thickness gauges, sonic testers. Web site: www.dakotainst.com

Daytona MIG   cutters
1821 Holsonback Dr   plasma
Daytona Beach, FL 32117   welders
800-331-9353; FAX: 904-274-1237
E-mail: ask@daytonamig.com

Mail order and open showroom. Monday-Friday 9 am to 5 pm, Saturday 9 am to 12 noon. The pioneers in providing welding and plasma cutting equipment to the auto hobbies/restorer and professional body shops. From portable machines to industrial heavy duty equipment, all consumables and accessories. Our technical sales department will help you choose the correct machine for your projects. Our technicians will help you maintain your equipment and achieve your project goals. Nobody offers you more. Web site: www.daytonamig.com

Deltran Corporation   battery chargers
801 US Hwy 92 E
Deland, FL 32724
904-736-7900; FAX: 904-736-9984

See full listing in **Section Two** under **batteries**

The Eastwood Company-Tools   plating & polishing
Box 296   powder coating
Malvern, PA 19355-0714   restoration aids
800-345-1178   rustproofing
FAX: 610-644-0560   sandblasters/welders

Daily 8 am to 9 pm EST. Powder coat at home with the innovative HotCoat™ Powder Coating System. See tools you never knew existed in Eastwood's extensive full-color catalog. Features specialty items for the automotive enthusiast like abrasive blasting cabinets, quality buffing equipment, durable welders, diagnostic equipment, specialty paints, general shop tools, metal working tools, books and videos, and much more. We can help you get it all together. Call or write for free catalog. Web site: www.eastwoodco.com

Enthusiast's Specialties   automobilia
350 Old Connecticut Path
Framingham, MA 01701
800-718-3999; FAX: 508-872-4914
E-mail: alvis1934@aol.com

See full listing in **Section Two** under **automobilia**

Fast Lane Products   chamois
PO Box 7000-50   drain tubs
Palos Verdes Peninsula, CA 90274   hand wringers
800-327-8669; FAX: 310-541-2235
E-mail: info@fastlaneproducts.com

See full listing in **Section Two** under **car care products**

W L Fuller Inc   woodworking tools
7A Cypress St
PO Box 8767
Warwick, RI 02888-0767
401-467-2900; FAX: 401-467-2905
E-mail: info@wlfuller.com

Mail order and open shop. Monday-Friday 8 am to 5 pm. Countersinks, counterbores, and drills. Immediate postpaid shipment on all stock sizes. Woodworking tools and sharpening service. Web site: www.wlfuller.com

Griot's Garage   car care products
3500-A 20th St E   paint
Tacoma, WA 98424   tools
800-345-5789; FAX: 888-252-2252

Direct mail catalog. Offer quality US and European tools, premium car care products, garage organizers, automotive paints, non-lifting concrete floor paint, the finest tool boxes, automotive accessories and collectibles, over 2,500 products for your garage. Call today for a free catalog. Web site: www.griotsgarage.com

HTP America Inc   welding tools
3200 Nordic Rd
Arlington Heights, IL 60005-4729
800-USA-WELD toll-free
FAX: 877-HTPS-FAX

Mail order and open shop. Monday-Friday 9 am to 5:30 pm. Selling mig welders, plasma cutters, metalworking tools, welding supplies and related equipment to body shops, garages, home restorers, street rodders and hobbyists. Web site: www.htpweld.com

Hydraulic Jack Inc   parts
PO Box 18   tools
Accord, NY 12404
914-626-2510; FAX: 914-626-5258

Mail order and open shop. Monday-Friday 8:30 am to 4 pm. Parts and tools for repairing hydraulic jacks and cylinders. Catalog, $3.

Jacobs Electronics   ignition systems
500 N Baird St
Midland, TX 79701
915-685-3345, 800-627-8800
FAX: 915-687-5951
E-mail: retsales@marshill.com

See full listing in **Section Two** under **ignition parts**

Kingsbury Dolly Co Inc   dollies
128 Kingsbury Rd
Walpole, NH 03608
800-413-6559; FAX: 603-756-4767
E-mail: sales@kingdolly.com

Save your back. Move heavy objects quick and easy with Kingsbury Shop Dollies. Motors, transmissions, anything heavy and if you need to move a car, you can do that too. Multi-purpose shop tool allows you to easily move up to 4,000 pounds with 4 dollies. Great for project cars, restoration jobs and more. Satisfaction guaranteed or your money back. 2-year warranty. Web site: www.kingdolly.com

Lake Buchanan Industries Inc Rt 1, Box 184-C Buchanan Dam, TX 78609 888-552-5278 toll-free 512-793-2867; FAX: 512-793-2869 E-mail: lbi:@tstar.net	**blasting cabinet**

Mail order and open shop. Monday-Friday 8 am to 5 pm.
Offering the Barrel Blaster™, an affordable abrasive blasting
cabinet for the automotive restorer, only $289. Web site:
www.barrelblaster.com

Mac's Custom Tie-Downs 105 Sanderson Rd Chehalis, WA 98532 800-666-1586 orders 360-748-1180; FAX: 360-748-1185	**automotive tie-downs**

See full listing in **Section Two** under **trailers**

Malm Chem Corp PO Box 300, Dept HVA Pound Ridge, NY 10576 914-764-5775; FAX: 914-764-5785 E-mail: jkolin@cloud9.net	**polish wax**

See full listing in **Section Two** under **car care products**

The Masters Company 30 Willow Dr Suite A Fort Thomas, KY 41075-2035 800-385-5811; FAX: 606-441-6765 E-mail: badger@cinternet.net	**parts tools**

Deal in automotive shop equipment, distributor testers, engine
and gas analyzers, etc. Buy, sell, repair, trade parts.

Mill Supply Inc PO Box 28400 Cleveland, OH 44128 800-888-5072; FAX: 888-781-2700 E-mail: info@millsupply.com	**clips fasteners panels**

See full listing in **Section Two** under **sheetmetal**

Myk's Tools 365 Sunnyvale St Coos Bay, OR 97420 541-267-6957; FAX: 541-267-5967	**engine hoists**

The engine hoist, Pivot Plate, is used to remove and replace a
complete V8 engine and transmission from all older cars and
trucks as well as street rods and race cars. It will work on Ford
flathead V8s, Corvette fuel injection and electronic fuel injected
engines of Ford and GM too.

Northern Auto Parts Warehouse Inc PO Box 3147 Sioux City, IA 51102 800-831-0884; FAX: 712-258-0088	**parts**

See full listing in **Section Two** under **engine parts**

Northern Tool & Equipment PO Box 1219 Burnsville, MN 55337-0219 800-533-5545	**engines generators hydraulics**

Mail order and open shop. Where the pros and handymen shop.
It's your #1 source for generators and engines, name brand
power, air and hand tools, air compressors and welders, log
splitters and chainsaws, lawn and garden equipment and accessories, pressure washers and spraying equipment, trailers, trailer parts and winches, hydraulics and more. Save up to 50%.
Web site: www.northern-online.com

PE/Snappin Turtle Tie-Down Straps 803 Petersburg Rd Carlisle, PA 17013 800-TIE-DOWN; FAX: 717-258-1348	**locks tie-down straps winches**

See full listing in **Section Two** under **trailers**

PK Lindsay Co Inc 63 Nottingham Rd Deerfield, NH 03037 800-258-3576; FAX: 800-843-2974	**paint removal rust removal**

See full listing in **Section Two** under **rust removal & stripping**

Production Tool Supply of Ohio 10801 Brookpark Rd Cleveland, OH 44130 216-265-0000 local FAX: 216-265-0094 800-362-0142 nationwide	**abrasives compressors cutting tools hand tools machinery shop supplies**

Mail order and open shop. Monday-Friday 8 am to 5 pm,
Saturday 8 am to 12 noon. Full stocking distributor of over
150,000 tools of all kinds, available at discounts of up to 70% off
list prices. 1,200-plus page catalog available free. Deal in tools,
abrasives, machine tools, compressors, cutting tools, woodworking tools, hand tools, shop supplies.Visa, MasterCard and COD
shipments daily.

Re-Flex Border Marker 138 Grant St Lexington, MA 02173 781-862-1343	**border markers posts**

See full listing in **Section Two** under **hardware**

Space Farms Zoo & Museum — museum, zoo
218 Rt 519
Sussex, NJ 07461
973-875-3223; FAX: 973-875-9397
E-mail: fpspace@warwick.net

See full listing in **Section Six** under **New Jersey**

Steck Manufacturing Co Inc — tools
1115 S Broadway
Dayton, OH 45408
800-227-8325; FAX: 937-222-6666

Mail order and open shop. Monday-Friday 8 am to 4 pm. Hand tools for collision repair, body restoration and painting. Also manufacture affordable 4-wheel alignment equipment and heavy pulling equipment.

Sunchaser Tools — metal-finishing kit, video
3202 E Foothill Blvd
Pasadena, CA 91107
626-795-1588; FAX: 626-795-6494

See full listing in **Section Two** under **restoration aids**

Superior Equipment — auto lifts, shop tools
703 W 53rd St N
Wichita, KS 67204
800-526-9992; FAX: 316-831-0154
E-mail: mail@superlifts.com

Mail order and open shop. Monday-Friday 8 am to 5 pm CST. Auto lifts, service equipment and shop tools. Web site: www.superlifts.com

TiP Tools & Equipment — abrasive blasters, air compressors, tools
7075 Route 446, PO Box 649
Canfield, OH 44406
330-533-3384 local
800-321-9260 US/Canada
FAX: 330-533-2876

See full listing in **Section Two** under **restoration aids**

Tru-Cut Automotive — car ramps, jacks, lug wrenches
75 Elm Ave
Salem, OH 44460-2627
800-634-7267; FAX: 330-332-5326
E-mail: trucut@mindspring.com

Mail order only. Makers of domestic lift and support products such as Ultra-Ramps™, car ramps, jack stands, scissor jacks, lug wrenches and garage accessories. Web site: www.autoramps.com

Valco Cincinnati Consumer Products Inc — adhesives, detailing products, sealants, tools
411 Circle Freeway Dr
Cincinnati, OH 45246
513-874-6550; FAX: 513-874-3612

Sole manufacturer of the Tube-Grip™, a patented 14-gauge steel tool which applies 10 times more pressure to a flexible tube than squeezing by hand, it allows you to squeeze 96% of the material out of the tube. In addition, Valco offers a complete line of high quality sealants, adhesives, detailers, lubricants and thread lockers for automotive applications. Web site: www.valcocinconsumerprod.com

Williams Lowbuck Tools Inc — tools
4175 California Ave
Norco, CA 91760
909-735-7848; FAX: 909-735-1210
E-mail: wlowbuck@aol.com

Mail order and open shop. Monday-Friday 9 am to 4 pm. Deal in metal fabricating tools for tubing and sheetmetal. Web site: www.lowbucktools.com

tops

California Convertible Co — top parts
1950 Lindsley Park Dr
San Marcos, CA 92069-3337
760-746-8211

Mail order and open shop. Monday-Friday 8 am to 5:30 pm. For American convertibles only. Top parts.

Caribou Canvas — convertible tops
26804 Vista Terr
Lake Forest, CA 92630
949-770-3136; FAX: 949-770-0815
E-mail: cariboulh@aol.com

Mail order and open shop. Monday-Friday 9:30 am to 5 pm PST. Manufacture canvas convertible tops for all sport, import and domestic automobiles. Specialists in Italian, British and German vehicle applications. Our products are available for worldwide shipping. Web site: www.caribou.cc

Classtique Upholstery Supply — carpet sets, headliners
PO Box 278-HMN
Isanti, MN 55040
612-444-3768, 612-444-4025
FAX: 612-444-9980

See full listing in **Section Two** under **interiors & interior parts**

Classtique Upholstery & Top Co — top kits, upholstery kits
PO Box 278 HK
Isanti, MN 55040
612-444-4025; FAX: 612-444-9980

See full listing in **Section One** under **Ford 1903-1931**

Convertible Service — convertible parts, manufacture, service, top mechanism
5126-HA Walnut Grove Ave
San Gabriel, CA 91776
800-333-1140, 626-285-2255
FAX: 626-285-9004

For domestic cars from 1946-present. Manufacture and sell convertible top mechanism replacement parts. 6 and 12-volt electric and hydraulic top lift cylinders and window lift cylinders, hose assemblies, top latches, relays, top switches, folding top frames. Distributor for Metro Molded Parts. Convertible top weatherstripping sets and weatherstripping and rubber parts in general. Most parts shipped same day. Overnight delivery available. Send $1 (to cover postage) and we'll send you our catalog of convertible parts. Web site: www.convertibleparts.com

Dom Corey Upholstery & Antique Auto — carpets/conv tops, dash covers, door panels, headliners, seats, upholstery
1 Arsene Way
Fairhaven Business Park
Fairhaven, MA 02719
508-997-6555

See full listing in **Section Two** under **interiors & interior parts**

Durabuilt Automotive Hydraulics — hose assemblies, pumps, top cylinders, valves
808 Meadows Ave
Canon City, CO 81212
PH/FAX: 719-275-1126
E-mail: durabuilt@ris.net

For over ten years we have provided quality hydraulic products to restoration shops, car owners and museums. Our components are on daily drivers and show winning vehicles throughout the world. Manufacture new pumps, valves, window cylinders, top cylinders and hose assemblies. Our rebuilt original pumps and valves perform and look like new. Can help with any 1930s-1990s American or European vehicle. All backed by the best warranty and competitive pricing.

Section Two Generalists

Hydro-E-Lectric
5475 Williamsburg Dr, Unit 8
Punta Gorda, FL 33982
800-343-4261

convertible top parts
power window parts

Carry canvas and vinyl tops, carpets, weatherstrip and a full line of convertible top and power window parts for US and foreign cars from 1946-present day. All parts are new. Please call for information.

Dave Knittel Upholstery
850 E Teton #7
Tucson, AZ 85706
PH/FAX: 520-746-1588

interiors
tops
upholstery

See full listing in **Section Two** under **upholstery**

Al Knoch Interiors
130 Montoya Rd
El Paso, TX 79932
800-880-8080; FAX: 915-581-1545
E-mail: alknoch@flash.net

carpets
interiors
tooling services
tops

See full listing in **Section One** under **Chevrolet**

Loga Enterprises
5399 Old Town Hall Rd
Eau Claire, WI 54701
715-832-7302

convertible tops
interior parts

See full listing in **Section One** under **Studebaker**

Markel's Auto Upholstery
1163 S Robertson Blvd
Los Angeles, CA 90035
310-274-1501

upholstery

See full listing in **Section Two** under **upholstery**

National Parts Depot
3101 SW 40th Blvd
Gainesville, FL 32608
800-874-7595 toll-free 24 hours
352-378-2473 local

accessories
restoration parts

See full listing in **Section Two** under **comprehensive parts**

Newport Upholstery Source
250 H St, Unit 8110
Blaine, WA 98231
604-990-0346; FAX: 604-990-9988

carpets
tops
upholstery

See full listing in **Section Two** under **upholstery**

Norm's Custom Shop
6897 E William St Ext
Bath, NY 14810
PH/FAX: 607-776-2357

interiors
tops

See full listing in **Section One** under **Cord**

NOS Locators
587 Pawtucket Ave
Pawtucket, RI 02860
401-725-5000

parts

See full listing in **Section One** under **MG**

Ray's Upholstering
600 N St Frances Cabrini Ave
Scranton, PA 18504
800-296-RAYS; FAX: 717-963-0415

partial/total
restoration

See full listing in **Section Two** under **restoration shops**

Ridgefield Auto Upholstery
34 Bailey Ave
Ridgefield, CT 06877
203-438-7583; FAX: 203-438-2666

interiors
tops

See full listing in **Section Two** under **interiors & interior parts**

Ron's Restorations Inc
2968-B Ask Kay Dr
Smyrna, GA 30082
770-438-6102; FAX: 770-438-0037

interior trim
restoration

See full listing in **Section One** under **Mercedes-Benz**

SL-Tech 230SL-250SL-280SL
1364 Portland Rd US Rt 1
Arundel/Kennebunkport, ME 04046
207-985-3001; FAX: 207-985-3011
E-mail: gernold@sltechw113.com

parts
restoration
service

See full listing in **Section One** under **Mercedes-Benz**

Smooth Line
2562 Riddle Run Rd
Tarentum, PA 15084
724-274-6002; FAX: 724-274-6121

body panels
removable hardtops

Mail order only. Monday-Friday 9 am to 5 pm. World's largest selection of removable hardtops for sports cars. Change your convertible into a GT coupe in minutes. Enjoy the best of both. Quiet and secure. New restoration body panels now available. Save. Austin-Healey, Fiats, Triumph, Datsun Z, MG, A, B, Midget. High-performance composites end rust forever. Premium quality. Fully guaranteed. Web site: www.smoothline.com

TMI Products Inc
191 Granite St
Corona, CA 91719
800-624-7960, 909-272-1996
FAX: 909-272-1584
E-mail: tmiprods@aol.com

classic car
interiors

See full listing in **Section One** under **Volkswagen**

Town Auto Top Co
111 Clinton Rd
Fairfield, NJ 07004
973-575-9333; FAX: 973-808-8366

convertible repairs
interiors

See full listing in **Section Two** under **restoration shops**

Ultimate Appearance Ltd
113 Arabian Trail
Smithfield, VA 23430
888-446-3078; FAX: 757-255-2620

cleaners
detailing products
detailing services
polish/wax

See full listing in **Section Two** under **car care products**

Ultimate Upholstery
14610 W Futura Dr
Sun City West, AZ 85375
602-975-4366

interiors
top restoration
upholstery

See full listing in **Section Two** under **restoration shops**

Victoria British Ltd
Box 14991
Lenexa, KS 66285-4991
800-255-0088, 913-599-3299

accessories
parts

See full listing in **Section One** under **MG**

World Upholstery & Trim
PO Box 2420
Camarillo, CA 93011
805-988-1848; FAX: 805-278-7886
E-mail: worlduph@mail.vcnet.com

carpet
tops
upholstery kits

See full listing in **Section Two** under **interiors & interior parts**

trailers

Alum-Line Inc — fabrication / manufacturing
PO Box 59
US Hwy 9 W
Cresco, IA 52136
319-547-3247; FAX: 319-547-5366
E-mail: alumline@sbtek.net.com

All aluminum open and enclosed car trailers. Aluminum truck beds and bodies, aluminum toolboxes. Fabrication and manufacturing. Web site: www.alum-line.com

Beam Distributors Trailer Sales — trailers
PO Box 524, 231 South St
Davidson, NC 28036
704-892-9853

Dealer United Express Line enclosed trailers. Large stock of enclosed trailers for all your automotive needs. Serving the old car hobby since 1968.

C & C Manufacturing Co — trailers
300 S Church St
Hazleton, PA 18201
717-454-0819; FAX: 717-454-5131

Mail order and open shop. Specializing in the manufacturing of custom car carriers to transport antique automobiles for the past 30 years.

Chernock Enterprises — trailers
PO Box 134
Airport Rd
Hazleton, PA 18201
570-455-1752; FAX: 570-455-7585
E-mail: jim@chernock.com

Enclosed and open car trailers, cargo and concession trailers custom built. International orders welcome. Factory authorized dealer for Carmate, Trailex aluminum trailers. Web site: www.chernock.com

Cobra Trailers — rollback trailers
PO Box 18105
Savannah, GA 31418
800-262-7286; FAX: 912-233-2937

Manufacture and custom build fully automatic rollback trailers with air ride suspension.

Glenn Curtiss Museum — museum
8419 St Rt 54
Hammondsport, NY 14840
607-569-2160; FAX: 607-569-2040

See full listing in **Section Six** under **New York**

D & D Trailers Inc — accessories / trailers
100 Lexington Ave
Trenton, NJ 08618
609-771-0001, 800-533-0442
FAX: 609-771-4479

Mail order and open shop. Monday-Saturday 8 am to 4:30 pm, other times by appointment. Custom built car carriers and utility trailers. Distributor of Wells Cargo enclosed trailers. Also carry tie-downs, winches and trailer parts. Registered trade name DEANDE™.

Galaxie Ltd — kits / model trailers
Box 655
Butler, WI 53007
414-673-6386, 414-790-9922
FAX: 414-673-6366

See full listing in **Section Two** under **models & toys**

Tommy Gale Trailer Sales & Service   trailers
Glassport-Elizabeth Rd
Elizabeth, PA 15037
412-384-3640; FAX: 412-384-8532

Open shop only. Monday-Friday 8:30 am to 5 pm, Saturday 8:30 am to 2 pm. Specialize in enclosed race, classic car, gooseneck and custom trailers. Open trailer from 5x8 to 53 ft long.

Haulmark Industries Inc   trailers
14054 CR #4
PO Box 281
Bristol, IN 46507
219-825-5867; FAX: 219-825-9816
E-mail: sales@haulmark.com

Manufacturer of enclosed trailers for vintage automobiles. Web site: www.haulmark.com

Hillsboro Trailers   trailers
220 Industrial Rd
Hillsboro, KS 67063
800-835-0209
E-mail: hii@gplains.com

Car trailers and cargo trailers. All aluminum construction, fully enclosed. Web site: www.gplains.com/hillsboro

Lazy B Trailer Sales Inc   parts / repairs / service
6040 St Rt 45
Bristolville, OH 44402
330-889-2353; FAX: 330-889-9630
E-mail: danny@lazybtrailers.com

Mail order and open shop. Monday-Friday 8 am to 5 pm, Saturday 9 am to 4 pm. Dealing in new and used steel and aluminum trailers, both open and enclosed. Have a complete parts and service facility capable of providing minor to major repairs and the capability to ship most parts directly to you. Can custom build a trailer to suit your needs. Call us for a quote. Web site: www.lazybtrailers.com

See our ad on page 425

Mac's Custom Tie-Downs   automotive tie-downs
105 Sanderson Rd
Chehalis, WA 98532
800-666-1586 orders
360-748-1180; FAX: 360-748-1185

A full range of tie-down equipment for all loads. Specializing in automotive tie-downs. Custom orders welcome.

Mobile Structures Inc/MSI Trailers   trailers
2405 Cassopolis St
PO Box 1405
Elkhart, IN 46514
800-348-8541; FAX: 219-264-4399
E-mail: billbeck@mobilestructures.com

Specializing in car and cargo trailers. Also have race, vendor and office trailers, modular buildings. Distributor for Haulmark, Pace American and United Expressline offering units in widths of 5', 6', 7', 8' & 8-1/2' and in lengths from 8' to 50'. Web site: www.mobilestructures.com

Nyles Haulmark Trailer Sales   car carriers
352 Macedon Center Rd
Fairport, NY 14450
716-223-6433

Open Monday-Friday 9 am to 5 pm, Saturday 9 am to 12 pm. Enclosed and open car carriers for vintage autos, race cars, snowmobiles. Major lines: Haulmark, Cargo Mate.

PE/Snappin Turtle Tie-Down Straps — locks, tie-down straps, winches
803 Petersburg Rd
Carlisle, PA 17013
800-TIE-DOWN; FAX: 717-258-1348

Mail order only. Tie-down straps, D-rings, wheel clocks, trailer hitches, trailer locks and electric winches. Specialize in antique and classic car tie-downs. Over 15 years serving the hobby. Call us for fast, friendly service. Web site: www.snappinturtle.com

Performance Shop — trailers
Ray Thorp
2078 Pleasant Valley Rd
Newark, DE 19702
302-368-9534; FAX: 302-368-0760

Open daily 7 am to 7 pm. Designing trailers, Lite car trailers, Hefty Hauler car trailers, E-Z Up Hauler and tilting deck car trailer, features no ramps. Also sell enclosed car and utility trailers with a 12 year warranty on the rubber roofing. Wrill build it your way, any size.

R-D-T Plans and Parts — car parts, trailer plans
PO Box 2272
Merced, CA 95344-0272
209-383-4441

Mail order and open shop. Monday-Friday 8 am to 5 pm. Trailer plans designed and sold. Also miscellaneous car parts for Packards, Cadillacs, Fords, Chevrolet and American underslung cars, along with Ferrari.

The Rampman — ramps
PO Box 718
New Kingstown, PA 17072
800-717-0326, 717-241-5474
FAX: 717-258-9009
E-mail: therampman@aol.com

See full listing in **Section Two** under **accessories**

Sloan's Kwik Load Inc — trailers
Rt 2, Box 100
Sherman, TX 75092
903-893-7133; FAX: 903-868-0448
E-mail: dsloan@gte.com

Trailer manufacturing and sales. Open, air, rollback trailers. Web site: www.kwikload.com

Timber Wolf Trailers Inc — trailers
Division of Leland Engineering
201 S Miller Dr
White Pigeon, MI 49099
616-483-2351; FAX: 616-483-2685
E-mail: info@timberwolftrailers.com

Manufacturer of cargo trailers, race car trailers, car haulers and custom trailers. Web site: www.timberwolftrailers.com

Trailers Ltd — trailers
308 W Washington
Morton, TX 79346
806-266-5646; FAX: 806-266-5846

Mail order and open shop. Monday-Saturday 9 am to 7 pm. Build custom-built enclosed trailers for transporting race cars, antique cars, show cars, etc.

Trailers of New England Inc — trailers
Boston Rd Rt 20
Palmer, MA 01069
413-289-1211; FAX: 413-289-1292

Mail order and open shop. Monday-Friday 8:30 am to 5 pm, Saturday 8:30 am to 12 noon. Specializing in Wells Cargo enclosed trailers, open trailers, trailer design and customizing, trailer parts, hitches and tie-down products.

Trailex Inc — aluminum/steel trailers
60 Industrial Park Dr
PO Box 553
Canfield, OH 44406
330-533-6814
800-282-5042, 877-TRAILEX toll-free
FAX: 330-533-9118
E-mail: trailex1@aol.com

Open Monday-Friday 8 am to 5 pm, Saturday 8 am to 12 noon. Trailers made from heat treated aluminum extrusions, anodized for lasting beauty. Also aluminum auto tow dollys. 10 different product lines of the world's only all aluminum, bolted, anodized trailers including our all new enclosed aluminum car trailer. A full line of steel trailers also available. We are the manufacturer, not just another dealer. Web site: www.trailex.com

Transport Designs Inc — trailers
240 Streibeigh Ln
Montoursville, PA 17754
570-368-1403; FAX: 570-368-2398
E-mail: boys4@csrlink.net

Factory direct sales. Monday-Friday 8 am to 5 pm, Saturday by appointment. Tag-a-long, goosenecks and semi-trailer styles. Enclosed only. Specializing in custom fabrication. Web site: www.dragnbreath.com

Wells Cargo Inc — trailers
PO Box 728-134
Elkhart, IN 46515
800-348-7553; FAX: 219-264-5938

Manufactures a full line of enclosed, steel-structured trailers for hauling all types of collector automobiles. 24 models from which to choose. Ball hitch trailers: 18 to 32 feet. 5th wheel, inverted 5th wheel and A-frame 5th wheel trailers: 24 to 48 feet. Payloads, 4,200 to 11,880 lbs. GVWR: 7,700 to 16,000 lbs. Choose from an impressive list of customizing options. Free "no obligation" quotes available. 3 year warranty program. Nationwide dealer network. Web site: www.wellscargo.com

See our ad on page 426

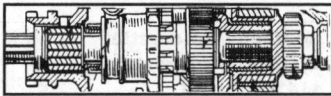 transmissions

356 Enterprises — parts
Vic & Barbara Skirmants
27244 Ryan Rd
Warren, MI 48092
810-575-9544; FAX: 810-558-3616

See full listing in **Section One** under **Porsche**

4-Speeds by Darrell — transmissions
PO Box 110
3 Water St
Vermilion, IL 61955
217-275-3743; FAX: 217-275-3515

Mail order and open shop. Monday-Friday 8 am to 5 pm, Saturday 8 am to 12 noon CST. Rebuilt transmissions. Show quality Borg-Warner T-10, M-21 and M-22, including all related parts. Specializes in build date transmissions for Corvette, Chevy 1958-up, Chevelle, Camaro, Buick, Pontiac and Oldsmobile.

AAdvanced Transmissions	rear axle service
15 Parker St	restoration
Worcester, MA 01610	ring/pinion
508-752-9674, 508-752-9679	trans parts/sales/
FAX: 508-842-0191	rebuilding/service

Mail order and open shop. Monday-Saturday 9 am to 6 pm. Standard transmission rebuilding since 1968. Rebuilt 3/4/5-speeds in stock. Muncie, Borg-Warner, Ford Toploader, GM Saginaw specialists. Complete units in stock. Worldwide sales, service. Customer cores accepted. RPS daily. AMC to Z-28.

American International Transmissions	differentials restoration
7145 E Earll Dr	
Scottsdale, AZ 85251	
602-946-5391	

Open shop only. Monday-Friday 8 am to 5 pm. Deal in transmission rebuilding and repair, differentials and restoration of classic cars.

American Restorations Unlimited TA	restoration parts
14 Meakin Ave, PO Box 34	
Rochelle Park, NJ 07662	
201-843-3567; FAX: 201-843-3238	
E-mail: amerrest@earthlink.net	

See full listing in **Section Two** under **glass**

Auto Restoration	transmission conversion kits
8150 S CR 1250 W	
Albany, IN 47320	
PH/FAX: 765-789-4037	

See full listing in **Section One** under **Ford 1903-1931**

Automotive Restorations Inc	clutch rebuilding
Stephen Babinsky	mechanical services
4 Center St	restorations
Bernardsville, NJ 07924	
908-766-6688; FAX: 908-766-6684	
E-mail: autorestnj@aol.com	

See full listing in **Section Two** under **restoration shops**

Be Happy Automatic Transmission Parts	trans rebuild kits
414 Stivers Rd	
Hillsboro, OH 45133	
800-416-2862; FAX: 937-442-6133	

Mail order only. Owner operated by David and Mona Crone. Dealing in automatic transmission rebuild kits, external dry-up kits and hard parts, 1940-1965. NOS, NORS, good used, Dynaflow, Dual path, Flightpitch, Hydramatic, Jetaway, Slim Jim, Roto 5, Powerglide, Turboglide, Powerflite, Torqueflite, 3-band, Ultramatic, etc. Technical assistance, exploded views, troubleshooting and repair literature. Orders for individual gaskets, seals, etc welcome. Free wholesale price list. We're open late for our West Coast customers. MasterCard, Visa, Discover, CODs accepted.

Dave Bean Engineering	parts
636 E St Charles St SR3H	
San Andreas, CA 95249	
209-754-5802; FAX: 209-754-5177	
E-mail: admin@davebean.com	

See full listing in **Section One** under **Lotus**

Bicknell Engine Company	parts
7055 Dayton Rd	repair
Enon, OH 45323	restoration
937-864-5224	

See full listing in **Section One** under **Buick/McLaughlin**

Bonk's Automotive Inc	automotive tools
4480 Lazelda Dr	
Milan, MI 48160	
800-207-6906; FAX: 734-434-0845	
E-mail: bonkers@bonkauto.com	

See full listing in **Section Two** under **tools**

California Pony Cars	parts
1906 Quaker Ridge Pl	
Ontario, CA 91761	
909-923-2804; FAX: 909-947-8593	
E-mail: 105232.3362@compuserve.com	

See full listing in **Section One** under **Mustang**

Carl's Ford Parts	muscle parts
23219 South St, Box 38	
Homeworth, OH 44634	
PH/FAX: 330-525-7291	

See full listing in **Section One** under **Mustang**

Classic Tube	brake lines
Division of Classic & Performance	choke tubes
Spec Inc	fuel lines
80 Rotech Dr	transmission lines
Lancaster, NY 14086	vacuum lines
800-TUBES-11 (882-3711)	
716-759-1800; FAX: 716-759-1014	

See full listing in **Section Two** under **brakes**

Coffey's Classic Transmissions	transmissions
2290 W Hicks Rd, Unit 42	
Hanger 30-1	
Ft Worth, TX 76111	
817-439-1611	

Mail order and open shop. Monday-Friday 8 am to 5:30 pm CST. Specializing in transmission parts and service for early model classic standard and automatic transmissions. Classic, vintage and racing transmissions, parts and service.

Coventry West Inc	assemblies
5936-A Peachtree Rd	Jaguar parts
Atlanta, GA 30341	
800-331-2193 toll-free	
770-451-3839 Atlanta	
FAX: 770-451-7561	

See full listing in **Section One** under **Jaguar**

David Edwards-Transmission Parts	auto trans kits
56 Dale St	auto trans parts
PO Box 245	
Needham Heights, MA 02494-0245	
PH/FAX: 781-449-2065	
E-mail: autotran2@aol.com	

Mail order only. SASE not required. Phone hours: Monday-Friday 6 pm to 11:30 pm; Saturday-Sunday by chance. For all automatic transmissions from 1946-present except Flightpitch and Ultramatics. Kits, bands, pumps, bushings, washers, drums and other miscellaneous parts in stock. Daily UPS shipments. Web site: http://members.aol.com/autotran

FATSCO Transmission Parts	parts
PO Box 635	transmissions
Pine Brook, NJ 07058-0635	
800-524-0485; FAX: 973-227-2487	

Mail order and open shop. Monday-Friday 8 am to 5 pm. Transmission parts. US automatic and manual transmission parts, 1946-present. Some parts for older manual transmissions.

Florida Caliper Manufacturers Inc
1450 SW 10th St #3
Delray Beach, FL 33444
561-272-5238

| brake systems |
| chassis parts |
| suspension parts |

See full listing in **Section One** under **Corvette**

JECC Inc
PO Box 616
West Paterson, NJ 07424
973-890-9682; FAX: 973-812-2724

| chassis parts |
| gaskets |
| transmissions |

See full listing in **Section One** under **Buick/McLaughlin**

Joyce's Model A & T Parts
PO Box 70
Manchaca, TX 78652-0070
512-282-1196

| new parts |
| NOS parts |
| rebuilt parts |

See full listing in **Section One** under **Ford 1903-1931**

Last Chance Repair & Restoration
PO Box 362A
Myers Rd
Shaftsbury, VT 05262

| repairs |
| restoration |

See full listing in **Section Two** under **restoration shops**

Lindley Restorations Ltd
10 S Sanatoga Rd
Pottstown, PA 19464
610-326-8484; FAX: 610-326-3845

| parts |
| sales |
| service |

See full listing in **Section One** under **Jaguar**

Lokar Inc
10924 Murdock Dr
Knoxville, TN 37932
423-966-2269; FAX: 423-671-1999
E-mail: lokarinc@aol.com

| performance parts |

See full listing in **Section Two** under **street rods**

Michael's Auto Parts
5875 NW Kaiser Rd
Portland, OR 97229
503-690-7750; FAX: 503-690-7735

| used Mercedes |
| parts only |

See full listing in **Section Five** under **Oregon**

Mid Valley Engineering
16637 N 21st St
Phoenix, AZ 85022
602-482-1251; FAX: 602-788-0812

| machine work |
| parts |
| restoration |

Mail order and open shop. Monday-Friday 8 am to 5 pm,
Saturday by appointment. Large inventory of new and antique
Hewland parts. Complete fabrication and machine shop facilities
for race car restoration. MVE Shur shifter side door pat pen for
T-10 transmissions.

Obsolete Chevrolet Parts Co
524 Hazel Ave
PO Box 68
Nashville, GA 31639-0068
800-248-8785; FAX: 912-686-3056
E-mail: obschevy@surfsouth.com

| engine parts |
| radiators |
| rubber parts |
| transmissions |

See full listing in **Section One** under **Chevrolet**

Orion Motors European Parts Inc | *parts*
10722 Jones Rd
Houston, TX 77065
800-736-6410, 281-894-1982
FAX: 281-849-1997
E-mail: orion-yugo@yugoparts.com

See full listing in **Section One** under **Alfa Romeo**

P-Ayr Products | *replicas*
719 Delaware St
Leavenworth, KS 66048
913-651-5543; FAX: 913-651-2084
E-mail: sales@payr.com

See full listing in **Section One** under **Chevrolet**

Packards & Collector Cars | *conversion kits*
425 E Laurel
Sierra Madre, CA 91024
626-355-4023, 714-539-8579
FAX: 626-355-4072

See full listing in **Section One** under **Packard**

Partwerks of Chicago | *parts / service*
718 S Prairie Rd
New Lenox, IL 60451
815-462-3000; FAX: 815-462-3006
E-mail: partwerks9@aol.com

See full listing in **Section Two** under **engine parts**

Street-Wise Performance | *differentials / parts / rebuild kits / transmissions*
Richie Mulligan
Box 105 Creek Rd
Tranquility, NJ 07879
973-786-6668 days
973-786-7133 evenings
FAX: 973-786-7861
E-mail: richie@goes.com

Mail order and open shop. Monday-Saturday 9 am to 6 pm. Used or rebuilt GM standard and performance 3, 4 and 5-speed gear boxes. Guaranteed, special dated units and parts. New/used gears, rebuilder's kits and directions. Factory/Hurst shifters, conversion parts. Rebuilt 1955-1980s GM 10/12-bolt positrac rear ends, r and p sets, carriers, axles. Over 25 years' individual experience. 20 years family operated. Huge inventory, same day shipping on most orders. Credit cards accepted. Free advice and referrals. Spring/Fall Englishtown swap meet spaces RK 58-60. Dealer/restorer inquiries welcomed.

Teddy's Garage | *parts / restoration / service*
8530 Louise Ave
Northridge, CA 91325
818-341-0505

See full listing in **Section One** under **Rolls-Royce/Bentley**

Transgo Performance | *shift kits*
2621 Merced Ave
El Monte, CA 91733
626-443-4953; FAX: 626-443-1079

Manufacturer of performance shift kits for GM, Ford and Chrysler automatic transmissions, also known as valve body modification kits.

John Ulrich | *parts*
450 Silver Ave
San Francisco, CA 94112
PH/FAX: 510-223-9587 days

See full listing in **Section One** under **Packard**

Universal Transmission Co | *transmission parts*
23361 Dequindre Rd
Hazel Park, MI 48030
800-882-4327; FAX: 248-398-2581

Dealing in standard transmission parts for American cars from Model A till tomorrow. A family owned business since 1948. Wholesale/retail.
See our ad on page 429

Vicarage Jaguar | *parts / restoration*
5333 Collins Ave, Suite 502
Miami Beach, FL 33140
305-866-9511; FAX: 305-866-5738
E-mail: vicarage@ix.netcom.com

See full listing in **Section One** under **Jaguar**

Dan Williams Toploader Transmissions | *transmissions*
206 E Dogwood Dr
Franklin, NC 28734
828-524-9085 noon to midnight
FAX: 828-524-4848

See full listing in **Section One** under **Ford 1954-up**

Zim's Autotechnik | *parts / service*
1804 Reliance Pkwy
Bedford, TX 76021
800-356-2964; FAX: 817-545-2002
E-mail: zimips@allzim.com

See full listing in **Section One** under **Porsche**

transport

A AAAdvantage Auto Transport Inc | *transport*
8920 S Hardy
Tempe, AZ 85284
800-233-4875
E-mail: webinfo@aaaadv.com

Mail order and open shop. Monday-Friday 7 am to 5 pm, Saturday 9 am to 12 pm MST. Transport of vehicles across the state or across the globe. Open or enclosed transport trucks. Provide the specialized care your car deserves. Web site: www.aaaadv.com

Auto Shipping of America | *transport*
Linda Quinn
1434 Greenfield Ave, Ste 104
Los Angeles, CA 90025
800-281-6999
E-mail: shipauto4u@aol.com

Auto transport of luxury, exotic, classic and all types of autos. State to state. Open and enclosed transport available. Fully insured, licensed, bonded. Domestic transport, based in Los Angeles, CA. References available. Call for a free quote.

Auto Transport Services | *transport*
5367 Fargo Rd
Avoca, MI 48006
810-324-2598; FAX: 810-324-6094

Transporting automobiles.

California Jaguar | *auto transport*
29109 Triunfo Dr
Agoura, CA 91301
800-335-2482; FAX: 818-707-3062

Coast to coast, door to door, open or enclosed transport. Cars, motorcycles, trucks, parts, boats.

Collector Car Transport   transport
Clifton, NJ 07012
PH/FAX: 973-815-1607

Locations in Clifton, NJ, and Kissimmee, FL. Enclosed and open transportation of antique, classic, new and sports cars. 48 states, ICC licensed and insured. Inspection services available. No stacking, new custom equipment, references gladly given. Remember, at Collector Car Transport your automobile is our only concern.

Collector's Carousel   appraisals
84 Warren Ave   sales
Westbrook, ME 04092   service
207-854-0343; FAX: 207-856-6913

See full listing in **Section Two** under **car dealers**

David Elliott   auto transport
11796 Franklin   car locator
Minocqua, WI 54548
715-356-1335

Auto transport and locator of western cars and parts. Transport cars from Wisconsin to Utah, Colorado, Arizona, Nevada, New Mexico, Texas or points near or between. Locator of all years western cars and trucks. Specializing in 1960s-1970s project cars and body shells.

Exotic Car Transport Inc   transport
880 C Maguire Rd
Ocoee, FL 34761
800-766-8797; FAX: 407-654-9951
E-mail: info@exoticcartransport.com

Nationwide transporter of exotic, vintage and luxury automobiles on enclosed carriers. Indoor storage available. Web site: www.exoticcartransport.com
See our ad on this page

Tommy Gale Trailer Sales & Service   trailers
Glassport-Elizabeth Rd
Elizabeth, PA 15037
412-464-0119; FAX: 412-384-8532

See full listing in **Section Two** under **trailers**

Sidney Hall Cars   transport
1591 Hall Rd
Clarkrange, TN 38553
931-863-5101

Transport vehicles to 48 states. Fully licensed and insured. Professional, courteous service. Timely pick up and delivery.

Intercity Lines Inc   transport
River Rd, Box 1299
Warren, MA 01083
800-221-3936; FAX: 413-436-9422
E-mail: info@intercitylines.com

Open Monday-Friday 9 am to 6 pm, Saturday 9 am to 12 noon. Specializing in enclosed transportation of collector cars throughout all 48 states and Canada. Web site: www.intercitylines.com

Interesting Parts Inc   appraisals
Paul TerHorst   gaskets
27526 N Owens Rd   parts
Mundelein, IL 60060   storage
PH/FAX: 847-949-1030   transport

See full listing in **Section Two** under **comprehensive parts**

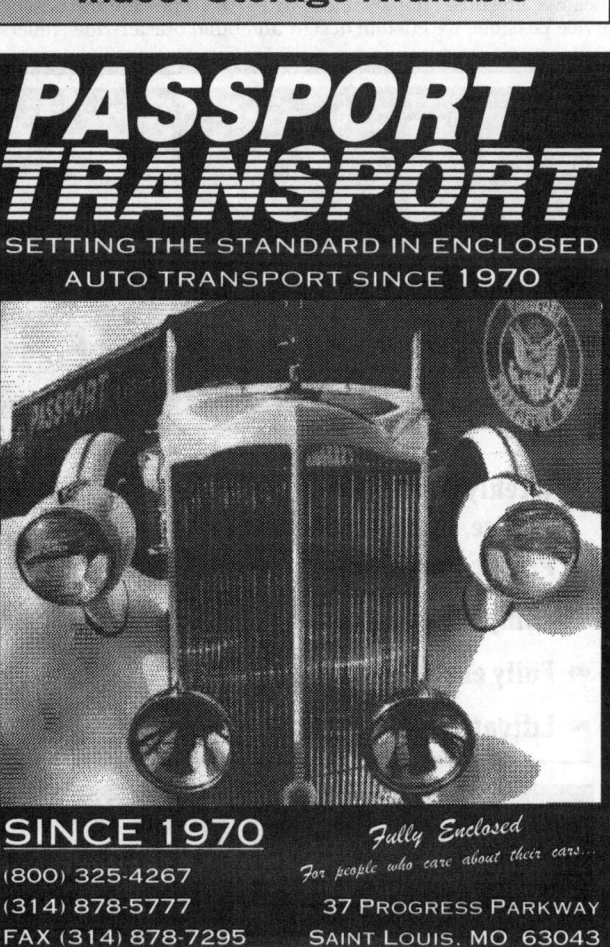

Section Two Generalists

Libbey's Classic Car Restoration Center 137 N Quinsigamond Ave Shrewsbury, MA 01545 PH/FAX: 508-792-1560	bodywork restoration service

See full listing in **Section Two** under **restoration shops**

Mac's Custom Tie-Downs 105 Sanderson Rd Chehalis, WA 98532 800-666-1586 orders 360-748-1180; FAX: 360-748-1185	automotive tie-downs

See full listing in **Section Two** under **trailers**

Mac's Euro Motorcars & Transport 1520 Burr Oak Rd Homewood, IL 60430 708-799-3469	Alfa Romeos parts transport

See full listing in **Section One** under **Alfa Romeo**

Paradise Classic Auto Appraisal 5894 Cornell Taylor, MI 48180 313-291-2758	appraisals transport

See full listing in **Section Two** under **appraisals**

Passport Transport Ltd 37 Progess Pkwy St Louis, MO 63043 800-325-4267; FAX: 314-878-7295	transport

Nationwide enclosed transportation of antique, classic and special interest cars. Over 100,000 vehicles transported nationwide since we "invented" this business in 1970. To provide the best service possible, we custom design and build our air-ride trailers specifically to handle the unique requirements of these vehicles. Passport Transport, the first and still the finest in enclosed auto transportation.

See our ad on page 431

The Rampman PO Box 718 New Kingstown, PA 17072 800-717-0326, 717-241-5474 FAX: 717-258-9009 E-mail: therampman@aol.com	ramps

See full listing in **Section Two** under **accessories**

Reward Service Inc 172 Overhill Rd Stormville, NY 12582 914-227-7647; FAX: 914-221-0293	appraisals restoration transportation

See full listing in **Section One** under **Jaguar**

Sea Expo Freight Services Inc 32 Somerville Rd Hewitt, NJ 07421 888-733-9766, 201-973-5700 FAX: 973-728-6060 E-mail: w.tmurphy@seaexpo.com	transporter

International transporter of motor vehicles, project cargo, car parts, general goods (export and import) worldwide.

Special Projects 27520 117th Ave SE Kent, WA 98031 800-CAR-HAUL (227-4285) FAX: 253-630-2506 E-mail: mrmspecialprojects@msn.com	transport

12 years' experience moving vintage, classic and special interest autos and trucks. Use small trucks and trailers, moving 2 vehicles

per truck. Your vehicle is moved direct, no reloading. Specialize in pre-1930 vehicles, racing cars, large cars (Packard, Cadillac, Pierce, etc), round-trip racing meets and car shows, basket cases with spare parts. Insured, honest and reliable.

Todd Stroud 1205 Farragut St NW Washington, DC 20011 301-526-1141, MD 202-722-5345; FAX: 202-722-2402	**auto transport**

Auto transport. 3 car flat bed trailer, new equipment. All 48 states, licensed, insured. Specializing in exotics and antiques. Reasonable rates, excellent service. Washington, DC, based.

Thomas C Sunday Inc PO Box 217 78 E Main St New Kingstown, PA 17072 800-541-6601; FAX: 717-697-0727	**transport**

Enclosed automobile transportation, weekly service coast to coast, including the Pacific Northwest, door-to-door service, lift-gate loading, competitive rates. Fully insured, special events, shows, races, auctions, etc.

See our ads on pages 432 and 627

Trailers Ltd 308 W Washington Morton, TX 79346 806-266-5646; FAX: 806-266-5846	**trailers**

See full listing in **Section Two** under **trailers**

Vintage Racing Services 1785 Barnum Ave Stratford, CT 06497 203-386-1736; FAX: 203-386-0486 E-mail: vrs@vintageracingservices.com	**storage** **track support** **transportation**

See full listing in **Section Two** under **racing**

trucks & tractors

Addison Generator Inc 21 W Main St Rear Freehold, NJ 07728 732-431-2438; FAX: 732-431-4503	**auto parts** **repairs** **supplies**

See full listing in **Section Two** under **electrical systems**

Advanced Maintenance Technologies Inc Box 250, Mountain Rd Stowe, VT 05672 802-253-7385; FAX: 802-253-7815 E-mail: info@advancedmaintenance.com	**filters** **lubricants**

See full listing in **Section Two** under **engine parts**

AMC Classic Appraisers 7963 Depew St Arvada, CO 80003 303-428-8760; FAX: 303-428-1070	**appraisals**

See full listing in **Section Two** under **appraisals**

Antiques Warehouse Michael J Welch 3700 Rt 6 Eastham, MA 02642 508-255-1437; FAX: 508-247-9166 E-mail: miketoys1@aol.com	**automobilia** **bikes** **toy trucks**

See full listing in **Section Two** under **models & toys**

Auto Transport Services 5367 Fargo Rd Avoca, MI 48006 810-324-2598; FAX: 810-324-6094	**transport**

See full listing in **Section Two** under **transport**

B & T Truck Parts 906 E Main St PO Box 799 Siloam Springs, AR 72761 501-524-5959; FAX: 501-524-5559	**pickup parts**

Specializing in 1960-1966 Chevrolet and GMC pickup truck parts. Body restoration. New, used and reproduction parts. Sheetmetal, weatherstripping, wiring harnesses, technical help.

Blint Equipment Inc 2204 E Lincolnway LaPorte, IN 46350 219-362-7021	**parts** **tractor rebuilding**

See full listing in **Section One** under **Ford 1954-up**

British T Shop Inc 165 Rt 82 Oakdale, CT 06370 860-889-0178; FAX: 860-889-6096	**car/tractor dealer** **parts** **service**

See full listing in **Section One** under **MG**

Section Two
Generalists

Brothers Truck Parts	accessories
4375 Prado Rd #105	parts
Corona, CA 91720	
800-977-2767; FAX: 909-808-9788	
E-mail: sales@brotherstrucks.com	

Mail order and open shop. Monday-Friday 8 am to 5 pm, Saturday 8 am to 12 pm PST. Specializing in 1947-1972 Chevy and GMC trucks restoration parts and custom accessories. Web site: brotherstrucks.com

See our ad on page 433

Carburetor Engineering	carburetor rebuilding
3324 E Colorado	distributor rebuilding
Pasadena, CA 91107	fuel pump rebuilding
626-795-3221	

See full listing in **Section Two** under **carburetors**

Jim Carter's Antique Truck Parts	truck parts
1508 E Alton	
Independence, MO 64055	
800-336-1913; FAX: 800-262-3749	
E-mail:	
jimcartertruck.parts@worldnet.att.ne	

See full listing in **Section One** under **Chevrolet**

Chevy Duty Pickup Parts	pickup parts
4319 NW Gateway	
Kansas City, MO 64150	
816-741-8029; FAX: 816-741-5255	
E-mail: trucks@sky.net	

See full listing in **Section One** under **Chevrolet**

Wood & Parts for Pickups

OFFERING MORE PARTS FOR YOUR PICKUP

CUSTOMIZING & RESTORATION FOR

FORD - '28 - '98 • CHEVY - GMC - '34 - '98

DODGE - '39 - '98

New! Show Deck Bed Liner

* Specializing in bed wood, steel and stainless skid strips, bolt sets and finishing supplies.
* Reproduction bed sides, front panels, tailgates and covers, roll pans, crossmembers, box angles, etc.
* Fiberglass front and rear fenders and runningboards.

Send for your NEW catalog - $4.00

BRUCE HORKEY'S WOOD & PARTS

 Rt. 4, Box 188H
Windom, MN 56101

507-831-5625 • FAX 507-831-0280

Cheyenne Pickup Parts	body panels
Box 959	bumpers
Noble, OK 73068	carpet
405-872-3399; FAX: 405-872-0385	weatherstripping

Specializing in new and reproduction parts for 1960-1987 Chevrolet full-size pickups and 1969-1991 Chevrolet full-size Blazers, including interior, exterior, chrome moldings, body panels, carpet, bumpers, weatherstripping, etc.

Clester's Auto Rubber Seals Inc	gloveboxes
PO Box 1113	molded rubber
Salisbury, NC 28145	parts
704-637-9979; FAX: 704-636-7390	weatherstripping

See full listing in **Section Two** under **rubber parts**

Coker Tire	tires
1317 Chestnut St	
Chattanooga, TN 37402	
800-251-6336 toll-free	
423-265-6368 local & international	
FAX: 423-756-5607	

See full listing in **Section Two** under **tires**

Dearborn Classics	accessories
PO Box 7649	restoration parts
Bend, OR 97708-7649	
800-252-7427; FAX: 800-500-7886	

See full listing in **Section One** under **Ford 1954-up**

Desert Valley Auto Parts	cars
22500 N 21st Ave	parts
Phoenix, AZ 85027	
800-905-8024, 602-780-8024	
FAX: 602-582-9141	
E-mail:	
rust-free-parts@worldnet.att.net	

See full listing in **Section Five** under **Arizona**

Dual Connection	models
Box 569	toys
Gibsonia, PA 15044	
724-898-9660; FAX: 724-898-9680	
E-mail: rich@dualconnection.com	

See full listing in **Section Two** under **models & toys**

Dusty Memories and Faded Glory	rentals
118 Oxford Hgts Rd	
Somerset, PA 15501-1134	
814-443-2393; FAX: 814-443-9452	

See full listing in **Section Two** under **military vehicles**

Early Wheel Co Inc	steel wheels
Box 1438	
Santa Ynez, CA 93460	
805-688-1187; FAX: 805-688-0257	

See full listing in **Section Two** under **wheels & wheelcovers**

Excelsweld USA/Cylinder Head Specialist	welding
1231 16th Ave	
Oakland, CA 94606	
800-743-4323; FAX: 510-534-1107	

See full listing in **Section Two** under **machine work**

Finders Service	parts finders
454-458 W Lincoln Hwy	
Chicago Heights, IL 60411-2463	
708-481-9685; FAX: 708-481-5837	
E-mail: findersvc@aol.com	

See full listing in **Section Two** under **car & parts locators**

The Finished Look	POR-15 products
PO Box 191413
Sacramento, CA 95819-1413
800-827-6715; FAX: 916-451-3984
E-mail: info@thefinishedlook.com

See full listing in **Section Two** under **rustproofing**

| Henry Ford Museum &
Greenfield Village	museum
20900 Oakwood Blvd
Dearborn, MI 48121-1970
313-271-1620; FAX: 313-982-6247

See full listing in **Section Six** under **Michigan**

| Fort Wayne Clutch & Driveline | axles
axleshafts
clutches
driveshafts |
| --- | --- |
2424 Goshen Rd
Fort Wayne, IN 46808
219-484-8505; FAX: 219-484-8605
E-mail: coca@mail.fwi.com

See full listing in **Section Two** under **clutches**

Fred's Truck Parts	parts
4811 S Palant
Tucson, AZ 85735
520-883-7151

See full listing in **Section One** under **Chevrolet**

| Fuller's Restoration Inc | repairs
restoration |
| --- | --- |
Old Airport Rd
Manchester Center, VT 05255
802-362-3643; FAX: 802-362-3360
E-mail: chevy@vermontel.com

See full listing in **Section Two** under **restoration shops**

Gambrinus Drivers Museum	brewery transport
2A Fontaine-Saint Pierre
B 5600
Romedenne Belgium
32-82678348; FAX: 32-82678348

See full listing in **Section Six** under **Belgium**

Gilbert's Early Chevy Pickup Parts	pickup parts
PO Box 1316
470 Rd 1 NW
Chino Valley, AZ 86323
PH/FAX: 520-636-5337
E-mail: gilb@goodnet.com

Specialize in reproduction and new parts for 1947-1966 Chevrolet and GMC pickups. Fast, friendly service.

| Great Lakes Auto "N" Truck
Restoration	parts
PO Box 251
Mayville, MI 48744
517-683-2614

See full listing in **Section One** under **Chevrolet**

Bruce Horkey's Wood & Parts	pickup parts
Rt 4 Box 188
Windom, MN 56101
507-831-5625; FAX: 507-831-0280

Mail order and open shop. Monday-Friday 8 am to 5 pm, Saturday by appointment. Replacement wood, metal and fiberglass pickup parts for 1928-1999 Ford, 1934-1999 Chevy/GMC, and 1939-1999 Dodge pickups.

See our ad on page 434

K C Obsolete Parts	parts
3343 N 61
Kansas City, KS 66104
913-334-9479; FAX: 913-788-2795

See full listing in **Section One** under **Ford 1954-up**

Kenask Spring Co	springs
307 Manhattan Ave
Jersey City, NJ 07307
201-653-4589

See full listing in **Section Two** under **suspension parts**

| Leigh & Sharon Knudson Truck
Light Sales | stoplights
truck lights
turn signals |
| --- | --- |
719 Ohms Way
Costa Mesa, CA 92627
949-645-5938; FAX: 949-646-6820
E-mail: catruckman@aol.com

See full listing in **Section Two** under **lighting equipment**

| LMC Truck | accessories
parts |
| --- | --- |
PO Box 14991
Lenexa, KS 66285
800-222-5664; FAX: 913-599-0323

See full listing in **Section One** under **Chevrolet**

Lokar Inc	performance parts
10924 Murdock Dr
Knoxville, TN 37932
423-966-2269; FAX: 423-671-1999
E-mail: lokarinc@aol.com

See full listing in **Section Two** under **street rods**

Long Road Productions	documentaries
1663 Hewins St
Ashley Falls, MA 01222
413-229-0474; FAX: 413-229-5903
E-mail: oldtrucks@longroadpro.com

See full listing in **Section Two** under **videos**

Lyme Pond Restorations	restoration
PO Box 202
Barnard, VT 05031
802-457-4657

See full listing in **Section Two** under **restoration shops**

Majestic Truck Parts	parts
17726 Dickerson
Dallas, TX 75252
972-248-6245; FAX: 972-380-8913
E-mail: majestictrk@juno.com

See full listing in **Section One** under **Chevrolet**

| MAR-K Quality Parts | bed parts
customizing parts
trim parts |
| --- | --- |
6625 W Wilshire, Ste 2
Oklahoma City, OK 73132
405-721-7945; FAX: 405-721-8906

Mail order and retail. Manufacturer and supplier for pickup truck parts for Chevy, Ford and Dodge. Includes bed parts, mouldings, rear pans and tailgate covers. Web site: www.mar-k.com

Michael's Classics Inc	Unimogs
954 Montauk Hwy
Bayport, NY 11705
516-363-4200; FAX: 516-363-9226
E-mail: info@unimognet.com

See full listing in **Section One** under **Mercedes-Benz**

Miracle of America Museum | museum
58176 Hwy 93
Polson, MT 59860
406-883-6804
E-mail: museum@cyberport.net

See full listing in **Section Six** under **Montana**

National Parts Locator Service | parts locator
636 East 6th St # 81
Ogden, UT 84404-2415
801-627-7210

See full listing in **Section Two** under **car & parts locators**

New Era Motors | restoration
11611 NE 50th Ave, Unit 6
Vancouver, WA 98686
360-573-8788

See full listing in **Section Two** under **woodwork**

North Yorkshire Motor Museum | museum
D T Mathewson
Roxby Garage, Pickering Rd
Thornton-le-Dale, North Yorkshire
England
01751 474455; FAX: 01944 758188

See full listing in **Section Six** under **England**

Nostalgia Productions Inc | shows, swap meets
268 Hillcrest Blvd
St Ignace, MI 49781
906-643-8087; FAX: 906-643-9784
E-mail: edreavie@nostalgia-prod.com

See full listing in **Section Two** under **auctions & events**

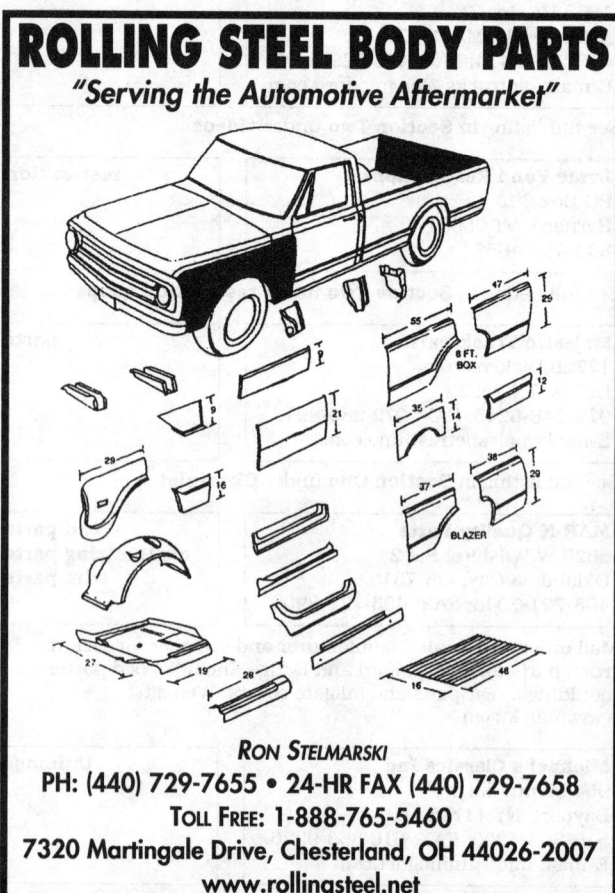

ROLLING STEEL BODY PARTS
"Serving the Automotive Aftermarket"

8 FT. BOX

BLAZER

RON STELMARSKI
PH: (440) 729-7655 • 24-HR FAX (440) 729-7658
TOLL FREE: 1-888-765-5460
7320 Martingale Drive, Chesterland, OH 44026-2007
www.rollingsteel.net

Obsolete Ford Parts Inc | parts
8701 S I-35
Oklahoma City, OK 73149
405-631-3933; FAX: 405-634-6815

See full listing in **Section One** under **Ford 1954-up**

On Mark International Inc | replicas
8923 S 43rd W Ave
Tulsa, OK 74132
918-446-7906; FAX: 918-445-1514
E-mail: onmark@ix.netcom.com

See full listing in **Section Two** under **models & toys**

Paragon Models & Art | artwork, models
1431-B SE 10th St
Cape Coral, FL 33990
941-458-0024; FAX: 941-574-4329
E-mail:
paragonmodels-art@worldnet.att.net

See full listing in **Section Two** under **models & toys**

Pick-ups Northwest | parts, trim
1430 Bickford Ave
Snohomish, WA 98290
360-568-9166; FAX: 360-568-1233

See full listing in **Section One** under **Chevrolet**

The Plateman | license plates
Jim Estrup
269 Webber Hill Rd
Kennebunk, ME 04043
207-985-4800; FAX: 207-985-TAGS

See full listing in **Section Two** under **license plates**

Power Effects® | exhaust systems
1800H Industrial Park Dr
Grand Haven, MI 49417
877-3POWRFX toll-free
616-847-4200
FAX: 616-847-4210

See full listing in **Section Two** under **exhaust systems**

Quik-Shelter | temporary garages
PO Box 1123
Orange, CT 06477
800-211-3730; FAX: 203-937-8897
E-mail: info@quikshelter.com

See full listing in **Section Two** under **car covers**

R-Mac Publications Inc | magazine
5439 SW US Hwy 41
Jasper, FL 32052
904-792-2480; FAX: 904-792-3230
E-mail: rbm@r-mac.com

See full listing in **Section Four** under **books & publications**

Recks & Relics Ford Trucks | truck parts
2675 Hamilton Mason Rd
Hamilton, OH 45011
513-868-3489
E-mail: truck@choice.net

See full listing in **Section One** under **Ford 1932-1953**

Redi-Strip Company | abrasive media, baking soda blasting, paint removal, rust removal
100 W Central Ave
Roselle, IL 60172
630-529-2442; FAX: 630-529-3626

See full listing in **Section Two** under **rust removal & stripping**

Richardson Restorations
1861 W Woodward Ave
Tulare, CA 93274
559-688-5002

custom work
repairs
restoration

See full listing in **Section Two** under **restoration shops**

Rock Valley Antique Auto Parts
Box 352
Rt 72 and Rothwell Rd
Stillman Valley, IL 61084
815-645-2271; FAX: 815-645-2740

gas tanks

See full listing in **Section One** under **Ford 1932-1953**

Rolling Steel Body Parts
7320 Martingale Dr
Chesterland, OH 44026-2007
888-765-5460; FAX: 440-729-7658
E-mail: rollingsteel@hotmail.com

body parts

See full listing in **Section Two** under **body parts**

Scotts Super Trucks
1972 Hwy 592 W
Penhold, AB Canada T0M 1R0
403-886-5572; FAX: 403-886-5577

parts

See full listing in **Section One** under **Chevrolet**

Simons Balancing & Machine Inc
1987 Ashley River Rd
Charleston, SC 29407
843-766-3911; FAX: 843-766-9003

machine work

See full listing in **Section Two** under **machine work**

Slim's Garage
PO Box 49
Seminary, MS 39479-0049
PH/FAX: 601-722-9861

garden tractors

Mail order and open shop. Weekdays 9 am to 5 pm. Specializing in garden tractors.

Stringbean's Pickup Parts
985 Cushon St
Johnstown, PA 15902
PH/FAX: 814-539-6440
E-mail: s-bean@surfshop.net

parts
service

See full listing in **Section One** under **Chevrolet**

Tabco Inc
11655 Chillicothe Rd
Chesterland, OH 44026-1994
216-921-5850; FAX: 216-921-5862

body parts

See full listing in **Section Two** under **sheetmetal**

This Old Truck Magazine
PO Box 500
Missouri City, TX 77459
800-310-7047 subscriptions
937-767-1433 publishing office
FAX: 937-767-2726
E-mail: antique@antiquepower.com

magazine

See full listing in **Section Four** under **periodicals**

Ultimate Spray-On Truck Bedliner
115 Garfield St
Sumas, WA 98295
800-989-9869; FAX: 604-864-0207
E-mail: info@ultimatelinings.com

bedliners

Open shop only. Spray-on polyurethane pickup truck bedliners.
Web site: www.ultimatelinings.com

Valley Motor Supply
1402 E Second St
Roswell, NM 88201
505-622-7450

accessories
parts

See full listing in **Section One** under **Ford 1954-up**

Vintage Motor and Machine
Gene French
1513 Webster Ct
Ft Collins, CO 80524
970-498-9224

auto components
fixtures
industrial
components

See full listing in **Section Two** under **machine work**

Vintage Motor Gaskets
W 604 19th
Spokane, WA 99203
509-747-9960, 509-747-0517
E-mail: dbrooke@ior.com

gaskets

See full listing in **Section Two** under **gaskets**

Wallace W Wade Specialty Tires
PO Box 560906
520 Regal Row
Dallas, TX 75356
800-666-TYRE, 214-688-0091
FAX: 214-634-8465

tires

See full listing in **Section Two** under **tires**

Wales Antique Chevy Truck Parts
143 Center
Carleton, MI 48117
734-654-8836

parts

See full listing in **Section One** under **Chevrolet**

Wesley Obsolete Parts
116 Memory Ln
Liberty, KY 42539
606-787-5293; FAX: 606-787-7252

parts

See full listing in **Section One** under **Ford 1954-up**

Widmann's Garage
1801 Liberty St
Hamilton, NJ 08629
609-392-1553; FAX: 609-392-1709

repairs
restorations

See full listing in **Section Two** under **restoration shops**

Willys America
PO Box 538
Cazadero, CA 95421
707-632-5258

parts
restoration

See full listing in **Section One** under **Willys**

trunks

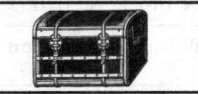

Auto Body Specialties Inc
Rt 66
Middlefield, CT 06455
888-277-1960 toll-free orders only
860-346-4989; FAX: 860-346-4987

accessories
body parts

See full listing in **Section Two** under **body parts**

Hooker Headers
1024 W Brooks St
Ontario, CA 91762
909-983-5871; FAX: 909-986-9860

exhaust systems

See full listing in **Section Two** under **exhaust systems**

Section Two
Generalists

National Parts Depot
3101 SW 40th Blvd
Gainesville, FL 32608
800-874-7595 toll-free 24 hours
352-378-2473 local

accessories
restoration parts

See full listing in **Section Two** under **comprehensive parts**

T-Bird Sanctuary
9997 SW Avery
Tualatin, OR 97062
503-692-9848; FAX: 503-692-9849

parts

See full listing in **Section One** under **Thunderbird**

Vintage Trunks
5 Brownstone Rd
East Granby, CT 06026-9705
860-658-0353
E-mail: john.desousa@snet.net

trunks

Mail order only. Plans and hardware for authentic wood construction of luggage trunks for Model As and other vintage autos. Drawing package contains prints, hardware listing and prices, history, instructions and fabric samples. Send SASE for information and price list. Have full line of trunk hardware on hand for your trunk restoration.

upholstery

AAC Restorations
Rt 1 Box 409
Mount Clare, WV 26408
304-622-2849

seat springs

Ace Antique Auto Restoration
65 S Service Rd
Plainview, NY 11803
516-752-6065; FAX: 516-752-1484

air conditioning
body rebuilding
restoration
wiring harnesses

See full listing in **Section Two** under **restoration shops**

All Seams Fine
23 Union St
Waterbury, VT 05676
800-244-7326 (SEAM)
802-244-8843

interior
restorations

Interior restorations, custom upholstery, carpet, headliner, panels, etc; convertible tops, antiques, late models, customs or street rods.

Arrow Fastener Co Inc
271 Mayhill St
Saddle Brook, NJ 07663

nail guns
rivet tools
staple guns

See full listing in **Section Two** under **tools**

Automotive Restorations Inc
Kent S Bain
1785 Barnum Ave
Stratford, CT 06614
203-377-6745; FAX: 203-386-0486
E-mail: carbain@compuserve.com

body fabrication
mechanical
painting
restorations
upholstery
woodwork

See full listing in **Section Two** under **restoration shops**

City Imports Ltd
166 Penrod Ct
Glen Burnie, MD 21061
410-768-6660; FAX: 410-768-5955

bodywork
car sales
restorations

See full listing in **Section One** under **Jaguar**

**Color-Plus Leather
Restoration System**
106 Harrier Ct, 3767 Sunrise Lake
Milford, PA 18337-9315
570-686-3158; FAX: 570-686-4161
E-mail: jpcolorplus@pikeonline.net

leather
conditioning
leather dye

See full listing in **Section Two** under **leather restoration**

**Comfy/Inter-American
Sheepskins Inc**
1346 Centinela Ave
West Los Angeles, CA 90025-1901
800-521-4014; FAX: 310-442-6080
E-mail: sales@comfysheep.com

floor mats
seat covers

See full listing in **Section Two** under **interiors & interior parts**

Custom Interiors
PO Box 51174
Indian Orchard, MA 01151
800-423-6053; FAX: 413-589-9178

carpets
headliners
upholstery

Mail order only. Interior parts. Manufacture seat upholstery for all makes domestic and foreign from 1928-1999. Also offer carpets, molded or cut and sewn and headliners too, to customize your project.

Dashhugger
PO Box 933
Clovis, CA 93613
559-298-4529; FAX: 559-298-3428
E-mail: sales@dashhugger.com

dashboard covers

See full listing in **Section Two** under **interiors & interior parts**

Doc's Jags
125 Baker Rd
Lake Bluff, IL 60044
847-367-5247; FAX: 847-367-6363
E-mail: docsjags@worldnet.att.net

appraisals
interiors
restoration

See full listing in **Section One** under **Jaguar**

Dr Vinyl and Assoc Ltd
9501 E 350 Hwy
Raytown, MO 64133
816-356-3312; FAX: 816-356-9049
E-mail: tbuckley@drvinyl.com

dent repair
interior repair
paint touch-up

See full listing in **Section Two** under **car care products**

East Coast Chevy Inc
Ol '55 Chevy Parts
4154A Skyron Dr
Doylestown, PA 18938
215-348-5568; FAX: 215-348-0560

custom work
parts
restoration

See full listing in **Section One** under **Chevrolet**

FEN Enterprises of New York Inc
PO Box 1559
1324 Rt 376
Wappingers Falls, NY 12590
914-462-5959, 914-462-5094
FAX: 914-462-8450

parts
restoration

See full listing in **Section One** under **Cadillac/LaSalle**

**Firewall Insulators & Quiet Ride
Solutions**
6333 Pacific Ave, Ste 523
Stockton, CA 95207
209-477-4840; FAX: 209-477-0918
E-mail: timcox@gotnet.net

auto insulation
firewall insulators
gloveboxes
sound deadening

Mail order only. Manufacture firewall insulator panels (upholstery) just like OEMs did originally. Currently have patterns for nearly 400 cars and trucks, 1928-1986, including Bitchin' firewalls for street rods. Also make specialty items including gloveboxes, heater plenum, air/defroster ducts, etc. If the pattern for your car is not available, send your old original for reproduction. Each insulator comes ready to install with insulation, all holes punched and detailed to look and fit just like the original. Standards are exacting and work is guaranteed. Also specialize in automotive insulation and sound deadening materials. Web site: quietride.com

See our ad on page 314

Garrett Leather Corp	upholstery
1360 Niagara St	
Buffalo, NY 14213	
800-342-7738; FAX: 716-882-9358	
E-mail: dduerr@garrettleather.com	

Offer premium Italian and German cowhide upholstery leather. Over 250 colors are in stock and ready for immediate shipment. Also carry 30 colors of shearling sheepskin and a complete line of nylon threads to match each of our leathers. Perforated leather is also available. Call today. Web site: www.garrettleather.com

Highway Classics	parts
949 N Cataract Ave, Unit J	
San Dimas, CA 91773	
909-592-8819; FAX: 909-592-4239	
E-mail: donnelson@earthlink.net	

See full listing in **Section One** under **Ford 1954-up**

Jerry's Classic Cars & Parts Inc	parts
4097 McRay Ave	restoration
Springdale, AR 72764	
800-828-4584; FAX: 501-750-1682	
E-mail: jcc@jerrysclassiccars.com	

See full listing in **Section One** under **Ford 1954-up**

Joyce's Model A & T Parts	new parts
PO Box 70	NOS parts
Manchaca, TX 78652-0070	rebuilt parts
512-282-1196	

See full listing in **Section One** under **Ford 1903-1931**

K & K Vintage Motorcars LC	restoration
9848 SW Frwy	sales
Houston, TX 77074	service
713-541-2281; FAX: 713-541-2286	

See full listing in **Section Two** under **restoration shops**

Keleen Leathers Inc	leather hides
10526 W Cermak Rd	
Westchester, IL 60154	
708-409-9800; FAX: 708-409-9801	

See full listing in **Section Two** under **interiors & interior parts**

Ken's Cougars	parts
PO Box 5380	
Edmond, OK 73083	
405-340-1636; FAX: 405-340-5877	

See full listing in **Section One** under **Mercury**

Dave Knittel Upholstery	interiors
850 E Teton #7	tops
Tucson, AZ 85706	upholstery
PH/FAX: 520-746-1588	

Deal in upholstery, convertible tops, interiors, rebuild seat backs, rebuilds frames and springs, carpeting, custom interiors, vans, boats, aircraft, custom cars and trucks, etc.

Koolmat	insulators
26258 Cranage Rd	
Olmsted Falls, OH 44138	
440-427-1888; FAX: 440-427-1889	
E-mail: koolmat1@gte.net	

See full listing in **Section Two** under **restoration aids**

Land Cruiser Solutions Inc	accessories
20 Thornell Rd	services
Newton, NH 03858	
603-382-3555; FAX: 603-378-0431	
E-mail: twbii@aol.com	

See full listing in **Section One** under **Toyota**

Lindley Restorations Ltd	parts
10 S Sanatoga Rd	sales
Pottstown, PA 19464	service
610-326-8484; FAX: 610-326-3845	

See full listing in **Section One** under **Jaguar**

Linearossa International Inc	parts
3931 SW 47th Ave	
Ft Lauderdale, FL 33314	
954-327-9888; FAX: 954-791-6555	

See full listing in **Section One** under **Fiat**

Memoryville USA Inc	restoration
1008 W 12th St	
Rolla, MO 65401	
573-364-1810	

See full listing in **Section Two** under **restoration shops**

Markel's Auto Upholstery	upholstery
1163 S Robertson Blvd	
Los Angeles, CA 90035	
310-274-1501	

All auto upholstery.

Morgan Oasis Garage	restoration
PO Box 1010	service
N 51 Terrace Rd	
Hoodsport, WA 98548	
360-877-5160	

See full listing in **Section One** under **Morgan**

National Parts Depot	accessories
3101 SW 40th Blvd	restoration parts
Gainesville, FL 32608	
800-874-7595 toll-free 24 hours	
352-378-2473 local	

See full listing in **Section Two** under **comprehensive parts**

Nationwide Auto Restoration	bodywork
1038 Watt St	paint
Jeffersonville, IN 47130	upholstery
812-280-0165; FAX: 812-280-8961	
E-mail: restore@unidial.com	

See full listing in **Section Two** under **restoration shops**

Newport Upholstery Source	carpets
250 H St, Unit 8110	tops
Blaine, WA 98231	upholstery
604-990-0346; FAX: 604-990-9988	

Your number one source for Wilton Wool carpet, Connolly leather, European vinyls and other high quality upholstery materials. Robbins Top distributor.

Original Auto Interiors | upholstery
7869 Trumble Rd
Columbus, MI 48063-3915
810-727-2486; FAX: 810-727-4344
E-mail: origauto@tir.com

Mail order and open shop. Monday-Friday 9 am to 5 pm EST.
Upholstery materials for vehicles from the 1950s-1980s. All
American made cars. Thunderbird seat covers 1961-1966, the
most original available. NOS seat covers for selected Mopars
1957-1964 and Mopar reproductions 1963-1976. OEM carpet
sets for most vehicles mid 1950s-present. Also available: headliners, floor mats, trunk mats, convertible tops and boots and
windlace.

Paul's Discount Jaguar Parts | parts
1124 NW 134th Ave
Sunrise
Fort Lauderdale, FL 33323
954-846-7976; FAX: 954-846-9450
E-mail: paulsjag@ix.netcom.com

See full listing in **Section One** under **Jaguar**

Performance Automotive Inc | accessories
1696 New London Tpke | car care
PO Box 10
Glastonbury, CT 06033
860-633-7868; FAX: 860-657-9110

See full listing in **Section Two** under **car care products**

Rick's First Generation Camaro | accessories
Parts & Accessories | parts
420 Athena Dr
Athens, GA 30601
800-359-7717; FAX: 706-548-8581
E-mail: firstgen@negia.net

See full listing in **Section One** under **Chevelle/Camaro**

Sailorette's Nautical Nook | covers
451 Davy Ln | interiors
Wilmington, IL 60481
815-476-1644; FAX: 815-476-2524

Monday-Friday 9 am to 5 pm, other times by appointment.
Custom handcrafted vehicle interiors which includes seat
reupholstering, door panels and carpets for old and new vehicles. Also specializing in custom covers for cars, trucks, motorcycles, marine covers, marine convertible tops.

SMS Auto Fabrics | upholstery
2325 SE 10th Ave
Portland, OR 97214
503-234-1175; FAX: 503-234-0651

See full listing in **Section Two** under **interiors & interior parts**

Strader Classics | parts
Bill Strader
2849 Locust Grove Rd
Elizabethtown, KY 42701
502-737-5294

See full listing in **Section One** under **Chevrolet**

Strange Motion Inc | customizing
14696 N 350th Ave | design
Cambridge, IL 61238 | fabrication
PH/FAX: 309-927-3346
E-mail: strange@netins.net

See full listing in **Section Two** under **street rods**

Tamraz's Parts Discount Warehouse | carpeting
10022 S Bode Rd | upholstery
Plainfield, IL 60544 | weatherstripping
630-904-4500; FAX: 630-904-2329

See full listing in **Section One** under **Chevelle/Camaro**

Thermax Inc | interior detailing
5385 Alpha Ave
Reno, NV 89506
800-247-7177; FAX: 702-972-4809

See full listing in **Section Two** under **car care products**

West Coast Metric Inc | apparel
24002 Frampton Ave | carpets
Harbor City, CA 90710 | plastic parts
310-325-0005; FAX: 310-325-9733 | rubber parts
E-mail: wcmi@earthlink.net

See full listing in **Section One** under **Volkswagen**

videos

Big Time Productions | video production
780 Munras Ave
Monterey, CA 93940
831-655-0409; FAX: 831-375-9102
E-mail: bigtime@redshift.com

Open shop only. Monday-Friday 10 am to 6 pm. Video production, post production and location services for Monterey County,
Laguna Seca Raceway and Big Sur Coast. Produce collector car

programming for cable, document restorations and shows nationwide. For hire to hobby or trade, formats for most budgets, Beta-SP to mini DV. Located downtown Monterey, near all historic weekend events.

British Car Films PO Box 13862 London N4 3WB England 800-454-8341 toll-free 011 44181-3744850 FAX: 011 44181-3744852 E-mail: british.car@virgin.net	**videos**

Mail order only. A unique series of documentary videos celebrating the history of seven of the most popular British car marques in America. The individual titles feature: Jaguar, MG, Triumph, Morris Minor, Mini, Land Rover and Rolls-Royce. Each movie contains a rich marriage of original footage which has been shot from coast to coast, along with a feast of fascinating archive material, much of which has not been seen for more than 30 years. This includes classic racing footage, New York Auto Show newsreels, old television advertisements, extraordinary owners, exclusive British car shows, highly modified cars, beautifully restored cars and much, much more.

Dalmar 11759 S Cleveland Ave, Suite 28 Ft Myers, FL 33907 941-275-6540; FAX: 941-275-1731 E-mail: dalmar@peganet.com	**electroplating plating supplies**

See full listing in **Section Two** under **plating & polishing**

GMC Solutions Robert English PO Box 675 Franklin, MA 02038-0675 508-520-3900; FAX: 508-520-7861 E-mail: oldcarkook@aol.com	**literature parts**

See full listing in **Section One** under **GMC**

The Gullwing Garage Ltd Bricklin SVI Specialists 5 Cimorelli Dr New Windsor, NY 12553-6201 914-561-0019 anytime	**appraisals literature parts service**

See full listing in **Section One** under **Bricklin**

Richard Hamilton 28 E 46th St Indianapolis, IN 46205 317-283-1902	**sales literature**

See full listing in **Section Two** under **literature dealers**

Hot Rod Nostalgia™ PO Box 249 West Point, CA 95255-0249 209-754-3697; FAX: 209-754-5521 E-mail: hvaa@hotrodnostalgia.com	**"magalog"**

See full listing in **Section Four** under **books & publications**

JHT Multi Media 5514 Lake Howell Rd Winter Park, FL 32792-1036 800-868-7492; FAX: 407-657-5233 E-mail: dhoward@jht.com	**videos**

Mail order only. Dealing in how-to videos. Web site: www.jht.com/autopaint

Long Road Productions 1663 Hewins St Ashley Falls, MA 01222 413-229-0474; FAX: 413-229-5903 E-mail: oldtrucks@longroadpro.com	**documentaries**

Mail order only. Specializing in video documentaries for heavy antique trucks and light trucks and vintage Mopars; also featuring cars and their owners; more titles forthcoming. Web site: www.longroadpro.com

MotorCam Media 138 N Alling Rd Tallmadge, OH 44278 800-240-1777; FAX: 330-633-3249 E-mail: carvideo@motorcam.com	**automotive videos**

Most comprehensive source of automotive video available anywhere. From histories to do-it-yourself, movies to motorsports. There's something for every auto buff. Call for free catalog. Web site: www.motorcam.com

MotorWeek 11767 Owings Mills Blvd Owings Mills, MD 21117 410-356-5600; FAX: 410-581-4113 E-mail: motorweek@mpt.org	**TV program**

See full listing in **Section Four** under **information sources**

Museum of the Spa-Francorchamps Track Old Abbey 4970 Stavelot Belgium PH/FAX: 080-8627-06	**museum**

See full listing in **Section Six** under **Belgium**

National Road-Zane Grey Museum 8850 East Pike Norwich, OH 43767 800-752-2602; FAX: 740-872-3510	**museum**

See full listing in **Section Six** under **Ohio**

Pikes Peak Auto Hill Climb Educational Museum 135 Manitou Ave Manitou Springs, CO 80829 719-685-4400; FAX: 719-685-5885 E-mail: ppihc@ppihc.com	**museum**

See full listing in **Section Six** under **Colorado**

Practical Images PO Box 245 Haddam, CT 06438-0245 860-704-0525 E-mail: practimages@snet.net	**int'l VHS video conversions photo scanning photography**

See full listing in **Section Two** under **photography**

Transport Books at DRB Motors Inc 16 Elrose Ave Toronto, ON Canada M9M 2H6 800-665-2665, 416-744-7675 FAX: 416-744-7696 E-mail: info@transportbooks.com	**books manuals periodicals videos**

See full listing in **Section Four** under **books & publications**

Yankee Candle Car Museum Yankee Candle Co Rt 5 South Deerfield, MA 01373 413-665-2020; FAX: 413-665-2399	**museum**

See full listing in **Section Six** under **Massachusetts**

water pumps

Automotive Friction
4621 SE 27th Ave
Portland, OR 97202
503-234-0606; FAX: 503-234-1026

brakes
clutches
water pumps

See full listing in **Section Two** under **clutches**

East Coast Jaguar
802B Naaman's Rd
Wilmington, DE 19810
302-475-7200; FAX: 302-475-9258
E-mail: ecjaguar@aol.com

parts
service

See full listing in **Section One** under **Jaguar**

Skip's Auto Parts
Skip Bollinger
1500 Northaven Dr
Gladstone, MO 64118
816-455-2337; FAX: 816-459-7547
E-mail: carpartman@aol.com

chassis parts
ignition parts
water pumps

Offer parts from 1938-present for various marques. Parts such as water pumps, reground camshafts, chassis parts, fuel pumps rebuilt for today's fuel with methanol, ignition parts and wiper motors, blades, arms. Fax and e-mail are the best as we are difficult to contact. Dealing globally, we are here at odd hours. Please leave your name including country and country code or state, area code and phone number, we will call you back on our nickel. Thank you for your consideration.

Superior Pump Exchange Co
12901 Crenshaw Blvd
Hawthorne, CA 90250-5511
310-676-4995
E-mail: autoh20@aol.com

water pumps

Mail order and open shop. Monday-Friday 8 am to 4 pm. Quality remanufactured automotive and industrial water pumps. Large inventory, all makes, models and years. Cars, trucks, forklifts, welders, farm equipment, etc.

wheels & wheelcovers

AKH Wheels
200 Broadview Rd
Ellensburg, WA 98926-2522
509-962-3390
E-mail: akhwheel@eburg.com

Rallye wheels
styled steel wheels
vintage aluminum

Mail order. Sale of vintage wheels, 1950s-1985. American Racing Torque Thrusts, 200S (Coke bottles), CP-200s, slots, etc. Aluminum wheels by Ansen, Mickey Thompson, Parnelli Jones, Appliance, Superior, Forsythe, ET, Fenton, Halibrand, Hurst and Radar Corp. Also have most factory styled steel and Rallye wheels from Ford, GM, Mercury, Dodge, Buick, Olds, Plymouth, Pontiac and AMC. Thousands of wheels available. For one rare wheel or a set. Reproduction wheels also available. Call!

American Arrow Corp
105 Kinross
Clawson, MI 48017
248-435-6115; FAX: 248-435-4670
E-mail: dsommer@greatid.com

chroming
mascots
wire wheel
rebuilding

See full listing in **Section Two** under **novelties**

Antique Wheels
1805 SW Pattulo Way
West Linn, OR 97068
503-638-5275

respoking

Respoking of wood and steel felloed wheels of all shapes and sizes of spokes. Only straight grain, FAS hickory wood used. Tracer lathing for uniformity and machine sandings for smoothness. Shipped with wood ready for paint or varnish.

Appleton Garage
PO Box B
West Rockport, ME 04865
207-594-2062

car dealer
parts
wheelcovers

Mail order and open shop. Monday-Friday 9 am to 4 pm. Have over 10,000 used/new wheelcovers and hubcaps for sale. Also sell GM cars, trucks and parts, 1960-1987. Specializing in 1962-1966 full-size Chevrolets, 1969-1972 Chevy/GMC pickups. Sorry, no catalog.

Big Boys Toys
Richard Boutin
Rt 67A Box 174A
North Bennington, VT 05257
800-286-1721; FAX: 802-447-0962

accessories
bodywork
tires
wheels

See full listing in **Section Two** under **accessories**

Tony D Branda Performance
Shelby and Mustang Parts
1434 E Pleasant Valley Blvd
Altoona, PA 16602
814-942-1869; FAX: 814-944-0801
E-mail: cobranda@aol.com

accessories
decals
emblems
sheetmetal
wheels

See full listing in **Section One** under **Mustang**

Budnik Wheels Inc
7412 Prince Dr
Huntington Beach, CA 92647
714-848-1996; FAX: 714-848-5051

aluminum wheels
steering wheels

Mail order and open shop. The finest quality billet aluminum wheels and steering wheels. Web site: www.budnik.com

Burr Nyberg Screw-on Hubcaps
198 Union Blvd #200
Denver, CO 80228
804-951-3294 days, VA
FAX: 303-988-7145
E-mail: e_burrnyberg@yahoo.com

hubcaps

See full listing in **Section Two** under **hubcaps**

California Classic Mustang
1102 Industrial Ave
Escondido, CA 92128
888-320-8929, 760-746-6580
FAX: 760-746-6581
E-mail: mmatt1965@aol.com

steel wheels

See full listing in **Section One** under **Mustang**

California Pony Cars
1906 Quaker Ridge Pl
Ontario, CA 91761
909-923-2804; FAX: 909-947-8593
E-mail: 105232.3362@compuserve.com

parts

See full listing in **Section One** under **Mustang**

California Wire Wheel
6922 Turnbridge Way
San Diego, CA 92119
619-698-8255; FAX: 619-589-9032

rechroming
tires
tubes
wheels

Mail order or appointment only. Specializing in wire wheel restoration of American, British and Italian wire wheels, (eg Franklin,

Duesenberg, Ferrari, MG, etc). Chrome, stainless, painted spokes and custom colors. New wire wheels for British cars tires, tubes, knock-off wheel hubs. MGs bought, sold, and refurbished. Die cast model car stockist specializing in British and European models. Model cars and die cast metal cars: 1/18, 1/43, 1/24 and 1/12 scales.

Calimer's Wheel Shop 30 E North St Waynesboro, PA 17268 717-762-5056; FAX: 717-762-5021	**wooden wheels**

Mail order and open shop. Monday-Friday 8 am to 5 pm. Rebuilding of wooden wheels using the customer's metal parts. Wheels made of hickory for years. Late 1890s-1930.

Sam Clark PO Box 1817 10960 Christenson Rd Lucerne Valley, CA 92356 PH/FAX: 760-248-9025 E-mail: sclark@lucernevalley.net	**wheel rims**

Producing ultra-quality wheel rims for Alco, Chadwick, Delauney-Belleville, Hispano-Suiza, Isotta-Fraschini, Locomobile, Lozier, Mercedes, Oldsmobile, Packard, Pope-Hartford, Thomas Flyer and other fine brass era autos. Since 1981.

Coker Tire 1317 Chestnut St Chattanooga, TN 37402 800-251-6336 toll-free 423-265-6368 local & international FAX: 423-756-5607	**tires**

See full listing in **Section Two** under **tires**.

Corvette Mike 1133 N Tustin Ave Anaheim, CA 92807 800-327-8388, 714-630-0700 FAX: 714-630-0777 E-mail: cvtmike@deltanet.com	**accessories** **parts** **sales** **service**

See full listing in **Section One** under **Corvette**.

Dayton Wheel Products 115 Compark Rd Dayton, OH 45459 800-862-6000, 937-438-0100 FAX: 937-438-9742	**parts** **restoration** **service**

Office open Monday-Friday 8 am to 5 pm. Wire wheel restoration for Dayton, Borrani, Kelsey-Hayes, Motor Wheel, Dunlop, etc. Also, manufacturer of replacement spline-drive wire wheels and quality knock-off and bolt-on wire wheels.

Buzz De Clerck 41760 Utica Rd Sterling Heights, MI 48313-3146 810-731-0765	**parts**

See full listing in **Section One** under **Lincoln**.

Early Wheel Co Inc Box 1438 Santa Ynez, CA 93460 805-688-1187; FAX: 805-688-0257	**steel wheels**

Mail order only. Manufacture steel wheels for the street rod, pickup and restoration market. Wheel widths from 5" to 14" wide. Hubcaps and trim rings available for our wheels. Web site: www.earlywheel.com

Enthusiast's Specialties 350 Old Connecticut Path Framingham, MA 01701 800-718-3999; FAX: 508-872-4914 E-mail: alvis1934@aol.com	**automobilia**

See full listing in **Section Two** under **automobilia**.

George's Auto & Tractor Sales Inc 1450 N Warren Rd North Jackson, OH 44451 330-538-3020; FAX: 330-538-3033	**Blue Dots/car dealer** **Dri-Wash metal polish** **upholstery cleaner** **New Castle batteries**

See full listing in **Section Two** under **car dealers**.

Grossmueller's Classic Corvette 55 Sitgreaves St Phillipsburg, NJ 08865 610-258-2028 FAX: 610-258-7013, PA E-mail: wfg@gccorvettes.com	**NOS parts** **used parts**

See full listing in **Section One** under **Corvette**.

Hubcap Jack Inc 1330 Market St Linwood, PA 19061 610-485-1155; FAX: 610-494-2989	**hubcaps** **wheelcovers**

Mail order and open shop. Monday-Friday 8 am to 5 pm, Saturday 9 am to 2 pm. Specializing in hubcaps and wheelcovers for cars, trucks, imports and classics.

Hubcap Mike 26242 Dimension Ste 150 Lake Forest, CA 92630 949-597-8120; FAX: 949-597-8123	**hubcaps** **wheelcovers**

Wheelcovers, hubcaps and trim rings, 1946-1996. Specializing in reproduction hubcaps for Chevy Rallye and 1968-1969 Ford GT wheels. Also baby moons, crossbars and much more. Same day shipping available on all orders. Money back satisfaction guarantee.

Italy's Famous Exhaust 2711 183rd St Redondo Beach, CA 90278 310-793-5985 E-mail: famous@earthlink.net	**exhaust systems** **wheels**

See full listing in **Section Two** under **exhaust systems**.

Iverson Automotive 14704 Karyl Dr Minnetonka, MN 55345 800-325-0480; FAX: 612-938-5707	**polishes** **pot metal** **restoration**

See full listing in **Section Two** under **plating & polishing**.

Roger Kraus Racing 2896 Grove Way Castro Valley, CA 94546 510-582-5031; FAX: 510-886-5605	**shocks** **tires** **wheels**

See full listing in **Section Two** under **tires**.

LMARR Disk Ltd PO Box 910 Glen Ellen, CA 95442-0910 707-938-9347; FAX: 707-938-3020 E-mail: lmarr@ibm.net	**wheel discs**

See full listing in **Section One** under **Rolls-Royce/Bentley**.

McGard Inc 3875 California Rd Orchard Park, NY 14127 716-662-8980; FAX: 716-662-8985 E-mail: jmondo@mcgard.com	**lug nuts** **wheel locks**

See full listing in **Section Two** under **locks & keys**.

National Parts Depot 3101 SW 40th Blvd Gainesville, FL 32608 800-874-7595 toll-free 24 hours 352-378-2473 local	**accessories** **restoration parts**

See full listing in **Section Two** under **comprehensive parts**.

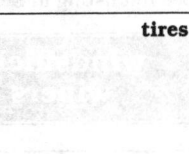

Section Two Generalists

OJ Rallye Automotive
PO Box 540
N 6808 Hwy OJ
Plymouth, WI 53073
920-893-2531; FAX: 920-893-6800
E-mail: ojrallye@excel.net

accessories
car care products
lighting parts

See full listing in **Section Two** under **lighting equipment**

Operations Plus
PO Box 26347
Santa Ana, CA 92799
PH/FAX: 714-962-2776
E-mail: aquacel@aquacel.com

accessories
parts

See full listing in **Section One** under **Cobra**

RD Enterprises Ltd
290 Raub Rd
Quakertown, PA 18951
215-538-9323; FAX: 215-538-0158
E-mail: rdent@rdent.com

parts

See full listing in **Section One** under **Lotus**

Southern Rods & Parts Inc
2125 Airport Rd
Gleer, SC 29651
864-848-0601; FAX: 864-801-0601

accessories
headlights
power windows
radiators

See full listing in **Section Two** under **street rods**

Stockton Wheel Service
648 W Fremont St
Stockton, CA 95203
209-464-7771, 800-395-9433
FAX: 209-464-4725
E-mail: sales@stocktonwheel.com

wheel repair

Mail order and open shop. Monday-Friday 8 am to 5 pm.
Specializing in wheel straightening and fabrication of GM and
Mopar Rallye wheels in various offsets and widths. Straighten
and repair all steel and aluminum wheels. Polishing and
chroming. Since 1883. Web site: www.stocktonwheel.com

Straw Church Speed Shop
602 Passaic St
Phillipsburg, NJ 08865
908-454-7487
E-mail: strawchurch_ss@hotmail.com

accessories
engine swaps
parts

See full listing in **Section Two** under **car & parts locators**

Al Trommers-Rare Auto Literature
614 Vanburenville Rd
Middletown, NY 10940

hubcaps/wheelcovers
license plates
literature/records

See full listing in **Section Two** under **literature dealers**

Ultra Wheel Co
6300 Valley View Ave
Buena Park, CA 90620
714-994-1444; FAX: 714-994-0723

custom wheels

Manufacturer only of custom wheels, one-piece, two-piece, composite wheels. Web site: www.ultrawheel.com

Valley Wire Wheel Service
14731 Lull St
Van Nuys, CA 91405
818-785-7237; FAX: 818-994-2042

wheel restoration
wheels

Mail order and open shop. Monday-Friday 8:30 am to 5:30 pm.
Restoration of all styles of wire, steel, aluminum and mag.
Straightening, truing, polishing, painting, powdercoating,
chrome. Since 1969, have been restoring wheels from daily drivers to concours. References upon request. Sell new and used
wheels and tires, custom jobs are no problem. Some antique
wheels in stock, also buy old wheels. Helping to keep them on
the road, call us, we're here to help.

**Wheel Repair Service of
New England**
317 Southbridge St, Rt 12
Auburn, MA 01501
508-832-4949; FAX: 508-832-3969

new wire wheels
wire wheel
restoration

Mail order and open shop. Wire wheel restoration specialists
since 1962. Replacement spokes available in bare, chrome or
polished stainless finishes. New Dayton wire wheels available to
fit most cars. Save up to 35% off factory prices.

Willies Antique Tires
5257 W Diversey Ave
Chicago, IL 60639
773-622-4037, 800-742-6226
FAX: 773-622-0623

tires
wire wheels

See full listing in **Section Two** under **tires**

Wirth's Custom Automotive
PO Box 5
505 Conner St
Prairie du Rocher, IL 62277
618-284-3359
E-mail: roywirth@htc.net

custom accessories
fender skirts
spinner hubcaps

See full listing in **Section Two** under **accessories**

windshield wipers

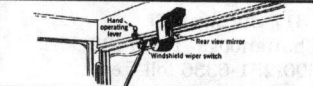

Bill's Speedometer Shop
109 Twinbrook Pl
Sidney, OH 45365
937-492-7800
E-mail: speedo@bright.net

repairs
restoration

See full listing in **Section Two** under **instruments**

**Clean Sweep-Vacuum Windshield
Wiper Motor Rebuilding**
760 Knight Hill Rd
Zillah, WA 98953
509-865-2481; FAX: 509-865-2189
E-mail: dkjaquith@prodigy.net

motors
repairs
wiper parts

Rebuilding vacuum windshield wiper motors of all makes. Also
rebuild hydro-wipe, hydraulically operated wiper motors on
1960s T-Birds and Lincolns.

East Coast Jaguar
802B Naaman's Rd
Wilmington, DE 19810
302-475-7200; FAX: 302-475-9258
E-mail: ecjaguar@aol.com

parts
service

See full listing in **Section One** under **Jaguar**

Bruce Falk
1105 Nichilson
Joliet, IL 60435
815-726-6455
E-mail: bbfalk@aol.com

parts

See full listing in **Section One** under **Chevrolet**

Ficken Wiper Service
Box 11
132 Calvert Ave
W Babylon, NY 11702
516-587-3332; FAX: 516-661-9125
E-mail: wiperman@aol.com

ignition parts
wiper parts

Mail order only. Phone hours: Monday-Friday 9 am to 5 pm.
Trico windshield wiper motors (vacuum), NOS or we can also
rebuild your vacuum motor. Arms, blades, linkages and repair
kits. Ignition tune-up parts. In business for 30 years. Money
back guarantee. Have booth at Hershey and Carlisle auto shows.
Hershey space GJ-45, Carlisle (Fall and Spring) I-105.

Grossmueller's Classic Corvette
55 Sitgreaves St
Phillipsburg, NJ 08865
610-258-2028
FAX: 610-258-7013, PA
E-mail: wfg@gccorvettes.com

NOS parts
used parts

See full listing in **Section One** under **Corvette**

K C Obsolete Parts
3343 N 61
Kansas City, KS 66104
913-334-9479; FAX: 913-788-2795

parts

See full listing in **Section One** under **Ford 1954-up**

J Pinto
31 Spruce
HC 1, Box F7
Swiftwater, PA 18370
570-839-3441
E-mail: lectri@yahoo.com

electric motors/
relays/switches/
solenoids repair

See full listing in **Section Two** under **electrical systems**

Skip's Auto Parts
Skip Bollinger
1500 Northaven Dr
Gladstone, MO 64118
816-455-2337; FAX: 816-459-7547
E-mail: carpartman@aol.com

chassis parts
ignition parts
water pumps

See full listing in **Section Two** under **water pumps**

Specialty Power Window
2087 Collier Rd
Forsyth, GA 31029
800-634-9801; FAX: 912-994-3124

power window kits
windshield wiper
kit

See full listing in **Section Two** under **street rods**

Star Classics Inc
7745 E Redfield #300
Scottsdale, AZ 85260
800-644-7827, 480-991-7495
FAX: 480-951-4096
E-mail: starcls@primenet.com

parts

See full listing in **Section One** under **Mercedes-Benz**

Tanson Enterprises
2508 J St, Dept HVA
Sacramento, CA 95816-4815
916-448-2950
FAX: 916-443-3269 *88
E-mail: tanson@pipeline.com

performance parts
restoration parts

See full listing in **Section One** under **Oldsmobile**

Windshield Wiper Service
9109 (Rear) E Garvey Ave
Rosemead, CA 91770
626-280-4546

parts
service

Mail order and open shop. Monday-Friday 9 am to 5 pm. Arms, blades and miscellaneous parts. Repair and rebuilding of vacuum and electric windshield wiper motors. Five day service.

wiring harnesses

Ace Antique Auto Restoration
65 S Service Rd
Plainview, NY 11803
516-752-6065; FAX: 516-752-1484

air conditioning
body rebuilding
restoration
wiring harnesses

See full listing in **Section Two** under **restoration shops**

American Autowire Systems Inc
150 Heller Pl #17W
Dept HVAA99
Bellmawr, NJ 08031
800-482-9473; FAX: 609-933-0805
E-mail: facfit@erols.com

battery cables
electrical systems
switches/components

See full listing in **Section Two** under **street rods**

Chev's of the 40's
2027 B St, Dept HVA
Washougal, WA 98671
800-999-CHEV (2438)
FAX: 360-835-7988

parts

See full listing in **Section One** under **Chevrolet**

Danchuk Mfg
3201 S Standard Ave
Santa Ana, CA 92705
714-751-1957; FAX: 714-850-1957
E-mail: info@danchuk.com

accessories
parts
restoration

See full listing in **Section One** under **Chevrolet**

Mike Drago Chevy Parts
141 E St Joseph St
Easton, PA 18042
PH/FAX: 610-252-5701
E-mail: dragomdcp@aol.com

Chevrolet parts

See full listing in **Section One** under **Chevrolet**

The El Camino Store
57 B Depot Rd
Goleta, CA 93117
805-681-8164; FAX: 805-681-8166
E-mail: ec@elcaminostore.com

parts

See full listing in **Section One** under **Chevelle/Camaro**

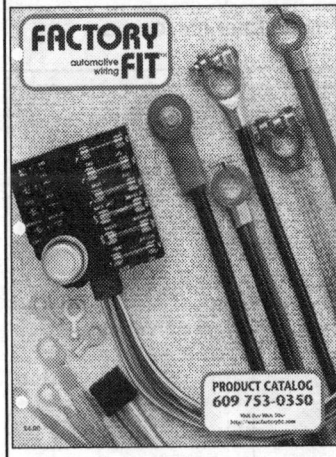

Ron Francis' Wire Works
167 Keystone Rd
Chester, PA 19013
800-292-1940 orders, 610-485-1937
E-mail: rfwwx@aol.com

fuel injection
harnesses
wiring accessories
wiring kits

Mail order only. Custom wiring kits for cars, trucks and kit cars. Fuel injection harnesses, wiring accessories. 72 page catalog filled with trick wiring and switches, $2. Web site: wire-works.com

K&D Enterprises
23117 E Echo Lake Rd
Snohomish, WA 98296-5426
425-788-0507; FAX: 360-668-2003
E-mail: tdb@halcyon.com

accessories
parts
restorations

See full listing in **Section One** under **Jensen**

National Parts Depot
3101 SW 40th Blvd
Gainesville, FL 32608
800-874-7595 toll-free 24 hours
352-378-2473 local

accessories
restoration parts

See full listing in **Section Two** under **comprehensive parts**

Passenger Car Supply
102 Cloverdale Rd
Swedesboro, NJ 08085
609-467-7966

parts

See full listing in **Section One** under **Chevrolet**

Rick's First Generation Camaro Parts & Accessories
420 Athena Dr
Athens, GA 30601
800-359-7717; FAX: 706-548-8581
E-mail: firstgen@negia.net

accessories
parts

See full listing in **Section One** under **Chevelle/Camaro**

woodgraining

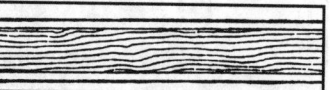

Adams Custom Engines Inc
806 Glendale Ave
Sparks, NV 89431-5720
775-358-8070; FAX: 775-358-8040

restorations

See full listing in **Section Two** under **restoration shops**

Automotive Specialties
11240 E Sligh Ave
Seffner, FL 33584
800-676-1928

restoration

See full listing in **Section Two** under **steering wheels**

RL Bailey Co
27902 45th Ave S
Auburn, WA 98001
PH/FAX: 253-854-5247
E-mail: rbailey2@gte.net

restorations
steering wheels
woodgraining

Woodgraining a specialty. Steering wheel restoration. Full service restoration shop. Insurance claims.

Classics Plus LTD
N7306 Lakeshore Dr
N Fond du Lac, WI 54937
888-923-1007

restoration

See full listing in **Section Two** under **steering wheels**

Dan's Restorations
PO Box 144
Snake Hill Rd
Sand Lake, NY 12153
518-674-2061

woodgraining

Mail order only. Authentic 18th Century woodgraining on dashboards and interior trim. Metal is carefully stripped, epoxy primed and a careful, multi-step process is used to create woodgrain and port structure. If there is a good sample of original graining, it is used as a guide to duplicate the grain and color in the new finish. Finished pieces are hand buffed to a soft luster as seen on fine marine woodwork.

Dash Graining by Mel Erikson
31 Meadow Rd
Kings Park, NY 11754
PH/FAX: 516-544-1102 days
516-360-7789 nights

dashboard
restoration

Mail order and open shop. 5 days a week 9 am to 6 pm. Active service in dashboard restoration for 15 years. Most business conducted by phone and UPS delivery. Phone estimates given. A hand process, matching original patterns as close to original as possible. Also restoration of some clock and speedometer faces. Can also restore exterior simulated wood for station wagons. Restoration of simulated wood finish on metal dashboards and interior trim for autos, 1920s-1950s.

Walter A Finner
11131 Etiwanda Ave
Northridge, CA 91326
818-363-6076

woodgraining

Mail order and open shop. Many years' experience. Many show car winners. Send SASE for information.

Gold Plated Emblems & Auto Accessories
2095 Pine Ridge Rd
Naples, FL 34109
800-231-7765, 941-592-5552
FAX: 941-597-0768
E-mail: sales@goldplated.com

plating equipment
wood dash kits

See full listing in **Section Two** under **plating & polishing**

Bill Gratkowski
515 N Petroleum St
Titusville, PA 16354
814-827-1782 eves
814-827-6111 days

woodgraining

Mail order and open shop. Have been doing woodgraining for 20 years, national show winning quality, low prices, quick turnaround, with references.

C D Hall
1217 Newport Ave
Long Beach, CA 90804-4014
PH/FAX: 562-494-5048

woodgraining

Mail order and professional open work shop. 9 am to 6 pm PST. Serving the West Coast and nationwide. Specializing in old time woodgraining faux finishes. Quality craftsmanship for your classics, woodies, hot rods, sports, antique interiors and exteriors. All work is done by hand with only fine artwork in mind. Most work completed in 3 to 4 weeks or less.

Bob Kennedy Woodgraining Service
8609 Ocean View
Whittier, CA 90605
562-693-8739

woodgraining

Mail order and open shop. Monday-Friday 8 am to 5 pm. Duplication of original grain.

Mar-Ke Woodgraining | woodgraining
1102 Hilltop Dr
Loveland, CO 80537
970-663-7803; FAX: 970-663-1138

Woodgraining dashes and moldings for autos, trucks. Metal or plastic trim pieces, original and custom. Specializing in burling.

Pilgrim's Auto Restorations | bodywork, metal fabrication, paint, restoration
3888 Hill Rd
Lakeport, CA 95453
707-262-1062; FAX: 707-263-6956
E-mail: pilgrims@pacific.net

See full listing in **Section Two** under **restoration shops**

woodwork

Arrow Fastener Co Inc | nail guns, rivet tools, staple guns
271 Mayhill St
Saddle Brook, NJ 07663

See full listing in **Section Two** under **tools**

Bassett Classic Restoration | parts, plating, restoration, service
2616 Sharon St, Suite D
Kenner, LA 70062
PH/FAX: 504-469-2982
(have auto switching device)

See full listing in **Section One** under **Rolls-Royce/Bentley**

Bicknell Engine Company | parts, repair, restoration
7055 Dayton Rd
Enon, OH 45323
937-864-5224

See full listing in **Section One** under **Buick/McLaughlin**

Bonnets Up | restoration
5736 Spring St
Clinton, MD 20735
301-297-4759

See full listing in **Section Two** under **coachbuilders & designers**

Calimer's Wheel Shop | wooden wheels
30 E North St
Waynesboro, PA 17268
717-762-5056; FAX: 717-762-5021

See full listing in **Section Two** under **wheels & wheelcovers**

Classic Wood Mfg | wood kits, wood replacement
1006 N Raleigh St
Greensboro, NC 27405
336-691-1344; FAX: 336-273-3074

Mail order and open shop. Monday-Friday 7:30 am to 5 pm EST, appointment advised. Ford Model T and A, Chevrolet 1927-1936, MG T Series and MGA wood kits from stock. Dealer program available to qualifying full-line new parts dealers. Custom made wood for other cars from your old pattern.

County Auto Restoration | bodywork, brakes, restoration, woodwork
6 Gavin Rd
Mt Vernon, NH 03057
603-673-4840

See full listing in **Section Two** under **restoration shops**

Chuck & Judy Cubel | wood parts
PO Box 278
Superior, AZ 85273
520-689-2734
FAX: 520-689-5815, 24 hours
E-mail: chuckjudy.cubel@cwix.com

See full listing in **Section One** under **Ford 1903-1931**

Dashboards Plus | restoration parts, wood dash overlays
336 Cottonwood Ave
Hartland, WI 53029
800-221-8161; FAX: 414-367-9474

See full listing in **Section One** under **Jaguar**

JB Donaldson Co | castings, steering wheels, wood parts
2533 W Cypress
Phoenix, AZ 85009
602-278-4505; FAX: 602-278-1112

See full listing in **Section Two** under **steering wheels**

Enfield Auto Restoration Inc | panel beating, restorations, Rolls-Royce parts, woodworking
4 Print Shop Rd
Enfield, CT 06082
860-749-7917; FAX: 860-749-2836

See full listing in **Section Two** under **restoration shops**

David J Entler Restorations | woodwork
10903 N Main St Ext
Glen Rock, PA 17327-8373
717-235-2112

Monday-Friday 8 am to 5 pm. Structural woodwork restoration for 1933-1936 General Motors bodies. Complete kits or individual pieces, coupes, sedans, trucks, roadsters, sedan deliveries. Rewooding of all bodies. Antique truck body fabrication. 17 years in business.

Glazier Pattern & Coachworks | coachwork, interior woodwork, restoration of wood bodied cars
3720 Loramie-Washington Rd
Houston, OH 45333
937-492-7355; FAX: 937-492-9987
E-mail: s.glazier.fam@juno.com

See full listing in **Section One** under **Chrysler**

Grey Hills Auto Restoration | restoration, service
PO Box 630
51 Vail Rd
Blairstown, NJ 07825
908-362-8232; FAX: 908-362-6796

See full listing in **Section Two** under **restoration shops**

Hatfield Restorations | restoration
PO Box 846
Canton, TX 75103
903-567-6742; FAX: 903-567-0645
E-mail: pathat@vzinet.com

See full listing in **Section Two** under **restoration shops**

Kwik Poly T Distributing Inc | restoration aids
24 St Henry Ct
St Charles, MO 63301
314-724-1065

See full listing in **Section Two** under **restoration aids**

M & T Manufacturing Co | convertible hold-down cables, wooden top bows
30 Hopkins Lane
Peace Dale, RI 02883
401-789-0472; FAX: 401-789-5650
E-mail: sales@mtmfg.com

Mail order only. Monday-Friday 9 am to 5 pm. Manufacturer of wooden top bows for classic convertible cars including VW, Jaguar, Mercedes, Rolls-Royce, old Fords and others. Also manufacturer of convertible hold-down cables. Distributor of domestic and foreign convertible tops and top cables.

Section Two Generalists

Madera Concepts
606 Olive St
Santa Barbara, CA 93101
800-800-1579, 805-962-1579
FAX: 805-962-7359
E-mail: jwayco@west.net

restoration
woodwork
woodwork repair

Woodwork restoration, reveneering and repair specialists. From chips and scratches to total basket cases, we've got you covered. Unsurpassed service, fastest turn-around time, 100 point Concours quality and expert color and veneer matching. OEM replacements for many European vehicles. Call to discuss any repairs you may need. Free phone estimates available on commonly repaired components. Over 1,600 exotic wooden dashboard and interior trim packages for late model cars and trucks. Automotive woodwork is all we do! Web site: www.maderaconcepts.com

Martin Carriage House
350 N Park Ave
Warren, OH 44481
330-395-8442

wood bodies

New all wood bodies for most pre-1912 automobiles. Repair work to save a good original body.

Memoryville USA Inc
1008 W 12th St
Rolla, MO 65401
573-364-1810

restoration

See full listing in **Section Two** under **restoration shops**

New Era Motors
11611 NE 50th Ave, Unit 6
Vancouver, WA 98686
360-573-8788

restoration

Mail order and open shop. Monday-Friday 8 am to 5 pm. Offer complete or partial restoration of any wood framed composite antique or classic automobile body, complete frame-off restorations also available. Seat spring duplicating services performed.

Oak Bows
122 Ramsey Ave
Chambersburg, PA 17201
717-264-2602

top bows

Steam bent top bows duplicating your original bow. All bows steam bent like the original, not glued. No danger of separation. Send patterns, sockets or old bows for duplication. All SASEs will be answered.

Paul's Discount Jaguar Parts
1124 NW 134th Ave
Sunrise
Fort Lauderdale, FL 33323
954-846-7976; FAX: 954-846-9450
E-mail: paulsjag@ix.netcom.com

parts

See full listing in **Section One** under **Jaguar**

Prestige Autowood
140 N Harrison Ave
Campbell, CA 95008
408-370-3705; FAX: 408-370-3792

dashboards

Mail order and open shop. Monday-Saturday 9 am to 6 pm. Manufacture both show quality and OEM replacement hardwood dashboards for Austin-Healey, Lotus, Jaguar, Morgan, MG, Sunbeam, Triumph and other British marques. America's most respected dashboard maker and have been for the past 20 years. Our dashboards will exceed the wildest expectations of the most discriminating customer.

Al Prueitt & Sons Inc
8 Winter Ave
PO Box 158
Glen Rock, PA 17327
717-428-1305, 800-766-0035
FAX: 717-235-4428

restoration
upholstery
woodworking

See full listing in **Section Two** under **restoration shops**

Reinholds Restorations
c/o Rick Reinhold
PO Box 178, 255 N Ridge Rd
Reinholds, PA 17569-0178
717-336-5617; FAX: 717-336-7050

appraisals
repairs
restoration

See full listing in **Section Two** under **restoration shops**

Silver Star Restorations
116 Highway 19
Topton, NC 28781
704-321-4268
E-mail: silverstar@main.nc.us

parts
restoration

See full listing in **Section One** under **Mercedes-Benz**

Vintage Woodworks
PO Box 49
Iola, WI 54945
715-445-3791

upholstery
woodwork

Shop address: Depot St, Iola, WI. All automotive woodworking specializing in Chrysler Town & Country cars. Reproduction parts for Town & Country cars. Custom upholstery work.

Willys Wood
35336 Chaucer Dr
North Ridgeville, OH 44039
440-327-2916

wood parts

See full listing in **Section One** under **Willys**

Wood Excel Ltd
1545 Green Hill Rd
Collegeville, PA 19426
610-584-1725

woodwork

Mail order and open shop. Monday-Friday 10 am to 6 pm. Repair veneer and refinish wood in automobiles including Rolls-Royce, Jaguar, Mercedes-Benz, Packard, Cadillac, Lincoln, etc. If possible, one piece is given free before any business is done.

The Wood N'Carr
3231 E 19th St
Signal Hill, CA 90804
562-498-8730; FAX: 562-985-3360
E-mail: suzyq22222@aol.com

wood parts
woodwork

Mail order and open shop. Monday-Friday 8 am to 4:30 pm. Automotive woodworking, specializing in woodies from stock to hot rod. Also replacement wood parts for 1932-1936 Ford V8 other than station wagon. In business for over 20 years. Work on all makes and models. Have expanded into a newer, bigger facility at a new location. Also garnish wood trims for Jag, Bentley, Rolls, Mercedes too. Web site: www.kars.com/showcase/woodn'carr/

The Woodie Works
245 VT Rt 7A
Arlington, VT 05250
PH/FAX: 802-375-9305
E-mail: dkwoodie@vermontel.com

woodworking

Mail order and open shop. Monday-Saturday 9 am to 6 pm. Complete woodworking shop dedicated to the preservation of the wooden vehicle. Provide a complete range of services including research and design, repair, reproduction, replacement and refinishing. New work or custom work is welcome, as are unusual marques, trucks and commercial vehicles. Complete patterns for 1933-1936 Ford wagons, 1949-1951 Ford wagons and 1941-1954 Chevrolet Cantrells in house. If your vehicle has wooden parts, you should be talking to us.

Tourguide:

Generalists

Planning a trip? Or perhaps you would just like to know what old-car resources are in your home territory. In either case, the tourguide to Section Two will help.

This tourguide offers you an alphabetical listing of old car generalists with open shops by state and foreign country. Simply turn to the page number indicated for complete information on the object of your visit, including hours of operation, complete address, and phone number.

316   Ridgefield Auto Upholstery, Ridgefield
233   Sports & Classics, Darien
213   Peter Tytla Artist, East Lyme
298   Vintage Glass USA, Tolland
361   Vintage Racing Services, Stratford

Delaware

266   Jess Auto Supply Co, Wilmington
426   Performance Shop, Newark

Florida

363   Antique Automobile Radio Inc, Palm Harbor
252   Berliner Classic Motorcars Inc, Dania
246   Bill & Brad's Tropical Formula, Clearwater
374   BMC Classics Inc, New Smyrna Beach
203   Car Critic, Naples
354   Chrome Masters, Tallahassee
376   Classics and Customs, Largo
376   Coach Builders Limited Inc, High Springs
241   Crane Cams Inc, Daytona Beach
420   Daytona MIG, Daytona Beach
226   Deltran Corporation, Deland
355   Gold Plated Emblems & Auto Accessories, Naples
219   Jerry Goldsmith Promos, Lakeland
379   Harbor Auto Restoration, Pompano Beach
231   Hoffman Automotive Distributor, Hilliard
266   IMCADO Manufacturing Co, Umatilla
360   Moroso Motorsports Park, Palm Beach Gardens
267   National Parts Depot, Gainesville
338   Paragon Models & Art, Cape Coral
356   Pot Metal Restorations, Tallahassee
356   Precision Pot Metal/Bussie Restoration Inc, Orange Park
255   Rader's Relics, Winter Park
356   Samson Technology Corporation, Davie
223   Scale Collectors USA, Miami
385   Chris Smith's Creative Workshop Motorcar Restoration, Dania
239   Ed Strain Inc, Pinellas Park
278   Ed Strain Inc, Pinellas Park
269   Vintage Car Corral, Gainesville

Georgia

202   Auto Appraisal Service, Augusta
251   Auto Quest Investment Cars Inc, Tifton
259   Cast Aluminum Repair, Conyers
375   Classic Car Works Ltd, Jasper
403   The Generation Gap, Byron
275   Jim Osborn Reproductions Inc, Lawrenceville
216   Red Baron's Antiques, Atlanta
413   Specialty Power Window, Forsyth

Illinois

427   4-Speeds by Darrell, Vermilion
420   A & I Supply, North Pekin
252   Chicago Car Exchange, Lake Bluff
230   Desert Dog Auto Parts Inc, Westchester
293   Gas Tank Renu, Rockford
421   HTP America Inc, Arlington Heights
305   Instrument Services Inc, Roscoe
305   International Speedometer, Brookfield
364   Marquette Radio, Orland Park
215   Dana Mecum Auctions Inc, Marengo
254   Memory Lane Motors Inc, Lake Bluff
282   Moline Engine Service Inc, Moline
383   Old Coach Works Restoration Inc, Yorkville
282   Partwerks of Chicago, New Lenox
408   Preserve Inc, Hamilton
393   Redi-Strip Company, Roselle
384   Restorations Unlimited II Inc, Cary
439   Sailorette's Nautical Nook, Wilmington

385   Sanders Antique Auto Restoration, Rockford
356   Star Chrome, Chicago
208   Sterling Restorations Inc, Sterling
420   Willies Antique Tires, Chicago
388   Wilson's Classic Auto, Congerville

Indiana

322   Collins Metal Spinning, New Palestine
420   Custom Bandsaw Blades, Muncie
262   Fort Wayne Clutch & Driveline, Fort Wayne
337   Grandpa's Attic, Goshen
381   LaVine Restorations Inc, Nappanee
382   Nationwide Auto Restoration, Jeffersonville
393   Pro-Strip, Fort Wayne

Iowa

372   Anderson Restoration, Kanawha
253   Duffy's Collectible Cars, Cedar Rapids
211   Guenther Graphics, LeClaire
330   Uhlenhopp Lock, Clarksville

Kansas

276   Fifth Avenue Graphics, Clay Center
266   Gowen Auto Parts, Coffeyville
422   Superior Equipment, Wichita

Kentucky

372   The Antique Auto Shop, Elsmere
403   Katen and Associates Inc, Lexington

Maine

442   Appleton Garage, West Rockport
337   Karl's Collectibles, Lewiston
382   McCann Auto Restoration, Houlton
215   McIntyre Auctions, East Dixfield
401   Thompson Hill Metalcraft, Berwick
217   J Wood & Co Auctioneers, Stockton Springs

Maryland

378   From Rust To Riches, Mt Airy
262   Quanta Restoration and Performance Products Rising Sun
328   TMC Publications, Baltimore

Massachusetts

427   AAdvanced Transmissions, Worcester
284   Aldrich Auto Supply Inc, Hatfield
358   AM Racing Inc, Danvers
264   Antique Auto Parts Cellar, South Weymouth
201   Antique & Special Interest Car Appraisals, Andover
335   Antiques Warehouse, Eastham
270   JJ Best & Co, Chatham
334   Commonwealth Automotive Restorations, Ashley Falls
311   Dom Corey Upholstery & Antique Auto , Fairhaven
320   Norman D'Amico, Clarksburg
204   Dearborn Automobile Co, Topsfield
235   DeVito Auto Restorations, Weston
392   Ecoclean 2000, Medfield
321   Richard Hurlburt, Greenfield
431   Intercity Lines Inc, Warren
380   Keilen's Auto Restoring, North Attleboro
285   Knight Automotive Engineering Inc, Gloucester
381   Libbey's Classic Car Restoration Center, Shrewsbury
305   Reynolds Speedometer Repair, Danvers
385   Paul Russell & Company, Essex
208   Steele's Appraisal, Maynard
427   Trailers of New England Inc, Palmer
391   Pat Walsh Restorations, Wakefield
444   Wheel Repair Service of New England, Auburn

Michigan
237 Allied Power Brake Co, Detroit
210 Antique Car Paintings, Dearborn Heights
335 Auto Zone, Birmingham
304 Bob's Speedometer Service, Farmington
341 British Only Motorcycles and Parts Inc, Garden City
333 Clark & Clark Specialty Products Inc, Holland
205 Russ Dentico's Sales & Auto Appraisal Consulting, Trenton
377 Deters Restorations, Temperance
415 Eaton Detroit Spring Service Co, Detroit
379 Hyde Auto Body, Auburn Hills
238 Inline Tube, Fraser
238 Muskegon Brake & Dist Co, Muskegon
282 Northwestern Auto Supply Inc, Grand Rapids
439 Original Auto Interiors, Columbus
233 Sherman & Associates Inc, Washington
329 Voss Motors Inc, Southfield
290 Waldron's Antique Exhaust Inc, Nottawa
213 Danny Whitfield, Automotive Artist, Rochester Hills

Minnesota
347 CJ Spray Inc, South St Paul
311 Classtique Upholstery Supply, Isanti
434 Bruce Horkey's Wood & Parts, Windom
355 Iverson Automotive, Minnetonka
281 Jackson's Oldtime Parts, Duluth
421 Northern Tool & Equipment, Burnsville
383 Odyssey Restorations Inc, Spring Lake Park
256 Yesterday's Auto Sales, Minneapolis

Mississippi
266 Wayne Hood, Grenada
436 Slim's Garage, Seminary

Missouri
353 A & A Plating Inc, Independence
256 The Carburetor Shop, Eldon
247 Dr Vinyl and Assoc Ltd, Raytown
407 Fiesta's Classic Car Center, St Louis
341 Harper's Moto Guzzi, Greenwood
367 Independence Porcelain Enamel, Independence
382 Memoryville USA Inc, Rolla
225 Paul's Rod & Bearing Ltd, Parkville
224 Scott Signal Co, Willard

Montana
241 Cam-Pro, Great Falls

Nebraska
202 Auto World Sales, Lincoln
217 Blast From the Past, Gretna
250 S & S Manufacturing Inc, South Sioux City
269 Speedway Motors Inc, Lincoln

Nevada
371 Adams Custom Engines Inc, Sparks

New Hampshire
376 County Auto Restoration, Mt Vernon
286 R & L Engines Inc, Dover
384 Redding Corp, George's Mills
384 Rick's Relics, Pittsburg

New Jersey
275 Addison Generator Inc, Freehold
362 American Honeycomb Radiator Mfg Co, Holmdel
296 American Restorations Unlimited TA, Rochelle Park
256 Arch Carburetor, Newark

373 Automotive Restorations Inc, Bernardsville
394 The Autoworks Ltd, Westwood
203 AVM Automotive Consulting, Montvale
373 Back-In-Time Automotive Restorations, Pompton Lakes
276 Robert D Bliss, Edison
331 Bob's Automotive Machine, Harrison
424 D & D Trailers Inc, Trenton
336 EWA & Miniature Cars USA Inc, Green Brook
428 FATSCO Transmission Parts, Pine Brook
379 Hibernia Auto Restorations Inc, Hibernia
349 Bill Hirsch Auto Parts, Newark
266 Kanter Auto Products, Boonton
416 Kenask Spring Co, Jersey City
196 NMW Products, Raritan
278 M Parker Autoworks Inc, Bellmawr
207 CT Peters Inc Appraisers, Red Bank
412 Rod-1 Shop, Pitman
385 Schaeffer & Long, Magnolia
245 Straw Church Speed Shop, Phillipsburg
429 Street-Wise Performance, Tranquility
287 Thul Auto Parts Inc, Plainfield
386 Town Auto Top Co, Fairfield
387 Widmann's Garage, Hamilton

New York
371 Ace Antique Auto Restoration, Plainview
191 Action Performance Inc, Bohemia
371 Adler's Antique Autos Inc, Stephentown
414 Apple Hydraulics Inc, Calverton
310 Auto-Mat Co, Hicksville
225 The Babbitt Pot, Fort Edward
252 Classic Cars & Parts, Lindenhurst
265 Joe Curto Inc, College Point
446 Dash Graining by Mel Erikson, Kings Park
394 Dependable RV & Auto Service, Lafayette
378 Edgerton Classics Ltd, Camden
219 Get It On Paper, Islip
362 Highland Radiator Inc, Highland
421 Hydraulic Jack Inc, Accord
238 Integrity Machine, Mount Sinai
247 KozaK® Auto Drywash® Inc, Batavia
221 l'art et l'automobile, East Hampton
359 Marcovicci-Wenz Engineering Inc, Ronkonkoma
426 Nyles Haulmark Trailer Sales, Fairport
406 Bill Peters, Rockville Centre
255 Retrospect Automotive, Huntington Station
300 R J & L Automotive Fasteners, Rochester
239 Rochester Clutch & Brake Co, Rochester
278 Rockland Auto Electric, Pearl River
224 Silver Image Photographics, Vestal
208 RL Smith Sales Inc, Rensselaer
224 Spirit Enterprises, Lockport

North Carolina
335 Asheville DieCast, Asheville
349 Automotive Paints Unlimited, Roxboro
388 Clester's Auto Rubber Seals Inc, Salisbury
257 The Old Carb Doctor, Nebo

Ohio
296 Airplane Plastics, Tipp City
374 Bastian Automotive Restoration, Fairfield
251 Jerry Bensinger, Hubbard
252 Bill's Collector Cars, South Point
375 Cars of the Past, Newbury
276 Certified Auto Electric Inc, Oakwood Village
355 CustomChrome Plating Inc, Grafton
355 D & D Plastic Chrome Plating, Toledo
312 Dave's Auto Restoration, Jefferson
442 Dayton Wheel Products, Dayton
306 Denmark Insurance Services, Beachwood

Washington

372 Antique & Classic Car Restorations, Oak Harbor
324 Automotive Bookstore, Seattle
203 Blair Collectors & Consultants, Seattle
211 Creative Wood Sculptures, Ferndale
448 New Era Motors, Vancouver
352 Nostalgic Reflections, Veradale
268 RB's Obsolete Automotive, Edmonds
437 Ultimate Spray-On Truck Bedliner, Sumas
209 USA of Yesterday, Tacoma
413 The V8 Store, Vancouver
269 Vintage Auto Parts Inc, Woodinville
328 Vintage Books, Vancouver

West Virginia

264 Antique Auto Parts, Elkview

Wisconsin

337 International House of Toys, Muskego
380 Ken's Klassics, Muscoda
323 OJ Rallye Automotive, Plymouth
363 Glen Ray Radiators Inc, Wausau
340 Town & Country Toys, Marshall
255 Valenti Classics Inc, Caledonia
387 Vintage Vehicles Co Inc, Wautoma

Australia

257 Midel Pty Ltd, Lakemba, NSW 2195
267 Obsolete Auto Parts Co, Kurrajong, NSW 2758
390 Old Auto Rubber Company, Dunheved, Sydney

Belgium

306 Classic Car Lobby, 4800 Verviers

Canada

323 Auto Nostalgia Enr, Mont St Gregoire, QC
336 The Collector's Guild, Kingston, ON

318 EVA Sports Cars, Vankleek Hill, ON
276 Ferris Auto Electric Ltd, North Bay, ON
382 Memory Lane Motors, Fenelon Falls, ON
268 Pre-Sixties Cars and Parts Ltd, South Guelph, ON
225 Precision Babbitt Service, Beamsville, ON
384 RM Auto Restoration Ltd, Blenheim, ON
268 Special Interest Cars, Oakville, ON
310 Zehr Insurance Brokers Ltd, New Hamburg, ON

Denmark

326 Kosters Motorboghandel, 8900 Randers

England

288 Double S Exhausts Ltd, Cullompton, Devon EX15 1BW
289 London Stainless Steel Exhaust Centre, London SW8 3NP
318 Woolies (I&C Woolstenholmes Ltd), Nr Peterborough PE6 8LD

Germany

325 International Automobile Archives, 85757 Karlsfeld

Italy

325 Giorgio Nada Editore, Vimodrone (Milan) 20090
326 Libreria Dell'Automobile, Milan 20121

Netherlands

362 Blaak Radiateurenbedryf, Heinenoord 3274LA

New Zealand

404 Mint Condition Auto Upholstery, Silverdale
386 Te Puke Vintage Auto Barn, Te Puke

Spain

324 Colleccio d'Automobils de Salvadore Claret, Girona

Switzerland

216 Oldtimer Galerie International, Toffen 3125

Section Three:
Clubs & Organizations

Since it began, the *Hemmings' Vintage Auto Almanac* has sought to present the most comprehensive list of old car hobby clubs and related organizations ever published. Here, with expanded listings and entries, the hobbyist will find six main categories:

Multi-marque clubs. Generally, these organizations welcome anyone with a sincere interest in the old car hobby. They are listed alphabetically by club name.

Marque clubs. These clubs specialize in serving enthusiasts of certain car makes. Some require ownership of the particular marque for membership. They are listed alphabetically by marque.

Registries. These are associations primarily interested in maintaining rosters of owners of particular marques, although some are also structured as actual clubs with activities, dues, events, etc. They are listed alphabetically by marque.

Specialty clubs. These are clubs with a specialized focus such as license plates, racing and other unique car subjects. They are listed alphabetically by club name.

Statewide and local clubs. These are organizations serving hobbyists within specific geographical area. They are listed alphabetically by state.

Legislative watch organizations. This is a listing of groups devoted to promoting and protecting the collector car hobby's interests in legislative matters. National organizations are listed first, followed by state/local groups. National and state/local groups are each listed alphabetically by organization name.

Multi-Marque Clubs

A Merry Car Club
Resp Nieuwlandt Peter
116 Langestraat
9300 Aalst Belgium
011-32-702861; FAX: 011-32-710653

Founded 1985. 250 members. Dedicated to the preservation, restoration and maintenance of American cars over 25 years old. Bi-monthly publication, Dutch/French, 40 pages, lots of stories, technical and humorous. 10 plus or minus meetings per year. Spare parts service and others. Dues: 2.100 BEF.

Aberdeen Antique and Classic Car Club Inc
10470 Hwy 382
Aberdeen, MS 39730
601-369-8245

Founded 1987. 15 families. Non-profit organization with the purpose of promoting the restoration and preservation of vehicles through car shows. Have an annual car show the 2nd Saturday of April each year and proceeds go to local charities at Christmas. Dues: $10/year.

American Car Club Hungary ACCH
Dolgozo u 11/B 3/10
Budapest H-1184 Hungary
00-36-1-2830883; FAX: 00-36-1-290-9643
E-mail: acch@mail.geocities.com

Founded 1995. 300 members. All information is on our web site. Dues: 3000/year HUF. Web site: www.geocities.com/motorcity/6151

American Station Wagon Owners Association
6110 Bethesda Way
Indianapolis, IN 46254-5060
317-291-0321
E-mail: aswoa@aol.com

Founded 1996. 350+ members. Dedicated to the enjoyment and preservation of this great vehicle and is open to all makes, models and fans of wagons. Members receive a quarterly, full color magazine, *The Wagon Roundup*. Free classified ads for all members. Club merchandise. 1999 Third National Convention in Charlotte, NC, is world's largest all station wagon show. Call or write for more information. Dues: $25/year.

American Truck Historical Society
300 Office Park Dr
Birmingham, AL 35223
205-870-0566; FAX: 205-870-3069
E-mail: aths@mindspring.com

For membership information, contact at the above address: Larry L Scheef, General Manager. Founded 1971. 21,000+ members. Maintains library and archives containing history, photos and films of the truck industry. Bi-monthly magazine, *Wheels of Time*. Annual *ATHS Show Time* color album, $20. Dues: $25/year US, $35/year Canada (US funds). Web site: www.aths.org

chapters:

Alabama   *Heart of Dixie Chapter*, Larry L Scheef, PO Box 531168, Birmingham, AL 35253-1168, 205-870-0566

Arizona   *Arizona Chapter*, Don Robertson, PO Box 125, Jerome, AZ 86331, 520-634-0053

     Northern Arizona Chapter, Joseph O Eisenman, 444 W Carondelet Rd, Prescott, AZ 86301, 520-778-1994

California   *Central California Chapter*, Terry D Fortier, PO Box 12004, Fresno, CA 93776, 559-275-0444

     Central Coast Chapter of California, Dan Theroux, 790 Thompson Ave, Nipomo, CA 93444, 805-929-3305

     Redwood Chapter, Dave Anderson, 795 Richardson Ln, Cotati, CA 94931, 707-792-0436

     San Diego Chapter, Rick Storrs, 1214 La Cresta Blvd, El Cajon, CA 92021, 619-448-8141

     Southern California Chapter, Steve Sackett, 25424 Jacklyn Ave, Moreno Valley, CA 92557, 909-247-6716

American Truck Historical Society chapters (continued)

Westside San Joaquin Valley Chapter, Leland Sparks, 13659 Badger Flat Rd, Los Banos, CA 93635, 209-826-9088

Colorado   *Intermountain West Chapter,* Ralph Selby, 3092 S Pennsylvania St, Englewood, CO 80110, 303-781-6109

Connecticut   *Nutmeg Chapter,* Al Newhouse, 74 Dunn Rd, Longmeadow, MA 01106, 413-567-1451

Florida   *Central Florida Chapter,* John E Gormican, 980 W McCormick Rd, Apopka, FL 32703-8957, 407-889-9252

South Florida Chapter, Cliff Gibson, 9725 SW 146th St, Miami, FL 33176, 305-251-5839 home, 305-825-5195 work

Georgia   *North Georgia Chapter,* Charles Adams, 1532 Adair Mill Rd, Cleveland, GA 30528, 706-865-5330

Idaho   *Snake River Chapter,* Guy Burnham, 12030 W Savage Dr, Boise, ID 83713-1751, 208-939-0216

Illinois   *Northwest Illinois Chapter,* Dale Olson, 2250 Wessman Pkwy, Cherry Valley, IL 61016, 815-332-4496

Windy City Chapter, Bill Schutt, 4106 Gilbert Ave, Western Springs, IL 60558-1236, 708-246-2406

Indiana   *Auburn Heritage Truck Chapter,* Levi Gleixner, 4120 Westlane Rd, Fort Wayne, IN 46815, 219-485-1895

Northwest Indiana Chapter, Curt Zehner, 1166 Salt Creek Rd, Burns Harbor, IN 46304, 219-787-8166

Iowa   *Central Iowa,* Dave Koehler, 817 S 3rd St, Winterset, IA 50273, 515-462-4806

Heartland Chapter, Mike Pagel, 1809 Mulberry Ave, Musentine, IA 52761, 319-263-8586

Kentucky   *Blue Grass Chapter,* Gene Bills, 1602 Cantrill Dr, Lexington, KY 40505, 606-299-0166

Derby City Chapter, Kenneth Rabeneck, 4411 Rudy Ln, Louisville, KY 40207, 502-897-5449

Maine   *Pine Tree Chapter,* George Sprowl Sr, PO Box 220, Searsmont, ME 04973, 207-342-5621

Maryland   *Baltimore-Washington Chapter,* Henry Fowler, 38777 Blossom Dr, Mechanicsville, MD 20659, 301-884-3390

Delmarva Chapter, Alan Daisey, RD 3 Box 485 Atlantic St, Fenwick Island, DE 19944, 302-539-5074

Mason-Dixon Chapter, Allen Bond, PO Box 62, Shepherdstown, WV 25443-0062, 304-876-6790

Massachusetts   *Antique Truck Club of New England Chapter,* James W Flett, 800 Pleasant St, Belmont, MA 02178, 617-484-8500

Michigan   *Michigan Chapter,* Warren Cooley, 505 W Ash St, Mason, MI 48854-1553, 517-676-5910

Southeast Michigan Chapter, Bob Ludwig, 5090 Timberview Ct, Saline, MI 48176, 734-429-0619

West Michigan Chapter, Robert Roelofs, 10333 Eastern Ave SE, Wayland, MI 49348, 616-698-2912

Minnesota   *Hiawathaland Chapter,* Joe Becker, 2401 Becker Dr, Albert Lea, MN 56007, 507-373-8513, 507-373-8598

Minnesota Metro Chapter, Jim McCarl, 5000 W 114th St, Bloomington, MN 55437-3417, 612-888-5868

Missouri   *Gateway Chapter,* Virgil Tucker, 1853 Jessie Cir, High Ridge, MO 63049-3821, 314-677-2207

Ozarks-4 State Chapter, Jim Steele, 1222 N Hillcrest Ave, Springfield, MO 65802-1134, 417-869-1348

Pony Express Chapter, Gary Rosa, 7117 Lundeen Dr, St Joseph, MO 64505, 816-390-9763

Three Trails Chapter, Dan McFarland, 29940 W 95th St, De Soto, KS 66018, 913-583-1974

Nevada   *Sierra Nevada Chapter,* Arch Libby, 220 Hercules Dr, Sparks, NV 89436-9213, 775-425-0644

New Hampshire   *Granite State Chapter,* Don Smith, PO Box 113, Barrington, NH 03825, 603-664-9761

New Jersey   *Metro Jersey Chapter,* Scott Baker, 10 South St, Mahwah, NJ 07430, 201-512-0056

South Jersey Shore Chapter, Cliff Sharp, PO Box 134, Mauricetown, NJ 08329-0114, 609-785-0431

New Mexico   *New Mexico Chapter,* Paul McLaughlin, 2720 Tennessee NE, Albuquerque, NM 87110, 505-296-2554

New York   *Central New York Chapter,* Ollie Farstler, 6564 Minoa Bridgeport Rd, East Syracuse, NY 13057, 315-656-7813

Hudson Mohawk Chapter, John A Wojtowicz, 14 Plant Rd, Clifton Park, NY 12065-4313, 518-371-6907

Long Island Chapter, Denis Ryan, 16 Wainscott Dr, Sound Beach, NY 11789-2339, 516-821-4845

Twin Tiers Chapter, Robert Messersmith, 949 Shirley Rd, Newark Valley, NY 13811, 607-642-8624

Western New York Chapter, George Pursel Jr, 9673 Linwood Rd, Le Roy, NY 14482, 716-768-6765

North Carolina   *Piedmont Carolina Chapter,* Nollie W Neill Jr, PO Box 38, Ennice, NC 28623-0038, 336-657-8083

Ohio   *Black Swamp Chapter,* Richard Flahiff, 6422 W US Rt 6, Gibsonburg, OH 43431, 419-638-3200

Buckeye Vintage Haulers, Dudley Debolt Jr, 8821 Winchester Rd, Carroll, OH 43112-9620, 614-837-7013

Northeast Ohio Chapter, Ted Straka, 8720 Chardon Rd, Kirtland, OH 44094, 440-256-3666

Oklahoma   *Heartland Sooner Chapter,* Andrew Seigel, 2130 S Owasso Ave, Tulsa, OK 74114, 918-583-1101

Oregon *Oregon Trail Chapter*, Ken Goudy, 15140 S Burkstrom Rd, Oregon City, OR 97045, 503-657-8359

State of Jefferson Chapter, Jack L Owen, 160 Hawkins Flat Rd, Crescent City, CA 95531, 707-458-3154

Pennsylvania *Philadelphia Chapter*, George Kaiser, 1137 Walnut St, Collingdale, PA 19023, 610-586-4759

Susquehanna Valley Chapter, Carl L Ellerman, RR 2 Box 226, Landisburg, PA 17040-9605, 717-789-3375

Rhode Island *Ocean State Vintage Haulers Chapter*, Antonio Forte, 55 Whipple Rd, Smithfield, RI 02917, 401-231-4651

South Carolina *Palmetto Central Chapter*, Robert McLeod, 141 Peachtree St, Gilbert, SC 29054, 803-892-3130

Tennessee *Chattanooga Chapter*, George A Grant, 4830 Woodland Cir, Hixson, TN 37343-4129, 423-875-5191

Music City Chapter, *James Waller, 4849 Lynn Dr, Nashville, TN 37211-4212, 615-781-8611*

Texas *Hi-Plains Chapter*, Glenn Lavender, 5339 Tradewinds, Amarillo, TX 79106, 806-379-8196

Vermont *Green Mountain Chapter*, Joe Phelan, 1335 Gulf Rd, Perkinsville, VT 05151, 802-263-5458; FAX: 802-263-5496; E-mail: grnmtaths@worldnet.att.net

Virginia *Shenandoah Valley Chapter*, Glenn D Martin, 107 Hickory Ln, Bridgewater, VA 22812-9556, 540-828-4728

Virginia Tidewater Chapter, Louis A Alberti, 7018 Basswood Rd, Frederick, MD 21703-7136, 301-682-8135

Washington *Blue Mountain Chapter*, Nick Plucker, Rt 1 Box 235, Touchet, WA 99360-9774, 509-394-2413

Inland Empire Chapter, Ric Hall, 1020 W Knox, Spokane, WA 99205, 509-328-3942

Northwest Chapter, Roy Friis, 6518 32nd Ave NW, Olympia, WA 98502-9519, 360-866-7716

Wisconsin *Beer City Chapter*, James Duclon, 10833 W Copeland Ave, Hales Corners, WI 53130, 414-425-3545

Southern Wisconsin Chapter, Danny Sheafor, Rt 3 Box 69, Richland Center, WI 53581, 608-647-2515

Wyoming *Wyoming Cowboy Chapter*, Robert Campbell, 4 Riggs Rd, Shoshoni, WY 82649, 307-856-5743

Australia *Australian Chapter*, Michael Owen, PO Box 224, Bayswater 3153, Victoria, 03 97296542

Canada *Alberta Chapter*, Byron Rutt, 15 Simon Fraser Blvd W, Lethbridge, AB T1K 4P9, 403-329-1481

BC Interior Chapter, Roger O Dillon, 430-1260 Raymer Ave, Kelowna, BC V1W 3S5, 250-862-8840

BC Pioneers Chapter, Richard Stevenson, 3940-254th St, Aldergrove, BC V4W 2R3, 604-856-7432

Saskatchewan Chapter, Lorne Hart, PO Box 295, Craik, SK S0G 0V0, 306-734-2832

Southwestern Ontario "Old Trucks & Friends" Chapter, Shirley White, 19608 Hurontario St, Caledon, ON L0N 1C0, 519-942-4033

Vancouver Island Chapter, Ed Petillion, PO Box 333, Shawnigan Lake, BC V0R 2W0, 250-743-7818

Antique Automobile Club of America
501 W Governor Road
PO Box 417
Hershey, PA 17033
717-534-1910 AACA
717-534-2082 library
FAX: 717-534-9101

Founded 1935. 55,000 members. Dedicated to the preservation, restoration and maintenance of automobiles and automotive history. Bi-monthly publication, *Antique Automobile*. Prospective membership sponsor not mandatory. Library and research center services available. AACA Museum Inc project well under way. Dues: $26/year (includes spouse).

regions:

Alabama *Boll Weevil Region*, Allen F Kahl, 6 Palomino Rd, Phenix City, AL 36869

Catahoula Junque Collectors Assoc Region, Paula Gould, 97 Model T Cir, Monroeville, AL 36460

Central Alabama Region, Marsha Killian, 527 Sheila Blvd, Prattville, AL 36066

Deep South Region, Edward Anderson, 3170 Meadow Ln, Mobile, AL 36608

Dixie Region, David H Boyd, 15041 Hwy 69 N, Northport, AL 35475

Muscle Shoals Region, Billy D Hendrix, 143 McGraw Cir, Anderson, AL 35610

North Alabama Region, Robert Larrabee, 6619 Robinhood Ln NW, Huntsville, AL 35806

Northeast Alabama Region, Kitta Vanpelt, 108 Tabor Ct, Gadsden, AL 35901

South Alabama Region, Minnie P Casey, 122 Casey St, Brewton, AL 36426

Tennessee Valley Region, Lloyd W Culp, 1819 Corrine Ave SW, Decatur, AL 35601

Alaska *Antique Auto Mushers of Alaska Region*, Kenneth O Stout, 6208 E 34th Ave, Anchorage, AK 99504

Vernon L Nash AAC of Fairbanks Region, William Chace, 2364 Lori Ln, North Pole, AK 99705

Arizona *AACME Region*, Karen Rodgers, PO Box 48477, Phoenix, AZ 85075

Metro Phoenix Region, Kathi Waterman, 909 W St John Rd, Phoenix, AZ 85023

Sedona Car Club Region, Joseph A Tulley Jr, 2320 Buckboard Rd, Sedona, AZ 86336

Tucson Region, Peter M Gariepy, 4910 E Bermuda St, Tucson, AZ 85712

Antique Automobile Club of America regions (*continued*)

California   *Antelope Valley Region*, Janet Best, 20502 W Ave D, Lancaster, CA 93536

Cabrillo Region, Jack Passey Jr, 425 Hecker Pass Rd, Watsonville, CA 95076

California Region, Lloyd D Riggs, 880 Hawthorne Dr, Walnut Creek, CA 94596

El Camino Region, Robert B Tinkey, 2108 Sandpoint Dr, Modesto, CA 95458

Foothills Region, Richard E Eckert, 1623 Ben Roe Dr, Los Altos, CA 94024-6241

Golden Gate Region, Randell W Sanders, 2 Bayhills Dr, San Rafael, CA 94903

Kern County Region, C E Trotter, 607 Vista Verde, Bakersfield, CA 93309

Korean Antique Automobile Region, Jchoo S Kimm, 3807 Wilshire Blvd #520, Los Angeles, CA 90010

Monterey Bay Classic European Motorcycle Club Region, Timothy D Riley, PO Box 7411, Spreckels, CA 93962

Mother Lode Region, Diantha Potter, PO Box 323, Columbia, CA 95310

Northern CA Antique Motorcycle Region, Lloyd Riggs, 880 Hawthorne Dr, Walnut Creek, CA 94546

Orange County Region, Kenneth A Brody, 19303 Barroso St, Rowland Heights, CA 91748

Palm Springs Region, Charles E Chappel, 992 W Hoffer St, Banning, CA 92220

Redwood Empire Region, Margaret Bawden, 7771 Healdsburg Ave #12, Sebastopol, CA 95472

Salinas Valley Region, Thomas J Huff, 22661 Murietta Rd, Salinas, CA 93908

San Diego Region, Sheldon Jurist, 6586 Salizar St, San Diego, CA 92111

San Diego Region, Fallbrook Vintage Car Chapter, Don Kramer, PO Box 68, Fallbrook, CA 92028

San Luis Obispo Region, John Osborne, 4240 Rancho Rd, Templeton, CA 93465

Santa Barbara Region, Dennis Ashley, 2736 Cuesta Rd, Santa Barbara, CA 93105

Santa Clarita Valley Region, Warren C Russell, 23649 Mill Valley Rd, Valencia, CA 91385

Southern California Region, Joe Pirrone, 2454 232nd St, Torrance, CA 90501

Southern California Region, Valley Chapter, John H Avans, 23614 Neargate Dr, Newhall, CA 91321

Southwestern Two-Wheelers Region, Harry A McGill, 1261 Emory St, Imperial Beach, CA 91932

Sun and Sand Region, Lloyd Miller, 41870 Yucca Ln, Bermuda Dunes, CA 92201

Valle Del Sur Region, Raymond Fairfield, 16481 Jackson Oaks Dr, Morgan Hill, CA 95037

Valley of the Flowers Region, Dott Brackin, 4408 Titan Ave, Lompoc, CA 93436

Colorado   *Poudre Valley Region*, Larry K Noller, PO Box 496, Wellington, CO 80549

Rocky Mountain Region, J D Bernard, 14706 E 134th Pl, Brighton, CO 80601

Rocky Mountain Region, Denver Chapter, Ted G Rossi, 1325 W 148th Ave, Westminster, CO 80020

Rocky Mountain Region, Ye Olde Auto Club Chapter, Robert L Durr, 1621 E 95th Ave, Thornton, CO 80229

Connecticut   *Central Connecticut Region*, George Scheyd, 97 Fleetwood Rd, Newington, CT 06111

Fairfield County Connecticut Region, William Seuch, 38 Rampart Rd, Norwalk, CT 06854

Gateway Antique Auto Club Region, Peter A Cavanna, 636 Hope St, Stamford, CT 06907

Housatonic Valley Region, Albert T Yankowski, 46 Rolling Ridge Rd, Shelton, CT 06484

Shoreline Antique Auto Club Region, Larry Burridge, 45 Essex Rd, Westbrook, CT 06498

Westerly-Pawcatuck Region, James Varas, 10 Marlin Dr, Pawcatuck, CT 06379

Delaware   *Brandywine Region*, Barry I Beck, 2722 Barnsley Rd, Wilmington, DE 19808

Florida   *Ancient City Region*, John Guarnieri, 410 23rd St, St Augustine, FL 32095

Azalea Region, Harry Burridge, 513 Emmett St, Palatka, FL 32177

Cape Canaveral Region, Arthur G Griffin Jr, 2556 Sellers Ln, Melbourne, FL 32940

Edison Region, John M Scoville, 3717 SW 21st Pl, Cape Coral, FL 33914

Florida Region, Richard T Gauchat, 737 Galloway Ct, Winter Springs, FL 32708

Florida West Coast Region, Frank Brown, 7400 Bay St NE, St Petersburg, FL 33702

Fort Lauderdale Region, Larry McPherson, 999 NE 37th St, Oakland Park, FL 33334

Highland Lakes Region, Robert H Harford, 501 Lake Josephine Shores, Sebring, FL 33872

Hillsborough Region, William Fernandez, 7214 Flowerfield Dr, Tampa, FL 33615

Indian River Region, A C Bowser, 49 Cache Cay Dr, Vero Beach, FL 32963

Kingdom of the Sun Region, Carol A Scoglio, 2506 NE 19th Ct, Ocala, FL 34470

Kissimmee-St Cloud Region, C Gordon Matthews, 715 Maryland Ave, St Cloud, FL 34769

Lemon Bay Region, David A Schramm, PO Box 5143, Englewood, FL 34224

Lemon Bay Region, Royal Palm Chapter, Richard F Ellsworth, PO Box 381151, Murdock, FL 33938

Lemon Bay Region, Venice Chapter, Betty J Poetker, 3267 Meadow Run Dr, Venice, FL 34293

Miracle Strip Region, Robert B Porter, 306 Greenwood Cir, Panama City, FL 32407

Naples-Marco Island Region, Dominic DiSarro, 3820 Groton Ct, Naples, FL 34112

North Central Florida Region, Sherwin N Karsh, 5918 CR 219, Melrose, FL 32666

Northeast Florida Region, Larry Smart, 1724 Debbie Ln, Orange Park, FL 32073

Peace River Region, William Hoyle, PO Box 510508, Punta Gorda, FL 33951

Richey Region, Robert H Snyder, 9903 San Mateo Way, Apt P H, Port Richey, FL 34668

South Florida Region, Bob B Mayer, 10285 SW 135th St, Miami, FL 33176

Space Coast Region, John W Larson, 1925 Fosse Way, Titusville, FL 32796

Sunshine Region, W Arnold Slight, 1197 Larchmont Dr, Englewood, FL 34223

Sunshine Region, Rare Birds of Florida Chapter, Ann M Bell, 4982 Hubner Cir, Sarasota, FL 34241

Suwannee River Region, Ralph P Towner, Rt 8 Box 739, Lake City, FL 32055

Tallahassee Region, Diane McCarthy, 7707 Cornucopia Ln, Tallahassee, FL 32308

Treasure Coast Region, Michael Mucci, 825 Krueger Pkwy, Stuart, FL 34996

Vintage Auto Club of Palm Beach Region, John Hiscock, 13721 Edith Rd, Loxahatchee, FL 33470

Vintage Wheels of Manatee County Region, Robert C Green, 5010 34th Ave E, Bradenton, FL 34208

Volusia Region, Jennie Pausewang, 2923 Paolini Dr, Deland, FL 32720

West Florida Region, Harold Jackson, 5597 Grande Lagoon Ct, Pensacola, FL 32507

Wheels in Motion Flagler County Region, Ronald Meyer, PO Box 1656, Flagler Beach, FL 32136

Georgia *Apple Country of North Georgia Region*, Roy W Smith, 22 Logan St, Ellijay, GA 30540

Artesian City Region, John B Kelly Jr, 104 Cornelia Dr, Americus, GA 31709

Athens, Georgia Region, Thomas E Cothran, 1361 Cole Dr, Carnesville, GA 30521

Brunswick-Golden Isles Region, Brian J Mallon, 124 Pine Valley, St Simons Island, GA 31522

Cherokee Region, Curtis Martin, 35 Walker Rd NW, Cartersville, GA 30121

Clocktower Region, Lynda Moulton, PO Box 2684, Rome, GA 30164

Coastal Georgia of Savannah Region, John A Pierce, 9 Pipers Pond Ln, Savannah, GA 31404

Gascar Region, Gerald Melchiors, 5066 Autumn Tr, Grovetown, GA 30813

Georgia-Alabama Region, Willis R Ball, 207 Woodfield Cir, Grange, GA 30240

Griffin Piedmont Region, Kenneth F Youngblood, 4732 W McIntosh Rd, Griffin, GA 30223

Middle Georgia Region, Marion Green, 309 Bonanza Dr, Bonaire, GA 31005

Northeast Georgia Antique Auto Region, Raymond E Collins, PO Box 28, Cleveland, GA 30528

Northwest Georgia Region, Bill Maddox, 507 Tyson Dr, Tunnel Hill, GA 30755

Pecan Region, Harry C Jayne III, PO Box 2037, Thomasville, GA 31799

Southeastern Region, Timothy W Harr, 611 Big Canoe, Jasper, GA 30143

Sowega Region, Lee West, 116 Flint River Heights Rd, Bainbridge, GA 31717

Tiftarea Region, Frank E Branch, 1215 N Wilson Ave, Tifton, GA 31794

West Georgia Region, Bill Crowley, 301 Spinks Rd, Temple, GA 30179

Hawaii *Aloha Region*, Art Medeiros, 3318 Hoolulu St, Honolulu, HI 96815

Illinois *Alden Ponds Region*, James F Blinder, 14518 O'Brien Rd, Harvard, IL 60033

Blackhawk Region, Robert G Meline, 8420 Winnebago Ln, Byron, IL 61010

Antique Automobile Club of America regions *(continued)*

Illinois Brass Touring Region, David G Weishaar, 25657 S Pinewood Ln, Monee, IL 60449

Illinois Region, Robert G Meline, 8420 Winnebago Ln, Byron, IL 61010

Illinois Region, Des Plaines Valley Chapter, Lee E Nelson, 522 S Washington St, Lockport, IL 60441

Illinois Region, Fox Valley Chapter, Wm Dale Woosley, 640 Eastview St, Elgin, IL 60120

Illinois Region, Gas & Brass Chapter, Donald H Sonichsen, 308 W Kentucky Rd, Beecher, IL 60401

Illinois Region, Momence Chapter, Robert Salm, 1447 Westminster Ln, Bourbonnais, IL 60914

Illinois Region, North Shore Chapter, James M Rubenstein, 2880 Idlewood Ln, Highland Park, IL 60035

Illinois Region, Silver Springs Chapter, Herschel M Cox, 812 Warren St, Earlville, IL 60518

Illinois Region, Waukegan Chapter, George Schurrer, 5502 Chasefield Cir, McHenry, IL 60050

Illinois Valley Region, Jim Saal, 622 N Church, Princeton, IL 61356

Mississippi Valley Region, Jim Scott, 3210 15th St A, Moline, IL 61265

Muddy T Region, Lyle Sheley, 3491 N Meridian Rd, Rockford, IL 61101

Southern Illinois Region, William L Morse, 396 May Apple Ln, Carbondale, IL 62901

Indiana *Snapper's Brass and Gas Touring Region*, Davis Staadt, 16617 Harper Rd, New Haven, IN 46744

White River Valley Region, James B Nelson, 820 Millerwood Dr, Lebanon, IN 46052

Iowa *Cedar Rapids Region*, Paul Kumley, 253 38th Dr SE, Apt 7, Cedar Rapids, IA 52403

Cedar Valley Region, Steven M Walker, 2534 W 9th St, Waterloo, IA 50702

Des Moines Region, Al D Edmond, 6900 Forest Ct, Des Moines, IA 50311

Iowa Great Lakes Region, Everett Amis, 2190 435th St, Greenville, IA 51343

Iowa Valley Region, Bruce A Platteter, 470 W Boise Ct, Riverside, IA 52327

Marshalltown Area Restorers Region, James C Willey, 1107 S 4th St, Marshalltown, IA 50158

Niappra Region, Vicki Anderson, 1235 Nash Ave, Kanawha, IA 50447

Niva Region, Jean Groth, 340 23rd SW, Mason City, IA 50401

North Idaho-Phans Region, Larry Cooke, 326 S Florence Ave, Sandpoint, ID 83864

Tall Corn Region, Wm B Shreve, PO Box 424, Boone, IA 50036

Kansas *Cherokee Strip Region*, Michael W Jarvis, 200 N A Street, Arkansas City, KS 67005

Lawrence Region, Michael Cormack, 715 Wellington Rd, Lawrence, KS 66049

Topeka Region, Kenneth E Lilley, 4031 NW Hoch Rd, Silver Lake, KS 66539

Kentucky *Blue Grass Region*, James N Fettig, 2045 Hancock Valley Dr, Winchester, KY 40391

Kyana Region, Carl Boyd, 4405 Westwood Dr, Crestwood, KY 40014

Lincoln Trail Region, Jerry T Mills, 6495 Bardstown Rd, Elizabethtown, KY 42701

Northern Kentucky Region, David G Fangman, 1145 Coram Ave, Covington, KY 41011

Southern Kentucky Region, Lynn A Goodman, 394 Martinsville Rd, Oakland, KY 42159

Twin Lakes Region, Howard Brandon, 1401 S 12th St, Murray, KY 42071

Louisiana *Louisiana Region*, Karen Kleinman, 24 Carriage Ln, Lake Charles, LA 70605

Louisiana Region, Baton Rouge Chapter, Charlie Matthews, 901 Sharp Rd, Baton Rouge, LA 70815

Louisiana Region, Central Louisiana Chapter, Dwight E Rashal, PO Box 285, Leesville, LA 71496

Louisiana Region, Contraband Chapter, Lee Roy Meaux, 225 Hazel St, Sulphur, LA 70663

Louisiana Region, Crescent City Chapter, John J Shaughnessy, PO Box 23503, New Orleans, LA 70183

Louisiana Region, Evangeline Chapter, Jo Ann Guilbeaux, 104 Greenfield Rd, Carencro, LA 70520

Louisiana Region, St Bernard Chapter, Curtis A Ducote, 1210 Hwy 39, Braithwaite, LA 70040

Maine *Maine Region*, Carl Barker, 107 Woodville Rd, Falmouth, ME 04105

Maryland *Accomack-Northhampton Region*, Robert L Ayres, 2831 Stockton Rd, Pocomoke City, MD 21851

Bay Country Region, Andrew R Wilhelm, 325 Dulin Clark Rd, Centreville, MD 21617

Chesapeake Region, Robert A Amos, 1116 Sleepy Dell Ct, Towson, MD 21286

Eastern Shore Region, Jack Wood, 10320 North Rd, Ocean City, MD 21841

Gettysburg Region, Arthur Rutledge, 3028 Blackrock Rd, Reisterstown, MD 21136

Harford Region, Bruce E Wheeler, 3610 Churchville Rd, Aberdeen, MD 21001

Model A Ford Foundation Region, Howard A Minners, 4700 Locust Hill Ct, Bethesda, MD 20814

National Capital Region, William R Thomas, 43124 Coles Dr, Hollywood, MD 20636

Queen City Region, Jeanne E Eaton, 10103 Town Creek Rd, Flintstone, MD 21530

Sugarloaf Mountain Region, Charles H Zierdt, 4100 Norbeck Rd, Rockville, MD 20853

Massachusetts *Connecticut Valley Region*, Willard Hick, 3 Iroquois Ln, Wilbraham, MA 01095

Massachusetts Region, Paul Lehtola, 307 Cherry St, Bridgewater, MA 02024

Michigan *Blue Water Region*, Brian C Campbell, 4222 Old Forge Dr, Fort Gratiot, MI 48059

Boyne Country Region, Samuel M Chipman, 04436 N Wildwood Harbor Rd, Boyne City, MI 49712

Flint Region, Larry Tremble, 6309 Van Vleet Rd, Swartz Creek, MI 48473

Inland Lakes Region, M G Randall, 508 Collingwood St, Houghton Lake, MI 48629

Irish Hills Region, George D McCaskey, 9217 Weston Rd, Morenci, MI 49256

Kalamazoo Valley Region, David Lyon, 27405 Shaw Rd, Lawton, MI 49065

Northwestern Michigan Region, Clarence V Smith, 1086 Rasho Rd, Traverse City, MI 49686

Saginaw Valley Region, Gerald F Evans, 2353 Richard Ave, Saginaw, MI 48603

St Joe Valley Region, Richard W Chandler, 68244 Cassoplis Rd, Cassopolis, MI 49031

West Michigan Region, Ryan E DeVries, 1048 Parkhust Ave, Grand Rapids, MI 49504

Wolverine State Region, Robert Scheffler, 19963 Sumpter, Belleville, MI 48111

Minnesota *Minnesota Region*, Gerald Broman, 5247 Lavaque Jct Rd, Hermantown, MN 55811

Minnesota Region, 412 Lakes Chapter, Duane P Wething, 1241 Summit Ave, Detroit Lakes, MN 56501

Minnesota Region, Arrowhead Chapter, Stephen W Blaede, 1896 W Chub Lake Rd, Carlton, MN 55718

Minnesota Region, Capitol City Chapter, Richard F Wolens, 6726 137th Ave NW, Anoka, MN 55303

Minnesota Region, Central Chapter, Richard M Morgan, 6739 Chicago Ave S, Minneapolis, MN 55423

Minnesota Region, Hiawatha Chapter, Lydia Hanson, 8311 County Rd SE, Chatfield, MN 55923

Minnesota Region, Little Crow Chapter, Russell N Johnson, 7230 159th St NE, Atwater, MN 56209

Minnesota Region, Pioneer Chapter, Paul L Dudek, 6021 Vernon Ave S, Minneapolis, MN 55436

Minnesota Region, Prairieland Chapter, Dennis A Johnson, 1126 N Washington St, New Ulm, MN 56073

Minnesota Region, River Bend Chapter, David T Borchert, Rt 1 Box 179, Kasota, MN 56050

Minnesota Region, Viking Chapter, Sherman Smith, PO Box 203, Winona, MN 55987

North Dakota Region, Ronald Moen, 523 13th St NW, East Grand Forks, MN 56721

Mississippi *Louisiana Region*, Slidell Antique Car Chapter, Walton M Jones PO Box 512, Waveland, MS 39576

Missouri *Gateway City Region*, Will Wack, 10525 E Watson Rd, St Louis, MO 63127

KC Metro Region, Robert M Hohimer, 1430 S Dodgion, Independence, MO 64055

Show Me Region, Dennis Mertz, PO Box 510439, St Louis, MO 63151

Nebraska *Siouxland Region*, Van Phillips, 120 Oakmont Dr, South Sioux City, NE 68776

Nevada *Northern Nevada Region*, Merlin T Sayre, 270 W Fairview St, Fallon, NV 89406

New Jersey *Ankokas Region*, Robert Schuman, 4 Severn Ct, Medford, NJ 08055

Curved Dash Olds Owners Club Region, Robert Giuliani, 72 Northwood Ave, Demarest, NJ 07627

Garden State Half Century Region, Clyde W Sorrell Jr, 80 Luke Ave, Bergenfield, NJ 07621

Garden State Model A Region, Joseph N Steiner, 200 Lafayette Ave, Magnolia, NJ 08049

Jersey Cape Region, Gerard A Desiderio, 6400 Landis Ave, Sea Isle City, NJ 08243

Mid-Jersey Region, Raymond Bouchard, 2 W Laurelwood Dr, Lawrenceville, NJ 08648

Antique Automobile Club of America regions *(continued)*

New Jersey Region, Louis C Holzberger, 8B Somerset Hills Village, Bernardsville, NJ 07924

New Jersey Region, Depression Vehicles Chapter, Doris M Werndly, 164 Bowden Rd, Cedar Grove, NJ 07009

New Jersey Region, Watchung Mountain Chapter, John Bedner, 82 Ravine Dr, Colonia, NJ 07067

South Jersey Region, Gary M Green, 22 Pedricktown Woodstown Rd, Pedricktown, NJ 08067

Staten Island Region, Fred Digiovanni, 41 Georgian Bay Dr, Morganville, NJ 07751

New Mexico *Eastern New Mexico Region*, Douglas Walker, 576 S Roosevelt Rd Y, Portales, NM 88130

Southeastern New Mexico Region, Ralph & Ruth Trice, 1734 Oriole Dr, Hobbs, NM 88240

Valley Vintage Motor Car Region, Phil Corbett, PO Box 1932, Roswell, NM 88202

New York *Algonquin Region*, Peter P Ferrante, 2402 Cty Rd 35, Bainbridge, NY 13733

Batavia Region, Gregory S Boehly, 31 Canterbury Ln, Bergen, NY 14416

Black River Valley Region, Frederick J Killian III, 241 Charles St, Watertown, NY 13601

Catskill Region, John DeCastro, 29 Pinehurst Dr, Liberty, NY 12754

Chautauqua Lake Region, James L Magee, 515 Kiantone Rd, Jamestown, NY 14701

Chemung Valley Region, Sandra M Pautz, 1444 W Water St, Elmira, NY 14905

Cooper's Cave Auto Enthusiasts Club Region, Martin Lemmo, 1 Southwoods Rd, Fort Edward, NY 12828

F R Porter Region, Janice L Sauter, 17 S Bicycle Path, Selden, NY 11784

Fingerlakes Region, James Vitale, RD 5 Beach Tree Rd, Auburn, NY 13021

Genesee Valley Antique Car Society Region, Edward L Franko, 724 Shanlee Dr, Webster, NY 14580

Greater New York Region, William Ragona, 75 Cedar Pl, Floral Park, NY 11001

Greenwood Lake Region, John F Kerwan Jr, 3 Kalvin Terr, Monroe, NY 10950

Iroquois Region, Thomas W Martin, 829 Zeggert Rd, Endicott, NY 13760

Lake Erie Region, Rosanne M Franco, 113 Cornwall Ave, Tonawanda, NY 14150

Livingston Region, Mark A Fisher, 5985 Co Rd 37, Springwater, NY 14560

Mid-Hudson Region, Carol Ann Champion, 323 New Hackensack Rd, Poughkeepsie, NY 12603

Onaquaga Region, Douglas Tucker, 3 Dodd Rd, Windsor, NY 13865

Oneida Lake Region, John F Perkis, 7971 Vernon Rd S, Cicero, NY 13039

Peconic Bay Region, Peter K Stokke, 2 Farmstead Ln, Water Mill, NY 11976

Ramapo Valley Region, Dr Stephen Lazar, 7 Arcadian Dr, Spring Valley, NY 10977

Rolling Antiquers OCC Norwich Region, Raymond C Hart, PO Box 168, Norwich, NY 13815

Schoharie Valley Region, Ronald Davis, RD 2 Box 935, Cobleskill, NY 12043

St Lawrence-Adirondack Region, David St Pier, 422 Lakeshore Dr, Norwood, NY 13668

Tioga Antique Auto Club Region, Dorothy Cheney, 12489 Main St, Berkshire, NY 13736

Vanderbilt Cup Region, Salvatore A Grenci, 425 Windmill Ave, North Babylon, NY 11704

Wayne Drumlins Antique Auto Region, George F Grube, 4845 Rt 96, Shortsville, NY 14548

Westchester New York Region, Richard E Marks, 2 Sudbury Dr, Yonkers, NY 10710

Whiteface Mountain Region, Edward D Rielly, RD 1 Box 1053, Westport, NY 12993

Wyoming Valley Region, James Fox, 18 High St, Attica, NY 14011

North Carolina *Foothills Region*, Raymond A Thomas, 5691 Country Ln, Stanley, NC 28164

Hornets Nest Region, Rodney Hawkins Jr, 4128 Little Mountain Rd, Gastonia, NC 28056

Mountaineer Region, Curtis Allison, 146 Allison Cove Rd, Sylva, NC 28779

North Carolina Region, Herb Oakes, 102 Converse Dr, Jacksonville, NC 28546

North Carolina Region, Alamance Chapter, Ernie Stoffel, 7565 N NC Hwy 62, Burlington, NC 27217

North Carolina Region, Brass-Nickel Touring Chapter, G Barker Edwards Jr, 116 E Front St, Clayton, NC 27520

North Carolina Region, Cape Fear Chapter, George J Weidenhammer, 3309 Tudor Ct, Wilmington, NC 28409

North Carolina Region, Coastal Plains Chapter, Preston Turner, 514 Main St, Washington, NC 27889

North Carolina Region, East Carolina Chapter, Jeff Breton, 153 Hickory Tree Ln, Angier, NC 27501

North Carolina Region, First Capital Antique Car Club Chapter, Larry Rucker, 718 Oakdale Ave, New Bern, NC 28562

North Carolina Region, Freshwater Chapter, William H Manke, Rt 5 Box 44, Hertford, NC 27944

North Carolina Region, Furnitureland Chapter, Arnold Gallimore, PO Box 482, Denton, NC 27239

North Carolina Region, General Greene Chapter, Don Ellis Jr, 4741 Kanora Dr, Julian, NC 27283

North Carolina Region, Hillbilly Chapter, Don Lewis Sprinkle, 9 Eller Ford Rd, Weaverville, NC 28787

North Carolina Region, Morehead City Chapter, Larry B Crowder, 1007 Oak Dr, Morehead, NC 28557

North Carolina Region, New River Chapter, Jeff Emery, 916 Lynchburg Dr, Jacksonville, NC 28546

North Carolina Region, Ol' Lightin' Rods Chapter, Dean Brown, 4842 S NC 41, Wallace, NC 28466

North Carolina Region, Old Salem Chapter, Larry C Shore, 751 Hallmark Dr, Rural Hall, NC 27045

North Carolina Region, San-Lee Chapter, Larry Wright, 1657 Post Office Rd, Sanford, NC 27330

North Carolina Region, Sandhills Chapter, Charles Bronk, 7 Highland Dr, Whispering Pines, NC 28327

North Carolina Region, Three Rivers Chapter, William Horton, 1114 Simpson St, Eden, NC 27288

North Carolina Region, Triangle Chapter, John Agayoff, 2612 Countrywood Rd, Raleigh, NC 27615

North Carolina Region, Uwharrie Chapter, Charles A Ford,11220 Stokes Ferry Rd, Gold Hill, NC 28071

Transylvania Region, Jerry M Arnold, PO Box 268, Brevard, NC 28712

Zooland Region, Jerry Rook, 5081 Burton Rd, Thomasville, NC 27360

North Dakota *Magic City Region*, Allen R Larson, 516 23rd St NW, Minot, ND 58703

North Dakota Region, Devils Lake Chapter, Glenn Lannoye, Rt 3 Box 424Z, Devils Lake, ND 58301

Ohio *FoMoCo Collectors Club of America Region*, Bill White, 1400 W Hill Dr, Gates Mills, OH 44040

Lakelands Region, Daryl R Timko, 5947 Everett Hull Rd, Fowler, OH 44418

Ohio Region, Ronald L Taylor, 6793 Bellefontaine Rd, Huber Hgts, OH 45424

Ohio Region, Canton Chapter, Timothy S Mast, PO Box 55, Mt Hope, OH 44660

Ohio Region, Central Chapter, William E Thomas, 5960 Stovertown Dr, Zanesville, OH 43701

Ohio Region, Commodore Perry Chapter, Alex C Heyd, 838 Poplar St, Elyria, OH 44035

Ohio Region, Meander Chapter, W B Smith, 1397 Doncaster Dr, Youngstown, OH 44511

Ohio Region, Northern Chapter, Dave W Grenier, 13130 Springblossom Tr, Chesterland, OH 44026

Ohio Region, Southern Chapter, J F Schreel, 3104 Catalpa Dr, Dayton, OH 45405

Ohio Region, Western Reserve Chapter, Robert J Marhefka, 1036 Sherman St, Geneva, OH 44041

Oklahoma *Cimmaron Region*, John Polluck, 19500 NE Meador Ln, Harrah, OK 73045

Enid Oklahoma Region, Gordon C Smith Jr, 1210 Indian Dr, Enid, OK 73703

Okie Region, Jerry Gibson, PO Box 271, Chickasha, OK 73018

Tulsa Region, Charlie Kukral, 14999 E 13th St, Tulsa, OK 74108

Pennsylvania *Allegheny Mountain Region*, John R O'Brien, 1887 Bellemead Dr, Altoona, PA 16602

Allegheny Mountain Region, Governor's Chapter, Scott Deno, 1723 Houserville Rd, State College, PA 16801

Anthracite Region, Joseph S Forish, 607 E Blaine St, McAdoo, PA 18237

Bus Transportation Region, Richard J Maguire, 426 S Third St, Ste 201, Lemoyne, PA 17043

Butler-Old Stone House Region, Edwin J Wilbert, 310 Cornetti Rd, Fenelton, PA 16034

Central Mountains Region, Roger O Menard, 11 W Pauline Dr, Clearfield, PA 16830

Coke Center Region, Joseph Roy Jr, 208 Perry St, Connellsville, PA 15425

Covered Bridge Region, Andrew C Tumicki Sr, 312 A Sundust Rd, Eighty Four, PA 15330

Delaware Valley Region, Michael J Jones Sr, 1361 Patrick Henry Dr, Phoenixville, PA 19460

Antique Automobile Club of America regions *(continued)*

Endless Mountains Region, Howard Crain, RD 2 Box 223, Towanda, PA 18848

Flood City Region, Dorothy S Wagner, 1305 Newbaker Dr, Johnstown, PA 15904

Fort Bedford Region, Donald M Hinish, 229 S Wood St, Bedford, PA 15522

Golden Triangle Region, William H Salvatora Jr, 251 Fassinger Rd, Evans City, PA 16033

Hershey Region, James C Koons, RD 3 Box 423, Palmyra, PA 17078

Keystone Region, Adam W Anderson, 30 S Madison Ave, Upper Darby, PA 19082

Kinzua Valley Region, David Jenkins, 112 Main St, Warren, PA 16365

Kiski Valley Region, Dale Frederick, 146 Lincoln St N, Vandergrift, PA 1569

Kit-Han-Ne Region, Russell E Clever Jr, 552 Main St, Ford City, PA 16226

Lanchester Region, Albert E Storrs Jr, 4 Main-Lin Dr, Coatesville, PA 19320

Laurel Highlands Region, Richard F Flickinger, 422 Summit Ave, Ligonier, PA 15658

Lehigh Valley Region, Joseph M Pokojni Sr, 37 Ridgewood Rd, Easton, PA 18045

Lower Bucks Region, James Cunnington, 1031 Whittier Ave, Bensalem, PA 19020

Mon Valley Region, James P McCune, 143 Adams St, Monongahela, PA 15063

New York State Allegheny Valley Region, James A Tilley, 35 Elk St, Coudersport, PA 16915

Northeastern Pennsylvania Region, Karen A Wolfe, 331 E Grand St, Nanticoke, PA 18634

Northwestern Pennsylvania Region, Sidney P Lewis, 4220 Depot Rd, Erie, PA 16510

Ontelaunee Region, Lester R Manwiller, RD 2 Box 2340, Fleetwood, PA 19522

Pennsylvania Dutch Region, Melvin U Burkholder, PO Box 195, Campbelltown, PA 17010

Pennsylvania Oil Region, William F Gratkowski, 515 N Petroleum St, Titusville, PA 16354

Pocono Region, Randy D Rutherford Sr, RD 1 Box 336B Lower Sees Hill Rd, Canadensis, PA 18325

Pottstown Region, Pierre G DeMauriac, 26 Elaine Dr, Boyertown, PA 19512

Presque Isle Region, Robert A Durst, 407 Stuart Way, Erie, PA 16509

Presque Isle Region, French Creek Valley Chapter, Dio M Yost, 9877 Free Rd, Conneaut Lake, PA 16316

Punxsutawney Region, Theodore O Dunmire, RD 2 Box 50, Indiana, PA 15701

Punxsutawney Region, Shannock Valley Car Club Chapter, Randy Duncan, 833 Rt 156 Hwy, Shelocta, PA 15774

Scranton Region, James Lyons, 31 Railroad St, Winton, PA 18403

Shenango Valley Region, Edward P Bailey Jr, 1343 Glenwood Dr, Sharon, PA 16146

Shikellamy Region, George O Campbell, 36 Effie Ave, Hughesville, PA 17737

Sugar Bush Region, Donald E Meese, 172 Lake Rd, Somerset, PA 15501

Susquehanna Valley Region, Richard L Powlus, 441 Second St, Nescopeck, PA 18635

Susquehannock Region, Ferd D Page Jr, 1016 Cherry St, Williamsport, PA 17701

Valley Forge Region, Alfred C Schneider, 334 E Signal Hill Rd, King of Prussia, PA 19406

Wayne-Pike Region, Carol Birdsall, PO Box 136, White Mills, PA 18473

Western Pennsylvania Region, Vincent P Altieri, 200 Bethany Dr, Greensburg, PA 15601

Wolf Creek Region, Michael D Urbassik, RR 1 Box 106, Polk, PA 16342

South Carolina   *Charleston-Lowcountry Region,* Charles T Hendrix, 1968 Westside St, Summerville, SC 29483

Chicora Region, Gus H Hardee, PO Box 1105, Conway, SC 29528

Coastal Carolina Region, Bill Gray, 9 Dolmane Dr, Charleston, SC 29407

Emerald City Region, Charles W Hatch, 1250 Jones St, Newberry, SC 29108

Peach Blossom Region, Mildred Mason, 579 Alamo St, Spartanburg, SC 29303

Piedmont Carolina Region, Ricky Thompson, 515 White's Rd, Gaffney, SC 29340

Sandlapper Region, Edward F Murphy, 1423 Corley Mill Rd, Lexington, SC 29072

Single Cylinder Cadillac Registry Region, Paul Ianuario, 311 Nature Tr Dr, Greer, SC 29651

South Carolina Region, Rein Brueggeman, 183 Lakeside Dr, Seneca, SC 29672

Sparkle City Region, C C Wheeler, 2004 Pine View Dr, Spartanburg, SC 29307

Swamp Fox Region, Charles A Robinson, 4569 W Belmont Cir, Florence, SC 29501

South Dakota   *South Dakota Region,* John Bergan, 2831 Sioux Conifer Rd, Watertown, SD 57201

Tennessee   *Battlefield Region,* Mike J Tschida, 4324 Columbia Pike, Franklin, TN 37064

Celebration City Region, James C Taylor, PO Box 502, Shelbyville, TN 37160

Cherokee Valley Region, Harold Miller, 151 Vermont Dr NW, Cleveland, TN 37312

Chickamauga Region, Jack Daugherty, 7627 Bishop Dr, Chattanooga, TN 37416

Clinton Region, Lee Ruble, 980 E Wolfe Valley Rd, Heiskell, TN 37754

Dan'l Boone Region, Howard K Osborne, 717 Yadkin St, Kingsport, TN 37660

Davy Crockett Region, Steven H Roberts, 1126 Hartman Ln, Greeneville, TN 37743

East Tennessee Region, Len Royston, 647 Miller Cir, Seymour, TN 37865

Mid-South Region, Roy E McLain, 4555 Hancock Dr, Memphis, TN 38116

Middle Tennessee Region, Bruce Hickerson, 3722 Lascassas Rd, Murfreesboro, TN 37130

Stones River Region, Deloris Stephenson, PO Box 11, Murfreesboro, TN 37130

Sumner County, Tennessee Region, T Wayne Stutts, 2416 Ravine Dr, Nashville, TN 37217

Tabacco Belt Region, Rudolph Reddick, 2505 Hickory Dr, Springfield, TN 37172

Tims Ford Region, Robert Morris, 944 Maxwell Rd, Belvidere, TN 37306

Walden Ridge Region, Fillmore Hendrickson, 917 Swan Pond Cir, Harriman, TN 37748

Texas   *Amarillo Region,* David N Patterson, 2521 12th Ave, Canyon, TX 79015

Big Spring Region, E L Hendon, 405 Westwood Ct, Lamesa, TX 79331

Central Texas Region, Victor L Donnell, 1801 Woods Loop, Driftwood, TX 78619

Deep East Texas Region, Wendall N Spreadbury, RR 13 Box 8600, Nacogdoches, TX 75961

Golden Crescent Region, B J Cornstubble, 403 N Main, Victoria, TX 77904

Gulf Coast Region, James Bartlett, 3620 Tartan Ln, Houston, TX 77025

Gulf Coast Region, Golden Triangle Chapter, Bobbie Reynolds 3241 Allison, Groves, TX 77619

Hill Country Region, Julius Neunhoffer, 2505 Lower Turtle Creek Rd, Kerrville, TX 78028

Northeast Texas Region, Troy F Parsons, 1104 CR 1031, Greenville, TX 75401

Red River Valley Honkers Region, John W Scharfe, PO Box 144, Paris, TX 75460

Rio Grande Valley Region, Robert W Doty Jr, 1701 Misty Ln, Weslaco, TX 78596

Snyder Wheels Region, Charlie Wilson, PO Box 795, Snyder, TX 79550

South Texas Region, John C Mosley, 9370 Teakwood Ln, Garden Ridge, TX 78266

Texas Region, J M Farrell, 326 Angus Rd, Waxahachie, TX 75167

West Texas Region, Ralph J Webb, 3401 W Golf Course Rd, Midland, TX 79703

Wichita Falls Region, Billy Rogers, 2018 Speedway, Wichita Falls, TX 76301

Wildflower Region, Odis Fuller, Rt 7 Box 7359, Belton, TX 76513

Wool Capital Region, Arlen Lohse, PO Box 61864, San Angelo, TX 76906

Virginia   *Appalachian Region,* George F Helms III, PO Box 607, Bristol, VA 24203

Bull Run Region, Gene E Welch, 1773 Macedonia Church Rd, White Post, VA 22663

Crater Antique Auto Club Region, Douglas R Strother, 1208 Wellington Rd, Colonial Hgts, VA 23834

Historic Fredericksburg Region, Ben E Schooler, 269 Truslow Rd, Falmouth, VA 22405

Historic Virginia Peninsula Region, Walter A Porter, 33 Hampshire Dr, Hampton, VA 23669

Lynchburg Region, Lennis P Wade, 1515 Langhorne Rd, Lynchburg, VA 24503

Martinsville-Danville Region, Ronald T Poteat, 235 Pioneer Tr, Collinsville, VA 24078

Mountain Empire Region, Elmer D Mottesheard, Box 82 Abby Ct, Dublin, VA 24084

North Carolina Region, North Cential Chapter, Jimmy C Lawson, 127 Martindale Dr, Danville, VA 24541

Northern Neck Region, Jackie B Ashburn, PO Box 295, White Stone, VA 22578

Piedmont Region, Richard D McIninch, 215 Stonet Creek W, Nellysford, VA 22958

Richmond Region, F M Fowlkes Jr, 106 Gaymont Rd, Richmond, VA 23229

Roanoke Valley Region, Robert M Pedigo, 2609 Parkview Dr, Vinton, VA 24179

Antique Automobile Club of America regions (continued)

Shenandoah Region, Duane Catlett, 5601 Middle Rd, Winchester, VA 22602

Tidewater Region, Robert L Parrish, 1221 Smokey Mountain Tr, Chesapeake, VA 23320

Tri-County Region, Hensel L Randall, Rt 1 Box 342, McGaheysville, VA 22840

Twin County Region, Charles Rudy, 212 Fish Pond Dr, Galax, VA 24333

Waynesboro-Staunton Region, John M Stone, RR 1 Box 683, Port Republic, VA 24471

Washington Evergreen Region, Dean R Lee, 16915 230th Ave SE, Maple Valley, WA 98038

Tacoma Region, Louis L Berquest, 2623 N 31st St, Tacoma, WA 98407

West Virginia Bluestone Region, Christopher Ziemnowicz, Concord Campus #2, Athens, WV 24712

Greenbrier Valley Region, David Hutsenpiller, HC71 Box 115A, Smoot, WV 24977

Huntington Region, Julian D Hensley, 3310 Brandon Rd, Huntington, WV 25704

Kanawha Valley Region, Glenn L Howard, 4112 Kanawha Ave, Charleston, WV 25304

Mason-Dixon Region, Paul J Rose, 5 Pembroke Grv, Charle Town, WV 25414

Mid-Ohio Valley Region, Guy Estep, 217 S 1st Ave, Paden City, WV 26159

Northern Panhandle Region, James E Bowery, 260 Park Addition, Wellsburg, WV 26070

West Virginia Region, Ivan L Austin, 106 Maplewood Dr, Fairmont, WV 26554

Wisconsin Minnesota Region, Dairyland Chapter, Henry Selle 1426 US Hwy 63, Turtle Lake, WI 54889

Northern Lakes Region, Gerald C Larson, 5426 Nature Rd, Rhinelander, WI 54501

Wisconsin Region, Walter A Wilde, 1840 N 68th St, Wauwatosa, WI 53213

Wyoming Big Horn Mountain Region, H O Thobaben II, 60 Cato Dr, Sheridan, WY 82801

Buzzard's Breath Touring Region, Daniel Binger, 3578 Essex Rd, Cheyenne, WY 82001

High Plains Region, Patricia K Simon, 2945 Spruce Dr, Cheyenne, WY 82001

High Plains Region, Laramie Hi Wheelers Chapter, Robert D Smith PO Box 152, Tie Siding, WY 82984

High Plains Region, Oak Spokes Chapter, Kenneth Barrow 1804 E 19th St, Cheyenne, WY 82001

Canada Lord Selkirk Region, T R Turner, 11 Woodgreen Pl, Winnipeg, MB R3J 1H4

Maple Leaf Region, David J Gurney, PO Box 809, Richmond, ON K0A 2Z0

Ontario Region, Arnold Kerry, Box 717, Port Perry, ON L9L 1A6

Central America Club de Autos Antiques de Costa Rica Region, Gaspar Ortuno Sr, PO Box 3641-1000, San Jose, Costa Rica

South America Colombia South America Region, Arturo Vayda, PO Box 49477, Medellin, Colombia

---

Antique Motorcycle Club of America Inc
Box 300
Sweetser, IN 46987
800-782-AMCA (2622)
FAX: 765-384-5700
E-mail: amc@comteck.com

For membership information, contact at the above address: Dick Winger, 765-384-5421. Founded 1954. Over 8,000 members. A non-profit organization devoted to the hobby of seeking out, preserving, restoring and exhibiting antique motorcycles, and to the exchange of fellowship and information. For owners and those interested in old motorcycles. Considered antique: 35 years old. Quarterly publication, The Antique Motorcycle. Dues: $20/year US, $28/year Canada, $40/year foreign. Web site: www.antiquemotorcycle.org

chapters:

Arkansas Louisiana Mississippi Oklahoma Texas Cherokee, MarianGuerin, 1144 Sycamore, San Marcos, TX 78666-7026

California Fort Sutter, Richard Ostrander, 3132 T St, Sacramento, CA 95816-7032

Los Angeles, Todd Bertrang, 15519 El Cajon St, Sylmar, CA 91342

Southern California, Tim Graber, 2058 Aliso Ave, Costa Mesa, CA 92627-2109

Colorado Rocky Mountain, Todd Vinzant, 16601 W 15th Ave, Golden, CO 80401-2809

Delaware Maryland Virginia Del Mar VA, William Hoover, 24973 Harrington Rd, Greensboro, MD 21639-1553

East Pennsylvania Perkiomen, Kathy Daya, 7 Pine Ln, Douglasville, PA 19518-1313

Florida Sunshine, Jerry Deutscher, 802 Elinor Way, Sanibel, FL 33957-6822

Georgia Dixie, Louie Hale, 1708 Indian Hills Ct, Augusta, GA 30906-9312

Illinois Indiana Wisconsin Prairie, Andy Anderson, PO Box 1028, Lake Zurich, IL 60047

Illinois Iowa Wisconsin Chief Blackhawk, Jack Gross, 2404 S Main St, Princeton, IL 61356

Illinois Missouri St Louis, Jack Latham, 9755 Four Corners Ln St Jacob, IL 62281-1043

Indiana Kentucky Ohio Ohio Valley, Kim Gadd, 3621 N Brownsville Rd, Brownsville, IN 47325

Indiana **Michigan/Ohio**	*Maumee Valley*, Wally Krzyzanowski, 7703 N 1200 W, North Judson, IN 46366-9737
Iowa **Nebraska**	*Omaha*, Connie Schlemmer, 1218 Wedgewood Dr, Council Bluffs, IA 51503
Kansas **Oklahoma**	*Sunflower*, Terry Sawyer, 1238 N Doris, Wichita, KS 67212-1947
Maryland **Virginia**	*Chesapeake*, Tom Finn, 37 Glenwood Ave, Catonsville, MD 21228-3429
Michigan/Ohio	*Lake Erie*, Terry Austin, 407 Keltner Ave, Akron, OH 44319-3831
Minnesota	*Viking*, Ralph Overholt, 6321 Rolf Ave, Edina, MN 55439-1434
New England	*Yankee*, Randy Walker, 7 S Maple St PO Box 296, Brookfield, MA 01506-0296
New Jersey	*Seaboard*, Bruce Venner, 383 Landing St, Mt Holly, NJ 08060-4525
New York	*Empire*, Tom Thomson, 475 CR 105A N, Savannah, NY 13146
North Carolina	*Blue Ridge*, Chris Wolf, PO Box 708, Indian Trails, NC 28079-0708
North **New Jersey**	*Colonial*, "Gentleman" Ray Dhue, 33 Colonial Way, New Providence, NJ 07974-1104
NW Indiana **SW Michigan**	*River Valley*, Tom Rickey, 52092 Cheryl Dr, Granger, IN 46530-9112
Oregon	*Oregon Trail*, Thomas Krise, 1615 Court St NE, Salem, OR 97301
Oregon **Washington**	*Evergreen*, Mike Kane, 6801 Stanton Pl NW, Seattle, WA 98117-6138
Pennsylvania	*Nashaminy Valley*, Charles Grafenstine, 1009 Honeysuckle Ave, Parkland, PA 19047-3842
South Dakota	*Great Plains*, Phil Mast, 48185-260th St, Corson, SD 57005-6609
Southern **Colorado**	*High Plains*, Zeke Rhodes, 305 Delaware Dr, Colorado Springs, CO 80909
Southwest **Virginia**	*Highlands*, Barry Wuergler, Rt 5 Box 279, Moneta, VA 24121
Tennessee	*Confederate*, Tina Schmalshof, 620 S Bellevue Blvd, Memphis, TN 38104-4533
Texas	*Tejas*, James Freeman, 924 Gay Ln, Arlington, TX 76012
Wisconsin	*Badger Heritage*, Roger Klopfenstein, N88 W17143 Main St, Menomonee Falls, WI 53051
Canada	*Buffalo*, Siggi Klann, 172 Harbison Ave W, Winnipeg, MB R2L 0A4
	Orcas, Peter Gagan, 14332 Magdalen, White Rock, BC V4B 2X2

Antique Truck Club of America Inc
PO Box 291
Hershey, PA 17033
717-533-9032

Founded 1971. 2,400 members. Open to owners of commercial vehicles or those who have an interest in the history, preservation, restoration and operation of antique commercial vehicles. *Double Clutch* magazine to members 6 times a year, free initial want and for sale ads to members. Dues: $25/year US, $30/year Canada, $35/year foreign.

chapters:

Connecticut	*Connecticut Yankees*, Matt Pfahl, PO Box 779, Georgetown, CT 06829, 203-544-8507

Delaware	*Northern Delaware Chapter*, Jack Smith, 35 Lynn Dr, Newark, DE 19711
Michigan	*Blue Water Chapter*, Richard Vanderworp, 2728 N Belle River, East China, MI 48054, 810-765-3473
New Jersey	*North Jersey Chapter*, Jack Moran, 284 Mt Hope Ave, Dover, NJ 07801
	South Jersey Shore Chapter, Lou Barber, PO Box 41, Leesburg, NJ 08327
	State Line Chapter, Robert J Abbott, 186 Rockland Ave, Norwood, NJ 07648, 201-768-4018
New York	*Finger Lakes Area Chapter*, Ray Hildreth, 2097 Rt 14 N, Lyons, NY 14489, 315-946-5006
	Long Island Chapter, Kevin Duffy, 50-42 195th St, Flushing, NY 11365, 718-357-7382
	Sound Shore Chapter, Angelo J Sposta, 52 Park Ave, Port Chester, NY 10573, 914-939-7910
North Carolina	*Western North Carolina Area Chapter*, Donald Kilpatrick Jr, 119 Maple St, Brevard, NC 28712, 828-883-4894
Pennsylvania	*Central Pennsylvania Chapter*, Tom Oehme, 7 Starlite Dr, Lititz, PA 17543, 717-626-1204
	Greater Lehigh Valley Chapter, Ron Young, 5411 N Halbea St, Bethlehem, PA 18017, 610-266-1947
	Greater Pittsburgh Area Chapter, Harvey Bush, RD 6 Box 118-A, Greensburg, PA 15601
	Keystone Chapter, Blair Hileman, 400 Tennyson Ave, Altoona, PA 16602, 814-943-9947
	Northeast Pennsylvania Chapter, Dave Lewis, 2709 Jackson St, Scranton, PA 18504, 717-344-1572
	Southeastern Pennsylvania Chapter, Al Whitcomb, 309 Euclid Ave, Ambler, PA 19002, 215-643-3517
Vermont	*Green Mountain Bulldawg Chapter*, Dave Zsido, 3 Haywood Ave, Rutland, VT 05701, 802-775-6576
Canada	*Eastern Ontario & Northern New York Chapter*, Mel Vice, 4501 Furguson Dr, Elizabethtown, ON K6T 1A9, 613-498-2909

Belltown Antique Car Club
PO Box 211
East Hampton, CT 06424

Founded 1968. 95 members. Open to anyone who enjoys old cars. Meetings 1st Wednesday of each month. Antique engine meet 4th Sunday in April, car show 1st Sunday in August. Dues: $10/year.

Borgward Owners' Club
77 New Hampshire Ave
Bay Shore
Long Island, NY 11706
PH/FAX: 516-BR-3-0458
alternate numbers:
775-348-8887, NV; FAX: 516-666-5446
E-mail: leftyny@aol.com or zarcoff@bcs1.telmex.net.mx

Founded 1974. 100 members. Open to owners of Borgward products: Borgward, Lloyd, Goliath, and to enthusiasts. Offers newsletter and an extensive stock of spares, some of which are made by special order. Get-togethers are arranged locally. Dues: $25/year.

British Car Club ASBL
Rue du College, BP 153
B-4800 Verviers Belgium
PH/FAX: 3287335122

Founded 1988. 2,500 members. Open to all British car lovers. Monthly magazine, *Gentleman Driver*, all you must know about British cars. Insurance scheme, spare parts and technical service, club shop, clubhouse for members. Dues: $30/year US.

British Sports Car Club
PO Box 43923
Louisville, KY 40253
812-923-7349, IN; FAX: 502-499-7491
E-mail: jim@budgetprint.win.net

Founded 1983. 100 members. Monthly newsletter, annual car show, monthly club and driving activities. Dues: $20/year. Web site: http://members.aol.com/lucaselec/cars.html

Brown County Cruisers Car Club
PO Box 113
Georgetown, OH 45121-0113
937-378-3945
E-mail: dfetters@comcomach.com

Founded 1986. 20 members. Meet once a month. No restrictions to join. Have one car show a year. Dues: $20 one time fee.

Cape Fear Classics Car and Truck Club
PO Box 997
Hope Mills, NC 28348
910-868-6312
E-mail: seanpfay@worldnet.att.net or
capefearcars@freeservers.com

Founded 1997. 350 members. Open to all classic car enthusiasts. Discounts from major restoration suppliers, monthly cruise-ins, multiple events sponsored year round. Newsletter, *Classic Quotes*, every six weeks with info on upcoming events and shows, special discounts on local and regional events, car of the month, etc. Dues: $20/year.

Cars of Yesteryear Inc
493 Citizens Rd
Newport, VT 05855
802-334-6079

Founded 1983. 100 members. Need only to have an interest in the promotion, appreciation and restoration of antique vehicles, classic car, street rods or any vehicle 15 years old of special interest. Dues: $10/year.

Chandler-Cleveland Motor Club
43 Wide Beach Rd
Irving, NY 14081
716-549-0729
E-mail: hansen_chandler@mindspring.com

Founded 1994. 110 members. Welcomes all Chandler-Cleveland owners and enthusiasts of Chandler or Cleveland cars. Newsletter 3 times a year with for sale and wanted sections. Dues: $10/year.

The Chrysler Cordoba Club & Registry
1402 N Adams Apt 3
Fredericksburg, TX 78624
830-997-0714 after 8 pm CST

Founded 1997. 420 members. Club and registry for 1975-1983 Chrysler Cordoba, 1979 Chrysler 300, 1975-1978 Dodge Charger, 1978-1979 Dodge Magnum, 1980-1983 Dodge Mirada and 1981-1983 Imperial. Send SASE for information and newsletter subscription fee. Dues: none. Web site: www.concentric.net/~440cuda/ccr.htm

Classic Car Club of America
1645 Des Plaines River Rd, Ste 7
Des Plaines, IL 60018
847-390-0443; FAX: 847-390-7118

Founded 1952. 5,500 members. Open to select makes and models of cars dating from 1925-1948. Dedicated to the collection, preservation and enjoyment of fine cars. Dues: $40/year.

regions:

Alabama	*Dixie*, Millard Young, PO Box 328, Piedmont, AL 36272, 205-447-9449 home, 205-447-9087 work; FAX: 205-447-9089
Arizona	*Arizona*, William Crumrine, 9956 E Ironwood Dr, Scottsdale, AZ 85258, 602-314-2066
California	*Northern California*, Phil Burton, 13680 Longridge Rd, Los Gatos, CA 95033, 408-353-3242 home
	San Diego/Palm Springs, Ed McCormick, 1521 Randall Ct, Los Angeles, CA 90065, 323-226-0250
	Southern California, Steve Snyder, 2446 E Orangeview, Orange, CA 92867, 714-279-0916
Colorado	*Colorado*, Harvey Delockroy, 12104 W 37th Pl, Wheatridge, CO 80033, 303-421-8203
Connecticut	*New England*, Frank Wemple, 10 Pine Ridge Dr, Andover, CT 06232, 860-742-6292 home
Florida	*Florida*, Edna Wieler, 420 Coconut Palm Rd, Vero Beach, FL 32963, 561-234-4111
	Gold Coast, Arthur Polacheck, 2056 Woodlake Cir, Deerfield Beach, FL 33442, 954-428-3815
Illinois	*Greater Illinois*, Dennis Sobieski, 5139 Lee Ave, Downers Grove, IL 60515, 630-969-4202 home
Indiana	*Indiana*, Bob Titlow, 6635 Sunset Ln, Indianapolis, IN 46260-4168, 317-257-6601
Maryland	*Chesapeake Bay*, Morton Y Bullock III, 320 N Wind Rd, Ruxton, MD 21204, 410-296-5048 home, 609-898-4230 summer home, NJ
Michigan	*Michigan*, Philip T Bray, 8858 Ferry Rd, Grosse Ile, MI 48138, 734-676-5520; FAX: 734-676-9438
Minnesota	*Upper Midwest*, Tom Brace, 1433 Idaho Ave W, St Paul, MN 55108, 651-644-1716 home
Missouri	*Spirit of St Louis*, Fred Guyton, 13 Westmoreland Pl, St Louis, MO 63108, 314-664-2451 home, 314-231-7318 work; FAX: 314-231-7433
New Jersey	*Delaware Valley*, Fred Allen, 385 Lebanon Rd, Millville, NJ 08332, 609-455-4310
	Metropolitan, Charles A Eggert Jr, Van Beuren Rd, Morristown, NJ 07960, 973-267-7102 home, 973-539-3200 work; FAX: 973-539-8448
New Mexico	*Rio Grande*, Michelle Ann Franowsky, PO Box 279, Corrales, NM 87048, 505-890-4461
Ohio	*Ohio*, Gary Rosenthal, 13569 Cty Line Rd, Chagrin Falls, OH 44022-4005, 440-423-1718 home, 440-449-040 work
Oklahoma	*Oil Belt*, Michael K Ross, 11180 S Pine, Guthrie, OK 73044, 405-282-2704 home, 405-348-0977 work

Oregon	*Oregon*, Jerry Hanauska, 7685 SW 84th Ave, Portland, OR 97223, 503-245-8845
Pennsylvania	*Western Pennsylvania*, Jon Leimkuchler, 1069 Tall Trees Dr, Pittsburgh, PA 15241, 412-257-1257 home, 412-622-2020 work
Texas	*Lone Star*, Don Scott, 84 Granburg Cir, San Antonio, TX 78218, 210-826-4831
	Northern Texas, Michael Ames, 3522 Polly Webb Rd, Arlington, TX 76017, 817-483-9270 home, 817-561-7530 work
Washington	*Pacific Northwest*, Bill Deibel, 6426 NE Windermere Rd, Seattle, WA 98105-2056, 206-522-7167; FAX: 206-985-1447
Wisconsin	*Wisconsin*, Warren Jensen, 2427 S 93rd St, West Allis, WI 53227, 414-545-4508

Classic Car Team Franken eV in DUS
Aeussere Brucker Str 70
Erlangen 91052 Germany
PH/FAX: +49-9131-304614
E-mail: classic-car-team@gmx.net

Founded 1993. 90 members. Located about 100 miles north of Munich. We welcome all American car and bike owners with pre-1975 vehicles and offer monthly meetings and newsletter, free worldwide event calendar, submembership of DUS and DEUVET (important German old car association), technical help, parts locating, restoration support. Dues: $50/year (65 DEM). Web site: http://cctf.home.pages.de

Club MCC
PO Box 3934
Evansville, IN 47737
812-425-4454; FAX: 812-425-5169
E-mail: services@myclassiccar.com

Founded 1997. 2,000+ members. Open to all automotive enthusiasts. Club MCC is a spin-off of the television show "My Classic Car Video Magazine" on TNN. The club offers a membership kit and benefits including discounts, a free subscription to *My Classic Car* magazine and special online privileges at its web site. Plus, a portion of all dues is donated to organizations lobbying to protect the automotive hobby. Club MCC also hosts the annual MCC Autofest each October in Evansville, Indiana, featuring an open car show and other events. Dues: $39/year US. Web site: www.myclassiccar.com

Club MCH Abitibi-Tem
PO Box 2127
Rouyn-Noranda, QC Canada J9X 5A5
819-797-3091; FAX: 819-797-8297
E-mail: diaron@sympatico.ca

Founded 1992. 412 members. Non-profit organization specializing in classic and antique vehicles, restoration help, car exhibitions, cruises and municipal charity events. Dues: $10/year.

Contemporary Historical Vehicle Assoc Inc
PO Box 493398
Redding, CA 96049

Founded 1967. 2,000 members. Recognizes all vehicles built since 1928, up to 20 years old. Activities are open to all cars, commercial vehicles, motorcycles and military land vehicles. Dues: $25/year domestic, $35/year foreign, $300/life membership.

Daytona-Super Bird Auto Club
13717 W Green Meadow Dr
New Berlin, WI 53151
414-786-8413
E-mail: dsac@execpc.com

Founded 1975. 500+ members. No restrictions, owners and admirers welcome to join. *Hightailer*, monthly newsletter

featuring historical articles, members cars, events and free advertising to club members; national and local events. Specializing in information exchange and registry for 1969 Dodge Charger Daytona, 1970 Plymouth Superbird, 1969 Dodge Charger 500, 1969 Ford Torino Talladega, 1969 Mercury Cyclone Spoiler. Dues: $18/year.

Deutscher Automobil Veteranen Club
Dachsstr 52
Wiesbaden D-65207 Germany
06122-12180; FAX: 06150-52243

Founded 1965. 1,250 members. 14 sections all over Germany. Monthly meetings, quarterly club news, open to all marques. Dues: 120 DM/year.

DUS-Dachverband US-Fahrzeugclubs Deutschland ev
Am Bueschel 5
Bobenheim Am Berg D-67273 Germany
0049-6353-2605; FAX: 0049-6353-2605

Founded 1995. 950 members. US cars only. 4 quarterly newsletters, membership includes membership in the Deuvet. The DUS works as a lobby for US car owners with the government and other authorities. Dues: $8/year, $15/ year DM.

Eastern Townships Vintage Automobile Club
PO Box 325
Lennoxville, QC Canada J1M 1Z5
819-562-8202

Founded 1977. 45 members. No restrictions to join. Friendship newsletter 2 weeks before meetings. One event per year, a car show plus a Christmas party. Dues: $10/year.

Frenchtown Auto Club
Rt 1 Box 439
Prairie du Chien, WI 53821
608-326-4544
E-mail: pdcvet@mhtc.net

Founded 1982. 20 members. Interest in cars needed to join. Monthly newsletter. Sponsors annual car show. Community service, roadside clean-up. Monthly meetings. Dues: $10/year.

Gateway Auto & Truck Club
2 Siesta Dr
West Wareham, MA 02576
508-295-0619

Founded 1991. 12+ members. Must have a love for the automobile and/or trucks. Dues: $20/year.

Gig Harbor Cruisers Automotive Club
PO Box 2642
Gig Harbor, WA 98335
253-265-3648; FAX: 253-851-1669
E-mail: ghcruisers@aol.com

Founded 1997. 120 members. All makes, models, years welcome, monthly newsletter (*Cruizletter*), host annual Cruise the Narrows Car Show, July 22, 2000. Dues: $25/year. Web site: www.members.tripod.com/~GHCruisers

Goodguys Rod & Custom Association
PO Box 424
Alamo, CA 94507
925-838-9876; FAX: 925-820-8241

Founded 1980. 45,000+ members. 20 events throughout the USA. Publisher of the giant sized *Goodtimes Gazette*. Dues: $25/year.

Great Autos of Yesteryear
PO Box 10856
Santa Ana, CA 92711-0856
E-mail: webmaster@greatautos.org

Founded 1983. 960+ members. Classic and special interest club welcoming all makes and models. Large contingent of Classic American Luxury Cars. Monthly newsletter, monthly events. Annual north/south meet, annual Concours for charity. Chapters in Los Angeles and San Diego. Mostly gay and lesbian membership. Dues: $30/year. Web site: www.greatautos.org

Happy Days Car Club
1323 8th Ave
Beaver Falls, PA 15010
724-843-6911 days, 724-843-4476 eves

Founded 1991. 25 members. No restrictions to join, Annual event, Happy Days Car Cruise, and flier. Dues: none.

Historical Vintage Car Club of Delaware
PO Box 43
Dover, DE 19903
302-422-7437; FAX: 302-422-3516

Founded 1969. 300 members. Purpose of club is to preserve and restore the antique vehicles. Sponsor shows, tours and trips for enjoyment of membership. Publish *Stovebolt* bi-monthly (six issues a year), free with membership, includes calendar of club events and other antique car activities of interest to club. Dues: $10/year.

Horseless Carriage Club of America
3311 Fairhaven Dr
Orange, CA 92866-1357
661-326-1023; FAX: 661-326-1260
E-mail: aopablo@aol.com

Founded 1937. 10,000 members. Membership offered to collectors, historians, anyone interested in early cars. Pioneer motor vehicles are the major interest of the HCCA and its members. Basically a touring club. *Horseless Carriage Gazette* is published 6 times a year. Annual national tours are limited to vehicles of 1915 or older vintage. Membership includes 6 yearly issues of the *Gazette*. Dues: $35/year per family. Web site: www.horseless.com

regions:

Arizona *Valley of the Sun*, Rosemary Cook, 4439 N 106th Ave, Phoenix, AZ 85039, 602-887-0757

California *Bay Area*, Phyllis Pottle, 1401 Iris St, Oakdale, CA 95361, 209-847-3636

Camping & Motoring Pioneers Register (affiliated), Roberta Watkins, 7990 Anders Cir, La Mesa, CA 91942, 619-460-9117

Central California, Robert W Strieter, 41041 Jean Rd W, Oakhurst, CA 93644, 209-642-2577

Central Coast, Wayne Stanfield, 940 Park Ave, Cayucos, CA 93430, 805-995-1677

El Cajon, Warren R Hoover, 6029 Malcolm Dr, San Diego, CA 92115, 619-582-4527

El Dorado, Joe J Anino, 10316 Newton Way, Rancho Cordova, CA 95670, 916-361-9864

EMF (affiliated), Paul Anthony, 5901 Azalea Ave, Bakersfield, CA 93306, 661-871-5043

Eureka, David A Goodman, 1626-A Hyland St, Bayside, CA 95524, 707-822-8594

Gold Country, Lloyd M Young, 506 Sacramento St, Nevada City, CA 95959-3010, 916-265-4444

Kern County, Paul Anthony, 5901 Azalea Ave, Bakersfield, CA 93306, 805-871-5043

La Jolla, Neil C LaRosa, 4757 Campanile Dr, San Diego, CA 92115, 619-582-7526

Modesto, Diane Noz, PO Box 365, Denair, CA 95316, 209-667-2061

Northern California, Robert C Hopkins Jr, 5637 Clairborne Way, Orangevale, CA 95662, 916-988-1518

Orange Empire, Larry J Hansen, 12423 Sibley St, Norwalk, CA 90650-6038, 562-921-5941

Pioneer Motorcycle (affiliated), Tom Holthaus, 878 N 10th, San Jose, CA 95112, 408-292-1232

Salinas Valley, Wayne D Earnest, 1113 San Ysidro Way, Salinas, CA 93901, 408-758-3902

San Diego, Gerald W Tabor, 6187 Mohler St, San Diego, CA 92120, 619-583-2059

San Francisco, Vincent Peck, 1878 Leimert Blvd, Oakland, CA 94602, 510-531-6687

Santa Clara Valley, Jeremy Wire, 15533 Kavin Ln, Monte Sereno, CA 95030, 408-395-0386

Santa Cruz, Sam Gurnee, 202 Lyle Ct, Aptos, CA 95003, 408-688-4926

Santa Rosa, L Warren Welsh, 5050 Hall Rd, Santa Rosa, CA 95401-5511, 707-545-9544

Shasta-Cascade, Robert Sanders, 1614 Del Mar Ave, Redding, CA 96003, 530-241-8681

Sonora, Paul G Kruetzfeldt, 16901 Yosemite Rd, Sonora, CA 95370-8220, 209-928-4040

Southern California, Dikk Jones, 4149 Lyman Ave, Covina, CA 91724, 626-339-1387

Stevens-Duryea Associates (affiliated), Warwick S Eastwood, 3565 Newhaven Rd, Pasadena, CA 91107, 626-351-8237

Temecula, Lesley H Von Nordheim, 1499 Via Feliz, Fallbrook, CA 92028, 760-723-2662

Tulare County, Barbara Pietroforte, 2113 S Church, Visalia, CA 93277, 209-734-9550

Western Gaslight 1 & 2-Cyl Touring Register (affiliated), John Morrison, 1450 Grand Ave, Piedmont, CA 94610, 510-655-6128

Wintons World Wide (affiliated), Roger C Allison, 5449 N Woodson, Fresno, CA 93711-2549, 209-439-8529

Colorado *Colorado*, Conrad C Fletcher, 2985 Indiana St, Golden, CO 80401-1463, 303-279-5655

Columbine, Marven Roth, 8106 Bruns Dr, Fort Collins, CO 80525-9353, 970-667-1964

Connecticut *Fairfield County*, William Seuch, 38 Rampart Rd, South Norwalk, CT 06854, 203-866-7618

Nutmeg, Arthur Wilkinson, 11 Indian Mountain Rd, Lakeville, CT 06039, 860-435-9282

Two-Cylinder Buick (affiliated), Robert Sahl, PO Box 460, Litchfield, CT 06759-0460, 860-567-4916

Florida   *Florida*, Charles R Kugel, 13920 Ruffner Ln, Sebastian, FL 32958-3421, 561-589-9651

Slow Spokes Manasota, Floyd E Fowler, 1622 Jewell Dr, Sarasota, FL 34240, 941-377-8335

Georgia   *Atlanta*, Robert G Reeves, 1895 Foxglove Ct, Tucker, GA 30084-6018, 770-939-3256

South Georgia, Steve Gordon, PO Drawer 2037, Thomasville, GA 31799, 912-226-2266

Idaho   *Southwestern Idaho*, Aileen Geer, 4044 Genesee Dr, Boise, ID 83709, 208-362-9313

Illinois   *Chicagoland*, Charles V Fabian, 10136 S Hoyne Ave, Chicago, IL 60643-2029, 773-445-0145

Meramech Hill, George Kaforski, 12806-A River Rd, Plano, IL 60545, 708-553-0790

Kansas   *Hutchinson*, Bernie Wray, 128 E Forest, South Hutchinson, KS 67501, 316-663-7107

Reo 1 & 2-Cylinder Registry (affiliated), Garyl Turley, 1313 N Gordon St, Wichita, KS 67203, 316-943-4513

Wichita, Verne Shirk, 1726 N Young, Wichita, KS 67212, 316-721-8868

Maryland   *Chesapeake Bay/Four Seasons*, Henry Petronis, 6561 Hopkins Neck Rd, Easton, MD 21601, 410-822-3963

Massachusetts   *Autoneers*, Donald Rising, 76 Treaty Elm Ln, Stow, MA 01775, 978-897-2466

Knox Motor Car Affiliated Register (affiliated), John Hess, 6 Concord Dr, East Longmeadow, MA 01028, 413-525-6782

Michigan   *Grand Rapids*, Robert L Dinger, 841 Parson St #O, Grandville, MI 49418, 616-457-9145

South Michigan Motorist, Guy Zaninovich, 4 Jay Lee Ct, Ann Arbor, MI 48108, 313-913-9762

Minnesota   *Twin Cities*, James R Forest, 4801 287th Ct NW, Isanti, MN 55040, 612-444-6230

Missouri   *Kansas City*, Rodney P Booth, 10135 Monticello Rd, Lenexa, KS 66227, 913-764-5668

St Louis, Gerald Perschbacher, 8868 Rock Forest Dr, St Louis, MO 63123, 314-849-5249

Nebraska   *Midwest Touring Association*, Merel Rex, 1625 W Berry Hill Dr, Norfolk, NE 68701, 402-371-2869

Omaha, Robert Moller, 2008 E Military Ave, Fremont, NE 68025, 402-271-4828

Nevada   *Nevada*, Clyde Jurey, 10 Sharon Dr, Wellington, NV 89444, 702-465-2147

New Jersey   *Antique Steam Touring Club (affiliated)*, Donald R Davidson, 48 Southern Blvd, Chatham, NJ 07928, 201-635-1647

Brighton Era Touring Affiliated Registry (affiliated), Robert Losco, 20 Spencer Ln, Warren, NJ 07059, 908-647-5435

North Jersey, Alan C Achtel, 536 Spring Valley Dr, Bridgewater, NJ 08807, 908-526-5197

New York   *Central New York*, Stephen D Bono, RR 1 Box 111, Bouckville, NY 13310, 315-893-7483

Long Island, Samuel Greco, 121 Sackville Rd, Garden City, NY 11530, 516-741-3284

Rochester, David Hess, 29 Maple Ave, Bloomfield, NY 14469, 716-657-7036

North Carolina   *North Carolina*, Bill H Brown, 3130 NC 150, Reidsville, NC 27320, 910-349-7740

North Dakota   *Fargo Red River Valley*, Jack Diemert, 532 21st St N, Fargo, ND 58102-4144, 701-232-4174

Ohio   *Lake Erie*, Sheldon Loewenthal, 7366 Hillendale Rd, Chesterland, OH 44026, 216-729-4258

White Steam Registry (affiliated), Henry Merkel, PO Box 220, Gates Mills, OH 44040, 216-449-0260

Oklahoma   *Sooner*, John H Witten, 7201 Spoon Terr, Edmond, OK 73003-1875, 405-844-2136

Tulsa, Joe D Smith, 5400 E Princeton St, Broken Arrow, OK 74014, 812-923-5965

Oregon   *Cadillac Single-Cylinder Register (affiliated)*, Jerome Hubert, 18714 NE Halsey, Portland, OR 97230, 503-666-2676

Crater Lake, F Joseph Petko, PO Box 135, Shady Cove, OR 97539, 541-664-1989

Eugene, Ron Robinson, 4030 Hilyard St, Eugene, OR 97405, 541-345-6303

Medford, Michael F McKey, 3306 S Pacific Hwy #88, Medford, OR 97501-8715, 541-512-9725

Oregon Pioneer, Dolores Byrnes, 4376 Viewcrest Rd S, Salem, OR 97302, 503-364-6646

Portland, Donald F Plumb, 8 Del Prado, Lake Oswego, OR 97035-1371, 503-635-4627

Pennsylvania   *Old Tyme Car Club*, Thomas S Heckman, 1-1/2 Earles Ln, Newtown Square, PA 19073, 215-353-5893

Pittsburgh, Richard F Wagner, 315 Chickasaw Ave, Pittsburgh, PA 15237-4708, 412-364-1921

Pullman Owners Register (affiliated), WFO Rosenmiller, 37 W Market St, York, PA 17401, 717-845-1974

Susquehanna, Paul H Vaughn Jr, 14 Clearview Rd, Willow Street, PA 17584, 717-464-4704

South Dakota   *Sioux Falls*, Todd Vetter, 1308 N Elmwood, Sioux Falls, SD 57104, 605-334-4772

Tennessee   *Circle South Touring Registry (affiliated)*, Alex Joyce, 4419 Chickering Ln, Nashville, TN 37122, 615-463-8880

Texas   *El Paso*, Donald R Meier, 6601 Overland Stage Rd, El Paso, TX 79938-8788, 915-855-6283

Electric Vehicle Registry (affiliated), Robert McDaniel, 3165 Hayter Rd, Abilene, TX 79603, 915-672-1307

Heart O'Texas, Bill Taylor, 715 W Karnes, Waco, TX 76706, 817-662-1528

North Texas, Bob Tarpenning, 3701 FM 2415, Cleburne, TX 76031, 817-641-1348

Utah   *Utah*, Bruce Boggess, 7415 Chapel Hill Cir, Midvale, UT 84047, 801-255-7473

Washington   *Greater Spokane*, Robert D Davis, E 1717 Trent, Spokane, WA 99202-2943, 509-534-7521

Section Three
Clubs & Organizations

Horseless Carriage Club of America regions *(continued)*

Olympia, Billie M Hyland, 6355 Lake Ave SW, Lakewood, WA 98499, 253-589-0911

Seattle-Tacoma, Gene Lander, 23906 78th Ave W, Edmonds, WA 98026-8822, 425-774-4760

Skagit/Snohomish, Candy Musolf, 23708 Locust Way #11-A, Bothell, WA 98021, 206-364-8089

Wisconsin Fox River Valley, John P Griesbach, N 5064 12 Corners Rd, Black Creek, WI 54106, 414-734-2699

Madison, Bill Gruber, PO Box 42, Plain, WI 53577, 608-646-3111

Argentina Club de Automoviles Historicos de Rosario, Juan Molinari, 3 de Febrero 312, 2000 Rosario, Sta Fe, 54 41-250040

Australia South Queensland, Noel D Adams, PO Box 183, Noosaville, Queensland 4566, 071-622-474

Canada Calgary, Leigh A Robertson, 323 Queen Anne Way SE, Calgary, AB T2S 4R7, 403-278-7934

Quebec, Gilbert Bureau, 1683 Alexis-Nihon, Ville St Laurent, QC H4R 2S6, 514-745-6278

Southern Ontario, Peter M McLay, 25 South St E, Aylmer, ON N5H 1P5, 519-773-2179

Vancouver, John Reilly, 8890 117th A St, North Delta, BC V4C 6C8, 604-590-7356

New Zealand Auckland, Dennis Scanlan, 18 Bristol Rd, Kumeu 1250 Auckland, 0-9-416-7692

Illini Collector Car Club
1911 N Duncan Rd
Champaign, IL 61822
217-355-1704; FAX: 217-355-9413
E-mail: mbalogh@balogh.com

Founded 1961. 100 members. Open to antique, special interest and classic car enthusiasts. Monthly newsletter, *The Roadmap*. Many annual events including a show in August. Dues: $15/year.

Israel Classic Car & Motorcycle Club
PO Box 39960
Tel Aviv 61398 Israel
+972-3-9793773; FAX: +972-3-9793774
E-mail: 5club@5club.org.il

Founded 1985. 1,400 members. Israel's only national car club. Classic and vintage cars and motorcycles of all makes. Weekly and monthly meetings and events. 3 annual shows. Monthly newsletter (in Hebrew) and quarterly publications (32 pages in Hebrew). Old cars museum and transportation archives. Dues: $50/year. Web site: 5club.org.il

Kent Island Cruisers Car Club
509 Victoria Dr
Stevensville, MD 21666-2625
410-643-4582

Founded 1994. 120+ members. No restrictions although the club is primarily made up of classic, street rods and antiques. Benefits include monthly newsletter and event information, discounts at some local stores, monthly membership meetings and summer cruise nights. Monthly newsletter with 12 pages of local events, classified ads, tech tips and other related information free with membership. Dues: $15/year.

King Kruisers Car Club
491 Allendale Rd #106
King of Prussia, PA 19406
610-265-2611; FAX: 610-962-0872

Founded 1995. Everyone welcome. Cruise nights 3rd Saturday of month, April-September. Local runs. Monthly newsletter. Dues: $20/year.

Klassy Kruzers Car Club
1 Kruzers Alley
Dunbar, WV 25064
304-768-7935

Founded 1989. 100 members. No restrictions to join. One meeting a month, two club cruise-ins, one car show, one cruise-in June 11, one cruise-in and show September 17-18, monthly newsletter. Dues: $12/year.

Kustom Kemps of America
Rt 1 Box 1714
Bill Hailey Dr
Cassville, MO 65625-9724
417-847-2940; FAX: 417-847-3647

Founded 1980. 10,000 members. 1935-1964 (Lead Sled Division) and 1965-present (Late Model Division). Publication, *Trendsetter Magazine*. Dues: $28/year.

Lake Region Car Club
PO Box 2
Revillo, SD 57259
605-623-4538; FAX: 605-623-4215
E-mail: alevisen@adhscats.org

Founded 1970. 25 members. Publish a bi-monthly newsletter, sponsor one car show a year, meet monthly (April-December) and take at least two driving tours each year. Dues: $10/year.

Lambda Car Club International
Delaware Valley Region
515 W Chelten Ave, Suite 1009
Philadelphia, PA 19144
610-688-6087
E-mail: devonwest@aol.com

Founded 1987. 50 members. A non-profit organization promoting fellowship among all peoples especially lesbians and gays interested in old and special interest motor vehicles. Annual international convention. Annual regional car show. Bi-monthly international newsletter. Monthly regional newsletter. Monthly socials and summer cruise-ins. Technical and social advisories. Dues: $30/year. Web site: www.classicar.com/clubs/lambdacarclub

The Mid-America Old Time Automobile Association
8 Jones Ln
Morrilton, AR 72110
PH/FAX: 501-727-5427

Founded 1959. 1,000 members in 29 affiliated clubs. The club recognizes automobiles built through 1972. *Antique Car Times* is published six times per year. Annual auto show and swap meet held the third weekend in June at the Museum of Automobiles on Petit Jean Mountain, Morrilton, Arkansas. Dues: $15/year.

Midwestern Council of Sports Car Clubs
3618 E 1769th Rd
Ottawa, IL 61350
815-434-9999; FAX: 815-434-9882
E-mail: rossf@interaccess.com

Founded 1958. 980 members. Sports car racing for vintage and current era cars. On-track driver schools (3/yr). Open track autocross/time trials. Wheel to wheel racing. Free introductory series in Rolling Meadows, IL. SASE for free info packet. Publications: *Klaxon* monthly newsletter, picture annual, annual rule book. Dues: $40/year. Web site: www.execpc.com/~mcscc

National Woodie Club
PO Box 6134
Lincoln, NE 68506
402-488-0990
E-mail: woodcar@tiac.net

Founded 1974. 2,650 members. Open to anyone interested in wood-bodied vehicles, original or modified. Ownership not required. Monthly magazine, *The Woodie Times*, with free ads to members 8 times per year, annual membership roster, regional chapters, tech advisors. Several regional and national events each year, in all parts of the country. Web site: www.classicar.com

chapters:

California	*Santa Cruz Woodies*, Andi Welles, 86 Hagemann Ct, Santa Cruz, CA 95062, 408-427-9433
	Southern California Woodies, Mark Gansel, PO Box 4533, San Clemente, CA 92674
Colorado	*Hi-Country Chapter*, John Blachowski, 2254 S Kingston Ct, Aurora, CO 80014, 303-338-9000
Illinois	*Lincoln Log Riders Club*, Michael Byrne, 13500 S Bell Rd, Lockport, IL 60441-8452, 708-301-7541
Massachusetts	*Yankee Wood Chapter*, Maria Maurer, PO Box 653, Dover, MA 02030, 508-785-1078
Virginia	*Capital District Chapter*, Jim Yergin, 5290 Old Alexandria Tpk, Warrenton, VA 20187-9358, 540-347-7342

Newfoundland Antique and Classic Car Club
PO Box 28147, Avalon Mall
St John's, NF Canada A1B 4J8
709-368-0865; FAX: 709-368-3436
E-mail: hillsci@nfld.com

Founded 1980. 112 members. Open to anyone. Registered vehicles must be antiques, 25 years old or older, vehicles 20-25 accepted by vote. Meet 2nd Wednesday evening, St John's Curling Club. Cruises every Thursday, A&W, weather permitting. Dues: $30/year. Web site: www.infonet.st-johns.nf.ca/naccc

Nor-Cal Galaxies/Mercurys
PO Box 6682
Concord, CA 94524-1682
925-825-2906; FAX: 925-684-2044
E-mail: rsheals@gte.net

Founded 1987. 85 memberships, 200 cars. Dedicated to the preservation, restoration and enjoyment of 1959-1970 Ford Galaxies and Mercurys, by expanding interest, exchanging information and assisting others in obtaining and restoring these cars. Also share the responsibility of fighting detrimental legislation aimed at removing classic cars from our roadways. Ownership is not a requirement. Club activities include outings, car shows, "Shop Days", holiday parties, monthly meetings. Newsletter is published monthly to inform members of meetings, activities and to share member car histories and technical information. Dues: $24/year.

Northeast Hemi Owners Assoc
74 Diller Ave
New Holland, PA 17557
717-354-0502

Founded 1976. 235 members. Open to all Mopars and AMC products. 2 meets a year, Memorial Day and Labor Day weekends. Newsletter, 6 issues a year. Dues: $25/year single, $30/year joint.

Old Car Club Inc
PO Box 462
Shrewsbury, MA 01545

Founded 1947. 90 members. No restrictions to join. Monthly newsletter, *Mudguard*. Mid-summer annual meet (car show, antique cars 25 years old or older, trophies). Dues: $15/year.

Old Cars Unlimited of Washington, DC
112 Rhode Island Ave NW
Washington, DC 20001
202-638-1771

Founded 1990. 30 members. Vehicles must be fifteen years old or older and must be in stock condition. Meetings 1st Monday each month. Dues: $25/year.

The Olde Tyme Auto Club
Station A Box 4534
Evansville, IN 47724-4534
812-474-1716
E-mail: deager1998@aol.com

Founded 1953. 130 members. Sponsor annual car show and swap meet 2nd weekend of June. 1999 was our 31st annual show. Dues: $15/year family.

Police Car Owners of America
15677 Hwy 62 W
Eureka Springs, AR 72632
501-253-4948; FAX: 501-253-4949

Founded 1991. 700 members worldwide. Open to all makes of police vehicles. Also to model builders. Members receive shoulder patch, decal, key ring, ID card and subscription to quarterly newsletter which features free advertising to members. State and regional chapters. Dues: $25/year US, $30/year Canada, $35/year overseas. Web site: www.policeguide.com/policecarclub.htm

chapters:

Arizona	David Gittner, 4701 N 68th St #107, Scottsdale, AZ 85251, 602-946-9570
California	Darryl Lindsay, PO Box 412, San Carlos, CA 94070, 415-592-7662
Connecticut	Thomas Weglarz Jr, 272 Woodbury Cir, Middletown, CT 06457, 203-343-0141
Georgia	Rick Thomas, PO Box 2403, Brunswick, GA 31521, 912-261-3695
Illinois	Greg Reynolds, 7112 W Summerdale, Chicago, IL 60656, 773-775-8031
Indiana	Edwin Sanow, 801 W 500 S, Boswell, IN 47921, 765-869-5815
Kansas	Jack Attig, 12990 V4 Rd, Hoyt, KS 66440-9064, 913-986-6426
Maryland	Victor E Colangelo, 1010 James St, Bel Air, MD 21014-2312, 410-638-6309
Michigan	Bob Johnson, 3726 Kane Rd, Carleton, MI 48117, 313-654-9327
Minnesota	Steve Pruitt, 316 S 6th St, Marshall, MN 56258, 507-532-5837
Missouri	*Eastern Missouri*, Dennis Sanchez, 1205 W Main St, Festus, MO 63028, 314-931-3644
	Western Missouri, Jim Cordell, 300 16th Ave S, Greenwood, MO 64034, 816-573-6248
Nebraska	Monty McCord, PO Box 133, Juniata, NE 68955, 402-751-2632
New Hampshire	Bill Robarge, 38 Peter Ct, Belmont, NH 03220, 603-527-1775

Police Car Owners of America chapters *(continued)*

New York/ Frank Goderre, 1561 Park St, Peekskill, NY
New Jersey 10566, 914-739-7943

Oklahoma Charles Primeaux, 4813 Newport Dr, Del City, OK 73115, 405-677-4952

Oregon Chris Watson, 145 Howard Pl, Grants Pass, OR 97526, 541-479-3858

Texas Ken T DeFoor, RR 5 Box 272, Dayton, TX 77535-9412, 713-820-7887

Wisconsin Bruce Hollander, 2129 S 107th St, West Allis, WI 53227, 414-545-5993

Canada *Eastern Canada*, Jason Williams, 162 Burns St #B, Strathroy, ON N7G 1E8, 519-246-1143

Western Canada, Sid Gough, Box 25, Irricana, AB T0M 1B0, 403-935-4216

Europe Rudiger Lotz, Johannesstrabe 1, 53225 Bonn, 01149-228-473765

Roaring 20's Antique & Classic Car Club Inc
PO Box 956
Cheshire, CT 06410
860-628-2309

Contact: Mary Gura. Founded 1969. 147 members. No restrictions to join. Dues: $21/year.

Topeka British Car Club
5231 NW Courtland
Topeka, KS 66618
785-246-2393
E-mail: mctriumph3467@juno.com

Founded 1992. 75 members. No membership restrictions. Monthly newsletter, *Knockoff News*. Monthly meetings and rallies. All British car enthusiasts welcomed.

Veteran Motor Car Club of America
4441 W Altadena Ave
Glendale, AZ 85304-3526
800-428-7327, 602-978-5622
FAX: 602-978-1106

For information, contact at the above address: Richard Rigby. Founded 1938. 5,700 members. Dues $35/year.

regions:

Arizona *NARHS Region*, Baja Arizona Chapter, Tedd deLong, President, PO Box 34, Valley Farms, AZ 85291, 520-723-5290

Southwest Region, Tedd deLong, Regional Director, PO Box 34, Valley Farms, AZ 85291, 520-723-5290

Southwest Region, Central Arizona Chapter, Bill Graves, President, PO Box 99, Camp Verde, AZ 86322-0099, 520-567-4347

Southwest Region, Coyote Chapter, Ron Sotardi, President, 3520 N Via San Juanito, Tucson, AZ 85749-8558, 520-749-8659

Southwest Region, Hummingbird Chapter, Harold Hawes, President, 5154 Calle Virada, Sierra Vista, AZ 85635, 520-458-8740

Southwest Region, Phoenix Chapter, Linda Butch, President, 4040 S Taylor, Tempe, AZ 85282, 602-897-7549

Southwest Region, Route 66 Car Club, Jim Roper, President, 2490 Carefree Cr, Flagstaff, AZ 86004, 520-527-9176

Southwest Region, Valley Roadrunners Chapter, John Tatro, President, 805 N 8th St #127, Avondale, AZ 85323, 602-932-4615

California *California Region*, Ray Williams, Regional Director, 12201 Gaston Rd, Madera, CA 93638, 209-645-5737

California Region, Los Angeles Chapter, Charles White, President, 2684 Turnbull Canyon Rd, Hacienda Heights, CA 91745, 310-693-5641

California Region, Nickel Age Touring Club, John Bertolotti, President, 150 Brooke Acres Dr, Los Gatos, CA 95032-6454, 408-358-6740

Colorado *Mountain Plains Region*, Colorado West Chapter, Richard Mendenhall, President, 289 Coulson Dr, Grand Junction, CO 81503, 970-243-2078

Mountain Plains Region, Denver Mile High Chapter, John Tuthill, President, 20413 W 56th, Rt 11, Golden, CO 80403, 303-279-8039

Mountain Plains Region, Loveland Chapter, Fred Krueger, President, 2794 N Empire Ave, Loveland, CO 80538, 970-669-6528

Mountain Plains Region, Montrose Chapter, Ralph Merwin, President, 9009 60.75 Rd, Montrose, CO 81401, 970-323-6641

Mountain Plains Region, Pikes Peak Chapter, John King, President, 2820 Avondale Dr, Colorado Springs, CO 80917, 719-573-5128

Mountain Plains Region, Pueblo-Arkansas Valley Chapter, Glen Wright, President, 824 Van Buren, Pueblo, CO 81004, 719-544-9686

Mountain Plains Region, Royal Gorge Chapter, Jim Fontana, President, 11609 Freemont Dr, Canon City, CO 81212, 719-275-6486

Florida *Florida Region*, Steve Wolf, Regional Director, 6720 SW 104 St, Miami, FL 33156, 305-665-9131

Florida Region, Citrus Capital Chapter, Richard T Gabrich, President, 8320 75th Ct, Vero Beach, FL 32967, 561-589-0242

Florida Region, Palm Beach County Chapter, Buddy Pierce, President, 7301 S Flagler Dr, West Palm Beach, FL 33405, 407-659-4854

Florida Region, Roadrunners Chapter, Earl Young, President, 533 67th St, Holmes Beach, FL 34217, 941-778-6731

Florida Region, Sun Coast Chapter, John Layzell, President, 2235 Magnolia Dr, North Miami Beach, FL 33145, 305-891-2059

Idaho *Bonneville Region*, Eastern Idaho Chapter, Lynn Erickson, President, 712 S 35th W, Idaho Falls, ID 83402, 208-522-4207

Bonneville Region, Magic Valley Chapter, Chuck Steinmetz, President, 951B S 1150 E, Eden, ID 83325, 208-825-5400

Bonneville Region, Tri-City Chapter, Sam Otero, President, 4656 Navajo St, Pocatello, ID 83204, 208-234-2917

Kansas *Mountain Plains Region*, Bob Bethell, Regional Director, PO Box 186, Alden, KS 67512, 316-534-3085

Mountain Plains Region, Kanza Chapter, Dean Davison, President, 309 W Truesdell, Lyons, KS 67554, 316-257-2914

Kentucky *Kentucky Region*, James E Poe, Regional Director, 3466 Mt Horeb Pike, Lexington, KY 40511, 606-255-0296

Kentucky Region, Bluegrass Chapter, Jane Johnson, President, 3456 Belvoir Dr, Lexington, KY 40502, 606-227-0327

Kentucky Region, Louisville Chapter, John H Caperton, President, 3112 Boxhill Ct, Louisville, KY 40222, 502-895-4127

Maryland *Midatlantic Region*, Charles Smith, Regional Director, 2030 Calvary Rd, Bel Air, MD 21015, 410-836-2705

Massachuetts *Connecticut Valley Region*, Willard Hick, Regional Director, 3 Iroquois Ln, Wilbraham, MA 01095, 413-596-4847

Massachusetts *New England Region*, Edmund F Leland III, Regional Director, 254 Great Pond Rd, North Andover, MA 01845, 508-688-4491

Michigan *Great Lakes Region*, Leon Zimkiewicz, Regional Director, 1480 Winter Ln, Brighton, MI 48114-8733, 810-227-6875

Great Lakes Region, Battle Creek Chapter, Glen Marentette, President, 675 Knollwood Dr, Battle Creek, MI 49015, 616-964-8966

Great Lakes Region, Blue Water Chapter, Robert G Burchill, President, 2316 17th Ave, Port Huron, MI 48060, 810-982-8210

Great Lakes Region, Brass and Gas Chapter, Wayne Funk, President, 14834 30 Mile Rd, Washington, MI 48095, 810-752-5341

Great Lakes Region, Brighton Chapter, Carl Sturgeon, President, 655 Burns Rd, Milford, MI 48381, 248-685-8806

Great Lakes Region, Detroit Chapter, Gray Robling, President, 24480 Lakeland, Farmington Hills, MI 48336, 248-478-6406

Great Lakes Region, Huron Valley Chapter, George Schaffer, President, 9317 Mapletree Dr, Plymouth, MI 48170, 313-453-7505

Great Lakes Region, Jackson Cascades Chapter, Leo E Warren, President, 3500 Hoyer Rd, Jackson, MI 49201, 517-764-3731

Great Lakes Region, Lakeshore Chapter, Ron Harris, President, 21916 Birchwood, St Clair Shores, MI 48082, 810-293-1284

Great Lakes Region, Lansing Chapter, James R Neal, President, 1069 Applegate, East Pointe, MI 48021, 810-779-4279

Missouri *Midwest Region*, Michael Welsh, Regional Director, 7501 Manchester Ave, Kansas City, MO 64138, 816-353-7890

Midwest Region, Heartland Chapter, Bob Collings, President, 19700 E 225th St, Harrisonville, MO 64701, 816-887-2319

Midwest Region, Kansas City Chapter, Don Oberholtz, President, 23903 Poindexter Dr, Lee's Summit, MO 64086, 816-537-6256

Midwest Region, Missouri Valley Chapter, Cooper Weeks, President, 3635 Belleview, Kansas City, MO 64111, 816-931-6230

Nevada *Western Region*, Art Foote, Regional Director, 3535 Freedom Ave, Las Vegas, NV 89121, 702-451-0026

Western Region, High Rollers Chapter, Gene Donley, President, 6349 Elmira Dr, Las Vegas, NV 89118, 702-876-5593

New Jersey *New York Region*, Edward Rowan, Regional Director, 161 Holland Rd, Far Hills, NJ 07931, 732-752-3636

New York Region, Garden State Chapter, Robert Giuliani, President, 72 Northwood Ave, Demarest, NJ 07627, 201-768-7973

New Mexico *Southwest Region*, Albuquerque Chapter, Joe Cifaratta, President, 186 Rincon Loop, Tijeras, NM 87059, 505-281-1933

New York *New York Region*, The Long Island Old Car Club, Charles Reylek, President, 67 Snedecor Ave, Bayport, NY 11705, 516-472-1154

New York Region, Niagara Frontier Chapter, Paul H Will Jr, President, 11965 Liberia Rd, East Aurora, NY 14052, 716-627-7857

Ohio *Buckeye-Keystone Region*, Walter Stockert, Regional Director, 985 Weber Ave SW, Strasburg, OH 44680, 330-878-5008

Buckeye-Keystone Region, Canton Chapter, Richard Barnhouse, President, 85 Haswell Cr, Strasburg, OH 44680, 303-878-7685

Buckeye-Keystone Region, Emerald Necklace Chapter, Scott Hartman, President, 14388 Trenton Ave, Strongsville, OH 44136, 216-238-0712

Great Lakes Region, Black Swamp Chapter, Tom Rectenwald, President, 25335 Hull Prairie Rd, Perrysburg, OH 43551, 419-874-5597

Great Lakes Region, Defiance Chapter, Jack Taylor, President, 15-280-F75, Bryan, OH 43506, 419-636-5873

Great Lakes Region, Toledo Chapter, Ralph Emery, President, 2608 Sequoia Rd, Toledo, OH 43617, 419-853-3882

Kentucky Region, Nickel Age Touring Chapter, John Tarleton, President, 449 W 5th St, Salem, OH 44460-2107, 330-332-0116

NARHS Region, Thomas F Saal, Regional Director, 1488 W Clifton, Lakewood, OH 44107, 216-521-3588

Ohio Valley Region, Tom Michael, Regional Director, 2267 Fairgreen Dr, Cincinnati, OH 45238, 513-922-6792

Tri-State Region, Albert Pavlik Jr, Regional Director, 1803 Norton Pl, Steubenville, OH 43952, 740-282-7197

Veteran Motor Car Club of America regions *(continued)*

Tri-State Region, Steel Valley Chapter, Robert H Kaine, President, 159 Gumps Ln, Wintersville, OH 43953, 740-264-7219

Rhode Island *New England Region,* Viking Chapter, Roger and Susan Paul, President, 43 Heritage Rd, North Kingston, RI 02852, 401-885-1190

South Dakota *Mountain Plains Region,* Gold Dust Chapter, Joan Lemer, President, PO Box 2973, Rapid City, SD 57709, 605-348-7529

Texas *Texoma Region,* Barbara Robbins, Regional Director, 10816 E Cottonwood Rd, Midland, TX 79707, 915-563-2258

Texoma Region, Bexar Touring Club, John Jones, President, PO Box 1705, Boerne, TX 78006, 830-537-4503

Texoma Region, Cowtown Touring Club, Mike Jones, President, PO Box 100397, Fort Worth, TX 76185, 817-738-4699

Texoma Region, Fredericksburg Vintage Car Club, E M "Tex" Anderson, President, 401 Highland Dr, Kerrville, TX 78028, 830-896-8075

Texoma Region, Key to the Hills Chapter, James E George, President, 25615 Dull Knife Tr, San Antonio, TX 78255, 210-755-4633

Texoma Region, Permian Basin Oil Burners, Cathy Womack, President, 6309 Mecca, Odessa, TX 79762, 915-366-2388

Utah *Bonneville Region,* Dr Robert Bryner, Regional Director, 144 E 300 N, Logan, UT 84321, 435-752-8166

Bonneville Region, Cache Valley Chapter, Craig Balls, President, 1097 Lamplighter Dr, Logan, UT 84321, 435-753-0514

Bonneville Region, Copper Classics Chapter, Chuck Sparrer, President, 5285 S Havenwood Ln, Salt Lake City, UT 84117, 801-278-0206

Bonneville Region, Utah Chapter, Kelly Purdum, President,4678 S Brown St, Murray, UT 84107, 801-272-2584

Washington *Northwest Region,* Mari Andrus, Regional Director, 70 Shadow Tr, Sequim, WA 98382, 360-681-0413

Northwest Region, Capital City Chapter, Roy Friis, President, 6518 32nd Ave NW, Olympia, WA 98502-9519, 360-866-7716

Northwest Region, Sequim Valley Chapter, Forrest Davis, President, PO Box 76, Sequim, WA 98382, 360-683-5871

Wyoming *Mountain Plains Region,* Oil Country Chapter, Steve Johnson, President, 721 W 57 St, Casper, WY 82601, 307-235-1051

The Vintage Car Club of New Zealand Inc
PO Box 2546
Christchurch New Zealand
03-366-4461; FAX: 03-366-0273
E-mail: admin@vcc.co.nz
or e-mail: beadedwheels@vcc.co.nz

Founded 1946. 6,100 members. Dedicated to the preservation of historic vehicles and New Zealand's motoring history. Members benefit from access to research material, parts, etc.

Approximately 150 events and meets annually, 36 branches throughout the country and a national magazine, *Beaded Wheels,* New Zealand's only veteran and vintage motoring magazine containing restoration and rally articles, technical tips and swap meet information. Subscription rate: $27.00 (o/s rates on application), 6 times/year. Dues: $50-$70/year, varies by region.

Vintage Wheels Antique Car Club
Rt 4, Box 165
Great Bend, KS 67530
316-793-7162

Founded 1975. 50 members. Dedicated to the preservation of and interest in antique and special interest vehicles. Dues: $20/year.

White Owners Register
1624 Perkins Dr
Arcadia, CA 91006
626-355-7679 evenings

Founded 1970. 300 members. Caters to owners of White, Indiana, Cletrac, Rollin, Templar, Rubay vehicles. Technical data shared. We cooperate with VWTA. Dues: none.

White Squirrel Cruisers
PO Box 14
Olney, IL 62450
618-393-7738; FAX: 618-395-4711
E-mail: gorace@omegabbs.com

Founded 1987. 20 members. Interest in automobiles, young or old. Newsletter, web page, 1 show, 3 cruises per year. Dues: $15/year. Web site: www.omegabbs.com/users.wsc

---

Willys-Overland-Knight Registry Inc
1440 Woodacre Dr
McLean, VA 22101-2535
703-533-0396

For membership information, contact at the above address: Duane Perrin. Founded 1960. 1,300 members. An organization of people interested in the Willys-Overland family of cars to 1942 and all Knight-engined vehicles and Stearns cars. Quarterly publication, *Starter.* Also monthly newsletter. Dues: $24/year US, $26/year Canada, $30/year all other countries.

Winamac Old Auto Club
PO Box 28
Crown Point, IN 46307
219-759-1638
E-mail: catbil@netnitco.net

Founded 1950. 125 members. Original restorations, monthly meetings, social activities, drive-outs, annual car show and swap meet, monthly newsletter on club activities. Dues: $12/year.

Ye Olde Car Club of Tri-Cities
PO Box 6873
Kennewick, WA 99336-0601
509-586-4933

Founded 1963. 170 members. No restrictions, just interest in old cars, enjoyment of association with others of similar interests. Monthly newsletter, *The Gas Gauge,* included in annual dues. Information available: *Hemmings Motor News, Old Car Weekly* magazine, *Old Car Value Guides.* Swap meet and car tours. Dues: $10/year.

Marque Clubs

Abarth Owners International
Box 1917
Thousand Oaks, CA 91360
818-707-2301

Founded 1963. 600/800 members. Publications, meets and events. AOI books available are 001 through 008, hardcover and color. Dues: $28/year.

The Abarth Register USA Inc
54 School St, Ste 102
Westbury, NY 11590-4469
516-876-8754; FAX: 516-538-7118

For membership information, contact at the above address: Gerald Rothman, Director. Founded 1973. 200 members. Vintage car club for Abarth and Cisitalia owners and enthusiasts. Do not have to own one to belong. Organized for the restoration, preservation and enjoyment of the Abarth and Cisitalia marques. Affiliated with Abarth Club of United Kingdom; Abarth Corsa Deutschland of Germany; Club Abarth, France; Club Abarth, Japan; Svenska Abarth Registret, Sweden; RIA, Registro Italiano Abarth, Italy. Quarterly newsletter. Club maintains excellent data base network of Abarth information and parts sources. Dues: $35/year US and foreign.

AC Owner's Club Ltd
11955 SW Faircrest St
Portland, OR 97225-4615
503-643-3225; FAX: 503-646-4009

For US registrar, contact at the above address: Jim Feldman. The world's largest organization of AC owners and enthusiasts. AC ownership not required. Monthly magazine.

Texas Hill Country Alfa Romeo Owners Club
PO Box 523
Alpine, TX 79831-0523
915-837-1717
E-mail: thc-aroc-usa@brooksdata.net

Founded 1982. 50 members. Club events and benefits include Hill Country tours, autocrosses, local and national monthly newsletters, technical info, AROC tech hotlines, tech sessions. Meetings in Austin or San Antonio. Dues: $45/year. Web site: www.brooksdata.net/personal/thc-aroc-usa

The Allard Owners Club
10 Brooklyn Ct
Woking
GU22 7TQ England
PH/FAX: +44 1483 773428
E-mail: 106752.2145@compuserve.com

For membership information, contact at the above address: Miss Michelle Wilson. Founded 1951 by Sydney Allard. Dedicated to the preservation and promotion of Allard cars. Dues: £25/year.

Alvis Owner Club of North America
140 Race St
PO Box 46
Bainbridge, PA 17502
PH/FAX: 717-426-3842

150 members. Dues: $10/year.

AMC World Clubs
7963 Depew St
Arvada, CO 80003-2527
303-428-8760; FAX: 303-428-1070

Founded 1974. 1,500 members. Comprised of the union of the Classic AMX Club International and American Motorsport International. AMC World Clubs is for those interested in AMC/AMX/Rambler/AMC-Jeep vehicles, 1954-1987. Telephone technical and restoration assistance six days a week. Large 28-32 page bi-monthly magazine. Dues: $30/year US, $35/year Canada and overseas.

American Motorsport International
7963 Depew St
Arvada, CO 80003-2527
303-428-8760; FAX: 303-428-1070

Founded 1987. International club for owners and enthusiasts of American Motors cars, 1955-1988. Large bi-monthly club publication. Parent organization is AMC World Clubs Inc. Telephone-tech and restoration help six days a week for members. Dues: $30/year US, $35/year Canada and overseas. Web site: www.amcwc.com

chapters:

Arizona — *The Arizona AMC Club*, c/o Mark Fletcher, 7257 W Paradise Dr, Peoria, AZ 85345

California — *American Motorsport of San Diego*, c/o Tony Zamisch, 977 Florida St, Imperial Beach, CA 91932

The South Bay AMC Club, c/o Pat Whiteside, 2348 Richland Ave, San Jose, CA 95125

Colorado — *The Pikes Peak AMC Club*, c/o Doug Eiriksen, 7935 Forest Hgts Cr, Colorado Springs, CO 80908

The Rocky Mountain AMC Club, c/o Werner Fruhwirth, 210 S Alcott St, Denver, CO 80219

Indiana — *The Hoosier Classic AMX/AMC Club*, c/o Harold Lehman, 3420 S 700 W, Pierceton, IN 46562

Nevada — *Southern Nevada American Motors Club*, c/o Larry R Leard, 7575 Hickman Ave, Las Vegas, NV 89129

New York — *The Hudson Valley American Motors Club*, c/o Joe Marsh, PO Box 165, Worcester, NY 12197

The Metropolitan NY & NJ Chapter, c/o Peter Statehes, 51 Twin Lawns Ave, Hicksville, NY 11801

Oregon — *American Motorsport of Portland*, c/o Max Frye, 14950 S Bradley Rd, Oregon City, OR 97045

Pennsylvania — *The Central Penn AMX/AMC Club*, c/o Bruce Rambler, 798 N Forge Rd, Palmyra, PA 17078

Washington — *American Motors Club Northwest*, c/o Al Barrie, PO Box 66672, Burien, WA 98166

Olympic Peninsula AMC Club, c/o Robert Bale, 5851 NE Lincoln Rd E, Poulsbo, WA 98370

Twin Harbors American Motors Club, c/o Mark Ogulnick, 3018 Sumner Ave, Hoquiam, WA 98550

Wisconsin — *The Wisconsin AMX/AMC Club*, c/o Jeff Sorenson, 2368 N 114th St, Milwaukee, WI 53226

Australia — *The Javelin Register of Australia (affiliated)*, c/o Craig Norling, 5 Two Bays Dr, Somerville, Victoria 3912

The American Rebels AMC Club
1614 Van Vranken Ave
Schenectady, NY 12308
518-372-4929
E-mail: ajg@nyserda.org

Founded 1990. 50 members. Organizers of the free AMC-Nash-Rambler Northeast Regional Car Show, held free of charge every last weekend in June at the Days Inn, Glenmont, NY, just off NYS Thruway exit #23. 8th annual show was June 26-27, 1999.

American Austin-Bantam Club
351 Wilson Rd
Willshire, OH 45898-9551
419-495-2569

Founded 1962. 700 members. Annual meet with judging. Club newsletters 6 times a year. Roster updates, technical assistance, leads of parts and vehicles for sale. Dues: $20/year per family, $25/year Canada and foreign, US funds.

Pacific Bantam Austin Club
1589 N Grand Oaks Ave
Pasadena, CA 91104
626-791-2617

For membership information, contact at the above address: Norm Booth. Founded 1969. 250 members. Club is open to American Austin, American Bantam and all pre-World War II British Austin Seven enthusiasts. 1999 dues: $15/year US, $20/year other countries; 2000 dues: $20/year US, $25/year other countries.

Amilcar Register
16 Holliland Croft
GT TEY Colchester C06 1BB
England
PH/FAX: 44-206-213683

Founded 1960. 120 members. Publish newsletter every 4 months. Rallies and social events in United Kingdom and Europe. Dues: £15/year.

Amphicar Car Club
Rue du College, BP-153
B-4800 Verviers Belgium
PH/FAX: 3287335122

Founded 1988. 20 members. No restriction to join. The club is open to all Amphicar lovers. Free newsletter. Dues: none.

International Amphicar Club
13 Bluebird Ln
Gloversville, NY 12078-9314
518-773-8877; FAX: 518-773-3370
E-mail: info@amphicar.com

Founded 1993. 280 members. Everybody welcome. Color bi-monthly newsletter. Annual convention. Free classifieds and much more. Float on in. Dues: $20/year US, $25/year Canada, $30/year foreign. Web site: amphicar.com

Classic AMX Club International
7963 Depew St
Arvada, CO 80003
303-428-8760; FAX: 303-428-1070

AMX

Founded 1973. 1,235 members. Open to owners and enthusiasts of the 1968, 1969, 1970 two passenger sport coupe. Large 28 page all AMC bi-monthly magazine. Telephone assistance on restoration, questions of originality, etc. Largest collection of AMX historical artifacts in the world. Dues: $30/year US, $35/year Canada and overseas. Web site: amcwc.com

chapters:

Arizona   *The Arizona AMC Club*, c/o Mark Fletcher, 7257 W Paradise Dr, Peoria, AZ 85345

California   *The South Bay AMC Club*, c/o Pat Whiteside, 2348 Richland Ave, San Jose, CA 95125

Indiana   *The Hoosier Classic AMX/AMC Club*, c/o Harold Lehman, 3420 S 700 W, Pierceton, IN 46562

Massachusetts   *The Classic AMX Club of New England*, c/o Tom Benvie, 5 Sachem Rock Ave, East Bridgewater, MA 02333

New Jersey   *The Mid-Atlantic Classic AMX Club*, c/o George Watts, 18 Berlin Cross Keys Rd, Williamstown, NJ 08094

New York   *The Metropolitan NY & NJ Chapter*, c/o Peter Stathes, 51 Twin Lawns Ave, Hicksville, NY 11801

Oregon   *The Classic AMX Club of Portland*, c/o Larry Lotter, 13575 SE 119th Dr, Clackamas, OR 97015

Pennsylvania   *The Central Penn AMX/AMC Club*, c/o Bruce Rambler, 798 N Forge Rd, Palmyra, PA 17078

Washington   *American Motors Club Northwest*, c/o Al Barrie, PO Box 66672, Burien, WA 98166

Olympic Peninsula AMC Club, c/o Robert Bale, 5851 NE Lincoln Rd E, Poulsbo, WA 98370

Twin Harbors American Motors Club, c/o Mark Ogulnick, 3018 Sumner Ave, Hoquiam, WA 98550

Wisconsin   *The Wisconsin AMX/AMC Club*, c/o Jeff Sorenson, 2368 N 114th St, Milwaukee, WI 53226

Australia   *The Classic AMX Club of Australia*, c/o Ray Sprague, 187 Adderly St, W Melbourne, Victoria 3003

Austin-Healey Club of America
PO Box 3220
Monroe, NC 28111-3220
877-5HEALEY toll-free

For membership information, contact at the above address: Edie Anderson. Founded 1961. Over 3,500 members. Club offers sevices for all Austin-Healeys and Austin-Healey Sprites. Monthly newsletter, *Harley Marque*. Dues: $40/January-July, $25/August-December, plus local club dues. International dues: $56 service, $76 air.

chapters:

Alabama   Rodney Martin, 85 Rifle Range Ridge, Wetumpka, AL 36092

California   *Central Valley*, David Nock, 1235 Eastridge Pl, Manteca, CA 95336

Golden Gate, John Trifari, 1160 LaRochelle Terr #B, Sunnyvale, CA 94089-1754

Colorado   *Rocky Mountain*, Marty VanScoyk, 8334 W Nevada Pl, Lakewood, CO 80226

DC (MD, VA)   *Capital*, Herman Farrer, 9012 Sudbury Rd, Silver Spring, MD 20901

Florida   *Orlando*, Michael Pinter, 522 Spring Club Dr, Altamonte Springs, FL 32714

Pensacola, Don Haugen, 9183 S Ponderosa, Mobile, AL 36575-7251

St John's, Bill Young, 208 St John's River Pl Ln, Switzerland, FL 32259

Tampa Bay, Marion Brantley, 2696 66th Terr S, St Petersburg, FL 33712

Georgia   *Central GA*, Len Thomas, 2140 Mountain Ln, Stone Mountain, GA 30087-1034

Illinois   *Illini*, Ed Kaler, 5624 S Washington, Hinsdale, IL 60521

Midwest, Bill Naretta, 404 Peach Tree Cir, Loves Park, IL 61111

Indiana   *Indianapolis*, Jim Richmond, 13088 Tarkington Common, Carmel, IN 46033

Northern Indiana, Jon Needler, 8308 S Anthony Blvd, Ft Wayne, IN 46816

Iowa   *Heartland Healey*, Darrell White, 408 Berry Ct, Port Byron, IL 61275

Kansas   Bill Maness, 4231 S Hocker Dr #13-100, Independence, MO 64055

Kentucky   *Bluegrass*, Mike Schneider, 110 N Rastetter, Louisville, KY 40206

Michigan   *SE Michigan*, Brian Thornton, 4618 Mandalay, Royal Oak, MI 48073-1624

Minnesota   Steve Rixen, 938 Becky Cir, Hudson, WI 54016

Missouri   *Gateway*, John Thousand, 9008 Crest Oak, Crestwood, MO 63126

Nebraska   *Flatwater*, Jerry Needham, 3728 Schuemann Dr, Omaha, NE 68123

New England/ Eastern New York   *Northeast*, Paul Dunnell, 299 River Rd, Chesterfield, NH 03466

New Mexico   *Roadrunner*, John Weinlein, PO Box 937, Cedar Crest, NM 87008

New York   *Niagara Frontier*, Rick Magro, 210 W Hazeltine Ave, Kenmore, NY 14217

North Carolina   *Carolinas*, Janis Pann, 322 E Houston St, Monroe, NC 28112

Triad, Gary Brierton, 9 Chestnut St, Lexington, NC 27292

Ohio   *Miami Valley*, Gregg Sipe, 2058 S Belleview Dr, Bellbrook, OH 45305

Mid-Ohio, Nancy Cole, 822 Mohawk St, Columbus, OH 43206-2604

NE Ohio, Bill Ebersole, 12535 Woodberry Ln, Strongsville, OH 44136

Ohio Valley, Don Klein, 1370 Karahill Dr, Cincinnati, OH 45240

Oklahoma   *Oklahoma AH Owners*, Chuck Anderson, 712 Miller Ave, Norman, OK 73069

Pennsylvania   *Three Rivers*, Tony Stakis, 218 Hoodridge Dr, Pittsburgh, PA 15234

Tennessee   *Middle TN*, Robbie Cook, 311 Winston Dr, Whitehouse, TN 37188

Smoky Mtn, Paulette Lownsdale, 417 Shawnee Pl, Loudon, TN 37774

Texas   *Gulf Coast*, Dave Edwards, Rt 1 Box 514, Washing-on-Braz, TX 77880

Northern Texas, Don Lenschow, Rt 2 Box 131, Boyd, TX 76023

Southern Texas, Brett Miller, 1006 Berrywood Dr, Austin, TX 78753-2426

Utah   *Bonneville*, Dave Maxwell, 1752 Paulista Way, Sandy, UT 84093

Virginia   *Tidewater*, Bill Parks, 25 Museum Dr, Newport News, VA 23601

Washington   Chuck Breckenridge, 7015 Olympic View Dr, Edmonds, WA 98026

Wisconsin   Leroy & Susan Joppa, PO Box 131, Laona, WI 54541-0131

Canada   *Bluewater*, Ken Williams, 2996 London Rd RR #1, Sarnia, ON N7T 7H2

Manitoba, Dave Gibson, 327 Ravelston Ave W, Winnipeg, MB R2C 1W3

Quebec, Roger Hamel, 317 Julie, St Eustache, QC J7P 3R8

Southern Ontario, Les Vass, 511 Guelph Line Ste 702, Burlington, ON L7R 3M3

Austin-Healey Sports and Touring Club
PO Box 3539
York, PA 17402
215-538-3813

Founded 1976. 400+ members. Most members are affiliated with one of six regions: Harrisburg, Lehigh Valley, Philadelphia, Brandywine, North Jersey and Long Island. Generally, regional activities are held monthly. A monthly magazine, *The Flash*, provides club and regional information. An all region event, Encounter, is usually held in August and is hosted by one of these regions. The club is dedicated to helping members enjoy the marque. Dues: $25/year. Web site: http://members.aol.com/ahstc

Mini Owners of New Jersey Car Club
24 Arrighi Dr
Warren, NJ 07059-5801
PH/FAX: 908-769-MINI
E-mail: miniac1@aol.com

Founded 1986. 150 members. A club for the Mini enthusiast. Also help people find Minis (1000s, Cooper S, etc) and parts for their Minis. A Mini is a small British auto created by Sir Alec Issigonis in 1959. Dues: $15/year.

DKW Club of America
260 Santa Margarita Ave
Menlo Park, CA 94025
650-321-6640; FAX: 650-329-0129
E-mail: jowett@best.com

AUTO UNION

See full listing in **Section Three** under **Marque Clubs**

Avanti Owners Association Int'l
PO Box 28788
Dallas, TX 75228
800-527-3452 US
214-709-6185 foreign

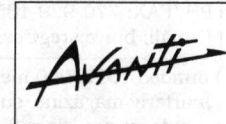

For membership information, contact, at the above address: Mr Sheldon Harrison, Membership Secretary. Founded 1963. 1,600 members. Open to all Avanti owners. Supports the Avanti marque from the 1963 Studebaker Avanti to the 1989 Avanti produced today. Ownership of an Avanti is not necessary to be a member. Publish *Avanti Quarterly* magazine, contains information on meets, member experiences, repairs, parts and cars for sale. Dues: $25/year.

Berkeley Newsletter
PO Box 162282
Austin, TX 78716-2282
512-327-6231
E-mail: gerronsh@aol.com

Founded 1990. 50 members. The only newsletter in North America devoted exclusively to Berkeley automobiles. Free ads to subscribers. Dues: $12/year.

Bitter Owners Club
Medina Garden Centre
Staplers Rd
Wootton IOW PO33 4RW England
PH/FAX: 0044-1983-883430

Founded 1988. 34 members. Publish *Best Bitter*, a bi-monthly magazine with 28-32 pages. Annual UK rally, representation at classic events, Bittermobilia range, sales/maintenance advice. Dues: £28/year (for US members).

BMW Car Club of America
2130 Massachusetts Ave
Cambridge, MA 02140
800-878-9292; FAX: 617-876-3424
E-mail: bmwcclub@aol.com

Founded 1969. 50,000 members. Open to BMW enthusiasts and owners. Benefits include monthly *Roundel*, our colorful, informative 130-plus page magazine featuring maintenance tips, test results of new products and exciting articles with tips on enhancing your BMW and ensuring its lasting value. Many of 60+ local chapters offer driving schools, tech sessions, rallies, autocrosses, social events and more. Dues: $35/year. Web site: www.bmwcca.org

The BMW CS Registry
c/o Art & Marilyn Wegweiser
5341 Gibson Hill Rd
Edinboro, PA 16412
814-734-5107
E-mail: awegweis@ncinter.net

Founded 1981. 350 members. No restrictions, for enthusiasts of the E9 Model and the E121 Model. Quarterly publication, $25 (included w/membership). Web site: www.bmwcsregistry.org

The BMW tii Register
Bob Murphy
6790 Monarda Ct
Houston, TX 77069
PH/FAX: 281-583-2676
E-mail: tiireg@aol.com

Founded 1981. 160 members. A special interest group for the BMW 2002tii. Quarterly newsletter, technical data and assistance. Past newsletters and manuals available. Group is dedicated to keeping the tii enjoyable and available. Dues: $15/2 years.

BMW Z Series Register
PO Box 81807
Conyers, GA 30013
PH/FAX: 770-929-1358
E-mail: bmwcsreg@earthlink.net

Founded 1997. 900 members. Must be BMW Z3 owner. Quarterly magazine, supplements on the off months which include events, classified and modification news. National Z3 Owners Homecoming September 2-5 at the BMW Z3 plant, Spartanburg, SC. Dues: $25/year. Web site: www.bmwregisters.com

Vintage BMW Motorcycle Owners Ltd
PO Box 67
Exeter, NH 03833
603-772-9799

For information, contact at the above address: Roland M Slabon, Editor. Founded 1972. 5,700 members. Devoted solely to the preservation, restoration, enjoyment and use of pre-1970 (vintage, antique and classic) BMW motorcycles. Extensive worldwide parts and publication service. Quarterly illustrated publication, *Vintage BMW Bulletin*. Dues $12/year. Web site: www.greatanswers.com/vintagebmw

Bricklin International Owners Club
Scott Hanisch, President
PO Box 2626
Grand Rapids, MI 49501-2626
FAX: 616-459-5915
E-mail: majordomo@autox.team.net

Membership inquiries: George Malaska, PO Box 564, Wakarusa, IN 46573. Founded 1975. 500 members. A non-profit club dedicated to the preservation and enjoyment of the Bricklin SV1, providing parts and service information. Two national meets per year and numerous regional functions. Quarterly magazine. Technical manuals. Dues: $35/year. Web site: http://129.189.4.248

American Bugatti Club
142 Berkeley St
Boston, MA 02116-5166
617-266-1217

Founded 1960. 300 members. Club encourages interest in Bugattis and provides network for members whereby they can learn more about each other and their cars. Open to Bugatti owners and genuine Bugatti enthusiasts. Publish a register of all known Bugattis in North America as well as the quarterly magazine *Pur Sang*. Inquiries regarding the Register or *Pur Sang* should be sent to the address above. Dues: $60/year USA and Canada, $65/year overseas, with a $10 initiation fee.

**1929 Silver Anniversary
Buick Club**
75 Oriole Pkwy
Toronto, ON Canada M4V 2E3
416-487-9522; FAX: 416-322-7475
E-mail: rolltop@compuserve.com

Founded 1987. 300 members. Ownership or interest in 1929 Buick preferred. *1929 Silver Anniversary Buick Newsletter*, published 4 times a year, 18 pages each issue with restoration information and want ads for parts. Dues: $15/year.

1937-38 Buick Club
1005 Rilma Ln
Los Altos, CA 94022
PH/FAX: 650-941-4587
E-mail: harrylogan@earthlink.net

Founded 1980. Over 600 members. International club devoted to restoration, preservation and enjoyment of 1937 and 1938 Buick automobiles. Open to those interested in 1937-1938 Buicks, not necessary to own one. Magazine published 6 times a year, *The Torque Tube*. Dues: $34/year US, $35/year Canada and Mexico, $40/year all others.

Buick Club of America
PO Box 401927
Hesperia, CA 92340-1927
760-947-2485; FAX: 760-947-2465
E-mail: natbuickclubval@juno.com

Founded 1966. 10,000 members. Founded for the preservation and restoration of those vehicles built by the Buick Motor

Division of General Motors Corporation. Dues: $30/year US, $48/year foreign. Web site: www.buickclub.org

chapters:

Arizona   *Southern Arizona*, Bob Gietl, 2890 N Sunrock Ln, Tucson, AZ 85745

Valley of the Sun, Greg Vair, PO Box 985, Phoenix, AZ 85001

California   *Buick Club of San Diego*, Lee Carroll, PO Box 87923, San Diego, CA 92138

Buick Club of the Redwoods, Rebecca Kisling, PO Box 1785, Rohnert Park, CA 94927, 707-575-1955

California Capitol, Jim Day, PO Box 601461, Sacramento, CA 95860

Inland Empire Road Masters, Larry Disney, 18343 Hibiscus Ave, Riverside, CA 92508, 909-780-9353

Los Angeles, Jim Moran, PO Box 10073, Canoga Park, CA 91309-1073

Northern California, Art Benton, 1704 Silverwood Rd, San Jose, CA 95124

Orange County, George Lux, 223 W Malvern, Fullerton, CA 92632

San Gabriel Valley, Preston Meyer, PO Box 2355, Pasadena, CA 91102-2355

Colorado   *Mile High*, Lou Scott, 4735 S Galapago, Englewood, CO 80110

Pike's Peak, Elmer "Gene" High, 14 Waltham Ave, Manitou Springs, CO 80829-1613, 719-685-0737

Rocky Mountain, Larry Pruegner, 2601 S County Rd 23 E, Berthoud, CO 80513

Connecticut   *Yankee (NE)*, Tony Vespolis, Nancy B Thompson 630 Middlebury Rd, Watertown, CT 06795

Delaware   *Delmarva (MA)*, Don Addor, 721 E State St, Millsboro, DE 19966

Florida   *Gulf Coast (SE)*, Al Bell, 4982 Hubner Cir, Sarasota, FL 34241

Space Coast (SE), Richard Gauchat, 737 Galloway Ct, Winter Springs, FL 32708, 407-695-4412

Sunshine State (SE), Mary Gay, 2129 E Carlton Dr, Orlando, FL 32806, 407-898-8376

Georgia   *Dixie (SE)*, Ernie Grant, 1211 Dover Pl SE, Conyers, GA 30013, 770-483-7732

Illinois   *Chicagoland (HL)*, Steve Kelly, PO Box 863, Arlington Heights, IL 60006, E-mail: kelly464@aol.com

Rock Valley (HL), Jon Thompson, 2604 Lorado Ln, Rockford, IL 61101

Indiana   *Central Indiana (GL)*, Ralph Colter, 2003 S Buckeye, Kokomo, IN 46902

Iowa   *Hawkeye (HL)*, Alan Oldfield, 7802 Thorndale Dr NE, Cedar Rapids, IA 52402-6980

Kansas   *Mid America (HL)*, Dan Ulam, 7511 N Hemple St, Kansas City, MO 64152-2247

Wheatland, Roger Kandt, PO Box 780999, Wichita, KS 67207

Maryland   *BOOM (MA)*, Craig Bober, 100 S Ritter Ln, Owings Mills, MD 21117

Massachusetts   *Central New England (NE)*, Kenneth Bourque, 1105 James St, Chicopee, MA 01022

Minuteman (NE), Charles Ross, Box 1795, Plymouth, MA 02362, Web site: www.tiac.net/users/laytin/buick/index.htm

Michigan   *Buicktown (GL)*, Judy Leets, 4287 Underhill Dr, Flint, MI 48506

Central Michigan (GL), Fran Pasch, 5801 Hughes Rd, Lansing, MI 48911-4717

Southeast Michigan (GL), Paul A Clark, 1695 Three Lakes Dr, Troy, MI 48098-1434

West Michigan (GL), Ben Birkbeck, 458 Maethy SE, Grand Rapids, MI 49548

Minnesota   *Fireball (HL)*, William Darrow, PO Box 24776, Edina, MN 55424

Gopher State (HL), Kevin Kinney, 458 Dunlop, St Paul, MN 55104, 612-646-2568

Missouri   *St Louis Gateway (HL)*, Paul Meyer, 4350 Rider Tr N, Earth City, MO 63045

Nebraska   *Crossroads (HL)*, Larry D Robb, 9346 Monroe St, Omaha, NE 68127

Nevada   *Southern Nevada*, Jack Krietzburg, 2845 Santa Margarita, Las Vegas, NV 89102

New Jersey   *Jersey Shore*, David Davis, 50 Pacific St, Edison, NJ 08817

North Jersey (NE), Ed Natale, 410 Russell Ave, Wyckoff, NJ 07481

South Jersey, Bill Henderson, 448 E Elmer Rd, Vineland, NJ 08360, 609-690-9177

New Mexico   *Roadrunner Buicks*, Ben Garland, 3101 Knudsen, Farmington, NM 87401

New York   *Central New York (GL)*, Dave Martin, 114 Byrne Pl, Syracuse, NY 13205

Finger Lakes (GL), James E Dierks, 417 Westminster Rd, Rochester, NY 14607-3231

Long Island (NE), Frank Coniglio, 57-23 162 St, Flushing, NY 11365

Niagara Frontier (GL), Dave Robinson, 44 Virginia Rd, Cheektowaga, NY 14225-1210

Ohio   *Akron-Canton (GL)*, Bryan Woodward, 323 E Paradise St, Orrville, OH 44667

Central Ohio (GL), Gary Goldenbogen, 1263 Ludlow Rd, Xenia, OH 45385

Glass City (GL), Dave Rex, 138 E Fifth, Perrysburg, OH 43557-2231

Northeast Ohio (GL), Dean Kriska, 955 Granger Rd, Medina, OH 44256

River Towne Road Masters (GL), Mike Harrington, 6397 Georgetown Rd, Fairfield, OH 45014

Buick Club of America chapters (continued)

Oregon

Pennsylvania

South Carolina

Tennessee

Texas

Virginia

Washington

Washington DC

Wisconsin

Youngstown Buicks of Yesteryear (GL), Cliff Moffett, 444 Laurelwood Dr SE, Warren, OH 44484

Portland Area, Bob Eyre, PO Box 14224, Portland, OR 97293-0224

Appalachian (GL), Chester Gaines, 122 Cherry Ave, Tyrone, PA 16686

Free Spirit (NE), Dennis Snell, 1424 Elliott Ave, Bethlehem, PA 18018

National Pike (GL), Charles Korey, 700 Red Barn Ct, Bethel Park, PA 15102

Northwest PA (GL), Charles Wise, 6112 Garries Hill Rd, Erie, PA 16506

Philadelphia '76 (NE), Joe Walker, 8116 Burholme Ave, Philadelphia, PA 19111

Carolina (SE), Willie Smith, Rt 3 Box 148, Abbeville, SC 29620

Music City (SE), Bob Fritz, 322 Jocelyn Hollow Cir, Nashville, TN 37205

Lone Star, Cecil Miles, 14021 Stoneshire, Houston, TX 77060

North Texas, Bill Lough, 3200 Hula, Mesquite, TX 75150

Northern Virginia (MA), Phillip Strassner, 433 Cavalier Rd, Rileyville, VA 22650

North Cascade, Keith Mitchell, 18122 NE 127th St, Redmond, WA 98052

Puget Sound, Lee Davis, 5323 SW 315th St, Federal Way, WA 98023

Metro (MA), John Nordin, 11511 Fairfax Station Rd, Fairfax Station, VA 22039

Cream City (HL), Bud Armstrong, 1926 Surrey Ln, Grafton, WI 53024, 414-377-7258

Dairyland (HL), James Meyers, E 5890 Co K, Algoma, WI 54201

regions:

South East Region (SE), Roddy Pierce, 432 E Pharr Rd, Decatur, GA 30030, 404-371-1999

Heartland Region (HL), Steve Ledger, 3022 Spruce Terr, Island Lake, IL 60042, 708-487-5340

Great Lakes Region (GL), Judy Leets, 4287 Underhill Dr, Flint, MI 48506, 810-736-2731

North East Region (NE), John G Heilig, 25 21st St, Jericho, NY 11753-2534, 516-931-4336

Mid-Atlantic Region (MA), Ben Berman, 13030 Farthingdale Dr, Herndon, VA 22071-2683, 713-437-6820

divisions:

Performance Division, John Gudaitis, 95 Joshua Ln, Coventry, CT 06238, 860-742-1341

Buick Driving Enthusiasts, Ken McClellan, 1457 Peachwood Dr, Flint, MI 48507, 810-232-1769

Reatta Division, Robert E Neuman, 6030 Bloss Ct, Swartz Creek, MI 48473-8877, 810-655-4202

other Buick clubs (non-affiliated with BCA):

1916-1917 Buick/McLaughlin Owners Group, c/o Dean Tyron, 2516 Laurelford Ln, Wake Forest, NC 27587

1937-1938 Buick Club, 1005 Rilma Ln, Los Altos, CA 94022

1953-1954 Buick Skylark Club, PO Box 57, Eagle Bay, NY 13331

Buick 1929 Club De Espana, Amador Vicente Amores, C Van Dulken #12 Urb Sitio De Calahonda29.647, Mijas Costa, Malaga

Buick Club of Australia, PO Box 177, Richmond, Victoria

Buick Club of Norway, PO Box 6565 Etterstad, 0606 Oslo

Buick Street Rod Association, 824 Kay Cir, Chattanooga, TN 37421

Compact Buick Club 1961-1963, PO Box 411, Tustin, CA 92681-0411

Marquette Owners Registry for Enthusiasts, c/o Don Holton, 803 Cedar St, Elmira, NY 14904-2643

McLaughlin Buick Club of Canada, 220 Industrial Pkwy S Unit 6, Aurora, ON L4G 3V6

New Zealand Buick, GJ Letica, 26 Dunraven Pl, Torbay Auckland 1310

Riviera Owners Association, PO Box 26344, Lakewood, CO 80226

Silver Anniversary Buick (1929), W E McLaughlin, 75 Oriole Pkwy, Toronto, ON M4V 2E3

The Buick Car Club of Australia, PO Box 168, Merrylands, New South Wales 2160

Buick Club of Germany (Pre '50 AAC)
c/o Rainer Hausgen
AM Wimmersberg 55
Erkrath D-40699 Germany
+49 (211) 9007383
FAX: +49 (211) 5626576
E-mail: buickclub@yahoo.com

Founded 1996. 110+ members. Interest and/or owner of classic Buick(s) 1903-1973. Free bi-monthly magazine, 2 meetings per year, 1 tour to Switzerland, club stand on Europe's largest classic car fair. Members are giving help to each other like a big family. No rules, no laws, just fun. Dues: 50/year DEM, $40/year US. Web site: http://buick.notrix.de

Buick GS Club of America
625 Pine Point Cir
Valdosta, GA 31602
912-244-0577

Founded 1982. 5,000 members. Dedicated to Buick owners who enjoy the performance of their cars. Emphasis is on racing as well as showing. Open to all Buick performance enthusiasts. Members receive the *GS X-tra* magazine containing performance build-ups, feature stories, tech tips, free classifieds and much more. GS Nationals held the first weekend of May. Dues: $35/year.

**New Zealand Buick
Enthusiasts Club**
26 Dunraven Pl
Torbay
North Shore City 1310 New Zealand
PH/FAX: 011-649-473-6856

Founded 1988. 130-160 members. Open to all Buick owners. Four magazines per year with stories, technical tips, dates of swap meets in New Zealand and United States plus member list every August. We also list member recommended suppliers of spare parts. Dues: $10/year local, $15/year overseas.

Riviera Owners Association
PO Box 26344
Lakewood, CO 80226
303-987-3712
E-mail: roa@ix.netcom.com

Founded 1984. 3,100 members. 1963-1999 Buick Riviera. 40 page color magazine, local events, annual international meet, library, technical help, part sources. Bi-monthly publication, *Riview*, features 1963-1999 Rivieras, technical tips, questions and answers, event listing and classifieds. Dues: $25/year US, $30/year foreign. Web site: www.rivowners.org

Allante Appreciation Group
PO Box 225
Edgewood, IL 62426
PH/FAX: 800-664-5224
E-mail: allante@pointers.com

Founded 1994. 1,550+ members. Eight newsletters per year. Internet homepage. Fax back service. Member library, national and local group meets and shows. Dues: $35/year. Web site: www.allante.org

Allante Owners' Association
140 Vintage Way, #456
Novato, CA 94945
888-ALLANTE toll-free
415-382-1973; FAX: 415-883-0203
E-mail: allantefan@aol.com

Founded 1991. 2,500+ members. *Allante Avenues* is a high quality, award winning quarterly magazine with many photos, technical information, regional events, accessory information and sales and resale Allantes and parts exchange. Visa, MasterCard and American Express. Subscription: $35/year without membership. Dues: $50/year. Web site: allante.com

Cadillac Club of North Jersey
20 Valley Ave, Ste D-2
Westwood, NJ 07675
PH/FAX: 201-263-0999

Founded 1991. 275 members. An active, local club dedicated to the preservation, restoration and enjoyment of Cadillacs over 15 years old. Parades, shows, monthly newsletter, weekly outdoor meetings during warm weather months. Dues: $20/year. Web site: www.tappedin.com/ccnj

Cadillac Drivers Club
5825 Vista Ave
Sacramento, CA 95824-1428
916-421-3193

Founded 1971. 113 members. No restrictions. Monthly newsletter with free ads. 6 tours per year. Club library for research on your car, 1941-1980. Service information, buyer/seller price information. Production numbers 1902-1980. Dues: $17.50/year.

Cadillac LaSalle Club Inc
PO Box 1916
Lenoir, NC 28645-1916
828-757-9919; FAX: 828-757-0367
E-mail: cadlasal@twave.net

For membership information, contact at the above address: Jay Ann Edmunds. Founded 1958. 6,200 members. Illustrated monthly magazine, *The Self Starter*, club directory. Director of Technical Service to help with members' problems. Local regions in most parts of the country. National and regional events, gift and life memberships, jewelry, memorabilia. Dues: $30/year US 2nd class mail, $40/year US 1st class mail, $40/year Mexico and Canada, $45/year foreign. Web site: www.cadillaclasalleclub.com

chapters:

Arizona	*Grand Canyon*, Jerry Morrissey, Director, 602-979-8870
	Saguaro Region (Tucson), Jim Little, Director, 520-797-4710
	Sonoran Desert (Scottsdale), Pete Hilgeman, Director, 602-488-1963
California	*Great Valley*, Robert Elsholz, Director, 209-463-0458
	Northern California, Marianne Martos, Director, 408-776-1373
	San Diego, George Bandy, Director, 619-445-0328
	Southern California (LA), Roy Schneider, Director, 626-445-1618
Colorado	*Rocky Mountain*, Rod Brewer, Director, 303-278-9939
Florida	*Florida Suncoast*, Scott Batchelder, Director, 727-320-0777
	South Florida, Edward Dauer, Director, 305-739-0978
Georgia	*Heart of Dixie (Prov)*, Chip Bryan, Director, 770-591-2318
	Peach State, Michael Posey, Director, 800-238-0359
Illinois	*West of the Lake (Chicago)*, William Buckingham, Director, 708-448-7237
Indiana	*Indiana*, Jeff Shivley, Director, 765-653-3180
Kansas	*Central Plains*, Joseph Kausse, Director, 316-942-4517
Maryland	*Potomac*, Nick Wilson, Director, 301-774-5154
Michigan	*Michigan Lake St Clair*, Steve Wolken, Director, 248-375-2793,
	West Michigan, Dave Martin, Director, 616-669-7825
Minnesota	*Northstar*, Donald Voss, Director, 612-479-1442
Missouri	*MO Valley (Kansas City)*, Roy Schaaf, Director, 816-796-8378
	St Louis, Tom Luebbert, Director, 314-921-3766
Nevada	*Las Vegas*, Hal Sheaks, Director, 702-243-0038
	Silver State (Northern Nevada), Laura Lea Evans, Director, 702-673-1843

Cadillac LaSalle Club Inc chapters *(continued)*

New Jersey	*Valley Forge*, John Hotz, Director, 609-429-0641
New York	*Long Island*, Vincent Florio, Director, 718-631-0250
	Lower Hudson (Prov), Ralph Bortugno, Director, 914-621-0634
	New York Capital District, Jim Cummings, Director, 518-399-6004
	Western New York, Roger Libby, Director, 716-872-4289
Ohio	*Buckeye*, Bob Andrews, Director, 513-777-4671
	Western Reserve (Cleveland), Carl J Schorr, Director, 216-291-0294
Oregon	*Mount Hood*, Ben Hetrick, Director, 503-761-2609
Pennsylvania	*Central Pennsylvania*, Frank Pinola, Director, 717-540-7711
	Pittsburgh, Jack & Pat Donovan, Co-Directors, 412-443-7298
	Upper Susquehanna, Ed Dougher, Director, 717-222-2351
Rhode Island	*New England*, Donald Rinaldi, Director, 401-438-2599
Texas	*Gulf Coast*, Steve Stewart, Director, 713-666-6576
	North Texas, Johnnie J Bills, Director, 972-878-0438
Virginia	*Hampton Roads*, Arthur Matthews, Director, 804-868-9717
Washington	*Pacific Northwest*, Robert Sondheim, Director, 206-283-4808
Wisconsin	*Badger*, Gene Bednar, Director, 414-462-6547

Classic Cadillac Club Deutschland eV
Windmuehlenstr 49
50129 Bergheim Germany
FAX: +49-2238-945407
E-mail: cccd@classiccars.de

Founded 1991. 180 members. Open to all Cadillac owners or owners to be. Bi-monthly newsletter, *The Standard*, some regional meetings and a national meeting every May. Dues: 120 DM/year Europe, 150 DM/year worldwide. Web site: http://classiccars.de/cccd

Checker Car Club of America
10530 W Alabama
Sun City, AZ 85351-3544
PH/FAX: 602-974-4987
E-mail: carclub@gte.net

For membership information, contact at the above address: Roy Dickinson. Founded 1982. Over 900 members. Open to anyone interested in Checkers. Publish quarterly newsletter, *Checkerboard News*, now includes members from all chapters, members contribute articles. Send for application. Dues: $20/year North America, $25/year foreign.

chapters:

California	*California Checker Club*, Kathryn Bassett, Editor & Memberships, 1080 N Holliston Ave, Pasadena, CA 91104-3014, E-mail: kathryn.bassett@switchboard.net

New York	*Big Apple Taxi & Checker Club*, Michael Angelich, President, 77 North St, Huntington Station, NY 11746, E-mail: michael-nyc-taxi@worldnet.att.net
Washington	*Northwest Checker Club*, Keith Routley, President, 843 NW 50th, Seattle, WA 98107, E-mail: 103416.254@compuserve.com

The 1965-66 Full-Size Chevrolet Club
15615 State Rd 23
Granger, IN 46530
219-272-6964

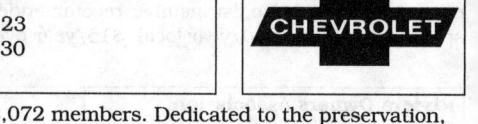

Founded 1983. 2,072 members. Dedicated to the preservation, restoration and recognition of 1965 and 1966 full-size Chevrolets. This is a social organization with the whole family in mind. Dues: $18/year.

Alamo Classic Chevy Club
6803 Cloverbend
San Antonio, TX 78238-1312
210-684-5399
E-mail: chevy26822@aol.com

Founded 1987. 45 members. No restrictions. Meeting last Wednesday of each month, 7 pm at Bun-n-Barrel on Austin Hwy. Newsletter, *Cruisin' News*, every month to all members. Dues: $20/year.

California Nomads
5842 E Parapet St
Long Beach, CA 90808-2726
562-421-5862

Founded 1969. 40 members. Single and family club. 1955-1957 Nomads and Safaris. Dues: $25/year.

Capital District Chevrolet Club Inc
20 Dussault Dr
Latham, NY 12110
518-783-8728 (club president)
518-355-5151 (membership)

Founded 1977. 85 members. Holiday parties, technical meetings, picnics, annual show, cruises, monthly meetings, family functions, guest speakers at monthly meetings. Need not own a vehicle currently. Vehicle years 1900-1997, cars, trucks and street rods welcome. Dues: $18/year single, $24/year family.

Chevrolet Nomad Association
8653 W Hwy 2
Cairo, NE 68824
402-393-7281; FAX: 308-385-2970
E-mail: chevymad@gionline.net

Founded 1988. 1,000 members. Preservation of 1955, 1956 and 1957 Chevy Nomads. Vehicle ownership not required. 8 mailings a year, free ads to members, tech assistance, one annual convention and show. 12th annual convention, July 8-14, 2000, Spokane, WA; for information contact: Skeeter Maxwell, 602-962-0174. Dues: $30/year US, $35/year Canada, $40/year foreign, US funds. Web site: www.chevynomadclub.com

Classic Chevy Cameo & GMC Suburban Pickup Club
4356 Riverview Dr
Port Allen, LA 70767-3808
225-383-8864
E-mail: dmayeaux@linknet.net

Founded 1988. 100 members. Open to anyone interested in Cameos, owners or not. Quarterly newsletter to inform and unite Cameo lovers. No scheduled meets at this time. Events will be announced later. Dues: $25/year.

Classic Chevy Club International Inc
PO Box 607188
Orlando, FL 32860
800-456-1957; FAX: 407-299-3341
E-mail: cciworld@aol.com

World's largest organization devoted to 1955-1972 Chevrolet cars and trucks. New, used, NOS, modified parts for Bel Air, Impala, Biscayne, and Caprice. Offer classic auto insurance and publish a full color monthly magazine with classifieds, feature cars, tech help and more. Call for more information or for one of our catalogues. Dues: $35/year. Web site: www.classicchevy.com

Cosworth Vega Owners Association
PO Box 5864
Pittsburgh, PA 15209
E-mail: cvoainc@aol.com

For information, contact at the above address: Michael Rupert, Membership VP. Founded 1979. Dedicated to promote and preserve the 1975-1976 Chevy Cosworth Vega as a collector car. 16 regional chapters. Annual national roundup in varing cities. Quarterly magazine, *Cosworth Vega Magazine*. Dues: $30/year, $75/three years.

Fifty 5 6 7 Club
2021 Wiggins Ave
Saskatoon, SK Canada S7J 1W2
306-343-0567; FAX: 306-343-5670

For membership information, contact at the above address: National Club Office. Founded 1974. 1,000 members. An organization for the support, promotion, restoration and preservation of the 1955-1956-1957 Chevrolets, including Chevrolet and GM trucks, Corvettes and Pontiacs. Owner or enthusiast. Dues: $45/year (G/S tax included).

Houston Classic Chevy Club
127 Bellaire Ct
Bellaire, TX 77401
713-667-4085
E-mail: amcclosk@aol.com

Founded 1989. 100 members. Dedicated to the preservation, restoration and enjoyment of 1955, 1956 and 1957 Chevrolet automobiles and trucks. Monthly newsletter and meeting. Cruises, picnics, shows and swap meets. Dues: $25/year.

Just Old Trucks of Austin, Texas
5209 Fort Mason Dr
Austin, TX 78745-2314
512-447-1446

Founded May 1991. 11 members. Interest in Chevy or GMC trucks to join. Affiliated with National Chevy/GMC Truck Assoc. Meetings are held once a month. 1918-1972 Chevy/GMC trucks of all sizes including sedan delivery.

Late Great Chevys
PO Box 607824
Orlando, FL 32860
407-886-1963; FAX: 407-886-7571
E-mail: chevy55-72@ao.net

Founded 1980. 10,500 members. Open to those interested in 1958-1972 Chevys. Monthly publication, *Late Great Chevys*. Restoration parts, free advertising. Subscription: $35/year 2nd class, $45/year 1st class. Web site: www.ao.net/chevy55-72

chapters:

California   *Inland Empire LGC*, Mike Garvin, President, 30908 E Sunset S, Redlands, CA 92373, 909-794-0888; E-mail: mikes@discover.net

South Coast LGC, Marty Tucker, President, 516 W Coolidge Dr, San Gabriel, CA 91775, 626-281-4484; E-mail: mtucker@webtv.net

Southern California LGC, Peter Potter, President, 735 Bonsall St, San Diego, CA 92114, 619-546-8809; E-mail: ag6186@aol.com

Tri Valley LGC, Jerome Ruzicka, President, 9850 Farralone Ave, Chatsworth, CA 91311-2746, 818-882-7724; E-mail: real409@aol.com

Colorado   *High Country Chevys*, Terry Steveson, President, 2815 S Winona Ct, Denver, CO 80236-2047, 303-255-2046

Connecticut   *Constitution State LGC*, Tom Jakups, President, PO Box 335, Southington, CT 06489, 860-233-5973

Delaware   *Delmarva LGC*, Donald Dunn, President, Rt 1 Box 489 BB, Delmar, DE 19940, 302-846-0398; E-mail: dunn@bware.com

Florida   *Chevy Circle*, Art Parsons, President, 714 Sunshine Dr, Delray Beach, FL 33444, 561-278-0147

Illinois   *Cool Cruisers*, Paul Combs, President, PO Box 11194, Springfield, IL 62791-1194, 217-698-3344; E-mail: cruisers@fgi.net

Lookingglass Corvette, Ed Chesnick, President, PO Box 82, Highland, IL 62249, 618-654-9919

Northern Illinois LGC, Dave Granger, President, 13119 W End Ln, Crestwood, IL 60445, 708-614-9423

Indiana   *Crown City Cruisers*, Max Weaver, President, 1229 S Main, Dunkirk, IN 47336, 765-768-1280

Hoosier LGC, Jerry Acheson, President, 2250 E Dudley Ave, Indianapolis, IN 46227, 317-570-9834; E-mail: jerryacheson@iquest.com

Kansas   *Mo-Kan LGC*, Harold McGlothlin, President, Box 457, Gardner, KS 66030, 816-390-8336

Louisiana   *LGC of Louisiana*, Greg Thomas, President, 7042 Bryce Canyon Dr, Greenwell Springs, LA 70739, 225-261-6834

Maryland   *LGC of Maryland*, Sandy McIntyre, President, 512 Ridgewell Way, Silver Spring, MD 20902, 301-680-0616; E-mail: smcintyre@usa.net

Massachusetts   *Greater Boston LGC*, Jay Davidson, President, 5 Vera Rd, Randolph, MA 02368, 781-963-7954

Michigan   *Southeast Michigan LGC*, Janet Schneider, President, 8395 Pine Cross Ln, Ann Arbor, MI 48103

Minnesota   *Gopher State Chevys*, Ed Grieman, President, PO Box 120561, New Brighton, MN 55112, 612-407-0385

Missouri   *Gateway City LGC Club*, John Thomure, President, PO Box 430063, Maplewood, MO 63143, 314-240-2008

Nebraska   *Heartland LGC*, Rick Lambert, President, 14005 Meredith Cir, Omaha, NE 68164, 402-493-3621; E-mail: lambert@radiks.net

New Jersey   *Jersey LGC*, Mike Berry, President, PO Box 1294, Hightstown, NJ 07716, 732-291-3553; E-mail: berrym@home.com

Late Great Chevys chapters *(continued)*

New York   *Long Island LGC,* Dave Doerrlamm, President, 1843 Louis Kossuth Ave, Ron Kon Koma, NY 11779-6424, 516-981-1273; E-mail: l8gr8t@webcentre.com

Nickel City LGC, Ken Knoll, President, 208 Warner Rd, Lancaster, NY 14086, 716-683-7242

North Carolina   *Tarheel LGC Club,* Jerry White, President, 9824 Tallwood Dr, Indian Trail, NC 28079, 704-786-8361; E-mail: sschevy@bellsouth.net

Ohio   *LGC of Northern Ohio,* Brian Zinner, President, 5287 E 117, Garfield Heights, OH 44125, 440-942-2068

Northwest Ohio Chevy Club, Mitch Siler, President, 357 Pine Ave, Dunkirk, OH 45836, 419-759-2834; E-mail: msiler@riverdale.woco.ohio.gov

Oklahoma   *LGC of Oklahoma City,* Dick Ransom, President, 8220 NW 25, Bethany, OK 73008, 405-737-0046

Oregon   *Central Oregon Classic Chevy Club,* Raymond Spongberg, President, PO Box 6343, Bend, OR 97708, 541-382-9370; E-mail: rsss@coinet.com

Emerald Empire LGC/BTC, Fred Mentze, President, PO Box 2232, Eugene, OR 97402, 541-747-6959

NW Oregon Chapter of LGC, Ron Vaw, President, PO Box 82507, Portland, OR 97202, 503-637-6630; E-mail: bekofam@juno.com

Pennsylvania   *East Penn LGC Club,* Linwood Stoudt, President, 2920 Bellview Rd, Cooplay, PA 18037, 215-679-2626

Tennessee   *Memphis Area LGC Club,* John Gaff, President, 1353 W Crestwood Dr, Memphis, TN 38119, 901-763-3501

Music City LGC Club, Jerry Tyrone, President, 773 Fitzpatrick Rd, Nashville, TN 37214, 615-885-4327

Texas   *Houston Area Chevrolet Club,* David Mondrik, President, PO Box 800222, Houston, TX 77280, 281-980-7337; E-mail: dfmondrik@shellus.com

LGC of Dallas, Danny Gill, President, PO Box 831751, Richardson, TX 75218, 972-243-6460; E-mail: rainbodan@worldnet.att.net

Virginia   *Old Dominion LGC,* Charles Reid, President, PO Box 14504, Richmond, VA 23234, 804-743-8294

Tidewater Late Great & YesterYear Chevys, Leo Boehm, President, 1209 Santeelah Ave, Chesapeake, VA 23325-3122, 757-420-1901

Washington   *Evergreen Chapter,* Ken Hopkins, President, PO Box 6191, Federal Way, WA 98063-6191, 206-243-8395; E-mail: royds58@email.msn.com

Inland Empire Lilac City LGC, Jim Corbett, President, PO Box 13068, Spokane, WA 99213, 509-927-1958

Olympic Chapter, Terry Scalena, President, PO Box 5093, Bremerton, WA 98312, 360-479-1693

Wisconsin   *North Central Classics & Customs,* Joe Drolschagen, President, N 5538 Norway Dr, Medford, WI 54451, 715-785-7117

Australia   *Old LGC Association Inc,* Adam Pownall, President, 20 Dinmore St Moorooka, Brisbane, Queensland 4105, 011617 3277-1830

Finland   *Finnish Impala Club,* Marcos Elvila, President, Aleksis Kivenkatu 76, 0052 Helsinki, +358-50-5522955; E-mail: esko.jarvi@polartst.fi

Germany   *Old World Chapter,* Gerhard Vielberth, President, Carl-Maria-von-Weber-Str 35, 93053 Regensburg, PH/FAX: 49 941-709349

New South Wales   *Late Great Chevrolet Association Inc,* Steve Dudgeon, President, PO Box 53, Peakhurst 2210, 02 989-72502

New Zealand   *Kiwi Classic Chevrolet Club,* Paul Baldwin, President, PO Box 15539 New Lynn, Auckland, E-mail: baldwin@ihug.co.nz

Norway   *Halden LGC,* Wilhelm Elders, President, Box 289, 1752 Halden, 47 6918-2630

Michiana Classic Chevy Club
PO Box 713
Elkhart, IN 46515
219-674-9198

Founded 1972. 42 members. Must own or have an interest in 1955, 1956 or 1957 Chevy. Family club. Meet once every third Sunday. Do a lot of things for charities in or around the areas. Monthly newsletter. Summer swap meet and a car show and winter swap meet. Lots of dances that club puts on. Have lots of fun as a group. Dues: $12/year.

Mid-Atlantic Nomad Association
337 Springdale Ave
York, PA 17403

Founded 1970. 200 members. Dedicated to the preservation, restoration and enjoyment of 1955-1957 Chevy Nomad wagons and Pontiac Safaris. Dues: $10/year.

National Impala Association
PO Box 968
2928 4th Ave
Spearfish, SD 57783
605-642-5864; FAX: 605-642-5868
E-mail: impala@blackhills.com

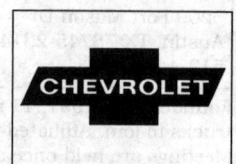

Founded 1980. 3,000 members worldwide. Bi-monthly publication. 1958-1969 full-size Chevrolets. Dues: $30/year second class, $40/year first class, $60/year overseas. Web site: impala.blackhills.com

---

National Monte Carlo Owner's Association Inc
PO Box 187
Independence, KY 41051
606-491-2378
E-mail: nmcoa@juno.com

Founded 1984. Dedicated to the preservation and restoration of the Monte Carlo. Bi-monthly magazine, *Class of Monte Carlo.* Free advertising in magazine to members. Annual convention. Dues: $30/year.

National Nostalgic Nova
PO Box 2344
York, PA 17405
717-252-4192; FAX: 717-252-1666

Founded 1982. 6,000 members. Members receive 48 page *Nova Times* magazine, free classified advertising. Three shows each year. Carry a complete line of parts for original and hot rod Novas. Dues: $30/year, $40/year Canada. Web site: www.nnnova.com

Obsolete Fleet Chevys
PO Box 13944
Salem, OR 97309
503-585-5578; FAX: 503-585-1856

Founded 1974. 60 members. Interest in the preservation and restoration of 1955-1957 Chevrolet cars, Corvettes and pickups. Meet once per month, 2nd Friday. *Fleet Sheet* is the monthly publication. Club activities include monthly events, caravaning to events, social events. Dues: $20/year.

Oklahoma Chevelle & El Camino Owners Assoc
PO Box 35441
Tulsa, OK 74153-0441
918-451-1657

Founded 1994. 100+ members. Dedicated to promoting interest in and preservation of 1964-1987 Chevelles and El Caminos. Dues: $20/year. Web site: www.okchevelle.com

Steel City Classics
701 Prestley Ave
Carnegie, PA 15106
412-276-0384

Founded 1976. 220 members. Monthly newsletter. 2 swap meets, spring and fall; 2 bus trips to Spring and Fall Carlisle; 2 membership parties/meetings, spring and fall; picnic, family oriented club, try to include everyone (kids model show at car show, kids judge cars at picnic). Began as 1955-1957 Chevy club, but in recent years expanded to include all Chevys. Dues: $18/year.

Vintage Chevrolet Club of America
PO Box 5387
Orange, CA 92613-5387
626-963-CHEV

Founded 1961. 8,000 members. Monthly magazine, *Generator & Distributor*. We meet through the year. Our express purpose is the restoring, preserving and enjoying of older Chevrolets.

Camaro Club of San Diego
PO Box 0416
La Mesa, CA 91944-0416
760-789-5151, 619-748-2612
E-mail: louheyn@aol.com

Founded 1993. 155 members. Monthly newsletter, monthly meetings, September car show (Fall Classic). Dues: $25/year single, $35/year family. Web site: www.angelfire.com/sd/camaroclub

Connecticut Chevelle Connection
PO Box 6094
Wolcott, CT 06716-0094
203-879-4016
E-mail: ctchevel@portone.com

Founded 1991. Over 200 members and growing. Our purpose is to encourage restoration and/or preservation and promote general interest in the 1964-1987 Chevrolet Chevelle, Malibu and El Camino. Monthly meetings, tech talks by guest speakers, parts

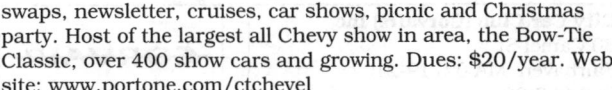

swaps, newsletter, cruises, car shows, picnic and Christmas party. Host of the largest all Chevy show in area, the Bow-Tie Classic, over 400 show cars and growing. Dues: $20/year. Web site: www.portone.com/ctchevel

Eastern Michigan Camaro Club
34113 Tonquish
Westland, MI 48185
734-728-2841
E-mail: superfest7@aol.com

Founded 1991. 50+ members. Fellowship, fun and information. No restrictions. Annual big event: Camaro Superfest at Domino's Farms in Ann Arbor, MI. All Camaros and owners welcome. Dues: $12/year. Web site: www.superfest7.com

International Camaro Club Inc
National Headquarters
2001 Pittston Ave
Scranton, PA 18505
570-585-4082

3,500+ members. Dedicated to serving the needs of the Camaro owner and enthusiast. Helps fellow members locate parts and supply ID, body tag info, etc. Open to owners and enthusiasts of 1967-present Camaros. Local/regional events, Annual Camaro Nationals, Pace Car Registry, 1967-1969 Registry for L78/L89 Camaros, we have a 1981 Yenko Turbo Z Registry. Recognizes Z10 coupes. Bi-monthly publication, *In the Fast Lane*. Dues: $20/year US, $25/year Canada, $35/year overseas (US funds please).

Maryland Chevelle Club
6030 Hunt Club Rd
Elkridge, MD 21075-5516
410-796-7725
E-mail: showcar402@aol.com

Founded 1985. 200+ members. Club is open to all who enjoy 1964-1972 Chevelles and El Caminos. Monthly meetings, cruises, picnics. Monthly newsletter. We also put on the largest Chevelle only show and swap meet on the East Coast. MCC is a associate chapter of ACES and NCOA. Dues: $25/year. Web site: www.clark/pub/chevelle/mcc.htm

National Chevelle Owners Association
7343-J W Friendly Ave
Greensboro, NC 27410
336-854-8935

Founded 1982. 7,000 members. Monthly color magazine, *The Chevelle Report*, features members' cars, tech tips, production data, factory photos and parts sources on 1964-1987 Chevelles and El Caminos. Dues: $30/year US, $40/year Canada, $55/year all other countries, US funds only. Web site: www.chevellereport.com

Pittsburgh Area Camaro Enthusiasts
PO Box 2361
Cranberry Twp, PA 16066
724-774-1418

Founded 1998. 30 members. Meets 2nd Wednesday of every month. Monthly newsletter. Dues: $20/year.

Central Pennsylvania Corvair Club
1751 Chesley Rd
York, PA 17403-4001
717-845-9347

Founded 1975. 90 members. Monthly meetings, tours, parades, shows and annual Mini-Convention. Monthly newsletter, *Action*. Dues: $10/year.

City Car Club (Corvairs) Inc
30 Camel St
Fairhaven, MA 02719-2102
508-993-2861

Founded in 1956 as a custom and hot rod club, became Corvair club in 1980. 27 members. Group of Corvair enthusiasts meeting every month to work on club members' cars and further Corvair interest. Monthly publication, *Vairgram*, free to members. Dues: $8/year.

Corvair Society of America (CORSA)
PO Box 607
Lemont, IL 60439-0607
630-257-6530; FAX: 630-257-5540
E-mail: corvair@corvair.org

Founded 1969. 6,000 members. Dedicated to the operation, preservation, restoration and enjoyment of the Corvair automobile and its derivatives. Monthly publication: *CORSA Communique*. Dues: $35/year US, $38/year Canadian, $48/year overseas, US funds please. Web site: www.corvair.org

chapters:

Alabama *Alabama Corvair Club*, 3112 Clayborne Rd, Dothan, AL 36303

Arizona *Cactus Corvair Club*, PO Box 11701, Phoenix, AZ 85061

Northern Arizona Corvair Club, 340 E David, Flagstaff, AZ 86001

Tucson Corvair Association, 4072 E 22nd St, Ste 197, Tucson, AZ 85711

Arkansas *Arkansas Corvair Club*, PO Box 627, Little Rock, AR 72203

California *Bakersfield Corvairs*, 10817 Sunset Canyon Dr, Bakersfield, CA 93311-2749

Central Coast CORSA, 3155 Nacimiento Lake Dr, Paso Robles, CA 93446-9773

Central Valley Corvairs, 3001 Lancelot Ln, Modesto, CA 95350-1408

Classic Corvairs of River City, 4391 Stockton Blvd, Sacramento, CA 95820

CORSA West of Los Angeles, PO Box 950023, Mission Hills, CA 91395

Corvanatics, 5000 Cascabel Rd, Atascadero, CA 93422-2302

Inland Empire Corvair Club, PO Box 52714, Riverside, CA 92517

Sacramento Corvair Tour Group, 9590 Appalachian Dr, Sacramento, CA 95827

San Diego Corvair Club, PO Box 23172, San Diego, CA 92193

San Joaquin Corvair Club, PO Box 4693, Fresno, CA 93744

Shasta Corvairs, 2922 Quartz Hill Rd, Redding, CA 96003

South Coast CORSA, PO Box 213, Redondo Beach, CA 90277-0213

Ventura County Corvairs, 1364 Cottonwood Ln, Fillmore, CA 93015

Vintage CORSA, PO Box 1180, Placentia, CA 92871-1180

Colorado *Group UltraVan*, 5537 Pioneer Rd, Boulder, CO 80301

Pikes Peak Corvair Club, PO Box 15034, Colorado Springs, CO 80935

Rocky Mountain CORSA, PO Box 27058, Denver, CO 80227

Connecticut *Connecticut CORSA*, PO Box 341, Georgetown, CT 06829-0341

Delaware *First State Corvair Club*, 1002 Stonewood Rd, Wilmington, DE 19810-3114

Florida *Central Florida Corvair*, 605 N Clayton, Mount Dora, FL 32757

First Coast Corvairs, PO Box 668, Yulee, FL 32041

Gulfcoast Corvairs, 2630 Webber St, Sarasota, FL 34239

Nature Coast Corvairs, 6735 W Rainhill Ct, Crystal River, FL 34429

Suncoast Corvairs, PO Box 788, Crystal Beach, FL 34681

West Florida Corvair Club, 2907 San Miguel, Milton, FL 32583

Georgia *Corvair Atlanta*, 2701 Old Jonesboro Rd, Fairburn, GA 30213

Idaho *Boise Basin Corvairs*, PO Box 16734, Boise, ID 83715

Illinois *Chicagoland Corvair Enthusiasts*, PO Box 704, Matteson, IL 60443-0704

Prairie Capital Corvair Association, PO Box 954, Springfield, IL 62705

Indiana *Mad Anthony Corvair Club*, 2323 Lima Valley Dr, Fort Wayne, IN 46818

Michiana Corvair Club, 2054 Carrbridge Ct, South Bend, IN 46614

Iowa *Iowa Corvair Enthusiasts*, 23 Gleason Dr, Iowa City, IA 52240-5854

Kentucky *Central Kentucky Corvair*, 300 Albany Rd, Lexington, KY 40503

Derby City Corvair, 7607 Marietta Ct, Louisville, KY 40258

Louisiana *New Orleans Corvair Enthusiasts*, PO Box 427, Denham Springs, LA 70727-0427

Maryland *Chesapeake Corvair*, PO Box 554, Forest Hill, MD 21050-0554

CORSA of Baltimore, 619 Round Oak Rd, Towson, MD 21204-3867

Group Corvair, 12710 Lode St, Bowie, MD 20720

Mid-Maryland Corvair Club, 8703 Antietam Dr, Walkersville, MD 21793-8020

Massachusetts *Bay State Corvairs*, 16 Darby Dr, Mansfield, MA 02048

City Car Club Corvairs, 30 Camel St, Fairhaven, MA 02719-2102

Colonial Corvair Club, 44 Columbia Rd, Arlington, MA 02174

Michigan   Detroit Area Corvair Club, 815 Madison, Birmingham, MI 48008

West Michigan Corvair Club, 7214 9 Mile Rd, Rockford, MI 49341

Minnesota   Corvair Minnesota, 3370 Library Ln, St Louis Park, MN 55426-4224

Missouri   Heart of America Corvair Owners' Association, 9802 Booth, Kansas City, MO 64134

Show-Me Corvair Club, 4067 Waterfall Dr, St Louis, MO 63034-0187

Nebraska   Corvair Midwest, 1522 W Manor Dr, Lincoln, NE 68506-1457

Nevada   Vegas Vairs, 4607 E Imperial Ave, Las Vegas, NV 89104-5816

New Hampshire   Central New Hampshire Corvair Association, PO Box 334, Contoocook, NH 03229

New Jersey   Delaware Valley Corvair Club, 1301 Union Landing Rd, Cinnaminson, NJ 08077

Lakewood-Monza Group, 14 Ashwood Dr, Brick, NJ 08723-3402

New Jersey Association of Corvair Enthusiasts, PO Box 631, Ridgewood, NJ 07451

New Mexico   Corvairs of New Mexico, 2226 Inez Dr NE, Albuquerque, NM 87110-4732

New York   Association of Corvair Nuts, 180 Prospect St, Spencerport, NY 14559

Capital District Corvair Club, PO Box 192, Rexford, NY 12148

Long Island Corvair Association, PO Box 1675, West Babylon, NY 11704

Niagara Frontier Corvair Club, PO Box 45, Buffalo, NY 14224

Resurrection Corvairs of Yonkers, 522 Saw Mill River Rd, Yonkers, NY 10701

North Carolina   CORSA/NC, 6715 Branson Mill Rd, Pleasant Garden, NC 27313

Ohio   Air 'Vair Group, 5474 SR 19, Galion, OH 44833

Corvair Club of Cincinnati, PO Box 40153, Cincinnati, OH 45240

Dayton Corvair Club, PO Box 3514, Dayton, OH 45401

Friends of Corvair, 7354 Middlebranch Ave NE, North Canton, OH 44721

Mid-Ohio Vair Force, 4673 Northwest Pkwy, Hilliard, OH 43026

North Coast Corvair Enthusiasts, 54 Kenilworth Ave, Painesville, OH 44077

Tri-State Corvairs, PO Box 581, Bryan, OH 43506

V-8 Registry, 4361 St Dominic Dr, Cincinnati, OH 45238

Vacationland Corvairs, 560 Lindberg Blvd, Berea, OH 44017-1418

Oklahoma   Green Country Corvair Group, PO Box 470022, Tulsa, OK 74147

Indian Nations Corvair Association, 3320 SE 24th St, Del City, OK 73115-1614

Oregon   CORSA Oregon, PO Box 1445, Portland, OR 97201

Southern Oregon Corvair Owners, 512 Fairmount St, Medford, OR 97501-2426

Pennsylvania   Central Pennsylvania Corvair Club, 3080 E Prospect Rd, York, PA 17402

Lehigh Valley Corvair Club, 137 American St, Whitehall, PA 18052

Philadelphia Corvair Association, 2545 Broder St 1st Fl, Allentown, PA 18103

Western Pennsylvania Corvair Club, 458 Whitestown Rd, Butler, PA 16001

South Carolina   Central Carolina CORSA, RR 03 Box 1195, Manning, SC 29102

CORSA South Carolina, PO Box 5559, Greenville, SC 29606

Lowcountry Corvair Association, PO Box 505, Ladson, SC 29456

Tennessee   East Tennessee Corvair Club, PO Box 928, Kingsport, TN 37660

Knoxville Area Corvair Club, PO Box 233, Knoxville, TN 37901

Upper Cumberland Corvair Club, 241 Palkway Dr, Cookeville, TN 38501

Texas   Alamo City Corvair Association, PO Box 291222, San Antonio, TX 78229

Corvair Houston, PO Box 2331, Houston, TX 77252-2331

Desert Corvair Club, PO Box 220108, El Paso, TX 79912-2108

Lone Star Corvair Club, RR 01 Box 15A, McDade, TX 78650

North Texas Corvair Association, 2701 W 15th St Box 153, Plano, TX 75075

Vermont   Vermont Independent Corvair Enthusiasts, PO Box 235, East Arlington, VT 05252

Virginia   Central Virginia Corvair Club, 8015 Driftwood Dr, Prince George, VA 23875

Northern Virginia Corvair Club, 13608 Smithwood Ct, Nokesville, VA 20181

Roanoke Valley Corvair Club, 2934 Rivermont Ave #30, Lynchburg, VA 24503

Tidewater Corvair Club, 2901 Cardo Pl, Virginia Beach, VA 23456

Washington   CORSA Northwest, PO Box 88, Renton, WA 98057-0088

Section Three
Clubs & Organizations

Corvair Society of America chapters (continued)

Inland Northwest Corvair Club, PO Box 132, Four Lakes, WA 99014-0132

West Virginia   *Wild Wonderful Corvair Club*, 140 Scott Acres, Scott Depot, WV 25560

Wisconsin   *Capital City Corvair Club*, 2795 Allegheny Dr, Madison, WI 53719

Milwaukee Corvair Club, 621 E State St, Milwaukee, WI 53202

Northeast Wisconsin Corvair Club, 2205 Sullivan Ave, Kaukauna, WI 54130-3455

Canada   *Western Canada CORSA*, 2378 Estevan Ave, Victoria, BC V8B 2S5

France   *Chevrolet Corvair Club of Paris*, 93 rue d'Angerville Les Granges le Roi, 91410 Dourdan

Netherlands   *Corvair Club Nederland*, Darwin Plantsoen 1, 1097 EX Amsterdam

Switzerland   *Swiss Corvair Club*, Bachtelenstrasse 39, CH-2450 Grenchen

First State Corvair Club Inc
1306 Friar Rd
Newark, DE 19713
302-737-3577

Founded 1982. 48 members. Annual show and banquet, monthly meetings and newsletters, various activities throughout the year. Dues: $12/year.

Aquia Creek Corvette Club
PO Box 986
Stafford, VA 22555
540-659-5234
E-mail: accclub@aol.com

Founded 1987. 65 members. Annual Corvettes of Carlisle tour, August 25-27, 2000. Monthly newsletter, very active membership. ACCC/NCCC dues: $35/year. Web site: http://members.aol.com/accclub/index.htm

Blue Ridge Corvette Club Inc
PO Box 1
Stuarts Draft, VA 24477
540-886-2433 after 6 pm

Founded 1977. 106 members. Must attend 2 club events and must be elected into club. Benefits, club car shows, club picnic, cruise-ins and road tours in the Blue Ridge Mountains (money raised goes to Blue Ridge area food bank). Monthly newsletter. Dues: $20/year. Web site: www.citymotors/net/brcc.htm

Boardwalk Corvettes of Atlantic City
PO Box 546
Brigantine Beach, NJ 08203-0546

Founded 1983. 45 members. Meetings 1st Thursday of each month, Oyster Creek Inn, Leeds Point, NJ. Club activities include weekend trips to Watkins Glen, Martha's Vineyard and various southern NJ locations. Three shows each year, an all Chevy show in June, a Corvette show on the Ocean City, NJ Boardwalk in September and a show in October at the historic town of Smithville. Club is open to all Corvette owners and enthusiasts. Dues: $40/year.

Boone Trail Corvette Club
74 Wilderness Ln
Defiance, MO 63341
314-798-2671
E-mail: ghellyer@westfordcom.com

Founded 1972. 120 members. Must be 18 years of age and own a Corvette. Sharing knowledge of Corvettes, monthly meetings, many events yearly and a monthly newsletter. Dues: $15/year individual, $25/year couple. Web site: www.boonetrail.com

Candlewood Valley Corvettes Inc
PO Box 2205
Danbury, CT 06813-2205
203-746-6709

Founded 1978. 120 members. Anyone who owns or is the primary driver of a Corvette is welcome to join our club. Members' benefits include local trade discounts, reduced cost on club sponsored events and numerous social activities. Social activities include brunches, dinners, rallies, car shows and cruises. Annual August car show. Dues: $20/year single, $25/year family.

Cascade Corvette Club
PO Box 363
Eugene, OR 97440
541-683-2538; FAX: 541-484-0882
E-mail: duckvett@sprynet.com

Open to all Corvette owners. Our activities include tours, auto crosses, car shows, rallies, picnics, technical sessions and many social events throughout the year. Meets on the second Friday of every month at Romania Chevrolet, located at 2020 Franklin Blvd, Eugene, Oregon. Guests are always welcome!

Circle City Corvette Club Inc
9320 E Prospect St
Indianapolis, IN 46239
317-898-2222; FAX: 317-89-VETTE
E-mail: philsvette@aol.com

Founded 1977. 46 members. Must own Corvette. Meetings 1st and 3rd Thursday at Blossom Chevrolet, 1800 N Shadeland Ave. Rally in June. Other events for charity. Area parades and high school homecomings. Dues: $65/year.

Classic Corvettes of Minnesota
PO Box 32123
Fridley, MN 55432
612-754-9987
E-mail: cruisin@classiccorvettesmn.com

Founded 1981. 346 members. Open to owners of Corvettes for 1953-present. Classic Corvettes of Minnesota is a Corvette club in the Minneapolis/St Paul and surrounding area. Various Corvette shows, Corvette cruises, picnics, dinners and assorted events each year. Visit our web site at: www.classiccorvettesmn.com or call our hotline, 612-754-9987. Dues: $35/year.

Classic Glass Corvette Club
PO Box 4936
Marietta, GA 30061
770-591-3578
E-mail: ronfloyd@mindspring.com

Founded 1983. 100 members. Primarily social oriented with monthly meetings and many activity events each year. Web site: http://members.aol.com/cgvettec

Clipper City Corvette Club
643B Broadway US Rt 1 S
Saugus, MA 01906
781-231-0478; FAX: 781-938-8833
E-mail: warren1020@aol.com

Paul Ferraro, President. Founded 1980. 44 members. Weekly summer cruises, Corvette weekends. One of the largest Corvette shows in New England, 1st Sunday in August. 25 cars with everything from straight axle classics to ZR1s, 1957s-1999s. Dues: $50/year per couple. Web site: http://people.ne.mediaone.net/cwarren/clippercitycorvettes.html

Club Corvette of Connecticut
PO Box 68
Monroe, CT 06468
203-387-9038; FAX: 203-389-0680
E-mail: rongoldbe@aol.com

Founded 1993. 285 members. No restrictions to join (but nice if you have a Corvette). Receive a newsletter (12 pages) once a month. We go to Corvette shows and have 3 cruise nights this year. Support other Corvette car shows in the Northeast whenever possible. Dues: $35/year per family. Web site: http://gdoc.com/ccc

Club Corvette Sweden
Box 2093
14102 Huddinge Sweden
046-11-59030; FAX: 046-11-58005
E-mail:
corvettemagasinet@clubcorvette.se
or manny@clubcorvette.se

Founded 1974. 1,000 members. Must be owner of a Corvette. Cheaper insurance available. *Corvette Magazine* is published quarterly, contains 48 pages; 6 major and 14-20 minor Corvette events a year. The club sponsors lots of events during the year, like homecomings, parades, film and video sessions, Corvette lectures, workshops, parties, barbecues, rallies, picnics, street and swap meets, beach parties, road tours, visits and participation in numerous automotive exhibitions. Dues: 675sek/year. Web site: www.clubcorvette.se

Corvette Club Norway
Boks 55 Bryn
0611 Oslo Norway
47-227-61170; FAX: 47-227-61176

Founded 1992. 200 members. Club for Corvette owners, meeting 10 times a year, quarterly publication. Dues: 350 NOK/year.

Corvette Club of America
PO Box 9879
Bowling Green, KY 42102
PH/FAX: 502-737-6022
E-mail: ccabg@ekx.infi.net

Founded 1988. 4,200+ members. No restrictions to membership. Publish bi-monthly newsletter, *Corvette Capers*, free with membership, 28 pages with info from Corvette plant, National Corvette Museum, tech advice by Gordon Killebrew, free members' swap show, discounts from over 100 vendors, updates on shows. National Convention, November 5-6-7, 1999, at Jekyll Island Collector Car Festival event in Jekyll Island, GA. Dues: $35/year. Web site: www.corvetteclubofamerica.com

Corvette Club of Delaware Valley
PO Box 397
Willow Grove, PA 19090
215-938-7722; FAX: 215-698-5888
E-mail: ccdv@ccdv.com

Founded 1958. 370+ members. Can be a member first year without a Corvette. Benefits include club discounts at various venders, technical seminars and problem solving assistance, newsletter *Gas Cap*, annual judged show since 1970 (1995 was

25th consecutive year) called The Cavalcade of Corvettes, other activities include charitable fund raising and shows, rallies, picnics, etc. Dues: $30/year. Web site: www.ccdv.com

Corvette Club of Michigan
PO Box 510330
Livonia, MI 48151
248-685-7145

Founded 1958. 300 members. Must be Corvette owner, 18 yrs of age or over and possessing a valid driver's license. Publication, *Slipstream*, is distributed 11 times a year and free to members; also a Corvette calendar, events, updates, articles, etc.

Corvette Club of Nova Scotia
RR 2
Wentworth, NS Canada B0M 1Z0
902-548-2068
E-mail:
brian.deb.palmer.corvettes.r.us
@ns.sympatico.ca

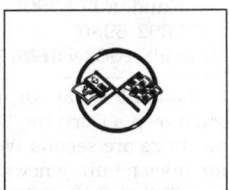

Founded 1974. 48 members. Interest in Corvettes required. Get to meet and go on drives with fellow enthusiasts. Club puts out a newsletter monthly from April-December. Dues: $35/year. Web site: www.geocities.com/motorcity/track/1629

Corvettes For Kids Inc
PO Box 23
Sassamansville, PA 19472
610-754-9149; FAX: 610-754-6476

Founded 1986. PA non-profit organization. Annual Corvette show second Sunday of August. Proceeds of which benefit local families of children with life threatening illnesses and disabling conditions.

The Corvettes of Lancaster
2275 Blue Valley Rd
Lancaster, OH 43130
740-746-8570, 614-833-ANGL

Founded 1972. 80 members. Must own a Corvette and enjoy driving on rallies, hosting cruises, helping to organize and work shows and help with the 13th annual Earth Angel Super Cruise and Car Show. Non-profit and charity event. Monthly newsletter. Dues: $15/year.

Corvettes of Southern California
PO Box 3603
Anaheim, CA 92803
714-776-6416

Founded 1956. 225 members. Must be registered owner of Corvette and 21 years old. Dues: $30/year.

Corvettes of the North
3403 Pelot Ln
Milladore, WI 54454
715-435-3707

Founded 1972. Over 70 members. Must own a Corvette and be over 18 years of age. Our club has many rallies, tours and other events throughout the year. We also host the Wisconsin Rapids Car Show weekend. Dues: $12/year.

Corvettes of Western Australia Inc
PO Box 88
Innaloo City WA 6918 Australia
08 9446 6243; FAX: 08 9446 1034

Founded 1982. 140 members. The purpose is to encourage the preservation, restoration and enjoyment of all Corvettes. Membership is available to all Corvette owners and enthusiasts. A non-profit organization, meets and events advised in our newsletter, *West Coast Vette Torque*. Dues: $40/year.

Corvettes Unlimited
PO Box 33433
Granada Hills, CA 91394-0059
818-368-9059

Founded 1966. 39 members. Must own a Corvette. Members compete in car shows, races, rallies and attend various Corvette functions. NCCC membership is included with insurance coverage for events.

Corvettes Unlimited Corvette Club Inc
1120 Fairmount Ave
Vineland, NJ 08360
609-692-8930
E-mail: red63vette@jnlk.com

Benjamin F Notaro Jr, President. Founded 1977. 250 members. Must own a Corvette. South Jersey's largest Corvette club. Meetings are second Wednesday of each month. Membership includes monthly newsletter, *Fiberglass Flyer* and club's magazine (3 times), *Cruisin' News*. Dues: $25/year couple. Web site: www.jnlk.com/corvettesunltd

Cyclone Corvettes Inc
3028 Northridge Pkwy
Ames, IA 50014-4581
515-292-0017

Founded 1978. 100 members. Only need interest in Corvettes. Monthly club newsletter, *Vettelines*. Meetings, social events and parties, road trips and cruises, car shows and competitive events, Funkhanas, road rallies. Receive membership packet, jacket patch, club parts discounts, camaraderie. Sponsor of annual All Iowa Corvette Fest. Dues: $20/year active, $10/year associate.

Essex County Corvette Club
177 Cameron Ave
Windsor ON Canada N9B 1Y5
519-258-2071; FAX: 519-258-2036
E-mail: eccc@wincom.net

Founded 1995. 30 members. Monthly newsletter with free buy and sell section. Yearly Corvette and all car show. Currently mail to Canada, USA and Spain. Dues: $50/year. Web site: www.thewing.com/eccc

Fort Lauderdale Corvette Club Inc
PO Box 491332
Fort Lauderdale, FL 33349

Founded 1991. 60 members. Must attend 3 meetings and 3 socials before being voted on. Belong to NCCC. Publish monthly newsletter, attends some major shows in force, local shows, rallies, drags and holds at least one social a month. Dues: $60/year.

The Heartbeat of America Corvette Club
4647 Ardmore
Sterling Heights, MI 48310
810-979-5968

Founded 1992. 55 members. Must own or have interest in the Corvette. Willing to work on charitable fund raisers. Dues: $50/year.

International Society Corvette Owners
PO Box 740614
Orange City, FL 32774
904-775-1203; FAX: 904-775-3042

Founded 1993. 3,000+/- members. Open to all Corvette enthusiasts. Bi-monthly newsletter, super Corvette insurance, two

annual events, conventions, St Ignace, MI, in September, Fort Pierce, FL in January. Certification, logo merchandise. Dues: $27/year.

Liberty Region Corvette Club
233 Jefferson Ave
Horsham, PA 19044
215-675-1460; FAX: 215-943-8302

Founded 1997. 100 members. Must be a Corvette owner. Fall Corvette show. *Vette Gazette* is the club newsletter. Caravans to dinner, shows, racing and other activities. Monthly general membership meetings 3rd Thursday of most months. Dues: $35/year, $55/year.

Majestic Glass Corvette Club
3147-D N Goldie Rd
Oak Harbor, WA 98277
E-mail: quackers@gte.net

Founded 1974. 55 members. Must own a Corvette, have valid driver's license and insurance, receive monthly newsletter, have average of 2 scheduled runs a month, 4 car shows a year, several weekend getaways. Dues: $25/year. Web site: www.geocities.com/~mgcc

Mid Alabama Corvette Club
PO Box 862
Alabaster, AL 35007
205-822-0403

Founded 1974. 105 members. Monthly meeting and newsletter. One annual show (charity). This is a drivers club, we promote and attend shows in the SE. Dues: $20/year.

Mid Maine Vettes
PO Box 265
Auburn, ME 04212-0265
207-782-8952

Founded 1979. 24 members. Must own Corvette. Publish monthly newletter, schedule various Corvette related activities during the year. Dues: $20/year.

Midwest Early Corvette Club
1606 N 85th St
Omaha, NE 68114
402-391-5270

Founded 1972. 100+ members. Open to anyone who owns or has an interest in Corvettes. Monthly meetings, socialize and share information, monthly newsletter. Annual swap meet and car show 1st Sunday in June, annual Halloween rally and party, All Corvette Show and other shows at malls, World of Wheels, etc. Dues: $9/year single, $12/year couple.

National Corvette Owners Association
900 S Washington St G13
Falls Church, VA 22046
703-533-7222; FAX: 703-533-1153
E-mail: ncoassoc@aol.com

Founded 1975. 15,500 members. For Corvette owners. Discounts on interior products, Chevy dealers, automotive outlets, Corvette auto insurance and more. Monthly publication, *For Vettes Only*. Dues: $39/year. Web site: www.ncoa-vettes.com

National Corvette Restorers Society
6291 Day Rd
Cincinnati, OH 45252-1334
513-385-8526, 513-385-6367
FAX: 513-385-8554
E-mail: info@ncrs.org

Founded 1974. 14,000 members. Membership is open to persons interested in the restoration, preservation and history of 1953-1982 Corvettes. 36 chapters in the US and foreign. Dues: $30/year US, $35/year Canada, $45/year foreign. Web site: www.ncrs.org

chapters:

Alabama *Southeast Chapter*, Jimmy McCutcheon, 3913 Oak Brook Cir, Birmingham, AL 35243, 205-967-8567

Tennessee Valley Chapter, Ed McComas, 113 Hotts Ln, Madison, AL 35758, 205-837-5675

Arizona *Southwest Chapter*, Abe Feder, 846 W Naranja, Mesa, AZ 85210, 602-839-5320

California *Northern California Chapter*, Bob Grauer, 8013 Kelok Way, Clayton, CA 94517, 925-672-2523

Southern California Chapter, Joyce Vario, 3957 Tivoli Ave, Los Angeles, CA 90066, 310-305-8174

Colorado *Rocky Mountain Chapter*, Dennis Kazmierzak, 7253 Sourdough Dr, Morrison, CO 80465, 303-697-8428

Western United States, Howard Loomis, 11131 Dobbins Run, Lafayette, CO 80026, 303-828-9210

Connecticut *Northeast Chapter*, Jerry Cribbs, 351 Wood Pond Rd, Cheshire, CT 06410, 203-272-4651

Florida *Florida Chapter*, Ed Augustine, 10462 Co Rd 561 A, Clermont, FL 34711, 352-394-6547

Illinois *Illinois Chapter*, Jay Stahl, 5229 High St, Roscoe, IL 61073, 815-623-7562

Indiana *Indiana Chapter*, Bill Bland, 4160 Woodland Stream, Greenwood, IN 46143, 317-535-7177

Iowa *Heartland Chapter*, Dick Bennett, 215 Northview, Waukee, IA 50263, 515-987-1410

Kansas *Kansas City Chapter*, Allen Kleinhenz, 14709 Slater, Overland Park, KS 66221, 913-685-2779

Kentucky *Kentucky Chapter*, Jerry Johnson, 3816 Heimbaugh Ln, Lexington, KY 40514, 606-223-2556

Louisiana *Louisiana Chapter*, James Youens, 805 E F St, Rayne, LA 70578, 318-334-9037

Maryland *Mason-Dixon Chapter*, Patricia Gongloff, 2113 Hampton Ct, Fallston, MD 21047, 410-879-8606

Massachusetts *New England Chapter*, Steve Cataldo, 71 Mill St, Middleton, MA 01949, 978-774-7405

Michigan *Michigan Chapter*, John Davin, 2220 Hickory Leaf Dr, Rochester Hills, MI 48309, 248-650-8363

Minnesota *North Central Chapter*, Ron Hendrickson, 860 Scenic Ct, Shoreview, MN 55126, 612-484-6306

Missouri *Saint Louis Chapter*, Bernie Myers, 1615 Forestview Ridge, Manchester, MO 63021, 314-530-0324

New Jersey *Central New Jersey Chapter*, Edward DiNapoli, 1150 Kearney Rd, North Brunswick, NJ 08902, 732-297-4280

New Mexico *New Mexico Chapter*, Paul Terry, 368 Bighorn Ridge Rd N, Albuquerque, NM 87122, 505-797-1388

New York *Adirondack Chapter*, Wayne Hammill, 18 Spa Dr, Saratoga Springs, NY 12866, 518-587-3269

Metro-Long Island Chapter, Sergio Fernendez, 3 Beech St, College Point, NY 11356, 718-762-2606

Western New York Chapter, Jim Miller, 258 Hillary Ln, Penfield, NY 14526, 716-377-5214

North Carolina *Carolinas Chapter*, Jimmy Gregg, PO Box 2692, Matthews, NC 28106, 704-847-5408

Ohio *Lake Erie Chapter*, Dan Cabot, 17111 Woodacre Dr, Chagrin Falls, OH 44023, 440-543-8364

Queen City Chapter, Tim Mickey, 7840 Hartford Hill Ln, Cincinnati, OH 45242, 513-984-8604

Oklahoma *Oklahoma Chapter*, Greg Hart, 10317 S Sandusky, Tulsa, OK 74137, 918-299-4824

Oregon *Northwest Chapter*, Bernie Schneider, 29637 SE Chase Rd, Gresham, OR 97080, 503-663-7887

Pennsylvania *Delaware Valley Chapter*, Dick Robinson, 1155 Goodman Dr, Fort Washington, PA 19034, 215-646-4495

Pittsburgh Tri-State Chapter, Tom Barr, 8 Cedarbrook Dr, Greensburg, PA 15601, 724-853-0306

Texas *Texas Chapter*, Tom O'Grady, 30 Southgate Dr, The Woodlands, TX 77380, 281-292-6522

Utah *Bonneville Chapter*, Cory Peterson, 294 E 1950 S, Bountiful, UT 84010, 801-298-4050

Virginia *Mid-Atlantic Chapter*, Bill Sangrey, 813 Lundberg Rd, Great Falls, VA 22066, 703-759-2160

Canada *Eastern United States*, Scott Sinclair, 153 Old King Rd, Bolton, ON L7E 5R7, 905-857-1463

Ontario Canada Chapter, Paul Dumas, 232 Tatlock Ct, Waterloo, ON N2L 5Y6, 519-885-1113

Quebec Canada Chapter, Michael Ward, 1741 Southmont St, St Bruno, QC J3V 4M1, 450-653-4110

United Kingdom *United Kingdom Chapter*, Barry Morris, 71 Green Ln St Albans, Hertfordshire AL3 6HE, 01895 672 419

National Council of Corvette Clubs Inc
3701 S 92nd St
Milwaukee, WI 53228-1611
800-245-VETT
E-mail: sezmajeb@execpc.com

Founded 1960. 13,000 members. A non-profit club dedicated to the enhancement, promotion and enjoyment of the Corvette. A service organization that provides communication and exchange of ideas between members and promotes activities on a national scale. Must own a Corvette to join. Quarterly publication, *Blue Bars*. Dues: $30/new membership, $20/renewal. Web site: www.corvettesnccc.org

New England Corvette Club
PO Box 5909
New Bedford, MA 02742
508-984-7291
E-mail: corvette@ici.net

Founded 1997. 38 members. Must own a Corvette. Club meets every month on second to last Tuesday of the month. Publish a monthly/weekly club newsletter, host Corvette shows and cruise nights. Dues: $35/year.

North Shore Corvettes of Mass
18 Heather Dr
Wilmington, MA 01887
978-658-9701
E-mail: billj@gis.net

Founded 1965. 88 members. Meetings are 3rd Thursday of month at Wakefield Elks, Wakefield, MA; Tuesday night cruise night at Uno's, May until September. Call for information. Dues: $25/year.
Web site: http://people.ne.mediaone.net/billyboy/nscm/index.html

Oceanside Vettes
23 Page Ave
Wiscasset, ME 04578
207-882-9617; FAX: 207-882-9086
E-mail: labaree@ibm.net

Founded 1997. Oceanside Vettes serves the state of Maine. Named for the famous Corvette weekend that was hosted in Maine for 17 years. Dedicated to fun, fellowship and sharing a common interest in Corvettes. Corvette ownership not required. The club hosts monthly meetings, social events and activities year round as well as an annual weekend event open to all Corvette clubs and enthusiasts.

Presque Isle Corvette Club
PO Box 604
Erie, PA 16512
814-838-6546; FAX: 814-899-6090
E-mail: apvette@aol.com

Founded 1972. 20 members. Must own a Corvette. 6 month probation period, monthly newsletter and meeting, annual car show, charity cruise in and various other activities. Dues: $36/year.

Rebel Corvette Club of the Bluegrass
857 Glen Abbey Cir
Lexington, KY 40509
606-263-3478

Founded 1981. 85 members. Must own a Corvette, meet the 1st Wednesday of each month, send a newsletter to each member every month, parties, drives, attend some major Corvette events (Mid America Fun Fest, Expo Knoxville, TN, homecoming, museum reunion Bowling Green, KY). Dues: $20/year per person, $30/year with spouse.

River Cities Corvette Club
9113 Stonecrest Dr
Louisville, KY 40272
502-935-2598; FAX: 502-935-2074

Founded 1986. 75 members. Must own Corvette. Publish local monthly newsletter. Volunteer car club for National Corvette Museum events. Dues: $30/year.

River City Corvette Club
6106 Turtle Pointe Dr
Hixson, TN 37343
423-843-0611
E-mail: letalley@juno.com

Founded 1983. 30 members. Do not have to own a Corvette, just be an enthusiast. Dues: $25/year.

Santa Clara Corvettes
PO Box 2634
Santa Clara, CA 95055

96 members. Must own a Corvette. Discounts from club sponsors and friendship, *First Class Glass* newsletter, meeting 1st Wednesday of the month, social events every month and Corvette Spectacular car show in September. Dues: $36/year. Web site: www.geocities.com/motorcity/7333/

Silver City Corvette Club
2 Golen Dr
North Dartmouth, MA 02747
PH/FAX: 508-991-4630
E-mail: bamvette88@aol.com

Founded 1983. 25 members. Attend most southeastern New England Corvette events. Monthly newsletter, *Silver Streak*. Dues: $30/year.

Solid Axle Corvette Club
Illinois Chapter
RR 1, Box 106
Chapin, IL 62628
217-457-2555
E-mail: saccmb@hotmail.com

Founded 1987. 30 members. Must have an interest in 1953-1962 Corvettes. Host regional in conjunction with Bloomington Gold show. Dues: $24/year. Web site: solidaxle.org

Solid Axle Corvette Club (SACC)
Box 2288
North Highlands, CA 95660-8288
916-991-7040
E-mail: sacc@bigfoot.com

Founded 1986. 800 members. A national club dedicated to enjoying the 1953-1962 Corvettes. Founder: Noland Adams. Membership is a family membership. Ownership is not required and dues include a subscription to quarterly magazine. Provides technical panel assistance with annual national convention and regional meets. Show locations are selected to provide activities for the whole family and suitable facilities for the Corvette. Dues: $24/year US, $30/year Canada, $40/year foreign. Web site: www.solidaxle.org

Spokane Corvette Club
PO Box 3032 TA
Spokane, WA 99220
509-922-8142; FAX: 509-495-8054

Founded 1966. 70 families. Corvette owners, monthly meetings, web site, newsletter, cruises. Dues: $40/year. Web site: ior.com/uscc

Steeltown Corvette Club
1707 Jancey St
Pittsburgh, PA 15206
412-361-3750

Founded 1972. 260 members. Open to all Corvette enthusiasts. Monthly meetings and newsletter. Annual car show, Christmas party, picnic, other events include cruises, drag racing, auto cross and road rallies. Numerous parties and fun driving events including weekend road trips. Dues: $20/year.

Three Rivers Corvette Club
PO Box 85
Library, PA 15129
412-343-7639

Founded 1980. 218 members. Anyone liking Corvettes is welcome, you don't have to own one to belong. Meetings second Wednesday of January, March, May, June, July, August, September and November. Cruising after the summer meetings. Dues: $20/year couple, $15/year single.

Thunder Vette Set
PO Box 483
Sierra Vista, AZ 85636
520-378-6498
E-mail: woodst@c2i2.com

Founded 1986. 48 members. Meet 1st Thursday every month at the VFW. Publish 6 issues a year club newsletter. Member NCCC and has 7 sanctioned events a year plus local club events. Dues: $12/year.

Treasure State Corvette Club
PO Box 6051
Helena, MT 59601
406-442-0650
E-mail: hamillmt@initco.net

Founded 1979. 37 members. Corvette interest only restriction. Newsletter once a month to members and other car clubs. Dues: $25/year single, $35/year couple.

Windy City Corvettes Inc
PO Box 353
Orland Park, IL 60462-0353
708-403-0129; FAX: 708-873-9519
E-mail: shadowlp@worldnet.att.net

Founded 1990. 175 members. Must own a Corvette (any year). Benefits: includes National Council of Corvettes membership, monthly club newsletter, quarterly NCCC magazine, events scheduled every weekend, liability insurance provided for all events and club activities. Dues: $40/year, $55/year couple. Web site: www.nlex.com/davec/windy.htm

Yakima Valley Vettes
PO Box 2373
Yakima, WA 98907
509-966-4462; FAX: 509-965-9681
E-mail: stngray@wolfenet.com

Founded 1973. 65 members. Must have Corvette to join. Have runs, events and monthly newsletter. Dues: $45/year.

Airflow Club of America
796 Santree Cir
Las Vegas, NV 89110-3939
PH/FAX: 702-438-4362

For membership information, contact at the above address: Bill Gordon. Founded 1962. 600 members. Should be Chrysler or DeSoto Airflow owner or enthusiast. Monthly newsletters including membership roster. National meets annually. Dues: $25/year US, $32/year outside North America (US funds).

California Chrysler Products Club
PO Box 2660
Castro Valley, CA 94546
510-889-0533
E-mail: ccpc1967@bigfoot.com

Founded 1967. 400 members. Dedicated to the preservation, restoration and enjoyment of Chrysler product cars and literature. Open to all years and models of Chrysler products. Publication, *Silver Dome Gazette*. Dues: $15/year. Web site: www.angelfire.com/ca/ccpc/index.html

Chrysler 300 Club Inc
PO Box 570309
Miami, FL 33257-0309
800-416-3443; FAX: 305-253-5978
E-mail: chrysler300@juno.com

Founded 1969. 900 members. No restrictions to join. Recognize all letter and non-letter 300 automobiles. Bi-monthly newsletter, *Brute Force*, technical advice, buy and sell ads for Chrysler parts and cars, articles submitted by members, historical articles on 300 cars. Reporting of National 300 meets and show calendar.

Visa/MasterCard accepted. Dues: $25/year US, $30/year Canada (US funds only), $35/year foreign.

Chrysler 300 Club International Inc
4900 Jonesville Rd
Jonesville, MI 49250
517-849-2783; FAX: 517-849-7445
E-mail:
crossram.motors@worldnet.att.net

For membership information, contact at the above address: Eleanor Riehl. Founded 1969. 950 members. Ownership of a 1955-1965 letter series 300 or a 1970 Hurst 300 preferred, but any interested person may join. Eight publications per year offering technical assistance, cars and parts locating assistance, classifieds as well as announcements of national and international meets. Dues: $20/year US and foreign. Web site: www.classicar.com/clubs/chrysler/300club.htm

Chrysler Product Owners Club Inc
809 Nelson St
Rockville, MD 20850-2052
301-340-7432
E-mail: tbuscemi@bwprotective.com

Tony Buscemi, President. Founded 1978. 350 members. Dedicated to the preservation, restoration and enjoyment of all Chrysler product automobiles including Chrysler, Imperial, Dodge, DeSoto, Plymouth, Maxwell and Chalmers. Technical advisors available to provide information on maintenance, restoration and parts location. Monthly technical seminar provides forum for problem solving and hands-on technical experience. Monthly newsletter lists events, club activities, technical advice and sources for parts. Free want/for sale ads to members. Dues: $18/year.

Chrysler Town and Country Owners Registry
John Slusar, Membership Chairman
3006 S 40th St
Milwaukee, WI 53215
414-384-1843
FAX: 216-228-0465, OH
E-mail: townandcountry@ameritech.net

Founded 1973. 350 members. Quarterly magazine, *Timber Tales*, annual registry, meets held in conjunction with WPC Club and National Woodie Club. Specializing in 1941-1950 Chrysler Town and Country cars, 1949-1950 Chrysler Royal wagons, 1983-1986 LeBaron Town and Country convertibles only. Dues: $30/year, $35/year 1st class.

Imperial Owners Association of Sacramento Valley
PO Box 254973
Sacramento, CA 95865-4973
916-481-3546, 916-687-8101

Founded 1982. 80 members. For owners of Imperials and Chrysler Imperials. 8 to 10 meetings, events or tours annually. Newsletter 6 times a year and special mailings. Members have advertising privileges. Statewide Imperial meet and show each year. Dues: $20/year US, $25/year foreign.

National Chrysler Products Club
c/o Edward W Botchie, President
160 Joyce Dr
Fayetteville, PA 17222
717-352-7673
E-mail: ncpc@ezonline.com

Founded 1979. 707 members. Purpose of the club: preservation, restoration and exhibition of Chrysler products cars and trucks with emphasis on friendship and family fun. Newsletter 7 times a year, national meet and regional meets. Dues: $20/year.

Citroen Car Club, Auckland Inc
PO Box 74393, Market Road
Auckland New Zealand
0061-9-307-7812
FAX: 0061-9-2784301

Founded 1964. 75 members. Cater to owners and people interested in all Citroen and Panhard models. Monthly club night and club event. Monthly newsletter and quarterly New Zealand magazine. Dues: $35/year.

Citroen Quarterly USA
PO Box 130030
Boston, MA 02113-0001
617-742-6604
E-mail: citq@aol.com

Founded 1976. Members nationwide. Provides source of Citroen information, camaraderie, national rendezvous. Membership includes a subscription to *Citroen Quarterly*, the journal of the Citroeniste, sample issue $5. Dues: $20/year, $25/year overseas airmail. Web site: http://members.aol.com/citq/citroenclub.html

Cooper Car Club
14 Biscayne Dr
Ramsey, NJ 07446
FAX: 201-825-8285

Founded 1987. 185 members. Worldwide organization to promote the use and restoration of Cooper cars. Also to recognize a place in motor racing history for Charles and John Cooper. Quarterly newsletter. Dues: $20/year.

Cushman Club of America
PO Box 661
Union Springs, AL 36089
334-738-3874
E-mail: ccoa@ustconline.net

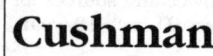

Founded 1981. 5,000 members. Bi-monthly member magazine, national meet. Dedicated to the restoration and preservation of Cushman Motor Scooters. Dues: $25/year.

DAF Club-America
293 Hudson St
Hackensack, NJ 07601
201-343-1252, 201-342-3684
FAX: 201-342-3568

Founded 1980. 10 members. West Coast address: 706 Monroe St, Santa Rosa, CA 95405. Club consists of owners of DAF cars and others with an interest in DAFs. Dedicated to the preservation of DAFs and promotion of the CVT transmission pioneered by DAF. Publication, *DAF Bulletin*. Dues: $10/year.

Daimler & Lanchester Owners' Club
PO Box 276
Sittingbourne
Kent ME9 7UJ England
PH/FAX: 0044 7000 356285
E-mail: daimleruk@aol.com

Founded 1964. 2,500 members. Enthusiast's club for all Daimlers, Lanchesters and BSAs (with fluid flywheel transmission). Prize winning monthly 36 page glossy journal. Offers free technical advice via model registrars, plus spare sourcing assistance. Full membership pack sent on request. Web site: daimler&lanchester.org.uk

Z Club of Georgia
333 England Pl
Marietta, GA 30066
770-926-2390; FAX: 770-428-2780
E-mail: hcostanzo@gowebway.com

Founded 1992. 300 members. Must own a Z or ZX. Discounts, rallies, autocross, road racing, monthly newsletter. Monthly

meeting 1st Tuesday at Hooter's, Jimmy Carter Blvd, Norcross, GA. Dues: $25/single, $30/family. Web site: georgiazclub.com

Club Delahaye
B P 15
59640 Dunkerque
France
3 28 29 68 68; FAX: 3 28 61 07 32

Two road meets in different towns in France each year as well as club sponsored dinners in Paris. Bulletin published four times a year. Dues: 500 francs/year.

DeLorean Midatlantic
515 W Chelten Ave, Suite 1009
Philadelphia, PA 19144
215-849-5160
E-mail: dmc1440@earthlink.net

Founded 1985. 125 members. All DeLorean enthusiasts welcome. Annual regional meet. Quarterly newsletter. Monthly techsocials, including free door adjustment social. Parts interchange list. Technical advisories. Dues: $12/year.

Pantera International
18586 Main St, Suite 100
Huntington Beach, CA 92648
714-848-6674; FAX: 714-843-5851

Founded 1973. Members worldwide. DeTomaso factory authorized. Ownership not required. Publishing quarterly color magazine and authoritative book. Your leading source for technical, collecting, restoration, vintage racing, historical, personality and feature car information. Many cars for sale. Annual convention in Monterey each August where we are the sole sponsoring club for the DeTomaso marque at the Concours Italiano. Club store has many DeTomaso theme items. Dues: $55/year US, $70/year foreign. Web site: www.panteracars.com

Pantera Owner's Club of America (POCA)
Shane Ingate
309 Playa Del Sur
La Jolla, CA 92037
619-454-4656; FAX: 619-456-2441
E-mail: membership@panteraclub.com

Founded 1973. 950 members. A not-for-profit organization, is the official factory recognized DeTomaso club in the United States. Through 15 regional chapters, POCA offers speed, social and technical events plus an annual fun rally in Las Vegas. Members receive an informative 32-page monthly newsletter and *Profiles*, the beautiful color quarterly magazine. Car ownership is not required for membership. Visa, MasterCard accepted. Dues: $60/year domestic, $75/year foreign. Web site: www.panteraclub.com

Divco Club of America
PO Box 1142
Kingston, WA 98346-1142
360-598-3938
E-mail: divcoclub@silverlink.net

Founded 1991. Over 500 members. Dedicated to the preservation and restoration of Divco trucks and vehicles. Open to all Divco enthusiasts. Newsletter provides information, parts sources, history, help and encouragement, free classifieds for members. For information contact: Les Bagley, Newsletter Editor. Dues: $18/year for individuals, other membership classes available. Web site: www.divco.org

DKW Club of America
260 Santa Margarita Ave
Menlo Park, CA 94025
650-321-6640; FAX: 650-329-0129
E-mail: jowett@best.com

For information, contact at the above address: Byron Brill.
Serving Auto Union and DKW owners and enthusiasts worldwide. Fun, informative newsletter, parts and information sources
and healthy doses of encouragement. Membership: $17/year
North America, $23/year elsewhere.

D.A.R.T.S.
PO Box 9
Wethersfield, CT 06129-0009
860-257-8434 evenings 8 pm-10 pm
E-mail: dartsclub@aol.com

Founded 1986. 375 members. A service club for high-performance 1967-1972 Dodge Darts and Demons. Quarterly newsletters provide events, technical information and restoration information. Free ads to buy and sell are encouraged to be used.
Dues: $10/year.

Dodge Brothers Club
PO Box 292
Eastpointe, MI 48021-0292
E-mail: bcogan@ameritech.net

Membership inquiries, contact at above address: Barry Cogan.
Founded 1983. 1,100 members. Open to anyone interested in
Dodge Brothers or Graham Brothers vehicles 1914-1938.
Ownership of vehicle is not required for membership.
Membership includes subscription to bi-monthly 32-page maga-
zine, annual meets at locations across the US and Canada.
Worldwide membership. Dues: $20/year US and Canada,
$26/year (US funds) foreign. Web site:
http://home.wkpowerlink.com/~dodgebrothers/
regions:
 Michigan   *Dodge Main Region*, John Connor, 11637
   Tahiti Dr, Sterling Heights, MI 48312

Dual Ghia Enthusiasts Club
Paul Sable
29 Forgedale Rd
Fleetwood, PA 19522
610-987-6923; FAX: 610-282-2254

Founded 1990. 65 members. Open to enthusiasts, owners of
Dual Ghias. A forum for exchange of information. Owner's registry and parts availability. Annual newsletter. Dues: none.

Edsel Owners Club of America Inc
816 Richard Ln
Danville, CA 94526
925-837-6410; FAX: 925-837-1602
E-mail: edsel94526@aol.com

For membership information, contact at the above address:
Harold Kleckner, Membership Vice President. Founded 1967.
1,000+ members worldwide. Edsel ownership not necessary.
Dues: $30/year US, $35/year Canada, $40/year foreign, US dol-
lars.

**North American English &
European Ford Registry**
PO Box 11415
Olympia, WA 98508
360-754-9585
E-mail: ifhp@aol.com

Founded 1991. 160 members. Now open to all English and
European Ford built vehicles. Bi-monthly newsletter, best classifieds for English Ford cars and parts in this hemisphere. Also
publish *Annual Roster and Survival Count*. Call or write for a
brochure and membership application. Web site:
www.geocities.com/motorcity/downs/2519

Ferrari Club of America
PO Box 720597
Atlanta, GA 30358
800-328-0444; FAX: 770-936-9392

Founded 1962. 4,500 members. Open to all Ferrari enthusiasts.
Quarterly magazine, monthly news bulletin, annual meet with
concours and track event. Club has 13 regions each hosting different events. Many regions have their own newsletter. A great
place to meet other people with Ferrari interests. Ferrari ownership is not mandatory. Dues: $85-$125/year. Web site:
ferrariclubofamerica.org

Ferraristi Vermont
19 Marble Ave Box 3
Burlington, VT 05401
802-658-1270 ext 201
FAX: 802-658-3873
E-mail: ferrarisvt@aol.com

Founded 1996. 100+ members. A social club for Ferrari owners
and enthusiasts. Monthly touring events May-October. Dues:
$50/year.

Rear Engine Fiat Club
PO Box 682
Sun Valley, CA 91353
818-768-3552

Founded 1988 by Jonathan Thompson of *Road & Track* for
lovers of rear engine Fiats and derivative cars. Four driving
events per year plus Fiat swap meet, car show. Quarterly
newsletter. Dues: $15/year US, $30/year international.

The 54 Ford Club of America
1517 N Wilmot #144
Tucson, AZ 85712
PH/FAX: 520-886-1184
E-mail: jstrobec@ix.netcom.com

Founded 1986. 520 members. Open to 1954 Ford owners and
those interested in 1954 Fords. Quarterly newsletter. Dues:
$15/year.

**Club del Ford V8-Republica
Argentina**
Lavalle 1454 P5 to OF3
Capital Federal 1048 Argentina
PH/FAX: 4371 8046
E-mail: yasmine@pinos.com

Contact: Gustavo Lafont, 4717 2814. Founded 1989. 150 members. V8 1932-1948. Meet every month. Main event is October
12. Club edits one magazine a year. Dues: $60/year.

Cowtown T's Inc
4424 Ideldell Dr
Fort Worth, TX 76116-7611
817-244-2340
E-mail: rggrunewald@juno.com

Founded 1982. 44 members. Monthly newsletter and meetings.
Open membership to anyone interested in the Ford Model T.
Dues: $15/year.

Crown Victoria Association
PO Box 6
Bryan, OH 43506
419-636-2475

Founded 1977. 1,650 members. Club recognizes all 1954-1956 Fords. Ownership of a car is not essential. Dues: $29/year US and Canada, $45/year foreign, US funds please. Web site: www.classicar.com/clubs/crownvictoria/index.htm

Early Bronco Registry
PO Box 1525
Poway, CA 92074-1525
619-530-2470; FAX: 619-530-2471
E-mail: ebremail@aol.com

Founded 1990. 700 members. International association, not-for-profit. Open to anyone interested in the 1966-1977 Ford Bronco. Publish *Horsing Around* monthly, includes tips, trips and classifieds. Dues: $25/year. Web site: www.earlybronco.com

The Early Ford V8 Club of America
PO Box 2122
San Leandro, CA 94577
PH/FAX: 925-606-1925
E-mail: fordv8club@aol.com

Founded 1963. 9,000+ members. 150 regions worldwide. Must be interested in Ford, Mercury or Lincoln products, 1932-1953. A national historical society dedicated to the restoration and preservation of Ford Motor Company vehicles from 1932-1953. Bi-monthly publication, *V8 Times*, is included with membership. Dues: $30/year single, $32/year joint. Web site: www.earlyfordv8.org

regions:

Arizona *Phoenix*, Phil Pittman, President, 328 E Rose Ln, Phoenix, AZ 85012, 970-533-7284

Southern Arizona, Jim LaDuc, President, 10580 E Pinal Vista, Tucson, AZ 85730, 520-419-6604

California *Atascadero*, Warren Hokinson, President, PO Box 1911, Atascadero, CA 93423, 805-466-4861

Baldy View, Carlos Wilhelm, President, PO Box 456, Upland, CA 91786, 909-886-9085

Big Valley, Eric Hinrichs, President, PO Box 693181, Stockton, CA 95269, 209-599-5460

Cable Car, Darrell LaFond, President, 42139 Camino Santa Barbara, Fremont, CA 94539, 510-656-5726

Central San Joaquin, Bill Laverty, President, PO Box 11364, Fresno, CA 93773, 209-683-7705

Diablo Valley, Jack Webb, President, PO Box 354, Danville, CA 94526, 925-757-8541

El Dorado, Don Haynes, President, PO Box 1821, Placerville, CA 95667, 530-644-3374

Golden Gate Charter, John Swanberg, President, PO Box 2364, Castro Valley, CA 94546, 650-341-0573

Mission Trail, Ken Check, President, PO Box 6864, San Jose, CA 95150, 408-923-5661

North Bay, Gary Zucha, President, c/o 126 Village Ct, Vacaville, CA 95687, 707-446-2988

Northern California, Dennis Rupp, President, 3 Brittany Ln, Chico, CA 95926, 530-895-1849

Palomar Mountain, Howard Simpson, President, PO Box 1169, Valley Center, CA 92082, 760-765-0653

Redwood Empire, Carol Rasmussen, President, PO Box 3302, Santa Rosa, CA 95404, 707-226-5256

Sacramento, Dan Schwartz, President, PO Box 60878, Sacramento, CA 95860, 916-962-3521

San Diego, Ed Hennig, President, PO Box 881107, San Diego, CA 92168, 925-789-2640

Santa Maria Valley, Marvin Nichols, President, 1119 S Speed St, Santa Maria, CA 93454, 805-349-3449

Southern California, Matthew Ettinger, President, PO Box 2294, Costa Mesa, CA 92626, 562-691-3620

Valley V-Eights, Rose Gott, President, 545 N Keystone St, Burbank, CA 91506, 818-767-6153

Ventura, Vince Barisic, President, PO Box 4600, Saticoy, CA 93007, 805-498-0250

Colorado *Hi-Country*, J R Marschall, President, PO Box 3137, Littleton, CO 80122, 303-460-0358

Connecticut *Connecticut*, Ted Ristau, President, 29 Hawthorne Dr, Norwalk, CT 06851, 203-847-0078

Florida *Birthplace of Speed*, Joe Gimpel Sr, President, 801-E Gatepark Dr, Daytona Beach, FL 32114, 904-257-9898

Central Florida, Cecil Goff, President, PO Box 855, Geneva, FL 32732, 407-349-9763

Gator V-8ers, John Carter, President, 8040 SW 135th St, Miami, FL 33546, 305-238-2052

Gulf Coast, George Mitchell, President, PO Box 106, Sanibel Island, FL 33957, 941-637-1813

Indian River, Paul D Munyon, President, 101 Jettie Terr, Port St Lucie, FL 34983, 561-871-1934

Palm Beach, Jack Breen, President, PO Box 12101, Lake Park, FL 33403, 561-684-4563

Suwannee River, Don Fales, President, 15250 NW 83rd Terr, Trenton, FL 32693, 352-493-0354

Georgia *Georgia*, Mitch Gwinn, President, 2622 Arlene Way, Atlanta, GA 30305, 770-493-7648

Idaho *Gem State*, Robert Poedy, President, 3901 Patton St, Boise, ID 83704, 208-325-8598

Illinois *Central Illinois*, Louis Taylor, President, PO Box 471, Pekin, IL 61554, 309-699-1796

Greater Rockford, Gary Hess, President, 306 E State, Rockford, IL 61008, 815-234-4067

Land of Lincoln, Don Tessendorf, President, 302 W Gray, Bloomington, IL 61701, 309-828-0787

Northern Illinois, Phyllis Witthdeft, President, PO Box 4076, Arlington Heights, IL 60006, 847-658-5912

Spoon River, Frank Walker, President, PO Box 67, Knoxville, IL 61448, 309-289-2425

Indiana *Indiana*, Debbie Sharp, President, Main PO Box 1381, Indianapolis, IN 46206, 317-243-3172

Northwest Indiana, Jim Brown, President, PO Box 1914, Highland, IN 46322, 219-942-4232

Iowa   *Cedar Valley*, Donald Shafer, President, 1435 Huntington Rd, Waterloo, IA 50701, 319-235-0451

Central Iowa, Jim Stanley, President, 3050 Meadow Rd, Adel, IA 50003, 515-993-3208

Quad City, PO Box 595, LeClaire, IA 52753

Kansas   *Wichita*, Verne Shirk, President, PO Box 1155, Wichita, KS 67201, 316-945-0893

Kentucky   *Central Kentucky Thoroughbred*, James Rogers, President, 926 Hanley Ln, Frankfort, KY 40601, 502-695-7080

Derby City, Robert Johnson, President, 8610 Michael Ray Dr, Louisville, KY 40219, 502-969-3058

Louisiana   *Bayou State*, Gerald Henson, President, 550 Choctaw Dr, Abita Springs, LA 70420, 504-867-4866

Maine   *Maine Coast*, Oscar Blue, President, 48 Tunk Rd, Steuben, ME 04680, 207-422-3987

Maryland   *National Capital*, Peggy Garrish, President, 27131 Ridge Rd, Damascus, MD 20872, 301-253-0320

Massachusetts   *New England*, John Caron, President, PO Box 974, Acton, MA 01720, 978-692-6063

Michigan   *Dearborn*, Jack Beggs, President, 2586 Cheswick, Troy, MI 48084, 248-646-5082

Southern Michigan, John Seelye, President, 4900 Churchill Rd, Leslie, MI 49251, 517-750-3405

Minnesota   *Twin Cities*, Jerry Felton, President, PO Box 20236, Minneapolis, MN 55420, 612-873-6754

Missouri   *Kansas City*, Dwight Norman, President, PO Box 411844, Kansas City, MO 64141, 913-478-3618

St Louis, John Walters, President, PO Box 623, Chesterfield, MO 63006, 314-432-0184

Montana   *Big Sky V8*, PO Box 252, Billings, MT 59103

Nebraska   *Cornhusker*, Charlotte Moyer, President, 14620 Eastbourne St, Waverly, NE 68462, 402-489-1689

Omaha, Mal Gardner, President, PO Box 540307, Omaha, NE 68154, 402-333-5380

Nevada   *Battle Born*, Chris Kiechler, President, PO Box 98, Carson City, NV 89702, 775-847-0389

New Jersey   *Garden State*, John Hunter, President, 11 Catalpa Rd, Morristown, NJ 07960, 973-263-5060

New Mexico   *Tumbleweed*, Jay Hertz, President, PO Box 21538, Albuquerque, NM 87154, 505-296-3137

New York   *Hudson Valley*, Richard Glasgow, President, 15 Greenvale Farms Rd, Poughkeepsie, NY 12603, 914-473-4071

Long Island, Wayne Duprez, President, PO Box 1204, Smithtown, NY 11787, 516-265-2597

Mohawk Valley, Ray Beebe, President, 1551 Hillsboro Rd, RD #2, Camden, NY 13316, 315-245-0728

Upstate NY, Gene Giuliano, President, PO Box 51, East Schodack, NY 12063, 518-477-6813

Western New York, Mark Moriarty, President, PO Box 13514, Rochester, NY 14613, 716-786-2876

North Carolina   *Blue Ridge V8*, James A Cashman, President, 246 Lakewood Dr, Wilkesboro, NC 28697, 336-921-3729

Central Carolina, Jay Temple, President, PO Box 628, Lexington, NC 27293, 336-956-4438

Piedmont, Ted Wilburn, President, 2508 Carriage Crossing Dr, Matthews, NC 28105, 704-847-8756

Ohio   *Northern Ohio*, Ron Wertz, President, PO Box 1074, Cuyahoga Falls, OH 44223, 330-533-4381

Ohio, Irvin Ziegler, President, PO Box 14671, Dayton, OH 45413, 513-851-4738

Oklahoma   *Oklahoma City*, Howard Shryock, President, 8417 Sandpiper Rd, Oklahoma City, OK 73132, 405-721-5821

Tulsa, Rick Claybaugh, President, PO Box 4109, Tulsa, OK 74159, 918-838-8354

Oregon   *Beaver State*, Daryl Hogan, President, 1815 Hill St SE, Albany, OR 97321, 503-928-4646

Columbia River, Chuck Harding, President, PO Box 8311, Portland, OR 97207, 503-647-5103

Crater Lake, Lou Dilda, President, 1709 Stratford Ave, Medford, OR 97504, 541-955-8953

Memory Lane, Dwain McPherson, President, PO Box 2291, Eugene, OR 97402, 503-688-7653

Mid-Willamette, Ron Hill, President, PO Box 12071, Salem, OR 97309, 503-393-1426

Umpqua Flatheads, Jack Zink, President, PO Box 1635, Roseburg, OR 97970, 541-672-1071

Pennsylvania   *Central Delaware Valley*, Matt Piotrowski, President, PO Box 721, Bensalem, PA 19020, 215-672-6629

Greater Pittsburgh, Ed Urbansky, President, PO Box 12852, Pittsburgh, PA 15241, 412-655-4095

Happy Valley Flatheads, Frank Vicente, President, PO Box 5301, Pleasant Gap, PA 16823, 804-360-0777

Hawk Mountain, Rick Siegel, President, PO Box 162, Blandon, PA 19510, 610-926-3061

Rhode Island   *Narragansett Bay*, Paul Sheehan, President, PO Box 3263, Newport, RI 02840, 401-846-2522

Tennessee   *East Tennessee*, Phil Vinson, President, 1836 Weaver Pike, Bristol, TN 37620, 423-764-0894

Volunteer, Kenneth Brown, President, PO Box 111311, Nashville, TN 37222, 931-598-9224

Texas   *Big Country*, Bill Smith, President, PO Box 3093, Abilene, TX 79604, 915-692-7967

The Early Ford V8 Club of America regions *(continued)*

Capitol City, Carl Henderson, President, PO Box 151032, Austin, TX 78715, 512-288-2628

Dallas, Ron Westwood, President, PO Box 460668, Garland, TX 75046, 972-396-5851

East Texas Lazy 8's, Lon Neighbors, President, Rt 4 Box 177A, Grand Saline, TX 75140, 903-763-2939

Golden Spread, Cecil Regier, President, PO Box 1782, Amarillo, TX 79105, 806-966-5479

Heart of Texas, Benny Huddleston, President, PO Box 125, Hewitt, TX 76643, 254-848-4958

Houston, Mark Costello, President, 18022 Moss Point Dr, Spring, TX 77379, 713-785-6908

Lone Star, Stacy Brown, President, PO Box 592, Arlington, TX 76010, 817-261-8502

Southern Texas, Alan Bentz, President, PO Box 202085, San Antonio, TX 78220, 830-276-3294

Utah *Great Salt Lake,* Gene Miller, President, 2926 Banbury Rd, Salt Lake City, UT 84121, 801-943-5893

Vermont *Twin-State,* John Woodruff, President, RR 1 Box 32, East Rudolph, VT 05041, 802-276-3058

Virginia *Northern Virginia,* David Westrate, President, PO Box 1195, Vienna, VA 22183, 703-620-9597

Southwest Virginia, Tom Richardson, President, 3919 Poplar Grove, Vinton, VA 24179, 703-890-3432

Virginia, Tommy Anderson, President, 1806 W Broad St, Richmond, VA 23220, 804-272-8432

Washington *Cascade,* Jerold Anderson, President, PO Box 3811, Federal Way, WA 98003, 206-226-1012

Inland Empire, Bob Sills, President, PO Box 176, Veradale, WA 99037, 509-928-3297

Puget Sound, Bill Meade, President, PO Box 12613, Seattle, WA 98111, 206-789-5534

Snohomish County, Mike Dermond, President, PO Box 12413, Mill Creek, WA 98082, 206-745-8877

Yakima Valley, Jerry Rowland, President, PO Box 5, Buena Vista, WA 98021, 509-829-5026

Wisconsin *Badger State,* William Storey, President, PO Box 302, Waterford, WI 53185, 414-338-0452

Australia *New South Wales,* Gordon Matthews, President, PO Box 13, Panania, New South Wales 2213, 46-35-38-48

Southern Australia, Graham Tonkin, President, PO Box 332, North Adelaide 5032

Victorian/Australia, Bryan Stephens, President, Mulgrave Bus Ctr PO Box 546, Victoria 3170

Canada *Southern Ontario,* Percy Bourne, President, PO Box 21023 290 Harwood Ave S, Ajax, ON L1H 7H2, 416-438-1491

Vancouver Fraser Valley, Yvette Decker, President, PO Box 602, Port Coquitlan, BC V3B 6H9, 604-576-2626

Vancouver Island, Bob Ainscough, President, PO Box 8433, Central PO, Victoria, BC V8W 3S1, 604-385-2287

Denmark *Danish,* Jess Nielsen, President, PO Box 1932-53, 4500 Nykoping SJ, 45 534-12453

England *Dagenham,* Chris Sanders, President, 12 Fairholm Gardens, Cranham, Upminster Essex RM1 41HJ, 040-22-22729

New Zealand *Northern New Zealand,* Doug Tutill, President, PO Box 97288 S Auckland Mail Ctr, Auckland, 64 09 410 7113

Southern Kiwi, Mike Barnes, President, PO Box 16-396, Christchurch, 03 3586168

Norway *Norway,* Harald Marthinsen, President, PO Box 2353 Bjoelsen, N-0406, Oslo, 47-669-11424

Sweden *Early Ford V8 of Sweden,* Jan Ryden, President, c/o J Almkvist-Folkungagatan 94, SE-11622 Stockholm, 08-55037570

Falcon Club of America
Northeast Chapter
73 Francis Rd
Glocester, RI 02857
401-934-2105
E-mail: falcon22@ix.netcom.com

Founded 1983. 120 members. Must be a member of parent club, Falcon Club of America. Bi-monthly newsletters, annual regional Falcon meet, cruises, Falcon related events. Specialize in services and activities for 1960-1970-1/2 Ford Falcon automobiles. Publication, *Northeast Falcon Newsletter,* free with membership, published 6 times a year, Falcon parts, sales and services. Dues: $8/year. Web site: www.falconclub.com

---

Ford Galaxie Club of America
PO Box 178
Hollister, MO 65672
870-429-8264
E-mail: galaxieclub@collector.org

Founded 1983. 1,400 members. FGCOA is an association dedicated to the restoration, preservation and enjoyment of the Galaxie passenger automobiles built by the Ford Motor Company from 1959-1974. Publish the *Galaxie Gazette* magazine on a bi-monthly basis. Dues: $25/year US, $30/year Canada and Mexico, $50/year others. Web site: www.galaxieclub.com

---

Ford Motorsports Enthusiasts
PO Box 1331
Dearborn, MI 48120-1331
313-438-2001
E-mail: teamfme@teamfme.com

Founded 1995. 1,214+ members. Regular members: full-time employee, retiree of Ford Motor Co, or member of immediate family of such. Associate members: subject to regulation by FME, if otherwise ineligible for regular membership and limited by percentage regulations of parent organization. Track days and FME discounts plus special annual events, in addition to monthly meetings with guest speakers. *First On Race Day* is published 4-6 times per year and is included in membership dues. Also *FME Business Directory* is published annually in April. Dues: $12/year. Web site: www.teamfme.com

---

Ford-Freak Club of Finland
PO Box 351
00531 Helsinki Finland
+358-40-5254114

Founded 1987. 200 members. For all US Ford fans. Keep up

good Ford humor, *Ford-Freak* magazine 4 times year. Meets: Nestori snow race, Freak's Peak, swap and meet. Dues: 100 FIM/year.

The Great Lakes Roadster Club
PO Box 302
Bath, OH 44210

For membership information, contact at the above address: Jerry A Barker.

Hawk MTV-8 Ford Club of Reading, PA
145 S Blainsport Rd
Reinholds, PA 17569
717-336-2735

Contact: Rick Slegel, President, Blandon, PA. Founded 1974. 75 members. Annual July 4th Fleetwood, PA, car show and flea market. Join club and belong to national club.

International Ford Retractable Club
PO Box 389
Marlboro, MA 01752
500-359-5857, OR
FAX: 508-481-9536

Founded 1971. 1,200 members. Promote the restoration, preservation and further interest in the 1957, 1958, 1959 Skyliner retractable hardtop produced by Ford Motor Co. Car ownership not required. Dues: $32/year US, $34/year Canada, $43/year foreign.

chapters:

Connecticut	*New England Chapter*, Carl Lasky, 954 Main St S, Woodbury, CT 06798
Illinois	*Gateway Chapter*, Bill Zimmerman, 916 W Hicks Hollow Rd, Edelstein, IL 61526
	Great Lakes Chapter, Richard Newendyke, 1509 E 33rd St, Sterling, IL 61081
Indiana	*Hoosier Chapter*, Dick Snider, 502 Spring Meadow Ct, Vincennes, IN 47591
Michigan	*Michigan-Ontario Chapter*, Howard Voigt, 631 Golf Crest Dr, Dearborn, MI 48124
Minnesota	*Northland Chapter*, Ron Anderson, 7308 James Ave S, Richfield, MN 55423
Nebraska	*Pathfinder Chapter*, Kiel Eliste, 1525 N Garfield, Fremont, NE 68025
North Carolina	*Virginia-Carolina Chapter*, Harry Lippard, 185 Majolica Rd, Salisbury, NC 28147
Ohio	*Buckeye Chapter*, Donna Simpson, 24769 Stein Rd, Creola, OH 45622
Pennsylvania	*East Coast Chapter*, Dick Trythall, 2175 Pottstown Pike, Pottstown, PA 19464
	Penn-Allegheny Chapter, Gloria Dudt, 104 McCrerey Rd, Claysville, PA 15323
South Carolina	*Southeastern Chapter*, Jerreld Price, PO Box 251, Hwy 221, Mayo, SC 29368

Iowa-Missouri Ford Club
512 E Franklin
Bloomfield, IA 52537
515-664-1025
E-mail: sdllpark@netins.net

Founded 1985. 15 members. Open to all Ford enthusiasts. Annual Ford Powered show, third weekend of August. Dues: $10/year.

Model A Ford Cabriolet Club
PO Box 515
Porter, TX 77365
281-429-2505

Founded 1980. 400 members. Quarterly publication, included in cost of dues. Club formed to provide a way to exchange information and parts among owners and enthusiasts of the cabriolet, a rare body style of the Model A Ford made from 1929-1931. Dues: $12/year US, Canada and Mexico, $14/year overseas.

Model A Ford Club of America
250 S Cypress
La Habra, CA 90631
562-697-2712, 562-697-2737
FAX: 562-690-7452
E-mail: mafcahq@aol.com

Founded 1957. 16,000 members. Interest in the Model A Ford. Technical information in the *Restore the Club* publication, national meets on the even year. Dedicated to the restoration and preservation of the Model A Ford. Over 300 chapters, 22 international chapters, 16 special interest and body style groups. The club is the largest car club in the world devoted to a single model. Dues: $30/year, $34/year foreign, $36/year foreign 1st class. Web site: www.mafca.com

chapters:

Alabama	*Gulf Coast Model A Club*, PO Box 1113, Robertsdale, AL 36567-1113
	Heart of Dixie A's, Gene Taylor, 26561 Martin Branch Rd, Madison, AL 35758
Alaska	*Alaskan A's*, 3612 Delores Dr, Eagle River, AK 99577
Arizona	*Ah-ooo-gah A's of Arizona*, PO Box 3502, Carefree, AZ 85377
	Arizona Traveling A's, 1212 E Alameda Dr, Tempe, AZ 85282, 602-968-3258
	Hi-Country A's of Arizona, PO Box 12211, Prescott, AZ 86304
	Model A Restorers Club of Arizona, PO Box 5255, Mesa, AZ 85201
	Patagonia T & A, PO Box 4481, Rio Rico, AZ 85648
	Phoenix Model A Club, PO Box 35702, Phoenix, AZ 85069, 602-993-8418
	Tucson, 2003 S 4th, Tucson, AZ 85713
Arkansas	*Fiftieth Anniversary*, c/o Doug Zahn, 16921 Crystal Valley Rd, Little Rock, AR 72210, 501-455-2562
	Natural State A Region, 127 Price St, Pea Ridge, AR 72751
	Texarkana A's, 213 Wood, Texarkana, AR 71854, 501-774-6477
California	*1929 Cabriolet Club*, 1045 Woodhaven, Spring Valley, CA 92077
	A-400 Group, 2912 McCray Rd, Lake Isabella, CA 93240, 760-379-7602
	Acorn A's, Box 2321, Castro Valley, CA 94546, 510-576-1612
	Adobe A Chapter, 1250 Orange St, Red Bluff, CA 96080
	Amador A's, PO Box 967, Pine Grove, CA 95665, 209-296-5104
	Angel City Chapter, Pat Worthy, 14017 Wilkie Ave, Gardena, CA 90249, 310-532-4371
	Auburn A's, Box 4345, Auburn, CA 95604, 916-367-2747
	Bakersfield Chapter, Box 1616, Bakersfield, CA 93302, 805-589-5795

Section Three Clubs & Organizations

Model A Ford Club of America chapters *(continued)*

Bay Area, 181 Alpine Way, San Bruno, CA 94066

Blossom Trail A's, PO Box 26, Reedley, CA 93654

Brake Away A's, 5121 Vernon Ave, Fremont, CA 94536, 415-656-8308

Butte-View A's, PO Box 1820 Tudor Rd, Yuba City, CA 95993-9516, 916-671-6634

CA Vehicle Foundation, c/o J Bengel, 2596 Warrego, Sacramento, CA 95826

Capistrano Valley A's, Box 614, San Juan Capistrano, CA 92693, 714-837-4178

Capitol A's, 2596 Warrego Way, Sacramento, CA 95826-2434, 916-484-7433

Central California Region, c/o Harry Coy, 4326 E Lane, Fresno, CA 93702

Charter Oak A's, Box 3696, Visalia, CA 93278-3696, 209-734-7348

Chico A's, 2674 Ceres Ave, Chico, CA 95973

Conejo Valley, PO Box 332, Newbury Park, CA 91319-0332, 805-499-1973

Cruisin' A's, Troy Farmer, PO Box 5346, Hemet, CA 92545, 714-927-7362

Cuesta Crankers, Norman M Harry, PO Box 714, San Luis Obispo, CA 93406, 805-489-4408

Delta Chapter, Box 7328, Stockton, CA 95267, 209-477-7449

Diablo A's, Box 6125, Concord, CA 94524, 925-689-7612

Diamond Tread, Box 4563, Downey, CA 90241, 310-927-7444

Eastern Sierra Model A Ford Club, 2727 Highland Dr, Bishop, CA 93514-3025

Eel River Valley A's, Box 688, Fortuna, CA 95540-0688, 707-443-6601

El Camino A's, PO Box 1754, San Mateo, CA 94401

Exclusive A's, 1549 Poppy Peak, Pasadena, CA 91105-2707, 213-254-0259

FAST, 39480 Colleen Way, Temecula, CA 92592-8438, 909-695-3713

Feather River A's, PO Box 1833, Quincy, CA 95971, 916-283-0503

Flying Quails, 595 El Camino Real, North Box 151, Salinas, CA 93907, 408-449-2834

Four Bangers, 20207 Stagg St, Canoga Park, CA 91306

Four Ever Four Cylinder A's, 39480 Colleen Way, Temecula, CA 92592-8438

Gateway A's, PO Box 1429, Merced, CA 95341-1429, 209-723-0834

Golden Feather MAC, PO Box 2351, Oroville, CA 95965, 530-533-3514

Gra-Neva Model A, Box 2415, Grass Valley, CA 95945, 916-272-4683

GRAMPA A's, Box 2201, Monterey, CA 93942, 408-624-1992

Hangtown A's, Box 2296, Placerville, CA 95667-2296, 916-622-0612

Happy Honkers, PO Box 1912, Porterville, CA 93258-1912, 209-781-2279

Harbor MARC, 2018 W 178th St, Torrance, CA 90504-4311

Heartland A's, PO Box 3665, Ontario, CA 91761

Henry's A's, Box 46, Livermore, CA 94550

Henry's Originals, Don Schade, 8821 La Entrade, Whittier, CA 90605

Humboldt Bay A's, PO Box 6664, Eureka, CA 95501

Jewel City, 1100 N Florence, Burbank, CA 91505

Johnies Broiler Flying A's, 7447 Firestone Blvd, Downey, CA 90241

Lake County A's, PO Box 634, Clearlake, CA 95422

Linden A's, PO Box 572, Linden, CA 95236, 209-887-3944

Los Amigos, 4833 Castana Ave, Lakewood, CA 90712

MAFC of Palm Springs, PO Box 3898, Palm Desert, CA 92261

Main Bearings, 2870 Brandt, La Verne, CA 91750

MARC/MAFCA San Diego, PO Box 19805, San Diego, CA 619-462-7256

Marin A's, Box 2864, San Rafael, CA 94901

Mariposa Four Bangers, 5840 Evergreen Ln, Mariposa, CA 95338

Modesto Area A's, PO Box 576073, Modesto, CA 95357, 209-838-7725

Mother Lode A's, PO Box 1500, Murphys, CA 95247-9636, 209-728-3306

Mountain Quail, Box 539, Loyalton, CA 96118, 916-993-4458

Mountain Road Rattlers, PO Box 3416, Oakhurst, CA 93644-3416

Napa Valley A's, Box 2656, Napa, CA 94558

Northern California Region, 1052 Maple Park Dr, Paradise, CA 95969

Oakdale A's, PO Box 60, Oakdale, CA 95361

Orange Blossom A's, PO Box 51824, Riverside, CA 92517

Orange County, PO Box 10595, Santa Ana, CA 92711, 714-633-0390

Palomar, PO Box 191, Carlsbad, CA 92018-0191, 619-438-2365

Paradise Valley, PO Box 1120, Rialto, CA 92377-1120, 714-888-0157

Phaeton Club, 1049 Don Pablo Dr, Arcadia, CA 91006, 818-447-6630

Pomono Valley, Box 2302, Pomona, CA 91766-2302, 714-983-4102

Queen Mary, 555 Forest Lake Dr, Brea, CA 92821

Redding Rambling A's, Box 3872, Redding, CA 96049

Reliable A's, Box 160322, Sacramento, CA 95816

San Fernando Valley, Box 2713, Van Nuys, CA 91404, 818-352-3670

Santa Anita A's, PO Box 660904, Arcadia, CA 91006-0904, 818-797-2048

Santa Barbara A's, PO Box 60358, Santa Barbara, CA 93160

Santa Clara Valley, PO Box 6072, San Jose, CA 95150, 408-867-2449

Santa Ynez Valley Model A Ford Club, 715 Kolding Ave, Solvang, CA 93463

Sierra, PO Box 2065, Fresno, CA 93718-2065, 209-434-7451

Sis-Q-A's, 523 N Oregon St, Yreka, CA 96097

Solano A's, PO Box 426, Elmira, CA 95625, 707-448-0585

Sonoma A's, Box 4052, Santa Rosa, CA 95402

Sonora A's, PO Box 382, Sonora, CA 95370-0382, 209-533-0419

Southern California Region, 8535 Lubec, Downey, CA 90240

Spark'n A's, 6394 Perrin Way, Carmichael, CA 95608

Tokay A's, PO Box 861, Lodi, CA 95241, 209-368-3175

Touring A's, 1777 Rosswood Dr, San Jose, CA 95124-5224, 408-266-6709

Towe Ford Museum of California, Library Copy, Mr Bengel, 2596 Warrego Way, Sacramento, CA 95826, 916-362-3183

US A's, PO Box 805, Cedar Ridge, CA 95924

Ventura County MAFC, PO Box 5584, Ventura, CA 93005

Whittier, PO Box 1908, Whittier, CA 90605, 562-927-7444

Colorado *Animas A's*, 6842 County Rd 203, Durango, CO 81301, 303-259-3519

Ford Model AA Truck Club, 1365 Cherryvale Rd, Boulder, CO 80303, 408-263-0692

MAFC of CO/Mile-Hi, PO Box 5554, Terminal Annex, Denver, CO 80217, 303-452-0496

Pike's Peak, PO Box 1929, Colorado Springs, CO 80901, 719-475-7499

Southern Colorado A's, PO Box 5221, Pueblo, CO 81002, 719-544-0176

Connecticut *Fairfield County A's*, 66 Glen Hill Rd, Wilton, CT 06897, 203-227-6911

MAFC of Connecticut, PO Box 508, Borad Brook, CT 06016, 203-658-0353

Northwestern Connecticut A's, c/o Dave Habersang, 65 Woodbridge Ln, Thomaston, CT 06787, 203-283-0743

Nutmeg A's, 162 Beardsley Pkwy, Trumbull, CT 06611

Florida *Columbia A's*,Pat Sama, RR 3, Box 4641, Ft White, FL 32038, 904-755-1479

First Coast, Karl Burghart 471 Sigsbee Rd, Orange Park, FL 32073, 904-269-3850

Model A's of Greater Orlando, 5029 Water Vista, Orlando, FL 32821, 407-354-3875

Moonport, 1975 N Tropical Tr, Merritt Island, FL 32953

Northwest Florida, James Parcelluzzi, 410 Marina Point Dr, Niceville, Fl 32578

Palm Beach A's, Bob Carpenter, 1340 Scottsdale Rd E, West Palm Beach, FL 33417, 561-471-1340

Panhandle A's, PO Box 411, Panama City, FL 32402

Georgia *Georgia Region*, PO Box 5, Lilburn, GA 30047, 404-923-4611

Shade Tree A's, 1110 Terrace Circle Dr, North Augusta, SC 29841-4349

Hawaii *Aloha Chapter*, Mr Mendonca, 301 Lunalilo Home Rd, Honolulu, HI 96825, 808-395-1788

Big Island Model A, PO Box 1321, Hilo, HI 96720

Idaho *Magic Valley Model A Ford Club*, 2339 Forest Vale Dr, Twin Falls, ID 83301

Snake River A's, 2349 9th Ave W, Vale, OR 97918-5045

Treasure Valley MAFC, c/o Bert Colwell, 4114 Hill Rd, Boise, ID 83703, 208-482-6416

Illinois *A's-R-Us*, PO Box 1108, Peotone, IL 60468

Chain O'Lakes, Box 420, Antioch, IL 60002

Chicagoland A's, 1201 W Glenn Ln, Mount Prospect, IL 60056

Corny A's, 201 William Dr, Normal, IL 61761

Fourever Fours, PO Box 6407, Peoria, IL 61601-6407

Naper A's, Box 245, Naperville, IL 60566, 708-420-0433

North Shore Model A's, 1764 Bowling Green, Lake Forest, IL 60045

Prairie A's, 309 Carrie Ave, Urbana, IL 61802

Rattling A's, PO Box 293, Columbia, IL 62236, 618-939-7321

Rock-Ford A's, PO Box 4001, Rockford, IL 61110

Salt Creek A's, 611 E Harding Ave, LaGrange Park, IL 60526, 708-354-9571

Sangamon Valley, Jerry Hasse, PO Box 4462, Springfield, IL 62708, 217-529-4279

Indiana *Sycamore* , 2904 Harrison Ave, Terre Haute, IN 47803

Iowa *Central Iowa MAFC*, PO Box 259, Des Moines, IA 50301

Hawk "A" Model A Club, PO Box 43, Marion, IA 52302

MAFC of Humbolt, 312 2nd St N, Humbolt, IA 50548, 712-297-8754

Kansas *Henry Leavenworth*, 3909 Shrine Park, Leavenworth, KS 66048

Plain Ol' A's, 5140 Long Dr, Shawnee, KS 66216, 913-268-7003

Wichita A's, PO Box 25, Wichita, KS 67201

Kentucky *Falls City*, 6495 Bardstown Rd, Elizabethtown, KY 42701

Louisiana *Acadiana A's*, Box 12401, New Iberia, LA 70562, 318-229-6722

Ark-La-Tex A's, 503 E Kings Hwy, Shreveport, LA 71105

Golden Gulf Model A Club, 616 18th St, Lake Charles, LA 70601, 318-477-5707

New Orleans A's, Webster Veade, PO Box 1674, Metairie, LA 70001, 504-626-8592

North Lake A's, PO Box 701, Covington, LA 70434

Red Stick A's, 20529 Liberty Rd, Pride, LA 70770, 504-383-7510

Maryland *Appalachian A's*, Rt 5, Box 111, Oakland, MD 21550

MAFC of Greater Baltimore, 5930 Old Washington Rd, Sykesville, MD 21784

Model A Ad Collectors, 4700 Locust Hill Ct, Bethesda, MD 20814

Massachusetts *Berkshire Co Antique*, 81 Westchester Ave, Pittsfield, MA 01201

Blackstone Valley A's, 2829 Providence Rd, Northbridge, MA 01534

Connecticut Valley Working A's, 15 Sycamore Terr, Agawam, MA 01001

Model A Ford Club of America chapters (continued)

MAFC of Cape Cod, 115 Windjammer Ln, Eastham, MA 02642

Massachusetts Bay, 183 Worcester St, Taunton, MA 02780

Minuteman, PO Box 545, Sudbury, MA 01776

Model A Fund Fundation Inc, PO Box 95151, Nonantum, MA 02495

Postal A's, 22 Burlington Rd, Bedford, MA 01730, 617-275-6737

Town Car Society, 197 Amity St, Amherst, MA 01002

Western Mass MARC, PO Box 784, Agawam, MA 01001-0784

Worcester County Model A, PO Box 36, North Oxford, MA 01537

Michigan *30-31 Dix Phaeton Club*, 47060 W Seven Mile Rd, Northville, MI 48167

Authentic A's, Don Bivens, 1205 S Ridge Rd, Canton, MI 48188-4793

Minnesota *Lady Slipper A's*, 110 6th St NE, Stewartville, MN 55976

Town Sedan Club, 9325 31st Ave N, New Hope, MN 55427

Twin City Model A Ford, 9270 Synducate Ave, Lexington, MN 55014, 612-888-7104

Mississippi *Mississippi Model A Ford Club*, Rt 1, Box 302A, Raleigh, MS 39153

Missouri *Heart of America*, 2100 Walnut St, Kansas City, MO 64108

Mid-Missouri Model A Restorers Club, 1407 Colonial Dr, Fulton, MO 65251, 314-581-0257

Show Me Model A Club, R#3, Box 292D, Cole Camp, MO 65325, 816-668-3583

Southwest Missouri, PO Box 9735, Springfield, MO 65801-9735

Montana *Big Sky A's*, Charles Bloom, 601 Pattee Canyon Rd, Missoula, MT 59803-1618, 406-728-4375

Nebraska *Cornhuskers*, 1150 Elba Ave, Lincoln, NE 68521

Golden Rod, 1605 Ave C, Cozad, NE 69130

Meadowlark, PO Box 6011, Omaha, NE 68106, 402-333-1391

Nevada *Battle Born A's*, 5880 Sun Valley Blvd, Sun Valley, NV 89433

Las Vegas Valley MAF, 5425 N Durango Dr, Las Vegas, NV 89129, 702-453-6769

Sagebrush, PO Box 1034, Carson City, NV 89702, 702-882-4005

Silver State A's, 829 Hillside Dr, Elko, NV 89801

New Hampshire *White Mountain Reg*, c/o Norman G Farmer, 16 Martin Rd, Weare, NH 03281

New Jersey *Cohanzick Region*, PO Box 1446, Millville, NJ 08332

MAFC of New Jersey, 649 Canistear Rd, Highland Lakes, NJ 07422

Watchung Valley MARC, PO Box 619, Falls Hills, NJ 07931, 908-758-0811

New Mexico *Poco Quatros*, PO Box 21058, Albuquerque, NM 87154-1058, 505-298-6927

New York *Adirondack A's*, PO Box 1246, Clifton Park, NY 12065, 518-877-5445

Chenango Model A'ers, 45 S Main St, Shervurne, NY 13460

Gowanda Model A's Box 131, Perrysburg, NY 14129

Iroquios A's, c/o Chester Kuhn, 4219 E Main St, Williamson, NY 14589

Lakeshore Model A, 2789 Chili Ave, Rochester, NY 14624-4827

Long Island, c/o Frank Ziegler, 2 Ellington Dr, East Northport, NY 11731

Model A's of Rockland, 3 Barbara Rd, New City, NY 10956

Mohican MAFCA Inc, c/o Sondra Roberts, 390 Mason Rd, Mohawk, NY 13407, 315-866-6876

New York City A's, 17 Midland Rd, Staten Island, NY 10308, 718-356-6290

Onondaga A Buffs, Canal Rd, Memphis, NY 13122

Queen City A's, 3883 Walden Ave, Lancaster, NY 14086

Southern Tier Model A's, Fred Blyer, 7 Crecent Dr, Apalachin, NY 13732, 607-754-0779

Spark & Throttle, 38-01 Little Neck Pkwy, Little Neck, NY 11363, 718-631-5870

Twin Tiers Vintage NY-PA, PO Box 100, Big Flats, NY 14814-0100

Westchester Chapter, 23 Main St, Mt Kisco, NY 10549

North Carolina *Eastern Carolina of MAFC*, c/o Roscoe Kirkland, PO Box 608, Battleboro, NC 23809

Queen City MAFC, 4511 Twin Oaks Pl, Charlotte, NC 28212

Thermal Belt, 465 McDade Rd, Forest City, NC 28043

Winston-Salem, 1821 Fannwood Cir, Winston-Salem, NC 27107

Ohio *Cabriolet Club*, 2481 Red Rock Blvd, Grove City, OH 43123

Cincinnati, 4239 School Section, Cincinnati, OH 45211

Dayton-Buckeye, PO Box 322, Englewood, OH 45322, 513-884-7438

Northern Ohio, 31870 Hiram Tr, Chagrin Falls, OH 44022-1324, 216-285-2711

Ohio Valley Region, PO Box 62303, Sharonville, OH 45241, 513-874-1609

Oklahoma *Okie A's Model A Ford*, 401 S Owen Dr, Mustang, OK 73064

Ouachita Model A Club, PO Box 463, Broken Bow, OK 74728, 405-584-2095

Sooner Model A Club, PO Box 83192, Oklahoma City, OK 73148

Territorial Model A, 609 Timberlane, Edmond, OK 73034

Tulsa, Box 691524, Tulsa, OK 74169, 918-743-6576

Oregon *Azalea A's*, Arthur Peary, 2350 Quines Creek Rd, Azalea, OR 97410

Beaver, 14655 NW Bonneville Loop, Beaverton, OR 97006-5540, 503-645-6346

Blue Mountain A's, Box 1724, Pendleton, OR 97801, 541-276-8801

DeLuxe Tudor Sedan Owners Group, Rick Black, 5595 Pioneer Rd, Medford, OR 97501

Enduring A's, PO Box 1428, Albany, OR 97321, 503-394-3054

Henry's Lady, PO Box 1442, Grants Pass, OR 97528

High Desert A's, PO Box 5602, Bend, OR 97708, 503-536-3878

McKenzie A's, Box 7271, Eugene, OR 97401, 503-746-2954

Myrtlewood A's, Box 996, Coos Bay, OR 97420

Northwest Regionional Group, 17470 SE Tickle Creek Rd, Boring, OR 97009

Williamette Valley, PO Box 3031, Salem, OR 97302, 503-399-7931

Pennsylvania *Beaver Valley*, 3763 37th St, Beaver Falls, PA 15010, 412-846-8822

Delaware Valley, 3447 Washington Ave, Brookhaven, PA 19015

Lehigh Valley, PO Box 90344, Allentown, PA 18018-3044

Mercer A's, PO Box 425, Pipersville, PA 18947

North Penn A's, 1651 N Wales Rd, Norristown, PA 19403

Steamtown A's, c/o Wayne Trivelpiece, 1251 Gravel Pond Rd, Clarks Summit, PA 18411, 717-586-0198

Steel CIty A's, 2159 Old Oakdale Rd, McDonald, PA 15057

Rhode Island *Little Rhody*, 622 Hatchery Rd, North Kingstown, RI 02852, 401-294-2268

South Carolina *Low Country Model A Club*, 1675 Wappoo Rd, Charleston, SC 29407-7634, 803-871-1556

Palmetto, 228 Continental Dr, West Colubia, SC 29170

Western Carolina Model A Ford Club, 6 Crestline Dr, Greenville, SC 29609, 803-244-6078

South Dakota *James Valley Chapter*, 759 Idaho Ave SE, Huron, SD 57350

Tennessee *Lookout A's*, 8701 St Johns Rd, Hixson, TX 37343, 615-842-0533

Memphis Model a Club, 691 Stratford Rd, Memphis, TN 38122, 901-683-2564

Middle Tennessee, Box 110424, Nashville, TN 37222-0424, 615-832-4422

Smoky Mountain, PO Box 3816, Knoxville, TN 37917

Texas *'31 Fordor Slant Windshield Group*, 6919 Cornelia Ln, Dallas, TX 75214

Abilene Model A Club, PO Box 2962, Abilene, TX 79604

Alabama, 7708 Briaridge Rd, Dallas, TX 75248

Alamo A's, 1319 Mount Vieja Dr, San Antonio, TX 78270-1617, 210-693-5140

Amarillo Long-Horns, PO Box 8336, Amarillo, TX 79114, 806-353-1786

Autumn Trails A's, 803 Lance Rd, Quitman, TX 75783, 903-763-2939

Blackland Model A Club, 6711 Finch Dr, Greenville, TX 75402

Bluebonnet, PO Box 1, Copperas Cove, TX 76522, 817-547-7408

Brazos Valley A's, RR 3, Box 612, Franklin, TX 77856

Capitol City A's, 1801 Stanley Ave, Austin, TX 78745

Coastal A's & Rods (CARS), PO Box 72387, Corpus Christi, TX 78472-2387, 512-993-2513

Concho Valley A's, 100 Glenmore Dr, San Angelo, TX 76903

Cross Timbers Model A Ford Club, PO Box 407, Hico, TX 76457

Dallas MAFC, Box 1028, Addison, TX 75001-1028, 972-394-8871

Devil's River A's, 124 E Garfield Ave, Del Rio, TX 78840, 512-298-2766

Fort Worth Model A Club, 6611 Anglin Dr, Fort Worth, TX 76119

Four States A's, 11 Azalea, Texarkana, TX 75503, 214-838-0630

Golden Triangle A's, PO Box 21185, Beaumont, TX 77702

Greater Houston Model A, 11318 Brandy Ln, Houston, TX 77044, 713-529-1839

International MAF Victoria Association, 11084 Windjammer, Frisco, TX 75034, 214-625-2922

Lone Star Model A Ford Club, PO Box 1049, Georgetown, TX 78627

MAFC of Cabriolet Club, PO Box 515, Porter, TX 77365, 713-572-2505

North Texas MAF Owners, PO Box 1192, Vernon, TX 76384

Oil City A's, PO Box 567, Luling, TX 78648, 512-875-3484

Piney Wood Model A Ford Club, 16203 Chipstead Dr, Spring, TX 77379

Plainview A's, PO Box 772, Plainview, TX 79072, 806-293-5862

Rio Grande Valley A's, PO Box 2371, McAllen, TX 78502-2371

Tex A's, Herman Garett, 10202 Moorberry Ln, Houston, TX 77043

Texas Model A Ford, c/o Ray Barth 16411, Heiden Cir, Spring, TX 77379

Texas Panhandle, PO Box 9602, Amarillo, TX 79105

Texas Road A O's, PO Box 449, Montgomery, TX 77356

Texoma Model A Club, PO Box 1055, Wichita Falls, TX 76307-1055

Tyler Model A Ford Club, PO Box 130953, Tyler, TX 75713-0953, 214-561-4741

Victoria A's, PO Box 441, Victoria, TX 77902

Woody Wagons, PO Box 341, McAllen, TX 78502

Utah *Beehive A's*, 3310 Taylor Ave, Ogden, UT 84403

Vermont *Green Mountain*, 4295 States Prison Hollow Rd, Monkton, VT 05443-9350

Virginia *Blue Ridge Model A's*, 940 Oak Dr, Christiansburg, VA 24079, 540-382-4746

Cape Henry MAFCA, 804 Davenport Ln, Virginia Beach, VA 23451, 757-340-5794

Colonial Virginia, PO Box 2044, Williamsburg, VA 23187-2044, 804-357-2660

George Washington, 3903 Old Lee Hwy (Rt 237), Fairfax, VA 22030

Lynchburg Model A, Glen Burroughs, Rt 1, Box 364-B, Madison Heights, VA 24572, 804-384-2488

Old Dominion, c/o Mary M Shepherd, 7207 Hermitage Rd, Richmond, VA 23228, 804-266-0883

Skyline, Rt 1, Box 226, Lyndhurst, VA 22980

Washington *Apple Valley*, Box 1205, Yakima, WA 98907

Section Three
Clubs & Organizations

Model A Ford Club of America chapters *(continued)*

Columbia Basin, Box 6904, Kennewick, WA 99336, 509-582-5527

Cowlitz Valley A's, 1006 N 7th Ave, Kelso, WA 98626, 425-423-3068

Evergreen, Box 15133, Wedgewood Station, Seattle, WA 98115-0133, 206-255-4038

Gallopin' Gertie, PO Box 14, Tacoma, WA 98401, 206-759-3461

Inland Empire A's, PO Box 614, Veradale, WA 99037-0614, 509-924-7763

Moon On A, 2214 Eighth St, Everett, WA 98201

Olympia Model A Club, PO Box 11478, Olympia, WA 98508-1478, 360-867-0454

Puget Sound Model A, 1818 Electric Ave, Bellingham, WA 98226

Spokes-N-Wheels, 640 Mountainview Rd, Grandview, WA 98930-9606

SW Wash Volcano A's, PO Box 87633, Vancouver, WA 98684-0663, 360-694-1618

Walla Walla Sweet A's, 1406 Shelton Rd, Walla Walla, WA 99362

Wisconsin   *Central Wisconsin*, Box 492, Wisconsin Rapids, WI 54494

Nickle A's, N1872 Manley Rd, Hortonville, WI 54944, 414-731-6271

Wisconsin, 11728 W North Ave, Wauwatosa, WI 53226, 414-332-2946

Argentina   *Club Ford de la Argentina*, Santa Fe 1394, (1059), Buenos Aires

Australia   *Model A Ford Club of South Australia*, PO Box 202, North Adelaide 5006, South Australia

Model A Ford Club of NSW Inc, PO Box 162, Panania NSW 2213

Model A Ford Club of Victoria, 79 Kathryn Rd, Knoxfield, Victoria 3180

Model A Restorers Club of Western Australia, 39 Sovereign Dr, Thornlie, Western, 6108

Model A Restorers of Australia, PO Box 320, Dickson ACT 2602

Belgium   *Ancient Ford Club of Belgium*, c/o Roger de Decker, 350 Mickesebaan, B2930, Brasschaat B-2930

Brazil   *Clube do Fordinho*, Rua Vasconcelos Drumond, 122 Ipiranga, Sao Paulo CEP 01548-000

Canada   *A Ford of London*, c/o Kathy Baker, 80 Blake St, Stratford, ON N5A 2C6, 519-451-4235

Canada Capital A's, 54 Perrin Ave, Nepean, ON K2J 2X5, 613-825-9136

Golden Bay A's, 1158 Redwood Ave, Winnepeg 14, MB R2X 0Y6

Model A Owners of Canada, Box 31 Post, Station A, Scarborough, ON M1K 5B9, 416-438-5939

Pacific Model A Club, 19759 28th Ave, Langley, BC V3A 4P5

Pembroke Chapter, PO Box 161, Pembroke, ON K8A 6X3

Scotia A's, S Ohio RR 2, Yarmouth, NS B0W 3E0

Stampede City, Box 22, Site 3, RR 12, Calgary, AB 73E 6W3, 403-242-9341

Totem Model A & T Ford Club, PO Box 18563-4857, Elliott, Delta, BC V4K 1J5, 604-980-1939

Van Isle A & B, 1939 Meadowbank Rd, Saanichton, BC V8M 1X9

Denmark   *Kobenhavns Ford A Club*, c/o Henrik Thostrup, Birkevoenget 16, 2880 Bagsvaerd, DK

England   *Model A Ford Club of Great Britain*, 10/14 Newland St, Coleford, Royal Forest of Dean, Gloucestershire GL16 8 AN

Germany   *Ford Model A Restorer*, Berliner Strasse 36, Berlin 10715

Japan   *Model A Club of Japan*, 2-15-13, Taira-Cho, Meguro-Ku, Tokyo

Mexico   *Model A Ford Club of Mexico*, Hacienda de Malpaso #127, Naucalpan Estado De Mexic, 53300

Netherlands   *A Ford CLub Nederland*, Zilveberkzoom 67, 2719 HX Zoetermeer

New Zealand   *Canterbury*, Box 4212, Christchurch

Foveaux Ford A Restorers Club, 166 George St, Invercargill

Hawkes Bay Model A Club, 688 Rotohiwi Rd, RD 2, Waipukurau

North Island Model A Ford Club, PO Box 57017, Owairaka, Auckland

Rebel A's, 492 Main Rd Hope, RR 1, Richmond, Nelson

Top of the South A's, PO Box 3260, Richmond, Nelson

Norway   *Eiker A Ford Club*, Sams Moveien 135, Hokksund 3300

Puerto Rico   *MAFC of Puerto Rico*, PO Box 195091, San Juan, PR 00919-5091

San Juan Model A Club, Escarlata 84, Urb, Munoz Rivera Guaynabo 00969

South Africa   *Early Ford Car Club*, 84 Provident St, Parow 7500, Cape Province, Republic South Africa

Sweden   *Svenska A-Fordarna*, Hogabergsgatan 43, 331 41 Varnamo

Uruguay   *Club Ford A del Uruguay*, Box 181, Yaguaron 1888 Y/O, Cerro Largo 1066, Montevideo

The Model A Ford Club of Great Britain
10-14 Newland St, Coleford
Royal Forest of Dean
Gloucestershire GL 16 8AN England
01594 834321; FAX: 01594 835456

For information, contact at the above address: Mike Cobell, Membership Registrar. Founded in 1988. 296 members. For owners and devotees of the Ford Model A and derivatives. Always like to hear from overseas enthusiasts.

Model A Restorer's Club
24800 Michigan Ave
Dearborn, MI 48124-1713
313-278-1455; FAX: 313-278-2624
E-mail: info@modelaford.org

Founded 1952. 9,800+ members. No restrictions to join. Must be a member to attend meets. Model A Ford owners, 1928-1931. Publish *Model A News* bi-monthly, which includes restoration and era fashions, club related items; parts, service, supplier's ads. Dues: $26/year (subscription included). Web site: www.modelaford.org

regions:

Alabama   *Alabama Region*, Richard Evens, 4640 Woodfield Ln, Trussville, AL 35173

Heart of Dixie A's, Harold Taylor, 26561 Martin Branch Rd, Madison, AL 35756

Arizona   *Four Cylinder Gang of Phoenix*, Gary Jones, 7717 N 46th Dr, Glendale, AZ 85301

Arkansas   *Natural State A Region*, Dick Knapp, 17644 Fox Hollow Rd, Garfield, AR 72732

California   *FAST Region*, Jim Brierley, 39480 Colleen Way, Temecula, CA 92592

Harbor Area Region, Richard Valot, 2018 W 178th St, Torrance, CA 90504

MARC of San Diego, Bob Willbanks, PO Box 15053, San Diego, CA 92175-5053

San Gabriel Valley Region, Michael Kniest, PO Box 29, San Gabriel, CA 91778-0029

Touring A's of California Region, Diane Dove, 1777 Rosswood Dr, San Jose, CA 95124-5224

Colorado   *Model A Ford Club of Colorado*, Charles Thomason, Terminal Annex PO Box 5554, Denver, CO 80217

The Ford Model AA Truck Club, Neil Wilson, 1365 Cherryvale Rd, Boulder, CO 80303

Connecticut   *Connecticut A Region*, Frederic Glabau, 20 Misty Mountain Rd, Kensington, CT 06037

The Blue Script Region, Barry Blake, PO Box 165, Stafford, CT 06075

Florida   *Citrus A Region*, Eugene Havey, PO Box 973, Lecanto, FL 34460

Crankin A Region, Harvey Willis, 392 Katrina St, De Leon Springs, FL 32130

First Coast Region, Henry Colemant, 744 Arran Ct, Orange Park, FL 32073

Gold Coast Region, Tony Spaich, 1290 NE 27 Ave, Pompano Beach, FL 33062

Lakeland Region, Steve Sopko, 419 E Belmar St, Lakeland, FL 33803

Model A's of Greater Orlando Region, Richard Hardman, 5029 Watervista Dr, Orlando, FL 32821

New Florida Region, James Kaphingst, 3813 Kenwood Ave, Tampa, FL 33611

Palm Beach Region, Bob Carpenter, 1340 Scottsdale Rd E, West Palm Beach, FL 33417

Sara-Mana Region, Gwen Albritton, 9620 State St Rd 72, Sarasota, FL 34241

Georgia   *Georgia Region*, Jones Layton, 26 Indian Tr SE, Cartersville, GA 30120

Griffin Georgia Region, E Marshall Pape, 790 Turner Rd, Williamson, GA 30292

Illinois   *Arling-Meadows A's Region*, Roy Bertola, 5406 Chateau Dr Unit 4, Rolling Meadows, IL 60008

Calumet Region, Craig Rith, 7621 Grant St, Darien, IL 60561

Fox Valley Region, Jack Anderson, PO Box 4, Geneva, IL 60134

Illinois Region, Joe Schutz, 3130 Boerderij Way, Woodstock, IL 60090

Joliet Region, Andy Honiotes, 29635 N Readman Ln, Wilmington, IL 60481

My First A Region, James Chiappetta, 2213 Northgate Ave, North Riverside, IL 60546

North Shore A's Region, Ken McPheeters, 400 E Illinois Rd, Lake Forest, IL 60045

Rock River Region, Hearold Montgomery, 14966 Norrish Rd, Morrison, IL 61270

Rock-Ford A Region, Dick Werckle, PO Box 4001, Rockford, IL 61110

Sangamon Valley Region, William Tarr, PO Box 4462, Springfield, IL 62708-4462

Starved Rock Region, Eldon Goldman, 211 E Van Buren St, Ottawa, IL 61350

Windy City A Region, Jerry Lyons, 19734 S 114th Ave, Mokena, IL 60448

Indiana   *Columbus Region*, Wayne Rosenbaum, 1710 Michigan St, Martinsville, IN 46151

Fountain City Region, Roger Adams, 719 Lee St, Connersville, IN 47331

Highland Indiana Region, Fred Jazyk, Box 1883, Highland, IN 46322

Hoosier A Region, Kenneth McClure, PO Box 1931, South Bend, IN 46624

Indiana Madison Region, Fred Wilkerson, 8108 W SR 56, Lexington, IN 47138

Indiana & Ohio Region, Dennys Stephens, 1649 W 9th St, Marion, IN 46953

Mid-Hoosier A Region, Bill Johnson, PO Box 764, Greenwood, IN 46142

Old Fort A Region, Robert Smith, 535 Iva St, Huntington, IN 46750

Sycamore A Region, Carrol Greiner, 2904 Harrison Ave, Terre Haute, IN 47803

Tri State Model A, John Tanner, 724 Cypress St, Newburgh, IN 47630

Iowa   *Central Iowa Region*, Dave Kingery, PO Box 259, Des Moines, IA 50301

Hawk A Region, Barbara Miller, Box 43, Marion, IA 52302

Kansas   *Wichita A Region*, Otto Praeger, PO Box 25, Wichita, KS 67201

Kentucky   *Central Kentucky Region*, John Yates, 445 Rogers Rd, Lancaster, KY 40444-9041

Falls City A Region, Emeric Howell, 6495 Bardstown Rd, Elizabethtown, KY 42701

Maryland   *Greater Baltimore Region*, William Alexander, 5930 Old Washinton Rd, Sykesville, MD 21784-8624

Model A Ad Collectors Region, Howard Minners, 4700 Locust Hill Ct, Bethesda, MD 20814

Southern Maryland Region, Gary Burley, PO Box 1553, California, MD 20619-9739

Massachusetts   *Massachusetts Bay Region*, John Freeman, 29 Ford Rd, Norton, MA 02766

Model A Restorer's Club regions: *(continued)*

Minuteman Region, Jo Johnson, PO Box 545, Sudbury, MA 01776

Model A Ford Foundation Region, Howard Minners, PO Box 95151, Nonantum, MA 02495

Postal A's Region, Aldie E Johnson Jr, 22 Burlington Rd, Bedford, MA 01730

Western Massachusetts Region, Wallace Franklin, PO Box 784, Agawam, MA 01001

Michigan   *1930-31 Deluxe Phaeton (180A) Region*, Don Bivens, 1205 S Ridge Rd, Canton, MI 48188

Au Sable Valley A Region, Gerald Sheick, 4876 Greenwood Rd, West Branch, MI 48661

Cherry Capitol Region, Bob Fitzgerald, c/o Fitzgerald 4903 Hoxie E, Cedar, MI 49621

Crank and Throttle Region, Thomas Fairles, 22640 27-1/2 Mile Rd, Springport, MI 49284

East Side A Region, John Paulina, PO Box 775, Royal Oak, MI 48068

Floral City A Region, Tony Meyers TTE, 4651 Bluebush Rd, Monroe, MI 48162

Grand A Region, Rick Sturim, PO Box 2831, Grand Rapids, MI 49501

Grape Country Region, Frank Southwell, 8044 W Q Ave, Kalamazoo, MI 49009

Livingston A Region, Norman Hall, 11201 Cherrylawn, Brighton, MI 48114

Mid Michigan A Region, Charles Crane, 3447 W Stoll Rd, Lansing, MI 48906

Motor Cities Region, Ron Jawernycky, 22031 Malden, Farmington Hills, MI 48336

Muskegon Portside A Region, Bob Glueck, 14385 Green St, Grand Haven, MI 49417

Oakleaf Region, Bill Franzel, 489 Parkview Blvd, Lake Orion, MI 48362

Script A Region, Duane Hazelton, 115 E River Rd, Mt Pleasant, MI 48858

Sparton Horn Region, Dick Cockran, PO Box 158, Clark Lake, MI 49234-0158

Sunrise Side Model A Ford Club, Larry Cornell, 4803 Kirchoff Rd, Alpena, MI 49707

Minnesota   *Town Sedan Region*, Werner Langenbach, 9325 31st Ave N, New Hope, MN 55427

Twin City Region, Joan Frisk, 9270 Syndicate Ave, Lexington, MN 55014

Missouri   *Heart of America Region*, Robert Frenthrop, 2100 Walnut St, Kansas City, MO 64108

Missouri Valley Region, Bob Beiser, 3609 Traci Ln, Byrnes Mill, MO 63051-1047

Southwest Missouri Model A Club, Jim Miller, PO Box 9735, Springfield, MO 65801-9735

Nebraska   *Meadowlark Region*, Butch Jorgensen, PO Box 6011, Omaha, NE 68106

Nevada   *Las Vegas Aces Model A's*, Eugene Tendvahl, 6727 W El Campo Grande, Las Vegas Valley, NV 89130

New Hampshire   *North Country Region*, George Hibbard, RR 3 Box 448, Claremont, NH 03743

New Jersey   *Keystone Region*, David Baldwin, 1235 Lower Ferry Rd, Trenton, NJ 08618-1405

Mid-Jersey Region, David Baldwin, 1235 Lower Ferry Rd, Trenton, NJ 08618

North Jersey Regional A's, John Karal, 17 Carlough Rd, Upper Saddle River, NJ 07458

New York   *Hudson Valley Region*, John Monforte Sr, 655 Rockcut Rd, Walden, NY 12586

Lakeshore Region, Art Drummond, 2789 Chili Ave, Rochester, NY 14624-4827

Long Island Region, Charles Cdiradvolo, 2 Ellington Dr, East Northport, NY 11731

Mohican Region, Sondra Roberts, 390 Mason Rd, Mohawk, NY 13407

Niagara Frontier Region, Dick Haynos, 1401 Stolle Rd, Elma, NY 14059

Southern Tier Region, Don Harrington, 7 Crescent Dr, Apalachin, NY 13732

Twin Tiers Vintage Ford Region, James Dix, PO Box 100, Big Flats, NY 14814

North Carolina   *Eastern Carolina Region*, Roscoe Kirklandton, PO Box 608, Battleboro, NC 27809

Fayetteville A Region, Philip Musselwhite, 853 E Great Marsh Church Rd, St Pauls, NC 28384

Old Timers Region, Tracy Williams, 1 Squirrel Hill Rd, Weaverville, NC 28787

Piedmont Region, John Avery, 142 East St, Jefferson, NC 28640

Queen City Region, Danny Phillips, 4511 Twin Oaks Pl, Charlotte, NC 28212

Tar Wheel A Region, Terry Babb, 1806 Dogwood Ln, Apex, NC 27502

Ohio   *Central Ohio Region*, Stewart Van Kirk, 128 Nob Hill Dr N, Gahanna, OH 43230

Dayton Buckeye Region, Joe Ayres, PO Box 322, Englewood, OH 45322

National Ford Tool Collectors, Ross Milne, 3300 Wheatcroft Dr, Cincinnati, OH 45239

Northern Ohio Region, Donald H Crum, 567 Vinewood Ave, Tallmadge, OH 44278

Ohio Valley Region, Dave Cradler, PO Box 62303, Sharonville, OH 45262-0203

Scattered A Region, Bruce Palmer, 10635 Lithopous Rd, Canal Winchester, OH 43110

Western Lake Erie Region, Dave Kevorkian, 5640 Cresthaven Ln, Toledo, OH 43614

Oklahoma   *NE Oklahoma Region*, James Meares, PO Box 690341, Tulsa, OK 74169-0341

Okie A Region, Mike Harnsberger, 401 S Owen Dr, Mustang, OK 73064

Oregon   *Oregon Trail Region*, Bruce Barnett, PO Box 5163, Aloha, OR 97006-5163

Willamette Valley Region, Tom Morrison, 5222 Cobb Ln S, Salem, OR 97302

Pennsylvania   *3 Rivers Region*, Ron Manges, RD 1 306 Grant St, Morgan, PA 15064

Active A's Region, James Upton, PO Box 90344, Allentown, PA 18109-0344

Delaware Valley Region, Michael Etling, PO Box 39047, Philadelphia, PA 19136

Lehigh Valley Region, James Upton, PO Box 90344, Allentown, PA 18109-0344

Mercer A's Region, Thomas Burrell, PO Box 425, Pipersville, PA 18947-0425

North Penn Region, David Whitmire, 1651 N Wales Rd, RD 3, Norristown, PA 19401

Running Board A's, Roger de Socarras, PO Box 580, Revere, PA 18953-0580

Susquehanna Valley Region, Randall Sierk, PO Box 4742, Lancaster, PA 17604-4742

Rhode Island   *Little Rhody Model A Ford Club*, Pat Howard, 622 Hatchery Rd, North Kingstown, RI 02852

South Carolina   *Foothills Region*, John Munn, 6 Crestline Dr, Greenville, SC 28726

Low Country Model A Club, Yvonne Coleman, 1675 Wappoo Rd, Charleston, SC 29407-7634

Shade Tree A Region, Ed Meloan, 1110 Terrace Cir Dr, North Augusta, SC 29841-4349

South Dakota   *South Dakota Territories Region*, Gary Haugan, 2428 Kenwood Manor, Sioux Falls, SD 57104

Tennessee   *East Tennessee Region*, Bob Terry, 256 Sycamore, Jonesborough, TN 37659

Ken-Tenn Region, Steve Vaughn, 902 High St, Union City, TN 38261

Mid Tennessee Region, Bill Dobson, PO Box 626, Ridgetop, TN 37152

Smokey Mountain Region, Ralph Morgan, PO Box 3816, Knoxville, TN 37917

Texas   *Capitol City A's*, Philip Garrett, 1801 Stanley Ave, Austin, TX 78745

Dallas Region, Don Gulliksen, PO Box 1028, Addison, TX 75001-1028

Fort Worth Region, David Smith, 6611 Anglin Dr, Fort Worth, TX 76119

Greater Houston Region, Bill Coleman, 11318 Brandy Ln, Houston, TX 77044-5858

International Model A Ford Victoria, Charlie Viosca, 11084 Windjammer, Frisco, TX 75034

Model A Ford Cabriolet Region, Larry Machacek, PO Box 515, Porter, TX 77365

Piney Wood Region, Bob Hitchcock, 17118 E Strack, Spring, TX 77379-8877

Victori A Region, Allen Maeker, PO Box 441, Victoria, TX 77902

Vermont   *The Green Mountain Region*, John Gaudette, 4295 States Prison Hollow Rd, Monkton, VT 05443-9350

Virginia   *Blue Ridge A Region*, Bud Akers, 2151 Childress Rd, Christiansburg, VA 24073

Cape Henry Region, Bill Goff III, 1113 W Revere Pt Rd, Virginia Beach, VA 23455

Colonial Virginia Region, Bill Lee, PO Box 2044, Williamsburg, VA 23187

Mount Vernon Region, Richard Clement, 3903 Old Lee Hwy, Fairfax, VA 22030

Southwestern Virginia, Donald Carbary, 843 Panacella Dr, Abingdon, VA 24210

Washington   *Emerald City Region*, Jim Barbee, 25050 SE 200 St, Maple Valley, WA 98038

Fun Timers Region, William Smart, Stan Shafer c/o 1804 Roosevelt, Yakima, WA 98902

Gallopin' Gerties Region, Ed Crosby, PO Box 14, Tacoma, WA 98401

South Puget Sound Region, Helen Pearman, 1136 E Eastside St, Olympia, WA 98506-1850

West Virginia   *Mountain Region*, Joe Davis, PO Box 3175, Clarksburg, WV 26302

Wisconsin   *Chippewa Valley A Region*, Charles Veicht, 22698 Cty Z, Cornell, WI 54732

Cream City A Region, Don Egner, 1807 Minnesota Ave, South Milwaukee, WI 53172

Nickel A Region, Gene Hegner, N 1872 Manley Rd, Hortonville, WI 54944

Wisconsin Region, Paul Sillman, W 8210 Doepke Rd, Waterloo, WI 53594

Canada   *Canada's Capital A Region*, Colin Lawson, 54 Perrin Ave, Nepean, ON K2J 2X5

Kingston Region, Terry Foley, 209 E St, Napanee, ON K7R 1S9

Model A Owners of Canada Inc, Ross Milne, PO Box 31 Postal Station A, Scarborough, ON M1K 5B9

Pacific Region, Phil Harden, 19759 28th Ave, Langley, BC V2Z 1Y1

Stampede City A Region, Paul Chudek, Box 22 Site 3 RR 12, Calgary, AB T3E 6W3

New Zealand   *Top of the South A's*, Gae Galway, PO Box 3260 Richmond, Nelson

Norway   *Norsk A Region*, Kare Lagstad, Postboks 1930 Vika 0125, Oslo 1

The Model T Ford Club International Inc
PO Box 276236
Boca Raton, FL 33427-6236
561-750-7170
E-mail: hgustav@aol.com

Founded 1952. 4,000 members. Model T Fords 1909-1927 (cars and trucks). Publish *Model T Times*, 6 issues per year, included with membership. Dues: $22/year US, $27/year Canada, $28/year elsewhere (all in US funds payable on a US bank). Web site: www.modelt.org
chapters:

Alabama *Heart of Dixie T's*, Vic Zannis, 2924 Ave W, Birmingham, AL 35208

Alaska *Frigid Ford T's*, Bruce Campbell, 14104 Hancock Dr, Anchorage, AK 99515

Colorado *Colorado High Peaks T's*, Benjy Kuehling, PO Box 541, Ouray, CO 81427

Connecticut *Informal T's*, Ronald St Amand, 69 Garfield Ave #2, East Hampton, MA 01027

Delaware *Delaware T's*, Duane G Eastburn, PO Box 221, Chatham, PA 19318

District of Columbia *Nation's Capital*, Erwin Mack, 8107 Chester St, Takoma Park, MD 20912

Florida *Central Florida*, Tom Henry, 2830 Ambergate Rd, Winter Park, FL 32792

Fun T's/Central Florida, Donald Lewis, 14830 Boland Ave, Spring Hill, FL 34610

Sunny T's of South Florida, Vince Chimera, 9508 NW 46th St, Sunrise, FL 33351

Treasure Coast T's, Robert Syverson, 2275 Sea Turtle Ln, Vero Beach, FL 32963

Wel-Ler T's of Miami, John Weller Jr, 5200 N Kendall Dr, Miami, FL 33156

Georgia *North Georgia T's*, Calvin Watts, PO Box 132, Fairmount, GA 30139

Illinois *Bismarck Tunklin T's*, Russell Potter, 206 South St Box 79, Bismarck, IL 61814

Crawling T's, Donald Krull, 2069 Knox Rd 150 E, Galesburg, IL 61401

Dupage Touring, Herbert Pasch, 8751 B High Point Rd E, Yorkville, IL 60560

Fox Valley, Maury Dyer, 117 Pecos Cir, Carpentersville, IL 60110

Gem City T's, Charles Rose, RR 1 Box 37-A, Fowler, IL 62338

Midwest, William Soop, 7516 Little Fawn Trace, Crystal Lake, IL 60012

Rockford, Valerie Schumacher, 11273 Edgemere Tr, Roscoe, IL 61073

Indiana *Circle City Model T Ford Club*, Rallie Murphy, 8441 New London Ct, Indianapolis, IN 46256

Indiana Travelin' T's, Joe M Batthauer, RR 1 Rd 700 W, Yorktown, IN 47396

Old Fort T's, Robert Summers, 12330 S Anthony Blvd, Fort Wayne, IN 46819

Temperamental T's of Indiana, John W Dennis, 239 S Division St, Auburn, IN 46706-1606

Tippewa, Ted Sturm, 4824 Hawthorne Ridge Rd, West Lafayette, IN 47906

Iowa *Nift's North Iowa*, Ford T's/Paul Larson, Box 212 Rt 1, Clear Lake, IA 50428

The Great River Flivver's, Fred Classon, 4405 Regency Pl, Davenport, IA 52806

Kentucky *Blue Grass T's of Kentucky*, F M Saulton, 104 Erskine Ln, Scott Depot, WV 25560

Noken T's, Donald Fitzgerald, 3460 Rocker Dr, Cincinnati, OH 45239

Ohio Valley of Kentucky, Owen "Jeep" Whitehouse Jr, 2419 S Hwy 53, La Grange, KY 40031

Louisana *New Orleans*, Allen Aucoin, 147 Moss Ln, River Ridge, LA 70123

Maryland *Chesapeake Bay T's*, James Golden, 2405 Belair Dr, Bowie, MD 20715

Heart of Maryland T's, Hunter Mauck, PO Box 251, Clarksburg, MD 20871

Maryland, Walter Stone, 3801 Mt Airy Dr, Mt Airy, MD 21771

Massachusetts *Pioneer Valley T's*, Joseph F Bergamini, 107 Fairway Village, Leeds, MA 01053

Michigan *Boilin T's*, Tom Fairles, 22640 27-1/2 Mile Rd, Springport, MI 49284

Borderline T's, Jack Zimmer, 1660 S Allen Rd, St Clair, MI 48079

Casual T's, Annie Fuller, 1431 Midwood, White Lake, MI 48386

Central Michigan T's, Jim Neal, 1069 Applegate Ln, East Lansing, MI 48823

Crankun T's, Bob Fitzgerald, 3357 S McGee Rd, Lake City, MI 49651

Huron Valley Cranks, Thomas Preston, 4270 Kingston Dr, Milan, MI 48160-9754

Model T Fliver's, Joseph Smotucha, N 4961 US Hwy 41, Wallace, MI 49893-9782

Tin Lizzie Travelers, Roger Kibby, 53717 Wilbur, Three Rivers, MI 49093

Tinkerin T's, Bill Smith, 8829 Circle E Dr, Farwell, MI 48622

Vehicle City T's, Hamilton Bagley, 5215 Belle River Rd, Attica, MI 48412

Washtenaw Nau Ties, Russ Payeur, 4747 Waterworks Rd, Saline, MI 48176

Western Michigan, Stan Windermuller, A-1164 Graafschap Rd, Holland, MI 49423

Minnesota *T Totalers*, Roy Newcomb, 16431 Dysprosium NW, Anoka, MN 55303

Missouri *Greater St Louis*, Marlet Ort, 7123 S Rock Hill Rd, Afton, MO 63123

Kansas City Chuggers, Hathon Fields, 3804 S Pleasant St, Independence, MO 64055

Nebraska   *Cornhusker Model T Ford Club*, Robert McKelvie, 15731 Weschester Cr, Omaha, NE 68118

Nebraskaland, Ken Chaney, 2221 S 37th St, Lincoln, NE 68506

New Hampshire   *New Hampshire Granite T'ers*, Karen Simmering, 121 South Rd, Hopkinton, NH 03229

New Jersey   *B & W T's*, John Jonas, 301 Whitaker St, Riverside, NJ 08075

New York   *Classic T & Antique*, Robert L Hark, 61 Pickford Ave, Kenmore, NY 14223

Niagara Frontier, Francis Licata, 6746 Akron Rd, Lockport, NY 14094

Twin Tiers, Bruce Bruckner, 5065 Co Rd 14, Odessa, NY 14869-9730

North Carolina   *Blue Ridge Riders*, William Guiney, 2113 Deerpath Ln, Hendersonville, NC 28739

Carolina T's, Edward Kendall, 4829 Currituck Dr, Charlotte, NC 28210

East Carolina T's, William A Eads, 923 Bonham Ave, Wilmington, NC 28403

Ohio   *Akron*, Dick Batchel, 4247 Ellsworth Rd, Stow, OH 44224

Greater Cleveland, Larry Hengenius, 18633 Ridge Rd, North Royalton, OH 44131

Maumee Valley T's, Gene Trzcinski, 10510 Eckel Jct Rd, Perrysburg, OH 43551

Southwest Ohio Model T, Joe Neer, 8150 Long Creek Dr, Centerville, OH 45458

Stark County, Thomas Michalek, 2021 Barnard Rd, Wooster, OH 44691

Tickin' T's of Central Ohio, Richard Baker, 3483 Trenton Rd, Columbus, OH 43232

Youngstown, Craig Bernard, 35 Fairview Ave, Canfield, OH 44406

Oklahoma   *Oklahoma Special T's*, David Baker, 10005 SE 44th St, Oklahoma City, OK 73150

Oregon   *Rose City of Oregon*, Keith Townsend, 5326 SE 22nd St, Gresham, OR 97080

Pennsylvania   *Tired T's*, Brian Jay Serfass, 2770 Sullivan Tr, Easton, PA 18040

South Dakota   *Black Hills Model T*, Les Schuchardt, 427 E Meier, Spearfish, SD 57783

Tennessee   *The Tennessee T's*, Larry Williams, 235 Mariah Church Ln, Waverly, TN 37185

Texas   *Cowtown T's*, Joe Stilwell, 3305 Lancelot Ct, Bedford, TX 76021

T Fords of Texas, James Deatherage, 606 River Springs Dr, Seguin, TX 78155

Texas Hill Country, Julius Neunhoffer, 2505 Lower Turtle Creek Rd, Kerrville, TX 78028

Texas Tin Lizzies, Ralph Reeder, PO Box 669, Dickinson, TX 77539

Virginia   *Central Virginia Model T*, Paul Carreras, 2206 Oakwood Ln, Richmond, VA 23228

Cranky T Chapter of Blue Ridge, John Harris, 2404 Windsor Ave, Roanoke, VA 24015

Shenandoah Valley Racket Ters, Bill Price, 1631 Stonyman Rd, Luray, VA 22835

Washington   *Carbon Canyon*, Larry Fairchild, PO Box 275, Carbonado, WA 98323

Graham Model A & Model T Club, Jerome "Sonny" Anseth, 19416 90th Ave E, Graham, WA 98338

Tacoma, Gerald Campbell, PO Box 88948, Steilacoon, WA 98388

West Virginia   *Cantankerous T's*, Howard Wright, PO Box 19, New Cumberland, WV 26047

Mountain State T's/WV, John McCoy, 980 Greendale Dr, Charleston, WV 25302

Wisconsin   *Central Wisconsin T's*, Dennis Lindeman, 2931 16th St S, Wisconsin Rapids, WI 54494

Greater Milwaukee, Kevin A Esser, 4241 N 69th St, Milwaukee, WI 53216

Ocooch Mt Chapter, Steve Stevenson, 18798 Deere Path Ln, Richland Center, WI 53581

"T"riffic T's, William Glass, 716 Miles St, Chippewa Falls, WI 54729

Australia   *Model T Ford Club of Australia*, PO Box 2658, North Parramatta NSW 2151

Model T Ford Club of Victoria, Roger Wotherspoon, PO Box 383 Chadstone Centre, Victoria 3148

Canada   *Ontario Region*, Des Spencer, Box 1566, Campbellford, ON K0L 1L0

Europe   *Halsinge Model T*, Sven-Olov Hansson, Alvagen 14 Kvissleby, 862 33

The Irish Model T Club, John Boland, Waterford Rd, New Ross, Co Wexford

South America   *The First Model T Club of Argentina*, c/o Jorge Eduardo Baez, Romulo Carbia 2897 B Poetal Lugones, Cordoba 5008

The Model T Ford Club of America
PO Box 743936
Dallas, TX 75374-3936
972-783-7531; FAX: 972-783-0575
E-mail: admin@mtfca.com

Founded 1965. 8,000 members. Dues: $22/year US, $27/year Canada, $28/year foreign (US funds please). Web site: mtfca.com

chapters:

Arizona   *Canyon Country Model T Club*, c/o Russ Furstnow, 4030 N Lugano Way, Flagstaff, AZ 86004

Model T Ford Club of Southern Arizona, c/o Frank Hoiles, 2121 N Nightshade Dr, Tucson, AZ 85715

Sun Country Model T Club, Box 56634, Phoenix, AZ 85079

The Model T Ford Club of America chapters *(continued)*

Tucson Touring T's, c/o Tom Russell, 2947 E 20th St, Tucson, AZ 85716

California   *Antelope Valley Chapter*, c/o T V Gorden, PO Box 2058, California City, CA 93504

Bay Area T's, c/o Rick Silvera, 2949 Los Altos Way, Antioch, CA 94509

Central Coast Model T Club, PO Box 1117, Templeton, CA 93465

Central Sierra Chapter, c/o Alex Lehman, 15715 Ave 13, Madera, CA 93637

Don Pedro Model T Club, c/o Jim W Ashby, 212 Crawford Rd, Modesto, CA 95356

Fiddletown Flivvers, c/o Jerry Welshans, PO Box 244, Fiddletown, CA 95629

Long Beach Model T Club, c/o Howard Genrich, 1830 Snowden Ave, Long Beach, CA 90815

Model T Ford Club of Kern County, Box 885, Bakersfield, CA 93302-0885

Model T Ford Club of San Diego, c/o Ruth Boswell-MacPherson, 1474 W 11th Ave, Escondido, CA 92029

Mother Lode Model T Ford Club, Box 4901, Auburn, CA 95603-0901

Northern California Model T Club, c/o Cliff Bennett, 740 Jane Ct, Martinez, CA 94553

Orange County Model T Ford Club, PO Box 1071, Westminster, CA 92684

Redwood Empire Model T Club, PO Box 6452, Santa Rosa, CA 95406

Riverside-Corona Chapter, PO Box 51177, Riverside, CA 92517

Sacramento Valley Model T Club, Box 492, Carmichael, CA 95608-0492

San Fernando Valley Chapter, c/o Clara Jo Ostergren, 8656 Balcom Ave, Northridge, CA 91325

Santa Clara Valley Model T Ford Club, PO Box 2081, Saratoga, CA 95070

South Bay Model T Ford Club, PO Box 797, Manhattan Beach, CA 90267-0797

Colorado   *Centennial Model T Club of Northern Colorado*, c/o David Brock, 6731 Holyoke Ct, Fort Collins, CO 80525

High Plains Model T Club, Box 366, Akron, CO 80720

Mile High Chapter, c/o Rick Holdaway, 6273 W 78th Ave, Arvada, CO 80003

Northeast Colorado Model T Club, c/o Deb Fritzler, 13945 Corene Rd, Sterling, CO 80751

Southern Colorado Model T Club, Box 5626, Pueblo, CO 81003

Connecticut   *Connecticut Crankin' Yanks*, c/o Will Revaz, 13 Scott Rd, Oxford, CT 06478-1553

Four Seasons Model T Association, c/o Grant Bombria, 11 Cards Mills Rd, Columbia, CT 06237

Florida   *Northeast Florida Chapter*, 844 River Rd, Orange Park, FL 32073

Sunny T's of South Florida, c/o Michael Madden, 1889 NW 22nd St, Pompano Beach, FL 33069

Idaho   *Western Idaho Model T Ford Club*, c/o Dwight Buck, 7668 Dry Lake Rd, Nampa, ID 83686

Illinois   *IL-IA-MO Chapter*, c/o Martin Alexander, PO Box 59, Queen City, MO 63561

Prairie State Model T Ford Club, 46-1300 Ave, Mt Pulaski, IL 62548

Indiana   *Indy 500 Chapter*, c/o Jack Daron, 10462 N Co Rd 950E, Brownsburg, IN 46112-9639

Iowa   *Early Chariots of Council Bluffs*, c/o Jerry Bogatz, 16 Lakewood Villa St, Council Bluffs, IA 51501

Heart of Iowa T's, c/o Thomas Gray, 3923 52nd St, Des Moines, IA 50310

Upper Iowa Vintage Ford Club, c/o Dave Dunlavy, 9274 Z St, Omaha, NE 68127

Kansas   *East Central Kansas T's*, c/o Bud Redding, 1938 Reaper Rd NE, Waverly, KS 66871

Flatland T's Model T Club, c/o Marion Shirk, 1529 N Charles, Wichita, KS 67203

Sunflower State Crankers, c/o Bill Wolf, 1221 MacArthur Rd, Great Bend, KS 67530

Kentucky   *Burley Belt Chapter*, c/o Jack Lemley, 340 Savannah Dr, Nicholasville, KY 40356

Golden Crossroads Chapter, c/o Ted Aschman, 214 Morningside Dr, Elizabethtown, KY 42701

Northern Kentucky Model T Club, c/o Bud Scudder, RR 3 Box 99, California, KY 41007

River City Chapter, c/o Carl Boyd, 4405 Westwood Dr, Crestwood, KY 40014

Somerset Chapter, c/o Andy Mounce, Box 1, Somerset, KY 42502

Maine   *Down East Chapter*, c/o John Anderson, 120 Intervale Rd, Temple, ME 04984

Maryland   *Blue and Gray Chapter*, c/o Connie Grimm, 21216 Chewsville Rd, Smithsburg, MD 21783

Massachusetts   *Central Mass Model T Club*, PO Box 371, Upton, MA 01568

Old Colony Model T Club, 130 Old Oaken Bucket Rd, Scituate, MA 02066

Western Massachusetts Model T Club, c/o Dan Krug, 5 South Rd, Westhampton, MA 01027

Yankee Ingenui T's, c/o George Livermore, 92 Miller St S, Lancaster, MA 01561

Minnesota   *Model T Club of Lake Minnetonka*, c/o Neil Blesi, 2064 Shadywood Rd, Wayzata, MN 55391

North Star State Chapter, c/o Ken Schult, 938 20th Ave N, South St Paul, MN 55075

Mississippi   *Magnolia State Model T Ford Club*, c/o Dean Spencer, 13516 Wilfred Seymour Rd, Ocean Springs, MS 39564

Missouri   *Greater St Louis Chapter*, c/o Pat Itterly, 12858 Crab Thicket, St Louis, MO 63131

Heart of the Ozarks Chapter, c/o Gail Seyl, 3555 W Republic Rd, Springfield, MO 65807

Kingdom of Callaway Chapter, c/o Vicki McDaniel, 5 Bartley Ln, Fulton, MO 65251

Montana   *Montana Cross Country Model T Association*, c/o Tony or Janet Cerovski, 1004 Sioux Rd, Helena, MT 59602

Rocky Mountain Model T Club, c/o Ralph Starr, 2108 Rattlesnake Rd, Missoula, MT 59802

Nebraska *Centennial T Club of Omaha*, c/o Lee Matson, 903 E 9th St, Schuyler, NE 68661

Nebraskaland Model T Club, c/o Steve Hughes, 8705 W Branched Oak Rd, Raymond, NE 68428

Nevada *Silver State Model T Ford Club*, c/o Jack Middleton, 620 Highland, Carson City, NV 89703

Southern Nevada Model T Club, 5617 Alfred Dr, Las Vegas, NV 89108

New Hampshire *Central New Hampshire Model T Club*, c/o David Simmering, 121 South Rd, Hopkinton, NH 03229

New Jersey *North Jersey Tinker T's*, c/o Gary Paulsen, 790 Franklin Tpke, Allendale, NJ 07401

T-Bones Chapter, c/o Jim Dowgin, Box 216, Dayton, NJ 08810

Tri-State Tin Lizzie Tourists, c/o Chris Paulsen, 790 Franklin Tpke, Allendale, NJ 07401

New Mexico *Tin Lizzies of Albuquerque*, PO Box 30473, Albuquerque, NM 87190-0473

New York *Capital District Chapter*, c/o William Clough, Box 27, Knox, NY 12107-0027

Central New York Chapter, c/o Steve Davis, RD 2 Box 842, West Winfield, NY 13491

Flivver Drivers Inc, c/o Douglas H Lockwood, 347 S Clinton St, Albion, NY 14411

NY-PA Twin T'ers Vintage Ford Club, c/o Bruce Bruckner, 5065 Co Rd 14, Odessa, NY 14869-9730

North Carolina *Blue Ridge Model T Club*, c/o Bill Guiney, 213 Deerpath Ln, Hendersonville, NC 28379

North Dakota *Viking Country Chapter*, c/o Reginald Urness, 3510 Belmont Rd, Grand Forks, ND 58201

Ohio *Model T Ford Club of Northwest Ohio*, c/o Jack A Putnam, 1215 Hancock Rd 28, Bluffton, OH 45817-9656

North Coast Bumps and Grinds Chapter, c/o Jerry Javorek, 27805 Sherwood Dr, Westlake, OH 44145

Ohio River Valley T's, c/o Lola Wells, 7359 Fallen Timber Rd, Lucasville, OH 45648

Southwest Ohio Model T Club, c/o Joe Neer, 8150 Longcreek Dr, Centerville, OH 45458-2109

Oklahoma *Model T Ford Club of Tulsa*, PO Box 691874, Tulsa, OK 74169-1874

Oregon *Northwest Vintage Speedster Club*, c/o Don Shreve, 8550 SW Holly Ln, Portland, OR 97223

Rose City Model T Ford Club, Box 3901, Portland, OR 97208

Williamette Valley Chapter, Box 13313, Salem, OR 97309

Pennsylvania *Valley Forge Chapter*, c/o Bob Arters, Box 65, Phoenixville, PA 19460-0065

Rhode Island *Model T Ford Owners of Southern New England*, c/o Bob Harrison, 135 Lynn Cir, East Greenwich, RI 02818

South Carolina *South Carolina Model T Ford Club*, c/o Ed Meloan, 1110 Terrace Cir Dr, North Augusta, SC 29841

South Dakota *Black Hills Model T Club*, c/o Les Schuchardt, Box 136, Spearfish, SD 57783

Dakota Hills Climbers Chapter, c/o David Grow, 13120 Mountain Park Rd, Rapid City, SD 57702

Texas *Cen-Tex Tin Lizzies*, PO Box 70, Manchaca, TX 78652

Cowtown Model T Ford Club, 4424 Idledell Dr, Fort Worth, TX 76116-7611

Dallas-Fort Worth Chapter, PO Box 835806, Richardson, TX 75083-5806

Paso Del Norte Model T Ford Club, c/o Vaughn Rodgers, 407 Lombardy, El Paso, TX 79922

Space City T's Chapter, c/o Dan McDonald, 6430 Neff St, Houston, TX 77074

Texas Model T Speedster Club, c/o Royce Peterson, 6471 Stichter, Dallas, TX 75230

Utah *Bonneville Chapter*, c/o Rex Zollinger, 1126 S 2183 E, Bountiful, UT 84010

Washington *Inland Empire Chapter*, PO Box 11708, Spokane, WA 99211-1708

Puget Sound Chapter, c/o Ray Steele, 17408 17th Pl NE, Shoreline, WA 98155

Three Rivers Chapter, Box 7083, Kennewick, WA 99336-7083

Wisconsin *Kettle Moraine Model T Ford Club*, c/o Burdella Miller, W211 N6876 Pheasant St, Menomonee Falls, WI 53051

Marshfield Model T Ford Club, c/o Dennis Rose, W5351 Co Rd N, Owen, WI 54460

Wisconsin Capital Model T Ford Club, Dennis Gorder, PO Box 440, Baraboo, WI 53913

Argentina *Primer Club del Ford T de Argentina*, c/o Jorge E Baez, Romulo Carbia 2897 Bo Poeta Lugones, 5008 Cordoba

Australia *Ford T Register of Australia*, PO Box 380, Hindmarsh SA 5007

Model T Ford Club of Australia, PO Box 2658, Parramatta NSW 2151

Model T Ford Club of Victoria, c/o Secretary, PO Box 383, Chadstone Centre PO, Victoria 3128

Austria *Model T Ford Club of Austria*, c/o Wolfgang Posch, Hochsatzeng 17, A-1140 Wien (Vienna)

Belgium *Ancient Ford Club of Belgium*, c/o Roger de Decker, 350 Micksebaan, B-2930 Brasschaat

Canada *Foothills Model T Ford Club*, c/o Reg Kober, 6119 Norfolk Dr NW, Calgary, AB T2K 5J8

Running Board Bandits, c/o Ralph Anderson, Rt 5 Box 11, Prince Albert, SK S6V 5R3

Sasketchewan Dus't Spokes Chapter, c/o Allan Clow, 16 Acadia Bay, Regina, SK S4S 4T6

The 2-4-T's Club, 1331 Readings Dr, Sydney, BC V8L 5K7

Great Britain *Model T Ford Register of Great Britain*, c/o Simon Meakin, Sunset View, Furze Ln Felthorpe, Norwich, Norfolk NR10 4UA

Holland *Ford T Register of Holland*, c/o A Martini, Postbus 2146, 1180 EC Amstelveen

New Zealand *Model T Ford Club of New Zealand*, c/o Rod McKenzie, 39 Francis Drake St, Waipukurau 4176

Section Three Clubs & Organizations

**Nifty Fifties Ford Club of
Northern Ohio**
PO Box 142
Macedonia, OH 44056

Founded 1976. 100 members. Limited to northeast Ohio.
Publication: *Nifty Fifties News*. Club events, local car shows,
general club news. Dues: $20/year.

Nor-Cal Fiestas
2135 Via Roma
Campbell, CA 95008
408-866-1390

Founded 1998. 2 members. Open to all northern California Ford
Fiesta enthusiasts. There is no newsletter due to lack of members. I hope to stay in contact by phone, mail and in person to
organize social events, parts swap meets, auto crosses and general sharing of Fiesta knowledge. Member input is very valuable.

Nor-Cal Ford Car Club Council
PO Box 6682
Concord, CA 94524-1682
925-684-3505; FAX: 925-684-2044
E-mail: mechamrs@pacbell.net

Founded 1997. 15 clubs. Organization of Ford car clubs formed
in northern California to sponsor Fun Ford Sunday. This show is
held annually each September at the Great Mall of the Bay Area,
Milpitas, site of the former Ford Assembly Plant. Through this
council, we network and support the member Ford clubs in their
activities and interests. Dues: $25 one time fee.

Northern Ohio Model A Club
1542 Gotthard St
Sugarcreek, OH 44681-9323
330-852-4700; FAX: 330-852-2100
E-mail: bhudec@aol.com

Founded 1972. 97 members. Open to anyone with an interest in
the Model A Ford. The club provides technical assistance and
information on the construction and operation of the Model A
Ford. The club offers monthly technical seminars, annual tours
and semi-annual driving events. The newsletter is published
monthly. Dues: $15/year.

Penn-Ohio Model A Ford Club
1542 Gotthard St
Sugarcreek, OH 44681-9323
330-852-4700; FAX: 330-852-2100
E-mail: bhudec@aol.com

Founded 1956. 550 members. Social and driving club. Open to
anyone with the interest of owning, preserving and driving the
Model A Ford. The club is comprised of 14 chapters across
northern Ohio and western Pennsylvania. Each chapter meets
once a month throughout the year. The club holds monthly driving events during the driving season, an annual tour and swap
meet/car show. Communications are provided by the clubs
newsletter, *The Quail Call*, published 9 times a year. Dues:
$20/year.
chapters:

Ohio *5 Points Chapter (Youngstown-Warren)*, Von
Wolfe, President, 3015 Renkenberger Rd,
Columbiana, OH 44408, 330-482-3012

Buckeye Chapter (Cleveland, OH area), Roy
Smolik, President, 6445 Beverly Dr, Parma,
OH 44130, 440-884-1760

Copus Hill Chapter (Ashland County area), Ken
Rachel, President, 619 Harter Ave, Mansfield,
OH 44907, 419-522-2798

Cranksters Chapter (Medina County area), Lou
Tull, President, 2957 Substation Rd, Medina,
OH 44256, 330-722-7336

Dixie Chapter (Mt Vernon, OH area), Dwayne
Roach, President, 5845 Cty Rd 121, Mt
Gilead, OH 43338, 419-768-3282

Flying Quail Chapter (Northwest Ohio), Brad
Bailey, President, 5360 Custar Rd, Delhler,
OH 43516, 419-278-3198

Mohican Chapter (Wooster, OH area), Buster
Smith, President, 1275 High View Dr,
Wadsworth, OH 44281, 330-336-5291

Newark Vibrators (Newark-Lancaster OH), Kim
Mudgett, President, 3085 E Pike, Zanesville,
OH 43701, 740-452-2517

Northeastern Ohio Chapter (NE Ohio area),
Tony Torre, President, 158 Sanford St,
Painesville, OH 44077, 440-352-2834

Rubber City Chapter (Akron, OH area), John
Menches, President, 3416 Saddleboro Dr,
Uniontown, OH 44685, 330-699-5951

Shelman Chapter (Mansfield, OH area), Arlene
Burks, President, 139 E Main St, Shelby, OH
44875, 419-347-7095

Tri-County Chapter (Canton-Dover area), Dave
Shanklin, President, 4698 Blacksnake Hill Rd
NE, Dover, OH 44622, 330-343-4006

Pennsylvania *Erie Chapter (Northwestern PA)*, Don Harvey,
President, 79 Townhall Rd E, Waterford, PA
16441, 814-864-0198

Keystone Chapter (Franklin-Titusville, PA),
Gordon Gebhardt, President, 4871 Watson Rd,
Erie, PA 16505, 814-833-9671

Shelby American Automobile Club
PO Box 788
Sharon, CT 06069
860-364-0449; FAX: 860-364-0769
E-mail: saac@discovernet.net

For information, contact at the above address: Rick Kopec.
Founded 1975. 6,200 members. Ownership not essential. Open
to all enthusiasts of high-performance Fords, Bosses, Panteras,
Griffiths, Mustangs, etc. Club magazine is the *The Shelby
American*. Dues: $47/year. Web site: saac.com
regions:

Alabama *Alabama Region*, John Farr, 764 Hwy 278 E,
Cullman, AL 35055, 256-734-2613; FAX:
256-775-6586; E-mail: saac4al@aol.com

California *COCOA/Los Angeles Area*, Lynn Park, 5140
Greencrest Rd, La Canada, CA 91011,
818-790-0427

COCOA/Orange County, Bob Stockwell, 3461
Wimbledon Way, Costa Mesa, CA 92626,
714-546-5670; E-mail: cocoa_oc@hotmail.com

LASAAC/Los Angeles Area, Mario Veltri, 236
24th St, Santa Monica, CA 90402,
310-387-3900 days, 310-395-9132 eves;
E-mail: gt350@lasaac.org; Web site:
www.lasaac.org

Northern California (NorCal) Region, Tom Fry,
Nor Cal SAAC PO Box 700789, San Jose, CA
95170, 408-987-7765 work; E-mail:
tom@amasco.com; Web site: www.norcal-
saac.org

Sacramento (River City) Region, Gary
Bettencourt, 5024 Camino Royale Dr,
Sacramento, CA 95823, 918-424-8748

SoCal Shelby Club, Dave Ham, 702 Regal Rd B-3, Encinitas, CA 92024, 619-438-1601

Colorado   *Colorado Region*, Bill Miller, 8223 W 62nd Pl, Arvada, CO 80004, 303-421-3009

Connecticut   *New England Region*, Carl Gagnon, PO Box 26, Windsor Locks, CT 06096, 880-623-1388; E-mail: saac.ner@snet.net

Florida   *Central Florida Region*, Randy Betsinger, 4517 Flagg St, Orlando, FL 32812, 407-273-9762

Florida Assn of Shelbys & Tigers, Todd Scranton, 5121 Palo Verde Pl, West Palm Beach, FL 33415, 407-683-8998

Georgia   *Shelby Cobra Owners Assn of the Southeast*, Kitty Wilmot, 115 Ansley Ct, Roswell, GA 30076, 404-992-1729

Hawaii   *Aloha Mustang & Shelby Club*, Don Johnston, PO Box 6216, Honolulu, HI 96818, 808-396-0723; E-mail: duck@pixi.com; Web site: www.aloha.net/~djhamma/mustcal.htm

Illinois   *Central Plains Region*, John De Reu, 623 E Orange St, Genesco, IL 61254-2020, 309-944-6118

Indiana   *Indiana Region*, Joyce Yates, 4005 Lower Schooner Rd, Nashville, IN 47448, 812-988-7146; FAX: 812-988-0146; E-mail: jcyates@indiana.edu

Iowa   *Mustang Club of Central Iowa*, Doug Dyar, 2714 NW 5th St, Ankeny, IA 50021, 515-964-2714

Kentucky   *Kentucky Region*, Tim or Sarah McAllister, 4721 Sunny Hill Dr, Crestwood, KY 40014, 502-984-8885

Maryland   *Maryland SAAC Group*, Jan Sochurek, President, 13747 Bottom Rd, Hydes, MD 21082-9753, 410-313-9757, 410-592-5583; E-mail: saacgroupmd@compuserve.com

Michigan   *Motor City Region*, Dean V Ricci, 30917 Dorais, Livonia, MI 48154, 313-980-3936 (recorded message, club hotline); E-mail: ricci@saac-mcr.com; Web site: www.saac.mcr.com

Western Michigan Region, Jack Redeker, PO Box 79, Spring Lake, MI 49456, 618-846-4136

Minnesota   *Upper Midwest Region*, Jerry Hansen, PO Box 600051, St Paul, MN 55106, 812-937-0323, 651-222-5022 club hotline; E-mail: dbegley@thecarsource.com; Web site: www.saa.net/pro/umrsaac/

Nebraska   *Mustang Car Club of Omaha*, Mark Meswarb, 2315 River Rd, Granbury, TX 76048, 402-533-2898

New Jersey   *New Jersey Region*, Vincent Liska, 128 Kimball St, Iselin, NJ 08830, 201-834-1044; E-mail: vinman@injersey.com

New York   *Adirondack Region*, Gordon Dinger, 21 Ponderosa Dr, Clifton Park, NY 12065, 518-383-8845

Hudson Valley Mustang Association, Ray Redner, 4 Windsor Ln, Cornwall, NY 12518, 914-534-1064 before 9 pm; E-mail: hvmustang@aol.com

Long Island Region, Gary Duprez, 25 Flamingo Dr, Smithtown, NY 11787, 518-381-8319

Shelby/Mustang Club of Rochester, Tom Zgrodnik, 64 Edgerton St, Rochester, NY 14607, 718-442-5953

Western New York Region, Dave Driggs, 4340 Reiter Rd, East Aurora, NY 14052, 718-852-4198

North Carolina   *North Carolina Region*, Bill & Cathy Harris, 8129 Cedarbrook Dr, Charlotte, NC 28215, 704-535-1228

Ohio   *Ohio SAAC Region*, Rod or Bev Harold, 6985 Leigh Ave NW, North Canton, OH 44720, 330-497-9883

Oklahoma   *Oklahoma Region*, Jim & Terry Wicks, 444 N Brown, Vinita, OK 74301, 918-256-7121

Oregon   *Northwest Region*, Fred Gehring, 414 S High St, Oregon City, OR 97045, 503-657-5595

Pennsylvania   *Central Pennsylvania Region*, Todd Eby, 2251 Nancy Lee Ave, Lebanon, PA 17042, 717-272-5428

Eastern Pennsylvania Region, Frank Boyer, 25 Powerline Rd, Boyertown, PA 19512, 215-889-4201

Lehigh Valley Region, Dan Reiter, 638 Arndt Rd, Forks Twp, PA 18040, 610-253-7107

Tennessee   *Tennessee Region*, Mark Craig, 200 Breckenridge, Franklin, TN 37067, 615-790-9944, 6-9 CST; E-mail: 2craigs@bellsouth.net

Texas   *Shelby Cobra Association of Texas*, Mike Shaw, 7809 Ivy Ln, Rowlett, TX 75089, 972-475-1294; E-mail: scatmail@airmail.net

Virginia   *Capitol Shelby Club*, Bob Jennings, 3817 Linda Ln, Annandale, VA 22004, 703-580-1773

Southeastern Virginia Region, Calvin Sanders, 6084 Knotts Creek Ln, Suffolk, VA 23435, 804-484-8995

Washington   *Washington SAAC*, Jeff Winchell, 206-781-1740; E-mail: jeff@winchell.com; Web site: http://ponycar.net/wasaac

Canada   *Western Canada Region*, Dale Warren, 604-538-1718

Washington Ford Retractable Club
8524 S 125th
Renton, WA 98055
206-772-5418

Founded 1978. 50 members. 6 newsletters, meetings and local car shows a year. Benefits: meet friends with same interest and exchange of parts. Dues: $10/year.

Alberta Mustangs Auto Club
PO Box 36092
Lakeview PO
Calgary AB Canada T3E 7C6

Founded 1979. 80 members. A non-profit organization made up of individuals and families who share a common interest in Mustangs, Cougars and special interest Fords. Membership entitles holder to bi-monthly newsletter, membership roster and discount at various retailers and on admission to club events. Major event is the Presidential Show and Shine held in June. Dues: $30/year, $25/year renewal. Web site: www.abmustang.com

Mustang Club of America
3588 Hwy 138, Ste 365
Stockbridge, GA 30281
PH/FAX: 770-477-1965
10 am to 5 pm

For membership information, contact at the above address:
National Headquarters. Founded 1976. Over 8,500 members and
110 regional groups. Should be an enthusiast of Ford Mustangs,
Bosses and Shelbys. Largest Mustang club in the world.
Visa/MasterCard accepted. Dues: $30/year US, $40/year
Canada, $65/year foreign.

regions:

Alabama   *Heart of Dixie Mustang Club*, Russ
Courtenmanche, President, 6853 Broonwood
Ln, Montgomery, AL 36109, 334-272-8753

Mobile Bay Mustang Club, John Kaeser,
President, 7688 Cornwallis St, Saraland, AL
36571, 334-675-7391

Model City Mustang Club, John Sudduth,
President, 320 Co Line Rd, Oxford, AL 36203,
256-835-1190

Rocket City Mustang Club, Joe Zielinski,
President, PO Box 5057, Huntsville, AL
35814, 256-859-7349

Arizona   *Copperstate Mustang Club*, Vinny Tuccillo,
President, 435 W Buena Vista Dr, Tempe, AZ
85284, 602-753-0110

Old Pueblo Mustang Club, David Hoverstock,
President, PO Box 17746, Tucson, AZ 85731,
520-298-5442

Arkansas   *Arkansas Valley Mustang Club*, Bill Whitman,
President, PO Box 6715, Fort Smith, AR
72906, 918-626-4986

Central Arkansas Mustangers, Charlotte
Fason, President, 2900 Spring St, Hot
Springs, AR 71901, 501-262-4209

NW Arkansas Mustang Club, Steve Sanders,
President, 2049 Reed Ave, Springdale, AR
72764, 501-750-6327

Ozarks Regional Mustang Club, Gary Richart,
President, 8 Crestview Rd, Harrison, AR
72601, 870-741-6854

California   *Diablo Valley Mustang Club*, Mike Weldon,
President, 1721 Geanne Cir, Martinez, CA
94553

Golden Hills Mustang Club, Dennis von Ting,
President, 624 Catalina Ct, Vacaville, CA
95687, 707-224-6835

Mustang Owners Club of California, Craig
Cunningham, President, PO Box 8261, Van
Nuys, CA 91406, 818-758-1826

Sacramento Area Mustang Club, Kevin
Williams, President, 4016 Bruce Way, North
Highland, CA 95660, 916-348-8105

Vintage Mustang Owners Association, Esteban
Chabolla, President, 1033 Rafael Dr, San
Jose, CA 95120, 408-997-6089

Colorado   *Front Range Mustang Club*, Tom Kay,
President, 1167 W 133rd Way, Westminster,
CO 80234, 303-451-9296

Delaware   *First State Mustangs*, Richard Langshaw,
President, 254 Sheats Ln, Middletown, DE
19709, 302-376-7289

Lower Delaware Mustang Club, Ernie Byanum,
President, PO Box 400, Felton, DE 19943,
302-284-8199

Florida   *Bay Mustang Club*, Tina Easterwood,
President, PO Box 1133, Panama City, FL
32402, 850-265-3203

Classic Mustang of Tampa, Chris Meyer,
President, PO Box 290493, Tampa, FL 33617,
813-961-3223

Emerald Coast Mustang Club, Ron Marx,
President, PO Box 4431, Fort Walton Beach,
FL 32549, 850-862-6916

Gold Coast Mustang Club, Larry Bedford,
President, PO Box 771091, Coral Springs, FL
33077, 954-752-5047

Gulf Coast Region Mustang Club, Ronald Trine,
President, 8911 Fowler Ave, Pensacola, FL
32534, 850-477-1144

Hernando County Mustang Association, Tony
Lagone, President, 25256 Plum St,
Brooksville, FL 34601, 904-796-0854

Imperial Mustangs of Polk County, Dave
LaRocco, President, 2106 Groveglen Ln N,
Lakeland, FL 33813, 941-644-4514

Magic City Mustangs Inc, George Barber,
President, 10981 SW 44th St, Miami, FL
33165, 305-221-6777

Mid Florida Mustang Club, Larry Goebel,
President, PO Box 2426, Orlando, FL 32802,
407-889-0799

Mustang Club of West Central Florida, Andrea
Waldron, President, 3939 37th St Ct W,
Bradenton, FL 34205

Southwest Florida Mustang Club, Steve
Keppen, President, 3101 Terrace Ave, Naples,
FL 33942, 813-939-7245

Space Coast Mustang Club, John McAvey,
President, 3437 Jay Tee Dr, Melbourne, FL
32901, 407-723-1486

Suncoast Mustang Club, Jim Carroll,
President, PO Box 4622, Clearwater, FL
34618, 813-884-8736

Surf Mustang of South Florida, Marc Schultz,
President, 124 SE 5th St N, Belle Glade, FL
33230, 561-996-5520

Georgia   *Central Savannah River Area Mustang Club*,
Steve Prewitt, President, PO Box 211726,
Augusta, GA 30917, 706-860-4535

Cherokee Regional Mustang Club, Randy
Powell, President, 248 Beason Rd SE,
Calhoun, GA 30701, 706-602-0535

Flag City Mustang Club, Hal Davis, President,
4258 Cordoba Ct, Macon, GA 31206,
912-781-1324

Georgia Regional Mustang Club, Charles
Lambert, President, 3911 Orange Wood Dr,
Marietta, GA 30062, 770-992-0343

Mustang Powerhouse of Atlanta, Kenneth
Washington, President, 9819 Owen Pkwy,
Jonesboro, GA 30236, 770-603-3494

Northeast Georgia Mustang Club, Reggie
Triggs, President, 320 Creekview Terr,
Alpharetta, GA 30005, 770-346-0776

Savannah Mustang Club, Johnny Moore, President, PO Box 13204, Savannah, GA 31416, 912-352-4643

Tara Mustang Club, Art Lowery, President, 1037 Warren Dr, Riverdale, GA 30296, 770-471-3517

Illinois   Central Illinois Mustangers, Chuck Brenner, President, 9 Indian Tr, Macomb, IL 61455, 309-836-6606

Northern Mustang Corral, Terry Hebert, President, 1200 King Arthur Ln, Bourbonnais, IL 60914, 815-932-5285

Rock Valley Mustang Club, Scott Fleming, President, 6079 Wild Rose Ln, Roscoe, IL 61073, 815-389-8828

Shiloh Valley Mustang Association, Scott Boisemenue, President, 22 Brittany Ln, Belleville, IL 62223, 618-235-4634

Southern Illinois Mustang Association, Jay Reid, President, 410 Francis St, Gillespie, IL 60233, 217-839-2058

Indiana   Falls City Mustang Club, Charlie Smith, President, PO Box 654, Jeffersonville, IN 47131, 812-283-6643

Michiana Mustangs, Victor Garrison, President, 8139 N Wilhelm Rd, Laporte, IN 46350, 219-326-8773

Mustang Club of Indianapolis, Jerry Sullivan, President, 2442 S Lockburn, Indianapolis, IN 46241, 317-244-2935

Old Fort Mustangers Club, John Baltes, President, PO Box 5082, Fort Wayne, IN 46895, 219-486-9074

Pony Express Mustang Club, Greg Stillwell, President, 1617 Wedeking, Evansville, IN 47708, 812-425-4794

Wabash Valley Mustang Club, Roy Chaney, President, PO Box 8441, Terre Haute, IN 47808, 317-832-2588

Iowa   Central Iowa Mustang Club, Roger Fee, President, 321 SW Logen St, Akeny, IA 50021, 515-765-8279

Kansas   S C Kansas Mustang Club, Craig Cantrell, President, 2467 Yellowstone Ct, Wichita, KS 67215, 316-721-9408

Vintage Mustang Club of Kansas City, Louis Fries, President, PO Box 40082, Overland Park, KS 66204, 816-331-9581

Kentucky   Bluegrass Mustang Club, Ken Pracht, President, 229 Lowry Ln, Lexington, KY 40503, 606-227-8559

Derby City Mustang Club, Gene Smith, President, 2510 Regal Rd, LaGrange, KY 40031, 502-241-8170

Louisana   Baton Rouge Mustangers, Steve Boivin, President, 1502 Woodmass, Baton Rouge, LA 70816, 504-272-5843

Cajun Mustangers, Rodney Breaux, President, 1216 Post Oak Rd #9, Sulphur, LA 70663, 318-625-2650

Classic Mustang Association of New Orleans, David Rouse, President, #3 Santa Anna, Jefferson, LA 70121

Michigan   Mustang Club of Mid-Michigan, Brian Sutherland, President, 976 W Saginaw Rd, Vassar, MI 48768, 517-823-8802

Mustang Owners Club of Southeastern Michigan, Francis Lundgren, President, PO Box 39088, Redford, MI 48239, 313-283-1849

Mississippi   Gumtree Mustang Club, Kenneth Hanks, President, 2135 Joann St, Tupelo, MS 38801

Mid Mississippi Mustangs, Su Rablin, President, 103 Spanish Ct, Clinton, MS 39056, 601-925-0717

Mississippi Coast Mustang Club, Mickey Penton, President, 82 Sealcrest Dr, Picayune, MS 39466, 228-798-3166

Missouri   Greater Ozarks Mustang Club, Robert Snook, President, PO Box 4725, Springfield, MO 65808, 417-883-5812

Mid America Mustangers, Linda Jirkovsky, President, PO Box 414913, Kansas City, MO 64141, 816-545-6689

Show-Me Mustang Club, Craig Anderson, President, 8458 Florence, Brentwood, MO 63114, 314-968-0722

New Jersey   Garden State Region Mustang Club, Sue Danner, President, 14 Hayward St, Bound Brook, NJ 08805, 732-469-4169

South Jersey Mustang Club, Victor Norberg, President, 1417 Rogers Ave, Vineland, NJ 08360, 609-696-3143

New Mexico   Rio Grande Mustang Club, Ramona Gallegos, President, 12825 Cedarbrook Ave NE, Albuquerque, NM 87111, 505-299-4573

New York   Adirondack Shelby-Mustang Club, John Watters, President, 49 Vosburgh Rd, Mechanicsville, NY 12118, 518-554-5390

Classic Mustang Long Island, Trudy Kent, President, PO Box 1011, North Massapequa, NY 11758, 516-798-6223

Twin Tiers Regional Group, Bill Griffith, President, 336 Castleman Rd, Vestal, NY 13850, 607-748-2168

North Carolina   Carolina Regional Mustang Club, James Ray, President, 5500 Bellerive St, Charlotte, NC 28277, 704-846-6117

Chrome Pony Mustang Club, Mark Cooper, President, 684 Methodist Church Rd, Elizabeth City, NC 27909, 919-264-4381

Eastern North Carolina Regional Mustang Club, Leslie Joyner, President, 301 S Caswell St, LaGrange, NC 25551, 252-566-3826

Gate City Triad Mustang Club, C Michael Briggs, President, 115 S Holden Rd, Greensboro, NC 27406, 336-854-2244

Heart of Carolina Mustang Club, Al Dulaney, President, 4312 Holly Run Rd, Apex, NC 27502, 919-387-4585

Sandhills Regional Mustang Club, Laurin Cooper, President, 5736 Sagamore Rd, Hope Mills, NC 28348, 910-425-9282

Southeastern North Carolina Regional Mustang Club, Robert O Smith, President, 495 Rivenbarktown Rd, Wallace, NC 28466, 910-285-4895

Mustang Club of America regions *(continued)*

Tarheel Mustang Club, Bill Weaver, President, 304 Fosterri Dr, Rocky Mount, NC 27801, 252-446-6639

Ohio   *Classic Mustang Club of Ohio*, Mark Morley, President, 1233 Colston Dr, Westerville, OH 43081, 614-895-7059

Mahoning Valley Mustangs, Nancy Evans, President, 14944 Palmyra Rd, Diamond, OH 44412, 330-538-2416

Northeastern Ohio Mustang Club, Steve Chimera, President, 4008 Lor-ron Ave, Kent, OH 44240, 330-678-2384

Tri-State Mustang Club, Farrel Buis, President, 399 Marycrest Dr, Cincinnati, OH 45237, 513-821-4928

Oklahoma   *Green Country Classic Mustangs*, Wayne Pense, President, PO Box 471361, Tulsa, OK 74147, 918-277-6732

Oklahoma Mustang Club, Bob Mollohan, President, 1602 Ridgecrest, El Reon, OK 73036, 405-262-6650

Pennsylvania   *Centre Region Mustang Club*, Dan Workman, President, PO Box 91, Lemont, PA 16851, 814-238-7792

First Pennsylvania Mustang Club, Scott Whitson, President, 354 Windsor Ave, Hatboro, PA 19040, 215-957-0834

Greater Pittsburgh Mustang Club, Christopher Fisher, President, 318 Circle Dr, Delmont, PA 15626, 724-468-5213

Lake Erie Mustang Owners Club, Bill Steger, President, 1137 Mission Dr, Erie, PA 16509, 814-864-3809

North Central Mustang Club, Rod Dieffenbacher, President, 315 Klump Rd, Cogan Station, PA 17728

Valley Forge Mustang Club, Jim Alberts, President, 1407 Whitford Rd, West Chester, PA 19380, 610-692-4815

Wyoming Valley Mustang & Ford, John Stefanick, President, 121 Lincoln Ave, West Wyoming, PA 18644, 717-287-3925

Puerto Rico   *Puerto Rico Mustang Club*, Luis F Lugo, President, GPO Box 3397, Aguadilla, PR 00605, 787-891-3266

Rhode Island   *Mustang Club of New England*, Jim Silverman, President, 72 Westhaven Dr, Brockton, MA 02401, 508-234-8848

South Carolina   *Carolina Stampede Mustang Club*, J W Lancaster, President, 404 Tower St, Duncan, SC 29334, 864-439-9377

Central South Carolina Regional Gruop, David Phillips, President, PO Box 232, Springfield, SC 29146, 803-258-3839

Eastern South Carolina Mustang Club, Gene Turner, President, 780 St Andrews Rd, Florence, SC 29501

Foothills Regional Group, Shawn Ratenski, President, 109 S Spearman Dr, Greer, SC 29651, 864-801-0892

South Carolina Coastal Region Mustang Club, Duane Helzer, President, 8008 Nantuckett, North Charleston, SC 29420, 803-553-7170

South Dakota   *Rapid Mustang Club*, Mark Weishaar, President, 125 MacArthur, Rapid City, SD 57701, 605-341-8877

Tennessee   *First Tennessee Regional Mustang Club*, Charles Mullins, President, 617 Rogers Ave, Kingsport, TN 37660, 423-246-6898

Golden Circle Mustang Club, James Mills, President, 100 Sharon Church Rd, Cedar Grove, TN 38231, 901-968-8617

Lakeway Mustang Club, Carl D Dunn, President, Rt 1 Box 40-1A, Rutledge, TN 37861, 423-828-4096

Music City Regional Group, Jim Chism, President, PO Box 780, Fairview, TN 37062, 615-446-0520

Mustangs of Memphis, Rick Duncan, President, 582 Dunwick Ct, Collierville, TN 38017, 901-854-9896

Tennessee Valley Mustang Club, Buddy Houser, President, PO Box 5294, Oak Ridge, TN 37831, 423-577-7743

Thunder Valley Mustang Club, Dale Wrinkle, President, 302 Hannah Ln, Hixson, TN 37343, 423-842-6054

Texas   *Coastal Bend Mustang Club*, Chuck Luckett, President, PO Box 72044, Corpus Christi, TX 78472, 512-850-8630

Mustang Club of Houston, Les Blankenship, President, 15034 Margison, Houston, TX 77084, 281-463-4245

North Texas Mustang Club, Jerry Flowers, President, PO Box 531374, Grand Prairie, TX 75053, 972-717-5969

San Antonio Mustang Club, Alan Hibler, President, 2107 Town Oak, San Antonio, TX 78232, 210-494-6154

South Texas Mustang Club, Henry Falcon, President, 601 N 43rd St, McAllen, TX 78501, 956-687-1674

Southeast Texas Mustang Club, Chris Cormier, President, 8496 Mitchell Rd, Lumberton, TX 77657, 409-755-4081

Texas Panhandle Mustang Club, Kathy Pruiett, President, PO Box 2574, Amarillo, TX 79105, 806-352-9357

Texoma Mustang Club, Bob Brown, President, 1908 Laurel Rd, Gainesville, TX 76240

Utah   *Northern Utah Mustang Owners*, Douglas Herman, President, 2727 S 625 W B 103, Bountiful, UT 84010

Vermont   *Green Mountain Mustang Club*, Wes Patnaude, President, 33 Eastry Ct, Charlotte, VT 05445, 802-425-4993

Virginia   *Central Virginia Mustang Club*, Kenny Fischer, President, 6506 Lothaire Ct, Richmond, VA 23234, 804-743-1490

Lynchburg Area Mustang Club, Peggy Tomlinson, President, 300 Westbury Dr, Lynchburg, VA 24502, 804-239-1594

Mustang Club of Tidewater, Doug Sample, President, 705 Erskine St, Hampton, VA 23666

National Capital Region Mustang Club, Val Wadsworth, President, 4886 Tobacco Way, Woodbridge, VA 22193-3222, 301-932-7684

Roanoke Valley Mustang Club, Linda Lancaster, President, 903 Camelot Dr, Apt 1, Salem, VA 24153, 540-343-7268

Shenandoah Valley Mustang Club, Bob Snyder, President, PO Box 2015, Winchester, VA 22601, 304-876-6830

Southeastern Virginia Mustang Club, Bobby Jenkins, President, 3113 Glastonbury Dr, Virginia Beach, VA 23456

Washington   *Mustangs Northwest,* Terry Green, President, 109 NE 170th, Seattle, WA 98155, 206-362-2128

Mustangs West Car Club, Debra Healy, President, PO Box 5876, Lacey, WA 98503, 360-943-5863

Pierce County Mustang Club, Dan Carmack, President, 306 Main St, Steilacoom, WA 98388, 253-274-1674

West Virginia   *Mid-Ohio Valley Mustang Club,* Russ Alton, President, 2306 Prunty St, Parkersburg, WV 26101, 304-428-4851

Wisconsin   *Badgerland Mustang Club,* Lawton Heilman, President, PO Box 45032, Madison, WI 53744, 608-635-7751

Western Wisconsin Regional, Herb Long, President, 755 W US Hwy 16, West Salem, WI 54669, 608-786-1142

Wisconsin Early Mustangers, Scott Moen, President, 2511 W Carrington Ave, Oak Creek, WI 53154, 414-567-2622

Wyoming   *Hoof Beats Mustang Club,* Kevin Anders, President, 4501 Rocky Point Dr, Gillette, WY 82718, 307-682-4339

Australia   *Mustang Owners Club of Australia,* Kevin Musgrave, President, 72 Eisemans Rd, Yarrambat, Victoria 3091

Canada   *Golden Horseshoe Mustang Association,* Mike Owens, President, 147 John Bowser Crescent, Newmarket, ON L3Y 7N4, 905-830-9488

Mustang Owners Club International
Paul McLaughlin
2720 Tennessee NE
Albuquerque, NM 87110
505-296-2554

Founded 1975. 500 members. Open to all Mustangs and Mustang enthusiasts from the earliest to the latest. Stock, restored, modified, race, etc, all welcomed. Large reference library available to answer questions pertaining to Mustangs. Newsletter, *The Pony Express.* Dues: $15/year US, $18/year foreign.

Mustang SVO Owners Association Inc
4234 I-75 Business Spur
Sault Ste Marie, MI 49783
705-525-7861 (SVO1)
FAX: 705-525-5178, Ontario, Canada
E-mail:
svooa.nationaloffice@sympatico.ca

Founded 1989. 400+ members. Dedicated to locating and documenting the SVO Mustang and serving the needs of SVO Mustang owners. Newsletter three times yearly. Collectible insurance appraisal service. National convention, technical support and modification support. Dues: $30/year. Web site: www.corral.net/svo/html

Sierra Mustang Club
PO Box 1793
Fair Oaks, CA 95628
916-967-6659; FAX: 916-967-6044

Founded 1981. 150 members. Need only be interested in the classic Mustang, monthly meetings and newsletters, displays, car shows, monthly events, discounts at many local Ford dealers and parts houses. Dues: $25/year. Web site: www.geocities.com/motorcity/factory/3629

Sonoma County Mustang Club
PO Box 8716
Santa Rosa, CA 95407
707-544-5852

Founded 1990. 50 members. Interest in Ford Mustangs (all years) and/or other Ford products. Meet 3rd Thursday of each month (except December) at 7:30 pm at Round Table Pizza Parlor, Occidental Rd (one block west of Stony Point), Santa Rosa, CA. Monthly newsletter or bulletin, monthly cruises, club sponsored Poker Run. Dues: $25/year family.

Stallions Gate Mustang & Ford Club Inc
4736 W Berenice Ave
Chicago, IL 60641
773-685-4748

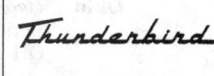

Founded 1993. 75 members. Club newsletter, parts and service discount with local vendors, club decal, free classified ads, annual club car show, weekly cruises, monthly meetings, social events and wearing apparel. Open to all Mustang and Ford owners. Dues: $25/year. Web site: www.stallionsgate.com

Chicagoland Thunderbird Club
107 S Highland Ave
Lombard, IL 60148
630-627-2866

Thunderbird

Founded 1982. 175 members. Thunderbird enthusiasts. Club open to cars 1958-present. Monthly publication, *Bird Word.* Monthly meetings. Free car shows. Car ownership not mandatory to join. Dues $25/year.

Classic Thunderbird Club International
1308 E 29th St, Dept HV
Signal Hill, CA 90806
562-426-2709
E-mail: office@ctci.org

Thunderbird

Founded 1961. 8,000 members. Dedicated to the 1955, 1956 and 1957 Thunderbirds. Publish magazine, *The Early Bird.* Sell manuals, posters, brochures to members only. 6 regional conventions this summer throughout USA and Canada. One international convention in the summer of 2000. Work with Ford Motor Co for continuance of parts. Everyone welcome to join. Dues: $25/year plus $15 initiation fee.

Heartland Vintage Thunderbird Club of America
2861 Comanche Dr
Kettering, OH 45420
PH/FAX: 937-235-9343
E-mail: tbirdclub@aol.com

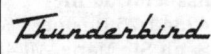

Thunderbird

Founded 1985. 2,600 members worldwide. National club dedicated to the preservation of all Thunderbirds 1958-1969. Monthly newsletter. Dues: $20/year US and Canada, $30/year overseas, US funds only. Web site: www.tbirdclub.com

regions:

Arkansas *Vintage Thunderbirds Central Kansas*, Greg Davis, President, 7220 Pontiac Dr N, Little Rock, AR 72116, 501-834-8964

Florida *Florida Vintage Thunderbirds*, Anton Leiter, President, 6000 Tomoka Dr, Orlando, FL 32809, 407-857-3796

Hawaii *Aloha State Thunderbird Club*, Ron Mata, President, 2370 Hoohoihoi St, Pearl City, HI 96782, 808-456-3740

Idaho *Idaho Vintage Thunderbird Club*, Ron Dietzler, President, 1212 W El Pelar Dr, Boise, ID 83702, 208-344-2133

Indiana *Hoosier Vintage Thunderbird Club*, Dave May, President, 4626 W 500 S, Marion, IN 46953, 317-384-7645

Kansas *Mid-Kansas Vintage Thunderbird Club*, Carol Kirkwood, President, 209 N St Clair, Wichita, KS 67203, 316-946-5668

T-Town Eastern Jayhawker Thunderbirds, Kevin Thomas, President, 1812 SW Ln, Topeka, KS 66604, 913-232-8852

Minnesota *Thunderbird Midwest*, Barry Blazevic, President, 8136 Narcissus Ln N, Maple Grove, MN 55311, 612-494-8477

Missouri *Kansas City Heartland Thunderbird Club*, Larry Cashen, President, 7719 Wornall RD, Kansas City, MO 64114, 816-941-4495

New Jersey *Garden State Latebirds*, Al Perilli, President, 2411 Columbia Ave, Ewing, NJ 08638, 609-882-3013

Ohio *Heartland-Ohio Vintage Thunderbird Club*, Ken Bender, President, 6700 Spokane Dr, Dayton, OH 45424, 937-236-4867

North Coast Latebirds, Dale Komives, President, 3700 Sweet Briar Dr, Medina, OH 44256, 330-239-2978

Oregon *Southern Oregon Thunderbird Club*, Byron Barr, President, 1011 NW Starlite PL, Grants Pass, OR 97526, 541-955-4548

Pennsylvania *Birds of Steel Thunderbird Club*, Bill McCloskey, President, 124 Linhurst Ave, Butler, PA 16001, 724-282-4352

Texas *Lone Star Vintage Thunderbird Club*, Bill Olsen, President, 324 Crestview, San Antonio, TX 78201, 210-735-3563

Washington *Heartland-Western Washington*, Erin Corey, President, 3216 180th Pl SW, Lynnwood, WA 98037, 425-775-9213

Australia *Thunderbird Owners Club of Australia*, Romeo Stellato, Director, 10 Munro Close Hampton Park 3976, Melbourne Victoria, 011-613-9799-1079

New Zealand *Heartland-New Zealand Thunderbirds*, Paul Joslen, Director, 81 Sneyde St Kaiapoi, Canterbury 8252, 64-3-327-8986

Long Island Thunderbird Club
737 Kearny Dr
North Woodmere, NY 11581
516-791-4940

Thunderbird

Founded 1994. 90 members. Meeting once a month, open to all people with interest in Thunderbirds. Social club with various activities such as cruises, weekend trips, scavenger hunts, picnic, rock and roll shows. Monthly award winning newsletter, *Bird Talk*. Strongly support the preservation of T-Birds. Dues: $25/year.

New England's Vintage Thunderbird Club Inc
c/o Don Seymour, President
5 Ridgewood Ln, Box 102
Farmington, NH 03835
603-859-3491 days
603-859-7818 eves
FAX: 603-859-3499
E-mail: beggan@ici.net

Thunderbird

Membership director: Tom Beggan, 170 Pheasant Ln, Manchester, NH 03109, PH: 603-647-7869. Founded 1991. 250+ members. NEVT is a non-profit club dedicated to the enjoyment and advancement of the motoring sport, with a special emphasis on the Ford Thunderbird. Club membership is open to all owners and enthusiasts interested in the restoration and preservation of Thunderbirds. Membership includes annual subscription to club newsletter, *The Bird's Nest*. Dues: $25/year. Web site: http://home.ici.net/customers/beggan

Tucson Thunderbird Club
3156 E President St
Tucson, AZ 85714
602-889-8634

Thunderbird

Founded 1976. 50 members. Chapter of CTCI, #103. Membership in CTCI is not required. Ownership is not required. Dues: $10/year.

Upstate New York Thunderbird Club Inc
7 Burton Rd
Greenwich, NY 12834
518-692-7815

Thunderbird

Founded 1981. 57 members. A member would benefit by meeting people across the state who are dedicated to preserving, restoring, driving and enjoying T-Birds, a monthly newsletter, meet once a month, annual general membership meeting, Syracuse, first Sunday in November. Dues: $23/year.

Vintage Thunderbird Club International
PO Box 2250
Dearborn, MI 48123-2250
316-794-8061 evenings/weekends
FAX: 316-794-8132
E-mail: tast@feist.com

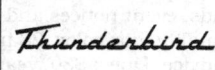

Founded 1968. 3,000 members worldwide. Enjoying and preserving the "personal luxury experience". Embracing all Thunderbirds, from 1958-today. Serving Thunderbird enthusiasts since 1968. Five regional/one international convention yearly. Chapters across the US and abroad. Award winning bimonthly *Thunderbird Scoop* magazine. Send for information/application or mail dues to above address. Dues: $26/year US and Canada, $45/year foreign. Web site: www.tbirdclub.net

chapters:

Arizona   *Central Arizona*, Larry Smith, 2101 E Michigan Ave, Phoenix, AZ 85022, 602-493-0143

California   *Funbirds of Southern California*, Don Felt, 6521 E Mantova St, Long Beach, CA 90815, 562-431-6357

Sunbirds of Palm Springs, Joe Arce, PO Box 1271, Palm Springs, CA 92263, 760-328-5063

Wunderbirds of San Diego, Don Maltman, 18878 Paradise Mtn Rd, Valley Center, CA 92082, 619-749-9073

Colorado   *Rocky Mountain Thunderbird Club*, John Saylor, 14057 E Hamilton Dr, Aurora, CO 80014-3946, 303-699-2604

Florida   *Space Coast Thunderbirds*, Irv Skov, 937 Buford St NW, Palm Bay, FL 32907, 407-728-1823

Sunshine State Vintage T-Bird Club, Nora Roberts, 3401 Elkridge Dr, Holiday, FL 34691, 813-938-1103

Vintage Thunderbirds of Florida, Dan Davis, 1409 Betty Ln S, Clearwater, FL 34617, 813-443-3190

Georgia   *North Georgia Vintage T-Bird Club*, Roger Lindros, 104 Paddock Tr, Peachtree City, GA 30269, 404-487-5096

Illinois   *Chicagoland Thunderbirds*, Wayne Warner, 170A S Highland Ave Apt A, Lombard, IL 60148, 630-627-2866

Land of Lincoln Thunderbirds, Terry Fletcher, 1020 W Walnut, Jacksonville, IL 62650, 217-245-5468

Indiana   *Vintage Thunderbird Club of Indiana*, James Maple, 2423 S Fishers Rd, Indianapolis, IN 46239, 317-356-6672

Iowa   *Mid America T-Birds of Iowa*, Gene Adkins, PO Box 4511, Brooklyn, IA 52211, 515-522-9467

Kansas   *Classic Thunderbird Club of Omaha*, Alan Tast, 1251 Reece Rd, Goddard, KS 67052, 316-794-8061

Kentucky   *Tri-State Thunderbirds*, Larry Sands, 1531 KY Hwy 144, Owensboro, KY 42303, 502-281-5817

Louisiana   *Acadian Thunderbirds*, J V Gale Jr, 1605 Nie Pkwy, New Orleans, LA 70131-1907, 504-368-1209

Michigan   *Water Wonderland Thunderbirds*, Tony Maisano, 3832 Nash, Troy, MI 48083, 248-689-2286

Western Michigan Thunderbird Club, Ed Elzinga, 17040 Ransom St, Holland, MI 49424, 616-399-6568

Minnesota   *Thunderbird Midwest*, Barry Blazevic, 8136 Narcissus Ln, Maple Grove, MN 55311, 612-494-8477

Missouri   *Gateway Thunderbirds*, William Larson, 1957 Miller Rd, Imperial, MO 63052, 314-464-1438

Vintage Thunderbirds of Kansas City, Timothy E Pundt, 609 E 72nd St, Kansas City, MO 64131-1613, 816-333-7346

Nevada   *Sierra Nevada Thunderbird Club*, Chuck MacLeod, 240 Bonnie Briar Pl, Reno, NV 89509, 702-826-7848

New Jersey   *Garden State Latebirds Inc*, Al Perilli, 2411 Columbia Ave, Ewing, NJ 08638-3021, 609-882-3013

New York   *Buffalo Thunderbird Club*, John Misso, 115 Schiller St, Buffalo, NY 14206, 716-897-4138

Long Island Thunderbirds, Joe Apicella, 100 Van Bomel Blvd, Oakdale, NY 11769-2075, 516-589-4620

North Carolina   *Carolinas*, Jim Cockerham, 710 Barney Ave, Winston-Salem, NC 27107, 919-788-8780

Oregon   *NW Vintage T-Bird Club of Oregon*, George Raeburn, 3147 NE Irving St, Portland, OR 97232, 503-232-8810

Pennsylvania   *Greater Pittsburgh Chapter*, Walter Kaczmarek, 118 Sycamore Dr, Pittsburgh, PA 15237, 412-487-6311

Rhode Island   *South Shores Thunderbirds*, Doug O'Neil, 81 Lawn St, Providence, RI 02908, 401-351-4034

Texas   *Capitol City Thunderbird Club*, Harold Clark, 8200 Pitter Pat Ln, Austin, TX 78736, 512-288-4524

North Texas Vintage Thunderbird Club, Charlotte Schubert, 606 Cliffside Dr, Richardson, TX 75080, 972-231-0090

South Texas Vintage Thunderbird Club, Kevin Bois, 12918 Hunters Moon, San Antonio, TX 78214, 210-690-3580

Vintage Thunderbirds of Houston, Bill Pastor, 615 E 10-1/2 St, Houston, TX 77008, 713-862-3556; E-mail: billypastor@pdq.net

Virginia   *Mid-Atlantic Chapter (MA, VA, PA)*, Stephen Cohen, 8190 Madrillon Ct, Vienna, VA 22182, 703-821-0055

Washington   *Inland Northwest Thunderbird Chapter*, Leonard Share, 3710 E 36th, Spokane, WA 99223, 509-448-1098

Pacific Northwest (WA, OR), Gary Nevius, 1724 214th St NE, Bothell, WA 98021-7632, 206-487-2228

Wisconsin   *Classic Thunderbird Club of Wisconsin*, James Rugg, W239 S5860 Hwy 164, Waukesha, WI 53186-9302, 414-544-0571

Australia   *Thunderbird Owners Club of Australia*, Brian Tomkins, 11 Reginald St, Rooty Hill NSW 2766, 02 625 8591

Vintage Thunderbird Club International chapters *(continued)*

Thunderbirds of Queensland, Mark O'Neill, 5 Vautin Way, Eagleby Queensland 4207, 07 3807 4207

Canada   *Club Renaissance Thunderbird Du Quebec,* Pierre Blais, 93 Brodeur St, Vaudreuil-Dorion, QC J7V 1R4, 514-455-9961

Okanagan Classic Thunderbird Club, Laurence Wilson, 1660 Simpson Ave, Kelowna, BC V1X 5Z4, 604-762-0602

Southern Ontario Thunderbird Club, Steve Town, 10012 Urlin Cres PO Box 92, Port Franks, ON N0H 2L0, 519-243-1193

Totem Classic Thunderbird Club, Dave Senechal, 33286 Robertson Ave, Abbotsford, BC V2S 1Z3, 604-853-3285

England   *Thunderbirds of England,* John T Cox, 8 Rock Rd, Peterborough PE1 3BU, 1733 342470

France   *Thunderbirds of France,* Jean Pierre Champagnol, 46 av Edouard Branly, 92370 Chaville, 33 1 47 50 52 1221

New Zealand   *New Zealands Sulfur City T-Birds,* Fred Rice, PO Box 820, Rotorua, 07 348 9389

Sweden   *Squarebird T-Bird Club of Sweden,* Ulf Gustafsson, Laxvagen 7, 175 39 Jarfalla, 46 8 580 19678

The H H Franklin Club
Home Office, Roy F Powers, Manager
Cazenovia College
Cazenovia, NY 13035
315-683-5376

Founded 1951. 850 members. Publications, technical information, national and regional meets. For all air cooled cars of the period to 1942. Dues: $30/year, $40/year foreign. Web site: www.hhfcmwr.com

---

Chevy & Geo Club
PO Box 11238
Chicago, IL 60611
773-769-6262; FAX: 773-769-3240
E-mail: chevyclub@hotmail.com

Founded 1992. 1,000 members. For enthusiasts of Tracker, Blazer, Storm, Metro, Prizm and Cavalier. Quarterly publication, *The Chevy & Geo World.* Annual convention. Dues: $25/year. Web site: www.chevyclub.com

---

H-Special Registry
PO Box 2653
Mission Viejo, CA 92690
E-mail: h07@earthlink.net

Founded 1995. 100+ participants. Dedicated to the preservation, restoration and enjoyment of 1975-1980 Chevrolet Monza, Pontiac Sunbird, Oldsmobile Starfire and Buick Skyhawk, including design and motorsports heritage. Newsletter, *H-Special Report.* Participants directory. Sections: H07 Registry, H27 Registry. Dues: none. Web site: http://home.earthlink.net/~h07/reg/main.htm

---

National Chevy/GMC Truck Association
PO Box 607458
Orlando, FL 32860
407-889-5549; FAX: 407-886-7571
E-mail: chevy55-72@ao.net

Founded 1989. Dedicated to the preservation and restoration of

all 1911-1972 Chevy/GMC trucks. In our official publication, *Pickups 'n Panels In Print,* subscribers have access to classified ads, event notices and it also features subscribers' trucks in this quality four color, 28 page publication. Free classified ads, tech advice. Dues: $30/year. Web site: www.ao.net/chev55-72

See our ad on page 578

See our ad on page 578

chapters:

California   *Central California Chevy/GMC Truck Association,* Richard Van Wyke, 1631 W Magill, Fresno, CA 93711, 209-431-3144

Central Coast Chevy/GMC Truck Club, Roy Yenne, 1135 Via Del Carmel, Santa Maria, CA 93455, 805-937-3591

Northern California Chevy/GMC Truck Club, Wayne Fredrickson, 5837 Soltero Dr, San Jose, CA 95123, 408-258-2985

Florida   *Classic GM Trucks of Central Florida,* Dennis Oakley, 11309 Porto Ct, Orlando, FL 32837-9045, 407-438-3655

Illinois   *Early Haulers Truck Club,* Vic Lombardo, 8918 Menard, Morton Grove, IL 60053, 847-966-0741

Louisiana   *Classic Chevy Cameo/GMC Suburban Pickup Club,* Dale Mayeaux, 4356 Riverview Dr, Port Allen, LA 70767-3808, 504-383-8864

Massachusetts   *Northeast Chevy/GMC Truck Club,* Bryant Stewart, PO Box 155, Millers Falls, MA 01349, 508-544-7714

Michigan   *Just Truck'n in Michigan,* Jerry Emmendnter, 21815 Gratiot Rd, Merrill, MI 48637, 517-643-5885

Minnesota   *Classic Chevy-GMC Truck Club of Minnesota,* Mark Berger, 11231 Norway St NW, Coon Rapids, MN 55448, 612-767-9606

Missouri   *Genuine Chevy/GMC Truck Club of KC,* Gaileen Jackson, 1606 N Main, Kansas City, MO 64155-1630, 816-734-5444

Nebraska   *Classic GM Truck Club,* John Ritchey, 3100 N 60th, Lincoln, NE 68507-2221, 402-464-7949

Texas   *Just Old Trucks, Austin Texas,* Terry M Stepan, 5209 Fort Mason Dr, Austin, TX 78745-2314, 512-447-1446

Pickups'n Panels of Dallas, Augie Holtkort, 1501 Sunnyslope, Carrollton, TX 75007, 972-550-8008

Washington   *Cameos Northwest,* Richard Skaugset, PO Box 862, Allyn, WA 98524, 425-486-5893

Canada   *Maple Leaf Chevy/GMC Truck Club,* Dale Billington, 7168 4th Line, RR 4, Milton, ON L9T 2X8, 905-878-0980

New Zealand   *Kiwi Classic Chevrolet Club,* Paul Baldwin, PO Box 15539, Auckland 1003, 09 8185168

Graham Brothers Truck & Bus Club
9894 Fairtree Dr
Strongsville, OH 44136
440-238-4956

GRAHAM

For membership information, contact at the above address: Edwin L Brinkman. Founded 1975. 215 members. 20-page owner's roster list available for $4 postpaid. Dues: none.

Graham Owners Club International
Terry Graham, Secretary
401 Center St
Huron, OH 44839-1609
419-433-5609
E-mail: grampaige@aol.com

Founded 1971. 600 members. Open to all the world for those dedicated to the preservation and restoration of all Graham built vehicles. The club provides great information through its quarterly publication, *The Supercharger*, and the many regional meets, as well as the annual international meet. Dues: $20/year US, $24/year other (US funds). Web site: www.mts.net/~rjsill

Hillman, Commer & Karrier Club
Capri House
Walton-On-Thomas
Surrey KT12 2LY England
(UK) 01932-269109

Founded 1991. 1,000 members. Club for Hillman, Commer and Karrier vehicles and all derivatives sold under Dodge, Plymouth, etc, plus Chrysler or Talbot badged Hunters, Avengers, Sunbeams and Sunbeam Lotus. Bi-monthly publication, *HCKC News*, free to members. Dues: £15/year.

Hudson-Essex-Terraplane Club
PO Box 715
Milford, IN 46542-0715

Founded 1959. 3,500 members. Bi-monthly magazine with free classifieds, club library, club store, four regional meets, one national meet, over 40 local chapters, parts locator, car registries, technical advisors. Also recognize the British built Railton and Brough-Superior. Ownership not required. Write for current dues.
Web site: www.classicar.com/clubs/hudson/hethome.htm
chapters:

Arizona	*Grand Canyon Chapter*, Jerry Crater, 1970 S Tumblewood Ln, Chandler, AZ 85248, 602-782-1008
California	*California Inland*, Craig Kistler, 1011 Cypress, La Habra, CA 90631
	Northern Cal, Alan Pryor, 1009 Santa Clara Ave, Alameda, CA 94501, 510-521-5052; E-mail: hudnut@jps.net
	Sacramento Valley, Larry Slocum, 7555 Circle Pkwy, Sacramento, CA 95823-3454, 916-421-6080
	Southern Cal, Ken Perkins Jr, 20543 Soledad St, Canyon Country, CA 91351, 805-298-9266; E-mail: doctorp99@earthlink.net
	Southwestern Borders, Pete Laughton, 10711 Prince Ln, La Mesa, CA 91941, 619-442-4811
Colorado	*Rocky Mountain*, Linden Welle, 421 Cheyenne St, Fort Morgan, CO 80701, 303-867-6589
Florida	*Orange Blossom Chapter*, Joe Stinnett, PO Box 223, Ocoee, FL 34761, 407-877-1047
Georgia	*Dixie*, John Upchurch, 107 Granite Bluff, Dahonega, GA 30533, 706-864-0164
Idaho	*Gem State*, Paul Johnson, 2503 Forest Glen, Post Falls, ID 83845, 208-773-7319
Illinois	*Central Mississippi Valley*, Bob Hoyle, 2076 IL, Pt 26, Dixon, IL 61021, 815-288-6140
	Chicago-Milwaukee, John Vanlier, 8215 Willow Dr, Palos Hills, IL 60465, 708-974-4513

	Gateway Chapter, Mike Norris, 1002 Hickory, Jerseyville, IL 62052, 618-498-6258
Indiana	*South Central*, Ross Woodbury, RR 3 Box 58-1, Elizabeth, IN 47117, 812-969-2612
	Southern Indiana, Douglass Wildrick, 9225 Indian Creek Rd S, Indianapolis, IN 46259, 317-862-4171
Iowa	*Central Iowa*, Jay DeJong, 2404 Hwy 163, Pella, IA 50219, 515-682-3375
Kansas	*Hudsonite Family Chapter*, Jerry Alcorn, 817 W Lincoln, Wellington, KS 67152, 316-488-2705
	Mo-Kan Hudson Family Chapter, James Durand, 4236 74th St, Meriden, KS 66512, 785-484-2756; E-mail: durand@inlandnet.net
Louisiana	*Red River Chapter*, Erwin Sanchez Flores, 1809 S Brookwood, Shreveport, LA 71118, 318-635-3304; E-mail: ehudson@softdisc.com
Maryland	*Chesapeake Bay*, Lewis Mendenhall, 3513 Oxwed Ct, Westminster, MD 21157, 410-795-4992; E-mail: essexadv@aol.com
Massachusetts	*Yankee*, Jerre Hoffman, 27 Howard St, Chicopee, MA 01013, 413-594-2368
Michigan	*Hudson Motor Car Co Home Chapter*, Bob Elton, 860 Edwards, Ann Arbor, MI 48103, 313-663-1020
Minnesota	*North Central*, Mary I Hestness, 5201-34th Ave S, Minneapolis, MN 55417, 612-724-9268
Montana	*Big Sky*, Michael Egeland, 324 N Main, Livingston, MT 59047, 800-507-7345
Nebraska	*Iowa-Nebraska*, Bob Dittrich, 112 N 2nd PO Box 126, Ceresco, NE 68017, 402-665-2132; E-mail: userrkd@aol.com
New Hampshire	*New England*, John Mann, 15 Fellows Rd, Sanbornville, NH 03872, 603-522-3039
New Jersey	*Garden State Chapter*, Charlie Becht, 32 Starlight Dr, Morristown, NJ 07960, 973-539-3144
New Mexico	*Southwest*, Leonard Murray, 1805 New Mexico Ave, Las Cruces, NM 88001, 505-523-2960
	Zia/New Mexico Chapter, Allen K Russell, 77 Turner Dr, Los Lunas, NM 87031 505-866-7180
New York	*Hudson Mohawk*, Bruce Smith, 42 Gilligan Rd, East Greenbush, NY 12061, 518-477-9740; E-mail: bsmith4777@aol.com
	Long Island, John Salemmo, 145 Sempton Blvd, Franklin Square, NY 11010, 516-481-1506
	Western New York/Ontario, Dick DeTaeye, 322 Stony Point Rd, Rochester, NY 14624, 716-594-2008
Ohio	*North Indiana-Ohio*, Noel Renner, 116 Hill, Box 363, Pleasant Hill, OH 45359, 513-676-5111
	Western Reserve, Joe Laurene, 3199 Rohrer Rd, Wadsworth, OH 44281, 330-336-7535; E-mail: hudson1955@aol.com
Oklahoma	*Dust Bowl*, Wanda Shelton, 117 S Stevens, Ponca City, OK 74601, 580-765-5839

Hudson-Essex-Terraplane Club chapters (continued)

Oregon   *Northwest*, Dick Riggs, 8549 NW Skyline, Portland, OR 97231, 503-286-2017

Pennsylvania   *Pennsylvania Dutch*, Carl Undercofler, RD Box 337 A, Woodland, PA 16881, 814-857-7748; E-mail: undercofler@clearnet.net

Tennessee   *Midsouth*, Billy Kemp, 267 Neely Sharp Rd, Adamsville, TN 38310, 901-632-4278 home, 901-632-5082 work

Texas   *North Texas*, Mark Huebert, 2309 Robin Hood Dr, Grand Prairie, TX 75050, 972-602-9751; E-mail: hhana@flash.net

South Texas, Breckenridge Wagner, Rt 5 Box 118, Brenham, TX 77833, 713-524-0712

Utah   *Deseret*, Dave Putnam, 490 E Mutton Hollow Dr, Kaysville, UT 48037, 801-544-9175

Virginia   *Dogwood Chapter*, Kathy Lester, 1246 Meadow Spring Rd, Bedford, VA 24523, 540-586-0443

Wyoming   *High Plains Chapter*, Bill Marcus, PO Box 404, Shoshoni, WY 82649, 307-876-2789

Australia   *Australia*, Phil Haxby, 216 Ryans Rd Eltham North, 3095 Victoria, E-mail: phaxby@melbpc.org.au

New South Wales, Les Pendlebury, Hudson AMC Group 19 Kay St, Carlingford 2118 NSW, E-mail: huddy@wr.com.au

Queensland, Bob Williams, 58 Long St, Cleveland 4163

South Australia, Ian Smith, 21 Bluebell Ct, Flagstaff Hill 5159

Western Australia, Dale Miller, 52 Orchid Dr, Roleystone 6111

New Zealand   *New Zealand Rep*, Geoffrey Clark, 72 Scotia St, Nelson

South Africa   *South African Rep*, Mike Davidson, PO Box 19805, Fishers Hill 1408

Smoky Mountain Heartland Chapter
6933 Sunstrand Dr
Knoxville, TN 37924-3754
E-mail: hudsonhornet@geocities.com

Founded 1986. 50 members. Must be member of National Hudson-Essex-Terraplane Club. Newsletter with free classifieds, 9-10 meetings per year including joint meets with other H-E-T Club chapters. Dues: $10/year. Web site: www.geocities.com/motorcity/downs/7192/index.html

Hupmobile Club Inc
158 Pond Rd
North Franklin, CT 06254
860-642-6697

Founded 1970. 600 members worldwide. Dedicated to the restoration, preservation and enjoyment of Hupmobiles, Hupp-Yeats and RCH automobiles. Publish *Hupp Herald* magazine, 3 times a year; *Hupmobile Parts Locator Bulletin*, bi-monthly. Dues: $20/year US and Canada, $25/year overseas (US funds).

Scout & International Motor Truck Association
PO Box 313
New Palestine, IN 46163
PH/FAX: 317-861-0495
E-mail: ihsimta@aol.com

Founded 1990. 1,100+ members. International Harvester trucks, pickups, Scouts. *International Happenings* magazine is published 6 times per year, features articles, member rigs, best buys, tech tips, member exchange. Dues: $30/year.

Iso & Bizzarrini Owners Club
2025 Drake Dr
Oakland, CA 94611
PH/FAX: 510-339-8347

Founded 1980. 200 members. Founded to promote the preservation and awareness of the marques. Membership includes quarterly magazine, *Griffon*, and bi-monthly newsletter, *Bresso Express*. No restrictions to join. Club sponsors meets and social gatherings, with an annual international meet at the Annual Monterey Historic Races. Dues: $35/year US, $45/year overseas.

Isuzu Trooper Owners Guild (ITOG)
26 Houston Dr
Pelham, AL 35124-2508
205-663-5800
E-mail: membership@itog.com

Founded 1995. 500+ members. The only worldwide owners group for all Isuzu built sport utility vehicles. Members receive ITOG sticker, ITOG lapel pin, 1 year subscription to *The ITOG Trooper* newsletter, discounts of 5-15% off genuine Isuzu and aftermarket parts and accessories and full access to our award winning web site. Dues: $15/year North America, $20/year world. Web site: www.itog.com

Jaguar Club of Connecticut
219 Greenwich Ave
New Haven, CT 06519
203-776-8148

Founded 1981. 135 members. No restrictions to join. Newsletter each month, *Purrings*. Events monthly. Dues: $20/year. Web site: http://welcome.to/thejaguarclubofct.com

Jaguar Clubs of North America Inc
Membership Dept
9685 McLeod Rd, RR 2
Chilliwack, BC Canada V2P 6H4
FAX: 604-794-3654
E-mail: parkhill@uniserve.com

Founded 1954. 5,500 members who belong to 51 local clubs in the US, Canada and Mexico which are affiliated with JCNA. JCNA sponsors championships in Concours d'Elegance, rally and slalom competition. The local clubs offer their own social, technical and other programs. Dues, which are paid to the local club, vary according to location and include JCNA membership, insurance and the bi-monthly *Jaguar Journal* magazine. Web site: www.jcna.com

chapters:

Arizona   *Jaguar Club of Central Arizona*, Howard Wolfley, 13810 N 50th St, Scottsdale, AZ 85254, 602-992-0662

Jaguar Club of Southern Arizona, Bob Keeler, 5721 N Paseo Niquel, Tucson, AZ 85718, 520-544-9280

California   *Classic Jaguar Assn*, Dr Robert Sutter MD, 1444 Key View, Corona Del Mar, CA 92625, 714-640-6722

Jaguar Associate Group, Bobby Yount, 5982 Post Oak Cir, San Jose, CA 95070-5403, 408-268-4508

Jaguar Owners Club/Los Angeles, Mark Mayuga, 5674 Magnolia Ave, Riverside, CA 92506, 909-328-9136

MAJORS, Steve Rege, 3425 Joanna Dr, Modesto, CA 95355, 209-529-6245

Sacramento Jaguar Club, John Kidwell, 3221 Kincaid Dr, Placerville, CA 95667, 916-621-2014

San Diego Jaguar Club, Norman C Bild, 344 Orange Ave, Coronado, CA 92118-1472, 619-435-0078

Colorado   *Rocky Mountain Jaguar Club*, Gary George, 2300 Linda Vista Dr, Lakewood, CO 80215-1263, 303-237-7031

Connecticut   *Jaguar Club of Southern New England*, Edward Messikian, 28 Mulcahy Dr, East Hartford, CT 06118, 860-568-5792

Florida   *Jaguar Clug of Florida*, Dan Middleton, 612 E Club Cir, Longwood, FL 32765, 407-774-0907

South Florida Jaguar Club, Richard Hartwell, 8730 NW 66th Ln, Parkland, FL 33067, 954-755-6945

Sun Coast Jaguar Club of Florida, Larry Ligas, 9082 66th St N, Pinellas Park, FL 33782, 727-545-1696

Illinois   *Jaguar Association of Greater Chicago*, Peter Fino, 21 W 180 N Ln, Tasca, IL 60143, 630-773-1096

Indiana   *Jaguar Assn Greater Indiana*, Steven L Jones, 8741 Bergeson Dr, Indianapolis, IN 46278, 317-875-5497

Kansas   *Great Plains Jaguar Owners Assn*, Jack Stamp, 606 N Brookfield, Wichita, KS 67206, 316-681-3045

Kentucky   *Jaguar Drivers Club Area 51*, Russel Phillips Jr, 3120 Grantham Way, Lexington, KY 40509, 606-263-2640

Louisiana   *Jaguar Club of New Orleans*, H Wayne Henry, 712 Ashland Dr, Pearl River, LA 70452, 504-863-3110

Michigan   *Jaguar Affiliates of Michigan*, John Brough, 3059 Mystic Valley Dr, White Lake, MI 48154, 248-684-6675

Missouri   *Heart of America Jaguar Club*, Dyle Wilson, 335 NW 36th Ave, Trenton, MO 64683, 660-856-6556

Jaguar Assn of Greater St Louis, Ray Unger, 8621 Lacelede Station Rd, St Louis, MO 63123, 314-849-8338

Nevada   *Greater Las Vegas Jaguar Club*, Chuck Plato, 10728 Esk Dr, Las Vegas, NV 89134, 702-233-5692

Reno Jaguar Club, Sam Dibitonto, 2301 Pioneer Dr, Reno, NV 89509, 702-826-5065

New Hampshire   *Jaguar Assn of New England*, David Roth, 180 Wheeler Rd, Hollis, NH 03049, 603-465-3787

New Jersey   *Jaguar Auto Group*, Paul A Delatush, 500 Old Dover Rd, Morris Plains, NJ 07950, 973-984-0422

New York   *Empire Division*, Charles Bordin, 9 Leatherstocking Ln, Scarsdale, NY 10583, 914-725-1274

Jaguar Aficio of Greater Buffalo, Cliff Schulz, 66 Patrice Terr, Williamsville, NY 14221, 716-634-7667

Jaguar Club of Central New York, Joanne Caslake, 1045 State Fair Blvd, Syracuse, NY 13209, 315-487-8276

Jaguar Drivers Club Long Island, Brian O'Keefe, 60 Curtis Pl, Bethpage, NY 11714, 516-433-8224

North Carolina   *Carolina Jaguar Club*, Dave Eckrote, 1443 Spring Hill Cir, Kernersville, NC 27284, 336-993-4740

Ohio   *Jaguar Assn of Central Ohio*, Eric Reindinger, 2201 Fernleaf Ln, Columbus, OH 43235, 614-766-5450

Jaguar Club of Ohio, Jon Krieger, 140 E Main St, Lexington, OH 44904, 419-884-0362

Oklahoma   *Central Oklahoma Jaguar Assn*, Mike Waldron, 2405 Colchester Dr, Edmond, OK 73034, 405-341-4117

Jaguar Club of Tulsa, Greg Timo, 11823 S 87th E Ave, Bixby, OK 74008, 918-369-5967

Oregon   *Jaguar Owners Club of Oregon*, Glen Enright, PO Box 2025, Beaverton, OR 97075, 503-538-8610

Pennsylvania   *Delaware Valley Jaguar Club*, Kurt Rappold, 116 Governor Markham Dr, Glen Mills, PA 19342-1033, 610-358-4055

Jaguar Club of Pittsburgh, Jack Terrick, 23 Shryll Hts, Greensburg, PA 15601, 412-837-7497

Jaguar Touring Club, Chris Acker, RR 1 Box 172-H, Montrose, PA 18801, 717-278-4159

South Carolina   *South Carolina Jaguar Society*, Barry Neil, 303 Bellerive Ln, Summerville, SC 29483, 843-832-8660

Texas   *Jaguar Club of Austin*, Rufus Coburn, 6509 Whitemarsh V Walk, Austin, TX 78746, 512-306-8195

Jaguar Club of Houston, Cleo Bay Jr, 407 Hickory Ridge, Seabrook, TX 77063, 281-244-0259

Jaguar Owners Assn of the Southwest, Steven Ward, 15818 Ranchita Dr, Dallas, TX 75248, 972-233-3738

San Antonio Jaguar Club, Bill Davis, 25211 Ada Mae, San Antonio, TX 78257, 210-698-1270

Utah   *Wasatch Mountain Jaguar*, John Green, PO Box 648, Farmington, UT 84025, 801-451-5776

Virginia   *National Capital Jaguar Owners Club*, Bruce Eisenhart, 15387 Twin Creeks Ct, Centreville, VA 22182, 703-802-4835

Jaguar Clubs of North America Inc chapters *(continued)*

Virginia Jaguar Club, Wayne Estrada, 1305 Rosecroft Rd, Richmond, VA 23229, 804-740-2957

Washington   *JDRC/NWA*, John Gleadle, 21726 NE 154th St, Woodinville, WA 98072, 425-788-1251

Wisconsin   *Wisconsin Jaguar Ltd*, Mike & Deb Korneli, 6236 Gilbert Cir, West Bend, WI 53095, 414-629-5314

Wisconsin Jaguar Ltd, Robert Budlow, 5320 Wind Point Rd, Racine, WI 53402, 414-639-1341

Canada   *Canadian XK Jaguar Register*, Edd Langelier, 12793 227B St, Maple Ridge, BC V2X 2Z4, 604-465-6506

Ontario Jaguar Owners Assn, Peter Harris, 8 Edenbridge Dr, Etobicoke, ON M9A 3E9, 416-233-2677

Ottawa Jaguar Club, Paul Davis, 1127 Albany Dr, Ottawa, ON K2C 2L1, 613-225-3449

Mexico   *Club Jaguar AC*, Benjamin Najar, Bosque de Duraznos #69-502, Bosques de las Lo 11700 DF, 01-525-596-8638

Association of Jensen Owners
140 Franklin Ave
Wyckoff, NJ 07481-3465
201-847-8549, 8 pm to 10 pm, EST
FAX: 201-847-8549, 9 am to 10 pm

Founded 1977. 800 members. No restricton. Communication with fellow Jensen owners; parts source; technical advice; *White Lady*, color publication, published quarterly; national meet annually. Dues: $40/year.

Jensen Interceptor Owners Club
PO Box 1572
Woodinville, WA 98072-1572
425-788-0507; FAX: 360-668-2003
E-mail: tdb@halcyon.com

Founded 1976. 500 members. *The Interceptor Premier* is published quarterly, international publication provides Jensen Interceptor owners with in depth technical articles and sources for parts and restoration. Dues: $25/year US, $35/year foreign. Web site: http://jioc.org

Jewett Owners Club
24005 Clawiter Rd
Hayward, CA 94545
510-785-1948

For membership information, contact at the above address: Terrell Shelley. Founded 1982. 30 members. Open to Jewett owners. Register of Jewett cars and clubs, parts, location and literature for all Jewett models. Information on request.

Kaiser Frazer Owner's Club International
PO Box 1014
Stroudsburg, PA 18360

Founded 1959. 1,800 members. Monthly news bulletin, quarterly magazine, various regional meets, annual national meet. Dues: $25/year US and Canada, $30/year foreign. Web site: http://members.tripod.com/~ben1937/kfoci.htm

The International King Midget Car Club
9409 W St Rt 571
Laura, OH 45337
PH/FAX: 937-698-5144
E-mail: katiekdot@aol.com or kmidgetcar@aol.com

Founded 1992. 200+ members. No restrictions to join. Benefits include meeting other King Midget owners and to preserve the history of the King Midget car. Publish 3 newsletters plus additional information throughout the year. There is an International King Midget Car Club Jamboree in August every year. Also, mini events such as parades or tours starting spring through fall. Dues: $15/year.

Kissel Kar Klub
147 N Rural St
Hartford, WI 53027
414-673-7999

For membership information, write to the above address. 197 members. Membership limited to owners of cars produced by the Kissel Motor Car Company, Hartford, WI (1906-1931), also to owners of their commercial vehicles including funeral cars, taxi cabs and fire trucks, and to personnel of the old company and family members who signify interest. Dues: none, donations accepted.

Lamborghini Owners' Club
Jim Kaminski
PO Box 7214
St Petersburg, FL 33734

Founded 1978. 1,000+ members. Oldest Lamborghini club in the world. Quarterly newsletter with technical tips, parts sources, meeting information, marque items for sale. Send for application form.

Dansk Lancia Register
Boserupvej 510
DK-3050 Humlebaek Denmark
PH/FAX: +45-49191129

Founded 1989. 80 members. Club for owners of Lancia cars. Technical aid and information. Rallies, meetings. Dues: 200 DKK/year.

Colorado Continental Convertible Club
385 S Olive Way
Denver, CO 80224-1354
PH/FAX: 303-322-2674
E-mail: wr77@com

Founded 1973. 60-75 members. Devoted to 1961-1967 Lincoln Continental 4-door convertibles. Anyone owning or interested in the 4-door convertibles is welcome. Trips, shows, parades, social functions, dealership displays and technical sessions. Publish bi-monthly *CCCC Comments*, included in membership. Information on club trips, shows, parades, social functions, members activities, technical tips, advertisement for persons or services for the cars, pictures of events and members and their cars. Dues: $25/year.

Lincoln and Continental Owners Club
PO Box 28788
Dallas, TX 75228-0788
800-527-3452, 972-709-6185
FAX: 972-296-7920

Founded 1953. Over 4,000 members. Dedicated to the enjoyment, preservation and restoration of all Lincolns and Continentals. Membership includes *Continental Comments* magazine, published bi-monthly. Three national meets annually. Dues: $30/year US, Canada and Mexico, $40/year other countries (US funds). Web site: www.lcoc.org

Lincoln Owners Club
PO Box 660
Lake Orion, MI 48361
248-693-4636

Organized in 1958. 500 members. Primarily interested in Lincolns built between 1920 and 1939, specifically models L, K, KA and KB. However, ownership of such a Lincoln is not necessary for membership, anyone interested in Lincolns is welcome. Dues: $25/year.

Lincoln Zephyr Owners Club
PO Box 422-H
Hazel Green, AL 35750
931-433-0065; FAX: 931-438-4742
E-mail: mead@vallnet.com

Founded 1968. 1,053 members. Bi-monthly issues of the award winning publication, *The Way of the Zephyr*. Western, central US and eastern meets each year, sites vary. Central and western chapters host regional events. Specializing in V12 engined Lincolns consisting of 1936-1948 Lincoln Zephyrs, 1941-1942 Lincoln Customs, 1940-1948 Lincoln Continentals. Dues: $29/year. Web site: http://personal.vallnet.com/lzoc

Road Race Lincoln Register (RRLR)
726 E Ind Pk Dr, #13
Manchester, NH 03109
603-666-4995

Founded 1972. 340 members. Must be interested in 1949-1957 Lincoln Premieres, Capris, Customs or Cosmopolitans and 1949-1951 "Baby" Lincolns on Mercury body shell, ownership not required. Publish a quarterly newsletter, *Viva Carrera*. Annual regional meets and have about 35 Canadian and overseas members. Dues: $19/year.

Club Elite (Lotus Type 14)
6238 Ralston Ave
Richmond, CA 94805-1519
PH/FAX: 510-232-7764

Founded 1971. 210 members. Open to any Lotus enthusiast. Annual register. Newsletters as available. Parts sources. Dues: $20/year US and Canada, $25/year foreign.

Lotus Ltd
PO Box L
College Park, MD 20741
PH/FAX: 301-982-4054
E-mail: lotusltd@lotuscarclub.org

Founded 1973. 1,500 members. The largest club for Lotus car enthusiasts in the US. The club is an entirely non-profit volunteer organization with over 13 affiliated local groups. Technical assistance. Monthly publication, *Lotus ReMarque*. Dues: $30/year new members, $20/year renewals in US, outside US add $5. Web site: www.lotuscarclub.org

Marmon Club
3044 Gainsborough Dr
Pasadena, CA 91107
626-449-2325

For membership information on Marmon and/or Roosevelt, contact at the above address: Duke Marston, Secretary. Founded 1970. 250 members. Annual directory of members and their Marmon and/or Roosevelt cars. Ownership not required for membership. Worldwide membership, bi-monthly publication. Dues: $20/year US, $25/year foreign (US funds, US bank).

The Maserati Club
PO Box 5300
Somerset, NJ 08875-5300
732-249-2177; FAX: 732-246-7570
E-mail: email@themaseraticlub.com

Founded 1986. 5,000 members. An international club with 4 US chapters and 1 Canadian chapter. Open to all Maserati enthusiasts. Publish *Il Tridente* quarterly magazine and hold over 35 events per year from New York to Denver and Toronto to Florida. Dues: $60/year. Web site: www.themaseraticlub.com

Maserati Owners Club of North America
14220 Saddlebow Ct
Reno, NV 89511
FAX: 702-853-7212
E-mail: rileysboss@worldnet.att.net

Founded 1979. 500 members. Club founded to benefit owners and the marque. Members receive technical information, parts info, quarterly newsletter, schedule of events, decals, patches, regalia, etc. Dues: $35/year.

Mazda Club
PO Box 11238
Chicago, IL 60611
773-769-6262; FAX: 773-769-3240
E-mail: mazdaclub@hotmail.com

For information, contact at the above address: Ernest Feliciano, President. Open to all Mazda owners including the RX-7, Miata, MX-6, 626 and MX-3. Technical advice, parts discounts and newsletters. Publication, *The Only Way*. Dues: $25/year. Web site: www.mazdaclub.com

Mazda RX-7 Club
1774 S Alvira St
Los Angeles, CA 90035
323-933-6993, 1 pm to 6 pm

Founded 1978. 1,400 members. A technical service club aimed at the enthusiast who does some of his own maintenance and would like to improve his RX-7 with performance and cosmetic accessories. Sample *Rotary Review*, $5. Dues: $30/year, $40/year foreign.

Miata Club of America
PO Box 2635
Alpharetta, GA 30023
770-205-8832; FAX: 770-205-8837
E-mail: svt@mindspring.com

Founded 1988. 25,000 members. No restrictions to join. *Miata Magazine*, 100 chapters and numerous events. Dues: $29/year US. Web site: www.miataclub.org

International 190SL Group Inc
3895 Bailey Ridge Dr
Woodbury, MN 55125
PH/FAX: 612-714-1211
E-mail: 190slgroup@mmm.pcc.org

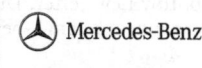

Founded 1983. 450 members. Bi-monthly newsletter, regional and national meets, technical support, camaraderie of other Mercedes 190SL enthusiasts. Dues: $30/year.

M-100 Group
4421 Greenville Ave
Dallas, TX 75206
PH/FAX: 214-368-3679
E-mail: hyattcheek@juno.com

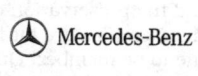

Founded 1991. 325 members. Dues: $30/year.

Mercedes-Benz 190SL Club e.V.
Wilfried Steer
Wittinger Strasse 154
29223 Celle Germany
05141-930190; FAX: 05141-381787

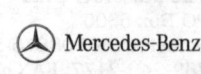

Founded 1989. 700 members. The club is specialized in the M-B 190SL type. We are accepted by the factory with worldwide memberships. At the moment we are organizing meetings, parts services (used and reproduction ones) and we do our own coloured magazine. Dues: DM120/year.

Mercedes-Benz 300SL Gullwing Group International
776 Cessna Ave
Chico, CA 95928
530-345-6701
E-mail: gestep3457@aol.com

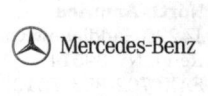

Founded 1961. 600 members. Open to owners of 300SL gull-wings and roadsters and those interested in them. Monthly publication *300 Star Letter*, tech tips, parts, projects, annual convention in different parts of US. Dues: $75/year US, $95/year Canada and foreign.

Mercedes-Benz Club of AmericaToronto Section
35 Birchcroft Rd
Etobicoke ON Canada M9A 2L5
PH/FAX: 416-233-6599
E-mail:
105601.1470@compuserve.com

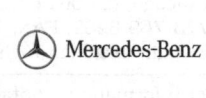

Founded 1990. 250 members. Must be an owner or have an interest in Mercedes-Benz and be a resident of Province of Ontario, Canada. Sections in Toronto and Ottawa, Ontario. Dues: $40/year US. Web site: www.themapleleafstar.com

Brewtown Cruisers Mercury Car Club
N21 W22139 Glenwood Ln
Waukesha, WI 53186
414-549-5646
E-mail: mercrews@aol.com

Founded 1980. 50 plus members. Open to all owners of 1949, 1950, 1951 Mercurys and Lincolns. Monthly meetings; annual show in May at The Nite Owl Drive-In; monthly newsletter, *Mercrews News*. Dues: $15/year.

Capri Club of Chicago
7158 W Armitage
Chicago, IL 60707
773-889-5197; FAX: 630-971-2875

For membership information, contact at the above address: Wayne H Tofel. Founded 1974. 45 members. Club functions include events, information and discounts for Capri owners. Monthly newsletter. Dues: $20/year. Web site: www.niagara.com/~bevc/ccc.htm

Carolina Cougar Club
5970 Fairview Rd, Ste 106
Charlotte, NC 28210
704-643-6430; FAX: 704-643-6425
E-mail: uscomm@bellsouth.net

Founded 1998. 28 members. Any family with an appreciation for and the preservation of the Mercury Cougar automobile. Memberships are for family members. You do not have to own one to be member. Quarterly publication, *Scratching Post,* is included in the membership. Publication has club meeting news, calendar of shows in the Carolina region, tech tips, letters from members. Dues: $10/year.

Chicagoland Mercury Club
PO Box 341
Crete, IL 60417
708-672-7864

Founded 1990. Membership still growing. To encourage appreciation of the Mercury motorcar. Dues: $20/year.

Cougar Club of America
Ron Crouch
1637 Skyline Dr
Norfolk, VA 23518

Founded 1980. 1,200 members. For enthusiasts of 1967-1973 Mercury Cougars. Quarterly publication. Dues: $25/year US, $30/year Canada and foreign.

CT Cougar Club
Richard Clark
75 Thayer Rd
Manchester, CT 06040
860-649-8520

Founded 1989. 40 members. Interest in or ownership of Mercury Cougars. Dedicated to the preservation of the 1967-1973 Mercury Cougar. Bi-monthly newsletters, cruises, meetings, picnics, rallies, car shows, swap meets and technical sessions. Dues: $12/year.

International Mercury Owners Association
6445 W Grand Ave
Chicago, IL 60707-3410
773-622-6445; FAX: 773-622-3602

Founded 1991. 950 members. Open to all Mercury enthusiasts. Quarterly publication, *Quicksilver*. Ads listed free to members (non-commercial). Dues: $35/year US and Canada, $40/year international.

Mercury Cyclone/Montego/Torino Registry
19 Glyn Dr
Newark, DE 19713-4016
302-737-4252 5 to 9:30 pm EST

Founded 1992. 120 members. This low key club registers all known 1964-1972 Cyclones, 1968-1974 Montegos and Torinos as well as 1970-1/2 Falcons. It doesn't matter if they are on the road or in a junkyard. Restoration help, classifieds, feature cars, history and info all put out in the *Registry Update,* 3 times per year. Specializing in 1970-1972 cars. Dues: $4/year. Web site: //home1.gte.net/76elite/index.html and/or now-online.com/cyclone

Mid-Century Mercury Car Club
1816 E Elmwood Dr
Lindenhurst, IL 60046
847-356-2255
E-mail:cruzinmerc@aol.com or
cwalter@kusd.kusd.edu

For more information, contact at the above address: Rusty Bethley. Founded 1977. 400 members. Ownership not required. Dedicated to the preservation of 1949-1951 Mercurys, custom or stock. Dues: $15/year US and Canada, $21/year foreign.

Metz Chain Gang
63 Commercial St
Honesdale, PA 18431
908-832-2186, NJ

Founded 1979. 100+ members. Interest in Metz cars only requirement. Ownership of a Metz vehicle a plus.

American MGB Association
PO Box 11401
Chicago, IL 60611-0401
800-723-MGMG, 773-878-5055
FAX: 773-769-3240
E-mail: info@mgclub.org

For membership information, contact at the above address: Frank Ochal, President. Founded 1975. 3,000 members. Open to MG owners and enthusiasts. North America's official registry for MGBs, MG Midgets, MGB/GT V8s and MG 1100/1300s. Publication, *AMGBA Octagon*. Dues: $30/year. Web site: www.mgclub.org

Central Ohio MG Owners
10260 Covan Dr
Westerville, OH 43082-9295
614-882-6191

Founded 1983. 185 members. A group of MG enthusiasts who welcome participation of all MG owners. The club encourages the preservation and driving of MGs and the opportunity to enjoy the friendship of other families involved in the hobby. Several events are held each year including tours, car shows, picnics and an annual Christmas party. A newsletter is published 5 times a year to keep members informed. Initiation fee, $3. Dues: $5/year.

Connecticut MG Club
240 New Harwinton Rd
Torrington, CT 06790
860-482-MGMG
E-mail: woofmg@snet.net

Founded 1987. 300+ members. Need to own or have an interest in MGs. Monthly newsletter, annual car show first Sunday in June for British cars, monthly meeting, various events throughout the year. Dues: $20/year.

Eastern New York MGA Club
Jon Rubel, President
3010 Avenue T
Brooklyn, NY 11229-4008
718-891-5776; FAX: call first
E-mail: eemgee@aol.com

Founded 1990. 100+ members. Club serves the entire MG community including MGTs, MGAs, MGBs, MGCs and MG Midgets in the New York, Long Island, New Jersey, Pennsylvania and Connecticut area. Award winning 40-page newsletter with full color pages is printed bi-monthly. Club hosts all British marque car shows, an annual gymkhana, superb tech sessions all through the winter months, picnics, an annual Winterfest dinner and more. Dues: $20/year.

Emerald Necklace MG Register
PO Box 81152
Cleveland, OH 44181
330-678-9394
E-mail: enmgr@sssnet.com

Founded 1980. 230 members. Serving the northern Ohio area and open to all MG enthusiasts. Monthly newsletter, tech sessions, rallies, special events and support for those who are octagonally inclined. Dues: $20/year.

Florida Suncoast MG Car Club
PO Box 0251
Tampa, FL 33601-0251

Founded 1980. 200 members. A social club organized to promote the knowledge, understanding and preservation of the MG. The club has monthly meetings, organizes a full calendar of car related activities, charitable endeavors, inter-club events, and publish a monthly newsletter. Membership is open to all MG car owners and individuals interested in the MG motor car. Dues: $20/year. Web site: http://members.aol.com/fsmgcc

MG Car Club Central Jersey Centre
PO Box 435
Convent Station, NJ 07961
973-267-3630; FAX: 973-731-0370
E-mail: swag11@worldnet.att.net

Founded 1963. 150 members. Call phone number listed for further information regarding time and place of monthly meetings, scheduled activities, etc. Dues include monthly newsletter, *Meshing Gears*. Dues: $20/year. Web site: www.geocities.com/~mgcarclub/

The MG Car Club Ltd
Kimber House, PO Box 251
Abingdon, Oxon, OX14 1FF England
01235-555552; FAX: 01235-533755
E-mail: mgcc@mgcars.org.uk

Founded 1930. Open to owners of all models of MGs. Operate throughout the world through 85 local chapters.

chapters:

California	*Abingdon Rough Riders*, A J Chalmers, 1231 12th Ave, San Francisco, CA 94122
	Long Beach, PO Box 8515, Long Beach, CA 90808-0515
	MG Owners, George Steneberg Jr, 9 Pomona Ave, El Cerrito, CA 94530
	Sacramento Valley, PO Box 2511, Fair Oaks, CA 95628
	TC Motoring Guild, PO Box 3452, Van Nuys, CA 91407
	Vintage MG Club of Southern California, Bob Zwart, 9 Redonda, Irvine, CA 92720-1955, 714-730-8140
Colorado	*Rocky Mountain Centre*, August Burgoon, 6467 S Brentwood Way, Littleton, CO 80123
Connecticut	*Southern Connecticut*, Joanne Raymond, 12 Old Redding Rd, West Redding, CT 06896
Florida	*Florida*, Jerome P Keuper, PO Box 394, Melbourne Beach, FL 32951
Georgia	*Peachtree MG Registry Ltd*, Esther Cooper, 130 Raymond Ct, Fayetteville, GA 30214, 770-460-9320
	Southeastern MG T-Register, Don Harmer, 3926 Harts Mill Ln, Atlanta, GA 30319
Illinois	*Chicagoland MGB Club*, James Evans, PO Box 455, Addison, IL 60101
	North American MGB Register, PO Box MGB, Akin, IL 62805, 800-626-4271 or 618-439-6464 outside US or Canada
Indiana	*MGA Twin Cam Registry*, Lyle York, 5105 Kingswood Ln, Anderson, IN 46011
Maryland	*MGs of Baltimore*, Richard G Liddick, 5237 Glen Arm Rd Glen Arm, Baltimore, MD 21057, 410-817-6862
Michigan	*Western Michigan OSH MGCC*, c/o John E Leese, 2129 Deer Hollow Dr SE, Grand Rapids, MI 49508
	Windsor-Detroit MGCC, Dan Bebaran, 1327 Austin, Lincoln Park, MI 48146-2002, 313-382-6715

The MG Car Club Ltd chapters *(continued)*

Missouri   *MGCC of St Louis*, 412 Glenmeadow, Balwin, MO 63011-3423

New York   *MG Car Club Long Island Centre*, c/o Blackwell, 177 Truberg Ave, North Patchogue, NY 11772, 516-475-2889

New York/Connecticut Chapter of NEMGTR, 4 The Circle, Warwick, NY 10990

Western New York, George R Herschell, 1286 Mill Creek Run, Webster, NY 14580

North Carolina   *American MGC Register*, Tom Boscarino, 19 R Mrton Ln, Asherville, NC 28806, PH/FAX: 828-258-0499; E-mail: tomb@main.nc.us

Metrolina MGCC, 320 Harvard Dr, Albemarle, NC 28001

North Carolina MGCC, Paul Linney, PO Box 12273, Raleigh, NC 27605

Ohio   *North American MMM Register*, Tom Metcalf, Registrar, Woodlands Cottage 1475 Township Rd 853, Ashland, OH 44805-4439, 419-289-6241

Southwestern Ohio, PO Box 32 Dabel Branch, Dayton, OH 45420

South Carolina   *British Motor Owners Club SE*, William W Sapp, PO Box 1274, Gramling, SC 29438

Texas   *Houston MGCC*, PO Box 441-1241, Houston, TX 77244-1241

Texas MG Register, c/o Kurt Miller, 2408 Emerald Cir, Southlake, TX 76092-3302

Washington   *Northwest*, PO Box 84284, Seattle, WA 98124-5584, 206-367-3512

Wisconsin   *Milwaukee Great Lakes MG Motorcar Group*, Wayne F Chandler, 11713 W Oxford Pl, Milwaukee, WI 53226

Australia   *Gold Coast MG Car Club Inc*, PO Box 1018 Southport, Queensland 4215

MGCC Canberra Inc, PO Box 600, Dickson ACT 2602

MGCC Geelong Inc, PO Box 296, Geelong 3220, Victoria

MGCC Hunter Reagion Inc, PO Box 503, Wallsend NSW 2287

MGCC Newcastle Inc, PO Box 62A, Newcastle NSW 2300

MGCC of New South Wales, GPO Box 5165, Sydney NSW 2001

MGCC of South Australia, 93 Chief St, Brompton SA 5007

MGCC of Tasmania Inc, GPO Box 5A, Hobart, Tasmania 7001

MGCC of Wagga Wagga Inc, PO Box 319, Kooringal NSW 2650

MGCC of Western Australia Inc, PO Box U1924 GPO, Perth WA 6001

MGCC Sunshine Coast Inc, PO Box 683 Buderim, Queensland 4556, E-mail: paulvangool@ozemail.com.au

MGCC Victoria, GPO Box 1989S, Melbourne 3001

Belgium   *MGCC Antwerp*, Guido Van Der Burgh, Van Den Berghelaan, B-2630 Aartselaar

MGCC Belgium, D Prove, Romain Clausstraat 17, 9041 Oostakker, 00-329-251-3525

Canada   *MGCC of Toronto*, Keith Holdsworth, PO Box 64 Station R, Toronto, ON M4G 3Z3, 416-410-5464; E-mail: keithh1@globalserve.net

North American MGA Register, Len Bonnay, 538 Alan Ave, Welland, ON L3C 2Y9

Czech Republic   *MGCC Czech Republic*, Radek Pelc, Palonky 608, 25301 Praha-Hostivice, 02-900-28-444; E-mail: rpelc@sun1.biomed.cas.cz

Denmark   *MGCC Danish Centre*, Peter Clausen, Ved Fortunen 1, DK 2800 Lyungby, 45-20-84-67-86

MGCC Danish Centre West, Soren Martin Soresen, Dyregard Overbyvej 13 As, 7130 Juelsminde, FAX: 45-75-69-02-11+

Finland   *MGCC Finland*, Tomi Lundell, Silvasti Stenbackinkatu 6 B 33, 00250 Helsinki, 358-50-5151038

France   *MGCC France*, Christoph Fleurent, Residence Le Belvedere 8 allee Sylvestre, 78250 Nievlan, 01-34-78-14-00

Germany   *MGCC Germany*, Norbert Lange, Klewerkoppel 20, 22335 Hamburg, 040-53-11-303

Holland   *MG T-Type Holland*, Siegrid Zwanenburg, Lange Uitwe 73, 3999 WK Tull en 't Waal

Ireland   *MGCC Eire*, Fred Lewis, Pineridge, Kilgobbin Rd, Stepaside, Co Dublin, 00353-129-56183

Italy   *MGCC Italy*, Fabio Filippello, Via Accademia dei Virtuosi 22, 00147 Roma, 0039-0330-626190; FAX: 0039-06-5940557; E-mail: mgcarclub@mclink.it

Luxembourg   *MGCC Luxembourg*, Ton Maathuis, 1 Rue Tomm, L-9454 Fouhren, 00352-834573

Netherlands   *MGA Type Owners Holland*, Theo Blankestijn, Burg v/d Boschlaan 37, 3956 DB Leersum, 31-343-45-29-90

MGCC Holland, Carrien Andriessen, Weena 290, 3012 NJ Rotterdam, 00-31-318-515-483 after 6 pm

New Zealand   *MGCC Auckland Inc*, PO Box 6483 Wellesley St, Auckland 1

MGCC Canterbury Centre Inc, PO Box 1775, Christchurch

MGCC Wellington Centre Inc, PO Box 3135, Wellington

Norway   *MGCC Norway*, Engveien 20, N-0487 Oslo

Portugal   *MGCC Portugal*, Luis Miguel, C DA Cunha TV Fabrica dos Pentes 17, R/C DTO 1250 Lisboa, 000-3511-38-30-791

Spain   *MGCC Catalunya Spain*, Josep Oriola, Bailen 15 08037, Barcelona, 93-459-46-97

Sweden   *MGCC Sweden*, Jan Borgfelt, Vasbystrandsvagen 38, S-184 95 Ljustero, ++46-435-770371

Switzerland   *MGCC Switzerland*, Wim Jetten, Postfach 346, CH-4021 Basel, 41-55-412-37-34

MG Car Club Ltd
Washington DC Centre
PO Box 6321
Arlington, VA 22206
703-207-9048
E-mail: schooler@erols.com

Founded 1951, incorporated in Washington DC, 1953. 215 members. One of the oldest US centres of the MG Car Club Ltd, UK. Membership open to all MG enthusiasts (MG ownership not a prerequisite). Host 35 events annually, they include: tech sessions, rallies, gymkhanas, caravans, membership meetings, car shows, etc. Publish *The Spark*, a 12-page club newsletter monthly. All events are free to members. Dues: $25/year. Web site: http://members.aol.com/mgccwdcc

MG Classics of Jacksonville
227 Hollywood Forest Dr
Orange Park, FL 32073
904-264-3676; FAX: 904-771-6871
E-mail: nwnel@mediaone.net

Founded 1971. 100+ members. Full membership restricted to owners of MG automobiles. Monthly meetings, monthly newsletter, car shows, tours, driving events. Sponsor the "Gathering of the Faithful South" every third year in Florida. Dues: $25/year.

MG Drivers Club
18 George's Pl
Clinton, NJ 08809-1334
PH/FAX: 908-713-6251
E-mail: marfmil@hotmail.com

Founded 1997. First US/Canada wide club open to all types of MGs. Open to anyone interested in the MG marque. Supporting existing registers and associations. Strong voice for car hobbyist rights. Discounts from major British car parts suppliers. Annual gathering, "The Drive-In". Expert technical advice. Our quarterly publication, *The Log Book*, covers all aspects of the MG marque, past, present and future as well as club news. Dues: $20/year. Web site: www.mgclub.com

MG Octagon Car Club
Unit 19, Hollins Business Centre
Rowley St
Stafford ST16 2RH England
01785 251014; FAX: 01785 248386

For membership information, contact at the above address: Harry Crutchley. Founded 1969. 2,200 members. Open to all, but full membership is given only to owners of pre-1956 MGs, so that we can give more personal service to our members. Dues: $42/year.

MG Vintage Racers Newsletter
Mark Palmer, Editor
253 Bridlepath Rd
Bethlehem, PA 18017
FAX: 610-954-9489

Founded 1981. 200 members. Must actively race a vintage MG (up to 1967) to join. Publish newsletter which consists of technical articles, letters, member profiles, competition reports, parts sources and race schedules. Fax or write for details. Joining fee: $10. Web site: www.geocities.com/motorcity/speedway/3282/mgvr.html

New England MG T Register Ltd
PO Drawer 220
Oneonta, NY 13820
607-432-6835; FAX: 607-432-334

For membership information, contact at the above address: Richard L Knudson. Founded 1963. 4,000 members. Regular membership is open only to owners of 1955 or older MGs powered by original type engine; all others may become associate members. Our bimonthly journal, *The Sacred Octagon*, is regard-

ed as the best source of MG historical material in the world. Dues: $35/year, plus $15 initiation fee. Web site: www.nemgt.org

North American MGA Register
(NAMGAR)
PO Box 11746
Albuquerque, NM 87192-0746
505-293-9085; FAX: 505-332-3116

Founded 1975. Over 2,000 members. Annual get-together, usually in July. Local chapters and meets. Bi-monthly magazine, *MGA!*. Parts sources, tech tips, includes Twin Cams, Magnettes, MGA powered variants. Dues: $25/year US, $40/year foreign. Web site: http://members.aol.com/namgarusa/mg.htm

The Philadelphia MG Club
1913-D Darby Rd
Havertown, PA 19083-2407
610-446-2073
E-mail: mgbgti@hotmail.com

Founded 1980. 100 members. No restrictions. Participate in car shows, road rallies (spring and fall MG vs Triumph rallies), tech sessions and car museum trips. Sponsor the MGs at Mercer British car show in October and have an annual Octagonal Holiday dinner in December. Publish a monthly newsletter, *The Nuffield News*. Dues: $20/year.

Central New York
Mopar Association
PO Box 3451
Syracuse, NY 13220-3451
315-638-1959; FAX: 315-699-9780
E-mail: gigawatt1@att.net

Founded 1988. 150 members. Monthly newsletter, annual car show to benefit National Marrow Donor program, spring and fall picnic, monthly meeting, cruises, etc. Member must like Mopars and have fun. Dues: $20/year. Web site: www.homestead.com/centralnewyorkmopar/main.html

The Coastal Empire Mopar Club
1432 Fort Argyle Rd
Savannah, GA 31419
912-748-2986
E-mail: mikeF17767@aol.com

Founded 1989. 15 members. Must own a Mopar product, annual car show for benefits, monthly newsletter, cruise-ins, monthly meetings, shows and events. Attend other shows and Mopar related events as a club within our region. Dues: $15/year.

Freddie Beach Mopars
1834 Woodstock Rd
Fredericton, NB Canada E3C 1L4
506-450-9074; FAX: 506-459-0708
E-mail: vallise@city.fredericton.nb.ca

Founded 1988. Prospective members must own or have an interest in any Mopar or AMC. Quarterly newsletter. Chyrco Muscle Show and Shine, every Father's Day weekend; Thunder on Freddie Beach, every Labor Day (Sunday); every Wednesday evening is Cruise to the Mall night from June-August. Dues: $20/year Canadian.

The Hoosier Mopar Association
PO Box 1892
Valparaiso, IN 46384
219-988-2493

Founded 1993. 136 members. Must own or have interest in classic Mopars (Chrysler, Dodge, Plymouth, Jeeps and AMCs). Monthly newsletter of club activities. Monthly meetings 3rd Tuesday of each month, 7 pm, Al's Diner, Valparaiso, IN. Mopar car show (swap and crafts), 2nd Saturday in September, 49er Drive-In. Dues: $24/year.

Lake Erie Tri-State Mopar
PO Box 35
Westfield, NY 14787
814-899-6732
E-mail: sl6jack@aol.com

Founded 1986. 90 members. Restrictions: own or have interest in Chrysler (Mopars) 1924-1993. Big car show and swap meet annually, monthly meeting or event, except winter. Bi-monthly newsletter. Dues: $20/year.

Mid-America E-body Mopar Club
PO Box 418
Onawa, IA 51040
712-423-2134; FAX: 712-423-2411
E-mail: ebodies@willinet.net

Founded 1998. 17 members. Open to owners and enthusiasts of 1970-1974 Plymouth Barracuda, Gran Coupe, Cuda, AAR and Dodge Challenger, SE, R/T, T/A models. Hope to have regional E-body meets in the future. Offer technical and restoration assistance. Publish *Broadcast Sheet* bi-monthly, includes member's features, detailing, restoration, technical tips, event coverage, production facts, historical information, etc. Dues: $25/year. Web site:
http://members.wbs.net/homepages/c/u/d/cudachallengerclub.html.

Mighty Mopars of Orlando
8956 Cherrystone Ln
Orlando, FL 32825-6427-46
407-282-1632
E-mail: gbarg@mpinet.net

Founded 1991. 150+ members. Must be a Mopar enthusiast. Multiple discounts; monthly newsletter; monthly cruise-in; spring parts extravaganza; fall Mopar car show; monthly family events. Dues: $15/year.
Web site: www.geocities.com/motorcity/flats/4561

Mopar Alley
2409 Villanueva Way
Mountain View, CA 94040
408-296-8186; FAX: 650-565-7931
E-mail: admin@moparalley.org

Founded 1990. 180 members. Monthly meetings and newsletter. Member discounts at select businesses. Yearly show and swap meet. Cruises and other events throughout the year. Dues: $25/year. Web site: www.moparalley.org

**Mopars Unlimited
Northwest Chapter**
PO Box 527
Burlington, WA 98233
360-422-7131; FAX: 360-755-9242

Founded 1984. 35 members. No restrictions to join, just need to show an interest in Mopars. Bi-monthly newsletter, discount car insurance, 10% discount at Year One, parts at cost plus 10% Tom Matson Dodge. Dues: $20/year.

Mr Norm's Sport Club
15774 S LaGrange Rd Suite 256
Orland Park, IL 60462-4766
905-508-0772; FAX: 905-508-0773
E-mail: sportclub@mrnorms.com

Founded 1963. Own, have owned or love Mopars? Here is your opportunity to return to the excitement of the muscle car era. Be a founding member of Mr Norm's Sport Club. When you join you receive a member exclusive shirt, sticker, card and a bi-monthly magazine filled with tech and how-to topics as well as nostalgic facts and photos. Members receive discounts on many parts, accessories, services and apparel from all the best Mopar related resources in North America. Dues: $29.95/year US. Web site: www.mrnorms.com

Northeast Mighty Mopar Club
19 Treasure Island Rd
Plainville, MA 02762
508-695-1583
E-mail: plymthpaul@aol.com

Founded 1984. 680 members. Must own or be a fan of Mopar, any year Mopars welcome. The club puts on at least one Mopar only show in each of the northeast states we cover. The club puts on a two day Mopar show, swap, banquet at a hotel in CT in August. Membership includes 6 newsletters (8 pages each) and a T-shirt. Dues: $25/year, $15/year renewal. Web site: http://members.aol.com/plymthpaul

Northern Mopars Auto Club
4416 16A St SW
Calgary AB Canada T2T 4L5
403-287-0765; FAX: 403-287-6787
Hemi Bob e-mail:
hemibob@shaw.wave.ca
Mark Levorson e-mail:
northern@mopars.org

Founded 1986. 285 members. For all Mopar enthusiasts (AMC, Dodge, Plymouth, Chrysler, DeSoto, etc). Bi-monthly newsletter containing a buy/sell, wanted section, free to members. Yearly show and swap (10th annual show August 14, 1999, Calgary, Alberta, Canada). Dues: $25/year Canadian. Web site: www.mopars.org

Power & Speed Racing Promotions
3612 W 50th
Fairway, KS 66205
913-831-9754; FAX: 913-831-0291
E-mail: mardi33@hotmail.com

Founded 1985. 400+ members. Open to Mopar enthusiasts. 2 shows a year, monthly cruise, 15th annual car show, June 12th and 13th; 13th annual show, race, swap and road course racing, September 25th and 26th at Heartland Park, Topeka, over 600 cars and 150 swap in 1998. Bi-monthly newsletter. Dues: $15/year. Web site: www.powerandspeed.com

**Winged Warriors/National B-body
Owner's Association (NBOA)**
216 12th St
Boone, IA 50036
515-432-3001, IA; 703-893-9370, VA
E-mail: hemi@willinet.net

Founded 1975. 500 members. Open to all 1962-1974 B-body performance Mopars, specializing in Daytonas, Superbirds and 1969 Charger 500s. Ownership is not required for membership. Knowledgeable staff of advisors to provide technical and restoration information to members. Monthly newsletter. Free classified ad section for members. Dues: $25/year US, $30/year outside US. Web site: www.superbird.com/wingedwarriors

Wisconsin Mopar Muscle Club
Bruce E Hinrichs
4210 Shawano Ave
Green Bay, WI 54313-7527
920-865-7447; FAX: 920-592-2188
E-mail: mr64dodge@sprynet.com

Founded 1981. 100+ members. Any make, model, year Mopar. Monthly newsletter, half-price at events to members, 3 shows and 2 swap meets annually, membership card, collectibles. Dues: $25/year. Web site: home.sprynet.com/sprynet/mr64dodg

WPC Club Inc
PO Box 3504
Kalamazoo, MI 49003-3504
FAX: 616-375-5535
E-mail: wpc@pacificcoast.net

Non-profit corporation dedicated to the preservation and enjoyment of Plymouth, Dodge, Chrysler, DeSoto, Imperials and related cars. *WPC News* is a monthly publication with feature articles and want/sale ads, plus other features. Subscription: $25/year, $29/year foreign. Web site: www.pacificcoast.net/~wpc/

See our ad on this page

regions:

Arizona   *Grand Canyon Region*, Gary Kuhstoss, President, PO Box 5537, Glendale, AZ 85312-5537

California   *Inland Empire Region*, Ed Powley, President, 11917 Cactus Ave, Bloomington, CA 92316-3802

Orange County Region, Howard Doering, President, 9682 Blanche Ave, Garden Grove, CA 92841

San Diego Region, Jim Jensen, President, PO Box 420, El Cajon, CA 92022-0420

San Fernando Valley Region, Aaron Kahlenberg, President, PO Box 57564, Sherman Oaks, CA 91413-2564

Colorado   *Rocky Mountain Region*, Wayne Maddox, President, 10755 E Dorado Ave, Englewood, CO 80111

Florida   *Florida West Coast Region*, Ralph Brueggeman, President, 145 Garman Ave, Davenport, FL 33837-9595

Sunshine State Region, Robert Good, President, 40020 Briarwood, Umatilla, FL 32784

Illinois   *Northern Illinois Region*, Guy Morice, President, 22 Eagle View Ln, Oswego, IL 60543

Michigan   *Great Lakes Region*, Pete Williams, President, 15561 Sherwood Ln, Fraser, MI 48026

West Michigan Region, Bob Toothman, President, 611 2nd St, Plainwell, MI 49080

Minnesota   *10,000 Lakes Region*, Bruce Knapp, President, 3212 Kentucky Ave S, Saint Louis Park, MN 55426-3419

Nebraska   *Greater Omaha Region*, Gail Hunt, President, 7701 Pacific St #215, Omaha, NE 68114

Nevada   *Silver State Region*, William Borton, President, PO Box 98019, Las Vegas, NV 89193-8019

New Jersey   *Garden State Region*, Don Piscitelli, President, 265 Hillcrest Rd, Boonton, NJ 07005

New Mexico   *New Mexico Region*, William B Fisher, President, 1521 Van Cleave Rd NW, Albuquerque, NM 87107

North Carolina   *Carolina Chrysler Club*, R David Lahr, President, 11410 April Day Ln, Charlotte, NC 28226

Ohio   *North Coast Region*, Eric Poti, President, 8626 Avery Rd, Broadview Heights, OH 44147

Oregon   *Columbia River Region*, Jeffrey Locke, President, 9308 SE Pardee, Portland, OR 97266

Pacific Wonderland Region, Tom Fox, President, 19305 SW Madeline St, Aloha, OR 97007-2912

Pennsylvania   *Liberty Bell Region*, Bruce Foelker, President, 918 N Broad St, Allentown, PA 18102

Tennessee   *Tennessee Valley Region*, Mike Bennett, President, PO Box 345, Hixson, TN 37343-0345

Texas   *Houston Region*, Gary P Hamel, President, 6914 Dillon St, Houston, TX 77061-3826

North Texas Region, Ken Angyal, 2905 Natches, Arlington, TX 76014

Texas Region, Bill Roberson, President, 225 N Santa Clara Rd, Marion, TX 78124-9747

Utah   *Great Salt Lake Region*, Richard E Stephens, President, 1042 E Cambridge, Kaysville, UT 84037

Washington   *Puget Sound Region*, Rob Baker, President, 18126 191st SW, Woodinville, WA 98072

Wisconsin   *Wisconsin Region*, Vince Doyle, President, 3155 Debra Ln, Racine, WI 53403

Canada   *Vancouver Island Region*, Mike Davies, President, 1151 Heald Ave, Victoria, BC V9A 5I7

Section Three
Clubs & Organizations

WPC Club Inc regions *(continued)*

Great Britain   *Chrysler Corp Club UK*, Peter Grist, President, 30 Purbrook Close Lordswood, Southampton, Hampshire S016 5NZ

Norway   *Norway Region*, Tor Elgil Danielson, President, Postboks 57, Bekkelaget, 0137 Oslo 1

Sweden   *Sweden Region*, Bo Bengtsson, President, c/o Stefan Farkas Sagdalsvandan 15, S-136 72 Haninge

Morgan Car Club, Washington DC
616 Gist Ave
Silver Spring, MD 20910
301-585-0121

Founded 1959. 325 members. No restrictions to join. Gathering of Morgan enthusiasts with frequent meetings, events, competitions, worldwide communications and historical files. Monthly publication, *The Rough Rider*. Dues: $25/year. Web site: www.morgandc.org

Morgan Motor Car Club
PO Box 50392
Dallas, TX 75250-0392
214-321-1648
E-mail: wmj3@airmail.net

Founded 1975. 50+/- members. No membership restrictions. Club activities center around interest in the Morgan automobile. Publish a monthly newsletter called the *Mog Log*. Participate in approximately 11 meetings and 7 social events annually. Dues: $20/year.

Morgan Three-Wheeler Club
W C Towner
56 Brick Hill Rd
Orleans, MA 02653
508-255-6432 eves
FAX: 508-255-9393

For membership information, contact at above address: Chris Towner. Founded 1947. 700+ members worldwide. Membership offers monthly bulletin, tech information, spares and other assistance.

Morgan Three-Wheeler Racing
138 Bridgeview Dr
San Francisco, CA 94124
415-824-2508; FAX: 415-954-4203
E-mail: redandrose@aol.com

Founded 1997. Information provided to other owners of Morgan Trikes to encourage racing in pre-war classes at tracks in the US. Dues: none.

Metropolitan Owners Club of North America
5009 Barton Rd
Madison, WI 53711
608-271-0457

Founded 1975. 2,500 members. Open to all Metropolitan enthusiasts and owners. National, regional and chapter meets. Monthly newsletter, *The Met Gazette*. Dues: $15/year, $27/2 years, $39/3 years, $200 lifetime; international rates in US dollars only: $22/year, $40/2 years, $60/3 years, $275 lifetime.

chapters:

Arizona   *Arizona*, Nancy Gnepper, 2520 W Chiricuaha, New River, AZ 85027

Arkansas   *Arkansas Razorbacks*, Robert Wade, 706 SW 3rd St, Bryant, AR 72022

California   *Central Valley (CA)*, Jim Shoemaker, 704 Ramona Ave, Modesto, CA 95350

Greater Bay Area Mets, Brian Cotariu, 17538 Garland Ct, Castro Valley, CA 94546

Greater San Diego Metropolitan Club, Karen Hughes, 4321 Maryland St, San Diego, CA 92103

Colorado   *Rocky Mountain Mets*, Suzanne & Roger Miller, 845 S Geneva St, Denver, CO 80231

Georgia   *Georgia Peach Met Club*, Arlan Zimmerman, 182 Jackson Rd SE, Milledgeville, GA 31061

Illinois   *Illini Mets*, Rita Bulow, 5213 W 105th St, Oaklawn, IL 60453

Indiana   *Hoosier Mets*, Bill Wood, 1200 W 300 N, Anderson, IN 46011

Kansas   *Central Kansas Metropolitan Club*, Ben Love, 4144 W 11th St, Wichita, KS 67212

Nash Met Club of Northeast Oklahoma, Frank Brewster, 219 S Penn, Independence, KS 67301

Kentucky   *Derby City Metropolitan Car Club (KY)*, Ralph Coultas, 3523 Huon Dr, Louisville, KY 40218

Maryland   *Maryland Metropolitan Club*, Tom Thompson, 2121 Cox Rd, Jarretsville, MD 21084

Massachusetts   *Yankee Mets (CT, ME, MA, NH, RI, VT)*, Paul A Meyers, PO Box 255, Hinsdale, MA 01235

Minnesota   *Mets From Minnesota Inc*, Jerry Christensen, 3810 Sheridan Ave N, Minneapolis, MN 55412

Missouri   *Unforgettable MO-Mets*, Wayne B Chapin, PO Box 466, Mt Vernon, MO 65712

Nebraska   *Midwest Mets*, John M Christ, 2341 S 35th St, Omaha, NE 68105

New Jersey   *The Metropolitan Mets (NY, NJ, CT)*, Chris Custin, 54 Chestnut Dr, Wayne, NJ 07470

New York   *Upstate New York Mets*, Leonard Hass Jr, 6366 Co Rt 4, Central Square, NY 13036

Ohio   *Buckeye Mets (Northern Ohio)*, Rose Kerekes, 1444 Parkhaven Row, Lakewood, OH 44107

Oregon   *Columbia-Willamette*, Dan Beltrami, 53055 SE Sylvan Dr, Sandy, OR 97055

Pennsylvania   *Glad We Met (Northwestern PA)*, Kent Mowery, 245 Beachgrove Dr, Erie, PA 16505

Metropolitan Motoring Club (PA), Les Keller, 225 W Main St, Annville, PA 17003

Tri-State Chapter (PA, DE, NJ), Sam Getty, 743 Agnes Ave, Rutledge, PA 19070

Texas   *Tex-Mets*, Ron Taylor, 3404 Sheffield Dr, Arlington, TX 76013

Virginia   *Old Dominion Metropolitan Club*, Bill Green, 295 Queens Lace Rd, Mechanicsville, VA 23111

Washington   *Pacific Northwest (WA, ID, AK, BC)*, Bobbie Woodruff, 2615 Delameter Rd, Castle Rock, WA 98611

Wisconsin   *Met Set (WI)*, Jerry Traeder, 8665 Rae Ct, Greendale, WI 53129

Canada   *BC Mets*, Joanne McDonald, PO Box 36, Fort Langley, BC V1M 2R4

Manitoba Metropolitan Car Club of Canada, Bob Pope, 7 Berens St, Winnipeg, MB R2C 2R4

The NSU Club of America
717 N 68th St
Seattle, WA 98103
206-784-5084

For membership information, contact at the above address: Jim Sykes. Quarterly 20+ page booklet. Dues: $15/year.

NSU Enthusiasts USA
c/o Terry Stuchlik
2909 Utah Pl
Alton, IL 62002
618-462-9195

Founded 1971. 100 members. Quarterly newsletter containing 24-28 pages. Annual meeting and occasional regional meetings. Dues: $15/year.

Oakland Owners Club International
767 McCoy Rd
Franklin Lakes, NJ 07417
201-337-1996; FAX: 201-847-4374
E-mail: norman_j_hutton@bd.com

Founded 1998. 20 members. Dedicated to the preservation, restoration and exhibition of all Oakland motor cars built by GM between 1907-1931, as well as the Oakland Highwheeler manufactured by the Oakland Ironworks of California. *The Oaklander* publication is sent bi-monthly. The only prerequisite for membership is the love of Oakland motor cars. Dues: $20/year US, $25/year international.

Curved Dash Oldsmobile Club
3455 Florida Ave N
Minneapolis, MN 55427
612-533-4280; FAX: 612-535-1421
E-mail: cdoclub@black-hole.com

Founded 1977. 400 members. Open to owners of 1901-1907 curved dash and other one-cylinder Oldsmobiles. Offers assistance in the proper restoration and reprints of historical documents. Also promotes usage of these cars. Six newsletters per year. Dues: $14/year.

Hurst/Olds Club of America, HMN
60520 Lamplighter Dr
New Hudson, MI 48165
FAX: 517-333-HO4U

Founded 1983. 600 members worldwide. A club for the Hurst/Olds enthusiasts. Seeks to perpetuate interest in and promote preservation of Hurst/Olds automobiles, which have been produced since 1968 by the Oldsmobile Division of the General Motors Corporation. Maintains Hurst/Olds registry and research library. Hold car shows annually across the US. Includes bi-monthly award winning publication, *Thunder & Lightning*. Dues: $25/year. Web site: www.hurstolds.com

National Antique Oldsmobile Club
13903 Roanoke St
Woodbridge, VA 22191-2416
703-491-7060
E-mail: paulthomas@iname.com

Founded 1981. 2,000 members. Anyone interested in the model year Oldsmobile from 1897-1964. Club membership is open to all. Publication is *Runabouts to Rockets*, published monthly, advertising is free for members. The high point of each year is our annual National meet and show restricted to 1897-1964 Oldsmobiles. We also have technical advisors on each model year to assist members with answers about their cars. Dues: $25/year US, $40/year Canada and Mexico, $50/year other countries. Web site: www.antiqueolds.org

Oldsmobile Club of America
PO Box 80318
Lansing, MI 48908-0318
517-663-1811; FAX: 517-663-1820

Founded 1971. 6,400 members. No restrictions. All years, no car necessary, just interest. Monthly publication, *Journey With Olds*. National meet annually, over 45 chapters. Chapter and regional meets all over the country. Dues: $30/year.

chapters:

Arizona Oldsmobile Club of Arizona, 1956 E Huntington Dr, Tempe, AZ 85282-2867

California 1957 Chapter, PO Box 661224, Arcadia, CA 91066

Northern California Chapter, 5762 Collier Canyon Rd, Livermore, CA 94550

Olds Club of Southern CA, PO Box 661224, Arcadia, CA 91066

Colorado Rocky Moutain Chapter, PO Box 54, Arvada, CO 80001-0054

Florida Olds Club of Florida, PO Box 80, Winter Park, FL 32790-0080

Georgia Dixie Oldsmobile Chapter, 2570 Hwy 29, Lawrenceville, GA 30044, E-mail: dixieolds@hotmail.com

Illinois Illinois Valley Oldsmobile Chapter, 816 13th St, Rockford, IL 61104

Indiana Indiana Olds Chapter, 11730 Mann Rd, Mooresville, IN 46158

Iowa Oldsmobile Club of Iowa, 14693 Fame Ave, Colfax, IA 50054

Kansas Toronado Chapter, PO Box 211, Council Grove, KS 66846

Kentucky Bluegrass Rockets, 3703 S Joyce Ann Ln, Alexandria, KY 41001

Derby City Olds Club, 136 Harding, Mt Washington, KY 40047

Maryland Oldsmobile Centennial Club, 7 Thomas Point Ct, Baltimore, MD 21234, Web site: www.erols.com/brad442/occ

Starfire/Jetstar I Chapter, 1713 Basil Way, Gambrills, MD 21054

Massachusetts Eastern Massachusetts GMO, PO Box 424, Danvers, MA 01923-2055

New England Olds Club, Box 603, Southampton, MA 01073-0603

Michigan Motor City Rockets, 45744 Cumberland, Shelby Twp, MI 48317

RE Olds Chapter, PO Box 80101, Lansing, MI 48908-0101

Minnesota Minnesota Olds Club, 13049 Herald Cir, Apple Valley, MN 55124

Missouri Archway Chapter, 11366 Birmingham Ct, St Louis, MO 63138

Heart of America Chapter, 3511 S Crane St, Independence, MO 64055-3511

Nebraska Great Plains Olds Club, PO Box 6724, Lincoln, NE 68506

New Jersey Olds Club of New Jersey, 382 Thurman Ave, West Berlin, NJ 08091

Oldsmobile Club of America chapters *(continued)*

Rallye 350 Chapter, 37 Georgia St, Cranford, NJ 07016

New Mexico   *Olds Club of New Mexico*, 1715 Geraldine Pl SE, Rio Rancho, NM 87124

New York   *LI & NYC Oldsmobile Club*, 527 S Pecan St, Lindenhurst, NY 11757

Western New York Olds Club, 50 Cramer St, North Tonawanda, NY 14120-4502, 716-692-1564; E-mail: tigerpaw65@aol.com

North Carolina   *Mid-Atlantic Chapter*, 1310 Victory St, Greensboro, NC 27407

Ohio   *Gem City Rockets Inc*, 2378 Brookdale Dr, Springfield, OH 45502

Greater Cincinnati/Northern KY Chapter, 6738 Springdale Rd, Cincinnati, OH 45247

Mid-Ohio Chapter, 1184 Fairview Ave, Columbus, OH 43212

Northern Ohio Chapter of OCA, 3887 Cumberland Dr, Austintown, OH 44515

Performance Chapter, 155 Sesame St, Springboro, OH 45066-3311

Oklahoma   *Oklahoma Oldsmobile Club*, 1008 SW 69th St, Oklahoma City, OK 73139

Pennsylvania   *Blue-Gray Chapter*, 6 Arwin Ave, Hummelstown, PA 17036-9215

Tennessee   *Music City Rockets*, 5036 Marchant Dr, Nashville, TN 37211

Smoky Mountain Olds Club, PO Box 1543, Powell, TN 37849

Texas   *North Texas Oldsmobile Club*, PO Box 38524, Dallas, TX 75238

Texas Gulf Coast Chapter, 2807 Hertiage Colony Dr, Webster, TX 77598

Utah   *Rendezvous Rockets*, 615 E Mutton Hollow Rd, Kaysville, UT 84037

Virginia   *Capitol City Rockets*, Box 331, McLean, VA 22101-0331

Eastern Virginia Oldsmobile Club, PO Box 34935, Richmond, VA 23234-0935

Washington   *Puget Sound Chapter*, PO Box 82042, Kenmore, WA 98028-0042

Wisconsin   *Olds Club of Wisconsin*, PO Box 435, Sturtevant, WI 53177

Oldsmobile Cutlass Coupes (73-77), N 24 W 26339 Wilderness Way, Pewaukee, WI 53072-4568

The Opel Association of North America
394 Mystic Ln
Wirtz, VA 23113
E-mail: oana@opel-na.com

Membership information: Charles D Goin, President, 804-379-9737. Founded 1985. 175 (regular) members, 150 (net-only) members. Bi-monthly newsletter. Annual events: Carlisle Imports, first of May, Carlisle, PA; Opels on the Lawn, late June,

Boston, MA; mid-July, Tacoma, WA; MOA picnic, late September, Richmond, VA; multiple events throughout the year, Colorado Springs area, CO. Six chapters: The Mid-Atlantic Opel Association, New England Opel Club, Rocky Mountain Opels, Pacific Northwest Opel Association, Great Lakes/Mid-West Opel Association, Central OK Opel Club. Dues: $35/year regular membership (mailed bi-monthly newsletter and net access), $20/2 years net membership (net access to web site and downloadable versions of newsletter). Web site: www.opel-na.com

---

Opel Kadett Coupe Club of Denmark
c/o Frank Kiessling
Landevejen 27, Toksvaerd
DK-4684 Holme-Olstrup Denmark
PH/FAX: +45-55-530100
best 11 am to 3 pm US Central time
E-mail: frank.kiessling@get2net.dk

Founded 1988. 50 members. No restrictions to join. Parts locator, annual meet first weekend every August, club magazine 4 times/year, small stock of parts, library with spare parts catalogues, workshop manuals, brochures, technical data, DIY articles, videos, etc. Cooperation with other Opel clubs worldwide. Parts sold, bought, exchanged and swapped. Ask for more information. Dues: 350 DKK/year.

Mississippi Valley Packards
602 S Franklin
Farmington, MO 63640
FAX: 314-783-5997
E-mail:
kchapman@mines.missouri.org

For membership information, contact: Ken Chapman, PO Box 681, Fredericktown, MO 63645. Founded 1976. 80 members. Ownership of a Packard is not required. Annual slide show and displays. Regional affiliate of PAC. Promotes the Packard with both social events and educational seminars or displays. Covers the St Louis area, eastern Missouri and southern Illinois. Publish a newsletter. Dues: $9/year.

Packard Automobile Classics Inc
dba The Packard Club
420 S Ludlow St
Dayton, OH 45402
972-709-6185
FAX: 972-296-7920, TX

Membership processing and info: PO Box 28788, Dallas, TX 75228-0788, PH: 800-527-3452; FAX: 972-296-7920. Founded 1953. 3,800 members. Annual nationwide membership meet. Monthly *Cormorant News* bulletin, quarterly *Packard Cormorant* magazine. Dues: $35/year US, $45/year Canada, $55/year Mexico, $95/year overseas, US funds.

Packard Truck Organization
1196 Mountain Rd
York Springs, PA 17372
717-528-4920

For membership information, contact at the above address: David B Lockard. Founded 1981. 50 members. Open to Packard truck owners. Interested in all materials relating to 1905-1923 Packard trucks. Quarterly publication. Annual meet in York Springs, PA (October). Technical assistance.

Packards International Motor Car Club
302 French St
Santa Ana, CA 92701
714-541-8431

Founded 1963. 2,500 members. Dedicated to the preservation and driving enjoyment of the Packard automobile. Publications as well as reproduction parts and literature. Publications: *Packards International* magazine and *News Counselor*, both quarterly. Dues: $35/year US, $40/year Canada and Mexico, $55/year overseas.

regions:

Arizona	*Arizona Region*, 3008 E Cheery Lynn Rd, Phoenix, AZ 85016
California	*Northern California Region*, 5717 Moddison Ave, Sacramento, CA 95819
	San Diego Region, 9030 Carroll Way #1, San Diego, CA 92121
	Southern California Region, PO Box 11192, Santa Ana, CA 92711
Ohio	*Midwest Region*, 365 St Leger Ave, Akron, OH 44305
Oregon	*Oregon Region*, PO Box 42127, Portland, OR 97242
Washington	*Northwest Region*, PO Box 88881, Seattle, WA 98188
Australia	*Australia Region*, c/o Pakard Automobile Club, 152 Bannockburn Rd, Turramurra 2074 NSW
Canada	*Alberta Region*, Box 40343 Highfield PO, Calgary, AB T2G 5G7

Patriot Truck Registry
8600 Buckboard
Lincoln, NE 68532
402-438-5839

PATRIOT

Founded 1988. 17 members. Members share information and parts for Patriot trucks manufactured in Lincoln, NE, during the years 1918-1925. Dues: none.

Peerless Motor Car Club Inc
5001 Femrite Dr
Madison, WI 53716
608-222-4528; FAX: 608-222-4693
E-mail: peerless19@aol.com

Peerless

Founded 1998. 120 members. Dedicated to the history, preservation and restoration of Peerless Motor cars. Peerless restoration pictures and stories, factory history, executive personnel profiles, want list and for sale list, repro literature, repro casting of parts, repro ads for all years Peerless. Repros of original Peerless Co-Operator. Publish bi-monthly newsletter, *Peerless Co-Operator*. Dues: $30/year US, $37/year overseas.

Pierce-Arrow Society Inc
135 Edgerton St
Rochester, NY 14607

PIERCE-ARROW

Founded 1957. 1,000 members. Technical and historical information provided for all Pierce vehicles including bicycles, cars, trucks, buses, trailers and motorcycles. Members receive four magazines, six service bulletins, a membership roster, a technical index and free advertising privileges each year. Several regions offer local activities. Dues: $25/year US. Web site: www.pierce-arrow.org

Plymouth Owners Club Inc
(formerly Plymouth 4 & 6-Cylinder Owners Club)
PO Box 416
Cavalier, ND 58220
701-549-3746; FAX: 701-549-3744
E-mail: benji@utma.com

PLYMOUTH

For membership information, contact at the above address: Jim Benjaminson. Founded 1957. 3,600 members. Open to 1928-1975 Plymouth passenger and Plymouth and Fargo commercial vehicles. Recognized by Chrysler Corporation. Publish bi-monthly magazine; sample issue, $2. Dues: $18/year (Canada and foreign must remit US funds).

regions:

Colorado	*Rocky Mountain Region*, Kenny Hammers, 4698 S Fountain Cr, Lakewood, CO 80127
Illinois	*Dairyland Region*, Ed & Julie Hovorka, 598 Banbury Rd, Mundelein, IL 60060
	Lincoln Land Region, Terry Lash, 1548 Weber, Edwardsville, IL 62025
Indiana	*Hoosier Region*, Stan W Peel, 5128 E Rowney, Indianapolis, IN 46203
Iowa	*Mid-Iowa Region*, John P Miller, 7109 Bellaire Ave, Des Moines, IA 50311
Maryland	*Mid-Atlantic Region*, Clayton Miller, 3345 Florence Rd, Woodbine, MD 21797
Massachusetts	*Colonial Region*, Betty Kibbe, 456 Holyoke St, Ludlow, MA 01056
Michigan	*Detroit Region*, Joseph B Lewis, 9145 Hazelton, Redford, MI 48239
Minnesota	*Tall Pines Region*, Carl Wegner, 19600 Cardinal Dr, Grand Rapids, MN 55744-6189
Missouri	*Heart of America Region*, Bop Bealmear, 7908 Maple, Raytown, MO 64138
	Missouri "Show Mr" Region, Tommy G Pike, 1602 E Dale, Springfield, MO 65803
Nebraska	*Prairie Region*, Shawn & Crystal Dewey, 2145 Main St, Crete, NE 68333
New Jersey	*Delaware Valley Region*, Dave Geise, 417 Tennessee Tr, Brown Mills, NJ 08015
North Carolina	*Carolina Region*, Thomas E Carroll, 181 Charles St, Forest City, NC 28043
Ohio	*Ohio Region*, Larry Schroeder, 9721 Shaw Rd, Spencer, OH 44275
Texas	*High Plains Region*, Roland Keenan, 1305 LaPaloma, Amarillo, TX 79106
	Lone Star Region, Thomas Heidorf, 19506 Oak Briar Dr, Humble, TX 77346
Virginia	*Old Dominion Region*, Bob Klinker, 1614 Mill Oak Dr, Virginia Beach, VA 23464
Canada	*Western Canada Region*, Trevor Landage, 75 Strathaven Cir SW, Calgary, AB T3J 2G2

Buckeye GTO Club
1500 Lourdes Dr
Cleveland, OH 44134
440-888-0416

PONTIAC.

Founded 1980. 25-30 members. Must own a GTO or have an interest in one. Monthly newsletter, 4 or 5 events per year with an estimated attendance of 100 per event, attend numerous cruises in and around the Cleveland area. Dues: $20/year.

Section Three Clubs & Organizations

Cactus GTOs Inc
c/o 17662 N 45th Ave
Glendale, AZ 85308
602-938-6802, 602-482-1620
E-mail: azautohobe@aol.com

Founded 1986. 80+ members. Club focuses on the preservation and fun of driving the Pontiac GTO (1964-1974). Also welcome LeMans and Tempest lovers too. Dues include a monthly newsletter. Activities throughout the year (car shows, breakfast cruises, club drag racing, etc). Dues: $12/year. Web site: http://members.aol.com/cactusgto

GTO Association of America
5829 Stroebel Rd
Saginaw, MI 48609
800-GTO-1964

Founded 1979. 3,000 members. Monthly magazine, *The Legend.* International convention each year hosted by local chapters, travels to differenct cities across US. Approximately 50 local chapters. Also, regional meets throughout summer. Dues: $30/year.
chapters:

Alabama *Deep South GTO's*, Bill Ondocsin, 133 South View Dr, Huntsville, AL 35806, 205-837-2426

Arizona *Cactus GTO's*, Steve Barcak, 1948 N Hamilton Pl, Chandler, AZ 85225

GTO Owners of Tucson, Tom Payton, 4320 S Silverbeech Ave, Tucson, AZ 85730, 520-790-5644

California *Golden Gate Goats*, John Mekisich, 435 W 25th Ave, San Mateo, CA 94403, 650-349-2095

Southern California Gathering of the Goats, Jack Blum, 1307 S Ardilla Ave, West Covina, CA 91790, 626-337-9563

Tri-Valley GTO Club, Tom Weed, 732 Alexander St, San Fernando, CA 91340, 818-361-5416

Colorado *Classic GTO Association Denver*, Linda Lawrence, PO Box 745092, Arvada, CO 80006, 303-423-GOAT

Northern Colorado GTO Association, Patty Gore, 2214 Franklin Rd, Fort Collins, CO 80524, 970-484-6463

Delaware *GTO Club of Delaware*, Frank Messick, 40 Worral Dr, Newark, DE 19711, 302-737-4657

Florida *Classic Pontiacs of Central Florida*, Bill Cocozza, PO Box 3151, Lakeland, FL 33802, 941-667-0293

Sunshine State GTO Association, Robert Hanley, 4376 N Mary Cir, Palm Beach Gardens, FL 33410, 561-622-0228

Georgia *Southeastern GTO Association*, David Trees, 2698 Pamela Dr, Snellville, GA 30078, 770-985-8128

Illinois *Cruisin Tigers GTO Club*, Jeff Hill, PO Box 7191, Buffalo Grove, IL 60089, 847-949-5733

Heart of Illinois GTO's, Steven Scobee, 2425 Maywood Ave, Pekin, IL 61554, 309-579-2485

Indiana *Indy GTO Association*, Bill Sanders, PO Box 487, Noblesville, IN 46061-0487, 317-849-3630

Northwest Indiana GTO's, Rick Losher, 3455 W State Rd, Fremont, IN 46737, 219-833-1275

Iowa *Pontiac Club of Iowa*, Mike Smith, PO Box 31065, Des Moines, IA 50310, 515-999-2544

Kansas *GR-888'R Wichita GTO Club*, Tom Wilhite, 200 W Washington, Derby, KS 67037, 316-788-0514

Kentucky *Louisville GTO Club Inc*, Mike Lickteig, PO Box 99185, Louisville, KY 40269, 502-937-3490

Maine *GTO Association of Maine*, C Huntington, 214 Atlantic Ave, Boothbay Harbor, ME 04538, 207-633-2904

Massachusetts *Pioneer Valley GTO Association*, David Gumlaw, 134 Lafayette St, Chicopee, MA 01020, 413-539-6525

Michigan *West Michigan Classic Pontiacs*, Gary Trama, 4285 E B Ave, Plainwell, MI 49080, 616-345-2202

Woodward GTO Tigers, Bill Schultz, 4677 Lockwood Dr, Washington, MI 48094, 810-783-5767

Minnesota *Land of Lakes GTO Club*, Lee Stagni, 14600 41st Ave N, Plymouth, MN 55446, 612-559-1797

Missouri *Gateway GTO Association*, Chris Simmons, 3 Trade Winds, St Peters, MO 63376, 314-397-8710

Montana *Big Sky GTO's*, Mark DeLong, 4416 Harvest Ln, Billings, MT 59106, 406-656-6254

Rocky Mountain Goats, Harry Gedna, 5750 Meadow Vista Dr, Florence, MT 59833, 406-273-6071

New Jersey *Delaware Valley Old Goat Club*, Steven Laughlin, PO Box 295, Hainesport, NJ 08057, 609-829-7696

Garden State GTO's, Bob Moore, 80 Burnt Meadow Rd, Ringwood, NJ 07456, 973-839-5150

New York *Electric City GTO's Inc*, Richard Konsella, PO Box 3724, Albany, NY 12203, 518-371-6047

GTO Association of Greater New York, David Barsky, 2682 Ford St, Brooklyn, NY 11235, 718-332-4479

Hudson Valley GTO Club, Bob Costabile, 5 Bridle Path, Newburgh, NY 12550, 914-761-1022

Western New York GTO Club, William Brown, 188 Bigelow Pl, Depew, NY 14043, 716-683-8539

North Carolina *Carolina Classic Pontiac Club*, Ken Simpson, 5361 Bedfordshire Ave, Harrisburg, NC 28075, 704-455-GOAT

Performance Pontiacs Carolinas, Jim Hill, 5005 Woodmark Dr, Greensboro, NC 27407, 336-454-4367

Tarheel Tigers GTO Club, Gary Anderson, 1126 Shadyside Dr, Raleigh, NC 27612, 919-848-1928

Ohio *Buckeye GTO's*, Randy Zinn, 6955 Wooster Pike Rd, Medina, OH 44256, 330-725-1069

GTO Association of Central Ohio, Jim Evans, 13791 Cable Rd, Pataskala, OH 43062, 740-927-5302

Ohio Valley GTO Association, John Hugentober, 3090 Shoemaker Rd, Lebanon, OH 45036, 513-932-GTOS

Oregon *Goat Herd GTO Club of Oregon*, Jim Gulley, PO Box 1071, Clackamas, OR 97015, 503-653-0291

Pennsylvania *GTO Association of Greater Pittsburgh*, Warren Hanbury, 108 Duquesne Ave, Dravosburg, PA 15034, 412-469-9842

GTO Association of Pennsylvania, Jim Darlington, 1065 Bushkill Dr, Easton, PA 18042, 610-258-0768

Susquehanna Valley GTO Tigers, Frank Fawber, 268 Campground Rd, Dillsburg, PA 17019, 717-432-3996

Texas *GTO Association of North Texas*, Roger Lachele, PO Box 794533, Dallas, TX 75379, 972-661-9677

Virginia *Greater Tidewater Owners Society*, Richard Holliday, 1200 1st Colonial Rd, Ste 204-G, Virginia Beach, VA 23454, 757-481-6337

Washington *Northwest GTO Legends*, Kevin Reed, 10004 114th Ave N, Kirkland, WA 98033, 425-827-8143

Radioactive Redskins Pontiac Club, Janice Pullen, PO Box 6234, Kennewick, WA 99336, 509-586-8401

West Virginia *Mountain Goats of West Virginia*, Stan Legge, 112 Riverview Ln, Beckley, WV 25801, 304-743-4710

Wild Wonderful West Virginia GTO's, Harold Morris, Rte 3, Box 34-A, Morgantown, WV 26505, 304-292-5056

Wisconsin *Gods Country GTO's*, Sheldon Hamilton, E-13183 Neuman Rd, Baraboo, WI 53913, 608-356-2832

Original GTO Club, Larry Lorenz, PO Box 14838, Milwaukee, WI 53218, 414-466-2300

Canada *The Classic GTO Club of Ontario*, Peter Mazzocato, 1022 Weir Rd S, Lynden, ON Canada L0R 1T0

The Judge GTO International Club
114 Prince George Dr
Hampton, VA 23669
757-838-2059

Founded 1982. 329 members. Open to owners and enthusiasts of 1969-1971 Pontiac GTO Judge. Quarterly publication, *The Judge's Chambers*. Yearly convention at Virginia Beach, VA. Dues $20/year.

Land of Lakes GTO Club Inc
PO Box 9844
North St Paul, MN 55109-9844
612-472-6481

Founded 1984. 200 members. Monthly newsletter, technical advisors, club library, monthly meetings, cruises, Cars For Kids car show, Land of Lakes Muscle Car Classic car show, technical seminars. Dues: $24/year.

Michigan Fiero Club
PO Box 1437
Dearborn, MI 48121-1437
313-274-8188
E-mail: sjb@tir.com

Founded 1993. 391 members. Monthly newsletter, monthly meeting, social car activities (shows and cruises). No restrictions, Fiero owners and enthusiasts always welcome. Dues: $25/year US, $35/year foreign. Web site: www.tir.com/jaski/mi-fiero.htm

National Firebird & T/A Club
PO Box 11238
Chicago, IL 60611-0238
773-769-6262; FAX: 773-769-3240
E-mail: firebirdtaclub@hotmail.com

Established 1984. North America's largest club for all year Firebirds and Trans Ams including the Formula, GTA and Firehawk. Web site: www.firebirdtaclub.com

Northern Illinois Fiero Enthusiasts Inc
6226 Trinity Dr
Lisle, IL 60532
630-305-9806
E-mail: jjh93@juno.com

Founded 1991. 400 members. Bi-monthly, award winning newsletter, *Fiero Focus*. Monthly events, our own car show called Fierorama, free to members, we are expecting over 125 Fieros this year, September 12. Parts discounts, mechanic referrals and much more. Dues: $20/year. Web site: www.xnet.com/~nife

Oakland-Pontiac Enthusiast Org
3520 Warringham Dr
Waterford, MI 48329-1380
248-623-7573; FAX: 248-623-6180
E-mail: 72602,344@compuserve.com

Founded 1971. 200 members. Interest in Oaklands and Pontiacs. Publish *Warrior*. Specializing in information for 1926-current Oaklands and Pontiacs. Dues: $10/year.

Pacific Northwest Pontiac Club
47525 SE Coalman Rd
Sandy, OR 97055
503-668-5416; FAX: 503-826-9019
E-mail: ohc6@pnnw.net

Founded 1978. 50-60 members. Monthly newsletter, *Wide Trackin News*, annual all Pontiac car show held last Sunday in August, annual club BBQ, Christmas dinner, tours, many other events. Dues: $20/year.

Pontiac-Oakland Club International Inc
PO Box 9569
Bradenton, FL 34206
941-750-9234; FAX: 941-747-1341

Founded 1972. 10,000+ members. One of the largest marque specific clubs in the country. An active and extensive local chapter network brings the club close to home for most of its members, something the club actively encourages and supports. *Smoke Signals*, POCI's monthly magazine, is one of the hobby's best, with lots of useful articles and a large classified ad section (free to members) with hundreds of Pontiac cars and parts for sale. Dues: $25/year US, $27/year Canada, $36/year foreign (US funds).

chapters:

Alabama *Alabama Chapter*, 8048 7th Ave N, Birmingham, AL 35206

Arizona *Arizona Chapter*, c/o Ross Whitehead, 5460 Calle Cayeus, Tucson, AZ 85741

Desert Renegades of Arizona, c/o Dave Bertramn, 8325 E Captain Dreyfus Ave, Scottsdale, AZ 85281

Arkansas *Arkansas River Chapter*, c/o Louie Reed, 675 S 28th, Rogers, AR 72758

California *Channel Islands Chapter*, c/o David McGarry, 5690 Aurora St, Ventura, CA 93003, 805-654-0401

Custom Safari Chapter, c/o Tom B Young, 204 Acacia Ln, Newbury Park, CA 91320

Northern Sierra-Cascade Chapter, c/o Gary Travis, 878 Deercreek Ln, Paradise, CA 95969-3262

Pontiacs of Central CA, c/o Joel Garret, 3155 Sylmar, Clovis, CA 93612, 209-292-9130

Sacramento Chapter, c/o Denise (Dee) Nelson, 7316 Dansfield Cir, North Highlands, CA 95660

San Diego Chapter, c/o Dave Keetch, 154 El Camino Pequeno, El Cajon, CA 92019

Southern California Chapter, c/o Gregg Miller, 1811 W Panoramic Dr, Corona, CA 91720

Colorado *Colorado Chapter*, c/o PO Box 56, Arvada, CO 80001

Connecticut *Nutmeg Chapter (CT)*, c/o Starr F Evans, Church Hill Rd, Washington Depot, CT 06794

Pontiac-Oakland Club International Inc chapters *(continued)*

Florida *Dixie Chapter,* c/o Ken Wales, 3201 Bliss Rd, Orange Park, FL 32065

Florida Chapter, c/o Joan Webb, 1104 39th St W, Bradenton, FL 34205

North Florida Ponchos, c/o Karen Miller, PO Box 35103, Panama City, FL 34212

Illinois *Early Times Chapter,* c/o Les Schwerdtner, 457 S Glencoe Ave, Decatur, IL 62522

Grand Prix Chapter, c/o Mike Schaudek, 357 Marvin Pl, Weeling, IL 60090, 708-537-0345

Illinois Chapter, c/o Carla Knotek, 15456 Scott Ct, Lockport, IL 60441, 815-838-7956

Pontiacs of Central Illinois Chapter, c/o Gary Mruz, 4511 Butler Dr, Decatur, IL 62526

Indiana *Hoosier Chapter (IN),* c/o Marilyn Dutoi, 64723 Miami Hwy, Bremen, IN 46506

Tri-State Arrowhead Cruisers Chapter, c/o Kelly Knaebel, 7121 North St, Newburgh, IN 47630

Iowa *Blackhawk Chapter (IL/IA),* c/o JJ Koehler, 30409 141st Ave W, Muscatine, IA 52761, 309-537-3696

Kansas *KC Arrowhead Chapter,* c/o Jean Day, 4517 W 75th, Prairie Village, KS 66208

Maine *All American Oakland Chapter,* c/o Arthur Archie, 22 Washington St, Millinocket, ME 04462, 207-732-8759

Massachusetts *Yankee Chapter (MA/ME),* c/o Donald Stuart, 70 Pine Ridge Dr, Bridgewater, MA 02324

Michigan *West Michigan Chapter,* c/o Wendell Miller, 8830 Taylor St, Zeeland, MI 49464

Minnesota *Pontiac Commercial and Professional Vehicle Chapter,* Paul Bergstrom, 1165 Cty Rd 83, Independence, MN 55359

Tomahawk Chapter (MN), Dave Bennett, 109 Crystal View Cir, Burnsville, MN 55306

Missouri *Arch Chapter (MO),* c/o Richard Lacavich, 808 Carman Woods Dr, Manchester, MO 63011

Greater Ozarks Chapter (MO), c/o Arthur Barrett, 211 W Alice, Mt Vernon, MO 65712, 417-466-3081

Nebraska *Nebraskaland Chapter,* c/o Chuck Merica, 4232 Harrison, Omaha, NE 68147

Nevada *Silver State Chapter,* c/o Russel Horning, 2265 Pennswood, Reno, NV 89509

New Hampshire *NOR-Eastern Chapter,* c/o PO Box 178, Newton Junction, NH 03859

New Jersey *Garden State Chapter (NJ),* c/o Stephen Kiellar, 118 Starr Pl, Wyckoff, NJ 07481

New York *Adirondack Green Mountain Chapter (Eastern NYS and VT),* c/o Michael L Moak, 150 Jewell Rd, Gansevoort, NY 12831

Finger Lakes Chapter (NY), c/o Debby Arend, 14 Judd Ln, Hilton, NY 14468

Long Island Chapter (NY), c/o Dave Worthington, PO Box 226, Aqueboque, NY 11931

Six Nations Chapter (NY), c/o Bob Klaisle, PO Box 2145, Syracuse, NY 13220

Western New York Chapter, c/o Brian Mertens, 50 Cramer St, North Tonawanda, NY 14120

North Carolina *Cape Fear Chapter,* c/o Jimmy Carter, 3690 Stag Park Rd, Burgaw, NC 28425, 910-259-6353

Piedmont Chapter, c/o Bill Sykes, 2312 N Centennial St, High Point, NC 27265, 336-883-2260

Ohio *North Coast Ohio Chapter,* c/o Marilyn Nicholas, 13896 Aquilla Rd, Burton, OH 44021

Northwest Ohio Chapter, c/o Ann Tasch, 16221 Martin Moline Rd, Grayton, OH 43432

Oklahoma *Indian Nations Chapter,* c/o Alma Robinson, 6783 E 25th Pl, Tulsa, OK 74129

Oregon *Emerald Valley Chapter,* c/o Rosie Henderson, 2084 Lemuri, Eugene, OR 97402

Pennsylvania *Keystone State Chapter (PA),* c/o Frank Kemp, 448 S Main St, Bechtelsville, PA 19505

Western Pennsylvania Chapter, c/o Gary F Gordan, 4507 W 7th Ave, Beaver Falls, PA 15010-2013

Rhode Island *Little Rhody Pontiac Chapter (RI),* c/o Robert Caliguiri, 80 Ingersoll Rd, Warwick, RI 02920

South Carolina *Palmetto Chapter,* c/o Erik Nagel, PO Box 65, Taylors, SC 29687

South Dakota *Empire Chapter,* c/o Kirk Lee, 3809 S Holbrook Ave, Sioux Falls, SD 57106

Tennessee *Little Indian Chapter,* c/o Greg Walters, PO Box 32588, Knoxville, TN 37930

Pontiacs of Tennessee, c/o Bob Woodside, 2230 Oakleaf Dr, Franklin, TN 37064

Sixty Owners Society Chapter, c/o Doug Bendle, PO Box 100333, Nashville, TN 37210

Texas *Lone Star Chapter (TX),* c/o Joe Rakoczy, 7208 Tumbleweed Ct, Colleyville, TX 76034

Southern Central Texas Chapter, c/o Jay Lord, PO Box 34654, San Antonio, TX 78265

Utah *Great Salt Lake Chapter,* c/o Kenny Gregrich, 59 N Broadway, Tooele, UT 84074, 801-882-5560

Virginia *National Capital Area,* c/o George Richardson, 1509 Baltimore Rd, Alexandria, VA 22308

Old Dominion Chapter (VA), c/o Michael L Abernathy, 1400 Fortingale Cir, Sandston, VA 23150

Star City Chapter, c/o Randy Hurt, PO Box 20652, Roanoke, VA 24018

Washington *Puget Sound Chapter,* c/o Karen E Housley, 21210 124th Ave SE, Kent, WA 98031

Wisconsin *Badger State Chapter (WI),* c/o David Keach, 1149 N 46th St, Milwaukee, WI 53208

Street Rod/Modified Chapter, c/o Ginny Simmons, 5209 84th St, Kenosha, WI 53142-2215, 414-694-2500

Royal Pontiac Club of America
PO Box 593
Keego Harbor, MI 48320
248-855-6291; FAX: 248-855-6299

Founded 1994. 185 members. Must be a Pontiac enthusiast. The club is dedicated to performance Pontiacs of all years. Club discounts at several retail auto suppliers. Tech information. Monthly newsletter. A seven event club drag racing series with awards dinner at end of season. Family fun. Participate in Woodward Dream Cruise. Ability to meet people that made these muscle cars the icon they are today. Dues: $20/year.

356 Registry Inc
Barbara Skirmants
27244 Ryan Rd
Warren, MI 48092
810-558-3692; FAX: 810-558-3616
E-mail: skirmant@mich.com

Founded 1974. 6,300 members. No restrictions to join, ownership is not required. Local and national events and a complete listing of local clubs, free classified ads to members. The most complete source of parts and suppliers for the Porsche 356 model car. Bi-monthly publication (on every odd numbered month), *356 Registry*, 50 page color cover magazine with 5-8 full feature color articles every year. Technical, mechanical and restoration articles. Historical information and book reviews. Literature and model collecting, vintage racing coverage. Visa/MasterCard. Dues: $25/year US, $35/year Canada and Mexico, $45/year international.

regions:

Arizona *Arizona Outlaws Porsche 356 Club*, Mike Wroughton, 19870 N 86th Ave, Peoria, AZ 85382, 602-362-8356; E-mail: mwroughton@aol.com

California *356 CAR*, Jim Hardie, 2282 D Sierra Blvd, Sacramento, CA 95825

Central Coast, Wes & Diane Morrill, 805-474-1401

Porsche 356 Club, Wayne Callaway, 2037 S Vineyard Ave, Ontario, CA 91761-8066

Colorado *Rocky Mountain Porsche 356 Club*, Al Gordon, 12773 Grizzly, Littleton, CO 80127, 303-979-1072

Connecticut *356 Southern Connecticut Register Ltd*, PO Box 35, Riverside, CT 06878, Web site: http://w3.nai.net/~edwardh/ed4yhtm

Florida *Florida Owners Group*, Rich Williams, 4570 47th St, Sarasota, FL 34235, 813-228-2901 ext 145 days, 941-355-4856 evenings/weekends

Georgia *Southern Owners Group*, Ray Ringler, 3755 Creek Stone Way, Marietta, GA 30068, E-mail: three56@aol.com

Illinois *356 Windige Stadt Klub*, Dale Moody, 19532 Governor's Hwy, Homewood, IL 60430, 708-798-2637

Massachusetts *Typ 356 Northeast*, Gary Resnick, 45 West Rd 1E, Orleans, MA 02653, 508-240-6909; E-mail: garyr.356@aol.com

Michigan *356 Motor Cities Gruppe*, Barbara Skirmants, 27244 Ryan Rd, Warren, MI 48092, 810-558-3692

Minnesota *Fahr North*, Phil Saari, 3374 Owasso St, Shoreview, MN 55126

Missouri *Groupe 356 St Louis Region*, Ted Melsheimer Sr, 10517 E Watson Rd, St Louis, MO 63127, 314-966-2131

Nevada *Sierra 356 Porsche Club*, Glenn Lewis, 2000 Royal Dr, Reno, NV 89503

Pennsylvania *356 Mid Atlantic*, Dan Haden, 143 W Carpenter Ln, Philadelphia, PA 19119

Texas *Lone Star 356 Club*, Mark Roth, 4915 S Main, Ste 109, Stafford, TX 77477, 281-277-9595; E-mail: mroth356@aol.com

Tub Club, Don Rutherford, 8006 Glen Albens Cir, Dallas, TX 75225, 214-365-9170; E-mail: don@rutherfords.net

Washington *356 Group Northwest*, Orr Potebnya, 1327 Tabitha Ct NW, Olympia, WA 98502

West Virginia *Potomac 356 Owner's Group*, Dan Rowzie, 800 S Samuel St, Charles Town, WV 25414-1416

Australia *Australian Porsche 356 Register*, PO Box 7356 St Kilda Rd, Melbourne, Victoria 3004

Canada *Maple Leaf 356 Club of Canada*, Dave Hinze, 2304 Weston Rd #1407, Weston, ON M9N 1Z3, 416-244-4759

New Zealand *356 Down Under*, PO Box 47-677 Ponsonby, Auckland

Porsche 356 Florida Owners Group
4570 47th St
Sarasota, FL 34235
813-228-2901, ext 145
E-mail: rich356fog@aol.com

Founded 1993. 120 members. Car ownership not required. Quarterly newsletter, 4-5 driving events per year, monthly local breakfasts, host of 356 Registry East Coast Holiday 1996. Dues: $10/year. Web site: www.356holiday.org

Porsche 914 Owners Association and 914-6 Club USA
100 S Sunrise Way, PMB 116H
Palm Springs, CA 92262
760-325-6583; FAX: 760-325-6583
E-mail: deeds@earthlink.net

Founded 1978. 2,000 members. An international organization with members in 20 countries. Members receive informative quarterly magazine, *Mid-Engined Views*, contains articles about 914 maintenance, restoration and history. Now combined with the 914-6 Club USA. Annual reunion June. Join us for Tour 2000, July 2000. Dues: $25/year US, $32/year overseas. Web site: http://home.earthlink.net/~deeds/

Renault Owner's Club of North America
13839 Old Highway 80
El Cajon, CA 92021
PH/FAX: 619-561-6687
E-mail: cdavid@dreamsoft.com

Founded 1991. 166 members. This is the only Renault club in the US. Join the North American network for Renault owners. Receive 1 year of the *Renault News*, published bi-monthly; monthly marketplace ads; yearly registry/directory; technical support, parts and documentation from other experienced Renault enthusiasts. Owners of Renault derivatives, such as Alpine, Eagle, Lotus, Matra, etc, are encouraged to join. Dues: $20/year. Web site: www.dreamsoft.com/renaultclub

REO Club of America Inc
115 Cherry Rd
Chesnee, SC 29323
864-461-2894

Founded 1973. 750 members. REO owners and enthusiasts. Send SASE when writing to club. Worldwide group dedicated to the preservation of the works of Ransom E Olds. Dues: $18/year.

chapters:

South Carolina *Carolinas Chapter*, John Barker, 115 Cherry Rd, Chesnee, SC 29323, 864-461-2894

Svenska Rileyregistret
c/o Erik Hamberg
Salagatan 41 A
SE-753 26 Uppsala Sweden
+46 18 12 82 83
E-mail:
erik.hamberg@huddinge.mail.telia.com

Founded 1977. 130 members. Newsletter 4 times a year, at least 1 rally each year. Open to everyone interested in Riley cars. Dues: SEK 100/year Sweden, SEK 125/year abroad.

Rolls-Royce Owner's Club Inc
191 Hempt Rd
Mechanicsburg, PA 17055
717-697-4671; FAX: 717-697-7820
E-mail: rroc.hq@rroc.org

Founded 1951. 6,700 members. Dedicated to the preservation, restoration and enjoyment of Rolls-Royce and Bentley motorcars. Dues: $45/year. Web site: rroc.org

Silver Ghost Association
1115 Western Blvd
Arlington, TX 76013
817-633-1422; FAX: 817-633-4389
E-mail:
76453.3543@compuserve.com

Founded 1986. 350 members. Newsletter, *The Tourer*, published quarterly, technical assistance by telephone or fax included with membership. Tech bible with 1,200+ pages of articles published about Silver Ghosts, club store, annual Wholly Ghost tour for Silver Ghosts only. Do not need to own a Silver Ghost to join. Dues: $40/year. Web site: www.rroc.org/regions/sga/

Rover Saloon Touring Club of America
733 S Providence Rd
Wallingford, PA 19086
610-872-2109
E-mail: rstca@clubs.hemmings.com or
glenwilson@worldnet.att.net or
smanwell@sprintmail.com or
rovercars@aol.com

Primary contacts: Glen Wilson and Steve Manwell. Founded 1998. 70 members. Open to anyone interested in Rover automobiles. Nearly all Rover models are already represented in our club including pre-war, P4, P5, P6, SD1 and Sterling models. RSTCA members will receive eleven issues of the British marque multi-club newspaper that will include a monthly column dedicated to the RSTCA. Dues: $15/year plus a one-time joining fee of $3 to partially offset the cost of the initial membership package. Web site: http://clubs.hemmings.com/rstca/

New England Sonett Club
PO Box 4362
Manchester, NH 03108
914-778-2469
E-mail: sonett@frontiernet.net

Founded 1980. 150 members US. Objectives include maintenance and preservation of Sonetts and vintage Saabs. Historical data, tech tips, quarterly newsletter. Dues: $18/year.

Saab Club of North America
7675 Bear Trap Jct
Saginaw, MN 55779
218-729-0826; FAX: 218-729-0827
E-mail: tim@saabclub.com

Founded 1973. 4,000 members. *NINES* magazine covers all Saabs from 2-stroke thru Turbo, features technical DIY, sources, news from Saab, history, classifieds. Annual convention in August. Dues: $30/year ($34/1st year). Web site: www.saabclub.com

The Sabra Connection
7040 N Navajo Ave
Milwaukee, WI 53217
414-352-8408

Sabra

An organization to share interest and information about the Sabra Sport automobile produced by Autocars of Haifa, Israel and Reliant of England between 1961 and 1963. Publication, *The Sabra Connection*.

Saxon Times
c/o Walter Prichard
5250 NW Highland Dr
Corvallis, OR 97330
541-752-6231
E-mail: prichard@proaxis.com

Saxon

Founded 1983. Approximately 90 members. Saxon automobiles, all years. Publication, *Saxon Times*, includes roster of owners, for sale and wanted cars and parts, factory literature.

SIMCA Car Club
644 Lincoln St
Amherst, OH 44001
440-988-9104 evenings
(no return calls)
E-mail:
us.simca.carclub@centuryinter.net

Founded 1985. Approximately 100 members in 15 countries. Dedicated to the restoration and preservation of SIMCA, Chrysler-SIMCA, and special-bodied SIMCA exotics from 1936-1982. Parts inventory, information sources and European connections. Monthly newsletter, *Vitesse*. Dues: $20/year. Web site: www.centuryinter.net/simca/

Squire SS-100 Registry
c/o Arthur Stahl
11826 S 51st St
Phoenix, AZ 85044-2313
602-893-9451; FAX: 602-705-6649
E-mail: squirepal@aol.com

Founded 1989. 42 members at present. Membership is restricted to ownership or intended ownership of the Squire SS-100 manufactured in Torino, Italy, by Intermeccanica in 1968-1972. Intended to find and list the owners of the fifty-odd Squire SS-100s that were produced in Italy in 1968-1972 by Intermeccanica. Monthly newsletter. Dues: $40/first year, $15/year thereafter. Web site: www.team.net/www//ktud/squir.html

Stevens-Duryea Associates
3565 Newhaven Rd
Pasadena, CA 91107
626-351-8237

For membership information, contact at the above address: Warwick Eastwood. Founded 1960. 100 members. Open only to owners of Stevens-Duryea automobiles. Dues: none.

Orange Empire Chapter, SDC
7812 Vicksburg Ave
Westchester, CA 90045
310-645-3438

Founded 1969. 147 members. A chapter of the Studebaker Drivers Club. Monthly meetings and newsletter, *Wheels & Deals*. Purpose is sharing information on parts, tips, activities and cars. Must be a member of the Studebaker Drivers Club to join chapter. Annual LaPalma show. Dues: $15/year.

Wisconsin Region Studebaker Drivers Club
PO Box 296
Allenton, WI 53002-0296
414-629-9969; FAX: 414-629-4171
E-mail: leighm@pmihwy.com

Founded 1968. 320 members. Dedicated to the preservation and operation of Studebaker vehicles, the exchange of technical information and the publication of information pertaining to Studebaker and affiliated companies. *The Studebaker Spokesman*, published bi-monthly. Host of the 36th International SDC Meet, June 18-24, 2000, Madison, WI. Dues: $15/year. Web site: http://studebaker.madison2000.org

The Stutz Club Inc
7400 Lantern Rd
Indianapolis, IN 46256
812-988-9325

For membership information, contact at the above number: John Kirkman, Membership VP. Founded 1988. 350 members. Membership open to all who have an interest in Stutz vehicles (Stutz and Blackhawk autos and fire engines, HCS autos and taxicabs, Stutz Pak-Age-Car and aircraft engine) or in history of the companies producing these marques and the man responsible, Harry Clayton Stutz. Quarterly publication, *Stutz News*. Annual meeting held with Grand Stutz car meet. Provides technical information, full current directory of members and vehicles. Dues: $35/year worldwide.

Subaru 360 Drivers' Club
1421 N Grady Ave
Tucson, AZ 85715
520-290-6492

Founded 1980. 350 members. Members help each other keep their Subaru 360s on the road and running on both cylinders. Quarterly newsletter. Dues: $6/year.

California Association of Tiger Owners
18771 Paseo Picasso
Irvine, CA 92612-3328
949-854-2561
E-mail: catmbr@best.com

Founded 1968. 1,000 members. Alpines welcome. Worldwide membership devoted to advancing the Sunbeam marque. Extensive parts supply. Dues: $25/year US, $27/year Canada, $35/year foreign. Web site: www.catmbr.org

Sunbeam Owners Group of San Diego
2250 Rosecrans
San Diego, CA 92106
619-223-0496

Founded 1986. 60 members. Active enthusiasts of Sunbeams and other Rootes Group cars. Monthly activities, monthly newsletter. Dues: $20/year.

Tatra Enthusiasts
16643 Rt 144
Mt Airy, MD 21771
301-854-5900, 410-442-3637
FAX: 301-854-5957
E-mail: tatrabill@aol.com

Tatra, the only cars to have a rear-engined air-cooled ohc V8. The club specializes in information, parts, service and anything pertaining to Tatra cars and trucks 1922-present. Also includes earlier Nesseldorfer vehicles.

New England Triumphs
6 Island Cove Rd
Eliot, ME 03903
207-439-3038
E-mail: grove@acornworld.net

Founded 1978. 220 members. Receive monthly newsletter, join in activities including rallies, tours, autocross throughout New England. Dues: $18/year.

TR8 Car Club of America
266 Linden St
Rochester, NY 14620
716-244-9693

Founded 1983. 350 members. Quarterly newsletter with technical data, news items, etc. Regalia and back issues of newsletters available. Dues: $15/year.

Triumph International Owners Club
PO Box 6676
Holliston, MA 01746-6676
508-429-4221; FAX: 508-429-6213
E-mail: johntioc@aol.com

Founded 1978. 2,600 members. Quarterly newsletter, patch and decal with membership. Annual rally. Founded to encourage riding, restoration and racing of Triumph motorcycles. Members worldwide. Dues: $18.50/year, US first class mail, $15.50/year, US third class bulk mail, $22/year, Canada first class mail, US funds, $27/year overseas airmail, US funds. For memberships outside US please use postal money orders, International Reply Coupons, MasterCard or Visa. Web site: www.tioc.com

Triumph Roadster Club
11, The Park
Carshalton, Surrey SM5 3BY
England
(UK) 0181 669 3965

Founded 1960. 500 members. Restricted to Triumph 1800 and 2000 roadster models 18TR and 20TR, manufactured between 1946 and 1949. Ten magazines or newsletters annually. Technical publications available. Dues: UK/EEC paid in £UK, £20/year; elsewhere paid in £UK, £25/year; other than in £UK, £30/year; except US and Canada paid to North American chapter, $41.25/year (US dollars).

chapters:

Australia   Glynn Ford, 30 Minyip Rd, Lara Lake Victoria 3212, PH/FAX: 03 5282 1725; E-mail: glyford@iaccess.com.au

Germany   Theo Dammerz, Feldstrasse 4, 47661 Issum-Sevelen, 02835 9541-11; FAX: 02835 9541-22

Holland   *Benelux*, Hans van Eeuwijk, Putterstraat 25, 5256 AM Heusden, 0416 665275; FAX: 0416 665276; E-mail: vaneeuijk@wxs.nl

New Zealand   Peter Faber, 123 Puriri Park Rd, Maunu, Wharangarei, 09 438 7613; FAX: 09 438 1733

Triumph Roadster Club chapters *(continued)*

North America   Mel Merzon, 5051 Greenleaf, Skokie, IL
60077-2172, PH/FAX: 847-677-7341; E-mail:
msm@navistor.com

Norway   *Scandinavia*, Kjell-Arne Hoel, Karlsvognen 5,
N-2300 Hamar, 6252 73 83; FAX: 6253 36 65

Vintage Triumph Register
15218 W Warren Ave
Dearborn, MI 48126
847-940-9347
E-mail: vtr~www@www.vtr.org

Founded 1974. 2,900 members. For owners and enthusiasts of
all Triumph automobiles. Membership includes quarterly magazine, free classified ads, technical information consultants and
more. Dues: $25/year, $30/year Canada, US funds. Web site:
www.vtr.org
zones:

Arizona   *Desert Centre Triumph Register*, John Lindly,
Editor, 6434 E Corrine Dr, Scottsdale, AZ
85254, 602-548-1915

Arkansas   *British Motoring Club of Arkansas*, Bob Ross,
VTR Liaison, PO Box 22865, Little Rock, AR
72221, 501-888-3396

California   *Central Coast Triumphs All British Car Club*,
C Darryl Struth, President, PO Box 503,
Ventura, CA 93002, 805-644-6211

*Southern California Triumph Owners
Association*, Bill Burroughs, VTR Liaison,
7250 McCool Ave, Westchester, CA 90045,
310-641-9204

Triumph Register of Southern California, Sue
Davis, VTR Liaison, 20929 Lassen St #112,
Chatsworth, CA 91311, 818-998-5753

Triumph Sports Car Club of San Diego, Leslie
Harpenau, Editor, PO Box 84342, San Diego,
CA 92138-0633, 619-484-6114

Triumph Travelers Sports Car Club, Jim
Sudduth, VTR Liaison, PO Box 60314,
Sunnyvale, CA 94088-0314, 510-649-7845

Colorado   *Rocky Mountain Triumph Club*, Glen Sorenson,
VTR Liaison, PO Box 300426, Denver, CO
80203-0426, 303-220-9742

Connecticut   *Connecticut Triumph Register*, Stan Malcolm,
Membership Director, 17 Caffyn Dr,
Marlborough, CT 06447, E-mail:
102654.3574@compuserve.com

Florida   *Central Florida Triumph Register*, Gary Hunter,
President, 293 Graham Ave, Oviedo, FL
32765

Gold Coast Triumph Club, Chad Jester,
President, PO Box 10451, Pompano Beach, FL
33061, 305-427-0534

Temple of Triumph, Robert L Jones, President,
Rt 4 Box 155, Westville, FL 32464,
850-956-2887

Triumph Club of North Florida, Walt Lanz, Vice
President, 1900 Kusaie Dr, Jacksonville, FL
32246, 904-646-0616

Triumph Standard Motor Club, Kent Stutler,
VTR Liaison, 8156 128th St N, Seminole, FL
33776, 813-397-4190

Georgia   *Georgia Triumph Association*, Don Burns, VTR
Liaison, 1824 Vermillion Bay Cir, Duluth, GA
30097, 404-623-9311

Idaho   *Northwest British Classics*, Donnel Schmidt,
VTR Liaison, 1924 Lakeside Ave, Coeur
d'Alene, ID 83814, 208-664-5062

Illinois   *Central Illinois Triumph Owners Association*,
Mark Joslyn, President, 1406 Winding Ln,
Champaign, IL 61820, 217-359-6792;
E-mail: mbjoslyn@prairienet.org

Illinois Sports Owners Association, Jack
Billimack, VTR Liaison, 23 Elmhurst Ave,
Crystal Lake, IL 60014, 815-459-4721;
E-mail: jbillimack@aol.com

Indiana   *Indiana Triumph Cars*, Thomas L Beaver, 7510
Allisonville Rd, Indianapolis, IN 46250,
317-848-3429

Iowa   *Hawkeye Triumphs Ltd*, Brian Fanton,
President, PO Box 81, Hiawatha, IA
52233-0081, 319-393-1192

**Kansas/
Missouri**   *Kansas City Triumphs*, Jay Smith, Director,
1315 NE 69th St, Gladstone, MO 64118,
E-mail: jsmith@mjharden.com

Kentucky   *British Sports Car Club Louisville*, Gordon &
Becky Carnes, 208 E Morrison St, Wilmore,
KY 40390, 502-267-8707

Louisiana   *British Motoring Club-New Orleans Inc*, Harold
O'Reilly, VTR Liaison, Box 13803, New
Orleans, LA 70185, 504-486-5837

Masssachusetts   *Western Massachusetts Triumph Association*,
Bob O'Donnel, President, 5 Louise Ave,
Easthampton, MA 01027, 413-527-2816

Michigan   *Detroit Triumph Sportscar Club*, Terry Walters,
President, 8972 Deborah Ct E, Livonia,
MI 48150

**Michigan/
Indiana**   *Michigan Triumph Association*, Joseph
Germay, 9349 S Westnedge, Kalamazoo, MI
49002, 616-327-9262

Minnesota   *Minnesota Triumphs*, Larry Sanderson, VTR
Liaison, PO Box 201054, Bloomington, MN
55420, 507-775-6940; E-mail:
sandolarry@aol.com

Mississippi   *English Motor Club-Central Mississippi Chapter
VTR*, Steve Collins, President, PO Box 5263,
Jackson, MS 39216, 601-856-3225

Missouri   *St Louis Triumph Owners Association*, David
Massey, President, 321 Peeke, Kirkwood, MO
63122, 314-966-6056

Nebraska   *Nebraska Triumph Drivers*, Bill Redinger,
Director, 1014 N 127th Ave, Omaha, NE
68154, 402-496-2006; E-mail:
aredinger@juno.com

Nevada   *British Auto Club of Las Vegas*, Isben Dow,
Editor, 2910 Boise St, Las Vegas, NV 89121,
702-641-9419

New England   *British Motorcars, FTR, Ltd of New England*,
Roger Jusseaume, Club Contact, 404 Spring
St PO Box 666, North Dighton, MA 02764-
0666, 508-679-8252

New England Triumphs, Frank Frett, Director,
598 S Almond St, Fall River, MA 02724,
508-672-1071

New Jersey   *British Motor Club of Southern New Jersey*, Ed Gaubert, Director, 13 Fox Hollow Dr, Cherry Hill, NJ 08003, 609-751-7773

New Jersey Triumph Association, George Hughes, PO Box 6, Gillette, NJ 07933, 908-788-1982; E-mail: jagshop@eclipse.net

New York   *Adirondack Triumph Association*, Rik Schlierer, VTR Liaison, PO Box 2207 Empire Station, Albany, NY 12220-2207, 516-356-5244

Finger Lakes Triumph Club, Russ Moore, President, 49 Caroline Depot Rd, Brooktondale, NY 14817, 607-539-7442

Long Island Triumph Association, Geoffrey Levy, Director, 14 Churchill Dr, Brentwood, NY 11717, 516-968-9772

Syracuse Area, Vincent Paul Hueber, 101 Vieau Dr, Syracuse, NY 13207, 315-475-8603

North Carolina   *Triumph Club of The Carolinas*, Bill Wood, President, 503 S Lindell Rd, Greensboro, NC 27403, 910-852-3301

Ohio   *Miami Valley Triumphs*, Frank Ciboch, President, 879 Heatherstone, Forest Park, OH 45240, 513-825-3500

North Coast Triumph Association, Al Kelly, President, 5891 St Rt 82, Hirma, OH 44234

Quad Cities British Auto Club, Beverly Floyd, 1996 Four Seasons, Akron, OH 44333

Oklahoma   *Central Oklahoma Vintage Triumph Register*, Glenn Danford, Membership, 329 NW 21st, Oklahoma City, OK 73101, 405-525-8631

Green Country Triumphs, Samuel R Clark, President, 13415 S 127th E Ave, Broken Arrow, OK 74011, 918-455-8993

Oregon   *Portland Triumph Owners Association*, Ray Marty, VTR Liaison, PO Box 5516, Portland, OR 97228, 503-645-6324

Pennsylvania   *British Car Club of the Lehigh Valley (BCCLV)*, Bob Snyder, VTR Liaison, 3397 Lanark Rd, Coopersburg, PA 18036, E-mail: rjsnydercpa@msn.com

Central Pennsylvania Triumph Club, Dick James, Membership, 23 Houston Dr, Mechanicsburg, PA 17055, 717-766-7407

Delaware Valley Triumphs Ltd, Frank Markowitz, VTR Liaison, 1430 Old West Chester Pike, West Chester, PA 19382, 610-431-0308

Keystone Triumphs Ltd, Bruce Strock, President, PO Box 490 3175 Center & Church Sts, Springtown, PA 18081-0490, 610-346-7304

Western Pennsylvania Triumph Association, Ed Woods, Membership, 105 Hawk Dr, Glenshaw, PA 15116, 412-486-4294

South Carolina   *Southeastern British Motorcar Owners Club*, Rick Morrison, President, c/o C Miller PO Box 1274, Gramling, SC 29348, 803-576-4228

Texas   *El Paso Triumph Club*, Charles Beck, 1641 Bert Green Dr, El Paso, TX 79936, 915-593-3584

Hill Country Triumph Club, Bob Kramer, Membership, 8006 Bernard St, Volente, TX 78641, 512-250-9498

Red River Triumph Club, Duncan Wood, President, 817-251-0912; E-mail: sheila_duncan@msn.com

South Texas Triumph Association, Kathie Hulka, Membership, 5306 La Cieniga, San Antonio, TX 78233, 512-650-4660

Texas Triumph Register, Len Myers, President, PO Box 40847, Houston, TX 77240-0847, 281-493-1476

Utah   *British Motor Club of Utah*, Jim Pivirotto, 1419 S 900 E, Salt Lake City, UT 84105, 801-486-0547

Vermont   *Vermont Centre of British Motorcars FTR, Ltd of New England*, Dave & Joyce Silveira, 4 Farmstead Dr, Shelburne, VT 05482, 802-985-2860

Virginia   *Blue Ridge Triumphs*, Bill Brooks, President, 3960 Bower Rd SW, Roanoke, VA 24018-2933, 540-989-3030

Richmond Triumph Register, Dean Tetterton, Membership, 8327 Avignon Dr, Richmond, VA 23235-4205, 804-320-6330

Tidewater Triumph Register, Martin Pachey, President, 3437 Petunia Cres, Virginia Beach, VA 20836, 757-468-9903; E-mail: martintr3-7@erols.com

Washington   *Tyee Triumph Club*, Jack Adams, VTR Liaison, PO Box 27668, Seattle, WA 98125-2668, 206-338-3366; E-mail: jackdian@juno.com

Washington DC   *Capital Triumph Register*, Keith Dunklee, Secretary, 3008 S 2nd St, Arlington, VA 22204, 703-521-2245

Wisconsin   *Vintage Triumphs of Wisconsin Ltd*, Jim Morris, President, 414-466-1252

Canada   *British Columbia Triumph Registry*, Daniel Brien, VTR Liaison, 32248 Autumn Ave, Abbotsford, BC V2T 1P3, 604-859-0149; E-mail: d_brien@pacificgroup.net

Ontario Triumph Club (Canada), Doug Bell, President, 166 Church St, Thamesford, ON N0M 2M0, 519-285-3158

Toronto Triumph Club, Don Mills, PO Box 39, Toronto, ON M3C 2R6, 416-638-6031

Tucker Automobile Club of America Inc
9509 Hinton Dr
Santee, CA 92071-2760
PH/FAX: 619-596-3028
E-mail: wep77@aol.com

TUCKER

450+ members. Monthly publication, *Tucker Topics*, is included in membership. Annual convention, mini-meets. Dues: $25/year US, $40/year foreign. Web site: tuckerclub.org

---

TVR Car Club North America
12512 Great Park Cir Apt 301
Germantown, MD 20876-5990
PH/FAX: 301-601-4945

For membership information, contact at the above address: Marq J Ruben. Founded 1971. 1,000 members. Open to all owners and enthusiasts of TVR and Griffith hand-built sports cars. Publication, *TVR Times*. Dues $30/year.

Vanden Plas Princess Register
16643 Rt 144
Lisbon, MD 21771
301-854-5900, 410-442-3637
FAX: 301-854-5957

Vanden Plas

Club for Princess limousines, sedans, hearses and ambulances from 1947-1968. Clearinghouse for information, parts, workshop and owner's manuals, repair help, Whitworth tools. Please provide chassis number in any correspondence. Large supply of original and reproduction parts including rubber seals, brake, suspension and body parts. 12 Princess parts cars on hand.

Virtual Vignale Gamine Club
PO Box 3059
Vlaardingen ZH 3130CB
Netherlands
+31-10-2470035
FAX: +31-10-2470036
E-mail: gamine@mixe.demon.nl

Vignale

Founded 1997. 20 members. Owners of a Vignale Gamine can subscribe to the Virtual Club. This club only exists on the internet and is aimed at reuniting all the remaining Gamines. Vignale Gamine owners and enthusiasts can subscribe to an e-mail newsletter. Web site: http://come.to/vignale

NEATO/Vintage VW Bus Club
PO Box 4190
Albuquerque, NM 87196
505-268-2220
E-mail: neato@rt66.com

Founded 1986. 1,200 members. For all owners and admirers of pre-1968 VW Type 2s/Transporters, buses, Kombis, campers, etc. Newsletter, chapters and meets all across North America. Publish member directory and old bus registry. Dues: $20/year.

South Eastern Volkswagen Club
257 Oak Trace Rd
Hahira, GA 31632
912-896-4957
E-mail: sgvw@geocities.com or
southeastvw@hotmail.com

Founded 1994. 150 members across the southeast. Must have a Volkswagen. Bi-monthly newsletter. Club sticker/shirts; get-togethers. Host several events throughout the year. Dues: $15/year. Web site: www.geocities.com/motorcity/5998

chapters:

Florida   *Daytona Chapter*, Richard Adamovic, 6173 Half Moon Dr, Port Orange, FL 32127, 904-761-1794; E-mail: radamovic@aol.com

Jacksonville Chapter, Hilltop Motors, 9557 Lem Turner Rd, Jacksonville, FL 32208, 904-768-9961; E-mail: grimondi@aol.com

St Augustine Chapter, Bruce Kahler, 212 Mayan Terr, St Augustine, FL 32084, 904-471-7705

Tallahasse Chapter, Joe Clark, 850-385-3959; E-mail: jclark@supernet.net

Georgia   *Atlanta Chapter*, Cheryl Houlton, 3009 Valley Brook Pl, Decatur, GA 30033, 404-296-2025; E-mail: dtrantham@mindspring.com

Three Rivers Volkswagen Club
409 Ave D
Forest Hills, PA 15221
412-734-5270 (24 hr hotline)
E-mail: prs@escm.com

Founded 1988. 100 members. Newsletter published 4 times per year. German Auto Expo last Sunday in September at Billco VW

in Wexford, PA, show and swap with food and music. Dues: $15/year. Web site: www.geocities.com/~3riversvwclub

Volvo Club of America
PO Box 16
Afton, NY 13730
607-639-2279; FAX: 607-639-2279

VOLVO

For information, write, phone or fax to the above address. Founded 1983. 3,500 members. National club of owners and enthusiasts of all Volvo automobiles. Membership benefits include: subscription to *Rolling* magazine, parts discounts, technical assistance, local chapters and regional and national meets. Dues: $25/year. Web site: www.vcoa.org

chapters:

Arizona   *Cactus Chapter*, Randall Pace, 14414 N 51st St, Scottsdale, AZ 85254, 602-953-0650

California   *North Bay (California)*, Lee Cordner, 313 Point San Pedro Rd, San Rafael, CA 94901, 415-455-9192

San Francisco/Northern California, David Spieler, 1908 California #7, Berkeley, CA 94703, 510-849-0961

Colorado   *Colorado/Rocky Mountain*, Gary Pittman, 1818 N Circle Dr, Colorado Springs, CO 80909, 719-635-7805

Delaware   *Delaware Valley*, Mel Rosenthal, 5 The Strand, New Castle, DE 19720, 302-322-8944

Florida   *Florida*, Dave Montgomery, 4424 Ortega Farms Cir, Jacksonville, FL 32210, 904-771-1154

Florida Nature Coast, The Garthes, 25373 Croom Rd, Brooksville, FL 34601-5007, 352-796-9490

Florida/Southwest, Bill or Pat Rose, 124 Trinidad St, Isles of Capri, FL 34113, 941-263-4505

Georgia   *Atlanta*, Kirk Houser, 501 Wexwood Dr, Riverdale, GA 30274, 770-477-1910

Bertone Register, Pat and Jon Evans, 1303 Swann Dr, Dalton, GA 30720, 706-226-0488

Maine   *Maine*, Tom Roane, RR 1 Box 1433, Limerick, ME 04048, 207-793-2418

Massachusetts   *Boston/Merrimack Valley*, Duncan LaBay, 4 Ferry Rd, Newburyport, MA 01950, 978-462-1607

Missouri   *Missouri/Southern Illinois*, Steve Patterson, 4714 Tennessee Ave, St Louis, MO 63111, 314-752-5331

New Jersey   *240 Classic Register*, Carl Bauske, 298 Pennington-Titusville Rd, Pennington, NJ 08534, 609-730-8124

Garden State Chapter, Tom Lamb, 6 Pergola St, Jamesburg, NJ 08831, 732-521-0253

New York   *New York Metro*, Howie Silverman, 207 Bayview Ave, Massapequa, NY 11758, 516-798-3618

Volvo PV Register, Mark Heyburn, PO Box 733, Vails Gate, NY 12584, 914-569-1390

North Carolina   *Blue Ridge*, Del Lance, 1008 Winwood Dr, Cary, NC 27511-4349, 919-380-0428

Ohio   *Southwest Ohio*, Chris Ward, PO Box 42, Willard, OH 44890, 914-935-2110

Oregon	*Pacific NW/SW Washington*, Amy Carlson, 4107A SE Washington St, Portland, OR 97214, 503-731-9960
Pennsylvania	*Philadelphia*, Michael Leslie, 29 Thomas Ave, Bryn Mawr, PA 19010, 610-525-4872
South Carolina	*South Carolina*, John Crabtree, 135 Ridge Glen, Simpsonville, SC 29680, 864-862-6737
Texas	*Texas*, Al Ringle, 3417 Forrester Ln, Waco, TX 76708, 254-753-1115
Virginia	*240 Limited Edition Register*, Ray Parsons, 1248 Bond St, Herndon, VA 22070, 703-742-8274
Washington	*Washington/Puget Sound*, Wes Urbanec, 128 Fifth Ave NW, Puyallup, WA 98371, 253-848-8958

Volvo Owners' Club
34 Lyonsgate Dr
Downsview, ON Canada M3H 1C8
416-633-6801

Founded 1976. 250 members from US, Canada, Europe, Brazil and Australia. Covers all Volvo models, old and new.

Mid-America Willys Club
18819 Valley Dr
Minnetonka, MN 55345
612-474-3867; FAX: 612-474-4526
E-mail: skids19@aol.com

Founded 1988. 1,325 members. Bi-monthly magazine, *Gasser Gossip*, yearly roster. No restrictions to join. Club focuses on Willys cars 1933-1942, from street rods to original to race cars. Dues: $30/year US, $33/year Canada, $35/year international. Web site: www.alistauto.com/mawillys

Midstates Jeepster Association
5905 N 300 W
Michigan City, IN 46360
219-326-5589; FAX: 219-324-9096
E-mail: wrightd1@csinet.net

Founded 1966. 360 families. Must have an interest in Jeepsters, 1948-1951. We encourage you to join. You will receive: information for the restoration and preservation of Jeepsters; access to classified advertising for items for sale and things wanted; notices of future meets where you can meet other Jeepster lovers; articles sent in by our members showing "what worked for me"; a roster of our 360+ family memberships. Publish monthly newsletter. Have two main meets each year, one in spring and one in fall. Encourage mini-meets in areas throughout the year for those that can't make our two main meets or just want to get together more often. Dues: $25/year, $3 one time application fee. Web site: http://members.tripod.com/~dan_wright/index-2.html

Willys-Overland Jeepster Club News
167 Worcester St
Taunton, MA 02780-2088
E-mail: jeepsterme@aol.com

Founded 1964. 600 members. Willys-Overland Jeepsters 1948-1951, members around USA, Canada, Scandinavia and Europe. Annual Founders Meet, meets around USA, monthly newsletter with free classified advertisments for members. Membership available to all who own, operate, restore, collect or otherwise have interest in this vehicle. Dues: $18/year US, outside US pays extra postage.

Zimmer Motor Car Club
1415 W Genesee St
Syracuse, NY 13204
315-422-7011 ext 125
FAX: 315-422-1721
E-mail: newtimes@rway.com

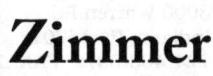

Founded 1995. 225 members. For all Zimmer motor car owners. Newsletters and information on Zimmers. Specializing in Zimmer Golden Spirits, 1980-1988 and 1998-1999. Free publication, *Zimmer Times*, published quarterly, information about Zimmer motor cars. Dues: none. Web site: www.rway.com/zimmer

Registries

North American Mini Moke Registry
1779 Kickapoo St
PO Box 9110
South Lake Tahoe, CA 96150
530-577-7895
E-mail: twobears@interserv.com

Founded 1982. 70 members. Need not own a Moke to join. No meetings, newsletter provides contact between owners. In contact with Mini Moke Club of England, Moke Club of Australia and exchange letters with Mini Clubs worldwide. Dues: $15/year.

The North American Bitter SC Registry
Richard Anderson, President
26 Brandywine
South Barrington, IL 60010
847-836-5006

4 members (total importation of the Bitter SC was approximately 300 cars). The North American Bitter Registry was originally formed in 1995 as part of the Opel Association of North America, due to the small number of Bitter SC coupes imported into the US and the non-existence of any club to help the owners of these rare and exotic cars. Our club gives assistance and helps owners have a place to get connected since the Bitter SC, while a custom car, was over 80% Opel parts and engineering. Have since become the Bitter SC Registry. Members of the Registry are encouraged to also join the Opel Association of North America to keep up with upcoming events and other information. The OANA also tries to add Bitter SC information into its newsletter when it has any. Dues: none.

Brabham Register
1611 Alvina Ave
Sacramento, CA 95822
916-454-1115

Brabham

Founded 1979. Formed to provide information to Brabham owners for use in the authentic restoration of the cars. Must own Brabham race car to join. Initiation fee: $30.

Bristol Register of New Zealand
61 Rothesay Bay Road
Rothesay Bay
Auckland, 10 New Zealand
PH/FAX: 64-9-478-7426
E-mail: bristol@clear.net.nz

Maintain a register of all Bristol and Bristol engined cars in New Zealand. Limited spares for Bristol 400-406 cars and 85-100-110-BS engines.

1932 Buick Registry
3000 Warren Rd
Indiana, PA 15701
724-463-3372; FAX: 724-463-8604

Founded 1974. 400 members. Open only to 1932 Buicks. Manufacture and sell reproduction parts for Buick 1925-1935. Disseminate information on 1932 model Buicks, including sales of literature. Free *1932 Buick Registry* newsletter. Printed parts list available for 1925-1935 Buicks, send SASE. Dues: none.

Marquette Owners Registry for Enthusiasts
Don Holton
803 Cedar St
Elmira, NY 14904-2643
607-734-5340
E-mail: topsdown@stny.rr.com

Founded 1996. Approximately 100 members. There are no restrictions to join. This is an international registry for owners of the Made by Buick Marquette. These were made for the 1930 model year but many are registered as 1929s. The publication is called *MORE* and is published approximately 3 times per year including the registry. We do hold an annual owners' meeting during the October AACA Fall Eastern Division National Show at Hershey, PA. Dues: $8/year US and Canada, $12/year international (US money order). Web site: http://home.stny.lrun.com/holtonfamily/marquette.html

Chalmers Automobile Registry
c/o Dave Hammond
110 Sourwood Dr
Hatboro, PA 19040-1922
215-672-0764
E-mail: dchamm@worldnet.att.net

Founded 1995. 85 owners (102 cars) listed in US, Canada and England. 48 active members. The purpose of the Chalmers Automobile Registry is to maintain an up-to-date record of all surviving Chalmers automobiles and to provide a means for information exchange between Chalmers owners. Newsletters are published irregularly based on membership questions and comments. Dues: none.

Clenet Registry
Donald C Royston
11311 Woodland Dr
Lutherville, MD 21093
410-825-2010

Clenet Registry has information regarding Clenet automobiles 1978-1997, listing of owners, etc.

De Vaux Registry
647 Ridgeview Dr
Corunna, MI 48817
517-743-5390

Registry of existing 1931-1932 De Vaux automobiles.

1939-1947 Dodge Truck Registry
c/o Dave Fenner
1625 Jason St
San Diego, CA 92154
619-575-1543; FAX: 619-571-3457
E-mail: dfenn@sdcoe.k12.ca.us

Founded 1998. 125+ members. Periodic newsletter is planned, annual truck show is planned during fall months. Dues: none.

1970 Dart Swinger 340's Registry
PO Box 9
Wethersfield, CT 06129-0009
860-257-8434 evenings
E-mail: dart1970@aol.com

Founded 1986. 500+ members. Must own a 1970 Dodge Dart Swinger 340. Verifies and locates all 13,785 1970 Dodge Dart Swinger 340's. Free information to help restore and preserve these cars. Newsletter subscription, $10/year for 4 quarterly issues. Dues: none.

Dodge Charger Registry
PO Box 184
Green Bay, VA 23942
804-223-1305

Founded 1986. 450 members. No restrictions to join. T-shirt, decal and quarterly newsletter available. Also free convention admission to any of our 5 shows. Dues: $25/year initial, $20/year renewal.

International Viper Registry
PO Box 914
Arkadelphia, AR 71923-0914
501-246-0015; FAX: 501-246-0762
E-mail: viperjay@iocc.com

Founded 1992. 750 members. Dedicated to the care, preservation and history of the Dodge Viper. Registration certificate, $15. Web site: www.viperclub.org/ivr

North American English & European Ford Registry
PO Box 11415
Olympia, WA 98508
360-754-9585
E-mail: ifhp@aol.com

See full listing in **Section Three** under **Marque Clubs**

Erskine Register
441 E St Clair
Almont, MI 48003
810-798-8600

For membership information, contact at the above address: Norman Hamilton, send SASE.

Topolino Register of North America
3301 Shetland Rd
Beavercreek, OH 45434
937-426-0098
E-mail: mike7353@aol.com

For information, contact at the above address: Mike Self. Founded 1969. 72 members. This is a register of Fiat 500 A/B/C, Simca 5, NSU-Fiat 500 owners and owners of Topolino-based vehicles, 1936-1955. Serves as a restoration, information and parts source exchange for owners. Register published periodically. Dues: none.

68 Ford Torino Indy Pace Car Registry
8032 E Hayne St
Tucson, AZ 85710-4213
520-886-8004; call for fax

Founded 1990. 20-25 members. Registry for 1968 Ford Torino Indy pace cars. Newsletter sometimes. Dues: none.

SHO Registry
PO Box 159
Carrollton, GA 30117
770-836-1474; FAX: 770-214-8864

Founded 1990. 2,800+ members. Formed to enhance the owner-

Section Three — Registries   Ford - Mercury **549**

ship of the Taurus SHO. Perhaps the finest high-performance sedan of this generation. Only enthusiasm is required. Publish a quarterly magazine. Dues: $35/year. Web site: www.shoregistry.com

1971-1973 Mustang High-Performance Coupe Registry
114 Dry Ave
Cary, NC 27511
E-mail: edandsusan@aol.com

For information, send SASE to the above address, Ed Tilley. Anyone owning a 1971-1973 Mustang coupe with engine code M, R, C, J or Q is eligible for inclusion. These are the 429 CJ, 429 CJ-R, 351 CJ, 351 HO and Boss 351 engines. No cost to join.

66-67-68 High Country Special Registry
6874 Benton Ct
Arvada, CO 80003-4244
303-424-3866

Founded 1980. Over 200 members. An information source for prospective buyers and owners of 1966, 1967, 1968 High Country Special Mustangs. Dues: none.

Mustang Special Order Paint Registry
c/o Tony Popish
6113 S Cherry Ct
Littleton, CO 80121
720-489-1504
E-mail: tpopish@aol.com

Founded 1994. 300 members. Interest in first generation Mustang history, especially dealing with special order paint Mustangs. Publish *Horse of a Different Color* for $9/4 issues. Dedicated to the special order paint Mustang, featuring color information, interviews with former FoMoCo employees, etc, for 1964-1/2 to 1973 Mustangs. Dues: none. Web site: http://members.aol.com/dsomustang/

Honda 600 Roster of Owners
c/o Bill Colford
7518 Westbrook Ave
San Diego, CA 92139
619-267-0485
E-mail: aahonda600@juno.com

No rules or regulations. A source of: reliable technical information, location of mechanics that "know" the Honda 600, restoration information and assistance, location of hard to find parts, information on the next gathering of the Honda 600 Group. No dues. No membership fee. Web site: www.freeyellow.com/members2/zcoupe/index/html

Inter-State Motor Car Registry 1909-1919
Jay Arendt, Registrar
13883 Tesson Ferry Rd
St Louis, MO 63128
314-849-3391; FAX: 314-326-0520

Inter-State

Founded 1994. 13 members. Open anytime day/night, weekends, etc, 8 am to 10 pm CST. Inter-State Motor Cars 1909-1919 registry for the free exchange of information, parts, services and publications. No restrictions to join, just an interest in the 1909-1919 Inter-State automobile, period publications upon request. Meets and events to be announced. Copies of Inter-State Motor Car publications available to all registry members.

The Jeep Registry Europe
Proosdyerveldweg 56-2
Ede 6712 AG The Netherlands
(31) 318-693690
FAX: (31) 318-693689
E-mail: jeep.registry.europe@wxs.nl

Founded 1992. 1,200+/- members. Quarterly newsletter. If you own any model Jeep, old or new, Bantam, Willys, Kaiser, AMC, Chrysler, military or civilian, then you should join The Jeep Registry. Dues: $22/year US, $30/year non-US address. Web site: http://members.aol.com/jeepreg1

The Jordan Register
2099 Pheasant Dr
Yuba City, CA 95993
530-673-7382

Founded 1983. 110 members. Celebrating Jordan Motor Car Company automobile collecting and restoring. Historical archives, tours and appreciation for this company's wonderful advertising. Quarterly magazine. Dues: $20/year.

Kaiser Darrin Owners Roster
734 Antram Rd
Somerset, PA 15501-8856
814-443-6468; FAX: 814-443-9452

Approximately 300 members. Club caters to owners of Kaiser Darrins. Publish *Darrin Roster* yearly. Roster includes information on car history, parts, restoration help, etc. The Kaiser Darrin Owners Roster operates with the Kaiser Frazer Owners Club International. Dues: none (donations).

Kellison & Astra Registry and Club eV
c/o Michael Dziedzic
Emdener Str 19
10551 Berlin Germany
0049 30 390 39944
FAX: 0049 30 390 39949
E-mail: kellisonre@aol.com

Kellison

The US contact: Hager Hedfield, 3402 Valley Creek Cir, Middleton, WI 53562. Founded 1996. The registry is for all actual and former owners. The club is looking for enthusiasts of Kellison and Astra too.

Manx Dune Buggy Club
PO Box 1491
Valley Center, CA 92082
760-749-6321; FAX: 760-751-0610
E-mail: manxclub@cts.com

Manx

See full listing in **Section Three** under **Specialty Clubs**

72/73 Mercury Montego GT Registry
11715 Winterpock Rd
Chesterfield, VA 23838
804-639-7289
E-mail: montegogt@aol.com

Founded 1998. 38 members. Promotes the preservation and restoration of these rare vehicles by being a link between various owners. Mails out a newsletter three times yearly. Dues: none. Web site: http://members.aol.com/montegogt/registry.html

Section Three
Clubs & Organizations

California MG T Register
4911 Winnetka Ave
Woodland Hills, CA 91364

For membership information, contact at the above address: Dick Riddle, 818-883-9681. Founded 1969. 200 members. All MG owners and enthusiasts are welcome to join. Monthly newsletter, tour or event and monthly meetings in Studio City, CA. Our purpose is to provide an association for owners of MG cars and to promote an interest in and perpetuation of these fine old cars. Dues include jacket patch and dash plaque. Dues: $20/year, $10 initiation fee.

Monteverdi Registry and Club eV
c/o Michael Dziedzic
Emdener Str 19
10551 Berlin Germany
0049 30 390 39944
FAX: 0049 30 390 39949
E-mail: monteg@aol.com

Founded 1983. The registry is for all actual and former owners. The club is looking for enthusiasts of Monteverdi GT-Cats, like the 375 high speed or the Safari, Sahara Jeep too.

Nordic 1955-1956 Mopar Register
PO Box 89
Borgenhaugen 1740 Norway
+4769167702; FAX: +4769167211
E-mail: mopar@of.telia.no

Founded 1994. 145 members. For owners and people interested in 1955-1956 Plymouth, Dodge, DeSoto, Chrysler and Imperial. Members' magazine 4 times a year, 3 meets each year. Cooperates with Mopar clubs all over the world. Dues: $20/year. Web site: www.shokstop.com/1955/nordic55.htm

Morris Minor Registry of North America
Tony Burgess
318 Hampton Park
Westerville, OH 43081-5723
614-899-2394; FAX: 614-899-2493
E-mail: morrisminr@aol.com

750 members nationwide and 34 regional representatives. Dedicated to the preservation, restoration and use of the postwar Morris Minor automobile. Bi-monthly newsletter, *Minor News*, contains technical tips, feature stories on cars and related topics, meet reports, calendar of events, club and car regalia, classified ads and much more. Car registration is free. Dues: $20/year US and Canada; $30/year overseas via airmail.

Muntz Registry
21303 NE 151st
Woodinville, WA 98072
425-788-6587; FAX: 425-844-2331
E-mail: bvmunsen@aol.com

Historical information and registration for Muntz Jet automobiles 1950-1954. *Muntz Registry* is published as requested and includes production history and owner's listing for Muntz Jet automobiles produced 1950-1954.

1948-1950 Packard Convertible Roster
84 Hoy Ave
Fords, NJ 08863
732-738-7859; FAX: 732-738-7625
E-mail: stellacapp@earthlink.net

Founded 1989. Seeking information on all 1948-1950 Packard Super Eight and Custom Eight convertibles. Send an SASE for roster form.

The Packard V-8 Roster, 1955-1956
84 Hoy Ave
Fords, NJ 08863
732-738-7859; FAX: 732-738-7625
E-mail: stellacapp@earthlink.net

For more information, contact at the above address: Stuart R Blond. Founded 1982. Roster for all 1955-1956 Packards and Clippers. Send an SASE for roster form.

1969-1971 Pontiac GTO The Judge Convertible Registry
1165 County Rd 83
Independence, MN 55359
612-479-2248
E-mail: parajada@aol.com

Founded 1993. 50 members. Providing a list of owners and enthusiasts of the Pontiac GTO "The Judge" convertibles (manufactured from 1969-1971).

Firehawk Association of America
c/o W Thomas
PO Box 96
Uniontown, PA 15401
724-437-6736
E-mail: fhawk149@bellatlantic.net

Founded 1994. 350 members. Registry, quarterly newsletter, includes new products, improvements, recalls, problems and members' articles and a sell and want section. Dues: $12/year. Web site: www.firehawk.com

The Association of Rootes Vehicle Owners
Capri House
Walton-On-Thames
Surrey, KT12 2LY England

An association of the owners of vehicles built and sold by the Rootes Group and their various subsidiary companies. Objective is to provide a means of communication and cooperation between these owners and maintain a watching brief on UK and European legislation affecting members' vehicles. Membership is open to owners and enthusiasts of Rootes vehicles. Publication, *ARVO News*. Dues: £14/year.

Scripps-Booth Register
735 W Lemon Ave
Monrovia, CA 91016-2507
626-358-7327
E-mail: scrippsbooth@earthlink.net

Founded 1982. 50 members. Free annual newsletter and register updates. Free copies of factory literature with car and engine serial number. Dues: free to owners. Web site: http://home.earthlink.net/~scrippsbooth/

Stephens Registry
Dick Farnsworth
1034 Henderson
Freeport, IL 61032
815-232-3825

STEPHENS

Sunbeam Rapier Registry of North America
3212 Orchard Cir
West Des Moines, IA 50266-2140
515-226-9475
E-mail: jmazour@aol.com

Founded 1992. A registry and club for the identification and preservation of Sunbeam Rapiers (Series I-V, 1955-1967). Publications: *Sunbeam Rapier Registry of North America* (1999)

and quarterly club newsletter, *Rapier News*. A free registry publication to each Rapier owner who participates in this registry. Dues: $16/year US, $19/year Canada.

Velie Register
1811 E Stella Ln
Phoenix, AZ 85016
602-274-6049
E-mail: velie@goodnet.com

Founded 1993. 200 members. Open to anyone. *Velie Vehicles and Their Vitals*, 55-page book, is the official register of Velie cars and trucks, 1909-1928. Publish 6-8 Velie newsletters per year. Dues: $10/year. Web site: www.goodnet.com/~velie

Vespa 400 Registry
100 Prince St
Fairfield, CT 06432
203-336-1505

Founded 1996. 100 members. Only interest in the Vespa 400 necessary. We keep a registry of cars and extra parts listings. Dues: none.

Victoria Registry
100 Prince St
Fairfield, CT 06432
203-336-1505

Founded 1996. 13 members. Only interest in the Victoria necessary. We keep a list of owners and spare parts. Dues: none.

Willys Aero Survival Count
952 Ashbury Heights Ct
Decatur, GA 30030-4177
404-288-8222
E-mail: aeroman@aol.com

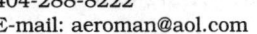

Founded 1981. 800 cars, 500 owners. This is not a club, it's really just a registry.

Zimmerman Registry
2081 Madelaine Ct
Los Altos, CA 94024
PH/FAX: 650-967-2908
E-mail: zmrmn@macconnect.com

Founded 1989. 42 members. Dedicated to the preservation and restoration of Zimmerman automobiles manufactured in Auburn, Indiana, from 1908-1915. Information exchanged between members by letter and fax. No meetings, publications or dues.

Specialty Clubs

Antique Auto Racing Association Inc
Alice Wertz, Secretary
8415 Herbert Rd
Canfield, OH 44406

Founded 1973. 300 members. Open to vintage race car owners and enthusiasts. Hold five meets each year. Provide the opportunity for vintage race car owners to participate in actual dirt track racing exhibitions. Dues: $25/year.

ARC Car/Truck Show
321 Tanglewood Lp
DeRidder, LA 70634
318-463-7336; FAX: 318-463-6221

Founded 1988. 50 members. Host annual car/truck show plus arts and crafts, swap meet and car corral. Show is sponsored for the Association of Retarded Citizens as an annual fund raiser. Dues: $15/year.

Atlantic Coast Old Timers Auto Racing Club
55 Hillard Rd
Old Bridge, NJ 08857
732-251-4148
E-mail: gewhite@crosslink.net

Newsletter address: c/o Gordon White, Box 129, Hardyville, VA 23070; membership: c/o Bradley Gray, 55 Hilliard Road, Old Bridge, NJ 08857. Founded 1983. 550 members, 250 cars. Dedicated to restoring and running antique American oval-track race cars. Also have an active program of searching out and preserving records of racing history. Monthly newsletter, *Pit Chatter*. Dues: $14/year. Web site: www.crosslink.net/~gewhite/

Automobile Objects d'art Club
252 N 7th St
Allentown, PA 18102
610-432-3355; FAX: 610-820-9368

For membership information, contact at the above address: David K Bausch. Founded 1983. 2 members. For people interested in early automobile objects d'art, paintings, prints, bronzes, etc.

Bent Axles
4522 Boardwalk Ln
Santa Maria, CA 93455
805-937-0555

Founded 1978. 80 families. Social club for the enjoyment of pre-1949 street rods, the only requirement needed for joining, with monthly cruises and get-togethers. *Bent Action* is the monthly newsletter. The annual cruise and Santa Maria style bar-b-que is held on the third weekend of July with about 200 street rods in attendance. Dues: $26/year.

Bow Tie Chevy Association
PO Box 608108
Orlando, FL 32860
407-880-1956; FAX: 407-886-7571
E-mail: chevy55-72@ao.net

Founded 1992. 3,000 members. Monthly magazine, *Bow Times*, (24-page full color magazine). Put on conventions around the US and Canada. Dues: $30/year. Web site: www.ao.net/chevy55-72/ chapters:

Arkansas	*CCC of North Arkansas*, Bobby Coble, PO Box 56, Gassville, AR 72635, 870-430-5219
	Heartbeat of the Ozarks, Randall Resh, 1766 N Main St, Cave Springs, AR 72718, 501-248-1133
California	*Central California CC*, Bob Smith, 6800 Zerillo Dr, Riverbank, CA 95367, 209-869-3222; E-mail: buffflo@msh
	Chevrolet Ltd Bakersfield, Dave Kielty, 6307 Brooklawn Way, Bakersfield, CA 93309, 805-589-0648
	Fresno Area CCC, Michelle Gregurich, Box 1141, Clovis, CA 93613-1141, 559-291-5340
	Golden State Classics, Harold Belcher, PO Box 939, Paso Robles, CA 93447, 805-238-2399
	Heartbeat Classic Chevys, Mike Harvey, PO Box 1697, Ramona, CA 92065, 760-789-2130
	Inland Empire Bowties, Sherry Beardsley, 4248 Monticello Ave, Riverside, CA 92503, 909-351-6955
	LA Classic Chevy Club, Jerry Mull, PO Box 45-1955, Los Angeles, CA 90045, 310-813-0841; E-mail: jerry@laccc.com

Bow Tie Chevy Association chapters (continued)

Orange County CCC, Wayne Branstetter, 6603 Vista Loma, Yorba Linda, CA 92886, 714-970-1957; E-mail: gwbran@ix.netcom.com

Redwood Empire CC, Greg Lamperti, PO Box 14175, Santa Rosa, CA 95402-6175, 707-588-9855

San Joaquin CCC, Rollin George, PO Box 1756, Visalia, CA 93291, 559-627-5353

Ventura County Chevys, Ted Hetherington, PO Box 309, Camarillo, CA 93011, 805-988-0330; E-mail: vcchevys@aol.com

Colorado *Rocky Mountain CCC*, Jerry Haselgren, PO Box 18882, Denver, CO 80218-0882, 303-477-6692

Florida *Capital City CCC*, Bill Cayson, PO Box 37175, Tallahassee, FL 32315, 850-385-0572

Cypress Classic Club, Lee Tanner, 1046 Sycamore St, Lakeland, FL 33815, 941-686-8803

Florida Gold Coast Classics, Lewis Slattery, 13901 SW 37 Ct, Davie, FL 33330, 954-475-0651

Kendall Classic Chevy Club, Steven Steele, 6920 SW 124th St, Miami, FL 33156, 305-238-2766; E-mail: acposter@gate.net

Treasure Coast CCC, Tom Beang, 133 Wide River Cove, Stuart, FL 34994, 561-335-5557; E-mail: chevyman@aol.com

Illinois *Greater Chicago CC*, David Tankersley, 331 N Cornell Apt C, Villa Park, IL 60181, 630-279-8046

Okaw Valley Classic Chevy, Dennis Ladrew, PO Box 1981, Fairview Heights, IL 62208, 618-632-8521

Tri-Chevy Association, Rodney Brockman, 24862 Ridge Rd, Elwood, IL 60421, 815-478-3633

Indiana *Central Indiana CC*, Bill Beaver, 623 Candlewood Dr, Marion, IN 46952, 765-457-3095

Michiana CCC, Raymond Statler Jr, PO Box 713, Elkhart, IN 46515, 219-264-7047

Iowa *NE Iowa Classic Chevys*, Charles Rokes, 511 Maple, Washburn, IA 50706, 319-296-2664

Spirit of the Fifties CCC, Pat Moore, Box 2762, Sioux City, IA 51106, 712-277-3884; E-mail: denny@willinet.net

Kansas *Chevy's Finest Classics*, Norman Puckett, 4710 S Euclid, Wichita, KS 67217, 316-522-2008

Golden Oldies CCC, Jim Lawson, PO Box 911, Olathe, KS 66061, 913-334-3956; E-mail: cjlawson@prodigy.net

Topeka Classic Chevy Club, Kenny Ray Sr, PO Box 2626, Topeka, KS 66601, 785-286-4413

Kentucky *Pennyrile Classic Car Club*, Steve Worsham, PO Box 1057, Hopkinsville, KY 42240, 502-269-2272

River City Classics of KY, Allen Jenkins, 815 Stringer Ln, Mt Washington, KY 40047, 502-538-4864

Louisianna *Crescent City Cruisers*, Walter Farrell, 1612 N Starrett Rd, Metairie, LA 70003-5748, 504-467-3451

Maine *Classic Chevys of Maine*, Everett Murphy, RR 1 Box 2305, Carmel, ME 04419, 207-848-5763

Maryland *Baltimore's Best CCC*, June Grammont, 904 Bob-El Dr, Westminster, MD 21157, 410-876-8898; E-mail: aprilg57@juno.com

Heart of Maryland CCC, Edwin Zimmerman Jr, 6502 B New London Rd, New Market, MD 21774, 301-865-5270

Mason-Dixon CCC, Sedrick Hurley Jr, PO Box 3371, Salisbury, MD 21802, 410-749-6476; E-mail: clasmommom@aol.com

Massachusetts *Baystate 55, 56, 57 Chevys*, Mark Hurt, PO Box 614, Springfield, MA 01101, 508-544-3201

NE Chevy/GMC Truck Club, Richard Stone, PO Box 155, Millers Falls, MA 01349, 508-754-8559

Michigan *Central Michigan Classic Cruisers*, Joe Twomey, 1212 Alpine Dr, Dewitt, MI 48820, 517-587-3529

Mid Michigan CCC, Beth Rodenborg, 3261 Hurley Rd, Midland, MI 48642, 517-893-3810

Oakland County CCC, Ward L Feather, 3472 Dallas St, Burton, MI 48519, 810-742-6998

Mississippi *Magnolia CCC*, James Pittman, PO Box 3973, Jackson, MS 39207, 601-372-6910

Missouri *CCC of Springfield*, Wendell Royster, PO Box 10111 GS, Springfield, MO 65808, 417-883-6541

Fabulous Fifties Inc, Ray Lorton, 575 Spring Glen, Ballwin, MO 63021, 314-227-1386; E-mail: rayl@michelob.wustl.edu

Heart of America Chevy Owners, Bob Greene, 303 Golden Ln, Independence, MO 64055, 816-254-3733

Montana *Treasure State Classics*, Frank Blaney, 817 Edith, Missoula, MT 59801, 406-454-1545; E-mail: milhouse@mssl.uswest.net

Nebraska *Chevrolet Classics Club Inc*, Omaha Council Bluffs, Milt Fricke Box 385, Omaha, NE 68101, 402-733-4170

Nevada *Southern Nevada CCC*, Don Nisley, PO Box 61311, Las Vegas, NV 89160, 702-593-5572; E-mail: nisleyd@skylink.net

New Jersey *Garden State Classics*, George S Braue, 52 Richard St, Dover, NJ 07801, 973-989-0698

New York *Adirondack CCC*, Douglas Hoffman, PO Box 270, Lake Placid, NY 12946, 518-523-2633; E-mail: akoffman@capital.net

Finger Lakes CCC, Jim Boehly, 48 Guinevere Dr, Rochester, NY 14626, 716-227-8105; E-mail: topchop1@aol.com

Mid-Atlantic Nomad Association, Jay Hammond, PO Box 195, Garrison, NY 10524, 302-322-1833; E-mail: pderham@hudson.highlands.com

Time Travelers of Western NY, Bruce Cox, PO Box 751, Tonawanda, NY 14150, 716-832-5633; E-mail: blcinluv@aol.com

North Dakota *Fifties Finest Classic Chevys*, Keith Gunderson, RR 1 Box 10, Cummings, ND 58223-9710, 701-436-5092

Ohio *Cruising the 50s CCC*, Robert Darney, 4875 Lower Elkton Rd, Leetonia, OH 44431, 330-482-9297

Eastgate CCC, Jeff Ansteatt, 3920 May St, Cincinnati, OH 45245, 513-753-7870

Lost in the 50s, Bill McGill, 403 Linway Ave NW, Massillon, OH 44646, 330-478-2198; E-mail: jmt@sssnet.com

Mid Ohio CCC, Fred Kaiser, PO Box 141285, Columbus, OH 43214, 614-875-0393

Northwest Ohio Chevy Club, Mitch Siler, 357 Pine Ave, Dunkirk, OH 45836, 419-759-2834; E-mail: msiler@riverdale.woco.ohio.gov

Toledo Metro CCC, John Pawlecki, 1434 Appomattox Dr, Maumee, OH 43537, 419-893-0675

Tri-State Classic Chevy, Randy Rhoden, 255 Hickman Rd, Minford, OH 45653, 740-820-8530

Oklahoma *CCC of Oklahoma*, Bill Jeffers, PO Box 35747, Tulsa, OK 74135, 918-645-2102; E-mail: bjef170945@aol.com

Oregon *Central Oregon CCC*, Raymond Spongberg, PO Box 634, Bend, OR 97708, 541-382-9370; E-mail: rsss@coinet.com

Emerald Empire Late Great & Bow Tie Chevys, Fred Mentze, PO Box 2322, Eugene, OR 97402, 541-747-6959

Emerald Valley CC, Thomas Jaff, PO Box 41989, Eugene, OR 97404, 541-689-4249

Obsolete Fleet Chevys, Harlan Warnick, PO Box 13944, Salem, OR 97309, 503-585-5578

Pennsylvania *Appalachian Golden Classics*, Bobby Etter, PO Box 167, Rouzerville, PA 17250, 717-762-2446

Blue Mountain CCC, William Warren, PO Box 857, White Hall, PA 18052, 717-897-6394

Keystone Tri-Five Classics, Mike Kissinger, 16 Conway Dr, Middletown, PA 17057, 717-957-3083; E-mail: kihm@epix.net

Steel City Classics, Augie Mauti, 701 Prestley St, Carnegie, PA 15106, 412-276-3519

White Rose CCC, Ralph Null, PO Box 7074, York, PA 17404, 717-246-3416

South Carolina CCC of Spartanburg, Ken Lawson, PO Box 4457, Spartanburg, SC 29305-4457, 864-827-4602

Tennessee *Memphis CC*, Charles McFarland, 1105 Sandra, Memphis, TN 38122, 901-327-6788

Poor Boys CCC, Henry Bullingrton Jr, PO Box 132, McEwen, TN 37101, 931-582-3038

Texas *CCC of Victoria*, Frank Garcia, 4806 Lone Tree Rd, Victoria, TX 77901, 512-578-9749

Central Texas CCC, Tom Porter, 2304 Mayfield Dr, Round Rock, TX 78681, 512-255-0118; E-mail: mtporter@flash.net

Corpus Christi CCC, Knox Graham, 7101 Brezina, Corpus Christi, TX 78413, 512-853-0582; E-mail: drmacaw@aol.com

Heart of Texas CCC, Mike Richmond, PO Box 1392, Waco, TX 76703, 254-750-5693

Houston CCC, Andy McCloskey, 127 Bellaire Ct, Bellaire, TX 77401, 713-667-4085; E-mail: amcclosk@aol.com

Washington *Bowtie Bunch*, Mike Ragan, 22509 SE 329th, Black Diamond, WA 98010, 253-848-3445; E-mail: vickmouse@aol.com

Ranier Classic Chevy Club, Robert Bolam, 28704 189th Pl SE, Kent, WA 98042, 253-631-3674; E-mail: bob.kathy.bolam@worldnet.att.net

VIP Classic Chevy Club, John Ziegler, 16811 SE 15th St, Vancouver, WA 98683, 360-892-4682

Wisconsin *Blue Ribbon CCC*, Mike Malterer, 1150 E Inman Pkwy, Beloit, WI 53511, 608-752-8622

Canada *Canadian CCC*, Scott Matthews, 426 Stanfield Dr, Oakville ON L6L 3P9, 905-825-0878; E-mail: amatthew@cgocable.net

CCC of Nova Scotia, Jeff Kempton, 106 Skyridge Ave, Lower Sackville, NS B4C 1R4, 902-865-3012

Coastal CCC, Martin VanZuylekom, PO Box 64030 555 Clarke Rd, Coquitlam, BC V3J 7V6, 604-941-8495

New Zealand *Kiwi Classic Chevrolet Club*, Paul Baldwin, PO Box 15539, New Lynn, Auckland, 818-5168; E-mail: baldwin@lhug.co.nz

Sweden *CCC of Sweden*, Jim Forseberg, PO Box 249, Uppsala SE-75105, 46-8-590-928-55

BridgeHampton Historical Society
PO Box 977
Bridgehampton, NY 11932
516-537-1088; FAX: 516-537-4225

Founded 1950. 350 members. Recreates annual in the street automobile races. Races open to all pre-1954 cars, membership to all. Dues: $10/year.

British Car Club of Charleston
Jack Lambert, President
1175 Mathis Ferry Rd H8
Mt Pleasant, SC 29464
843-849-9707 (home); FAX: 843-577-2061

Founded 1983. Approximately 85 members. Open to all British marques. Hold the annual British Car Day in June. Publish *The Windscreen*, a monthly publication. Dues: $20/year.

British Motoring Club Inc
4200 Wares Ferry Rd
Montgomery, AL 36109
334-279-0971
E-mail: fishdoctor@aol.com

Founded 1992. 84 members. Must be a British car lover. Meet 2nd Monday each month. One driving event each month and one car show a year. Monthly newsletter. Dues: $10/year.

Central Ohio Antique Fire Apparatus Assn
293 Lyncroft Dr
Gahanna, OH 43230
614-471-2120

Founded 1986. 100 members. Meeting monthly, 1st Monday. Host annual antique fire engine muster. Dues: $12.50/year.

Chris-Craft Antique Boat Club
217 S Adams St
Tallahassee, FL 32301
850-224-BOAT; FAX: 850-224-1033
E-mail: wwright@nettally.com

2,700 members. Monday-Friday 9 am to 5 pm. Open to anyone interested in antique or classic Chris Crafts, 1920-1972. Benefits include subscription to quarterly magazine, group insurance, online discussion group, archival information, library access. Quarterly publication, *Brass Bell*, includes calendar of events, member profiles, boat reviews, helpful hints, reports on current events, free classified ads for members. Dues: $25/year. Web site: www.chris-craft.org

"Classics" Car Club Inc
720 Iowa Ave
Onawa, IA 51040
712-423-3837; FAX: 712-423-2411
E-mail: classics@willinet.net

Founded 1976. 83 members. Open to classic, custom, special interest auto enthusiasts. Annual Graffiti Night, 3rd Saturday in June; annual swap meet, 3rd Sunday in August; various cruise nights, parties, get-togethers throughout the year. Bi-monthly publication, *Cruisin' News*, includes club and area event coverage, member's features, meeting reports/club business, technical and how-to articles, new products, etc. Dues: $15/year. Web site: www.alistauto.com/classiccars/

Cole Motor Car Club of America
201 Rising St
Davison, MI 48423
810-658-5373, 810-636-7221
FAX: 810-653-9419
E-mail: leroycole2@aol.com

Leroy D Cole, President. Founded 1990. 72 members. Open membership. *Cole Bulletin* is published 2-4 times per year and gives news on members and their cars, club meets and historical articles. Dues: $12/year.

Country Cruisers Car Club
1624 155th St
Manchester, IA 52057
319-927-4676

Founded 1992. 38 members. Must have specialty car or classic car. Annual car show at Dele Co fairgrounds, August 13, 2000. Our main charity is Special Olympics. Other donations go to Operation Santa Claus, food pantry, March of Dimes. Dues: $20/year.

Electric Car Owner's Society
167 Concord St
Brooklyn Hgts, NY 11201
718-797-4311, ext 3262; FAX: 718-596-4852
E-mail: fdidik@ddgn.com

Founded 1984. 520 members. BBS, special electric car database CD-ROM, electric car library and registry. $25 donation requested. Web site: www.didik.com

Filching Manor Motor Club
Paul Foulkes-Halbard
Filching Wannock Eastbourne
Polegate Sussex BN26 5QA England
011 441323 487838, 011 441323 487124
FAX: 011 441323 486331

Founded 1987. 150 members. Membership by invitation or recommendation. Meets throughout the year.

Foothills Street Rod Association
c/o 47 Malibou Rd SW
Calgary, AB Canada T2V 1W9
403-259-4764; FAX: 403-253-1412

Founded 1968. 100+ members. Interest in pre-1954 vehicles. Dues: $20/year.

Friends of the Crawford Auto-Aviation Museum
10825 E Blvd
Cleveland, OH 44106
216-721-5722; FAX: 216-721-0645

Founded 1964. 300 members. The Friends of the Crawford Auto-Aviation Museum (CAAM) promotes and supports the Museum through social activities, volunteerism and fund raising. In addition to sharing the company of other enthusiasts, Friends have the opportunity to work with the collection artifacts and to participate in Museum program development. Friends' raffle proceeds have purchased five vehicles for the Museum and funded restoration projects. Membership in the Friends of the CAAM is open to members of the Western Reserve Historical Society. Dues: $40/year.

Group Ultra Van
W Christy Barden
5537 Pioneer Rd
Boulder, CO 80301-3048
303-530-1288

Founded 1981. 200 members. 360 Ultra Vans were built from 1962-1969. They are 22-foot motor homes, 8 feet high and 8 feet wide, weight from 3,200 pounds to 4,200 pounds. Club assists in preserving these classics. Quarterly publication, *Whales on Wheels*, contains technical information on Ultra Vans. Dues: $6/year. Web site: www.onu.edu/~kwildman/ultravan.html

Guldstrand Racing Association
11924 W Jefferson Blvd
Culver City, CA 90230
310-391-7108; FAX: 310-391-7424
E-mail: geiauto@aol.com

Founded 1968. 160+ members. GRA meets second Thursday of every month, 7:30 pm, Guldstrand Eng Inc, Culver City, CA. Solo I and II special race events. Dues: $25/year.

Heartland Vintage Truck Club
425 E North St
DuQuoin, IL 62832
618-542-6554
E-mail: phoenix@cybalink.com

Founded 1997. 15 members. Classic trucks 1972 or older, any make or model. Bi-monthly newsletter, club get-together (picnic) held twice per year. Dues: $10/year.

Historic Vehicle Society of Ontario
PO Box 221
Harrow, ON Canada N0R 1G0
519-776-6909; FAX: 519-776-8321

Chartered 1959. 98 members. Monthly publication, *Through the Windshield*. Benefits include free admission to 12 annual events, April-October. Must attend three meetings, must be recommended and sponsored by a current member in good standing. Dues: $25/year.

Hoosier Model Car Association
1019 N Tuxedo St
Indianapolis, IN 46201
317-264-9387

Founded 1979. 20 members. For builders and collectors, any marque, scale or building style. Serving central Indiana area. Annual swap meet and involvement in local shows. Monthly newsletter. Dues: $12/year.

Lincoln Highway Association
111 S Elm St
PO Box 308
Franklin Grove, IL 61031
815-456-3030
E-mail: lnchq@essex1.com

Founded 1992. 1,000 members. 501(c)3 not for profit organization. Promoting and preserving the Lincoln Hwy, annual conference. 1999 was held in Rochelle, IL, on June 15-19, 1999. Quarterly publication, *The Lincoln Highway Forum*. Dues: $25/year individual, $30/year family.

chapters:

California	Carmel Barry-Schweyer, 12190 Holly Vista Way, Auburn, CA 95603, 916-885-7476
Illinois	Ruth B Frantz, PO Box 27, Sugar Grove, IL 60554, 630-466-4382; E-mail: rbfrantz@aol.com
Indiana	Sidney B Pepe, 13423 Tonkel Rd, Fort Wayne, IN 46845-9223, 219-627-2437
Iowa	Robert Ausberger, 987 P Ave, Jefferson, IA 50129, 515-386-4521
Nebraska	Bob Stubblefield, 7300 Willow Rd, Sheldon, NE 68876, PH/FAX: 308-647-6554
Nevada	Leon C Schegg, Box 2146, Truckee, CA 96160, 530-587-7654; E-mail: schegg@sierra.net
New Jersey	Keith Hixon, 207 Lexington Dr, Little Egg Harbor, NJ 08087, 609-296-3255
New York	Douglas Pappas, 100 E Hartsdale Rd #6EE, Hartsdale, NY 10530, 914-472-7954; E-mail: dougp001@aol.com
Ohio	Bob C Lichty, 555 Market St S, Canton, OH 44702, 330-456-7869 home, 330-455-3666 work; E-mail: rrubin@neo.lrun.com
Pennsylvania	Kevin Patrick, 747 Croyland Ave, Indiana, PA 15701, 724-463-0289; FAX: 724-357-6479; E-mail: kpatrick@grove.iup.edu
Utah	Jesse G Petersen, 56 Bench Mark Village, Tooele, UT 84074, 435-882-6581
Wyoming	Chris Plummer, PO Box 836, Lyman, WY 82937, 307-787-6541; E-mail: cplummer@union-tel.com

Local Cruisers Car Club
19 Circle Dr
Rockaway, NJ 07866
973-625-8408; FAX: 973-625-4683
E-mail: smokey225@aol.com

Founded 1994. 40+ members. You must have an antique or rare vintage car or working on one. Free breakfast meeting each month, get-togethers to make a club presence at certain shows or cruise nights. Monthly newsletter, T-shirts, jackets, sweatshirts available. Sponsoring our own car show (annual). Dues: $60/year per person, $120/year per couple.

Long Island Street Rod Association
66 Bridge St
Central Islip, NY 11722
516-520-0161; FAX: 516-582-6885

Founded 1965. 150+ members. Must own a street rod. Monthly newsletter, *LISRA Newsletter*, included in membership. 3 annual car shows/swap meets. Dues: $24/year.

Mac's Pack
429 Co Rd 332
Bertram, TX 78605
512-355-3618
E-mail: camac@bigfoot.com

Founded 1987. To become a member, you must help put on an event or showing in two events, we put on several events. Hill Country Cruise and Poker Run and our Spring Dust-Off in the spring, also a free show in August at a local winery called the Grape Stomp.

Mad Dogs & Englishmen
630 E Cork St
Kalamazoo, MI 49001
616-344-5555; FAX: 616-344-8431

Founded 1991. 40 members. No restrictions, all makes of cars welcome to belong to club. Major event: Mad Dogs & Englishmen British car fair. Car show in July, all British marques welcome at show, 1998 was eighth year. Dues: $10/year.

Manx Dune Buggy Club
PO Box 1491
Valley Center, CA 92082
760-749-6321; FAX: 760-751-0610
E-mail: manxclub@cts.com

Founded 1994. 1,000 members internationally. Open to all owners of street-legal dune buggies and a registry for any Meyers kit car. There is a quarterly newsletter, *Manx Mania*, with announcements about future meets and events. Dues: $25/year. Registry: $5/year. Web site: www.manxclub.com

Massachusetts Antique Fire Apparatus Association
Robert Noseworthy, Secretary
PO Box 3332
Peabody, MA 01960
978-664-4533
E-mail: paulromano@pipeline.com

Paul Romano, President, 781-334-3132 days, 781-334-3573 evenings. Founded 1976. 200 members. Open to persons interested in the development and history of motorized fire apparatus. Monthly publication, *The Box Alarm*. Dues: $15/year.

Massena Olde Car Club Inc
PO Box 465
Massena, NY 13662
315-769-6739
E-mail: ranmac@slic.com

Founded 1997. 70 members. The club is open to all. Meet every Thursday night (May-October) at the Massena Dairy Queen. The club helps to raise money for charity and other organizations. Dues: $10/year.

The Microcar and Minicar Club
PO Box 43137
Upper Montclair, NJ 07043
973-366-1410

Founded 1991. 900+ members. Successor to the Heinkel-Messerschmitt-Isetta Club. Dedicated to the enjoyment and preservation of all small and unusual cars. Our quarterly magazine, *Minutia*, features news, technical information, parts sources and classified advertisements. Nationwide events and club representatives. Monthly meetings in Hackensack, NJ. Dues: $20/year US and Canada, $30/year overseas.

Mid-Michigan Antique Fire Apparatus Association
2910 Meister Ln
Lansing, MI 48906-9010
517-676-5910

Founded 1983. 40 members. No membership restrictions other than having an interest in fire apparatus history and preservation. Fire apparatus ownership is not required. Members participate in a number of parades and musters throughout the year. We also tour area fire depts and hold meetings at different fire stations. Dues: $10/year.

Midwest Mopar Club-Sioux Empire Chapter
26471 467th Ave
Sioux Falls, SD 57107
605-334-9161; FAX: 605-331-6065
E-mail: 79volare@gateway.net

Founded 1986. 50 members. Open to all Mopar and Mopar powered vehicles. Monthly newsletter and subscription to *Chrysler Power* magazine included in membership. Host the annual Moparama at Tufty Dodge in Sioux Falls in September each year. Dues: $25/year.

Military Vehicle Preservation Assoc
PO Box 520378
Independence, MO 64052
816-737-5111; FAX: 816-737-5423
E-mail: mvpa-hq@mvpa.org

Founded 1976. 8,500 members. MVPA is a not-for-profit organization dedicated to the restoration and preservation of military transport. 10 magazines per year with 100s of ads, MV events, color photos, technical and historic articles. Host to the largest annual swap meet and military vehicle display in the United States. Web site: www.mvpa.org

See our ad on page 572

Motor Bus Society Inc
PO Box 251
Paramus, NJ 07653-0251
E-mail: mct@shore.net

Founded 1948. 1,100 members. Collect and publish the colorful and fascinating history of the bus industry. Two quarterly publications (8 per year both publications), *Motor Coach Age* and *Motor Coach Today*. Dues: $30/year US; $35/year Canada, $40/year overseas.

National Belchfire Owner's Club
Box 5502
Concord, CA 94524
510-228-7821; FAX: 510-228-1410

45 members. A national tongue-in-cheek club for professional auto writers to promote the lighter side of the automobile world. Now open to writers who write for fun too. Also open to contemporary writers post-dating 1965. Name comes from a series of cartoons by the late George Lichty. One meeting per year at San Francisco Auto Show. Purpose is to roast auto celebrities and each other. Qualified auto journalists are invited to apply. Must verify having written for money before 1965 by dated clips. Dues: none.

National Historic Route 66 Federation
PO Box 423 Dept H
Tujunga, CA 91043-0423
PH/FAX: 818-352-7232
E-mail: national66@national66.com

Founded 1994. Over 1,600 members around the world. Dedicated to preserving America's most famous highway. Members receive quarterly magazine and access to Route 66 maps, guides, books, videos, etc. Web site: www.national66.com

NZ Military Vehicle Collectors Club Inc
c/o President John Campbell
96 Whitney St, Avondale
Auckland New Zealand
09-8287850; FAX: 07-8569319

Founded 1979. 160 family members. Open to anyone interested in the collection and restoration of military vehicles. Monthly magazine. Local monthly meetings and April national meet. 11 branches throughout New Zealand. We participate in off-road events, displays, air shows, camp outs and swapping of ideas and information. Dues: NZ $40/year.

Old Town Cruisers
PO Box 1104
Van Buren, AR 72957
501-782-9909, 501-452-1476

Founded 1992. 24 members. Annual car show to be held September 11-12, 1999 and September 9-10, 2000, pre-1960, entry fee: $20. Contact: Butch Gilyard at the above phone number. Pre-registration until September 1st. Our show is held in historical downtown Van Buren, AR. Lots of antique shopping for the ladies. Dues: $40/year.

Pachecho, Martinea & Port Costa Sewing Circle, Book Review Society & Street Racing Association
Box 5502
Concord, CA 94524
510-228-7821; FAX: 510-228-1410

Founded 1983. 1,301 members. Club meets twice each year to review the past year in the auto world and to roast dignitaries. Meets held at San Francisco Auto Show and Los Angeles Auto Show each year.

Pittsburgh Vintage Grand Prix Association
PO Box 2243
Pittsburgh, PA 15230
412-734-5853; FAX: 412-221-1923
E-mail: pvgpa@trfn.clpgh.org

Founded 1983. 1,600 members. All volunteer organization holds annual vintage races and largest collector car show in western Pennsylvania every 3rd weekend in July. All proceeds benefit Autism Society of Pittsburgh and Allegheny Valley School. Web site: http://trfn.clpgh.org/pvgpa

Professional Car Society
PO Box 9636
Columbus, OH 43209-9636
614-237-2350
E-mail: b1ruff@gcfn.org

Founded 1976. 1,300 members. Dedicated to the preservation and appreciation of vintage funeral, ambulance, livery and related vehicles on passenger car chassis. Car ownership not required. Quarterly magazine, *The Professional Car*, with industry news, historical articles, club news, personal ads, lots of photos, regular features: Owner's Pride, Limopage, Marketplace; biennial directory, annual international meet. Dues: $20/year. Web site: www.professionalcar.org

chapters:

California   *Southern California Chapter*, 432 E Fairmount Rd, Burbank, CA 91501

Florida	*Florida Chapter*, 428 E Orange St, Tarpon Springs, FL 34689
Georgia	*Peachtree Chapter*, 3680 Regent Dr, Kennesaw, GA 30144
Illinois	*Illini Chapter*, 1401 24th Pl, Sterling, IL 61081
Maryland	*Association for Preservation of Historical Ambulances*, 3922 W Watersville Rd, Mt Airy, MD 21771
	Mid-Atlantic Chapter, PO Box 123, Fulton, MD 20759-0123
Michigan	*Great Lakes Chapter*, 3440 Fuller Ave, Grand Rapids, MI 49505
Minnesota	*Northland Chapter*, 1167 Grand Ave, St Paul, MN 55105
New Hampshire	*New England Chapter*, 175 S Main St, Franklin, NH 03235
New Jersey	*Northeast Chapter*, 369 Chestnut St, Stirling, NJ 07980-1101
Ohio	*Ohio Chapter*, 2116 Creekview Ct, Reynoldsburg, OH 43068
Oklahoma	*South Central Chapter*, PO Box 9295, Tulsa, OK 74157-9295
Pennsylvania	*Tri-State Chapter*, 416 4th Ave Apt 1, Tarentum, PA 15084-1853
Tennessee	*Southeastern Chapter*, 7613 Water Tower Rd, Knoxville, TN 37920
Texas	*Lone Star State Chapter*, PO Box 741, Justin, TX 76247-0741
Wisconsin	*Wisconsin Chapter*, PO Box 154, Blanchardville, WI 53516-0154
Canada	*Trillium Chapter*, RR 4, Chatham, ON N7M 5J4
England	*British Ambulance Society*, 21 Victoria Rd, Horley, Surrey RH6 9BN
	Classic Hearse Register, 121 St Mary's Crescent, Basildon, Essex SS13 2AS
Germany	*German Chapter*, Rablstrasse 40, DE-81669 Munchen

Puget Sound British Automotive Society
17610 NE 8th Pl
Bellevue, WA 98008
425-644-7874; FAX: 425-747-0205
E-mail: ataub@worldnet.att.net

Founded 1989. 450 members. Club's purpose is the sponsorship of the Western Washington All British Field Meet. A car show and swap meet for all British marques with over 500 entrants, held annually, third Saturday of July in Redmond, WA. Web site: www.abfm,com

Relics & Rods Car Club
PO Box 1516
Lake Havasu City, AZ 86405
PH/FAX: 520-855-0933

Founded 1978. 170 members. Must be 1959 or earlier car or truck. We are the hosts of Run to the Sun car show, approximately 1,000 cars enter. Call for fax number. Dues: $30/year. Web site: www,relicsandrods.com

South Jersey Street Rod Association
PO Box 63
Williamstown, NJ 08094
609-629-9754

Founded 1974. 30 members. Must own pre-1948 modified vehicle, attend 3 meetings and help and participate in our annual street rod event every September. Dues: $24/year.

Southern Mopar Association
c/o Larry Jordan
5781 Aljon Dr
Theodore, AL 36582
334-653-5154

Founded 1988. 30 members. Established for the preservation and restoration of Chrysler products. You do not have to own a car or truck to join, Meets monthly and has an annual Mopar show in Mobile, AL. Proceeds of show are given to charity. Dues: $15/year.

Sportscar Vintage Racing Association
1 Maple St
Hanover, NH 03755
603-640-6161; FAX: 603-640-6130
E-mail: pbench@valley.net

Founded 1976. 1,900 members. SVRA is one of the largest organizations presenting vintage race events for historically significant race cars in North America. SVRA organized its first event in 1976 and has grown into an international organization with 1,900 members in 43 states, Canada and several foreign countries. Dues: $75/year and $100/year.

St Joe Valley Street Rods
PO Box 137
Mishawaka, IN 46544

Founded 1971. 25 members. Dues: $60/year.

Steam Automobile Club of America Inc
1227 W Voorhees St
Danville, IL 61832
217-442-0268; FAX: 217-442-3299
E-mail: jreynol@aol.com

Founded 1958. 850 members. Open to all steam automobile enthusiasts. A non-profit organization dedicated to the preservation of steam auto history and to the development of modern steam automobiles. Quarterly publication, *Steam Automobile Bulletin*. Dues: $15/year US funds. Web site: http://members.aol.com/jreynol/sacaarc.htm

Street Machines of Rochester
409 Bennington Dr
Rochester, NY 14616
716-663-0393

Founded 1974. 127 members. No restrictions for our club. Discount on parts and accessories. Not-for-profit organization, meets monthly and sponsors 1 or more monthly events, usually free or at reduced rates and a monthly newsletter is mailed out. Dues: $42/year. Web site: www.frontiernet.net/~pferrera

Street Machines of Table Rock Lake
HC 3 Box 4250
Reed's Spring, MO 65737
417-338-5233; FAX: 417-338-2179
E-mail: billbob42@.com

Founded 1996. 60 members. Dues: $25/year.

Tarrant County Street Rod Association
5801 Graham
Fort Worth, TX 76114
817-626-2708

Founded 1971. 25 members. You must own a 1948 or earlier model vehicle with some modifications. We meet the first Sunday of each month at members' homes. Dues: $5/monthly.

Texas Joy Ride
2622 Micliff
Houston, TX 77068
281-444-8680; FAX: 281-444-0687

Founded 1988. Joy Williams, founder. Rod run.

Toy Car Collectors Club
33290 W 14 Mile, #454
West Bloomfield, MI 48322
248-682-0272; FAX: 248-682-5782
E-mail: fossohl@aol.com

Founded 1993. 164 members. A club for collectors of all miniature vehicles, all manufactures, materials, scales, types, eras, etc. Services: quarterly magazine, *Toy Car Magazine*, free copy of *Model Car Directory 1992*, monthly meetings (Detroit area), annual convention. *Model Car Directory* is a book of lists: auctioneers, books, catalogs, clubs, codes, contests, conventions, dealers, dictionary, individuals, magazines, manufacturers, museums, scales, shows, videos, etc. Dues: $15/year. Web site: www.unicycling.com/toycar

Tri-Chevy Association
1831 Roberts St
Wilmington, IL 60481
815-476-4130

Founded 1972. Interested in 1955-1956-1957 Chevy preservation. Second Sunday of June car show and swap meet. Monthly meeting every 3rd Saturday or Sunday. Dues: $15/year.

Tucson Miniature Auto Club
Lou Pariseau, President
1111 E Limberlost Dr 164
Tucson, AZ 85719

Founded 1976. 87 members. Open to anyone 16 years and older. Monthly newsletter, monthly meetings. 380 table toy show in March. Open to collectors of any wheeled vehicles. Dues: $10/year.

The Tuna Club Inc
c/o CAR Products Inc
120 Bosworth St
West Springfield, MA 01089
413-733-0599

Founded 1985. 10 members. Must be a car enthusiast and willing to donate time to the annual Tuned by Tuna car show and swap meet, held 3rd Sunday of every August, benefiting the Shriners Hospital for Children. Over 500 show cars and 20,000 people attend. It is held at Smith and Wesson, 2100 Roosevelt Ave, Springfield, Massachusetts. Dues: none.

United Detroit Car Modelers
13856 Roxanne Rd
Sterling Heights, MI 48312-5673
810-268-3479
E-mail: paully@home.com

Founded 1991. 13 members. Membership open to all. For builders and collectors. Semi-monthly publication, *Model Car Action*. Monthly club meetings that include model building how-to. Club located in NE Detroit suburb. New members wanted. Dues: voluntary pay.

Valley Cruisers Car Club
PO Box 1184
Gardnerville, NV 89410
PH/FAX: 702-265-2256
E-mail: preed@nanosecond.com

Founded 1989. 110 members. No restrictions other than a love of cars/vehicles, 1969 and older. Family oriented non-profit group going on cruises, tours and outings throughout the year. We host main street event Show and Shine yearly as a money maker and donate the profits back to the community. 1999 show was August 20, 21, 22, open to the public. Dues: $15/year.

West Coast Kustoms
PO Box 8028
Moreno Valley, CA 92552
909-488-0413

Founded 1982. 1,800+ members. Open to those who remember how it was in the 1950s to early 1960s when Kustoms, rods and classics cruised to the local drive-ins and diners, as well as, Kustoms, classics and rod owners and admirers. Dues: $20/year.

Winchester Speedway Old Timers' Club Inc
PO Box 291
Urbana, OH 43078
937-652-2145; FAX: 937-652-2147

Founded 1972. 500 members. Held annual Winchester Speedway Old Timers' convention/exhibition at Winchester Speedway, Winchester, IN, August 14-15, 1999. Vintage race car owners, drivers, mechanics and fans are encouraged to join. Membership includes newsletter 4 times/year. Dues: $10/year includes spouse.

Women's Committee of the Crawford Auto-Aviation Museum
10825 E Blvd
Cleveland, OH 44106
216-721-5722; FAX: 216-721-0645

Founded 1964. 35 members. The Women's Committee of the Crawford Auto-Aviation Museum (CAAM) endeavors to promote the Museum, assists the Museum's educational programs and, through fundraising, augment its collection. Activities include the Millionaire's Run, Concours d'Ordinaire, holiday staff luncheon and seasonal decorating. The Women's Committee purchased the CAAM's 1948 Chrysler Town and funded restoration of the Museum's 1932 Peerless V16 prototype. Women's Committee membership is open to all members of the Western Reserve Historical Society. Dues: $55/year.

State Clubs

Gadsden Antique Automobile Club   Alabama
113 Buckingham Pl
Gadsden, AL 35904
205-547-7143

Founded 1966. Over 100 members. Independent organization, family oriented and dedicated to preservation of antique and special interest automobiles. Annual invitational meet for over 30 years.

Arizona Bus Club   Arizona
3121 E Yucca
Phoenix, AZ 85028-2616
PH/FAX: 602-867-7672
E-mail: vwstuff@uswest.net

200+ members. Monthly meetings, car shows, swap meets. Largest VW club in Arizona. All VWs and family welcome. Web site: www.mindspring.com/~deasterw/jess/jess.html

Prescott Antique Auto Club PO Box 2654 Prescott, AZ 86302 520-778-3604 E-mail: paac@northlink.com	**Arizona**

Founded 1970. 250 members. Oldest and biggest car club in northern Arizona. Monthly newsletter, annual swap meet and show the first weekend in August. Dues: $20/year.

Northwest Arkansas Corvette Club PO Box 124 Fayetteville, AR 72702 501-271-0210 E-mail: jmbell@specent.com	**Arkansas**

Founded 1996. 100 members. Open to all Corvette owners. Dues: $30/year. Web site: www2.arkansas.net/~jyount/

Early Iron of Ukiah Inc PO Box 107 Ukiah, CA 95482 707-463-2483; FAX: 707-263-3223 E-mail: hansenfamily@saber.net	**California**

124 members. Pre-1959, monthly newsletter, monthly outings, annual Fabulous Flashback Car Show and Poker Run held in late September. Dues: $24/year.

Meadow Valley Kruisers John Marvin PO Box 1484 445 Pineleaf Dr Quincy, CA 95971-1484 530-283-1555	**California**

Founded 1992. The Meadow Valley Kruisers believe in search, rescue and daily driving of Buick, Cadillac and Ford cars of the 1950s and 1960s. In the process we always have spare parts and information to share with others of like interests. Call or write anytime. Dues: none.

Litchfield Hills Historical Automobile Club 16 Calhoun St Torrington, CT 06790 860-482-4500	**Connecticut**

Contact: Glenn Royals at the above address or telephone. Founded 1956. 55 members. Annual auto show and swap meet is held at the Goshen fairgrounds, Rt 63 North, Goshen, CT, 3rd Sunday in August, rain or shine. Dues: $10/year.

50s & 60s Cruisin' Car Club PO Box 22001 St Petersburg, FL 33742-2001	**Florida**

Founded 1994. 140 members. Dedicated to the preservation of 1950s and 1960s cars, trucks, motorcycles and all types of collectibles from the 1950s and 1960s. Special feature: the club meets every weekend via our syndicated 1950s and 1960s Cruizin' Rock 'n' Roll radio show which is heard on great radio stations across USA. Club members buy, sell, trade cars, trucks, motorcycles, parts, services and all types of 50s and 60s collectibles during special feature segments. For club membership application, send a self addressed stamped envelope to the club address. Write for details. Dues: none.

All British Car Club of Vol Co FL 3261 Buckland St Deltona, FL 32738 904-789-5749; FAX: 904-789-7948 E-mail: peggco@aol.com	**Florida**

Founded 1993. 122 members. Our club is open to all British cars and to those who have an interest in the restoration and preservation of the British car and the enjoyment of the car. Our club is a chapter of NAMGAR (North American MGA Registry).

Monthly publication, *British Connection*, which gives a list of activities, wanted and classifieds, general club information and tech tips. Dues: $10/year (single), $16/year (married). Web site: geocities.com/motorcity/downs4777

Avanti Club of Florida John Ebstein, Chapter AOAI 319 Toledo St Sebastian, FL 32958 561-388-5379 E-mail: rdoty32958@aol.com	**Florida**

Founded 1994. 120 members. Must be a member of National organization, Avanti Owners Association International (AOAI). Hobby for owners of Avanti automobiles for 1963 and 1964, Studebaker Avantis through 1990, Avanti IIs or for people interested in their history. Publish *Florida Avanti News* 6 times a year, included with membership. Newsletter lists local and national events, items for sale, history of owners' cars. Dues: $12/year.

Central Florida Ford Club 619 Durango Loop St Davenport, FL 33837 941-424-4224	**Florida**

Founded 1997. 10 members. Open to all Ford cars and trucks, any year. Eventually we will be publishing a bi-monthly newsletter. Also trying to tie into The Performance Ford Club of America, PFCA. Dues: none.

Cool Cruisers of Naples, FL PO Box 9290 Naples, FL 34101-9290 941-598-9793 E-mail: denimpala@yahoo.com	**Florida**

Contact: Dennis "Impala" Popick. Founded 1989. 200 members. Family oriented car club that works to subsidize children's charities in Collier County, FL. Dues: $40/year initial, $30/year family.

Florida Keys Corvette Club PO Box 420807 Summerland Key, FL 33042-0807 305-872-9641; FAX: 305-872-4093 E-mail: racinvet@aol.com	**Florida**

Founded 1992. 30 members. Meets 2nd Tuesday of every month in alternating locations, also southernmost Corvette club in continental US, specialties, cruising the Islands, cruise-ins and annual Corvettes in Paradise show in November. Publication: *Keyvette Redliner*, available thru membership, published bi-monthly, includes car care information, calendar of events, social happenings within the club, person profiles, web sites. Dues: $25/year. Web site: members.aol.com/racinvet/fkcc.html

Rods 'N Classics 610 Manatee Dr SW Ruskin, FL 33570 813-645-9101	**Florida**

Founded 1997. 11 members. No restrictions. All classics, customs and rods welcome. Informal get-togethers for information and magazine swapping, no newsletter, one cumulation bulletin of accumulated tech, custom, engine information to new members. Dues: $6/year.

Suncoast British Car Club | **Florida**
7767 N Holiday Dr
Sarasota, FL 34231
941-922-6462

Founded 1990. 80+ members. No restrictions to join, just an interest in British cars. Monthly newsletter, annual rally, monthly meeting 2nd Wednesday of the month. Dues $30/year.

Good Neighbors Auto Club | **Georgia**
2221 Blue Ridge Hwy
Blairsville, GA 30512
706-745-2596

Founded 1983. 100 members. Fun run, 1st Saturday in May; car show, 3rd Saturday in October; cruise night, 3rd Saturday May-September. Dues: $12/year.

Peach State Nova Club | **Georgia**
PO Box 1393
Lilburn, GA 30048-1393
770-921-5422

Founded 1988. 75 members. Monthly meeting 2nd Sunday of each month. Also monthly newsletter. Dues: $15/year individual, $18/year husband and spouse.

Idaho Vintage Motorcycle Club | **Idaho**
10346 Foxbrush Ct
Boise, ID 83709-7407
208-362-0319
E-mail: norton99@micron.net

Founded 1977. 110 members. Open to all interested. Newsletter 5-6 times per year. Want ads are free to members. Largest vintage bike show in the Northwest in late March. Dues: $5/year.

Centerville Antique Auto Touring Society | **Illinois**
PO Box 33
Woodstock, IL 60098-0033
815-338-2204

Founded 1981. 60 members. Must have an interest in old vehicles to join. Monthly newsletter, picnics, tours and overnighters. Dues: $18/year.

Collector Car Club of Greater Belleville Area | **Illinois**
30 Troy-O'Fallon Rd
Troy, IL 62294
618-667-3958

Founded 1980. 98 members. No restrictions. Entertainment at all monthly meetings, monthly publication, *The Spotlight*, 6 shows and numerous annual events. Dues: $12/year.

Dekalb-Sycamore Vintage Auto Club | **Illinois**
15623 Derbyline Rd
Genoa, IL 60135
815-784-5623

Founded 1973. 58 members. No restrictions to join. Club newsletter once a month; meet first Sunday of the month; annual car show in August. Dues: $10/year.

North Shore Rods, Southside | **Illinois**
318 Charlestown Dr
Bolingbrook, IL 60440
630-739-3324; FAX: 708-788-7038
E-mail: dave46@freewwweb.com

Founded 1975. 36 members. No restrictions. Must enjoy working with others, involvement with our charity car show and other events, we work to earn money for our selected charities. Meet 1st Saturday of every month.

Rustic Auto Club of Pontiac Inc | **Illinois**
PO Box 482
Pontiac, IL 61764
815-844-5783 days
FAX: 815-844-6179 days

Founded 1968. 33 members. Anyone with interest in old vehicles can join. The club has sponsored the Hang Loose 1950s and 1960s weekend for 13 years. The event is the biggest in the area and includes a car show, craft booths, food and a cruise-in. The club has restored a 1920s gas station and has built an old fashioned root beer stand, both are used throughout the summer for numerous activities. Dues: $10/year new, $5/year renew.

4 Wheels to Freedom | **Indiana**
PO Box 342
Shelbyville, IN 46176
812-523-4484
E-mail: brian_rowda@toyota.com

Founded 1976. 50 families. Ownership of a four-wheel drive vehicle is required. Organized as a non-profit organization for the purpose of providing social, educational and recreational activities, events including trail rides, swap meets and parades. Monthly publication, *Winchline,* and meet on the first Sunday of the month at 6 pm in Shelbyville, IN. Dues: $25/year.

Central Indiana Vintage Vehicles | **Indiana**
PO Box 635
Noblesville, IN 46060
317-773-5480; FAX: 317-773-0551
E-mail: slpyhollow@aol.com

Founded 1988. 73 members. No restrictions to join. Monthly newsletter, activities, yearly car show. Dues: $15/year.

Cruisin Classics Inc | **Indiana**
401 E Grimes
Bloomington, IN 47401
812-336-4278

Founded 1993. 100 members. No alcoholic beverages. Newsletter, 2 car shows per year. Dues: $20/year.

Hoosier Volks Club | **Indiana**
8694 Bell St
Crown Point, IN 46307
219-365-6973; FAX: 219-365-4925
E-mail: pspi@jorsm.com

Founded 1996. 80+ members. All Volkswagens welcome, air and watercooled. Dues include membership to the Volkswagen Club of America. Monthly meetings and events. The Hoosier Volks newsletter is called *Fahrverg"news"en.* The Volkswagen Club of America newsletter is called *The Autoist.* Car shows, fix-it days, car cruises, fund raisers for charities. Dues: $31/year (first year only, dues are reduced after first year).

Michiana Antique Auto Club Inc | **Indiana**
910 State St
La Porte, IN 46350
PH/FAX: 219-393-3332

Founded 1967. 75 members. No restrictions other than the desire to preserve and enjoy antique and special interest automobiles. Annual swap meet and car show on the Sunday of Memorial Day weekend, 200 plus cars shown and attendance of 2,000 plus. We publish a newsletter monthly and have outings every month to drive our cars. Dues: $20/year.

Pioneer Auto Club | **Indiana**
Haynes-Apperson Chapter
1500 N Reed Rd
Kokomo, IN 46901-2592
765-455-3053, 765-454-9999
FAX: 765-454-9956

Founded 1950. 130 members. Home of the Haynes and

Apperson cars. Dedicated to the preservation and restoration of antique cars. Dues: $20/year individual.

Hawkeye Area Classic Chevy Club PO Box 8755 Cedar Rapids, IA 52408 319-622-3293 E-mail: dnsjanda@webtv.net	**Iowa**

Founded 1977. 21 members. Monthly newsletter, annual car show, spring and fall cruises, tech sessions, specializing in preservation, restoration and enjoyment of 1955, 1956 and 1957 Chevrolets, Corvettes and trucks. Need not own one to join. Dues: $10/year.

Ottawa Antique Car Club 2451 Oregon Rd Ottawa, KS 66067 785-242-2036	**Kansas**

Founded 1969. 20 members. Dues: $10/year.

Southern Knights of Central Kentucky Car Club 2214 Leestown Rd Frankfort, KY 40601 502-695-0831 E-mail: tingle@dcr.net	**Kentucky**

Founded 1989. 40 families. Open to old and young car enthusiasts. Two car shows yearly, meet 1st Sunday of every month, monthly newsletter. Non-profit organization. Dues: $12/year.

Florida Parishes Vintage Car Club PO Box 38 Ponchatoula, LA 70454 504-386-3714	**Louisiana**

Founded 1977. 47 member families. Applicants must be voted in by members. Affiliated with Mid-America Old Time Automobile Association (MOTAA). Dues: $10/year.

Antique Motor Club of Greater Baltimore Inc 208 Brightside Ave Pikesville, MD 21208-4806 410-484-1715	**Maryland**

For membership information, contact at the above address: Maurleen Buttery. Founded 1968. 650 members. Offers activities which every member of the family can participate in and enjoy. No judging. Activities are open to the general public. Publication, *Olde Jalopy News*. Dues: $17/year.

Convertible Owners Club of Greater Baltimore 208 Brightside Ave Pikesville, MD 21208-4806 410-484-1715, 410-337-0697	**Maryland**

Founded 1985. 100 members. Convertible owners (both antique and modern) enjoying their cars by participating in parades, exhibits, promotions, movies, etc. Newsletter, *Top Down News*. Dues: $6/year.

Mid-Maryland Ford Club Inc PO Box 3171 Frederick, MD 21705-3171 301-663-6903; FAX: 301-694-7624 E-mail: mmfc@x-press.net	**Maryland**

Founded 1993. 142 members (Maryland, Pennsylvania, Virginia, West Virginia, DC). National award-winning newsletter, *The Ford Express*, 12 issues, contains full page of calendar of events listings of local and regional shows and 26 Ford flyers, etc. The club unites Ford enthusiasts from the five-state area of Ford, Mercury and Lincoln cars and trucks, from antique to modified or any Ford powered vehicles. Dues: $15/year double, $10/year single. Web site: x-press.net/mmfc

Street Cars of Desire Car Club David C Cohen, President PO Box 831 Cockeysville, MD 21030 410-628-6262 E-mail: stonman@hotmail.com	**Maryland**

Founded 1990. 138 families. Open membership, American made cars. Fun car club that has donated over $350,000 to charity since 1990. Monthly meetings and newsletter. Holds largest indoor car show for charity in December of each year at Timonium fairgrounds. Dues: $20/year. Web site: www.streetcarsofdesire.com

Maynard Area Auto Club PO Box 633 Maynard, MA 01754 978-897-3445; FAX: 978-897-3175 E-mail: jmalcolm@juno.com	**Massachusetts**

Founded 1988. 200 members (closed). No restrictions, 1 show each year, monthly newsletter. Dues: $20/year.

Plymouth County Auto Club PO Box 88 Carver, MA 02330 Pete: 508-866-4633 Chuck: 508-866-2709 E-mail: mercury47@capecod.net	**Massachusetts**

Founded 1981. 40 members. Monthly meetings, summer get-togethers and cruises. Family oriented. All makes and car lovers. Dues: $20/year.

Spindles Auto Club c/o 17 Sycamore Rd Squantum, MA 02171-1336 617-472-3572 E-mail: deskjet894@worldnet.att.net	**Massachusetts**

Founded 1957. Currently have a building with 25 cars inside. Yearly car show (over 500 vehicles) with a portion of the proceeds to benefit local charities on the Sunday of Labor Day weekend (September 5, 1999), Marshfield fairgrounds, Marshfield, MA. Dues: (start at) $25/year. Web site: http://members.tripod.com/spindlescarclub

Wachusett Old Car Club PO Box 414 Holden, MA 01520 508-421-6565	**Massachusetts**

Founded 1952. 70 members. You should have an interest in old cars, their history and preservation. Meet monthly and sponsor one of the best classic car shows in New England during the last full weekend in September each year. Dues: $10/year.

Capitol City Old Car Club PO Box 16075 Lansing, MI 48910 517-663-1785	**Michigan**

Founded 1962. 150+ members. No restrictions. Monthly newsletter, annual spectacular Memorial Day weekend car show, swap meet. Monthly meetings (3rd Thursday), great club house, Father's Day nursing home tour, overnighter, mystery run, awards banquet, cruise-ins, much fun for all. Dues: $14.50/year single, $16.50/year family. Web site: www.uvona.com/ccocc/

Granite City Street Machines
Gary Hartgers
822 N 10th Ave Unit 5
Sartell, MN 56377
PH/FAX: 320-255-5352

Minnesota

Founded 1996. 20 members. Group of people interested in cars. Car show each May. Members MSMA, Minnesota Street Machine Assoc. Newsletter, *White Line Flyer*. State club has approximately 200+ members.

Jaguar Club of Minnesota
5610 Woodcrest Dr
Minneapolis, MN 55424
612-927-8126

Minnesota

Founded 1977. 100+ members. Open to owners or enthusiasts of Jaguar cars. Dues: $35/year.

Phantoms of Red Wing
PO Box 195
Red Wing, MN 55066
651-388-1800; FAX: 651-267-0809

Minnesota

Founded 1998. 50 members. Quarterly newsletter, sponsor organizations receive advertising. Members receive discounts at local businesses. Dues: $25/year.

St Cloud Antique Auto Club
PO Box 704
St Cloud, MN 56302-0704

Minnesota

For membership information, contact at the above address: Pantowners, attn: Secretary. Founded 1971. 263 members. Our club nickname of "Pantowners" is named after the Pan automobile made in St Cloud from 1917-1919. Family centered club. Monthly meetings and newsletter, summer tours, car show and swap meet each August, always the third Sunday, over 500 cars and 400 swappers. Smaller shows and tours throughout the year. Welcome all antique, pioneer or collector car enthusiasts. Dues: $10/year.

Twin Cities Roadsters
9811 Hamilton Rd
Eden Prairie, MN 55344
612-941-2918; FAX: 612-941-8315
E-mail: v8ford@juno.com

Minnesota

Founded 1969. 25 members. Must have pre-1949 roadster or other open car, be invited, sponsored and voted upon. Dues: none.

Willmar Car Club
PO Box 428
Willmar, MN 56201

Minnesota

Founded 1979. 40 members. No restrictions, monthly newsletters, annual banquet, monthly meetings, sponsor monthly car buffs breakfasts at area restaurants, annual car show and swap meet. Publication, *The Polishing Rag*, included in membership, published monthly, includes calendar of events, classified ads, features on club members or vehicles, theme features and general information for club members. Dues: $10/year single, $15/year family.

Wright County Car Club
PO Box 662
Buffalo, MN 55313
612-682-3772

Minnesota

For membership information, write to the above address. Founded 1986. 100 families. No restrictions. Monthly meetings and newsletter. Parades, cruises, picnics and other family oriented outings. Car show and swap meet every June. Breakfast first Saturday and meeting third Tuesday of each month. Dues: $15/year.

Montana Street Rod Association
PO Box 991
Livingston, MT 59047
406-222-1084
E-mail: jcopenhaver@mcn.net

Montana

Founded 1974. 100 members. 25th year. Meet quarterly. Purpose is to promote street rodding and other auto related activities and provide sounding board for all clubs and interested street rodders in the state to discuss common problems. Dues: $10/year. Web site: www.mcn.net/~jcopenhaver/

Amoskeag Reserve Engine Co
PO Box 307
Lebanon, NH 03766
603-632-4998

New Hampshire

Founded 1984. 110 members. Chapter of the Society for the Preservation and Appreciation of Antique Motorized Fire Apparatus in America. Bi-monthly meetings held on the second Friday of the month at various locations around the state. Annual meet and show. Bi-monthly newsletter. Dues: $15/year.

New Hampshire Mustang Club
c/o Tom Cannon
8 Sycamore St
Hudson, NH 03051-4733
PH/FAX: 603-594-0838
E-mail: tjc1965@aol.com

New Hampshire

Founded 1988. 182 members. Ownership not required. Nonprofit organization devoted to Ford Mustangs, past and present. Monthly meets, newsletter, shows, rallies, etc. Monthly publication, *New Hampshire Mustang*, free with membership. Dues: $25/year.

Unforgettable Autos of Mid-Jersey
PO Box 423
Dunellen, NJ 08812

New Jersey

Founded 1986. 60+ members. Attend 2 meetings and join. Receive technical assistance, receive monthly newsletter. Run 2 shows and a banquet each year. Dues: $25/year.

British Car Club of Western New York
c/o Sally Genco
11560 Genesee St
Alden, NY 14004
716-937-6986; FAX: 716-937-3534
E-mail: sscraps@aol.com

New York

Founded 1990. 250+/- members. Open to all who have interest in any of the British marques. A very social organization, our membership is as diverse as our cars. Meet monthly at the Rose Garden Restaurant on Wehrle Dr in Williamsville, adding many other events in season (runs, dinners, tech sessions, picnics). EuroCar Day is held on the second Sunday in June, unique to western New York, draws 150 fabulous European cars from as far away as Toronto, the Finger Lakes, Ohio and Pennsylvania. Dues: $15/year single, $20/year family.

Long Island Motor Touring Club Inc
PO Box 412
West Islip, NY 11795-0412
PH/FAX: 516-422-1353

New York

Founded 1957. 83 families are members. Pre-WW II, 1942 and older, multi-marque, annual picnic, annual anniversary, Christmas/holiday parties. Monthly 10-page newsletter, monthly meeting 2nd Thursday except December. Annual flea market and show, monthly tour or event and youth events. Dues: $20/year family or single.

Saugerties Antique Auto Club Inc	New York
PO Box 111	
Saugerties, NY 12477	
914-679-6810; FAX: 914-679-8517	

Founded 1957. 56 members. No restrictions to join, just a sincere interest in preserving and restoring antique, classic and special interest vehicles and their history. Sponsor a yearly show the second Sunday in August, this year being our 42nd one. Dues: $7.50/year single, $10/year family.

North Carolina Studebaker Drivers Club	North Carolina
1448 Triplett Rd	
Cleveland, NC 27013	
704-528-6623	
E-mail: avanti@vvi.net	

Founded 1971. 175 active members. Member of National Studebaker Drivers Club is a local club requirement. Six newsletters per year. Tickets to Spring Autofare in Charlotte. Monthly meetings across state. Dues: $10/year.

Dakota Western Auto Club	North Dakota
Ken Praus	
976 Elm Ave	
Dickinson, ND 58601	
701-225-8097	

Founded 1977. 55 members. Open to anyone with an interest and love of the automobile. Car show held in June at Medora, North Dakota. Also hosts Wendy's Big Classic auto show and swap meet, held the 3rd Sunday in July at Wal-Mart parking lot in Dickinson, ND, no fee. Dues: $10/year.

North Dakota Street Rod Association	North Dakota
PO Box 459	
Bismarck, ND 58502	
701-255-6382, 701-222-2069	
FAX: 701-222-0736	
E-mail: ndsra@btigate.com	

Founded 1985. 500 members. Six newsletters per year, annual Christmas party, co-sponsor rodding events in North Dakota. Dues: $10/year.

Valley Vintage Car Club	North Dakota
Box 2682	
Fargo, ND 58107	
Steve: 701-235-9107	
Kurt Ketterl, President:	
218-483-3268	
(February 1999-January 2000)	

Founded 1973. 90 members. Newsletter, fall car show, monthly meetings, summer family events. Club accepts vehicles of all types including pickups, street rods, restored, special interest, sports cars and trucks. Dues: $10/year.

British Car Club of Greater Cincinnati	Ohio
PO Box 772	
West Chester, OH 45071-0772	
513-779-0317	
E-mail: bccgc@aol.com	

Founded 1988. 110 members. Open to all British cars. Monthly newsletter, sponsors two car shows per year, monthly meetings, 2nd Wednesday of the month. Dues: $20/year. Web site: http://members.aol.com/bccgc/index.html

Buckeye Ramblin' Rods	Ohio
958 E Milltown Rd	
Wooster, OH 44691	
330-345-6971	

Founded 1979. 20+ members. No restrictions except interest in antique cars. Meet once a month at Freelander Park, Wednesdays at 7 pm, June-October; Greenleaf restaurant Sundays at 7 pm, November-May. Host Runt Roast 3rd weekend August; also downtown cruises, June, July, August. Dues: $12/year.

Car Coddlers Club of Ohio Inc	Ohio
PO Box 2094	
Sandusky, OH 44871-2094	
419-935-0286; FAX: 419-935-1635	

Founded 1963. 470 members. Monthly newsletter, sponsor several car shows, 3 trophy meets. Primarily antique, classic and collectible cars. Tours, picnics. Dues: $10/year.

Mahoning Valley Old Car Club	Ohio
1498 Brantford Blvd	
Youngstown, OH 44509	
330-792-6807	

Founded 1977. 120 members. Must have an interest in old cars. We take part in parades, car shows, nursing home shows. Our club has a monthly newsletter membership book; also an annual car show that we use the money to help the needy. Dues: $15/year (single), $20/year (couple).

Mid-Ohio Ford Club	Ohio
5262 Broadview Rd	
Columbus, OH 43230	
614-475-3585; FAX: 614-475-3589	

Founded 1985. 160 members. Do a lot of charity work. Take trips, rent drag strip for 1/2 day (4 times a year), monthly newsletter. All Ford show in June, all Ford swap meet first weekend of April. No restrictions at all to join, just like old cars and trucks, do favor Ford, Lincoln and Mercury. Dues: $12/year. Web site: www.springswap.com

Y-City Custom Car Association	Ohio
Attn Ken McPeck	
2090 Shady Ln	
Zanesville, OH 43701	
740-454-0347	

Founded 1969. 10 members. Helps and assists several historic organizations and area Jaycee clubs in organizing and co-producing antique auto and truck shows and cruise-in car shows. Encourages socializing and fellowship among car owners at these annual events.

Central Pennsylvania Street Machines	Pennsylvania
310 Wright St	
Flemington, PA 17745-3829	
717-748-7070	

Founded 1991. 50 members. Ownership of a vehicle is not a requirement. Family oriented organization and exist solely for the people of this club so that they can share their interests with others in the area. Our club is run for and by the people. It serves through an elected board of directors and officers. Informative newsletter, technical advice, enjoyable monthly meetings and an annual auto and truck show with proceeds to benefit local charity. Dues: $10/year.

Chester County Antique Car Club	Pennsylvania
PO Box 1014	
Exton, PA 19341	
E-mail: oakes@worldaxes	

Founded 1951. 200+ members. Approval by board of directors needed to join. Monthly membership meetings, club activities throughout the year, monthly newsletter. Oldest non-national club in Pennsylvania. Dues: $20/year.

Historical Car Club of Pennsylvania PO Box 688 Havertown, PA 19083 610-325-4264; FAX: 610-325-2022 E-mail: mail@spokenwheel.com	**Pennsylvania**

Founded 1949. 600 members. *Spokenwheel* is a publication of HCCP. Fall meet at the Delaware County Community College, October 17, 1999. Dues: $10/year. Web site: www.spokenwheel.com

Pittsburgh CARS 1008 Wren Dr Kennedy Twp, PA 15136 412-331-7153	**Pennsylvania**

Founded 1991. 150 members. To have an interest in classics, antiques, rods and specialty CARS. Monthly newsletter, numerous cruises or car show, picnic, Christmas party, etc. Dues: $20/year.

The Wanderers Car Club 2620 Old Elizabeth Rd West Mifflin, PA 15122 412-466-8626	**Pennsylvania**

Founded 1991. 100+ members. Must be a car lover. Newsletter, event schedules, car cruises, club picnics and parties. Anti-litter campaign, car shows, rod runs. Dues: $20 to join, $10/year. regions:

California	*The Wanderers Car Club of Central California*, Lynn Hubbard, President, 1908 Belle Terr, Bakersfield, CA 93304
Florida	*The Wanderers Car Club of Central Florida*, Lloyd Odell, President, 8615 E Derby Oaks Dr, Floral City, FL 34436
New York	*The Wanderers Car Club of New York*, Dolly Hunter, Secretary, PO Box 677, Mt Vision, NY 13810
Wisconsin	*The Wanderers Car Club of Wisconsin*, David Burdis, President, 2537 Back Rd, Burlington, WI 53105

Rhode Island Chevy Owners Association 100 Balch St Pawtucket, RI 02861 401-728-7059 eves E-mail: chevyprez@aol.com	**Rhode Island**

Founded 1990. 78 members. Must be 18 years old and own 1 Chevrolet vehicle of any year. Sponsors of the All Chevy Show held the last Sunday of every June. Monthly newsletter, various year round family activities. Open to car and truck owners. Dues: $20/year.

West Tennessee Antique Car Club 595 Liberty Claybrook Rd Beech Bluff, TN 38313-9335 901-427-6633 E-mail: denmartin@juno.com	**Tennessee**

Founded 1964. 50 members. Open to any individual or family with an interest in original and restored antique cars. Monthly meetings, occasional tours, annual car show second Saturday in May. Dues: $10/year.

Alamo City Historical Car Club 4827 Casa Bello San Antonio, TX 78233 210-599-1258 E-mail: ndl100@aol.com	**Texas**

Founded 1954. 113 members. Open to all owners of any car 20 years or older. Monthly newsletter. Hosts annual car show, tours, parades and lots of fun. Dues: $15/year.

Caprock Classic Car Club Inc PO Box 53352 Lubbock, TX 79424 806-794-3389; FAX: 806-798-1598 E-mail: mjo.martin@juno.com	**Texas**

Founded 1992. 160 members. Monthly newsletter, charity car show and also Rock and Roll Nostalgia car cruise and car show, both in the summer. All car enthusiasts are encouraged to join. Meet on the 2nd Thursday at Garden and Arts Center, 4215 S University Ave. Call or write for dates on above shows. Dues: $25/year. Web site: www.ccccinc.org

Summer Knights Inc PO Box 38342 Dallas, TX 75238 214-341-3706; FAX: 972-801-3928 E-mail: tjohnson@cyberramp.net	**Texas**

35 families. All makes, models of antique, classic and muscle cars, trucks. Monthly car show (April-September) and toy drive and food drive car shows in October. Dues: $25/year.

West Texas Cruisers PO Box 9716 Midland, TX 79708 915-620-0536; FAX: 915-520-7886 E-mail: laryhill@nwol.net	**Texas**

Founded 1991. 150 members. All car nuts welcome. You don't even have to own a car to join, but you must love cars. Now meeting in our own building, 1st and 3rd Tuesdays, monthly, 7 pm, 2901 Frances, Midland, TX. Public welcome. Dues: $24/year.

Now & Then Vehicles Club Inc of Southern Vermont 1138 US Rt 5 Dummerston, VT 05346 802-257-3053	**Vermont**

Founded 1978. 50 families. Interest in history or preservation of autos. Family oriented club endeavoring to inform and enrich our understanding of the history and kinds of motor vehicles from the early flivvers through the modern performance cars. The club sponsors a car show and other events to enhance the enjoyment of members of "special interest" cars and trucks. Dues: $10/year.

Bremerton Auto Club 3230 View Crest Dr NE Bremerton, WA 98310-9785 360-373-5358	**Washington**

Founded 1976. 30 members. Anyone interested in pre-1970 vehicles can join. Do not need to own a collectible vehicle. Dues: $10/year.

The Friendly OK Car Club 48 Wagon Trail Rd Tonasket, WA 98855 509-826-4631, 509-826-3154	**Washington**

Founded 1994. 120 members. Car show and swap meet 3rd weekend in May. Dues: $10/year.

Northwoods Cruisers 408 W Leather Ave Tomahawk, WI 54487 715-453-1955	**Wisconsin**

Founded 1994. 45 members. Sponsors Main Street Memories, an annual car show and craft fair conducted on Sunday of Memorial Day weekend. Also have cruises, poker runs, picnics, etc. All activities revolve around vintage automobiles and trucks.

Section Three
Clubs & Organizations

All types, years and makes available. Dues: $10/year single, $15/year couple, $20/year family.

RACE Car Club	**Wisconsin**
c/o Lee Soda	
PO Box 598	
Ripon, WI 54971	
920-748-5800	

Founded 1989. 80 members. Monthly newsletter, meet 2nd Wednesday of each month, car and truck show 3rd weekend of May. Club is open to all makes with various activities, cruises, etc throughout the year. Dues: $15/year.

Rods-N-Relics Car Club Ltd	**Wisconsin**
PO Box 737	
Cedarburg, WI 53012	
414-242-7792	

Meetings are the first Thursday evening of each month in Cedarburg, WI. Events: annual 1950s sock hop each January, annual car show (Grafton, WI) each July, annual holiday party each December, plus road rallies, parades, cruises and custard stand outings. No restrictions. If you own a rod, a relic, a classic or even an ordinary car, truck or motorcycle, or if you crave to someday own one, you are welcome to join. Charities: Ozaukee County (WI) schools, Ozaukee County Humane Society and Southeast Wisconsin Health Education Center. Dues: $25/year.

Voitures Anciennes Du Quebec Inc	**Canada**
24 Ave Jaffa	
Candiac, QC Canada J5R 3R3	
514-990-9111; FAX: 514-635-2294	

Almost 2,000 members. Association regrouping owners and amateurs of antiques and classic cars. Our mission is to preserve the authenticity and origin of an antique in its most condition. Publisher of a French 32-page monthly magazine (largest in North America). Organizer of many events and shows throughout the Province of Quebec. For car owners (20 years and up). Dues: $45/year Canada, $67/year US and Europe.

Legislative Watch Organizations

National

AACA Legislative
Russell Fisher
21525 Lancelot Dr
Brookfield, WI 53045
414-781-5130; FAX: 414-781-7780

Founded 1935. Membership includes 50+ states. Interested in legislation centered around the automobile, the hobby and its preservation. Have a networking system for states to assist the hobby and club members. Publications: *Rummage Box News* and *Antique Automobile* magazine with information on state and federal automobile legislation.

Automotive Restoration Market Organization (ARMO)
PO Box 4910
Diamond Bar, CA 91765-0910
909-396-0289; FAX: 909-860-0184

For information, contact at the above address: Lee Lasky. ARMO, a council of the Specialty Equipment Market Association (SEMA), was created for the purpose of meeting the legislative, educational and communications needs of the automotive restoration industry. Through cooperative action, ARMO works to address those legislative and/or regulatory issues which may impact on the restoration industry and strives to ensure the viability of the industry/hobby. Any business or club serving the automotive restoration industry or the collector-car hobby is invited to join.

Clean Air Performance Professionals (CAPP)
84 Hoy Ave
Fords, NJ 08863
732-738-7859; FAX: 732-738-7625
E-mail: stellacapp@earthlink.net

Founded 1991. Less than 500 members. CAPP is an award-winning international coalition interested in personal property and the environment. CAPP was created to promote common sense in vehicle inspection and maintenance programs. Dues: $60/year.

Council of Vehicle Associations/
Classic Vehicle Advocate Group Inc
aka COVA/CVAG Inc
Butch DeZuzio, President
PO Box 2136
West Paterson, NJ 07424-3311
800-CARS-166, 973-881-8838
FAX: 973-279-3779
E-mail: info@covacvag.org

For complete listing of chapters, contact at the above address: Butch DeZuzio. Founded 1992. Representing over 85,000 hobbyists. COVA/CVAG Inc is a not for profit organization, devoted to the interests of all individuals, clubs, organizations and companies involved in the automotive, truck, motorcycle hobby/industry. All members receive the fact and information filled monthly newsletter. When fighting for your rights, remember: "If not you, who? If not now, when?". Dues: $25/year or more. Web site: www.covacvag.org

chapters (partial listing):

Arizona *Arizona Automobile Hobbyist Council*, PO Box 26057, Phoenix, AZ 85068-6057

Grand Canyon State Chapter, Studebaker Driver's Club, c/o Chris Collins, 2410 W Freeway Ln, Phoenix, AZ 85021

Southwestern America Vehicle Enthusiasts, SAVE, PO Box 18353, Tucson, AZ 85731-8353

California *COVA/CVAG Inc*, Los Angeles County Rep, Brandon Brooks, 4550 Longridge Ave, Sherman Oaks, CA 91423, 818-784-9690

Florida *Antique Automobile Club of Cape Canaveral*, PO Box 1611, Cocoa, FL 32922, 407-724-6015

Florida Sun Coast MG Car Club Inc, Attn: Bruce Rauch, PO Box 0251, Tampa, FL 33601

Treasure Coast Vintage Car Club, c/o Dweight Geiger, 518 N River Point Dr, Stuart, FL 34994, 561-283-4433

Georgia *Vintage Thunderbird Club International*, c/o Stephen Longaker, 2565 New College Way, Cumming, GA 30041

Iowa *Southeast Iowa Antique Car Club*, c/o Robert Carleton, 17841 50th St, Morning Sun, IA 52640-9427

Illinois *Fox Valley Model A Ford Club*, c/o Jack Anderson, PO Box 4, Geneva, IL 60134, 630-584-2380

Kane County Car Club, Norma Wissing, 824 Hillview Ave, West Chicago, IL 60185-2916, 630-231-4606

Salt Creek Chapter Model A Ford Club of America, c/o Michael Schomer Sr, 6155 Pershing Ave, Downers Grove, IL 60516-1724

Windy City Chapter American Truck Historical Society, c/o John E Kutska, Treasurer, 4334 DuBois Blvd, Brookfield, IL 60513-2222, 708-485-1961

COVA/CVAG Inc chapters *(continued)*

Indiana *United Four Wheel Drive Assoc*, PO Box 3553, Evansville, IN 47734

Kentucky *Iron City Antique Auto Club*, c/o Carl E Virgin, 1308 Sparks St, Flatwoods, KY 41139, 606-836-5040

Michigan *Citizens Against Repressive Zoning (CARZ)*, Jack Down, PO Box 536, Haslett, MI 48840-0536, 517-351-6751

COVA/CVAG Inc, Michigan State Rep, J Steven Kiraly, 7844 Enzian Rd, Delton, MI 49046-9716, 616-664-5888

Floral City A's Region Model A Restorers Club, c/o Roger Van Houten, 1876 E Hurd Rd, Monroe, MI 48162-9308

Oldsmobile Club of America Inc, Greg Childs, President, PO Box 80318, Lansing, MI 48909-0318

Missouri *Heart of America 364 Corvair Owners Assoc*, 9802 Booth, Kansas City, MO 64134

Mississippi *Antique Vehicle Club of Mississippi*, c/o Bob Jackman, 2206 Scenic Dr, Brandon, MS 39296-5792, 601-919-0791

New Jersey *Antique Motoring Club of Monmouth County*, c/o Tom Nobile, 2 Wyoming Dr, Hazlett, NJ 07730, 732-739-0704

Bergen County Cruisers, c/o Tommy, 170 Preston St, Ridgefield Park, NJ 07660, 201-641-1716

Cadillac Club of North Jersey Inc, c/o Richard W Bankart, 20 Valley Ave, Ste D-2, Westwood, NJ 07675-3601, 201-263-0999

COVA/CVAG Inc, Central Jersey State Rep, Ben Deutschman, Bldg 11 Apt A-1, Redfield Village, Metuchen, NJ 08840-3033, 732-549-0188

COVA/CVAG Inc, North Jersey State Rep, Steven Falker, 53 W Gouverneur Ave, Rutherford, NJ 07070-2627, 201-460-4592

NJ Open Road Thunderbird Club, c/o Richard Martin, PO Box 565, Hewitt, NJ 07421, 201-728-8652

NJ VORC, Jere Duffett, 17 Larsen Park Dr, Medford, NJ 08055, 609-983-8246

North Jersey Thunderbird Association, Ezra Hinkle, 7 Carol Pl, Wayne, NJ 07470, 973-694-9597

Trans Am Formulas-Firebirds of America, 2486 Vauxhall Rd, Union, NJ 07083-5024, 908-851-2063

Tri-County Cruisers, c/o Frank, PO Box 3671, Wayne, NJ 07470, 973-956-1309

New York *Antique Automobile Club of America Livingston Region*, W R Laidlaw, 3475 North Rd, Geneseo, NY 14454

COVA/CVAG Inc, New York State Rep, Richard Golanec, 6 Rockland Ave, Port Chester, NY 10573, 914-937-6486

Niagara Frontier Classic Car Club, c/o Bill Parks, 40 Henley Rd, Buffalo, NY 14216, 716-834-7494

Ohio *Car Coddlers Club of Ohio*, c/o Norman Abston, 3994 Bullhead Rd, Willard, OH 44890, 419-935-0286

COVA of Ohio, c/o Glenn Miller, 17190 US Rt 20A, West Unity, OH 43570, 419-636-4604

Penn-Ohio A Ford Club, c/o Cliff Naugle, 17502 Laverne Ave, Cleveland, OH 44135-1944, 216-671-9917

Scioto Model A Ford Club, 3389 Calumet St, Columbus, OH 43214-4105

Oregon *COVA/CVAG Inc*, Oregon State Rep, Dick Larrowe, PO Box 1239, Sandy, OR 97055, 503-668-4096

Pennsylvania *Classy Cruisers Club*, Cliff Babin, President, PO Box 3122, Bethlehem, PA 18017, 610-866-9019

Texas *Texas Vehicle Club Council*, c/o Troy Mennis, 604 Evans Dr, Euless, TX 76040-3906, 817-283-6942

Wisconsin *COVA/CVAG Inc*, Wisconsin State Rep, Richard H Dorsey, 5114 St Rd 44, Oshkosh, WI 54904, 920-589-4652

COVA/CVAG Inc, Wisconsin State Rep, Vincent Ruffolo, 2104 Washington Rd, Kenosha, WI 53140-5335, 414-658-2600

Wisconsin Auto Clubs in Association Inc (1972), 5114 State Rd 44, Oshkosh, WI 54904, 920-589-4652

Wyoming *Big Horn Mountain Region of AACA*, H O "Toby" Thobaben II, President, PO Box 5063, Sheridan, WY 82801, 307-672-2600

Motorsports Parts Manufacturers Council (MPMC)
PO Box 4910
Diamond Bar, CA 91765-0910
909-396-0289; FAX: 909-860-0184

For more information, contact at the above address: Lee Lasky. MPMC is a council of the Specialty Equipment Market Association (SEMA), established specially for companies engaged in manufacturing performance parts used in sanctioned racing applications. Dedicated to addressing industry-specific issues and to promoting and preserving the motorsports parts industry. All companies that meet at least two of these criteria are eligible and encouraged to become involved. Membership is open to all companies that manufacture, assemble and/or design performance products.

National Motorists Assn
402 W 2nd St
Waunakee, WI 53597-1342
608-849-6000
800-882-2785 membership information
FAX: 608-849-8697
E-mail: nma@motorists.org

Founded 1982. 7,000 members. Represent the interests of American drivers. Promote rational traffic regulation, motorist courtesy and work to eliminate abusive insurance company practices, speed traps and other infringements of motorists' rights. Strong grass roots organization. State chapter coordinators. State and national lobbying. Political campaign involvement. Editorials and news releases. Bi-monthly national newsletter. Quarterly statewide newsletters. Dues: $29/year individual, $39/year family, $65/year business. Web site: www.motorists.org

chapters:

Alaska Lawrence D Wood, State Chapter Coordinator PO Box 1789, Palmer, AK 99645-1789, 907-746-4981; E-mail: lwood@akcache.com; Web site: www.motorists.org/ak

Arizona Steve Bacs, State Chapter Coordinator 6587 W Irma Ln, Glendale, AZ 85308, 602-572-0349 home; E-mail: abacs@cmxinc.com

California Jim Thomas, 244 Summit Dr, Corte Madera, CA 94925, 415-924-2184 home/work; FAX: 415-927-4902

Connecticut Sheldon Wishmick, State Chapter Coordinator 94 Stagecoach Ln, Newington, CT 06111, PH/FAX: 860-666-1006 home, 860-667-3649 work; E-mail: ctnma@aol.com; Web site: www.motorists.org/ct

Greg Amy, Milford, CT 06460-6728, 203-874-1403; E-mail: ct@motorists.org

Delaware Robert L Hickerson III, 35 Yosemite Dr, Bear, DE 19701-3806, 302-836-5921 home (until 9 pm), 302-540-6848 cellular; E-mail: rhckrsn@aol.com

Florida Gregory F Mauz, Delray Beach, FL 33444, 561-243-0920

Ralph Robinson, Sarasota, FL 34239, 941-349-6636; FAX: 941-922-2152

Georgia David Carr, Marietta, GA 30062, 770-640-8209 home, 770-714-5662 cellular; E-mail: cbr1100x@gw.total-web.net

Maryland Bill Gawthrop, 1504 Chapman Rd, Crofton, MD 21114, 410-451-2610; E-mail: gawthrop@aol.com

Charles Terlizzi, PO Box 1408, Olney, MD 20830, 301-570-8492; E-mail: charter9@idt.net

Massachusetts John Carr, Newton, MA 02466, 617-630-5264; E-mail: jfc@tiac.net; Web site: www.motorists.org/ma

Ivan Sever, Needham, MA 02492-4318, 781-449-7231 home; E-mail: ma@motorists.org

Michigan Parker Thomas, State Chapter Coordinator 2906 Laurel Dr, Commerce, MI 48382, 248-553-1286 work; FAX: 248-553-5205; E-mail: mi@motorists.org; Web site: www.motorists.org/mi

Steve Purdy, Williamston, MI 48895, 517-655-3591

Minnesota Thomas K Trecker, State Chapter Coordinator 885 Govern Cir, Eagan, MN 55123, 651-406-9405; FAX: 651-406-9403; E-mail: ttreck@aol.com; Web site: www.motorists.org/mn

Missouri Jeffrey Barnes, Independence, MO 64055-3047, 816-519-0748 cellular; E-mail: jefabarnes@yahoo.com

Nevada Chad Dornsife, Zephyr Cove, NV 89448, 702-588-6325; E-mail: chad@hwysafety.com

New Jersey Stephen G Carrellas, State Chapter Coordinator 35 Sycamore Ave, Berkeley Heights, NJ 07922, 908-464-7943; E-mail: nj@motorists.org; Web site: www.motorists.org/nj

New York Andrew Gregory, Schenectady, NY 12306, 518-346-2547; E-mail: ny_nma_scc@msn.com

Casey W Raskob III, Croton-On-Hudson, NY 10520, PH/FAX: 914-271-5383 home days; E-mail: speedlaw@bestweb.net

North Carolina Henry B Stowe, High Point, NC 27263, 910-434-4998; E-mail: h_stowe@northstate.net

Ohio David Sweeney, Akron, OH 44312, 330-860-2399; E-mail: sweeneyd@pgg.mcdermott.com; Web site: www.motorists.org/oh

Oregon Bennet K Langlotz, State Chapter Coordinator 2850 SW Fairmont Blvd, Portland, OR 97201, 503-275-9100; FAX: 503-275-9109; E-mail: langlotz@teleport.com; Web site: www.motorists.org/or

Rhode Island Thomas Frank, State Chapter Coordinator PO Box 267, Newport, RI 02840, PH/FAX: 401-849-3974; E-mail: ri@motorists.org

South Carolina Matthew Hayduk, State Chapter Coordinator 102 Ansley Ct, Greer, SC 29650-2700, 864-268-9829 home; E-mail: matt@plusweb.net

Texas Luke Ball, State Chapter Coordinator 15517 Weldon Dr, Houston, TX 77032, PH/FAX: 281-987-3898; E-mail: lball@gateway.net

Virginia Mike McGuire, Falls Church, VA 22043-1314, 703-893-9370 home; E-mail: mcguirem@ofo.psb.bls.gov

West Virginia James M Mullins Jr, State Chapter Coordinator 329 Riverside Dr, Logan, WV 25601-4033, 304-752-3156 home (after 3 pm); E-mail: jimmullins@newwave.net; Web site: www.motorists.org/wv

---

Specialty Equipment Market Association (SEMA)
1575 S Valley Vista Dr
PO Box 4910
Diamond Bar, CA 91765
909-396-0289 ext 113
FAX: 909-860-0184

Founded 1963. 3,400 members including manufacturers, distributors, retailers, installers, restylers, jobbers, restorers, car dealers, race facilities, and others. SEMA is a trade association that represents the producers and marketers of specialty equipment products and services for the automotive aftermarket. SEMA's mission is to help members' businesses succeed and prosper. Web site: www.sema.org

Street Rod Marketing Alliance (SRMA)
PO Box 4910
Diamond Bar, CA 91765
909-396-0289; FAX: 909-860-0184
E-mail: leel@sema.org

SRMA is a council of the Specialty Equipment Market Association (SEMA). Dedicated to addressing the challenges facing this segment of the automotive aftermarket and to preserving and promoting the street rod industry. SRMA members are the manufacturers, builders/fabricators, dealers, car clubs and enthusiast publications that make up the street rod industry. Focuses on industry-specific issues, developing effective strategies and programs that will assist members in improving their businesses. Special attention is given to addressing those legislative and/or regulatory matters which affect the rodding industry.

Vehicle Preservation Society
PO Box 9800
San Diego, CA 92169
619-449-1010; FAX: 619-449-6388
E-mail: director@vehicles.cc

See full listing in **Section Two** under **appraisals**

State and Local

Arizona Automotive Hobbyist Council
PO Box 26057
Phoenix, AZ 85068-6057
602-945-2423

Founded 1973. 8,000 to 10,000 members. No restrictions. Formed to stop government harassment of the automotive hobbyist. List car shows and other events. Publish *Council Journal* 9 times a year. Dues: $12.50/year individual, club membership from $30-up/year.

Citizens Against Repressive Zoning
PO Box 536
Haslett, MI 48840-0536
517-351-6751; FAX: 517-339-4926
E-mail: malzoning@aol.com

Founded 1988. 300 members. Michigan incorporated foundation. Publish a bi-monthly newsletter. Concerned with nuisance zoning zealots who abuse civil and PTO property rights of individual collectors, salvage yards, rechrome shops, repaint shops and auto storage yards. Currently 70 bulletins on rights and fighting methods, $45; $55 with membership; $15 membership only. Send SASE for information.

DC Council of Car Clubs
6629 32nd St NW
Washington, DC 20015
202-966-2737
E-mail: lackie@ix.netcom.com

Founded 1977. Consists of 10 clubs. Irregularly distribute *Washington Area Legislative News* to area clubs in DC, Maryland and Virginia. Drafted existing DC Historic Motor Vehicle License Law in 1978. Dues: none, contributions welcome.

Eastern Nebraska, Western Iowa Car Council
12559 O St
Omaha, NE 68137
402-895-0629
E-mail: phigh@inetnebr.com

Contact: Paul High. Founded 1970. 76 clubs. Open to any organized area car club. Holds annual spring swap meet, state fairgrounds, Lincoln, NE; fall swap meet, AK Sarben, Omaha, NE. Dues: 25¢ per club member.

Legislative Council of Motor Vehicle Clubs
PO Box 291
Hershey, PA 17033
717-533-9032

Legislative watchdog organization which monitors prospective legislation relevant to antique and collectible vehicles in Pennsylvania.

Tri-River Car Club Council
3 Cherry Valley Rd
Pittsburgh, PA 15221
412-243-0403

Founded 1993. 43 clubs and 15 individual members. No restrictions. Benefits include benefactor of new collectible license plate we had approved, eliminated CET from PA; judges for local shows, etc. Dues: $40/year club, $15/year individual.

United Street Rods of Idaho
2165 Bruneau Dr
Boise, ID 83709
PH/FAX: 208-377-0344
E-mail: megglest@micron.net

Founded 1979. 1,400 members. No restrictions to join. Automotive hobby organization for legislative watch and lobbying to improve laws that encourage street rod, classic and vintage car continued use. Yearly events calendar. Dues: $5/year. Web site: netnow.micron.net/~kevack/usri.htm

Washington Car Club Council
PO Box 2054
Everett, WA 98203
425-776-8529
E-mail: thekellyz@nsn.com

Contacts: Don Berry or Don Kelly. Founded 1988. 33,000 members. Must have an interest in the automotive hobby. Serves Washington State in the promotion of laws that affect car owners. Dues: $50/year.

Wisconsin Car Clubs Alliance (WCCA)
PO Box 562
Menomonee Falls, WI 53052-0562
414-255-5385

Founded 1989. 60 members. An alliance of car clubs. Each club has one vote, no matter how large or small. We are a watchdog group for legislation for and against our hobby. Also offer an individual membership, they can come to any meeting (2 a year), get our newsletter but have no vote. *WCCA Newsletter* comes with membership once a month, it contains any information we can get on things that affect our hobby, also list our members' car shows, swap meets and any other event they sponsor. Dues: $20/year club, $15/year individual.

Section Four:
Publications & Information Sources

156 listings

This section contains publications for car collectors as well as sources of information, photos, technical data, restoration information, and historical data. It does not include literature dealers, which are found both in Section One under marque specialists and Section Two under literature generalists. There are five categories.

Information Sources. These are businesses or individuals offering specific or general information which may be purchased.

Books & Publications. In this category are publishers and other suppliers of books, single pamphlets, and magazine back issues.

Periodicals. Included here are magazines and other publications to which the hobbyists may subscribe. Many are also available in the form of back issues. Subscription prices were current when the publishers submitted listings, but may have increased by the time the *Almanac* reaches you.

Newsletters ordinarily deal with investment/market condition aspects of car collecting and related fields.

Research & Reference Libraries. Includes private and public archives, libraries, specialized collections and reference sources. Many are not open to the general public and may require special arrangements to visit. Most libraries and other organizations will charge for finding and sending research material. When writing to them, be as specific as possible. Don't for instance, ask them to "send everything you have on 1951 XYZ's." The more precise you are in your request the better the response will be.

Information Sources

1958 Thunderbird Convertible Registry
Bill Van Ess
2306 Post Dr NE
Belmont, MI 49306
616-364-1973; FAX: 616-363-2870

book

See full listing in **Section One** under **Thunderbird**

AACA Library & Research Center
501 W Governor Rd
PO Box 417
Hershey, PA 17033
717-534-2082

research library

See full listing in **Section Four** under **research & reference libraries**

Automotive Information Clearinghouse
PO Box 1746
La Mesa, CA 91944
619-447-7200
FAX: 619-447-8080, include address

information source

America's largest stocking warehouse for original manufacturer's publications. Shop, owner's, parts manuals, sales brochures and more. Totally computerized. 10 second quotes. 34 years' experience.

Bimmer Magazine
42 Digital Dr #5
Novato, CA 94949
415-382-0580; FAX: 415-382-0587

magazine

See full listing in **Section Four** under **periodicals**

The CM Booth Collection of Historic Vehicles
Falstaff Antiques
63-67 High St
Rolvenden Kent TN17 4LP England
01580-241234

museum

See full listing in **Section Six** under **England**

Bill Boudway
105 Deerfield Dr
Canandaigua, NY 14424-2409
716-394-6172

restoration info

See full listing in **Section One** under **Packard**

British Car Films
PO Box 13862
London N4 3WB England
800-454-8341 toll-free
011 44181-3744850
FAX: 011 44181-3744852
E-mail: british.car@virgin.net

videos

See full listing in **Section Two** under **videos**

"Check The Oil!" Magazine
PO Box 937
Powell, OH 43065-0937
614-848-5038; FAX: 614-436-4760

magazine

See full listing in **Section Two** under **petroliana**

Classic Motorbooks
PO Box 1/HMN
729 Prospect Ave
Osceola, WI 54020
800-826-6600; FAX: 715-294-4448

books
videos

See full listing in **Section Four** under **books & publications**

Clean Air Performance Professionals (CAPP) 84 Hoy Ave Fords, NJ 08863 732-738-7859; FAX: 732-738-7625 E-mail: stellacapp@earthlink.net	**legislative watch organization**

See full listing in **Section Three** under **legislative watch organizations**

Collector Car & Truck Market Guide 41 N Main St North Grafton, MA 01536 508-839-6707; FAX: 508-839-6266 E-mail: vmr@vmrintl.com	**price guide**

See full listing in **Section Four** under **periodicals**

DeTomaso Registry Bill Van Ess 2306 Post Dr NE Belmont, MI 49306 616-364-1973; FAX: 616-363-2870	**book**

See full listing in **Section One** under **DeTomaso/Pantera**

Eastern New York MGA Club Newsletter Jon Rubel, President 3010 Avenue T Brooklyn, NY 11229-4008 718-891-5776; FAX: call first E-mail: eemgee@aol.com	**publication**

See full listing in **Section Four** under **newsletters**

Excellence Magazine 42 Digital Dr #5 Novato, CA 94949 415-382-0580; FAX: 415-382-0587	**magazine**

See full listing in **Section Four** under **periodicals**

Forza Magazine 42 Digital Dr #5 Novato, CA 94949 415-382-0580; FAX: 415-382-0587	**magazine**

See full listing in **Section Four** under **periodicals**

Bob Francis Auto Writer & Historian 1108 W Jackson St Tupelo, MS 38801 601-844-6070 E-mail: bigbob@ebicom.net	**history research trivia**

Mail order only. Will attempt to report on history of any make or model car. No technical questions, no questions about repair, etc. Usually give the "whole nine yards" when answering questions. Pictures available, reasonable rates, satisfaction. Automotive history books available, 2 books on automotive dates and chronology of events, 1st one $16.95 ppd, 2nd (most recent), $23.95 ppd. *Wonderful World of (Little Known) Automotive History* (mini-stories and trivia), 6x8-1/2", 226 pages. Volume 1, $18 postpaid anywhere.

Arthur Freakes Capri House Walton-On-Thames Surrey KT12 2LY England PH/FAX: (UK) 01932 269109	**researcher writer**

Motoring writer, historian, researcher. Editor of *HCKC News*, *Rootes Group Vehicles*, and *The Mitchamian*. Research and information on Rootes Group, Hillman, Commer for motor vehicle publications.

Hemmings' Vintage Auto Almanac©   Fourteenth Edition

GMC Solutions Robert English PO Box 675 Franklin, MA 02038-0675 508-520-3900; FAX: 508-520-7861 E-mail: oldcarkook@aol.com	**literature parts**

See full listing in **Section One** under **GMC**

Greater Manchester Fire Service Museum Maclure Rd Rochdale Lancashire OL11 1DN England 01706 341221	**museum**

See full listing in **Section Six** under **England**

Leon Henry Inc 455 Central Ave, Dept HVA Scarsdale, NY 10583 914-723-3176; FAX: 914-723-0205 E-mail: lhenryinc@aol.com	**list brokers package inserts**

Full service package insert/mailing list broker/manager. In our 43rd year. Our brokers can place your inserts into merchandise packages, statements, co-ops, ride-alongs, card decks, sample kits, etc, to target your prospective customer. We are managers for package insert programs including Ecklers Corvette Parts, Performance Products & Summit Racing Equipment. Let us put inserts into your packages. Web site: www.leonhenryinc.com

The Italian Car Registry 3305 Valley Vista Rd Walnut Creek, CA 94598-3943 925-458-1163	**information source**

Mail order only. An information exchange for Italian built and coachbuilt cars on any chassis. The only worldwide registry for Italian cars of any make. Extensive production information already compiled for Abarth, Alfa Romeo, Allemano, Arnolt, ASA, Bandini, Bertone, Bizzarini, Cisitalia, DeTomaso, Dual Ghia, Ermini, Ferrari, Fiat, Ghia, Giannini, Giaur, Intermeccanica, Iso, Isotta-Fraschini, Italia, Lamborghini, Lancia, Maserati, Michelotti, Moretti, Nardi, Nash-Healey, OM, Osca, Osella, Otas, Pininfarina, Siata, Stabilimenti Farina, Stanguellini, Taraschi, Touring, Vignale, Volpini, Zagato and more. Legal SASE for information.

Jaguar Cars Archives 555 MacArthur Blvd Mahwah, NJ 07430 201-818-8144; FAX: 201-818-0281	**research**

Mail order only. On-site research by appointment only. Provides individual vehicle research from Jaguar/Daimler build records for owners only. Fee includes JDHT certificate. Other holdings include Jaguar parts, service and owner's manuals, technical/service bulletins, paint/trim information, marketing, advertising and photographic collection. Send SASE to receive a form for vehicle or other technical research or for a list of items for sale (please specify).

Eliot James Enterprises Inc PO Box 3986 Dana Point, CA 92629-8986 949-661-0889; FAX: 949-661-1901	**development info**

See full listing in **Section Four** under **books & publications**

Main Attractions PO Box 4923 Chatsworth, CA 91311 818-709-9855; FAX: 818-998-0906	**posters videos**

Hot rod, classic car, drag racing, early NASCAR and biker flicks on video. *Thunder Road, Big Wheel, Drag Strip Girl, Hell on Wheels, Funny Car Summer, Stock Car Memories, Fireball 500, Hot Rod to Hell*, and thousands more available. Send $5 for the wildest 112-page catalog ever!

Mopar Collector's Guide Magazine — magazine
10067 El Camino Ave
Baton Rouge, LA 70815
504-274-0609; FAX: 504-274-9033
E-mail: mcgpub@mcg-pub.com

See full listing in **Section One** under **Mopar**

MotorWeek — TV program
11767 Owings Mills Blvd
Owings Mills, MD 21117
410-356-5600; FAX: 410-581-4113
E-mail: motorweek@mpt.org

Mail order only. Weekly TV program, *MotorWeek*. Television's original automotive magazine can be seen on more than 250 public television stations. It also appears weekly on Speedvision. Check local listings for the time and date in your area. Web sites: www.pbs.org or www.mpt.org/motorweek

Petroleum Collectibles Monthly — periodical
411 Forest St
LaGrange, OH 44050
440-355-6608; FAX: 440-355-4955

See full listing in **Section Four** under **periodicals**

William D Siuru Jr, PhD PE — information source
4050 Dolphin Cir
Colorado Springs, CO 80918
719-528-1980; FAX: 719-264-1303
E-mail: siuru@pcisys.net

Mail order only. Research and technical consultation for all makes of cars. Also advice on collector cars as investments. Freelance automotive journalist.

Richard Spiegelman Productions Inc — photography slides
19 Guild Hall Dr
Scarborough, ON Canada M1R 3Z7
416-759-1644
E-mail: carphoto@interlog.com or carphoto@yahoo.com

Photography, large slide file on old cars, color slide, 4x5 transparencies, slide shows, film productions.

Sports Car International — magazine
42 Digital Dr #5
Novato, CA 94949
415-382-0580; FAX: 415-382-0587

See full listing in **Section Four** under **periodicals**

Sting-Ray City — periodical
PO Box 13343
Scottsdale, AZ 85267-3343
602-348-9912
E-mail: rohns@doitnow.com

Newsletter catering to the Schwinn Sting-Ray enthusiast. Facts, features and classified ads for Schwinn Sting-Ray bicycles manufactured from 1963 to the late 1970s. Publishes *Sting-Ray City News*, bi-monthly publication. Subscription: $12/year, sample issue $2. Also publishes *Klassified*, monthly newsletter with Schwinn Sting-Ray ads only. Subscription: $15/year.

Sunburst Technology — electronic technical consultant
PO Box 598
Lithia Springs, GA 30122
770-949-2979; FAX: 770-942-6091
E-mail: sunburst2000@juno.com

Sunburst Technology can customize your electrical, electronic and micro processor controls for: auto, home and shop. A Sunburst multi parameter controller can be designed to monitor, control or adapt your machine to operate the way you want. As a technical consultant, manufacturer, Sunburst can write custom software programs to control almost any electro mechanical powered options. Let Sunburst design your next application for engine, electrical options, alarms/monitoring and power drives. Call, we can help.

This Old Truck Magazine — magazine
PO Box 500
Missouri City, TX 77459
800-310-7047 subscriptions
937-767-1433 publishing office
FAX: 937-767-2726
E-mail: antique@antiquepower.com

See full listing in **Section Four** under **periodicals**

Thunderbird Information eXchange — newsletter
8421 E Cortez St
Scottsdale, AZ 85260
602-948-3996

See full listing in **Section One** under **Thunderbird**

University Motors Ltd — events line/bench service restoration
6490 E Fulton
Ada, MI 49301
616-682-0800; FAX: 616-682-0801

See full listing in **Section One** under **MG**

Vintage Jag Works — consulting how-to articles
1390 W Hwy 26
Blackfoot, ID 83221
208-684-4767; FAX: 208-684-3386
E-mail: walt@vintagejag.com

See full listing in **Section One** under **Jaguar**

Vintage Parts 411 — books
4909 Ruffner St
San Diego, CA 92111
800-MOTORHEAD
FAX: 619-467-0777
E-mail: cars@vintageparts.com

Mail order only. *Vintage Part Sources* is updated annually. Publishing highly organized books on where to find parts for specific old cars. 16 different editions for different cars (full-size Chevy, GTO, Mustang, Mopar). Separate sections for dealers specializing in parts for body, interior, trim, engine, rubber, suspension, as well as literature. The book also contains parts restoration specialists and a nationwide listing of salvage yards specializing in old cars. Guaranteed to find any part or your money back. $16.95 plus shipping per book. Web site: www.vintageparts.com

Wolverine Video — videos
300 Stonecliffe Aisle
Irvine, CA 92612-5728
949-854-5171; FAX: 949-854-2154

Wolverine Video takes you to the center of the great American car culture. Crank up the volume and the noise of whinning blowers, gear driven cams and throbbing open headers fills the air. The colors are vibrant and true as Bitchin' hot rods, dusty dry lakes racers, way cool customs, outlaw's bikes, knarly woodys, illustrated lowriders appear for hours to your delight and amusement. This is the magic of Wolverine Video. Web site: www.carculture69.com

Section Four Publications

Books & Publications

1958 Thunderbird Convertible Registry
book

Bill Van Ess
2306 Post Dr NE
Belmont, MI 49306
616-364-1973; FAX: 616-363-2870

See full listing in **Section One** under **Thunderbird**

ADP Hollander
interchange info manuals

14800 28th Ave N #190
Plymouth, MN 55447
800-761-9266; FAX: 800-825-1124
E-mail: hollander@autonet.net

See full listing in **Section Two** under **car & parts locators**

Archway Press Inc
garage blueprints

19 W 44th St
New York, NY 10036
800-374-4766; FAX: 212-869-5215
E-mail: archway@mindspring.com

Protect Your Vintage Beauty (and gain affordable loft/living space). Fully illustrated brochure describes 20 garage/loft plans for 2 to 5 cars. Professional building blueprints available for every plan. Call or write to order. Web site: www.archwaypress.com

Auto Interchange Systems
books

Doug Johnson
PO Box 12385
Las Vegas, NV 89112
702-454-9170

Mail order. Interchange parts manuals covering 1950-1965 Ford, GM, Chrysler and 1963-1974 Ford products. 15 day money back guarantee. Web site: www.autocars.com

Auto Review Publishing
publications

5 Rowan Oak Ln
Columbia, IL 62236
618-281-3311
E-mail: autrev@aol.com

Publisher of automotive restoration and historical books. Recent titles include: *Restorer's Classic Car* shop manual; *AA Truck* supplement to *Restorer's Model A* shop manual. Upcoming books include: *Fleetwood, The Company and the Coachcraft*. Price list and information available upon request. The Auto Review was established in 1906. Web site: http://users.aol.com/fordmoval/schild.html

Auto Zone
books magazines models videos

33202 Woodward Ave
Birmingham, MI 48009
800-647-7288; FAX: 248-646-5381
E-mail: info@azautozone.com

See full listing in **Section Two** under **models & toys**

Section Four Publications

Bentley Publishers | **books**
1734 Massachusetts Ave | **manuals**
Cambridge, MA 02138-1804
800-423-4595; FAX: 617-876-9235
E-mail: sales@rb.com

Bentley Publishers is the authoritative source for official factory service information and enthusiasts books on a multitude of automotive topics including parts identification, high-performance tuning, fuel injection, aerodynamics, engineering, vintage racing and competition driving. Bentley has books and service manuals for Volkswagen, Audi, BMW, Bosch, Saab, Volvo, Alfa Romeo, MG, Austin-Healey, Jaguar, Land Rover, Range Rover, MG, Triumph, Morris Minor, Jeep, Ford, Chevrolet and Toyota. Web site: www.rb.com

BritBooks | **books**
PO Box 321
Otego, NY 13825
PH/FAX: 607-988-7956
E-mail: britbook@dmcom.net

BritBooks catalog, free. Published annually. 32 page catalog of books on British sports cars. We have a large selection of new and out of print books. Our prices are always competitive. Please write or call for our catalog. Web site: www.britbook.com

British Car Magazine | **magazine**
343 Second St, Suite H
Los Altos, CA 94022-3639
650-949-9680; FAX: 650-949-9685
E-mail: britcarmag@aol.com

See full listing in **Section Four** under **periodicals**

Michael Bruce Associates Inc | **publication**
PO Box 396
Powell, OH 43065
740-965-4859

Corvette and Camaro publications: *Corvette Black Book*, *Camaro White Book*.

Cadillac Motor Books | **books**
PO Box 7
Temple City, CA 91780
626-445-1618

See full listing in **Section One** under **Cadillac/LaSalle**

"Check The Oil!" Magazine | **magazine**
PO Box 937
Powell, OH 43065-0937
614-848-5038; FAX: 614-436-4760

See full listing in **Section Two** under **petroliana**

Classic Motorbooks | **books**
PO Box 1/HMN | **videos**
729 Prospect Ave
Osceola, WI 54020
800-826-6600; FAX: 715-294-4448

Monday-Friday 8 am to 4:30 pm. The world's largest selection of automotive literature. Motorbooks is a long established publisher and mail order company offering thousands of books on repair, restoration, racing, buying, driving and general marque studies and histories. We also offer a wide selection of videos and auto related items. Our 120 page catalog is only $3.95 or free with every order.

See our ad on this page

The Classic Motorist | **automotive books**
PO Box 363 | **literature**
Rotterdam Junction, NY 12150-0363 | **motoring accessories**

See full listing in **Section Two** under **automobilia**

Coin-Op Classics | **coin-op books**
17844 Toiyabe St | **coin-op machines**
Fountain Valley, CA 92708
714-968-3020; FAX: 714-963-1716
E-mail: pmovsesian@aol.com

Publisher and book seller of coin-op books, buy/sell coin-op machines (slots, arcades), games, furniture for game rooms. Web site: coin-opclassics.com

Colleccio d'Automobils de | **books**
Salvador Claret | **catalogs**
17410 Sils | **literature**
Girona Spain | **photos**
972-853036; FAX: 972-853502
E-mail: sclaret@logiccontrol.es

See full listing in **Section Two** under **literature dealers**

Alfred Cosentino Solo Books | **books**
Box 1917 | **publication**
Thousand Oaks, CA 91360
818-707-2301

Mail order only. Federal Express, air cargo, truck, sea freight. *Abarth Owners International*, published semi-annually, about Abarth, Abarth Fiat auto activities, plus books on Abarth, Ferrari and Fiat group.

The Davis Registry
4073 Ruby
Ypsilanti, MI 48197-9317
734-434-5581, 313-662-1001
E-mail: kfnut@umich.edu

periodical
quarterly bulletin

Serves as a worldwide clearinghouse for information regarding history, technical background, up-keep, restoration, preservation, current events, prices and any other aspect of the aluminum bodied three-wheeled Davis automobile built by the Davis Motorcar Co, 4055 Woodley Ave, Van Nuys, CA, from 1947 to 1949. Sells authentic Davis literature, T-shirts, videos. Sample copy $2 postpaid. Quarterly publication. Subscription: $8/year. Checks payable to Tom Wilson. Web site: www.suarezweb.com/davis.htm

DeTomaso Registry
Bill Van Ess
2306 Post Dr NE
Belmont, MI 49306
616-364-1973; FAX: 616-363-2870

book

See full listing in **Section One** under **DeTomaso/Pantera**

Dragonwyck Publishing Inc
PO Box 385
Contoocook, NH 03229
603-746-5606; FAX: 603-746-4260

books
magazines

Open Monday-Friday 8 am to 6 pm. Publishes *The Packard Cormorant* magazine and offers back issues.

The Evergreen Press
9 Camino Arroyo Pl
Palm Desert, CA 92260
760-569-1880; FAX: 760-773-5255
E-mail: evpress@aol.com

books

Publisher and distributor of well illustrated hardcover books. Each is a photographic record of a specific marque. Each contains approximately 1,000 clear, sharp photos (b/w and color) illustrating model changes on a year-by-year basis.

Bob Francis Auto Writer & Historian
1108 W Jackson St
Tupelo, MS 38801
601-844-6070
E-mail: bigbob@ebicom.net

history research
trivia

See full listing in **Section Four** under **information sources**

Giorgio Nada Editore
Via Treves 15/17
Vimodrone (Milan) 20090 Italy
++39-02-27301126
FAX: ++39-02-27301454
E-mail: nadamail@sii.it

motoring books

See full listing in **Section Two** under **literature dealers**

Hemmings Motor News Sunoco Filling Station
216 Main St
Bennington, VT 05201
HMN Customer Service:
1-800-CAR-HERE ext 550
HMN Sunoco Filling Station:
802-447-9652

books, videos
HMN caps, t-shirts
HMN sweatshirts
HMN tote bags
HMN truck banks
Free Vintage
Vehicle Display

"Old-tyme" Filling Station/Book Store/Gift Shop open 7 am to 10 pm every day but Christmas. Offers a variety of automotive books and videos, plus *Hemmings Motor News* caps, clothing, gifts, and automobilia. Located at Hemmings Motor News Sunoco Filling Station in downtown Bennington. Call or write for Free Mail Order Catalog of *HMN* products or visit our web site: www.hemmings.com

Hot Rod Nostalgia™
PO Box 249
West Point, CA 95255-0249
209-754-3697; FAX: 209-754-5521
E-mail: hvaa@hotrodnostalgia.com

"magalog"

Hot Rod Nostalgia is published annually. Dave Wallace's fourth nostalgia "magalog" is expanded to 60 pages of gearhead gifts, editorials, artist profiles and humor. Pro and sportsman racers of the 1950s, 1960s and 1970s are featured in books, videos, prints, posters and 200 action photos. Send $5 or charge by phone. Web site: www.hotrodnostalgia.com
See our ad on page 220

Eliot James Enterprises Inc
PO Box 3986
Dana Point, CA 92629-8986
949-661-0889; FAX: 949-661-1901

development info

EJE offers products and services to help hobbyists profit from their hobby as well as create and protect new ideas for their hobby and profit from them through licensing or starting a business. Web site: www.bugstik.com

Jack Juratovic
819 Absequami Trail
Lake Orion, MI 48362
PH/FAX: 248-814-0627

artwork
magazine

See full listing in **Section Two** under **artwork**

The Klemantaski Collection
65 High Ridge Rd, Suite 219
Stamford, CT 06905
PH/FAX: 203-968-2970
E-mail: klemcoll@aol.com

books
photography

See full listing in **Section Two** under **photography**

Lamm Morada Publishing Co Inc
Box 7607
Stockton, CA 95207
209-931-1056; FAX: 209-931-5777

books

Publish books for auto enthusiasts. Latest: *A Century of Automotive Style* and *Fabulous Firebird*. $64.95 postpaid.

Libreria Dell'Automobile
International Motoring Book Shop
Corso Venezia 43
Milan 20121 Italy
++39-02-76006624
FAX: ++39-02-27301454
E-mail: nadamail@sii.it

car books
motorcycle books

See full listing in **Section Two** under **literature dealers**

MG Magazine Inc
PO Box 85020
Fort Wayne, IN 46885-5020
888-870-4993, 616-375-4073, MI
FAX: 219-485-0845
E-mail: mgmag2000@aol.com

automobilia
books
magazine

Mail order only. *MG Magazine Inc*, quarterly magazine specific to MG cars and their owners for all MG cars from 1924-present. Official publication for MG enthusiasts since 1979. Covers the history, people and models that made the marque famous. Features include Moto Gravure, tech tips, event schedules, humor, restorations, vintage racing and more. Subscription: $25/year, $45/2 years, $65/3 years.

Mid-America Auction Services
2277 W Hwy 36, Ste 214
St Paul, MN 55113
612-633-9655; FAX: 612-633-3212
E-mail: midauction@aol.com

auctions

See full listing in **Section Two** under **auctions & events**

Mopar Collector's Guide Magazine	magazine

10067 El Camino Ave
Baton Rouge, LA 70815
504-274-0609; FAX: 504-274-9033
E-mail: mcgpub@mcg-pub.com

See full listing in **Section One** under **Mopar**

MotorCam Media	automotive videos

138 N Alling Rd
Tallmadge, OH 44278
800-240-1777; FAX: 330-633-3249
E-mail: carvideo@motorcam.com

See full listing in **Section Two** under **videos**

NADA Appraisal Guides	appraisal guides

PO Box 7800
Costa Mesa, CA 92628
800-966-6232; FAX: 714-556-8715

NADA Classic, Collectible & Special Interest Car Appraisal Guide, 70 years of used values for all cars and trucks 1930-1979 including used values on exotic cars 1946-1999. The most comprehensive guide available today! Complete model listings, optional equipment, engine information, vehicle weight and three values (low-average-high) based on vehicle condition. Updated January-May-September. Subscription: $40/year. Web site: www.nadaguides.com

National Parts Depot	accessories restoration parts

3101 SW 40th Blvd
Gainesville, FL 32608
800-874-7595 toll-free 24 hours
352-378-2473 local

See full listing in **Section Two** under **comprehensive parts**

Oil Company Collectibles Inc	books gasoline globes signs

PO Box 556
LaGrange, OH 44050
440-355-6608; FAX: 440-355-4955
E-mail: scottpcm@aol.com

See full listing in **Section Two** under **automobilia**

Petroleum Collectibles Monthly	periodical

411 Forest St
LaGrange, OH 44050
440-355-6608; FAX: 440-355-4955

See full listing in **Section Four** under **periodicals**

PM Research Inc	books models

4110 Niles Hill Rd
Wellsville, NY 14895
716-593-3169; FAX: 716-593-5637

See full listing in **Section Two** under **models & toys**

Portrayal Press	books manuals

PO Box 1190
Andover, NJ 07821
PH/FAX: 973-579-5781

Mail order only. Publishes and sells manuals and books for older jeeps, Dodge military trucks and other military trucks (WW II to modern) and tracked military vehicles such as tanks. 56 page full size catalog mailed first class for $3 (overseas $5). Dennis R Spence, owner. Web site: www.portrayal.com

Promotionals 1934-1983 Dealership Vehicles in Miniature	price guide

2696 Brookmar
York, PA 17404
PH/FAX: 717-792-4936

See full listing in **Section Two** under **automobilia**

R-Mac Publications Inc	magazine

5439 SW US Hwy 41
Jasper, FL 32052
904-792-2480; FAX: 904-792-3230
E-mail: rbm@r-mac.com

The *Automotive Reference Digest* includes technical information, photographs, specifications, repair tips, etc, as taken from original and often rare sources including sales and shop manuals, operator and owner's manuals, catalogs, etc. Heavy emphasis will be placed on reader supplied information plus rare texts, manuals, catalogs and photographs included in the R-Mac archives. The *Digest* will replace supplements to *ALF*, Mack and Ford fire apparatus books. Subscription: $30/year, 6 issues. Web site: www.r-mac.com

Ed Rouze	painting guide book

406 Sheila Blvd
Prattville, AL 36066
334-365-2381

See full listing in **Section Two** under **painting**

Steve Smith Autosports Publications	books

PO Box 11631
Santa Ana, CA 92711
714-639-7681; FAX: 714-639-9741

Mail order only. Publisher of automotive technical books such as *Street Rod Building Skills, Practical Engine Swapping, How to Build a Repro Rod, Racing the Small Block Chevy*, etc. 245 titles available. Free catalog. Web site: www.ssapubl.com

Spyder Enterprises Inc	accessories artwork automobilia books

RFD 1682
Laurel Hollow, NY 11791-9644
516-367-1616; FAX: 516-367-3260
E-mail: singer356@aol.com

See full listing in **Section One** under **Porsche**

Tech-Art Publications	books

Jason Houston
Box 753
Ranchero Mirage, CA 92270
760-862-1979

Mail order only. We publish soft-bound books on promotional car models, plus newsletters for same. SASE required.

Transport Books at DRB Motors Inc	books manuals periodicals videos

16 Elrose Ave
Toronto, ON Canada M9M 2H6
800-665-2665, 416-744-7675
FAX: 416-744-7696
E-mail: info@transportbooks.com

Mail, e-mail, phone order and retail store. Monday-Saturday 10 am to 5 pm, closed holidays. Cars, bikes, boats, planes, trucks, tractors, tanks, trains. Canada's largest selection of transportation books and videos. Choose from 10,000+ histories, biographies, gift books, repair manuals, racing and driving books, videos and art from Canada and around the world. Magazines include *Hemmings, Old Autos* and *Wheels & Tracks*. Visit our store, just off Highway 401. Visit our web site catalog and location map. Web site: www.transportbooks.com

Vintage Parts 411	books

4909 Ruffner St
San Diego, CA 92111
800-MOTORHEAD
FAX: 619-467-0777
E-mail: cars@vintageparts.com

See full listing in **Section Four** under **information sources**

T E Warth Esq Automotive Books — **books**
Lumberyard Shops
Marine on St Croix, MN 55047
612-433-5744; FAX: 612-433-5012
E-mail: tew@bitstream.net

Office open by chance or appointment. Deal in pictorial, history and technical books relating to automobiles, trucks, motorcycles, tractors, models, racing, etc; out of print and rare. No manuals, handbooks or sales literature.

Vic Zannis — **book**
735 Montgomery Hwy Box 337H
Birmingham, AL 35216
205-788-7752
E-mail: viczannis@aol.com

Mail order only. *Rebuilding the Model T Ford Power Plant*, a guide designed to let the owner with average mechanical ability rebuild his own Model T Ford engine and transmission. Includes plans for pouring and line boring bearings and recharging magnets. Price: $23.50 ppd. Web site:
http://members.aol.com/viczannis/pages/t-book.htm

Periodicals

America's Most Wanted Publishing — **periodical**
PO Box 17107
Little Rock, AR 72222
501-660-4030; FAX: 501-614-8017
E-mail: amwc1@aol.com

Publishes *America's Most Wanted to Buy* bi-monthly. Packed with wanted to buy ads from collectors in all areas. Subscription: $12.95/year. Web site: www.mostwantedtobuy.com

Auto Retro — **periodical**
BP 58
77211 Avon Cedex France
01-331-60-715555
FAX: 01-331-60-72-22-37
E-mail: autoretro@elvea.fr

Auto Retro is a monthly publication specializing in popular and classic cars, four color, about 120 pages, news, various features, ads. Subscription: 370*f*/year.

AutoWire.Net — **web site**
PO Box 1011
San Mateo, CA 94403
650-340-8669; FAX: 650-340-9473
E-mail: autowire@pacbell.net

Automotive Article Communication Network, a web site about cars, trucks, sport utility vehicles, classic car auctions, events and automotive information. Web site: www.autowire.net

Bimmer Magazine — **magazine**
42 Digital Dr #5
Novato, CA 94949
415-382-0580; FAX: 415-382-0587

Bimmer is a new, full-color magazine about BMWs. Critical reviews and drive reports put you in the driver's seat of these cars, from the latest models to the classics. Each bi-monthly issue brings you everything, good and bad, about BMW. Subscription (6 issues): $14.99/year; $21/year foreign USD.

British Car Magazine — **magazine**
343 Second St, Suite H
Los Altos, CA 94022-3639
650-949-9680; FAX: 650-949-9685
E-mail: britcarmag@aol.com

Since 1985. Publish *British Car Magazine* bi-monthly. The only American magazine exclusively for British car enthusiasts, owners, restorers and industry devoted to the use and appreciation of classic and contemporary British cars, including marque profiles, photo essays, history, technical advice, humor, calendars and report on North American events and sources for parts and services. Subscription: $22.95/year US, $26/year Canada; $39.95/two years US, $46/two years Canada.

Car Toy Collectibles Magazine — **magazine**
7950 Deering Ave
Canoga Park, CA 91304-5063
818-887-0550; FAX: 818-884-1343
E-mail: mail@challengeweb.com

Car Toy Collectibles is published 9 times a year. Nationally distributed via newsstand and subscriptions. Covers all aspects of toy cars and trucks from vintage metal and tin to the latest die cast releases from all major manufacturers in all scales. Glossy picture-book quality. Subscription (9 issues): $19.95/year. Web site: www.challengeweb.com

Cars & Parts Magazine — **periodical**
PO Box 482
Sidney, OH 45365
800-448-3611, 937-498-0803
FAX: 937-498-0808

Cars & Parts is a monthly magazine with full-color editorial features on collector cars, restoration, salvage yards, shows and swap meets, display advertising and large classified ad section with vintage cars, parts and related items for sale and wanted. Subscription: $26.95/year US, $41.95/year foreign; second class: $46.95/year US; first class: $66.95/year foreign, airmail. Web site: www.carsandparts.com

"Check The Oil!" Magazine PO Box 937 Powell, OH 43065-0937 614-848-5038; FAX: 614-436-4760	**magazine**

See full listing in **Section Two** under **petroliana**

The Classic Motorist PO Box 363 Rotterdam Junction, NY 12150-0363	**automotive books** **literature** **motoring accessories**

See full listing in **Section Two** under **automobilia**

Collector Car & Truck Market Guide 41 N Main St North Grafton, MA 01536 508-839-6707; FAX: 508-839-6266 E-mail: vmr@vmrintl.com	**price guide**

The only complete market guide in the hobby. Editorial features include auction reports and commentary, market analysis and vehicle market profiles. Lists current pricing for over 12,000 1946-1979 domestic and import cars and trucks. Extensive engine, transmission and optional equipment listings for every vehicle. Used worldwide by appraisers, auction firms, insurance and finance firms, investors and enthusiasts. Subscription: $16.95/year. Web site: www.vmrintl.com

Cruisin' Style Magazine 324 8th Ave W #103 Palmetto, FL 34221 941-729-6669; FAX: 941-729-7773 E-mail: chop48@gte.net	**magazine**

Cruisin' Style is published monthly in Florida with the custom and classic car enthusiast in mind. We feature informative articles on everything related to our hobby, car owners and their toys. Plus we have a section covering all Florida races. Also in each issue: car shows, car clubs, new products, classifieds, business directory, race news and much more. *Cruisin' Style* magazine is the #1 magazine of its type in the southeastern United States. Subscription: $14.95/year. Web site: www.cruisinstyle.com

See our ad on page 576

The Davis Registry 4073 Ruby Ypsilanti, MI 48197-9317 734-434-5581, 313-662-1001 E-mail: kfnut@umich.edu	**periodical** **quarterly bulletin**

See full listing in **Section Four** under **books & publications**

Deals On Wheels PO Box 205 Sioux Falls, SD 57101 605-338-7666; FAX: 605-338-5337	**periodical**

Monthly publication, *Deals On Wheels*. Buy/sell/trade specializing in clean, easy to read photo ads from across the US and Canada. All types of vehicles are for sale from Ferraris to restorable antique autos. Subscription: $15.95/year. Web site: www.dealsonwheels.com

Elvea-la Vie de l'Auto BP 88 77303 Fontainebleau Cedex France 01-331-60-715555 FAX: 01-331-60-72-22-37 E-mail: iva@elvea.fr	**magazine**

The leader of the French classic car magazines. Every week it contains everything you have to know when you own a classic car: events, news and a lot of ads to buy or sell anything about cars; about 50 pages. Subscription: 520ƒ/year.

EWA & Miniature Cars USA Inc 205 US Hwy 22 Green Brook, NJ 08812-1909 732-424-7811; FAX: 732-424-7814 E-mail: ewa@ewacars.com	**books** **models** **subscriptions** **videos**

See full listing in **Section Two** under **models & toys**

Excellence Magazine 42 Digital Dr #5 Novato, CA 94949 415-382-0580; FAX: 415-382-0587	**magazine**

Excellence is a magazine about Porsches. Each full color issue brings you the latest news and information about Porsche along with technical features. *Excellence* also includes an extensive classified section. Subscription (8 issues): $20/year; $27/year foreign USD.

Forza Magazine 42 Digital Dr #5 Novato, CA 94949 415-382-0580; FAX: 415-382-0587	**magazine**

Forza is a bi-monthly magazine about Ferraris. Each full color issue is packed with the latest Ferrari news and information from around the world. Subscription (6 issues): $19.95/year; $27/year foreign USD.

Fournier Enterprises Inc 1884 Thunderbird Dr Troy, MI 48084-5428 248-362-3722, 800-501-3722 FAX: 248-362-2866	**publication**

Metal Crafter's News is a bi-monthly publication. Every issue includes tips and techniques, new construction, tools and products, metal work history, projects and patterns and more hard to find metal work info. Subscription: $19.95/6 issues. Web site: fournierenterprises.com

GN Wheels & Deals PO Box 2138 Oroville, CA 95965 530-533-2134; FAX: 530-533-1531 E-mail: gnwd@quiknet.com	**periodical**

Wheels & Deals, a free weekly pictorial automotive publication with circulation of over 80,000 a week, covering 24 counties of northern CA. Pictures of new, used, old autos, boats, bikes and heavy equipment. A free events calendar listing and stories on auto shows, etc. Web site: www.wheelanddeal.com

Grassroots Motorsports 425 Parque Dr Ormond Beach, FL 32174 904-673-4148; FAX: 904-673-6040	**periodical**

Glossy, colorful national publication *Grassroots Motorsports*, for amateur motor sports enthusiasts. Autocross rally vintage and road race news, events, personalities and car preparation tips. Published bi-monthly. Free sample copy. Subscription: $14.97/year. Web site: www.grmotorsports.com

HCKC News Capri House Walton-On-Thomas Surrey KT12 2LY England	**magazine**

Bi-monthly magazine for Hillman, Commer and Karrier and derivatives of these makes of vehicles, many of which were sold under Sunbeam or Dodge badges in USA and Canada. Subscription: £15/year.

Hemmings Motor News
PO Box 100
Bennington, VT 05201
1-800-CAR-HERE ext 550
802-447-9550
FAX: 802-447-1561
E-mail: hmnmail@hemmings.com

The monthly "bible" of the collector-car hobby

"The bible" of the collector-car hobby, monthly trading place, 98% paid hobby advertising with world's largest paid circulation to old car hobbyists (nearly 300,000), and publishing world's largest number of hobby advertisements (averaging over 800 pages monthly), including any-&-all antique, vintage, muscle, and special-interest collector cars, trucks, motorcycles, custom cars, &c, plus parts, literature, services, automobilia, &c, without limitations. One year subscriptions: Fourth class mail: $26.95 USA; $58.00 Canada. First class mail: $65.00 USA; $88.00 Canada; $88 Mexico. US funds only. Airmail to other countries (inquire for current rates). Wholesale terms available. Visitors welcome at HMN Sunoco Filling Station/Book Store/Gift Shop, 7 am to 10 pm everyday but Christmas. Web site: www.hemmings.com

Late Great Chevrolet Association
Robert Snowden
PO Box 607824
Orlando, FL 32860
407-886-1963; FAX: 407-886-7571
E-mail: chevy55-72@ao.net

magazine

Mail order and open shop. Monday-Friday 8 am to 5 pm. Dedicated to the restoration and preservation of all 1958-1972 Chevrolets. Specializing in 1958-1972 Chevrolet parts and monthly magazine publication, *Late Great Chevys*, approx 32 pg, color/b-w. The magazine displays our members' automobiles along with their story. Also provides restoration help, club events, general information on events around the US. Subscription: $35/year second class, $45/year first class, $60/year airmail. Web site: www.ao.net/chevy55-72

The Latest Scoop-Auto Enthusiast Calendar
PO Box 7477
Loveland, CO 80537-0477
970-686-6155

periodical

Handy guide for automotive enthusiasts and businesses providing you with the most up-to-date information on car-related events taking place in the Rocky Mountain Region of CO, WY, NE, KS, OK, TX, NM, AZ and UT. Published 9 times a year. Send for free sample issue. Visa, MasterCard and American Express accepted. Subscription: $12/year, $23/2 years, outside US add $8 per year.

Military Vehicles Magazine
12-H3 Indian Head Rd
Morristown, NJ 07960
973-285-0716; FAX: 973-539-5934
E-mail: mvehicle@aol.com

publication

Bi-monthly magazine about historic military vehicles: military jeeps, trucks, armor, etc. Features restoration, maintenance articles, advertising, events calendar. 136 pages per issue. Subscription: $18/year, $29/two years, sample copy $5, US only; foreign $40/year airmail.

Mobilia
PO Box 575
Middlebury, VT 05753
802-388-3071; FAX: 802-388-2215
E-mail: info@mobilia.com

periodical

Publication name: *Mobilia*. Marketplace for toys, models and automobilia. Tabloid format. Contains news, auction results, event listings, price guides, new model releases, 18,000 model buyer's guide, items for sale and wanted. Printed monthly. Subscription: $19.97/year. Web site: mobilia.com

Mopar Collector's Guide Magazine
10067 El Camino Ave
Baton Rouge, LA 70815
504-274-0609; FAX: 504-274-9033
E-mail: mcgpub@mcg-pub.com

magazine

See full listing in **Section One** under **Mopar**

Musclecar Review
3816 Industry Blvd
Lakeland, FL 33811
941-644-0449; FAX: 941-648-1187

periodical

Puts the latest Detroit iron against the earth-shaking muscle cars of the past, or takes readers' favorite cars to the track for "shootouts and showdowns". Plus loads of restoration, repair and maintenance information, parts and service sources, news on national muscle car events and more. Subscription: $16.97/year.

Old Cars Price Guide
700 E State St
Iola, WI 54990
800-258-0929 subscriptions only
715-445-2214; FAX: 715-445-4087

price guide

The hobby's most respected source for collector car values, featuring over 135,000 individual prices for models manufactured from 1901-1988. All values are presented according to the 1-to-6 conditional grading system, with numerous photos. Visa, MasterCard, Discover or American Express accepted. Published bi-monthly. Subscription: $18.95/year. Web site: www.krause.com

Old Cars Weekly News & Marketplace
700 E State St, Dept 8FT
Iola, WI 54990
800-258-0929 subscriptions only
715-445-2214; FAX: 715-445-4087

periodical

The old car hobby's weekly source for up-to-date hobby news, restoration tips, auction reports, events calendar, plus new buy and sell opportunities in display and classified advertising for collector cars and parts. Visa, MasterCard, Discover or American

Express accepted. Published weekly. Subscription: $37.98/year.
Web site: www.krause.com

Petroleum Collectibles Monthly	periodical
PO Box 556 LaGrange, OH 44050 440-355-6608; FAX: 440-355-4955	

Publication: *Petroleum Collectibles Monthly*. Most comprehensive magazine covering all aspects of collecting gas pumps, globes, signs, cans, etc. Auctions, ads, historical, discoveries, color photos, Q&A and more. Subscription: $29.95/year US, $38.50/year Canada, $65.95/year international. Web site: www.pcmpublishing.com

R-Mac Publications Inc	magazine
5439 SW US Hwy 41 Jasper, FL 32052 904-792-2480; FAX: 904-792-3230 E-mail: rbm@r-mac.com	

See full listing in **Section Four** under **books & publications**

Retroviseur	periodical
Chateau de la Magdeleine 77920 Samois s/Seine France (01) 331-60-71-55-55 FAX: (01) 331-60-72-22-37 E-mail: retrovis@elvea.fr	

Retroviseur is a monthly publication specializing in classic cars; four color, about 150 pages, news, various features, ads. Subscription: 455f/year.

Skinned Knuckles	periodical
175 May Ave Monrovia, CA 91016 626-358-6255 E-mail: skpubs@earthlink.net	

A monthly publication devoted to the restoration, operation and maintenance of all authentic collector vehicles. Subscription: $20/year domestic, $23/year foreign.

Southern Wheels Magazine	magazine
6739 Ringgold Rd #B Chattanooga, TX 37412 423-899-4300; FAX: 706-375-7711, GA E-mail: sowheels@aol.com	

Southern Wheels Magazine is a monthly magazine for restorers and car builders. Your source for parts and services, plus restoration articles and tech tips. Monthly car quiz. Published by restoration specialist Bill Johnson. Subscription: $7.99/year. Web site: www.southernwheels.com

Special Interest Autos	periodical
PO Box 196 Bennington, VT 05201 1-800-CAR-HERE, ext 550 802-447-9550; FAX: 802-447-1561	

A bi-monthly magazine featuring collector cars from 1920-1980. In-depth, thoroughly researched articles and road tests. Over 100 photos in each issue. Authoritative information throughout. Most back issues available. One year (6 issues) subscription, $19.95 US, $21.95 foreign. Ask about our retail dealer program. Wholesale terms available. To view sample articles, visit our web site: www.hemmings.com

Specialty Car Marketplace	periodical
PO Box 205 Sioux Falls, SD 57101 605-338-7666; FAX: 605-338-5337	

Monthly publication, *Specialty Car*. Buy/sell/trade publication. All types of vehicles kit cars, muscle cars, trucks, motorcycles are available for sale in full color or black and white photos. Ads listed from across the US and Canada. Subscription: $12.95/year. Web site: www.dealsonwheels.com

Sports Car International	magazine
42 Digital Dr #5 Novato, CA 94949 415-382-0580; FAX: 415-382-0587	

Sports Car International is a full color magazine featuring performance and sports cars from around the world. The critical reviews give you a unique perspective on each car. News reports keep you abreast of the latest information on the cars you want to hear about, not minivans. Subscription (6 issues): $14.99/year; $21/year foreign USD.

The Registry	periodical
Pine Grove Stanley, VA 22851 540-778-3728; FAX: 540-778-2402 E-mail: britregstry@aol.com or oldwregistry@aol.com	

The Registry is a monthly magazine. British and European cars, parts, services, also club news, tech information, club calendar. Marque Spotlight each month highlights model development, history, production numbers, etc. Write or call for free sample issue. Free private ads anytime. Subscription: $8.95/year.

TheAlternate	periodical
PO Box 239-393 Grantville, PA 17028-0229 717-469-0777; FAX: 717-469-1388	

A monthly publication for vintage motor racing enthusiasts with a touch of history. Most stories are written by the oldtimers who were there. Our classified ads offer cars, parts, books, etc for vintage racing buyers and sellers. Subscription: $18/year; $33/year foreign (US funds).

This Old Truck Magazine | magazine
PO Box 500
Missouri City, TX 77459
800-310-7047 subscriptions
937-767-1433 publishing office
FAX: 937-767-2726
E-mail: antique@antiquepower.com

Devoted to the preservation of all makes and vintages of antique trucks, station wagons, pickups and commercial vehicles. Includes color photos, restoration tips, truck company history, plus free classified ads for subscribers. Publishes *This Old Truck* bi-monthly. Subscription: $24.95/year US and Canada, $39.95/year foreign. Web site: www.thisoldtruck.com

See our ad on page 579

See our ad on page 579

Transport Books at DRB Motors Inc | books manuals periodicals videos
16 Elrose Ave
Toronto, ON Canada M9M 2H6
800-665-2665, 416-744-7675
FAX: 416-744-7696
E-mail: info@transportbooks.com

See full listing in **Section Four** under **books & publications**

Triumph World Magazine | periodical
PO Box 75
Tadworth
Surrey KT20 7XF England
01737 814311; FAX: 01737 814591
E-mail: triumphworld@chp.ltd.uk

See full listing in **Section One** under **Triumph**

Truck, Race, Cycle and Rec | periodical
PO Box 205
Sioux Falls, SD 57101
605-338-7666; FAX: 605-338-5337

Monthly publication, *Truck, Race, Cycle & Rec*. Buy/sell/trade publication. Specializing in trucks, race cars, motorcycles and repairable autos. Ads are available with photos and are placed from across the US and Canada. Subscription: $15.95/year. Web site: www.truckracecycle.com

Vette Vues Magazine | magazine
PO Box 741596
Orange City, FL 32774
904-775-8454; FAX: 904-775-3042
E-mail: comments@vettevues.com

Publishes *Vette Vues* magazine monthly, Corvette related magazine. Subscription: $21.95/year. Web site: www.vette-vues.com

Victory Lane | periodical
2460 Park Blvd
Palo Alto, CA 94306
650-321-1411; FAX: 650-321-4426
E-mail: victory@best.com

Monthly news magazine covering vintage auto racing in US and international. Features include race reports with results, columns by insiders, technical articles, event schedules, vintage race car classifieds, marque histories, collector car stories and more. Subscription: $39.95/year. Web site: www.victorylane.com

Walneck's Classic Cycle Trader | magazine
PO Box 2576
Norfolk, VA 23501
757-640-4000; FAX: 757-314-2508

Monthly magazine, *Walneck's Classic Cycle-Trader*. In print for 20 years, over 200 pages of color and black and white classic motorcycles for sale. Also included, many old road tests for references. A free sample for the asking. Subscription: $29/year. Web site: www.traderonline.com

Newsletters

1956 Studebaker Golden Hawk Owners Register | information exchange
31700 Wekiva River Rd
Sorrento, FL 32776-9233
E-mail: 56sghor@prodigy.net

See full listing in **Section One** under **Studebaker**

The 60 Oldsmobile Club | newsletter
Dick Major
10895 E Hibma Rd
Tustin, MI 49688
616-825-2891; FAX: 616-825-8324
E-mail: dmajor@netonecom.net

See full listing in **Section One** under **Oldsmobile**

600 Headquarters | advice parts service
Miles Chappell
PO Box 1262
Felton, CA 95018
PH/FAX: 408-336-4600
E-mail: z600guru@ix.netcom.com

See full listing in **Section One** under **Honda**

Blackhawk Automotive Museum | museum newsletter
3700 Blackhawk Plaza Cir
Danville, CA 94506
925-736-2277, 925-736-2280
FAX: 925-736-4818
E-mail: museum@blackhawkauto.org

See full listing in **Section Six** under **California**

Clean Air Performance Professionals (CAPP) | legislative watch organization
84 Hoy Ave
Fords, NJ 08863
732-738-7859; FAX: 732-738-7625
E-mail: stellacapp@earthlink.net

See full listing in **Section Three** under **legislative watch organizations**

Eastern New York MGA Club Newsletter | publication
Jon Rubel, President
3010 Avenue T
Brooklyn, NY 11229-4008
718-891-5776; FAX: call first
E-mail: eemgee@aol.com

Catering to owners of all MGs in the NY, NJ, PA and CT area. Bi-monthly award winning 40-page newsletter is really a magazine. It includes four pages in full color, superb technical and restoration articles, human interest stories, editorials, letters to the editor, coverage of local car events and tech sessions, complete calendar of events covering the northeast and more. Subscription included with annual club membership of $20.

International Ford History Project | newsletter
PO Box 11415
Olympia, WA 98508
360-754-9585
E-mail: ifhp@aol.com

The International Ford History Project was founded in 1997 and publishes *The Universal Car* on an occasional basis. The purpose of the IFHP and its newsletter is to promote fellowship and the international free flow of information among those interested in the development of the Ford Motor Company and its products, worldwide. Subscription: $10/year for 4 issues, $14/year outside US and Canada. Web site: www.geocities.com/motorcity/2519

Mercedes-Benz Market Letter	**newsletter**
aka SL Market Letter	
2020 Girard Ave S	
Minneapolis, MN 55405	
612-377-0155; FAX: 612-377-0157	
E-mail: slmarket@aol.com	

Specializes in Mercedes-Benz special models only. Especially SL Models 1954-1996 and SLC, SEC. All convertibles, coupes and 6.3, 6.9 and 600. Subscription based collation of price trends, restoration and parts sources and rare Mercedes-Benz models offered for sale. Now in 16th year. 18 issues per year. Subscription: $87/year; 9 issue trial offer, $47. Web site: www.slmarket.com

National Chevy Assoc	**parts**
947 Arcade Street	
St Paul, MN 55106	
612-778-9522; FAX: 800-785-5354	

See full listing in **Section One** under **Chevrolet**

Research & Reference Libraries

AACA Library & Research Center	**research library**
501 W Governor Rd	
PO Box 417	
Hershey, PA 17033	
717-534-2082	

Open Monday-Friday 8:30 am to 3:45 pm. Library located adjacent to AACA National Headquarters. Collection contains books, periodicals, sales literature, manuals, wiring diagrams, paint chips, etc, 1895-present.

Automobile Reference Collection	**information source**
Free Library of Philadelphia	
1901 Vine St	
Philadelphia, PA 19103-1189	
215-686-5404; FAX: 215-686-5426	
E-mail: refarc@library.phila.gov	

Open year round. Monday-Friday 9 am to 5 pm. Major collection of automotive literature located in one of the country's major public libraries. Web site: www.library.phila.gov

Clean Air Performance Professionals (CAPP)	**legislative watch organization**
84 Hoy Ave	
Fords, NJ 08863	
732-738-7859; FAX: 732-738-7625	
E-mail: stellacapp@earthlink.net	

See full listing in **Section Three** under **legislative watch organizations**

Ralph Dunwoodie Research and Information	**research information**
5935 Calico Dr	
Sun Valley, NV 89433-6910	
775-673-3811	

Car and truck histories researched. Extensive library from 1895-present. Research of all phases of automobile and truck information for writers, restorers, historians and enthusiasts.

Henry Ford Museum & Greenfield Village	**museum**
20900 Oakwood Blvd	
Dearborn, MI 48121-1970	
313-271-1620; FAX: 313-982-6247	

See full listing in **Section Six** under **Michigan**

Duncan F Holmes	**research library**
493 King Philip St	
Fall River, MA 02724	
508-672-0071	

Automotive research library. GM, Ford, Chrysler, all independent manufacturers of 1949-1967 model years, earlier years on some cars. Over 7,500 original magazine and newspaper ads on file. Over 500 original owner's manuals, over 500 original dealer sales catalogs. New items constantly being added. Duplicate items offered for sale. Can Xerox most items at nominal cost.

International Motorsports Hall of Fame	**museum**
3198 Speedway Blvd	
PO Box 1018	
Talladega, AL 35161	
256-362-5002; FAX: 256-362-5684	
E-mail: imhof@coosavalley.net	

See full listing in **Section Six** under **Alabama**

National Bicycle Museum Velorama	**museum**
Waalkade 107 6511 XR	
Nijmegen Netherlands	
024-3225851; FAX: 024-3607177	

See full listing in **Section Six** under **Netherlands**

Chris Smith's Creative Workshop Motorcar Restoration	**parts restoration service**
118 NW Park St	
Dania, FL 33004	
954-920-3303; FAX: 954-920-9950	
E-mail: restor1st@aol.com	

See full listing in **Section Two** under **restoration shops**

Topper Luback's Historical Library	**library**
458 W Fourteen St 2A	
Chicago Heights, IL 60411	

Mail order only. Replacement OEM genuine parts, specializing 1959-1965. Research publications for a nominal charge, retail sales only. Scooter literature including service manual, parts catalog, owners manual, keys cut from code or from original lock.

Virginia Museum of Transportation Inc	**museum**
303 Norfolk Ave	
Roanoke, VA 24016	
540-342-5670; FAX: 540-342-6898	
E-mail: info@vmt.org	

See full listing in **Section Six** under **Virginia**

Wayne County Historical Museum	**museum research**
1150 North A St	
Richmond, IN 47374	
765-962-5756; FAX: 765-939-0909	

See full listing in **Section Six** under **Indiana**

Hemmings' Vintage Auto Almanac©   Fourteenth Edition

Sometimes the search is just as interesting as the item sought, and for those who'd like to track down a car or a needed part where it was once laid to rest, the *Almanac* presents this state-by-state listing of salvage yards. Check the individual listings for era or marque special-ties. Many of the yards will not ship parts and require a personal visit. Be sure to phone ahead or check business hours carefully before making a long drive, as some of the yards operate on irregular schedules.

Alabama

Vintage Automobiles 1261 Old Hackleburg Rd Hackleburg, AL 35564	205-935-3649

Mail order and open by appointment only. 1930-1948 Ford parts. 1933-1952 Dodge parts, mainly original running gear parts. Some body parts, mechanical parts, wheels, transmissions, etc.

Alaska

Binder's Auto Restoration and Salvage PO Box 1144 1 Mile Maud Rd Palmer, AK 99645	907-745-4670 FAX: 907-745-5510

Mail order, SASE required. Salvage yard open by appointment only. Specializing in 1960-present Cadillac cars only. Complete line of used parts and some NOS. No part too small. Shipping worldwide. MasterCard and Visa accepted. Complete and partial restorations. Car transporting local and long distance. Please call between 6 pm to 9 pm local time for free advice.

Arizona

British Car Service 2854 N Stone Ave Tucson, AZ 85705 E-mail: bcs@liveline.com	520-882-7026 FAX: 520-882-7053

Mail order and open shop. Monday-Friday 8 am to 5:30 pm, Saturday 9 am to 3 pm. Specializing in rust-free British cars and parts from the 1950s to the present. We also offer complete machine shop services and distributor rebuilding as well as a full service maintenance and restoration facility for British cars. New parts for all British and European cars available. E-mail inquiries encouraged or see our web site: www.britishcarservice.com

Desert Valley Auto Parts 22500 N 21st Ave Phoenix, AZ 85027 E-mail: rust-free-parts@worldnet.att.net	**800-905-8024** **602-780-8024** **FAX: 602-582-9141**

Mail order and open shop. Monday-Friday 8 am to 5:30 pm, Saturday 8 am to 2 pm. Rust-free Arizona parts. 80 full acres of classic and hard to find parts or cars for restoration projects, from the 1950s to the 1980s. Quality parts, dependable service and competitive prices guaranteed. New classics arrive daily to our existing inventory of thousands. Daily shipping worldwide via UPS and freight. No part too large or too small. Visa/MasterCard accepted. Web site: www.dvap.com
See our ad on page 583

Hoctor's Hidden Valley Auto Parts 21046 N Rio Bravo Rd Maricopa, AZ 85239	**520-568-2945** **602-252-2122** **602-252-6137** **FAX: 602-258-0951**

Mail order and open shop. Monday-Friday 8 am to 5 pm, Saturday 9 am to 3 pm. 80 acres of rust-free foreign and American autos and trucks. Just over 8,000 cars for parts. From 1920s-1980s, mostly 1950s, 1960s. Also 2 other Phoenix stores for convenience. Shipping worldwide. Send specific list of needs w/SASE or call.

Wiseman's Auto Salvage 900 W Cottonwood Ln Casa Grande, AZ 85222	**520-836-7960** **FAX: 520-836-7960**

Mail order and open shop. Monday-Friday 8 am to 5:30 pm, Saturday 9 am to 1 pm. Arizona desert salvage yard. 2,500 cars and trucks for parts. All types of auto and truck parts. Good, used, guaranteed. 1920s-1970s. Browsers welcome. Sale of used auto and truck parts. SASE please. MasterCard, Visa, Discover card. Web site: www.wisemansalvage.com

California

Aase Bros Inc 701 E Cypress St Anaheim, CA 92805 E-mail: sales@aasebros.com	**714-956-2419** **FAX: 714-956-2635**

Open Monday-Thursday 8:30 am to 5 pm, Friday 8:30 am to 4 pm. Specializing in Porsche, Mercedes and BMW parts. Our 2-1/2 acre yard always has more than 200 corrosion-free southern California cars. Our warehouse is loaded with new, used and reconditioned parts. Web site: www.aasebros.com

American Auto & Truck Dismantlers 12172 Truman St San Fernando, CA 91340	**818-365-3908**

Mail order and open shop. Monday-Friday 8:30 am to 5 pm, Saturday 9 am to 4 pm. Salvage yard specializing in 1955-1957 Chev cars; 1958-1989 all GM cars and trucks; 1967-1989 Camaros; 1964-1972 Chevelles.

Buick Bonery 6970 Stamper Way Sacramento, CA 95828	**916-381-5271** **FAX: 916-381-0702**

See full listing in **Section One** under **Buick/McLaughlin**

Mercedes Auto Recycling 225C Salinas Rd Watsonville, CA 95076 E-mail: admin@mercedesrecycling.com	**800-264-2111** **831-786-0536** **FAX: 831-786-0545**

Mail order and open shop. Monday-Friday 9 am to 6 pm PST. Specializing in Mercedes-Benz late 1960s-early 1990s. Mercedes repair shop and dismantlers. Web site: www.mercedesrecycling.com

Pearson's Auto Dismantling & Used Cars 2343 Hwy 49 Mariposa, CA 95338	**209-742-7442**

Open Friday-Saturday only 8:30 am to 5:30 pm. A G Pearson, owner. Specializing in all cars 1959 and older. Also has some 1959 and newer used cars and parts in stock. Enclose an SASE.

Connecticut

Mostly Mustangs Inc 55 Alling St Hamden, CT 06517	**203-562-8804** **FAX: 203-562-4891**

See full listing in **Section One** under **Mustang**

Royals' Garage 16-24 Calhoun St Torrington, CT 06790	**860-489-4500**

See full listing in **Section One** under **Corvette**

Leo Winakor and Sons Inc 470 Forsyth Rd Salem, CT 06420	**860-859-0471**

Open Saturday-Sunday 10 am to 2 pm. Specializing in old car parts 1926-1987.

Florida

Anderson Automotive 1604 E Busch Blvd Tampa, FL 33612 813-932-4611; FAX: 813-932-5025	**813-932-4611** **FAX: 813-932-5025**

See full listing in **Section One** under **Oldsmobile**

Collectors Choice Antique Auto Parts PO Box 7605 Sarasota, FL 34278 E-mail: choiceparts@home.com	**941-923-4514**

Mail order only. All makes and models of American cars, 1930s-up.

Mustang Village 8833 Fowler Ave Pensacola, FL 32534 E-mail: rmcneal@aol.com	**850-477-8056** **FAX: 850-484-4244**

Specializing in Mustangs 1964-1/2 and up.

Georgia

Bayless Inc 1111 Via Bayless Marietta, GA 30066-2770	**800-241-1446** **order line US/Canada** **770-928-1446** **FAX: 770-928-1342**

See full listing in **Section One** under **Fiat**

Fiat Lancia Heaven Bayless Inc 1111 Via Bayless Marietta, GA 30066-2770	**800-241-1446** **770-928-1446** **FAX: 770-928-1342**

Exclusive Fiat, Lancia, Yugo salvage yard.

Old Car City USA 3098 Hwy 411 NE White, GA 30184	**770-382-6141** **FAX: 770-387-2122**

Est 1931. Call for time. Selling all restorable cars, pickups. Pre-1972 all American cars. Also parts cars. Videos of OCC USA, $19.95 plus $3 s&h.

Illinois

Sylvester McWorthy 5723 A Illinois Rt 84 Thomson, IL 61285	**815-259-5797**

We have disposed of all automobiles. We still have a lot of older auto parts, such as, transmissions, radiators, heaters, carburetors, small parts, starters and generators 1940-1960. We also have some new parts, gaskets, GMC and Chevrolet truck parts, ignition parts, new mufflers and tailpipes, bottom window channels, 6 volt sealed beam conversion kits for Ford and Chev, much more. Bearings, wheelcovers in sets, large collection of original hubcaps, other chrome trim for wheels. Working alone, and may be a little slow answering your calls.

Gus Miller Box 604 Heyworth, IL 61745	**309-473-2979** **FAX: 309-473-2979**

Open by appointment only. 10 acres of cars and parts from the forties, fifties and sixties for sale. All FOB. No mail orders.

Indiana

Webb's Classic Auto Parts 5084 W State Rd 114 Huntington, IN 46750 219-344-1714; FAX: 219-344-1754	**219-344-1714** **FAX: 219-344-1754**

See full listing in **Section One** under **AMC**

Kansas

Easy Jack & Sons Antique Auto Parts Store 2725 S Milford Lake Rd Junction City, KS 66441-8446	**785-238-7541** **785-238-7161** **FAX: 785-238-8714**

Open Monday-Friday 8 am to 5:30 pm, Saturday 8 am to 2 pm CST. Specializing in 1912-1985 parts and vehicles. Over 80 different makes and brands available. Store and yard covers over twenty acres. Hundreds of restorable vehicles. Millions of parts. Buying and selling antique and collector type vehicles and parts since 1963. Located six miles west of Junction City on Interstate #70, at Milford Lake Road exit #290. We accept MasterCard/Visa/Discover. SASE for more information.

Bob Lint Motor Shop PO Box 87 101 Main St Danville, KS 67036	**316-962-5247**

Mail order and open shop. Monday-Friday 8 am to 5 pm, Saturday 8 am to 12 pm. Thousands of parts, mostly Ford and Chevrolet, Plymouth, Buick, Studebaker, A and T Fords, lots of truck parts. Many 1920s and 1930s wire wheels, old car parts, also tires. Many old car radiators & hubcaps. Also have complete old cars and trucks, NOS tires, used transmissions, rear ends, motors, brake shoes, generators & starters, etc. In business for 45 years same location.

Louisiana

Fannaly's Auto Exchange 41403 S Range Rd PO Box 23 Ponchatoula, LA 70454	**504-386-3714**

Mail order and shop open by appointment. Approximately 400

parts cars. Cadillacs, Buicks 1939-1970, Mopar, NOS parts, obsolete marques, Blue Crown spark plugs. Antique and contemporary cars and trucks. Antique parts, both used and NOS.

Maine

Classic Ford Sales PO Box 60 East Dixfield, ME 04227 E-mail: classicford@quickconnect.com	**207-562-4443** **FAX: 207-562-4576**

Mail order and open shop. Monday-Friday 9 am to 5 pm, closed Saturday. Ford products only, 1949-1972 full size, Thunderbird, Lincoln, Mercury, Falcon, Fairlane, Comet, F100, quality used parts with some NOS. Web site: www.classicford.com

Maryland

Driving Passion Ltd USA Marc Tuwiner 7132 Chilton Ct Clarksville, MD 21029 E-mail: mt.tees@erols.com	**301-596-9078** **Fax: 301-596-9078**

See full listing in **Section One** under **Cadillac/LaSalle**

Smith Brothers' Auto Parts 2316 Snydersburg Rd Hampstead, MD 21074 410-374-6781	**410-374-6781** **410-239-8514**

Open 6 days 8 am to 5 pm. Approximately 500 cars from 1946-1980, some muscle cars from 1965-1972. Ford driveline parts 1935-up.

Section Five Salvage Yards

TMC Publications
5817 Park Heights Ave
Baltimore, MD 21215

410-367-4490
FAX: 410-466-3566

See full listing in **Section Two** under **literature dealers**

Massachusetts

Independent Salvage Source
508 Myricks St
PO Box 620
East Taunton, MA 02718
E-mail: admin@ind-salvage.com

301-262-0641, MD
FAX: 301-262-2488

National sales of insurance total losses and donated vehicles for parts and rebuilding. Classic, exotic and antique vehicles. Web site: ind-salvage.com

See our ad on page 585

R E Pierce
47 Stone Rd
Wendell Depot, MA 01380
978-544-7442; FAX: 978-544-2978
E-mail: robin@billsgate.com

978-544-7442
FAX: 978-544-2978

See full listing in **Section One** under **Volvo**

Michigan

Bob's Auto Parts
6390 N Lapeer Rd
Fostoria, MI 48435

810-793-7500

Mail order and open shop. Monday, Wednesday, Friday 9 am to 5 pm; Saturday 9 am to 12 pm. Phone for appointment or send SASE for information. 2,000 cars in yard. New and used classic and antique auto parts. Owner semi-retired. Customer may go into yard with owner or employee. Parts are removed by employees only. 40 years at same location, 60 miles north of Detroit on M-24 at M-90.

Michigan Corvette Recyclers
11995 US 223
Riga, MI 49276
800-533-4650; FAX: 517-486-4124

800-533-4650
FAX: 517-486-4124

See full listing in **Section One** under **Corvette**

Minnesota

ADP Hollander
14800 28th Ave N #190
Plymouth, MN 55447
E-mail: holland@autonet.net

800-761-9266
FAX: 800-825-1124

See full listing in **Section Two** under **car & parts locators**

Bill's Auto Parts
310 7th Ave
Newport, MN 55055

612-459-9733

Mail order and open shop. Monday-Friday 8 am to 5:30 pm, Saturday 8 am to 12 pm. Auto parts dismantling and recycling. Used parts only, all years, makes and models 1930-1980s.

Doug's Auto Parts
900 North Hwy 59
PO Box 811
Marshall, MN 56258

507-537-1488
FAX: 507-537-0519

Doug's Auto Parts, Douglas J Mosch, owner. Celebrating 25 years in business, 1973-1998. Specializing in 1949-1953 Mercurys, 1928-1959 Fords, 1937-1969 Chevys. Many good complete restorable cars including coupes and convertibles. Buick, Olds, Pontiac and others included. We like solid and rust-free cars like everyone else does. Also gas pumps, both visible and electric, old signs, other collectibles.

Hemmings' Vintage Auto Almanac©   Fourteenth Edition

Missouri

J & M Vintage Auto
2 Mi W Goodman on B Hwy
Goodman, MO 64843

417-364-7203

Open Tuesday-Friday 8 am to 5 pm, Saturday 8 am to 3 pm, closed Sunday-Monday. 1,600 cars, 1930-1972. Customers may browse unassisted.

Montana

Freman's Auto
138 Kountz Rd
Whitehall, MT 59759

406-287-5436
FAX: 406-287-9103

See full listing in **Section Two** under **car dealers**

Medicine Bow Motors Inc
343 One Horse Creek Rd
Florence, MT 59833

406-273-0002

See full listing in **Section Two** under **car dealers**

New Hampshire

Parts of the Past
Rt 2, Box 118A
Canaan, NH 03741

603-523-4524
FAX: 603-523-4524
*49

Mail order and open shop. Monday-Friday, weekends by appointment. 1924-1972 General Motors, Ford, Mopar, Hudson, Kaiser-Fraser, Edsel, Graham, Mercury, Nash, Packard, Studebaker, Lincoln, LaSalle parts. "If I don't have it, I will try to find it." Sale of parts, pieces and whole cars and restorable antiques.

New Mexico

Discount Auto Parts
4703 Broadway SE
Albuquerque, NM 87105

505-877-6782

Mail order and open shop. Monday-Friday 8 am to 5:30 pm. Salvage yard. Specialist in Volkswagen and Audi.

Route 66 Reutilization
1357 Historic Rt 66 E
Tijeras, NM 87059

505-286-2222
FAX: 505-281-6555

Storage yard. Sell vintage autos and trucks, parts and Route 66 memorabilia.

New York

Adler's Antique Autos Inc
801 NY Rt 43
Stephentown, NY 12168
E-mail: advdesign1@aol.com

518-733-5749

Over 600 1935-1980 Chevrolets. Specializing in 1947-1955 Chevrolet Advance Design trucks. Parts vehicles and restoration projects, shipping service available. Browsers welcome to the outdoor museum. Complete restoration facility. All work and parts guaranteed. Towing available. In business over 27 years.

Halpin Used Auto & Truck Parts
1093 Rt 123
Mayfield, NY 12117
E-mail: junkyard2064@webtv.net

518-863-4906

Mail order and open shop. Monday-Saturday 8 am to 4 pm. We deal in used and NOS auto and truck parts, 1930-present. We ship UPS and deliver. If we don't have it, we will try to locate it for you. No part too small, we sell anything you need. Large selection of taillights, all years. In business since 1972.

Maffucci Sales Company Inc
RD 1 Box 60, Rt 9 W
Athens, NY 12015
E-mail: maffuccisales@mindspring.com

518-943-0100
FAX: 518-943-4534

See full listing in **Section One** under **Lincoln**

Reardon Enterprises
Box 1633, Rt 28
Mohawk, NY 13407

315-866-3072

Mail order and open shop. Weekends and evenings open 24 hours. Large selection of 1928-1960 GM parts cars, plus oddballs. Trucks too. Antique motorcycles, gas pumps, oil filters, fan belts, memorabilia. Cars bought and traded as well as antique snowmobiles.

Tucker's Auto Salvage
Raymond A Tucker
5121 St Rt 11
Burke, NY 12917

518-483-5478

Open Monday-Friday 8 am to 5 pm, Saturday 8 am to 12 pm. Cars and parts, sandblasting, body and mechanical restoration.

Ohio

Alotta Auto Parts
8426 Upper Miamisburg Rd
Miamisburg, OH 45342
E-mail: unc8426joe@aol.com

937-866-1849
FAX: 937-866-6431

Mail order and open shop. Monday-Friday 8:30 am to 5 pm, Saturday 8:30 am to 2 pm. Six acre salvage yard with cars and parts. Specializing in 1950s and 1960s autos and light trucks. NOS and used parts. COD shipping available.

Files Auto Wrecking
936 Scoville-North Rd
Vienna, OH 44473

330-539-5114

Mail order and open weekends including Sundays. All makes and models, 1950s, 1960s, 1970s. We are located in northeast Ohio, near Interstates 80 and 76, Rts 11 and 82.

Rode's Restoration
1406 Lohr Rd
Galion, OH 44833
E-mail: rodes@bright.net

419-468-5182
FAX: 419-462-1753

See full listing in **Section One** under **Mustang**

Oklahoma

East West Auto Parts Inc
4605 Dawson Rd
Tulsa, OK 74115

800-447-2886
FAX: 918-832-7900

Mail order only. All General Motors parts: Pontiac, Chevrolet, Oldsmobile, Buick, Cadillac and GMC. Have a 17 acre facility with over 950 cars and trucks ranging in years from 1946-1988. Also have parts for European imports: Saab, Volvo, Volkswagen and Opel. Oklahoma based mail order business with over 50 years of combined experience. Ship parts anywhere. Sorry, no catalogs. Credit cards accepted. Web site: www.eastwestautoparts.com

Hauf Antique & Classic Cars & Pickups
Box 547
Stillwater, OK 74076

405-372-1585
FAX: 405-372-1586

Open Tuesday-Friday 8 am to 5 pm, weekends by appointment. Specialize in classic, antique cars and pickups.

North Yale Auto Parts
Rt 1, Box 707
Sperry, OK 74073

918-288-7218
800-256-6927
(NYAP)
FAX: 918-288-7223

Mail order and open shop. Monday-Friday 8 am to 5 pm.

Specializes in 1950-1980s Chevys, Chryslers, Fords, Cadillac. New and used body fillers for most GM cars. Nationwide parts locating of new, used, aftermarket parts, ask for Bobby.

Oregon

Michael's Auto Parts
5875 NW Kaiser Rd
Portland, OR 97229

503-690-7750
FAX: 503-690-7735

Mail order. Monday-Friday 9 am to 5 pm, Saturday 12 pm to 5 pm. Used Mercedes parts. Models 1956-1980, body styles roundbody, 107, 108, 109, 110, 111, 113, 114, 115, 116, 121, 123, 126 2 and 4-door. Reasonable prices. Rust-free sheetmetal, glass, chrome, grilles, bumpers, a/c units, manifolds, heads, transmissions, interiors, etc. Specialize in 111 coupes. Satisfaction guaranteed. Web site: www.mercedesusedparts.com

Pennsylvania

Barton Auto Wrecking
175 School Dr
Waynesburg, PA 15370
E-mail: bartons@greenepa.net

724-627-3351

Open Monday-Friday 8 am to 5 pm EST, Saturday 8 am to 2 pm, closed Sundays. Our salvage yard specializes in foreign and domestic automobiles from the 1970s, 1980s and 1990s. We are located 50 miles south of Pittsburgh and have been a family owned business since 1937. As 3rd generation salvage yard operators, we are well known for our fast, friendly and courteous customer service. At Barton Auto Wrecking no part is too big or too small. Feel free to take advantage of our new e-mail and web page. Web site: www.bartonautowrecking.com

Corvair Ranch Inc
1079 Bon-Ox Rd
Gettysburg, PA 17325

717-624-2805
FAX: 717-624-1196

See full listing in **Section One** under **Corvair**

Ed Lucke's Auto Parts
RR 2, Box 2883
Glenville, PA 17329

717-235-2866

Open Monday-Friday 9 am to 5 pm, Saturday 9 am to 12 noon. 1,200 to 1,500 vehicles, many parts already removed. Parts for 1939-1956 Packards, 1939-present Chryslers and 1949-present Fords and GMs.

Rhode Island

B & B Cylinder Head Inc
320 Washington St
West Warwick, RI 02893

401-828-4900

See full listing in **Section Two** under **engine parts**

South Dakota

Dakota Studebaker Parts
RR 1, Box 103A
Armour, SD 57313

605-724-2527

See full listing in **Section One** under **Studebaker**

Wayne's Auto Salvage
RR 3, Box 41
Winner, SD 57580-9204

605-842-2054

Mail order and open shop. Monday-Saturday 9 am to 6 pm. Twenty acres of cars from the forties, fifties and sixties. A few from the thirties. Cars and pickups. Sell complete vehicles or parts. Mechanics shop.

Tennessee

Kelley's Korner
22 14th St
Bristol, TN 37620

423-968-5583

See full listing in **Section One** under **Studebaker**

Volunteer State Chevy Parts
Hwy 41 S
PO Box 10
Greenbrier, TN 37073

615-643-4583
FAX: 615-643-5100

See full listing in **Section One** under **Chevrolet**

Texas

South Side Salvage
Rt 2, Box 8
Wellington, TX 79095

806-447-2391

Open Monday-Friday 8 am to 5 pm, Saturday 8 am to 12 noon. Specializing in old and rebuildable vehicles and parts. Over 40 years at same location. Owner: Marshall Peters, 806-447-2490 home. Ready to retire, will sell entire business.

Virginia

Old Dominion Mustang/Camaro
509 S Washington Hwy, Rt 1
Ashland, VA 23005

804-798-3348
FAX: 804-798-5105

See full listing in **Section One** under **Mustang**

Philbates Auto Wrecking Inc
PO Box 28
Hwy 249
New Kent, VA 23124

804-843-9787
804-843-2884

Mail order sales. Open Monday-Friday 9 am to 5 pm, Saturday 9 am to 2 pm. Parts for 1940-1982 cars. Over 6,000 autos in stock at all times. Old, odd, collector autos our specialty. Browsers welcome.

Bill Thomsen
1118 Wooded Acres Ln
Moneta, VA 24121

540-297-1200

Mail order and open shop by appointment only, phone hours vary, call up to 9:30 pm EST. Small private salvage yard specializing in 1953-1973 full-size Chevrolet cars. Primarily mail out shipping worldwide. Hundreds of used hard to find parts. Consistently adding to inventory.

West Virginia

Antique Auto Parts
PO Box 64
60 View Dr
Elkview, WV 25071

304-965-1821

See full listing in **Section Two** under **comprehensive parts**

Wisconsin

Zeb's Salvage
N3181 Bernitt Rd
Tigerton, WI 54486

715-754-5885

Open Monday-Friday 8 am to 5 pm, Saturday 8 am to 3 pm. Have about 1,000 parts cars, mid-1920s to late 1980s. Ship small parts only.

Australia

Old Tin Australia
PO Box 26
Wendouree Victoria 3355 Australia

03 5339 FORD
FAX: 03 5339 9900

Australian utilities made by Ford and Chev from 1928-1952.

Canada

Scotts Super Trucks
1972 Hwy 592 W
Penhold, AB Canada T0M 1R0

403-886-5572
FAX: 403-886-5577

See full listing in **Section One** under **Chevrolet**

Section Six:
Museums

Auto museums are like scotch whiskey. Some are better than others, but there really are no bad ones. For the hobbyist seeking a car or auto-related exhibit close to home or on a vacation trip, museums are listed under state categories.

When planning a visit to a museum, be sure you've checked its exhibition hours as well as the months of the year when it is open. Some operate all year, but others are only open seasonally, generally in the spring, summer, and early fall. Some listed here are private museums and are open only by appointment.

Most every museum charges admission. Some, however, will offer group rates for clubs wishing to tour their collections. Many of the entries list the person in charge of the museum, and he or she should be contacted, in advance, to arrange a group visit. Some of the museums operate in conjunction with other exhibition attractions, while a few also serve as the showrooms for vintage car dealers. The latter group may be stretching the definition of a museum a bit far, but the hobbyist may find such displays interesting in their own right.

Alabama

International Motorsports Hall of Fame 3198 Speedway Blvd PO Box 1018 Talladega, AL 35161 E-mail: imhof@coosavalley.net	**256-362-5002** **FAX: 256-362-5684**

Open year round. Daily 8:30 am to 5 pm. Located 45 miles east of Birmingham and 95 miles west of Atlanta, International Motorsports Hall of Fame contains vehicles and memorabilia from all forms of racing. In addition to historic race cars, there are muscle cars, classics and prototypes. There is also memorabilia such as helmets, uniforms, trophies, photos, paintings and programs. There is a full gift shop, a 55-seat theater, video racing simulators and a comprehensive motorsports research library. Exhibit includes stock cars, Indy cars, drag racers, motorcycles, power boats, karts, sprint cars. Web site: historyonwheels.com

Mercedes-Benz Visitor Center PO Box 100 Tuscaloosa, AL 35403-0100	**888-2TOUR-MB** **205-507-2262** **FAX: 205-507-2255**

See full listing in **Section One** under **Mercedes-Benz**

Arizona

Franklin Museum 3420 N Vine Ave Tucson, AZ 85719 E-mail: hhff2@aol.com	**520-326-8038** **FAX: 520-326-6100**

Open September-May, Wednesday-Friday 10 am to 4 pm or by appointment. Documents Franklin Company products 1892-1976, with 19 restored or original cars on display in a western desert setting with other make vehicles, art and automobilia. The Tom Hubbard collection of classic Franklins on exhibit. Web site: www.hhfcmwr.com

Hall of Flame Museum of Firefighting 6101 E Van Buren St Phoenix, AZ 85008 E-mail: petermolloy@hallofflame.org	**602-275-3473** **FAX: 602-275-0896**

Open year round. Monday-Saturday 9 am to 5 pm, Sunday 12 noon to 4 pm. Nation's largest firefighting museum, with almost 90 restored pieces of fire apparatus in 33,000 square feet of air conditioned galleries. Hand, horse drawn and motorized pieces from the US, England, Germany and France. Membership. Web site: www.hallofflame.org

Arkansas

Good Old Days Vintage Motorcar Museum Main St PO Box 311 Hardy, AR 72542	**870-856-4884** **FAX: 870-856-4885**

Open year round. Monday-Saturday 9 am to 5 pm, Sunday 12:30 pm to 5 pm. Over 50 cars on display plus automobilia dating back to early 1900s. Gift shop with memorabilia, souvenirs and models of all kinds. Cars from the teens, 1920s, 1930s, 1940s and 1950s. A wide variety of vehicles.

The Last Precinct Police Museum 15677 Hwy 62 W Eureka Springs, AR 72632	**501-253-4948** **FAX: 501-253-4949**

Open year round. Tuesday-Saturday 10 am to 6 pm, Sunday by appointment. A police museum featuring 150 years of law enforcement history including: 5 decades of police cars and motorcycles, uniforms, badges, equipment from around the world. Largest private collection of police cars on display in the US. Movie memorabilia, old west displays. Also, large gift shop. Exhibit includes: last one of 12 Z-28 Camaros (1979) built for CHP, Bluesmobile, Dick Tracy squad car, propane powered police car. Web site: www.policeguide.com/policemuseum.htm

The Museum of Automobiles 8 Jones Ln Morrilton, AR 72110	**501-727-5427** **FAX: 501-727-5427**

Open daily 10 am to 5 pm. Buddy Hoelzeman, director. Exhibits include antique and classic cars on loan from private collectors. An auto fair and swap meet is held the third weekend in June with auto judging, style shows and driving events. In addition, a fall swap meet is held the fourth week of September. The museum serves as national headquarters for the Mid-America Old Time Auto Assoc (MOTAA).

California

Blackhawk Automotive Museum 3700 Blackhawk Plaza Cir Danville, CA 94506 E-mail: museum@blackhawkauto.org	**925-736-2277** **925-736-2280** **FAX: 925-736-4818**

Open Wednesday-Sunday 10 am to 5 pm PST. Admission is charged and group tours are available. Located 45 miles southeast of San Francisco in Danville, CA, the Blackhawk Automotive Museum presents and displays historically significant and artistically inspired automobiles, automotive art and related artifacts from the very earliest to the contemporary for public enjoyment and educational enrichment. The 100,000 square foot multi-level glass and granite architectural masterpiece showcases an ever-changing exhibition of over 120 of the world's greatest autos dating from the 1890s. The Automotive Art wing features *Moving Inspiration*, a rotating exhibition of nearly 1,000 artifacts in an amazing variety of media from the automobile's first 110 years. The museum's shop and bookstore is open during museum hours and has a large selection of automotive books, posters, models and kits. The museum and its facilities are totally wheelchair accessible. Web site: www.blackhawkauto.org

Bob's Radio & TV Service 238 Ocean View Pismo Beach, CA 93449	**805-773-8200**

See full listing in **Section Two** under **radios**

Ed Cholakian Enterprises Inc dba All Cadillacs of the 40's and 50's 12811 Foothill Blvd Sylmar, CA 91342	**818-361-1147** **800-808-1147** **FAX: 818-361-9738**

See full listing in **Section One** under **Cadillac/LaSalle**

JA Cooley Museum 4233 Park Blvd San Diego, CA 92103	**619-296-3112**

Open year round. Monday-Saturday 10 am to 5 pm. 18 antique vehicles. 1886 Benz, 1992 Benz, 1899 Mobile, 1903 Olds, 1904-1905-1913 Cadillacs, 1907 International, 1907 Brush, plus much more. Old phonographs, toys, trains, tools, clocks, cameras, and much more. Exhibit includes: Stevens Duryea used by President Wilson and XP2000 concept Buick.

Hays Antique Truck Museum 1962 Hays Ln PO Box 2347 Woodland, CA 95776-2347 E-mail: hatm@wheel.dcn.davis.ca.us	**530-666-1044** **FAX: 530-666-5777**

Open year round. Daily 10 am to 5 pm. Founded 1982. Non-profit public benefit corporation formed for the preservation and display of antique trucks. Over a hundred antique trucks representing a large number of makes dating from 1903 to mid-1950s are on display. The history of the trucking industry is shown through a variety of displays. A quarterly newsletter, *Old Truck Town News*, is published and mailed to the museum's members. There are various classes of membership in addition to a subscription only support. Web site: www.dcn.davis.ca.us/~hatm/

Muffler Museum Box 1917 Thousand Oaks, CA 91360	**818-707-2301**

Open by appointment. The only muffler museum. 10,000 on view. Maximum guarantee 10 years (not warranty).

Petersen Automotive Museum 6060 Wilshire Blvd Los Angeles, CA 90036	**323-930-CARS** **(2277)** **FAX: 323-930-6642**

Open all year. Tuesday-Sunday 10 am to 6 pm. A member of the Natural History Museum Group. Largest, most definitive automotive museum in North America. Dedicated to the interpretive study of the automobile and its influence on American life and culture. Three levels of exhibits, secure parking and large gift shop. Venue for car shows, auctions and 3rd party social events. Features include Hollywood star cars, motorcycles, petroliana, automotive themed art and our hands-on interactive children's discovery center. Web site: www.petersen.org

San Diego Automotive Museum 2080 Pan American Plaza Balboa Park San Diego, CA 92101	**619-231-2886** **FAX: 619-231-9869**

Open year round. Daily 10 am to 4:30 pm (last admission 4 pm); summer hours, 10 am to 5:30 pm (last admission 5 pm). A breath taking array of rare and exotic automobiles and a world

class motorcycle display with feature shows changing 2-3 times a year. Also special interest shows during the year including the annual "Motorcycles in the Park Show". Call for current show information. Full service gift shop. Museum membership available ($25 a year) providing many car enthusiast benefits, including free entry to museum and guest passes, updates on museum activities and invitations to special events.

Towe Auto Museum 2200 Front St Sacramento, CA 95818	**916-442-6802** **FAX: 916-442-2646**

Open daily 10 am to 6 pm (closed Thanksgiving, Christmas and New Year's Day). Be dazzled by chrome headlights and two-toned glistening paint as you hit the high road to the new Towe Auto Museum. Come see the history of the automobile in America; our motoring heritage which is brought to life by the dreams of hope, desire and fantasy stimulated by our passion for automobiles. The Museum now shows its collector cars in a series of exhibits built around these dream themes. Free parking, gift shop, group rates, special evening functions, located south of Old Sacramento, a block off Broadway.

Colorado

AMC Historical and Artifact Collection 7963 Depew St Arvada, CO 80003-2527	**PH/FAX:** **303-428-8760**

Open year round. Monday-Saturday by appointment only. A collection of literature, books, magazines, scale models, toys and other historical artifacts of American Motors Corporation, 1949-1988.

Pikes Peak Auto Hill Climb Educational Museum 135 Manitou Ave Manitou Springs, CO 80829 E-mail: ppihc@ppihc.com	**719-685-4400** **FAX: 719-685-5885**

Open year round. Daily 9 am to 5 pm, Sunday 12 pm to 5 pm. The museum contains cars and motorcycles from the Pikes Peak International Hill Climb, the "Race to the Clouds" that started in 1916. The race held on July 4 is the highest and most spectacular motorsports event in the world. The museum includes actual cars that have competed and won, including a 1918 Pierce-Arrow, a 1920 Lexington and Bobby Unser's open wheel race car, as well as photographs, memorabilia, videos and a gift shop. Web site: www.ppihc.com

Connecticut

Connecticut Fire Museum PO Box 297 Warehouse Point, CT 06088	**860-623-4732**

Open April-June and September-October Saturday-Sunday 11 am to 4 pm; July-August Saturday-Sunday 11 am to 5 pm. Dedicated to the preservation and appreciation of antique fire apparatus and associated equipment. A non-profit and historical association organized in 1968, incorporated in 1971 and opened in 1975. The collection equipment ranges from a fire sleigh circa 1894 to a 1967 Walter airport crash truck. In addition, fire truck models and fire alarm equipment are displayed. Membership: $10/year. Send SASE for a copy of museum brochure and application.

Florida

Elliott Museum 825 NE Ocean Blvd Stuart, FL 34996 E-mail: elliottmuseum@cwix.com	**561-225-1961** **FAX: 561-225-2333**

Open year around 10-4, except major holidays. Americana 1900-1950 featuring 24 antique cars (1902-1950), spotlighting automotive inventions of Sterling and Harmon Elliott. Exhibits include antique and classic automobiles, motorcycles, bicycles. Web site: www.goodnature.org/elliottmuseum

Don Garlits Attractions 13700 SW 16th Ave Ocala, FL 34473	352-245-8661 FAX: 352-245-6895

Open daily 9 am to 5 pm, closed Christmas. Garlits Auto Attractions offers a unique variety of vehicles from 1908 to the 1970s in the antique collection. Our drag racing exhibit traces the sport from the 1940s to the present day record breakers. Call for more information. Web site: www.garlits.com

Georgia

Auto Quest Investment Cars Inc 710 W 7th St PO Box 22 Tifton, GA 31793 E-mail: info@auto-quest.com	912-382-4750 FAX: 912-382-4752

See full listing in **Section Two** under **car dealers**

Museo Abarth 1111 Via Bayless Marietta, GA 30066-2770	770-928-1446

Open Monday-Friday 9 am to 5 pm, except holidays. Admission free. Display of original Abarth, Fiat and Lancia memorabilia.

Illinois

Hartung's Automotive Museum 3623 W Lake St Glenview, IL 60025	847-724-4354

Auto museum, call for hours. License plate and auto museum with over 100 antique autos, trucks and motorcycles on exhibit. Vehicles on display include 75 antique bicycles, 28 motorcycles from 1901-1941; Whizzers, sidecars and scooters; Ford Model As, Ts, V8s, plus many other automobiles. License plate collection contains plates from 50 states and Canada. Also promotional model cars, auto hubcaps, radiator emblems, etc. Also police badge collection.

Max Nordeen's Wheels Museum 6400 N 400 Ave Alpha, IL 61413	309-334-2589

Open May, September, October weekends only; June, July, August closed Monday only; 9 am to 4 pm, other days by appointment. A variety of vehicles, show cases of automobilia, 83 pedal cars, trucks, tractors, etc. Show cases of rare and unusual, Indian relics, war items, railroad items, steam, farm machinery, adv mirrors, world fair souvenirs. The list goes on and on. Exhibition car: 1942 Lincoln Mark I conv, only 136 built, one of 28 left, only one in Illinois.

Volo Antique Auto Museum 27582 Volo Village Rd Volo, IL 60073	815-385-3644 FAX: 815-385-0703

Open daily 10 am to 5 pm. Located 13 miles west of I-94 on Volo Village Rd, one traffic light north of Rt 120. Exhibits include approximately 200 restored collector cars, automobilia gift shop. Exquisite homemade food and 3 giant antique malls to browse. We buy, sell and appraise collector cars. Admission: adults, $4.50; seniors and children ages 6-12, $2.50; under 6, free. Group rates by advance reservation. Web site: www.volocars.com

Wheels Through Time Museum Rt 1 Waltonville Rd Mt Vernon, IL 62864 E-mail: daleshd@dales-hd.com	PH/FAX: 618-244-5470

Open year round. Monday-Friday 9 am to 5 pm, Saturday 9 am to 4 pm. One of the very few places in the country where such a volume of privately owned motorcycles can be viewed by the public at no charge and where such a wealth of information on the early days of motorcycling can be gained. Web site: www.dales-hd.com

Indiana

Auburn Cord Duesenberg Museum 1600 S Wayne St Auburn, IN 46706	219-925-1444 FAX: 219-925-6266

Open year round. Daily 9 am to 5 pm. Robert Sbarge, Executive Director. More than 100 automobiles on exhibit, featuring Auburns, Cords and Duesenbergs. The Museum is housed in the 1930 art deco factory showrooms of the Auburn Automobile Company. Autos on exhibit include the earliest Auburn known to exist and a cross section of all types of collector cars. Discount admission for any old car club member. Museum store, banquet facilities. Auburn Cord Duesenberg festival, Labor Day weekend. Web site: http://welcome.to/acd.museum

Elwood Haynes Museum 1915 S Webster Kokomo, IN 46902-2040	765-456-7500

Open year round. Tuesday-Saturday 1 pm to 4 pm, Sunday 1 pm to 5 pm. The museum is located in the home of inventor Elwood Haynes. 1st floor Haynes history, 2nd floor industrial history, basement movie "On The Road" (documentary). There are 4 Haynes cars on the premises, 1905-1924: 1905 Haynes Model L, 1923 Haynes roadster, 1924 Haynes touring car, 1916 Haynes.

Historical Military Armor Museum 2330 Crystal St Anderson, IN 46012	765-649-TANK FAX: 765-642-0262

Open year round. Tuesday, Thursday, Saturday 1 pm to 4 pm, other times by appointment. History of Armor from WW I to current issue (light tanks, jeeps, trucks). 35 pieces of armor, etc, on display. Vintage military vehicle rally held each July (call for details).

Miller Auto Museum Inc 2130 Middlebury St Elkhart, IN 46516 E-mail: millermuseum@earthlink.net	219-522-0539 FAX: 219-522-0358

Open year round. Monday-Friday 10 am to 4 pm, last weekend of each month 12 pm to 4 pm. Forty uniquely displayed antique and award winning classic autos along with miscellaneous auto memorabilia, collectibles, vintage clothing and antiques. Many National winners on display.

Studebaker National Museum 525 S Main St South Bend, IN 46601	219-235-9714

Open Monday-Saturday 9 am to 5 pm; Sunday 12 pm to 5 pm. Admission fee. Depicts 112 years of Studebaker transportation history. Collection includes wagons, carriages, automobiles and trucks produced by Studebaker, and industrial treasures of northern Indiana. Also features Hands-On Science and Technology Center.

Wayne County Historical Museum 1150 North A St Richmond, IN 47374	765-962-5756 FAX: 765-939-0909

Open February-mid December Tuesday-Friday 9 am to 4 pm, Saturday-Sunday 1 pm to 4 pm. Features curiosities from around the world. Authentic Egyptian mummy, Davis airplane, Wooten desk, pioneer life exhibits, Gaar-Scott steam engine, early automobile collection that includes six Richmond made cars. 1908 Wescott, 1909 Richmond, 1920 Pilot, 1918 Davis, 1925 Davis, 1939 Crosley. Plus: 1912 Baker Electric, 1921 Detroit Electric, 1906 Detroit, 1909 Maxwell, 1914 Model T Ford, 1926 Dodge, 1926 Model T Ford fire engine, 1929 Ahrens Fox fire engine.

Iowa

National Sprint Car Hall of Fame & Museum PO Box 542 Knoxville, IA 50138 E-mail: sprintcarhof@lisco.net	515-842-6176 FAX: 515-842-6177

Open year round. Monday-Friday 10 am to 6 pm, Saturdays 10 am to 5 pm, Sundays 12 pm to 5 pm. The world's only museum dedicated to preserving the history of the sport of big car, super modified and sprint car racing. Handicapped accessible. Gift shop. Group tours available. All cars on loan and rotated yearly. Web site: knoxvilleiowa.com

Olson-Linn Museum 323 East 4th Villisca, IA 50864	712-826-2756 FAX: 712-826-2756

Open year round. Daily 9 am to 4 pm. Specializing in antique cars, trucks and tractors, pre-1930s. Also many other primitives. Exhibition of 1917 Cole 8 (Cloverleaf), 1909 2-cylinder Maxwell, several other makes 1909-1930.

Kansas

Kansas State Historical Society 6425 SW 6th Ave Topeka, KS 66615-1099 E-mail: btarr@kshs.org	785-272-8681 FAX: 785-272-8682

Open year round. Monday-Saturday 9 am to 4:30 pm, Sunday 12:30 pm to 4:30 pm. General history museum for the State of Kansas. Featuring 1910 Thomas, 1908 Great Smith and 1955 Ford F600 farm truck (off-exhibit). Web site: www.kshs.org

Kentucky

The National Corvette Museum 350 Corvette Dr Bowling Green, KY 42101-9134 E-mail: lisa@corvettemuseum.com	800-53-VETTE FAX: 270-781-5286

Open 7 days a week. Features changing displays/exhibits of over 60 Corvettes to celebrate the invention of the Corvette, preserve its past, present and future and serve as an educational model for all.

Rineyville Sandblasting Model A Ford Museum 179 Arvel Wise Ln Elizabethtown, KY 42701	502-862-4671

Open year round by phone or by chance. Ernest J Pyzocha, curator and proprietor. Located off Hwy 1538 between Fort Knox and Elizabethtown, KY. 6,000 sq ft warehouse packed with nearly 40 unrestored Model A Ford cars and trucks of various body styles. Also license plate collection, porcelain signs, tools, new, used and NOS parts, accessories and much, much more. Admission $2.

Maine

Boothbay Railway Village Rt 27 PO Box 123 Boothbay, ME 04537	207-633-4727

Open daily mid-June to mid-October 9:30 am to 5 pm. Turn of century village containing historical exhibits including Thorndike and Freeport railroad stations, Boothbay Town Hall, general store, blacksmith shop, filling station. Ride on a coal-fired, narrow gauge steam train to an exceptional antique vehicle display housing more than 50 vehicles from 1907-1949. Web site: http://lincoln.midcoast.com/~railvill

Cole Land Transportation Museum 405 Perry Rd Bangor, ME 04401 E-mail: mail@colemuseum.com	207-990-3600 FAX: 207-990-2653

Open May 1-November 11, daily 9 am to 5 pm. Home of Maine State World War II Memorial. 200 Maine land transportation vehicles; 2,000 photos of life in early Maine communities; military artifacts from Civil War to Desert Storm, including vehicles, weapons, uniforms, etc. If it moved over land in this century or last, it is probably represented here, from roller skates to a locomotive. Covered bridge, 72'x15', 1840s design; trucks and cars include 1912 Reo, 1913 Stanley Steamer to 1964 Tank-Van; 1923 Packard, 1931 Reo Royale coupe, 1928 Buick, 1941 Pontiac, etc. Web site: www.colemuseum.org

Stanley Museum School St Kingfield, ME 04947 E-mail: stanleym@somtel.org	207-265-2729 FAX: 207-265-4700

Open year round. May 1-October 31, Tuesday-Sunday 1 pm to 4 pm; November 1-April 30, Monday-Friday 8 am to 12 pm and 1 pm to 5 pm; other times by appointment. Stanley Museum preserves, interprets and promotes the Stanley family tradition of Yankee ingenuity and creativity in photography, steam car transportation and the arts through its collections, publications and educational programs and activities. Membership levels from $25/individual through $2,500/lifetime. Members receive quarterly newsletter with historical and technical articles, free museum admission, 10% off gift shop items and advance event notification. On exhibit: 1910 Stanley Model 70, 1916 Stanley Model 725, 1905 Stanley Model CX. Web site: www.stanleymuseum.org

Maryland

Fire Museum of Maryland 1301 York Rd Lutherville, MD 21093 E-mail: firemuseumofmaryland@erols.com	410-321-7500 FAX: 410-769-8433

Open weekends May-October, Saturday 11 am to 4 pm, Sunday 1 pm to 5 pm (please call in advance); open Wednesday-Friday June-August, 11 am to 4 pm. The Fire Museum of Maryland is America's premier collection of fire fighting apparatus dating from 1806. More than 40 hand-pulled, horse drawn & motorized vehicles are on display. Web site: members.home.net/firemu/

Massachusetts

Heritage Plantation of Sandwich JK Lilly III Automobile Museum 67 Grove St Sandwich, MA 02563-2147 E-mail: museumcc@aol.com	508-888-3300 info: 508-888-1222 FAX: 508-888-9535

Open May to mid-October daily 10 am to 5 pm. Museum of Americana and Gardens on 76 acres. Antique Automobile Museum with 36 vintage and classic cars. Shown in a replica of a Shaker round barn. Stars of the collection are 1930 Duesenberg originally owned by Gary Cooper, 1932 Auburn boattail speedster and 1915 Stutz Bearcat. Military museum and art museum. Picnic area. Admission. Web site: www.heritageplantation.org

Museum of Transportation 15 Newton St Brookline, MA 02445	617-522-6547 FAX: 617-524-0170

Open year round. Tuesday-Sunday. New England's premier auto museum with a changing exhibits program, monthly lecture series and a full calendar of car club events. Web site: www.mot.org

Waltham Museum | **781-893-8017**
17 Noonan St
Waltham, MA 02453

Open March-December. Sunday 1 pm to 4:30 pm. A museum on the history of Waltham, Massachusetts. Bi-monthly newsletter to members. Special focus on the Metz automobile, Orient Buckboard and Waltham Watch Co. Exhibit includes 1903 Orient Buckboard, 1913 and 1915 Metz.

Yankee Candle Car Museum | **413-665-2020**
Yankee Candle Co Rt 5 | **FAX: 413-665-2399**
South Deerfield, MA 01373

Open year round. Daily 9:30 am to 6 pm, closed Thanksgiving and Christmas. Car museum is a world class collection of more than 80 American and European automobiles. Our 20,000 sq ft museum features an array of automobiles from the hottest sports cars to the coolest and most regal automobiles. Museum store is stocked with hats, T-shirts, model cars, books, videotapes and much more. Call for admission prices.

Michigan

Henry Ford Museum & | **313-271-1620**
Greenfield Village | **FAX: 313-982-6247**
20900 Oakwood Blvd
Dearborn, MI 48121-1970

Open year round. Daily 9 am to 5 pm, closed Thanksgiving and Christmas. Henry Ford Museum and Greenfield Village provides unique educational experiences based on authentic objects, stories and lives from America's traditions of integrity, resourcefulness and innovation. 9th Motor Muster, June 17-18, 2000, vehicles 1933-1969; 50th annual Old Car Festival (the longest, continuous running car show in North America), September 9-10, 2000, vehicles 1932 and earlier. Exhibit includes: 1896 Duryea motor wagon, 1st American production car; "Old 16" 1906 Locomobile, 1st American car to win an international auto race, 1908 Vanderbilt cup; 1961 Lincoln limousine JFK was assassinated in. Automobile in American Life exhibit, 100 car display, from its earliest beginnings to modern day. Web site: www.hfmgv.org

Gilmore-Classic Car Club of | **616-671-5089**
America Museum | **FAX: 616-671-5843**
6865 Hickory Rd
Hickory Corners, MI 49060
E-mail:
gcccam@gilmorecarmuseum.org

Open daily 10 am to 5 pm, early May-late October. A transportation museum run in cooperation with the Classic Car Club of America Museum, dedicated to preserving and displaying the historical significance of the automobile industry. 130 cars displayed in several exquisite barns situated on ninety manicured acres. Cars featured include Packard, Cadillac, Tucker, Duesenberg, Corvette and cars made in Kalamazoo. Web site: www.gilmorecarmuseum.org/

Alfred P Sloan Museum | **810-760-1169**
1221 E Kearsley St | **FAX: 810-760-5339**
Flint, MI 48503

Open Monday-Friday 10 am to 5 pm, Saturday-Sunday 12 pm to 5 pm. Major new exhibition, "Flint and the American Dream", traces the dramatic history of Flint, MI, in the 20th century, from the birth of General Motors to the present. Changing automotive gallery. Automotive archives available to researchers by appointment. Visit our Annual Summer Auto Fair, the fourth weekend in June, over 1,000 vehicles displayed on the grounds of the Flint Cultural Center.

Yesterday's Collection | **734-668-6304**
5899 Jackson Rd
Ann Arbor, MI 48103

Open year round. Monday-Saturday 10 am to 9 pm, Sunday 12 noon to 9 pm. Restored gasoline pumps, signs, oil dispensers, some cars. Gift shop, ice cream parlor.

Mississippi

Classique Cars Unlimited | **800-543-8691**
7005 Turkey Bayou Rd | **228-467-9633**
PO Box 249 | **FAX: 228-467-9207**
Lakeshore, MS 39558
E-mail: parts@datasync.com

See full listing in **Section One** under **Lincoln**

Missouri

Auto World Car Museum by Backer | **573-642-2080**
Business 54 N | **573-642-5344**
PO Box 135 | **FAX: 573-642-0685**
Fulton, MO 65251
E-mail: webacker@ktis.net

Open daily 10 am to 4 pm March-December, closed Easter, Thanksgiving, Christmas and New Years. 90 rare vehicles including Wills St Claire, Scripps-Booth, Stanley Steamer, DeLorean and a 1986 Pulse (only 60 were made). Vintage fire trucks and tractors. Unique gift shop.

Memoryville USA Inc | **573-364-1810**
Jct I-44 & Hwy 63 N
Rolla, MO 65401

Open year round. Daily 9 am to 5:30 pm. In business for 30 years. Have over 100 cars under roof from 1902 horseless carriage cars to muscle cars of the 1960s and 1970s including one of the largest restoration shops in the US. Feature a recreation of Rolla, Missouri, at the turn of the century, complete with authentic antiques and memorabilia and a gift shop where you will find a wide assortment of items from antique furniture to historic Route 66 items.

Museum of Transportation | **314-965-7998**
St Louis County Parks & Recreation | **FAX: 314-965-0242**
3015 Barrett Station Rd
St Louis, MO 63122

Open daily 9 am to 5 pm, closed New Year's, Thanksgiving and Christmas. Exhibits include 1901 St Louis automobile, 1906 Ford Model N, 1907 Anderson high-wheeler, 1963 Chrysler Turbine car (operational), 1960 Dia Dia/Darrin dream car as well as locomotives, rail cars, busses, trucks, street cars and horse drawn vehicles. Admission: adults $4, children 5-12, $1.50, children under 5, free and senior citizens, $1.50.

Patee House Museum | **816-232-8206**
12th & Penn, Box 1022 | **FAX: 816-232-8206**
St Joseph, MO 64502

Open weekends only November-March, Monday- Saturday 10 am to 4 pm, Sunday 1 pm to 5 pm April-October. Served as the Pony Express headquarters in 1860. Focus is on transportation and communications. Newsletter published 10 times yearly and sent to members. Also, operate the Jesse James home where the outlaw was gunned down in 1882, just two blocks away. Exhibits include Franklin, Flint, Model T, Federal truck, fire trucks and Sprinter. Web site: www.stjoseph.net/ponyexpress

St Louis Car Museum & Sales | **314-993-1330**
1575 Woodson Rd | **FAX: 314-993-1540**
St Louis, MO 63114

Open year round. Monday-Saturday 9 am to 5 pm, Sunday 11 am to 5 pm. Largest car museum in the midwest with over 150 cars displayed in a showroom covering 65,000 sq ft. Wide variety of cars from nearly every era including some that are one of a kind. Many of our cars are on consignment for sale. We also offer storage of classic cars. We also have a large automobile memorabilia shop, including T-shirts, hats, signs, books, videos, and the largest selection of die cast cars in the midwest. Exhibition cars include: 26th Anniversary Lamborghini Countach, 1969 Corvair w/12 miles, last one built off assembly line and Steed Stealth motorcycle. Web site: http://stlouiscarmuseum

Section Six
Museums

Montana

Miracle of America Museum
58176 Hwy 93
Polson, MT 59860
E-mail: museum@cyberport.net

406-883-6804
406-883-6264

Open year round. Daily 8 am to 8 pm summer, 8 am to 5 pm winter. Focus stresses America's progress from the walking plow to walking on the moon. Memorial displays include Veterans' tribute, DUI victims' memorial, Mt Fiddlers Hall of Fame. Between 20 to 30 vehicles in each section, motorcycles, autos, military trucks, etc. Web site: cyberport.net/museum

Old Prison Museums
Montana Auto Museum
1106 Main St
Deer Lodge, MT 59727

406-846-3111
406-846-3114
FAX: 406-846-3156

Open daily 8 am to 8 pm, Memorial Day through Labor Day; shorter hours after Labor Day. Features 100-plus cars on rotating exhibit. In 1999, the museum will feature muscle cars and Mustangs in addition to the museum's always changing collection.

Nebraska

Sandhills Museum
440 Valentine St
Valentine, NE 69201

402-376-3293

Open by appointment. Located on West Highway 20. Exhibits include: 16 antique cars from 1900-1928, in running order; bar room piano; band box and other musical items; 2-headed calf; band saw; firearms; Indian artifacts; broom making machine; moonshine still; barb wire collection; glassware; all types of lamps.

Harold Warp Pioneer Village Foundation
PO Box 68
Minden, NE 68959-0068

308-832-1181
800-445-4447
(out of state)
FAX: 308-832-2750

Open year round. Daily 8 pm to sundown. 50,000 historic items from every field of human endeavor. 26 buildings. Authentic originals arranged in their order of development to show visually the history of our country. 350 antique autos on display. Restaurant, motel, camping, all within walking distance. Stay overnight, come back next day, same admission fee. Write for more information. Pioneer Village® is a registered trademark of the Harold Warp Pioneer Village Foundation. Web site: www.pioneer-village.org

Nevada

Imperial Palace Auto Collection
3535 Las Vegas Blvd S
Las Vegas, NV 89109
E-mail: ipauto@ipautocollection.com

702-794-3174
FAX: 702-369-7430

Open year round. Daily 9:30 am to 11:30 pm. One of the largest privately owned collections in the world and cited by *Car & Driver* magazine as one of the world's ten best. On display in a plush, gallery-like setting are over 200 antique, classic and special interest automobiles, including the world's largest collection of Model J Duesenbergs. It also features a unique gift shop with a wide selection of automotive memorabilia and books. Located at the Imperial Palace Hotel and Casino, Center Strip, on the fifth floor of the parking structure. Web site: www.ipautocollection.com

National Automobile Museum
The Harrah Collection
10 Lake St S
Reno, NV 89501-1558

775-333-9300
FAX: 775-333-9309

Open Monday-Saturday 9:30 am to 5:30 pm, Sunday 10 am to 4 pm, closed Thanksgiving and Christmas. The museum exhibits over 220 antique, classic, vintage and special interest automobiles in 4 galleries and on 4 authentic street scenes representing

each quarter of the 20th Century. Features include a unique multi-media theatre presentation; multi-media time lines chronicling the automobile; museum store; and riverside cafe. World-famous automotive library offers research by mail. Museum is available in the evenings for group and convention activities. Web site: www.automuseum.org

New Jersey

Space Farms Zoo & Museum
218 Rt 519
Sussex, NJ 07461
E-mail: fpspace@warwick.net

973-875-3223
FAX: 973-875-9397

Open May 1st-October 31st daily 9 am to 6 pm. 100 acre complex. Over 500 animals, 50 antique cars, old wagons, sleds, 2,500 old firearms, Indian museum, tools, children's toys and much more. Special cars: Kaiser Darrin, Premiere, Reo, Chevy, Ford, Dodge, Willys and motorcycles. Web site: http://spacefarms

New York

The Buffalo Transportation Museum
263 Michigan Ave at Seneca
Buffalo, NY 14204

716-853-0084

Months open (to be announced). Featuring Pierce-Arrow, Thomas Flyer, Buffalo made autos and memorabilia.

Glenn Curtiss Museum
8419 St Rt 54
Hammondsport, NY 14840

607-569-2160
FAX: 607-569-2040

Open January-March, Wednesday-Sunday; April-December, daily 10 am to 4 pm. Focus on aviation/motorcycling pioneer Glenn Curtiss and on turn-of-the-century life. Early aircraft, early motorcycles, early engines, exhibits on daily life, open workshop, annual classic motorcycle weekend. Exhibition cars of special note include: 1918 Buick opera coupe, 1904 Orient Buckboard, 1937 Curtiss Aerocar travel trailer, Curtiss motorcycles.

Hall of Fame & Classic Car Museum, DIRT
PO Box 240
1 Speedway Dr
Weedsport, NY 13166

315-834-6606
FAX: 315-834-9734

Open April-Labor Day Monday-Saturday 10 am to 5 pm, Sunday 12 pm to 7 pm; September-December Monday-Friday 10 am to 5 pm, Saturday-Sunday 11 am to 4 pm; closed January-March. Dozens of classic cars on display throughout the showroom. Our classic car finder's network assists in selling, buying and locating classic cars. A classic car corral located outdoors adds to the rare and continuously changing models already shown. Rarity can easily be found. Web site: www.dirtmotorsports.com

Museum of Automobile History
321 N Clinton St
Syracuse, NY 13202

315-478-CARS
FAX: 315-432-8256

Open year round. Wednesday-Sunday 10 am to 5 pm. The largest museum of its kind in the world. Over 10,000 objects on display devoted to the history of automobiles, trucks and motorcycles from the 19th century to the present. Web site: www.autolit.com

Northeast Classic Car Museum
NYS Rt 23
24 Rexford St
Norwich, NY 13815
E-mail: neccm@ascent.net

607-334-AUTO
(334-2886)
FAX: 607-336-6745

Open year round. Daily 10 am to 5 pm. Fabulous 100 car Staley collection of classic and antique cars, very rare, one-of-a-kind or among very few known. The exhibit provides historical context about this unique collection. Fascinating examples of early technological advances, plus unusual models and famous manufacturers that shaped our countries automotive heritage. Exhibits include Duesenberg, Auburn, Cord, Packard, Stutz, plus the world's largest collection of Franklins (1902-1934). Admission: regular adult $7, seniors $6, students $3.50, members free, group discounts. Web site: www.ascent.net/neccm

Old Rhinebeck Aerodrome 44 Stone Church Rd Rhinebeck, NY 12572	**914-758-8610** **FAX: 914-758-6481**

Open May 15-October 31, 10 am to 5 pm. Living museum of vintage airplanes featuring WWI and earlier aircraft in weekend air shows, air museums and airplane rides. Features 1909 Renault, 1916 Packard moving van, 1918 GMC WWI ambulance, 1911 Baker Electric, 1911 International Auto Buggy, 1911 Hupmobile, 1910 Maxwell runabout, 1913 Brewster Town Car, 1916 Studebaker, 1914, 1919, 1927 Ford Model Ts, 1920 Buick, 1916 Royal Enfield motorcycle, 1917 Indian motorcycle, 1936 Indian motorcycle used in conjunction with weekend air shows. New air show schedule: every Saturday and Sunday mid-June through mid-October, at 2:00 pm. Great meeting place for an outing, especially for vintage car clubs. Web site: www.oldrhinebeck.org

Wilson Historical Society-Car Museum Lake St Wilson, NY 14172	**716-751-9886**

Open April-December Sundays 2 pm to 4 pm. Exhibits include 14 classic and collector cars.

North Carolina

Backing Up Classics Motor Car Museum 4545 Hwy 29 (Concord Pkwy) Concord, NC 28075 E-mail: buc@vnet.net	**704-788-9494** **FAX: 704-788-9495**

Open daily year round 9 am to 5:30 pm, closed Christmas and Thanksgiving. 50 motor vehicles on display with special focus on 1950s, classic and race cars. Web site: www.backingupclassics.com

North Dakota

Cass County Historical Society 1351 W Main Ave PO Box 719 West Fargo, ND 58078	**701-282-2822** **FAX: 701-282-7606**

Open Memorial Day weekend through September daily 9 am to 5 pm. Located within the historic village of Bonanzaville, this vintage auto museum contains more than 80 cars including a 1902 Oldsmobile, Model Ts through 1927, to a 1964-1/2 Mustang convertible. Also featured at Bonanzaville are main street businesses, log cabins, Bonanza farm homes, country school and church.

Ohio

Canton Classic Car Museum Market Ave S at 6th St SW Canton, OH 44702	**330-455-3603** **FAX: 330-455-0363**

Open year round. Daily 10 am to 5 pm. 40 cars focusing on pre-war classics. Cars range from 1911 Model T to 1981 DeLorean. Many memorabilia items, gift shop and more. Exhibition cars include: 1914 Benham, 1922 Holmes, 1937 Packard 1508 V12 carved side hearse.

Carillon Historical Park 2001 S Patterson Blvd Dayton, OH 45409 E-mail: chpdayton@aol.com	**937-293-2841** **FAX: 937-293-5798**

Open May 1-October 31, Tuesday-Saturday 9:30 am to 5 pm, Sunday 12 pm to 5 pm. 20 buildings on a 65-acre site. Auto related exhibits include a 1908 Stoddard-Dayton, 1910

Speedwell, 1923 Maxwell, 1910 Courier, 1914 Davis and 1918 Cleveland motorcycles located in the Dayton sales building; a 1912 Cadillac, Charles Kettering and Delco exhibits inside Deeds Barn, and a 1924 Sun Oil Company Station. Web site: www.activedayton.com/community

The Citizens Motorcar Company America's Packard Museum 420 S Ludlow St Dayton, OH 45420	**937-226-1917**

Open Monday-Friday 12 pm to 5 pm, Saturday-Sunday 1 pm to 5 pm. America's only Packard dealership operating as a museum. *Car Collector* magazine says it's one of the ten best small museums in the United States. Elegant Packards in an art deco showroom. World's largest collection of Packard only automobiles, artwork and artifacts. Don't miss America's Packard Museum.

Crawford Auto-Aviation Museum 10825 East Boulevard Cleveland, OH 44106	**216-721-5722** **FAX: 216-721-0645**

Open 12 months, Monday-Saturday 10 am to 5 pm, Sunday 12 pm to 5 pm. Over 150 automobiles, airplanes, bicycles, specializing in Cleveland built automobiles. 1st Cleveland car (1898 Winton) to last Cleveland car (1932 Peerless). Special exhibition. White Motors, Crawfords' Cleveland, Cleveland air races. Web site: www.wrhs.org

Motorcycle Hall of Fame Museum 13515 Yarmouth Dr Pickerington, OH 43147 E-mail: afitch@ama-cycle.org	**614-882-2782 info** **614-856-1900 office** **FAX: 614-856-1920**

Open year round. Monday-Friday 9 am to 5 pm, Saturday-Sunday 9 am to 5 pm March-October, special summer holiday hours, closed weekends November-February. Exhibits depict the development of motorcycling in America with rotating themes. The 26,000 sq ft facility usually has 100 motorcycles on display. The museum also maintains archives pertaining to the history of motorcycling and a Hall of Fame honoring the heroes of the sport. The museum features a gift shop, refreshment vending area and covered motorcycle parking, all on a beautiful 23 acre wooded site. Web site: www.ama-cycle.org

National Packard Museum 1899 Mahoning Ave NW Warren, OH 44483	**330-394-8484**

Closed Mondays and holidays, Tuesday-Saturday 11 am to 5 pm, Sunday 1 pm to 5 pm. Packard's birthplace, family, Packard Electric, Packard Motor Car Company archives. 15 to 20 Packard cars, 1900-1958. Large gift shop, bi-monthly newsletter. Membership to the Association: $25/year. Web site: www.packardmuseum.org

National Road-Zane Grey Museum 8850 East Pike Norwich, OH 43767	**800-752-2602** **FAX: 740-872-3510**

Open March-November, Wednesday-Sunday 9:30 am to 5 pm. The museum features three subject areas. Featured are the National Road, America's First Highway, Western novel writer Zane Grey and Zanesville, Ohio, art pottery. Exhibition cars of special note: 1899 Locomobile, 1914 Chevrolet Royal Mail and 1915 Ford depot hack. Web site: www.ohiohistory.org/places/nat/road

Oklahoma

Mac's Antique Car Museum 1319 E 4th St Tulsa, OK 74120	**918-583-7400** **FAX: 918-583-3108**

Open Saturday-Sunday 12 pm to 5 pm. An impressive collection of over 50 fully restored classic automobiles. The collection includes Packards (Twin Six, Super Eight and V12s), LaSalles, Cadillacs, Rolls-Royces, Fords, Chevrolets, Dodge and Chrysler and others dating primarily from the 1920s and 1930s. The 19,200 square foot facility is climate controlled, handicapped accessible and conveniently located near downtown Tulsa. Group tours welcome. Banquet facilities available.

Oregon

Tillamook County Pioneer Museum 2106 2nd St Tillamook, OR 97141	**503-842-4553** **FAX: 503-842-4553**

Open Monday-Saturday 8 am to 5 pm, Sunday 12 noon to 5 pm. Open all holidays except Thanksgiving and Christmas. History museum and large natural history collection. Exhibits include 1902 Holsman, 1909 Buick.

Pennsylvania

Swigart Museum Box 214 Museum Park Huntingdon, PA 16652 E-mail: cars@swigartmuseum.com	**814-643-0885** **FAX: 814-643-2857**

Open Memorial Day-October. Admission: adults, $4; children 6-12, $2; senior citizen and group rates available. William E Swigart Jr, owner. Located three miles east of Huntingdon, PA, on US Rt 22. One of the foremost collections of antique cars including 3 Duesenbergs, Dupont, Scripps-Booth, Carroll, Herbie-The Love Bug and two Tuckers-The Tin Goose and #13. Plus a memorable collection of toys, lights, clothing and a large collection of license plates and emblems. Web site: www.swigartmuseum.com

South Dakota

Pioneer Auto Museum and Antique Town PO Box 76 I-90 Exit 192 Murdo, SD 57559 E-mail: pas@pioneerautoshow.com	**605-669-2691** **FAX: 605-669-3217**

Open June-August 7 am to 10 pm; March-May and September-October 9 am to 6 pm. Dave Geisler, manager. Located at I-90, Exit 192 and US Highways 16 and 83 in Murdo. Exhibits include over 250 antique and classic cars from a 1902 Oldsmobile to a 1970 Superbird. Also several other exhibits of different modes of transportation from covered wagons to trains. Motorcycles on display include Elvis Presley's motorcycle. We have added muscle cars and a 1950s display. Joined with Pioneer Hallmark, KFC Food Court and Super 8. Web site: www.pioneerautoshow.com

Telstar Mustang-Shelby-Cobra Restorations & Museum 1300-1400 S Kimball St Mitchell, SD 57301	**605-996-6550**

Open year round upon request. Exhibits every year, model and body style of Shelbys, Boss 302s and Boss 429s, AC Cobras, fastbacks, GTs, convertibles.

Tennessee

International Towing & Recovery Museum 401 Broad St Chattanooga, TN 37402	**423-267-3132** **FAX: 423-267-3132**

Open year round. Weekdays 10 am to 4:30 pm, weekends 11 am to 5 pm. The museum displays antique vehicles with a variety of antique wreckers and tow trucks. The Hall of Fame honors individuals from around the world who have made contributions to the towing and recovery industry. Other memorabilia and artifacts are on display from the earliest inventions. Exhibitions of special interest include 1913 Locomobile w/Holmes 485 wrecker and 1929 Chrysler w/Weaver 3 ton auto crane.

Texas

Central Texas Museum of Automotive History PO Box 160 Hwy 304 Rosanky, TX 78953	**512-237-2635**

Open April 1-September 30, Wednesday-Saturday 10 am to 5 pm, Sunday 1:30 pm to 5 pm; October 1-March 31, Friday-Saturday 10 am to 5 pm, Sunday 1:30 pm to 5 pm. Central Texas Museum of Automotive History is dedicated to the collection, restoration and preservation of historic automobiles, accessories and related items. There are usually 120-125 vehicles on display. Also included are European estate cars, town cars, limousines and sports cars. Other displays include a large number of gasoline and oil pumps, automobile and oil company signs, accessories, automobile models and automotive toys. Web site: www.tourtexas/rosanky

GAF Auto Museum 340 W Tyler St Longview, TX 75601	**903-758-0002** **800-234-0124** **FAX: 903-758-0133**

Open Monday-Friday 8 am to 5 pm. No admission charge. 55 autos from 1916-1976. Auto memorabilia. Original drawings by Herb Newport, automobile designer. Old car parts, 1920s-1960s.

Pate Museum of Transportation PO Box 711 Fort Worth, TX 76101	**817-332-1161** **FAX: 817-336-8441**

Open daily except Monday. Jim Peel, curator. Located on Highway 377 between Fort Worth and Cresson. Exhibits include antique and special interest automobiles, aircraft and missiles and a 1,500-volume library.

Utah

Classic Cars International Museum Displays & Sales 335 W 7th St So Salt Lake City, UT 84101	**801-322-5186** **801-582-6883** **FAX: 801-322-5509**

Open year round. Monday-Friday 9 am to 4 pm. Special hours available by phone appointment. Over 200 antique and classic cars on display. Select units for sale to rotate cars. Classics range from Rolls-Royces to Rickenbackers, Cords, Hupmobiles, Essex, LaSalles, Packards, Pierce-Arrows, V16s, V12s, 1903-1960 classics. Approximately 50 classics on sale year round to rotate displays. Web site: www.classicarmuseumsales.com

Vermont

Hildene PO Box 377 Historic Rt 7A Manchester, VT 05254 E-mail: info@hildene.org	**802-362-1788** **FAX: 802-362-1564**

Open May-October daily, 9:30 am to 4 pm. Former 412 acre estate of Robert Todd Lincoln. A 1928 Franklin once owned by Jesse Lincoln Randolph is on display. Annual antique and classic car show second weekend in June. Web site: www.hildene.org

Virginia

Roaring Twenties Antique Car Museum Route 1, Box 576 Hood, VA 22723 E-mail: roaringtwnties@ns.gemlink.com	**540-948-6290** **FAX: 540-948-3744**

Open Sunday 1 pm to 6 pm from June-October, other times by appointment. Located in Madison County on State Route 230 between I-29 and 33. John Dudley, owner. Exhibits include cars from the 1920s and 1930s, trucks, stationary engines, horse-drawn equipment, farm tools, household goods and other Americana. Examples of Carter, Stephens, Cleveland, Star, Hupmobile, Paige, Essex and Nash cars are on display. Cars and parts for sale. Web site: http://maxpages.com/carmuseum

Virginia Museum of Transportation Inc 303 Norfolk Ave Roanoke, VA 24016 E-mail: info@vmt.org	**540-342-5670** **FAX: 540-342-6898**

Open year round. Monday-Saturday 10 am to 5 pm, Sunday 12 pm to 5 pm, closed on certain holidays as well as on Mondays in January and February. Auto Gallery opening in 2000. Currently exhibiting vintage cars, carriages, buses, trucks, trolleys, locomotives and rail cars. Also exhibiting model layouts, models, historic and interactive exhibits. Library and archives for research by appointment. Special events including annual Cool Wheels Festival in August. Memberships available at various levels. Special exhibits showcase VWs, Studebakers, Porsches, Harley-Davidsons, Packards, customized creations, street rods, stock cars, antique automobiles and more. Web site: www.vmt.org

See our ad on this page

Washington

Carr's One of a Kind in the World Museum 5225 N Freya St Spokane, WA 99207	**509-489-8859** **800-350-6469** **FAX: 509-489-8859**

Open year round. Saturday-Sunday 1 pm to 4 pm. Showcasing under chandeliers such wondrous cars as JFK and Jackie's private 62 Lincoln, Jackie Gleason's personal limo, Elvis' 1973 Mark IV and hundreds of beautiful Asian treasurers. $1,000,000 entertainment for only $5. This is a hands-on museum. All may sit in the precise seats that were occupied by JFK, Jackie, Marilyn, Elvis, Jackie Gleason and the June Taylor Dancers. A subsidiary of Trom Publications.

Wisconsin

Alfa Heaven Inc 2698 Nolan Rd Aniwa, WI 54408-9667	**715-449-2141**

See full listing in **Section One** under **Alfa Romeo**

Hartford Heritage Auto Museum 147 N Rural St Hartford, WI 53027	**414-673-7999**

Open year round except holidays. Features Kissel automobiles, Nash, along with Pierce-Arrow, Locomobiles, Terraplanes and various pieces of fire fighting equipment. Also displays gasoline pumps and gasoline and steam engines. Museum houses 90 vehicles of all kinds in its 40,000 square feet of display area. Admissions: $5 adults, $4 seniors and students, $2 children 8 to 15, free to children under 8.

Brooks Stevens Auto Collection Inc 10325 N Port Washington Rd Mequon, WI 53092 E-mail: apjb@prodigy.net	**414-241-4185** **FAX: 414-241-4166**

Open year round. Monday-Friday 9 am to 5 pm. A museum with 65 to 70 autos. A repair and service facility and a restoration shop for autos of all years, makes and models. On exhibit: one of a kinds and Excaliburs along with many other autos. Web site: www.execpc.com/~kyrie

Zunker's Antique Auto Museum 3722 MacArthur Dr Manitowoc, WI 54220	**920-684-4005**

Open May-September 10 am to 5 pm, by appointment after September. Auto museum and other displays. Doll collection and children's lunchboxes. Old gas station and cycles. Over 40 autos.

Australia

Raverty's Motor Museum 23-33 Ogilvie Ave Echuca Victoria 3564 Australia	**03 54 822730**

Open most days 10 am to 4 pm. Display of over 100 veteran, vintage, classic and historic vehicles, cars and trucks. Pierce-Arrow, Gardner, Yellow Cab, Fords, Chevrolets.

York Motor Museum Pty Ltd 116-119 Avon Terr York 6302 Australia	**0061896411288** **FAX:** **0061896411818**

Open year round 9 am to 5 pm. Superb display of veteran vintage, classic, historic racing, motorcycles, motoring memorabilia. Over 100 exhibits housed in beautiful buildings in historic town.

Austria

Das osterr. Motorradmuseum Museumgasse 6 A-3730 Eggenburg Austria	**43 2984 2151** **FAX: 43 2984 2119**

Open year round. Monday-Friday 8 am to 4 pm, Saturday-Sunday and holidays 10 am to 5 pm. Largest motorcycle muse-

Section Six Museums

um in Austria with 300 vehicles on show. Own departments of Austrian motorcycles, English, German and international motorcycles. Racing bike dept. The most exclusive and expensive bikes from Brough Superior to MV Agusta.

Belgium

Automuseum Oldtimer Tempelare 12 (Road Ypres-Furnes) Reninge 8647 Belgium	32 57 40 04 32 FAX: 32 57 40 11 64

Open Monday 1:30 pm to 6:15 pm, Tuesday-Friday 1 pm to 6:15 pm, Saturday 10:30 am to 5:15 pm, closed Sunday and bank holidays. On the N8 road between Ypres and Furnes (Leper and Veurne) 130 km west of Brussels, towards the French border (40 km east of Lille, France). Collection of 95 cars from 1899-1970 and 25 motorcycles. Cars: 1898 Decauville, 1906 Werner, 1912 Unic, 1930 Minerva, 1924 FN, 1931 Pierce-Arrow, 1936 NSU-Fiat, 1938 BMW 327, 1953 Hotchkiss Tour de France, 1953 Peugeot 203 Tour de France, 1986 Range Rover Paris-Dakar. Motorbikes: 1938 Ariel, 1974 Suzuki Wankel. Cafeteria with snacks.

Autoworld ASBL Parc Du Cinquantenaire, 11 1000 Brussels Belgium E-mail: autoworld@skynet.be	32-2-7364165 FAX: 32-2-7365136

Open April-September 10 am to 6 pm, October-March 10 am to 5 pm. Old timer's museum. More than 400 vehicles. Guided tours on request, shop and restaurant, booking of reception rooms, large free car park. Web site: www.autoworld.be

Gambrinus Drivers Museum 2A Fontaine-Saint Pierre B 5600 Romedenne Belgium	32-82678348 Fax: 32-82678348

Open April 1-November 1, 11 am to 7 pm. Dedicated to beer and brewery transport. Different displays about the European firms such as Mercedes-Benz, Volvo, Scania, Renault, and others. 20 different trucks from the UK, USA, Switzerland, France and Germany. Exhibition of petrol, steam and electric trucks used in breweries. Also a bar with 50 different beers from Belgium.

Mahymobiles Rue Erna 3 Leuze-Hainaut-B7900 Belgium	32-69-663416 FAX: 32-9-2822231

Opening spring 2000. About 750 cars will be on show, trucks and motorcycles. Library (23 tons of paper) and restoration shop. Cars are mostly not restored yet. Oldest vehicle on exhibit: Rochet-Schneider 1894; latest: NSX prototype 1992.

Museum of the Spa- Francorchamps Track Old Abbey 4970 Stavelot Belgium	PH/FAX: 080-8627-06

Open year round. 10 am to 12:30 pm, 2 pm to 5:30 pm, open until 4:30 pm in winter. An exhibition of race cars in the old Abbey (in a conservation area), near the famous race track. Photos, bookshop, scale models, video films and many documents which call up the world famous track.

Canada

Nova Scotia Museum of Industry PO Box 2590 147 N Foord St Stellarton, NS Canada B0K 1S0 E-mail: industry@gov.ns.ca	902-755-5425 FAX: 902-755-7045

Open year round. Allows the visitor to experience the fascinating human story of industry in Nova Scotia. Each visitor receives a time card so they may punch in and travel back through the working lives of our Nova Scotian ancestors. Visitors can work a steam engine, feel waterpower, hook a rag mat, build a model car on an assembly line. Samson, Canada's oldest steam locomotive, 1899 "Victorian" horseless carriage, 1912 McKay car, 1963 Volvo.

Reynolds-Alberta Museum Box 6360 (1km west on Hwy 13) Wetaskiwin, AB Canada T9A 2G1 E-mail: ram@mcd.gov.ab.ca or ram.library@ccinet.ab.ca	800-661-4726 403-361-1351 FAX: 403-361-1239

Open daily 9 am to 5 pm winter, 9 am to 7 pm summer. The Reynolds-Alberta Museum interprets the history of ground and air transportation, agriculture and industry from the 1890s-1950s. Collection of over 1,400 vintage automobiles, trucks, aircraft and agricultural machinery. 60,000 sq ft exhibit hall with over 100 major artifacts on display. Vehicles in collection include: 1929 Duesenberg phaeton Royale Model J214, 1927 LaSalle convertible coupe, 1913 Locomobile sport phaeton, 1918 National V12 sport phaeton, 1912 Hupp-Yeats electric coach. Museum is also home to Canada's Aviation Hall of Fame. Web site: www.gov.ab.ca/~mcd/mhs/ram/ram.htm

Reynolds Museum 4110 57th St Wetaskiwin, AB Canada T9A 2B6 E-mail: srsl@incentre.net	780-352-6201 FAX: 780-352-4666

Open daily May 15-Labor Day. Stanley G Reynolds, President. Located on Highway 2A in Wetaskiwin. Exhibits include antique airplanes, cars, tractors, steam engines, trucks, fire engines and military vehicles museum.

Saskatchewan Western Development Museum 2935 Melville St Saskatoon, SK Canada S7J 5A6	306-934-1400 FAX: 306-934-4467

Open daily 9 am to 5 pm; Yorkton Museum closed in winter. Head office at above address, branches at North Battleford, Saskatoon, Moose Jaw and Yorkton. Moose Jaw Museum features exhibits on transportation theme. All museums display vintage automobiles.

Southwestern Ontario Heritage Village County Rd 23 (Arner Townline) Harrow, ON Canada N0R 1G0	519-776-6909 FAX: 519-776-8321

Open April-June and September-mid-November Wednesday-Sunday 10 am to 5 pm, July and August daily 10 am to 5 pm. Large collection of vintage automobiles and early transportation devices. Have 5 fire trucks (4 in working condition). Exhibit includes: 1895 Shamrock, 1904 horse drawn Mitchell hearse, 1992 Viper, first Viper registered in Canada, first to be made to Canadian specs. Web site: www.swoheritagesites.org

Western Development Museum History of Transportation 50 Diefenbaker Dr, Box 185 Moose Jaw, SK Canada S6H 4B8 E-mail: wdm.mj@sk.sympatico.ca	306-693-5989 FAX: 306-693-0511

Open year round. Daily 9 am to 6 pm (closed Mondays January-March). History of Transportation, an extensive collection of automobiles, buggies, planes and locomotives as well as related artifacts. Classy cars on exhibit. Located at the junction of Highways 1 and 2. Web site: www.wdmuseum.sk.ca

Channel Islands

Jersey Motor Museum St Peter's Village Jersey JE3 7AG Channel Islands	01534-482966

Open March-late October daily 10 am to 5 pm. Veteran and vin-

tage cars, motorcycles, Allied and German military vehicles of WW II, aero engines, models, memorabilia and accessory displays. Cars on display: Rolls-Royce Phantom III used by General Montgomery, also Sir Winston Churchill's car.

Czech Republic

Skoda Auto Museum Vaclava Klementa 294 29360 Mlada Boleslav Czech Republic E-mail: museum@skoda-auto.cz	**00420-326-831138** **FAX:** **00420-326-832028**

Open daily 9 am to 5 pm, except December 24 and December 31. Exposition: 100 years of Skoda, motor gallery, how a car is produced. Conference halls: Laurin and Klement for 600 people; Hieronimus I and II for 20-80 people; Kolowrat for 16 people. Factory tours for visitors under the age of 15. Restoration workshop a part of the museum. Admission: 36 Kc adults, 18 Kc children. Rallye bar open from 9 till 8. Visitors service: Petra Fadrhonsova, PH: 00420-326-831134, FAX: 00420-326-832039, e-mail: petra.fadrhonsova@skoda-auto.cz Web site: www.skoda-auto.cz/history

Technical Museum Zahumenni 369 Koprivnice 742 21 Czech Republic E-mail: regmuko@tatramuseum.cz	**PH/FAX:** **+420-656-721415**

Open Tuesday-Sunday. Winter hours: 9 am to 4 pm; summer hours: 9 am to 5 pm. Tatra cars, trucks, railroad carriages, aircraft, chassis, engines, etc. Seven audio/video boxes with the Tatra history from 1850 till this time. Replica of the first car Prasident (1897) and the first truck (1898) manufactured in former Austrian-Hungary monarchy. Web site: www.tatramuseum.cz

Denmark

Jysk Automobilmuseum 8883 Gjern Denmark	**86-87-50-50**

Open April 1-May 15 Saturday-Sunday and holidays 10 am to 5 pm, May 16-September 15 daily 10 am to 5 pm, September 16-October 31 Saturday-Sunday 10 am to 5 pm. 140 vehicles, 68 different makes from the period 1900-1948, primarily cars and motorcycles, but also trucks and fire engines.

England

Beamish, The North of England **Open Air Museum** Beamish Co Durham DH9 0RG England E-mail: beamish@neoam.demon.co.uk	**01207 231811** **FAX: 01207 290933**

Open year round. Summer hours: 10 am to 5 pm; winter hours: closed Mondays and Fridays, times vary according to season. Open Air Museum illustrating life in the North of England in the early 1800s and 1900s in The Town, Colliery Village, Home Farm, Railway Station and Pockerley Manor, including period "Motor and Cycle Works" with showroom, spares department and workshop. Exhibit includes: 1906 Armstrong Whitworth, 1914 Model T Ford, several restored motorcycles. Web site: www.merlins.demon.co.uk/beamish

Bentley Wildfowl & Motor Museum Halland Nr Lewes East Sussex BN8 5AF England E-mail: barrysutherland@pavilion.co.uk	**01825-840573** **FAX: 01825-841322**

Open mid March-October 31 daily 10:30 am to 5 pm. Veteran, Edwardian and vintage vehicles, all privately owned.

The CM Booth Collection of **Historic Vehicles** Falstaff Antiques 63-67 High St Rolvenden Kent TN17 4LP England	**01580-241234**

Open year round. Monday-Saturday 10 am to 6 pm. Specializing in Morgan 3-wheel cars, 11 normally on display, other interesting cars, motorcycles, cycles, 1936 Bampton Caravan, much automobilia, toy and model cars. Books, restoration, information and museum for 1910-1952 Morgan 3-wheelers.

British Cycling Museum The Old Station Camelford Cornwall PL32 9TZ England	**PH/FAX:** **01840-212811**

Open year round. Sunday-Thursday 10 am to 5 pm. The nation's foremost museum of cycling history. Showing over 300 various cycles and cycling memorabilia from 1818-present day. Web site: www.chycor.co.uk

Canterbury Motor Museum 11 Cogans Terr Canterbury Kent CT1 3SJ United Kingdom	**01227-451718**

Open April-October. Please telephone to view. Privately owned collection of veteran and vintage cars, stationary engines and automobilia.

Castle Point Transport Museum 105 Point Rd Canvey Island Essex SS8 7TD England E-mail: glynis@topolino.demon.co.uk	**01268 684272**

Open April-October. Sundays 10 am to 5 pm. Approximately 35 commercial vehicles, mainly buses and coaches, spanning the years 1929-1972. Condition ranging from the fully restored to those in need of complete restoration. Newsletter for members of the Castle Point Transport Museum Society, founded in 1979, approximately 100 members. Dues: £6/year UK. Web site: www.topolino.demon.co.uk/

Cobbaton Combat Collection Chittlehampton Umberleigh N Devon EX37 9RZ England E-mail: cobbaton_combat@yahoo.com	**PH/FAX:** **01769-540740**

Open year round. Mainly 1939-1945 British and Canadian vehicles and civilian displays. Over 50 vehicles and artillery pieces plus some Warsaw pact. Militaria shop. Churchill, Sexton, Daimler and Morris on display. Web site: www.ndia.ndirect.co.uk/cobbaton

Cockermouth Motor Museum The Maltings Brewery Ln Cockermouth Cumbria England	**01900 824448**

Open March-October daily 10 am to 4 pm. A superb collection of vehicles (40 cars and 20 motorcycles), from 1912-1992. Exhibits include the east Africa winning rally car from 1972.

Cotswold Motor Museum & Toy **Collection** The Old Mill Bourton on the Water Gloucestershire GL542BY England	**1451-821255**

Open February-November daily 10 am to 6 pm. Along with many cars and motorcycles, Britain's largest display of period signs, automobilia and toys including pedal cars.

Donington Grand Prix Collection
Donington Pk
Castle Donington, Derby
Derbyshire DE74 2RP England

01332-811027
FAX: 01332-812829

Open year round. Daily 10 am to 5 pm, closed Christmas and New Year's. The world's largest collection of single seater racing cars. See Senna's car which won the 1993 European Grand Prix at Donington, plus many more. Ascari's Ferrari, Mansell's Red 5, Makkinew's West and Vanwall's on exhibit.

Dover Transport Museum
Old Park, Whitfield
Dover
Kent England

01304 204612
01304 822409
FAX: 01303 253628

Open Easter to end of September. Sunday 10:30 am to 5 pm. Road vehicles of all types from bicycles to buses. Model railway and tramway. Local transport history. Hundreds of models. Maritime room, Bygone shops and 1930s garage.

Filching Manor Motor Museum
Filching Wannock Eastbourne
Polegate
Sussex BN26 5QA England

011 441323 487838
011 441323 487124
FAX:
011 441323 486331

Open April-October Thursday-Sunday 10:30 am to 4 pm. 100 cars: 1893 Benz to Damion Hills, Arrow Grand Prix car of 1997. Specializing in sports and racing cars. Bugattis, Amilcar, Mercedes 1904, Paul McCartney's Hispano-Suiza on display.

Geeson Bros Motorcycle Museum & Workshop
2-6 Water Ln
South Witham
Grantham Lincs NG33 5 PH
England

01572 767280
01572 768195

Open April 4, May 30, August 29, October 3, November 11, December 27, January 2, 10:30 am to 5 pm. 85 British motorcycles dating back to 1913. All restored to new condition, workshop open to show work in progress and serve refreshments.

Greater Manchester Fire Service Museum
Maclure Rd
Rochdale Lancashire OL11 1DN
England

01706 341221

Open year round by prior arrangement. The official museum of the Greater Manchester County fire service. Portrays the history of firefighting in UK generally and particularly Manchester area. 17 fire appliances from 1741-1957 plus uniforms, equipment, models, photos. Archives. Exhibit includes New Sham manual 1741, Dennis-Metz 125 ft turntable ladder/aerial truck.

Heritage Motor Centre
Banbury Rd
Gaydon
Warwichshire CV35 0BJ England

0044 1926 641188
FAX:
0044 1926 641555

Open year round. April-October 10 am to 6 pm, November-March 10 am to 4:30 pm, closed December 24, 25, 26, 31, 1999, and January 1, 2000. Home of the largest collection of historic British cars in the world. Houses 200 vehicles charting the development of the British motor industry from the 1890s-present day. The collection includes the world famous marques of Rover, Austin, Morris, Wolseley, Riley, Standard, Triumph, MG and Austin-Healey. Attractions also include 4-wheel drive demonstration circuit, quad bike, children's roadway, cafe and gift shop. Many special events held throughout the year, please call for further details. Admission: adults, £6; seniors, £5; children (up to 16 years), £4; under age 5 free; group rates available (20 people and over); family ticket (2 adults and 3 children), £17. Web site: www.stratford.co.uk/bmiht

Jaguar Daimler Heritage Trust
Browns Ln
Allesley, Coventry CV5 9DR England

0044 (0) 1203 402121
FAX:
0044 (0) 1203 405581

See full listing in **Section One** under **Jaguar**

Keighley Bus Museum Trust Limited
47 Brantfell Dr
Burnley
Lancashire BB12 8AW England

01282-413179

Open year round. Tuesday and Thursday evenings, Sunday 10 am to 5 pm. A collection of fifty buses and coaches from 1931-1970s, many under active restoration. Free bus services run on open days and other special occasions.

Lakeland Motor Museum
Holker Hall Cark-in-Cartmel
Grange-over-Lands
Cumbria LA11 7PL England

PH/FAX: 015395
58509

Open April-October Sunday-Friday 10:30 am to 4:45 pm, closed Saturday. Over 150 classic and vintage cars, motorcycles, tractors, cycles and engines plus rare automobilia and the Campbell legend. Bluebird exhibition.

Llangollen Motor Museum
Pentrefelin
Llangollen
Denbighshire LL20 8EE England

01987860324

Open February-November Tuesday-Sunday 10 am to 5 pm. A collection of cars, motorbikes, toys and memorabilia dating from 1920s-1960s plus an exhibition depicting the history of Canals in Britain. 1922 GP Sunbeam and 1925 Vauxhall 30/98 on display.

Sammy Miller Motorcycle Museum
Bashley Cross Rd
New Milton
Hampshire BH25 5SZ England

01425 620777
FAX: 01425 619696

Open year round. 10 am to 4:30 pm. Sammy Miller is a legend in his own lifetime. He is still winning competitions, 47 years after his first victory. The Museum houses the finest collection of fully restored motorcycles in Europe including factory racers and exotic prototypes. The tea rooms, craft shops and animals are open all year. Web site: www.sammymiller.co.uk

The Museum of Science & Industry in Manchester
Liverpool Rd
Castlefield
Manchester M34FP England
E-mail: curatorial@mussci.u-net.com

+44 (0) 161-832-2244
FAX:
+44 (0) 161-834-5135

Open daily 10 am to 5 pm. The museum is based in the world's first passenger railway station dating from 1830. Exhibits include working stationary steam engines, land and air transport, industrial and scientific collections, all related to Manchester's industrial past. Manchester made vehicles including early Rolls-Royce and Crossleys. Web site: www.mussci.org.uk

National Motor Museum
John Montagu Building
Beaulieu, Brockenhurst
Hampshire, SO42 7ZN England
E-mail: beaulieu@tcp.co.uk

01590-612345
FAX: 01590-612624

Open daily (except Christmas Day) 10 am to 6 pm Easter-September, 10 am to 5 pm October-Easter. The National Motor Museum is one of the finest in the world and tells the story of motoring on the roads of Great Britain from 1895-present day. There are over 250 vehicles on show including four land speed record breaking cars. Excellent reference, photographic and film libraries. Web site: www.beaulieu.co.uk

National Motorcycle Museum
Coventry Rd
Bickenhill
Solihull, West Midlands B92 0EJ
England

+44 01675 443311
FAX:
+44 01675 443310

Open year round. Daily 10 am to 6 pm, except Christmas Eve, Christmas Day, Boxing Day. A breathtaking collection of British motorcycles is on view at the purpose built National Motorcycle

Museum complex, founded to ensure over sixty years of British motorcycle design and construction are not lost to future generations. Exhibit includes British motorcycles from 1898 onwards.

The National Tramway Museum Crich, Matlock Derbyshire DE4 5DP England	**01773 852565** **FAX: 01773 852326**

Open January-March Tuesdays for pre-booked schools and groups only 10:30 am to 3 pm, Sundays 11 am to 3 pm; April-August daily 10 am to 5:30 pm (6:30 pm bank holiday weekends); September-October daily 10 am to 5:30 pm (Starlight Special event until 7:30 pm); November-December Tuesdays for pre-booked schools and groups only 10:30 am to 3 pm, Sundays 11 am to 3 pm. Fully operational vintage tramway, indoor and outdoor attractions. Drivers of classic vehicles built and registered before January 1, 1968, admitted free if vehicle is parked in the Museum Street for a minimum of 3 hours. Web site: www.tramway.co.uk

North Yorkshire Motor Museum D T Mathewson Roxby Garage, Pickering Rd Thornton-le-Dale, North Yorkshire England	**01751 474455** **FAX: 01944 758188**

Open year round. Daily 10 am to 4 pm, closed Christmas Day. Classic and vintage cars, motorbikes, commercials and memorabilia. Owned and run by a family of enthusiasts.

The Ramsgate Motor Museum Westcliff Hall Ramsgate, Kent England	**01843 581948**

Open April-November 10:30 am to 6 pm. A private collection displaying 65 cars and 50 motorcycles from 1900-1970s. Exhibit includes bullnose MG saloon, Phoenix, Zedel, Arrol Johnson.

REME Museum of Technology Isaac Newton Rd Arborfield, Reading Berkshire RG2 9NJ England E-mail: reme-museum@gtnet.gov.uk	**0118-976-3567** **FAX: 0118-976-3563**

Open year round. Telephone for opening times. History of British Army's Corps of Royal Electrical and Mechanical Engineers and its role repairing military equipment. Displays include part of a total collection of over 100 military vehicles. Web site: www.eldred.demon.co.uk/reme-museum/index.htm

Sandringham House Museum & Grounds Sandringham Nr King's Lynn Norfolk PE35 6EN England	**01553-772675** **FAX: 01485-541571**

Open daily 11 am to 5 pm Easter-mid July and early August-October. Converted stables and coach houses in the grounds of her Majesty Queen Elizabeth IIs country home containing collections of vintage royal vehicles and carriages, limousines and miniature cars. 1900 Daimler phaeton, the first car owned by the British Royal family on display.

Skopos Motor Museum Alexandra Hills, Alexandra Rd Batley West Yorkshire WA7 6JA England	**01924-444423**

Open year round. Daily 10 am to 5 pm. Over 60 of the finest examples of motoring history, from the 200 mph F40 Ferrari to the world's first car: the 1885 Benz Patent motor wagon. 4-1/2 litre blower Bentley once owned by Ian Fleming (James Bond) on exhibit.

The Tank Museum Bovington Dorset BH20 6JG England E-mail: admin@tankmuseum.co.uk	**00 44 1929 405096**

Open year round. Daily 10 am to 5 pm. Tank and AFV from evolution to present day. 150 exhibits on display. Web site: www.tankmuseum.co.uk

West of England Transport Collection 15, Land Park Chulmleigh Devon EX18 7BH England	**01769 580811**

Annual opening day in Winkleigh, Devon, Sunday, October 3, 1999, otherwise by prior appointment, 10 am to 4 pm. Large collection of mainly west country buses, coaches, commercial vehicles and much related memorabilia items concerning bus operation from the twenties to the sixties. Quantities of early engines, transmissions, etc held. Bus exhibit includes: Leyland, AEC, Guy, Bristol, Austin.

Whitewebbs Museum of Transport Whitewebbs Rd Enfield Middlesex EN2 9HW England	**181-367-1898** **FAX: 181-363-1904**

Open year round. 4th Sunday of the month, 10 am to 5 pm. Museum run and funded by Enfield and District Veteran Vehicle Trust (local old car club). Can be open by appointment at other times. Call before visiting. Cars and motorcycles, unique 1912 Belsize Motor fire engine on exhibit.

Germany

Auto-und Spielzeugmuseum Boxenstop Brunnenstr 18 D-72074 Tuebingen Germany	**0707 11929020** **FAX: 0707 11929099**

Open April-October Wednesday-Sunday, November-March Sundays only, 10 am-12 pm and 2 pm-5 pm. It's a collection of race and sportscars and toys. We have several race bikes on display. Exhibits include Maserati 4CL from 1939, Porsche Carrera 6 from 1966, Bugatti Type 37 from 1928 and so on.

Automuseum Story St Adriansplatz 5 31167 Bockenem-Story Germany	**05067 759** **FAX: 05067 69296**

Open March 15-October 31, Saturday-Sunday 10 am to 6 pm. A special epoch of motorization, the recommencement after the second World War. More than 130 small and economical vehicles with an engine capacity under 700cc like BMW Isetta, Messerschmitt, Kleinschnittger, Zundapp Janus and more than 130 motorcycles and scooter. The collection comprises German, British, French and other European microcars.

Deutsches Museum Museumsinsel 1 D-80538 Munchen Germany	**089 2179-1** **089 2179-260** **089 2179-255** **FAX: 089 2179-324**

Open daily from 9 am to 5 pm, closed January 1, Shrove Tuesday, Good Friday, May 1, Corpus Christi, November 1, December 24, 25, 31. The Deutsches Museum covers the development of science and technology from its origins to the present day. It shows 55 automobiles, 25 sectioned cars and 40 motorcycles. On exhibit is the first motor vehicle, Karl Benz' three-wheeler 1886. Web site: www.deutsches-musuem.de/

Motorcycle Museum (Motorrad Museum) Lengericher Str 49479 Ibbenburen Germany	**05451-6454**

Open April-October Saturday 2 pm-6 pm, Sunday 10 am-6 pm, other days by special request. More than 150 motorcycles are waiting for you in an old school. They cover a wide range reaching from the ordinary from 1882 to the heaviest motorcycle ever produced in Germany, the Munch Mammut. Experts will enjoy rarities like the watercooled Diel from 1927.

Museum fur Post und Kommunikation Frankfurt am Main Schaumainkai 53 60596 Frankfurt Germany	069 60 60-0 FAX: 069 60 60-1 23

Open year round. Tuesday-Sunday 9 am to 5 pm. The Museum of Post and Communication is the former Museum of the German Postmaster General. It shows several historical commercial vehicles (trucks, buses, vans).

Stiftung AutoMuseum Volkswagen Dieselstr 35 Wolfsburg 38446 Germany	05361 52071 FAX: 05361 52010

Open year round. 7 days a week. Specializing in Volkswagen/Auto Union cars for all models of the Volkswagen AG. Jazz concerts, cabaret events. Publication: *Ein Wolfsburger Erlebnis.* Sales brochure, gift shop.

Hungary

Auto Muzeuma Haris (Bross) Testverek 1117 Budapest XI, Moricz Zsigmond Korter 12 Hungary	01 (1) 3656893

Private collection. Antique cars and motorcycles, 1875-1900. On exhibit are Hungarian history cars and Hungarien-Marklin cars toy series. Experimental cars 45 pieces: fire cars series, police, lorries, Vandenlence and racing cars 1/20. MSM-Haris Marc! MCA.BUDAPEST. Forma-1. Club.

Ireland

Museum of Irish Transport Scotts Hotel Gardens, Killarney Co. Kerry Ireland E-mail: kevin@kygems.iol.ie	353-64-34677 FAX: 353-64-31582

Open April-October daily 10 am to 6 pm. Exhibition of veteran, vintage and classic cars, cycles, motorcycles, carriages and automobilia. Fire fighting equipment. Special exhibits include 1902 Oldsmobile, 1904 Germain, 1907 Silver Stream and 1900 Argyll. Fascinating collection of American number plates.

National Transport Museum Howth Demesne Howth Co Dublin Ireland	00-353-1-8320427

Open October-May weekends 2 pm to 5 pm (including bank holidays), June-September daily 2 pm to 5 pm. Ireland's only comprehensive collection of public service and commercial road transport. Approximately 150 vehicles at present. Members are drawn from all walks of life, people interested in commercial vehicles. Our major publication is *The Winged Wheel*, a history of CIE (the National transport company).

Route 66 American Automobile Collection 94 Dundrum Rd Newcastle, Co Down BT33 0LN Northern Ireland UK	013967-25223 FAX: 013967-23302

Open Easter-September daily 10:30 am to 6 pm, October-Easter weekends only 2 pm to 6 pm. Route 66 is a collection of American classics dating from the 1930s-1990s with accent on the fifties. Together with American memorabilia, juke boxes, video cinema, souvenir shop, snacks. Wheelchair accessible. Exhibits include 1939 Hupmobile Skylark, 1/2 scale model Batmobile. Web site: www.yell.co.uk/sites/route66/

Italy

Museo Dell'Automobile "C Biscaretti Di Ruffia" Corso Unita'D'Italia 40 Torino 10126 Italy	011 677-666 FAX: 011 6647-148

Open year round. Tuesday-Sunday 10 am to 6:30 pm. National automobile museum.

Museo Ford Gratton-Museo Dell'Automobile E Della Technica Via Gorizia N 150 Farra D'Isonzo-Go 34070 Italy	0481 888404 0481 520121 FAX: 0481 20643

Open year round. Monday-Friday 9 am to 1 pm. Ford automobiles, motorcycles, radios, Edison gramophone. Exhibits include how Ford got started and produced the Model T.

Japan

Transportation Museum 25 Kanda=Sudacho 1-Chome Chiyoda-ku Tokyo 101-0041 Japan E-mail: gakugei@kouhaku.or.jp	03-3251-8481 FAX: 03-3251-8489

Open year round. Tuesday-Sunday 9:30 am to 5 pm (admission until 4:30 pm). In the Transportation Museum original vehicles and models of all sorts of means of transportation on land, on the seas and in the air are collected and exhibited. On exhibit: first JNR (Japanese National Railways) bus, type TGE-MP, 1930. Web site: www.kouhaku.or.jp

Monaco

Collection de Voitures Anciennes de SAS Le Prince Rainier III de Monaco Les Terrasses de Fontvieille MC 98000 Monaco	377 92 05 28 56 FAX: 377 92 05 96 09

Open year round. 10 am to 6 pm. 105 cars. 5500 m2. The personal collection of SAS Le Prince Rainier III de Monaco: Bugatti which won the first 1929 Monaco Grand Prix, Packard Eight, RR Phantom I, Silver Ghost, Twenty, Lincoln, Cadillac, Humber, Napier, Delahaye 135, Cisitalia, Hispano Suiza Coupe Chauffeur transformable H6B.

New Zealand

Te Puke Vintage Auto Barn 26 Young Rd Te Puke New Zealand	PH/FAX: 07 5736547

Open daily 9 am to 5 pm. Over 70 vintage and classic vehicles, all in working condition and regularly used.

Yaldhurst Museum of Transport and Science School Rd Yaldhurst RD 6 Christchurch New Zealand E-mail: museum@ihug.co.nz	64 03 3427914 FAX: 64 03 3427916

Open every day except Christmas, 10 am to 5 pm; night tours by arrangement, 5 pm to 9 pm. The museum first opened in 1968 and features vintage and classic cars, motorcycles, racing cars, horsedrawn carriages, fire engines, replica fire station, military and naval equipment, tractors, farm machinery, education center and more. Exhibit includes: 1938 International car coupe, one of five ever made in that era. Web site: http://members.xoom.com.carmuseum

Netherlands

Autotron PO Box 142 (Graafsebaan 133) A 50 Motorway 's-Hertogenbosch- Nijmegen Rosmalen 5240 AC (56248 NL) Netherlands E-mail: info@autotron.nl	0031-73-5233300 FAX: 0031-73-5216795

Open daily June 4-October 31, 1999, 10 am to 5 pm. Vintage and classic cars, more than 100 in new AutoDome. Presentation of automotive industry, their vision on the future. Situated in leisure park with theme transport, lots of attractions for children. Lots of car events. Web site: www.autotron.nl

Den Hartogh Ford Museum Haarlemmerstraat 36 Hillegom 2181HC Netherlands E-mail: hartford@xs4all.nl	0031-252-518-118 FAX: 0031-252-517-615

Open Wednesday-Sunday 10 am to 5 pm; restaurant open 10 am to 5 pm. The brand new Den Hartogh Ford Museum is the world's largest one dedicated to Ford automobiles. It measures 5,000 m2 and consists of three halls, which house the main exhibition, a cinema, conference rooms. Of course, the museum's great pride consists of 170 vintage Ford models, all of which are in mint condition and can safely be driven on the road. Our models range from T Fords to Lincolns, sedans, sportscars, trucks, etc. 15 Lincolns (handmade, 1920s-1930s), some Model S/Model N 1906, 1907, 1908. Web site: www.classics.nl

Het Nationaal Autobielmuseum Steurweg 8 Raamsdonksveer 4941VR Netherlands	31-162-585400 FAX: 31-162-519480

Open April-October, Tuesday-Sunday 10 am to 5 pm. The Dutch National Motor Museum provides a complete picture of the history of the automobile, from every period and from every corner of the world. The museum not only houses an important collection of motor cars but also important examples of other modes of transportation.

Internationaal Museum 1939-1945 Dingeweg 1 9981 NC Uithuizen Netherlands E-mail: mus39-45@tref.nl	*31 595-434100 FAX: *31 595-431837

Open April 1-October 31 daily 9 am to 6 pm. Soft skin and armoured military vehicles from parabike up to and including Sherman tank, restored to full running order, documents, photographs, models, uniforms, equipment, guns, utilities and telecommunication sets. Maybach German WW II staff car on display. Web site: www.tref.nl/noord-groningen'cultuurenvrijetijd'

National Bicycle Museum Velorama Waalkade 107 6511 XR Nijmegen Netherlands	024-3225851 FAX: 024-3607177

Open year round (closed December 25 and January 1). Sunday 11 am to 5 pm, other days 10 am to 5 pm. We are a museum specializing in historical bicycles, parts of bicycles and everything that has to do with bicycles. Museum Velorama has an extensive library with publications, information, documentation concerning bicycles, companies, etc.

Oldtimermuseum De Rijke De Pinnepot 23 Ind area De Pinnepot Oostvoorne 3233 LP Netherlands	+31(0)181-483876 FAX: +31(0)181-486143

Open April 1-October 29 Saturday-Sunday 12 pm to 5 pm, July 1-October 29 also open every Wednesday 12 pm to 5 pm. Approximately 200 cars, all kinds of makes and models, the oldest ones date from 1904.

Portanje's Vespa Scooter & **Nostalgia Collection** Stationsweg 41 3981AB Bunnik Netherlands E-mail: k.portanje@consunet.nl	PH/FAX: +31-30-6563838

Private collection open by appointment. The collection contains pre-war, military and mainly Vespa motor scooters plus posters, photos and Vespa Club memorabilia of the 1950s/1960s. 6 days Vespa (1951), Paris Dakar Vespa (1980) early Vespa (1947), etc on display.

Norway

The Motor Museum at Strommen **Storsenter** Stoperivegen 5 N-2010 Strommen Norway	47-63-80-23-10 Fax: 47-63-80-23-10 cellular: 47-91-85-57-52

Open year round. Daily 12 pm to 4 pm. The museum reflects the 20th century, with small environments of furniture, utensils, etc. 30-40 veteran cars/trucks, 20 motorcycles and cycles from approx 1900-approx 1970 link the exhibits. Vehicles are changed annually. A small shop sells coffee, mineral water, books, toy cars and so on. The museum is situated just outside one of Norway's largest malls, with more than 100 shops and restaurants, lots of free parking available. Strommen is located approximately 20 km (12 miles) east of Oslo City.

Norsk Kjoretoy-Historisk Museum Lilletorget 1 2615 Lillehammer Norge Norway	61 25 62 65

The Norwegian Museum of Historical Vehicles is Norway's first and only museum for vehicles and shows the development from the first vehicles and wagons to the car of today. Presents Norwegian car history from the Oldsmobile rebuilt just after the turn of the century to the Troll Car which ended Norwegian car production at the end of the fifties. The museum's section for horsedrawn vehicles includes sleighs, gigs, carrioles and vans.

Scotland

Argyll Motoring Heritage Centre Argyll Works, Main St Alexandria G83 0UG Scotland	PH/FAX: +44(0)1389607862

Open year round. Daily 10 am to 6 pm. Housed in the magnificent splendor of the 1906 Argyll Motor Works. Once Europe's largest car factory, this historic A graded building has a 700 ft frontage in Italian marble and sandstone with an entrance hall copied from the Paris Opera House. See amongst others: a 1910 Argyll car, an audio-visual exhibition on all aspects of motoring and Scottish driver Colin McRae's 1995 World Championship Rally car. Scottish Tourist Board commended.

Moray Motor Museum Bridge St Elgin Moray 1030 2DE Scotland	01343 542933 FAX: 01343 546315

Open April-October daily 11 am to 5 pm. Veteran, vintage and classic cars and motorbikes. Exhibit includes: Jaguars, Astons, Alfa Romeo, Bentley.

Myreton Motor Museum Michael J Mutch, Curator Aberlady East Lothian EH32 0PZ Scotland	01875-870288

Open year round. Daily from 10 am. A diverse collection of motor cars from 1880. Motorcycles, cycles, commercials and World War II military vehicles. Aero and motor engines, period enamel advertising, posters, period models and all manner of ephemera. 1896 Leon Bollee, 1899 General Electric, 1900 Locomobile (original, unrestored) on display.

Sweden

Gotlands Veteran Car Museum Kneippbygatan 8 62148 Visby Sweden E-mail: jan.janthe@alfa.telenordia.se	**0498/264666** **FAX: 0498/264833**

Open June-August daily 10 am to 8 pm. Cars, motorcycles, cycles and tractors worthwhile seeing. Including go-carts, track and RC cars/boats, minicar track, antique slot machine hall, antique country shop/petro station, cafe. On display: Rolls-Royce, Amphicar, A Ford 3w coupe, cycles from 1862-mc, tractor, locomobile-the oldest in Sweden.

The Motor Museum in Torsang Skomsarby 81 78194 Borlange Sweden E-mail: s-e.autoparts@ebox.tninet.se	**+46 243 60573** **FAX: +46 243 221298**

Open May to mid-summer and September weekends 12 pm to 6 pm; mid-summer to August daily 12 pm to 6 pm. Motorcycles from early century (1902) up to the 1950s, the base being many older, pre-10, in very good unrestored condition. A toy collection of 3-400 items and enamel signs, an authentic Swedish village store with original packages and items of what could be found in a store yesterday. On exhibit: 1916 Scania Vabis, fire chief car, under restoration in the museum.

Smalands Bil, Musik°Leksaksmuseum Hjortsjo 33017 Rydaholm Sweden	**0472-20005**

Open May-October daily 10 am to 6 pm. Automobiles, motorcycles, mopeds, toys, Meccanical Music instrument, old museum church, antik and coffee shop. On exhibit: Roll-Royce, Bentley Speed Six, cars from 1901-1969.

Svedino's Automobile and Aviation Museum Ugglarp SE-31050 Sloinge Sweden E-mail: svedinos@algonet.se	**+46 346 43187** **FAX: +46-31-144848**

Open daily June, July and August 10 am to 4 pm. 140 vintage cars, mainly 1900-1950. 30 aircrafts. Web site: www.algonet.se/~svedinos

Tidaholms Museum S-52283 Tidaholm Sweden	**00946-502-16192** **FAX:** **00946-502-14329**

Open May-August, Tuesday, Thursday-Sunday 2 pm to 6 pm, Wednesday 2 pm to 7 pm; September-April, Tuesday, Sunday 2 pm to 5 pm, Wednesday 2 pm to 7 pm. A company called Tidaholms Bruk in Sweden produced some 1,000 motor vehicles between 1903 and 1934. Some of these vehicles have been saved and are shown at Tidaholms Museum. On exhibit: a truck from 1927, a bus from 1925 and 6 firefighting vehicles.

Visby Bilmuseum Skogsholm S-62190 Visby Sweden	**0498-278161** **FAX: 0498-203390**

Open daily June 15-June 30, 1 pm to 5 pm; July 1-July 31, 10 am to 6 pm; August 1-August 15, 1 pm to 5 pm. 35 veteran cars 1904-1964, 35 motorcycles 1910-1960. On exhibit: Selve Motorwagen 1920, Stutz Bulldog 1920, Calthorpe 1913, Opel Doktorwagen 1907.

Uruguay

Automovil Club Del Uruguay's Museum Colonia Y Y1 Montevideo Uruguay	**5982 9024792** **FAX: 5982 9021406**

Open February-December Tuesday-Sunday 5 pm to 9 pm. Always 40 or more cars being exhibited from an 1899 Delin to a 1967 Rago. Entrance is free.

Wales

National Cycle Exhibition The Automobile Palace Temple St Llandrindod Wells Powys Mid Wales LD1 5DL Wales	**01597-825531**

Open year round. Daily 10 am to 4 pm. Large displays of bicycles from 1818-1999. An amazing exhibition that will fascinate and entertain you. Walk through the lanes of bicycle history.

FC: Full Classic
NC: Non-Classic
Please apply to CCCA: Call or write with specifics on the vehicle.
Note: 1925-48 Custom-bodied cars not listed should apply to CCCA.

Classic Cars 1925-1948 Classic Car Club of America

The term "classic car" is one that has been so distorted and abused over the past twenty years or so that it might be handy to those seeking a single authoritative list of Classic Cars to include this in the *Almanac*. This group of cars and no others can truly be called "Classic"; as defined and chosen through the years by the Classic Car Club of America.

Our thanks to the Classic Car Club of America, Suite 7, 1645 Des Plaines River Rd., Des Plaines, IL 60018. PH: 847-390-0443. See their free listing on page 468.

A

AC..FC
Adler..............................please apply to CCCA
Alfa Romeo...FC
Alvis, Speed 20, Speed 25 and 4.3 Litre..............FC
   Others..........................please apply to CCCA
Amilcar...........................please apply to CCCA
Armstrong Siddeley.................please apply to CCCA
Aston-Martin, all 1927-39.............................FC
   Others..........................please apply to CCCA
Auburn, all 8 and 12-cyl.............................FC
Austro-Daimler.......................................FC

B

Ballot.............................please apply to CCCA
Bentley..FC
Benz..............................please apply to CCCA
Blackhawk..FC
BMW, 327, 328, 327/318 and 335.......................FC
Brewster, all Heart Front Fords......................FC
   Others..........................please apply to CCCA
Brough Superior...................please apply to CCCA
Bucciali, TAV 8, TAV 30, TAV 12 and Double Huit..FC
   Others..........................please apply to CCCA

Bugatti, all except type 52.........................FC
Buick, 1931-42 90 Series............................FC
   All others.......................................NC
   Custom-bodied....................please apply to CCCA

C

Cadillac, all 1925-35...............................FC
   All 12s and 16s..................................FC
   1936-48, all 63, 65, 67, 70, 72, 75, 80, 85, 90 Series
   ....FC
   1938-47 60 Special...............................FC
   1940-47 all 62 series............................FC
   All others.......................................NC
Chenard-Walcker...................please apply to CCCA
Chrysler, 1926-30 Imperial 80, 1929 Imperial L, 1931-37 Imperial series CG, CH, CL and CW..............FC
   Newports and Thunderbolts........................FC
   1934 CX..FC
   1935 C-3...FC
   1936 C-11..FC
   1937-48 Custom Imperial, Crown Imperial Series C-15, C-20, C-24, C-27, C-33, C-37, C-40..........FC
   All others.......................................NC
Cord..FC
Cunningham, Series V6, V7, V8, V9...................FC

D

Dagmar, 6-80..FC
Daimler, all 8-cyl and 12-cyl.......................FC
   Others...........................please apply to CCCA
Darracq, 8-cyl and 4-litre 6-cyl....................FC
   Others...NC
Delage, Model D-8...................................FC
4-Cylinder cars.....................................NC
   Others...........................please apply to CCCA
Delahaye, Series 135, 145, 165......................FC
4-Cylinder cars.....................................NC
   Others...........................please apply to CCCA
Delaunay Belleville, 6-cyl..........................FC
   Others...NC
Doble...FC
Dorris..FC
Duesenberg..FC
duPont..FC

E

Excelsior.....................................please apply to CCCA

F

Farman.......................................please apply to CCCA
Fiat...please apply to CCCA
FN...please apply to CCCA
Franklin, all models except 1933-34 Olympic.........FC
Frazer Nash................................please apply to CCCA

G

Graham, 1930-31 Series 137................................FC
Graham-Paige, 1929-30 Series 837.......................NC
   Custom-bodied.....................please apply to CCCA

H

Hispano-Suiza, all French models, Spanish models
   T56, T56BIS, T64.......................................FC
Horch...FC
Hotchkiss..................................please apply to CCCA
Hudson, 1929 Series L...FC
   Custom-bodied.....................please apply to CCCA
Humber......................................please apply to CCCA

I

Invicta...FC
Isotta Fraschini...FC
Itala..FC

J

Jaguar, 1946-48 2-1/2 Litre, 3-1/2 Litre (Mark IV)..FC
   4-Cylinder cars...NC
Jensen......................................please apply to CCCA
Jordan, Speedway Series 'Z'..................................FC
   All others..NC
Julian...FC

K

Kissel, 1925-26, 1927 8-75, 1928 8-90 and
   8-90 White Eagle, 1929-31 8-126.......................FC
   All others..NC

L

Lagonda, all models except 1933-40 Rapier............FC
Lanchester.................................please apply to CCCA
Lancia.......................................please apply to CCCA
LaSalle, 1927-33...FC
Lincoln, all L, KA, KB and K, 1941 168 H,
   1942 268 H...FC
Lincoln Continental ....FC
Locomobile, all Models 48 and 90, 1927-29 Model 8-
80, 1929 8-88...FC
   All others...NC

M

Marmon, all 16-cyl, 1925-26 74, 1927 75, 1928 E75,
   1930 Big 8, 1931 88 and Big 8 ....FC
   Others...NC
Maserati....................................please apply to CCCA
Maybach...FC
McFarlan TV6 and 8 ....FC
Mercedes...FC
Mercedes-Benz, all 230 and up, K, S, SS, SSK,
   SSKL, Grosser and Mannheim..............................FC
Mercer...FC
MG, 1935-39 SA, 1938-39 WA..................................FC
Minerva, all except 4-cyl.......................................FC

N

NAG..please apply to CCCA
Nash, 1931 Series 8-90, 1932 series 9-90, Advanced
   8 and Ambassador 8, 1933-34 Ambassador 8 .....FC
   All others...NC

P

Packard, all Sixes and Eights, 1925-34...................FC
   All 12-cylinder models...FC
   1935 Models 1200 thru 1205, 1207 and 1208......FC
   1936 Models 1400 thru 1405, 1407 and 1408......FC
   1937 Models 1500 thru 1502 and 1506 thru 1508 FC
   1938 Models 1603 thru 1605, 1607 and 1608.....FC
   1939 Models 1703, 1705, 1707 and 1708...........FC
   1940 Models 1803, 1804, 1805, 1806, 1807 and
   1808 ....FC
   1941 Models 1903, 1904, 1905, 1906, 1907 and
   1908 ....FC
   1942 Models 2023, 2003, 2004, 2005, 2055, 2006,

2007 and 2008 ....FC
1946-47 Models 2103, 2106 and 2126 ....FC
  All Darrin-bodied ....FC
  All other models..NC
  Custom-bodied ....please apply to CCCA
Peerless, 1925 Series 67, 1926-28 Series 69, 1930-31
  Custom 8, 1932 Deluxe Custom 8 ....FC
  Others ....NC
Peugeot.....................................please apply to CCCA
Pierce-Arrow ....FC

R

Railton......................................please apply to CCCA
Raymond Mays ....please apply to CCCA
Renault, 45 hp...FC
Reo, 1931-33 8-31, 8-35, 8-52, Royale Custom 8,
  1934 N1, N2, and 8-52 ....FC
Revere...FC
Riley..please apply to CCCA
Roamer, 1925 8-88, 6-54e, 4-75, 4-85e; 1926 4-75e,
  4-85e and 8-88; 1927-29 8-88; 1929 and
  1930 8-120 ....FC
Rochet Schneider......................please apply to CCCA
Rohr..please apply to CCCA
Rolls-Royce ....FC
Ruxton...FC

S

Squire..FC
SS and SS Jaguar, 1932-40 SS 1, SS 90, SS
  Jaguar and SS Jaguar 100 ....FC
Stearns-Knight ....FC
Stevens-Duryea ....FC
Steyr.......................................please apply to CCCA
Studebaker, 1929-33 President, except Model 82 ....FC
  All others..NC
Stutz..FC
Sunbeam, 8-cyl and 3 Litre twin cam ....FC

T

Talbot, 105C and 110C..FC
Talbot Lago, 150C...FC
Tatra.......................................please apply to CCCA
Triumph, Dolomite 8 and Gloria 6 ....FC

V

Vauxhall, 25-70 and 30-98 ....FC
Voisin ....FC

W

Wills Sainte Claire..FC
Willys-Knight, Series 66, 66A, 66B custom bodied only
  ....please apply to CCCA

None of the above Classic Marques are acceptable in race car configuration.

Statement of Policy
"Race Car Configuration,"
March 10, 1993

As of March 10, 1993, the Classic Car Club of America will no longer accept any automobile which is in a "race car configuration." The race car configuration is a vehicle which is missing some or all of the following: fenders, lights, windshield, windshield wipers, bumpers, top. It may be without doors, or reverse gear or starting motor. It may not have an exhaust system other than a straight pipe, nor have proper instrumentation or upholstery. In short, it would not be considered a legal, road worthy vehicle which is licensable in a majority of the states.

Certified Milestone Cars, 1945-1972

There's also continual debate over the meaning of "Milestone" cars. Like Classics, they do have a precise meaning. Basically, they're post-WWII Classic Cars — cars of superior design or engineering or performance or innovation or craftsmanship — or a combination of these characteristics. Following is the list of Milestones courtesy of the Milestone Car Society of California Inc, 1255 La Brea Dr., Thousand Oaks, CA 91362, PH: 805-497-1955.

FC: Full Classic
NC: Non-Classic
Please apply to CCCA: Call or write with specifics on the vehicle.

A

AC Ace 1954-61
AC Aceca 1955-61
AC Buckland Open Tourer 1949
AC (Shelby) Cobra 1962-67
Alfa Romeo Giulietta Spider 1956-64
Alfa Romeo Giulietta-Giulia Sprint Speciale ... 1959-61
Alfa Romeo 6C 2500 Super Sport 1949
Allard Series J2, K2, K3 1946-56
AMX, 2-seater 1968-70
Apollo 1963-66
Arnolt Bristol 1952-62
Aston Martin 1948-63
Aston Martin DB4, DB5, DB6 (all) 1964-67
Austin-Healey 100/100M 1953-56
Austin-Healey 100-6 1956-59
Austin-Healey 3000 1959-67
Austin/Morris Mini 1959-70

B

Bentley (all) 1946-67
BMW 507 1957-59
BMW 2800 CS 1969-71
Bugatti Type 101 1951
Buick Riviera 1949; 1963-70
Buick Skylark 1953-54

C

Cadillac Eldorado 1953-58
Cadillac Eldorado 1967-70
Cadillac Eldorado Brougham 1957-58
Cadillac 60 Special 1948-49
Cadillac 61 Coupe (Fastback) 1948-49

Cadillac 62 Sedanet/Convertible/deVille 1948-49
Cadillac 75 Sedan/Limo 1946-70
Chevrolet Bel Air, V8, Hardtop and Convertible ....
.... 1955-57
Chevrolet Camaro SS/RS, V8 and Z-28 1967-69
Chevrolet Corvette 1953-70
Chevrolet Impala Sport Coupe/Convertible 1958
Chevrolet Nomad 1955-57
Chrysler 300 Letter Series 1955-65
Chrysler 300 Hurst 1970
Chrysler Town & Country 1946-50
Cisitalia GT (Pininfarina) 1946-49
Citroen Chapron 1960-70
Citroen DS and ID 19 1955-64
Citroen SM 1970
Continental Convertible 1958-60
Continental Mark II 1956-57
Continental Mark III 1969-70
Corvair Monza 1960-64
Corvair Monza Spyder 1962-64
Corvair Monza & Corsa 1965-69
Crosley Hotshot/SS 1950-52
Cunningham 1951-55

D

Daimler DE-36 (Custom built) 1949-53
Daimler 2.5 Special Sport Convertible 1949-53
Delage D-6 Sedan 1946-49
Delahaye Type 135, 175, 180 1946-51
DeSoto Adventurer 1956-58
Deutsch-Bonnet GT 1950-61
Devin SS 1958-62
Dodge Charger R/T and Daytona 1968-70
Dodge Coronet R/T 1967-70
Dual Ghia 1956-58

E

Excalibur II Series I 1965-69

F

Facel Vega, V8 1954-64
Ferrari, V12 (all front engined) 1947-70
Ford Crestline Skyliner 1954
Ford Crown Victoria Skyliner 1955-56
Ford Mustang Boss 302/Mach I 1969-70
Ford Mustang GT/GTA, V8 1965-67
Ford Skyliner (Retractable) 1957-59
Ford Sportsman 1946-48
Ford Thunderbird 1955-60
Frazer Manhattan 1947-50

G

Gaylord 1955-57

H

Healey Silverstone 1949-50
Hudson (all)..1948-49
Hudson Hornet 1951-54

I

Imperial...1955-56

J

Jaguar XK 120..1945-54
Jaguar Mark V Drophead 1951
Jaguar Mark VII and 1954 Mark VII M...........1951-54
Jaguar XK 140..1954-57
Jaguar Mark VIII..1956-57
Jaguar Mark IX...1958-61
Jaguar Mark X..1962-64
Jaguar XK 150..1958-61
Jaguar 3.4/3.8 Sedans 1957-64
Jaguar E-Type...1961-67

K

Kaiser Darrin 161..1954
Kaiser Deluxe/Deluxe Virginian 1951-52
Kaiser Dragon 1951-53
Kaiser Manhattan 1954-55
Kaiser Vagabond 1949-50
Kaiser Virginian (Hardtop)...............................1949-50
Kurtis 500S & 500KK...1953-55
Kurtis 500M & 500X...1953-55

L

Lagonda, V12 1948-49
Lagonda, 2.5 Liter Drophead Coupe 1949-53
Lancia Aurelia B.20 and B.20 Coupe 1951-59
Lancia Aurelia B.24 Spyder and Convertible ..1953-59
Lancia Flaminia GT 2-Passenger Coupe or Convertible
....1961-63
Lancia Flaminia Zagato 1959-64
Lancia Flavia Coupe..1962-66
Lea Francis 2.5 Liter Eighteen Sports.............1950-54
Lincoln Capri 1952-54
Lincoln Continental..1946-48
Lincoln Continental..1961-67
Lincoln Continental Custom Limos (Lehmann-
  Peterson) 1963-67
Lotus Elite...1958-63

M

Maserati A6/1500, A6G/2000/A6GCS Berlinetta ....
....1946-57
Maserati 3500/3700 GT.....................................1957-64
Maserati Ghibli, Mexico, Indy, 5000 GT 1959-70
Maserati Quattroporte 1963-69
Maserati Sebring, Mistral 1965-70
MG Series TC 1946-49
MG Series TD 1950-53
MGA Twin Cam 1958-62
Mercedes-Benz 190 SL 1955-62
Mercedes-Benz 220A Coupe and Convertible..............
....1951-54
Mercedes-Benz 220S/220 SE Coupe and Convertible..
....1956-65
Mercedes-Benz 230 SL Coupe and Convertible...........
....1963-67
Mercedes-Benz 250 SE/SL Coupe and Convertible......
....1965-67
Mercedes-Benz 280 SL 1969-70
Mercedes-Benz 300S/SE/SL Coupe and Convertible...
....1952-64
Mercedes-Benz 300 SE Coupe and Convertible ....
....1965-67
Mercedes-Benz 300 SEL 6.3 1969-70
Mercedes-Benz 600 1964
Mercedes-Benz 600, SWB/LWB 1965-70
Mercury Cougar XR-7...1967-68
Mercury Sportsman..1946
Mercury Sun Valley..1954-55
Morgan 4/4 1955-70
Morgan Plus Four...1950-67
Muntz Jet..1950-54

N

Nash Healey 1951-54
NSU Wankel Spyder 1964

O

OSCA MT-4 1948-56
Oldsmobile 88 (Coupe, Convertible, Holiday) ..1949-50
Oldsmobile 98 Holiday Hardtop.........................1949
Oldsmobile 442 1964-70
Oldsmobile Fiesta 1953
Oldsmobile Toronado...1966-67

P

Packard Caribbean...1953-56
Packard Custom (Clipper and Custom Eight) ....
....1946-50
Packard Pacific/Convertible................................1954
Packard Panther Daytona....................................1954

Packard Patrician/400 1951-56
Panhard Dyna 1946-67
Pegaso (all) 1951-58
Plymouth Barracuda Formula S 1965-69
Plymouth Fury 1956-58
Plymouth Roadrunner & Superbird...............1968-70
Plymouth Satellite SS & GTX........................1965-70
Pontiac GTO 1964-69
Pontiac Safari 1955-57
Porsche Series 356 1949-64
Porsche 356C 1965

R

Riley 2.5 (RMA, RME) 1945-55
Rolls-Royce (all) 1947-67
Rover 2000/2000 TC....................................1964-70

S

Shelby 350GT & 500GT................................1965-67
Studebaker Avanti......................................1963-64
Studebaker Convertible (all) 1947-49
Studebaker Gran Turismo Hawk....................1962-64
Studebaker President Speedster 1955
Studebaker Starlight Coupe (all)....................1947-49
Studebaker Starlight Coupe (Six and V8) 1953-54
Studebaker Starliner Hardtop (Six and V8).....1953-54
Sunbeam Tiger 1965-67

T

Talbot Lago 4.5 (all) 1946-54
Triumph TR2/TR3...1953-63
Tucker..1948

V

Volkswagen Karmann Ghia 1956-70
Volvo P.1800S, E, & ES Series........................1961-70

W

Willys Overland Jeepster 1948-51
Woodill Wildfire 1952-58

US Vehicle Makes Past to Present

One of the most fascinating lists, and one which is changing even today, is the long, long list of makes of cars built in the US during the past century. There are literally thousands of them from every corner of the nation, distilled and diminished by competition and changing markets into the small handful of volume manufacturers of motorcars left today. This list, large as it is, is not totally complete as more and more tinkerers and backyard geniuses who built cars through the decades are discovered and documented by automotive historians. But it's a hefty list nonetheless and one which we think you'll enjoy browsing through.

A

A.B.C. ....1908 and 1922
Abenaque 1900
Abendroth and Root 1907
Abbott 1909-1916
Abbott-Cleveland 1917
Abbott-Detroit 1909
Abbott-Downing 1919
A.C. 1938
Acadia 1904
Acason 1915
Ace 1920-1922
A.C.F. 1926
Acme 1902-1911
Acorn 1925
Adams ....1911 and 1924
Adams-Farwell 1904-1913
Adelphia 1921
Adette 1947
Adria 1921-1922
Advance 1909
A.E.C. 1914-1916
Aero 1921
Aerocar ....1905-1906 and 1948
Aerotype 1921
Ahrens-Fox 1927
Airphibian 1946-1952
Air Scout 1947
Airway 1949
Ajax Electric 1901-1903
Ajax ....1914 and 1923-1925
Akron 1901
Alamobile 1902
Aland 1917
Albany 1907
Alco 1909-1912
Aldo 1910
Alden-Sampson 1904-1909

All American 1919
Allegheny 1908
Allen 1914-1922
Allen and Clark 1908
Allen Cyclecar 1914
Alith 1908
Allen-Kingston 1907-1909
Allis-Chalmers 1914-1917
All Steel 1915-1916
Alma 1908
Alpena 1910-1914
Alsace 1920-1921
Alter 1916-1917
Altha 1905
Altham ....1897 and 1898
Amalgamated 1905
Ambassador 1921-1922
Amco 1920
American ....
    ...1901, 1905-1914, 1916-1918, 1922-1925 and 1937
American Austin 1930
American-Bantam 1937
American Beauty 1916
American Benham 1917
American Berliet 1906
American Chocolate 1903
American Coulthard 1907
American Electric 1899-1900
American Fiat 1912
American Gas 1902-1903
American-LaFrance 1910
American Mercedes 1903
American Mors 1903
American Napier 1904
American Populaire 1904
American Power Carriage 1900
American Simplex 1908
American Steam Car 1935
American Steamer 1922-1923
American Southern 1921
American Tri-Car 1912
American Underslung 1908
American Voiturette 1900
Americar 1941
Ames ....1895, 1898 and 1912-1915
Amesbury 1898
Amex 1895
Amplex 1908-1915
Ams-Sterling 1917
Anchor 1909
Anderson ....1908 and 1916-1926
Anger 1913
Angus 1908
Anheuser-Busch 1905
Anhut 1909
Anthony 1897
Apex 1920
Apell 1911
Appel 1915
Appelo 1973
Apperson 1902-1926
Apple 1917

Appleton	1922
Apollo	1906
Arbenz	1911-1919
Arcadia	1911
Ardsley	1905
Argo-Borland	1914
Argo-Case	1916
Argo Electric	1912-1917
Argo-Gas	1914
Argonne	1920
Ariel	1906
Aristos	1913
Armlader	1914
Arnold Electric	1895
Arrow	1914
Arrow Cyclecar	1914
Artzberger Steamer	1864
Astor	1925
Astra	1920
Astre	1975-1977
Atlantic	1915
Atlas	1907-1913
Auburn	1903-1936
Auglaize	1911
Aultman	1901
Aurora	1907
Austin	1903-1922
Auto-Acetylene	1899
Autobain	1900
Auto-Bug	1910
Autobuggy	1907
Autocar	1899-1911
Auto Cycle	1913
Auto Dynamic	1901
Auto Fore Carriage	1900-1901
Auto-Go	1900
Automatic	1908 and 1921
Automobile Voiturette	1900-1902
Automote	1900
Automotor	1901-1904
Autoplane	1947
Auto-Tricar	1914
Auto Two	1900
Auto Vehicle	1903
Avanti	1963-present
Avery	1921

B

Babcock	1909-1913
Babcock Electric	1906-1911
Bachelles	1901
Backhus	1925
Bacon	1925
Badger	1911-1912
Bailey	1907-1916
Baker-Electric	1899-1917
Baker Steam	1917-1924
Balboa	1924
Baldner	1902-1903
Baldwin	1900

Ball	1902
Ball Steam	1900
Balzer	1900
Banker	1905
Banker Electric	1905
Bantam	1914
Barbarino	1923
Barley	1922-1924
Barlow	1922
Barnes	1907-1912
Barnhart	1905
Barrett & Perret	1895
Barrow	1896
Barrows Motor Vehicle	1897
Bartholomew	1901-1903
Barver	1925
Bateman	1917
Bates	1903
Bauer	1914
Bauroth	1899
Bayard	1903
Bay State	1906-1907 and 1922-1924
Beacon	1933
Beacon Flyer	1908
Beardsley	1901 and 1914-1917
Beau-Chamberlain	1905
Beaver	1920
Beck	1947
Beebe	1907
Beggs	1918-1922
B.E.L.	1921-1923
Belden	1907-1911
Belfontains	1907
Bell	1907 and 1915-1922
Bellmay	1904
Belmont	1904, 1908, 1910 and 1912-1916
Bemmel & Burham	1898
Bendix	1907
Bendix-Ames	1911
Benham	1914
Ben-Hur	1908-1917
Benner	1908-1909
Benson	1913
Bentley	1907
Benton Harbor Motor	1896
Berg	1902-1903
Bergdoll	1908-1911
Berkshire	1904-1911
Berwick Electric	1926
Bessemer	1904
Bertolet	1908-1912
Best	1900
Bethlehem	1904-1908
Betz	1919
Beverly	1904
Bewis	1915
Bewman	1912
Beyster	1910-1911
Beyster By-Autogo	1904
B.F.S.	1908
Biddle	1916-1922
Biddle-Murray	1906

Bierderman	1915
Bimel	1917
Binney-Burnham	1888-1902
Birch	1916-1923
Bird	1911
Birmingham	1921-1922
Birnel	1911
Black	1899 and 1908
Black Crow	1905 and 1909-1910
Black Diamond	1904
Blackhawk	1902-1905 and 1928-1929
Blair	1915
Blaisdell	1903
Blakeslee	1906
Blemline	1898
Bliss	1906
B.L.M.	1907-1909
Block	1905
Block Bros.	1905
Blomstrom	1904-1908
Blood	1903 and 1914
Bluebird	1910
Blumberg	1918
Bob Cat	1923
Bobbi-Car	1945
Boggs	1903
Boisselot	1901-1906
Bolte	1901
Borbein	1905
Borland	1913-1914
Boss	1903
Boston	1900 and 1903
Boston and Amesbury	1902
Boston High Wheel	1908
Bour-Davis	1916-1922
Bournonville	1914
Bouton and Bateman	1899
Bowman	1921-1922
Boynton	1922
Bradfield	1929
Bradley	1920
Bramwell	1900-1902
Bramwell-Robinson	1899
Brasie	1915
Brecht	1902-1903
Breer	1900
Breeze and Lawrence	1905
Breman	1908
Brennan	1908
Brew and Hatcher	1904-1905
Brewster	1915-1937
Bridgeport	1922
Briggs	1914
Briggs and Stratton	1920-1923
Briggs-Detroiter	1912
Brighton	1896 and 1914
Brightwood	1912
Brintel	1912
Briscoe	1914-1921
Bristol	1903 and 1908
Broc	1909-1917
Brock	1920

Brockville-Atlas	1911
Brockway	1912
Brodesser	1909
Brogan	1948
Brook	1920-1921
Brooks	1908 and 1925
Brower	1890
Brown	1898, 1914 and 1916
Brown-Burtt	1904
Brownell	1910
Brownie	1915-1916
Browniekar	1908-1910
Brunn	1906
Brunner	1910
Brunswick	1916
Brush	1907-1911
Bruss	1907
Buck	1925
Buckeye	1901 and 1906-1912
Buckeye Gas Buggy	1895
Buckles	1914
Buckmobile	1903-1907
Buffalo	1900-1907
Buffalo Electric	1901-1907
Buffington	1900
Buffman	1900
Buffum	1901-1909
Buford	11915
Buggyaut	1895 and 1908
Buggycar	1908-1909
Bugmobile	1907
Buick	1903-present
Bundy	1895
Burdick	1909-1910
Burg	1910
Burns	1910
Burroughs	1914-1916
Bus	1917-1924
Bush	1909 and 1917
Busser	1915
Buzmobile	1917
Byrider	1908-1909

C

Cadillac	1903-present
California	1902 and 1912-1914
California Cyclecar	1914
Californian	1916
Calvert	1927
Cameron	1905-1907 and 1909-1921
Campbell	1916-1921
Canda	1901
Cannon	1904
Canton	1906
Capital	1902
Capps	1908
Car Deluxe	1907
Car Nation	1913
Carbon	1902
Cardway	1923

Carhart..1871
Carhartt 1911
Carlisle 1900
Carlson..1904-1911
Carovan 1948
Carpenter 1895
Carqueville-MacDonald........................1930
Carrison 1908
Carroll ....1908, 1912-1918 and 1920-1922
Cartecar 1907-1911
Carter ....1901 and 1903
Cartermobile......................................1924
Carter Twin Engine.............................1909
Carthage 1924
Cartone..1905
Casco..1926
Case 1909-1927
Caseler 1901
Casward-Dard 1924
Cato..1907
Cavac-Plymouth 1910
Cavalier 1927
C.B...1917
Ceco 1914
Celt..1927
Centaur 1902
Central 1905
Century ....1901, 1903 and 1911-1912
Century Tourist 1901
C.F...1908
C.G. Gay 1915
C.G.V...1902
Chadwick 1905-1912
Chalmers 1908-1923
Chalmers Detroit 1907
Champion..............1902, 1909-1910 and 1919-1926
Champion Electric 1899-1901
Chandler...1913
Chapman.....................................1899 and 1901
Charter Car 1904
Charter Oak......................................1917
Chase 1910
Chatham 1906
Checker Cab 1921
Chelfant...1906-1912
Chelsea...1901-1904
Chevrolet 1911-present
Chicago.................1898, 1906 and 1914-1916
Chicago Commercial 1905
Chicago Electric..............................1914-1917
Chicago Motor Buggy............................1908
Chicago Steam....................................1906
Chief ....1908 and 1947
Christie...1904-1906
Christman 1901-1902
Christopher 1908
Chrysler.....................................1924-present
Church ....1903 and 1913
Churchfield 1911-1913
Cincinnati...1903
Cino 1909-1913
Cinov 1909-1912

Cistalia 1948
Clapps Motor 1898
Clark...1901-1902
Clark Electric.................................1906-1910
Clark Hatfield 1908-1909
Clark Steamer 1900-1909
Clarke Carter 1900-1906
Clarkmobile 1903-1906
Clarkspeed..1928
Classie...1917-1920
Clear and Durham...............................1905
Cleburne..1912
Clegg..1885
Clement 1903
Clendon 1908
Clermont..................................1903 and 1922
Cleveland..............1902-1906, 1909 and 1919-1926
Climber..1919-1923
Clinton..1923
Cloughley 1902-1903
Club Car 1911
Clyde 1919
Clymer 1908
Coates 1921-1922
Coates-Goshen 1908-1910
Coey 1911
Coffon...1898
Cogswell 1912
Colburn..1906-1911
Colby..1911-1914
Cole 1910-1925
Collins ....1901 and 1920
Colly 1900
Colonial ....1907 and 1921-1922
Colonial Electric.................................1912
Colt ....1908 and 1971
Columbia..............1892-1913 and 1916-1925
Columbia Dauman 1900
Columbia Electric 1898-1906
Columbia Knight..................................1916
Columbian Electric 1915
Columbus................1903-1905 and 1906-1909
Comet ....1907, 1914 and 1917-1923
Comet 3 Wheel...................................1947
Comet Cyclecar..................................1914
Commander ....1921 and 1923
Commerce 1916
Commercial 1903
Commodore 1921
Commonwealth 1917-1922
Compound.....................................1904-1906
Concord...1916
Conklin Electric..................................1895
Connersville.......................................1914
Conover 1907
Conrad Steam.....................................1900
Consolidated......................................1904
Continental......1907, 1909-1912, 1914 and 1933-1934
Cook...1908
Cooley...1900
Copley Minor 1917
Coppock...1907

Corbin	1903-1912
Corbitt	1907-1916
Cord	1929-1932 and 1936-1937
Cordoba	1976
Corinthian	1922
Corl	1911
Corliss	1917
Cornelian	1913-1915
Cornish	1917-1919
Correja	1911-1914
Cort	1914
Cortez	1947
Corweg	1905
Coscob	1900
Cosmopolitan	1907-1910 and 1951
Cotay	1921
Cotta	1901
Couch	1899-1900
Couch Steamer	1900
County Club	1903
Couple-Gear	1905
Courier	1904-1912 and 1919-1924
Covert	1902-1907
Covert Motorette	1902
Coyote	1909
C.P.	1908
Craig Toledo	1906-1907
Crane	1912-1914
Crane and Breed	1912-1917
Crane-Simplex	1923-1924
Crawford	1902-1924
Crescent	1905-1908 and 1914-1915
Crest	1902
Crestmobile	1901-1904
Cricket	1913-1915 and 1971-1973
Criterion	1912
Crock	1909
Croesus Jr.	1906
Crompton	1903-1905
Crosley	1940
Cross Steam Carriage	1895
Crother-Duryea	1915
Crow	1915
Crowdus	1901-1903
Crow-Elkhart	1914-1925
Crown	1907 and 1915
Crown High Wheel	1897
Crown Magnetic	1907
Crowther-Duryea	1915-1917
Croxton	1911-1914
Croxton Keeton	1909-1912
Cruiser	1918
Crusader	1923
Cucmobile	1907
Cull	1901
Culver	1905
Cunningham	1911
Cunningham Steamer	1900-1907
Curtis	1921
Custer	1921
Cutting	1910-1912
C.V.I.	1907

Cyclecar	1901
Cyclemobile	1920
Cycleplane	1914-1915

D

D.A.C.	1923
Dagmar	1922-1927
Daley	1893
Dalton	1911
Dan Patch	1911
Daniels	1916-1924
Darby	1909
Darling	1901-1902 and 1917
Darrow	1903
Dart	1922
Dartmobile	1922
Davenport	1902-1903
Davids	1902
Da Vinci	1925
Davis	1914, 1919-1928 and 1947-1950
Dawson	1904
Day	1911-1914
Day Utility	1911
Dayton	1904 and 1909-1911
Dayton Electric	1911
Dayton Steam	1900
Deal	1911
Decker	1902-1903
De Cross	1914
De Dion Bouton	1888-1904
Deemaster	1923
Deemotor	1923
Deere	1906-1909
Deere Clark	1906
Deering	1915
Deering Magnetic	1917-1919
Defiance	1919
Dekalb	1919
De La Vergne Motor Drag	1896
Delcar	1947-1949
Delling Steamer	1924-1927
Delmore	1923
Deltal	1914
De Mar	1949
De Mars Electric	1905
De Mot	1905 and 1909-1911
De Motte	1904
Denby	1922
Deneen	1916
De Rair	1911
Desberon Steamer	1901-1902
De Shaum	1908
Deshaw	1906
De Soto	1928-1960
De Tamble	1909-1912
Detroit	1900, 1905, 1916 and 1922
Detroit Air Cooled	1923
Detroit Dearborn	1909-1910
Detroit Electric	1907-1938
Detroit Steamer	1922

Detroiter 1912
De Vaux...1931-1932
Dewabout 1899
Dey Electric 1894
Dial..1923
Diamond 1907
Diamond Arrow 1909
Diamond T.......................................1905-1911
Diana 1924-1928
Diebel...1900-1901
Diehl..1923
Differential 1921
Dile..1914-1916
Direct Drive 1907
Disbrow 1917-1918
Dispatch...1912-1922
Divco Twin 1946
Dixie ....1912 and 1917
Dixie Flyer 1915-1924
Dixie Tourist...................................1908-1909
Dixon...1922
Doble 1914-1931
Dodge 1914-present
Dodgeson 1926
Dodo 1909
Dolson 1904-1907
Dorris 1906-1926
Dort..1915-1925
Douglas 1918-1922
Dover 1929
Dowagiac 1908
Downing 1914
Downing Detroit....................................1913
Dragon...1921
Dragon Steam.................................1906-1908
Drake 1921-1922
Drexel 1916-1917
Driggs...1915-1916
Drummond......................................1915-1916
Duck..1913
Dudgeon Steam 1866
Dudley 1914
Duer ....1907-1909 and 1925
Duesenberg 1921-1937
Dumont 1909-1912
Dunn...1914-1917
Duplex...1909
Dupont 1915-1923
Duquesne 1913-1916
Durable 1902
Durant...1921-1932
Durocar 1908-1910
Duryea 1895-1913
Duryea Gem 1916
Dusseau 1912
Dyke 1903
Dymaxion 1933

E

Eagle..............1905-1906, 1908-1909, 1914 and 1924
Eagle Cyclecar 1914-1915
Eagle Electric..................................1915-1917
Eagle Macaober 1917
Eagle Rotary 1917
Earl 1907-1909, 1916-1924
Eastman 1897
Eastman Steam 1900
Easton 1907
Easton Electric 1898
Eaton...1910
Eaton Electric 1898
ECK 1903-1909
Eclipse..1901-1902
Economy.....................1906 and 1917-1919
Economy Car 1914
Eddy Electric 1902
Edsel 1958-1960
Edwards Knight................................1912-1914
E.H.V...1903
Eichstaedt 1902
E.I.M...1916
Eisenhuth...1896
Elberon Steam 1903
Elbert 1915
Elcar...1908-1930
Elco 1915-1916
Eldorado 1969
Eldridge 1906
Electra 1913
Electric Vehicle 1897
Electric Wagon 1895
Electrobat 1895
Electrocar 1922
Electronomic...1901
Elgin...1914-1924
Elinor 1903
Elite..1909-1919
Elite Steamer 1901
Elk..1912
Elkhart 1908-1922
Elliott..1899-1902
Ellis Electric 1901
Ellsworth 1917
Elmore..1900-1911
Elrick 1896
Elston 1895
Elwell-Parker 1909
Elysee 1926
Emancipator 1909
Emerson 1907
Emerson and Fisher 1896
E.M.F. 1909-1912
Empire.....................1898-1901 and 1910-1919
Empire State..1901
Empress 1906
Endurance Steamer...........................1922-1923
Engelhardt..1901

Enger..1909-1917
Enterprise..1901
Entyre...1911
Entz..1914
Erie....................................1897 and 1916-1921
Erskine..1926-1930
Ernst...1896
Erving...1911-1913
Essex...1918-1932
Euclid..1907
Eureka....................................1908 and 1909-1914
Evans..1904
Evans Steam...1887
Evansville..1907-1909
Everitt..1909-1911
Everybodys...1908-1909
Ewing...1908-1910

F

Facto...1920
Fageol...1916-1917
Fairbanks-Morse..1909
Fairmont...1906 and 1978
F.A.L...1909
Falcar..1908, 1910 and 1922
Falcon......................................1909-1911 and 1922
Falcon Knight..1927-1928
Famose..1909
Fanning Electric..1902-1904
Farmack..1916
Farmobile..1906-1907
Farner...1922-1924
Fauber...1900 and 1914
Fay..1912
Fedelia...1903
Federal..1907-1909
Federal Steam...1905
Fee...1908
Felton..1914
Fergus...1915-1922
Ferris..1920-1923
Findley...1910-1912
Firestone Columbus..1906-1911
Fischer..................................1902-1904 and 1914
Fish..1908
Fisher..1914
Fitzjohn..1946
Flagler..1914
Flanders..1911-1912
Flanders Electric...1914
Flexbi...1904
Flexibel..1935
Flint.....................1902-1904 and 1922-1927
Flyer..1913-1914
Foos..1913
Ford...1903-present
Forest..1908
Forest City..1906
Forster Six...1920
Fort Pitt..1908-1909

Foster Steam..1898-1905
Fostoria..............................1906-1907 and 1916
Four Traction...1907
Fox...1921-1925
Frankford..1922
Franklin...1901-1934
Frayer..1905
Frayer Miller...1905-1909
Frazer..1945-1951
Fredonia...1902-1904
Fredrickson..1914
Freeman..1900-1903
Fremont..1922-1923
French...1903
Friedberd..1908
Friedman...1900-1903
Friend..1921-1923
Fritchie Electric...1907-1917
Frontenac....................1909-1911, 1917 and 1922
Frontmobile..1917
F.R.P...1915-1917
F.S..1908
Fuller..1907-1911
Fulton..1908 and 1948
F.W.D...1911

G

Gabriel...1912
Gadabout..1914-1915
Gaeth...1902-1906
Gaethmobile...1902
Gale..1906
Galt..1914
Gardner..1919-1931
Garford...1907-1913
Garvin..1900
Gas Au Lac..1905-1906
Gas Engine...1905
Gasmobile..1900
Gasoline Motor..1897
Gawley..1895
Gaylord..1910-1913
Gearless...1908 and 1920
Geer Steam..1900
Gem...1917
General...1903
General Cab..1929
General Electric...1899
General Vehicle..1906
Genesee..1911-1912
Geneva....................................1901-1909 and 1917
German American..1902
Geronimo...1917-1921
Gersix..1921
Ghent...1918
Gibbs Electric...1903
Gibson..1899
Gifford Pettitt...1907
Gillette...1916
G.J.C...1909-1915

Gleason ....1910-1912 and 1914
Glide 1902-1919
Globe 1921-1922
Glover 1921
Golden State 1928
Goldeneagle 1906
Goodspeed 1922
Gorson..1907
Graham 1903
Graham-Paige.......................................1927-1941
Grant...1914-1923
Gray ....1916 and 1922-1925
Gray-Dort 1917
Great Eagle..1911-1914
Great Smith 1911
Great Southern.......................................1910-1914
Great Western 1909-1916
Greeley 1903
Gregory 1948
Gregory Front Drive 1922
Greyhound 1914
Griffith...1962-1966
Grinnel Electric 1910-1915
Griswold 1907
Grout Steam 1899-1912
Guilder 1922
Gurley..1901
Guy Vaughn 1912
Gyroscope..1914

H

Hackett...1916-1919
H.A.L. 1918
Hale...1917
Hall...1903
Hall Gasoline 1895
Halladay ....1908-1912 and 1919-1921
Halsey..1901
Hamilton..1909
Hamilton Holmes...................................1920-1921
Hammer 1905
Hammer Sommer...1905
Handley 1921-1923
Handley-Knight 1921-1922
Hanger...1916
Hanover..1922-1924
Hansen 1902
Hanson..1917-1923
Harding 1916
Hardy 1904
Hare 1918
Harper 1907
Harrie 1925
Harrigan 1922
Harris Six 1923
Harrisburg...1922
Harrison 1904-1907
Harroun..1917-1922
Hart Kraft 1908
Hartman..1898

Harvard 1916
Harvey 1914
Hasbrouck 1900
Haseltine 1916
Hassler 1917
Hatfield..1906-1908
Hathaway 1924
Haupt 1909
Havers 1912-1914
Haviland 1895
Havoc 1914
Hawkeye 1923
Hawley 1907
Hay Berg...1907-1908
Haydock 1907
Haynes 1904-1925
Haynes-Apperson 1898-1904
Hayward 1913
Hazard 1914-1915
H. Brothers 1908
H.C.S. 1920-1925
Healy 1912-1916
Heine-Velox ....1906-1909 and 1921
Henderson...1912-1915
Henley Steam...1899
Henney..1921-1931
Henrietta 1901
Henry...1911
Henry J. 1950-1954
Hercules 1914
Hercules Electric...1902
Herff Brooks 1915
Hermes 1915
Herreshoff...1909-1914
Herschell-Spillman 1904-1907
Herschmann...1906
Hertel 1895-1900
Hertz..1925
Hess Steam..1902
Hewitt...1905-1910
Hewitt Linstrom 1900
Heymann...1898-1899
Hicks 1900
Highlander...1922
Hill 1907-1908
Hill Locomotor 1895
Hillsdale...1908
Hilton 1908
Hines 1908
Hobbie 1909
Hoffman 1902-1904
Hoffman Steam 1902
Hol Tan 1908
Holden 1915
Holland Steam 1905
Holley 1900-1903
Hollier..1915
Holly.....................1900 and 1916-1917
Holmes ....1908 and 1918-1923
Holsman 1903-1911
Holyoke Steam..1901-1903
Homer Laughlin 1916

Hopkins	1902
Hoppenstand	1948
Houpt-Rockwell	1910-1912
Howard	1901, 1903-1905 and 1914
Howard Gasoline Wagon	1895
Howey	1903
Hudson	1909-1957
Hupmobile	1908-1940
Hupp-Yeats	1911-1919
Hydro Carbon	1901
Hydromotor	1917
Hylander	1922

I

Ideal	1902, 1903, 1909-1914
Ideal Electric	1909
I.H.C.	1911
Illinois	1910-1914
Imp	1914-1915 and 1955
Imperial	1903-1904, 1907-1916 and 1928
Ingram Hatch	1917-1918
Innes	1921-1922
International	1900
International Harvester	1907-1911 and 1961-1984
Interstate	1909-1918
Iroquois	1904-1908
Izzer	1910

J

Jackson	1903-1923
Jacquet Flyer	1921
James	1909
Janney	1906
Jarvis Huntington	1912
Jeannin	1908-1909
Jeep	1963-present
Jeffery	1914-1917
Jenkins	1907-1912
Jewel	1906-1909
Jewett	1923-1926
Johnson	1905-1912
Jones	1915-1920
Jones Corbin	1902-1907
Jonz	1908-1911
Jordan	1916-1931
J.P.L.	1913-1914
Julian	1922 and 1925

K

Kaiser	1945-1955
Kalamazoo	1922
Kankakee	1919
Kansas City	1909
Karbach	1908
Kato	1907

Kauffman	1909-1912
Kavin	1905
K.D.	1914
Kearns	1908-1916
Keasler	1916
Keating	1899
Keene Electric	1900-1901
Keene Steam	1948
Keeton	1908-1914
Keller Chief	1947
Keller Kar	1914 and 1927
Kenmore	1909-1912
Kennedy	1898-1903 and 1915-1918
Kensington	1899-1904
Kent	1916-1917
Kenworthy	1920-1922
Kermath	1907-1908
Kermet	1900
Kessler	1921-1922
Keystone	1909-1910 and 1915
Kiblinger	1907-1909
Kidder	1901
Kimball	1910-1912
King	1896 and 1910-1924
King Midget	1946-1969
King Remick	1910
Kissell	1906-1931
Kline Kar	1910-1923
Kling	1907
Klink	1907-1909
Knickerbocker	1901-1903
Knox	1900-1915
Koppin	1914
Kreuger	1904-1905
K.R.I.T.	1909-1916
Kunz	1902-1906
Kurtis	1948-1955
Kurtz	1921-1923

L

L and E	1922-1931
Laconia	1914
Lads Car	1912-1914
Lafayette	1920-1924 and 1934-1939
Lambert	1904-1917
Lane Steamer	1899
Lanpher	1909-1912
Lansden Electric	1906-1908
La Petite	1905
La Salle	1927-1940
Lauth Jergens	1907-1910
Law	1905
Leach	1899-1901 and 1920-1923
Leader	1905-1912
Lehigh	1912
Lende	1908-1909
Lenox	1911-1918
Lenox Electric	1908-1909
Lescina	1916
Lewis	1899-1902, 1914-1916 and 1937

Lewis Six 1913
Lexington.............................1909-1928
Liberty 1916-1924
Lima 1915
Limited 1911
Lincoln.................1908, 1914 and 1920-present
Lion 1909-1912
Little 1912-1915
Littlemac 1930-1931
Locomobile 1899-1929
Logan 1903-1908
London 1921-1924
Lone Star 1920-1922
Loomis.................................1896-1904
Lorraine...............1907-1908 and 1920-1922
Los Angeles............................1913-1915
Lowell 1908
Lozier.................................1905-1917
Lutz Steam 1917
Luverne 1903-1918
Luxor Cab.............................1920
Lyman 1903-1904
Lyman and Burnham 1903-1904
Lyon Atlas 1912-1913
Lyon Knight...........................1914-1915

M

MacDonald 1923
Mackle-Thompson 1903
MacNaughton 1907
Macomber.............................1917
Macon 1915-1917
Madison...............................1915-1918
Magnolia..............................1902
Mahoning 1904-1905
Maibohm 1916-1922
Mais...................................1911
Majestic 1917
Malcolm 1915
Maltby 1900-1902
Manexall 1921
Manhattan 1905
Manistee 1912
Mann 1895
Maplebay 1908
Marathon..............................1908-1915
Marble Swift 1902-1905
Marion.................................1904-1915
Marion Handley.......................1916-1919
Maritime...............................1913-1914
Mark Electric 1897
Marlboro Steam 1899-1902
Marmon................................1902-1933
Marquette ....1912 and 1929-1931
Marr 1903-1904
Marsh..............1898-1899, 1905 and 1920-1921
Marshall 1919-1921
Martin.................1920, 1926-1928 and 1931
Marvel.................................1907
Maryland 1900-1901

Mason 1906-1910
Mason Steamer.......................1898-1899
Massachusetts.........................1901
Massilon 1909
Master 1918
Mather 1901
Matheson 1903-1912
Maxwell Briscoe.......................1904-1925
Maytag.................................1910-1911
McCue 1909-1911
McCullough 1899
McFarlan 1910-1928
McGill 1922
McIntyre 1909-1915
McKay Steam..........................1900-1902
McLaughlin 1908-1922
McLean 1910
Mecca 1914-1916
Melbourne 1922
Menard.................................1908-1910
Menges 1908
Mercer ....1910-1925 and 1931
Merchant 1914
Mercury..............1904, 1914, 1918 and 1938-present
Merit..................................1920-1923
Merkel 1905-1906
Merz 1914-1915
Meteor....1898, 1902-1903, 1904-1908 and 1914-1921
Metropol 1913-1914
Metropolitan ....1922 and 1954-1961
Metz 1909-1922
Michigan...............................1908-1914
Middleby...............................1908-1913
Midland 1908-1913
Mier 1908-1909
Milburn Electric.......................1914-1922
Militaire 1916-1922
Miller ....1912-1913 and 1915-1932
Miller Steam 1896
Milwaukee Steam 1900-1902
Minneapolis 1915
Mino 1914
Mitchell 1903-1923
Mobile Steam..........................1899-1903
Model 1903-1909
Modoc 1913
Moehn 1895
Mogul 1912
Mohawk.............1903-1904 and 1914-1915
Mohler 1901
Moline 1904-1913
Moline Knight 1914-1920
Moller 1920-1921
Monarch ....1908 and 1914-1917
Monarch Canada.......................1946-1961
Moncrieff 1901-1902
Monitor................................1916
Monroe 1914-1924
Moody.................................1900-1903
Mooers 1900
Moon 1905-1930
Moore ....1906-1907 and 1916-1921

Mora	1906-1911
Morlock	1903
Morris Salom	1895-1897
Morrison Electric	1891
Morse	1904-1909 and 1909-1916
Motorette	1910-1912
Moyea	1902-1904
Moyer	1909-1915
M.P.M.	1914-1915
Mueller	1895-1900
Multiplex	1912-1913
Munson	1899-1902
Murdaugh	1901
Murray	1902-1903 and 1916-1918
Murray Mac	1921-1928
Mustang	1948-1949

N

Napoleon	1916-1917
Nash	1917-1957
National	1900-1924
Navajo	1953-1955
Navarre	1921
Nelson	1917-1921
Neuman Electric	1922
Neustadt Perry	1902-1907
Nevada	1908
Neville	1910
Newcomb	1921
New Departure Cab	1904
New England	1898-1900
New England Electric	1899-1901
New Haven	1904
New York	1928-1929
Niagara	1903-1907 and 1915-1916
Nichols	1908
Noble	1902
Noma	1919-1923
Northern	1902-1909
Northway	1921
Norwalk	1910-1922
Novara	1917
Nyberg	1912-1914

O

Oakland	1907-1931
Oakman	1898
Oakman Hertel	1902
Obertine	1915
O'Connor	1916
Odelot	1916
Ofeldt	1899-1902
Ogren	1915-1923
Ohio	1909-1913
Ohio Electric	1910-1918
Okey	1907-1908
Oldfield	1917-1922

Oldsmobile	1897-present
Oliver	1905
Olympian	1917-1921
Omaha	1912-1913
Only	1909-1915
Orient	1901-1905
Ormond	1904-1905
Orson	1908-1909
Otto	1909-1912
Overholt	1912
Overland	1903-1929 and 1939
Overman Steam	1899-1900
O We Go	1914-1915
Owen	1910-1914
Owen Magnetic	1914-1922
Owen Schoeneck	1915-1916
Owen Thomas	1909
Oxford	1913-1915

P

Pacific	1914
Pacific Special	1914
Packard	1899-1958
Packet	1916-1917
Page	1907 and 1923-1924
Paige	1908-1927
Pak Age Car	1935-1938
Palmer	1906
Palmer Singer	1907-1914
Pan	1918-1922
Pan American	1902 and 1917-1922
Panda	1955-1956
Panther	1962-1963
Paragon	1905-1907 and 1922
Parenti	1920-1922
Parker	1921-1923
Parkin	1908
Parry	1910-1912
Parsons Electric	1905-1906
Partin Palmer	1913-1917
Paterson	1908-1923
Pathfinder	1911-1918
Patriot	1922
Patterson Greenfield	1916-1918
Patton Electric	1890
Patton Gas	1890
Pawtucket Steam	1900-1901
Payne Modern	1906-1909
Peabody	1907
Peck	1897
Peerless	1900-1931
Peninsular	1915
Penn	1911-1913
Pennington	1894-1902
Pennsy	1916-1919
Pennsylvania	1907-1911
People's	1901
Perfection	1906-1908
P.E.T.	1914
Peter Pan	1914-1915

Peters 1921-1922
Petrel 1908-1912
Phelps 1903-1905
Phianna 1916-1922
Philadelphia...................................1924
Phipps 1901-1912
Pickard 1908-1912
Piedmont 1917-1922
Pierce-Arrow 1901-1938
Pierce Racine 1904-1909
Piggins 1909
Pilgrim 1914-1918
Pilliod 1915-1918
Pilot 1909-1924
Pioneer 1909-1911
Pitcher 1920
Pittsburgh 1909-1911
Plass Motor....................................1895
Playboy 1946-1951
Plymouth ....1910 and 1928-present
P.M.C. 1908
Pomeroy..1902
Ponder 1923
Pontiac.................1902-1908 and 1926-present
Pope Hartford 1904-1914
Pope Robinson...........................1903-1904
Pope Toledo 1904-1909
Pope Tribune 1904-1906
Pope Waverly Electric 1904-1907
Poppy Car.......................................1917
Porter 1919-1922
Porter Steam..............................1900-1901
Port Huron....................................1922
Portland..1914
Postal 1907-1908
Powercar...................................1909-1912
Prado.......................................1920-1922
Pratt 1907
Pratt Elkhart 1911-1917
Preferred.......................................1920
Premier....................................1903-1925
Premocar...................................1921-1923
Prescott Steam 1901-1905
Pridemore..................................1914-1915
Primo......................................1910-1912
Prince 1902
Princess...................................1914-1918
Princeton..................................1923-1924
Publix 1947-1948
Pullman....................................1903-1917
Pungs Finch 1904-1910
Pup..1947
Puritan Steam 1902-1903

Q

Queen.......................................1904-1906
Quick 1899-1900
Quinlan 1904

R

R and L Electric........................1922-1928
R and V Knight..........................1920-1924
R.A.C.......................................1910-1911
Racine 1909-1911
Radford...........................1895 and 1903
Rae ....1898 and 1902
Railsbach..1914
Rainier 1905-1911
Raleigh 1921-1922
Rambler.....................................1902-1913
Randall Steam...........................1902-1903
Rand Harvey Steam 1899
Randolph Steam...............................1910
Ranger ....1907 and 1920-1922
Ranlet 1900
Rapid 1903
Ras Electric 1898
Rauch & Lang...........................1905-1928
Rayfield 1911-1915
R.C.H.......................................1912-1916
Read 1912-1915
Reading 1913-1914
Reading Steamer 1901-1902
Real 1914-1915
Reber 1902-1903
Red Bug.....................................1924-1930
Red Jacket......................................1904
Red Wing 1909
Reed 1909
Rees..1921
Reese 1887
Reeves ....1896-1898 and 1905-1912
Regal 1907-1918
Regas.......................................1903-1905
Reinertsen 1901
Relay 1903-1904
Reliable Dayton 1906-1909
Reliance....................................1904-1906
Remal Steam 1923
Remington 1914-1916
Reo 1905-1936
Republic....................................1910-1916
Re Vere.....................................1918-1926
Rex 1914-1915
Reya 1917
Reynolds...................................1899-1901
Richard.....................................1914-1919
Richards....................................1896-1903
Richelieu 1922-1923
Richmond..................................1904-1917
Rickenbacker.............................1922-1927
Ricketts 1909-1911
Riddle.......................................1916-1926
Rider Lewis 1908-1911
Riess Royal.....................................1921
Riker Electric.............................1897-1902
Riley and Cowley...............................1902
Ripper...1903

Ritz	1914-1915
R.O.	1911
Roadable	1946
Roader	1911-1912
Road Cart	1896
Roamer	1916-1929
Robe	1923
Roberts	1904 and 1915
Robie	1914
Robinson	1900-1902
Robson	1909
Roche	1924-1925
Rochester Steam	1901-1902
Rock Falls	1919-1925
Rockaway	1902-1903
Rocket	1903
Rockne	1932-1933
Rockwell	1910-1911
Rodgers	1921
Roebling	1909
Rogers	1895 and 1911-1912
Rogers and Hanford	1902
Rogers Steam	1903
Rollin	1924-1925
Rolls-Royce	1921-1935
Roman	1909
Romer	1921
Roosevelt	1929-1930
Roper Steamer	1860-1896
Ross	1915-1918
Ross Steam	1906-1909
Rotary	1904-1905 and 1922
Rowe	1908 and 1910
Rowena Front Drive	1926
Royal Electric	1904-1905
Royal Tourist	1904-1911
Ruggmobile	1922
Ruler	1917
Rumley	1920
Rushmobile	1901-1903
Russell	1903-1904 and 1921
Russell-Knight	1914
Rutenber	1902
Ruxton	1929-1930
Ryder	1900

S

S and M	1913
S and S Hearse	1924-1929
Saf T Cab	1926-1928
Saginaw	1916
Salisbury	1895
Salter	1909-1913
Salvador	1914
Sampson	1911
Samuels Electric	1899
Sandusky	1913
Santos	1902-1904
Saturn	1991-present
Savage	1914

Saxon	1914-1922
Sayers	1917-1924
Scarab	1935
Schacht	1904-1913
Schaum	1900-1903
Schebler	1908
Schleicher	1895
Schlosser	1912
Schnader	1907
Schoening	1895
Schwarz	1899-1900
Scootmobile	1947
Scott	1901
Scott Newcomb	1921
Scout	1914
Scripps-Booth	1912-1922
Seabury	1904-1905
Seagrave	1914
Searchmont	1900-1903
Sears Motor Buggy	1908-1912
Sebring	1910-1912
Seely Steam	1905
Sekine	1923
Selden	1907-1914
Sellers	1908-1912
Senator	1906-1910
Seneca	1917-1924
Serpentina	1915
Serrifile	1921
Servitor	1907
Seven Little Buffaloes	1909
Severin	1920-1921
S.G.V.	1911-1915
Shad Wyck	1917-1918
Shain	1902-1903
Sharon	1915
Sharp Arrow	1908-1910
Sharp Steam	1901
Shatwells Steam	1901-1903
Shavers Steam	1895
Shaw	1920-1921
Shaw Wick	1917-1919
Shawmut	1906-1908
Shelby	1903
Sheridan	1921
Shoemaker	1906-1907
Sibley	1911
Sibley Curtiss	1911-1912
Sigma	1914
Signel	1915
Silent	1912
Silent Knight	1905-1907
Silver Knight	1914-1919
Simmons Stream	1895
Simms Light Four	1920
Simplex	1907-1919
Simplex Crane	1915-1919
Simplicity	1907-1911
Simplo	1908-1909
Sinclair Scott	1908
Singer	1914-1920
Single Center	1906-1908

Sintz 1902-1904
S.J.R. 1915-1916
Skelton 1920-1922
Skene 1900-1901
Slater 1909
Smisor 1899
Smith 1905
Smith and Mabley Simplex 1904-1907
Smith Motor Buggy 1896
Smith Motor Wheel 1916-1919
Smith Spring Motor 1896
S.N. 1921
Snyder 1906-1908
Sommer 1904-1905
South Bend 1913-1914
Southern 1906-1908
Southern Six 1921
Sovereign 1906-1907
Spacke 1919
Spartan 1910
Spaulding ....1902-1903 and 1910-1916
Special 1904
Speedway 1905-1906
Speedwell 1907-1914
Spencer 1921-1922
Spencer Steam ....1862 and 1901
Sperling 1921-1923
Sperry 1899-1901
Sphinx 1914-1916
Spicer 1902
Spiller 1900
Spoerer 1908-1914
Sprague 1896
Springer 1903-1905
Springfield Electric 1908
Springfield Steam 1900-1901
Sprite 1914
Spurr 1901
Squires Steamer 1899
S.S.E. 1917
Stafford 1908-1914
Stammobile Steam 1900-1901
Standard 1900, 1902,
    1904-1905, 1909-1910, 1915, 1916-1922 and 1948
Standard Electric O 1911
Standard Steamer ....1900 and 1911-1915
Stanley Steamer 1897-1927
Stanley Whitney 1899
Stanton Steam 1901
Stanwood 1920-1922
Staples 1900
Star ....
    ...1902-1904, 1907-1908, 1909-1911 and 1922-1928
Starin 1903-1904
States 1914-1915
Staver 1907-1914
Steam Vehicle 1900
Steamobile 1901-1902
Stearns 1901-1929
Stearns Steam Car 1898
Steco 1914
Steel Swallow 1907-1908

Stageman 1915
Stein Koenig 1926
Steinhart Jensen 1908
Steinmetz 1922-1923
Stephens 1917-1924
Sterling ....1909-1911 and 1914-1916
Sterling Knight 1920-1922
Sterling Steam 1901-1902
Stetson 1916
Stevens 1899
Stevens-Duryea 1901-1927
Stewart ....1895 and 1915-1916
Stewart Coates Steam 1922
Stickney 1914
Stilson 1907-1909
St. Joe 1909
St. John 1903
St. Louis ....1899-1901, 1903-1907 and 1922
Stoddard Dayton 1904-1913
Storck Steam 1902
Storms Electric 1915
Stout 1946
Stout Scarab 1932-1936
Stranahan 1906
Strathmore 1899-1901
Strattan Premier 1923
Streator 1902
Stringer Steary 1899-1902
Strong and Rogers 1900
Strouse Steam 1915
Strouss 1897
Studebaker 1902-1966
Sturgis 1897
Sturtevant 1905-1907
Stutz 1911-1935
Stuyvesant 1911-1912
Suburban 1911-1912
Success 1906-1909
Sultan 1908-1912
Summit 1907-1909
Sun 1916-1917
Sunset 1900-1913
Super Cooled 1923
Super Kar 1947
Superior 1914
Supreme 1917-1922
Sweany Steam 1895
Synnestvedt 1904-1905
Syracuse Electric 1899-1903

T

Tait Electric 1923
Tally Ho 1914
Tarkington 1922-1923
Tasco 1947
Taunton 1901-1903
Taylor 1895
Templar 1917-1924
Temple 1899
Templeton 1910

Terraplane 1933-1937
Terwilliger Steam 1904
Tex...1915
Texan 1920-1922
Texmobile..1920-1921
Thomas 1903-1918
Thomas Detroit..1906-1908
Thompson 1901-1907
Thomson Electric...1901
Thorobred 1901
Thresher Electric...1900
Tiffany 1913-1914
Tiger 1914-1915
Tiley..1904-1913
Tincher 1903-1909
Tinkham 1899
Tjaarda 1935
Toledo Steamer...1901-1903
Tonawanda 1900
Toquet 1905
Torbensen 1902-1906
Touraine 1912-1916
Tourist...1902-1910
Tower..1899
Trabold ....1898 and 1905
Tractobile Steam...1900-1902
Trask Detroit...1922-1923
Traveler ...1907, 1910-1911, 1913-1914 and 1924-1925
Trebert..1907-1908
Triangle 1918
Tribune..1913
Tri Moto..1900-1901
Trinity Steam...1900-1901
Triumph 1907-1912
Trumbull 1914-1915
Tucker 1948
Tulsa...1917-1922
Turner 1900
Twin City 1914
Twombly..1913-1915
Twyford ....1899-1902 and 1904-1907

U

Ultimate...1914
Union..1902-1909 and 1912
United..1914
United Power 1901
Unito 1909
Universal ....1910 and 1914
University 1907
Unwin..1921-1922
Upton ....1902-1903 and 1905-1907
U.S. 1908
U.S. Electric 1899-1903
U.S. Long Distance 1900-1904
U.S. Motor Vehicle......................................1899-1900

V

Valley..1908
Van..1911-1912
Van Wagoner 1899
Vandergrift..1907
Van Dyke...1912
Vanell Steam 1895
Vanette 1946
Vaughan...........................1910-1914 and 1921-1923
V.E. Electric..1903-1904
Veerac...1905
Velie 1909-1929
Vernon...1918-1921
Verrett 1895
Vestal 1914
Victor...1913-1917
Victor Steam 1899-1903
Victoria 1900
Victory...1920-1921
Viking ....1907-1908 and 1929-1930
Vim Cyclecar...1914
Virginian..1911-1912
Vixen 1914-1916
Vogel..1909
Vogue 1921-1922
Vulcan..1913-1915

W

Waco 1915-1917
Wagenhals..1910-1915
Wagner 1900-1901
Wahl...1913-1914
Waldron...1908-1911
Walker ....1895 and 1905
Wall..1900-1903
Walter..1902-1906
Waltham ....1898, 1905-1908 and 1922
Walther..1903
Walworth 1904-1905
Ward Electric...1914-1916
Ward Leonard 1903
Ware 1861
Warren 1909-1914
Warren Detroit...1910-1913
Warwick 1901-1905
Washburn 1896-1902
Washington ....1908-1909, 1911-1923 and 1925
Wasp 1919-1924
Waterloo 1903-1905
Waterman...1900
Waters 1900-1903
Watrous..1905
Watt Steam 1910
Waukeshaw 1906-1910
Waverley Electric 1898-1916
Wayne 1904-1908
Webb Jay Steam...1908

Weeks	1908
Welch	1903-1911
Welch and Lawson	1895
Welch Detroit	1910-1911
West Gasoline	1895
Westcott	1909-1925
Western	1901
Westfield Steam	1901-1903
Westinghouse	1905-1907
Weston	1899-1903
W.F.S.	1912
Whaley Henriette	1900
Wharton	1922-1923
Wheeler	1900-1902
Whippet	1927-1931
White	1900-1918
White Star	1909-1911
Whiting	1910-1912
Whitney	1896-1899
Wichita	1920-1921
Wick	1902-1903
Wilcox	1910-1913
Wildman	1902
Willard	1903-1905
Williams	1905
Wills St. Claire	1921-1927
Willys	1916-1955
Willys-Knight	1914-1933
Wilson	1906
Windsor	1929-1930
Wing	1896 and 1922
Winkler	1911
Winner	1907-1909
Winther	1921-1923
Winton	1896-1924
Wisconsin	1899

Witt	1912
Wizard	1914
Wolfe	1907-1909
Wolverine	1904-1906, 1917-1919 and 1927-1928
Wonder	1907-1909
Woodruff	1902-1903
Woods	1899-1918
Woods Electric	1901
Woods Mobilette	1913-1916
Worth	1906-1910
Worthington	1904-1905
Wright	1904 and 1910-1911

X

Xenia	1914

Y

Yale	1902-1905 and 1916-1918
Yates	1914
Yellow Cab	1915-1930
York	1905

Z

Zeitler	1917
Zent	1900-1906
Zentmobile	1903
Zimmer	1908-1988 and 1997-present
Zimmerman	1908-1915
Zip	1913-1914

Section Seven Lists

Index to this Almanac

This index is a complete roster of all listings appearing in the *Almanac*. The page number indicated will direct you to the main listing for that supplier or organization.

Please note that numerical names (e.g. 1932 Buick Registry) and symbols (& for example) come before alphabetical names.

Also, vendors who use their own names are alphabetized by their last names. However, to make reading the index easier, we have printed the vendor's full name in its proper order. In addition, vendors who use a nickname or title as part of their business name are listed under that nickname or title — so that you find Mopar Jack Dyson under "M" rather than "D".

Index

Index

Index

Index

Index

Index

Index

Index

Index

Index

Index

S

Index

X

Y

Z

Index

Index to Display Advertisers

This index is a complete roster of all display advertisers appearing in the *Almanac*. The page number indicated will direct you to the main listing for that supplier or organization.

Please note that symbols (& for example) come before alphabetical names.

Also, advertisers who use their own names are alphabetized by their last names. However, to make reading the index easier, we have printed the advertiser's full name in its proper order. In addition, advertisers who use a nickname or title as part of their business name are listed under that nickname or title — so that you find Mopar Jack Dyson under "M" rather than "D".

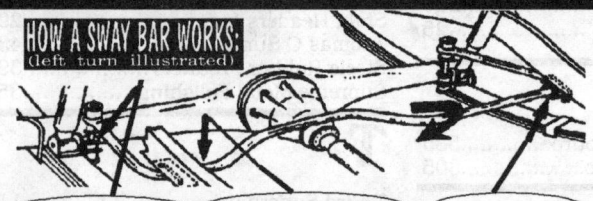

Hemmings' Vintage Auto Almanac©   Fourteenth Edition